THE ALMANAC OF AMERICAN EMPLOYERS 2022

The Only Guide to America's Hottest, Fastest-Growing Major Corporations

Jack W. Plunkett

Published by:
Plunkett Research®, Ltd., Houston, Texas
www.plunkettresearch.com

THE ALMANAC OF AMERICAN EMPLOYERS 2022

Editor and Publisher:
Jack W. Plunkett

Executive Editor and Database Manager:
Martha Burgher Plunkett

Senior Editor and Researchers:
Isaac Snider
Michael Cappelli

Editors, Researchers and Assistants:
Keith Carnes
Blake Lee
Ekaterina Lyubomirova
Annie Paynter
Gina Sprenkel

Information Technology Manager:
Rebeca Tijiboy

Special Thanks to:
U.S. Department of Labor
Bureau of Labor Statistics
U.S. Department of Commerce
Bureau of Economic Analysis, National Technical Information Service

Plunkett Research®, Ltd.
P. O. Drawer 541737, Houston, Texas 77254 USA
Phone: 713.932.0000   Fax: 713.932.7080
www.plunkettresearch.com

Plunkett Research®, Ltd.
P. O. Drawer 541737
Houston, Texas 77254-1737
Phone: 713.932.0000, Fax: 713.932.7080 www.plunkettresearch.com

ISBN13 # 978-1-62831-601-8 (eBook Edition # 978-1-62831-955-2)

THE ALMANAC OF AMERICAN EMPLOYERS 2022

CONTENTS

Continued on the next page

Continued from the previous page

INTRODUCTION

THE ALMANAC OF AMERICAN EMPLOYERS is an easy-to-use solution to what would otherwise be a complicated problem: How can you tell, among America's giant companies, which firms are most likely to be hiring? Among those firms, which are the best to work for? No other source provides this book's easy-to-understand comparisons of growth, treatment of employees, salaries, benefits, pension plans, profit sharing and many other items of great importance to job seekers.

Especially helpful is the way in which THE ALMANAC OF AMERICAN EMPLOYERS enables readers with no business background to readily compare the growth potential and benefit plans of large employers. You'll see the mid-term financial record of each firm, along with the impact of earnings, sales and growth plans on each company's potential to provide employment opportunities.

Information is presented in a way that addresses the differing interests of individual employees. You'll find separate listings for dozens of categories of data that you may want to consider. While this book is aimed primarily at job seekers, it will also be of tremendous value to researchers, marketing executives and personnel professionals. THE ALMANAC OF AMERICAN EMPLOYERS is the premier guide to the most successful employers in the nation, their policies and their performance.

THE ALMANAC OF AMERICAN EMPLOYERS is your opportunity to gain valuable knowledge in a matter of minutes. Five hundred of the biggest, most successful corporate employers in America are analyzed in this book. Tens of thousands of pieces of information, gathered from a wide variety of sources, have been researched for these corporations and are presented here in a form that can be easily understood by job seekers of all types.

Thanks to THE ALMANAC OF AMERICAN EMPLOYERS' exclusive data system, potentially confusing considerations have been reduced to simple groups of focused data. By scanning the data groups and the long list of unique indexes, you can find the right employers to fit your personal needs.

The AMERICAN EMPLOYERS 500 are among the best major growth companies to work for in America. Which companies offer the best benefits, are the biggest employers or earn the most profits? Where are these companies operating? All of these things and more are made easy for the reader to determine.

Thousands of observations are made that will be of great interest to prospective employees. For many of the firms, you'll find comments about such items as plans for growth, increases or decreases in the number of employees and charitable programs. You'll also find notes about corporate culture and special programs for the convenience of employees, such as health and recreation facilities, on-site child care, job training or career paths. Finally, you'll find basic information on each company, including the home office address and telephone number; regional, national and international locations; a description of the business; and a list of selected subsidiaries and trade names. In addition, you will find fax numbers and Internet addresses.

Whether you are currently employed by one of these corporate giants or are considering applying for a job with one, you will be able to see how each company compares with the others, even if you don't have the slightest understanding of accounting, finance or employee benefits.

Whatever your purpose for researching corporate employers, you'll find this book to be an indispensable guide. Nonetheless, as is true with all resources, this volume has limitations that the reader should be aware of:

- Financial data and other corporate information can change quickly. A book of this type can be no more current than the data that was available as of the time of editing. Consequently, the financial picture, management and ownership of the firm(s) you are studying may have changed since the date of this book. For example, this almanac includes the most up-to-date sales figures and profits available to the editors as of mid-2021. This means that we have typically used corporate financial data as of the end of 2020.

- Corporate mergers, changes in corporate financial ratings or stability, acquisitions and downsizing are occurring at a very rapid rate. Such events may have created significant change, subsequent to the publishing of this book, within a company you are studying.

- Some of the companies in THE AMERICAN EMPLOYERS 500 are so large in scope and in variety of business endeavors conducted within a parent organization that we have been unable to completely list all subsidiaries, affiliations, divisions and activities within a firm's corporate structure.

- This volume is intended to be a general guide to major employers in numerous industries. That means that researchers should look to this book for an overview and, when conducting in-depth research, should contact the specific corporations and related industry associations in question for the very latest changes and data. Where possible, we have listed contact information, telephone numbers and Internet addresses for pertinent companies, government agencies and industry associations so that the reader may get further details without unnecessary delay.

- We have used exhaustive efforts to locate and fairly present accurate and complete data. However, when using this book or any other source for business and industry information, the reader should use caution and due diligence by conducting further research where it seems appropriate. We wish you success in your endeavors, and we trust that your experience with this book will be both satisfactory and productive.

- To obtain the best results and to best understand the fields in the company profiles, you should first read the chapter titled "How to Use This Book."

Good luck in your job search. Be patient, do your research and use this book as an important start in the right direction.

Jack W. Plunkett
Houston, Texas
October 2021

HOW TO USE THIS BOOK

Dozens of excellent books already exist to help you choose a career, write a resume, apply for a job and so on. That is not the purpose of THE ALMANAC OF AMERICAN EMPLOYERS. Instead, this book's job is to help you sort through America's giant corporate employers to determine which may be the best for you, or to see how your current employer compares to others. Whether you are entering the job market and looking for your first position, or you are thinking about switching companies in mid-career to find more promising vistas, this book will be a valuable guide.

The two primary sections of the book are devoted first to general information for job seekers (trends analysis and advice on conducting employer research, along with resources, statistics and contacts), followed by the "Individual Data Listings" for THE AMERICAN EMPLOYERS 500. If time permits, you should begin your research in the front chapters of this book. Also, you will find lengthy indexes in Chapter 5 and in the back of the book.

GENERAL INFORMATION FOR JOB SEEKERS

Chapter 1: Major Trends Affecting Job Seekers. This chapter presents an encapsulated view of the major trends in business and the economy that are creating rapid changes in the employment picture at large corporations.

Chapter 2: Statistics. This chapter presents in-depth statistics on employment by education level, sex and race, along with unemployment rates, the fastest-growing occupations and more.

Chapter 3: Research—7 Keys for Job Seekers. This chapter provides a definitive list of items that job seekers should look for when conducting research into major corporate employers.

Chapter 4: Important Contacts for Job Seekers. This chapter covers contacts for important government agencies, professional societies, industry associations, job banks, reference sources and more. Included are Internet sites and contact addresses for a wide variety of job search uses.

THE AMERICAN EMPLOYERS 500

Chapter 5: THE AMERICAN EMPLOYERS 500: Who They Are and How They Were Chosen.

The companies compared in this book were chosen from nearly all industries, on a nationwide basis. They were individually chosen from the largest U.S. employers, based on selected types of business and industry sectors. For a complete description, see Chapter 5.

Individual Data Listings:

Look at one of the companies in THE AMERICAN EMPLOYERS 500's Individual Data Listings. You'll find the following information fields:

Company Name:

The company profiles are in alphabetical order by company name. If you don't find the company you are seeking, it may be a subsidiary or division of one of the firms covered in this book. Try looking it up in the Index by Subsidiaries, Brand Names and Selected Affiliations in the back of the book.

Industry Code:

Industry Group Code: An NAIC code used to group companies within like segments.

Types of Business:

A listing of the primary types of business specialties conducted by the firm.

Brands/Divisions/Affiliations:

Major brand names, operating divisions or subsidiaries of the firm, as well as major corporate affiliations—such as another firm that owns a significant portion of the company's stock. A complete Index by Subsidiaries, Brand Names and Selected Affiliations is in the back of the book.

Contacts:

The names and titles up to 27 top officers of the company are listed, including human resources contacts.

Growth Plans/ Special Features:

Listed here are observations regarding the firm's strategy, hiring plans, plans for growth and product development, along with general information regarding a company's business and prospects.

Financial Data:

Revenue (2020 or the latest fiscal year available to the editors, plus up to five previous years): This figure represents consolidated worldwide sales from all operations. These numbers may be estimates.

R&D Expense (2020 or the latest fiscal year available to the editors, plus up to five previous years): This figure represents expenses associated with the research and development of a company's goods or services. These numbers may be estimates.

Operating Income (2020 or the latest fiscal year available to the editors, plus up to five previous years): This figure represents the amount of profit realized from annual operations after deducting operating expenses including costs of goods sold, wages and depreciation. These numbers may be estimates.

Operating Margin % (2020 or the latest fiscal year available to the editors, plus up to five previous

years): This figure is a ratio derived by dividing operating income by net revenues. It is a measurement of a firm's pricing strategy and operating efficiency. These numbers may be estimates.

SGA Expense (2020 or the latest fiscal year available to the editors, plus up to five previous years): This figure represents the sum of selling, general and administrative expenses of a company, including costs such as warranty, advertising, interest, personnel, utilities, office space rent, etc. These numbers may be estimates.

Net Income (2020 or the latest fiscal year available to the editors, plus up to five previous years): This figure represents consolidated, after-tax net profit from all operations. These numbers may be estimates.

Operating Cash Flow (2020 or the latest fiscal year available to the editors, plus up to five previous years): This figure is a measure of the amount of cash generated by a firm's normal business operations. It is calculated as net income before depreciation and after income taxes, adjusted for working capital. It is a prime indicator of a company's ability to generate enough cash to pay its bills. These numbers may be estimates.

Capital Expenditure (2020 or the latest fiscal year available to the editors, plus up to five previous years): This figure represents funds used for investment in or improvement of physical assets such as offices, equipment or factories and the purchase or creation of new facilities and/or equipment. These numbers may be estimates.

EBITDA (2020 or the latest fiscal year available to the editors, plus up to five previous years): This figure is an acronym for earnings before interest, taxes, depreciation and amortization. It represents a company's financial performance calculated as revenue minus expenses (excluding taxes, depreciation and interest), and is a prime indicator of profitability. These numbers may be estimates.

Return on Assets % (2020 or the latest fiscal year available to the editors, plus up to five previous years): This figure is an indicator of the profitability of a company relative to its total assets. It is calculated by dividing annual net earnings by total assets. These numbers may be estimates.

Return on Equity % (2020 or the latest fiscal year available to the editors, plus up to five previous years): This figure is a measurement of net income as a percentage of shareholders' equity. It is also called the rate of return on the ownership interest. It is a vital indicator of the quality of a company's operations. These numbers may be estimates.

Debt to Equity (2020 or the latest fiscal year available to the editors, plus up to five previous years): A ratio of the company's long-term debt to its shareholders' equity. This is an indicator of the overall financial leverage of the firm. These numbers may be estimates.

Address:

The firm's full headquarters address, the headquarters telephone, plus toll-free and fax numbers where available. Also provided is the internet address.

Stock Ticker, Exchange: When available, the unique stock market symbol used to identify this firm's common stock for trading and tracking purposes is indicated. Where appropriate, this field may contain "private" or "subsidiary" rather than a ticker symbol. If the firm is a publicly-held company headquartered outside of the U.S., its international ticker and exchange are given.

Total Number of Employees: The approximate total number of employees, worldwide, as of the end of 2020 (or the latest data available to the editors).

Parent Company: If the firm is a subsidiary, its parent company is listed.

Salaries/Bonuses:

(The following descriptions generally apply to U.S. employers only.)

Highest Executive Salary: The highest executive salary paid, typically a 2020 amount (or the latest year available to the editors) and typically paid to the Chief Executive Officer.

Highest Executive Bonus: The apparent bonus, if any, paid to the above person.

Second Highest Executive Salary: The next-highest executive salary paid, typically a 2020 amount (or the latest year available to the editors) and typically paid to the President or Chief Operating Officer.

Second Highest Executive Bonus: The apparent bonus, if any, paid to the above person.

Other Thoughts:

Estimated Female Officers or Directors: It is difficult to obtain this information on an exact basis, and employers generally do not disclose the data in a public way. However, we have indicated what our best efforts reveal to be the apparent number of women who either are in the posts of corporate officers or sit on the board of directors. There is a wide variance from company to company.

Hot Spot for Advancement for Women/Minorities: A "Y" in appropriate fields indicates "Yes." These are firms that appear either to have posted a substantial number of women and/or minorities to high posts or that appear to have a good record of going out of their way to recruit, train, promote and retain women or minorities. (See the Index of Hot Spots For Women and Minorities in the back of the book.) This information may change frequently and can be difficult to obtain and verify. Consequently, the reader should use caution and conduct further investigation where appropriate.

Chapter 1

MAJOR TRENDS AFFECTING JOB SEEKERS

Major trends sweeping through business and the economy that affect job seekers of all types:

1) The Coronavirus and the U.S. Job Market Overview
2) Cost Control Remains a Major Concern at Employers/Consolidation Through Mergers Continues
3) The Sharing & Gig Economy's Effect on Employment, Work Life and Careers
4) Technology Continues to Create Sweeping Changes in the Workplace
5) Continued Growth in Outsourcing, Including Supply Chain and Logistics Services
6) Offshoring and the Reshoring of American Manufacturing
7) Older Americans Will Delay Retirement and Work Longer/Many Employers Find Older Employees Desirable
8) Employment Sectors that Will Offer an Above-Average Number of Job Opportunities:

Employment Sectors that Will Offer an Above-Average Number of Job Opportunities:

- Biotechnology, including Vaccines
- Consumer Products
- Cybersecurity, Digital Customer ID Tools
- Delivery Services
- Electronic Games
- Energy Conservation Products and Services
- Health Care Technology, Including Electronic Health Records
- Health Foods, Organic Foods, Enhanced Foods
- Home Building
- Insurance
- Internet Services, Server Hosting, Cloud Computing
- Internet of Things: Connected Devices, Remote Wireless Sensors and their Networks, Machine to Machine Communications
- Logistics and Warehousing Services (3PL), Particularly in Support of E-Commerce
- Online Search Services & Social Media, with Advertising Revenues
- Online-based Business and Consumer Sales and Services, including E-Commerce
- Outsourcing, Including Outsourced Business and Computer Services
- Payments Technologies (Online and Cashless, Digital Payments)
- Pets: Services and Products
- Pharmaceuticals (Drugs, including Vaccines)
- Restaurants—Quick Service
- Retail: Select Stores in Home Centers, Supermarkets and Discount Stores
- Robotics and Factory Automation
- Software—Artificial Intelligence
- Software—Data Analytics
- Software—Mobile Apps
- Software-as-a-Service (SaaS)
- Solar Energy Cells Installation & Maintenance
- Water Filtration and Conservation Equipment
- Wireless and Cellular Communications

1) The Coronavirus and the U.S. Job Market Overview

The Coronavirus epidemic altered the employment landscape dramatically. Large numbers of outstanding companies were forced to lay off employees due to both a rapid decline in revenues and uncertainty about the future. Hardest hit were the entertainment, restaurant, retail and travel sectors. At the same time, some sectors enjoyed soaring growth. Interest rates plummeted, causing a massive jump in business at mortgage companies as homeowners sought to refinance their loans. Home sales, including vacation homes, soared when people sought comfortable surroundings for their newly established work-from-home routines. Supermarkets and food-delivery services boomed. Cloud computing firms, cybersecurity companies and digital payments firms, such as Square and PayPal, were also dramatically boosted.

By late 2021, thanks to immense federal government stimulus plans and the widespread adoption of Coronavirus vaccines, the U.S. economy was roaring ahead in most sectors, creating vast numbers of job openings. Nearly all industries were complaining about large shortages of qualified workers, wages were rising and some industries were offering generous sign-on bonuses. Many industries were suffering shortages of parts and inventory. In September 2021, the unemployment rate was down to a modest 4.8%.

One of the most important changes in business and related employment has been the acceleration of long-term trends, in a manner that saw years' worth of business change occurring over a matter of months. The most noticeable of these trends was a boom in ecommerce of nearly all types. Technology-driven services of many other types were accelerated, from remote telemedicine to remote online education.

At Plunkett Research, we believe that consumer and business habits have permanently changed in many ways as a result of this global pandemic. The trend towards shopping via e-commerce means more jobs in website management, logistics, warehousing and delivery services (but fewer jobs in retail stores). On-demand delivery of groceries and meals will remain strong.

The work-at-home trend will endure in many types of sales, administrative and support jobs. This is an evolving trend, with employers attempting to maintain high productivity and efficiency, while accommodating employees' interests in working from home. Many workers are now in hybrid mode, going to the office a couple of days a week, and working remotely the rest of the time. This has serious career implications. For example, are workers who show up in the office more likely to get choice assignments and promotions?

Jobseekers also have vital decisions to make regarding whether or not to take the Coronavirus vaccine. Many employers are now requiring evidence of the vaccine—to obtain or keep a job in some cases, or to work in the office instead of at home. Many jobseekers are putting their vaccine status on their resumes, hoping that will give them an edge over non-vaccinated people.

The travel industry suffered miserably as a result of the Coronavirus, and hotels, cruises and airlines have undergone structural changes and a long-term reduction in business as a result. While leisure travel is popular again, business travel remains very soft.

Job seekers who want good positions with good pay must be extremely well prepared for the process of seeking a job. A large part of the preparation requires meaningful research into prospective employers and the industries in which they operate. The fact remains that several million

Americans consider themselves underemployed, and many of them will be looking for better jobs. Competition for the most desirable positions will remain fierce. Many companies receive hundreds or even thousands of resumes for every job opening. Simply sending in a resume and hoping for the best is nowhere near enough for a successful job search.

The good news is that a select set of employers and growth companies will offer superb job opportunities. Sectors such as cloud computing and ecommerce will continue to grow and hire. A few companies with exciting new technologies or cost-saving services will see terrific growth.

Solid companies that do a terrific job of providing the day-to-day needs of consumers and business will continue to hire—Costco and Amazon.com are good examples. Other industry sectors that fall into this category include insurance firms, such as USAA and The Progressive Corporation, along with online services and apps that provide efficient or new ways for consumers and businesses to make purchases, gather data or view entertainment and news.

Growing numbers of consumers prefer to buy from firms that sell goods and services online, offering avoidance of contact with crowds, savings of time, money and car travel. This boosts companies like Amazon.com that offer low prices combined with deep selections and great customer service. Virtually all major retailers, including giants like Wal-Mart and Home Depot, are working hard to provide better online services and choices to their customers. All major supermarkets are enabling online ordering and many offer home delivery.

Americans who find themselves in the market for a job will need to understand the changes surging through the economy in order to determine which companies to pursue and which to avoid. The U.S. employment market has evolved dramatically, and job seekers must be both knowledgeable and nimble in order to position themselves to find promising careers. There will be excellent opportunities for those who are diligent in seeking top employers in most business sectors.

Economic Factors Affecting the Job Market

Business Productivity: Productivity growth has been positive in recent years, but the increases have been very modest. That is, business can be produced—whether it is goods or services—by utilizing fewer workers than before. This will be extremely beneficial to the U.S. economy in the long run. Productivity is boosted by new technologies (such as the use of robotics or artificial intelligence), improved management methods and other factors, sometimes as simple as reorganizing the staff and redesigning the workflow to increase output. (It can also receive a quick boost from restrained corporate hiring.) If rising productivity occurs along with rapidly rising sales and profits, then the job market improves.

> _Corporate Revenues:_ A trend of rising revenues encourages hiring. Unfortunately, dropping revenues or an uncertain outlook for the future, typically lead to layoffs and hiring freezes.
>
> _Corporate Profits_: When profits increase sharply, companies are inclined to increase both investment and hiring. Hiring is strongest when corporate revenues, and accompanying profits, show significant growth, encouraging executives to forecast an extended period of increased demand for their products and services. Losses, or simply drops in profits, lead to hiring freezes, often to layoffs.

It is vital for the job seeker to use the best reference tools possible in order to seek out employers that offer a reasonable balance of financial stability, opportunities for advancement and good pay. Excellent job opportunities always exist if you know where to look.

In particular, companies that offer products or services that save time and/or money will prosper—for example, many types of companies that offer services that help businesses operate more efficiently, will be hiring. Meanwhile, large companies that are not increasing their overall numbers of employees will nonetheless be hiring on a regular basis due to normal attrition—that is, the loss of employees due to retirement, relocation or other personal circumstances. Massive companies like Walgreen's or Kroger typically need to hire tens of thousands of workers yearly due to normal attrition. At the same time, hiring will be boosted by the numbers of Americans who are turning retirement age and either quitting work or reducing their hours through part-time work.

2) Cost Control Remains a Top Concern at Employers/Consolidation Through Mergers Continues

For many years, executives have been focusing on cost control as a means to boost profits and financial stability. The Coronavirus will accelerate this need at most types of companies. Employee costs are always a focus, as employers seek to boost the overall productivity of their work forces. Often, companies merge with others in order to seek operating efficiencies or gain access to needed capital. Financing is readily available for large corporate mergers and acquisitions, and the number of mergers has been high. A consolidation of companies via a merger may enable the firms to combine customer bases, administrative staff, sales offices and production facilities, while cutting employees who hold duplicated jobs, in hopes of thereby creating more efficient, more profitable firms. Mergers may be spurred by economic difficulties and falling profits, or they may involve large firms seeking to acquire companies that bring advantages that may boost growth and accelerate profits. For example, online leaders Amazon, Facebook and Google have acquired numerous firms in order to bring in new technologies.

Even in a period of vibrant economic growth, good managers continue to seek ways to control costs, including payroll costs. Because they face tough, global competition, manufacturing firms are frequently involved in such mergers. Good jobs in the U.S. manufacturing sector can be found, despite intense competition from manufacturers in China and other offshore markets. Overall, U.S. factories are running with fewer people per unit of output, thanks to immense investments in factory automation and robotics.

A small, but significant, number of firms are "reshoring" some of their manufacturing, by making products at American plants that were previously manufactured in overseas facilities. Even the American textile industry, which was hit hard by layoffs and bankruptcies during the late 1900s, is enjoying a modest rebound. This is positive, but it has not led to large numbers of job openings. However, the Coronavirus is causing many companies to reconsider the former habits of reliance on overseas supply chains and work forces. This will provide a boost to the reshoring movement.

Some of the statistical loss in manufacturing employment has been exaggerated by the fact that many firms now outsource a good deal of their non-manufacturing operations to services companies. For example, many computer departments, company cafeterias, distribution centers and engineering needs are now outsourced to companies that specialize in such work, thus dramatically reducing the number of in-house jobs at manufacturing firms. This is the long-term trend of outsourcing in action.

Also, companies in both manufacturing and service sectors have caught on to management by teams, vastly enhanced supply chain technology (such as the use of the internet for ordering and tracking components), along with networked management, distribution and manufacturing systems, which all add up to the fact that fewer mid-management, white-collar types are needed to communicate with the people doing the day-to-day work. Production workers have been encouraged to communicate among themselves. In many cases, workers are taking on unprecedented responsibilities, setting their own goals and schedules, tracking costs and output, thereby boosting profits. Historically, these were the tasks of middle managers. Today, vast numbers of those management jobs have been eliminated. Businesses without factories are also undergoing re-engineering and leaps in productivity, often through the streamlining of processes through the use of better computers and software.

3) The Sharing & Gig Economy's Effect on Employment, Work Life and Careers

The sharing economy is disrupting the nature of work, employment and entrepreneurship. Most sharing/gig economy workers are working as independent, contract workers, not employees. This means that they do not qualify for company-provided benefits such as health coverage or retirement plans. Many of them conduct work for two or more sharing economy firms. That is, a worker might drive for Uber at night, do installations for TaskRabbit on weekends and shop for Instacart on weekdays. They may vary the schedule according to the demand level, which can be constantly monitored via smartphone.

In one-on-one interviews, Plunkett Research has found that many sharing/gig workers consider themselves to be "entrepreneurs." While they may not have created a new company that employs others or makes products, they nonetheless work for themselves, independently, using their own tools or vehicles and setting their own schedules. In that regard, they are literally running a business, in the same way that a one-man plumbing shop is a business.

Working independently in the sharing/gig economy generally requires no specialized education, and no licensing beyond a drivers' license. This type of work lends itself very well to people, such as retirees or students, who only want to work part-time, or who want a part-time sideline in addition to a regular job. One study (MBO Partners) found that 49% of part-time independent workers also had a full-time traditional job.

MBO Partners publishes an annual report "The State of Independence in America," that studies the independent worker market. MBO estimated the 2020 level of independent workers in the U.S. at 38.2 million, down from 2019's 41.1 million, and forecasts that number to grow to 47.8 million by 2023. (Their total includes three categories of independent worker: full-time, part-time and occasional. Many of these people have multiple jobs.) For 2020, independent workers generated approximately $1.21 trillion in revenue, or 5.6% of U.S. GDP.

There is a significant debate underway in many nations as to whether or not people working as Uber drivers, Instacart shoppers and similar agents are actually employees, rather than contract workers. Legislative reform may well be attempted on large scale in this regard. In some cases, class action lawsuits have been filed by the contract workers. If governments rule that such workers are employees, it would have a massive effect on the business models of sharing economy firms. In the U.S., for example, it would mean that firms were subject to paying payroll taxes such as Social Security, and were subject to very high levels of labor, safety, health and anti-discrimination laws. This debate will likely continue for many years to come, and may well lead to legal reform in some nations. Another outcome may be the formation of contractor workers' unions or union-like organizations that might demand better pay or working conditions. The "Independent Drivers Guild" now exists in New York City, representing tens of thousands of local Uber drivers, but not quite acting as a true labor union.

Over time, there could conceivably be massive changes within gig-based companies of all types. Multiple laws and regulations that protect employees and regulate the ways in which firms must treat them could come into effect, such as minimum wage, unemployment coverage, employer's liability, OSHA, EEOC and a long list of additional rules. On the other hand, there is already intense competition among gig economy employers, such as Uber and Lyft, to find and hire new workers. Sign-on bonuses, incentives, perks and better revenue share for workers are now common. Better treatment and pay may have the effect of neutralizing calls to turn contract workers into true employees.

4) Technology Continues to Create Sweeping Changes in the Workplace

Technology has introduced vast changes throughout industries of all types, greatly boosting productivity and reallocating (or eliminating) workers. A major cause of change for employees, and therefore job seekers, is the tidal wave of new technologies that continues to revolutionize the workplace at all levels. Prospering companies are using new ways to communicate with customers, automate back-office tasks and factory operations, and push ahead with research and development. There is a never-ending stream of technological innovation. For example, employers long ago harnessed the power of networked desktop computers. Today, they are rapidly adopting the use of mobile computing devices such as tablets, internet-based telephone systems (VOIP and unified communication systems), voice-recognition software, cloud computing and video conferencing technologies.

The trend of using new practices and technologies while cutting layers of management is largely about communication. This is true whether it is communication between the top offices and the factory floor, communication with customers, communication between the computers in one corporate office with those in another, or communication from the sales department to the warehouse and the supply chain.

These new technologies mean continuous retraining for much of the workforce. Job seekers who want the best posts must have the training and skills that will let them utilize new technologies effectively. Workforce training is a critical need nationwide.

Jobs in America are shifting to new categories of work based on technologies that didn't exist a few decades ago. For example, the job title "social media manager" emerged in recent years. Services firms, as well as manufacturers, are placing more and more employees in recently created technical and service positions, while many of the tasks once performed in-house are now provided by outsourced services providers. In the telecommunications industry, digital technology has completely changed the list of job titles while enabling phone service providers to reduce the ratio of employees to customers. In the meantime, hundreds of thousands of jobs have been created at cellular telephone companies. Now, internet-based telephony, competition from cable providers, fiber to the premises and wireless networks such as Wi-Fi and LTE continue to force telecommunications firms to evolve.

Another excellent example: Retailing, shipping and warehousing are undergoing a technology revolution due to the introduction of Radio Frequency Identification Tags (RFID). This breakthrough in inventory management is based on the placement of digitized product data within product packaging, combined with the use of special sensors in stores and warehouses that can automatically read that data. These sensors can alert a central inventory management system of product movement and the need to restock inventory. From loading docks to shelves to cash registers to parking lots, RFID sensors will eventually track the movement of each pallet or individual item. Many bar codes will eventually be replaced by RFIDs. RFID can even eliminate the need to scan each item at checkout in a retail store. Checkout stations will be equipped with sensors that read RFID-based data such as product code and price, and then automatically calculate purchase totals. Benefits can include less shoplifting and few inventory errors. Another benefit is that firms will be able to reduce overall inventory thanks to better tracking.

As online ordering, tracking and inventory management continue to become more sophisticated and cost-effective, purchasing executives at firms of all types and sizes will accelerate the use of internet-based systems for management of their supply chains. There are significant opportunities here for e-commerce services and software companies. Likewise, there is great promise for third-party logistics (3PL) companies that combine the power of internet-based information with strategically located warehouses to fulfill the inventory needs of manufacturers. Robots are being used to a rapidly growing extent in picking inventory within warehouses prior to shipment. Amazon.com is a leader in this regard.

Manufacturing is undergoing its own technology revolution. This is often referred to as factory automation. Advanced technology used with great success on the factory floor includes computer-driven machine tools that require highly skilled operators, along with robotic assemblers that are capable of working nonstop, 24/7 to create and assemble parts into finished goods.

Over the mid-term, massive changes in business and industry will be caused through rapid adoption of processes and systems based on artificial intelligence (AI). AI enables software to identify patterns in digital data, as well as in images such as digital photos/video of people, places and things. AI and a process known as machine learning means that more and more task that are currently handled by humans will be processed by computers. It remains to be seen how quickly, and to what extent, this will have broad effects on the workplace and hiring.

5) Continued Growth in Outsourcing, Including Supply Chain and Logistics Services

Part of the re-engineering process at employers has been a boom in "outsourcing," or the use of outside specialty firms to do chores that firms formerly performed through in-house departments. One of the largest fields of outsourcing growth has long been in computer departments. IBM and Accenture are among the global leaders in this area. Cloud computing (the use of outsourced, remote servers to run computer functions) is the latest major trend in this regard, and cloud services firms are enjoying soaring growth.

However, many other business functions are commonly outsourced. ServiceMaster takes over janitorial tasks, building management and maintenance functions for giant corporate office campuses and industrial facilities. Another company outsources all of the food warehousing and distribution for nationwide restaurant chains. Why? Because it can run trucks and warehouses more efficiently while its clients concentrate on running restaurants.

While the 1960s, '70s and '80s saw many firms frantically trying to do all tasks in-house, recent trends are quite different. As a period noted for rising productivity and efficiency, the 1990s and 2000s combined were an era of specialization and focus. Companies may do a better job by focusing on their core tasks, while allowing outside firms to provide support and maintenance needs. That trend will continue to be powerful over the long term. Outsourcing, which rapidly gained popularity, will persist in leading the way to higher efficiency and profits. Many outsourced services companies continue to grow, and they will create (and displace) large numbers of jobs.

One of the fastest-growing fields in outsourcing has been supply chain and logistics management. Companies offering services in this field include giant transportation companies like FedEx and UPS. "Supply chain" refers to the entire set of providers of supplies and services that are involved in creating and delivering a component or end product. For example, for an automobile manufacturer like Ford, the supply chain includes companies that make tires, batteries, interior components and engine parts, as well as the trucks and trains that ship these parts and the warehouses that hold them. This supply chain supports Ford's own manufacturing and assembly plants. At the end of Ford's business chain lie the automobile dealers that receive completed cars and deliver them to the end customers. Another example: For a clothing store chain like The Gap, the supply chain includes clothing designers, clothing manufacturers and the warehouses and transportation systems that deliver completed clothes to the stores. The Gap's supply chain is located across dozens of nations.

Logistics is the art of moving goods through the supply chain. Supply chains are so complex and so critical to a company's operations that there are countless ways to automate, improve efficiencies and cut costs. Many manufacturers and retailers are outsourcing all or part of their logistics needs to firms that specialize in creating efficiencies and saving costs. Logistics and supply chain companies have been growing rapidly over the past several years, and creating large numbers of jobs. A concept you should be familiar with is Third Party Logistics ("3PL"), a system whereby a specialist firm in logistics provides a variety of transportation, warehousing and logistics-related services to its clients. These tasks were previously performed in-house by the client. When 3PL services are provided within the client's own facilities, it can also be referred to as "Insourcing." In other words, you might find yourself working for UPS at a site within a distribution company that has no other ties to UPS.

Robotics and Artificial Intelligence (AI) are already having a significant effect on the way that warehouses and distribution centers are operated, including those of outsourced 3PL (third party logistics) companies. This means higher capital investment, but lower overall management and manpower requirements.

6) Offshoring and the Reshoring of American Manufacturing

Competition from workers in such nations as Mexico, Indonesia, Thailand and, in particular, China, has been fierce. For several decades, America's manufacturing employment was declining while a vast amount of manufacturing has been sent overseas by U.S. firms.

Today, however, some U.S. industries are experiencing reshoring, or the practice of moving formerly offshored tasks back to America. As wages rise in countries such as China and India, a number of manufacturers are rethinking offshoring, taking into account higher productivity rates among American workers. Supply chain problems encountered during the Coronavirus pandemic may accelerate this trend.

This is not to say that vast numbers of manufacturing jobs are going to return to America. Many of the newest factories are relying on advanced technologies instead of large workforces. Robots and artificial intelligence are driving today's most modern factories. An additional, informal classification of robots is collaborative robots, or "cobots." This refers to robots that work closely alongside human workers, with the intent of making repetitive tasks easier and faster to complete.

Another factor fueling reshoring is energy costs, which continue to be lower in the U.S. than in many other countries. Savings through low energy costs can be further augmented by increased manufacturing efficiency. This is due to the growing adoption of robotics. 3-D printing (additive manufacturing) is another technology that is significantly lowering prototyping and product design costs.

While lower employee wages have been a factor in some offshoring, proximity to growing foreign markets is another. Giant multinational companies ranging from Apple to Kraft to General Motors find that a vast portion of their business now lies overseas, often in the rapidly growing, emerging nations. Many of the world's largest companies find that they need to have local operations throughout the world.

Globalization has a profound effect on Americans—consumer prices become lower, while the U.S. job market changes considerably. Consumer goods are quite inexpensive due to the vast variety of items the U.S. imports from other nations, and prices for many categories of these goods have declined dramatically. Americans can purchase consumer electronics like DVD players and color televisions at extremely low prices, and the price of many types of apparel is much lower thanks to globalization. For example, over 90% of the shoes sold in America are manufactured in low cost nations, especially China.

Consider the rapid globalization of the automobile industry. The entire global automobile sector is dominated by only a handful of companies, including Toyota, GM, Ford, Daimler, Honda, Volkswagen and Nissan, as well as the increasingly successful Korean automakers Kia and Hyundai. Car manufacturers in China are becoming more dominant as well. Car manufacturers commonly have engineering teams collaborating from offices in multiple nations, while parts and components may be imported from a wide variety of suppliers in various countries to undergo final assembly at home.

American companies in many industry sectors have been merging and consolidating on a global basis at a rapid clip. That consolidation will continue. One benefit is that U.S. firms can enter into foreign markets through international acquisitions.

U.S. firms hold leadership positions in several key product and service sectors vital to the rest of the world, including health technology, computers, e-commerce, software and entertainment of all types.

7) Older Americans Will Delay Retirement and Work Longer/Many Employers Find Older Employees Desirable

Certain large employers, particularly national retail chains, have discovered that older workers provide a terrific pool of potential employees. This may be positive for older workers, but to younger job seekers it means more competition for work.

Many members of the immense Baby Boom generation are not planning to retire any time soon. This trend is accelerated by the fact that today's senior citizens will enjoy much longer life spans than earlier generations. Many will continue to work simply because they want to remain active, contributing members of society.

The phrase "Baby Boomer" generally refers to the 78 million Americans born from 1946 to 1964. The term evolved to describe the children of soldiers and war industry workers who were involved in World War II. When those veterans and workers returned to civilian life, they started or added to families in large numbers. As a result, this generation is one of the largest demographic segments in the U.S. Baby Boomers make more than 20% of the U.S. population.

Not long ago, 2011 marked the year when millions began turning traditional retirement age (65). As Baby Boomers continue to age, America will be experiencing extremely rapid growth in the senior portion of the population. Many Baby Boomers will leave their traditional, long-term jobs and turn to part-time work. Others will continue in their full-time jobs as long as possible.

By the early 2000s, many employers were already developing human resources strategies aimed at hiring or retaining older workers. On the lower end of the pay scale, retailers like Home Depot, a firm that has been known to need tens of thousands of new hires each year, have found older people to be ideal employees. They have knowledge that is extremely useful for providing advice and service to shoppers. They are experienced workers who understand the need to show up on time.

On the higher end of the employment scale, older workers with long-term experience in scientific and engineering tasks will be vital in keeping the gears of business and industry turning. During the 2000s boom, when the airline industry saw good growth, rules were altered in the U.S. to enable commercial airline pilots to keep flying until age 65, instead of facing forced retirement at age 60 as they had in the past.

Industrial firms are dealing with this challenge along two lines: First, how to document and pass along the immense treasure of work-related knowledge that these employees have, and second, how to keep these employees interested in working later into their lives.

8) Employment Sectors that Will Offer an Above-Average Number of Job Opportunities

Job seekers should remain aware of the fact that certain industries will have above-average likelihood to offer job openings. This is due to a number of circumstances, including shifts in consumer tastes and requirements, normal employee turnover and attrition, structural changes within industries, global economic conditions and national policies and priorities.

Below is a list of industries particularly recommended to job seekers.

Employment Sectors that Will Offer an Above-Average Number of Job Opportunities:
- Biotechnology, including Vaccines
- Consumer Products
- Cybersecurity, Digital Customer ID Tools
- Delivery Services
- Electronic Games
- Energy Conservation Products and Services
- Health Care Technology, Including Electronic Health Records
- Health Foods, Organic Foods, Enhanced Foods
- Home Building
- Insurance
- Internet Services, Server Hosting, Cloud Computing
- Internet of Things: Connected Devices, Remote Wireless Sensors and their Networks, Machine to Machine Communications
- Logistics and Warehousing Services (3PL), Particularly in Support of E-Commerce
- Online Search Services & Social Media, with Advertising Revenues
- Online-based Business and Consumer Sales and Services, including E-Commerce
- Outsourcing, Including Outsourced Business and Computer Services
- Payments Technologies (Online and Cashless, Digital Payments)
- Pets: Services and Products
- Pharmaceuticals (Drugs, including Vaccines)
- Restaurants—Quick Service
- Retail: Select Stores in Home Centers, Supermarkets and Discount Stores
- Robotics and Factory Automation
- Software—Artificial Intelligence
- Software—Data Analytics
- Software—Mobile Apps
- Software-as-a-Service (SaaS)
- Solar Energy Cells Installation & Maintenance
- Water Filtration and Conservation Equipment
- Wireless and Cellular Communications

Chapter 2

STATISTICS

Contents:

U.S. Employment Statistics Overview: 2020-2021

(Labor Counts In Thousands; Seasonally Adjusted)

	Jul-20	*May-21*	*Jun-21*	*Jul-21*
Civilian Labor Force, Total	159,870	160,935	159,932	152,645
Employed	143,532	151,620	151,602	152,645
Unemployed	16,338	9,316	9,484	8,702
Persons 16 Years of Age and Over, Not in Labor Force	100,503	100,275	100,253	100,123
Unemployment Rate, 16 years and over	10.2%	5.8%	5.9%	5.4%
Adult Men (20 years and over)	9.4%	5.9%	5.9%	5.4%
Adult Women (20 years and over)	10.5%	5.4%	5.5%	5.0%
Teenagers (16 to 19 years)	19.3%	9.6%	9.9%	9.6%
White	9.2%	5.1%	5.2%	4.8%
Black or African American	14.6%	9.1%	9.2%	8.2%
Asian	12.0%	5.5%	5.8%	5.3%
Hispanic or Latino	12.9%	7.3%	7.4%	6.6%
Average Hourly Earnings, Private Industry	$29.37	$30.31	$30.43	$30.54
Weekly Earnings, Private Industry	$1,016.20	$1,054.79	$1,058.96	$1,062.79
Average Work Week, Private Industry (Hours)	34.6	34.8	34.8	34.8
Employment by Selected Industry (Over-the-month change, in thousands)				
Total nonfarm	1,726	614	938	943.0
Total private	1,523	555	769	703.0
Goods-producing	60	16	45	44.0
Mining and logging	-4	4	11	6.0
Construction	26	-24	-5	11.0
Manufacturing	38	36	39	27.0
Private service-providing	1,463	539	724	659.0
Wholesale trade	-20	15	27	2.8
Retail trade	240	60	73	-5.5
Transportation and warehousing	50	15	20	49.7
Utilities	1	-1	0	-0.1
Information	-10	20	4	24.0
Financial activities	12	2	-1	22.0
Professional and business services	147	50	75	60.0
Education and health services	214	46	60	87.0
Health care and social assistance	201	13	7	46.8
Leisure and hospitality	666	319	394	380.0
Other services	163	13	73	39.0
Government	203	59	169	240.0

Source: U.S. Bureau of Labor Statistics
Plunkett Research,® Ltd.
www.plunkettresearch.com

U.S. Civilian Labor Force:
1997-July 2021

(Persons 16 & Older; In Thousands)

Year	Civilian Workforce Level
1997	136,297
1998	137,673
1999	139,368
2000	142,583
2001	143,734
2002	144,863
2003	146,510
2004	147,401
2005	149,320
2006	151,428
2007	153,124
2008	154,287
2009	154,142
2010	153,889
2011	153,617
2012	154,975
2013	155,389
2014	155,922
2015	157,130
2016	159,187
2017	160,320
2018	162,075
2019	163,539
2020	160,742
Jul-21	161,347

Note: The civilian labor force consists of employed and unemployed people actively seeking work, but it does not include any Armed Forces personnel.

Source: U.S. Bureau of Labor Statistics

Plunkett Research,® Ltd.

www.plunkettresearch.com

Employment by Major Industry Sector: 2009, 2019 & Projected 2029

Industry Sector	Employment (in Thousands)			Change (in Thousands)		Percent Distribution			Compound Annual Rate of Change	
	2009	2019	2029	2009-19	2019-29	2009	2019	2029	2009-19	2019-29
Total[1]	143,036.4	162,795.6	168,834.7	19,759.2	6,039.1	100.0	100.0	100.0	1.3	0.4
Nonagriculture wage & salary[2]	132,029.2	151,709.7	158,115.6	19,680.5	6,405.9	92.3	93.2	93.7	1.4	0.4
Goods-producing, excluding agriculture	18,507.7	21,016.3	20,964.9	2,508.6	-51.4	12.9	12.9	12.4	1.3	0.0
Mining	643.3	684.6	777.8	41.3	93.2	0.4	0.4	0.5	0.6	1.3
Construction	6,016.5	7,492.2	7,792.4	1,475.7	300.2	4.2	4.6	4.6	2.2	0.4
Manufacturing	11,847.9	12,839.5	12,394.7	991.6	-444.8	8.3	7.9	7.3	0.8	-0.4
Services-providing	113,521.5	130,693.4	137,150.7	17,171.9	6,457.3	79.4	80.3	81.2	1.4	0.5
Utilities	560.1	549.0	506.7	-11.1	-42.3	0.4	0.3	0.3	-0.2	-0.8
Wholesale trade	5,520.9	5,903.4	5,801.3	382.5	-102.1	3.9	3.6	3.4	0.7	-0.2
Retail trade	14,527.6	15,644.2	15,275.9	1,116.6	-368.3	10.2	9.6	9.0	0.7	-0.2
Transportation & warehousing	4,224.7	5,618.1	5,944.1	1,393.4	326.0	3.0	3.5	3.5	2.9	0.6
Information	2,803.8	2,859.4	2,853.2	55.6	-6.2	2.0	1.8	1.7	0.2	0.0
Financial activities	7,838.0	8,746.0	8,799.9	908.0	53.9	5.5	5.4	5.2	1.1	0.1
Professional & business services	16,633.8	21,313.1	22,831.4	4,679.3	1,518.3	11.6	13.1	13.5	2.5	0.7
Educational services	3,090.5	3,764.5	4,230.0	674.0	465.5	2.2	2.3	2.5	2.0	1.2
Health care & social assistance	16,539.8	20,412.6	23,491.7	3,872.8	3,079.1	11.6	12.5	13.9	2.1	1.4
Leisure & hospitality	13,077.5	16,575.9	17,691.5	3,498.4	1,115.6	9.1	10.2	10.5	2.4	0.7
Other services	6,150.1	6,713.8	6,994.7	563.7	280.9	4.3	4.1	4.1	0.9	0.4
Federal government	2,832.0	2,834.0	2,650.4	2.0	-183.6	2.0	1.7	1.6	0.0	-0.7
State & local government	19,722.7	19,759.4	20,080.0	36.7	320.6	13.8	12.1	11.9	0.0	0.2
Agriculture, forestry, fishing & hunting[3]	2,011.9	2,303.6	2,265.1	291.7	-38.6	1.4	1.4	1.3	1.4	-0.2
Agriculture wage & salary	1,175.7	1,565.2	1,600.5	389.5	35.3	0.8	1.0	0.9	2.9	0.2
Agriculture self-employed & unpaid family workers	836.2	738.4	664.5	-97.8	-73.9	0.6	0.5	0.4	-1.2	-1.0
Nonagriculture self-employed & unpaid family workers	8,995.3	8,782.3	8,454.1	-213.0	-328.2	6.3	5.4	5.0	-0.2	-0.4

[1] Employment data for wage and salary workers are from the BLS Current Employment Statistics survey, which counts jobs, whereas self-employed, unpaid family workers, and agriculture, forestry, fishing, and hunting are from the Current Population Survey (household survey), which counts workers.

[2] Includes wage and salary data from the Current Employment Statistics survey, except private households, which is from the Current Populations Survey. Logging workers are excluded.

[3] Includes agriculture, forestry, fishing, and hunting data from the Current Population Survey, except logging, which is from Current Employment Statistics survey. Government wage and salary workers are excluded.

Source: U.S. Bureau of Labor Statistics
Plunkett Research,® Ltd.
www.plunkettresearch.com

Number of People Employed and Unemployed, U.S.: July 2020 vs. July 2021

(Persons 16 & Older; Numbers In Thousands; Not Seasonally Adjusted)

Occupation	Employed		Unemployed		Unemp. Rates (%)	
	Jul-20	Jul-21	Jul-20	Jul-21	Jul-20	Jul-21
Total*	**144,492**	**153,596**	**16,882**	**9,221**	**10.5**	**5.7**
Management, professional and related	62,494	64,179	4,400	2,203	6.6	3.3
Management, business and financial operations	26,928	28,000	1,460	753	5.1	2.6
Professional and related	35,566	36,180	2,940	1,450	7.6	3.9
Service	21,929	25,695	4,249	2,053	16.2	7.4
Sales and office	29,472	29,527	3,384	1,748	10.3	5.6
Sales and related	14,234	14,378	1,734	916	10.9	6.0
Office and administrative support	15,238	15,149	1,650	832	9.8	5.2
Natural resources, construction and maintenance	13,183	14,549	1,339	957	9.2	6.2
Farming, fishing and forestry	983	1,129	78	116	7.3	9.3
Construction and extraction	7,675	8,312	876	660	10.2	7.4
Installation, maintenance and repair	4,524	5,107	386	180	7.9	3.4
Production, transportation and material moving	17,414	19,646	2,753	1,559	13.7	7.4
Production	7,315	8,254	928	490	11.3	5.6
Transportation and material moving	10,100	11,392	1,825	1,070	15.3	8.6

* Persons with no previous work experience and persons whose last job was in the Armed Forces are included in the unemployed total.

Note: Updated population controls are introduced annually with the release of January data.

Source: U.S. Bureau of Labor Statistics
Plunkett Research,® Ltd.
www.plunkettresearch.com

U.S. Labor Force Ages 16 to 24 Years Old by School Enrollment, Educational Attainment, Sex, Race & Ethnicity: October 2020

(Numbers in Thousands, Latest Year Available)	Civilian non-institutional population	Total in Labor Force	Percent of Populace	Employed		Unemployed		Not in Labor Force
				Total	Percent of Populace	Number	Rate (%)	
Total, 16 to 24 years	37,468	20,597	55	18,264	48.7	2,334	11.3	16,870
Educational Attainment								
Enrolled in school	21,012	7,564	36.0	6,710	31.9	855	11.3	13,448
Enrolled in high school[1]	9,214	2,097	22.8	1,832	19.9	266	12.7	7,116
Men	4,757	991	20.8	826	17.4	165	16.6	3,766
Women	4,456	1,106	24.8	1,005	22.6	101	9.1	3,350
White	6,704	1,657	24.7	1,481	22.1	176	10.6	5,047
Black or African American	1,416	275	19.4	212	14.9	64	23.1	1,141
Asian	512	68	13.3	62	12.1	6	-	444
Hispanic or Latino ethnicity	440	51	11.6	47	10.7	4	-	389
Enrolled in college	11,798	5,467	46.3	4,878	41.3	589	10.8	6,331
Enrolled in 2-year college	2,703	1,503	55.6	1,324	49.0	178	11.9	1,200
Enrolled in 4-year college	9,095	3,964	43.6	3,554	39.1	410	10.4	5,131
Full-time students	10,395	4,316	41.5	3,865	37.2	451	10.4	6,079
Part-time students	1,403	1,151	82.0	1,013	72.2	138	12.0	252
Men	5,530	2,548	46.1	2,405	43.5	143	5.6	2,982
Women	6,544	3,252	49.7	2,931	44.8	321	9.9	3,292
White	8,495	4,165	49.0	3,790	44.6	375	9.0	4,330
Black or African American	1,589	689	43.4	579	36.5	110	16.0	899
Asian	1,185	393	33.2	332	28.0	61	15.6	792
Hispanic or Latino ethnicity	2,492	1,337	53.7	1,192	47.8	145	10.9	1,155
Not enrolled in school	16,456	13,033	79.2	11,554	70.2	1,479	11.3	3,423
16 to 19 years	3,396	2,284	67.3	1,957	57.6	327	14.3	1,112
20 to 24 years	13,059	10,748	82.3	9,597	73.5	1,152	10.7	2,311
Sex								
Men	8,796	7,256	82.5	6,367	72.4	889	12.3	1,540
Less than a high school diploma	1,165	778	66.8	699	59.9	80	10.2	387
High school graduates, no college[2]	4,414	3,597	81.5	3,100	70.2	498	13.8	817
Some college or associate degree	1,997	1,749	87.6	1,534	76.8	215	12.3	248
Bachelor's degree and higher[3]	1,219	1,131	92.8	1,034	84.8	97	8.6	88
Women	7,659	5,777	75.4	5,187	67.7	590	10.2	1,883
Less than a high school diploma	814	382	47.0	339	41.7	43	11.2	432
High school graduates, no college[2]	3,229	2,305	71.4	2,028	62.8	277	12.0	923
Some college or associate degree	2,038	1,656	81.3	1,499	73.6	157	9.5	382
Bachelor's degree and higher[3]	1,579	1,433	90.8	1,320	83.6	113	7.9	146
Race								
White	12,259	9,865	80.5	8,908	72.7	958	9.7	2,394
Black or African American	2,482	1,876	75.6	1,498	60.4	378	20.1	606
Asian	649	503	77.5	460	70.8	44	8.7	146
Hispanic or Latino ethnicity	4,172	3,157	75.7	2,809	67.3	348	11.0	1,015

Note: Detail for the above race groups (White, Black or African American, and Asian) do not sum to totals because data are not presented for all races. Persons whose ethnicity is identified as Hispanic or Latino may be of any race. Updated population controls are introduced annually with the release of January data. Dash indicates no data or data that do not meet publication criteria (values not shown where base is less than 75,000).

[1] Includes a small number of persons who are in grades below high school. [2] Includes persons with a high school diploma or equivalent. [3] Includes persons with bachelor's, master's, professional, and doctoral degrees.

Source: U.S. Bureau of Labor Statistics

Plunkett Research,® Ltd.

www.plunkettresearch.com

Retirement Benefits in the U.S.: Access, Participation and Take-Up Rates, March 2020

(All workers = 100 percent)

Characteristics	Private Industry			State/Local Government		
	Access	Particip-ation	Take-up Rate[1]	Access	Particip-ation	Take-up Rate[1]
All workers	67%	51%	76%	91%	83%	90%
Worker Characteristics						
Management, professional and related	84%	71%	85%	94%	84%	90%
Service	41%	25%	61%	85%	78%	92%
Sales and office	73%	52%	71%	91%	83%	91%
Natural resources, construction and maintenance	61%	48%	78%	97%	92%	94%
Production, transportation and material moving	70%	54%	77%	90%	83%	91%
Full time	77%	61%	80%	99%	90%	91%
Part time	39%	20%	52%	45%	39%	87%
Union	91%	82%	89%	97%	89%	91%
Nonunion	65%	48%	74%	86%	78%	90%
Wage percentiles[2]						
Lowest 25 percent	42%	22%	52%	78%	69%	89%
Lowest 10 percent	29%	14%	48%	70%	61%	87%
Second 25 percent	67%	48%	72%	94%	85%	91%
Third 25 percent	79%	64%	81%	98%	89%	91%
Highest 25 percent	88%	78%	89%	97%	88%	91%
Highest 10 percent	90%	81%	90%	96%	87%	90%
Establishment Characteristics						
1 to 99 workers	53%	37%	69%	88%	83%	95%
1 to 49 workers	49%	34%	69%	85%	80%	94%
50 to 99 workers	69%	46%	68%	91%	87%	95%
100 workers or more	83%	67%	81%	92%	83%	89%
100 to 499 workers	80%	60%	76%	91%	84%	92%
500 workers or more	88%	77%	88%	93%	82%	88%

Note: Benefits may include defined benefit pension plans as well as defined contribution retirement plans. Workers are considered as having access or as participating if they have access to or participate in at least one of these plan types. Farm and private household workers, the self-employed and Federal government workers are excluded from the survey.

[1] The take-up rate is a rounded estimate of the percentage of workers with access to a plan who participate in the plan.

[2] Surveyed occupations are classified into wage categories based on the average wage for the occupation, which may include workers with earnings both above and below the threshold. The categories were formed using percentile estimates generated using wage data for March 2019.

Source: U.S. Bureau of Labor Statistics
Plunkett Research,® Ltd.
www.plunkettresearch.com

Top 30 U.S. Occupations by Numerical Change in Job Growth: 2019-2029

(By Thousands of Employees)

Occupation	Employment		Change, 2019-29		Median annual wage, 2020*
	2019	2029	Number	Percent	
Total, all occupations	162,795.6	168,834.7	6,039.2	3.7	$41,950
Wind turbine service technicians	7.0	11.3	4.3	60.7	$56,230
Nurse practitioners	211.3	322.0	110.7	52.4	$111,680
Solar photovoltaic installers	12.0	18.1	6.1	50.5	$46,470
Occupational therapy assistants	47.1	63.5	16.3	34.6	$62,940
Statisticians	42.7	57.5	14.8	34.6	$92,270
Home health and personal care aides	3,439.7	4,599.2	1159.5	33.7	$27,080
Physical therapist assistants	98.7	130.9	32.2	32.6	$59,770
Medical and health services managers	422.3	555.5	133.2	31.5	$104,280
Physician assistants	125.5	164.8	39.3	31.3	$115,390
Information security analysts	131.0	171.9	40.9	31.2	$103,590
Data scientists and mathematical science occupations, all other	33.2	43.4	10.3	30.9	$98,230
Derrick operators, oil and gas	12.0	15.7	3.7	30.5	$47,920
Rotary drill operators, oil and gas	20.9	26.6	5.6	26.9	$53,820
Roustabouts, oil and gas	58.5	73.1	14.7	25.1	$39,420
Speech-language pathologists	162.6	203.1	40.5	24.9	$80,480
Operations research analysts	105.1	131.3	26.1	24.8	$86,200
Substance abuse, behavioral disorder, and mental health counselors	319.4	398.4	79.0	24.7	$47,660
Forest fire inspectors and prevention specialists	2.3	2.8	0.5	24.3	$42,150
Cooks, restaurant	1,417.3	1,744.6	327.3	23.1	$28,800
Animal caretakers	300.7	369.5	68.8	22.9	$26,080
Service unit operators, oil and gas	51.7	63.6	11.8	22.9	$47,380
Marriage and family therapists	66.2	80.9	14.8	22.3	$51,340
Computer numerically controlled tool programmers	25.7	31.3	5.6	21.9	$57,740
Film and video editors	38.3	46.5	8.3	21.6	$67,250
Software developers and software quality assurance analysts and testers	1,469.2	1,785.2	316.0	21.5	$110,140
Genetic counselors	2.6	3.2	0.6	21.5	$85,700
Physical therapist aides	50.6	61.3	10.8	21.3	$28,450
Massage therapists	166.7	201.1	34.4	20.6	$43,620
Health specialties teachers, postsecondary	254.0	306.1	52.1	20.5	$99,090
Helpers--extraction workers	16.9	20.3	3.4	20.2	$37,860

* Data are from the Occupational Employment Statistics program, U.S. Bureau of Labor Statistics. Wage data cover non-farm wage and salary workers and do not cover the self-employed, owners and partners in unincorporated firms, or household workers.

Source: U.S. Bureau of Labor Statistics
Plunkett Research,® Ltd.
www.plunkettresearch.com

Top 30 U.S. Fastest Growing Occupations by Percent Change in Job Growth: 2019-2029

(Employment in Thousands)

Occupation	Employment 2019	Employment 2029	Change, 2019-29 Number	Change, 2019-29 Percent	Median annual wage, 2020*
Total, all occupations	162,795.6	168,834.7	6,039.2	3.7	$41,950
Wind turbine service technicians	7.0	11.3	4.3	60.7	$56,230
Nurse practitioners	211.3	322.0	110.7	52.4	$111,680
Solar photovoltaic installers	12.0	18.1	6.1	50.5	$46,470
Occupational therapy assistants	47.1	63.5	16.3	34.6	$62,940
Statisticians	42.7	57.5	14.8	34.6	$92,270
Home health and personal care aides	3,439.7	4,599.2	1,159.5	33.7	$27,080
Physical therapist assistants	98.7	130.9	32.2	32.6	$59,770
Medical and health services managers	422.3	555.5	133.2	31.5	$104,280
Physician assistants	125.5	164.8	39.3	31.3	$115,390
Information security analysts	131.0	171.9	40.9	31.2	$103,590
Data scientists and mathematical science occupations, all other	33.2	43.4	10.3	30.9	$98,230
Derrick operators, oil and gas	12.0	15.7	3.7	30.5	$47,920
Rotary drill operators, oil and gas	20.9	26.6	5.6	26.9	$53,820
Roustabouts, oil and gas	58.5	73.1	14.7	25.1	$39,420
Speech-language pathologists	162.6	203.1	40.5	24.9	$80,480
Operations research analysts	105.1	131.3	26.1	24.8	$86,200
Substance abuse, behavioral disorder, and mental health counselors	319.4	398.4	79.0	24.7	$47,660
Forest fire inspectors and prevention specialists	2.3	2.8	0.5	24.3	$42,150
Cooks, restaurant	1,417.3	1,744.6	327.3	23.1	$28,800
Animal caretakers	300.7	369.5	68.8	22.9	$26,080
Service unit operators, oil and gas	51.7	63.6	11.8	22.9	$47,380
Marriage and family therapists	66.2	80.9	14.8	22.3	$51,340
Computer numerically controlled tool programmers	25.7	31.3	5.6	21.9	$57,740
Film and video editors	38.3	46.5	8.3	21.6	$67,250
Software developers and software quality assurance analysts and testers	1,469.2	1,785.2	316.0	21.5	$110,140
Genetic counselors	2.6	3.2	0.6	21.5	$85,700
Physical therapist aides	50.6	61.3	10.8	21.3	$28,450
Massage therapists	166.7	201.1	34.4	20.6	$43,620
Health specialties teachers, postsecondary	254.0	306.1	52.1	20.5	$99,090
Helpers--extraction workers	16.9	20.3	3.4	20.2	$37,860

* Data are from the Occupational Employment Statistics program, U.S. Bureau of Labor Statistics. Wage data cover non-farm wage and salary workers and do not cover the self-employed, owners and partners in unincorporated firms, or household workers.

Occupations with the Largest Expected Employment Increases, U.S.: 2019-2029

(By Increase in Number Employed, in Thousands)

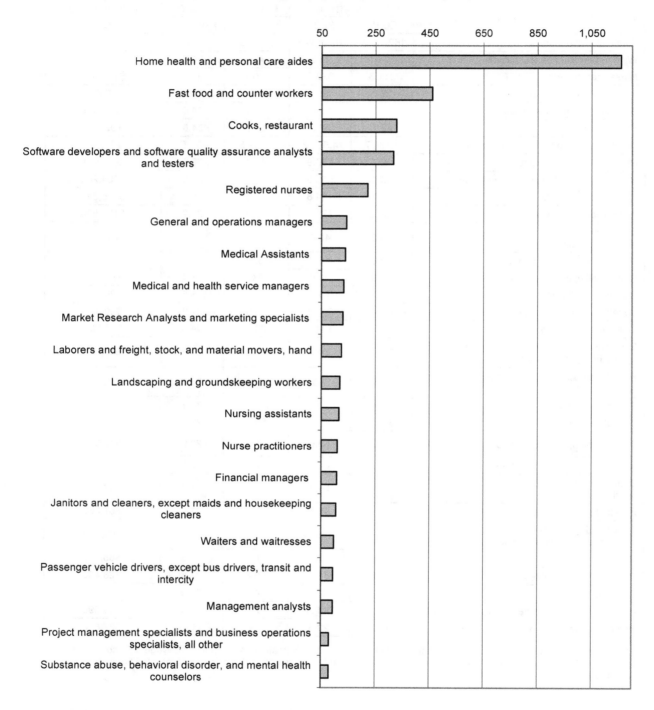

Source: U.S. Bureau of Labor Statistics
Plunkett Research,® Ltd.
www.plunkettresearch.com

Occupations with the Fastest Expected Decline, U.S.: 2019-2029

(In Thousands)

Occupation	Employment		Change, 2019-29		Median Annual Wage, 2019*
	2019	2029	Number	Percent	
Total, all occupations	161,037.7	169,435.9	8.4	5.2	39,810
Locomotive firers	0.5	0.2	-0.4	-68.3	—
Respiratory therapy technicians	9.3	3.9	-5.3	-57.5	—
Parking enforcement workers	8.6	5.4	-3.1	-36.7	40,920
Word processors and typists	60.4	40.0	-20.4	-33.8	40,340
Watch repairers	3.0	2.1	-0.9	-29.6	42,520
Electronic equipment installers and repairers, motor vehicles	11.0	7.9	-3.1	-28.6	37,380
Telephone operators	5.7	4.1	-1.6	-28.4	35,750
Cutters and trimmers, hand	10.7	7.7	-3.0	-28.4	30,200
Postmasters and mail superintendents	13.3	9.6	-3.7	-27.5	76,900
Mine shuttle car operators	1.7	1.3	-0.4	-25.3	—
Computer operators	36.8	28.0	-8.9	-24.1	—
Switchboard operators, including answering service	73.4	55.9	-17.5	-23.8	30,610
Postal service mail sorters, processors, and processing machine operators	99.7	76.0	-23.7	-23.8	60,140
Data entry keyers	187.3	143.9	-43.4	-23.2	33,490
Aircraft structure, surfaces, rigging, and systems assemblers	45.1	35.2	-9.9	-22.0	54,210
Coil winders, tapers, and finishers	12.3	9.7	-2.7	-21.6	36,520
Photographic process workers and processing machine operators	17.1	13.4	-3.6	-21.3	32,280
Pressers, textile, garment, and related materials	39.9	31.4	-8.5	-21.2	24,190
Legal secretaries	180.1	142.5	-37.6	-20.9	47,300
Prepress technicians and workers	29.9	23.7	-6.2	-20.8	40,510
Milling and planing machine setters, operators, and tenders, metal and plastic	19.8	15.7	-4.1	-20.7	43,210
Drilling and boring machine tool setters, operators, and tenders, metal and plastic	11.6	9.2	-2.4	-20.5	38,910
Postal service clerks	75.7	60.7	-15.0	-19.8	48,330
Postal service mail carriers	328.7	263.7	-65.1	-19.8	51,310
Executive secretaries and executive administrative assistants	622.5	499.4	-123.0	-19.8	60,890
Forging machine setters, operators, and tenders, metal and plastic	18.6	15.0	-3.6	-19.5	39,670
Textile bleaching and dyeing machine operators and tenders	9.7	7.9	-1.9	-19.4	29,460
Timing device assemblers and adjusters	0.8	0.6	-0.2	-19.3	35,080
Grinding and polishing workers, hand	30.7	24.8	-5.9	-19.2	30,600
Textile knitting and weaving machine setters, operators, and tenders	22.1	17.9	-4.2	-18.9	29,980

* Data are from the Occupational Employment Statistics program, U.S. Bureau of Labor Statistics. Wage data cover non-farm wage and salary workers and do not cover the self-employed, owners and partners in unincorporated firms, or household workers.

Chapter 3

RESEARCH: 7 KEYS FOR JOB SEEKERS

How to use your library, college placement office, the internet and other resources
to become well-informed about a company and its industry
before you ask for an interview

Research is the key to finding appropriate job openings, targeting the best possible employers and performing well when you go to job interviews. Learn what's unique about a company compared to other firms in its industry. Learn why it's prospering–or why it isn't. Where is this company going? Is it favored by stock investors? Is it privately-owned by a family, or has it been acquired by private equity investors who plan to resell it over the mid-term? What are its hottest-selling products and services? Is it investing in research and new facilities so that it may prosper in the future? Also, as many people who have been laid off from failing firms have learned the hard way, determining a company's level of financial stability can be one of the most important factors in making a career decision.

The more you're willing to dig deep at the library or your college's career planning office, and the more adept you are at using the internet for research, the better your chances of success in a job search. If you are willing to ask questions of knowledgeable businesspeople and of employees who currently work for your target employers, you will enhance your job search even further. The two secrets to successful job research are tenacity and focus. Know what to look for and where to find it.

Once you've landed an interview, you should research both the prospective employer and its industry even further. In this manner, you'll know what questions to ask before you agree to take the job, and you'll present yourself as a knowledgeable potential hire who is truly interested in the company and its business.

Here are the seven keys for research that can lead you to a great employer:

1) Financial Stability
Check bond ratings, credit ratings, debt level, growth in sales and growth in profits, along with the views of stock analysts and business journalists.

2) Growth Plans
Look for new plants, stores or offices to be opened; new technologies, products or divisions to be launched; or plans for strategic acquisitions. (See 3, 4 and 5 below.) Is the employer's growth strategy focused primarily on offshoring work to overseas locations or outsourcing work to outside services providers? Or, does it have a balanced growth strategy that will create good opportunities in its American operations?

3) Research and Development Programs
If the company is a major manufacturer or a technology-based firm, then you should investigate how it invests in R&D (research and development). Is its research and development budget growing? For many types of companies, research is a vital investment in the future.

4) Product Launch and Production
Does the company have the ability to successfully launch new products and services (see 5 below) or to invest in and utilize cutting-edge technologies needed to maintain a competitive edge?

5) Marketing and Distribution Methods
Does the firm utilize an in-house sales force? Does it work through outside dealers and distribution partners? What are its advertising methods? Is it increasing its market share, or are competitors taking customers away? Is the company growing its international sales? Is it adept at using the internet as a powerful sales tool? Is it successful at selling into vital international markets?

6) Employee Benefits

Are wealth-building benefit plans offered? Will the company match all or part of your deposits to a 401(k) savings plan? Check for tuition reimbursement, pension plans, profit sharing, stock ownership plans, discount stock purchase plans, stock options or performance-based bonuses.

7) Quality-of-Work Factors

Does the company offer working from home, continual training, wellness programs, child care, elder care support, promote-from-within policies, flexible work schedules, performance reviews, product discounts or on-site health clubs? Is it a corporate culture that fits your lifestyle?

As a serious job seeker, you should conduct in-depth research and make detailed notes about these key factors for each firm you are considering. Then compare each company's finances, plans and programs to others in the same industry. You'll begin to see what makes some firms outstanding and why those outstanding companies are the best places to make a career investment.

Your research goal should be twofold: First, determine whether this is a firm you want to work for. Are the salaries and benefits appealing? Are layoffs likely? Is it planning to expand its workforce in lower-cost nations like India and then lay off U.S. employees? Or, is the company planning to increase its number of U.S.-based facilities and boost its domestic employment? Is the firm growing steadily? A growing company will offer opportunities for you to advance when it launches new locations, services, technologies or product lines. Second, develop a personal understanding of both the company and its industry so you can better sell yourself as a potential employee.

Other Considerations:

Women and Minorities:

Certain industries have a greater tendency to offer advancement opportunities for women or minorities. Historically, the banking and insurance segments have tended to promote both women and minorities, as have retailing, electric utilities, apparel, consumer goods, packaged food and beverages, education, publishing and telephone companies.

Some technology companies have been terrific places for women who want to advance, and many tech companies, such as Hewlett-Packard, IBM, Yahoo, Xerox and eBay, have been known to post women to CEO spots.

Black Enterprise magazine publishes an annual list of the "Power in the Boardroom: Registry of Black Corporate Board Members," (see www.blackenterprise.com). Meanwhile, the Executive Leadership Council, www.elcinfo.com, a Washington, D.C.-based nonprofit group that conducts programs aimed at filling more executive posts with African Americans, has a unique statistic to report. Its membership is composed of senior-level black executives who have jobs that are no more than three levels below the CEO spot at Fortune 500 companies. When the group was founded in 1986, it had only a handful of members. Today, its membership is comprised of hundreds of people employed in high-level executive jobs at major corporations (about one-third of them are women).

The Hispanic Association on Corporate Responsibility (www.hacr.org) promotes Hispanic advancement in the areas of employment, procurement, philanthropy and governance. Another nonprofit agency, National Hispanic Corporate Achievers (hispanicachievers.org), provides an educational forum for Hispanics working for Fortune 1000 companies.

Tips on Using Business Magazines, Newspapers and Trade Journals to Find Job Leads and Do Employer Research

Many job seekers overlook the tremendous advantages offered by industry magazines (called "trade journals") and other publications when conducting research.

Industry-specific trade journals frequently have classified ads in the back that list job openings. An example of a great magazine to study is American Banker, which can be found at major libraries. Additional information is available at www.americanbanker.com.

Journalists at trade journals and business newspapers continuously interview industry-leading executives regarding their companies' growth plans. New projects and company expansion plans described in these articles provide terrific job leads.

You can also get great contact information from these publications. Read the latest business stories about companies and industries that interest you and you will learn vital information. Best of all, you can glean from stories and interviews the names and titles of executives who lead projects, divisions and subsidiaries.

There are literally hundreds of these trade journals—at least one for each industry sector and sometimes dozens covering the largest industries.

Other great resources include business newspapers such as the Dallas/Ft. Worth Business Journal, The Wall Street Journal, the business pages of major newspapers like The New York Times and publications written for major investors like Investor's Business Daily. At www.bizjournals.com, you can gain access to news stories from business journals from all over the U.S.

Quality-of-Life Benefits:

Many companies offer benefits that help employees balance their personal and professional lives. The concept is that employees who are healthy and comfortable with their personal and family lives make better, more productive employees. To that end, many companies include fitness programs and family services such as extended maternity leaves and child care or elder care, whether on-site or off-site in the form of referral services. Other popular family-friendly benefits include flextime, flexible benefits spending accounts, adoption assistance and telecommuting. In many cases, benefits are listed on employers' web sites.

Work-Life has become a popular phrase for family-friendly benefits and programs among major employers such as Intel, Abbott Laboratories, Baxter International and Aramark. For additional information, you can study such organizations at WorldatWork (formerly the Alliance for Work-Life Progress) site at www.worldatwork.org.

Growth Potential and Job Stability:

A firm's growth potential should be among your top priorities. Companies are always trying to maintain or increase productivity, or the ratio of revenues per employee. If a company's sales are sliding, or if it is running out of cash, the job picture starts to collapse. A little extra research into a company's finances and true potential for growth might save you from a future layoff.

Of course, employers sometimes must resort to layoffs due to conditions outside of their control. The devastating economic recession that officially ran from late 2007 through early 2009 led to millions of layoffs in America. Even worse was the massive level of layoffs at the onset of the Coronavirus pandemic. Although 2021 was seeing massive hiring programs across a wide number of industries, the total number of workers in hospitality, including restaurants, hotels and cruise lines, is still below pre-Coronavirus days. Restaurants, for the most part, have been aggressively seeking new workers, but face shortages of applicants.

As a job seeker, you're forced to look out for your own best interests while you sort through thousands of potential employers in dozens of industries. This means that good research is vital. For example, if you put salary at the top of your list, you may have the wrong priorities. From time to time, some of the highest-paying firms have been among those cutting the largest numbers of employees. If you are looking for job stability, your biggest challenge is to pick companies that are more likely to hire now and less likely to have layoffs in the future. That's why a firm's growth outlook should be one of your guiding lights.

However, the goal is *internal* growth caused by expanding sales. Generally less appealing are firms that post a quick spike in growth through big mergers. (In many cases, merged companies lay off people who suddenly find themselves filling jobs duplicated in newly consolidated offices. Also, companies that grow excessively through acquisitions may be taking on loads of debt that can become hard to handle later. However, there are occasional exceptions to this rule, where firms are enjoying soaring demand for products or services and find it difficult to hire quickly enough to keep up.) Companies

that are growing rapidly through internal expansion include those opening new stores, distribution centers or offices, developing exciting new products, moving into new markets (including international markets) and creating hot new technologies, retail formats or services. Those types of expansion frequently mean great career opportunities, including the chance for rapid job promotion.

If you're tenacious, you can find opportunities where others will find only rejection. Identifying real prospects for growth takes more than a quick glance.

Here's an extremely important point for you to remember: You should also look for opportunities in growing divisions that serve special niches, even when the company as a whole is cutting jobs. For example, a firm's online division may be growing, even while its traditional business units are shrinking.

Additional key factors for strong corporate growth, and thereby the best job prospects, include:

1) Companies or divisions with a growing share of a promising market.

Management's ability to anticipate or create change in the marketplace makes for a growing company with great prospects. For example, Sam Walton revolutionized the department store business by realizing that consumers want everyday low prices on name-brand merchandise. He created Wal-Mart, while competitor Sears suffered by maintaining an old-fashioned policy of special sales events on private-label goods. Wal-Mart rapidly became one of the largest creators of new jobs in the private sector. Sears was forced to close multiple stores and slash its employee ranks.

Microsoft made its way to the top with unique products serving a soaring market when it developed highly functional software for personal computers. The software giant created thousands of millionaire employees through the immense increase in the value of its stock plans. HEB, an innovative grocer in Texas, has evolved continually over the decades, constantly introducing improvements to store layouts, and even creating an exciting new HEB Marketplace concept that is a retail industry leader. HEB has large numbers of job openings of many types on a continuous basis.

The point to these stories is that you shouldn't invest your career in a company with mediocre prospects. With perseverance, you can target your own list of employers that are posting growth due to competitive advantages or growing market demand. Your best bets are companies taking reasonable risks in order to move ahead. Those risks may include investments in advertising, research and development, new technology, improved techniques on the manufacturing floor, testing of new products and the opening of new retail store formats. For example, Genentech, now owned by drug giant Roche Holding, became a leader in the biotechnology field by risking vast amounts on research. Also, don't overlook the potential of the export market—many American firms find much of their growth by creating products and services that enjoy demand overseas as well as in the U.S.

2) Sales and profits: past and present.

The companies most likely to move along at a good clip are those with an exciting mid-term history. Firms with an average annual growth in sales of 10% to 15% or more over the past several years are generally very promising. Many small and mid-size firms grow at much faster rates and find themselves hiring continuously.

3) Beware of fads.

Unfortunately, a few companies post meteoric growth in businesses that turn out to be mere fads. The restaurant industry suffers from this problem on a regular basis. In recent years, companies selling bagels, frozen yogurt, rotisserie chicken and the like enjoyed impressive, nationwide growth only to collapse like a house of cards a couple of years later.

How to Find and Use Expert Opinions:

Superior sources used by sophisticated job researchers include reports written by: 1) analysts; 2) professional researchers and executives; and 3) journalists at business magazines and industry-specific web sites. Many major libraries have large collections of industry-specific "trade magazines" that can give you vital clues that competing job seekers will overlook. Virtually every industry is covered by one or two major websites and trade magazines that will give you leads to growing companies. Many articles in these resources contain the names of executives you may want to contact. Also, some trade magazines publish help-wanted ads in the back. It's easy to do an online search for trade magazines and industry-specific websites, and many of them are filled with extremely useful information. For example, a recent search on Google for "pet industry trade magazine" quickly turned up leads to the top magazines for that sector.

Next, move on to reports from experts. Marketing and investment professionals are looking for some of the same clues you should use as a job seeker, and reports written by full-time analysts who cover specific companies or industries can help you find firms that are growing and hiring. Search the internet for white papers, industry reports and studies that cover your industry of interest.

Professionally written market research can be found at Marketresearch.com, www.marketresearch.com. This market research broker charges varying fees for access to the reports. However, many of the reports are reasonably priced, and the insight you gain into industries, markets and leading companies can be extremely helpful. Web sites such as this offer the ability to search for reports by a wide variety of criteria, including company name and industry.

Internet Research Tip:

Be sure to create Google "Alerts" to follow your targeted employers and profession. Google will email results to you daily.

By going to the "more" link at the top of the Google home page, and then selecting "even more" from the drop-down list, you can access Google's "Alerts" tool. Here you can arrange to receive email updates on topics of your choice. For example, you can set a general alert about an industry or locale: sales jobs in California, for example. Or something like: opportunities in the American wireless industry. Or even: sales jobs at automobile dealers.

You can use alerts to track specific jobs or employers. For example: openings at Intel. Or: regional sales manager opening Los Angeles. Finally, don't forget that you may want to put a search phrase within quotes to get an exact match to part of your phrase. For example: "loan officer" wanted.

Other Basic Resources:

Annual Reports/10-Ks/S-1s: Companies that sell their stocks to the public, including most of the firms covered in this book, publish annual reports that contain a wealth of information. Annual reports and 10-Ks cover yearly results, financial statements, management practices and other vital information for publicly held firms. S-1s provide the same type of information on companies that are selling stock to the public for the first time. You can find copies of these reports at large libraries. Online, the best place to acquire this information is at typically at the "Investors" tab on the website of the company you are researching. Alternately, try the site of the U.S. Securities and Exchange Commission. They have a user-friendly service that enables you to search for companies and access their financial reports at www.sec.gov. (Look for the "Filings & Forms" section, and then see "Search for Company Filings.") Look especially at the five-year "summary financial statement" in the back of these reports. Also, look for growth in sales and earnings. If these are falling, dig deeper to find out why. Faltering sales or profits can lead to layoffs or to a merger with another firm (which could result in deep job cuts).

Also, you can find a wealth of financial information on publicly-traded firms at Yahoo! Finance, http://finance.yahoo.com.

See Chapter 4, "Important Contacts for Job Seekers," for additional places to get basic corporate data.

Tips on Utilizing Financial Documents Filed by Publicly Held Firms

(Access these documents at the Securities Exchange Commission, www.sec.gov.)

10-K (also called Annual Report on Form 10-K): This is an annual filing required by federal law. It follows a standard format. Information includes a complete description of the business, risk factors, historical financial data and much more. It is vital reading for job seekers. You will find that these documents are written in dry, legal language, but they contain a wealth of information.

DEF 14A Proxy Statement: This is an annual document that gives shareholders certain options to consider at their annual meeting. It names the firm's board of directors and top management. It also gives the dollar value and description of salaries, bonuses, pension plans, stock options and other benefits enjoyed by the company's five highest-paid officers. Job seekers can learn a great deal about a firm's management, pay and benefits from this document. Included is a list of the people or organizations that own more than 5% of the company's stock.

S-1: This is a new registration document for companies that are going public for the first time. In other words, they are creating an IPO (initial public offering). The information includes all of the data found in the 10-K and proxy statement filed annually by companies that have been public for more than one year.

10-Q: This is a quarterly report detailing a company's latest sales, profits and balance sheet.

Press Releases: Most mid-size to large companies issue a continual stream of press releases about new products, technologies and locations; new executive appointments; community activities and a wide variety of other company developments. The best place to find these is online, at the "News" tab on the company's own web site. You can also search popular business press release services such as www.prnewswire.com and www.businesswire.com.

More Ways to Research an Employer's Financial Stability and Growth Plans:

1) Check out its bond rating.

There's no sense in trying to become a financial analyst on your own. Use internet searches to look for the bond ratings of potential employers. These ratings are based on a company's ability to pay principal and interest when due. If you're considering a major corporation with a bond rating of less than BB (an indicator that a company's debt is riskier than "investment grade"), you should do a lot more investigating before you continue chasing a job at that company.

2) Talk to vendors and current employees.

Talk to employees who work for the employer, or talk to people who do business with it. No one knows what's really going on better than people who are on the scene. If there are problems that are not known by the media, or if there are exciting new developments that have not yet been announced, you may find out a lot just by asking around. While you're at it, ask about corporate culture—how well are employees treated?

Popular Job-Search Internet Sites

CareerBuilder   www.careerbuilder.com
(As of 2020, CareerBuilder was offering special, Coronavirus-era tools for job seekers)
Monster   www.monster.com
Indeed   www.indeed.com

Tips on Finding Information on Privately Held Employers

Our subscription service, Plunkett Research Online, and our printed Plunkett's industry almanacs, are among the world's most highly regarded sources of profiles of privately-held companies. Check with your library to see if you have access to these tools.

Study back-issue indexes and archives to major newspapers to see what journalists are reporting about a prospective private employer. Many libraries have recent issues of *The Wall Street Journal, The New York Times* and other important business newspapers. At major public and university libraries, you may be able to access online databases like ProQuest. These databases have excellent search engines that lead you into online archives of the best publications, including *The Wall Street Journal*, as well as many trade magazines and local business journals.

For smaller firms, go online and try American Journalism Review at www.newslink.org, where you'll be able to search news sites including hometown newspapers across the nation. Likewise, search local business newspapers at www.bizjournals.com, where you'll find links to dozens of major business weeklies like the *Houston Business Journal.*

Finally, consider investing in a credit report. If you really want reassurance, go to Experian SmartBusinessReports, www.smartbusinessreports.com. You can use its links to order a credit report on the employer. These reports are reasonably priced, and they can help you determine whether the company is paying its bills on time or has other problems. This could be vital in helping you determine whether to accept a job at a privately-held firm.

---

3) Use Internet search engines.

Look up your firm and industry in an internet search engine such as Google. (You may need to click on "News" instead of relying on a general web search.) There, you may find unusual articles that were recently written about a company's product breakthroughs, treatment of women or minorities, human interest stories, training programs or stories written from other unique slants.

4) Study other business books and guides.

Search at a library or at an online bookseller like Amazon.com for recent books regarding major companies. For example, if you want to apply to biotech leader Genentech for a job, don't fail to read *The Billion Dollar Molecule: One Company's Quest for the Perfect Drug*. With a little research, you can turn up many other excellent books about specific companies, from banks like Bank of America to publishers like Gannett.

Great Places for Industry Research

Plunkett Research, www.plunkettresearch.com. Go to the specific industry of your choice to see an overview of trends and statistics. At our subscription service, www.plunkettresearchonline.com, subscribers have access to thousands of pages of industry analysis, statistics, contacts and company profiles, along with multiple search and export tools.

Vault.com, www.vault.com. This site publishes insights about careers with hundreds of leading firms.

---

5) Explore industry-specific web sites.

In particular, study the leading industry associations for the sector in which you want to work. You will find listings of hundreds of the most important organizations, professional societies and resources, personally selected by our editors, in the almanacs published by Plunkett Research, Ltd., and in the contacts databases at Plunkett Research Online.

6) Research benefits and pension plans.

For additional information about corporate pension plans, start with the government agency charged with protecting and regulating pensions: the Pension Benefit Guaranty Corporation, 1200 K St. NW, Washington, D.C. 20005-4026, 202-326-4000, www.pbgc.gov. They can answer certain questions over the telephone.

The U.S. Department of Labor publishes a useful site titled Consumer Information on Retirement Plans, https://www.dol.gov/general/topic/retirement/consumerinf pension.

The Social Security Administration, 800-772-1213, www.ssa.gov, can provide you with information regarding your potential Social Security benefits.

NOTE: Generally, employees covered by wealth-building benefit plans do not fully own ("vest in") funds contributed on their behalf by the employer until as many as five years of service with that employer have passed. All pension plans are voluntary—that is, employers are not obligated to offer pensions.

Pension Plans: The type and generosity of these plans vary widely from firm to firm. Caution: Some employers refer to plans as "pension" or "retirement" plans when they are actually 401(k) savings plans that require a contribution by the employee.

Defined Benefit Pension Plans: Pension plans that do not require a contribution from the employee are infrequently offered. However, a few companies, particularly larger employers in high-profit-margin industries, offer defined benefit pension plans where the employee is guaranteed to receive a set pension benefit upon retirement. The amount of the benefit is determined by the years of service with the company and the employee's salary during the later years of employment. The longer a person works for the employer, the higher the retirement benefit. These defined benefit plans are funded entirely by the employer. The benefits, up to a reasonable limit, are guaranteed by the Federal Government's Pension Benefit Guaranty Corporation. These plans are not portable—if you leave the company, you cannot transfer your benefits into a different plan. Instead, upon retirement you will receive the benefits that vested during your service with the company. If your employer offers a pension plan, it must give you a "summary plan description" within 90 days of the date you join the plan. You can also request a "summary annual report" of the plan, and once every 12 months you may request an "individual benefit statement" accounting of your interest in the plan.

Defined Contribution Plans: These are quite different. They do not guarantee a certain amount of pension benefit. Instead, they set out circumstances under which the employer will make a contribution to a plan on your behalf. The most common example is the 401(k) savings plan. Pension benefits are not guaranteed under these plans.

Cash Balance Pension Plans: These plans were recently invented. They are hybrid plans—part defined benefit and part defined contribution. Many employers have converted their older defined benefit plans into cash balance plans. The employer makes deposits (or credits a given amount of money) on the employee's behalf, usually based on a percentage of pay. Employee accounts grow based on a predetermined interest benchmark, such as the interest rate on Treasury Bonds. There are some advantages to these plans, particularly for younger workers: a) The benefits, up to a reasonable limit, are guaranteed by the Pension Benefit Guaranty Corporation. b) Benefits are portable—they can be moved to another plan when the employee changes companies. c) Younger workers and those who spend a shorter number of years with an employer may receive higher benefits than they would under a traditional defined benefit plan.

ESOP Stock Plan (Employees' Stock Ownership Plan): This type of plan is becoming rare, but it can be of great value to employees. Typically, the plan borrows money from a bank and uses those funds to purchase a large block of the corporation's stock. The corporation makes contributions to the plan over a period of time, and the stock purchase loan is eventually paid off. The value of the plan grows significantly as long as the market price of the stock holds up. Qualified employees are allocated a share of the plan based on their length of service and their level of salary. Under federal regulations, participants in ESOPs are allowed to diversify their account holdings in set percentages that rise as the employee ages and gains years of service with the company. In this manner, not all of the employee's assets are tied up in the employer's stock.

Savings Plan, 401(k): Under this type of plan, employees make a tax-deferred deposit into an account. In the best plans, the company makes annual matching donations to the employees' accounts, typically in some proportion to deposits made by the employees themselves. A good plan will match one-half of employee deposits of up to 6% of wages. For example, an employee earning $50,000 yearly might deposit $3,000 (6%) into the plan. The company will match one-half of the employee's deposit, or $1,500. The plan grows on a tax-deferred basis, similar to an IRA. A very generous plan will match 100% of employee deposits. However, some plans do not call for the employer to make a matching deposit at all. Other plans call for a matching contribution to be made at the discretion of the firm's board of directors. Actual terms of these plans vary widely from firm to firm. Generally, these savings plans allow employees to deposit as much as 15% of salary into the plan on a tax-deferred basis. However, the portion that the company uses to calculate its matching deposit is generally limited to a maximum of 6%. Employees should take care to diversify the holdings in their 401(k) accounts, and most people should seek professional guidance or investment management for their accounts. (Note: when profits are down, many employers exercise their right to suspend their contributions to 401(k)s. Employees may continue to make contributions, but they will not be matched by the employer in these cases.)

Stock Purchase Plan: Qualified employees may purchase the company's common stock at a price below its market value under a specific plan. Typically, the employee is limited to investing a small percentage of wages in this plan. The discount may range from 5% to 15%. Some of these plans allow for deposits to be made through regular monthly payroll deductions. However, new accounting rules for corporations, along with other factors, are leading many companies to curtail these plans—dropping the discount allowed, cutting the maximum yearly stock purchase or otherwise making the plans less generous or appealing.

Profit Sharing: Qualified employees are awarded an annual amount equal to some portion of a company's profits. In a very generous plan, the pool of money awarded to employees would be 15% of profits. Typically, this money is deposited into a long-term retirement account. Caution: Some employers refer to plans as "profit sharing" when they are actually 401(k) savings plans. True profit sharing plans are rarely offered.

Plunkett Research Online and Plunkett's Industry Reference Books:

1) Internet-Based Services: Plunkett Research Online is a reference service that is subscribed to by the nation's leading university placement offices, libraries and information offices. You can use it to filter prospective employers by location, industry, size and more. You can then export contact information for those companies into spreadsheets or text files. In addition, you can use the site to research the latest editions of our industry analysis. Many additional tools for job seekers are included. For an extensive online tour, see www.plunkettresearch.com.

2) Plunkett's Industry Almanacs: Plunkett Research also publishes industry-specific almanacs for the world's most vital industries. They are available in both printed and eBook editions. These are top-notch resources for job seekers.

Industry-Specific Books from Plunkett Research:

- Plunkett's Advertising & Branding Industry Almanac
- Plunkett's Aerospace, Aircraft, Satellites & Drones Industry Almanac
- Plunkett's Airline, Hotel & Travel Industry Almanac
- Plunkett's Almanac of Middle Market Companies
- Plunkett's Apparel, Shoes & Textiles Industry Almanac
- Plunkett's Artificial Intelligence (AI) & Machine Learning Industry Almanac
- Plunkett's Automobile Industry Almanac
- Plunkett's Banking, Mortgages & Credit Industry Almanac
- Plunkett's Biotech, Pharmaceuticals & Genetics Industry Almanac
- Plunkett's Chemicals, Coatings & Plastics Industry Almanac
- Plunkett's Computers, Hardware & Software Industry Almanac
- Plunkett's Consulting Industry Almanac
- Plunkett's Consumer Products, Cosmetics, Hair & Personal Services Industry Almanac
- Plunkett's Cybersecurity, Digital ID & Online Fraud Industry Almanac
- Plunkett's E-Commerce & Internet Business Almanac
- Plunkett's Education, EdTech and MOOCs Industry Almanac
- Plunkett's Energy Industry Almanac
- Plunkett's Engineering & Research Industry Almanac
- Plunkett's Entertainment. Movie, Publishing & Media Industry Almanac

- Plunkett's FinTech, Cryptocurrency & Electronic Payments Industry Almanac
- Plunkett's Food Industry Almanac
- Plunkett's Games, Apps & Social Media Industry Almanac
- Plunkett's Green Technology Industry Almanac
- Plunkett's Health Care Industry Almanac
- Plunkett's Insurance Industry Almanac
- Plunkett's Internet of Things (IoT) & Data Analytics Industry Almanac
- Plunkett's Investment & Securities Industry Almanac
- Plunkett's Manufacturing, Automation & Robotics Industry Almanac
- Plunkett's Outsourcing & Offshoring Industry Almanac
- Plunkett's Real Estate & Construction Industry Almanac
- Plunkett's Solar Power, Wind Power & Renewable Energy Industry Almanac
- Plunkett's Restaurant & Hospitality Industry Almanac
- Plunkett's Retail Industry Almanac
- Plunkett's Sharing & Gig Economy, Freelance Workers & On-Demand Delivery Almanac
- Plunkett's Sports & Recreation Industry Almanac
- Plunkett's Telecommunications Industry Almanac
- Plunkett's Transportation, Supply Chain & Logistics Industry Almanac
- Plunkett's Wireless & Cellular Telephone Industry Almanac

Publications from Plunkett Research Written Especially for Job Seekers:

- The Almanac of American Employers
- Plunkett's Companion to the Almanac of American Employers

Our books will give you in-depth coverage of specific industries and the leading firms in those industries, along with trends and developments in technology and services. You will find these books in public and academic libraries, college placement offices, human resources offices, corporate libraries and government agency libraries. For sample chapters and additional details, you can preview as well as purchase these books at www.plunkettresearch.com.

The Almanac of American Employers provides profiles and detailed listings of 500 hand-picked, U.S. employers of 2,500 employees or more in size

Plunkett's Companion to The Almanac of American Employers is our book that provides profiles on 500 additional, rapidly growing corporate employers. This companion book covers smaller firms than those in the main volume of *The Almanac of American Employers*.

Chapter 4

IMPORTANT CONTACTS FOR JOB SEEKERS

Contents:

1) Accountants & CPAs Associations
2) Advertising/Marketing Associations
3) Aerospace & Defense Industry Associations
4) Airline & Air Cargo Industry Associations
5) Alternative Energy-Ethanol
6) Alternative Energy-Solar
7) Alternative Energy-Wind
8) Banking Industry Associations
9) Biotechnology & Biological Industry Associations
10) Booksellers Associations
11) Broadcasting, Cable, Radio & TV Associations
12) Careers-Airlines/Flying
13) Careers-Apparel
14) Careers-Banking
15) Careers-Biotech
16) Careers-Computers/Technology
17) Careers-Contract & Freelance
18) Careers-First Time Jobs/New Grads
19) Careers-General Job Listings
20) Careers-Health Care
21) Careers-Job Listings for Seniors
22) Careers-Job Listings Hong Kong, China, Singapore, Asia
23) Careers-Job Reference Tools
24) Careers-Restaurants
25) Careers-Science
26) Careers-Sports
27) Careers-Video Games Industry
28) Chemicals Industry Associations
29) Communications Professional Associations
30) Computer & Electronics Industry Associations
31) Consulting Industry Associations
32) Consulting Industry Resources
33) Corporate Information Resources
34) Disabling Conditions
35) Electronic Health Records/Continuity of Care Records
36) Energy Associations-Electric Power
37) Energy Associations-Natural Gas
38) Energy Associations-Other
39) Energy Associations-Petroleum, Exploration, Production, etc.
40) Engineering, Research & Scientific Associations
41) Entertainment & Amusement Associations-General
42) Film & Theater Associations
43) Fitness Industry Associations
44) Food Industry Associations, General
45) Food Industry Resources, General
46) Food Processor Industry Associations
47) Food Service Industry Associations
48) Games Industry Associations
49) Grocery Industry Associations
50) Health & Nutrition Associations
51) Health Care Business & Professional Associations
52) Health Insurance Industry Associations
53) Hearing & Speech
54) Hotel/Lodging Associations
55) Human Resources Industry Associations
56) Industry Research/Market Research
57) Insurance Industry Associations
58) Insurance Industry Associations-Agents & Brokers
59) Investment Industry Associations
60) Magazines, Business & Financial
61) MBA Resources
62) Online Recruiting & Employment ASPs & Solutions
63) Outsourcing Industry Associations
64) Pensions, Benefits & 401(k) Associations
65) Pensions, Benefits & 401(k) Resources
66) Pharmaceutical Industry Associations (Drug Industry)
67) Pilots Associations
68) Printers & Publishers Associations
69) Real Estate Industry Associations
70) Recording & Music Associations
71) Satellite Industry Associations
72) Satellite-Related Professional Organizations

73) Securities Industry Associations
74) Software Industry Associations
75) Stocks & Financial Markets Data
76) Telecommunications Industry Associations
77) Temporary Staffing Firms
78) Testing Resources
79) Textile & Fabric Industry Associations
80) Travel Business & Professional Associations
81) Travel Industry Associations
82) U.S. Government Agencies
83) Water Technologies & Resources
84) Wireless & Cellular Industry Associations
85) Writers, Photographers & Editors Associations

1)   Accountants & CPA Associations

American Institute of CPAs (AICPA)
1211 Ave. of the Americas
New York, NY 10036-8775 US
Phone: 212-596-6200
Fax: 800-362-5066
Toll Free: 888-777-7077
E-mail Address: *service@aicpa.org*
Web Address: www.aicpa.org
American Institute of CPAs (AICPA) represents nearly 370,000 members in 128 countries involved in the accounting profession. Its web site provides information and news for CPAs, news from the organization and a search for accounting firms.

Council of Petroleum Accountants Societies, Inc. (COPAS)
445 Union Blvd., Ste. 207
Lakewood, CO 80228 USA
Phone: 303-300-1131
Toll Free: 877-992-6727
Web Address: www.copas.org
The Council of Petroleum Accountants Societies, Inc. (COPAS) provides a forum for discussing and solving the variety of problems related to accounting for oil and gas. COPAS also provides valuable educational materials related to oil and gas accounting.

International Accounting Standards Board (IASB)
30 Cannon St.
London, EC4M 6XH UK
Phone: 44-20-7246-6410
Fax: 44-20-7246-6411
E-mail Address: info@ifrs.org

Web Address: www.ifrs.org
The International Accounting Standards Board (IASB) website hosts an electronic subscription service to the International Financial Reporting (IFRS) Standards as well access to IFRS summaries.

2)   Advertising/Marketing Associations

4A's (American Association of Advertising Agencies)
1065 Ave. of the Americas, Fl. 16
New York, NY 10018 USA
Phone: 212-682-2500
Web Address: www.aaaa.org
The 4A's (American Association of Advertising Agencies) is the national trade association representing the advertising agency industry in the U.S.

American Institute of Graphic Arts (AIGA)
222 Broadway
New York, NY 10038 USA
Phone: 212-807-1990
Web Address: www.aiga.org
The American Institute of Graphic Arts (AIGA) strives to further excellence in communication design, both as a strategic tool for business and as a cultural force.

American Marketing Association (AMA)
130 E. Randolph St., Fl. 22
Chicago, IL 60601 USA
Phone: 312-542-9000
Fax: 312-542-9001
Toll Free: 800-262-1150
Web Address: www.ama.org
The American Marketing Association (AMA) serves marketing professionals in both business and education and serves all levels of marketing practitioners, educators and students.

Association of National Advertisers
155 E 44th St.
New York, NY 10017 USA
Phone: 212-697-5950
Fax: 212-687-7310
Web Address: www.ana.net
The Association of National Advertisers', which absorbed the Data & Marketing Association, mission is to drive growth for marketing professionals, for brands and businesses, and for the industry.

She Runs It
1460 Broadway
New York, NY 10036 USA
Phone: 212-221-7969
E-mail Address: info@sherunsit.org
Web Address: www.sherunsit.org

She Runs It, formerly known as Advertising Women of New York, is designed to encourage and promote women's role in the advertising industry, the club held classes and dinners with presentations on advertising best practices, and gave scholarships to encourage girls to pursue degrees in advertising.

3)   Aerospace & Defense Industry Associations

American Institute of Aeronautics and Astronautics (AIAA)
12700 Sunrise Valley Dr., Ste. 200
Reston, VA 20191-5807 USA
Phone: 703-264-7500
Fax: 703-264-7551
Toll Free: 800-639-2422
E-mail Address: custserv@aiaa.org
Web Address: www.aiaa.org
The American Institute of Aeronautics and Astronautics (AIAA) is a nonprofit society aimed at advancing the arts, sciences and technology of aeronautics and astronautics. The institute represents the U.S. in the International Astronautical Federation and the International Council on the Aeronautical Sciences.

4)   Airline & Air Cargo Industry Associations

International Air Transport Association (IATA)
800 Place Victoria
P.O. Box 113
Montreal, QC H4Z 1M1 Canada
Phone: 514-874-0202
Web Address: www.iata.org
The International Air Transport Association (IATA) represents about 260 airlines in order to offer the highest standards of passenger and cargo service.

5)   Alternative Energy-Ethanol

Renewable Fuels Association (RFA)
425 3rd St. SW, Ste. 1150
Washington, DC 20024 USA
Phone: 202-289-3835
Fax: 202-289-7519
Web Address: www.ethanolrfa.org
The Renewable Fuels Association (RFA) is a trade organization representing the ethanol industry. It publishes a wealth of useful information, including a listing of biorefineries and monthly U.S. fuel ethanol production and demand.

6) Alternative Energy-Solar

Solar Energy Industries Association (SEIA)
1425 K St. NW, Ste. 1000
Washington, DC 20005 USA
Phone: 202-682-0556
E-mail Address: info@seia.org
Web Address: www.seia.org
Established in 1974, the Solar Energy Industries Association is the American trade association of the solar energy industry. Among its operations is a web site that provides news for the solar energy industry, links to related products and companies and solar energy statistics.

7) Alternative Energy-Wind

American Wind Energy Association (AWEA)
1501 M St. NW, Ste. 900
Washington, DC 20005 USA
Phone: 202-383-2500
Fax: 202-383-2505
E-mail Address: stats@awea.org
Web Address: www.awea.org
The American Wind Energy Association (AWEA) promotes wind energy as a clean source of electricity worldwide. Its website provides excellent resources for research, including an online library, discussions of legislation, and descriptions of wind technologies.

8) Banking Industry Associations

American Bankers Association (ABA)
1120 Connecticut Ave. NW
Washington, DC 20036 USA
Toll Free: 800-226-5377
E-mail Address: custserv@aba.com
Web Address: www.aba.com
The American Bankers Association (ABA) represents banks of all sizes on issues of national importance for financial institutions and their customers. The site offers financial information and solutions, financial news and member access to further advice and content.

9) Biotechnology & Biological Industry Associations

Biotechnology Industry Organization (BIO)
1201 Maryland Ave. SW, Ste. 900
Washington, DC 20024 USA
Phone: 202-962-9200
Fax: 202-488-6301
E-mail Address: info@bio.org
Web Address: www.bio.org
The Biotechnology Industry Organization (BIO) represents members involved in the research and development of health care, agricultural, industrial and environmental biotechnology products. BIO has both small and large member organizations.

10) Booksellers Associations

American Booksellers Association, Inc.
333 Westchester Ave., Ste. S202
White Plains, NY 10604 USA
Phone: 914-406-7500
Fax: 914-417-4013
Toll Free: 800-637-0037
E-mail Address: info@bookweb.org
Web Address: www.bookweb.org
The American Booksellers Association is a nonprofit association representing independent bookstores in the United States.

11) Broadcasting, Cable, Radio & TV Associations

Academy of Television Arts and Sciences
5220 Lankershim Blvd.
North Hollywood, CA 91601-3109 USA
Phone: 818-754-2800
Web Address: www.emmys.tv
The Academy of Television Arts and Sciences is a nonprofit corporation devoted to the advancement of telecommunications arts and sciences and to fostering creative leadership in the telecommunications industry. It is one of three organizations that administer the Emmy Awards. It is responsible for prime time Emmys.

Alliance for Women in Media
2365 Harrodsburg Rd., A325
Lexington, KY 40504 USA
Phone: 202-750-3664
Fax: 202-750-3664
E-mail Address: info@allwomeninmedia.org
Web Address: www.allwomeninmedia.org/
The Alliance for Women in Media, formerly the American Women in Radio and Television (AWRT), founded in 1951, is a national nonprofit organization dedicated to advancing the role of women in electronic media and related fields.

Association of America's Public Television Stations (APTS)
1225 S. Clark St., Ste. 1425
Arlington, VA 22202 USA
Phone: 202-654-4200
Fax: 202-654-4236
E-mail Address: kwblunt@apts.org
Web Address: www.apts.org
The Association of America's Public Television Stations (APTS) is a nonprofit membership organization formed to support the continued growth and development of strong and financially sound noncommercial television service for the American public.

Broadcast Education Association (BEA)
1 M St. SE
Washington, DC 20003 USA
Phone: 202-602-0584
Fax: 202-609-9940
E-mail Address: help@beaweb.org
Web Address: www.beaweb.org
The Broadcast Education Association (BEA) is the professional association for professors, industry professionals and graduate students interested in teaching and research related to electronic media and multimedia enterprises.

National Academy of Television Arts and Sciences
450 Park Ave. S., Fl. 3
New York, NY 10016 USA
Phone: 212-586-8424
Fax: 212-246-8129
E-mail Address: ppillitteri@emmyonline.tv
Web Address: www.emmyonline.org
The National Academy of Television Arts and Sciences is dedicated to the advancement of the arts and sciences of television and the promotion of creative leadership for artistic, educational and technical achievements within the television industry. It is responsible for awarding the Emmy Awards.

National Association of Broadcasters (NAB)
1 M St. SE
Washington, DC 20003 USA
Phone: 202-429-5300
Toll Free: 800-622-3976
E-mail Address: nab@nab.org
Web Address: www.nab.org
The National Association of Broadcasters (NAB) represents broadcasters for radio and television. The organization also provides benefits to employees of member companies and to individuals and companies that provide products and services to the electronic media industries.

National Association of Television Program Executives (NATPE)
12534 Valley View St., Ste. 326
Garden Grove, CA 92845-2006 USA
Phone: 310-453-4440
E-mail Address: jpbommel@natpe.org
Web Address: www.natpe.com

The National Association of Television Program Executives (NATPE) is the leading association for content professionals in the global television industry. It is dedicated to the growth of video content development, creations, production, financing and distribution across various platforms by providing education and networking opportunities to its members.

National Cable and Telecommunications Association (NCTA)
25 Massachusetts Ave. NW, Ste. 100
Washington, DC 20001-1413 USA
Phone: 202-222-2300
Fax: 202-222-2514
E-mail Address: info@ncta.com
Web Address: www.ncta.com
The National Cable and Telecommunications Association (NCTA) is the principal trade association of the cable television industry in the United States. It represents cable operators as well as over 200 cable program networks that produce TV shows.

Radio Television Digital News Association (RTDNA)
529 14th St. NW, Ste. 1240
Washington, DC 20045 USA
Phone: 202-662-7257
Fax: 202-223-4007
E-mail Address: mikec@rtdna.org
Web Address: www.rtdna.org
The Radio Television Digital News Association (RTDNA), formerly the Radio-Television News Directors Association (RTNDA), is the world's largest professional organization exclusively committed to professionals in electronic journalism.

Screen Actor's Guild, American Federation of Television and Radio Artists (SAG-AFTRA)
5757 Wilshire Blvd., Fl. 7
Los Angeles, CA 90036-3600 USA
Phone: 323-634-8100
Fax: 323-549-6792
Toll Free: 855-724-2387
E-mail Address: info@sagaftra.org
Web Address: www.sagaftra.org
The Screen Actors Guild, American Federation of Television and Radio Artists (SAG-AFTRA), a product of the merger of the Screen Actors Guild (SAG) and the American Federation of Television and Radio Artists (AFTRA), is a national labor union representing actors and other professional performers and broadcasters in television, radio, sound recordings, non-broadcast/industrial programming and new technologies such

as interactive programming and CD-ROMs.

Women in Cable & Telecommunications (WICT)
2000 K St., Ste. 350
Washington, DC 20006 USA
Phone: 202-827-4794
Fax: 202-450-5596
E-mail Address: membership@wict.org
Web Address: www.wict.org
Women in Cable & Telecommunications (WICT) exists to advance the position and influence of women in media through leadership programs and services at both the national and local level.

12) Careers-Airlines/Flying

Aviation/Aerospace/Defense Jobs Page
920 Morgan St., Ste. T
Des Moines, IA 50309 USA
Fax: 515-243-5384
Toll Free: 800-292-7731
E-mail Address: customerservice@nationjob.com
Web Address: www.nationjob.com/aviation
The Aviation/Aerospace Jobs Page, a division of NationJob, Inc., features detailed aviation and aerospace job listings and company profiles.

AviationJobSearch.com
7955 NW 12th St., Ste. 401
Miami, FL 33126 USA
Phone: 786-433-7120 ext. 203
Fax: 305-716-4064
E-mail Address: info@aviationjobsearch.com
Web Address: www.aviationjobsearch.com
AviationJobSearch.com lists jobs related to the airline industry.

Avjobs, Inc.
9609 S. University Blvd., Unit 630830
Littleton, CO 80163-3032 USA
Phone: 303-683-2322
Fax: 303-683-5239
E-mail Address: info@avjobs.com
Web Address: www.avjobs.com
Avjobs, Inc. is a group of employers dedicated to helping individuals obtain aviation, airline, aerospace and airport careers.

Flightdeck Recruitment Ltd.
15 High St., W. Mersea
Colchester, Essex CO5 8QA UK
E-mail Address: contact@flightdeckrecruitment.com
Web Address: www.flightdeckrecruitment.com

Flightdeck Recruitment Ltd. provides a link between aviation recruiters who are looking for flight deck crew and pilots or flight engineers who are seeking employment.

13) Careers-Apparel

24 Seven Fashion Recruitment
120 Wooster St., Fl. 4
New York, NY 10012 USA
Phone: 212-966-4426
Fax: 212-966-2313
E-mail Address: newyork@24seventalent.com
Web Address: www.24seventalent.com
24 Seven Fashion Recruitment is an employment agency serving the fashion, beauty, entertainment, advertising, marketing and retail industries.

Fashion Career Center
950 Tower Ln., Fl. 6
Foster City, CA 94404 USA
Web Address: www.fashioncareercenter.com
The Fashion Career Center site provides employees and employers with a place to meet and access information about employment in the fashion industry. The FashionCareerCenter.com web site offers links to fashion jobs and fashion schools, as well as offering fashion career advice.

14) Careers-Banking

National Banking & Financial Service Network (NBFSN)
3075 Brickhouse Ct.
Virginia Beach, VA 23452-6860 USA
Phone: 757-463-5766
Fax: 757-340-0826
E-mail Address: smurrell@nbn-jobs.com
Web Address: www.nbn-jobs.com/
The National Banking & Financial Service Network (NBFSN) is made up of recruiting firms in the banking and financial services marketplace. The web site provides job listings.

15) Careers-Biotech

BiotechEmployment.com
E-mail Address: jobs@Biotechemployment.com
Web Address: www.biotechemployment.com
BiotechEmployment.com is an online resource for job seekers in biotechnology. The site's features include resume posting, job search agents and employer profiles. It is part of the eJobstores.com, Inc., which includes the Health Care Job Store sites.

Chase Group (The)
10975 Grandview Dr., Ste. 100
Overland Park, KS 66210 USA
Phone: 913-663-3100
Fax: 913-663-3131
E-mail Address: chase@chasegroup.com
Web Address: www.chasegroup.com
The Chase Group is an executive search firm specializing in biomedical and pharmaceutical placement.

16) Careers-Computers/ Technology

ComputerJobs.com, Inc.
675 Alpha Dr., Ste. E
Highland Heights, OH 44143 USA
Toll Free: 800-850-0045
Web Address: www.computerjobs.com
ComputerJobs.com, Inc. is an employment web site that offers users a links to computer-related job opportunities organized by skill and market.

Dice.com
6465 S. Greenwood Plaza Blvd., Ste. 400
Centennial, CO 80111 USA
Phone: 515-280-1144
Fax: 515-280-1452
Toll Free: 888-321-3423
E-mail Address: techsupport@dice.com
Web Address: www.dice.com
Dice.com provides free employment services for IT jobs. The site includes advanced job searches by geographic location and category, availability announcements and resume postings, as well as employer profiles, a recruiter's page and career links. It is maintained by Dice Holdings, Inc., a publicly traded company.

Institute for Electrical and Electronics Engineers (IEEE) Job Site
445 Hoes Ln.
Piscataway, NJ 08855-1331 USA
Phone: 732-981-0060
Toll Free: 800-678-4333
E-mail Address: candidatejobsite@ieee.org
Web Address: careers.ieee.org
The Institute for Electrical and Electronics Engineers (IEEE) Job Site provides a host of employment services for technical professionals, employers and recruiters. The site offers job listings by geographic area, a resume bank and links to employment services.

Pencom Systems, Inc.
152 Remsen St.
Brooklyn, NY 11201 USA
Phone: 718-923-1111

Fax: 718-923-6065
E-mail Address: tom@pencom.com
Web Address: www.pencom.com
Pencom Systems, Inc., an open system recruiting company, hosts a career web site geared toward high-technology and scientific professionals, featuring an interactive salary survey, career advisor, job listings and technology resources. Its focus is the financial services industry within the New York City area.

17) Careers-Contract & Freelance

Guru.com
5001 Baum Blvd., Ste. 760
Pittsburgh, PA 15213 USA
Toll Free: 888-678-0136
Web Address: www.guru.com
Guru.com provides contract job access for freelancers and contract workers, in fields ranging from interior design to architecture, marketing and web design, among others. Employers can post projects, and freelancers can offer bids on prospective jobs. Many tools are provided to enable freelancers to be completely informed about the scope of the work needed.

18) Careers-First Time Jobs/New Grads

CollegeGrad.com, Inc.
950 Tower Ln., Fl. 6
Foster City, CA 94404 USA
E-mail Address: info@quinstreet.com
Web Address: www.collegegrad.com
CollegeGrad.com, Inc. offers in-depth resources for college students and recent grads seeking entry-level jobs.

National Association of Colleges and Employers (NACE)
62 Highland Ave.
Bethlehem, PA 18017-9085 USA
Phone: 610-868-1421
E-mail Address: customerservice@naceweb.org
Web Address: www.naceweb.org
The National Association of Colleges and Employers (NACE) is a premier U.S. organization representing college placement offices and corporate recruiters who focus on hiring new grads.

19) Careers-General Job Listings

6FigureJobs
25 3rd St., Ste. 230
Stamford, CT 06905 USA

Phone: 203-326-8777
Toll Free: 800-605-5154
E-mail Address: info@6figurejobs.com
Web Address: www.6figurejobs.com
6FigureJobs offers executives a database of high-level positions. Membership is free for qualified individuals.

CareerBuilder, Inc.
200 N La Salle Dr., Ste. 1100
Chicago, IL 60601 USA
Phone: 773-527-3600
Fax: 773-353-2452
Toll Free: 800-891-8880
Web Address: www.careerbuilder.com
CareerBuilder, Inc. focuses on the needs of companies and also provides a database of job openings. The site has over 1 million jobs posted by 300,000 employers, and receives an average 23 million unique visitors monthly. The company also operates online career centers for 140 newspapers and 9,000 online partners. Resumes are sent directly to the company, and applicants can set up a special e-mail account for job-seeking purposes. CareerBuilder is primarily a joint venture between three newspaper giants: The McClatchy Company, Gannett Co., Inc. and Tribune Company.

CareerOneStop
Toll Free: 877-872-5627
E-mail Address: info@careeronestop.org
Web Address: www.careeronestop.org
CareerOneStop is operated by the employment commissions of various state agencies. It contains job listings in both the private and government sectors, as well as a wide variety of useful career resources and workforce information. CareerOneStop is sponsored by the U.S. Department of Labor.

Careers Organization (The)
4300 Horton St.
Emeryville, CA 94608 USA
Phone: 510-761-5805
Web Address: www.careers.org
The Career Organization is an online career resource center with links to jobs and other career-related web sites, as well as information regarding colleges and online degree programs.

CollegeRecruiter.com
3109 W. 50th St., Ste. 121
Minneapolis, MN 55410-2102 USA
Phone: 952-848-2211
Web Address: www.collegerecruiter.com
CollegeRecruiter.com provides college students with internship, part-time and summer job listings. Recent graduates can search for career opportunities by category and location.

ContractJobHunter
C. E. Publications, Inc.
P.O. Box 3006
Bothell, WA 98041-3006 USA
Phone: 425-806-5200
Fax: 425-806-5585
E-mail Address: staff@cjhunter.com
Web Address: cjhunter.com
ContractJobHunter is a web-based version
of the magazine Contract Employment
Weekly Online. It posts job listings and
links to contract firms in the engineering,
IT and technical fields. Libraries for
reference materials and resume writing
guidelines are also offered. The site is a
service of C. E. Publications, Inc.

eFinancialCareers
1040 Ave. of the Americas, Ste. 16B
New York, NY 10018 USA
Phone: 212-370-8502
Web Address:
www.efinancialcareers.com
eFinancialCareers.com provides
employment listings in the finance
industry, as well as job tools such as
salary surveys, resume writing assistance
and industry news. It is owned DHI
Group, Inc.

EmploymentGuide
4460 Corporation Ln., Ste. 317
Virginia Beach, VA 23462 USA
Toll Free: 877-876-4039
Web Address:
www.employmentguide.com
EmploymentGuide offers general career
resources along with lists of position
openings, company profiles and a resume
database. It also circulates a free print
publication.

EscapeArtist International
300 Caye Financial Center, Coconut Dr.
P.O. Box 11
San Pedro, Belize
Web Address: www.escapeartist.com
EscapeArtist.com provides job searches
for overseas positions, as well as
international working condition resources
and immigration information. It's an
online resource offering information,
analysis and insights for international
expat community in areas of business
opportunities, employment, asset
protection, investments and international
real estate.

ExecuNet, Inc.
295 Westport Ave.
Norwalk, CT 06851 USA
Toll Free: 800-637-3126
E-mail Address:
member.services@execunet.com
Web Address: www.execunet.com

ExecuNet, Inc. is an executive career
management information and contact
service. It's a private career network for
executives at the senior level offering
career advancement, recruitment,
coaching and advisory and peer
networking opportunities.

HigherEdJobs.com
328 Innovation Blvd., Ste. 235
State College, PA 16803 USA
Phone: 814-861-3080
Fax: 914-861-3082
E-mail Address:
jobseeker@higheredjobs.com
Web Address: www.higheredjobs.com
HigherEdJobs.com lists job vacancies in
colleges and universities.

IMDiversity, Inc.
201 St. Charles Ave., Ste. 2502
New Orleans, LA 70170 USA
Phone: 281-265-2472
Fax: 281-265-2476
E-mail Address: admin@indiversity.com
Web Address: www.imdiversity.com
IMDiversity, Inc. provides job listings and
career development information for
minorities in the U.S., with a particular
focus on African Americans, Asian
Americans and Pacific Islanders,
Latino/Hispanic Americans, Native
Americans and women.

Indeed.com
6433 Champion Grandview Way, Bldg. 1
Austin, TX 78750 USA
Web Address: www.indeed.com
Indeed.com provides extensive lists of
jobs of all types, with links directly to the
employers. It covers over 60 countries,
including the U.S., Canada, India,
Mexico.

Job Search USA
E-mail Address:
contactjsu@jobsearchusa.org
Web Address: www.jobsearchusa.org
Job Search USA is a major job posting
site that contains job opportunities
classified by a variety of keywords.

Jobs in Logistics
Toll Free: 877-562-7678
Web Address: www.jobsinlogistics.com
Jobs in Logistics is an online job board,
which provides contacts for job seekers in
the transportation, manufacturing, freight
forwarding, warehousing, purchasing,
inventory management and logistics
fields.

JobSearchUSA.org
Web Address: www.jobsearchusa.org

Founded in 2006, Job Search USA is an
all-purpose job search web site offering
job listings from various organizations
including not for profits, small businesses,
corporations and educational institutions.
Job Search USA was developed from the
concept of integrating the best features,
design practices and privacy principles of
the leading US job search websites.

LaborMarketInfo (LMI)
Employment Development Dept.
P.O. Box 826880, MIC 57
Sacramento, CA 94280-0001 USA
Phone: 916-262-2162
Fax: 916-262-2352
Web Address:
www.labormarketinfo.edd.ca.gov
LaborMarketInfo (LMI) provides job
seekers and employers a wide range of
resources, namely the ability to find,
access and use labor market information
and services. It provides statistics for
employment demographics on both a local
and regional level, as well as career
searching tools for California residents.
The web site is sponsored by California's
Employment Development Office.

MediaBistro.com
825 Eighth Ave., Fl. 29
New York, NY 10019 USA
E-mail Address:
support@mediabistro.com
Web Address: www.mediabistro.com
MediaBistro.com provides news and
information on current events relating to
the media industry. It also offers an array
of employment resources, including job
listings within the industry.

Monster Worldwide, Inc.
622 Third Ave., Fl. 39
New York, NY 10017 USA
Phone: 212-351-7000
Fax: 646-658-0540
E-mail Address: ir@monster.com
Web Address: www.monster.com
Monster Worldwide, Inc., parent company
of Monster.com, provides online career
and personnel services. The firm operates
in over 40 countries.

MyResumeAgent.com
24 Railroad St.
Kennedy Information, LLC
Keene, NH 03431 USA
Phone: 603-357-8104
Toll Free: 800-531-0007
E-mail Address:
customerservice@kennedyinfo.com
Web Address: www.myresumeagent.com
MyResumeAgent.com allows senior-level
professionals to have their resumes sent to
executive placement firms for a fee. The

site is owned by Kennedy Information, Inc.

NationJob, Inc.
920 Morgan St., Ste. T
Des Moines, IA 50309 USA
Fax: 515-243-5384
Toll Free: 888-292-7731
E-mail Address:
customerservice@nationjob.com
Web Address: www.nationjob.com
NationJob.com is an online job search portal. The web site allows users to search through listings or develop a profile of the ideal job based on the criterion of location, industry, salary; and, if they provide an e-mail address, wait for appropriate listings to be sent to them through the firm's PJScout feature.

NETSHARE, Inc.
359 Bel Marin Keys, Ste. 24
Novato, CA 94949 USA
Toll Free: 800-241-5642
E-mail Address: netshare@netshare.com
Web Address: www.netshare.com
Netshare provides access to exclusive listings of executive jobs that pay $100,000 and up.

Net-Temps, Inc.
55 Middlesex St., Ste. 220
North Chelmsford, MA 01863 USA
Fax: 978-251-7250
Toll Free: 800-307-0062
E-mail Address: service@net-temps.com
Web Address: www.net-temps.com
Net-Temps, Inc. offers a web site, operated by professional career consultants, that features job listings and job seeking tips.

Recruiters Online Network
E-mail Address: rossi.tony@comcast.net
Web Address: www.recruitersonline.com
The Recruiters Online Network provides job postings from thousands of recruiters, Careers Online Magazine, a resume database, as well as other career resources.

USAJOBS
USAJOBS Program Office
1900 E St. NW, Ste. 6500
Washington, DC 20415-0001 USA
Phone: 818-934-6600
Web Address: www.usajobs.gov
USAJOBS, a program of the U.S. Office of Personnel Management, is the official job site for the U.S. Federal Government. It provides a comprehensive list of U.S. government jobs, allowing users to search for employment by location; agency; type of work; or by senior executive positions. It also has special employment sections

for individuals with disabilities, veterans and recent college graduates; an information center, offering resume and interview tips and other information; and allows users to create a profile and post a resume.

20) Careers-Health Care

Health Care Source
100 Sylvan Rd., Ste. 100
Woburn, MA 01801 USA
Phone: 781-368-1033
Fax: 800-829-6600
Toll Free: 800-869-5200
E-mail Address:
support@healthcaresource.com
Web Address: www.healthcaresource.com
Health Care Source is a leading provider of talent management, recruitment and employment services for healthcare providers. It offers a comprehensive suite of solutions, which includes features, such as applicant tracking and onboarding, recruitment optimization, reference checking, behavioral assessments, merit planning, employee performance and eLearning courseware among others.

MedicalWorkers.com
Web Address: www.medicalworkers.com
MedicalWorkers.com is an employment site for medical and health care professionals.

Medzilla, Inc.
P.O. Box 1710
Marysville, WA 98270 USA
Phone: 360-657-5681
Fax: 425-279-5427
E-mail Address: info@medzilla.com
Web Address: www.medzilla.com
Medzilla, Inc.'s web site offers job searches, salary surveys, a search agent and information on employment in the biotech, pharmaceuticals, healthcare and science sectors.

Monster Career Advice-Healthcare
133 Boston Post Rd.
Weston, MA 02493 USA
Phone: 978-461-8000
Fax: 978-461-8100
Toll Free: 800-666-7837
Web Address: career-advice.monster.com/Healthcare/job-category-3975.aspx
Monster Career Advice-Healthcare, a service of Monster Worldwide, Inc., provides industry-related articles, job listings, job searches and search agents for the medical field.

NationJob Network-Medical and Health Care Jobs Page
920 Morgan St., Ste. T
Des Moines, IA 50309 USA
Fax: 515-243-5384
Toll Free: 800-292-7731
E-mail Address:
customerservice@nationjob.com
Web Address:
www.nationjob.com/medical
The NationJob Network-Medical and Health Care Jobs Page offers information and listings for health care employment.

Nurse-Recruiter.com
113 Cherry St., Ste. 26760
Seattle, WA 98104 USA
Phone: 1-800-243-3407
Fax: 1-866-608-1781
Toll Free: 877-562-7966
Web Address: www.nurse-recruiter.com
Nurse-Recruiter.com is an online job portal devoted to bringing health care employers and the nursing community together.

PracticeLink
415 2nd Ave.
Hinton, WV 25951 USA
Toll Free: 800-776-8383
E-mail Address:
helpdesk@practicelink.com
Web Address: www.practicelink.com
PracticeLink, one of the largest physician employment web sites, is a free service with over 1.7 million page views each month. There are more than 5,000 hospitals, medical groups, private practices and health systems, posting over 20,000 physician job opportunities on the web site.

RPh on the Go USA, Inc.
8430 West Bryn Mawr Ave., Ste. 1150
Chicago, IL 60631 USA
Phone: 847-588-7170
Fax: 904-632-5692
Toll Free: 800-553-7359
Web Address: www.rphonthego.com
RPh on the Go USA, Inc. places temporary and permanent qualified professionals in the pharmacy community. This pharmacy staffing firm offers access to more than 160,000 pharmacy professionals and matches the right pharmacy personnel to help meet clients' needs.

21) Careers-Job Listings for Seniors

Senior Job Bank
NHC Group, Inc.
P.O. Box 508

Marlborough, MA 01752 USA
Toll Free: 866-562-2627
E-mail Address:
publisher@seniorjobbank.org
Web Address: www.seniorjobbank.org
The Senior Job Bank web site offers an
easy, effective and free method for senior
citizens to find occasional, part-time,
flexible, temporary or full-time jobs. The
site is owned and managed by NHC
Group, Inc.

Seniors4Hire.org
7071 Warner Ave. F466
Huntington Beach, CA 92647 USA
Phone: 714-848-0996
Fax: 714-848-5445
Toll Free: 800-906-7107
E-mail Address: info@seniors4hire.org
Web Address: www.seniors4hire.org
Seniors4Hire.org is an online career
center with job postings, employment
resources and information on community
service employment programs for older
workers, retirees and senior citizens. The
site is owned and operated by The
Forward Group.

YourEncore
20 N. Meridian St., Ste. 800
Indianapolis, IN 46204 USA
Phone: 317-226-9301
Fax: 317-226-9312
E-mail Address: info@yourencore.com
Web Address: www.yourencore.com
YourEncore is a program that seeks to
employ retirees by matching them with
member companies. The web site utilizes
retirees mainly in the areas of
engineering, science and product
development.

**22) Careers-Job Listings Hong
Kong, China, Singapore,
Asia**

CareerJet
Web Address: www.careerjet.hk
CareerJet provides excellent search tools
leading to job listings in Hong Kong,
China and throughout Asia.

Careers@Gov
Web Address: www.careers.gov.sg
Careers@Gov is the government-
sponsored job search site within
Singapore.

CT Good Jobs
Web Address: www.ctgoodjobs.hk
CT Good Jobs provides easy to use job
listings. It also offers online communities
in such areas as retail, human resources
and finance.

HeadHunt
Web Address: www.headhunt.com.sg/
HeadHunt bills itself as an executive job
search site for Singapore.

JobMarket
Web Address: www.jobmarket.com.hk
JobMarket features a very detailed
advanced search option.

JobsCentral Singapore
Web Address: http://jobscentral.com.sg/
JobsCentral Singapore is maintained by
CareerBuilder.

jobsDB
Web Address: http://hk.jobsdb.com/hk
jobsDB provides well organized job
listings in Hong Kong, Indonesia,
Malaysia, Philippines, Singapore,
Thailand and China.

JobStreet
Web Address: www.jobstreet.sg
JobStreet is an extensive job search site
focused in positions within Singapore.

Monster Hong Kong
Web Address: www.monster.com.hk/
Monster Hong Kong provides easy online
access to thousands of jobs in Hong Kong,
Macau, Mainland China and Taiwan.

Monster Singapore
Web Address: www.monster.com.sg/
Monster Singapore is specific to the
Singapore area.

Recruit
Web Address: www.recruit.com.hk
Recruit provides job news, job tips
employer new and job listings in the Hong
Kong area.

Singapore Jobs Online
Web Address:
www.singaporejobsonline.com/
Singapore Jobs Online enables job
searches within Singapore for a wide
variety of job categories.

STJobs
Web Address: www.stjobs.sg/site/index
STJobs is an extensive web site offering
job search within Singapore and the
surrounding area.

**23) Careers-Job Reference
Tools**

CareerXroads (CXR)
7 Clark Ct.
Kendall Park, NJ 08824-1810 USA
Phone: 732-821-6652

E-mail Address: mmc@careerxroads.com
Web Address: www.careerxroads.com
CareerXroads (CXR) publishes an annual
guide on job and resume web sites. It was
cofounded by Gerry Crispin and Mark
Mehler.

Job-Hunt.org
186 Main St.
NETability, Inc.
Marlborough, MA 01752 USA
Phone: 508-624-6261
E-mail Address: info@job-hunt.org
Web Address: www.job-hunt.org
Job-Hunt.org, rather than collecting
resumes or posting job vacancies, offers a
vast list of job listing web sites and links
to helpful job search tools. It is owned by
NETability, Inc.

jobipedia.org
E-mail Address: info@jobipedia.org
Web Address: www.jobipedia.org
jobipedia.org is a public service provided
by the HR Policy Association to help new
entrants into the workforce find jobs.
Every answer you read on jobipedia was
written by someone from a large employer
who actually hires employees for a living.

MBA Career Services Council (CSC)
P.O. Box 47478
Tampa, FL 33646-7478 USA
Phone: 813-220-3191
Fax: 813-319-4952
E-mail Address:
execdirector@mbacsc.org
Web Address: www.mbacsc.org
The MBA Career Services Council (CSC)
is a global professional association for
individuals in the field of MBA career
services and those that recruit directly
from graduate management programs.

Vault.com, Inc.
132 W. 31st St., Fl. 16
New York, NY 10001 USA
Fax: 212-366-6117
Toll Free: 800-535-2074
E-mail Address:
customerservice@vault.com
Web Address: www.vault.com
Vault.com, Inc. is a comprehensive career
web site for employers and employees,
with job postings and valuable
information on a wide variety of
industries. Its features and content are
largely geared toward MBA degree
holders.

What Color is Your Parachute?
E-mail Address:
rnbolles@jobhuntersbible.com
Web Address: www.jobhuntersbible.com

The What Color is Your Parachute? official web site, JobHuntersBible.com, is based on the Job-Hunting on the Internet chapter of Richard (Dick) Bolle's best-selling book. Designed to aid job hunters and career changers who want to use the Internet as part of their job search, the site provides links to job listing, resume, career counseling, contacts and research sites.

24) Careers-Restaurants

FoodService.com
24 W. Camelback Rd., Ste. 104
Phoenix, AZ 85013 USA
Phone: 602-381-3663
Web Address: www.foodservice.com
FoodService.com, managed and run by Food Service Interactive, LLC, offers web site design and job search services for the food service industry.

Resources in Food, Inc. (RIF)
417 S Lincolnway, Ste. B
North Aurora, IL 60542 USA
Phone: 630-801-0469
Fax: 630-357-7548
Toll Free: 877-743-1100
E-mail Address: jgrimm@rifood.com
Web Address: www.rifood.com
Resources in Food (RIF) provides professional management placement for the hospitality, food manufacturing, food services, restaurants and wholesale grocery industry.

25) Careers-Science

Chem Jobs
730 E. Cypress Ave.
Monrovia, CA 91016 USA
Phone: 626-930-0808
Fax: 626-930-0102
E-mail Address: info@chemindustry.com
Web Address: www.chemjobs.net
Chem Jobs is a leading Internet site for job seekers in chemistry and related fields, with a particular focus on chemists, biochemists, pharmaceutical scientists and chemical engineers. The web site is powered by Chemindustry.com.

New Scientist Jobs
25 Bedford St.
London, WC2E 9ES UK
Phone: 617-283-3213
E-mail Address: nssales@newscientist.com
Web Address: jobs.newscientist.com
New Scientist Jobs is a web site produced by the publishers of New Scientist Magazine that connects jobseekers and employers in the bioscience fields. The

site includes a job search engine and a free-of-charge e-mail job alert service.

Science Careers
Phone: 202-312-6375
Web Address: jobs.sciencecareers.org
Science Careers is a web site that contains many useful categories of links, including employment newsgroups, scientific journals, hob postings and placement agencies. It also links to sites containing information regarding internship and fellowship opportunities for high school students, undergrads, graduates, doctoral and post-doctoral students.

26) Careers-Sports

Jobs in Sports
1719 Penman Rd
Jacksonville Beach, FL 32250 USA
Web Address: www.jobsinsports.com
Jobs in Sports is an employment web site that provides job listings in areas including sports marketing, sports media, sales, health and fitness, computers and administration, as well as other job resources.

Sports Careers
Web Address: www.sportscareers.com
Sports Careers offers a range of services to help individuals and employers in the sports industry, including job listings, a resume bank, industry contacts and salary information.

Sports Job Board
Web Address: www.sportsjobboard.com
The Sports Job Board is an employment web site for the sports industry.

Work in Sports LLC
7010 E. Chauncey Ln., Ste. 115
Phoenix, AZ 85054 USA
Phone: 480-905-7221
Fax: 480-905-7231
Toll Free: 855-220-5627
Web Address: www.workinsports.com
Work in Sports LLC is an online employment resource for the sports industry that posts hundreds of jobs on its web site.

27) Careers-Video Games Industry

GameJobs
Web Address: www.gamejobs.com
GameJobs.com is independently owned and operated by the Crest Group, LLC, the managers of the Entertainment Consumers Association (ECA), a non-profit membership association. It offers

both employers and job seekers in the interactive entertainment industry access to online tools and resources, such as post resume and job openings to accomplish their respective goals.

Video Game Jobs-About.com Career Planning
Web Address: http://careerplanning.about.com/od/occupations/a/videogamecareer.htm
A useful page on About.com that contains advice and links for people interested in working in the video games industry.

28) Chemicals Industry Associations

American Chemical Society (ACS)
1155 16th St. NW
Washington, DC 20036 USA
Phone: 202-872-4600
Toll Free: 800-333-9511
E-mail Address: service@acs.org
Web Address: www.acs.org
The American Chemical Society (ACS) is a nonprofit organization aimed at promoting the understanding of chemistry and chemical sciences. It represents a wide range of disciplines including chemistry, chemical engineering and other technical fields.

29) Communications Professional Associations

Association for Women In Communications (AWC)
1717 E Republic Rd., Ste. A
Springfield, MO 65804 USA
Phone: 417-886-8606
Fax: 417-886-3685
E-mail Address: members@womcom.org
Web Address: www.womcom.org
The Association for Women In Communications (AWC) is a professional organization that works for the advancement of women across all communications disciplines by recognizing excellence, promoting leadership and positioning its members at the forefront of the communications industry.

Health and Science Communications Association (HeSCA)
P.O. Box 31323
Omaha, NE 68132 USA
Phone: 402-915-5373
E-mail Address: hesca@hesca.org
Web Address: hesca.net
The Health and Science Communications Association (HeSCA) is an organization of communications professionals

committed to sharing knowledge and resources in the health sciences arena.

Health Industry Business Communications Council (HIBCC)

2525 E. Arizona Biltmore Cir., Ste. 127
Phoenix, AZ 85016 USA
Phone: 602-381-1091
Fax: 602-381-1093
E-mail Address: info@hibcc.org
Web Address: www.hibcc.org
The Health Industry Business
Communications Council (HIBCC) seeks
to facilitate electronic communications by
developing appropriate standards for
information exchange among all health
care trading partners.

International Association of Business Communicators (IABC)

330 N Wabash Ave., Ste. 2000
Chicago, IL 60611 USA
Phone: 312-321-6868
Toll Free: 800-776-4222
E-mail Address:
member_relations@iabc.com
Web Address: www.iabc.com
The International Association of Business
Communicators (IABC) is the leading
resource for effective business
communication practices.

30) Computer & Electronics Industry Associations

Electronics Technicians Association international (ETA International)

5 Depot St.
Greencastle, IN 46135 USA
Phone: 765-653-8262
Fax: 765-653-4287
Toll Free: 800-288-3824
E-mail Address: eta@eta-i.org
Web Address: www.eta-i.org
The Electronics Technicians Association
International (ETA International) is a
nonprofit professional association for
electronics technicians worldwide. The
organization provides recognized
professional credentials for electronics
technicians.

Semiconductor Industry Association (SIA)

1101 K St. NW, Ste. 450
Washington, DC 20005 USA
Phone: 202-446-1700
Fax: 202-216-9745
Toll Free: 866-756-0715
Web Address: www.semiconductors.org
The Semiconductor Industry Association
(SIA) is a trade association representing
the semiconductor industry in the U.S.
Through its coalition of more than 60

companies, SIA members represent
roughly 80% of semiconductor production
in the U.S. The coalition aims to advance
the competitiveness of the chip industry
and shape public policy on issues
particular to the industry.

31) Consulting Industry Associations

Association of Internal Management Consultants (AIMC)

720 N. Collier Blvd., Ste. 201
Marco Island, FL 34145 USA
Phone: 239-642-0580
Web Address: www.aimc.org
The Association of Internal Management
Consultants (AIMC) is a professional
association representing in-house
management consultants. Members work
in for-profit corporations, government
agencies, educational institutions and
nonprofit organizations.

Association of Management Consulting Firms (AMCF)

370 Lexington Ave., Ste. 2209
New York, NY 10017 USA
Phone: 212-262-3055
Fax: 212-262-3054
E-mail Address: info@amcf.org
Web Address: www.amcf.org
The Association of Management
Consulting Firms (AMCF) is a recognized
leader in promoting the management
consulting industry. AMCF represents a
diverse list of international members,
from large, multinational companies to
small, regional firms.

Institute of Management Consultants USA (IMC)

631 U.S. Highway One, Ste. 400
North Palm Beach, FL 33408 USA
Phone: 561-472-0833
Toll Free: 800-837-7321
Web Address: www.imcusa.org
The Institute of Management Consultants
USA (IMC) certifies management
consultants in accordance with the strict
international standards of the International
Council of Management Consulting
Institutes.

Investment Management Consultant Association (IMCA)

5619 DTC Pkwy., Ste. 500
Greenwood Village, CO 80111 USA
Phone: 303-770-3377
Fax: 303-770-1812
E-mail Address: imca@imca.org
Web Address: www.imca.org
The Investment Management Consultant
Association (IMCA) provides information

and communication for investment
management consultants.

32) Consulting Industry Resources

Consulting Magazine

120 Broadway, Fl.5
New York, NY 10271 USA
Phone: 877-256-2472
Web Address: www.consultingmag.com
Consulting Magazine is a leading online
publication for the consulting industry,
and features information on consulting
careers, thought leadership and corporate
strategies. The web site is owned and
operated by ALM Media, LLC.

33) Corporate Information Resources

Business Journals (The)

120 W. Morehead St., Ste. 400
Charlotte, NC 28202 USA
Toll Free: 866-853-3661
E-mail Address:
gmurchison@bizjournals.com
Web Address: www.bizjournals.com
Bizjournals.com is the online media
division of American City Business
Journals, the publisher of dozens of
leading city business journals nationwide.
It provides access to research into the
latest news regarding companies both
small and large. The organization
maintains 42 websites and 64 print
publications and sponsors over 700 annual
industry events.

Business Wire

101 California St., Fl. 20
San Francisco, CA 94111 USA
Phone: 415-986-4422
Fax: 415-788-5335
Toll Free: 800-227-0845
E-mail Address: info@businesswire.com
Web Address: www.businesswire.com
Business Wire offers news releases,
industry- and company-specific news, top
headlines, conference calls, IPOs on the
Internet, media services and access to
tradeshownews.com and BW Connect
On-line through its informative and
continuously updated web site.

Edgar Online, Inc.

35 W. Wacker Dr.
Chicago, IL 60601 USA
Phone: 301-287-0300
Fax: 301-287-0390
Toll Free: 800-823-5304
Web Address: www.edgar-online.com
Edgar Online, Inc. is a gateway and
search tool for viewing corporate

documents, such as annual reports on Form 10-K, filed with the U.S. Securities and Exchange Commission.

PR Newswire Association LLC
200 Vesey St., Fl. 19
New York, NY 10281 USA
Fax: 800-793-9313
Toll Free: 800-776-8090
E-mail Address:
mediainquiries@cision.com
Web Address: www.prnewswire.com
PR Newswire Association LLC provides comprehensive communications services for public relations and investor relations professionals, ranging from information distribution and market intelligence to the creation of online multimedia content and investor relations web sites. Users can also view recent corporate press releases from companies across the globe. The Association is owned by United Business Media plc.

Silicon Investor
E-mail Address:
si.admin@siliconinvestor.com
Web Address: www.siliconinvestor.com
Silicon Investor is focused on providing information about technology companies. Its web site serves as a financial discussion forum and offers quotes, profiles and charts.

34) Disabling Conditions

Job Accommodation Network (JAN)
P.O. Box 6080
Morgantown, WV 26506-6080 USA
Phone: 304-293-7186
Fax: 304-293-5407
Toll Free: 800-526-7234
E-mail Address: jan@askjan.org
Web Address: askjan.org
The Job Accommodation Network (JAN) is a free consulting service that provides guidance and information about job accommodations, the Americans with Disabilities Act and the employability of people with disabilities.

35) Electronic Health Records/Continuity of Care Records

American Health Information Management Association (AHIMA)
233 N. Michigan Ave., Fl. 21
Chicago, IL 60601-5809 USA
Phone: 312-233-1100
Fax: 312-233-1090
Toll Free: 800-335-5535
E-mail Address: info@ahima.org
Web Address: www.ahima.org

The American Health Information Management Association (AHIMA) is a professional association that consists health information management professionals who work throughout the health care industry.

American Medical Informatics Association (AMIA)
4720 Montgomery Ln., Ste. 500
Bethesda, MD 20814 USA
Phone: 301-657-1291
Fax: 301-657-1296
Web Address: www.amia.org
The American Medical Informatics Association (AMIA) is a membership organization of individuals, institutions and corporations dedicated to developing and using information technologies to improve health care.

College of Healthcare Information Management Executives (CHIME)
710 Avis Dr., Ste. 200
Ann Arbor, MI 48108 USA
Phone: 734-665-0000
Fax: 734-665-4922
E-mail Address: staff@cio-chime.org
Web Address: www.cio-chime.org
College of Healthcare Information Management Executives (CHIME) was formed with the dual objective of serving the professional development needs of health care CIOs and advocating the more effective use of information management within health care.

Healthcare Information and Management Systems Society (HIMSS)
33 W Monroe St., Ste. 1700
Chicago, IL 60603-5616 USA
Phone: 312-664-4467
Fax: 312-664-6143
Web Address: www.himss.org
The Healthcare Information and Management Systems Society (HIMSS) provides leadership in the optimal use of technology, information and management systems for the betterment of health care.

36) Energy Associations- Electric Power

American Public Power Association (APPA)
2451 Crystal Dr., Ste. 1000
Arlington, VA 22202-4804 USA
Phone: 202-467-2900
E-mail Address: info@PublicPower.org
Web Address: www.publicpower.org
The American Public Power Association (APPA) is a nonprofit service organization for the country's community-owned electric utilities, dedicated to

advancing the public policy interests of its members and their consumers.

Edison Electric Institute (EEI)
701 Pennsylvania Ave. NW
Washington, DC 20004-2696 USA
Phone: 202-508-5000
E-mail Address: feedback@eei.org
Web Address: www.eei.org
The Edison Electric Institute (EEI) is an association of U.S. shareholder-owned electric companies as well as worldwide affiliates and industry associates. Its web site provides energy news and a link to Electric Perspectives magazine.

Women's International Network of Utility Professionals (WINUP)
2795 East Bidwell St., Ste. 100-209
Folsom, CA 95630 USA
Phone: 916-425-8780
E-mail Address: winup@att.net
Web Address: www.winup.org
The Women's International Network of Utility Professionals (WINUP) provides networking and support for women in the utility industry.

37) Energy Associations- Natural Gas

American Gas Association (AGA)
400 N. Capitol St. NW, Ste. 450
Washington, DC 20001 USA
Phone: 202-824-7000
Web Address: www.aga.org
The American Gas Association (AGA) represents a large number of natural gas providers, advocating for these companies and providing a broad range of programs and services for members.

38) Energy Associations-Other

American Association of Blacks in Energy
1625 K St. NW, Ste. 450
Washington, DC 20006 USA
Phone: 202-371-9530
Fax: 202-371-9218
E-mail Address: info@aabe.org
Web Address: www.aabe.org
The American Association of Blacks in Energy is dedicated to ensuring the input of African Americans and other minorities in discussions and developments of energy policies, regulations, research and development technologies and environmental issues.

39) Energy Associations- Petroleum, Exploration, Production, etc.

American Association of Professional Landmen (AAPL)
800 Fournier St.
Fort Worth, TX 76102 USA
Phone: 817-847-7700
Fax: 817-847-7704
E-mail Address: aapl@landman.org
Web Address: www.landman.org
The American Association of Professional Landmen (AAPL) promotes the highest standards of performance for all land professionals and seeks to advance their stature and to encourage sound stewardship of energy and mineral resources.

American Petroleum Institute (API)
1220 L St. NW
Washington, DC 20005-4070 USA
Phone: 202-682-8000
Web Address: www.api.org
American Petroleum Institute (API) represents U.S. oil and gas industries and its web site includes in-depth sections for energy consumers and energy professionals.

Independent Petroleum Association of America (IPAA)
1201 15th St. NW, Ste. 300
Washington, DC 20005 USA
Phone: 202-857-4722
Fax: 202-857-4799
E-mail Address: nkirby@ipaa.org
Web Address: www.ipaa.org
The Independent Petroleum Association of America (IPAA) provides a forum for the exploration and production segment of the independent oil and natural gas business. It also provides information on the domestic exploration and production industry.

International Association of Drilling Contractors (IADC)
10370 Richmond Ave., Ste. 760
Houston, TX 77042 USA
Phone: 713-292-1945
Fax: 713-292-1946
E-mail Address: info@iadc.org
Web Address: www.iadc.org
The International Association of Drilling Contractors (IADC) represents the worldwide oil and gas drilling industry and promotes commitment to safety, preservation of the environment and advances in drilling technology.

40) Engineering, Research & Scientific Associations

American Association of Petroleum Geologists (AAPG)
1444 S. Boulder Ave.
Tulsa, OK 74119 USA
Phone: 918-584-2555
Fax: 918-560-2665
Toll Free: 800-364-2274
Web Address: www.aapg.org
The American Association of Petroleum Geologists (AAPG) is an international geological organization that supports educational and scientific programs and projects related to geosciences.

American Institute of Chemical Engineers (AIChE)
120 Wall St., Fl. 23
New York, NY 10005-4020 USA
Phone: 203-702-7660
Fax: 203-775-5177
Toll Free: 800-242-4363
Web Address: www.aiche.org
The American Institute of Chemical Engineers (AIChE) provides leadership in advancing the chemical engineering profession. The organization, which is comprised of more than 50,000 members from over 100 countries, provides informational resources to chemical engineers.

American Society for Healthcare Engineering (ASHE)
155 N. Wacker Dr., Ste. 400
Chicago, IL 60606 USA
Phone: 312-422-3800
Fax: 312-422-4571
E-mail Address: ashe@aha.org
Web Address: www.ashe.org
The American Society for Healthcare Engineering (ASHE) is the advocate and resource for continuous improvement in the health care engineering and facilities management professions. It is devoted to professionals who design, build, maintain and operate hospitals and other healthcare facilities.

American Society of Agricultural and Biological Engineers (ASABE)
2950 Niles Rd.
St. Joseph, MI 49085 USA
Phone: 269-429-0300
Fax: 269-429-3852
Toll Free: 800-371-2723
E-mail Address: hq@asabe.org
Web Address: www.asabe.org
The American Society of Agricultural and Biological Engineers (ASABE) is a nonprofit professional and technical organization interested in engineering knowledge and technology for food and agriculture and associated industries.

American Society of Civil Engineers (ASCE)
1801 Alexander Bell Dr.
Reston, VA 20191-4400 USA
Phone: 703-295-6300
Toll Free: 800-548-2723
Web Address: www.asce.org
The American Society of Civil Engineers (ASCE) is a leading professional organization serving civil engineers. It ensures safer buildings, water systems and other civil engineering works by developing technical codes and standards.

American Society of Safety Engineers (ASSE)
520 N. Northwest Hwy
Park Ridge, IL 60068 USA
Phone: 847-699-2929
E-mail Address: customerservice@asse.org
Web Address: www.asse.org
The American Society of Safety Engineers (ASSE) is the world's oldest and largest professional safety organization. It manages, supervises and consults on safety, health and environmental issues in industry, insurance, government and education.

Association of Federal Communications Consulting Engineers (AFCCE)
P.O. Box 19333
Washington, DC 20036 USA
Web Address: www.afcce.org
The Association of Federal Communications Consulting Engineers (AFCCE) is a professional organization of individuals who regularly assist clients on technical issues before the Federal Communications Commission (FCC).

Institute of Industrial Engineers (IIE)
3577 Parkway Ln., Ste. 200
Norcross, GA 30092 USA
Phone: 770-449-0460
Fax: 770-441-3295
Toll Free: 800-494-0460
E-mail Address: cs@iienet.org
Web Address: www.iienet2.org
The Institute of Industrial Engineers (IIE) is an international, non-profit association dedicated to the education, development, training and research in the field of industrial engineering.

National Society of Professional Engineers (NSPE)
1420 King St.
Alexandria, VA 22314-2794 USA
Fax: 703-836-4875
Toll Free: 888-285-6773

Web Address: www.nspe.org
The National Society of Professional Engineers (NSPE) represents individual engineering professionals and licensed engineers across all disciplines. NSPE serves approximately 45,000 members and has more than 500 chapters.

Society of Automotive Engineers (SAE)
755 W. Big Beaver, Ste. 1600
Troy, MA 48084 USA
Phone: 248-273-2455
Fax: 248-273-2494
Toll Free: 877-606-7323
E-mail Address: automotive_hq@sae.org
Web Address: www.sae.org
The Society of Automotive Engineers (SAE) is a resource for technical information and expertise used in designing, building, maintaining and operating self-propelled vehicles for use on land, sea, air or space.

Society of Broadcast Engineers, Inc. (SBE)
9102 N. Meridian St., Ste. 150
Indianapolis, IN 46260 USA
Phone: 317-846-9000
E-mail Address: jporay@sbe.org
Web Address: www.sbe.org
The Society of Broadcast Engineers (SBE) exists to increase knowledge of broadcast engineering and promote its interests, as well as to continue the education of professionals in the industry.

Society of Cable Telecommunications Engineers (SCTE)
140 Philips Rd.
Exton, PA 19341-1318 USA
Phone: 610-363-6888
Fax: 610-884-7237
Toll Free: 800-542-5040
E-mail Address: info@scte.org
Web Address: www.scte.org
The Society of Cable Telecommunications Engineers (SCTE) is a nonprofit professional association dedicated to advancing the careers and serving the industry of telecommunications professionals by providing technical training, certification and information resources.

Society of Hispanic Professional Engineers (SHPE)
13181 Crossroads Pkwy. N., Ste. 450
City of Industry, CA 91746 USA
Phone: 323-725-3970
Fax: 323-725-0316
E-mail Address: shpenational@shpe.org
Web Address: oneshpe.shpe.org
The Society of Hispanic Professional Engineers (SHPE) is a national nonprofit organization that promotes Hispanics in science, engineering and math.

Society of Manufacturing Engineers (SME)
One SME Dr.
Dearborn, MI 48121 USA
Phone: 313-425-3000
Fax: 313-425-3400
Toll Free: 800-733-4763
E-mail Address: communications@sme.org
Web Address: www.sme.org
The Society of Manufacturing Engineers (SME) is a leading professional organization serving engineers in the manufacturing industries.

Society of Motion Picture and Television Engineers (SMPTE)
455 Hamilton Ave., Ste. 601
White Plains, NY 10601 USA
Phone: 914-761-1100
Fax: 914-206-4216
E-mail Address: marketing@smpte.org
Web Address: www.smpte.org
The Society of Motion Picture and Television Engineers (SMPTE) is the leading technical society for the motion imaging industry. The firm publishes recommended practice and engineering guidelines, as well the SMPTE Journal.

Society of Women Engineers (SWE)
230 N La Salle St., Ste. 1675
Chicago, IL 60601 USA
Toll Free: 877-793-4636
E-mail Address: hq@swe.org
Web Address: societyofwomenengineers.swe.org
The Society of Women Engineers (SWE) is a nonprofit educational and service organization of female engineers.

SPIE
1000 20th St.
Bellingham, WA 98225-6705 USA
Phone: 360-676-3290
Fax: 360-647-1445
Toll Free: 888-504-8171
E-mail Address: customerservice@spie.org
Web Address: www.spie.org
SPIE is a nonprofit technical society aimed at the advancement and dissemination of knowledge in optics, photonics and imaging.

41) Entertainment & Amusement Associations-General

International Association of Amusement Parks and Attractions (IAAPA)
4155 W. Taft Vineland Rd.
Orlando, FL 32837 USA
Phone: 321-319-7600
Fax: 321-319-7690
E-mail Address: iaapa@iaapa.org
Web Address: www.iaapa.org
The International Association of Amusement Parks and Attractions (IAAPA) is dedicated to the preservation and prosperity of the amusement industry.

International Live Events Association (ILEA)
7918 Jones Branch Dr., Ste. 300
McLean, VA 22102 USA
Phone: 571-685-8010
Fax: 703-506-3266
Toll Free: 800-688-3266
E-mail Address: info@ileahub.com
Web Address: www.ileahub.com
The International Live Events Association (ILEA) advances the live events industry by creating an inclusive global community dedicated to personal and business development, and inspiration to elevate all professionals engaged in live events. The ILEA collaborates with key stakeholders to promote the importance of industry standards.

42) Film & Theater Associations

Academy of Motion Picture Arts and Sciences (AMPAS)
8949 Wilshire Blvd.
Beverly Hills, CA 90211-1972 USA
Phone: 310-247-3000
Fax: 310-859-9619
Web Address: www.oscars.org
The Academy of Motion Picture Arts and Sciences (AMPAS) is a professional honorary organization, founded to advance the arts and sciences of motion pictures. Besides hosting the Academy Awards and selecting the winners of the Oscars, AMPAS organizes smaller events highlighting the art of filmmaking, including lectures and seminars, and is currently building the Academy Museum of Motion Pictures.

Alliance of Motion Picture and Television Producers (AMPTP)
15301 Ventura Blvd., Bldg. E
Sherman Oaks, CA 91403 USA
Phone: 818-995-3600
Web Address: www.amptp.org

The Alliance of Motion Picture and Television Producers (AMPTP) is the primary trade association with respect to labor issues in the motion picture and television industry.

American Cinema Editors, Inc. (ACE)
5555 Melrose Ave.
Marx Brothers Bldg., Ste. 108
Los Angeles, CA 90038 USA
Phone: 323-956-2900
E-mail Address: amercinema@earthlink.net
Web Address: www.americancinemaeditors.org
American Cinema Editors (ACE) is an honorary society of motion picture editors that seeks to advance the art and science of the editing profession.

American Society of Cinematographers (ASC)
1782 N. Orange Dr.
Hollywood, CA 90028 USA
Phone: 323-969-4333
Fax: 323-882-6391
Toll Free: 800-448-0145
E-mail Address: office@theasc.com
Web Address: www.theasc.com
The American Society of Cinematographers (ASC) is a trade association for cinematographers in the motion picture industry.

Art Directors Guild (ADG)
11969 Ventura Blvd., Fl. 2
Studio City, CA 91604 USA
Phone: 818-762-9995
Fax: 818-762-9997
E-mail Address: nick@artdirectors.org
Web Address: www.adg.org
The Art Directors Guild (ADG) represents the creative talents that conceive and manage the background and settings for most films and television projects.

Association of Cinema and Video Laboratories (ACVL)
Phone: 805-427-2620
E-mail Address: peterbulcke@hotmail.com
Web Address: www.acvl.org
The Association of Cinema and Video Laboratories (ACVL) is an international organization whose members are pledged to the highest possible standards of service to the film and video industries.

Independent Film & Television Alliance (IFTA)
10850 Wilshire Blvd., Fl. 9
Los Angeles, CA 90024-4311 USA
Phone: 310-446-1000
Fax: 310-446-1600
E-mail Address: info@ifta-online.org

Web Address: www.ifta-online.org
The Independent Film & Television Alliance (IFTA), formerly the American Film Marketing Association (AFMA), is a trade association whose mission is to provide the independent film and television industry with high-quality, market-oriented services and worldwide representation.

International Alliance of Theatrical Stage Employees (IATSE)
207 W. 25th St., Fl. 4
New York, NY 10001 USA
Phone: 212-730-1770
Fax: 212-730-7809
E-mail Address: webmaster@iatse-intl.org
Web Address: www.iatse-intl.org
The International Alliance of Theatrical Stage Employees (IATSE) is the labor union representing technicians, artisans and crafts workers in the entertainment industry, including live theater, film and television production and trade shows.

International Animated Film Society (ASIFA-Hollywood)
2114 W. Burbank Blvd.
Burbank, CA 91506 USA
Phone: 818-842-8330
E-mail Address: info@asifa-hollywood.org
Web Address: www.asifa-hollywood.org
International Animated Film Society (ASIFA-Hollywood) is a nonprofit organization dedicated to the advancement of the art of animation.

International Documentary Association (IDA)
3600 Wilshire Blvd., Ste. 1810
Los Angeles, CA 90010 USA
Phone: 213-232-1660
Fax: 213-232-1669
E-mail Address: info@documentary.org
Web Address: www.documentary.org
The International Documentary Association (IDA) is a nonprofit member service organization, providing publications, benefits and a public forum to its members for issues regarding nonfiction film, video and multimedia.

Motion Picture Association of America (MPAA)
15301 Ventura Blvd., Bldg. E
Sherman Oaks, CA 91403 USA
Phone: 818-995-6600
Fax: 818-285-4403
E-mail Address: ContactUs@mpaa.org
Web Address: www.mpaa.org
The Motion Picture Association of America (MPAA) serves as the voice and

advocate of the U.S. motion picture, home video and television industries.

Motion Picture Editors Guild (MPEG)
7715 Sunset Blvd., Ste. 200
Hollywood, CA 90046 USA
Phone: 323-876-4770
Fax: 323-876-0861
Toll Free: 800-705-8700
E-mail Address: social@editorsguild.com
Web Address: www.editorsguild.com
The Motion Picture Editors Guild's (MPEG) web site provides an online directory of editors, a discussion forum and links to related magazines and other organizations that serve the motion picture industry.

Producers Guild of America, Inc. (PGA)
11150 W. Olympic Blvd., Ste. 980
Los Angeles, CA 90064 USA
Phone: 310-358-9020
Fax: 310-358-9520
E-mail Address: info@producersguild.org
Web Address: www.producersguild.org
The Producers Guild of America, Inc. (PGA) is a nonprofit organization for career professionals who initiate, create, coordinate, supervise and control all aspects of the motion picture and television production processes.

Women In Film (WIF)
4221 Wilshire Blvd., Ste. 130
Los Angeles, CA 90010 USA
Phone: 323-935-2211
Fax: 323-935-2212
E-mail Address: info@wif.org
Web Address: www.wif.org
Women In Film (WIF) strives to empower, promote and mentor women in the entertainment, communication and media industries through a network of contacts, educational programs and events.

43) Fitness Industry Associations

American Fitness Professionals and Associates (AFPA)
1601 Long Beach Blvd.
P.O. Box 214
Ship Bottom, NJ 08008 USA
Phone: 609-978-7583
Fax: 609-978-7582
Toll Free: 800-494-7782
E-mail Address: afpa@afpafitness.com
Web Address: www.afpafitness.com
American Fitness Professionals and Associates (AFPA) offers health and fitness professionals certification programs, continuing education courses,

home correspondence courses and regional conventions.

44) Food Industry Associations, General

Institute of Food Technologies (IFT)
525 W. Van Buren, Ste. 1000
Chicago, IL 60607 USA
Phone: 312-782-8424
Fax: 312-782-8348
Toll Free: 800-438-3663
E-mail Address: info@ift.org
Web Address: www.ift.org
The Institute of Food Technologies (IFT) is devoted to the advancement of the science and technology of food through the exchange of knowledge. The site also provides information and resources for job seekers in the food industry. Members work in food science, food technology and related professions in industry, academia and government.

45) Food Industry Resources, General

Food Manufacturing
199 E. Badger Rd., Ste. 101
Madison, WI 53713 USA
Phone: 973-920-7761
E-mail Address:
abmprogrequests@advantagemedia.com
Web Address:
www.foodmanufacturing.com
Food Manufacturing is a trade magazine for companies and employees in the food manufacturing industry. It is published by Advantage Business Media.

46) Food Processor Industry Associations

Grocery Manufacturers Association (GMA)
1350 I St. NW, Ste. 300
Washington, DC 20005 USA
Phone: 202-639-5900
Fax: 202-639-5932
E-mail Address: info@gmaonline.org
Web Address: www.gmaonline.org
The Grocery Manufacturers Association (GMA), formerly the National Food Products Association (NFPA), is the voice of the food, beverage and consumer products industry on scientific and public policy issues involving food safety, food security, nutrition, technical and regulatory matters and consumer affairs.

National Frozen and Refrigerated Foods Association (NFRA)
4755 Linglestown Rd., Ste. 300

Harrisburg, PA 17112 USA
Phone: 717-657-8601
Fax: 717-657-9862
E-mail Address: info@nfraweb.org
Web Address: www.nfraweb.org
The National Frozen and Refrigerated Foods Association (NFRA) promotes the sales and consumption of refrigerated and frozen foods through education, research, training, sales planning and menu development, providing a forum for industry dialogue. It represents manufacturers, sales agents, suppliers, local associations, retailers, wholesalers, distributors and logistic providers involved in the frozen and refrigerated food industry.

47) Food Service Industry Associations

International Flight Services Association (IFSA)
1100 Fry Rd., Ste. 300
Atlanta, GA 30342 USA
Phone: 404-303-2969
E-mail Address:
ifsa@kellencompany.com
Web Address: www.ifsanet.com
The International Flight Services Association (IFSA), formerly the International Inflight Food Service Association, informs the public with respect to educational and career opportunities within the multi-billion-dollar inflight and railway food service industry. IFSA is managed by the Kellen Company.

48) Games Industry Associations

Entertainment Software Association (ESA)
601 Massachusetts Ave. NW, Ste. 300
Washington, DC 20001 USA
Phone: 202-223-2400
E-mail Address: esa@theesa.com
Web Address: www.theesa.com
The Entertainment Software Association (ESA) is a U.S. trade association for companies that publish video and computer games for consoles, personal computers and the Internet. The ESA owns the E3 Media & Business Summit, a major invitation-only annual trade show for the video game industry.

Fantasy Sports & Gaming Association (FSGA)
600 N. Lake Shore Dr.
Chicago, IL 60611 USA
Phone: 312-771-7019
E-mail Address: megan@fsga.org

Web Address: www.fsga.org
The Fantasy Sports & Gaming Association (FSGA), formerly the Fantasy Sports Trade Association, was founded in 1997 to provide a forum for interaction between companies in a unique and growing fantasy sports industry. FSGA represents more than 300 member companies.

Game Manufacturers Association (GAMA)
258 E. Campus View Blvd.
Columbus, OH 43235 USA
Phone: 614-255-4500
Fax: 614-255-4499
E-mail Address: ed@gama.org
Web Address: www.gama.org
The Game Manufacturers Association (GAMA) is an international non-profit trade association serving the hobby games industry. It hosts two annual events, the GAMA Trade Show and Origins Game Fair, and publishes a quarterly information newsletter, GAMATimes.

International Game Developers Association (IGDA)
1 Eglinton Ave. E., Ste. 705
Toronto, ON M4P 3A1 Canada
Phone: 856-423-2990
E-mail Address: info@igda.org
Web Address: www.igda.org
The International Game Developers Association (IGDA) represents members involved in the video game production industry. The firm aims to promote professional development within the gaming industry and advocates for issues that affect the game developer community, including anti-censorship issues.

49) Grocery Industry Associations

National Grocers Association (NGA)
1005 N. Glebe Rd., Ste. 250
Arlington, VA 22201-5758 USA
Phone: 703-516-0700
Fax: 703-516-0115
E-mail Address:
feedback@nationalgrocers.org
Web Address: www.nationalgrocers.org
The National Grocers Association (NGA) is a national trade association representing retail and wholesale grocers that comprise the independent sector of the food distribution industry.

50) Health & Nutrition Associations

Academy of Nutrition and Dietetics
120 S. Riverside Plz., Ste. 2190
Chicago, IL 60606-6995 USA
Phone: 312-899-0040
Toll Free: 800-877-1600
E-mail Address: foundation@eatright.org
Web Address: www.eatright.org
The Academy of Nutrition and Dietetics,
formerly known as the American Dietetic
Association (ADA) is the world's largest
organization of food and nutrition
professionals, with nearly 65,000
members. In addition to services for its
professional members, this organization's
web site offers consumers a respected
source for food and nutrition information.

51) Health Care Business & Professional Associations

Advanced Medical Technology Association (AdvaMed)
701 Pennsylvania Ave. NW, Ste. 800
Washington, DC 20004-2654 USA
Phone: 202-783-8700
Fax: 202-783-8750
E-mail Address: info@advamed.org
Web Address: www.advamed.org
The Advanced Medical Technology
Association (AdvaMed) strives to be the
advocate for a legal, regulatory and
economic climate that advances global
health care by assuring worldwide access
to the benefits of medical technology.

American Academy of Nursing (AAN)
1000 Vermont Ave., Ste. 910
Washington, DC 20005 USA
Phone: 202-777-1170
E-mail Address: info@aannet.org
Web Address: www.aannet.org
The American Academy of Nursing
(AAN) works to enhance nursing
profession by advancing health policy and
practice and generate, synthesize and
disseminate nursing knowledge.

American Association of Medical Assistants (AAMA)
20 N. Wacker Dr., Ste. 1575
Chicago, IL 60606 USA
Phone: 312-899-1500
Fax: 312-899-1259
Toll Free: 800-228-2262
Web Address: www.aama-ntl.org
The American Association of Medical
Assistants (AAMA) seeks to promote the
professional identity and stature of its
members and the medical assisting
profession through education and
credentialing.

American College of Health Care Administrators (ACHCA)
1101 Connecticut Ave. NW, Ste. 450
Washington, DC 20036 USA
Phone: 800-561-3148
Fax: 800-561-3148
E-mail Address: info@achca.org
Web Address: www.achca.org
The American College of Health Care
Administrators (ACHCA) offers
educational programming, professional
certification and career development
opportunities for health care
administrators.

American College of Healthcare Executives (ACHE)
300 S. Riverside Plaza, Ste. 1900
Chicago, IL 60606-6698 USA
Phone: 312-424-2800
Fax: 312-424-0023
E-mail Address: contact@ache.org
Web Address: www.ache.org
The American College of Healthcare
Executives (ACHE) is an international
professional society of health care
executives that offers certification and
educational programs.

American Dental Association (ADA)
211 E. Chicago Ave.
Chicago, IL 60611-2678 USA
Phone: 312-440-2500
Web Address: www.ada.org
The American Dental Association (ADA)
is a nonprofit professional association of
dentists committed to enhancing public's
oral health with a focus on ethics, science
and professional advancement.

American Medical Technologists (AMT)
10700 W. Higgins Rd., Ste. 150
Rosemont, IL 60018 USA
Phone: 847-823-5169
Fax: 847-823-0458
E-mail Address:
mail@americanmedtech.org
Web Address: www.americanmedtech.org
American Medical Technologists (AMT)
is a nationally and internationally
recognized nonprofit certification agency
and professional membership association
representing allied health professionals.
Its members include laboratory health
professionals, as well as medical and
dental office professionals.

American Medical Women's Association (AMWA)
1100 E. Woodfield Rd., Ste. 350
Schaumberg, IL 60173 USA
Phone: 847-517-2801
Fax: 847-517-7229
Toll Free: 866-564-2483

E-mail Address:
associatedirector@amwa-doc.org
Web Address: www.amwa-doc.org
The American Medical Women's
Association (AMWA) is an organization
of women physicians and medical
students dedicated to serving as the
unique voice for women's health and the
advancement of women in medicine.

American Occupational Therapy Association, Inc. (AOTA)
6116 Executive Blvd., Ste. 200
North Bethesda, MD 20852-4929 USA
Phone: 301-652-6611
Fax: 301-652-7711
Toll Free: 800-377-8555
Web Address: www.aota.org
The American Occupational Therapy
Association, Inc. (AOTA) advances the
quality, availability, use and support of
occupational therapy through standard-
setting, advocacy, education and research
on behalf of its members and the public.

American Organization of Nurse Executives (AONE)
155 N. Wacker Dr., Ste. 400
Chicago, IL 60606 USA
Phone: 312-422-2800
E-mail Address: aone@aha.org
Web Address: www.aone.org
The American Organization of Nurse
Executives (AONE) is a national
organization focused on advancing
nursing practice and patient care through
leadership, professional development,
advocacy and research.

American Public Health Association (APHA)
800 I St. NW
Washington, DC 20001-3710 USA
Phone: 202-777-2742
Fax: 202-777-2534
Web Address: www.apha.org
The American Public Health Association
(APHA) is an association of individuals
and organizations working to improve the
public's health and to achieve equity in
health status for all.

American School Health Association (ASHA)
7918 Jones Branch Dr., Ste. 300
McLean, VA 22102 USA
Phone: 703-506-7675
Fax: 703-506-3266
E-mail Address: info@ashaweb.org
Web Address: www.ashaweb.org
The American School Health Association
(ASHA) advocates high-quality school
health instruction, health services and a
healthy school environment.

Dental Trade Alliance (DTA)
4350 N. Fairfax Dr., Ste. 220
Arlington, VA 22203 USA
Phone: 703-379-7755
Fax: 703-931-9429
Web Address:
www.dentaltradealliance.org
The Dental Trade Alliance (DTA)
represents dental manufacturers, dental
dealers and dental laboratories.

**Health Industry Distributors
Association (HIDA)**
310 Montgomery St.
Alexandria, VA 22314-1516 USA
Phone: 703-549-4432
Fax: 703-549-6495
E-mail Address: rowan@hida.org
Web Address: www.hida.org
The Health Industry Distributors
Association (HIDA) is the international
trade association representing medical
products distributors.

**Healthcare Financial Management
Association (HFMA)**
3 Westbrook Corp. Ctr., Ste. 600
Westchester, IL 60154 USA
Phone: 708-531-9600
Fax: 708-531-0032
Toll Free: 800-252-4362
E-mail Address: inquiry@hfma.org
Web Address: www.hfma.org
The Healthcare Financial Management
Association (HFMA) is one of the nation's
leading personal membership
organizations for health care financial
management executives and leaders.

**Medical Device Manufacturers
Association (MDMA)**
1333 H St., Ste. 400 W.
Washington, DC 20005 USA
Phone: 202-354-7171
Web Address: www.medicaldevices.org
The Medical Device Manufacturers
Association (MDMA) is a national trade
association that represents independent
manufacturers of medical devices,
diagnostic products and health care
information systems.

**Medical Group Management
Association (MGMA)**
104 Inverness Terrace E.
Englewood, CO 80112-5306 USA
Phone: 303-799-1111
Toll Free: 877-275-6462
E-mail Address: hkohtz@mgma.com
Web Address: www.mgma.com
Medical Group Management Association
(MGMA) is one of the nation's principal
voices for medical group practice. It
represents over 33,000 administrators and
executives in 18,000 healthcare

organizations in which 385,000
physicians practice.

**National Association of Health Services
Executives (NAHSE)**
1050 Connecticut Ave. NW, Fl. 5
Washington, DC 20036 USA
Phone: 202-772-1030
Fax: 202-772-1072
Web Address: www.nahse.org
The National Association of Health
Services Executives (NAHSE) is a
nonprofit association of black health care
executives who promote the advancement
and development of black health care
leaders and elevate the quality of health
care services rendered to minority and
underserved communities.

**Regulatory Affairs Professionals
Society (RAPS)**
5635 Fishers Ln., Ste. 550
Rockville, MD 20852 USA
Phone: 301-770-2920 ext.200
Fax: 301-841-7956
E-mail Address: raps@raps.org
Web Address: www.raps.org
The Regulatory Affairs Professionals
Society (RAPS) is an international
professional society representing the
health care regulatory affairs profession
and individual professionals worldwide.

52) Health Insurance Industry Associations

**America's Health Insurance Plans
(AHIP)**
601 Pennsylvania Ave. NW
S. Bldg., Ste. 500
Washington, DC 20004 USA
Phone: 202-778-3200
Fax: 202-331-7487
E-mail Address: ahip@ahip.org
Web Address: www.ahip.org
America's Health Insurance Plans (AHIP)
is a prominent trade association
representing the health care insurance
community. Its members offer health and
supplemental benefits through employer-
sponsored coverage, the individual
insurance market, and public programs
such as Medicare and Medicaid.

53) Hearing & Speech

Hearing Industries Association (HIA)
777 6th St. NW, Ste. 09-114
Washington, DC 20001 USA
Phone: 202-975-0905
Fax: 202-216-9646
E-mail Address: mjones@bostrom.com
Web Address: www.hearing.org

The Hearing Industries Association (HIA)
represents and unifies the many aspects of
the hearing industry.

54) Hotel/Lodging Associations

**American Hotel and Lodging
Association**
1250 I St., NW, Ste. 1100
Washington, DC 20005-3931 USA
Phone: 202-289-3100
Fax: 202-289-3199
E-mail Address:
informationcenter@ahla.com
Web Address: www.ahla.com
The American Hotel and Lodging
Association is a federation of state
lodging associations throughout the U.S.

55) Human Resources Industry Associations

**Association for Talent Development
(ATD) (The)**
1640 King St.
Alexandria, VA 22313-1443 USA
Phone: 703-683-8100
Fax: 703-299-8723
Toll Free: 800-628-2783
E-mail Address: customercare@td.org
Web Address: www.td.org
The Association for Talent Development
(ATD), formerly American Society for
Training & Development (ASTD) is
dedicated to those professionals in the
fields of training and development. It
provides resources such as research,
analysis, benchmarking, online
information, books and other publications
to training and development professional,
educators and students. Additionally, the
association brings professional together in
conferences, workshops and online, while
also offering professional development
opportunities, certificate programs and
Certified Professional in Learning and
Performance (CPLP) credential.

HR Policy Association
1001 19th St. N., Ste. 1002
Arlington, VA 22209 USA
Phone: 202-789-8670
Fax: 202-789-0064
E-mail Address: info@hrpolicy.org
Web Address: www.hrpolicy.org
HR Policy Association is a public policy
organization of chief human resource
officers from major employers. The
association brings together HR
professionals at the highest level of
corporations to discuss changes in public
policy, and to lay out a vision and
advocate for competitive workplace

initiatives that promote job growth and employment security.

Society for Human Resource Management (SHRM)
1800 Duke St.
Alexandria, VA 22314 USA
Phone: 703-548-3440
Fax: 703-535-6490
Toll Free: 800-283-7476
E-mail Address: shrm@shrm.org
Web Address: www.shrm.org
The Society for Human Resource Management (SHRM) addresses the interests and needs of HR professionals through advocacy, publications, research and other resource materials. The organization has 575 affiliate chapters, both in the U.S. and internationally, serving over 5,000 members in approximately 160 countries.

56) Industry Research/Market Research

Forrester Research
60 Acorn Park Dr.
Cambridge, MA 02140 USA
Phone: 617-613-5730
Toll Free: 866-367-7378
E-mail Address: press@forrester.com
Web Address: www.forrester.com
Forrester Research is a publicly traded company that identifies and analyzes emerging trends in technology and their impact on business. Among the firm's specialties are the financial services, retail, health care, entertainment, automotive and information technology industries.

MarketResearch.com
6116 Executive Blvd., Ste. 550
Rockville, MD 20852 USA
Phone: 240-747-3093
Fax: 240-747-3004
Toll Free: 800-298-5699
E-mail Address: customerservice@marketresearch.com
Web Address: www.marketresearch.com
MarketResearch.com is a leading broker for professional market research and industry analysis. Users are able to search the company's database of research publications including data on global industries, companies, products and trends.

Plunkett Research, Ltd.
P.O. Drawer 541737
Houston, TX 77254-1737 USA
Phone: 713-932-0000
Fax: 713-932-7080

E-mail Address: customersupport@plunkettresearch.com
Web Address: www.plunkettresearch.com
Plunkett Research, Ltd. is a leading provider of market research, industry trends analysis and business statistics. Since 1985, it has served clients worldwide, including corporations, universities, libraries, consultants and government agencies. At the firm's web site, visitors can view product information and pricing and access a large amount of basic market information on industries such as financial services, InfoTech, ecommerce, health care and biotech.

57) Insurance Industry Associations

American Property Casualty Insurance Association (PCIAA)
8700 West Bryn Mawr Ave., Ste. 1200S
Chicago, IL 60631-3512 USA
Phone: 847-297-7800
Fax: 947-297-5064
E-mail Address: susan.sheperd@apci.org
Web Address: www.pciaa.net
The American Property Casualty Insurance Association (PCIAA), which is the formation of the Propery Casualty Insurers (PCI) and the American Insurance Association (AIA), is an advocacy group that informs members' on public policy positions in all 50 states and on Capitol Hill, and to keep our members current on the information that is critical to their businesses.

58) Insurance Industry Associations-Agents & Brokers

Council of Insurance Agents & Brokers (CIAB)
701 Pennsylvania Ave. NW, Ste. 750
Washington, DC 20004 USA
Phone: 202-783-4400
Fax: 202-783-4410
E-mail Address: ciab@ciab.com
Web Address: www.ciab.com
The Council of Insurance Agents & Brokers (CIAB) is an association for commercial insurance and employee benefits intermediaries in the U.S. and abroad.

Independent Insurance Agents & Brokers of America, Inc. (IIABA)
127 S. Peyton St.
Alexandria, VA 22314 USA
Fax: 703-683-7556
Toll Free: 800-221-7917
E-mail Address: info@iiaba.org

Web Address: www.independentagent.com
Independent Insurance Agents & Brokers of America (IIABA) represents its over 300,000 members who are independent insurance agents and brokers.

Professional Insurance Agents (PIA)
25 Chamberlain St.
P.O. Box 997
Glenmont, NY 12077-0997 USA
Fax: 888-225-6935
Toll Free: 800-424-4244
E-mail Address: pia@pia.org
Web Address: www.piaonline.org
Professional Insurance Agents (PIA) is a group of voluntary, membership-based trade associations representing professional, independent property and casualty insurance agents.

59) Investment Industry Associations

Securities Industry and Financial Markets Association (SIFMA)
120 Broadway, Fl. 35
New York, NY 10271-0080 USA
Phone: 212-313-1200
Fax: 212-313-1301
E-mail Address: inquiry@sifma.org
Web Address: www.sifma.org
The Securities Industry and Financial Markets Association (SIFMA), formed by the merger of the Securities Industry Association (SIA) and the Bond Market Association, brings together the shared interests of more than 650 securities and bond industry firms to accomplish common goals.

60) Magazines, Business & Financial

Bloomberg Businessweek Online
731 Lexington Ave.
New York, NY 10022 USA
Phone: 212-318-2000
Fax: 917-369-5000
Web Address: www.businessweek.com
Business Week Online offers an investor service, global business advice, technology news, small business guides, career information, business school advice, daily news briefs and more.

Forbes Online
60 5th Ave.
New York, NY 10011 USA
Phone: 212-620-2200
E-mail Address: customerservice@forbes.com
Web Address: www.forbes.com

Forbes Online offers varied stock information, news and commentary on business, technology and personal finance, as well as financial calculators and advice.

Fortune
1271 Ave. of the Americas
Rockefeller Ctr.
New York, NY 10020-1393 USA
Phone: 212-522-8528
Web Address: http://fortune.com/
Fortune, one of the world's premiere business magazines, contains news, business profiles and information on investing, careers, small business, technology and other details of U.S. and international business. Fortune is a publication of Cable News Network (CNN), a Time Warner company.

Investor's Business Daily (IBD)
12655 Beatrice St.
Los Angeles, CA 90066 USA
Phone: 310-448-6000
Toll Free: 800-831-2525
Web Address: www.investors.com
Investor's Business Daily (IBD) offers subscribers information and articles on the stock market, educational resources, advice from analyst William O'Neil, personal portfolios and updates on events and workshops.

Wall Street Journal Online (The)
1211 Ave. of the Americas
New York, NY 10036 USA
Phone: 609-514-0870
Toll Free: 800-568-7625
E-mail Address: support@wsj.com
Web Address: www.wsj.com
The outstanding resources of The Wall Street Journal are available online for a nominal fee.

61) MBA Resources

MBA Depot
Web Address: www.mbadepot.com
MBA Depot is an online community and information portal for MBAs, potential MBA program applicants and business professionals.

62) Online Recruiting & Employment ASPs & Solutions

Hrsoft
2200 Lucien Way, Ste. 201
Maitland, FL 32751 USA
Phone: 407-475-5500
Fax: 407-475-5502
Toll Free: 866-953-8800

E-mail Address: Michael.Noland@HRsoft.com
Web Address: www.hrsoft.com
HRsoft, formerly Workstream, Inc., creates workforce management solutions through a combination of technology and services designed to integrate an organization.

Insala
2005 NE Green Oaks Blvd., Ste. 110
Arlington, TX 76006 USA
Phone: 817-355-0939
Fax: 817-355-0746
E-mail Address: info@insala.com
Web Address: www.insala.com
Insala provides job search software solutions for the outplacement industry.

Kenexa
650 E. Swedesford Rd., Fl. 2
Wayne, PA 19087 USA
Phone: 877-971-9171
Fax: 610-971-9181
Toll Free: 800-391-9557
E-mail Address: contactus@kenexa.com
Web Address: www.kenexa.com
Kenexa is a back-end recruiting and job-posting service that is used by many companies in building a workforce. Products and services include recruitment software solutions, talent consulting and recruitment process management.

63) Outsourcing Industry Associations

International Association of Outsourcing Professionals (IAOP)
2600 South Rd., Ste. 44-240
Poughkeepsie, NY 12601 USA
Phone: 845-452-0600
Fax: 845-452-6988
E-mail Address: memberservices@iaop.org
Web Address: www.iaop.org
The International Association of Outsourcing Professionals (IAOP) represents outsourcing leaders and experts from companies of all sizes and industries around the world.

64) Pensions, Benefits & 401(k) Associations

Plan Sponsor Council of America (PSCA)
20 N. Wacker Dr., Ste. 3164
Chicago, IL 60606 USA
Phone: 312-419-1863
Fax: 312-419-1864
E-mail Address: psca@psca.org
Web Address: www.psca.org

The Plan Sponsor Council of America (PSCA), formerly the Profit Sharing/401(k) Council of America (PSCA). is a national nonprofit association of 1,200 companies and their 6 million employees. The group expresses its members' interests to federal policymakers and offers practical, cost-effective assistance with profit sharing and 401(k) plan design, administration, investment, compliance and communication. Its web site offers a thorough glossary, statistics and educational material.

65) Pensions, Benefits & 401(k) Resources

Employee Benefits Security Administration (EBSA)
200 Constitution Ave. NW
Washington, DC 20210 USA
Toll Free: 866-444-3272
Web Address: www.dol.gov/ebsa
The Employee Benefits Security Administration (EBSA) is a division of the U.S. Department of Labor, whose web site features a wealth of benefits information for both employers and employees. Included are the answers to such questions as to how a company's bankruptcy will affect its employees and what one should know about pension rights.

Pension Benefit Guarantee Corporation (PBGC)
1200 K St. NW, Ste. 9429
Washington, DC 20005-4026 USA
Phone: 202-326-4000
Fax: 202-326-4047
Toll Free: 800-400-7242
E-mail Address: webmaster@pbgc.gov
Web Address: www.pbgc.gov
The Pension Benefit Guarantee Corporation (PBGC) is a U.S. Government agency that guarantees a portion of the retirement incomes of about 41 million American workers in about 24,000 private defined benefit pension plans. Its web site contains information regarding this guarantee, along with information on retirement planning and links to several related organizations.

66) Pharmaceutical Industry Associations (Drug Industry)

American Pharmacists Association (AphA)
2215 Constitution Ave. NW
Washington, DC 20037 USA
Phone: 202-628-4410

Fax: 202-783-2351
Toll Free: 800-237-2742
E-mail Address: infocenter@aphanet.org
Web Address: www.pharmacist.com
American Pharmaceutical Association
(APhA), formerly American
Pharmaceutical Association is a national
professional society that provides news
and information to pharmacists. Its
membership includes over 62,000
practicing pharmacists, pharmaceutical
scientists, student pharmacists and
pharmacy technicians.

**Pharmaceutical Research and
Manufacturers of America (PhRMA)**
950 F St. NW, Ste. 300
Washington, DC 20004 USA
Phone: 202-835-3400
Web Address: www.phrma.org
Pharmaceutical Research and
Manufacturers of America (PhRMA)
represents the nation's leading research-
based pharmaceutical and biotechnology
companies.

67) Pilots Associations

Airline Pilots Association (ALPA)
1625 Massachusetts Ave NW
Washington, DC 20036 USA
Phone: 703-689-2270
E-mail Address: media@alpa.org
Web Address: www.alpa.org
The Airline Pilots Association (ALPA) is
an association for professional airline
pilots in the United States, in Canada and
internationally. ALPA provides airline
safety, security, pilot assistance,
representation and advocacy to its
members.

68) Printers & Publishers Associations

Idealliance
1800 Diagonal Rd., Ste. 320
Alexandria, VA 22314-2862 USA
Phone: 703-837-1070
Fax: 703-837-1072
Web Address: www.idealliance.org
Idealliance, which merged with Epicomm,
is a global graphic communications
industry non-profit association with
eleven (11) strategically located offices
around the world. Idealliance serves
brands, OEMs, service providers in print
and packaging, content and media
creators, creative agencies and design
teams, material suppliers, and technology
developers.

**In-Plant Printing and Mailing
Association (IPMA)**
103 N Jefferson St.
Kearney, MO 64060 USA
Phone: 816-919-1691
Fax: 816-902-4766
E-mail Address: ipmainfo@ipma.org
Web Address: www.ipma.org
The In-Plant Printing and Mailing
Association (IPMA), formerly the
International Publishing Management
Association, is an exclusive not-for-profit
organization dedicated to assisting in-
house corporate publishing and
distribution professionals.

**MPA-The Association of Magazine
Media**
1211 Connecticut Ave. NW, Ste. 610
Washington, DC 20036 USA
Phone: 202-296-7277
E-mail Address: mpa@magazine.org
Web Address: www.magazine.org
MPA-The Association of Magazine
Media (formerly the Magazine Publishers
of America, Inc.) is the industry
association for consumer magazines in all
formats, including printed, mobile and
online.

**Newspaper Association of America
(NAA)**
4401 Fairfax Dr., Ste. 300
Arlington, VA 22203 USA
Phone: 571-366-1000
Fax: 571-366-1195
E-mail Address:
info@newsmediaalliance.org
Web Address:
www.newsmediaalliance.org
The Newspaper Association of America
(NAA) is a nonprofit organization
representing the newspaper industry.

69) Real Estate Industry Associations

**Institute of Real Estate Management
(IREM)**
430 N. Michigan Ave.
Chicago, IL 60611 USA
Fax: 800-338-4736
Toll Free: 800-837-0706
E-mail Address: getinfo@irem.org
Web Address: www.irem.org
The Institute of Real Estate Management
(IREM) seeks to educate real estate
managers, certify their competence and
professionalism, serve as an advocate on
issues affecting the real estate
management industry and enhance its
members' professional competence so
they can better identify and meet the
needs of those who use their services.

NAREC
6348 N. Milwaukee Ave., Ste. 103
Chicago, IL 60606 USA
Phone: 773-283-6362
E-mail Address: info@narec.org
Web Address: narec.org
NAREC, formerly PeerSpan and, prior to
that, the National Association of Real
Estate Companies, is composed of
representatives of publicly and privately
owned real estate companies, significant
subsidiaries of publicly owned companies
and public accounting firms.

**National Association of Real Estate
Brokers (NAREB)**
9831 Greenbelt Rd., Ste. 309
Lanham, MD 20706 USA
Phone: 301-552-9340
Fax: 301-552-9216
E-mail Address: info@nareb.com
Web Address: www.nareb.com
The National Association of Real Estate
Brokers (NAREB) is a national trade
organization dedicated to bringing
together the nation's minority
professionals in the real estate industry.

National Association of Realtors (NAR)
430 N. Michigan Ave.
Chicago, IL 606-4087 USA
Toll Free: 800-874-6500
Web Address: www.realtor.org
The National Association of Realtors
(NAR) is composed of realtors involved
in residential and commercial real estate
as brokers, salespeople, property
managers, appraisers and counselors and
in other areas of the industry. NAR also
sponsors Realtor.com, operated by Move,
Inc.

Women's Council of Realtors (WCR)
430 N. Michigan Ave.
Chicago, IL 60611 USA
Fax: 312-329-3290
Toll Free: 800-245-8512
E-mail Address: wcr@wcr.org
Web Address: www.wcr.org
The Women's Council of Realtors (WCR)
is a community of women real estate
professionals. It promotes the professional
growth of its members through
networking, leadership development,
resources, infrastructure and accessibility

70) Recording & Music Associations

**American Federation of Musicians
(AFM)**
1501 Broadway, Fl. 9
New York, NY 10036 USA
Phone: 212-869-1330

Fax: 212-764-6134
Toll Free: 800-762-3444
Web Address: www.afm.org
The American Federation of Musicians
(AFM) is the largest union in the world
for music professionals, serving musicians
throughout the U.S. and Canada.

**American Society of Composers,
Authors & Publishers (ASCAP)**
250 West 57th St.
New York, NY 10107 USA
Phone: 212-621-6000
Fax: 212-621-6595
Web Address: www.ascap.com
American Society of Composers, Authors
& Publishers (ASCAP) is a membership
association of U.S. composers,
songwriters and publishers of every kind
of music, with hundreds of thousands of
members worldwide.

**Content Delivery & Storage Association
(CDSA)**
39 N. Bayles Ave.
Port Washington, NY 11050 USA
Phone: 917-513-5963
E-mail Address:
kbrewer@CDSAonline.org
Web Address: www.cdsaonline.org
The Content Delivery & Storage
Association (CDSA), formerly the
International Recording Media
Association, is a worldwide trade
association for organizations involved in
every facet of recording media, including
entertainment, information and software
content storage. CDSA is under the
management of the Media &
Entertainment Services Alliance (MESA).

**International Association of Audio
Information Services (IAAIS)**
1294 E 1600 Rd.
Lawrence, KS 66046 USA
Toll Free: 800-280-5325
E-mail Address:
IAAISMember@gmail.com
Web Address: www.iaais.org
International Association of Audio
Information Services (IAAIS) is an
organization that provides audio access to
information for people who are print-
disabled.

**Music Publisher's Association of the
United States (MPA)**
243 5th Ave., Ste. 236
New York, NY 10016 USA
Phone: 212-327-4044
E-mail Address: admin@mpa.org
Web Address: mpa.org
The Music Publisher's Association of the
United States (MPA) serves as a forum
for publishers to deal with the music

industry's vital issues and is actively
involved in supporting and advancing
compliance with copyright law,
combating copyright infringement and
exploring the need for further reform.

**Recording Industry Association of
America (RIAA)**
1025 F St. NW, Fl. 10
Washington, DC 20004 USA
Phone: 202-775-0101
Web Address: www.riaa.com
The Recording Industry Association of
America (RIAA) is the trade group that
represents the U.S. recording industry.

Songwriters Guild of America
5120 Virginia Way, Ste. C22
Brentwood, TN 37027 USA
Phone: 615-742-9945
Fax: 615-630-7501
Toll Free: 800-524-6742
Web Address: www.songwritersguild.com
The Songwriters Guild of America is the
nation's largest and oldest songwriters'
organization, providing its members with
information and programs to further their
careers and understanding of the music
industry.

**71) Satellite Industry
Associations**

**Satellite Broadcasting &
Communications Association (SBCA)**
230 Washington Ave., Ste. 101
Albany, NY 12203 USA
Phone: 202-349-3620
Fax: 202-349-3621
Toll Free: 800-541-5981
E-mail Address: info@sbca.org
Web Address: www.sbca.com
The Satellite Broadcasting &
Communications Association (SBCA) is
the national trade organization
representing all segments of the satellite
consumer services industry in America.

**72) Satellite-Related
Professional Organizations**

**Society of Satellite Professionals
International (SSPI)**
250 Park Ave., Fl. 7
The New York Information Technology
Ctr.
New York, NY 10177 USA
Phone: 212-809-5199
Fax: 212-825-0075
E-mail Address: rbell@sspi.org
Web Address: www.sspi.org
The Society of Satellite Professionals
International (SSPI) is a nonprofit

member-benefit society that serves
satellite professionals worldwide.

**73) Securities Industry
Associations**

**North American Securities
Administrators Association, Inc.
(NASAA)**
750 First St. NE, Ste. 1140
Washington, DC 20002 USA
Phone: 202-737-0900
Fax: 202-783-3571
E-mail Address: ri@nasaa.org
Web Address: www.nasaa.org
The North American Securities
Administrators Association (NASAA) is
the oldest international organization
committed to investor protection. Its web
site provides information on franchising
and raising capital, as well as state blue
sky securities laws and resources for small
investment advisors.

**74) Software Industry
Associations**

**Software & Information Industry
Association (SIIA)**
1090 Vermont Ave. NW, Fl. 6
Washington, DC 20005-4095 USA
Phone: 202-289-7442
Fax: 202-289-7097
Web Address: www.siia.net
The Software & Information Industry
Association (SIIA) is a principal trade
association for the software and digital
content industry.

**75) Stocks & Financial Markets
Data**

Reuters.com
3 Times Sq.
New York, NY 10036 USA
Phone: 646-223-6890
Web Address: www.reuters.com
Reuters.com, a service of Thomson
Reuters, offers information on business
and world markets, political and
international news and company-specific
stock information.

Yahoo! Finance
701 1st Ave.
Yahoo! Inc.
Sunnyvale, CA 94089 USA
Phone: 408-349-3300
Web Address: finance.yahoo.com
Yahoo! Finance provides a wealth of links
and a supreme search guide. Users can
find just about any financial information
concerning both U.S. and world markets.

Tax, insurance information, financial news and community research can be conducted through this site, as can searches for other aspects of the financial world.

76) Telecommunications Industry Associations

INCOMPAS
1100 G St. NW, Ste. 800
Washington, DC 20005 USA
Phone: 202-296-6650
E-mail Address: gnorris@comptel.org
Web Address: www.incompas.org
CompTel is a trade organization representing voice, data and video communications service providers and their supplier partners. Members are supported through education, networking, policy advocacy and trade shows.

National Association of Telecommunications Officers and Advisors (NATOA)
3213 Duke St., Ste. 695
Alexandria, VA 22314 USA
Phone: 703-519-8035
Fax: 703-997-7080
E-mail Address: info@natoa.org
Web Address: www.natoa.org
The National Association of Telecommunications Officers and Advisors (NATOA) works to support and serve the telecommunications industry's interests and the needs of local governments.

Telecommunications Industry Association (TIA)
1310 N. Courthouse Rd., Ste. 890
Arlington, VA 22201 USA
Phone: 703-907-7700
Fax: 703-907-7727
E-mail Address: smontgomery@tiaonline.org
Web Address: www.tiaonline.org
The Telecommunications Industry Association (TIA) is a leading trade association in the information, communications and entertainment technology industry. TIA focuses on market development, trade promotion, trade shows, domestic and international advocacy, standards development and enabling e-business.

United States Telecom Association (USTelecom)
601 New Jersey Ave. NW, Ste. 600
Washington, DC 20001 USA
Phone: 202-326-7300
Fax: 202-315-3603
E-mail Address: membership@ustelecom.org
Web Address: www.ustelecom.org
The United States Telecom Association (USTelecom) is a trade association representing service providers and suppliers for the telecom industry.

77) Temporary Staffing Firms

Adecco
Saegereistrasse 10
Glattbrugg, CH-8152 Switzerland
Phone: 41-44-878-88-88
Fax: 41-44-829-88-06
E-mail Address: press.office@adecco.com
Web Address: www.adecco.com
Adecco maintains human resources and staffing services offices in 70 countries. It provides temporary and permanent personnel.

Advantage Resourcing, Inc.
220 Norwood Park S.
Norwood, MA 02062 USA
Phone: 781-251-8000
Toll Free: 800-343-4314
E-mail Address: M
Web Address: www.hirethinking.com
Advantage Resourcing, Inc., formerly Radia Holdings, Inc., provides integrated human resources services throughout Japan, North America, Europe and Australia. It is one of the largest staffing providers, with over 350 branches and satellite offices.

Allegis Group
7301 Parkway Dr.
Hanover, MD 21076 USA
Toll Free: 800-927-8090
Web Address: www.allegisgroup.com
The Allegis Group provides technical, professional and industrial recruiting and staffing services. Allegis specializes in information technology staffing services. The firm operates in the United Kingdom, Germany and The Netherlands as Aerotek and TEKsystems, and in India as Allegis Group India. Aerotek provides staffing solutions for aviation, engineering, automotive and scientific personnel markets.

CDI Corporation
1735 Market St., Ste. 200
Philadelphia, PA 190103 USA
Phone: 215-636-1240
E-mail Address: engineeringsolutions@cdicorp.com
Web Address: www.cdicorp.com
CDI Corporation specializes in engineering and information technology staffing services. Company segments include CDI IT Solutions, specializing in information technology; CDI Engineering Solutions, specializing in engineering outsourcing services; AndersElite Limited, operating in the United Kingdom and Australia; and MRINetwork, specializing in executive recruitment.

Express Employment Professionals
9701 Boardwalk Blvd.
Oklahoma City, OK 73162 USA
Phone: 405-840-5000
Toll Free: 888-923-3797
Web Address: www.expresspros.com
Express Employment Professionals operates through a network of over 550 locations in the United States, Canada, South Africa and Australia. Services include temporary and flexible staffing, evaluation and direct hire, professional and contract staffing, human resource services and online payroll processing (U.S. only).

Glotel Inc.
8700 W. Bryn Mawr Ave., Ste. 400N
Chicago, IL 60631 USA
Phone: 312-612-7480
E-mail Address: info@glotelinc.com
Web Address: www.glotel.com
Glotel is a global technology staffing and managed projects solutions company specializing in the placement of contract and permanent personnel within all areas of technology. Glotel has a network of offices throughout Europe, the U.S. and Asia-Pacific.

Harvey Nash
110 Bishopgate
London, EC2N 4AY UK
Phone: 44-20-7333-0033
Fax: 44-20-7333-0032
E-mail Address: info@harveynash.com
Web Address: www.harveynash.com
Harvey Nash provides professional recruitment, interim executive leadership services and outsourcing services. The firm specializes in information technology staffing on a permanent and contract basis in US, UK and Europe. It also offers outsourcing services including offshore software development services, information technology systems management, workforce risk management and managed services for network administration.

Hays plc
250 Euston Rd.
London, NW1 2AF UK
Phone: 44-20-7383-2266
Fax: 44-20-7388-4367

E-mail Address:
customersercive@hays.com
Web Address: www.hays.com
Hays plc is a global leader in specialist recruitment. It places professional candidates in permanent, temporary and interim positions across numerous fields, including accountancy and finance; education; health care; IT and telecom; manufacturing and engineering; pharmaceuticals; professional services; retail, sales and marketing; and support services.

Hudson Highland Group, Inc.
1325 Avenue of the Americas, Fl. 12
New York, NY 10019 USA
Phone: 212-351-7400
Fax: 212-351-7401
Web Address: www.hudson.com
Hudson Highland Group, Inc. provides permanent recruitment, contract and human resources consulting and inclusion solutions. Services range from single placements to total outsourced solutions. The company employs professionals serving clients and candidates in 20 countries.

Kelly Services, Inc.
999 W. Big Beaver Rd.
Troy, MI 48084-4782 USA
Phone: 248-362-4444
E-mail Address: kfirst@kellyservices.com
Web Address: www.kellyservices.com
Kelly Services is a workforce solutions company offering a wide range of outsourcing and consulting services, as well as quality staffing on a temporary, temporary-to-hire and direct-hire basis both locally and worldwide.

Kforce, Inc.
1001 E. Palm Ave.
Tampa, FL 33605 USA
Toll Free: 800-395-5575
E-mail Address:
internalstaffing@kforce.com
Web Address: www.kforce.com
Kforce, Inc. is one of America's largest temporary placement firms, with more than 70 offices in 44 cities across the U.S. It specializes in employees for the following types of jobs: finance and accounting, scientific, technology, health care, clinical research, mortgages, title insurance and real estate.

Labor Ready, Inc.
1015 A St.
Tacoma, WA 98402 USA
Phone: 253-383-9101
Fax: 877-733-0399
Toll Free: 877-733-0430

E-mail Address:
customercare@laborready.com
Web Address: www.laborready.com
Labor Ready, Inc. specializes in temporary staffing in construction, manufacturing, hospitality services, transportation, landscaping, warehousing, retail and more with almost 700 branches throughout the U.S., Canada and Puerto Rico.

Manpower, Inc.
100 Manpower Pl.
Milwaukee, WI 53212 USA
Phone: 414-961-1000
Fax: 414-906-7822
E-mail Address:
Britt.Zarling@manpowergroup.com
Web Address: www.manpower.com
One of the largest temporary staffing providers in the world, Manpower places approximately 2 million workers annually in a variety of positions around the world.

Michael Page International plc
Page House, 1 Dashwood Lang Rd.
Addlestone, Weybridge
Surrey, KT15 2QW UK
Phone: 44-207-831-2000
Web Address: www.michaelpage.co.uk
Michael Page International is one of the world's leading professional recruitment consultancies specializing in the placement of candidates in permanent, contract, temporary and interim positions. The Group has operations in the US, UK, Continental Europe, Asia-Pacific and a regional presence in France and Australia. In the US, the firm's focus is on the areas of financial services, supply chain, executive searches, marketing, legal and administrative support.

Pasona Group Inc. (Japan)
Otemachi 2-6-4 Chiyoda-ku
Tokyo, 100-8228 Japan
Web Address: www.pasonagroup.co.jp
Pasona, Inc. provides personnel services, ranging from temporary staffing/contracting, placement/recruiting and outplacement to outsourcing and training.

Randstad USA
2015 S. Park Pl.
Atlanta, GA 30339 USA
Phone: 770-937-7000
Fax: 770-937-7100
Toll Free: 877-922-2468
E-mail Address: info@us.randstad.com
Web Address: www.us.randstad.com
Randstad provides staffing services in the office, industrial, technical, creative and professional markets. It specializes in temporary and permanent staffing;

recruitment and consultant services; and human resource services. It operates in 83 countries, primarily in Europe, Asia and the U.S. Brands include Capac, Yacht, and Tempo-Team.

Robert Half International Inc. (RHI)
2884 Sand Hill Rd.
Menlo Park, CA 94025 USA
Phone: 650-234-6000
E-mail Address: webmaster@rhi.com
Web Address: www.rhi.com
Robert Half International Inc. (RHI) specializes in accounting and finance positions. It also places workers in administrative, information technology, legal, advertising and marketing positions on temporary or permanent bases.

Robert Walters plc
11 Slingsby Pl.
St. Martin's Courtyard
London, WC2E 9AB UK
Phone: 44-20-7379-3333
Fax: 44-20-7509-8714
E-mail Address:
london@robertwalters.com
Web Address: www.robertwalters.com
Robert Walters PLC is a professional recruitment specialist, outsourcing and human resource consultant. The firm provides services for the temporary, contract and permanent placement of individuals in the sectors of finance, operations, legal, information technology, marketing and administration support. It has offices in 24 countries including the US.

Spherion Corporation
33625 Cumberland Blvd., Ste. 600
Atlanta, GA 30339 USA
Phone: 954-308-6266
E-mail Address: gailferro@spherion.com
Web Address: www.spherion.com
Spherion Corp., a subsidiary of SFN Group, provides temporary staffing, recruitment and employee consulting, primarily in administrative, clerical, customer service and light industrial fields.

Synergie SA (France)
11 Ave. du Colonel Bonnet
Paris, 75016 France
Phone: 44-14-90-20
Fax: 45-25-97-10
Web Address: www.synergie.fr
Synergie provides human resource management services that include temporary placement, consulting and training. The firm is most active in France, but also operates through a network of 550 agencies in throughout Europe and Canada.

Tempstaff Co., Ltd. (Japan)
Shinjuku Maynds Twr. 2-1-1
Yoyogi, Shibuya-ku
Tokyo, 151-0053 Japan
Phone: 81-3-5350-1212
Web Address: www.tempstaff.co.jp
Tempstaff Co., Ltd. provides temporary
and permanent placement and recruiting
and outsourcing services. It has 263
offices in Japan and 12 overseas offices
located in Los Angeles, Seattle, Shanghai,
Suzhou, Guangzhou, Hong Kong, Taiwan,
Korea, Singapore and Indonesia.

Volt Information Sciences, Inc.
50 Charles Lindbergh Blvd., Ste. 206
Uniondale, NY 11553 USA
Phone: 516-228-6700
Web Address: www.volt.com
Volt Information Sciences, Inc. provides
temporary staffing services, professional
search, managed services programs,
vendor management systems and
recruitment process outsourcing, as well
as a wealth of additional support services,
in North and South America, Europe and
Asia through approximately 400
locations.

78)   Testing Resources

CPP, Inc.
1055 Joaquin Rd., Ste. 200
Mountain View, CA 94043 USA
Phone: 650-969-8901
Fax: 650-969-8608
Toll Free: 800-624-1765
E-mail Address: custserv@cpp.com
Web Address: www.cpp.com
CPP, Inc. (formerly known as Consulting
Psychologists Press) publishes the
Meyers-Briggs Type Indicator, Strong
Inventory Test and other psychological
assessment-related products. CPP also
provides information about the tests and,
through division Davies-Black Publishing,
offers business-related books and
services, including those covering career
management and leadership development.

79)   Textile & Fabric Industry Associations

International Textile and Apparel Association (ITAA)
P.O. Box 70687
Knoxville, TN 37938-0687 USA
Phone: 865-992-1535
E-mail Address: info@itaaonline.org
Web Address: www.itaaonline.org
The International Textile and Apparel
Association (ITAA) is a nonprofit
educational and scientific corporation
dedicated to providing opportunities to

scholars in the retail, textile and apparel
industries.

80)   Travel Business & Professional Associations

American Society of Travel Agents (ASTA)
675 N Washington St., Ste. 490
Alexandria, VA 22314 USA
Phone: 703-739-2782
Toll Free: 800-275-2782
E-mail Address: askasta@asta.org
Web Address: www.asta.org
The American Society of Travel Agents
(ASTA) is one of the world's largest
associations of travel professionals.

Association of Retail Travel Agents (ARTA)
3014 N. Hayden Rd., Ste. 115
Scottsdale, AZ 85251 USA
Fax: 866-743-2087
Toll Free: 866-369-8969
Web Address: www.arta.travel
The Association of Retail Travel Agents
(ARTA) is one of the largest nonprofit
associations in North America to
exclusively represent travel agents.

Association of Travel Marketing Executives (ATME)
P.O. Box 3176
West Tisbury, MA 02575 USA
Phone: 508-693-0550
Fax: 508-693-0115
E-mail Address: kzern@atme.org
Web Address: www.atme.org
The Association of Travel Marketing
Executives (ATME) is a global
professional association of senior-level
travel marketing executives dedicated to
providing cutting-edge information,
education and opportunities for
meaningful networking with peers.

National Society of Minorities in Hospitality
7400 E. Orchard Rd., Ste. 375S
Greenwood Village, CO 80111 USA
Phone: 303-502-5354
Fax: 720-496-4974
E-mail Address: hq@nsmh.org
Web Address: www.nsmh.org
The National Society of Minorities in
Hospitality strives to establish a working
relationship between the hospitality
industry and minority students.

Network of Executive Women in Hospitality, Inc. (NEWH)
P.O. Box 322
Shawano, WI 54166 USA
Phone: 715-526-5267

Fax: 800-693-6394
Toll Free: 800-593-6394
Web Address: www.newh.org
The Network of Executive Women in
Hospitality, Inc. (NEWH) brings together
professionals from all facets of the
hospitality industry by providing
opportunities for education, professional
development and networking. Although
primarily a U.S.-based organization,
NEWH does have international chapters
in Toronto and London.

Society of Incentive and Travel Executives
330 N. Wabash, Ste. 2000
Chicago, IL 60611 USA
Phone: 312-321-5148
Fax: 312-527-6783
E-mail Address: site@siteglobal.com
Web Address: www.site-intl.org
The Society of Incentive and Travel
Executives is a worldwide organization of
business professionals dedicated to the
recognition and development of
motivational and performance
improvement strategies in the travel
industry.

81)   Travel Industry Associations

Destination Marketing Association International
2025 M St. NW, Ste. 500
Washington, DC 20036 USA
Phone: 202-296-7888
Fax: 202-296-7889
E-mail Address:
info@destinationmarketing.org
Web Address:
www.destinationmarketing.org
The Destination Marketing Association
International, formerly the International
Association of Convention & Visitor
Bureaus, strives to enhance the
professionalism, effectiveness and image
of destination management organizations
worldwide. Its members include
professionals, industry partners, students
and educators from roughly 15 countries.

International Association of Conference Centers (IACC)
35 E. Wacker Dr., Ste. 850
Chicago, IL 60601 USA
Phone: 312-224-2580
Fax: 312-644-8557
E-mail Address: info@iacconline.org
Web Address: www.iacconline.com
The International Association of
Conference Centers (IACC) is a nonprofit,
facilities-based organization founded to
promote a greater awareness and

understanding of the unique features of conference centers around the world.

National Tour Association (NTA)
101 Prosperous Pl., Ste. 350
Lexington, KY 40509 USA
Phone: 859-264-6540
Fax: 859-266-6570
Toll Free: 800-682-8886
E-mail Address:
NTAwashington@gmail.com
Web Address: www.ntaonline.com
The National Tour Association (NTA) is an association for travel professionals who have an interest in the packaged travel sector of the industry.

U.S. Travel Association
1100 New York Ave. NW, Ste. 450
Washington, DC 20005-3934 USA
Phone: 202-408-8422
Fax: 202-408-1255
E-mail Address: feedback@ustravel.org
Web Address: www.ustravel.org
The U.S. Travel Association is the result of a merger between the Travel Industry Association (TIA) and the Travel Business Roundtable. It is a nonprofit association that represents and speaks for the common interests and concerns of all components of the U.S. travel industry.

---

82) U.S. Government Agencies

Bureau of Economic Analysis (BEA)
4600 Silver Hill Rd.
Washington, DC 20233 USA
Phone: 301-278-9004
E-mail Address:
customerservice@bea.gov
Web Address: www.bea.gov
The Bureau of Economic Analysis (BEA), is an agency of the U.S. Department of Commerce, is the nation's economic accountant, preparing estimates that illuminate key national, international and regional aspects of the U.S. economy.

Bureau of Labor Statistics (BLS)
2 Massachusetts Ave. NE
Washington, DC 20212-0001 USA
Phone: 202-691-5200
Fax: 202-691-7890
Toll Free: 800-877-8339
E-mail Address: blsdata_staff@bls.gov
Web Address: stats.bls.gov
The Bureau of Labor Statistics (BLS) is the principal fact-finding agency for the Federal Government in the field of labor economics and statistics. It is an independent national statistical agency that collects, processes, analyzes and disseminates statistical data to the American public, U.S. Congress, other

federal agencies, state and local governments, business and labor. The BLS also serves as a statistical resource to the Department of Labor.

Equal Employment Opportunity Commission (EEOC)
131 M St. NE
Washington, DC 20507-0100 USA
Phone: 202-663-4900
Fax: 202-633-4679
Toll Free: 800-669-4000
E-mail Address: info@eeoc.gov
Web Address: www.eeoc.gov
The Equal Employment Opportunity Commission (EEOC) is a Federal Government agency focused on practices and programs that foster equal opportunity at work and elsewhere. Its web site features details about various protective laws regarding employment. It also provides information on how to file a discrimination claim.

FedStats Web Address:
fedstats.sites.usa.gov/
FedStats compiles information for statistics from over 100 U.S. federal agencies. Visitors can sort the information by agency, geography and topic, as well as perform searches.

National Labor Relations Board (NLRB)
1015 Half St. SE
Washington, DC 20570-0001 USA
Phone: 2002-273-1000
Toll Free: 866-667-6572
Web Address: www.nlrb.gov
The National Labor Relations Board (NLRB) provides case reports on labor disputes, searchable by company or union.

U.S. Census Bureau
4600 Silver Hill Rd.
Washington, DC 20233-8800 USA
Phone: 301-763-4636
Toll Free: 800-923-8282
E-mail Address: pio@census.gov
Web Address: www.census.gov
The U.S. Census Bureau is the official collector of data about the people and economy of the U.S. Founded in 1790, it provides official social, demographic and economic information. In addition to the Population & Housing Census, which it conducts every 10 years, the U.S. Census Bureau numerous other surveys annually.

U.S. Department of Commerce (DOC)
1401 Constitution Ave. NW
Washington, DC 20230 USA
Phone: 202-482-2000
E-mail Address: TheSec@doc.gov
Web Address: www.commerce.gov

The U.S. Department of Commerce (DOC) regulates trade and provides valuable economic analysis of the economy.

U.S. Department of Labor (DOL)
200 Constitution Ave. NW
Washington, DC 20210 USA
Phone: 202-693-4676
Toll Free: 866-487-2365
Web Address: www.dol.gov
The U.S. Department of Labor (DOL) is the government agency responsible for labor regulations. The Department of Labor's goal is to foster, promote, and develop the welfare of the wage earners, job seekers, and retirees of the United States; improve working conditions; advance opportunities for profitable employment; and assure work-related benefits and rights.

U.S. Securities and Exchange Commission (SEC)
100 F St. NE
Washington, DC 20549 USA
Phone: 202-942-8088
Fax: 202-772-9295
Toll Free: 800-732-0330
E-mail Address: help@sec.gov
Web Address: www.sec.gov
The U.S. Securities and Exchange Commission (SEC) is a nonpartisan, quasi-judicial regulatory agency responsible for administering federal securities laws. These laws are designed to protect investors in securities markets and ensure that they have access to disclosure of all material information concerning publicly traded securities. Visitors to the web site can access the EDGAR database of corporate financial and business information.

---

83) Water Technologies & Resources

American Water Resources Association (AWRA)
P.O. Box 1626
Middleburg, VA 20118 USA
Phone: 540-687-8390
Fax: 540-687-8395
E-mail Address: info@awra.org
Web Address: www.awra.org
The American Water Resources Association (AWRA) represents the interests of professionals involved in water resources and provides a platform for education, research, information exchange on water related issues.

84) Wireless & Cellular Industry Associations

Cellular Telecommunications & Internet Association (CTIA)
1400 16th St. NW, Ste. 600
Washington, DC 20036 USA
Phone: 202-785-0081
Web Address: www.ctia.org
The Cellular Telecommunications & Internet Association (CTIA) is an international nonprofit membership organization that represents a variety of wireless communications sectors including cellular service providers, manufacturers, wireless data and Internet companies. CTIA's industry committees study spectrum allocation, homeland security, taxation, safety and emerging technology.

Wireless Communications Association International (WCAI)
1333 H St. NW, Ste. 700 W
Washington, DC 20005-4754 USA
Phone: 202-452-7823
Web Address:
www.wcainternational.com/
The Wireless Communications Association International (WCAI) is a nonprofit trade association representing the wireless broadband industry.

85) Writers, Photographers & Editors Associations

American Society of Journalists and Authors, Inc. (ASJA)
355 Lexington Ave., Fl. 15
New York, NY 10017 USA
Phone: 212-997-0947
Web Address: www.asja.org
The American Society of Journalists and Authors (ASJA) is one of the nation's leading organizations of independent nonfiction writers.

American Society of Magazine Editors (ASME)
P.O. Box 112
New York, NY 10163 USA
Phone: 212-872-3737
E-mail Address: asme@asme.media
Web Address: www.asme.media
The American Society of Magazine Editors (ASME) is a professional organization for editors of print and online magazines. ASME is part of the Magazine Publishers of America (MPA).

International Women's Writing Guild (IWWG)
5 Penn Plaza, Fl. 19
New York, NY 10001 USA
Phone: 617-792-7272
E-mail Address:
iwwgquestions@gmail.com
Web Address: www.iwwg.com
The International Women's Writing Guild (IWWG) is a network for the personal and professional empowerment of women through writing.

National Association of Hispanic Journalists (NAHJ)
1050 Connecticut Ave. NW, Fl. 10
Washington, DC 20036 USA
Phone: 202-662-7145
E-mail Address: nahj@nahj.org
Web Address: www.nahj.org
The National Association of Hispanic Journalists (NAHJ) is dedicated to the recognition and professional advancement of Hispanics in the news industry.

National Association of Science Writers, Inc. (NASW)
P.O. Box 7905
Berkley, CA 94707 USA
Phone: 510-647-9500
E-mail Address: webmaster@nasw.org
Web Address: www.nasw.org
The National Association of Science Writers (NASW) exists to foster the dissemination of accurate information regarding science through all media devoted to informing the public.

National Federation of Press Women (NFPW)
140B Purcellville Gateway Dr., Ste. 120
Purcellville, VA 20132 USA
Phone: 571-295-5900
E-mail Address: info@nfpw.org
Web Address: www.nfpw.org
The National Federation of Press Women (NFPW) is an organization of female professional journalists and communicators.

National Writers Union (NWU)
256 W. 38th St., Ste. 703
New York, NY 10018 USA
Phone: 212-254-0279
Fax: 212-254-0673
E-mail Address: nwu@nwu.org
Web Address: www.nwu.org
The National Writers Union (NWU) is a labor union that represents freelance writers in all genres, formats and media. It is committed to improving the economic and working conditions of freelance writers.

News Leaders Association (NLA)
209 Reynolds Journalism Institute
Missouri School of Journalism
Columbia, MO 65211 USA
Phone: 573-884-2405
Fax: 573-884-3824
E-mail Address: contact@newsleaders.org
Web Address: newsleaders.org
The American Society of News Editors and the Associated Press Media Editors have merged to become the News Leaders Association (NLA). NLA aims to foster and develop the highest standards of trustworthy, truth-seeking journalism; to advocate for open, honest and transparent government; to fight for free speech and an independent press; to nurture the next generation of news leaders committed to spreading knowledge that informs democracy.

Society of Children's Book Writers and Illustrators (SCBWI)
6363 Wilshire Blvd.
Los Angeles, CA 90048 USA
Phone: 323-782-1010
Fax: 323-782-1892
E-mail Address: scbwi@scbwi.org
Web Address: www.scbwi.org
The Society of Children's Book Writers and Illustrators (SCBWI) serves people who write, illustrate or share a vital interest in children's literature, including publishers, librarians, booksellers and agents.

Chapter 5

THE AMERICAN EMPLOYERS 500:
WHO THEY ARE AND
HOW THEY WERE CHOSEN

Note: financial data given for each of the AMERICAN EMPLOYERS 500 firms is for the year ended December 31, 2020 or the latest figures available to the editors. Telephone numbers, addresses, contact names, Internet addresses and other vital facts were collected in the fall of 2021.

The companies chosen to be listed in THE ALMANAC OF AMERICAN EMPLOYERS are not the same as the "Fortune 500" or any other list of corporations. The AMERICAN EMPLOYERS 500 were chosen specifically for their likelihood to provide new job openings to the greatest number of employees. Complete information about each firm can be found in the "Individual Data Listings," beginning about the middle of this book. They are in alphabetical order.

THE AMERICAN EMPLOYERS 500 includes companies from all parts of the United States and from nearly all industry segments: selected financial services firms, retailers, service companies, wholesalers and distributors, and others, as well as industrial companies, technology firms and manufacturers.

Simply stated, the list contains 500 of the largest, most successful employers in the United States today. In particular, the list contains companies that we have hand-selected to have qualities that we feel will be of greatest interest to job seekers of today who are looking for opportunities to obtain employment with major corporations.

In order to make this reference guide as useful as possible, we are selecting companies for this list by focusing on the type of business, the industry sector served and a company's competitive advantage. To a lesser extent, we are also considering the most recent year's financial performance. We consider industry sector to be a major factor, because some sectors may not offer good career prospects today. Consequently, we have deleted some well-known companies due to the state of their particular markets.

To be included in our list, the firms were selected based on the following criteria:

1) U.S.-based companies. (However, a small number of companies may be subsidiaries of foreign-based firms. Also, a small number of the firms are major U.S. employers that utilize headquarters addresses in other nations.)

2) 2,500 employees or more.

3) These are almost exclusively for-profit companies. However, a small number are major, non-profit health care companies.

4) Selected Type of Business and/or Industry Sector. Companies were chosen based on our analysis of the business potential of their products, services and industrial sectors in light of today's economic conditions and the effects of globalization and technological changes.

The companies were chosen in this manner for the following reasons:

500 COMPANIES so there is a broad base among which to make comparisons and from which you can study potential employers.

LARGER EMPLOYERS (2,500 or more employees) so the information can pertain to as many employees as reasonably possible, and so the companies ranked will tend to create large numbers of job openings. Also, large companies historically have offered significantly higher wages, better benefits and better training than small employers.

FOR-PROFIT so that job seekers using THE ALMANAC OF AMERICAN EMPLOYERS can choose positions in the profit-seeking, private sector, where incentive plans may be available to motivate and reward them, such as profit sharing, stock ownership, bonuses, stock options and the high pay and prestige of top executive posts.

COMPANIES THAT OPERATE IN PROMISING BUSINESS SECTORS because:
1) Companies that are stable or enjoying growing business are much more likely to have job openings. Corporate stability is more important to job seekers today than ever before due to the wave of layoffs and downsizing that continues to sweep through the U.S. (See Chapter 1, "Major Trends Affecting Job Seekers.")
2) These companies are much more likely to offer advancement opportunities. Current employees will benefit from promote-from-within policies when new plants, new stores, new product lines or new offices are opened.

Obviously, some companies are better to work for than others, depending on what you value. Creating this annual list is an arduous task. Generally, our results are very good, but we do occasionally select a company that soon develops problems or announces a layoff. The world of business constantly goes through major changes, and unforeseen events often occur. Nonetheless, it is not easy for a firm to be selected for the AMERICAN EMPLOYERS 500, and the mere presence of a company on the list can be taken as evidence that it has excelled in many ways. To start with, it has to have generated enough business to employ thousands of people–never a simple task. Also, many of these

firms are among the dominant companies in their industries.

INDEX OF COMPANIES WITHIN INDUSTRY GROUPS

The industry codes shown below are based on the 2012 NAIC code system (NAIC is used by many analysts as a replacement for older SIC codes because NAIC is more specific to today's industry sectors, see www.census.gov/NAICS). Companies are given a primary NAIC code, reflecting the main line of business of each firm.

Industry Group/Company	Industry Code	2020 Sales	2020 Profits
Agricultural Equipment or Machinery (Farm Implement) Manufacturing			
Deere & Company (John Deere)	333111	35,258,998,784	2,751,000,064
Aircraft Manufacturing (Aerospace), including Passenger Airliners and Military Aircraft,			
General Dynamics Corporation	336411	37,924,999,168	3,167,000,064
Gulfstream Aerospace Corporation	336411	9,313,258,500	
Lockheed Martin Corporation	336411	65,398,001,664	6,832,999,936
Northrop Grumman Corporation	336411	36,799,000,576	3,188,999,936
Textron Inc	336411	11,651,000,320	309,000,000
Aluminum Production, Alumina Refining and Aluminum Form Production			
Alcoa Corporation	331313	9,285,999,616	-170,000,000
Ambulatory Health Care Services, Other			
Magellan Health Inc	621999	4,577,530,880	382,335,008
Asset Management			
BlackRock Inc	523920	16,204,999,680	4,931,999,744
Fidelity Investments Financial Services	523920	21,000,000,000	7,200,000,000
State Street Corporation	523920	10,622,999,552	2,420,000,000
T Rowe Price Group Inc	523920	6,206,700,032	2,372,699,904
TIAA	523920	32,661,000,000	604,000,000
Vanguard Group Inc (The)	523920	4,576,000,000	
Automobile (Car) and Light Truck Dealers (New)			
Group 1 Automotive Inc	441110	10,851,800,064	286,500,000
Penske Automotive Group Inc	441110	20,443,899,904	543,600,000
Automobile (Car) and Light Truck Dealers (Used)			
CarMax Inc	441120	20,319,987,712	888,433,024
Automobile (Car) and Other Motor Vehicle Wholesale Distribution			
JM Family Enterprises Inc	423110	15,087,500,000	
Automobile (Car) and Truck Parts, Components and Systems Manufacturing, Including Gasoline Engines, Interiors and Electronics,			
East Penn Manufacturing Company Inc	336300	1,530,090,844	
LKQ Corporation	336300	11,628,829,696	638,422,976
Automobile (Car) Manufacturing (incl. Autonomous or Self-Driving)			
Ford Motor Company	336111	127,144,001,536	-1,279,000,064
General Motors Company (GM)	336111	122,484,998,144	6,426,999,808
Tesla Inc	336111	31,536,001,024	690,000,000
Automobile (Car) Parts and Supplies Distributors (Wholesale Distribution)			
Genuine Parts Company	423120	16,537,433,088	-29,102,000

Industry Group/Company	Industry Code	2020 Sales	2020 Profits
Bakeries (Including Breads, Cookies, Cakes, Tortillas and Other Baked Goods) and Pasta Manufacturing			
Flowers Foods Inc	311800	4,387,991,040	152,318,000
Beer, Wine and Alcoholic Beverage Wholesalers, Distribution and Distributors			
Southern Glazers Wine & Spirits LLC	424800	20,304,375,000	
Beer, Wine and Liquor Stores			
Goody Goody Liquor Inc	445310	296,076,375	
Building Material Dealers			
84 Lumber Company	444190	4,700,000,000	
BMC Stock Holdings Inc	444190		
Ferguson Enterprises Inc	444190	18,816,950,000	
Cable TV Programming, Cable Networks and Subscription Video			
Discovery Inc	515210	10,670,999,552	1,219,000,064
Netflix Inc	515210	24,996,055,040	2,761,394,944
Candy and Chocolate Manufacturing (From Cocao Beans)			
Mars Incorporated	311351	40,425,229,688	
Russell Stover Candies Inc	311351	360,000,000	
Car Repair (Repair and Maintenance of Automobiles and Trucks)			
Monro Inc	811100	1,256,524,032	58,024,000
Cereal Manufacturing			
General Mills Inc	311230	17,626,599,424	2,181,199,872
Kellogg Company	311230	13,770,000,384	1,251,000,064
Chips (Tortilla, Potato and Corn), Popcorn and Pretzel Manufacturing			
Frito-Lay North America Inc	311919	18,189,000,000	5,340,000,000
Chocolate Candy Manufacturing (From Purchased Chocolate)			
Hershey Company (The)	311352	8,149,719,040	1,278,707,968
Cloud, Data Processing, Business Process Outsourcing (BPO) and Internet Content Hosting Services			
GoDaddy Inc	518210	3,316,699,904	-495,100,000
Newfold Digital Inc	518210	833,250,000	
Coffee Shops, Doughnut Shops, Ice Cream Parlors, Canteens and Snack Bars			
Starbucks Corporation	722515	23,517,999,104	928,300,032
Commercial and Institutional Building Construction			
Clark Construction Group LLC	236220	5,565,000,000	
Gilbane Inc	236220	6,360,000,000	
McCarthy Building Companies Inc	236220	4,118,100,000	
Turner Corporation (The)	236220	13,992,000,000	
Commercial Banks (Banking)			
Bank of America Corporation	522110	86,266,003,456	17,894,000,640
Bank of New York Mellon Corporation	522110	15,505,999,872	3,616,999,936
Citigroup Inc	522110	75,493,998,592	11,047,000,064
JPMorgan Chase & Co Inc	522110	119,542,996,992	29,130,999,808
US Bancorp (US Bank)	522110	23,225,999,360	4,959,000,064
Wells Fargo & Company	522110	72,339,996,672	3,300,999,936

Industry Group/Company	Industry Code	2020 Sales	2020 Profits
Computer and Data Systems Design, Consulting and Integration Services			
CACI International Inc	541512	5,720,041,984	321,480,000
Cognizant Technology Solutions Corporation	541512	16,652,000,256	1,392,000,000
Concentrix Corporation	541512	4,719,534,080	164,811,008
HTC Global Services Inc	541512	760,000,000	
Kratos Defense & Security Solutions Inc	541512	747,699,968	79,600,000
ManTech International Corporation	541512	2,518,384,128	120,530,000
MAXIMUS Inc	541512	3,461,537,024	214,508,992
Publicis Sapient	541512	1,877,871,996	
Science Applications International Corporation (SAIC)	541512	6,378,999,808	226,000,000
Sykes Enterprises Incorporated	541512	1,710,260,992	56,432,000
Computer Disks (Discs) and Drives, including Magnetic and Optical Storage Media Manufacturing			
NetApp Inc	334112	5,411,999,744	819,000,000
Computer Manufacturing, Including PCs, Laptops, Mainframes and Tablets			
Dell Technologies Inc	334111	92,154,003,456	4,616,000,000
Computer Networking & Related Equipment Manufacturing (may incl. Internet of Things, IoT)			
Cisco Systems Inc	334210A	49,301,000,192	11,214,000,128
Fortinet Inc	334210A	2,594,400,000	488,500,000
Juniper Networks Inc	334210A	4,445,100,032	257,800,000
Computer Peripherals and Accessories, including Printers, Monitors and Terminals Manufacturing			
Datalogic SpA	334118	586,242,816	16,594,175
Logitech International SA	334118	2,975,851,008	449,723,008
Computer Programming and Custom Software Development and Consulting			
EPAM Systems Inc	541511	2,659,478,016	327,160,000
Computer Software, Accounting, Banking & Financial			
Concur Technologies Inc	511210Q	1,848,510,000	69,273,000
DocuSign Inc	511210Q	973,971,008	-208,359,008
Intuit Inc	511210Q	7,679,000,064	1,826,000,000
Jack Henry & Associates Inc	511210Q	1,697,067,008	296,668,000
SS&C Technologies Holdings Inc	511210Q	4,667,899,904	625,200,000
Computer Software, Business Management & ERP			
BMC Software Inc	511210H	2,178,000,000	
Microsoft Corporation	511210H	143,015,002,112	44,280,999,936
Oracle Corporation	511210H	39,068,000,256	10,135,000,064
Oracle NetSuite	511210H	1,008,291,375	
SAS Institute Inc	511210H	3,000,000,000	
Workday Inc	511210H	3,627,205,888	-480,673,984
Computer Software, Electronic Games, Apps & Entertainment			
Activision Blizzard Inc	511210G	8,086,000,128	2,196,999,936
Take-Two Interactive Software Inc	511210G	3,088,969,984	404,459,008
Computer Software, Healthcare & Biotechnology			
Allscripts Healthcare Solutions Inc	511210D	1,502,700,032	700,406,976
Cerner Corporation	511210D	5,505,787,904	780,088,000

Industry Group/Company	Industry Code	2020 Sales	2020 Profits
Epic Systems Corporation	511210D	3,300,000,000	
Computer Software, Multimedia, Graphics & Publishing			
Adobe Inc	511210F	12,867,999,744	5,260,000,256
Computer Software, Network Management, System Testing, & Storage			
Citrix Systems Inc	511210B	3,236,699,904	504,446,016
F5 Networks Inc	511210B	2,350,821,888	307,440,992
Nutanix Inc	511210B	1,307,682,048	-872,883,008
ServiceNow Inc	511210B	4,519,483,904	118,503,000
Splunk Inc	511210B	2,358,926,080	-336,668,000
VMware Inc	511210B	10,810,999,808	6,412,000,256
Computer Software, Operating Systems, Languages & Development Tools, Artificial Intelligence (AI)			
Red Hat Inc	511210I	3,315,000,000	
Computer Software, Product Lifecycle, Engineering, Design & CAD			
ANSYS Inc	511210N	1,681,297,024	433,887,008
Cadence Design Systems Inc	511210N	2,682,891,008	590,643,968
National Instruments Corporation	511210N	1,286,670,976	143,659,008
Synopsys Inc	511210N	3,685,281,024	664,347,008
Computer Software, Sales & Customer Relationship Management			
salesforce.com Inc	511210K	17,098,000,384	126,000,000
Computer Software, Security & Anti-Virus			
FireEye Inc	511210E	940,584,000	-207,303,008
McAfee Corp	511210E	2,905,999,872	-289,000,000
NortonLifeLock Inc	511210E	2,489,999,872	3,887,000,064
Palo Alto Networks Inc	511210E	3,408,399,872	-267,000,000
SecureWorks Corporation	511210E	552,764,992	-31,666,000
Computers, Peripherals, Software and Accessories Distribution			
Anixter International Inc	423430	9,287,879,731	
Arrow Electronics Inc	423430	28,673,363,968	584,438,016
Avnet Inc	423430	17,634,332,672	-31,081,000
CDW Corporation	423430	18,467,500,032	788,499,968
Insight Enterprises Inc	423430	8,340,578,816	172,640,000
SYNNEX Corporation	423430	24,675,563,520	529,160,000
Tech Data Corporation	423430		
Connectors for Electronics Manufacturing			
Belden Inc	334417	1,862,716,032	-55,162,000
Molex LLC	334417	4,095,000,000	
Construction Equipment and Machinery Manufacturing			
Caterpillar Inc	333120	41,748,000,768	2,998,000,128
Terex Corporation	333120	3,076,400,128	-10,600,000
Construction of Telecommunications Lines and Systems & Electric Power Lines and Systems			
American Tower Corporation (REIT)	237130	8,041,500,160	1,690,599,936
Crown Castle International Corp	237130	5,840,000,000	1,056,000,000
Consulting Services, Human Resources			
Mercer LLC	541612	4,828,320,000	

Industry Group/Company	Industry Code	2020 Sales	2020 Profits
Consulting Services: Process, Physical Distribution and Logistics			
Kenco Group Inc	541614	753,816,000	
Consumer Electronics and Appliances Rental			
Rent-A-Center Inc	532210	2,814,191,104	208,115,008
Contract Electronics Manufacturing Services (CEM) and Printed Circuits Assembly			
Jabil Inc	334418	27,266,437,120	53,912,000
Sanmina Corporation	334418	6,960,370,176	139,712,992
Cookie and Cracker Manufacturing			
Mondelez International Inc	311821	26,581,000,192	3,555,000,064
Cosmetics; Soaps, Detergents & Cleansers; and Personal Care and Consumer Products, Perfumes & Colognes Manufacturing			
SC Johnson & Son Inc	325600	6,489,000,000	
Couriers, Express, Gig Economy and Overnight Delivery			
FedEx Corporation	492110	69,217,001,472	1,286,000,000
FedEx Ground	492110	22,733,000,000	2,014,000,000
United Parcel Service Inc (UPS)	492110	84,627,996,672	1,343,000,064
CPA Firms (Certified Public Accountants), Accounting			
Deloitte LLP	541211	23,157,000,000	
EY LLP	541211	17,187,000,000	
Grant Thornton LLP	541211	1,920,000,000	
KPMG LLP	541211	11,220,000,000	
PricewaterhouseCoopers (PwC)	541211	43,032,000,000	
Credit Bureaus and Credit Rating Agencies			
Moody's Corporation	561450	5,370,999,808	1,778,000,000
Credit Card Processing, Online Payment Processing, EFT, ACH and Clearinghouses			
American Express Company	522320	34,857,000,960	3,135,000,064
Fidelity National Information Services Inc	522320	12,551,999,488	158,000,000
Fiserv Inc	522320	14,851,999,744	958,000,000
Heartland Payment Systems Inc	522320	4,137,241,500	
MasterCard Incorporated	522320	15,301,000,192	6,410,999,808
PayPal Holdings Inc	522320	21,454,000,128	4,201,999,872
Square Inc	522320	9,497,578,496	213,104,992
Visa Inc	522320	21,845,999,616	10,865,999,872
Dairy, Milk and Cheese Product Manufacturing			
Schreiber Foods Inc	311500	6,058,690,980	
Dialysis Centers			
DaVita Inc	621492	11,550,604,288	773,641,984
Discount Department Stores			
99 Cents Only Stores LLC	452112	2,364,289,200	
Dollar General Corporation	452112	27,753,973,760	1,712,555,008
Dollar Tree Inc	452112	23,610,800,128	827,000,000
Distributors of Telecommunications Equipment, Telephones, Cellphones and Electronics Components (Wholesale Distribution)			
Brightstar Corporation	423690	11,576,250,000	

Industry Group/Company	Industry Code	2020 Sales	2020 Profits
Electric Motor and Power & Motor Generator Manufacturing			
Regal-Beloit Corporation	335312	2,907,000,064	189,300,000
Electric Power Distribution			
Eversource Energy	221122	8,904,429,568	1,205,166,976
Electric Signal, Electricity, and Semiconductor Test and Measuring Equipment Manufacturing			
Itron Inc	334515	2,173,349,888	-57,955,000
Electrical Contractors and Other Wiring Installation Contractors			
EMCOR Group Inc	238210	8,797,061,120	132,943,000
Electricity Control Panels, Circuit Breakers and Power Switches Equipment (Switchgear) Manufacturing			
Broadcom Inc	335313	23,887,998,976	2,960,000,000
Engineering Services, Including Civil, Mechanical, Electronic, Computer and Environmental Engineering			
Black & Veatch Holding Company	541330	3,586,275,000	
Burns & McDonnell Inc	541330	5,300,000,000	
McDermott International Ltd	541330		
Parsons Corporation	541330	3,918,946,048	98,541,000
Factory Automation, Robots (Robotics) Industrial Process, Thermostat, Flow Meter and Environmental Quality Monitoring and Control Manufacturing (incl. Artificial Intelligence, AI)			
Ametek Inc	334513	4,540,028,928	872,438,976
II-VI Incorporated	334513	2,380,070,912	-67,029,000
Rockwell Automation Inc	334513	6,329,800,192	1,023,400,000
Roper Technologies Inc	334513	5,527,099,904	949,699,968
Woodward Inc	334513	2,495,664,896	240,395,008
Fiber Optic Cable, Connectors and Related Products Manufacturing			
Amphenol Corporation	335921	8,598,899,712	1,203,399,936
CommScope Holding Company Inc	335921	8,435,899,904	-573,400,000
Financial Data Publishing - Print & Online			
Bloomberg LP	511120A	11,000,000,000	
FactSet Research Systems Inc	511120A	1,494,110,976	372,937,984
Flour, Grain & Corn Milling and Cooking Oils (Including Vegetable, Canola, Olive, Peanut & Soy) Manufacturing			
Archer-Daniels-Midland Company (ADM)	311200	64,355,000,320	1,772,000,000
Cargill Incorporated	311200	114,600,000,000	4,128,040,000
Food and Groceries Distributors (Packaged and Fresh Food Products, Meat, Vegetables and Grocery Wholesale Distribution)			
Ben E Keith Company	424400	3,755,500,000	
Golden State Foods Corporation	424400	5,000,000,000	
Fossil Fuel Electric Power Generation			
AES Corporation (The)	221112	9,660,000,256	46,000,000
Ameren Corporation	221112	5,793,999,872	871,000,000
Berkshire Hathaway Energy Company	221112	20,952,000,000	6,943,000,000
CenterPoint Energy Inc	221112	7,417,999,872	-773,000,000
Dominion Energy Inc	221112	14,172,000,256	-401,000,000

Industry Group/Company	Industry Code	2020 Sales	2020 Profits
DTE Energy Company	221112	12,177,000,448	1,368,000,000
Duke Energy Corporation	221112	23,868,000,256	1,376,999,936
Edison International	221112	13,578,000,384	871,000,000
FirstEnergy Corporation	221112	10,789,999,616	1,079,000,064
Georgia Power Company	221112	8,309,000,000	1,575,000,000
Sempra Energy	221112	11,370,000,384	3,932,999,936
Southern California Edison Company	221112	13,546,000,000	942,000,000
Southern Company	221112	20,374,999,040	3,134,000,128
Frozen Foods, Specialty Manufacturing			
Conagra Brands Inc	311412	11,054,399,488	840,099,968
Fruit and Vegetable Canning (Including Juices and Sauces)			
B&G Foods Inc	311421	1,967,908,992	131,988,000
JM Smucker Company (The)	311421	7,800,999,936	779,500,032
Kraft Heinz Company (The)	311421	26,185,000,960	356,000,000
Funeral Homes and Funeral Services			
Carriage Services Inc	812210	329,448,000	16,090,000
Service Corporation International Inc	812210	3,511,508,992	515,907,008
Furniture Manufacturing, Household Upholstered			
Ashley Furniture Industries Inc	337121	6,500,000,000	
General Grocery Products Distributors (Groceries Wholesale Distribution, Excluding Meats, Frozen Foods and Vegetables)			
C&S Wholesale Grocers Inc	424410	29,767,500,000	
McLane Company Inc	424410	46,840,000,000	
United Natural Foods Inc	424410	26,514,266,112	-274,140,000
Hardware Stores			
Tractor Supply Company	444130	10,620,352,512	748,958,016
Health Insurance and Medical Insurance Underwriters (Direct Carriers), including Group Health, Supplemental Health and HMOs			
aetnaCVSHealth	524114	75,467,000,000	
AFLAC Incorporated	524114	22,115,999,744	4,777,999,872
Amerigroup Corporation	524114	11,210,000,000	
Anthem Inc	524114	121,867,001,856	4,572,000,256
Blue Shield of California	524114	21,806,000,000	680,000,000
Centene Corporation	524114	111,115,001,856	1,808,000,000
Cigna Corporation	524114	160,576,995,328	8,457,999,872
Health Care Service Corporation (HCSC)	524114	47,300,000,000	
Humana Inc	524114	77,155,000,320	3,367,000,064
Molina Healthcare Inc	524114	19,423,000,576	673,000,000
UnitedHealth Group Inc	524114	255,638,994,944	15,402,999,808
WellCare Health Plans Inc	524114	36,644,650,000	
Heavy Construction, Including Civil Engineering-Construction, Major Construction Projects, Land Subdivision, Infrastructure, Utilities, Highways and Bridges			
Bechtel Group Inc	237000	17,600,000,000	
Fluor Corporation	237000	15,668,476,928	-435,046,016
Jacobs Engineering Group Inc	237000	13,566,974,976	491,844,992

Industry Group/Company	Industry Code	2020 Sales	2020 Profits
KBR Inc	237000	5,767,000,064	-72,000,000
Heavy Duty Truck (including Buses) Manufacturing			
REV Group Inc	336120	2,277,600,000	-30,500,000
Highway, Street, Tunnel & Bridge Construction (Infrastructure)			
AECOM	237310	13,239,975,936	-186,370,000
Kiewit Corporation	237310	12,500,000,000	
Home Centers, Building Materials			
Home Depot Inc (The)	444110	110,224,998,400	11,242,000,384
Lowes Companies Inc	444110	72,148,000,768	4,280,999,936
Menard Inc	444110	10,762,500,000	
Home Health Care Services			
Amedisys Inc	621610	2,071,518,976	183,608,000
Chemed Corporation	621610	2,079,582,976	319,465,984
Envision Healthcare Corporation	621610	8,478,750,000	
LHC Group Inc	621610	2,063,203,968	111,596,000
Hospitals, General Medical and Surgical			
AdventHealth	622110	10,230,000,000	
Baylor Scott & White Health	622110	1,158,505,975	-136,407,231
Cleveland Clinic Foundation (The)	622110	10,627,906,000	1,325,244,000
HCA Healthcare Inc	622110	51,533,000,704	3,753,999,872
Houston Methodist	622110	3,859,500,000	
Kaiser Permanente	622110	88,700,000,000	6,400,000,000
Mass General Brigham Incorporated	622110	13,020,000,000	
Mayo Clinic	622110	13,910,000,000	1,971,000,000
Memorial Hermann Healthcare System	622110	5,747,742,387	
Sutter Health Inc	622110	13,220,000,000	200,000,000
Universal Health Services Inc	622110	11,558,896,640	943,953,024
Hospitals, Psychiatric and Substance Abuse			
Acadia Healthcare Company Inc	622210	2,089,928,960	-672,131,968
Hospitals, Specialty			
Memorial Sloan Kettering Cancer Center	622310	5,407,196,000	-417,172,000
Household Dishwasher, Disposal, Trash Compactor and Water Heater Manufacturing			
AO Smith Corporation	335228	2,895,300,096	344,900,000
Hydroelectric Power Generation			
Bonneville Power Administration	221111	3,683,700,000	245,700,000
PG&E Corporation	221111	18,468,999,168	-1,304,000,000
Puget Energy Inc	221111	3,326,450,000	182,717,000
Insurance Claims Administration and Services			
athenahealth Inc	524292	1,465,750,000	
Internet Search Engines, Online Publishing, Sharing, Gig and Consumer Services, Online Radio, TV and Entertainment Sites and Social Media			
Alphabet Inc (Google)	519130	182,527,000,576	40,269,000,704
Facebook Inc	519130	85,964,996,608	29,145,999,360
IAC/InterActiveCorp	519130	3,047,681,024	269,726,016
LinkedIn Corporation	519130	7,140,000,000	
YouTube LLC	519130	19,772,000,000	

Industry Group/Company	Industry Code	2020 Sales	2020 Profits
Zillow Group Inc	519130	3,339,816,960	-162,115,008
Investment Banking, and Related Stock Brokerage and Investment Services			
Goldman Sachs Group Inc (The)	523110	47,979,999,232	9,459,000,320
Legg Mason Inc	523110		
Merrill	523110	15,300,000,000	
Morgan Stanley	523110	45,269,000,192	10,995,999,744
Raymond James Financial Inc	523110	7,888,999,936	818,000,000
Stifel Financial Corp	523110	3,696,101,120	503,472,000
Iron and Steel Mills and Ferroalloy Manufacturing			
United States Steel Corporation	331110	9,740,999,680	-1,164,999,936
Life Insurance and Annuity Underwriters (Direct Carriers)			
Hartford Financial Services Group Inc (The)	524113	20,320,000,000	1,736,999,936
John Hancock Financial	524113	8,487,706,500	
Lincoln National Corporation	524113	17,556,000,768	499,000,000
MassMutual Financial Group	524113	23,259,000,000	128,000,000
MetLife Inc	524113	67,841,998,848	5,407,000,064
Mutual of Omaha Insurance Company	524113	10,306,206,441	844,799,395
New York Life Insurance Company	524113	32,054,000,000	1,501,000,000
Northwestern Mutual Life Insurance Company (The)	524113	31,124,000,000	425,000,000
Principal Financial Group Inc	524113	14,741,699,584	1,395,800,064
Prudential Financial Inc	524113	57,032,998,912	-374,000,000
Local Messengers and Food Delivery, Gig Economy			
DoorDash Inc	492210	2,886,000,128	-461,000,000
GrubHub Inc	492210	1,819,981,952	-155,860,992
Management Consulting and General Business Consulting (including Human Resources)			
AT Kearney Inc	541610	1,456,000,000	
Bain & Company Inc	541610	4,600,000,000	
Booz Allen Hamilton Holding Corporation	541610	7,463,840,768	482,603,008
Boston Consulting Group Inc (The, BCG)	541610	8,600,000,000	
FTI Consulting Inc	541610	2,461,274,880	210,682,000
McKinsey & Company Inc	541610	10,900,000,000	
North Highland Company (The)	541610	555,000,000	
Oliver Wyman Group	541610	2,069,280,000	
Protiviti Inc	541610	1,144,000,000	
Strategy&	541610	1,528,800,000	
Market Research, Business Intelligence and Opinion Polling			
Gartner Inc	541910	4,099,403,008	266,744,992
Nielsen Holdings plc	541910	6,289,999,872	-6,000,000
Meat Packing and Processing, Including Beef, Pork and Lamb			
Smithfield Foods Inc	311612	16,446,543,750	
Medical Diagnostics, Reagents, Assays and Test Kits Manufacturing			
Bio-Rad Laboratories Inc	325413	2,545,626,112	3,806,266,880
Hycor Biomedical LLC	325413	4,417,497,000	
Illumina Inc	325413	3,239,000,064	656,000,000
PerkinElmer Inc	325413	3,782,745,088	727,886,976

Industry Group/Company	Industry Code	2020 Sales	2020 Profits
Medical Equipment and Supplies Manufacturing			
3M Company	339100	32,184,000,512	5,384,000,000
Align Technology Inc	339100	2,471,941,120	1,775,888,000
Baxter International Inc	339100	11,672,999,936	1,102,000,000
Becton Dickinson and Company	339100	17,116,999,680	874,000,000
Cooper Companies Inc (The)	339100	2,430,899,968	238,400,000
Dentsply Sirona Inc	339100	3,342,000,128	-83,000,000
Edwards Lifesciences Corporation	339100	4,386,299,904	823,400,000
Hill-Rom Holdings Inc	339100	2,880,999,936	223,000,000
Stryker Corporation	339100	14,350,999,552	1,599,000,064
Medical Imaging and Electromedical (Medical Devices) Equipment, including MRI, Ultrasound, Pacemakers, EKG and CAT			
Beckman Coulter Inc	334510	6,232,950,000	
Danaher Corporation	334510	22,283,999,232	3,646,000,128
IDEXX Laboratories Inc	334510	2,706,654,976	581,776,000
Philips Healthcare	334510	24,021,030,000	
ResMed Inc	334510	2,957,012,992	621,673,984
Varian Medical Systems Inc	334510		
Medical Laboratories			
Laboratory Corporation of America Holdings	621511	13,978,500,096	1,556,099,968
Quest Diagnostics Incorporated	621511	9,436,999,680	1,431,000,064
Medical, Dental and Hospital Equipment and Supplies (Medical Devices) Wholesale Distribution			
Thermo Fisher Scientific Inc	423450	32,217,999,360	6,375,000,064
Metal Can Manufacturing			
Ball Corporation	332431	11,781,000,192	585,000,000
Crown Holdings Inc	332431	11,575,000,064	579,000,000
Metal Window and Door Manufacturing			
Griffon Corporation	332321	2,407,522,048	53,429,000
Missile (Aerospace Defense) and Space Vehicle Manufacturing			
SpaceX (Space Exploration Technologies Corporation)	336414	1,200,000,000	
Mobile, Modular & Prefabricated Homes and Buildings Manufacturing			
Clayton Homes Inc	321992	8,600,000,000	1,250,000,000
Skyline Champion Corporation	321992	1,369,730,048	58,160,000
Natural Gas Utilities			
MDU Resources Group Inc	221210	5,532,749,824	390,204,992
NiSource Inc	221210	4,681,699,840	-17,600,000
New Home Builders (Production, For-Sale Home Builders)			
DR Horton Inc	236117	20,311,099,392	2,373,700,096
Lennar Corporation	236117	22,488,854,528	2,465,036,032
NVR Inc	236117	7,545,852,928	901,248,000
PulteGroup Inc	236117	11,036,082,176	1,406,839,040
Toll Brothers Inc	236117	7,077,659,136	446,624,000
Nuclear Electric Power Generation			
Exelon Corporation	221113		

Industry Group/Company	Industry Code	2020 Sales	2020 Profits
Online Sales, B2C Ecommerce, Sharing Economy Platforms			
Amazon.com Inc	454111	386,063,990,784	21,330,999,296
Chewy Inc (Chewy.com)	454111	4,846,743,040	-252,370,000
Fanatics Inc	454111	2,887,500,000	
Wayfair LLC	454111	14,145,156,096	184,996,000
Paints and Coatings Manufacturing			
RPM International Inc	325510	5,506,994,176	304,384,992
Sherwin-Williams Company (The)	325510	18,361,700,352	2,030,400,000
Paper Mills and Paper Manufacturing (Excluding Newsprint)			
Georgia-Pacific LLC	322121	13,440,000,000	
Pawn Shops and Specialty Short-Term Financing			
FirstCash Inc	522298	1,631,283,968	106,579,000
Personal Care Products; Consumer Products; Cosmetics and Makeup; Fragrances and Perfumes; and Hair Care Products Manufacturing			
Procter & Gamble Company (The)	325620	70,950,002,688	13,027,000,320
Pet and Pet Supplies Stores			
Petco Animal Supplies Inc	453910	4,574,062,500	
PetSmart Inc	453910	6,150,000,000	
Petrochemicals Manufacturing			
Lubrizol Corporation (The)	325110	5,950,000,000	
Westlake Chemical Corporation	325110	7,504,000,000	330,000,000
Pharmaceuticals and Druggists' Merchandise Distributors			
AmerisourceBergen Corporation	424210	189,893,918,720	-3,408,716,032
Cardinal Health Inc	424210	152,921,997,312	-3,696,000,000
McKesson Corporation	424210	231,051,001,856	900,000,000
Pharmaceuticals, Biopharmaceuticals, Generics and Drug Manufacturing			
Abbott Laboratories	325412	34,608,001,024	4,495,000,064
AbbVie Inc	325412	45,803,999,232	4,616,000,000
Alexion Pharmaceuticals Inc	325412	6,069,899,776	603,400,000
Amgen Inc	325412	25,423,998,976	7,264,000,000
Biogen Inc	325412	13,444,599,808	4,000,600,064
BioMarin Pharmaceutical Inc	325412	1,860,461,056	859,100,032
Bristol-Myers Squibb Company	325412	42,517,999,616	-9,015,000,064
DUSA Pharmaceuticals Inc	325412	104,284,000	7,387,310
Eli Lilly and Company	325412	24,539,799,552	6,193,699,840
Genentech Inc	325412	21,840,000,000	
Gilead Sciences Inc	325412	24,689,000,448	123,000,000
Johnson & Johnson	325412	82,584,002,560	14,714,000,384
Merck & Co Inc	325412	47,993,999,360	7,066,999,808
Pfizer Inc	325412	41,907,998,720	9,616,000,000
Regeneron Pharmaceuticals Inc	325412	8,497,099,776	3,513,200,128
Sanofi Genzyme	325412	13,443,100,000	
Pharmacies and Drug Stores			
CVS Health Corporation	446110	268,706,004,992	7,178,999,808
Walgreens Boots Alliance Inc	446110	139,537,006,592	456,000,000

Industry Group/Company	Industry Code	2020 Sales	2020 Profits
Plastic Product Manufacturing, Miscellaneous, Including Trash Containers, Household Items			
Cornerstone Building Brands Inc	326199	4,617,369,088	-482,777,984
Owens Corning	326199	7,055,000,064	-383,000,000
Plastics (Including Packaging Materials, Pipe, Laminated & Unlaminated Film & Sheet, Foam and Bottles) Product Manufacturing			
Berry Global Group Inc	326100	11,708,999,680	559,000,000
Plastics Material and Resin Manufacturing			
Celanese Corporation	325211	5,655,000,064	1,984,999,936
Plumbing Contractors, and Heating and Air Conditioning (HVAC) Contractors			
Comfort Systems USA Inc	238220	2,856,658,944	150,139,008
Poultry (Including Chicken, Duck & Turkey) Processing and Packaging			
Pilgrims Pride Corporation	311615	12,091,900,928	94,757,000
Sanderson Farms Inc	311615	3,564,267,008	28,274,000
Tyson Foods Inc	311615	43,185,000,448	2,140,000,000
Power-Driven Handtool Manufacturing			
Stanley Black & Decker Inc	333991	14,534,599,680	1,233,799,936
Pressed and Blown Glass and Glassware (except Glass Packaging Containers) Manufacturing			
Corning Incorporated	327212	11,303,000,064	512,000,000
Primary Battery Manufacturing			
Spectrum Brands Holdings Inc	335912	3,964,199,936	97,800,000
Property and Casualty (P&C) Insurance Underwriters (Direct Carriers)			
Allstate Corporation (The)	524126	44,791,001,088	5,576,000,000
American Financial Group Inc	524126	7,810,999,808	732,000,000
American International Group Inc (AIG)	524126	43,839,000,576	-5,944,000,000
Berkshire Hathaway Inc (Holding Co)	524126	286,256,005,120	42,521,001,984
Liberty Mutual Group Inc	524126	43,796,000,000	760,000,000
Nationwide Mutual Insurance Company	524126	48,067,500,000	
State Farm Insurance Companies	524126	78,900,000,000	3,700,000,000
Travelers Companies Inc (The)	524126	31,981,000,704	2,696,999,936
USAA	524126	36,296,000,000	3,915,000,000
Radar, Navigation, Sonar, Space Vehicle Guidance, Flight Systems and Marine Instrument Manufacturing			
Collins Aerospace	334511	19,288,000,000	1,466,000,000
Trimble Inc	334511	3,147,699,968	389,900,000
Radio, Television and Other Electronics Stores			
Best Buy Co Inc	443142	43,638,001,664	1,540,999,936
Railroad Cars, Subways, Trams, Trolleys, Engines and Locomotives Manufacturing			
Greenbrier Companies Inc (The)	336510	2,792,188,928	48,967,000
Trinity Industries Inc	336510	1,999,399,936	-147,300,000
Wabtec Corporation	336510	7,556,100,096	414,400,000
Railroads, Passenger and Freight, Long Distance			
BNSF (Burlington Northern Santa Fe LLC)	482111	20,181,000,000	5,161,000,000
Kansas City Southern	482111	2,632,600,064	617,000,000

Industry Group/Company	Industry Code	2020 Sales	2020 Profits
Union Pacific Corporation	482111	19,533,000,704	5,349,000,192
Recreational Vehicle (RV) Trailer and Camper Manufacturing			
Jayco Inc	336214	2,072,264,512	
Thor Industries Inc	336214	8,167,932,928	222,974,000
Recreational Vehicle Dealers			
Camping World Holdings Inc	441210	5,446,590,976	122,345,000
Restaurants, Fast-Food, Pizza Delivery, Takeout and Family			
Burger King Worldwide Inc	722513	20,038,000,000	832,000,000
Chick-fil-A Inc	722513	13,700,000,000	
Chipotle Mexican Grill Inc	722513	5,984,633,856	355,766,016
Dominos Pizza Inc	722513	4,117,411,072	491,296,000
In-N-Out Burgers Inc	722513	982,437,750	
McDonalds Corporation	722513	19,207,800,832	4,730,500,096
Shake Shack Inc	722513	522,867,008	-42,158,000
Sonic Corp	722513	448,875,000	
Yum! Brands Inc	722513	5,651,999,744	904,000,000
Sanitary Paper Product Manufacturing (Including Hygienic)			
Kimberly-Clark Corporation	322291	19,139,999,744	2,352,000,000
Scientific Research and Development (R&D) in Life Sciences, Medical Devices, Biotechnology and Pharmaceuticals (Drugs)			
Charles River Laboratories International Inc	541711	2,923,932,928	364,304,000
Curia Inc	541711	801,360,000	
IQVIA Holdings Inc	541711	11,358,999,552	279,000,000
PAREXEL International Corporation	541711	2,665,000,000	
PPD Inc	541711	4,681,474,048	153,691,008
PRA Health Sciences Inc	541711	3,183,365,120	197,043,008
Syneos Health Inc	541711	4,415,776,768	192,787,008
Secondary Market Financing			
Fannie Mae (Federal National Mortgage Association)	522294	23,733,999,616	11,804,999,680
Freddie Mac (Federal Home Loan Mortgage Corporation)	522294	16,659,000,320	7,326,000,128
Securities Brokerage, Discount Brokers and Online Stock Brokers			
Charles Schwab Corporation (The)	523120	11,690,999,808	3,299,000,064
E*Trade Financial LLC	523120	3,030,300,134	
Edward D Jones & Co LP	523120	1,006,300,000	1,285,000,000
TD Ameritrade Holding Corporation	523120	5,989,440,000	2,252,160,000
Semiconductor and Solar Cell Manufacturing, Including Chips, Memory, LEDs, Transistors and Integrated Circuits, Artificial Intelligence (AI), & Internet of Things (IoT)			
Advanced Micro Devices Inc (AMD)	334413	9,763,000,320	2,489,999,872
AVX Corporation	334413	1,827,625,751	277,249,251
Diodes Incorporated	334413	1,229,214,976	98,088,000
Intel Corporation	334413	77,866,999,808	20,899,000,320
KEMET Corporation	334413	1,260,000,000	
Microchip Technology Incorporated	334413	5,274,200,064	570,600,000

Industry Group/Company	Industry Code	2020 Sales	2020 Profits
NVIDIA Corporation	334413	10,917,999,616	2,796,000,000
Qualcomm Incorporated	334413	23,530,999,808	5,198,000,128
Texas Instruments Incorporated	334413	14,460,999,680	5,594,999,808
Xilinx Inc	334413	3,162,665,984	792,721,024
Semiconductor Manufacturing Equipment and Systems (Including Etching, Wafer Processing & Surface Mount) Manufacturing			
Applied Materials Inc	333242	17,201,999,872	3,619,000,064
KLA Corporation	333242	5,806,424,064	1,216,785,024
Lam Research Corporation	333242	10,044,735,488	2,251,752,960
Soap and Other Detergent Manufacturing			
Church & Dwight Company Inc	325611	4,895,799,808	785,900,032
Clorox Company (The)	325611	6,720,999,936	939,000,000
Colgate-Palmolive Company	325611	16,471,000,064	2,695,000,064
Ecolab Inc	325611	11,790,199,808	-1,205,100,032
NCH Corporation	325611	1,169,792,400	
Soft Drinks (Including Bottled Carbonated and Flavored Water, Bottled Coffee & Tea, Sodas, Pop and Energy Drinks) Manufacturing			
Coca-Cola Bottling Consolidated Inc	312111	5,007,356,928	172,492,992
Monster Beverage Corporation	312111	4,598,638,080	1,409,593,984
Solar Cell Manufacturing			
First Solar Inc	334413A	2,711,332,096	398,355,008
SunPower Corporation	334413A	1,124,829,056	475,048,000
Solar Electric Power Generation (Solar Energy)			
Sunrun Inc	221114	922,190,976	-173,394,000
Vivint Solar Inc	221114	360,000,000	
Solid Waste Collection, Treatment, Disposal and Recycling			
Republic Services Inc	562111	10,153,600,000	967,200,000
Specialty Canned Foods (Including Soups & Ethnic Foods)			
Campbell Soup Company	311422	8,691,000,320	1,628,000,000
Specialty Chemicals Manufacturing, Including Fragrances, Silicones, Biodiesel and Enzymes,			
Dow Inc	325199	38,542,000,128	1,224,999,936
Spices, Seasonings, Salad Dressing, Mayonnaise, Mustard and Condiments Manufacturing			
McCormick & Company Incorporated	311940	5,601,299,968	747,400,000
Sporting Goods Stores			
Academy Sports & Outdoors Inc	451110	4,829,897,216	120,043,000
Bass Pro Shops Inc	451110	5,675,670,000	
Cabelas Inc	451110	5,093,550,000	
Dicks Sporting Goods Inc	451110	8,750,742,528	297,462,016
REI (Recreational Equipment Inc)	451110	2,754,714,000	-33,543,000
Supermarkets and Grocery (except Convenience) Stores			
Albertsons Companies Inc	445110	62,455,099,392	466,400,000
Associated Wholesale Grocers Inc	445110	10,634,379,000	284,394,000
Giant Eagle Inc	445110	10,679,090,625	
Golub Corporation	445110	3,982,125,000	

Industry Group/Company	Industry Code	2020 Sales	2020 Profits
Harris Teeter Supermarkets Inc	445110	5,876,325,000	
HEB Grocery Company LP	445110	29,000,000,000	
Hy-Vee Inc	445110	11,550,000,000	
Ingles Markets Incorporated	445110	4,610,609,152	178,601,440
Kroger Co (The)	445110	122,285,998,080	1,659,000,064
Meijer Inc	445110	18,726,750,000	
Publix Super Markets Inc	445110	44,863,507,000	3,971,838,000
Roundys Supermarkets Inc	445110	4,793,862,938	
Safeway Inc	445110	43,625,400,000	
Saker ShopRites Inc	445110	2,128,698,731	
Southeastern Grocers LLC	445110	9,250,625,000	
SpartanNash Company	445110	9,348,485,120	75,914,000
Sprouts Farmers Market Inc	445110	6,468,759,040	287,449,984
Supervalu Inc	445110	16,530,000,000	
Trader Joes Company Inc	445110	14,246,475,000	
Wegmans Food Markets Inc	445110	10,497,500,000	
Weis Markets Inc	445110	4,112,601,088	118,917,000
Whole Foods Market Inc	445110	18,977,516,250	
WinCo Foods Inc	445110	6,615,493,500	
Telecommunications, Telephone and Network Equipment Manufacturing, including PBX, Routers, Switches, Internet of Things (IoT), and Handsets Manufacturing			
Ciena Corporation	334210	3,532,156,928	361,291,008
Plantronics Inc	334210	1,696,989,952	-827,182,016
Tellabs Inc	334210	1,610,256,375	
Telephone, Internet Access, Broadband, Data Networks, Server Facilities and Telecommunications Services Industry			
AT&T Inc	517110	171,759,992,832	-5,176,000,000
Comcast Corporation	517110	103,564,001,280	10,533,999,616
Equinix Inc	517110	5,998,544,896	369,776,992
J2 Global Inc	517110	1,489,592,960	150,668,000
Rackspace Technology Inc	517110	2,707,099,904	-245,800,000
Verizon Communications Inc	517110	128,292,003,840	17,801,000,960
Third-Party Logistics (3PL), Supply Chain and Freight Forwarding			
CH Robinson Worldwide Inc	488510	16,207,106,048	506,420,992
Expeditors International of Washington Inc	488510	10,116,481,024	696,140,032
FedEx Supply Chain	488510	1,652,757,750	
XPO Logistics Inc	488510	16,252,000,256	110,000,000
Tire and Tube Wholesale Distribution			
American Tire Distributors Inc	423130	4,800,000,000	
Tire Stores			
Discount Tire Company	441320	4,608,000,000	
Title Insurance Underwriters (Direct Carriers)			
Fidelity National Financial Inc	524127	10,778,000,384	1,427,000,064
First American Financial Corporation	524127	7,080,949,248	696,428,992
Stewart Information Services Corporation	524127	2,288,432,128	154,904,992

Industry Group/Company	Industry Code	2020 Sales	2020 Profits
Truck, Utility Trailer and RV (Recreational Vehicle) Rental and Leasing			
AMERCO (U-Haul)	532120	3,978,867,968	442,048,000
Trucking and Freight-Long Distance, Full Truckload (FTL)			
JB Hunt Transport Services Inc	484121	9,636,573,184	506,035,008
Trucking and Freight-Long Distance, Less Than Truckload (LTL)			
Averitt Express Inc	484122	1,202,500,000	
Estes Express Lines Inc	484122	2,844,000,000	
FedEx Freight	484122	7,102,000,000	580,000,000
Old Dominion Freight Line Inc	484122	4,015,129,088	672,681,984
Roadrunner Transportation Systems Inc	484122		
Yellow Corporation	484122	4,513,699,840	-53,500,000
Vaccines, Skin Replacement Products and Biologicals Manufacturing			
Zoetis Inc	325414	6,674,999,808	1,638,000,000
Venture Capital, Private Equity Investment and Hedge Funds			
Blackstone Group Inc (The)	523910	5,966,306,816	1,045,363,008
Veterinary Services			
VCA Inc	541940	3,213,000,000	
Warehouse Clubs and Super Stores			
Costco Wholesale Corporation	452910	166,761,005,056	4,001,999,872
PriceSmart Inc	452910	3,329,188,096	78,109,000
Sams Club	452910	59,284,975,000	1,580,800,000
Target Corporation	452910	78,111,997,952	3,280,999,936
Walmart Inc	452910	523,963,990,016	14,881,000,448
Waste Collection, Recycling, Treatment and Remediation Services			
Waste Management Inc	562000	15,217,999,872	1,496,000,000
Wet Corn Milling			
Ingredion Incorporated	311221	5,986,999,808	348,000,000
Wind Electric Power Generation (Wind Energy)			
NextEra Energy Inc	221115	17,997,000,704	2,919,000,064
Wine Manufacturing (including Wineries with Vineyards)			
Constellation Brands Inc	312130	8,343,499,776	-11,800,000
E & J Gallo Winery	312130	5,093,550,000	
Wireless Communications and Radio and TV Broadcasting Equipment Manufacturing, including Cellphones (Handsets) and Internet of Things (IoT)			
Apple Inc	334220	274,515,001,344	57,410,998,272
L3Harris Technologies Inc	334220	18,193,999,872	1,119,000,064
Lumentum Operations LLC	334220	1,678,600,000	135,500,000
ViaSat Inc	334220	2,309,238,016	-212,000
Viavi Solutions Inc	334220	1,136,300,032	28,700,000
Wireless Telecommunications Carriers (except Satellite)			
AT&T Mobility LLC	517210	72,564,000,000	22,372,000,000
T-Mobile US Inc	517210	68,396,998,656	3,064,000,000
United States Cellular Corporation	517210	4,036,999,936	229,000,000

Plunkett Research, Ltd.

79

Industry Group/Company	Industry Code	2020 Sales	2020 Profits
Wooden Kitchen Cabinets & Countertops Manufacturing			
Fortune Brands Home & Security Inc	337110	6,090,299,904	553,100,032

ALPHABETICAL INDEX

FedEx Supply Chain
Ferguson Enterprises Inc
Fidelity Investments Financial Services
Fidelity National Financial Inc
Fidelity National Information Services Inc
FireEye Inc
First American Financial Corporation
First Solar Inc
FirstCash Inc
FirstEnergy Corporation
Fiserv Inc
Flowers Foods Inc
Fluor Corporation
Ford Motor Company
Fortinet Inc
Fortune Brands Home & Security Inc
Freddie Mac (Federal Home Loan
Mortgage Corporation)
Frito-Lay North America Inc
FTI Consulting Inc
Gartner Inc
Genentech Inc
General Dynamics Corporation
General Mills Inc
General Motors Company (GM)
Genuine Parts Company
Georgia Power Company
Georgia-Pacific LLC
Giant Eagle Inc
Gilbane Inc
Gilead Sciences Inc
GoDaddy Inc
Golden State Foods Corporation
Goldman Sachs Group Inc (The)
Golub Corporation
Goody Goody Liquor Inc
Grant Thornton LLP
Greenbrier Companies Inc (The)
Griffon Corporation
Group 1 Automotive Inc
GrubHub Inc
Gulfstream Aerospace Corporation
Harris Teeter Supermarkets Inc
Hartford Financial Services Group Inc
(The)
HCA Healthcare Inc
Health Care Service Corporation (HCSC)
Heartland Payment Systems Inc
HEB Grocery Company LP
Hershey Company (The)
Hill-Rom Holdings Inc
Home Depot Inc (The)
Houston Methodist
HTC Global Services Inc
Humana Inc
Hycor Biomedical LLC
Hy-Vee Inc
IAC/InterActiveCorp
IDEXX Laboratories Inc
II-VI Incorporated
Illumina Inc
Ingles Markets Incorporated
Ingredion Incorporated
In-N-Out Burgers Inc
Insight Enterprises Inc

Intel Corporation
Intuit Inc
IQVIA Holdings Inc
Itron Inc
J2 Global Inc
Jabil Inc
Jack Henry & Associates Inc
Jacobs Engineering Group Inc
Jayco Inc
JB Hunt Transport Services Inc
JM Family Enterprises Inc
JM Smucker Company (The)
John Hancock Financial
Johnson & Johnson
JPMorgan Chase & Co Inc
Juniper Networks Inc
Kaiser Permanente
Kansas City Southern
KBR Inc
Kellogg Company
KEMET Corporation
Kenco Group Inc
Kiewit Corporation
Kimberly-Clark Corporation
KLA Corporation
KPMG LLP
Kraft Heinz Company (The)
Kratos Defense & Security Solutions Inc
Kroger Co (The)
L3Harris Technologies Inc
Laboratory Corporation of America
Holdings
Lam Research Corporation
Legg Mason Inc
Lennar Corporation
LHC Group Inc
Liberty Mutual Group Inc
Lincoln National Corporation
LinkedIn Corporation
LKQ Corporation
Lockheed Martin Corporation
Logitech International SA
Lowes Companies Inc
Lubrizol Corporation (The)
Lumentum Operations LLC
Magellan Health Inc
ManTech International Corporation
Mars Incorporated
Mass General Brigham Incorporated
MassMutual Financial Group
MasterCard Incorporated
MAXIMUS Inc
Mayo Clinic
McAfee Corp
McCarthy Building Companies Inc
McCormick & Company Incorporated
McDermott International Ltd
McDonalds Corporation
McKesson Corporation
McKinsey & Company Inc
McLane Company Inc
MDU Resources Group Inc
Meijer Inc
Memorial Hermann Healthcare System
Memorial Sloan Kettering Cancer Center

Menard Inc
Mercer LLC
Merck & Co Inc
Merrill
MetLife Inc
Microchip Technology Incorporated
Microsoft Corporation
Molex LLC
Molina Healthcare Inc
Mondelez International Inc
Monro Inc
Monster Beverage Corporation
Moody's Corporation
Morgan Stanley
Mutual of Omaha Insurance Company
National Instruments Corporation
Nationwide Mutual Insurance Company
NCH Corporation
NetApp Inc
Netflix Inc
New York Life Insurance Company
Newfold Digital Inc
NextEra Energy Inc
Nielsen Holdings plc
NiSource Inc
North Highland Company (The)
Northrop Grumman Corporation
Northwestern Mutual Life Insurance
Company (The)
NortonLifeLock Inc
Nutanix Inc
NVIDIA Corporation
NVR Inc
Old Dominion Freight Line Inc
Oliver Wyman Group
Oracle Corporation
Oracle NetSuite
Owens Corning
Palo Alto Networks Inc
PAREXEL International Corporation
Parsons Corporation
PayPal Holdings Inc
Penske Automotive Group Inc
PerkinElmer Inc
Petco Animal Supplies Inc
PetSmart Inc
Pfizer Inc
PG&E Corporation
Philips Healthcare
Pilgrims Pride Corporation
Plantronics Inc
PPD Inc
PRA Health Sciences Inc
PriceSmart Inc
PricewaterhouseCoopers (PwC)
Principal Financial Group Inc
Procter & Gamble Company (The)
Protiviti Inc
Prudential Financial Inc
Publicis Sapient
Publix Super Markets Inc
Puget Energy Inc
PulteGroup Inc
Qualcomm Incorporated
Quest Diagnostics Incorporated

Rackspace Technology Inc
Raymond James Financial Inc
Red Hat Inc
Regal-Beloit Corporation
Regeneron Pharmaceuticals Inc
REI (Recreational Equipment Inc)
Rent-A-Center Inc
Republic Services Inc
ResMed Inc
REV Group Inc
Roadrunner Transportation Systems Inc
Rockwell Automation Inc
Roper Technologies Inc
Roundys Supermarkets Inc
RPM International Inc
Russell Stover Candies Inc
Safeway Inc
Saker ShopRites Inc
salesforce.com Inc
Sams Club
Sanderson Farms Inc
Sanmina Corporation
Sanofi Genzyme
SAS Institute Inc
SC Johnson & Son Inc
Schreiber Foods Inc
Science Applications International
Corporation (SAIC)
SecureWorks Corporation
Sempra Energy
Service Corporation International Inc
ServiceNow Inc
Shake Shack Inc
Sherwin-Williams Company (The)
Skyline Champion Corporation
Smithfield Foods Inc
Sonic Corp
Southeastern Grocers LLC
Southern California Edison Company
Southern Company
Southern Glazers Wine & Spirits LLC
SpaceX (Space Exploration Technologies
Corporation)
SpartanNash Company
Spectrum Brands Holdings Inc
Splunk Inc
Sprouts Farmers Market Inc
Square Inc
SS&C Technologies Holdings Inc
Stanley Black & Decker Inc
Starbucks Corporation
State Farm Insurance Companies
State Street Corporation
Stewart Information Services Corporation
Stifel Financial Corp
Strategy&
Stryker Corporation
SunPower Corporation
Sunrun Inc
Supervalu Inc
Sutter Health Inc
Sykes Enterprises Incorporated
Syneos Health Inc
SYNNEX Corporation
Synopsys Inc

T Rowe Price Group Inc
Take-Two Interactive Software Inc
Target Corporation
TD Ameritrade Holding Corporation
Tech Data Corporation
Tellabs Inc
Terex Corporation
Tesla Inc
Texas Instruments Incorporated
Textron Inc
Thermo Fisher Scientific Inc
Thor Industries Inc
TIAA
T-Mobile US Inc
Toll Brothers Inc
Tractor Supply Company
Trader Joes Company Inc
Travelers Companies Inc (The)
Trimble Inc
Trinity Industries Inc
Turner Corporation (The)
Tyson Foods Inc
Union Pacific Corporation
United Natural Foods Inc
United Parcel Service Inc (UPS)
United States Cellular Corporation
United States Steel Corporation
UnitedHealth Group Inc
Universal Health Services Inc
US Bancorp (US Bank)
USAA
Vanguard Group Inc (The)
Varian Medical Systems Inc
VCA Inc
Verizon Communications Inc
ViaSat Inc
Viavi Solutions Inc
Visa Inc
Vivint Solar Inc
VMware Inc
Wabtec Corporation
Walgreens Boots Alliance Inc
Walmart Inc
Waste Management Inc
Wayfair LLC
Wegmans Food Markets Inc
Weis Markets Inc
WellCare Health Plans Inc
Wells Fargo & Company
Westlake Chemical Corporation
Whole Foods Market Inc
WinCo Foods Inc
Woodward Inc
Workday Inc
Xilinx Inc
XPO Logistics Inc
Yellow Corporation
YouTube LLC
Yum! Brands Inc
Zillow Group Inc
Zoetis Inc

INDEX OF U.S. HEADQUARTERS LOCATION BY STATE

To help you locate members of THE AMERICAN EMPLOYERS 500 geographically, the city and state of the headquarters of each company are in the following index.

ARIZONA

Align Technology Inc; Tempe
Avnet Inc; Phoenix
Discount Tire Company; Scottsdale
First Solar Inc; Tempe
GoDaddy Inc; Tempe
Insight Enterprises Inc; Tempe
Magellan Health Inc; Scottsdale
Microchip Technology Incorporated; Chandler
NortonLifeLock Inc; Tempe
PetSmart Inc; Phoenix
Republic Services Inc; Phoenix
Sprouts Farmers Market Inc; Phoenix
Viavi Solutions Inc; Scottsdale

ARKANSAS

JB Hunt Transport Services Inc; Lowell
Sams Club; Bentonville
Tyson Foods Inc; Springdale
Walmart Inc; Bentonville

CALIFORNIA

99 Cents Only Stores LLC; City of Commerce
Activision Blizzard Inc; Santa Monica
Adobe Inc; San Jose
Advanced Micro Devices Inc (AMD); Santa Clara
AECOM; Los Angeles
Alphabet Inc (Google); Mountain View
Amgen Inc; Thousand Oaks
Apple Inc; Cupertino
Applied Materials Inc; Santa Clara
Beckman Coulter Inc; Brea
BioMarin Pharmaceutical Inc; San Rafael
Bio-Rad Laboratories Inc; Hercules
Blue Shield of California; Oakland
Broadcom Inc; San Jose
Cadence Design Systems Inc; San Jose
Chipotle Mexican Grill Inc; Newport
Cisco Systems Inc; San Jose
Clorox Company (The); Oakland
Concentrix Corporation; Freemont
Cooper Companies Inc (The); Pleasanton
DocuSign Inc; San Francisco
DoorDash Inc; San Francisco
E & J Gallo Winery; Modesto
Edison International; Rosemead
Edwards Lifesciences Corporation; Irvine
Equinix Inc; Redwood City
Facebook Inc; Menlo Park
FireEye Inc; Milpitas

First American Financial Corporation; Santa Ana
Fortinet Inc; Sunnyvale
Genentech Inc; South San Francisco
Gilead Sciences Inc; Foster City
Golden State Foods Corporation; Irvine
Hycor Biomedical LLC; Garden Grove
Illumina Inc; San Diego
In-N-Out Burgers Inc; Irvine
Intel Corporation; Santa Clara
Intuit Inc; Mountain View
J2 Global Inc; Los Angeles
Juniper Networks Inc; Sunnyvale
Kaiser Permanente; Oakland
KLA Corporation; Milpitas
Lam Research Corporation; Fremont
LinkedIn Corporation; Sunnyvale
Logitech International SA; Newark
Lumentum Operations LLC; San Jose
McAfee Corp; San Jose
Molina Healthcare Inc; Long Beach
Monster Beverage Corporation; Corona
NetApp Inc; Sunnyvale
Netflix Inc; Los Gatos
Nutanix Inc; San Jose
NVIDIA Corporation; Santa Clara
Oracle Corporation; Redwood City
Palo Alto Networks Inc; Santa Clara
PayPal Holdings Inc; San Jose
Petco Animal Supplies Inc; San Diego
PG&E Corporation; San Francisco
Plantronics Inc; Santa Cruz
PriceSmart Inc; San Diego
Protiviti Inc; Menlo Park
Qualcomm Incorporated; San Diego
ResMed Inc; San Diego
Safeway Inc; Pleasanton
salesforce.com Inc; San Francisco
Sanmina Corporation; San Jose
Sempra Energy; San Diego
ServiceNow Inc; Santa Clara
Southern California Edison Company; Rosemead
SpaceX (Space Exploration Technologies Corporation); Hawthorne
Splunk Inc; San Francisco
Square Inc; San Francisco
SunPower Corporation; San Jose
Sunrun Inc; San Francisco
Sutter Health Inc; Sacramento
SYNNEX Corporation; Fremont
Synopsys Inc; Mountain View
Tesla Inc; Palo Alto
Trader Joes Company Inc; Monrovia
Trimble Inc; Sunnyvale
Varian Medical Systems Inc; Palo Alto
VCA Inc; Los Angeles
ViaSat Inc; Carlsbad
Visa Inc; San Francisco
VMware Inc; Palo Alto
Wells Fargo & Company; San Francisco
Workday Inc; Pleasanton
Xilinx Inc; San Jose
YouTube LLC; San Bruno

COLORADO

Arrow Electronics Inc; Centennial
Ball Corporation; Westminster
DaVita Inc; Denver
Pilgrims Pride Corporation; Greeley
Woodward Inc; Fort Collins

CONNECTICUT

aetnaCVSHealth; Hartford
Amphenol Corporation; Wallingford
Cigna Corporation; Bloomfield
EMCOR Group Inc; Norwalk
FactSet Research Systems Inc; Norwalk
Gartner Inc; Stamford
Hartford Financial Services Group Inc (The); Hartford
SS&C Technologies Holdings Inc; Windsor
Stanley Black & Decker Inc; New Britain
Terex Corporation; Norwalk
XPO Logistics Inc; Greenwich

DISTRICT OF COLUMBIA

Fannie Mae (Federal National Mortgage Association); Washington
FTI Consulting Inc; Washington

FLORIDA

AdventHealth; Altamonte Springs
Burger King Worldwide Inc; Miami
Chewy Inc (Chewy.com); Dania Beach
Citrix Systems Inc; Fort Lauderdale
Fanatics Inc; Jacksonville
Fidelity National Financial Inc; Jacksonville
Fidelity National Information Services Inc; Jacksonville
Jabil Inc; St. Petersburg
JM Family Enterprises Inc; Deerfield Beach
L3Harris Technologies Inc; Melbourne
Lennar Corporation; Miami
Newfold Digital Inc; Jacksonville
NextEra Energy Inc; Juno Beach
Publix Super Markets Inc; Lakeland
Raymond James Financial Inc; St. Petersburg
Roper Technologies Inc; Sarasota
Southeastern Grocers LLC; Jacksonville
Southern Glazers Wine & Spirits LLC; Miami
Sykes Enterprises Incorporated; Tampa
Tech Data Corporation; Clearwater
WellCare Health Plans Inc; Tampa

GEORGIA

AFLAC Incorporated; Columbus
AT&T Mobility LLC; Atlanta
Chick-fil-A Inc; Atlanta
Flowers Foods Inc; Thomasville
Genuine Parts Company; Atlanta
Georgia Power Company; Atlanta
Georgia-Pacific LLC; Atlanta
Gulfstream Aerospace Corporation; Savannah

Heartland Payment Systems Inc; Atlanta
Home Depot Inc (The); Atlanta
North Highland Company (The); Atlanta
PulteGroup Inc; Atlanta
SecureWorks Corporation; Atlanta
Southern Company; Atlanta
United Parcel Service Inc (UPS); Atlanta

IDAHO
Albertsons Companies Inc; Boise
WinCo Foods Inc; Boise

ILLINOIS
Abbott Laboratories; Abbott Park
AbbVie Inc; North Chicago
Allscripts Healthcare Solutions Inc; Chicago
Allstate Corporation (The); Northbrook
Anixter International Inc; Glenview
Archer-Daniels-Midland Company (ADM); Chicago
AT Kearney Inc; Chicago
Baxter International Inc; Deerfield
Camping World Holdings Inc; Lincolnshire
Caterpillar Inc; Deerfield
CDW Corporation; Lincolnshire
Conagra Brands Inc; Chicago
Deere & Company (John Deere); Moline
Exelon Corporation; Chicago
Fortune Brands Home & Security Inc; Deerfield
Grant Thornton LLP; Chicago
GrubHub Inc; Chicago
Health Care Service Corporation (HCSC); Chicago
Hill-Rom Holdings Inc; Chicago
Ingredion Incorporated; Westchester
LKQ Corporation; Chicago
McDonalds Corporation; Chicago
Molex LLC; Lisle
Mondelez International Inc; Chicago
Roadrunner Transportation Systems Inc; Downers Grove
State Farm Insurance Companies; Bloomington
United States Cellular Corporation; Chicago
Walgreens Boots Alliance Inc; Deerfield

INDIANA
Anthem Inc; Indianapolis
Berry Global Group Inc; Evansville
Eli Lilly and Company; Indianapolis
Jayco Inc; Middlebury
NiSource Inc; Merrillville
Thor Industries Inc; Elkhart

IOWA
Berkshire Hathaway Energy Company; Des Moines
Hy-Vee Inc; West Des Moines
Principal Financial Group Inc; Des Moines

KANSAS
Associated Wholesale Grocers Inc; Kansas City
Black & Veatch Holding Company; Overland Park
Yellow Corporation; Overland Park

KENTUCKY
Humana Inc; Louisville
Yum! Brands Inc; Louisville

LOUISIANA
Amedisys Inc; Baton Rouge
LHC Group Inc; Lafayette

MAINE
IDEXX Laboratories Inc; Westbrook

MARYLAND
Ciena Corporation; Hanover
Clark Construction Group LLC; Bethesda
Discovery Inc; Silver Spring
Legg Mason Inc; Baltimore
Lockheed Martin Corporation; Bethesda
McCormick & Company Incorporated; Hunt Valley
T Rowe Price Group Inc; Baltimore

MASSACHUSETTS
Alexion Pharmaceuticals Inc; Boston
American Tower Corporation (REIT); Boston
athenahealth Inc; Watertown
Bain & Company Inc; Boston
Biogen Inc; Cambridge
Boston Consulting Group Inc (The, BCG); Boston
Charles River Laboratories International Inc; Wilmington
DUSA Pharmaceuticals Inc; Wilmington
Eversource Energy; Springfield
Fidelity Investments Financial Services; Boston
John Hancock Financial; Boston
Liberty Mutual Group Inc; Boston
Mass General Brigham Incorporated; Boston
MassMutual Financial Group; Springfield
PAREXEL International Corporation; Newton
PerkinElmer Inc; Waltham
Philips Healthcare; Cambridge
Publicis Sapient; Boston
Sanofi Genzyme; Cambridge
State Street Corporation; Boston
Thermo Fisher Scientific Inc; Waltham
Wayfair LLC; Boston

MICHIGAN
Dominos Pizza Inc; Ann Arbor
Dow Inc; Midland
DTE Energy Company; Detroit
Ford Motor Company; Dearborn
General Motors Company (GM); Detroit
HTC Global Services Inc; Troy

Kellogg Company; Battle Creek
Meijer Inc; Grand Rapids
Penske Automotive Group Inc; Bloomfield Hills
Skyline Champion Corporation; Troy
SpartanNash Company; Grand Rapids
Stryker Corporation; Kalamazoo

MINNESOTA
3M Company; St. Paul
Best Buy Co Inc; Richfield
Cargill Incorporated; Minneapolis
CH Robinson Worldwide Inc; Eden Prairie
Ecolab Inc; St. Paul
General Mills Inc; Minneapolis
Mayo Clinic; Rochester
Supervalu Inc; Eden Prairie
Target Corporation; Minneapolis
UnitedHealth Group Inc; Minnetonka
US Bancorp (US Bank); Minneapolis

MISSISSIPPI
Sanderson Farms Inc; Laurel

MISSOURI
Ameren Corporation; St. Louis
Bass Pro Shops Inc; Springfield
Belden Inc; St. Louis
Burns & McDonnell Inc; Kansas City
Centene Corporation; St. Louis
Cerner Corporation; North Kansas City
Edward D Jones & Co LP; Des Peres
Jack Henry & Associates Inc; Monett
Kansas City Southern; Kansas City
McCarthy Building Companies Inc; St. Louis
Russell Stover Candies Inc; Kansas City
Stifel Financial Corp; St. Louis

NEBRASKA
Berkshire Hathaway Inc (Holding Co); Omaha
Cabelas Inc; Sidney
Kiewit Corporation; Omaha
Mutual of Omaha Insurance Company; Omaha
TD Ameritrade Holding Corporation; Omaha
Union Pacific Corporation; Omaha

NEVADA
AMERCO (U-Haul); Reno

NEW HAMPSHIRE
C&S Wholesale Grocers Inc; Keene

NEW JERSEY
B&G Foods Inc; Parsippany
Becton Dickinson and Company; Franklin Lakes
Campbell Soup Company; Camden
Church & Dwight Company Inc; Ewing
Cognizant Technology Solutions Corporation; Teaneck

Johnson & Johnson; New Brunswick
Merck & Co Inc; Kenilworth
Prudential Financial Inc; Newark
Quest Diagnostics Incorporated; Secaucus
Saker ShopRites Inc; Freehold
Zoetis Inc; Parsippany

NEW YORK
American Express Company; New York
American International Group Inc (AIG); New York
Bank of New York Mellon Corporation; New York
BlackRock Inc; New York
Blackstone Group Inc (The); New York
Bloomberg LP; New York
Bristol-Myers Squibb Company; New York
Citigroup Inc; New York
Colgate-Palmolive Company; New York
Constellation Brands Inc; Victor
Corning Incorporated; Corning
Curia Inc; Albany
Deloitte LLP; New York
EY LLP; New York
Goldman Sachs Group Inc (The); New York
Golub Corporation; Schenectady
Griffon Corporation; New York
IAC/InterActiveCorp; New York
JPMorgan Chase & Co Inc; New York
KPMG LLP; New York
MasterCard Incorporated; Purchase
McKinsey & Company Inc; New York
Memorial Sloan Kettering Cancer Center; New York
Mercer LLC; New York
Merrill; New York
MetLife Inc; New York
Monro Inc; Rochester
Moody's Corporation; New York
Morgan Stanley; New York
New York Life Insurance Company; New York
Nielsen Holdings plc; New York
Oliver Wyman Group; New York
Pfizer Inc; New York
PricewaterhouseCoopers (PwC); New York
Regeneron Pharmaceuticals Inc; Tarrytown
Shake Shack Inc; New York
Strategy&; New York
Take-Two Interactive Software Inc; New York
TIAA; New York
Travelers Companies Inc (The); New York
Turner Corporation (The); New York
Verizon Communications Inc; New York
Wegmans Food Markets Inc; Rochester

NORTH CAROLINA
American Tire Distributors Inc; Huntersville
Bank of America Corporation; Charlotte
BMC Stock Holdings Inc; Raleigh
Coca-Cola Bottling Consolidated Inc; Charlotte
Collins Aerospace; Charlotte
CommScope Holding Company Inc; Hickory
Cornerstone Building Brands Inc; Cary
Dentsply Sirona Inc; Charlotte
Duke Energy Corporation; Charlotte
Harris Teeter Supermarkets Inc; Matthews
Ingles Markets Incorporated; Asheville
IQVIA Holdings Inc; Durham
Laboratory Corporation of America Holdings; Burlington
Lowes Companies Inc; Mooresville
Old Dominion Freight Line Inc; Thomasville
PPD Inc; Wilmington
PRA Health Sciences Inc; Raleigh
Red Hat Inc; Raleigh
SAS Institute Inc; Cary
Syneos Health Inc; Morrisville

NORTH DAKOTA
MDU Resources Group Inc; Bismarck

OHIO
American Financial Group Inc; Cincinnati
Cardinal Health Inc; Dublin
Chemed Corporation; Cincinnati
Cleveland Clinic Foundation (The); Cleveland
FirstEnergy Corporation; Akron
JM Smucker Company (The); Orrville
Kroger Co (The); Cincinnati
Lubrizol Corporation (The); Wickliffe
Nationwide Mutual Insurance Company; Columbus
Owens Corning; Toledo
Procter & Gamble Company (The); Cincinnati
RPM International Inc; Medina
Sherwin-Williams Company (The); Cleveland

OKLAHOMA
Sonic Corp; Oklahoma City

OREGON
Bonneville Power Administration; Portland
Datalogic SpA; Bologna
Greenbrier Companies Inc (The); Lake Oswego

PENNSYLVANIA
84 Lumber Company; Eighty Four
Alcoa Corporation; Pittsburge
AmerisourceBergen Corporation; Conshohocken
Ametek Inc; Berwyn
ANSYS Inc; Canonsburg
Comcast Corporation; Philadelphia
Crown Holdings Inc; Yardley
Dicks Sporting Goods Inc; Coraopolis
East Penn Manufacturing Company Inc; Lyon Station
EPAM Systems Inc; Newtown
FedEx Ground; Coraopolis
FedEx Supply Chain; Cranberry Township
Giant Eagle Inc; Pittsburgh
Hershey Company (The); Hershey
II-VI Incorporated; Saxonburg
Kraft Heinz Company (The); Pittsburgh
Lincoln National Corporation; Radnor
Toll Brothers Inc; Horsham
United States Steel Corporation; Pittsburgh
Universal Health Services Inc; King Of Prussia
Vanguard Group Inc (The); Malvern
Wabtec Corporation; Pittsburgh
Weis Markets Inc; Sunbury

RHODE ISLAND
CVS Health Corporation; Woonsocket
Gilbane Inc; Providence
Textron Inc; Providence
United Natural Foods Inc; Providence

SOUTH CAROLINA
AVX Corporation; Fountain Inn
KEMET Corporation; Simpsonville

TENNESSEE
Acadia Healthcare Company Inc; Franklin
Averitt Express Inc; Cookeville
Clayton Homes Inc; Maryville
Dollar General Corporation; Goodlettsville
Envision Healthcare Corporation; Nashville
FedEx Corporation; Memphis
FedEx Freight; Memphis
HCA Healthcare Inc; Nashville
Kenco Group Inc; Chattanooga
Tractor Supply Company; Brentwood

TEXAS
Academy Sports & Outdoors Inc; Katy
AT&T Inc; Dallas
Baylor Scott & White Health; Dallas
Ben E Keith Company; Fort Worth
BMC Software Inc; Houston
BNSF (Burlington Northern Santa Fe LLC); Fort Worth
Brightstar Corporation; Southlake
Carriage Services Inc; Houston
Celanese Corporation; Irving
CenterPoint Energy Inc; Houston
Charles Schwab Corporation (The); Westlake
Comfort Systems USA Inc; Houston
Crown Castle International Corp; Houston
Dell Technologies Inc; Round Rock
Diodes Incorporated; Plano
DR Horton Inc; Arlington
FirstCash Inc; Fort Worth
Fluor Corporation; Irving
Frito-Lay North America Inc; Plano
Goody Goody Liquor Inc; Dallas
Group 1 Automotive Inc; Houston
HEB Grocery Company LP; San Antonio
Houston Methodist; Houston
Jacobs Engineering Group Inc; Dallas
KBR Inc; Houston
Kimberly-Clark Corporation; Dallas

Kratos Defense & Security Solutions Inc;
Round Rock
McDermott International Ltd; Houston
McKesson Corporation; Irving
McLane Company Inc; Temple
Memorial Hermann Healthcare System;
Houston
National Instruments Corporation; Austin
NCH Corporation; Irving
Oracle NetSuite; Austin
Rackspace Technology Inc; San Antonio
Rent-A-Center Inc; Plano
Service Corporation International Inc;
Houston
Stewart Information Services Corporation;
Houston
Tellabs Inc; Carrollton
Texas Instruments Incorporated; Dallas
Trinity Industries Inc; Dallas
USAA; San Antonio
Waste Management Inc; Houston
Westlake Chemical Corporation; Houston
Whole Foods Market Inc; Austin

UTAH
Vivint Solar Inc; Lehi

VIRGINIA
AES Corporation (The); Arlington
Amerigroup Corporation; Virginia Beach
Bechtel Group Inc; Reston
Booz Allen Hamilton Holding Corporation;
McLean
CACI International Inc; Arlington
CarMax Inc; Richmond
Dollar Tree Inc; Chesapeake
Dominion Energy Inc; Richmond
E*Trade Financial LLC; Arlington
Estes Express Lines Inc; Richmond
Ferguson Enterprises Inc; Newport News
Freddie Mac (Federal Home Loan
Mortgage Corporation); McLean
General Dynamics Corporation; Renton
ManTech International Corporation;
Herndon
Mars Incorporated; McLean
MAXIMUS Inc; Reston
Northrop Grumman Corporation; Falls
Church
NVR Inc; Reston
Parsons Corporation; Centreville
Science Applications International
Corporation (SAIC); Reston
Smithfield Foods Inc; Smithfield

WASHINGTON
Amazon.com Inc; Seattle
Concur Technologies Inc; Bellevue
Costco Wholesale Corporation; Issaquah
Danaher Corporation; Washington
Expeditors International of Washington
Inc; Seattle

F5 Networks Inc; Seattle
Itron Inc; Liberty Lake
Microsoft Corporation; Redmond
Puget Energy Inc; Bellevue
REI (Recreational Equipment Inc); Kent
Starbucks Corporation; Seattle
T-Mobile US Inc; Bellevue
Zillow Group Inc; Seattle

WISCONSIN
AO Smith Corporation; Milwaukee
Ashley Furniture Industries Inc; Arcadia
Epic Systems Corporation; Verona
Fiserv Inc; Brookfield
Menard Inc; Eau Claire
Northwestern Mutual Life Insurance
Company (The); Milwaukee
Regal-Beloit Corporation; Beloit
REV Group Inc; Brookfield
Rockwell Automation Inc; Milwaukee
Roundys Supermarkets Inc; Milwaukee
SC Johnson & Son Inc; Racine
Schreiber Foods Inc; Green Bay
Spectrum Brands Holdings Inc; Middleton

Individual Data
Profiles
On Each Of
The AMERICAN EMPLOYERS 500

3M Company

NAIC Code: 339100

TYPES OF BUSINESS:

Health Care Products
Specialty Materials & Textiles
Industrial Products
Safety, Security & Protection Products
Display & Graphics Products
Consumer & Office Products
Electronics & Communications Products
Fuel Cell Technology

BRANDS/DIVISIONS/AFFILIATES:

3M Purification Inc
Thinsulate
Scotch
Command
Filtrete

CONTACTS: Note: Officers with more than one job title may be intentionally listed here more than once.

Michael Roman, CEO
Jon Lindekugel, Sr. VP, Divisional
Theresa Reinseth, Chief Accounting Officer
John Banovetz, Chief Technology Officer
Joaquin Delgado, Executive VP, Divisional
Julie Bushman, Executive VP, Divisional
Michael Vale, Executive VP, Divisional
Mojdeh Poul, Executive VP, Divisional
Ashish Khandpur, Executive VP, Divisional
Paul Keel, Executive VP, Divisional
James Bauman, Executive VP, Divisional
Ivan Fong, General Counsel
Inge Thulin, President
Eric Hammes, Senior VP, Divisional
Kristen Ludgate, Senior VP, Divisional
Denise Rutherford, Senior VP, Divisional

GROWTH PLANS/SPECIAL FEATURES:

3M Company is involved in the research, manufacturing and marketing of a variety of products. Its operations are organized in five segments: industrial, safety and graphics, electronics and energy, healthcare and consumer. The industrial segment serves the automotive, electronics, appliance, paper, printing, food, beverage and construction markets. Its major industrial products include Thinsulate acoustic insulation and 3M paint finishing and detail products. Also, 3M Purification, Inc. provides a line of filtration products. The safety and graphics segment serves a range of markets, with major product offerings including personal protection, traffic safety, border and civil security solutions, commercial graphics sheeting, architectural surface and lighting solutions, cleaning products and roofing granules for asphalt shingles. The electronics and energy segment serves customers with telecommunications networks, electrical products, power generation and distribution and infrastructure protection. Major products include LCD computers and televisions, hand-held mobile devices, notebook PCs and automotive displays. The healthcare segment serves medical clinics, hospitals, pharmaceuticals, dental and orthodontic practitioners, health information systems and food manufacturing and testing. Products include medical and surgical supplies, skin health, and infection prevention. The consumer segment serves markets such as consumer retail, office retail, home improvement and building maintenance. Major products include the Scotch tape, Command adhesive and Filtrete filtration family lines of products. 3M has more than 100,000 patents worldwide. During 2020, 3M company sold substantially all of its drug delivery business to an affiliate of Altaris Capital Partners, LLC, for approximately $650 million.

3M offers its employees medical and dental insurance, tuition reimbursement, flexible spending accounts, disability coverage, a 401(k), adoption assistance and more.

FINANCIAL DATA: Note: Data for latest year may not have been available at press time.

In U.S. $	2020	2019	2018	2017	2016	2015
Revenue	32,184,000,000	32,136,000,000	32,765,000,000	31,657,000,000	30,109,000,000	30,274,000,000
R&D Expense	1,878,000,000	1,911,000,000	1,821,000,000	1,850,000,000	1,735,000,000	1,763,000,000
Operating Income	6,822,000,000	6,128,000,000	6,733,000,000	7,234,000,000	7,223,000,000	6,946,000,000
Operating Margin %		.19%	.20%	.23%	.24%	.23%
SGA Expense	6,879,000,000	6,961,000,000	7,529,000,000	6,572,000,000	6,111,000,000	6,182,000,000
Net Income	5,384,000,000	4,570,000,000	5,349,000,000	4,858,000,000	5,050,000,000	4,833,000,000
Operating Cash Flow	8,113,000,000	7,070,000,000	6,439,000,000	6,240,000,000	6,662,000,000	6,420,000,000
Capital Expenditure	1,501,000,000	1,699,000,000	1,577,000,000	1,373,000,000	1,420,000,000	1,461,000,000
EBITDA	9,151,000,000	7,753,000,000	8,838,000,000	9,414,000,000	8,726,000,000	8,407,000,000
Return on Assets %		.11%	.14%	.14%	.15%	.15%
Return on Equity %		.46%	.50%	.44%	.46%	.39%
Debt to Equity		1.812	1.377	1.051	1.041	0.752

CONTACT INFORMATION:

Phone: 651 733-1110   Fax: 651 733-9973
Toll-Free: 800-364-3577
Address: 3M Center, St. Paul, MN 55144 United States

STOCK TICKER/OTHER:

Stock Ticker: MMM   Exchange: NYS
Employees: 95,000   Fiscal Year Ends: 12/31
Parent Company:

SALARIES/BONUSES:

Top Exec. Salary: $ Bonus: $
Second Exec. Salary: $ Bonus: $

OTHER THOUGHTS:

Estimated Female Officers or Directors: 7
Hot Spot for Advancement for Women/Minorities: Y

84 Lumber Company

www.84lumber.com

NAIC Code: 444190

TYPES OF BUSINESS:

Hardware Stores
Building Materials
Construction Financing
Builder's Insurance
Travel Agency

BRANDS/DIVISIONS/AFFILIATES:

84 Lumber Travel
84 Federal Sales
Maggies Management LLC

CONTACTS: Note: Officers with more than one job title may be intentionally listed here more than once.

Maggie Hardy Magerko, CEO
Amy Smiley, VP-Mktg.

GROWTH PLANS/SPECIAL FEATURES:

84 Lumber Company is a supplier of building materials, equipment and expertise to professional homebuilders, commercial contractors, remodelers and individuals. The company operates over 250 locations in 30 states including door shops, installation centers, engineered wood product shops and component manufacturing facilities, which offer lumber, plywood, insulation, trim, molding, flooring, siding, drywall, trusses, roofing, skylights, engineered lumber, hardware, doors and windows. 84 Lumber also offers a variety of services, such as turn-key installation and onsite management services. The company's manufacturing division builds metal plate connected roof and floor trusses and wall panels. 84 Lumber Travel is a full-service accredited travel agency offering no-fee service to professional contractors and other 84 Lumber customers. Through a team of professionals, the firm's 84 Federal Sales provides national homebuilders, who construct multi-family and single-family units for commercial sales, with geographic information and quotes. The firm offers builder's risk, general liability, workers compensation, commercial auto and personal insurance through Maggie's Management, LLC. 84 Lumber's installation services include framing, roofing, insulation, windows, doors, trip and siding. The firm will support the customer throughout the home building process, including budgeting, package pricing on 84 Lumber homes/blueprints, tailoring a materials package and more.

The company offers its employees life, disability, medical, mental and dental insurance; a 401(k) plan; a profit sharing plan; and training and development programs.

FINANCIAL DATA: Note: Data for latest year may not have been available at press time.

In U.S. $	2020	2019	2018	2017	2016	2015
Revenue	4,700,000,000	3,900,000,000	3,860,000,000	3,000,000,000	2,860,000,000	2,500,000,000
R&D Expense						
Operating Income						
Operating Margin %						
SGA Expense						
Net Income						
Operating Cash Flow						
Capital Expenditure						
EBITDA						
Return on Assets %						
Return on Equity %						
Debt to Equity						

CONTACT INFORMATION:

Phone: 724-228-8820   Fax: 724-228-8058
Toll-Free:
Address: 1019 Rte. 519, Eighty Four, PA 15330 United States

SALARIES/BONUSES:

Top Exec. Salary: $ Bonus: $
Second Exec. Salary: $ Bonus: $

STOCK TICKER/OTHER:

Stock Ticker: Private   Exchange:
Employees: 6,000   Fiscal Year Ends: 12/31
Parent Company:

OTHER THOUGHTS:

Estimated Female Officers or Directors: 1
Hot Spot for Advancement for Women/Minorities:

99 Cents Only Stores LLC

www.99only.com

NAIC Code: 452112

TYPES OF BUSINESS:

Dollar Stores
Wholesale Distribution
Discount General Merchandise

BRANDS/DIVISIONS/AFFILIATES:

Number Holdings Inc

CONTACTS: *Note: Officers with more than one job title may be intentionally listed here more than once.*

Barry J. Feld, CEO
Jason Kidd, Pres.
Ashok Walia, CFO
Mike Kvitko, Chief Merchandising Officer
Michael Fung, Interim Chief Admin. Officer
Russell Wolpert, Chief Legal Officer

GROWTH PLANS/SPECIAL FEATURES:

99 Cents Only Stores, LLC is a general merchandise retailer that markets value priced, primarily consumable goods at a 99 cents or less price point for most items. The company's more than 350 stores sell a wide variety of name brand products, with an average store size of approximately 21,000 square feet. The firm has locations in four U.S. states: California, Texas, Arizona and Nevada. Its two distribution centers are located in California and Texas. Stores are located in a variety of areas including shopping centers, freestanding buildings or in central downtown locations. The company's plethora of merchandise includes staple food items such as produce, deli, alcoholic and non-alcoholic beverages and refrigerated and frozen food products. In addition, its stores offer health and beauty items, household products and cleaning supplies, house wares and kitchen items, pet products, gardening and outdoor items, hardware, stationery, party goods and seasonal items and electronics and entertainment products. The company also offers consumers quality closeout merchandise at a substantial retail discount. The majority of product offerings are recognizable name brand merchandise, including items from 3M, Colgate-Palmolive, Frito-Lay, Dole, General Mills, Hershey Foods, Energizer Battery, Johnson & Johnson and Kraft. Moreover, 99 Cents Only Stores sell merchandise through its bargain wholesale division at prices generally below normal wholesale levels to local, regional and national discount, drug and grocery store chains. The merchandise is sold to independent retailers, distributors and exporters. The wholesale division allows the company to purchase products in larger volumes at more favorable prices. 99 Cents Only Stores is a subsidiary of Number Holdings, Inc.

99 Cents Only Stores offer comprehensive benefits, retirement options and employee assistance programs.

FINANCIAL DATA: *Note: Data for latest year may not have been available at press time.*

In U.S. $	2020	2019	2018	2017	2016	2015
Revenue	2,364,289,200	2,273,355,000	2,165,100,000	2,062,000,000	2,003,995,000	1,926,949,000
R&D Expense						
Operating Income						
Operating Margin %						
SGA Expense						
Net Income				-118,200,000	-241,226,000	5,502,000
Operating Cash Flow						
Capital Expenditure						
EBITDA						
Return on Assets %						
Return on Equity %						
Debt to Equity						

CONTACT INFORMATION:

Phone: 323-980-8145   Fax:
Toll-Free:
Address: 4000 Union Pacific Ave., City of Commerce, CA 90023 United States

STOCK TICKER/OTHER:

Stock Ticker: Private
Employees: 17,000
Parent Company: Number Holdings Inc

Exchange:
Fiscal Year Ends: 03/31

SALARIES/BONUSES:

Top Exec. Salary: $ Bonus: $
Second Exec. Salary: $ Bonus: $

OTHER THOUGHTS:

Estimated Female Officers or Directors:
Hot Spot for Advancement for Women/Minorities:

Abbott Laboratories

www.abbott.com

NAIC Code: 325412

TYPES OF BUSINESS:

Nutritional Products Manufacturing
Immunoassays
Diagnostics
Consumer Health Products
Medical & Surgical Devices
Generic Pharmaceutical Products
LASIK Devices

BRANDS/DIVISIONS/AFFILIATES:

BinaxNOW

CONTACTS: Note: Officers with more than one job title may be intentionally listed here more than once.

Miles White, CEO
Jaime Contreras, Sr. VP, Divisional
Brian Yoor, CFO
Robert Funck, Chief Accounting Officer
Robert Ford, COO
Andrew Lane, Executive VP, Divisional
Stephen Fussell, Executive VP, Divisional
John Capek, Executive VP, Divisional
Brian Blaser, Executive VP, Divisional
Daniel Salvadori, Executive VP, Divisional
Hubert Allen, Executive VP
Roger Bird, Senior VP, Divisional
Jared Watkin, Senior VP, Divisional
Sharon Bracken, Senior VP, Divisional
Sammy Karam, Senior VP, Divisional

GROWTH PLANS/SPECIAL FEATURES:

Abbott Laboratories develops, manufactures and sells healthcare products and technologies in over 150 countries. The firm operates in four product segments: established pharmaceuticals, diagnostic, nutritional and medical devices. Established pharmaceuticals include a line of branded generic pharmaceuticals manufactured worldwide and marketed and sold outside the U.S. in emerging markets. These products are primarily sold directly to wholesalers, distributors, government agencies, healthcare facilities, pharmacies and independent retailers. This segment's principal therapeutic offerings include gastroenterology, women's health, cardiovascular, metabolic, pain, central nervous system, respiratory and vaccination products. The diagnostics segment includes systems and tests manufactured, marketed and sold worldwide to blood banks, hospitals, commercial laboratories, clinics, physicians' offices, government agencies, alternate care testing sites and plasma protein therapeutic companies from Abbot-owned distribution centers, public warehouses and third-party distributors. This segment's products include core laboratory systems in the areas of immunoassay, clinical chemistry, hematology and transfusions; molecular diagnostics systems; point of care systems; rapid diagnostic systems; and informatics and automation solutions for use in laboratories. The nutritional segment offers a line of pediatric and adult nutritional products manufactured, marketed and sold worldwide. This segment's products include various forms of prepared infant formula and follow-on formula; adult and other pediatric nutritional products; and nutritional products used in enteral feeding in healthcare institutions. The medical devices segment products include broad line of rhythm management, electrophysiology, heart failure, vascular and structural heart devices for the treatment of cardiovascular diseases, and diabetes care products for people with diabetes, as well as neuromodulation devices for the management of chronic pain and movement disorders. During 2020, due to the COVID-19 pandemic, the FDA issued Emergency Use Authorizations for Abbott diagnostic tests. In April 2021, Abbott began shipping its BinaxNOW COVID-19 Ag Self Test to retailers in the U.S.

Abbott offers its employees comprehensive benefits.

FINANCIAL DATA: Note: Data for latest year may not have been available at press time.

In U.S. $	2020	2019	2018	2017	2016	2015
Revenue	34,608,000,000	31,904,000,000	30,578,000,000	27,390,000,000	20,853,000,000	20,405,000,000
R&D Expense	2,420,000,000	2,440,000,000	2,300,000,000	2,235,000,000	1,422,000,000	1,405,000,000
Operating Income	5,357,000,000	4,532,000,000	3,650,000,000	1,726,000,000	3,185,000,000	2,867,000,000
Operating Margin %		.14%	.12%	.06%	.15%	.14%
SGA Expense	9,696,000,000	9,765,000,000	9,744,000,000	9,117,000,000	6,672,000,000	6,785,000,000
Net Income	4,495,000,000	3,687,000,000	2,368,000,000	477,000,000	1,400,000,000	4,423,000,000
Operating Cash Flow	7,901,000,000	6,136,000,000	6,300,000,000	5,570,000,000	3,203,000,000	2,966,000,000
Capital Expenditure	2,177,000,000	1,638,000,000	1,394,000,000	1,135,000,000	1,121,000,000	1,110,000,000
EBITDA	8,841,000,000	7,761,000,000	6,977,000,000	6,156,000,000	3,197,000,000	4,818,000,000
Return on Assets %		.05%	.03%	.01%	.03%	.11%
Return on Equity %		.12%	.08%	.02%	.07%	.21%
Debt to Equity		0.56	0.634	0.881	1.007	0.277

CONTACT INFORMATION:

Phone: 847 937-6100   Fax: 847 937-1511
Toll-Free:
Address: 100 Abbott Park Rd., Abbott Park, IL 60064-6400 United States

STOCK TICKER/OTHER:

Stock Ticker: ABT
Employees: 107,000
Parent Company:

Exchange: NYS
Fiscal Year Ends: 12/31

SALARIES/BONUSES:

Top Exec. Salary: $ Bonus: $
Second Exec. Salary: $ Bonus: $

OTHER THOUGHTS:

Estimated Female Officers or Directors: 5
Hot Spot for Advancement for Women/Minorities: Y

Sales, profits and employees may be estimates. Financial information, benefits and other data can change quickly and may vary from those stated here.

AbbVie Inc
NAIC Code: 325412

www.abbvie.com

TYPES OF BUSINESS:
Pharmaceuticals Manufacturing
Biopharmaceutical Production
Biopharmaceutical Development

BRANDS/DIVISIONS/AFFILIATES:
HUMIRA
IMBRUVICA
MAVYRET
Botox
Lumigan
Lo Loestrin

CONTACTS: Note: Officers with more than one job title may be intentionally listed here more than once.
Richard Gonzalez, CEO
Robert Michael, CFO
Brian Durkin, Chief Accounting Officer
Laura Schumacher, Chief Legal Officer
Azita Saleki-Gerhardt, Executive VP, Divisional
William Chase, Executive VP, Divisional
Timothy Richmond, Executive VP
Henry Gosebruch, Executive VP
Carlos Alban, Other Executive Officer
Michael Severino, President
Jeffrey Stewart, Senior VP, Divisional
Nicholas Donoghoe, Senior VP, Divisional

GROWTH PLANS/SPECIAL FEATURES:
AbbVie, Inc. is a global biopharmaceutical manufacturing and research firm. The company discovers and develops innovative medicines, with focus areas including immunology, oncology, neuroscience, eye care, virology, women's health, gastroenterology and Allergan aesthetics. AbbVie investigates both small and large molecule approaches, and its research efforts are partnered with external collaborations across industry, academia and healthcare authorities. The firm's leading drugs include HUMIRA, a biologic therapy; IMBRUVICA, an oral therapy that inhibits a protein called Bruton's tyrosine kinase for the treatment of lymphoma-related issues and more; MAVYRET, for the treatment of patients with chronic HCV genotype 1-6 infection without cirrhosis; Botox, for temporary improvement in the appearance of moderate to severe glabellar lines, crow's feet and forehead lines in adults; and Botox Therapeutic, for the treatment of overactive bladder, urinary incontinence and the prophylaxis of headaches; Lumigan, for the reduction of elevated intraocular pressure; and Lo Loestrin, for prevention of pregnancy. Other key products include treatments for patients with hepatitis C virus, metabolic and hormone products, endocrinology products, endometriosis products, and anemia caused by uterine fibroid products. The company operates research centers in Abbott Park and North Chicago, Illinois; Redwood City, South San Francisco and Sunnyvale, California; Worcester and Cambridge, Massachusetts; and Ludwigshafen, Germany. AbbVie's products are generally sold worldwide directly to wholesalers, distributors, government agencies, health care facilities, specialty pharmacies and independent retailers.

Depending on the country, AbbVie offers healthcare and retirement benefits, life and disability insurance and a variety of incentives and employee assistance programs.

FINANCIAL DATA: Note: Data for latest year may not have been available at press time.

In U.S. $	2020	2019	2018	2017	2016	2015
Revenue	45,804,000,000	33,266,000,000	32,753,000,000	28,216,000,000	25,638,000,000	22,859,000,000
R&D Expense	6,557,000,000	6,407,000,000	10,329,000,000	4,982,000,000	4,366,000,000	4,285,000,000
Operating Income	12,561,000,000	13,368,000,000	6,807,000,000	9,919,000,000	9,584,000,000	7,687,000,000
Operating Margin %		.40%	.21%	.35%	.37%	.34%
SGA Expense	11,299,000,000	6,942,000,000	7,399,000,000	6,275,000,000	5,855,000,000	6,387,000,000
Net Income	4,616,000,000	7,882,000,000	5,687,000,000	5,309,000,000	5,953,000,000	5,144,000,000
Operating Cash Flow	17,588,000,000	13,324,000,000	13,427,000,000	9,959,999,000	7,041,000,000	7,535,000,000
Capital Expenditure	798,000,000	552,000,000	638,000,000	529,000,000	479,000,000	532,000,000
EBITDA	12,323,000,000	12,227,000,000	8,310,000,000	10,378,000,000	10,120,000,000	8,200,000,000
Return on Assets %		.11%	.09%	.08%	.10%	.13%
Return on Equity %				1.09%	1.38%	1.81%
Debt to Equity				6.073	7.86	7.412

CONTACT INFORMATION:
Phone: 847-932-7900   Fax:
Toll-Free: 800-255-5162
Address: 1 N. Waukegan Rd., North Chicago, IL 60064 United States

STOCK TICKER/OTHER:
Stock Ticker: ABBV
Employees: 47,000
Parent Company:

Exchange: NYS
Fiscal Year Ends: 12/31

SALARIES/BONUSES:
Top Exec. Salary: $ Bonus: $
Second Exec. Salary: $ Bonus: $

OTHER THOUGHTS:
Estimated Female Officers or Directors:
Hot Spot for Advancement for Women/Minorities:

Academy Sports & Outdoors Inc

www.academy.com

NAIC Code: 451110

TYPES OF BUSINESS:

Sporting Goods Stores
Apparel
Footwear
Outdoor Sports Gear
Hunting Licenses

BRANDS/DIVISIONS/AFFILIATES:

CONTACTS: *Note: Officers with more than one job title may be intentionally listed here more than once.*

Ken Hicks, CEO
Michael Mullican, CFO
Steven P. Lawrence, Exec. Pres., Retail Oper.
Steven P. Lawrence, Chief Merchandising Officer
Beth Menuer, Exec. VP-Footwear
Robert Frennea, Exec. VP-Apparel
Kevin Chapman, Exec. VP-Stores

GROWTH PLANS/SPECIAL FEATURES:

Academy Sports & Outdoors, Inc. is a leading full-line sporting goods and outdoor recreation retailer in the U.S. The company operates nearly 260 stores throughout 16 states including Alabama, Arkansas, Florida, Georgia, Illinois, Indiana, Kansas, Kentucky, Louisiana, Mississippi, Missouri, North Carolina, Oklahoma, South Carolina, Tennessee and Texas. Its retail operations also include a full ecommerce retail store. Academy Sports offers a broad selection of sporting equipment, apparel and footwear. The stores, which range in size from 40,000 to over 130,000 square feet, are laid out in a racetrack format with soft goods on the inside, including branded and private label athletic and casual apparel; and hard goods, such as camping, hunting, fishing, marine, footwear and fitness and sporting goods on the outside. The company distributes merchandise to its stores from its distribution centers located in Katy, Texas; Twiggs County, Georgia; and Cookeville, Tennessee. These centers use sophisticated sorting and logistical equipment to fill the product needs of the retail customers they serve, as well as to fulfill ecommerce orders.

Academy Sports offers its employees comprehensive health benefits, retirement options, life and disability coverage and a variety of employee assistance plans and programs.

FINANCIAL DATA: *Note: Data for latest year may not have been available at press time.*

In U.S. $	2020	2019	2018	2017	2016	2015
Revenue	4,829,897,000	4,783,893,000	4,835,582,000			
R&D Expense						
Operating Income	179,421,000	128,950,000	157,321,000			
Operating Margin %						
SGA Expense	1,251,733,000	1,239,002,000	1,241,643,000			
Net Income	120,043,000	21,442,000	58,501,000			
Operating Cash Flow	263,669,000	198,481,000	83,355,000			
Capital Expenditure	62,818,000	107,905,000	132,126,000			
EBITDA	341,421,000	264,827,000	299,342,000			
Return on Assets %						
Return on Equity %						
Debt to Equity						

CONTACT INFORMATION:

Phone: 281-646-5200   Fax: 281-646-5000
Toll-Free: 888-922-2336
Address: 1800 N. Mason Rd., Katy, TX 77449 United States

STOCK TICKER/OTHER:

Stock Ticker: ASO   Exchange: NAS
Employees: 22,430   Fiscal Year Ends: 01/30
Parent Company:

SALARIES/BONUSES:

Top Exec. Salary: $ Bonus: $
Second Exec. Salary: $ Bonus: $

OTHER THOUGHTS:

Estimated Female Officers or Directors: 1
Hot Spot for Advancement for Women/Minorities:

Acadia Healthcare Company Inc

www.acadiahealthcare.com

NAIC Code: 622210

TYPES OF BUSINESS:

Psychiatric and Substance Abuse Hospitals
Residential Treatment Facilities
Behavioral Health Care Centers

BRANDS/DIVISIONS/AFFILIATES:

CONTACTS: *Note: Officers with more than one job title may be intentionally listed here more than once.*

Debra Osteen, CEO
David Duckworth, CFO
Reeve Waud, Chairman of the Board
Ronald Fincher, COO
Christopher Howard, Executive VP

GROWTH PLANS/SPECIAL FEATURES:

Acadia Healthcare Company, Inc. provides inpatient behavioral healthcare services via 299 facilities with more than 10,100 licensed beds in 40 U.S. states and in Puerto Rico. Acadia provides psychiatric and chemical dependency services in a variety of settings, including psychiatric hospitals, residential treatment centers, outpatient clinics and therapeutic school-based programs. Treatment specializes in helping children, teenagers and adults suffering from mental health disorders and/or alcohol and drug addiction. Acadia operates through four types of facilities: acute inpatient psychiatric facilities, residential treatment centers, outpatient community-based services and specialty. Acute inpatient psychiatric facilities help stabilize patients that are either a threat to themselves or to others, and have 24-hour observation, daily intervention and residential treatment centers. Residential treatment centers treat patients with behavioral disorders in a non-hospital setting, and balance therapy activities with social, academic and other activities. Certain residential treatment centers provide group home and therapeutic foster care programs. Outpatient community-based services are usually divided between children and adolescents (7-18 years of age) and young children (three months to six years old). Community-based programs provide therapeutic treatment to minors who have clinically-defined emotional, psychiatric or chemical dependency disorders while enabling the youth to remain at home and within their community. Specialty treatment facilities include residential recovery facilities, eating disorder facilities and comprehensive treatment centers (CTCs) for addictive disorders, co-occurring mental disorders and detoxification. Acadia's U.K. operations work under the Partnerships in Care (PiC) name. During 2021, Acadia Healthcare formed a joint venture with Bronson Healthcare, which will build a new 96-bed facility in Battle Creek, Michigan, expected to open in early 2023. That same year, Acadia sold its U.K. facilities.

FINANCIAL DATA: *Note: Data for latest year may not have been available at press time.*

In U.S. $	2020	2019	2018	2017	2016	2015
Revenue	2,089,929,000	3,107,462,000	3,012,442,000	2,836,316,000	2,810,914,000	1,794,492,000
R&D Expense						
Operating Income	332,787,000	404,532,000	412,743,000	437,882,000	445,142,000	320,810,000
Operating Margin %		.13%	.14%	.15%	.16%	.18%
SGA Expense	157,851,000	323,212,000	307,707,000	272,998,000	258,834,000	148,991,000
Net Income	-672,132,000	108,923,000	-175,750,000	199,835,000	6,143,000	112,554,000
Operating Cash Flow	658,807,000	332,904,000	414,080,000	399,577,000	361,478,000	240,403,000
Capital Expenditure	216,615,000	284,682,000	341,462,000	274,177,000	307,472,000	276,047,000
EBITDA	437,158,000	487,126,000	175,288,000	555,815,000	349,383,000	335,045,000
Return on Assets %		.02%	-.03%	.03%	.00%	.03%
Return on Equity %		.05%	-.07%	.08%	.00%	.09%
Debt to Equity		1.44	1.354	1.246	1.501	1.304

CONTACT INFORMATION:

Phone: 615 861-6000   Fax: 615 261-9685
Toll-Free:
Address: 6100 Tower Circle, Ste. 1000, Franklin, TN 37067 United States

STOCK TICKER/OTHER:

Stock Ticker: ACHC   Exchange: NAS
Employees: 42,200   Fiscal Year Ends: 12/31
Parent Company:

SALARIES/BONUSES:

Top Exec. Salary: $ Bonus: $
Second Exec. Salary: $ Bonus: $

OTHER THOUGHTS:

Estimated Female Officers or Directors:
Hot Spot for Advancement for Women/Minorities:

Activision Blizzard Inc

www.activisionblizzard.com

NAIC Code: 511210G

TYPES OF BUSINESS:

Electronic Games, Apps & Entertainment
League-Based, Live Gaming Competition
Apps
TV Distribution of Gaming Events
Merchandising
Licensing Game Content for Movies
Licensing Content to Comic Books

BRANDS/DIVISIONS/AFFILIATES:

Activision Publishing Inc
Blizzard Entertainment Inc
King Digital Entertainment
Call of Duty
BlizzardBattle.net
Overwatch League
World of Warcraft
Starcraft

CONTACTS: Note: Officers with more than one job title may be intentionally listed here more than once.

Riccardo Zacconi, CEO, Subsidiary
Robert Kotick, CEO
Dennis Durkin, CFO
Brian Kelly, Chairman of the Board
Stephen Wereb, Chief Accounting Officer
Christopher Walther, Chief Legal Officer
Collister Johnson, COO
Brian Stolz, Other Executive Officer

GROWTH PLANS/SPECIAL FEATURES:

Activision Blizzard, Inc. is a global developer and publisher of interactive entertainment content and services for use on video game consoles, personal computers (PCs) and mobile devices. Activision also operates eSports leagues and offer digital advertising within its content. The company has three segments: Activision Publishing, Inc.; Blizzard Entertainment, Inc.; and Kind Digital Entertainment. Activision Publishing develops and publishes interactive software products and entertainment content, particularly for the console platforms; delivering content through retail and digital channels, including full-game and in-game sales, as well as by licensing software to third-party or related-party companies that distribute Activision products. This segment's key product franchise is Call of Duty, a first-person shooter for the console and PC platforms. Blizzard develops and publishes interactive software products and entertainment content, particularly for the PC platform; delivering content through retail and digital channels, including subscriptions, full-game and in-game sales, as well as by licensing software to third-party or related-party companies that distribute Blizzard products. BlizzardBattle.net is an online game service that facilitates digital distribution of Blizzard content and selected Activision content, online social connectivity, and the creation of user-generated content. Blizzard also includes the activities of: Overwatch League, a global professional eSports league with city-based teams; and the major league gaming business, which is responsible for various eSports events and serves as a multi-platform network for Activision Blizzard eSports content. Blizzard's key product franchise includes World of Warcraft, StarCraft, Diablo, Hearthstone and Overwatch. King Digital develops and publishes interactive entertainment content and services, primarily on mobile platforms such as Google, Inc.'s Android and Apple Inc's iOS. It also distributes its content and services on PCs, primarily via Facebook. King's games are free to play, and its key product franchises include Candy Crush, Farm Heroes and Bubble Witch.

FINANCIAL DATA: Note: Data for latest year may not have been available at press time.

In U.S. $	2020	2019	2018	2017	2016	2015
Revenue	8,086,000,000	6,489,000,000	7,500,000,000	7,017,000,000	6,608,000,000	4,664,000,000
R&D Expense	1,150,000,000	998,000,000	1,101,000,000	1,069,000,000	958,000,000	646,000,000
Operating Income	2,828,000,000	1,739,000,000	1,988,000,000	1,309,000,000	1,412,000,000	1,319,000,000
Operating Margin %		.27%	.27%	.19%	.21%	.28%
SGA Expense	1,848,000,000	1,658,000,000	1,894,000,000	2,138,000,000	1,844,000,000	1,114,000,000
Net Income	2,197,000,000	1,503,000,000	1,813,000,000	273,000,000	966,000,000	892,000,000
Operating Cash Flow	2,252,000,000	1,831,000,000	1,790,000,000	2,213,000,000	2,155,000,000	1,192,000,000
Capital Expenditure	78,000,000	116,000,000	131,000,000	155,000,000	136,000,000	111,000,000
EBITDA	3,161,000,000	2,276,000,000	2,986,000,000	2,508,000,000	2,562,000,000	1,813,000,000
Return on Assets %		.08%	.10%	.02%	.06%	.06%
Return on Equity %		.12%	.17%	.03%	.11%	.12%
Debt to Equity		0.209	0.235	0.464	0.536	0.506

CONTACT INFORMATION:

Phone: 310 255-2000   Fax: 310 255-2100
Toll-Free:
Address: 3100 Ocean Park Blvd., Santa Monica, CA 90405 United States

STOCK TICKER/OTHER:

Stock Ticker: ATVI
Employees: 9,200
Parent Company:

Exchange: NAS
Fiscal Year Ends: 12/31

SALARIES/BONUSES:

Top Exec. Salary: $ Bonus: $
Second Exec. Salary: $ Bonus: $

OTHER THOUGHTS:

Estimated Female Officers or Directors:
Hot Spot for Advancement for Women/Minorities:

Adobe Inc

NAIC Code: 511210F

TYPES OF BUSINESS:

Computer Software, Multimedia, Graphics & Publishing
Document Management Software
Photo Editing & Management Software
Graphic Design Software

BRANDS/DIVISIONS/AFFILIATES:

Adobe Experience Cloud
Adobe LiveCycle
Adobe Connect
Workfront

CONTACTS: Note: Officers with more than one job title may be intentionally listed here more than once.

Shantanu Narayen, CEO
John Murphy, CFO
Mark Garfield, Chief Accounting Officer
Ann Lewnes, Chief Marketing Officer
Abhay Parasnis, Chief Technology Officer
John Warnock, Co-Founder
Charles Geschke, Director
Matthew Thompson, Executive VP, Divisional
Donna Morris, Executive VP, Divisional
Scott Belsky, Executive VP, Divisional
Dana Rao, Executive VP
Bryan Lamkin, Executive VP
Bradley Rencher, Executive VP

GROWTH PLANS/SPECIAL FEATURES:

Adobe, Inc. is one of the largest software companies in the world. The company operates in three segments, namely digital media, digital experience and publishing, with a current focus on investing in digital media and digital experience, its two strategic growth areas. Digital media provides products, services and solutions that enable individuals, teams and enterprises to create, publish and promote their content anywhere. Its customers include content creators, web designers, app developers and digital media professional, as well as management in marketing departments and agencies, companies and publishers. Customers also include workers who create, collaborate and distribute documents. The digital experience segment provides solutions and services for creating, managing, executing, measuring and optimizing digital marketing and advertising campaigns across multiple channels. Its customers include marketers, advertisers, agencies, publishers, merchandisers, web analysts, marketing executives, information management executives, product development executives and sales and support executives. Every year, this division processes trillions of data transactions via its analytics products, which provides customers with a data platform that can be used to gain insight and optimize digital experiences through the Adobe Experience Cloud. By combining the creativity of the digital media business and the science of the digital experience offerings, Adobe helps customers more efficiently and effectively make, manage, measure and monetize their content across all channels. Last, the publishing segment contains legacy products and services that address diverse market opportunities such as eLearning solutions, technical document publishing, web application development and high-end printing. This division offers Adobe LiveCycle, an enterprise document and forms platform; and Adobe Connect, a web conferencing platform. In December 2020, Adobe acquired Workfront, a work management platform for marketers with more than 3,000 customers and one million users.

Adobe offers its employees comprehensive benefits.

FINANCIAL DATA: Note: Data for latest year may not have been available at press time.

In U.S. $	2020	2019	2018	2017	2016	2015
Revenue	12,868,000,000	11,171,300,000	9,030,008,000	7,301,505,000	5,854,430,000	4,795,511,000
R&D Expense	2,188,000,000	1,930,228,000	1,537,812,000	1,224,059,000	975,987,000	862,730,000
Operating Income	4,237,000,000	3,268,121,000	2,840,369,000	2,168,095,000	1,492,094,000	904,654,000
Operating Margin %		.29%	.31%	.30%	.25%	.19%
SGA Expense	4,559,000,000	4,124,984,000	3,365,727,000	2,822,298,000	2,487,907,000	2,215,161,000
Net Income	5,260,000,000	2,951,458,000	2,590,774,000	1,693,954,000	1,168,782,000	629,551,000
Operating Cash Flow	5,727,000,000	4,421,813,000	4,029,304,000	2,912,853,000	2,199,728,000	1,469,502,000
Capital Expenditure	419,000,000	394,479,000	266,579,000	178,122,000	203,805,000	184,936,000
EBITDA	5,049,000,000	4,098,624,000	3,229,610,000	2,538,040,000	1,837,115,000	1,277,438,000
Return on Assets %		.15%	.16%	.12%	.10%	.06%
Return on Equity %		.30%	.29%	.21%	.16%	.09%
Debt to Equity		0.094	0.441	0.222	0.256	0.272

CONTACT INFORMATION:

Phone: 408 536-6000   Fax: 408 536-6799
Toll-Free: 800-833-6687
Address: 345 Park Ave., San Jose, CA 95110-2704 United States

STOCK TICKER/OTHER:

Stock Ticker: ADBE
Employees: 22,516
Parent Company:

Exchange: NAS
Fiscal Year Ends: 11/30

SALARIES/BONUSES:

Top Exec. Salary: $ Bonus: $
Second Exec. Salary: $ Bonus: $

OTHER THOUGHTS:

Estimated Female Officers or Directors: 5
Hot Spot for Advancement for Women/Minorities: Y

Advanced Micro Devices Inc (AMD)

www.amd.com

NAIC Code: 334413

TYPES OF BUSINESS:

Microprocessors
Semiconductors
Chipsets
Wafer Manufacturing
Multimedia Graphics

BRANDS/DIVISIONS/AFFILIATES:

AMD
ATI
Athlon
EPYC
Radeon
Ryzen
Threadripper

CONTACTS: *Note: Officers with more than one job title may be intentionally listed here more than once.*

Lisa Su, CEO
Devinder Kumar, CFO
Darla Smith, Chief Accounting Officer
Mark Papermaster, Chief Technology Officer
John Caldwell, Director
Sandeep Chennakeshu, Executive VP, Divisional
Forrest Norrod, General Manager, Divisional
Darren Grasby, Other Executive Officer
Harry Wolin, Senior VP

GROWTH PLANS/SPECIAL FEATURES:

Advanced Micro Devices, Inc. (AMD) is a global semiconductor company that provides processing products for the computing, graphics and consumer electronics markets. AMD operates through two segments. The computing and graphics segment primarily includes desktop and notebook processors and chipsets, discrete and integrated graphics processing units (GPUs), data center and professional GPUs and development services. The enterprise, embedded and semi-custom segment primarily includes server and embedded processors, semi-custom system-on-chip (SoC) products, development services and technology for game consoles. The company's x86 microprocessors are primarily offered as standalone devices or as incorporated into an accelerated processing unit (APU), chipsets, discrete/integrated GPUs and professional GPUs. A microprocessor is an integrated circuit (IC) that serves as the CPU of a computer, and generally consists of hundreds of millions or billions of transistors that process date in a serial fashion, and control other devices in the system, acting as the brain of the computer. A GPU is a programmable logic chip that helps render images, animations and video. An APU is a processing unit that integrates a CPU and a GPU onto one chip, along with other special-purpose components. This integration enhances system performance by offloading selected tasks to the best-suited component (the CPU of GPU) to optimize component use, increasing the speed of data flow via shared memory while also improving energy efficiency. AMD's server and embedded processors and semi-custom system-on-a-chip (SoC) products and technology are utilized in game consoles. AMD also license portions of its intellectual property. Trademarks of the firm include AMD, ATI, Athlon, EPYC, Radeon, Ryzen and Threadripper, as well as combinations of these. In October 2020, AMD agreed to acquire rival chip maker Xilinx Inc. for $35 billion. The planned purchase still must pass regulatory scrutiny.

FINANCIAL DATA: *Note: Data for latest year may not have been available at press time.*

In U.S. $	2020	2019	2018	2017	2016	2015
Revenue	9,763,000,000	6,731,000,000	6,475,000,000	5,329,000,000	4,272,000,000	3,991,000,000
R&D Expense	1,983,000,000	1,547,000,000	1,434,000,000	1,160,000,000	1,008,000,000	947,000,000
Operating Income	1,369,000,000	631,000,000	451,000,000	204,000,000	-382,000,000	-352,000,000
Operating Margin %		.09%	.07%	.04%	- .09%	- .09%
SGA Expense	995,000,000	750,000,000	562,000,000	511,000,000	460,000,000	482,000,000
Net Income	2,490,000,000	341,000,000	337,000,000	43,000,000	-497,000,000	-660,000,000
Operating Cash Flow	1,071,000,000	493,000,000	34,000,000	68,000,000	90,000,000	-226,000,000
Capital Expenditure	294,000,000	217,000,000	163,000,000	113,000,000	77,000,000	96,000,000
EBITDA	1,676,000,000	724,000,000	621,000,000	339,000,000	-159,000,000	-319,000,000
Return on Assets %		.06%	.08%	.01%	- .15%	- .19%
Return on Equity %		.17%	.36%	.08%	-248.50%	
Debt to Equity		0.242	0.88	2.169	3.45	

CONTACT INFORMATION:

Phone: 408 749-4000   Fax:
Toll-Free:
Address: 2485 Augustine Dr., Santa Clara, CA 95054 United States

STOCK TICKER/OTHER:

Stock Ticker: AMD
Employees: 12,600
Parent Company:

Exchange: NAS
Fiscal Year Ends: 12/31

SALARIES/BONUSES:

Top Exec. Salary: $ Bonus: $
Second Exec. Salary: $ Bonus: $

OTHER THOUGHTS:

Estimated Female Officers or Directors: 3
Hot Spot for Advancement for Women/Minorities: Y

AdventHealth

NAIC Code: 622110

TYPES OF BUSINESS:

General Medical and Surgical Hospitals
Nursing Homes
Home Health Care Services

BRANDS/DIVISIONS/AFFILIATES:

Seventh-day Adventist Church

CONTACTS: Note: Officers with more than one job title may be intentionally listed here more than once.

Terry Shaw, CEO
Paul Rathbun, CFO
Olesea Azevedo, Chief Human Resources Officer
Brent G. Snyder, CIO
Robert R. Henderschedt, Sr. VP-Admin.
Jeffrey S. Bromme, Chief Legal Officer
Sandra K. Johnson, VP-Bus. Dev., Risk Mgmt. & Compliance
Womack H. Rucker, Jr., VP-Corp. Rel.
Lewis Seifert, Sr. VP-Finance
Amanda Brady, Chief Acct. Officer
Amy L. Zbaraschuk, VP-Finance
T.L. Trimble, VP-Legal Svcs.
Ted Hamilton, VP-Medical Mission
Carlene Jamerson, Sr. VP
Ron Smith, Chmn.
John Brownlow, Sr. VP-Managed Care
Celeste M. West, VP-Supply Chain Mgmt.

GROWTH PLANS/SPECIAL FEATURES:

AdventHealth is sponsored by the Seventh-day Adventist Church and is one of the largest nonprofit Protestant healthcare organizations in the U.S. The firm operates nearly 50 hospitals and hundreds of care sites in diverse markets throughout nine states. The company serves millions of patients annually through its more than 80,000 caregivers. Adventist Health's services span bariatric/weight care, behavioral health, cancer, children's care, diabetes, digestive, emergency/urgent, heart/vascular, home care, hospice care, imaging services, lab services, men's health, mother and baby care, neurology/neurosurgical care, orthopedic, pain, primary care, senior care, skilled nursing, sleep care, spine, sports medicine, rehab, surgical care, transplant care, wellness care, women's health and wound care. The firm is guided by its Christian mission, combining disease treatment, preventative medicine, education and advocacy of a wholesome lifestyle. Hospitals within the health group provide a wide range of free or reduced-price services in their communities, including free medical vans and community clinics, free screening and education programs, debt forgiveness, abuse shelters and programs for the homeless and jobless.

FINANCIAL DATA: Note: Data for latest year may not have been available at press time.

In U.S. $	2020	2019	2018	2017	2016	2015
Revenue	10,230,000,000	11,000,000,000	10,000,000,000	9,699,947,345	9,651,689,000	9,116,187,000
R&D Expense						
Operating Income						
Operating Margin %						
SGA Expense						
Net Income				229,800,000	89,559,000	-131,403,000
Operating Cash Flow						
Capital Expenditure						
EBITDA						
Return on Assets %						
Return on Equity %						
Debt to Equity						

CONTACT INFORMATION:

Phone: 407-357-1000   Fax:
Toll-Free:
Address: 900 Hope Way, Altamonte Springs, FL 32714 United States

STOCK TICKER/OTHER:

Stock Ticker: Nonprofit   Exchange:
Employees: 80,000   Fiscal Year Ends: 12/31
Parent Company:

SALARIES/BONUSES:

Top Exec. Salary: $ Bonus: $
Second Exec. Salary: $ Bonus: $

OTHER THOUGHTS:

Estimated Female Officers or Directors: 6
Hot Spot for Advancement for Women/Minorities: Y

AECOM
NAIC Code: 237310

www.aecom.com

TYPES OF BUSINESS:
Engineering & Design Services
Transportation Projects
Environmental Projects
Building Projects
Consulting
Water Projects
Energy Projects

BRANDS/DIVISIONS/AFFILIATES:

GROWTH PLANS/SPECIAL FEATURES:
AECOM is an infrastructure consulting firm for public and private sector clients. The company's expertise spans transportation, buildings, water, energy and the environment, offering specialized professional services throughout the project lifecycle, from planning, design and engineering to consulting and construction management. During 2020, AECOM sold its management services business to American Securities LLC and Lindsay Goldberg LLC. In early-2021, the firm sold its power construction business to CriticalPoint Capital LLC; and sold its civil infrastructure construction business to affiliates of Oroco Capital.

CONTACTS: *Note: Officers with more than one job title may be intentionally listed here more than once.*
Lara Poloni, CEO, Geographical
Daniel Tishman, CEO, Subsidiary
Michael Burke, CEO
Randall Wotring, COO
W. Rudd, Executive VP
Carla Christofferson, Executive VP
Mary Finch, Executive VP
John Vollmer, President, Divisional
Daniel McQuade, President, Divisional
Fredrick Werner, President, Divisional
Steve Morriss, President, Geographical
Chuan-Sheng Chiao, President, Geographical

FINANCIAL DATA: *Note: Data for latest year may not have been available at press time.*

In U.S. $	2020	2019	2018	2017	2016	2015
Revenue	13,239,980,000	20,173,330,000	20,155,510,000	18,203,400,000	17,410,820,000	17,989,880,000
R&D Expense						
Operating Income	521,025,000	665,322,000	514,862,000	550,411,000	527,736,000	421,213,000
Operating Margin %		.03%	.03%	.03%	.03%	.02%
SGA Expense	188,535,000	148,123,000	135,787,000	133,309,000	115,088,000	113,975,000
Net Income	-186,370,000	-261,050,000	136,468,000	339,390,000	96,109,000	-154,845,000
Operating Cash Flow	329,622,000	777,616,000	774,553,000	696,654,000	814,155,000	764,433,000
Capital Expenditure	114,591,000	100,664,000	113,279,000	86,354,000	191,386,000	69,426,000
EBITDA	629,893,000	303,059,000	712,573,000	939,123,000	782,447,000	747,422,000
Return on Assets %		- .02%	.01%	.02%	.01%	- .02%
Return on Equity %		- .07%	.03%	.09%	.03%	- .06%
Debt to Equity		0.89	0.851	0.926	1.116	1.305

CONTACT INFORMATION:
Phone: 213 593-8100   Fax: 213 593-8730
Toll-Free:
Address: 300 S. Grand Ave., Ste. 900, Los Angeles, CA 90071 United States

STOCK TICKER/OTHER:
Stock Ticker: ACM
Employees: 86,000
Parent Company:

Exchange: NYS
Fiscal Year Ends: 09/30

SALARIES/BONUSES:
Top Exec. Salary: $ Bonus: $
Second Exec. Salary: $ Bonus: $

OTHER THOUGHTS:
Estimated Female Officers or Directors: 6
Hot Spot for Advancement for Women/Minorities: Y

AES Corporation (The)

NAIC Code: 221112

TYPES OF BUSINESS:

Utilities-Electricity
Wind Generation
Contract Power Generation

BRANDS/DIVISIONS/AFFILIATES:

AES Tiete SA

CONTACTS: *Note: Officers with more than one job title may be intentionally listed here more than once.*

Andres Gluski, CEO
Gustavo Pimenta, CFO
Sarah Blake, Chief Accounting Officer
Sanjeev Addala, Chief Information Officer
Leonardo Moreno, Chief Risk Officer
Paul Freedman, General Counsel
Letitia Mendoza, Other Executive Officer
Julian Nebreda, President, Divisional
Juan Rubiolo, President, Divisional
Lisa Krueger, President, Divisional
Manuel Dubuc, Senior VP, Divisional
Bernerd Santos, Senior VP

GROWTH PLANS/SPECIAL FEATURES:

The AES Corporation operates in the global power industry in 14 countries worldwide. It has a capacity of approximately 30,400 megawatts (MW) in operation and 3,000 MW under construction. AES is organized into four market-oriented service business units: U.S. and utilities (U.S., Puerto Rico and El Salvador), South America (Chile, Colombia, Argentina and Brazil), MCAC (Mexico, Central America and the Caribbean) and Eurasia (Europe and Asia). Within these geographical service business units are two lines of business: generation, in which AES owns and/or operates power plants to generate and sell power to customers such as utilities, industrial users and other intermediaries; and utilities, in which AES owns and/or operates utilities to generate or purchase, distribute, transmit and sell electricity to end-user customers in the residential, commercial, industrial and governmental sectors within a defined service area. The U.S. and utilities unit is comprised of 30 generation facilities with a generation capacity of 9,896 MW, and six utility companies with a generation capacity of 34,363 gigawatt hours (GWH). This division has eight plants under construction with a generating capacity expected of about 1,950 MW. The South America unit has 54 generation facilities with a generation capacity of 12,568 MW, and 10 plants under construction with an expected generation capacity of 1,005 MW. The MCAC unit has 16 generation facilities with a generation capacity of 3,476 MW, and one plant under construction with an expected generation capacity of 50 MW. Last, the Eurasia unit has 10 generation facilities with a generation capacity of 4,531 MW. In July2020, AES an additional 18.5% in AES Tiete S.A., increasing its ownership to 43%, from BNDES Participacoes S.A.

FINANCIAL DATA: *Note: Data for latest year may not have been available at press time.*

In U.S. $	2020	2019	2018	2017	2016	2015
Revenue	9,660,000,000	10,189,000,000	10,736,000,000	10,530,000,000	13,586,000,000	14,963,000,000
R&D Expense						
Operating Income	2,528,000,000	2,153,000,000	2,374,000,000	2,249,000,000	2,187,000,000	2,670,000,000
Operating Margin %		.21%	.22%	.21%	.16%	.18%
SGA Expense	165,000,000	196,000,000	192,000,000	215,000,000	194,000,000	196,000,000
Net Income	46,000,000	303,000,000	1,203,000,000	-1,161,000,000	-1,130,000,000	306,000,000
Operating Cash Flow	2,755,000,000	2,466,000,000	2,343,000,000	2,489,000,000	2,884,000,000	2,134,000,000
Capital Expenditure	1,900,000,000	2,405,000,000	2,121,000,000	2,177,000,000	2,345,000,000	2,308,000,000
EBITDA	2,594,000,000	3,096,000,000	4,077,000,000	3,110,000,000	2,744,000,000	3,702,000,000
Return on Assets %		.01%	.04%	-.03%	-.03%	.01%
Return on Equity %		.10%	.42%	-.44%	-.38%	.08%
Debt to Equity		6.11	5.498	7.222	6.858	5.804

CONTACT INFORMATION:

Phone: 703 522-1315   Fax:
Toll-Free:
Address: 4300 Wilson Blvd., Arlington, VA 22203 United States

STOCK TICKER/OTHER:

Stock Ticker: AES
Employees: 8,200
Parent Company:

Exchange: NYS
Fiscal Year Ends: 12/31

SALARIES/BONUSES:

Top Exec. Salary: $ Bonus: $
Second Exec. Salary: $ Bonus: $

OTHER THOUGHTS:

Estimated Female Officers or Directors: 2
Hot Spot for Advancement for Women/Minorities: Y

aetnaCVSHealth

www.aetnacvshealth.com

NAIC Code: 524114

TYPES OF BUSINESS:

Insurance-Medical & Health
Health Care Benefits
Dental Benefits
Medicare Plans
Life Insurance

BRANDS/DIVISIONS/AFFILIATES:

CVS Health Corporation
CVS Health
CVS Pharmacy Inc
MinuteClinic LLC
Aetna Inc
Aetna Life Insurance Company
Aetna Health Inc

CONTACTS: Note: Officers with more than one job title may be intentionally listed here more than once.

Daniel Finke, Pres.
Shawn Guertin, CFO
Francis Soistman, Executive VP, Divisional
Margaret McCarthy, Executive VP, Divisional
Richard Jelinek, Executive VP, Divisional
Thomas Sabatino, Executive VP

GROWTH PLANS/SPECIAL FEATURES:

AetnaCVSHealth represents the health care benefits segment of CVS Health Corporation, offering solutions to employers and government businesses, serving more than 34 million members. Aetna Inc, CVS Health, CVS Pharmacy Inc. and MinuteClinic LLC are part of the CVS Health family of companies. Aetna is the brand name for products and services provided by Aetna Life Insurance Company and its affiliates. Health plans are offered or underwritten or administered by Coventry Health Plan of Florida Inc., Aetna Health Inc. (Georgia), Aetna Health of Utah Inc., Aetna Health Inc. (Pennsylvania), or Aetna Health Inc. (Texas). Health benefits and health insurance plans contain exclusive exclusions and limitations. Affordable Care Act (ACA) plans cover essential benefits such as hospitalization, preventive care and mental health services. some plans offer extras such as dental and vision. Open enrollment for ACA begins November 1 and closes January 15. Aetna offers a Medicare plan with hospital, medical, prescription coverage and other benefits, as well as individual and family plans.

FINANCIAL DATA: Note: Data for latest year may not have been available at press time.

In U.S. $	2020	2019	2018	2017	2016	2015
Revenue	75,467,000,000	69,604,000,000	61,500,000,000	60,535,001,088	63,154,999,296	60,336,500,736
R&D Expense						
Operating Income						
Operating Margin %						
SGA Expense						
Net Income		4,400,000,000	4,000,000,000	1,904,000,000	2,271,000,064	2,390,200,064
Operating Cash Flow						
Capital Expenditure						
EBITDA						
Return on Assets %						
Return on Equity %						
Debt to Equity						

CONTACT INFORMATION:

Phone: 860 273-0123   Fax:
Toll-Free: 800-872-3862
Address: 151 Farmington Ave., Hartford, CT 06156 United States

STOCK TICKER/OTHER:

Stock Ticker: Subsidiary   Exchange:
Employees: 49,500   Fiscal Year Ends: 12/31
Parent Company: CVS Health Corporation

SALARIES/BONUSES:

Top Exec. Salary: $ Bonus: $
Second Exec. Salary: $ Bonus: $

OTHER THOUGHTS:

Estimated Female Officers or Directors: 8
Hot Spot for Advancement for Women/Minorities: Y

AFLAC Incorporated

NAIC Code: 524114

TYPES OF BUSINESS:

Insurance-Supplemental & Specialty Health
Life Insurance
Cancer Insurance
Long-Term Care Insurance
Accident & Disability Insurance
Vision Plans
Dental Plans

BRANDS/DIVISIONS/AFFILIATES:

Aflac Life Insurance Japan Ltd
One Day Pay
American Family Life Assurance Company
Continental American Insurance Company
Aflac Group Insurance/AGI
Tier One Insurance Company

CONTACTS: *Note: Officers with more than one job title may be intentionally listed here more than once.*

Daniel Amos, CEO
James Daniels, CFO, Divisional
June Howard, Chief Accounting Officer
Masatoshi Koide, COO, Divisional
Eric Kirsch, Executive VP, Subsidiary
Frederick Crawford, Executive VP
Audrey Tillman, Executive VP
Koji Ariyoshi, Executive VP
Richard Williams, Executive VP
Albert Riggieri, Other Corporate Officer
Teresa White, President, Divisional
Charles Lake, President, Subsidiary
Max Broden, Senior VP

GROWTH PLANS/SPECIAL FEATURES:

AFLAC Incorporated provides supplemental insurance to more than 50 million people through its subsidiaries in Japan and the U.S. In short, the firm pays cash when policyholders get sick or injured. Aflac Life Insurance Japan Ltd. is the leading provider of medical and cancer insurance in Japan, where it insures one in four households. Through its One Day Pay initiative in the U.S. (for eligible claims), AFLAC can process, approve and electronically send funds to claimants for quick access to cash in one business day. AFLAC helps protect its customers from asset loss, income loss and supplemental medical expenses. In the U.S., AFLAC is a leader in voluntary insurance sales at the work site, including short-term disability, life insurance, accident insurance, cancer coverage, critical illness coverage, hospital intensive care, hospital indemnity, dental care and vision care. U.S. subsidiaries are collectively referred to as Aflac U.S., and include American Family Life Assurance Company of Columbus, Continental American Insurance Company (branded as Aflac Group Insurance/AGI), American Family Life Assurance Company of New York and Tier One Insurance Company. Aflac Japan's revenues accounted for 82% of the company's total revenues at June 30, 2021, with Aflac U.S. accounting for the remainder.

FINANCIAL DATA: *Note: Data for latest year may not have been available at press time.*

In U.S. $	2020	2019	2018	2017	2016	2015
Revenue	22,116,000,000	22,223,000,000	21,689,000,000	21,600,000,000	22,380,000,000	20,845,000,000
R&D Expense						
Operating Income						
Operating Margin %						
SGA Expense						
Net Income	4,778,000,000	3,304,000,000	2,920,000,000	4,604,000,000	2,659,000,000	2,533,000,000
Operating Cash Flow	5,958,000,000	5,455,000,000	6,014,000,000	6,128,000,000	5,987,000,000	6,776,000,000
Capital Expenditure						
EBITDA						
Return on Assets %		.02%	.02%	.03%	.02%	.02%
Return on Equity %		.13%	.12%	.20%	.14%	.14%
Debt to Equity		0.227	0.246	0.215	0.262	0.283

CONTACT INFORMATION:

Phone: 706 323-3431   Fax:
Toll-Free: 800-235-2667
Address: 1932 Wynnton Rd., Columbus, GA 31999 United States

STOCK TICKER/OTHER:

Stock Ticker: AFL   Exchange: NYS
Employees: 11,729   Fiscal Year Ends: 12/31
Parent Company:

SALARIES/BONUSES:

Top Exec. Salary: $ Bonus: $
Second Exec. Salary: $ Bonus: $

OTHER THOUGHTS:

Estimated Female Officers or Directors: 8
Hot Spot for Advancement for Women/Minorities: Y

Albertsons Companies Inc

www.albertsonscompanies.com

NAIC Code: 445110

TYPES OF BUSINESS:

Grocery Stores/Supermarkets
Pharmacy
Fuel Centers
Home Delivery
Online Services

BRANDS/DIVISIONS/AFFILIATES:

Cerberus Capital Management
Kimco Realty
SUPERVALU
Safeway
Vons
Tom Thumb
Randalls
Pavilions

CONTACTS: Note: Officers with more than one job title may be intentionally listed here more than once.

Jim Donald, CEO
Susan Morris, Exec. VP-COO
Robert Dimond, CFO
Shane Sampson, Chief Mktg. & Merchandising Officer
Andrew J. Scoggin, Exec. VP-Human Resources
Anuj Dhanda, CIO
Shane Dorcheus, Pres., Southwest Div.
Wayne Denningham, Pres., Southern
Dennis Bassler, Pres., Northwest Div.
Susan Morris, Pres., Intermountain Div.
Bob Miller, Chmn.

GROWTH PLANS/SPECIAL FEATURES:

Albertsons Companies, Inc. is one of the largest U.S. based retailers of food and drugs. The firm operates more than 2,250 stores in 34 states under 20 well-known banners, including Albertsons, Safeway, Vons, Jewel-Osco, Shaw's, ACME, Tom Thumb, Randalls, United Supermarkets, Pavilions, Star Market, Haggen and Carrs. The firm operates in many metropolitan areas in the U.S. Most stores contain pharmacies and some have an adjacent fuel center. The firm serves, on average, 34 million customers every week. The pharmacy services offered by Albertsons include health screenings, immunizations and a pharmacy products discount card as well as drug interaction information provided through its website. As of September 2020, approximately 1,725 pharmacies are located in-store, nearly 400 fuel centers are at select locations, and Albertsons Companies operates 22 distribution centers and 20 manufacturing facilities. Albertsons is owned by a consortium led Cerberus Capital Management and includes Kimco Realty and grocery chain SUPERVALU. In October 2020, Albertsons Companies was the successful bidder for 27 Kings Food Market and Balducci's Food Lover's Market locations at auction, which was still subject to regulatory and court approvals. Upon the successful completion of the transaction, the stores would become part of the mid-Atlantic division, which operates ACME and Safeway stores.

Albertsons Companies offers its employees a benefit package that includes health and wellness plans.

FINANCIAL DATA: Note: Data for latest year may not have been available at press time.

In U.S. $	2020	2019	2018	2017	2016	2015
Revenue	62,455,100,000	60,534,500,000	59,924,600,000	59,678,200,000	58,734,000,000	
R&D Expense						
Operating Income	952,300,000	787,300,000	137,400,000	640,500,000	401,700,000	
Operating Margin %	.02%	.01%	.00%	.01%	.01%	
SGA Expense	16,641,900,000	16,107,300,000	16,223,700,000	16,000,000,000	15,660,000,000	
Net Income	466,400,000	131,100,000	46,300,000	-373,300,000	-502,200,000	
Operating Cash Flow	1,903,900,000	1,687,900,000	1,018,800,000	1,813,500,000	901,600,000	
Capital Expenditure	1,475,100,000	1,362,600,000	1,547,000,000	1,414,900,000	960,000,000	
EBITDA	3,540,000,000	2,591,400,000	1,855,400,000	2,345,000,000	2,015,400,000	
Return on Assets %	.02%	.01%	.00%	- .02%	- .02%	
Return on Equity %	.25%	.09%	.03%	- .25%	- .27%	
Debt to Equity	6.10	7.195	8.373	8.766	7.371	

CONTACT INFORMATION:

Phone: 208-395-6200   Fax: 208-395-6349
Toll-Free: 877-932-7948
Address: 250 Parkcenter Blvd., Boise, ID 83706 United States

STOCK TICKER/OTHER:

Stock Ticker: ACI
Employees: 300,000
Parent Company:

Exchange: NYS
Fiscal Year Ends: 01/31

SALARIES/BONUSES:

Top Exec. Salary: $ Bonus: $
Second Exec. Salary: $ Bonus: $

OTHER THOUGHTS:

Estimated Female Officers or Directors: 1
Hot Spot for Advancement for Women/Minorities:

Alcoa Corporation
NAIC Code: 331313

TYPES OF BUSINESS:
Primary & Fabricated Aluminum
Bauxite Mining
Vinyl Siding
Industrial Fasteners
Building & Construction Materials

BRANDS/DIVISIONS/AFFILIATES:
Alcoa World Alumina and Chemicals

CONTACTS: *Note: Officers with more than one job title may be intentionally listed here more than once.*
Roy Harvey, CEO
Michael Morris, Chairman of the Board
Molly Beerman, Chief Accounting Officer
Leigh Ann Fisher, Chief Administrative Officer
John Slaven, Chief Strategy Officer
William Oplinger, Executive VP
Jeffrey Heeter, Executive VP
Garret Dixon, President, Divisional
Michael Parker, President, Divisional
Timothy Reyes, President, Divisional

GROWTH PLANS/SPECIAL FEATURES:
Alcoa Corporation is a global industry leader in the production of bauxite, alumina, and aluminum, with a strong portfolio of value-added cast and rolled products, as well as substantial energy assets. The company is active in all major aspects of the aluminum industry, including bauxite mining, alumina refining, aluminum smelting and fabrication, recycling and technology. Alcoa is a global company with 28 operating locations across nine countries. The firm's operations consist of three reportable segments: bauxite, alumina and aluminum. The bauxite and alumina segments primarily consist of a series of affiliated operating entities held in Alcoa World Alumina and Chemicals, a global, unincorporated joint venture between Alcoa and Alumina Limited. The aluminum segment consists of Alco's aluminum smelting, casting and rolling businesses, along with the majority of the energy business. Aluminum metal is produced by refining alumina oxide from bauxite into alumina, which is then smelted into aluminum and can be cast and rolled into many shapes and forms. Alumina is an intermediary product. Joint ventures of Alcoa include: Alcoa World Alumina and Chemicals, which has a number of affiliated entities that own, operate or have an interest in bauxite mines and alumina refineries, as well as certain aluminum smelters in seven countries; and a Ma'aden-affilated joint venture owns and operates a bauxite mine with a capacity of 4 million dry metric tons per year (mtpy), an alumina factory with a capacity of 1.8 million mtpy, an aluminum smelter with a capacity of ingot, slab and billet of 740,000 million mtpy, and a rolling mill with a capacity of 460,000 million mtpy. During the first half of 2021, Alcoa sold its Warrick rolling mill to Kaiser Aluminum Corporation for $670 million; and sold its Eastalco smelter site for $100 million.

FINANCIAL DATA: *Note: Data for latest year may not have been available at press time.*

In U.S. $	2020	2019	2018	2017	2016	2015
Revenue	9,286,000,000	10,433,000,000	13,403,000,000	11,652,000,000	9,318,000,000	11,199,000,000
R&D Expense	27,000,000	27,000,000	31,000,000	32,000,000	33,000,000	69,000,000
Operating Income	428,000,000	732,000,000	2,196,000,000	1,496,000,000	187,000,000	958,000,000
Operating Margin %		.07%	.16%	.13%	.02%	.09%
SGA Expense	206,000,000	280,000,000	248,000,000	284,000,000	359,000,000	353,000,000
Net Income	-170,000,000	-1,125,000,000	227,000,000	217,000,000	-400,000,000	-863,000,000
Operating Cash Flow	394,000,000	686,000,000	448,000,000	1,224,000,000	-311,000,000	875,000,000
Capital Expenditure	353,000,000	379,000,000	399,000,000	405,000,000	404,000,000	391,000,000
EBITDA	972,000,000	396,000,000	2,452,000,000	2,015,000,000	799,000,000	713,000,000
Return on Assets %		-.07%	.01%	.01%	-.02%	-.05%
Return on Equity %		-.24%	.05%	.04%	-.05%	-.09%
Debt to Equity		0.462	0.334	0.307	0.252	0.022

CONTACT INFORMATION:
Phone: 412-315-2900   Fax:
Toll-Free:
Address: 201 Isabella St., Ste. 500, Pittsburge, PA 15212-5858 United States

STOCK TICKER/OTHER:
Stock Ticker: AA
Employees: 13,800
Parent Company:

Exchange: NYS
Fiscal Year Ends: 12/31

SALARIES/BONUSES:
Top Exec. Salary: $ Bonus: $
Second Exec. Salary: $ Bonus: $

OTHER THOUGHTS:
Estimated Female Officers or Directors: 4
Hot Spot for Advancement for Women/Minorities: Y

Alexion Pharmaceuticals Inc

www.alexion.com

NAIC Code: 325412

TYPES OF BUSINESS:

Therapeutic Products
Hematologic Diseases
Neurological Diseases
Oncology
Autoimmune Disorders

BRANDS/DIVISIONS/AFFILIATES:

Ultomiris
Soliris
Strensiq
Kanuma
Andexxa

CONTACTS: *Note: Officers with more than one job title may be intentionally listed here more than once.*

Ludwig Hantson, CEO
Paul Clancy, CFO
Indrani Franchini, Chief Compliance Officer
David Brennan, Director
Ellen Chiniara, Executive VP
John Orloff, Executive VP
Brian Goff, Executive VP
Anne-Marie Law, Executive VP
Daniel Bazarko, Senior VP

GROWTH PLANS/SPECIAL FEATURES:

Alexion Pharmaceuticals, Inc. is a biopharmaceutical company that discovers, develops and commercializes therapeutic products for rare diseases. The company focuses its research on novel molecules and targets in the complement cascade, with core therapeutic areas consisting of hematology, nephrology, neurology and metabolic disorders. Alexion has five marketed products: Ultomiris (ravulizumab-cwvz), Soliris (eculizumab), Strensiq (asfotase alfa), Kanuma (sebelipase alfa) and Andexxa. Ultomiris is designed to inhibit a specific aspect of the complement component of the immune system and thereby treat inflammation associated with chronic disorders. Ultomiris is approved by the U.S. Food and Drug Administration (FDA) as a treatment for adults with paroxysmal nocturnal hemoglobinuria (PNH), a life-threatening, ultra-rare genetic blood disorder that destroys red blood cells. Like Ultomiris, Soliris is designed to inhibit a specific aspect within the immune system and is a humanized monoclonal antibody that blocks terminal complement activity. Soliris is approved for the treatment of PNH and for the treatment of atypical hemolytic uremic syndrome (aHUS) in several countries. aHUS is an ultra-rare genetic disease that forms blood clots in small blood vessels throughout the body. Strensiq is a targeted enzyme replacement therapy approved for patients with hypophosphatasia (HPP) and is designed to directly address underlying causes of HPP by aiming to restore the genetically defective metabolic process, thereby preventing or reversing the severe complications in patients with the disease. Kanuma is a recombinant form of the human lysosomal acid lipase (LAL) enzyme and is approved for the treatment for patients with LAL deficiency (LAL-D). LAL-D is a life-threatening, ultra-rare disease associated with premature mortality and significant morbidity. Last, Andexxa is an FDA-approved reversal agent for patients treated with rivaroxaban or apixaban for uncontrollable bleeding. In May 2021, Alexion announced shareholder approval to be acquired by AstraZeneca. The transaction was slated to close by year's end.

FINANCIAL DATA: *Note: Data for latest year may not have been available at press time.*

In U.S. $	2020	2019	2018	2017	2016	2015
Revenue	6,069,899,776	4,991,099,904	4,131,200,000	3,551,099,904	3,084,000,000	2,604,047,104
R&D Expense						
Operating Income						
Operating Margin %						
SGA Expense						
Net Income	603,400,000	2,404,300,032	77,600,000	443,300,000	399,000,000	144,384,992
Operating Cash Flow						
Capital Expenditure						
EBITDA						
Return on Assets %						
Return on Equity %						
Debt to Equity						

CONTACT INFORMATION:

Phone: 203 272-2596   Fax: 203 271-8198
Toll-Free:
Address: 121 Seaport Blvd., Boston, MA 02210 United States

STOCK TICKER/OTHER:

Stock Ticker: ALXN
Employees: 3,837
Parent Company:

Exchange: NAS
Fiscal Year Ends: 12/31

SALARIES/BONUSES:

Top Exec. Salary: $ Bonus: $
Second Exec. Salary: $ Bonus: $

OTHER THOUGHTS:

Estimated Female Officers or Directors: 2
Hot Spot for Advancement for Women/Minorities: Y

Sales, profits and employees may be estimates. Financial information, benefits and other data can change quickly and may vary from those stated here.

Align Technology Inc

NAIC Code: 339100

www.aligntech.com

TYPES OF BUSINESS:

Orthodontic Equipment
Dental Alignment Products
Oral Scanners
Digital Services
Dentistry
Orthodontics
Dental Records Storage
Product Manufacturing

BRANDS/DIVISIONS/AFFILIATES:

Invisalign
ClinCheck
Vivera Retainers
Invisalign Comprehensive Package
Mandibular Advancement
iTero
OrthoCAD
exocad Global Holdings GmbH

CONTACTS: *Note: Officers with more than one job title may be intentionally listed here more than once.*

Joseph Hogan, CEO
John Morici, CFO
Charles Larkin, Chairman of the Board
Roger George, Chief Legal Officer
Raphael Pascaud, Chief Marketing Officer
Vamsi Pudipeddi, Chief Marketing Officer
Zelko Relic, Chief Technology Officer
Yuval Shaked, Managing Director, Divisional
Jennifer Olson, Managing Director, Divisional
Julie Tay, Managing Director, Geographical
Simon Beard, Managing Director, Geographical
Stuart Hockridge, Senior VP, Divisional
Sreelakshmi Kolli, Senior VP, Divisional
Emory Wright, Senior VP, Divisional

GROWTH PLANS/SPECIAL FEATURES:

Align Technology, Inc. (ATI) designs, manufactures and markets a system of clear aligner therapy, intra-oral scanners and CAD/CAM (computer-aided design and computer-aided manufacturing) digital services used in dentistry, orthodontics and dental records storage. The company operates in two segments: clear aligner and scanners and services. Clear aligner produces Invisalign for the treatment of malocclusion (misalignment of the teeth). Invisalign is series of doctor prescribed, custom manufactured, clear plastic removable orthodontic aligners. Customized systems are designed in conjunction with the ClinCheck software program, which works off an original mold of the patient's mouth and makes incremental adjustments that eventually lead to total alignment. Upon completion of the treatment, the patient may be prescribed a single clear retainer product or one of the company's Vivera Retainers. Invisalign Comprehensive Package replaces, yet includes, the features of both Invisalign Full and Invisalign Teen treatments, but also encompasses the Mandibular Advancement feature, which is used for a wide range of malocclusion and orthodontic needs. Scanners and CAD/CAM services utilize intra-oral scanning to create a 3D image of a patient's teeth using a handheld intra-oral scanner inside the mouth, as opposed to the traditional methods of taking a mold or physical impression. The company's iTero scanner is used by dental professionals and/or labs for restorative and orthodontic digital procedures as well as Invisalign digital impression submission. It stands as the only intra-oral scanner system in the market based on parallel confocal imaging, which can capture 100,000 points of laser light in perfect focus. These images are used in the OrthoCAD program, which aid in the fabrication of veneers, inlays, onlays, crowns, bridges and implant abutment; Invisalign digital impressions; and digital records storage.

FINANCIAL DATA: *Note: Data for latest year may not have been available at press time.*

In U.S. $	2020	2019	2018	2017	2016	2015
Revenue	2,471,941,000	2,406,796,000	1,966,492,000	1,473,413,000	1,079,874,000	845,486,000
R&D Expense	175,307,000	157,361,000	128,899,000	97,559,000	75,720,000	61,237,000
Operating Income	387,171,000	514,483,000	466,564,000	353,611,000	248,921,000	188,634,000
Operating Margin %		.21%	.24%	.24%	.23%	.22%
SGA Expense	1,200,757,000	1,072,053,000	852,404,000	665,777,000	490,653,000	390,239,000
Net Income	1,775,888,000	442,776,000	400,235,000	231,418,000	189,682,000	144,020,000
Operating Cash Flow	662,174,000	747,270,000	554,681,000	438,539,000	247,654,000	237,997,000
Capital Expenditure	154,916,000	149,707,000	223,312,000	195,695,000	70,576,000	53,451,000
EBITDA	480,709,000	593,473,000	521,291,000	391,350,000	272,923,000	206,638,000
Return on Assets %		.19%	.21%	.15%	.15%	.13%
Return on Equity %		.34%	.33%	.22%	.21%	.18%
Debt to Equity		0.032				

CONTACT INFORMATION:

Phone: 602-742-2000   Fax:
Toll-Free:
Address: 410 N. Scottsdale Rd., Ste. 1300, Tempe, AZ 85281 United States

STOCK TICKER/OTHER:

Stock Ticker: ALGN
Employees: 18,070
Parent Company:

Exchange: NAS
Fiscal Year Ends: 12/31

SALARIES/BONUSES:

Top Exec. Salary: $ Bonus: $
Second Exec. Salary: $ Bonus: $

OTHER THOUGHTS:

Estimated Female Officers or Directors: 2
Hot Spot for Advancement for Women/Minorities:

Allscripts Healthcare Solutions Inc

www.allscripts.com

NAIC Code: 511210D

TYPES OF BUSINESS:

Computer Software, Healthcare & Biotechnology
Interactive Education Services
Clinical Software
Electronic Records Systems
Care Management Software

BRANDS/DIVISIONS/AFFILIATES:

Sunrise
Paragon
Allscripts TouchWorks EHR
Allscripts Professional EHR
Veradigm
FollowMyHealth
Allscripts CareInMotion
2bPrecise

CONTACTS: Note: Officers with more than one job title may be intentionally listed here more than once.

Paul Black, CEO
Dennis Olis, CFO
Brian Farley, Chief Administrative Officer
Michael Klayko, Director
Lisa Khorey, Executive VP
Richard Poulton, President

GROWTH PLANS/SPECIAL FEATURES:

Allscripts Healthcare Solutions, Inc. provides clinical software, connectivity and information solutions for physicians and healthcare providers. The firm provides software solutions to physicians, hospitals, governments, health systems, health plans, life-sciences companies, retail clinics, retail pharmacies, pharmacy benefit managers, insurance companies, employer wellness clinics, post-acute organizations, consumers and lab companies. The company's electronic health records (EHR) solutions are built on an open platform with advanced clinical decision support via analysis and insights. EHR brands include Sunrise, Paragon, Allscripts TouchWorks EHR and Allscripts Professional EHR. Payer and life sciences solutions include the Veradigm brand of integrated data systems and services, which combine data-driven clinical insights with actionable tools for clinical workflow, research, analytics and media. Consumer solutions include the FollowMyHealth platform, for patient engagement via telehealth and remote patient monitoring. Financial management solutions support revenue cycle, claims management, budgeting and analytic functions for healthcare organizations. These tools can help change clinician behavior to improve patient flow, increase quality, advance outcomes, optimize referral networks, decrease leakage and reduce costs. Population health management solutions includes Allscripts CareInMotion, a community-connected population health management platform that delivers care coordination, connectivity, data aggregation and analytics. 2bPrecise is a precision medicine solution for enabling a personalized approach regarding diagnostic, therapeutic and preventive interventions. Allscripts offers customizable professional and managed service offerings, from hosting, consulting, optimization and managed IT services to revenue cycle services. Allscripts' facilities are primarily located in the U.S., but the company also maintains facilities in Canada, India, Israel and the U.K.

Allscripts offers its employees medical, dental and vision insurance; flex spending accounts; 401(k); adoption assistance; and education assistance.

FINANCIAL DATA: Note: Data for latest year may not have been available at press time.

In U.S. $	2020	2019	2018	2017	2016	2015
Revenue	1,502,700,000	1,771,677,000	1,749,962,000	1,806,342,000	1,549,899,000	1,386,393,000
R&D Expense	206,061,000	254,509,000	268,409,000	220,219,000	187,906,000	184,791,000
Operating Income	-55,911,000	12,081,000	-21,420,000	41,917,000	64,421,000	33,427,000
Operating Margin %		.01%	-.01%	.02%	.04%	.02%
SGA Expense	389,941,000	419,774,000	450,967,000	486,271,000	392,865,000	339,175,000
Net Income	700,407,000	-182,178,000	363,740,000	-196,459,000	-25,652,000	-2,226,000
Operating Cash Flow	-106,715,000	46,254,000	67,891,000	279,415,000	269,004,000	211,579,000
Capital Expenditure	105,018,000	130,436,000	144,617,000	185,271,000	137,982,000	67,586,000
EBITDA	97,782,000	66,296,000	256,398,000	96,398,000	220,523,000	191,544,000
Return on Assets %		-.06%	.10%	-.05%	-.01%	.00%
Return on Equity %		-.13%	.27%	-.17%	-.02%	.00%
Debt to Equity		0.503	0.418	1.373	1.059	0.435

CONTACT INFORMATION:

Phone: 866 358-6869   Fax:
Toll-Free: 800-654-0889
Address: 222 Merchandise Mart Plz., Ste. 2024, Chicago, IL 60654 United States

STOCK TICKER/OTHER:

Stock Ticker: MDRX
Employees: 8,400
Parent Company:

Exchange: NAS
Fiscal Year Ends: 12/31

SALARIES/BONUSES:

Top Exec. Salary: $ Bonus: $
Second Exec. Salary: $ Bonus: $

OTHER THOUGHTS:

Estimated Female Officers or Directors: 2
Hot Spot for Advancement for Women/Minorities: Y

Sales, profits and employees may be estimates. Financial information, benefits and other data can change quickly and may vary from those stated here.

Plunkett Research, Ltd.

Allstate Corporation (The)
NAIC Code: 524126

www.allstate.com

TYPES OF BUSINESS:
Insurance, Direct Property & Casualty
Auto Insurance
Homeowners Insurance
Life Insurance
Business Insurance

BRANDS/DIVISIONS/AFFILIATES:
Allstate Insurance Company
Allstate Protection
Allstate
Esurance
Encompass
SquareTrade
InfoArmor
Allstate Roadside Services

CONTACTS: Note: Officers with more than one job title may be intentionally listed here more than once.
Thomas Wilson, CEO
Mario Rizzo, CFO
Suren Gupta, Executive VP, Subsidiary
Elizabeth Brady, Executive VP, Subsidiary
John Dugenske, Executive VP, Subsidiary
Susan Lees, Executive VP
Jesse Merten, Executive VP
Glenn Shapiro, President, Divisional
Don Civgin, President, Divisional
Mary Jane Fortin, President, Subsidiary
Eric Ferren, Senior VP
Steven Shebik, Vice Chairman

GROWTH PLANS/SPECIAL FEATURES:
The Allstate Corporation is a holding company for Allstate Insurance Company, through which it principally conducts its business. The firm is engaged in the personal property and casualty insurance business as well as the home, auto, life insurance, retirement and investment products market. Allstate provides insurance products, with more than 113 million proprietary policies, through a distribution network that utilizes 10,800 exclusive agencies and financial specialists primarily in the U.S. The company conducts its business through seven business segments: Allstate Protection, Services Businesses, Allstate Life, Allstate Benefits, Allstate Annuities, discontinued lines and coverages and corporate/other. Allstate Protection includes Allstate, Encompass and Esurance brands and Answer Financial. The segment offers private passenger auto, homeowners, other personal lines and small commercial insurance products through agencies and directly through contact centers and the internet. The Services Businesses include SquareTrade, Arity, InfoArmor, Allstate Roadside Services and Allstate Dealer Services. Allstate Life offers traditional, interest-sensitive and variable life insurance products through Allstate exclusive agencies and exclusive financial specialists. Allstate Benefits offers voluntary benefits products, including life, accident, critical illness, short-term disability and other health products sold through workplace enrolling independent agents and Allstate exclusive agencies. Allstate Annuities consist of deferred fixed annuities and immediate fixed annuities (including standard and sub-standard structured settlements) in run-off. The discontinued lines and coverages segment includes results from property-liability insurance coverage that the company no longer writes, as well as results for certain commercial and other business in run-off. The corporate/other segment oversees holding company activities and certain non-insurance operations. In mid-2020, Allstate agreed to acquire National General Holdings Corp., which offers property and casualty and accident and health products.

Allstate offers comprehensive employee benefits, retirement options and assistance programs.

FINANCIAL DATA: Note: Data for latest year may not have been available at press time.

In U.S. $	2020	2019	2018	2017	2016	2015
Revenue	44,791,000,000	44,675,000,000	39,815,000,000	38,524,000,000	36,534,000,000	35,653,000,000
R&D Expense						
Operating Income						
Operating Margin %						
SGA Expense	5,681,000,000	5,804,000,000	5,869,000,000	4,658,000,000	4,106,000,000	4,081,000,000
Net Income	5,576,000,000	4,847,000,000	2,252,000,000	3,189,000,000	1,877,000,000	2,171,000,000
Operating Cash Flow	5,491,000,000	5,129,000,000	5,175,000,000	4,314,000,000	3,993,000,000	3,616,000,000
Capital Expenditure	308,000,000	433,000,000	277,000,000	299,000,000	313,000,000	303,000,000
EBITDA						
Return on Assets %		.04%	.02%	.03%	.02%	.02%
Return on Equity %		.22%	.10%	.16%	.09%	.11%
Debt to Equity		0.279	0.333	0.305	0.337	0.28

CONTACT INFORMATION:
Phone: 847 402-5000   Fax: 847 402-2351
Toll-Free: 800-255-7828
Address: 2775 Sanders Rd., Northbrook, IL 60062 United States

STOCK TICKER/OTHER:
Stock Ticker: ALL
Employees: 46,290
Parent Company:

Exchange: NYS
Fiscal Year Ends: 12/31

SALARIES/BONUSES:
Top Exec. Salary: $ Bonus: $
Second Exec. Salary: $ Bonus: $

OTHER THOUGHTS:
Estimated Female Officers or Directors: 4
Hot Spot for Advancement for Women/Minorities: Y

Alphabet Inc (Google)

NAIC Code: 519130

www.google.com

TYPES OF BUSINESS:

Search Engine-Internet
Paid Search Listing Advertising Services
Online Software and Productivity Tools
Online Video and Photo Services
Travel Booking
Web Analytical Tools
Venture Capital
Online Ad Exchanges

BRANDS/DIVISIONS/AFFILIATES:

DV 360
AdX
Android
Analytics 360
DoubleClick
YouTube
Google Ad Manager
AdMob

CONTACTS: *Note: Officers with more than one job title may be intentionally listed here more than once.*

Sundar Pichai, CEO, Subsidiary
Larry Page, CEO
Ruth Porat, CFO
John Hennessy, Chairman of the Board
Amie OToole, Chief Accounting Officer
David Drummond, Chief Legal Officer
Sergey Brin, Director

GROWTH PLANS/SPECIAL FEATURES:

Alphabet, Inc. owns a collection of businesses, the largest of which is Google, LLC, an information company offering a leading online search and advertising platform. Google is the leader in the online search and advertising business. Alphabet states that its primary job is to make the internet available to as many people as possible and does this by tailoring hardware and software experiences that suit the needs of emerging markets, mainly through Android and Chrome. Google's core products include Search, Android, Maps, Chrome, YouTube, GooglePlay and Gmail, each of which have more than 1 billion monthly active users. Within Google, Alphabet's investments in machine learning are what enable the firm to continually innovate and build Google products, making them smarter and more useful over time. Machine learning also dramatically improves the energy efficiency of the company's data centers. For advertisers, Google offers a full suite of tools to bid on and analyze the results of online ads, both fixed and mobile. These tools include DoubleClick, the Google Ad Manager, Google AdMob and Google AdSense. Alphabet's other businesses include Access, Calico, CapitalG, GV, Nest, Verily, Waymo and X, all of which are not primarily engaged in the company's main internet offerings. Across these businesses, machine learning has the capability of doing things like helping self-driving cars better detect and respond to others on the road, or aiding clinicians in detecting diabetic retinopathy. Therefore, these firms utilize technology to try and solve big problems across many industries. They are early-stage businesses with the goal to become thriving ones in the medium- to long-term.

FINANCIAL DATA: *Note: Data for latest year may not have been available at press time.*

In U.S. $	2020	2019	2018	2017	2016	2015
Revenue	182,527,000,000	161,857,000,000	136,819,000,000	110,855,000,000	90,272,000,000	74,989,000,000
R&D Expense	27,573,000,000	26,018,000,000	21,419,000,000	16,625,000,000	13,948,000,000	12,282,000,000
Operating Income	41,224,000,000	35,928,000,000	31,392,000,000	28,882,000,000	23,716,000,000	19,360,000,000
Operating Margin %		.22%	.23%	.26%	.26%	.26%
SGA Expense	28,998,000,000	28,015,000,000	24,459,000,000	19,765,000,000	17,470,000,000	15,183,000,000
Net Income	40,269,000,000	34,343,000,000	30,736,000,000	12,662,000,000	19,478,000,000	16,348,000,000
Operating Cash Flow	65,124,000,000	54,520,000,000	47,971,000,000	37,091,000,000	36,036,000,000	26,024,000,000
Capital Expenditure	22,281,000,000	23,548,000,000	25,139,000,000	13,184,000,000	10,212,000,000	9,915,000,000
EBITDA	61,914,000,000	51,506,000,000	44,062,000,000	34,217,000,000	30,418,000,000	24,818,000,000
Return on Assets %		.14%	.14%	.07%	.12%	.11%
Return on Equity %		.18%	.19%	.09%	.15%	.14%
Debt to Equity		0.073	0.023	0.026	0.028	0.017

CONTACT INFORMATION:

Phone: 650 253-0000   Fax: 650 253-0001
Toll-Free:
Address: 1600 Amphitheatre Pkwy., Mountain View, CA 94043 United States

STOCK TICKER/OTHER:

Stock Ticker: GOOGL   Exchange: NAS
Employees: 135,301   Fiscal Year Ends: 12/31
Parent Company:

SALARIES/BONUSES:

Top Exec. Salary: $ Bonus: $
Second Exec. Salary: $ Bonus: $

OTHER THOUGHTS:

Estimated Female Officers or Directors: 3
Hot Spot for Advancement for Women/Minorities: Y

Amazon.com Inc
NAIC Code: 454111

TYPES OF BUSINESS:
Online Retailing and Related Services
Robotics
Cloud Computing Services
Logistics Services
Retail Supermarkets & Grocery Delivery
Online Household Goods Retail
Online Auto & Industrial Retail
E-Commerce Support & Hosting

BRANDS/DIVISIONS/AFFILIATES:
Amazon Web Services (AWS)
Amazon Marketplace
Amazon Prime
Echo
Whole Foods Market
Amazon Go
Amazon Go Grocery
Zoox

CONTACTS: *Note: Officers with more than one job title may be intentionally listed here more than once.*
Andrew Jassy, CEO, Divisional
Jeffrey Wilke, CEO, Divisional
Jeffrey Bezos, CEO
Brian Olsavsky, CFO
Shelley Reynolds, Chief Accounting Officer
David Zapolsky, General Counsel
Jeffrey Blackburn, Senior VP, Divisional

GROWTH PLANS/SPECIAL FEATURES:
Amazon.com, Inc. is an internet consumer-shopping site that offers millions of new, used, refurbished and collectible items in categories such as books, movies, music and games, electronics and computers, home and garden, toys, children's goods, grocery, apparel and jewelry, health and beauty, sports, outdoors, digital downloads, tools and auto and industrial. The company, which serves more than 50 million members, operates in three segments: North America (which generates more than 60% of annual revenue), international (26%) and Amazon Web Services (AWS) (12%), which offers computing, storage, database and other service offerings globally for start-ups, enterprises, government agencies and academic institutions. The Amazon Marketplace and Merchants programs allow third parties to integrate their products on Amazon websites and provide related fulfillment and advertising services to third-party merchants; allow customers to shop for products owned by third parties using Amazon's features and technologies; and enable customers to complete transactions that include multiple sellers in a single checkout process. Amazon Prime memberships afford members a host of perks including free two-day shipping, streaming music and video, delivery from participating restaurants and much more. The company also sells proprietary electronic devices, including eReaders, tablets, TVs and phones; as well as the Echo personal digital assistant. The firm serves authors and independent publishers with Kindle Direct Publishing, an online platform that lets independent authors and publishers choose a 70% royalty option and make their books available in the Kindle Store. Subsidiary Whole Foods Market is a supermarket chain featuring foods without artificial preservatives, colors, flavors, sweeteners and hydrogenated fats, with stores throughout the U.S and internationally. Amazon Go and Amazon Go Grocery stores use cameras and sensors to detect items that a shopper purchases. During 2020, Amazon acquired Zoox, a designer and manufacturer of the robotaxi, capable of operating up to 75 miles per hour. In May 2021, the firm agreed to acquire MGM Holdings, Inc. for $6.5 billion.

FINANCIAL DATA: *Note: Data for latest year may not have been available at press time.*

In U.S. $	2020	2019	2018	2017	2016	2015
Revenue	386,064,000,000	280,522,000,000	232,887,000,000	177,866,000,000	135,987,000,000	107,006,000,000
R&D Expense						
Operating Income	22,899,000,000	14,541,000,000	12,421,000,000	4,106,000,000	4,186,000,000	2,233,000,000
Operating Margin %		.05%	.05%	.02%	.03%	.02%
SGA Expense	71,416,000,000	60,012,000,000	46,987,000,000	36,363,000,000	25,750,000,000	19,541,000,000
Net Income	21,331,000,000	11,588,000,000	10,073,000,000	3,033,000,000	2,371,000,000	596,000,000
Operating Cash Flow	66,064,000,000	38,514,000,000	30,723,000,000	18,434,000,000	16,443,000,000	11,920,000,000
Capital Expenditure	40,140,000,000	16,861,000,000	13,427,000,000	11,955,000,000	6,737,000,000	4,589,000,000
EBITDA	51,076,000,000	37,365,000,000	28,019,000,000	16,132,000,000	12,492,000,000	8,308,000,000
Return on Assets %		.06%	.07%	.03%	.03%	.01%
Return on Equity %		.22%	.28%	.13%	.15%	.05%
Debt to Equity		1.018	0.914	1.369	0.789	1.06

CONTACT INFORMATION:
Phone: 206 266-1000   Fax:
Toll-Free:
Address: 410 Terry Ave. N., Seattle, WA 98109 United States

STOCK TICKER/OTHER:
Stock Ticker: AMZN
Employees: 1,298,000
Parent Company:

Exchange: NAS
Fiscal Year Ends: 12/31

SALARIES/BONUSES:
Top Exec. Salary: $ Bonus: $
Second Exec. Salary: $ Bonus: $

OTHER THOUGHTS:
Estimated Female Officers or Directors: 3
Hot Spot for Advancement for Women/Minorities: Y

Amedisys Inc

www.amedisys.com

NAIC Code: 621610

TYPES OF BUSINESS:

Home Health Care Services
Home Health Care
Hospice Care
Personal Assistance Care

BRANDS/DIVISIONS/AFFILIATES:

CONTACTS: Note: Officers with more than one job title may be intentionally listed here more than once.

Donald Washburn, Chairman of the Board
Scott Ginn, Chief Accounting Officer
Michael North, Chief Information Officer
Christopher Gerard, COO
Paul Kusserow, Director
David Kemmerly, General Counsel
David Pearce, Other Executive Officer
Sharon Brunecz, Other Executive Officer

GROWTH PLANS/SPECIAL FEATURES:

Amedisys, Inc. is a healthcare services company focused on providing care in the home. The firm serves patients across 39 U.S. states through three business segments: home health, hospice and personal care. The home health segment provides care to a variety of patients: those recovering from surgery or illness, those living with chronic diseases, and to those who want to prevent being re-admitted in a hospital. This division includes more than 320 care centers located in 34 U.S. states and the District of Columbia. Within these care centers, Amedisys deploys skilled nurses, rehabilitation therapists and social workers. The hospice segment provides comfort and support for those dealing with a terminal illness. It is a benevolent form of care that promotes dignity and affirms quality of life for the patient, family members and other loved ones. Those eligible for hospice care include individuals with heart disease, pulmonary disease, Alzheimer's, HIV/AIDS or cancer, if they have a life expectancy of six months or less. Amedisys operates 180 Medicare-certified hospice care centers throughout the country. Last, the personal care segment provides assistance with the essential activities of daily living, enabling patients to maintain a sense of independence.

FINANCIAL DATA: Note: Data for latest year may not have been available at press time.

In U.S. $	2020	2019	2018	2017	2016	2015
Revenue	2,071,519,000	1,955,633,000	1,662,578,000	1,533,680,000	1,437,454,000	1,280,541,000
R&D Expense						
Operating Income	223,420,000	178,942,000	155,148,000	108,559,000	61,772,000	68,102,000
Operating Margin %		.09%	.09%	.07%	.04%	.05%
SGA Expense	668,300,000	607,926,000	501,306,000	482,213,000	503,430,000	452,435,000
Net Income	183,608,000	126,833,000	119,346,000	30,301,000	37,261,000	-3,021,000
Operating Cash Flow	288,952,000	202,000,000	223,483,000	105,731,000	62,259,000	107,785,000
Capital Expenditure	5,332,000	7,888,000	6,558,000	10,707,000	15,717,000	21,429,000
EBITDA	289,799,000	239,258,000	179,619,000	102,955,000	86,408,000	30,511,000
Return on Assets %		.13%	.16%	.04%	.05%	.00%
Return on Equity %		.23%	.24%	.06%	.09%	-.01%
Debt to Equity		0.45	0.012	0.152	0.191	0.232

CONTACT INFORMATION:

Phone: 225 292-2031   Fax:
Toll-Free: 800-467-2662
Address: 3854 American Way, Ste. A, Baton Rouge, LA 70816 United States

STOCK TICKER/OTHER:

Stock Ticker: AMED
Employees: 21,000
Parent Company:

Exchange: NAS
Fiscal Year Ends: 12/31

SALARIES/BONUSES:

Top Exec. Salary: $ Bonus: $
Second Exec. Salary: $ Bonus: $

OTHER THOUGHTS:

Estimated Female Officers or Directors: 3
Hot Spot for Advancement for Women/Minorities: Y

AMERCO (U-Haul)

NAIC Code: 532120

www.amerco.com

TYPES OF BUSINESS:

Truck Rental & Leasing Services
Moving & Storage Services & Supplies
Property & Casualty Insurance
Life Insurance
Annuities
Self-Storage Properties
Propane Tank Refilling
Car Sharing Services

BRANDS/DIVISIONS/AFFILIATES:

U-Haul International Inc
Amerco Real Estate Company
Repwest Insurance Company
Oxford Life Insurance Company
Uhaul.com
Safemove
Safetow
Safestor

CONTACTS: Note: Officers with more than one job title may be intentionally listed here more than once.

Jason Berg, CFO
Edward Shoen, Chairman of the Board
Samuel Shoen, Director
Laurence Derespino, General Counsel
Mark Haydukovich, President, Subsidiary
John Taylor, President, Subsidiary
Carlos Vizcarra, President, Subsidiary
Douglas Bell, President, Subsidiary

GROWTH PLANS/SPECIAL FEATURES:

AMERCO is a holding company operating through four primary subsidiaries: U-Haul International, Inc.; Amerco Real Estate Company; Repwest Insurance Company; and Oxford Life Insurance Company. Accordingly, the firm has three reportable business segments: moving and storage, property and casualty insurance and life insurance. Moving and storage consists of U-Haul, with its rental equipment fleet of trucks, trailers and tow dollies offered at 1,745 company operated locations in the U.S. and Canada, as well as independent dealer outlets. It also provides furniture pads, utility dollies and hand trucks; sells a wide selection of moving supplies; and offers protection packages for moving and storage. U-Haul owns approximately 176,000 trucks, 127,000 trailers and 41,000 towing devices. The firm's Uhaul.com online reservation portal allows its self-storage customers to make reservations, access all U-Haul storage centers and affiliate partners. This segment is also operated by Amerco Real Estate Company, which manages 774,000 rentable rooms comprising 66.7 million square feet of rentable storage space located in North America. The property and casualty insurance segment, operated by Repwest Insurance Company, provides loss adjusting and claims handling for U-Haul through regional offices across North America. This segment also underwrites components of the Safemove, Safemove Plus, Safetow, Safestor and Safestor Mobile protection packages to U-Haul customers. The life insurance segment, operated by Oxford Life Insurance Company, provides life and health insurance products primarily to the senior market through the direct writing and reinsuring of life insurance, Medicare supplement and annuity policies.

FINANCIAL DATA: Note: Data for latest year may not have been available at press time.

In U.S. $	2020	2019	2018	2017	2016	2015
Revenue	3,978,868,000	3,768,707,000	3,601,114,000	3,421,767,000	3,275,656,000	
R&D Expense						
Operating Income	570,589,000	649,499,000	593,419,000	768,481,000	890,086,000	
Operating Margin %	.14%	.16%	.16%	.22%	.26%	
SGA Expense	201,718,000	133,435,000	219,271,000	220,053,000	217,216,000	
Net Income	442,048,000	370,857,000	790,583,000	398,424,000	489,001,000	
Operating Cash Flow	1,075,513,000	975,583,000	936,328,000	1,020,061,000	1,041,063,000	
Capital Expenditure	2,309,406,000	1,869,968,000	1,363,745,000	1,419,505,000	1,509,154,000	
EBITDA	1,198,767,000	1,197,254,000	1,315,521,000	1,219,839,000	1,252,972,000	
Return on Assets %	.03%	.03%	.08%	.05%	.07%	
Return on Equity %	.11%	.10%	.26%	.16%	.24%	
Debt to Equity	1.12	1.128	1.031	1.245	1.194	

CONTACT INFORMATION:

Phone: 775-688-6300   Fax: 775 688-6338
Toll-Free:
Address: 5555 Kietzke Ln., Ste. 100, Reno, NV 89511 United States

STOCK TICKER/OTHER:

Stock Ticker: UHAL   Exchange: NAS
Employees: 29,800   Fiscal Year Ends: 03/31
Parent Company:

SALARIES/BONUSES:

Top Exec. Salary: $ Bonus: $
Second Exec. Salary: $ Bonus: $

OTHER THOUGHTS:

Estimated Female Officers or Directors: 1
Hot Spot for Advancement for Women/Minorities:

Ameren Corporation

NAIC Code: 221112

TYPES OF BUSINESS:

Utilities-Electricity & Natural Gas
Electrical Generation & Distribution
Natural Gas Purchasing & Distribution
Investment Services
Energy Marketing

BRANDS/DIVISIONS/AFFILIATES:

Union Electric Company (Ameren Missouir)
Ameren Illinois Company
Ameren Transmission Company of Illinois
Midcontinent Independent Sys Operator Inc (MISO)

CONTACTS: *Note: Officers with more than one job title may be intentionally listed here more than once.*

Warner Baxter, CEO
Mark Birk, Senior VP, Subsidiary
Martin Lyons, CFO
Michael Moehn, Chairman of the Board, Subsidiary
Richard Mark, Chairman of the Board, Subsidiary
Shawn Schukar, Chairman of the Board, Subsidiary
Bruce Steinke, Chief Accounting Officer
Chonda Nwamu, Deputy General Counsel
Gregory Nelson, General Counsel
Bhavani Amirthalingam, Other Executive Officer
Fadi Diya, Other Executive Officer
Mark Lindgren, Other Executive Officer
Mary Heger, Senior VP, Subsidiary

GROWTH PLANS/SPECIAL FEATURES:

Ameren Corporation is a public utility holding company serving approximately 2.4 million electric customers and 900,000 natural gas customers across 64,000 square miles throughout Illinois and Missouri. Its utility operations are conducted through three primary subsidiaries: Union Electric Company (dba Ameren Missouri), Ameren Illinois Company and Ameren Transmission Company of Illinois (ATXI). Ameren Missouri operates a rate-regulated electric generation, transmission and distribution business, as well as a rate-regulated natural gas distribution in the state of Missouri. Ameren Illinois operates rate-regulated electric transmission, electric distribution and natural gas distribution in Illinois. ATXI operates a Federal Energy Regulatory Commission (FERC) rate-regulated electric transmission business; and operates the Spoon River project. Ameren also operates two Midcontinent Independent System Operator, Inc. (MISO) balancing authority areas: AMMO and AMIL. The AMMO balancing authority area includes the load and energy centers of Ameren Missouri and has a peak demand of 7,363 megawatts (MW). The AMIL balancing authority area includes the load of Ameren Illinois and has a peak demand of 8,735 MW. The Ameren transmission system directly connects with 15 other balancing authority areas for the exchange of electric energy. Power generation sources include coal, nuclear, natural gas and renewable energy (hydroelectric, methane gas and solar).

Ameren offers comprehensive benefits, retirement options and employee assistance programs.

FINANCIAL DATA: *Note: Data for latest year may not have been available at press time.*

In U.S. $	2020	2019	2018	2017	2016	2015
Revenue	5,794,000,000	5,910,000,000	6,291,000,000	6,177,000,000	6,076,000,000	6,098,000,000
R&D Expense						
Operating Income	1,300,000,000	1,267,000,000	1,357,000,000	1,458,000,000	1,381,000,000	1,259,000,000
Operating Margin %		.21%	.22%	.24%	.23%	.21%
SGA Expense						
Net Income	871,000,000	828,000,000	815,000,000	523,000,000	653,000,000	630,000,000
Operating Cash Flow	1,727,000,000	2,170,000,000	2,170,000,000	2,104,000,000	2,123,000,000	2,017,000,000
Capital Expenditure	3,299,000,000	2,442,000,000	2,338,000,000	2,195,000,000	2,131,000,000	1,969,000,000
EBITDA	2,604,000,000	2,478,000,000	2,492,000,000	2,448,000,000	2,346,000,000	2,177,000,000
Return on Assets %		.03%	.03%	.02%	.03%	.03%
Return on Equity %		.11%	.11%	.07%	.09%	.09%
Debt to Equity		1.106	1.03	0.987	0.928	0.99

CONTACT INFORMATION:

Phone: 314 621-3222   Fax: 314 621-2888
Toll-Free:
Address: 1901 Chouteau Ave., St. Louis, MO 63103 United States

SALARIES/BONUSES:

Top Exec. Salary: $ Bonus: $
Second Exec. Salary: $ Bonus: $

STOCK TICKER/OTHER:

Stock Ticker: AEE   Exchange: NYS
Employees: 9,323   Fiscal Year Ends: 12/31
Parent Company:

OTHER THOUGHTS:

Estimated Female Officers or Directors: 2
Hot Spot for Advancement for Women/Minorities:

American Express Company

www.americanexpress.com

NAIC Code: 522320

TYPES OF BUSINESS:
Credit Card Processing and Issuing
Travel-Related Services
Lending & Financing
Transaction Services
Bank Holding Company
International Banking Services
Expense Management
Magazine Publishing

BRANDS/DIVISIONS/AFFILIATES:
American Express Travel Related Services Co Inc
American Express Global Business Travel
Kabbage Inc

CONTACTS: *Note: Officers with more than one job title may be intentionally listed here more than once.*
Stephen Squeri, CEO
Jeffrey Campbell, CFO
Richard Petrino, Chief Accounting Officer
Marc Gordon, Chief Information Officer
Laureen Seeger, Chief Legal Officer
Elizabeth Rutledge, Chief Marketing Officer
Denise Pickett, Chief Risk Officer
Michael ONeill, Other Executive Officer
Paul Fabara, President, Divisional
Anre Williams, President, Divisional
Douglas Buckminster, President, Divisional
Anna Marrs, President, Divisional

GROWTH PLANS/SPECIAL FEATURES:
American Express Company (AmEx), a bank holding company, is a leading global payments and travel firm. Its principal products are charge and credit payment card products and travel-related services. The firm primarily operates through subsidiary American Express Travel Related Services Company, Inc. AmEx's business is organized into two main segments: global consumer services and global commercial services. Together, these segments offer a range of products and services that include: charge card, credit card and other payment and financing products; merchant acquisition and processing, servicing and settlement, and point-of-sale marketing and information products and services for merchants; network services; other fee services, such as fraud prevention services and the design and operation of customer loyalty programs; expense management products and services; and travel-related services. AmEx's products and serves are sold globally to diverse customer groups through various channels, including mobile and online applications, third-party vendors and business partners, direct mail, telephone, in-house sales teams and direct response advertising. Business travel-related services are offered through the firm's non-consolidated joint venture, American Express Global Business Travel. In late-2020, AmEx acquired Kabbage Inc., a financial technology company that provides checking accounts for small businesses in the U.S., as well as credit lines of $1,000 to $150,000 via Kabbage's automated underwriting software. As of mid-2021, AmEx's former global merchant and network services segment was merged into its global consumer services segment.

FINANCIAL DATA: *Note: Data for latest year may not have been available at press time.*

In U.S. $	2020	2019	2018	2017	2016	2015
Revenue	34,857,000,000	41,334,000,000	38,538,000,000	32,032,000,000	32,204,000,000	31,739,000,000
R&D Expense						
Operating Income						
Operating Margin %						
SGA Expense	12,465,000,000	13,025,000,000	11,720,000,000	8,475,000,000	8,909,000,000	8,085,000,000
Net Income	3,135,000,000	6,759,000,000	6,921,000,000	2,736,000,000	5,408,000,000	5,163,000,000
Operating Cash Flow	5,591,000,000	13,632,000,000	8,930,000,000	13,540,000,000	8,224,000,000	10,972,000,000
Capital Expenditure	1,478,000,000	1,645,000,000	1,310,000,000	1,062,000,000	1,375,000,000	1,341,000,000
EBITDA						
Return on Assets %		.03%	.04%	.02%	.03%	.03%
Return on Equity %		.29%	.34%	.14%	.26%	.24%
Debt to Equity		2.507	2.621	3.062	2.292	2.325

CONTACT INFORMATION:
Phone: 212 640-2000   Fax: 212 640-2458
Toll-Free: 800-528-4800
Address: 200 Vesey St., New York, NY 10285 United States

STOCK TICKER/OTHER:
Stock Ticker: AXP   Exchange: NYS
Employees: 63,700   Fiscal Year Ends: 12/31
Parent Company:

SALARIES/BONUSES:
Top Exec. Salary: $ Bonus: $
Second Exec. Salary: $ Bonus: $

OTHER THOUGHTS:
Estimated Female Officers or Directors: 4
Hot Spot for Advancement for Women/Minorities: Y

American Financial Group Inc

www.afginc.com

NAIC Code: 524126

TYPES OF BUSINESS:

Insurance, Direct Property & Casualty
Property and Casualty Insurance
Specialized Commercial Insurance
Transportation Insurance
Specialty Financial Services

BRANDS/DIVISIONS/AFFILIATES:

Great American Insurance Group

GROWTH PLANS/SPECIAL FEATURES:

American Financial Group, Inc. (AFG) is a holding company
that offers property and casualty (P&C) insurance services
through its subsidiaries. Great American Insurance Group
provides P&C insurance, with a focus on specialized
commercial products for businesses. AFG's specialty P&C
division is comprised of over 30 diversified businesses that
offer coverages in three major groupings: property and
transportation, specialty casualty and specialty financial. It
handles underwriting, claims and policy servicing, and enables
business customers to develop distribution strategies and
relationships in the markets they serve. During 2021, AFG sold
its annuity business to Massachusetts Mutual Life Insurance
Company, including its two insurance subsidiaries Annuity
Investors Life Insurance Company and Manhattan National Life
Insurance Company.

AFG offers its employees medical, dental, vision, disability and
life coverage; paid time off; and onsite fitness centers.

CONTACTS: Note: Officers with more than one job title may be intentionally listed here more than once.

Karl Grafe, Assistant General Counsel
Joseph Consolino, CFO
Michelle Gillis, Chief Administrative Officer
Carl Lindner, Co-CEO
S. Lindner, Co-CEO
John Berding, Director
Vito Peraino, General Counsel

FINANCIAL DATA: Note: Data for latest year may not have been available at press time.

In U.S. $	2020	2019	2018	2017	2016	2015
Revenue	7,811,000,000	8,237,000,000	7,150,000,000	6,865,000,000	6,498,000,000	6,145,000,000
R&D Expense						
Operating Income						
Operating Margin %						
SGA Expense						
Net Income	732,000,000	897,000,000	530,000,000	475,000,000	649,000,000	352,000,000
Operating Cash Flow	2,183,000,000	2,456,000,000	2,083,000,000	1,804,000,000	1,150,000,000	1,357,000,000
Capital Expenditure						
EBITDA						
Return on Assets %		.01%	.01%	.01%	.01%	.01%
Return on Equity %		.16%	.10%	.09%	.14%	.07%
Debt to Equity		0.235	0.262	0.244	0.261	0.222

CONTACT INFORMATION:

Phone: 513 579-2121   Fax: 513 412-0200
Toll-Free:
Address: 301 E. 4th St., Cincinnati, OH 45202 United States

STOCK TICKER/OTHER:

Stock Ticker: AFG
Employees: 6,500
Parent Company:

Exchange: NYS
Fiscal Year Ends: 12/31

SALARIES/BONUSES:

Top Exec. Salary: $ Bonus: $
Second Exec. Salary: $ Bonus: $

OTHER THOUGHTS:

Estimated Female Officers or Directors: 3
Hot Spot for Advancement for Women/Minorities: Y

American International Group Inc (AIG)   www.aig.com

NAIC Code: 524126

TYPES OF BUSINESS:

Insurance, Direct Property & Casualty
Life Insurance
Commercial Insurance
Property Insurance

BRANDS/DIVISIONS/AFFILIATES:

American Home Assurance Company
Lexington Insurance Company
AIG General Insurance Company Ltd
AIG Europe Limited
American General Life Insurance Company
Variable Annuity Life Insurance Company (The)
United States Life Insurance Company (The)
National Union Fire Insurance Co. of Pittsburgh

CONTACTS: *Note: Officers with more than one job title may be intentionally listed here more than once.*

Peter Zaffino, CEO, Divisional
Naohiro Mouri, Executive VP
Kevinm Hogan, CEO, Divisional
Brian Duperreault, CEO
Mark Lyons, CFO
Douglas Steenland, Chairman of the Board
John Repko, Chief Information Officer
Douglas Dachille, Chief Investment Officer
Alessandrea Quane, Chief Risk Officer
Seraina Macia, Executive VP
Thomas Leonardi, Executive VP, Divisional
Thomas Leonardi, Executive VP, Divisional
Lucy Fato, Executive VP

GROWTH PLANS/SPECIAL FEATURES:

American International Group, Inc. (AIG) is an international insurance organization serving customers in more than 80 countries. AIG distributes insurance products and services across the geographic regions of the Americas (the U.S., Canada, Mexico, South America, the Caribbean and Bermuda), Asia Pacific (Japan, China, Korea, Singapore, Malaysia, Thailand, Australia, Indonesia and others) and EMEA (the U.K., Continental Europe, Russian Federation, India, Middle East and Africa). AIG primarily operates through two segments: General Insurance and Life & Retirement. General Insurance is a leading provider of insurance products and services for commercial and personal insurance customers. It includes one of the world's most far-reaching property casualty networks. Operating companies within this segment include: National Union Fire Insurance Company of Pittsburgh, Pa.; American Home Assurance Company; Lexington Insurance Company; AIG General Insurance Company, Ltd.; AIG Asia Pacific Insurance, Pte, Ltd.; and AIG Europe Limited. Life and Retirement is a franchise that brings together a broad portfolio of life insurance, retirement and institutional products offered through an extensive, multichannel distribution network. Operating companies within this segment include American General Life Insurance Company, The Variable Annuity Life Insurance Company and The United States Life Insurance Company in the City of New York. In October 2020, AIG announced its intention to separate its Life & Retirement business from itself.

FINANCIAL DATA: *Note: Data for latest year may not have been available at press time.*

In U.S. $	2020	2019	2018	2017	2016	2015
Revenue	43,839,000,000	49,792,000,000	47,481,000,000	49,930,000,000	52,754,000,000	58,925,000,000
R&D Expense						
Operating Income						
Operating Margin %						
SGA Expense	8,396,000,000	8,537,000,000	9,302,000,000	9,107,000,000	10,989,000,000	12,686,000,000
Net Income	-5,944,000,000	3,348,000,000	-6,000,000	-6,084,000,000	-849,000,000	2,196,000,000
Operating Cash Flow	1,038,000,000	-928,000,000	61,000,000	-8,585,000,000	2,383,000,000	2,877,000,000
Capital Expenditure						
EBITDA						
Return on Assets %		.01%	.00%	-.01%	.00%	.00%
Return on Equity %		.05%	.00%	-.09%	-.01%	.02%
Debt to Equity		0.542	0.613	0.485	0.405	0.327

CONTACT INFORMATION:

Phone: 212 770-7000   Fax: 212 344-6828
Toll-Free: 877-638-4244
Address: 180 Maiden Ln., New York, NY 10038 United States

STOCK TICKER/OTHER:

Stock Ticker: AIG   Exchange: NYS
Employees: 46,000   Fiscal Year Ends: 12/31
Parent Company:

SALARIES/BONUSES:

Top Exec. Salary: $ Bonus: $
Second Exec. Salary: $ Bonus: $

OTHER THOUGHTS:

Estimated Female Officers or Directors: 10
Hot Spot for Advancement for Women/Minorities: Y

American Tire Distributors Inc

www.atd-us.com

NAIC Code: 423130

TYPES OF BUSINESS:

Tires & Related Products, Distribution
Tire Manufacturer
Replacement Tires
Tire Distribution Centers
Retail
Tire Dealers
Ecommerce

BRANDS/DIVISIONS/AFFILIATES:

American Tire Distributors Holdings Inc
ATDOnline
TireBuyer.com

CONTACTS: *Note: Officers with more than one job title may be intentionally listed here more than once.*

Stuart Schuette, CEO
Michael Gaither, General Counsel
Phillip Marrett, Exec. VP-Product Planning & Positioning
Daniel Brown, Pres., Tire Pros

GROWTH PLANS/SPECIAL FEATURES:

American Tire Distributors, Inc. (ATD) is one of the nation's largest suppliers of tires and wheels as well as tools and other automotive service equipment. The company serves the replacement tire market through approximately 145 distribution centers in Canada and the U.S., and a fleet of delivery vehicles, delivering products to approximately 80,000 customers. ATD distributes more than 40 million replacement tires each year. ATD offers its tire retailers and service shop clients various tires for passenger vehicles and light trucks, tractor-trailers, buses, farm machinery and specialty and recreational vehicles. The company carries brands including Michelin, Continental, BFGoodrich and Bridgestone. Its wheel division offers rims in a range of sizes for passenger vehicles and light trucks. The firm maintains ATDOnline, which offers dealers access to prices, availability and the ability to place orders 24 hours a day, seven days a week; and TireBuyer.com, where customers can buy tires and wheels as well as choose a dealer location for installation. TireBuyer.com also allows potential purchasers to view tires and wheels on their particular vehicle, using the website's 3D visualizer. ATD operates as a subsidiary of American Tire Distributors Holdings, Inc.

FINANCIAL DATA: *Note: Data for latest year may not have been available at press time.*

In U.S. $	2020	2019	2018	2017	2016	2015
Revenue	4,800,000,000	5,286,750,000	5,565,000,000	5,300,000,000	5,000,000,000	4,800,000,000
R&D Expense						
Operating Income						
Operating Margin %						
SGA Expense						
Net Income						
Operating Cash Flow						
Capital Expenditure						
EBITDA						
Return on Assets %						
Return on Equity %						
Debt to Equity						

CONTACT INFORMATION:

Phone: 704-992-2000   Fax: 704-992-1384
Toll-Free: 800-222-1167
Address: 12200 Herbert Wayne Ct., Ste. 150, Huntersville, NC 28070
United States

STOCK TICKER/OTHER:

Stock Ticker: Subsidiary   Exchange:
Employees: 5,000   Fiscal Year Ends: 10/01
Parent Company: American Tire Distributors Holdings Inc

SALARIES/BONUSES:

Top Exec. Salary: $ Bonus: $
Second Exec. Salary: $ Bonus: $

OTHER THOUGHTS:

Estimated Female Officers or Directors:
Hot Spot for Advancement for Women/Minorities:

American Tower Corporation (REIT)

www.americantower.com

NAIC Code: 237130

TYPES OF BUSINESS:

Cellular Service Antenna Towers
Antenna Site Leasing
Radio & TV Broadcast Towers
Network Development & Consulting
Antenna Site Leasing

BRANDS/DIVISIONS/AFFILIATES:

American Towers LLC
SpectraSite Communications LLC
American Tower International Inc
Telxius Tower

CONTACTS: *Note: Officers with more than one job title may be intentionally listed here more than once.*

James Taiclet, CEO
Thomas Bartlett, CFO
Robert Meyer, Chief Accounting Officer
Edmund DiSanto, Chief Administrative Officer
William Hess, Executive VP
Steven Vondran, Executive VP
Olivier Puech, Executive VP
Amit Sharma, Executive VP

GROWTH PLANS/SPECIAL FEATURES:

American Tower Corporation (AMT) is a global real estate investment trust (REIT) and an independent owner, operator and developer of multitenant communications real estate. AMT's primary business is the leasing of space on communications sites to wireless service providers, radio and television broadcast companies, wireless data providers, government agencies and municipalities, and tenants in other industries. The firm also offers tower-related services in the U.S., such as site acquisition, zoning, permitting and structural analysis. AMT's principal domestic operating subsidiaries are American Towers, LLC and SpectraSite Communications, LLC. International operations are conducted through American Tower International, Inc., which in turn conducts operations through its various international subsidiaries and joint ventures. As of July 2021, AMT's communications real estate portfolio consisted of 214,000 communications sites spread throughout North America (U.S. and Mexico), Asia, Europe/Middle East/Africa and Latin America. In June 2021, AMT closed both tranches of its Telxius Tower acquisition agreement with Telefonica SA. The first tranche comprised nearly 20,000 communications sites in Germany and Spain, and the second tranche comprised over 7,000 communications sites in Brazil, Peru, Chile and Argentina.

FINANCIAL DATA: *Note: Data for latest year may not have been available at press time.*

In U.S. $	2020	2019	2018	2017	2016	2015
Revenue	8,041,500,000	7,580,300,000	7,440,100,000	6,663,900,000	5,785,668,000	4,771,516,000
R&D Expense						
Operating Income	3,127,600,000	2,688,400,000	1,905,000,000	1,998,400,000	1,853,029,000	1,612,789,000
Operating Margin %		.35%	.26%	.30%	.32%	.34%
SGA Expense	778,700,000	730,400,000	733,200,000	637,000,000	543,395,000	497,835,000
Net Income	1,690,600,000	1,887,800,000	1,236,400,000	1,238,900,000	956,425,000	685,074,000
Operating Cash Flow	3,881,400,000	3,752,600,000	3,748,300,000	2,925,600,000	2,703,604,000	2,183,052,000
Capital Expenditure	1,031,700,000	991,300,000	913,200,000	803,600,000	682,505,000	728,753,000
EBITDA	4,496,900,000	4,509,000,000	4,092,100,000	3,722,800,000	3,369,783,000	2,712,059,000
Return on Assets %		.05%	.04%	.04%	.03%	.02%
Return on Equity %		.36%	.21%	.18%	.13%	.11%
Debt to Equity		5.467	3.449	3.113	2.705	2.566

CONTACT INFORMATION:

Phone: 617 375-7500   Fax: 617 375-7575
Toll-Free: 877-282-7483
Address: 116 Huntington Ave., Boston, MA 02116 United States

STOCK TICKER/OTHER:

Stock Ticker: AMT
Employees: 5,618
Parent Company:

Exchange: NYS
Fiscal Year Ends: 12/31

SALARIES/BONUSES:

Top Exec. Salary: $ Bonus: $
Second Exec. Salary: $ Bonus: $

OTHER THOUGHTS:

Estimated Female Officers or Directors: 3
Hot Spot for Advancement for Women/Minorities: Y

Amerigroup Corporation

www.amerigroup.com

NAIC Code: 524114

TYPES OF BUSINESS:
Managed Health Care
State-Sponsored Health Benefits

BRANDS/DIVISIONS/AFFILIATES:
Anthem Inc

CONTACTS: Note: Officers with more than one job title may be intentionally listed here more than once.
Felicia F. Norwood, Exec. VP-Anthem
Richard C. Zoretic, Exec. VP
Mary T. McCluskey, Exec. VP
Jack Young, VP
Ken Aversa, Sr. VP-Customer Svc. Oper., Medicaid, WellPoint
Georgia Dodds Foley, Chief Compliance Officer, Medicaid, WellPoint
John E. Little, Interim Sr. VP-Gov't Affairs, WellPoint
Aileen McCormick, CEO-Western Region, Medicaid, WellPoint

GROWTH PLANS/SPECIAL FEATURES:
Amerigroup Corporation is the state-sponsored program services division of health benefits company Anthem, Inc. These programs include Medicaid, Family Care and the Children's Health Insurance Program (CHIP), across all states. Amerigroup also offers Medicare plans throughout the U.S. The firm reduces costs for families and state governments by combining social and behavioral health services to help members obtain health care. Amerigroup's provider networks consist of: hospitals; and physicians, including primary care physicians, specialists and ancillary providers. The company connects members to the services and supports they need for physical health, mental health and substance abuse. It addresses members' psychosocial needs and goals for housing, education/employment, transportation and meaningful participation in the community. Amerigroup works with individuals with intellectual and developmental disabilities, children and youth in foster care, individuals with mental health and substance abuse needs, individuals who need long-term services and support, and children with special needs.

FINANCIAL DATA: Note: Data for latest year may not have been available at press time.

In U.S. $	2020	2019	2018	2017	2016	2015
Revenue	11,210,000,000	11,800,000,000	11,500,000,000	11,000,000,000	10,500,000,000	10,000,000,000
R&D Expense						
Operating Income						
Operating Margin %						
SGA Expense						
Net Income						
Operating Cash Flow						
Capital Expenditure						
EBITDA						
Return on Assets %						
Return on Equity %						
Debt to Equity						

CONTACT INFORMATION:
Phone: 757 490-6900 Fax:
Toll-Free: 800-600-4441
Address: 4425 Corporation Ln., Virginia Beach, VA 23462 United States

STOCK TICKER/OTHER:
Stock Ticker: Subsidiary
Employees: 8,000
Parent Company: Anthem Inc
Exchange:
Fiscal Year Ends: 12/31

SALARIES/BONUSES:
Top Exec. Salary: $ Bonus: $
Second Exec. Salary: $ Bonus: $

OTHER THOUGHTS:
Estimated Female Officers or Directors: 3
Hot Spot for Advancement for Women/Minorities: Y

AmerisourceBergen Corporation

www.amerisourcebergen.com

NAIC Code: 424210

TYPES OF BUSINESS:

Drug Distribution
Pharmacy Management & Consulting Services
Packaging Solutions
Information Technology
Healthcare Equipment

BRANDS/DIVISIONS/AFFILIATES:

AmerisourceBergen Consulting Services
MWI
World Courier

CONTACTS: *Note: Officers with more than one job title may be intentionally listed here more than once.*

Steven Collis, CEO
Lazarus Krikorian, Chief Accounting Officer
Gina Clark, Chief Administrative Officer
Kathy Gaddes, Chief Compliance Officer
Dale Danilewitz, Chief Information Officer
John Chou, Chief Legal Officer
James Cleary, Executive VP
Robert Mauch, Executive VP

GROWTH PLANS/SPECIAL FEATURES:

AmerisourceBergen Corporation is one of the largest wholesale distributors of pharmaceutical products and services to a wide variety of health care providers and pharmacies. The firm offers brand name and generic pharmaceuticals, supplies and equipment and serves the U.S., Canada and selected global markets. The company's operations are divided into two segments: pharmaceutical distribution services (PDS) and other. PDS provides drug distributes a comprehensive offering of brand-name, specialty brand-name and generic pharmaceuticals, over-the-counter healthcare products, home healthcare supplies and equipment, outsourced compounded sterile preparations and related services to a wide variety of healthcare providers, including acute care hospitals and health systems, independent and chain retail pharmacies, mail order pharmacies, medical clinics, long-term care and alternate site pharmacies and other customers. Through a number of operating businesses, the PDS reportable segment provides pharmaceutical distribution (including plasma and other blood products, injectible pharmaceuticals, vaccines and other specialty pharmaceutical products) and additional services to physicians who specialize in a variety of disease states, especially oncology, and to other healthcare providers, including hospitals and dialysis clinics. Additionally, the PDS provides data analytics, outcomes research and additional services for biotechnology and pharmaceutical manufacturers. The other segment oversees: AmerisourceBergen Consulting Services (ABCS), which provides commercialization support services such as reimbursement support programs, outcomes research, contract field staffing, patient assistance and copay assistance programs; MWI, a leading animal health distribution company in the U.S. and in the U.K.; and World Courier, which is a global specialty transportation and logistics provider for the biopharmaceutical industry serving more than 50 countries. During 2021, AmerisourceBergen acquired the majority of Walgreens Boots Alliance, Inc.'s healthcare businesses for $6.275 billion in cash.

Employee benefits include comprehensive health benefits, 401(k), employee stock purchase program, life and disability insurance, adoption assistance and more.

FINANCIAL DATA: *Note: Data for latest year may not have been available at press time.*

In U.S. $	2020	2019	2018	2017	2016	2015
Revenue	189,893,900,000	179,589,100,000	167,939,600,000	153,143,800,000	146,849,700,000	135,961,800,000
R&D Expense						
Operating Income	2,033,605,000	2,012,397,000	1,686,889,000	2,019,669,000	1,816,634,000	1,367,988,000
Operating Margin %		.01%	.01%	.01%	.01%	.01%
SGA Expense	2,767,217,000	2,663,508,000	2,460,301,000	2,128,730,000	2,091,237,000	1,918,045,000
Net Income	-3,408,716,000	855,365,000	1,658,405,000	364,484,000	1,427,929,000	-134,887,000
Operating Cash Flow	2,207,040,000	2,344,023,000	1,411,388,000	1,504,138,000	3,178,497,000	3,920,379,000
Capital Expenditure	369,677,000	310,222,000	336,411,000	466,397,000	464,616,000	231,585,000
EBITDA	-4,727,296,000	1,660,092,000	1,877,172,000	1,499,260,000	1,927,425,000	625,735,000
Return on Assets %		.02%	.05%	.01%	.05%	-.01%
Return on Equity %		.29%	.66%	.17%	1.03%	-.10%
Debt to Equity		1.401	1.418	1.661	1.688	5.514

CONTACT INFORMATION:

Phone: 610 727-7000   Fax: 610 647-0141
Toll-Free: 800-829-3132
Address: 1 West First Ave., Conshohocken, PA 19428-1800 United States

STOCK TICKER/OTHER:

Stock Ticker: ABC   Exchange: NYS
Employees: 22,000   Fiscal Year Ends: 09/30
Parent Company:

SALARIES/BONUSES:

Top Exec. Salary: $ Bonus: $
Second Exec. Salary: $ Bonus: $

OTHER THOUGHTS:

Estimated Female Officers or Directors: 7
Hot Spot for Advancement for Women/Minorities: Y

Sales, profits and employees may be estimates. Financial information, benefits and other data can change quickly and may vary from those stated here.

Ametek Inc

NAIC Code: 334513

www.ametek.com

TYPES OF BUSINESS:

Monitoring, Testing, Calibration and Display Electronic Device
Manufacturing
ElectromechanicalÂ Device Manufacturing

BRANDS/DIVISIONS/AFFILIATES:

Magnetrol International
Crank Software
EGS Automation

CONTACTS: *Note: Officers with more than one job title may be intentionally listed here more than once.*

David Zapico, CEO
William Burke, CFO
Thomas Montgomery, Chief Accounting Officer
Ronald Oscher, Chief Administrative Officer
Tony Ciampitti, President, Divisional
Timothy Jones, President, Divisional
John Hardin, President, Divisional
Thomas Marecic, President, Divisional

GROWTH PLANS/SPECIAL FEATURES:

Ametek, Inc. is a manufacturer of electronic instruments and electromechanical devices, with operations across the globe. The company markets its products through two operating groups: the electronic instruments group (EIG) and the electromechanical group (EMG). EIG builds monitoring, testing, calibration and display devices for the process, aerospace, industrial and power markets. The group makes significant use of distributors and sales representatives in marketing its products as well as direct sales in some of its more technically sophisticated products. EIG has operating facilities in the U.S., the U.K., Germany, Canada, China, Denmark, Finland, France, Switzerland, Argentina, Austria and Mexico. EIG also shares facilities with EMG in Brazil, China and Mexico. EMG is a supplier of electromechanical devices. This division produces highly engineered electromechanical connectors for hermetic (moisture-proof) applications, specialty metals for niche markets and brushless air-moving motors, blowers and heat exchangers. EMG has operating facilities in the U.S., the U.K., China, Germany, France, Italy, Mexico, Serbia, Brazil, the Czech Republic, Malaysia and Taiwan. AMETEK owns numerous unexpired U.S. patents and foreign patents, including counterparts of its more important U.S. patents, in the major industrial countries of the world. In March 2021, Ametek completed three acquisitions: Magnetrol International, Crank Software and EGS Automation, each of which provide Ametek with unique capabilities that strategically expand its presence in growth areas. Magnetrol and Crank offer advanced analytical, monitoring, testing, calibrating and display instruments, and will merge into the EIG group; and EGS offers thermal management systems and automation and engineering solutions and will merge into the EMG group.

FINANCIAL DATA: *Note: Data for latest year may not have been available at press time.*

In U.S. $	2020	2019	2018	2017	2016	2015
Revenue	4,540,029,000	5,158,557,000	4,845,872,000	4,300,170,000	3,840,087,000	3,974,295,000
R&D Expense						
Operating Income	1,027,884,000	1,177,380,000	1,075,540,000	915,094,000	801,897,000	907,716,000
Operating Margin %		.23%	.22%	.21%	.21%	.23%
SGA Expense	515,630,000	610,280,000	584,022,000	533,645,000	462,970,000	448,592,000
Net Income	872,439,000	861,297,000	777,933,000	681,470,000	512,158,000	590,859,000
Operating Cash Flow	1,280,980,000	1,114,422,000	925,518,000	833,259,000	756,835,000	672,540,000
Capital Expenditure	74,199,000	102,346,000	82,076,000	75,074,000	63,280,000	69,083,000
EBITDA	1,423,646,000	1,392,271,000	1,269,415,000	1,077,985,000	967,123,000	1,047,635,000
Return on Assets %		.09%	.09%	.09%	.07%	.09%
Return on Equity %		.18%	.19%	.19%	.16%	.18%
Debt to Equity		0.444	0.536	0.463	0.633	0.478

CONTACT INFORMATION:

Phone: 610 647-2121   Fax:
Toll-Free:
Address: 1100 Cassatt Rd., Berwyn, PA 19312-1177 United States

STOCK TICKER/OTHER:

Stock Ticker: AME
Employees: 18,100
Parent Company:

Exchange: NYS
Fiscal Year Ends: 12/31

SALARIES/BONUSES:

Top Exec. Salary: $ Bonus: $
Second Exec. Salary: $ Bonus: $

OTHER THOUGHTS:

Estimated Female Officers or Directors:
Hot Spot for Advancement for Women/Minorities:

Amgen Inc

NAIC Code: 325412

www.amgen.com

TYPES OF BUSINESS:

Drugs-Diversified
Oncology Drugs
Nephrology Drugs
Inflammation Drugs
Neurology Drugs

BRANDS/DIVISIONS/AFFILIATES:

ENBREL
Prolia
Neulasta
Otezla
XGEVA
Aranesp
KYPROLIS
Repatha

CONTACTS: *Note: Officers with more than one job title may be intentionally listed here more than once.*

Robert Bradway, CEO
David Meline, CFO
Murdo Gordon, Executive VP, Divisional
David Reese, Executive VP, Divisional
Esteban Santos, Executive VP, Divisional
Cynthia Patton, Other Executive Officer
Lori Johnston, Senior VP, Divisional
David Piacquad, Senior VP, Divisional
Jonathan Graham, Senior VP

GROWTH PLANS/SPECIAL FEATURES:

Amgen, Inc. is a global biotechnology medicines company that discovers, develops, manufactures and markets human therapeutics based on cellular and molecular biology. Amgen's current pipeline products in Phase 3 include, but are not limited to: EVENITY, a humanized monoclonal antibody that inhibits the action of sclerostin for male osteoporosis; KYPROLIS, a proteasome inhibitor for multiple myeloma; Omecamtiv Mecarbil, a small molecule activator of cardiac myosin for the treatment of chronic heart failure; and Tezepelumab, a human monoclonal antibody that inhibits the action of thymic stromal lymphopoietin for severe asthma and atopic dermatitis. During 2020, Amgen's largest marketed product was ENBREL (21%), which is used in indications for the treatment of adult patients with types of rheumatoid arthritis and psoriasis. Prolia is second (11%) and approved for different indications, patient populations, doses and frequencies of administration, but primarily used for the treatment of post-menopausal women with osteoporosis at high risk of fracture. Other leading products include Neulasta, Otezla, XGEVA, Aranesp, KYPROLIS, and Repatha. A substantial majority of Amgen's U.S. product sales is made to three pharmaceutical product wholesaler distributors, including AmerisourceBergen, McKesson and Cardinal Health. In May 2021, the FDA accepted Amgen's supplemental new drug application for Otezla (apremilast) for adults with mild-to-moderate plaque psoriasis.

Amgen offers its employees health, disability and life insurance; paid time off; home and auto insurance; tuition reimbursement; childcare services; telecommuting options; and recreation/fitness classes.

FINANCIAL DATA: *Note: Data for latest year may not have been available at press time.*

In U.S. $	2020	2019	2018	2017	2016	2015
Revenue	25,424,000,000	23,362,000,000	23,747,000,000	22,849,000,000	22,991,000,000	21,662,000,000
R&D Expense	4,207,000,000	4,116,000,000	3,737,000,000	3,562,000,000	3,840,000,000	4,070,000,000
Operating Income	9,139,000,000	9,674,000,000	10,263,000,000	9,973,000,000	9,794,000,000	8,470,000,000
Operating Margin %		.41%	.43%	.44%	.43%	.39%
SGA Expense	5,730,000,000	5,150,000,000	5,332,000,000	4,870,000,000	5,062,000,000	4,846,000,000
Net Income	7,264,000,000	7,842,000,000	8,394,000,000	1,979,000,000	7,722,000,000	6,939,000,000
Operating Cash Flow	10,497,000,000	9,150,000,000	11,296,000,000	11,177,000,000	10,354,000,000	9,077,000,000
Capital Expenditure	608,000,000	618,000,000	738,000,000	664,000,000	837,000,000	649,000,000
EBITDA	12,996,000,000	12,633,000,000	12,883,000,000	12,856,000,000	12,528,000,000	11,181,000,000
Return on Assets %		.12%	.11%	.03%	.10%	.10%
Return on Equity %		.71%	.44%	.07%	.27%	.26%
Debt to Equity		2.786	2.361	1.355	1.011	1.044

CONTACT INFORMATION:

Phone: 805 447-1000   Fax: 805 447-1010
Toll-Free: 800-772-6436
Address: 1 Amgen Center Dr., Thousand Oaks, CA 91320 United States

STOCK TICKER/OTHER:

Stock Ticker: AMGN   Exchange: NAS
Employees: 19,200   Fiscal Year Ends: 12/31
Parent Company:

SALARIES/BONUSES:

Top Exec. Salary: $ Bonus: $
Second Exec. Salary: $ Bonus: $

OTHER THOUGHTS:

Estimated Female Officers or Directors: 4
Hot Spot for Advancement for Women/Minorities: Y

Amphenol Corporation

www.amphenol.com

NAIC Code: 335921

TYPES OF BUSINESS:

Cables & Connectors
Fiber Optic Cable
Interconnect Systems

BRANDS/DIVISIONS/AFFILIATES:

MTS Systems Corporation

CONTACTS: Note: Officers with more than one job title may be intentionally listed here more than once.

Richard Norwitt, CEO
Craig Lampo, CFO
Martin Loeffler, Director
Lance DAmico, General Counsel
Zachary Raley, General Manager, Divisional
Luc Walter, General Manager, Divisional
William Doherty, General Manager, Divisional
Martin Booker, General Manager, Divisional
Richard Gu, General Manager, Divisional
David Silverman, Senior VP, Divisional
Jean-Luc Gavelle, Vice President
Dieter Ehrmanntraut, Vice President

GROWTH PLANS/SPECIAL FEATURES:

Amphenol Corporation is a leading global designer, manufacturer and marketer of electrical, electronic and fiber optic connectors, interconnect systems and coaxial and flat-ribbon cable. The company has two operating segments: interconnect products and assemblies, and cable products and solutions. Interconnect products and assemblies include connectors, which when attached to an electrical, electronic or fiber optic cable; a printed circuit board; or other device, facilitate transmission of power or signal. Value-add systems generally consist of a system of cable, flexible circuits or printed circuit boards and connectors for linking electronic equipment. The cable products and solutions segment primarily designs, manufacturers and markets cable, value-added products and components for use primarily in the broadband communications and information technology markets as well as certain applications in other markets. Amphenol's interconnect products and assemblies are intended for the following primary industry and end markets, accounting for 96% of 2020 net sales, and include automotive, broadband communications, industrial, information technology, data communications, military, mobile devices and mobile networks. Cable products and solutions account for the remaining 4% of annual net sales, with its primary markets including automotive, broadband communications, industrial, information technology, data communications and mobile networks. Amphenol has international manufacturing and assembly facilities in the Americas, Europe, Asia and Africa. In April 2021, Amphenol acquired MTS Systems Corporation, a global supplier of precision sensors.

FINANCIAL DATA: Note: Data for latest year may not have been available at press time.

In U.S. $	2020	2019	2018	2017	2016	2015
Revenue	8,598,900,000	8,225,400,000	8,202,000,000	7,011,300,000	6,286,400,000	5,568,700,000
R&D Expense						
Operating Income	1,649,900,000	1,644,600,000	1,695,400,000	1,431,600,000	1,241,800,000	1,110,400,000
Operating Margin %		.20%	.21%	.20%	.20%	.20%
SGA Expense	1,014,200,000	971,400,000	959,500,000	878,300,000	798,200,000	669,100,000
Net Income	1,203,400,000	1,155,000,000	1,205,000,000	650,500,000	822,900,000	763,500,000
Operating Cash Flow	1,592,000,000	1,502,300,000	1,112,700,000	1,144,200,000	1,077,600,000	1,030,500,000
Capital Expenditure	276,800,000	295,000,000	310,600,000	226,600,000	190,800,000	172,100,000
EBITDA	1,950,100,000	1,925,600,000	1,989,800,000	1,671,500,000	1,430,700,000	1,292,700,000
Return on Assets %		.11%	.12%	.07%	.10%	.11%
Return on Equity %		.27%	.30%	.17%	.24%	.25%
Debt to Equity		0.707	0.699	0.888	0.717	0.869

CONTACT INFORMATION:

Phone: 203 265-8900   Fax: 203 265-8516
Toll-Free: 877-267-4366
Address: 358 Hall Ave., Wallingford, CT 06492 United States

STOCK TICKER/OTHER:

Stock Ticker: APH   Exchange: NYS
Employees: 62,000   Fiscal Year Ends: 12/31
Parent Company:

SALARIES/BONUSES:

Top Exec. Salary: $ Bonus: $
Second Exec. Salary: $ Bonus: $

OTHER THOUGHTS:

Estimated Female Officers or Directors: 1
Hot Spot for Advancement for Women/Minorities:

Anixter International Inc

www.anixter.com

NAIC Code: 423430

TYPES OF BUSINESS:

Wire & Cable Distribution
C Class Inventory Component Distribution
Connectivity Parts Distribution

BRANDS/DIVISIONS/AFFILIATES:

WESCO International Inc

CONTACTS: Note: Officers with more than one job title may be intentionally listed here more than once.

William Galvin, CEO
Theodore Dosch, CFO
Rodney Smith, Executive VP, Divisional
Robert Graham, Executive VP, Divisional
William Geary, Executive VP, Divisional
Orlando McGee, Executive VP, Divisional
Justin Choi, Executive VP

GROWTH PLANS/SPECIAL FEATURES:

Anixter International, Inc. is a leading global distributor of data, voice, video and security network communication products and one of the largest North American distributors of specialty wire and cable products. With more than 300 sales and warehouse locations in over 50 countries, the firm sells nearly 600,000 products, such as transmission media (copper and fiber optic cable) and connectivity, support, supply and security surveillance products as well as C-class inventory components (small parts used in manufacturing such as nuts and bolts) to original equipment manufacturers (OEMs). These products, used to connect personal computers, peripheral equipment, mainframe equipment, security equipment and various networks to each other, are incorporated into enterprise networks, physical security networks, central switching offices, web hosting sites and remote transmission sites. In addition, Anixter provides industrial wire and cable products, including electrical and electronic wire and cable, control and instrumentation cable and coaxial cable, used in a wide variety of maintenance, repair and construction-related applications. During 2020, Anixter International was acquired by WESCO International, Inc., and ceased from public trading.

FINANCIAL DATA: Note: Data for latest year may not have been available at press time.

In U.S. $	2020	2019	2018	2017	2016	2015
Revenue	9,287,879,731	8,845,599,744	8,400,200,192	7,927,399,936	7,622,799,872	6,190,499,840
R&D Expense						
Operating Income						
Operating Margin %						
SGA Expense						
Net Income		262,900,000	156,300,000	109,000,000	120,500,000	127,600,000
Operating Cash Flow						
Capital Expenditure						
EBITDA						
Return on Assets %						
Return on Equity %						
Debt to Equity						

CONTACT INFORMATION:

Phone: 224-521-8000   Fax: 224-521-8100
Toll-Free: 800-323-8167
Address: 2301 Patriot Blvd., Glenview, IL 60026 United States

STOCK TICKER/OTHER:

Stock Ticker: Subsidiary   Exchange:
Employees: 9,400   Fiscal Year Ends: 12/31
Parent Company: WESCO International Inc

SALARIES/BONUSES:

Top Exec. Salary: $ Bonus: $
Second Exec. Salary: $ Bonus: $

OTHER THOUGHTS:

Estimated Female Officers or Directors: 2
Hot Spot for Advancement for Women/Minorities: Y

ANSYS Inc

www.ansys.com

NAIC Code: 511210N

TYPES OF BUSINESS:

Software-Engineering, Design & Testing
MEMS Design Software

BRANDS/DIVISIONS/AFFILIATES:

ANSYS Workbench
Pervasive Engineering Simulation
ANSYS ACT
Lumerical Inc.
Analytical Graphics, Inc.

CONTACTS: *Note: Officers with more than one job title may be intentionally listed here more than once.*

Maria Shields, CFO
Ronald Hovsepian, Chairman of the Board
Prithviraj Banerjee, Chief Technology Officer
Ajei Gopal, Director
Janet Lee, General Counsel
Richard Mahoney, Senior VP, Divisional
Matthew Zack, Vice President, Divisional
Shane Emswiler, Vice President, Divisional

GROWTH PLANS/SPECIAL FEATURES:

ANSYS, Inc. develops, markets and supports engineering simulation software and technologies. The company's software enables users to analyze designs directly on the desktop, providing a platform for efficient product development, from design to testing and validation. ANSYS distributes its products through a network of channel partners in more than 40 countries and through its own direct sales offices worldwide. The company's products are used in many industries, including aerospace, electronics, automotive, energy, manufacturing, biomedical and defense. ANSYS' software can be divided into several product lines. ANSYS Workbench enables customers to simulate engineering designs using computer-aided design (CAD) technology. The Workbench platform includes Pervasive Engineering Simulation, a solution for simulation-based process and data managed challenges. This solution enables an organization to address issues associated with simulation data, including backup and archival, traceability and audit trail, process automation, collaboration and capture of engineering expertise and intellectual property protection. ANSYS ACT allows users to modify the user interface, process simulation data or embed third-party applications to create specialized tools based on ANSYS Workbench. The firm's high-performance computing product suite enables enhanced insight into product performance and improves the productivity of the design process. Finally, ANSYS' geometry handling solutions for engineering simulation integrates with direct interfaces to all major CAD systems, supports additional readers and translators, and comprises an integrated geometry modeler exclusively for analysis purposes. In March 2020, ANSYS announced it will acquire Lumerical, Inc., which will add photonics products and a multiphysics portfolio to ANSYS' offerings. In October 2020, ANSYS announced it will acquire Analytical Graphics, Inc., a provider of mission-driven simulation, modeling, testing and analysis software for aerospace, defense, telecommunication and intelligence applications.

FINANCIAL DATA: *Note: Data for latest year may not have been available at press time.*

In U.S. $	2020	2019	2018	2017	2016	2015
Revenue	1,681,297,000	1,515,892,000	1,293,636,000	1,095,250,000	988,465,000	942,753,000
R&D Expense	355,371,000	298,210,000	233,802,000	202,746,000	183,093,000	168,831,000
Operating Income	496,356,000	515,040,000	476,574,000	390,728,000	376,242,000	353,679,000
Operating Margin %		.34%	.37%	.36%	.38%	.38%
SGA Expense	587,707,000	521,200,000	413,580,000	338,640,000	269,515,000	253,603,000
Net Income	433,887,000	451,295,000	419,375,000	259,251,000	265,636,000	252,521,000
Operating Cash Flow	547,310,000	499,936,000	486,437,000	430,438,000	356,827,000	367,523,000
Capital Expenditure	35,370,000	44,940,000	21,762,000	19,149,000	12,443,000	16,145,000
EBITDA	611,159,000	605,019,000	535,829,000	458,406,000	450,123,000	434,760,000
Return on Assets %		.11%	.14%	.09%	.10%	.09%
Return on Equity %		.15%	.17%	.12%	.12%	.11%
Debt to Equity		0.149				

CONTACT INFORMATION:

Phone: 724 746-3304   Fax: 724 514-9494
Toll-Free: 866-267-9724
Address: 2600 ANSYS Dr., Canonsburg, PA 15317 United States

STOCK TICKER/OTHER:

Stock Ticker: ANSS
Employees: 4,100
Parent Company:

Exchange: NAS
Fiscal Year Ends: 12/31

SALARIES/BONUSES:

Top Exec. Salary: $ Bonus: $
Second Exec. Salary: $ Bonus: $

OTHER THOUGHTS:

Estimated Female Officers or Directors: 4
Hot Spot for Advancement for Women/Minorities: Y

Anthem Inc

NAIC Code: 524114

www.antheminc.com

TYPES OF BUSINESS:

Health Insurance
Health Maintenance Organizations (HMOs)
Point-of-Service Plans
Dental and Vision Plans
Plan Management (ASO) for Self-Insured Organizations
Prescription Plans
Wellness Programs
Medicare Administrative Services

BRANDS/DIVISIONS/AFFILIATES:

Blue Cross and Blue Shield Association
Aim Specialty Health
CareMore
Freedom Health
HealthSun
Optimum HealthCare
IngenioRx
myNEXUS Inc

CONTACTS: Note: Officers with more than one job title may be intentionally listed here more than once.

Gail Boudreaux, CEO
John Gallina, CFO
Elizabeth Tallett, Chairman of the Board
Ronald Penczek, Chief Accounting Officer
Gloria McCarthy, Chief Administrative Officer
Thomas Zielinski, Executive VP
Leah Stark, Executive VP
Felicia Norwood, Executive VP
Prakash Patel, Executive VP
Peter Haytaian, Executive VP

GROWTH PLANS/SPECIAL FEATURES:

Anthem, Inc. is a health benefits company, serving more than 43 million medical members through its affiliated health plans (as of mid-2021). Through its affiliated companies, Anthem services more than 116 million people. The firm is an independent licensee of the Blue Cross and Blue Shield Association, an association of independent health benefit plans, and also serves customers throughout the country under the Aim Specialty Health, America's 1st Choice, Amerigroup, Aspire Health, CareMore, Freedom Health, HealthLink, HealthSun, Optimum HealthCare, Simply Healthcare and UniCare brands. Anthem also provides pharmacy benefits management services through its IngenioRx subsidiary. Anthem is licensed to conduct insurance operations in all 50 U.S. states and the District of Columbia through its subsidiaries. Anthem offers a broad spectrum of network-based managed care plans to large group, small group, individual, Medicaid and Medicare markets. Managed care plans include preferred provider organizations (PPOs), health maintenance organizations (HMOs), point-of-service (POS) plans, traditional indemnity plans and other hybrid plans. The firm also offers hospital only and limited benefit products, as well as an array of managed care services to self-funded customers, including claims processing, stop loss insurance, actuarial services, provider network access, medical cost management, disease management, wellness programs and other administrative services. Anthem provides specialty and other insurance products and services such as dental, vision, life and disability benefits, radiology benefit management and analytics-driven personal healthcare. The firm provides services to the federal government in connection with the Federal Employee Program (FEP). During 2021, Anthem acquired myNEXUS, Inc. a home-based nursing management company for payors; and acquired MMM Holdings, LLC and its Medicare Advantage plan MMM Healthcare LLC, as well as affiliated companies and Medicaid plan.

Anthem offers comprehensive health benefits, retirement plans and a variety of employee assistance programs.

FINANCIAL DATA: Note: Data for latest year may not have been available at press time.

In U.S. $	2020	2019	2018	2017	2016	2015
Revenue	121,867,000,000	104,213,000,000	92,105,000,000	90,039,400,000	84,863,000,000	79,156,500,000
R&D Expense						
Operating Income						
Operating Margin %						
SGA Expense	17,450,000,000	13,364,000,000	14,020,000,000	12,649,600,000	12,557,900,000	12,534,800,000
Net Income	4,572,000,000	4,807,000,000	3,750,000,000	3,842,800,000	2,469,800,000	2,560,000,000
Operating Cash Flow	10,688,000,000	6,061,000,000	3,827,000,000	4,184,800,000	3,204,500,000	4,116,000,000
Capital Expenditure	1,021,000,000	1,077,000,000	1,208,000,000	799,500,000	583,600,000	638,200,000
EBITDA						
Return on Assets %		.06%	.05%	.06%	.04%	.04%
Return on Equity %		.16%	.14%	.15%	.10%	.11%
Debt to Equity		0.561	0.603	0.656	0.572	0.665

CONTACT INFORMATION:

Phone: 317 488-6000   Fax:
Toll-Free: 800-331-1476
Address: 220 Virginia Ave., Indianapolis, IN 46204 United States

STOCK TICKER/OTHER:

Stock Ticker: ANTM   Exchange: NYS
Employees: 70,600   Fiscal Year Ends: 12/31
Parent Company:

SALARIES/BONUSES:

Top Exec. Salary: $ Bonus: $
Second Exec. Salary: $ Bonus: $

OTHER THOUGHTS:

Estimated Female Officers or Directors: 1
Hot Spot for Advancement for Women/Minorities: Y

AO Smith Corporation

NAIC Code: 335228

www.aosmith.com

TYPES OF BUSINESS:

Water Heaters
Water Boilers
Solar Water Heating Systems

BRANDS/DIVISIONS/AFFILIATES:

AO Smith
American Water Heaters
Aquasana
Clean Water Testing
Evolve
GSW
Hague Quality Water
John Wood

CONTACTS: *Note: Officers with more than one job title may be intentionally listed here more than once.*

William Vallett, CEO, Subsidiary
Ajita Rajendra, CEO
John Kita, CFO
Daniel Kempken, Chief Accounting Officer
Peter Martineau, Chief Information Officer
Robert Heideman, Chief Technology Officer
James Stern, Executive VP
Kevin Wheeler, General Manager, Geographical
Wei Ding, General Manager, Subsidiary
Paul Dana, President, Subsidiary
Wilfridus Brouwer, President, Subsidiary
Charles Lauber, Senior VP, Divisional
Mark Petrarca, Senior VP, Divisional

GROWTH PLANS/SPECIAL FEATURES:

A.O. Smith Corporation is a manufacturer of water heating equipment serving a diverse mix of residential, commercial and industrial end markets. The firm markets its products under several brand names, including AO Smith, American Water Heaters, Aquasana, Clean Water Testing, CustomCare, Evolve, GSW, Hague Quality Water, John Wood, Lochinvar, Mineral Right, Reliance Water Heaters, among others. The company operates in two segments: North America and rest of the world. The North America segment markets products mainly in the U.S. In addition, it manufactures and markets specialty commercial condensing and non-condensing boilers and water system tanks. The rest of the world segment does business in China, Europe and India. It manufactures and markets water treatment products, primarily for Asia. Both segments manufacture and market comprehensive lines of residential gas, gas tankless and electric water heaters. The firm's residential and commercial water heaters come in sizes ranging from 2.5-gallon (point-of-use) models to 2,500-gallon models with varying efficiency ranges. It offers electric, natural gas and liquid propane models as well as solar tank units. Typical applications include restaurants, hotels and motels, office buildings, laundries, car washes and small businesses. The company's commercial and residential boilers come in capacities ranging from 40,000 British Thermal Units (BTUs) to 6.0 million BTUs. The boilers are used in hospitals, schools, hotels and other large commercial buildings. Other products include expansion tanks, commercial solar water heating systems, swimming pool and spa heaters and related products and parts.

FINANCIAL DATA: *Note: Data for latest year may not have been available at press time.*

In U.S. $	2020	2019	2018	2017	2016	2015
Revenue	2,895,300,000	2,992,700,000	3,187,900,000	2,996,700,000	2,685,900,000	2,536,500,000
R&D Expense						
Operating Income	447,900,000	465,100,000	551,700,000	520,500,000	460,400,000	399,100,000
Operating Margin %		.16%	.17%	.17%	.17%	.16%
SGA Expense	660,300,000	715,600,000	753,800,000	718,200,000	658,900,000	610,700,000
Net Income	344,900,000	370,000,000	444,200,000	296,500,000	326,500,000	282,900,000
Operating Cash Flow	562,100,000	456,200,000	448,900,000	326,400,000	446,600,000	344,400,000
Capital Expenditure	56,800,000	64,400,000	85,200,000	94,200,000	80,700,000	72,700,000
EBITDA	531,200,000	561,400,000	638,100,000	601,000,000	534,900,000	472,900,000
Return on Assets %		.12%	.14%	.10%	.12%	.11%
Return on Equity %		.22%	.26%	.19%	.22%	.20%
Debt to Equity		0.19	0.129	0.244	0.209	0.164

CONTACT INFORMATION:

Phone: 414 359-4000   Fax:
Toll-Free:
Address: 11270 W. Park Pl., Milwaukee, WI 53224-9508 United States

STOCK TICKER/OTHER:

Stock Ticker: AOS
Employees: 13,900
Parent Company:

Exchange: NYS
Fiscal Year Ends: 12/31

SALARIES/BONUSES:

Top Exec. Salary: $ Bonus: $
Second Exec. Salary: $ Bonus: $

OTHER THOUGHTS:

Estimated Female Officers or Directors:
Hot Spot for Advancement for Women/Minorities:

Apple Inc
NAIC Code: 334220

TYPES OF BUSINESS:
Electronics Design and Manufacturing
Software
Computers and Tablets
Retail Stores
Smartphones
Online Music Store
Apps Store
Home Entertainment Software & Systems

BRANDS/DIVISIONS/AFFILIATES:
iPhone
iPad
Apple Watch
Apple TV
iOS
watchOS
HomePod
AirPods

CONTACTS: Note: Officers with more than one job title may be intentionally listed here more than once.
Timothy Cook, CEO
Luca Maestri, CFO
Arthur Levinson, Chairman of the Board
Chris Kondo, Chief Accounting Officer
Jeffery Williams, COO
Katherine Adams, General Counsel
Angela Ahrendts, Senior VP, Divisional
Deirdre O'Brien, Senior VP, Divisional

GROWTH PLANS/SPECIAL FEATURES:
Apple, Inc. designs, manufactures and markets personal computers, portable digital music players and mobile communication devices and sells a variety of related software, services, peripherals and networking applications. The company's products and services include iPhone, iPad, Mac, Apple Watch, Apple TV; a portfolio of consumer and professional software applications; iOS, macOS, watchOS and tvOS operating systems; iCloud, Apple Pay and a variety of accessory, service and support offerings. iPhone is the company's line of smartphones based on its iOS operating system. iCloud stores music, photos, contacts, calendars, mail, documents and more, keeping them up-to-date and available across multiple iOS devices, Mac and Windows personal computers and Apple TV. Other products include apple-branded and third-party accessories; the HomePod wireless speaker; AirPods wireless headphone; and iPod touch, a flash memory-based digital music and medial player that works with the iTunes store, App Store, iBooks store and Apple Music (collectively referred to as digital content and services) for purchasing and playing digital content and apps. The firm has brick and mortar stores worldwide, but also sells its products worldwide through online stores and direct sales force, as well as through third-party cellular network carriers, wholesalers, retailers and value-added resellers.

Apple offers employees comprehensive health benefits, retirement plans and various employee assistance programs.

FINANCIAL DATA: Note: Data for latest year may not have been available at press time.

In U.S. $	2020	2019	2018	2017	2016	2015
Revenue	274,515,000,000	260,174,000,000	265,595,000,000	229,234,000,000	215,639,000,000	233,715,000,000
R&D Expense	18,752,000,000	16,217,000,000	14,236,000,000	11,581,000,000	10,045,000,000	8,067,000,000
Operating Income	66,288,000,000	63,930,000,000	70,898,000,000	61,344,000,000	60,024,000,000	71,230,000,000
Operating Margin %		.25%	.27%	.27%	.28%	.30%
SGA Expense	19,916,000,000	18,245,000,000	16,705,000,000	15,261,000,000	14,194,000,000	14,329,000,000
Net Income	57,411,000,000	55,256,000,000	59,531,000,000	48,351,000,000	45,687,000,000	53,394,000,000
Operating Cash Flow	80,674,000,000	69,391,000,000	77,434,000,000	63,598,000,000	65,824,000,000	81,266,000,000
Capital Expenditure	7,309,000,000	10,495,000,000	13,313,000,000	12,795,000,000	13,548,000,000	11,488,000,000
EBITDA	81,020,000,000	81,860,000,000	87,046,000,000	76,569,000,000	73,333,000,000	84,505,000,000
Return on Assets %		.16%	.16%	.14%	.15%	.20%
Return on Equity %		.56%	.49%	.37%	.37%	.46%
Debt to Equity		1.015	0.875	0.725	0.588	0.448

CONTACT INFORMATION:
Phone: 408 996-1010   Fax: 408 974-2483
Toll-Free: 800-692-7753
Address: One Apple Park Way, Cupertino, CA 95014 United States

STOCK TICKER/OTHER:
Stock Ticker: AAPL   Exchange: NAS
Employees: 147,000   Fiscal Year Ends: 09/30
Parent Company:

SALARIES/BONUSES:
Top Exec. Salary: $ Bonus: $
Second Exec. Salary: $ Bonus: $

OTHER THOUGHTS:
Estimated Female Officers or Directors:
Hot Spot for Advancement for Women/Minorities:

Applied Materials Inc

www.appliedmaterials.com

NAIC Code: 333242

TYPES OF BUSINESS:

Semiconductor Manufacturing Equipment
LCD Display Technology Equipment
Automation Software
Energy Generation & Conversion Technologies

BRANDS/DIVISIONS/AFFILIATES:

CONTACTS: Note: Officers with more than one job title may be intentionally listed here more than once.

Gary Dickerson, CEO
Daniel Durn, CFO
James Morgan, Chairman Emeritus
Charles Read, Chief Accounting Officer
Omkaram Nalamasu, Chief Technology Officer
Thomas Iannotti, Director
Thomas Larkins, General Counsel
Ali Salehpour, Senior VP
Steve Ghanayem, Senior VP, Divisional
Prabu Raja, Senior VP, Divisional
Ginetto Addiego, Senior VP, Divisional

GROWTH PLANS/SPECIAL FEATURES:

Applied Materials, Inc. (AMI), a global leader in the semiconductor industry, provides manufacturing equipment, services and software to the global semiconductor, flat panel display, solar photovoltaic (PV) and related industries. AMI operates in three segments: semiconductor systems, applied global services and display and adjacent markets. The semiconductor systems division develops, manufactures and sells a range of manufacturing equipment used to fabricate semiconductor chips or integrated circuits. Technologies found in this segment are transistor and interconnect, patterning and packaging, and imaging and process control. The applied global services segment provides integrated solutions to optimize equipment and fab performance and productivity, including spares, upgrades, services, remanufactured earlier generation equipment and factory automation software for semiconductor, display and other products. Its services encompass the following components: fabrication services, automation systems and software, sub-fabrication systems and equipment, parts programs and abatement control systems. The display and adjacent market segment is comprised of products for manufacturing liquid crystal displays (LCDs), organic light-emitting diodes (OLEDs), and other display technologies for TVs, personal computers (PCs), tablets, smart phones, and other consumer-oriented devices as well as equipment for flexible substrates. The segment offers a variety of technologies and products, including: array testing, defect review, chemical vapor deposition, physical vapor deposition and flexible technologies. In late-2020, AMI and BE Semiconductor Industries NV announced an agreement to develop an equipment solution for die-based hybrid bonding, an emerging chip-to-chip interconnect technology that enables heterogenous chip and subsystem designs for applications including high-performance computing, artificial intelligence (AI) and 5G.

Applied Materials offers comprehensive benefits, retirement options and employee assistance programs.

FINANCIAL DATA: Note: Data for latest year may not have been available at press time.

In U.S. $	2020	2019	2018	2017	2016	2015
Revenue	17,202,000,000	14,608,000,000	17,253,000,000	14,537,000,000	10,825,000,000	9,659,000,000
R&D Expense	2,234,000,000	2,054,000,000	2,019,000,000	1,774,000,000	1,540,000,000	1,451,000,000
Operating Income	4,365,000,000	3,350,000,000	4,796,000,000	3,868,000,000	2,152,000,000	1,618,000,000
Operating Margin %		.23%	.28%	.27%	.20%	.17%
SGA Expense	1,093,000,000	982,000,000	1,002,000,000	890,000,000	819,000,000	883,000,000
Net Income	3,619,000,000	2,706,000,000	3,313,000,000	3,434,000,000	1,721,000,000	1,377,000,000
Operating Cash Flow	3,804,000,000	3,247,000,000	3,787,000,000	3,609,000,000	2,466,000,000	1,163,000,000
Capital Expenditure	422,000,000	441,000,000	622,000,000	345,000,000	253,000,000	215,000,000
EBITDA	4,782,000,000	3,869,000,000	5,385,000,000	4,336,000,000	2,557,000,000	2,072,000,000
Return on Assets %		.15%	.18%	.20%	.12%	.10%
Return on Equity %		.36%	.41%	.41%	.23%	.18%
Debt to Equity		0.574	0.776	0.567	0.436	0.439

CONTACT INFORMATION:

Phone: 408 727-5555   Fax: 408 727-9943
Toll-Free:
Address: 3050 Bowers Ave., Santa Clara, CA 95052 United States

STOCK TICKER/OTHER:

Stock Ticker: AMAT
Employees: 24,000
Parent Company:

Exchange: NAS
Fiscal Year Ends: 10/31

SALARIES/BONUSES:

Top Exec. Salary: $ Bonus: $
Second Exec. Salary: $ Bonus: $

OTHER THOUGHTS:

Estimated Female Officers or Directors: 2
Hot Spot for Advancement for Women/Minorities: Y

Archer-Daniels-Midland Company (ADM)   www.adm.com
NAIC Code: 311200

TYPES OF BUSINESS:
Food Processing-Oilseeds, Corn & Wheat
Agricultural Services
Nutraceuticals
Transportation Services
Biodiesel
Natural Plastics
Chocolate
Corn Syrups

BRANDS/DIVISIONS/AFFILIATES:
Pacificor
Wilmar International Limited
Hungrana Ltd
Almidones Mexicanos SA
Neovia SAS
Florida Chemical Company
Ziegler Group (The)
Gleadell Agriculture Ltd

CONTACTS: Note: Officers with more than one job title may be intentionally listed here more than once.
Thuy-Nga Vo, Assistant Secretary
Gregory Morris, Pres., Divisional
Juan Luciano, CEO
Ray Young, CFO
John Stott, Chief Accounting Officer
Kristy Folkwein, Chief Information Officer
Stefano Rettore, Chief Risk Officer
Todd Werpy, Chief Technology Officer
D. Findlay, General Counsel
Benjamin Bard, Other Executive Officer
Patricia Logan, Other Executive Officer
Ismael Roig, Other Executive Officer
Pierre Duprat, President, Divisional
Christopher Cuddy, President, Divisional
Vincent Macciocchi, President, Divisional
Joseph Taets, President, Divisional

GROWTH PLANS/SPECIAL FEATURES:
Archer-Daniels-Midland Company (ADM) produces food and beverage ingredients, and other products made from a variety of agricultural products. ADM operates through three business segments, including Ag services and oilseeds, carbohydrate solutions, and nutrition. The Ag services and oilseeds segment includes global activities related to the origination, merchandising, transportation and storage of agricultural raw materials, and the crushing and further processing of oilseeds such as soybeans and soft seeds (cottonseed, sunflower seed, canola, rapeseed and flaxseed) into vegetable oils and protein meals. Oilseeds products produced and marketed by this division include ingredients for food, feed, energy and industrial customers. Joint ventures within this segment include Pacificor, Wilmar International Limited, Stratas Foods LLC, Edible Oils Limited, Olenex Sarl, and SoyVen. The carbohydrate solutions segment engages in corn and wheat wet and dry milling and other activities. This division converts corn and wheat into products and ingredients used in the food and beverage industry, including sweeteners, corn and wheat starches, syrup, glucose, wheat flour and dextrose. Joint ventures within this segment include Hungrana Ltd., Almidones Mexicanos SA, Red Star Yeast Company LLC, and Aston Foods and Food Ingredients. Last, the nutrition segment serves customer needs for food, beverages, health and wellness, and more by manufacturing, selling and distributing a wide array of products such as plant-based proteins, natural flavor ingredients, flavor systems, natural colors, emulsifiers, soluble fibers, polyols, hydrocolloids, probiotics, prebiotics, enzymes, botanical extracts and other specialty food and feed ingredients. Subsidiaries in this segment include Neovia SAS, Florida Chemical Company, The Ziegler Group, and Gleadell Agriculture Ltd.

ADM offers its employees comprehensive health and financial benefits and learning/development opportunities.

FINANCIAL DATA: Note: Data for latest year may not have been available at press time.

In U.S. $	2020	2019	2018	2017	2016	2015
Revenue	64,355,000,000	64,656,000,000	64,341,000,000	60,828,000,000	62,346,000,000	67,702,000,000
R&D Expense						
Operating Income	1,766,000,000	1,654,000,000	2,016,000,000	1,513,000,000	1,639,000,000	2,010,000,000
Operating Margin %		.03%	.03%	.02%	.03%	.03%
SGA Expense	2,687,000,000	2,493,000,000	2,165,000,000	1,993,000,000	2,045,000,000	2,010,000,000
Net Income	1,772,000,000	1,379,000,000	1,810,000,000	1,595,000,000	1,279,000,000	1,849,000,000
Operating Cash Flow	-2,386,000,000	-5,452,000,000	-4,784,000,000	2,211,000,000	1,475,000,000	2,481,000,000
Capital Expenditure	823,000,000	828,000,000	842,000,000	1,049,000,000	882,000,000	1,125,000,000
EBITDA	3,198,000,000	2,983,000,000	3,365,000,000	2,863,000,000	3,015,000,000	3,474,000,000
Return on Assets %		.03%	.04%	.04%	.03%	.04%
Return on Equity %		.07%	.10%	.09%	.07%	.10%
Debt to Equity		0.399	0.406	0.362	0.379	0.323

CONTACT INFORMATION:
Phone: 312-634-8100   Fax:
Toll-Free: 800-637-5843
Address: 77 West Wacker Dr., Ste. 4600, Chicago, IL 60601 United States

STOCK TICKER/OTHER:
Stock Ticker: ADM
Employees: 38,100
Parent Company:

Exchange: NYS
Fiscal Year Ends: 12/31

SALARIES/BONUSES:
Top Exec. Salary: $ Bonus: $
Second Exec. Salary: $ Bonus: $

OTHER THOUGHTS:
Estimated Female Officers or Directors: 4
Hot Spot for Advancement for Women/Minorities: Y

Arrow Electronics Inc
www.arrow.com

NAIC Code: 423430

TYPES OF BUSINESS:
Electronic Components-Distributor
Computer Products-Distributor
Technical Support Services
Supply Chain Services
Design Services
Materials Planning
Assembly Services
Inventory Management

BRANDS/DIVISIONS/AFFILIATES:

CONTACTS: Note: Officers with more than one job title may be intentionally listed here more than once.
Michael Long, CEO
Sean J. Kerins, COO
Christopher Stansbury, CFO
Richard Seidlitz, Chief Accounting Officer
Vincent Melvin, Chief Information Officer
Gregory Tarpinian, Chief Legal Officer
Mary Morris, Chief Strategy Officer
Matthew Anderson, Other Executive Officer
Chuck Kostalnick, Other Executive Officer
Gretchen Zech, Other Executive Officer
Sean Kerins, President, Divisional
Andy King, President, Divisional

GROWTH PLANS/SPECIAL FEATURES:
Arrow Electronics, Inc. is a global provider of products, services and solutions to industrial and commercial users of electronic components and enterprise computing software. Products and solutions include materials planning, new product design services, programming and assembly services, inventory management, reverse logistics, electronics asset disposition (EAD) and a variety of online supply chain tools. Arrow serves as a supply channel partner for over 175,000 original equipment manufacturers (OEMs), contract manufacturers and commercial customers through a global network of over 300 sales facilities and 49 distribution centers serving over 80 countries. Its operations are divided into two segments: global enterprise computing solutions (ECS), representing 30% of sales, and the global components business, 70%. The global ECS segment distributes enterprise IT products, such as servers, software and storage devices, as well as midrange computing products, services and solutions to value added retailers (VARs) in North America and Europe, the Middle East and Africa (EMEA). This segment also provides unified communications products and related services in North America. The global components business segment distributes electronics components and related products to customers in North and South America, EMEA and the Asia-Pacific. Its sales consist of semiconductors; passive, electro-mechanical and interconnect products, such as capacitors, resistors, potentiometers, power supplies, relays, switches and connectors; and computing, memory and other products.

FINANCIAL DATA: Note: Data for latest year may not have been available at press time.

In U.S. $	2020	2019	2018	2017	2016	2015
Revenue	28,673,360,000	28,916,850,000	29,676,770,000	26,812,510,000	23,825,260,000	23,282,020,000
R&D Expense						
Operating Income	915,022,000	916,979,000	1,211,477,000	1,040,744,000	932,141,000	893,247,000
Operating Margin %		.03%	.04%	.04%	.04%	.04%
SGA Expense	2,087,050,000	2,191,612,000	2,303,051,000	2,162,996,000	2,052,863,000	1,986,249,000
Net Income	584,438,000	-204,087,000	716,195,000	401,962,000	522,750,000	497,726,000
Operating Cash Flow	1,359,843,000	857,995,000	272,690,000	124,557,000	355,806,000	655,079,000
Capital Expenditure	124,298,000	150,807,000	155,336,000	203,949,000	164,695,000	154,800,000
EBITDA	1,085,527,000	281,703,000	1,310,528,000	1,011,697,000	1,025,307,000	983,338,000
Return on Assets %		-.01%	.04%	.03%	.04%	.04%
Return on Equity %		-.04%	.14%	.09%	.12%	.12%
Debt to Equity		0.549	0.608	0.592	0.611	0.575

CONTACT INFORMATION:
Phone: 300 824-4000   Fax:
Toll-Free:
Address: 9201 E. Dry Creek Rd., Centennial, CO 80112 United States

STOCK TICKER/OTHER:
Stock Ticker: ARW
Employees: 19,600
Parent Company:

Exchange: NYS
Fiscal Year Ends: 12/31

SALARIES/BONUSES:
Top Exec. Salary: $ Bonus: $
Second Exec. Salary: $ Bonus: $

OTHER THOUGHTS:
Estimated Female Officers or Directors: 4
Hot Spot for Advancement for Women/Minorities: Y

Ashley Furniture Industries Inc

www.ashleyfurniture.com

NAIC Code: 337121

TYPES OF BUSINESS:

Furniture Manufacturing & Distribution
Franchising of Furniture Stores
Mattresses

BRANDS/DIVISIONS/AFFILIATES:

Ashley Furniture HomeStores

CONTACTS: Note: Officers with more than one job title may be intentionally listed here more than once.

Todd R. Wanek, CEO
Gino Mangione, Corp. Controller
Ronald G. Wanek, Chmn.

GROWTH PLANS/SPECIAL FEATURES:

Ashley Furniture Industries, Inc. is one of the nation's largest furniture manufacturers. The firm manufactures and imports upholstered, leather and hardwood furniture for living rooms, home offices and dining rooms as well as bedding and other furniture for bedrooms. Its products include stationary upholstered and leather furniture, recliners, sectionals, chairs, desks, dining room sets, entertainment centers, curios, lamps and tables. The firm is known for its glossy finish Millennium line of furniture as well as its Ashley Sleep brand mattresses. Ashley retails its furniture through licensed operating agreements with 1,000 independently owned and operated Ashley Furniture HomeStores in addition to third-party furniture retailers. Ashley Furniture HomeStores market only Ashley products and maintain locations in more than 35 countries, but the company offers its product assortments to 6,000+ retail partners with over 20,000 storefronts in 123 countries. Ashley has manufacturing and distribution facilities worldwide. More than one-half of its furniture is made in the U.S., with the balance imported from Asia. While its sofa and chair frames are made in the U.S., the fabric is cut and sewn in Asia. The company operates its own fleet of delivery trucks.

The company offers employees medical, life, disability and dental insurance; 401(k); tuition reimbursement; and a profit sharing plan.

FINANCIAL DATA: Note: Data for latest year may not have been available at press time.

In U.S. $	2020	2019	2018	2017	2016	2015
Revenue	6,500,000,000	5,000,000,000	4,700,000,000	4,815,000,000	4,600,000,000	4,150,000,000
R&D Expense						
Operating Income						
Operating Margin %						
SGA Expense						
Net Income						
Operating Cash Flow						
Capital Expenditure						
EBITDA						
Return on Assets %						
Return on Equity %						
Debt to Equity						

CONTACT INFORMATION:

Phone: 608-323-3377   Fax: 608-323-6008
Toll-Free:
Address: One Ashley Way, Arcadia, WI 54612 United States

STOCK TICKER/OTHER:

Stock Ticker: Private   Exchange:
Employees: 22,500   Fiscal Year Ends: 12/31
Parent Company:

SALARIES/BONUSES:

Top Exec. Salary: $ Bonus: $
Second Exec. Salary: $ Bonus: $

OTHER THOUGHTS:

Estimated Female Officers or Directors:
Hot Spot for Advancement for Women/Minorities:

Associated Wholesale Grocers Inc   www.awginc.com
NAIC Code: 445110

TYPES OF BUSINESS:
Grocery Stores, Retail
In-Store Pharmacies
Bakeries
Delis
Wholesale Grocery Distribution
Retail Support Services

BRANDS/DIVISIONS/AFFILIATES:
Country Mart
Price Chopper
Sun Fresh
Thriftway
Apple Market
CashSaver
IGA
Valu Merchandisers Company

CONTACTS: *Note: Officers with more than one job title may be intentionally listed here more than once.*
David Smith, CEO
Steve Dillard, VP-Corp. Sales Dev.
Barry Queen, Chmn.

GROWTH PLANS/SPECIAL FEATURES:
Associated Wholesale Grocers, Inc. (AWG) is a grocery co-operative. The firm supplies more than 3,800 stores throughout the U.S. AWG has developed several different store concepts depending on which market area the store is located. Country Mart is a warehouse-oriented, low-price store designed for small towns and rural areas. Price Chopper stores are among the company's most successful concepts, with large amounts of floor space, low prices, in-store pharmacies, salad bars, seafood and poultry departments, full-service bakeries and delis. Sun Fresh is an upscale store generally located in high-density residential areas and is focused on providing high-quality fresh foods. Thriftway is a convenient neighborhood store located in small and medium-sized market areas. Apple Market stores focus on providing high-quality perishables in a warm atmosphere and large store format. CashSaver stores attempt to combine savings without sacrificing quality in small to medium-sized markets. Finally, IGA is the world's largest voluntary supermarket network. Valu Merchandisers Company, AWG's wholesale distribution subsidiary, carries roughly 43,000 items, including health and beauty care products, specialty foods and dollar grocery items, general merchandise items and seasonal and promotional products. The subsidiary sells its products to stores in 35 states. The firm's services division offers programs focusing on advertising, training, print shop, store engineering, design and decor, electronic data exchange, real estate reclamation and retail systems support.

FINANCIAL DATA: *Note: Data for latest year may not have been available at press time.*

In U.S. $	2020	2019	2018	2017	2016	2015
Revenue	10,634,379,000	9,666,303,000	9,614,686,000	9,703,821,000	9,183,802,000	8,935,915,000
R&D Expense						
Operating Income						
Operating Margin %						
SGA Expense						
Net Income	284,394,000	215,381,000	212,845,000	199,103,000	189,907,000	198,919,000
Operating Cash Flow						
Capital Expenditure						
EBITDA						
Return on Assets %						
Return on Equity %						
Debt to Equity						

CONTACT INFORMATION:
Phone: 913-288-1000   Fax: 913-288-1587
Toll-Free:
Address: 5000 Kansas Ave., Kansas City, KS 66106 United States

STOCK TICKER/OTHER:
Stock Ticker: Private   Exchange:
Employees: 21,000   Fiscal Year Ends: 12/31
Parent Company:

SALARIES/BONUSES:
Top Exec. Salary: $ Bonus: $
Second Exec. Salary: $ Bonus: $

OTHER THOUGHTS:
Estimated Female Officers or Directors:
Hot Spot for Advancement for Women/Minorities:

Sales, profits and employees may be estimates. Financial information, benefits and other data can change quickly and may vary from those stated here.

AT Kearney Inc

NAIC Code: 541610

www.kearney.com

TYPES OF BUSINESS:

Management Consulting
Technology Consulting
Retail Consulting
Government Consulting
Manufacturing Consulting
Transportation Consulting
Supply Chain Consulting
Industry Research & Publications

BRANDS/DIVISIONS/AFFILIATES:

Kearney
Global Business Policy Council

GROWTH PLANS/SPECIAL FEATURES:

A.T. Kearney, Inc., operating as Kearney, is a global consulting firm involved in a wide variety of industries. It works alongside clients to create bespoke, collaborative, analytical and entrepreneurial solutions. Kearney specializes in transformation services, mergers/acquisitions, digital, procurement, operations/performance, strategy, top-line, analytics, leadership, change, organization and Global Business Policy Council services and solutions. The Global Business Policy Council was designed to give a select companies prescient information on global market trends. Industries served by the company include energy, chemicals, metals, mining, public sector, financial services, health, aerospace, defense, communications, media, technology, infrastructure, transportation, travel, private equity, industrial goods, automotive consumer goods and retail. Kearney maintains offices in major business centers in over 40 countries.

CONTACTS: *Note: Officers with more than one job title may be intentionally listed here more than once.*

Christine Laurens, CFO
Abby Klanecky, CMO
Stephen Parker, Chief Human Resources Officer
Daniel Mahler, Head-The Americas
Luca Rossi, Head-EMEA
Laura Gurski, Head-Global Practices
Alex Liu, Chmn.
John Kurtz, Head-Asia Pacific

FINANCIAL DATA: *Note: Data for latest year may not have been available at press time.*

In U.S. $	2020	2019	2018	2017	2016	2015
Revenue	1,456,000,000	1,400,000,000	1,300,000,000	1,100,000,000	1,120,000,000	1,150,000,000
R&D Expense						
Operating Income						
Operating Margin %						
SGA Expense						
Net Income						
Operating Cash Flow						
Capital Expenditure						
EBITDA						
Return on Assets %						
Return on Equity %						
Debt to Equity						

CONTACT INFORMATION:

Phone: 312-648-0111   Fax: 312-223-6200
Toll-Free:
Address: 227 W. Monroe St., Chicago, IL 60606 United States

STOCK TICKER/OTHER:

Stock Ticker: Private   Exchange:
Employees: 3,500   Fiscal Year Ends: 12/31
Parent Company:

SALARIES/BONUSES:

Top Exec. Salary: $ Bonus: $
Second Exec. Salary: $ Bonus: $

OTHER THOUGHTS:

Estimated Female Officers or Directors: 1
Hot Spot for Advancement for Women/Minorities:

AT&T Inc

NAIC Code: 517110

TYPES OF BUSINESS:

Local Telephone Service
Wireless Telecommunications
Long-Distance Telephone Service
Corporate Telecom, Backbone & Wholesale Services
Internet Access
Entertainment & Television via Internet
Satellite TV
VOIP

BRANDS/DIVISIONS/AFFILIATES:

WanerMedia
Xandr
AT&T
Cricket
AT&T PREPAID
Home Box Office Inc (HBO)
Warner Bros Entertainment Inc
Vrio

CONTACTS: Note: Officers with more than one job title may be intentionally listed here more than once.

Brian Lesser, CEO, Divisional
John Stankey, CEO, Subsidiary
John Donovan, CEO, Subsidiary
Lori Lee, CEO, Subsidiary
Randall Stephenson, CEO
John Stephens, CFO
David Huntley, Chief Compliance Officer
David McAtee, General Counsel
William Blase, Senior Executive VP, Divisional

GROWTH PLANS/SPECIAL FEATURES:

AT&T, Inc. is one of the world's largest providers of diversified telecommunications services. The company and its subsidiaries offers communications, digital entertainment services and products to consumers in the U.S., Mexico and Latin America, as well as to businesses and other providers of telecommunications services worldwide. AT&T also owns and operates three regional sports networks. Services and products include wireless communications, data/broadband and internet services, digital video services, local and long-distance telephone services, telecommunications equipment, managed networking and wholesale services. The company operates through four business segments: communication, generating over 75% of operating revenues; WarnerMedia; Latin America; and Xandr. The communications segment provides mobile, broadband, video and other communications services to over 166 million U.S.-based consumers, and products and services are marketed under the AT&T, Cricket, AT&T PREPAID and DIRECTV brand names. The WanerMedia segment consists of the operations of Home Box Office, Inc. (HBO); Turner Broadcasting System, Inc. (Turner); and Warner Bros Entertainment, Inc. Together these firms create premium content, operate one of the largest TV and film studios and own a vast library of entertainment. The Latin America business provides entertainment and wireless services outside the U.S. through its Vrio segment, which provides video services in Latin America, and its Mexico segment, which provides wireless service and equipment to customers in Mexico. The Xandr segment provides advertising services using data (on an anonymous basis) from the firm's more than 170 million customer relationships to develop digital advertising that is more relevant to consumers. In November 2020, AT&T completed its sale of its wireless and wireline operations in Puerto Rico and the U.S. Virgin Islands to Liberty Latin America for $1.95 billion. The following month, the firm agreed to sell its Crunchyroll anime business to Sony's Funimation Global Group, LLC.

FINANCIAL DATA: Note: Data for latest year may not have been available at press time.

In U.S. $	2020	2019	2018	2017	2016	2015
Revenue	171,760,000,000	181,193,000,000	170,756,000,000	160,546,000,000	163,786,000,000	146,801,000,000
R&D Expense						
Operating Income	25,285,000,000	29,413,000,000	26,142,000,000	23,863,000,000	24,708,000,000	24,785,000,000
Operating Margin %		.16%	.15%	.15%	.15%	.17%
SGA Expense	38,039,000,000	39,422,000,000	36,765,000,000	34,917,000,000	36,347,000,000	32,954,000,000
Net Income	-5,176,000,000	13,903,000,000	19,370,000,000	29,450,000,000	12,976,000,000	13,345,000,000
Operating Cash Flow	43,130,000,000	48,668,000,000	43,602,000,000	39,151,000,000	39,344,000,000	35,880,000,000
Capital Expenditure	15,675,000,000	19,435,000,000	20,758,000,000	20,647,000,000	21,516,000,000	19,218,000,000
EBITDA	42,188,000,000	64,694,000,000	65,032,000,000	45,826,000,000	50,569,000,000	46,828,000,000
Return on Assets %		.03%	.04%	.07%	.03%	.04%
Return on Equity %		.08%	.12%	.22%	.11%	.13%
Debt to Equity		0.94	0.903	0.894	0.923	0.966

CONTACT INFORMATION:

Phone: 210 821-4105   Fax:
Toll-Free:
Address: 208 S. Akard St., Dallas, TX 75202 United States

STOCK TICKER/OTHER:

Stock Ticker: T
Employees: 230,000
Parent Company:

Exchange: NYS
Fiscal Year Ends: 12/31

SALARIES/BONUSES:

Top Exec. Salary: $ Bonus: $
Second Exec. Salary: $ Bonus: $

OTHER THOUGHTS:

Estimated Female Officers or Directors: 4
Hot Spot for Advancement for Women/Minorities: Y

AT&T Mobility LLC

NAIC Code: 517210

www.att.com/wireless

TYPES OF BUSINESS:

Mobile Phone and Wireless Services
Wireless Data Services
Cell Phone Services

BRANDS/DIVISIONS/AFFILIATES:

AT&T Inc
AT&T Wireless

GROWTH PLANS/SPECIAL FEATURES:

AT&T Mobility, LLC, also referred to as AT&T Wireless, is a leading wireless telecommunications service provider predominantly serving the U.S. The wholly-owned subsidiary of AT&T, Inc. provides wireless voice and data services to consumer and wholesale subscribers. AT&T Mobility offers a comprehensive range of nationwide wireless voice and data communications services in a variety of pricing plans, including postpaid and prepaid service plans. The firm provides 5G services in select locations throughout the U.S., which offers seamless connection and ultra-fast speeds at home, business or on-the-go. AT&T also offers 5G phones and devices for 5G connection and compatibility.

CONTACTS:
Note: Officers with more than one job title may be intentionally listed here more than once.

John T. Stankey, CEO-Corporate
Ralph de la Vega, Pres.

FINANCIAL DATA:
Note: Data for latest year may not have been available at press time.

In U.S. $	2020	2019	2018	2017	2016	2015
Revenue	72,564,000,000	71,056,000,000	70,521,000,000	70,259,000,000	72,587,000,000	73,705,000,000
R&D Expense						
Operating Income						
Operating Margin %						
SGA Expense						
Net Income	22,372,000,000	22,321,000,000	21,568,000,000	20,204,000,000	20,743,000,000	19,803,000,000
Operating Cash Flow						
Capital Expenditure						
EBITDA						
Return on Assets %						
Return on Equity %						
Debt to Equity						

CONTACT INFORMATION:

Phone: 404-236-7895 Fax:
Toll-Free:
Address: 1025 Lenox Park Blvd., Atlanta, GA 30319 United States

STOCK TICKER/OTHER:

Stock Ticker: Subsidiary Exchange:
Employees: 40,000 Fiscal Year Ends: 12/31
Parent Company: AT&T Inc

SALARIES/BONUSES:

Top Exec. Salary: $ Bonus: $
Second Exec. Salary: $ Bonus: $

OTHER THOUGHTS:

Estimated Female Officers or Directors:
Hot Spot for Advancement for Women/Minorities:

athenahealth Inc

www.athenahealth.com

NAIC Code: 524292

TYPES OF BUSINESS:

Outsourced Health Reimbursement Services
Patient Information Management
Billing & Collection Services for Health Care Providers
Automated Messaging
Telehealth Solutions

BRANDS/DIVISIONS/AFFILIATES:

Veritas Capital
Evergreen Coast Capital
Virence Health Technologies

GROWTH PLANS/SPECIAL FEATURES:

athenahealth, Inc. is a provider of network-enabled services and mobile applications for medical groups and health systems. Services and solutions provided by the company include electronic health records, medical billing, patient engagement, care coordination, enterprise revenue cycle, telehealth, mobile capabilities and advisory services. athenahealth primarily serves obstetrics/gynecology groups, orthopedic groups, federally-qualified health centers (FQHCs), health plans, member-centric organizations, startups and ancillary service providers. The company offers an embedded telehealth solution, ranging from scheduling to billing, for both clinicians and patients. athenahealth is privately-held by Veritas Capital and Evergreen Coast Capital. The firm is combined with Veritas' Virence Health Technologies, but operates under the athenahealth brand.

athenahealth offers comprehensive benefits to its employees.

CONTACTS: Note: Officers with more than one job title may be intentionally listed here more than once.

Bob Segert, CEO
Karl Salnoske, Sr. VP-Oper. & Cloud Engineering
Jeffrey Immelt, Chairman of the Board
Luis Borgen, CFO
William J. Conway, Chief Sales Officer
Fran Lawler, Chief Human Resources Officer
Paul Brient, Chief Product Officer
Stephen Kahane, Other Corporate Officer
Kyle Armbrester, Other Executive Officer
Jonathan Porter, Other Executive Officer
Simon Mouyal, CMO

FINANCIAL DATA: Note: Data for latest year may not have been available at press time.

In U.S. $	2020	2019	2018	2017	2016	2015
Revenue	1,465,750,000	1,430,000,000	1,300,000,000	1,220,300,032	1,082,899,968	924,728,000
R&D Expense						
Operating Income						
Operating Margin %						
SGA Expense						
Net Income		55,245,240	54,162,000	53,100,000	21,000,000	14,027,000
Operating Cash Flow						
Capital Expenditure						
EBITDA						
Return on Assets %						
Return on Equity %						
Debt to Equity						

CONTACT INFORMATION:

Phone: 617 402-1000   Fax: 617 402-1099
Toll-Free: 800-981-5084
Address: 311 Arsenal St., Watertown, MA 02472 United States

STOCK TICKER/OTHER:

Stock Ticker: Private
Employees: 5,305
Parent Company: Veritas Capital

Exchange:
Fiscal Year Ends: 12/31

SALARIES/BONUSES:

Top Exec. Salary: $ Bonus: $
Second Exec. Salary: $ Bonus: $

OTHER THOUGHTS:

Estimated Female Officers or Directors: 1
Hot Spot for Advancement for Women/Minorities:

Averitt Express Inc

www.averittexpress.com

NAIC Code: 484122

TYPES OF BUSINESS:

General Freight Trucking, Less than Truckload
Logistics Services
Freight Forwarding Services
Supply Chain Management
Express Freight Trucking
Air Freight
LTL Freight
International Shipping

BRANDS/DIVISIONS/AFFILIATES:

Reliance Network (The)
ATOM System

CONTACTS: *Note: Officers with more than one job title may be intentionally listed here more than once.*

Gary D. Sasser, CEO
Wayne Spain, COO
Johnny Fields, CFO
Phil Pierce, Exec. VP-Mktg. & Sales
Gary D. Sasser, Chmn.

GROWTH PLANS/SPECIAL FEATURES:

Averitt Express, Inc. is a full-service transportation and logistics services provider with service centers and thousands of delivery points throughtout the U.S., Canada, Mexico and the Caribbean. It serves over 300 international destinations in more than 100 countries by way of air, sea or ground. Averitt has 4,600 tractors and nearly 15,000 trailers in its ground fleet. The firm's services include less-than-truckload (LTL), truckload, expedited, international ocean/air, supply chain management and warehousing. Its regional LTL services cover the entire Southeastern area of the U.S., while its membership in The Reliance Network provides full coverage to North America. Expedited services include various options, such as emergency air, emergency ground and a blended mode, which combines services in a cost-effective manner. Additionally, it offers 24-hour expedited ground or air transport. International ocean/air services include less-than-container load (LCL) or full container load (FCL) shipments, LTL, truckload, freight forwarding, consolidation and distribution as well as its Asia-Memphis express service, which loads containers in Asia and delivers straight to its distribution center in Memphis, Tennessee. The supply chain management division supplies facility operations, dedicated fleet operations, transport network design and operation as well as complete transport management. Its supply chain management technology solutions include the ATOM System, which provides scalable features such as multi-carrier shipment management, bill auditing and shipping network optimization. Its warehousing and other services are provided through a network of 143 service center, port facilities and supply chain sites across the U.S.

Averitt Express, Inc. offers employees a benefits package that includes medical, dental, vision and prescription packages; a savings plan; a profit-sharing plan; and life and disability insurance.

FINANCIAL DATA: *Note: Data for latest year may not have been available at press time.*

In U.S. $	2020	2019	2018	2017	2016	2015
Revenue	1,202,500,000	1,300,000,000	1,146,970,000	1,091,450,000	1,078,436,000	1,078,000,000
R&D Expense						
Operating Income						
Operating Margin %						
SGA Expense						
Net Income						
Operating Cash Flow						
Capital Expenditure						
EBITDA						
Return on Assets %						
Return on Equity %						
Debt to Equity						

CONTACT INFORMATION:

Phone: 931-526-3306   Fax: 931-520-5603
Toll-Free: 800-283-7488
Address: 1415 Neal St., Cookeville, TN 38502 United States

STOCK TICKER/OTHER:

Stock Ticker: Private
Employees: 9,500
Parent Company:

Exchange:
Fiscal Year Ends: 12/31

SALARIES/BONUSES:

Top Exec. Salary: $ Bonus: $
Second Exec. Salary: $ Bonus: $

OTHER THOUGHTS:

Estimated Female Officers or Directors:
Hot Spot for Advancement for Women/Minorities:

Avnet Inc

NAIC Code: 423430

TYPES OF BUSINESS:

Components-Distributor
Marketing Services
Supply Chain Advisory Services

BRANDS/DIVISIONS/AFFILIATES:

Premier Farnell Ltd
element14
Witekio

CONTACTS: Note: Officers with more than one job title may be intentionally listed here more than once.

Phil Gallagher, CEO
Beth McMullen, Global VP, Operations
Tom Liguori, CFO
Dayna Badhorn, Global VP, Corporate Marketing
Ken Arnold, Chief People Officer
Max Chan, CIO
MaryAnn Miller, Other Corporate Officer
Therese Bassett, Other Executive Officer
Peter Bartolotta, Other Executive Officer
Michael O'Neill, Other Executive Officer
Philip Gallagher, President, Divisional

GROWTH PLANS/SPECIAL FEATURES:

Avnet, Inc. is one of the world's largest value-added distributors of electronic components. The firm creates a link in the technology supply chain that connects electronic component manufacturers with a global customer base primarily comprised of original equipment manufacturers (OEMs), electronic manufacturing services (EMS) providers and original design manufacturers (ODMs). The company works with over 1,400 technology suppliers to serve 2.1 million customers in more than 125 countries. Avnet operates through two primary groups: electronic components and Premier Farnell Ltd. Both groups have operations in the Americas, Europe, the Middle East, Africa, Asia, Australia and New Zealand. The electronics components group markets and sells semiconductors, electronic components and other integrated components from leading electronic component manufacturers. These products and services cater to a diverse customer base, serving end-markets such as automotive, communications, computer hardware/peripherals, industrial, manufacturing, medical equipment and defense and aerospace. Premier Farnell globally distributes a comprehensive portfolio of electronic components, typically in small order quantities, primarily to support design engineers, maintenance and test engineers, makers and entrepreneurs as they develop technology products. Premier Farnell operates element14, an online engineering community of more than 500,000 active user members from which purchasers and engineers can access peers, experts, technical information and proprietary tools in relation to the latest products, services and development software. Witekio is under the Avent umbrella; offers expertise in software and embedded systems that help developers overcome the technical challenges and complexity of developing Internet of Things (IoT) solutions.

Avnet employees receive life, AD&D, disability, travel accident, medical, dental and vision insurance; flexible spending accounts; a pension plan; a 401(k); an employee stock purchase plan; and tuition reimbursement.

FINANCIAL DATA: Note: Data for latest year may not have been available at press time.

In U.S. $	2020	2019	2018	2017	2016	2015
Revenue	17,634,330,000	19,518,590,000	19,036,890,000	17,439,960,000	26,219,280,000	
R&D Expense						
Operating Income	221,334,000	611,451,000	557,081,000	598,815,000	866,987,000	
Operating Margin %		.03%	.03%	.03%	.03%	
SGA Expense	1,842,122,000	1,874,651,000	1,970,103,000	1,770,627,000	2,170,524,000	
Net Income	-31,081,000	176,337,000	-156,424,000	525,278,000	506,531,000	
Operating Cash Flow	730,182,000	534,770,000	253,485,000	-368,691,000	224,315,000	
Capital Expenditure	73,516,000	122,690,000	155,873,000	120,397,000	147,548,000	
EBITDA	237,530,000	557,984,000	482,474,000	572,455,000	896,043,000	
Return on Assets %		.02%	-.02%	.05%	.05%	
Return on Equity %		.04%	-.03%	.11%	.11%	
Debt to Equity		0.343	0.318	0.334	0.285	

CONTACT INFORMATION:

Phone: 480 643-2000   Fax: 480 643-7370
Toll-Free: 800-409-1483
Address: 2211 S. 47th St., Phoenix, AZ 85034 United States

STOCK TICKER/OTHER:

Stock Ticker: AVT
Employees: 14,600
Parent Company:

Exchange: NAS
Fiscal Year Ends: 06/30

SALARIES/BONUSES:

Top Exec. Salary: $ Bonus: $
Second Exec. Salary: $ Bonus: $

OTHER THOUGHTS:

Estimated Female Officers or Directors: 2
Hot Spot for Advancement for Women/Minorities: Y

AVX Corporation

NAIC Code: 334413

TYPES OF BUSINESS:

Electronic Equipment-Capacitors
Advanced Electronic Components
Interconnect Sensors
Antenna Solutions
Manufacturing
Circuit Protection
Inductors
Thermistors

BRANDS/DIVISIONS/AFFILIATES:

Kyocera Corporation

GROWTH PLANS/SPECIAL FEATURES:

AVX Corporation is a manufacturer and international supplier of advanced electronic components and interconnect sensor, control and antenna solutions. The company has more than 30 research, design, manufacturing and customer support facilities in 16 countries worldwide. Other products and solutions include circuit protection, diodes, filters, inductors, modules, passive micro components, resistive products, radio frequency (RF) and microwave products, thermistors and more. AVX's delivery and production capabilities are used to suit its customer's inventory requirements, and its global engineering teams develop new-to-market product solutions specifically designed to fulfill their unique application requirements. The firm serves the automotive, industrial, medical, military, consumer electronics, communications and transportation markets. AVX operates as a subsidiary of Kyocera Corporation.

CONTACTS: *Note: Officers with more than one job title may be intentionally listed here more than once.*

John Sarvis, CEO
Michael Hufnagel, CFO
Evan Slavitt, General Counsel
Eric Pratt, Senior VP, Divisional
S. King, Senior VP, Divisional
Alexander Schenkel, Senior VP, Divisional
Steven Sturgeon, Senior VP, Divisional

FINANCIAL DATA: *Note: Data for latest year may not have been available at press time.*

In U.S. $	2020	2019	2018	2017	2016	2015
Revenue	1,827,625,751	1,791,789,952	1,562,473,984	1,312,660,992	1,195,528,960	1,353,228,032
R&D Expense						
Operating Income						
Operating Margin %						
SGA Expense						
Net Income	277,249,251	271,812,992	4,910,000	125,785,000	101,535,000	225,871,008
Operating Cash Flow						
Capital Expenditure						
EBITDA						
Return on Assets %						
Return on Equity %						
Debt to Equity						

CONTACT INFORMATION:

Phone: 864 967-2150   Fax:
Toll-Free:
Address: 1 AVX Blvd., Fountain Inn, SC 29644-9039 United States

STOCK TICKER/OTHER:

Stock Ticker: Subsidiary   Exchange:
Employees: 10,800   Fiscal Year Ends: 03/31
Parent Company: Kyocera Corporation

SALARIES/BONUSES:

Top Exec. Salary: $ Bonus: $
Second Exec. Salary: $ Bonus: $

OTHER THOUGHTS:

Estimated Female Officers or Directors: 1
Hot Spot for Advancement for Women/Minorities:

B&G Foods Inc

www.bgfoods.com

NAIC Code: 311421

TYPES OF BUSINESS:
Food Products Manufacturing
Shelf-Stable Products
Seasonings
Processed Meat Products

BRANDS/DIVISIONS/AFFILIATES:
Ortega
Green Giant
B&G
Maple Grove Farms of Vermont
Regina
Don Pepino
Crisco

CONTACTS: Note: Officers with more than one job title may be intentionally listed here more than once.
Kenneth Romanzi, CEO
Bruce Wacha, CFO
Stephen Sherrill, Chairman of the Board
Michael Adasczik, Chief Accounting Officer
Scott Lerner, Chief Compliance Officer
William Herbes, Executive VP, Divisional
Eric Hart, Executive VP, Divisional
Erich Fritz, Executive VP
Jordan Greenberg, Executive VP
Ellen Schum, Executive VP

GROWTH PLANS/SPECIAL FEATURES:
B&G Foods, Inc. manufactures, sells and distributes more than 50 brand-named foods with long shelf lives throughout the U.S, Canada and Puerto Rico. The firm produces a range of spreads, syrups, condiments, seasonings, canned goods and other processed foods under numerous national and regional brands. Some of its many product lines include Ortega taco shells, seasonings, dinner kits, taco sauce, peppers, refried beans, salsa and related food products; Green Giant vegetables; B&G pickles, olives, sauerkraut and relishes; Maple Grove Farms of Vermont salad dressings, marinades, syrups, confections and pancake mixes; Dash-branded spices and seasonings; Polaner fruit-based spreads and jarred wet spices; Emeril's seasonings, salad dressings, marinades, pepper sauces, barbecue sauces and pasta sauces; Regina vinegar and cooking wines; Cream of Wheat and Cream of Rice products; Don Pepino pizza and spaghetti sauces; and Grandma's molasses. The firm sells its products to supermarket chains, foodservice outlets, mass merchants, warehouse clubs, dollar stores, drug store chains and specialty food distributors. In December 2020, B&G Foods acquired the Crisco brand of oils and shortening from The J.M. Smucker Co. for $550 million in cash, including the manufacturing facility and warehouse in Cincinnati, Ohio.

FINANCIAL DATA: Note: Data for latest year may not have been available at press time.

In U.S. $	2020	2019	2018	2017	2016	2015
Revenue	1,967,909,000	1,660,414,000	1,700,764,000	1,668,056,000	1,391,257,000	966,358,000
R&D Expense						
Operating Income	276,438,000	203,836,000	163,768,000	239,402,000	259,400,000	172,370,000
Operating Margin %		.12%	.10%	.14%	.19%	.18%
SGA Expense	186,191,000	160,745,000	167,389,000	205,234,000	174,759,000	105,939,000
Net Income	131,988,000	76,389,000	172,435,000	217,463,000	109,425,000	69,090,000
Operating Cash Flow	281,477,000	46,504,000	209,456,000	37,799,000	289,661,000	128,479,000
Capital Expenditure	26,748,000	42,355,000	41,627,000	59,802,000	42,418,000	18,574,000
EBITDA	354,656,000	273,948,000	384,250,000	289,018,000	288,788,000	201,023,000
Return on Assets %		.02%	.05%	.07%	.04%	.03%
Return on Equity %		.09%	.19%	.26%	.18%	.17%
Debt to Equity		2.346	1.818	2.518	2.183	3.771

CONTACT INFORMATION:
Phone: 973 401-6500   Fax: 973 364-1037
Toll-Free: 866-211-8151
Address: Four Gatehall Dr., Parsippany, NJ 07054 United States

STOCK TICKER/OTHER:
Stock Ticker: BGS
Employees: 3,207
Parent Company:

Exchange: NYS
Fiscal Year Ends: 12/31

SALARIES/BONUSES:
Top Exec. Salary: $ Bonus: $
Second Exec. Salary: $ Bonus: $

OTHER THOUGHTS:
Estimated Female Officers or Directors: 1
Hot Spot for Advancement for Women/Minorities: Y

Bain & Company Inc

NAIC Code: 541610

TYPES OF BUSINESS:

Management Consulting
Management Consulting
Digital Transformation
Analytics

BRANDS/DIVISIONS/AFFILIATES:

Results Delivery
Bain Media Lab

CONTACTS: *Note: Officers with more than one job title may be intentionally listed here more than once.*

Manny Maceda, Managing Dir.
Dave Johnson, Managing Dir.-The Americas
Dale Cottrell, Managing Dir.-Asia Pacific
Orit Gadiesh, Chmn.
Paul Meehan, Managing Dir.-EMEA

GROWTH PLANS/SPECIAL FEATURES:

Bain & Company, Inc. is a global provider of management consulting services. The firm advises clients on their most critical issues and opportunities, including strategy, marketing, organization, operations, information technology (IT), digital transformation, digital strategy, advanced analytics, transformations, sustainability, corporate finance and mergers and acquisitions, across all industries and geographies. Bain & Company's approach to change management is through its Results Delivery platform, which helps clients measure and manage risk and overcome the odds to realize results. The company has worked with the majority of the Global 500, as well as major regional and local organizations, nonprofits and private equity funds representing 75% of global equity capital. Bain Media Lab is the firm's business unit engaged in creating digital products and related services, combining breakthrough technologies with powerful data sets. Headquartered in Massachusetts, USA, Bain & Company has offices across North and South America, Europe, Africa, Asia and Australia.

Bain tends to hire college graduates with either liberal arts degrees, MBA degrees or both. Positions often involve extensive travel and sometimes major relocation, the costs of which are reimbursed by Bain.

FINANCIAL DATA: *Note: Data for latest year may not have been available at press time.*

In U.S. $	2020	2019	2018	2017	2016	2015
Revenue	4,600,000,000	4,300,000,000	3,800,000,000	2,700,000,000	2,500,000,000	2,300,000,000
R&D Expense						
Operating Income						
Operating Margin %						
SGA Expense						
Net Income						
Operating Cash Flow						
Capital Expenditure						
EBITDA						
Return on Assets %						
Return on Equity %						
Debt to Equity						

CONTACT INFORMATION:

Phone: 617-572-2000   Fax: 617-572-2427
Toll-Free:
Address: 131 Dartmouth St., Boston, MA 02116 United States

SALARIES/BONUSES:

Top Exec. Salary: $ Bonus: $
Second Exec. Salary: $ Bonus: $

STOCK TICKER/OTHER:

Stock Ticker: Private   Exchange:
Employees: 8,000   Fiscal Year Ends: 12/31
Parent Company:

OTHER THOUGHTS:

Estimated Female Officers or Directors: 1
Hot Spot for Advancement for Women/Minorities:

Ball Corporation

www.ball.com

NAIC Code: 332431

TYPES OF BUSINESS:

Metal Can Manufacturing
Civil Space Systems
Defense Systems
Commercial Space Systems
Metal Food and Household Products Packaging
Radio Frequency and Microwave Technology
Metal Beverage Packaging

BRANDS/DIVISIONS/AFFILIATES:

Tubex Industria E Comercio de Embalagens Ltda

CONTACTS: Note: Officers with more than one job title may be intentionally listed here more than once.

John Hayes, CEO
Scott Morrison, CFO
Nate Carey, Chief Accounting Officer
Daniel Fisher, COO, Geographical
Charles Baker, General Counsel
Robert Strain, President, Subsidiary
Lisa Pauley, Senior VP, Divisional
Jeffrey Knobel, Treasurer

GROWTH PLANS/SPECIAL FEATURES:

Ball Corporation is a leading manufacturer of metal packaging for the food and beverage, personal care and household products industries. It also supplies aerospace and other technologies and services to governmental and commercial customers within Ball's aerospace segment. The firm's packaging businesses are responsible for 85% of the company's net sales, with the remaining 15% by the aerospace business. Ball's largest product line is aluminum beverage containers; but the company also produces aerosol containers, extruded aluminum aerosol containers and aluminum slugs. The packaging products are primarily sold to large multinational beverage, personal care and household products companies, including The Coca-Cola Company and its affiliated bottlers, Anheuser-Busch InBev nv/sa, among others. The aerospace business designs, develops and manufactures innovative aerospace systems for civil, commercial and national cyber security aerospace markets. It produces spacecraft, instruments and sensors, radio frequency systems and components, data exploitation solutions and a variety of advanced aerospace technologies and products that enable deep space missions. In 2020, Ball Corporation completed its acquisition of Tubex Industria E Comercio de Embalagens Ltda, an aluminum aerosol packaging business with a plant near Sao Paolo, Brazil. In mid-2021, Ball Corporation announced plans to build new aluminum beverage packaging plants in the U.K. and Russia, each of which would produce billions of cans each year across a range of formats and sizes, and provide up to 200 jobs. Production is expected to begin by 2023.

FINANCIAL DATA: Note: Data for latest year may not have been available at press time.

In U.S. $	2020	2019	2018	2017	2016	2015
Revenue	11,781,000,000	11,474,000,000	11,635,000,000	10,983,000,000	9,061,000,000	7,997,000,000
R&D Expense						
Operating Income	1,265,000,000	1,176,000,000	1,126,000,000	1,023,000,000	800,000,000	799,900,000
Operating Margin %		.10%	.10%	.09%	.09%	.10%
SGA Expense	525,000,000	417,000,000	478,000,000	514,000,000	512,000,000	451,300,000
Net Income	585,000,000	566,000,000	454,000,000	374,000,000	263,000,000	280,900,000
Operating Cash Flow	1,432,000,000	1,548,000,000	1,566,000,000	1,478,000,000	194,000,000	1,006,700,000
Capital Expenditure	1,113,000,000	598,000,000	816,000,000	556,000,000	606,000,000	527,900,000
EBITDA	1,630,000,000	1,603,000,000	1,636,000,000	1,528,000,000	807,000,000	774,200,000
Return on Assets %		.03%	.03%	.02%	.02%	.03%
Return on Equity %		.18%	.12%	.10%	.11%	.25%
Debt to Equity		2.21	1.883	1.654	2.128	4.039

CONTACT INFORMATION:

Phone: 303 469-3131   Fax: 303 460-2127
Toll-Free:
Address: 9200 West 108th Cir., Westminster, CO 80021 United States

STOCK TICKER/OTHER:

Stock Ticker: BLL
Employees: 18,300
Parent Company:

Exchange: NYS
Fiscal Year Ends: 12/31

SALARIES/BONUSES:

Top Exec. Salary: $ Bonus: $
Second Exec. Salary: $ Bonus: $

OTHER THOUGHTS:

Estimated Female Officers or Directors: 2
Hot Spot for Advancement for Women/Minorities: Y

Bank of America Corporation

www.bankofamerica.com

NAIC Code: 522110

TYPES OF BUSINESS:

Banking
Asset Management
Investment & Brokerage Services
Mortgages
Credit Cards
Insurance Agency

BRANDS/DIVISIONS/AFFILIATES:

CONTACTS: *Note: Officers with more than one job title may be intentionally listed here more than once.*

Brian Moynihan, CEO
Sheri Bronstein, Other Executive Officer
Paul Donofrio, CFO
Rudolf Bless, Chief Accounting Officer
Andrea Smith, Chief Administrative Officer
Geoffrey Greener, Chief Risk Officer
Catherine Bessant, Chief Technology Officer
Thomas Montag, COO
David Leitch, General Counsel
Dean Athanasia, President, Divisional
Kathleen Knox, President, Subsidiary
Andrew Sieg, President, Subsidiary

GROWTH PLANS/SPECIAL FEATURES:

Bank of America Corporation is a bank holding and a financial holding company, through which its subsidiaries provide a diversified range of related services on a global basis. The company operates through four primary business segments: consumer banking, global wealth and investment management (GWIM), global banking and global markets. Consumer banking provides deposit and lending services, as well as small business client management services, consumer and small business credit card services, debit card services, consumer vehicle lending and home loan options. GWIM offers Merrill Lynch branded global wealth management, as well as U.S. trust services and private wealth management services. Global banking offers investment banking, global corporate banking, global commercial banking and business banking services. The global markets segment offers fixed income and equity market products. Other activities by Bank of America include asset and liability management (ALM), equity investments, international consumer cards, merchant services, liquidating services, residual expense allocation services and more.

Bank of America offers its employees benefits including tuition and adoption reimbursement; medical, dental and vision insurance plans; employee assistance programs; and health care and dependent care flexible spending accounts.

FINANCIAL DATA: *Note: Data for latest year may not have been available at press time.*

In U.S. $	2020	2019	2018	2017	2016	2015
Revenue	86,266,000,000	91,244,000,000	91,247,000,000	87,352,000,000	83,701,000,000	82,246,000,000
R&D Expense						
Operating Income						
Operating Margin %						
SGA Expense	46,378,000,000	46,715,000,000	45,911,000,000	47,154,000,000	46,408,000,000	47,962,000,000
Net Income	17,894,000,000	27,430,000,000	28,147,000,000	18,232,000,000	17,906,000,000	15,888,000,000
Operating Cash Flow	37,993,000,000	61,777,000,000	39,520,000,000	10,403,000,000	18,306,000,000	27,730,000,000
Capital Expenditure						
EBITDA						
Return on Assets %		.01%	.01%	.01%	.01%	.01%
Return on Equity %		.11%	.11%	.07%	.07%	.06%
Debt to Equity		0.998	0.944	0.929	0.897	1.012

CONTACT INFORMATION:

Phone: 704 386-5681   Fax:
Toll-Free: 800-432-1000
Address: 100 N. Tryon St., Charlotte, NC 28255 United States

STOCK TICKER/OTHER:

Stock Ticker: BAC
Employees: 213,000
Parent Company:

Exchange: NYS
Fiscal Year Ends: 12/31

SALARIES/BONUSES:

Top Exec. Salary: $ Bonus: $
Second Exec. Salary: $ Bonus: $

OTHER THOUGHTS:

Estimated Female Officers or Directors: 8
Hot Spot for Advancement for Women/Minorities: Y

Bank of New York Mellon Corporation

www.bnymellon.com

NAIC Code: 522110

TYPES OF BUSINESS:

Asset Management & Securities Services
Investment & Wealth Management
Private Banking
Shareowner Services
Broker-Dealer Services
Issuer Services
Treasury Services

BRANDS/DIVISIONS/AFFILIATES:

Bank of New York Mellon (The)
BNY Mellon National Association
Bank of New York Mellon Trust Company, NA (The)
BNY Mellon Trust of Delaware
BNY Mellon Investment Servicing Trust Co
BNY Mellon Trust Company of Illinois
Pershing LLC

CONTACTS: Note: Officers with more than one job title may be intentionally listed here more than once.

Lester Owens, Sr. VP
Roman Regelman, Other Corporate Officer
Hani Kablawi, CEO, Divisional
Francis Salla, CEO, Divisional
Mitchell Harris, CEO, Divisional
Thomas Gibbons, CEO, Divisional
Charles Scharf, CEO
Michael Santomassimo, CFO
Kurtis Kurimsky, Chief Accounting Officer
Bridget Engle, Chief Information Officer
James Wiener, Chief Risk Officer
J. Mccarthy, General Counsel
Akash Shah, Other Corporate Officer
Monique Herena, Other Exec. Officer

GROWTH PLANS/SPECIAL FEATURES:

Bank of New York Mellon Corporation (BNYM) is a global investment company providing asset management and securities services for individual investors, institutions and corporations in 35 countries and more than 100 markets. In addition, BNYM offers financial solutions for individuals, including investment and wealth management, private banking and shareowner services. The company works with consultants and advisors to help them select the services that best meet their customers' needs. The firm has two principal banking subsidiaries: The Bank of New York Mellon and BNY Mellon, National Association (NA), which provide trust and custody activities, investment management services, banking services and various securities-related activities. Additionally, the firm has four other U.S. bank and/or trust company subsidiaries concentrating on trust products and services across the nation: The Bank of New York Mellon Trust Company NA, BNY Mellon Trust of Delaware, BNY Mellon Investment Servicing Trust Company and BNY Mellon Trust Company of Illinois. Most of the asset management businesses are direct or indirect non-bank subsidiaries of BNY Mellon. Through Pershing, LLC, the firm offers broker-dealer and advisor services. Pershing is a provider of clearing, execution and financial business solutions to institutional and retail financial organizations and independent registered investment advisors. BNYM's issuer service offerings include global corporate trust services, depositary receipt services and shareowner services. The company also offers treasury services. BNYM has approximately $1.9 trillion in assets under management and $37.1 trillion in assets under administration or custody. Customers include corporations, foundations, governments, unions, endowments, mutual funds and high-net-worth individuals.

Employees are offered medical, vision and dental health plans; life insurance; and an array of retirement plans varying by location.

FINANCIAL DATA: Note: Data for latest year may not have been available at press time.

In U.S. $	2020	2019	2018	2017	2016	2015
Revenue	15,506,000,000	16,170,000,000	16,040,000,000	15,401,000,000	14,832,000,000	14,813,000,000
R&D Expense						
Operating Income						
Operating Margin %						
SGA Expense	5,966,000,000	6,063,000,000	6,145,000,000	5,972,000,000	5,733,000,000	5,837,000,000
Net Income	3,617,000,000	4,441,000,000	4,266,000,000	4,090,000,000	3,547,000,000	3,158,000,000
Operating Cash Flow	5,038,000,000	96,000,000	5,996,000,000	4,641,000,000	6,246,000,000	4,127,000,000
Capital Expenditure	1,222,000,000	1,210,000,000	1,108,000,000	1,197,000,000	825,000,000	601,000,000
EBITDA						
Return on Assets %		.01%	.01%	.01%	.01%	.01%
Return on Equity %		.11%	.11%	.11%	.10%	.08%
Debt to Equity		0.725	0.786	0.742	0.694	0.607

CONTACT INFORMATION:

Phone: 212 495-1784   Fax:
Toll-Free:
Address: 240 Greenwich St., New York, NY 10286 United States

STOCK TICKER/OTHER:

Stock Ticker: BK
Employees: 48,400
Parent Company:

Exchange: NYS
Fiscal Year Ends: 12/31

SALARIES/BONUSES:

Top Exec. Salary: $ Bonus: $
Second Exec. Salary: $ Bonus: $

OTHER THOUGHTS:

Estimated Female Officers or Directors: 6
Hot Spot for Advancement for Women/Minorities: Y

Sales, profits and employees may be estimates. Financial information, benefits and other data can change quickly and may vary from those stated here.

Bass Pro Shops Inc

NAIC Code: 451110

TYPES OF BUSINESS:

Sporting Goods, Retail
Sport Boats
Hunting & Fishing Equipment
Catalog & Online Sales
Outdoor Apparel
Resort Operations
Television Production

BRANDS/DIVISIONS/AFFILIATES:

Bass Pro Shops
RedHead
Offshore Angler
White River Fly Shops
Tracker Marine Group
American Rod & Gun
Wonders of Wildlife
Big Cedar Lodge

CONTACTS: *Note: Officers with more than one job title may be intentionally listed here more than once.*

John L. Morris, CEO
Martin G. MacDonald, Dir.-Conservation

GROWTH PLANS/SPECIAL FEATURES:

Bass Pro Shops, Inc. is a leader in sporting goods retail. The company markets its products through over 90 Bass Pro Shops retail stores in the U.S. and Canada, as well as through mail-order catalog and ecommerce sites. The firm provides outdoor recreational products, including specialty apparel, and also aims to inspire environmental conservation among its customers. Products include boats and campers as well as fishing, hunting, camping, automobile and marine supplies. Many of these stores have a variety of unique features and attractions to draw more customers, including restaurants, snack bars, archery ranges, aquariums, waterfalls and video arcades. Aside from its stores, the company sells goods over the internet and through catalogs/sales flyers under the Bass Pro Shops, RedHead, Offshore Angler and White River Fly Shops brand names. Its wholesale operations consist of Tracker Marine Group, a leader in sport boat manufacturing, and American Rod & Gun, one of the largest wholesale hunting and fishing distributors in the country. In addition to offering a variety of hunting and fishing trips and contests, Bass Pro runs the Wonders of Wildlife facility, a museum and conservation education center near its corporate headquarters, and Big Cedar Lodge, an outdoors-themed vacation spot in Missouri located near the company's own nature park, Dogwood Canyon Adventure Park. The company also produces a weekly television program on The Outdoor Channel and an international radio show.

FINANCIAL DATA: *Note: Data for latest year may not have been available at press time.*

In U.S. $	2020	2019	2018	2017	2016	2015
Revenue	5,675,670,000	5,159,700,000	4,914,000,000	4,680,000,000	4,620,000,000	4,500,000,000
R&D Expense						
Operating Income						
Operating Margin %						
SGA Expense						
Net Income						
Operating Cash Flow						
Capital Expenditure						
EBITDA						
Return on Assets %						
Return on Equity %						
Debt to Equity						

CONTACT INFORMATION:

Phone: 417-873-5000   Fax: 417-873-5060
Toll-Free: 800-227-7776
Address: 2500 E. Kearney St., Springfield, MO 65898 United States

STOCK TICKER/OTHER:

Stock Ticker: Private   Exchange:
Employees: 40,000   Fiscal Year Ends: 12/31
Parent Company:

SALARIES/BONUSES:

Top Exec. Salary: $ Bonus: $
Second Exec. Salary: $ Bonus: $

OTHER THOUGHTS:

Estimated Female Officers or Directors:
Hot Spot for Advancement for Women/Minorities:

Baxter International Inc

www.baxter.com

NAIC Code: 339100

TYPES OF BUSINESS:

Medical Equipment Manufacturing
Supplies-Intravenous & Renal Dialysis Systems
Medication Delivery Products & IV Fluids
Biopharmaceutical Products
Plasma Collection & Processing
Vaccines
Software
Contract Research

BRANDS/DIVISIONS/AFFILIATES:

Cheetah Medical inc
Seprafilm

CONTACTS: Note: Officers with more than one job title may be intentionally listed here more than once.

Jose Almeida, CEO
James Saccaro, CFO
Brian Stevens, Chief Accounting Officer
Sean Martin, General Counsel
Andrew Frye, President, Geographical
Giuseppe Accogli, President, Geographical
Cristiano Franzi, President, Geographical
Scott Pleau, Senior VP, Divisional
Jeanne Mason, Senior VP, Divisional

GROWTH PLANS/SPECIAL FEATURES:

Baxter International, Inc., through its subsidiaries, provides a broad portfolio of essential healthcare products. These offerings include: acute and chronic dialysis therapies; sterile intravenous (IV) solutions; infusion systems and devices; parenteral nutrition therapies; inhaled anesthetics; generic injectable pharmaceuticals; and surgical hemostat and sealant products. In addition, Baxter's renal portfolio addresses the needs of patients with kidney failure or kidney disease. This portfolio includes innovative technologies and therapies for peritoneal dialysis, in-center and home hemodialysis, continuous renal replacement therapy, multi-organ extracorporeal support therapy, and additional dialysis services. Baxter's scientists are currently pursuing a range of next-generation monitors, dialyzers, devices, dialysis solutions and connectivity technology for home patients. Baxter manufactures its products in several countries, and sells them in more than 100 countries worldwide. The majority of the firm's revenues (approximately 60%) are generated outside the U.S., with an international presence including operations in Europe (Eastern and Central Europe), the Middle East, Africa, Asia-Pacific, Latin America and Canada. Each of these regions provide a wide range of essential healthcare products across the company's entire portfolio. Baxter maintains manufacturing facilities worldwide. During 2020, Baxter International acquired Cheetah Medical, Inc., a provider of non-invasive hemodynamic monitoring technologies; and acquired Sanofi's Seprafilm adhesion barrier product line, complementing Baxter's hemostat and sealant portfolio used in surgery procedures.

FINANCIAL DATA: Note: Data for latest year may not have been available at press time.

In U.S. $	2020	2019	2018	2017	2016	2015
Revenue	11,673,000,000	11,362,000,000	11,127,000,000	10,561,000,000	10,163,000,000	9,968,000,000
R&D Expense	521,000,000	595,000,000	655,000,000	617,000,000	647,000,000	603,000,000
Operating Income	1,551,000,000	876,000,000	1,647,000,000	1,258,000,000	724,000,000	449,000,000
Operating Margin %		.08%	.15%	.12%	.07%	.05%
SGA Expense	2,515,000,000	3,290,000,000	2,569,000,000	2,587,000,000	2,739,000,000	3,094,000,000
Net Income	1,102,000,000	1,001,000,000	1,624,000,000	717,000,000	4,965,000,000	968,000,000
Operating Cash Flow	1,868,000,000	2,104,000,000	2,096,000,000	1,837,000,000	1,654,000,000	1,647,000,000
Capital Expenditure	709,000,000	696,000,000	681,000,000	634,000,000	719,000,000	911,000,000
EBITDA	2,268,000,000	1,870,000,000	2,571,000,000	2,063,000,000	5,843,000,000	1,333,000,000
Return on Assets %		.06%	.10%	.04%	.27%	.04%
Return on Equity %		.13%	.19%	.08%	.58%	.11%
Debt to Equity		0.675	0.446	0.385	0.335	0.445

CONTACT INFORMATION:

Phone: 847 948-2000   Fax: 847 948-2964
Toll-Free: 800-422-9837
Address: 1 Baxter Pkwy., Deerfield, IL 60015 United States

SALARIES/BONUSES:

Top Exec. Salary: $ Bonus: $
Second Exec. Salary: $ Bonus: $

STOCK TICKER/OTHER:

Stock Ticker: BAX
Employees: 50,000
Parent Company:

Exchange: NYS
Fiscal Year Ends: 12/31

OTHER THOUGHTS:

Estimated Female Officers or Directors: 6
Hot Spot for Advancement for Women/Minorities: Y

Baylor Scott & White Health

NAIC Code: 622110

www.bswhealth.com

TYPES OF BUSINESS:

General Medical and Surgical Hospitals
Long-Term Care
Retirement & Nursing Homes
Retail Pharmacies
Rehabilitation Services

BRANDS/DIVISIONS/AFFILIATES:

Baylor Health Care System
Scott & White Healthcare
MyBSWHealth
FollowMyHealth

CONTACTS: Note: Officers with more than one job title may be intentionally listed here more than once.

Pete McCanna, CEO
Jennifer Mitzner, CFO
Nikki Moll, Sr. VP-Mktg. & Communications
Nakesha Lopez, Chief Human Resources Officer
Matthew Chambers, CIO
Alejandro Arroliga, Chief Medical Officer

GROWTH PLANS/SPECIAL FEATURES:

Baylor Scott & White Health is a non-profit healthcare system in Texas, and created through the 2013 combination of Baylor Health Care System and Scott & White Healthcare. Today, Baylor Scott & White includes 52 hospitals, more than 800 patient care sites and over 7,300 active physicians. The firm provides full-range, inpatient, outpatient, rehabilitation and emergency medical services, serving more than 7.5 million patients each year. Specialties include allergy, anesthesiology, back and neck care, behavioral and psychological health, breast imaging, cancer care, dentistry, diabetes, ear/nose/throat, genetics, heart/vascular, hospice, infectious diseases, kidney disease, lung care, men's health, neuroscience, pediatric care, pharmacy, rheumatology, sleep disorders, surgical services, transplants, urology, weight loss surgery and more. Appointments can be made by phone and online, and patient registration and billing can also be completed online. MyBSWHealth and FollowMyHealth enable patients to access their personal health records, set or change appointments, view test results and communicate with providers from any computer, tablet or smartphone device. Insurance products are available including a variety of health plans as well as dental and life insurance.

FINANCIAL DATA: Note: Data for latest year may not have been available at press time.

In U.S. $	2020	2019	2018	2017	2016	2015
Revenue	1,158,505,975	982,475,378	960,710,546	946,738,753	938,248,557	877,345,140
R&D Expense						
Operating Income						
Operating Margin %						
SGA Expense						
Net Income	-136,407,231	-17,194,766	-23,838,306	-16,448,684	7,205,412	-17,805,755
Operating Cash Flow						
Capital Expenditure						
EBITDA						
Return on Assets %						
Return on Equity %						
Debt to Equity						

CONTACT INFORMATION:

Phone: 254-724-2111   Fax:
Toll-Free: 844-279-3627
Address: 301 N. Washington Ave., Dallas, TX 75246 United States

STOCK TICKER/OTHER:

Stock Ticker: Nonprofit
Employees: 49,000
Parent Company:

Exchange:
Fiscal Year Ends: 06/30

SALARIES/BONUSES:

Top Exec. Salary: $ Bonus: $
Second Exec. Salary: $ Bonus: $

OTHER THOUGHTS:

Estimated Female Officers or Directors:
Hot Spot for Advancement for Women/Minorities:

Sales, profits and employees may be estimates. Financial information, benefits and other data can change quickly and may vary from those stated here.

Bechtel Group Inc

NAIC Code: 237000

www.bechtel.com

TYPES OF BUSINESS:

Heavy Construction
Civic Engineering
Procurement
Infrastructure
Defense
Chemicals
Water Solutions
Advanced Energy Solutions

BRANDS/DIVISIONS/AFFILIATES:

CONTACTS: *Note: Officers with more than one job title may be intentionally listed here more than once.*

Brendan Bechtel, CEO
Craig Albert, Pres.
Catherine Hunt Ryan, CFO
Justin Zaccaria, Chief Human Resources Officer
Michael Bailey, General Counsel
Charlene Wheeless, Head-Corp. Affairs
Anette Sparks, Controller
Steve Katzman, Pres., Asia
Jose Ivo, Pres., Americas
Charlene Wheeless, Head-Sustainability Svcs.
Michael Wilkinson, Head-Risk Mgmt.
Brendan Bechtel, Chmn.
David Welch, Pres., EMEA

GROWTH PLANS/SPECIAL FEATURES:

Bechtel Group, Inc. is one of the world's largest engineering companies. The privately-owned firm offers engineering, procurement and construction management services (EPC), with a broad project portfolio including road and rail systems, airports and seaports, nuclear power plants, petrochemical facilities, mines, defense and aerospace facilities, environmental cleanup projects, telecommunication networks, pipelines and oil fields development. Bechtel has seven areas of expertise: infrastructure; defense & nuclear security; environmental cleanup; chemicals; water; energy; and mining & metals. The infrastructure segment oversees projects pertaining to wired and wireless telecommunications, power, ports, harbors, bridges, airports and airport systems, commercial and light-industrial buildings, wireless sites, railroads, rapid-transit and rail systems. The defense & nuclear security segment includes missile defense infrastructure, scientific and national security facility operations, commercial and U.S. navy nuclear reactor services and chemical weapons dematerialization projects. The environmental cleanup segment offers cleanup & remediation, waste processing & disposal and decontamination & decommissioning services. The chemicals segment helps customers that create facilities to produce finished polymers and other end-products such as ethylene, polyethylene, polypropylene, butylenes, polyester and polyethylene terephthalate (PET), and polyvinyl chloride. It assists with process design packages and technology through licensors for polyethylene, polypropylene, vinyls and other products. The energy segment offers solutions in areas such as advanced fuels, carbon capture, combined/simple cycle, emissions retrofits, energy technologies, hydrogen, liquefied natural gas (LNG), nuclear power and transmission and storage. The water segment offers large-scale conveyance & tunneling, industrial water solutions, water planning for new cities and hydroelectric power & pumped storage solutions. Last, the mining & metal segment encompasses mining and metal projects across six continents, including procurement, construction, engineering and solutions for mining of coal, ferrous, industrial and nonferrous metals.

Bechtel Group offers its employees comprehensive health and retirement benefits.

FINANCIAL DATA: *Note: Data for latest year may not have been available at press time.*

In U.S. $	2020	2019	2018	2017	2016	2015
Revenue	17,600,000,000	21,800,000,000	25,500,000,000	25,900,000,000	32,900,000,000	32,300,000,000
R&D Expense						
Operating Income						
Operating Margin %						
SGA Expense						
Net Income						
Operating Cash Flow						
Capital Expenditure						
EBITDA						
Return on Assets %						
Return on Equity %						
Debt to Equity						

CONTACT INFORMATION:

Phone: 571-392-6300   Fax:
Toll-Free:
Address: 12011 Sunset Hills Rd, Reston, VA 20190 United States

STOCK TICKER/OTHER:

Stock Ticker: Private   Exchange:
Employees: 38,000   Fiscal Year Ends: 12/31
Parent Company:

SALARIES/BONUSES:

Top Exec. Salary: $ Bonus: $
Second Exec. Salary: $ Bonus: $

OTHER THOUGHTS:

Estimated Female Officers or Directors: 4
Hot Spot for Advancement for Women/Minorities: Y

Sales, profits and employees may be estimates. Financial information, benefits and other data can change quickly and may vary from those stated here.

Beckman Coulter Inc

NAIC Code: 334510

www.beckmancoulter.com

TYPES OF BUSINESS:

Electromedical and Electrotherapeutic Apparatus Manufacturing
Chemistry Systems
Genetic Analysis/Nucleic Acid Testing
Biomedical Research Supplies
Immunoassay Systems
Cellular Systems
Discovery & Automation Systems

BRANDS/DIVISIONS/AFFILIATES:

Danaher Corporation
Access SARS-CoV-2 IgM

CONTACTS: *Note: Officers with more than one job title may be intentionally listed here more than once.*

Julie Sawyer-Montgomery, Pres.
Marianne Ovesen, Sr. VP-Global Oper.
Chris Hagen, VP-Global Mktg.
Mickey Blanks, Sr. VP-Human Resources & Communications
Pedro Diaz, Dir.-Research
John Blackwood, Sr. VP-Product Mgmt.
Jeff Linton, Sr. VP
Ken Hyek, Dir.-Service Oper.
Allan Harris, Sr. VP-Strategy & Bus. Dev.
Jerry Battenberg, VP-Finance
Clair O'Donovan, Sr. VP-Quality & Regulatory Affairs
Jennifer Honeycutt, Pres., Life Sciences
Richard Creager, Sr. VP
Michael K. Samoszuk, VP
Brian Burnett, Sr. VP-Global Oper.

GROWTH PLANS/SPECIAL FEATURES:

Beckman Coulter, Inc., a wholly-owned subsidiary of Danaher Corporation, designs, develops, manufactures and markets clinical diagnostic products and laboratory solutions. The company's products and solutions are used in clinical settings worldwide to deliver test result. Disciplines of the firm encompass automation, blood banking, clinical chemistry, clinical centrifugation, clinical information management tools, hematology, immunoassay, microbiology, protein chemistry and urinalysis. Diagnostic solutions include sepsis diagnosis and management, early sepsis indicator, cardiovascular disease, reproductive health, anemia, drug monitoring & detection and life sciences. Beckman's Access SARS-CoV-2 Immunoglobulin M (IgM) assay is an antibody test that demonstrated 99.9% specificity against 1,400 negative samples and 98.3% sensitivity at 15-30 days post-symptom onset. Access SARS-CoV-2 IgG II received U.S. Emergency Use Authorization from the U.S. Food and Drug Administration in 2021, which measures a patient's level of antibodies in response to a previous SARS-CoV-2 infection and provides a qualitative and numerical result of antibodies in arbitrary units. Headquartered in California, the firm has additional centers in Minnesota and Florida.

Beckman offers its employees medical, dental and vision coverage; a wellness program; a 401(k) and company retirement plan; life insurance; disability income protection; credit union membership; and employee discounts.

FINANCIAL DATA: *Note: Data for latest year may not have been available at press time.*

In U.S. $	2020	2019	2018	2017	2016	2015
Revenue	6,232,950,000	6,561,000,000	6,257,000,000	5,839,000,000	5,050,000,000	5,000,000,000
R&D Expense						
Operating Income						
Operating Margin %						
SGA Expense						
Net Income						
Operating Cash Flow						
Capital Expenditure						
EBITDA						
Return on Assets %						
Return on Equity %						
Debt to Equity						

CONTACT INFORMATION:

Phone: 714-993-5321   Fax: 800-232-3828
Toll-Free: 800-526-3821
Address: 250 S. Kraemer Blvd., Brea, CA 92821 United States

STOCK TICKER/OTHER:

Stock Ticker: Subsidiary   Exchange:
Employees: 11,000   Fiscal Year Ends: 12/31
Parent Company: Danaher Corporation

SALARIES/BONUSES:

Top Exec. Salary: $ Bonus: $
Second Exec. Salary: $ Bonus: $

OTHER THOUGHTS:

Estimated Female Officers or Directors: 5
Hot Spot for Advancement for Women/Minorities: Y

Becton Dickinson and Company

www.bd.com

NAIC Code: 339100

TYPES OF BUSINESS:

Medical Equipment-Injection/Infusion
Drug Delivery Systems
Infusion Therapy Products
Diabetes Care Products
Surgical Products
Microbiology Products
Diagnostic Products
Consulting Services

BRANDS/DIVISIONS/AFFILIATES:

BD Medical
BD Life Sciences
BD Interventional
V Muller

CONTACTS: Note: Officers with more than one job title may be intentionally listed here more than once.

Vincent Forlenza, CEO
Roland Goette, Executive VP
Christopher Reidy, CFO
Charles Bodner, Chief Accounting Officer
James Borzi, Executive VP, Divisional
Betty Larson, Executive VP, Divisional
Samrat Khichi, Executive VP
Alberto Mas, Executive VP
Patrick Kaltenbach, Executive VP
Simon Campion, Executive VP
James Lim, Executive VP
Thomas Polen, President
Gary DeFazio, Secretary

GROWTH PLANS/SPECIAL FEATURES:

Becton, Dickinson and Company (BD) is a global medical technology company engaged in the development, manufacture and sale of medical supplies, devices, laboratory equipment and diagnostic products. These offerings are primarily used by healthcare institutions, life science researchers, clinical laboratories, the pharmaceutical industry and the general public. The company operates in three worldwide business segments: BD Medical, BD Life Sciences and BD Interventional. BD Medical's principal product lines include a broad range of medication delivery solutions, medication management solutions, diabetes care solutions and pharmaceutical systems. BD Life Sciences offers products for safe collection and transport of diagnostics specimens, and instruments and reagent systems to detect infectious diseases, healthcare-associated infections and cancers. This division produces research and clinical tools that facilitate the study of cells, and the components of cells, to gain a better understanding of normal and disease processes. This information is used to aid the discovery and development of new drugs and vaccines, among other purposes. Last, the BD Interventional segment provides vascular, urology, oncology and surgical specialty products intended to be used once and then discarded or are either temporarily or permanently implanted. V. Muller-trademarked surgical laparoscopic instrumentation products are an exception to these temporary offerings. Manufacturing operations outside the U.S. include Bosnia/Herzegovina, Brazil, Canada, China, Dominican Republic, France, Germany, Hungary, India, Ireland, Israel, Italy, Japan, Malaysia, Mexico, Netherlands, Singapore, Spain and the U.K. Products are marketed and distributed in the U.S. and internationally through distribution channels, and directly to end-users by BD and independent sales representatives. In late-2020, BD acquired the medical business assets of Cubex LLC, expanding its automated dispensing portfolio; and announced plans to invest $1.2 billion in pre-fillable syringe manufacturing capacity over the next four years.

BD offers its employees comprehensive benefits.

FINANCIAL DATA: Note: Data for latest year may not have been available at press time.

In U.S. $	2020	2019	2018	2017	2016	2015
Revenue	17,117,000,000	17,290,000,000	15,983,000,000	12,093,000,000	12,483,000,000	10,282,000,000
R&D Expense	1,096,000,000	1,062,000,000	1,006,000,000	774,000,000	828,000,000	632,000,000
Operating Income	1,800,000,000	2,238,000,000	2,241,000,000	1,833,000,000	2,158,000,000	1,500,000,000
Operating Margin %		.13%	.14%	.15%	.17%	.15%
SGA Expense	4,318,000,000	4,334,000,000	4,015,000,000	2,925,000,000	3,005,000,000	2,563,000,000
Net Income	874,000,000	1,233,000,000	311,000,000	1,100,000,000	976,000,000	695,000,000
Operating Cash Flow	3,539,000,000	3,328,000,000	2,865,000,000	2,550,000,000	2,559,000,000	1,729,000,000
Capital Expenditure	810,000,000	957,000,000	895,000,000	727,000,000	718,000,000	633,000,000
EBITDA	3,667,000,000	4,068,000,000	3,857,000,000	2,585,000,000	2,576,000,000	2,001,000,000
Return on Assets %		.02%	.00%	.03%	.04%	.04%
Return on Equity %		.05%	.01%	.10%	.13%	.11%
Debt to Equity		0.858	0.90	1.442	1.382	1.587

CONTACT INFORMATION:

Phone: 201 847-6800   Fax:
Toll-Free: 800-284-6845
Address: 1 Becton Dr., Franklin Lakes, NJ 07417 United States

STOCK TICKER/OTHER:

Stock Ticker: BDX
Employees: 72,000
Parent Company:

Exchange: NYS
Fiscal Year Ends: 09/30

SALARIES/BONUSES:

Top Exec. Salary: $ Bonus: $
Second Exec. Salary: $ Bonus: $

OTHER THOUGHTS:

Estimated Female Officers or Directors: 6
Hot Spot for Advancement for Women/Minorities: Y

Belden Inc

NAIC Code: 334417

www.belden.com

TYPES OF BUSINESS:

Cable & Wire Connectors Manufacturing
Electronic Products
Broadcasting Equipment
Aerospace & Automotive Electronics
Enclosures

BRANDS/DIVISIONS/AFFILIATES:

OTN Systems NV

CONTACTS: Note: Officers with more than one job title may be intentionally listed here more than once.

John Stroup, CEO
Doug Zink, Chief Accounting Officer
Henk Derksen, CFO
Douglas Zink, Chief Accounting Officer
Dhrupad Trivedi, Chief Technology Officer
Roel Vestjens, Executive VP, Divisional
Glenn Pennycook, Executive VP, Divisional
Brian Anderson, General Counsel
Dean McKenna, Senior VP, Divisional
Ross Rosenberg, Senior VP, Divisional
Leo Kulmaczewski, Senior VP, Divisional
Paul Turner, Senior VP, Divisional

GROWTH PLANS/SPECIAL FEATURES:

Belden, Inc. is an innovative signal transmission solutions company operating through two business segments: enterprise solutions and industrial solutions. Enterprise solutions provides in-network infrastructure solutions, as well as cabling and connectivity solutions for broadcast, commercial audio/video and security applications. This division serves customers in markets such as healthcare, education, financial, government and corporate enterprises, as well as end-markets, including sport venues, broadcast studios and academic campuses and facilities. Enterprise product lines include copper cable and related connectivity solutions, fiber cable and related connectivity solutions, and racks and enclosures. These products are used in applications such as local area networks, data centers, access control and building automation. The industrial solutions segment provides high-performance networking components and machine connectivity products. These products include physical network and fieldbus infrastructure components and on-machine connectivity systems customized to end-user and original equipment manufacturer (OEM) needs. They are used in applications such as network and fieldbus infrastructure, sensor and actuator connectivity; and power, control and data transmission. Belden has manufacturing facilities in the U.S., and manufacturing and other operating facilities in Brazil, Canada, China, India, Japan, Mexico and St. Kitts, as well as in various countries in Europe. Approximately 45% of the firm's 2020 sales were to customers outside the U.S. In February 2020, Belden announced the signing of a definitive agreement to sell its live media business (Grass Valley) to Black Dragon Capital, a private equity firm with a focus on technology investment opportunities in disrupted industries. In early-2021, Belden acquired OTN Systems NV, a Belgium-based provider of automation networking infrastructure solutions..

FINANCIAL DATA: Note: Data for latest year may not have been available at press time.

In U.S. $	2020	2019	2018	2017	2016	2015
Revenue	1,862,716,000	2,131,278,000	2,585,368,000	2,388,643,000	2,356,672,000	2,309,222,000
R&D Expense	107,296,000	94,360,000	140,585,000	134,330,000	140,601,000	148,311,000
Operating Income	125,410,000	207,207,000	243,080,000	234,690,000	247,784,000	138,783,000
Operating Margin %		.10%	.09%	.10%	.11%	.06%
SGA Expense	366,188,000	417,329,000	525,918,000	461,022,000	494,224,000	527,288,000
Net Income	-55,162,000	-377,015,000	160,894,000	93,210,000	128,003,000	66,204,000
Operating Cash Flow	173,364,000	276,893,000	289,220,000	255,300,000	314,794,000	236,410,000
Capital Expenditure	90,215,000	110,002,000	97,847,000	64,261,000	53,974,000	54,969,000
EBITDA	233,702,000	347,483,000	430,521,000	331,899,000	367,104,000	290,895,000
Return on Assets %		-.11%	.03%	.02%	.03%	.02%
Return on Equity %		-.34%	.09%	.04%	.10%	.08%
Debt to Equity		1.558	1.055	1.088	1.109	2.124

CONTACT INFORMATION:

Phone: 314 854-8000   Fax: 314 854-8001
Toll-Free: 800-235-3361
Address: 1 N. Brentwood Blvd., 15/Fl, St. Louis, MO 63105 United States

STOCK TICKER/OTHER:

Stock Ticker: BDC   Exchange: NYS
Employees: 7,000   Fiscal Year Ends: 12/31
Parent Company:

SALARIES/BONUSES:

Top Exec. Salary: $ Bonus: $
Second Exec. Salary: $ Bonus: $

OTHER THOUGHTS:

Estimated Female Officers or Directors: 2
Hot Spot for Advancement for Women/Minorities: Y

Ben E Keith Company

www.benekeith.com

NAIC Code: 424400

TYPES OF BUSINESS:

Food & Beverage Distribution
Food Service
Beverage Distribution

BRANDS/DIVISIONS/AFFILIATES:

Keith Kitchen Essentials

CONTACTS: Note: Officers with more than one job title may be intentionally listed here more than once.

John Howard Hallam, CEO
Robert Hallam Jr., Pres.
John Howard Hallam, Chmn.

GROWTH PLANS/SPECIAL FEATURES:

Ben E. Keith Company is a food service products and premium beverage distributor, serving retailers throughout the U.S. The company operates through two divisions, food service and beverage. The food service division has operations in New Mexico, Texas, Oklahoma, Arkansas and Alabama, with products including both national brands as well as Ben E. Keith's own exclusive brands. Product categories include frozen foods, produce, dairy, poultry, seafood, fresh and frozen meats, disposables and restaurant equipment and supplies. Brands offered in this division include Bridgford, Cortona and Keith Kitchen Essentials, among many others. The food division caters to a broad range of clients including formal and casual restaurants, schools, hotels, health care and other food distribution facilities. The beverage division services several counties throughout the state of Texas on behalf of Anheuser Busch, and has statewide distribution for most import and craft brands. The beverage division operates through more than 20 distribution facilities and offers products such as wines, ciders and soft drinks, in addition to beer. Brands offered by the division include the Budweiser brand family, Busch family, Bud light brand family, Michelob Ultra, 11 Below Brewing, Altstadt Brewery, Beck's, Carlsberg, Double Horn Brewing Company, Goose Island and Saint Arnold, among others. In late-2020, Ben E. Keith Company announced a partnership with a new San Antonio craft beer developer, Viva Brewery, to distribute Viva in 49 southern Texas counties.

FINANCIAL DATA: Note: Data for latest year may not have been available at press time.

In U.S. $	2020	2019	2018	2017	2016	2015
Revenue	3,755,500,000	3,700,000,000	3,500,000,000	3,850,000,000	3,800,000,000	3,400,000,000
R&D Expense						
Operating Income						
Operating Margin %						
SGA Expense						
Net Income						
Operating Cash Flow						
Capital Expenditure						
EBITDA						
Return on Assets %						
Return on Equity %						
Debt to Equity						

CONTACT INFORMATION:

Phone: 817-877-5700   Fax:
Toll-Free:
Address: 601 E. 7th St., Fort Worth, TX 76102 United States

STOCK TICKER/OTHER:

Stock Ticker: Private   Exchange:
Employees: 4,000   Fiscal Year Ends: 12/31
Parent Company:

SALARIES/BONUSES:

Top Exec. Salary: $ Bonus: $
Second Exec. Salary: $ Bonus: $

OTHER THOUGHTS:

Estimated Female Officers or Directors:
Hot Spot for Advancement for Women/Minorities:

Berkshire Hathaway Energy Company

www.berkshirehathawayenergyco.com
NAIC Code: 221112

TYPES OF BUSINESS:
Utilities-Electricity & Natural Gas
Pipelines
Wind Generation
Hydroelectric Generation
Thermal Solar Generation
Real Estate Brokerage
Solar Power

BRANDS/DIVISIONS/AFFILIATES:
Berkshire Hathaway Inc
PacifiCorp
MidAmerican Energy Company
NV Energy Inc
Northern Powergrid
Northern Natural Gas Company
Kern River Gas Transmission Company
BHE Renewables

CONTACTS: *Note: Officers with more than one job title may be intentionally listed here more than once.*
William J. Fehrman, CEO
Calvin D. Haack, CFO
Maureen E. Sammon, Chief Admin. Officer
Douglas L. Anderson, General Counsel
Gregory E. Abel, Chmn.

GROWTH PLANS/SPECIAL FEATURES:
Berkshire Hathaway Energy Company generates, transmits, stores, distributes and supplies energy through its subsidiaries. The company has 10 primary subsidiaries. PacifiCorp serves roughly 1.9 million customers, operating in two business units: Rocky Mountain Power, which delivers electricity in Wyoming, Utah and Idaho; and Pacific Power, delivering electricity in Oregon, Washington and California. MidAmerican Energy Company generates, transmits and sells electricity, and supplies natural gas to more than 1.5 million customers in Illinois, Nebraska, Iowa and South Dakota. NV Energy, Inc. has approximately 1.24 million customers in Nevada, serving approximately 90% of the state with electricity. Northern Powergrid offers 3.9 million users' electricity in the Northeastern part of England. Northern Natural Gas Company owns a 16,300-mile interstate natural gas pipeline system extending from Texas to the upper Midwest, serving 81 utility companies. Kern River Gas Transmission Company owns 1,700 miles of interstate pipeline and delivers natural gas to Nevada, Utah and California. BHE Renewables' 4,654 megawatts total capacity of owned and under construction clean energy includes: 1,536 MW solar; 1,665 MW wind; 345 MW geothermal; and 138 MW hydro. AltaLink is the largest regulated transmission company with an 81,850-square-mile (212,000 square kilometers) service area, supplying electricity to more than 85% of the population in Alberta. BHE U.S. Transmission provides transmission solutions for wholesale customers, owning more than 1,000 miles of lines. Last, HomeServices of America, Inc. is a leading U.S. residential real estate brokerage firm, with over 911 sales offices throughout the country. Berkshire Hathaway Energy is a wholly owned subsidiary of Berkshire Hathaway, Inc. In July 2020, the agreed to acquire Dominion Energy's natural gas transmission and storage business for approximately $9.7 billion.

Berkshire offers comprehensive benefits, retirement options and employee incentives.

FINANCIAL DATA: *Note: Data for latest year may not have been available at press time.*

In U.S. $	2020	2019	2018	2017	2016	2015
Revenue	20,952,000,000	19,844,000,000	19,787,000,000	18,614,000,000	17,422,000,000	17,880,000,000
R&D Expense						
Operating Income						
Operating Margin %						
SGA Expense						
Net Income	6,943,000,000	2,950,000,000	2,568,000,000	2,910,000,000	2,570,000,000	2,400,000,000
Operating Cash Flow						
Capital Expenditure						
EBITDA						
Return on Assets %						
Return on Equity %						
Debt to Equity						

CONTACT INFORMATION:
Phone: 515-242-3022   Fax:
Toll-Free:
Address: 666 Grand Ave., Des Moines, IA 50306-0657 United States

STOCK TICKER/OTHER:
Stock Ticker: Subsidiary   Exchange:
Employees: 23,800   Fiscal Year Ends: 12/31
Parent Company: Berkshire Hathaway Inc

SALARIES/BONUSES:
Top Exec. Salary: $ Bonus: $
Second Exec. Salary: $ Bonus: $

OTHER THOUGHTS:
Estimated Female Officers or Directors: 1
Hot Spot for Advancement for Women/Minorities:

Berkshire Hathaway Inc (Holding Co)   www.berkshirehathaway.com
NAIC Code: 524126

TYPES OF BUSINESS:
Insurance--Property & Casualty, Specialty, Surety
Retail Operations
Foodservice Operations
Building Products & Services
Apparel & Footwear
Technology Training
Manufactured Housing & RVs
Business Jet Flexible Ownership Services

BRANDS/DIVISIONS/AFFILIATES:
GEICO Corporation
Berkshire Hathaway Reinsurance Group
Berkshire Hathaway Primary Group
Burlington Northern Santa Fe
Berkshire Hathaway Energy Company
Precision Castparts Corp
Clayton Homes Inc
McLane Company Inc

CONTACTS: Note: Officers with more than one job title may be intentionally listed here more than once.
Warren Buffett, CEO
Marc Hamburg, CFO
Daniel Jaksich, Chief Accounting Officer
Charles Munger, Director
Gregory Abel, Director
Ajit Jain, Director

GROWTH PLANS/SPECIAL FEATURES:
Berkshire Hathaway, Inc. is a holding company that owns subsidiaries engaged in diverse business activities, most importantly insurance and reinsurance. Berkshire provides property and casualty insurance and reinsurance, as well as life, accident and health reinsurance, through U.S. and foreign businesses. The company conducts its insurance underwriting business through three subsidiary divisions. First, GEICO Corporation mainly provides private passenger auto insurance to individuals in all 50 U.S. states and Washington, D.C. Second, Berkshire Hathaway Reinsurance Group underwrites excess-of-loss and quota-share reinsurance for insurers and reinsurers. Third, Berkshire Hathaway Primary Group offers insurance for property and casualty. Other businesses and subsidiaries include, but are not limited to: Burlington Northern Santa Fe, which operates a leading railroad system in North America through BNSF Railway Company; Berkshire Hathaway Energy Company, a global energy company with subsidiaries that generate, transmit, store, distribute and supply energy; Precision Castparts Corp., which manufactures complex metal components and products and provides high-quality investment castings, forgings, fasteners/fastener systems and aerostructures for critical aerospace and power/energy applications; Clayton Homes, Inc., a housing company utilizing manufactured, modular and site build methods; McLane Company, Inc., which provides wholesale distribution services in all 50 states to customers that include convenience stores, discount retailers, wholesale clubs, drug stores, military bases, quick service restaurants and casual dining restaurants; FlightSafety International, Inc., a provider of professional aviation training services; XTRA Corporation, a transportation equipment lessor operating under the XTRA Lease brand name; and See's Candies, which produces boxed chocolates and other confectionery products, operating approximately 250 retail and discount stores primarily in California and other western states.

FINANCIAL DATA: Note: Data for latest year may not have been available at press time.

In U.S. $	2020	2019	2018	2017	2016	2015
Revenue	286,256,000,000	327,223,000,000	225,382,000,000	242,137,000,000	223,604,000,000	210,821,000,000
R&D Expense						
Operating Income						
Operating Margin %						
SGA Expense	23,329,000,000	23,325,000,000	22,299,000,000	18,181,000,000	18,217,000,000	15,309,000,000
Net Income	42,521,000,000	81,417,000,000	4,021,000,000	44,940,000,000	24,074,000,000	24,083,000,000
Operating Cash Flow	39,773,000,000	38,687,000,000	37,400,000,000	45,776,000,000	32,535,000,000	31,491,000,000
Capital Expenditure	13,012,000,000	15,979,000,000	14,537,000,000	11,708,000,000	12,954,000,000	16,082,000,000
EBITDA						
Return on Assets %		.11%	.01%	.07%	.04%	.04%
Return on Equity %		.21%	.01%	.14%	.09%	.10%
Debt to Equity		0.232	0.267	0.276	0.352	0.322

CONTACT INFORMATION:
Phone: 402 346-1400   Fax: 402 346-3375
Toll-Free:
Address: 3555 Farnam St., Omaha, NE 68131 United States

STOCK TICKER/OTHER:
Stock Ticker: BRK.A   Exchange: NYS
Employees: 360,000   Fiscal Year Ends: 12/31
Parent Company:

SALARIES/BONUSES:
Top Exec. Salary: $ Bonus: $
Second Exec. Salary: $ Bonus: $

OTHER THOUGHTS:
Estimated Female Officers or Directors:
Hot Spot for Advancement for Women/Minorities:

Berry Global Group Inc

NAIC Code: 326100

TYPES OF BUSINESS:

Injection Molded Packaging
Open-Top Containers
Closures
Consumer Products
Plastic Housewares
Thermoforming

BRANDS/DIVISIONS/AFFILIATES:

Berry Global Inc

CONTACTS: *Note: Officers with more than one job title may be intentionally listed here more than once.*

Thomas Salmon, CEO
Mark Miles, CFO
James Till, Chief Accounting Officer
Jason Greene, Chief Legal Officer
Curtis Begle, President, Divisional
Jean-Marc Galvez, President, Divisional
Michael Hill, President, Divisional

GROWTH PLANS/SPECIAL FEATURES:

Berry Global Group, Inc., operating through Berry Global, Inc., is a leading manufacturer of non-woven, flexible and rigid products that are used every day within the consumer and industrial end markets. Berry has operations that span over 295 locations on six continents. The firm operates through four business segments: consumer packaging international, consumer packaging North America, engineered materials, and health, hygiene and specialties. Consumer packaging international primarily consists of the following product groups: recycling, with capabilities to recycle rigid and flexible end-of-life materials from industrial and consumer sources; bottles and cannisters, manufacturing narrow neck blow molded and injection-stretch molded packaging solutions; containers, manufacturing injection molded and thermoformed pails, jars and tubs; closures and dispensing systems, manufacturing closures, dispensing systems and applications; pharmaceutical devices and packaging, manufacturing inhalers and dose counters as well as containers and closures for over-the-counter and prescription medicines; polythene films, manufacturing films for diverse end-markets; and technical components, manufacturing complex high-precision molds and molded components for materials handling and specialty vehicles markets. Consumer packaging North America operates in the U.S. and manufactures containers, pails, lightweight polypropylene beverage cups and lids, closures, overcaps, bottles, prescription vials and tubes. The engineered materials segment is comprised of the following product groups: stretch and shrink films, converter films, institutional can liners, tape products, food and consumer films, retail bags, polyvinyl chloride (PVC) films and agriculture films. Last, the health, hygiene and specialties segment consists of the following product groups: health, manufacturing medical garment materials, surgical drapes, cleaning wipes and face masks; hygiene, manufacturing components for diapers and other absorbent hygiene products, elastic films, laminates and substrates; and specialties, manufacturing an array of products and components for geosynthetics and filtration products servicing the specialty industrial markets.

FINANCIAL DATA: *Note: Data for latest year may not have been available at press time.*

In U.S. $	2020	2019	2018	2017	2016	2015
Revenue	11,709,000,000	8,878,000,000	7,869,000,000	7,095,000,000	6,489,000,000	4,881,000,000
R&D Expense						
Operating Income	1,258,000,000	842,000,000	797,000,000	756,000,000	613,000,000	421,000,000
Operating Margin %		.09%	.10%	.11%	.09%	.09%
SGA Expense	850,000,000	583,000,000	480,000,000	494,000,000	531,000,000	357,000,000
Net Income	559,000,000	404,000,000	496,000,000	340,000,000	236,000,000	86,000,000
Operating Cash Flow	1,530,000,000	1,201,000,000	1,004,000,000	975,000,000	857,000,000	637,000,000
Capital Expenditure	583,000,000	399,000,000	336,000,000	269,000,000	288,000,000	180,000,000
EBITDA	1,993,000,000	1,432,000,000	1,274,000,000	1,239,000,000	1,124,000,000	663,000,000
Return on Assets %		.03%	.06%	.04%	.04%	.02%
Return on Equity %		.27%	.41%	.55%	3.15%	
Debt to Equity		6.96	4.057	5.542	26.202	

CONTACT INFORMATION:

Phone: 812 424-2904   Fax:
Toll-Free:
Address: 101 Oakley St., Evansville, IN 47710 United States

STOCK TICKER/OTHER:

Stock Ticker: BERY
Employees: 47,000
Parent Company:

Exchange: NYS
Fiscal Year Ends: 09/26

SALARIES/BONUSES:

Top Exec. Salary: $ Bonus: $
Second Exec. Salary: $ Bonus: $

OTHER THOUGHTS:

Estimated Female Officers or Directors:
Hot Spot for Advancement for Women/Minorities:

Best Buy Co Inc

www.bestbuy.com

NAIC Code: 443142

TYPES OF BUSINESS:

Consumer Electronics Stores
Retail Music & Video Sales
Personal Computers
Office Supplies
Cell Phones and Accessories
Appliances
Cameras
Consumer Electronics Installation & Service

BRANDS/DIVISIONS/AFFILIATES:

bestbuy.com
Best Buy Direct
Best Buy Express
Geek Squad
Magnolia
Pacific Kitchen and Home
bestbuy.ca
greatcall.com

CONTACTS: *Note: Officers with more than one job title may be intentionally listed here more than once.*

Corie Barry, CEO
Hubert Joly, Chairman of the Board
Mathew Watson, Chief Accounting Officer
Todd Hartman, Chief Compliance Officer
Michael Mohan, COO
Brian Tilzer, Other Executive Officer
Kamy Scarlett, Other Executive Officer

GROWTH PLANS/SPECIAL FEATURES:

Best Buy Co., Inc. is a leading provider of technology products, services and solutions. The company offers these products and solutions through Best Buy stores, Geek Squad agents, ecommerce channels and mobile apps. Retail operations are located in the U.S. and Canada. Best Buy Co. operates its business through two segments: domestic and international. The domestic segment is comprised of the U.S. operations, including brand names such as Best Buy, bestbuy.com, greatcall.com, Best Buy Direct, Best Buy Express, Geek Squad, CST, GreatCall, Magnolia and Pacific Kitchen and Home. The international segment is comprised of all operations in Canada and Mexico, including brand names such as Best Buy, Best Buy Express, Geek Squad and the domain names bestbuy.ca and bestbuy.com.mx. Both segment's development of merchandise and service offerings, pricing and promotions, procurement and supply chain, online and mobile application operations, marketing and advertising and labor deployment across all channels are centrally managed. The company has field operations that support retail teams from corporate as well as regional office locations. Best Buy's merchandise and services consist of the following: consumer electronics, including digital imaging, health/fitness, home automation, home theater and portable audio devices; computing and mobile phones, including computers, laptops, tablets, eReaders, mobile phones, networking and wearables; entertainment, including drones, gaming hardware/software, movies, music, technology toys, virtual reality and other software; appliances, including dishwashers, laundry, ovens, refrigerators, blenders, coffee makers and much more; and services, including consultation, delivery, design, educational classes, installation, memberships, protection plans, repair, set-up and tech support. During 2021, Best Buy announced it was exiting the Mexico market, and expected to cease operations there sometime in 2022.

Employee benefits include medical, dental, vision, life and disability insurance; 401(k); and various assistance programs.

FINANCIAL DATA: *Note: Data for latest year may not have been available at press time.*

In U.S. $	2020	2019	2018	2017	2016	2015
Revenue	43,638,000,000	42,879,000,000	42,151,000,000	39,403,000,000	39,528,000,000	
R&D Expense						
Operating Income	2,050,000,000	1,946,000,000	1,853,000,000	1,893,000,000	1,573,000,000	
Operating Margin %	.05%	.05%	.04%	.05%	.04%	
SGA Expense	7,998,000,000	8,015,000,000	8,023,000,000	7,547,000,000	7,618,000,000	
Net Income	1,541,000,000	1,464,000,000	1,000,000,000	1,228,000,000	897,000,000	
Operating Cash Flow	2,565,000,000	2,408,000,000	2,141,000,000	2,545,000,000	1,322,000,000	
Capital Expenditure	743,000,000	819,000,000	688,000,000	582,000,000	649,000,000	
EBITDA	2,869,000,000	2,731,000,000	2,575,000,000	2,542,000,000	2,047,000,000	
Return on Assets %	.11%	.11%	.07%	.09%	.06%	
Return on Equity %	.45%	.42%	.24%	.27%	.19%	
Debt to Equity	0.976	0.403	0.225	0.281	0.306	

CONTACT INFORMATION:

Phone: 612 291-1000   Fax: 612 292-4001
Toll-Free:
Address: 7601 Penn Ave. S., Richfield, MN 55423 United States

STOCK TICKER/OTHER:

Stock Ticker: BBY   Exchange: NYS
Employees: 102,000   Fiscal Year Ends: 02/28
Parent Company:

SALARIES/BONUSES:

Top Exec. Salary: $ Bonus: $
Second Exec. Salary: $ Bonus: $

OTHER THOUGHTS:

Estimated Female Officers or Directors: 5
Hot Spot for Advancement for Women/Minorities: Y

Sales, profits and employees may be estimates. Financial information, benefits and other data can change quickly and may vary from those stated here.

Biogen Inc

NAIC Code: 325412

TYPES OF BUSINESS:

Drugs-Immunology, Neurology & Oncology
Autoimmune & Inflammatory Disease Treatments
Drugs-Multiple Sclerosis
Drugs-Cancer

BRANDS/DIVISIONS/AFFILIATES:

TECFIDERA
AVONEX
PLEGRIDY
SPINRAZA
FUMADERM
RITUXAN
GAZYVA
OCREVUS

CONTACTS: *Note: Officers with more than one job title may be intentionally listed here more than once.*

Michel Vounatsos, CEO
Jeffrey Capello, CFO
Gregory Covino, Chief Accounting Officer
Alfred Sandrock, Chief Medical Officer
Stelios Papadopoulos, Director
Michael Ehlers, Executive VP, Divisional
Paul McKenzie, Executive VP, Divisional
Kenneth Dipietro, Executive VP, Divisional
Adriana Karaboutis, Executive VP, Divisional
Chirfi Guindo, Executive VP
Ginger Gregory, Executive VP
Susan Alexander, Executive VP

GROWTH PLANS/SPECIAL FEATURES:

Biogen, Inc. is a biotechnology company focused on discovering, developing, manufacturing and marketing therapies for people living with serious neurological and neurodegenerative diseases. The company's core growth areas in relation to these diseases include multiple sclerosis (MS), neuroimmunology, Alzheimer's disease, dementia, movement disorders, and neuromuscular disorders such as spinal muscular atrophy (SMA) and amyotrophic lateral sclerosis (ALS). Biogen announced plans to invest in emerging growth areas such as pain, ophthalmology, neuropsychiatry and acute neurology, as well as discovering potential treatments for rare and genetic disorders. The firm also manufactures and commercializes biosimilars of advanced biologics. Biogen's marketed products include: TECFIDERA, AVONEX, PLEGRIDY, TYSABRI, VUMERITY and FAMPRYA for the treatment of MS; SPINRAZA for the treatment of SMA; and FUMADERM for the treatment of severe plaque psoriasis. In addition, the company has certain business and financial rights with respect to: RITUXAN and RITUXAN HYCELA for the treatment of non-Hodgkin's lymphoma and chronic lymphocytic leukemia (CLL) and other conditions; GAZYVA for the treatment of CLL and follicular lymphoma; OCREVUS for the treatment of primary progressive MS and relapsing MS; and other potential anti-CD20 therapies under a collaboration agreement with Genentech, Inc., which is wholly-owned by Roche Group. In order to support its future growth and drug development pipeline, Biogen announced plans to expand its large molecule production capacity by building a large-scale biologics manufacturing facility in Solothurn, Switzerland, which was expected to be partially operational by mid-2021.

Biogen offers its employees medical, dental and vision insurance; tuition reimbursement; flexible spending accounts; and an employee assistance program.

FINANCIAL DATA: *Note: Data for latest year may not have been available at press time.*

In U.S. $	2020	2019	2018	2017	2016	2015
Revenue	13,444,600,000	14,377,900,000	13,452,900,000	12,273,900,000	11,448,800,000	10,763,800,000
R&D Expense	3,990,900,000	2,280,600,000	2,597,200,000	2,253,600,000	1,973,300,000	2,012,800,000
Operating Income	4,446,300,000	7,035,700,000	6,000,800,000	5,527,800,000	5,653,100,000	5,014,900,000
Operating Margin %		.49%	.45%	.45%	.49%	.47%
SGA Expense	2,504,500,000	2,374,700,000	2,106,300,000	1,935,500,000	1,947,900,000	2,113,100,000
Net Income	4,000,600,000	5,888,500,000	4,430,700,000	2,539,100,000	3,702,800,000	3,547,000,000
Operating Cash Flow	4,229,800,000	7,078,600,000	6,187,700,000	4,551,000,000	4,522,400,000	3,716,100,000
Capital Expenditure	551,800,000	669,500,000	886,100,000	1,962,800,000	727,700,000	643,000,000
EBITDA	5,734,800,000	7,993,900,000	7,116,800,000	6,460,600,000	5,875,700,000	5,463,200,000
Return on Assets %		.22%	.18%	.11%	.17%	.21%
Return on Equity %		.45%	.35%	.21%	.34%	.35%
Debt to Equity		0.365	0.455	0.471	0.536	0.696

CONTACT INFORMATION:

Phone: 617-679-2000   Fax: 619 679-2617
Toll-Free:
Address: 225 Binney St., Cambridge, MA 02142 United States

STOCK TICKER/OTHER:

Stock Ticker: BIIB   Exchange: NAS
Employees: 7,400   Fiscal Year Ends: 12/31
Parent Company:

SALARIES/BONUSES:

Top Exec. Salary: $ Bonus: $
Second Exec. Salary: $ Bonus: $

OTHER THOUGHTS:

Estimated Female Officers or Directors: 4
Hot Spot for Advancement for Women/Minorities: Y

BioMarin Pharmaceutical Inc

www.bmrn.com/index.php

NAIC Code: 325412

TYPES OF BUSINESS:

Biopharmaceutical Product Development
Biotechnology
Drug Development
Clinical Testing
Therapy Commercialization

BRANDS/DIVISIONS/AFFILIATES:

Aldurazyme
Brineura
Kuvan
Palynziq
Naglazyme
Vimizim
Valoctocogene Roxaparvovec
Vosoritide

CONTACTS: *Note: Officers with more than one job title may be intentionally listed here more than once.*

Jean-Jacques Bienaime, CEO
Daniel Spiegelman, CFO
Brian Mueller, Chief Accounting Officer
Robert Baffi, Executive VP, Divisional
G. Davis, Executive VP
Jeffrey Ajer, Executive VP
Henry Fuchs, President, Divisional

GROWTH PLANS/SPECIAL FEATURES:

BioMarin Pharmaceutical, Inc. is a global biotechnology company that develops and commercializes innovative therapies for people with serious and life-threatening rare diseases and medical conditions. BioMarin's current commercial products include: Aldurazyme (laronidase), for the treatment of mucopolysaccharidosis Type I (MPS I); Brineura (cerlinponase alfa), for the treatment of late infantile neuronal ceroid lipofuscinosis Type 2 (CLN2); Kuvan (sapropterin dihydrochloride), for the treatment of phylketonuria (PKU); Palynziq (pegvaliase-pqpz), for adult patients with PKU; Naglazyme (galsuffase), for the treatment of MPS VI; and Vimizim (elosulfase alpha), for the treatment of MPS IV Type A. Major product candidates in development include: Valoctocogene roxaparvovec, in Phase 3 clinical trials for the treatment of severe hemophilia A; Vosoritide, in Phase 3 clinical trials for the treatment of achondroplasia; and BMN 307, in Phase Â½ clinical trials for the treatment of PKU. In February 2021, BioMarin announced that the U.S. Food and Drug Administration granted priority review designation for its new drug application (NDA) for Vosoritide for the treatment of children with achondroplasia. The FDA Prescription Drug User Fee Act target action date was August 20, 2021. That July, the European Medicines Agency validated BioMarin's marketing authorization application for Valoctocogene roxaparvovec to treat severe hemophilia A.

Employee benefits include medical, dental, vision, life and AD&D insurance as well as a 401(k).

FINANCIAL DATA: *Note: Data for latest year may not have been available at press time.*

In U.S. $	2020	2019	2018	2017	2016	2015
Revenue	1,860,461,000	1,704,048,000	1,491,212,000	1,313,646,000	1,116,854,000	889,895,000
R&D Expense	628,116,000	715,007,000	696,328,000	610,753,000	661,905,000	634,806,000
Operating Income	-91,827,000	-125,457,000	-173,524,000	-139,700,000	-204,311,000	-281,500,000
Operating Margin %		-.07%	-.12%	-.11%	-.18%	-.32%
SGA Expense	737,700,000	680,924,000	604,353,000	554,336,000	476,593,000	402,271,000
Net Income	859,100,000	-23,848,000	-77,211,000	-117,042,000	-630,210,000	-171,799,000
Operating Cash Flow	85,365,000	48,262,000	20,208,000	-8,757,000	-227,837,000	-221,689,000
Capital Expenditure	137,519,000	163,406,000	144,620,000	199,219,000	148,380,000	227,653,000
EBITDA	92,159,000	31,918,000	-6,980,000	90,968,000	-698,006,000	-72,587,000
Return on Assets %		-.01%	-.02%	-.03%	-.16%	-.06%
Return on Equity %		-.01%	-.03%	-.04%	-.24%	-.09%
Debt to Equity		0.156	0.28	0.29	0.239	0.276

CONTACT INFORMATION:

Phone: 415 506-6700   Fax: 415 382-7889
Toll-Free:
Address: 770 Lindaro St., San Rafael, CA 94901 United States

SALARIES/BONUSES:

Top Exec. Salary: $ Bonus: $
Second Exec. Salary: $ Bonus: $

STOCK TICKER/OTHER:

Stock Ticker: BMRN   Exchange: NAS
Employees: 3,059   Fiscal Year Ends: 12/31
Parent Company:

OTHER THOUGHTS:

Estimated Female Officers or Directors: 1
Hot Spot for Advancement for Women/Minorities:

Bio-Rad Laboratories Inc

NAIC Code: 325413

www.bio-rad.com

TYPES OF BUSINESS:

Clinical Diagnostics Products
Diagnostics Products
Manufacture
Distribution
Reagents
Laboratory Instruments
Diagnostics Tests
Biological Materials

BRANDS/DIVISIONS/AFFILIATES:

CONTACTS: Note: Officers with more than one job title may be intentionally listed here more than once.

Norman Schwartz, CEO
Ilan Daskal, CFO
James Stark, Chief Accounting Officer
Andrew Last, COO
Michael Crowley, Executive VP, Divisional
Timothy Ernst, Executive VP
Giovanni Magni, Executive VP
Annette Tumolo, Executive VP
John Hertia, Executive VP
Ronald Hutton, Executive VP

GROWTH PLANS/SPECIAL FEATURES:

Bio-Rad Laboratories, Inc. is a multinational manufacturer and distributor of its own life science research and clinical diagnostics products. Bio-Rad supplies the life science research, healthcare, analytical chemistry and other markets with a range of products and systems used to separate complex chemical and biological materials and to identify, analyze and purify their components. The firm has direct distribution channels in over 36 countries outside the U.S. via subsidiaries whose focus is sales, customer service and product distribution. Bio-Rad operates its business through two segments: life science and clinical diagnostics, which generated 49% and 51% of net sales in 2020. The life science segment develops, manufactures and markets approximately 6,000 reagents, apparatus and laboratory instruments. Many of these products are used in research techniques, biopharmaceutical production processes and food testing regimes. The clinical diagnostics segment designs, manufactures, sells and supports test systems, informatics systems, test kits and specialized quality controls that serve clinical laboratories in the global diagnostics market. These products currently address specific niches within the in vitro diagnostics (IVD) test market. This division supplies more than 3,000 different products that cover 300+ clinical diagnostic tests to the IVD test market. Bio-Rad utilizes a wide variety of chemicals, biological materials, electronic components, machined metal parts, optical parts, computing and peripheral devices, most of which are available from numerous sources. Bio-Rad owns over 2,200 U.S. and international patents and numerous trademarks.

FINANCIAL DATA: Note: Data for latest year may not have been available at press time.

In U.S. $	2020	2019	2018	2017	2016	2015
Revenue	2,545,626,000	2,311,659,000	2,289,415,000	2,160,153,000	2,068,172,000	2,019,441,000
R&D Expense	226,598,000	202,710,000	199,196,000	250,301,000	205,864,000	192,972,000
Operating Income	410,957,000	229,661,000	189,172,000	128,156,000	115,499,000	166,708,000
Operating Margin %		.10%	.08%	.06%	.06%	.08%
SGA Expense	800,267,000	824,625,000	834,783,000	808,942,000	816,724,000	761,990,000
Net Income	3,806,267,000	1,758,675,000	365,614,000	122,249,000	28,125,000	113,093,000
Operating Cash Flow	575,328,000	457,897,000	285,494,000	103,885,000	216,433,000	186,210,000
Capital Expenditure	98,920,000	98,532,000	129,828,000	115,127,000	141,571,000	113,372,000
EBITDA	5,067,599,000	2,418,697,000	674,721,000	268,419,000	206,402,000	299,339,000
Return on Assets %		.26%	.07%	.03%	.01%	.03%
Return on Equity %		.36%	.11%	.04%	.01%	.05%
Debt to Equity		0.033	0.109	0.148	0.168	0.175

CONTACT INFORMATION:

Phone: 510 724-7000   Fax: 510 741-5817
Toll-Free: 800-424-6723
Address: 1000 Alfred Nobel Dr., Hercules, CA 94547 United States

SALARIES/BONUSES:

Top Exec. Salary: $ Bonus: $
Second Exec. Salary: $ Bonus: $

STOCK TICKER/OTHER:

Stock Ticker: BIO   Exchange: NYS
Employees: 8,120   Fiscal Year Ends: 12/31
Parent Company:

OTHER THOUGHTS:

Estimated Female Officers or Directors: 3
Hot Spot for Advancement for Women/Minorities: Y

Black & Veatch Holding Company

www.bv.com

NAIC Code: 541330

TYPES OF BUSINESS:

Heavy & Civil Engineering, Construction
Infrastructure & Energy Services
Environmental & Hydrologic Engineering
Consulting Services
IT Services
Power Plant Engineering and Construction
Asset Management
Project Development

BRANDS/DIVISIONS/AFFILIATES:

Black & Veatch Construction Inc
Overland Contracting
Atonix Digital
Diode Ventures

CONTACTS: Note: Officers with more than one job title may be intentionally listed here more than once.

Steven L. Edwards, CEO
Martin G. Travers, Pres.
Ken Williams, CFO
Patty Corcoran, Chief Human Resources Officer
Irvin Bishop, Jr., CIO
James R. Lewis, Chief Admin. Officer
Timothy W. Triplett, General Counsel
Cindy Wallis-Lage, Pres., Water
O.H. Oskvig, CEO-Energy Business
William R. Van Dyke, Pres., Federal Svcs.
Steven L. Edwards, Chmn.
Hoe Wai Cheong, Sr. VP-Water-Asia Pacific
John E. Murphy, Pres., Construction & Procurement

GROWTH PLANS/SPECIAL FEATURES:

Black & Veatch Holding Company (B&V) is an employee-owned engineering, procurement, consulting and construction company, with more than 100 offices worldwide. The company specializes in the following markets: commercial, connected communities, data centers, management consulting, food and beverage, industrial and manufacturing, governments, mining, oil/gas, power utilities, telecommunications, transportation and water. B&V divides its service offerings into 10 categories. Asset management services span from single asset evaluation to enterprise optimization and efficiency, with specific services including: ISO 55000 assessment and implementation, enterprise asset management system implementation, capital prioritization and risk management. Consulting services include advanced metering infrastructure, customer engagement, operations, infrastructure investment, infrastructure transactions, utility rates and regulatory support. Engineering solutions ensures project performance in relation to power generation, power delivery, oil/gas, water supply challenges and integrated broadband/telecommunications. Master Planning, offering sustainable infrastructure solutions with data analytics for business-decision purposes about investing and optimization. Program management, providing services for reducing risk and managing large-scale capital programs or multiple-site distributed infrastructure programs. Construction services focus on power, water, telecommunications, non-union shops and more through Black & Veatch Construction, Inc. and Overland Contractng. Data analytic services includes software subsidiary Atonix Digital, which focuses on cloud-based software development, sales and delivery. Environmental services consist of integrated solutions that address current environmental needs and future environmental risks. Procurement provides proposal support, global sourcing, procurement management, preparation of request for proposal packages, evaluation, contract administration and more. Last, project development services include working directly with project developers, entrepreneurs and city and utility planners throughout the development process. Subsidiary Diode Ventures provides end-to-end asset development solutions.

FINANCIAL DATA: Note: Data for latest year may not have been available at press time.

In U.S. $	2020	2019	2018	2017	2016	2015
Revenue	3,586,275,000	3,622,500,000	3,500,000,000	3,400,000,000	3,200,000,000	3,030,000,000
R&D Expense						
Operating Income						
Operating Margin %						
SGA Expense						
Net Income						
Operating Cash Flow						
Capital Expenditure						
EBITDA						
Return on Assets %						
Return on Equity %						
Debt to Equity						

CONTACT INFORMATION:

Phone: 913-458-2000   Fax: 913-458-2934
Toll-Free:
Address: 11401 Lamar Ave., Overland Park, KS 66211 United States

SALARIES/BONUSES:

Top Exec. Salary: $ Bonus: $
Second Exec. Salary: $ Bonus: $

STOCK TICKER/OTHER:

Stock Ticker: Private   Exchange:
Employees: 10,000   Fiscal Year Ends: 12/31
Parent Company:

OTHER THOUGHTS:

Estimated Female Officers or Directors: 4
Hot Spot for Advancement for Women/Minorities: Y

BlackRock Inc

NAIC Code: 523920

TYPES OF BUSINESS:

Investment Management
Risk Management Services
Investment System Services

BRANDS/DIVISIONS/AFFILIATES:

Aladdin
iShares
BlackRock Investment Institute

CONTACTS: *Note: Officers with more than one job title may be intentionally listed here more than once.*

Laurence Fink, CEO
Jeffrey Smith, Other Corporate Officer
Marc Comerchero, Chief Accounting Officer
Christopher Meade, Chief Legal Officer
Robert Goldstein, COO
Robert Kapito, Director
Mark McCombe, Other Corporate Officer
J. Kushel, Other Corporate Officer
Rachel Lord, Other Corporate Officer
Mark Wiedman, Other Corporate Officer
Geraldine Buckingham, Other Corporate Officer

GROWTH PLANS/SPECIAL FEATURES:

BlackRock, Inc. and its subsidiaries form one of the largest investment management firms in the U.S., with about $8 trillion worth of assets under management as of the end of 2020. The company manages offices 32 states in the U.S. as well as Canada, Mexico, Brazil, Chile and Colombia which serve clients in over 100 countries. The firm acts as a fiduciary on behalf of institutional and individual investors worldwide through a variety of fixed income, cash management, equity and balanced and alternative investment accounts and funds. The company also provides risk management, investment system outsourcing and financial advisory services. BlackRock's Aladdin platform is an operating system for investment managers that combines risk analytics with portfolio management, trading and operations tools. Its clients include a diverse group of taxable, tax-exempt and official institutions, retail investors and high-net-worth individuals globally. Institutional clients include pension funds, official institutions, foundations, endowments and charities, insurance companies, banks, sub-advisory relationships and private banks. Products are offered directly through intermediaries that include open-end and closed-end mutual funds, iShares exchange-traded funds (ETFs), collective investment funds and separate accounts. The firm's global platform, BlackRock Investment Institute, leverages its expertise in markets, asset classes and client segments to produce information that makes the company's portfolio managers better investors. In November 2020, BlackRock announced that it has entered into a definitive agreement to acquire Aperio, a pioneer in customizing tax-optimized index equity separately managed accounts, from Golden Gate Capital.

FINANCIAL DATA: *Note: Data for latest year may not have been available at press time.*

In U.S. $	2020	2019	2018	2017	2016	2015
Revenue	16,205,000,000	14,539,000,000	14,198,000,000	12,491,000,000	11,155,000,000	11,401,000,000
R&D Expense						
Operating Income	6,313,000,000	5,635,000,000	5,598,000,000	5,272,000,000	4,646,000,000	4,664,000,000
Operating Margin %		.39%	.39%	.42%	.42%	.41%
SGA Expense	1,847,000,000	1,674,000,000	1,557,000,000	1,462,000,000	1,301,000,000	1,380,000,000
Net Income	4,932,000,000	4,476,000,000	4,305,000,000	4,970,000,000	3,172,000,000	3,345,000,000
Operating Cash Flow	3,743,000,000	2,884,000,000	3,075,000,000	3,828,000,000	2,154,000,000	3,004,000,000
Capital Expenditure	194,000,000	254,000,000	204,000,000	155,000,000	119,000,000	221,000,000
EBITDA	7,087,000,000	6,395,000,000	5,782,000,000	5,722,000,000	4,894,000,000	5,053,000,000
Return on Assets %		.03%	.02%	.02%	.01%	.01%
Return on Equity %		.14%	.13%	.16%	.11%	.12%
Debt to Equity		0.148	0.156	0.158	0.169	0.173

CONTACT INFORMATION:

Phone: 212 810-5300   Fax: 212 754-3123
Toll-Free:
Address: 40 E. 52nd St., New York, NY 10022 United States

STOCK TICKER/OTHER:

Stock Ticker: BLK   Exchange: NYS
Employees: 16,500   Fiscal Year Ends: 12/31
Parent Company:

SALARIES/BONUSES:

Top Exec. Salary: $ Bonus: $
Second Exec. Salary: $ Bonus: $

OTHER THOUGHTS:

Estimated Female Officers or Directors: 5
Hot Spot for Advancement for Women/Minorities: Y

Blackstone Group Inc (The)

www.blackstone.com

NAIC Code: 523910

TYPES OF BUSINESS:

Private Equity Investments
Real Estate Investments
Financial & Restructuring Advising
Mutual Funds Investments
Hedge Fund Investments
Fund Placement Services
Credit Business
Advisory Services

BRANDS/DIVISIONS/AFFILIATES:

Blackstone Capital Partners
Blackstone Real Estate Partners
Blackstone Real Estate Debt Strategies
Blackstone Alternative Asset Management
GSO Capital Partners LP
Ancestry

CONTACTS: Note: Officers with more than one job title may be intentionally listed here more than once.

Stephen Schwarzman, CEO
Michael Chae, CFO
Christopher Striano, Chief Accounting Officer
John Finley, Chief Legal Officer
Jonathan Gray, COO
Hamilton James, Director
Joan Solotar, Other Corporate Officer

GROWTH PLANS/SPECIAL FEATURES:

The Blackstone Group Inc., together with its consolidated subsidiaries, is a leading global alternative asset manager, with approximately $571.1 billion in assets under management (AUM). Blackstone's businesses include vehicles focused on private equity, real estate, hedge fund solutions, non-investment grade credit, secondary private equity funds of funds and multi-asset class strategies. The firm also provides capital markets services. Its business segments include: private equity, real estate, hedge fund solutions and credit. The private equity segment manages $182.9 billion AUM, and focuses on identifying, managing and creating lasting value for clients. This division's corporate private equity unit consists of corporate private equity funds, Blackstone Capital Partners funds and sector-focused corporate private equity funds. The real estate segment manages $163.2 billion AUM, with investments in North America, Europe, Asia and Latin America. Its Blackstone Real Estate Partners funds are geographically diversified and target a range of opportunistic real estate and related investments. The Blackstone Real Estate Debt Strategies platform targets debt investment opportunities collateralized by commercial real estate. The hedge fund solutions segment manages $80.7 million AUM and is primarily comprised of Blackstone Alternative Asset Management, a discretionary allocator to hedge funds, managing a range of commingled and customized hedge fund of fund solutions. Last, the credit segment manages $144.3 billion AUM and consists of GSO Capital Partners LP, a leveraged finance-focused alternative asset manager that operates worldwide. Its investment funds include loans and securities of non-investment grade companies spread across the capital structure, including senior debt, subordinated debt, preferred stock and common equity. In 2020, Blackstone agreed to acquire Takeda Consumer Healthcare Company Limited, DCI and a majority stake in HealthEdge; acquired genealogy provider Ancestry; and sold its stakes in Cheniere Energy Partners L.P., Rothesay Life and De Nora.

FINANCIAL DATA: Note: Data for latest year may not have been available at press time.

In U.S. $	2020	2019	2018	2017	2016	2015
Revenue	5,966,307,000	7,421,451,000	6,860,991,000	5,911,231,000	4,389,138,000	4,197,289,000
R&D Expense						
Operating Income						
Operating Margin %						
SGA Expense	724,646,000	697,146,000	673,359,000	599,103,000	572,490,000	655,602,000
Net Income	1,045,363,000	2,049,682,000	1,541,788,000	1,470,830,000	1,039,235,000	709,789,000
Operating Cash Flow	1,935,945,000	1,963,107,000	45,742,000	-2,448,740,000	-541,286,000	2,397,043,000
Capital Expenditure	111,650,000	60,280,000	18,377,000	24,347,000	21,826,000	59,247,000
EBITDA						
Return on Assets %		.07%	.05%	.05%	.04%	.03%
Return on Equity %		.31%	.24%	.22%	.16%	.11%
Debt to Equity		1.658	1.56	2.232	1.372	0.976

CONTACT INFORMATION:

Phone: 212 583-5000   Fax:
Toll-Free:
Address: 345 Park Ave., New York, NY 10154 United States

STOCK TICKER/OTHER:

Stock Ticker: BX   Exchange: NYS
Employees: 3,165   Fiscal Year Ends: 12/31
Parent Company:

SALARIES/BONUSES:

Top Exec. Salary: $ Bonus: $
Second Exec. Salary: $ Bonus: $

OTHER THOUGHTS:

Estimated Female Officers or Directors: 2
Hot Spot for Advancement for Women/Minorities: Y

Bloomberg LP

NAIC Code: 511120A

www.bloomberg.com

TYPES OF BUSINESS:

Financial Data and News Publishing
Magazine Publishing
Management Software
Multimedia Presentation Services
Broadcast Television
Radio Broadcasting
Electronic Exchange Systems
Economic Data

BRANDS/DIVISIONS/AFFILIATES:

Bloomberg Terminal
Bloomberg Tradebook LLC
Bloomberg Briefs
Bloomberg Indexes
Bloomberg Government
Bloomberg New Energy Finance Limited
Bloomberg Business
Bloomberg Television

CONTACTS: Note: Officers with more than one job title may be intentionally listed here more than once.

Michael Bloomberg, CEO
Jason Schechter, Chief Communications Officer
Matthew Winkler, Editor-in-Chief, Bloomberg News
Thomas Secunda, Vice Chmn.
Peter Grauer, Chmn.

GROWTH PLANS/SPECIAL FEATURES:

Bloomberg LP is an information services, news and media company, serving the financial services industry, government offices and agencies, corporations and news organizations. The company operates in five segments: communications, financial products, industry products, media and media services. Communications provides press announcements involving Bloomberg through its worldwide press contact centers, including the Americas, Europe/Middle East/Africa and Asia Pacific. Financial products are comprised of the Bloomberg Terminal, a platform for financial professionals who need real-time data, news and analytics to make fast and informed decisions; and the Bloomberg Tradebook, LLC, a global agency broker that provides anonymous direct market access and algorithmic trading to more than 110 global liquidity venues across 40+ countries. This division also includes Bloomberg Briefs, Bloomberg Indexes, Bloomberg SEF (swap execution facility) and Bloomberg Institute. Industry products include Bloomberg Government, a web-based information service for professionals who interact with the federal government; Bloomberg Law/BNA and Bloomberg Big Law for legal, tax and regulatory professionals; and Bloomberg New Energy Finance Limited for decision-makers in the energy system. Media delivers business and political news through Bloomberg Business, Bloomberg Politics, Bloomberg View, Bloomberg Television, Bloomberg Radio, Bloomberg Mobile Apps and news bureaus. Media Services includes advertising and media distribution services. Bloomberg LP's news and analytics solutions allow enterprise customers to access, integrate, distribute and manage data and information across organizations.

FINANCIAL DATA: Note: Data for latest year may not have been available at press time.

In U.S. $	2020	2019	2018	2017	2016	2015
Revenue	11,000,000,000	10,500,000,000	10,000,000,000	9,658,000,000	9,400,000,000	9,184,000,000
R&D Expense						
Operating Income						
Operating Margin %						
SGA Expense						
Net Income						
Operating Cash Flow						
Capital Expenditure						
EBITDA						
Return on Assets %						
Return on Equity %						
Debt to Equity						

CONTACT INFORMATION:

Phone: 212-318-2000   Fax: 917-369-5000
Toll-Free:
Address: 731 Lexington Ave., New York, NY 10022 United States

STOCK TICKER/OTHER:

Stock Ticker: Private
Employees: 21,000
Parent Company:

Exchange:
Fiscal Year Ends: 12/31

SALARIES/BONUSES:

Top Exec. Salary: $ Bonus: $
Second Exec. Salary: $ Bonus: $

OTHER THOUGHTS:

Estimated Female Officers or Directors: 8
Hot Spot for Advancement for Women/Minorities: Y

Blue Shield of California
NAIC Code: 524114

www.blueshieldca.com

TYPES OF BUSINESS:
Insurance-Medical & Health, HMOs & PPOs
Managed Care
Life Insurance
Dental Insurance
Health Insurance
Health Maintenance Organization

BRANDS/DIVISIONS/AFFILIATES:
Blue Cross and Blue Shield Association
Blue Shield of California Life & Health Insurance
Blue Shield of California Foundation

CONTACTS: *Note: Officers with more than one job title may be intentionally listed here more than once.*
Paul S. Markovich, CEO
Sarah Iselin, COO
Sandra Clarke, CFO
Jeffrey Robertson, Sr. VP-Mktg. & Consumer Growth
Mary O'Hara, Exec. VP-People
Marcus Thygeson, Chief Health Officer
Lisa Davis, CIO
Seth A. Jacobs, General Counsel
Steve Shivinsky, VP-Corp. Comm.
Tom Brophy, VP-Finance & Treas. Svcs.
Ed Cymerys, Chief Actuary
Juan Davila, Exec. VP-Health Care Quality & Affordability
Rob Geyer, Sr. VP-Customer Quality
Kirsten Gorsuch, Sr. VP-External Affairs
Kristina Leslie, Chmn.

GROWTH PLANS/SPECIAL FEATURES:
Blue Shield of California (BSC) is a nonprofit mutual benefit corporation and a member of the Blue Cross Blue Shield Association, serving approximately 4.5 million members. The firm offers insurance plans including health maintenance organizations (HMOs) and preferred provider organizations (PPOs), as well as dental and Medicare supplemental through its offices in California. BSC works with HMO physicians and specialists, PPO physicians and specialists, HMO hospitals and PPO hospitals. The company also offers executive medical reimbursement, life and vision insurance and short-term health plans through Blue Shield of California Life & Health Insurance Company (Blue Shield Life). The Blue Shield of California Foundation provides charitable contributions and conducts research and supports programs with an emphasis on domestic violence prevention and medical technology assessments. BSC also offers plans for self-employed California workers not covered by employer-sponsored health plans, as well as low cost PPO plans for individuals. The company offers an enhanced small group dental benefit for pregnant women to reduce risks of periodontal disease and pregnancy gingivitis and is expanding dental coverage options with four new dental PPO plans for small groups.

BSC offers its employees medical, dental and vision coverage; life insurance; disability insurance; tuition reimbursement; flexible spending accounts; discounts on entertainment and chiropractic and massage therapy; income protection benefits; a 401(k) sa

FINANCIAL DATA: *Note: Data for latest year may not have been available at press time.*

In U.S. $	2020	2019	2018	2017	2016	2015
Revenue	21,806,000,000	21,086,000,000	20,632,000,000	17,684,000,000	17,598,000,000	14,836,000,000
R&D Expense						
Operating Income						
Operating Margin %						
SGA Expense						
Net Income	680,000,000	573,000,000	413,000,000	296,000,000	67,000,000	115,000,000
Operating Cash Flow						
Capital Expenditure						
EBITDA						
Return on Assets %						
Return on Equity %						
Debt to Equity						

CONTACT INFORMATION:
Phone: 510-607-2000   Fax:
Toll-Free:
Address: 601 12th St., Oakland, CA 94607 United States

SALARIES/BONUSES:
Top Exec. Salary: $ Bonus: $
Second Exec. Salary: $ Bonus: $

STOCK TICKER/OTHER:
Stock Ticker: Nonprofit   Exchange:
Employees: 7,500   Fiscal Year Ends: 12/31
Parent Company:

OTHER THOUGHTS:
Estimated Female Officers or Directors: 14
Hot Spot for Advancement for Women/Minorities: Y

BMC Software Inc

NAIC Code: 511210H

TYPES OF BUSINESS:

Computer Software, Mainframe Related
Systems Management Software
e-Business Software
Consulting & Training Services

BRANDS/DIVISIONS/AFFILIATES:

KKR & Co LP

CONTACTS: *Note: Officers with more than one job title may be intentionally listed here more than once.*

Ayman Sayed, CEO
Michelle Carbone, Sr. VP-Oper.
Marc Rothman, CFO
Saar Shwartz, CMO
Eric Olmo, Sr. VP-People & Spaces
Ali Siddiqui, Chief Product Officer
Hollie Castro, Sr. VP-Admin.
Patrick K. Tagtow, General Counsel
Steve Goddard, Sr. VP-Bus. Oper.
Ken Berryman, Sr. VP-Strategy & Corp. Dev.
Ann Duhon, Mgr.-Comm.
Derrick Vializ, VP-Investor Rel.
T. Cory Bleuer, Chief Acct. Officer
Patrick K. Tagtow, Chief Compliance Officer
Paul Avenant, Sr. VP-Solutions
Ram Chakravarti, CTO

GROWTH PLANS/SPECIAL FEATURES:

BMC Software, Inc. is a software vendor company that provides system management, service management and automation solutions primarily for large companies. The company's software products span mainframe systems, IT service management, cloud management, IT operations, digital, chatbot, software-as-a-service (SaaS)-based solutions, workflow orchestration workload automation and IT automation. BMC's solutions are grouped into six categories: multi-cloud management, security and compliance, artificial intelligence and machine learning, automation and DevOps, IT optimization and service management. Multi-cloud management solutions include multi-cloud cost control, asset visibility, cloud performance management, automation across clouds, cloud security, cloud migration and services management across clouds. Security and compliance solutions include building a SecOps strategy, ensuring GDPR compliance, remediating vulnerabilities and managing policies and compliance. AI & machine learning solutions include cognitive service management, AI application to IT, big data insights, and acceleration via self-managing mainframe. Automation and DevOps solutions include automating workloads, file transfers, application deployment and data centers. IT optimization solutions cover IT infrastructure, cloud spend, applications performance, mainframe costs and database performance. Last, service management solutions offer transformation, modernization, IT asset visibility and digital workplace enhancement.

FINANCIAL DATA: *Note: Data for latest year may not have been available at press time.*

In U.S. $	2020	2019	2018	2017	2016	2015
Revenue	2,178,000,000	2,200,000,000	2,000,000,000	2,500,000,000	2,300,000,000	2,250,000,000
R&D Expense						
Operating Income						
Operating Margin %						
SGA Expense						
Net Income						
Operating Cash Flow						
Capital Expenditure						
EBITDA						
Return on Assets %						
Return on Equity %						
Debt to Equity						

CONTACT INFORMATION:

Phone: 713 918-8800   Fax: 713 918-8000
Toll-Free: 800-793-4262
Address: 2103 Citywest Blvd., Houston, TX 77042 United States

STOCK TICKER/OTHER:

Stock Ticker: Subsidiary   Exchange:
Employees: 6,000   Fiscal Year Ends: 03/31
Parent Company: KKR & Co LP

SALARIES/BONUSES:

Top Exec. Salary: $ Bonus: $
Second Exec. Salary: $ Bonus: $

OTHER THOUGHTS:

Estimated Female Officers or Directors: 2
Hot Spot for Advancement for Women/Minorities: Y

BMC Stock Holdings Inc

www.buildwithbmc.com

NAIC Code: 444190

TYPES OF BUSINESS:

Building Materials & Hardware Stores, Retail
Building & Construction Services

BRANDS/DIVISIONS/AFFILIATES:

BMC
Ready-Frame
BMC Design
BMC Timber Truss

CONTACTS: Note: Officers with more than one job title may be intentionally listed here more than once.

David Flitman, CEO
James Major, CFO
David Bullock, Director
Mike Farmer, Executive VP, Divisional
Lisa Hamblet, Executive VP, Divisional
Timothy Johnson, Executive VP

GROWTH PLANS/SPECIAL FEATURES:

BMC Stock Holdings, Inc. is a diversified lumber and building materials distributor and solutions provider that sells to new construction, repair and remodeling contractors. The company carries a wide range of products via operations in 18 U.S. states. Its primary products include lumber, lumber sheet goods, millwork, doors, flooring, windows, structural components (engineered wood products, trusses and wall panels) and other exterior products. BMC's solution-based services include design, product specification, installation and installation management services. The firm also offers a broad range of products sourced through a network of suppliers, which together with various solution-based services, represent approximately 50% of the construction cost of a typical new home. BMC serves its customers from more than 150 locations, which include 110 distribution and retail operations, 48 millwork fabrication operations and 53 truss, panel and engineered wood products floor operations. Brands of the company include BMC, Ready-Frame, BMC Design and BMC Timber Truss. In August 2020 BMC and Builders FirstSource, Inc. announced that they have entered into a definitive merger agreement under which the two will combine in an all-stock merger transaction. The combined company will operate under the name Builders FirstSource, Inc. and will be headquartered in Dallas, TX.

FINANCIAL DATA: Note: Data for latest year may not have been available at press time.

In U.S. $	2020	2019	2018	2017	2016	2015
Revenue		3,626,593,024	3,682,447,872	3,365,967,872	3,093,743,104	1,576,745,984
R&D Expense						
Operating Income						
Operating Margin %						
SGA Expense						
Net Income		109,845,000	119,738,000	57,425,000	30,880,000	-4,831,000
Operating Cash Flow						
Capital Expenditure						
EBITDA						
Return on Assets %						
Return on Equity %						
Debt to Equity						

CONTACT INFORMATION:

Phone: 919-431-1000 Fax:
Toll-Free:
Address: 8020 Arco Corporate Drive, Ste. 400, Raleigh, NC 27617
United States

STOCK TICKER/OTHER:

Stock Ticker: BMCH
Employees: 10,200
Parent Company:

Exchange: NAS
Fiscal Year Ends: 12/31

SALARIES/BONUSES:

Top Exec. Salary: $ Bonus: $
Second Exec. Salary: $ Bonus: $

OTHER THOUGHTS:

Estimated Female Officers or Directors: 2
Hot Spot for Advancement for Women/Minorities:

BNSF (Burlington Northern Santa Fe LLC)   www.bnsf.com
NAIC Code: 482111

TYPES OF BUSINESS:
Line-Haul Railroads
Railroad Infrastructure Management
Locomotive Operation
Intermodal Hubs
Real Estate Development Services

BRANDS/DIVISIONS/AFFILIATES:
Berkshire Hathaway Inc
BSNF Railway Company

CONTACTS: Note: Officers with more than one job title may be intentionally listed here more than once.
Kathryn Farmer, CEO
Julie A. Piggott, CFO
Stevan B. Bobb, Exec. VP
Dean Wise, VP-Network Strategy
Richard Weicher, General Counsel-Regulatory
Charles W. Shewmake, General Counsel
Gregory C. Fox, Exec. VP-Oper.
Julie A. Piggott, VP-Planning & Studies
Zak Andersen, VP-Corp. Rel.
David Stropes, VP-Corp. Audit Services
Julie A. Piggott, Controller
Roger Nober, Exec. VP-Law & Secretary
Michael R. Annis, VP-Tax
Judy Carter, VP-Compliance & Audit
Dean H. Wise, VP-Network Strategy
Paul W. Bischler, Chief Sourcing Officer

GROWTH PLANS/SPECIAL FEATURES:
Burlington Northern Santa Fe, LLC (BNSF), a subsidiary of Berkshire Hathaway, Inc., is engaged in the freight rail transportation business. BNSF, through its primary subsidiary, BNSF Railway Company, controls one of North America's largest railroad systems, operating approximately 32,500 route miles of track that pass through 28 states and three Canadian provinces. The railway is a product of nearly 400 railroads acquired over the past 160 years. BNSF Railway operates various facilities and equipment, including approximately 8,000 locomotives. It also operates 25 intermodal hubs and serves more than 40 ports. In addition to major cities and ports, the company serves smaller markets through partnerships with numerous shortline partners. The railway transports consumer, industrial and agricultural freight products. Intermodal or consumer products include truck trailers and containers, canned goods, sugar, automotive goods and low-sulfur coal. Industrial products include construction, building, petroleum, forest products, metals, minerals, chemicals and plastic products. Agricultural products include wheat, corn, bulk foods, soybeans, oil seeds and meals, feeds, barley, oats and rye, flour and mill products, sorghum, oils, specialty grains, malt, ethanol and fertilizer. As a supplement to railway revenues, the company also offers economic and real estate development services. Annually, the firm delivers over 1.1 million carloads of agricultural products, nearly 2 million carloads of industrial products, 1.8 million coal shipments and more than 5 million intermodal shipments (truck trailers or containers).

BNSF offers its employees comprehensive health benefits, retirement options and a range of employee assistance plans and programs.

FINANCIAL DATA: Note: Data for latest year may not have been available at press time.

In U.S. $	2020	2019	2018	2017	2016	2015
Revenue	20,181,000,000	22,745,000,000	22,999,000,000	21,387,000,000	19,829,000,000	21,967,000,000
R&D Expense						
Operating Income						
Operating Margin %						
SGA Expense						
Net Income	5,161,000,000	5,481,000,000	5,219,000,000	3,959,000,000	3,569,000,000	4,248,000,000
Operating Cash Flow						
Capital Expenditure						
EBITDA						
Return on Assets %						
Return on Equity %						
Debt to Equity						

CONTACT INFORMATION:
Phone: 817-352-1000   Fax: 817-352-7171
Toll-Free: 800-795-2673
Address: 2650 Lou Menk Dr., Fort Worth, TX 76131-2830 United States

STOCK TICKER/OTHER:
Stock Ticker: Subsidiary   Exchange:
Employees: 35,000   Fiscal Year Ends: 12/31
Parent Company: Berkshire Hathaway Inc

SALARIES/BONUSES:
Top Exec. Salary: $ Bonus: $
Second Exec. Salary: $ Bonus: $

OTHER THOUGHTS:
Estimated Female Officers or Directors: 3
Hot Spot for Advancement for Women/Minorities: Y

Bonneville Power Administration

www.bpa.gov

NAIC Code: 221111

TYPES OF BUSINESS:
Hydroelectric Power Generation & Transmission
Transmission Lines
Power Marketing & Distribution

BRANDS/DIVISIONS/AFFILIATES:

CONTACTS: Note: Officers with more than one job title may be intentionally listed here more than once.
John Hairston, Acting CEO
Tom McDonald, Acting COO
Michelle Manary, CFO
Ben Berry, CIO
Randy Roach, General Counsel
Cathy Ehli, Exec. VP-Corp. Strategy
Elliot Mainzer, Deputy Administrator
Greg Delwiche, Sr. VP-Power Svcs.
Larry Bekkedahl, Sr. VP-Transmission Svcs.
John Hairston, Exec. VP-Internal Bus. Svcs.

GROWTH PLANS/SPECIAL FEATURES:
Bonneville Power Administration (BPA), a division of the U.S. Department of Energy, markets and transmits wholesale electricity at cost to the Pacific Northwest's public utilities, public utility districts, municipal districts, public cooperatives, private utilities and a few large industrial customers. Its service territory covers 300,000 square miles and includes large portions of Washington, Idaho and Oregon and smaller portions of California, Utah, Nevada, Montana and Wyoming. Some of the firm's customers buy all of their power from BPA, while others supplement their supply with non-federal power. The company's electricity comes largely from the Federal Columbia River Power System (CRPS), a system of 31 hydroelectric plants on the Columbia River and its tributaries, which it operates with the U.S. Army Corps of Engineers and U.S. Bureau of Reclamation. It also purchases power from one private nuclear plant and several non-federal hydroelectric plants and wind energy generation facilities. When the Northwest has heavy snow and rain, the CRPS can generate more electricity than its customers need, offering surplus energy to its primary customers first and then to utilities and municipalities outside the region. BPA provides approximately 28% of the electricity used in the Northwest and operates over 75% of the region's high-voltage transmission grid. The company also operates large interregional transmission lines that connect to Canada, California, the Southwest and eastern Montana.

BPA offers its employees health care, retirement and savings plans, subsidized public transportation, child and eldercare and onsite fitness centers at Portland and Vancouver locations and fitness reimbursement programs for field employees.

FINANCIAL DATA: Note: Data for latest year may not have been available at press time.

In U.S. $	2020	2019	2018	2017	2016	2015
Revenue	3,683,700,000	3,655,900,000	3,710,300,000	3,596,800,000	3,432,600,000	3,404,432,000
R&D Expense						
Operating Income						
Operating Margin %						
SGA Expense						
Net Income	245,700,000	247,600,000	470,600,000	338,600,000	277,200,000	404,654,000
Operating Cash Flow						
Capital Expenditure						
EBITDA						
Return on Assets %						
Return on Equity %						
Debt to Equity						

CONTACT INFORMATION:
Phone: 503-230-3000   Fax: 503-230-5884
Toll-Free: 800-282-3713
Address: 905 NE 11th Ave., Portland, OR 97232 United States

STOCK TICKER/OTHER:
Stock Ticker: Government-Owned   Exchange:
Employees: 2,793   Fiscal Year Ends: 09/30
Parent Company:

SALARIES/BONUSES:
Top Exec. Salary: $ Bonus: $
Second Exec. Salary: $ Bonus: $

OTHER THOUGHTS:
Estimated Female Officers or Directors: 3
Hot Spot for Advancement for Women/Minorities: Y

Sales, profits and employees may be estimates. Financial information, benefits and other data can change quickly and may vary from those stated here.

Booz Allen Hamilton Holding Corporation

www.boozallen.com

NAIC Code: 541610

TYPES OF BUSINESS:

Strategy Consulting
Engineering & IT Consulting
Supply Chain Management
Industry Research & Publications
War Gaming & Strategic Simulation

BRANDS/DIVISIONS/AFFILIATES:

Carlyle Group (The)

CONTACTS: *Note: Officers with more than one job title may be intentionally listed here more than once.*

Horacio Rozanski, CEO
Lloyd Howell, CFO
Ralph Shrader, Chairman of the Board
Nancy Laben, Chief Legal Officer
Gary Labovich, Executive VP
Kristine Anderson, Executive VP
Christopher Ling, Executive VP
Karen Dahut, Executive VP
Joseph Mahaffee, Executive VP
Angela Messer, Executive VP
Susan Penfield, Executive VP
Elizabeth Thompson, Executive VP

GROWTH PLANS/SPECIAL FEATURES:

Booz Allen Hamilton Holding Corporation (BAH), founded in 1914, provides management and technology consulting, engineering, analytics, digital solutions, mission operations and cyber expertise to U.S. and international governments, major corporations and nonprofit organizations. Specific markets served by BAH include civil government, commercial, defense, intelligence, international, energy, resources, utilities, financial services, health, homeland security, law enforcement and transportation. In addition, BAH is engaged in incubating and developing digital, cyber, artificial intelligent (AI) and immersive solutions in order to solve future problems via technology, software and other solutions for its clients. Investment firm, The Carlyle Group, maintains a majority interest in the company. In June 2021, BAH acquired Liberty IT Solutions, LLC, a digital firm that drives transformation across the federal IT ecosystem with robust, modern software development capabilities including Agile, DevSecOps, and application programming interfaces (APIs) as well as cloud and low-code/no-code (LCNC) solutions implementation.

Booz Allen Hamilton offers employees dental, medical and vision insurance; life insurance; medical flexible spending accounts; tuition assistance; an employee assistance program; and health and wellness programs.

FINANCIAL DATA: *Note: Data for latest year may not have been available at press time.*

In U.S. $	2020	2019	2018	2017	2016	2015
Revenue	7,463,841,000	6,704,037,000	6,171,853,000	5,804,284,000	5,405,738,000	
R&D Expense						
Operating Income	669,202,000	602,394,000	520,085,000	484,247,000	444,584,000	
Operating Margin %	.09%	.09%	.08%	.08%	.08%	
SGA Expense	3,334,378,000	2,932,602,000	2,719,909,000	2,568,511,000	2,319,592,000	
Net Income	482,603,000	418,529,000	305,111,000	252,490,000	294,094,000	
Operating Cash Flow	551,428,000	499,610,000	369,143,000	382,277,000	249,234,000	
Capital Expenditure	128,079,000	94,681,000	78,437,000	53,919,000	66,635,000	
EBITDA	750,693,000	668,443,000	579,668,000	533,742,000	511,813,000	
Return on Assets %	.11%	.11%	.09%	.08%	.10%	
Return on Equity %	.63%	.68%	.54%	.51%	.98%	
Debt to Equity	2.66	2.52	3.165	2.563	3.634	

CONTACT INFORMATION:

Phone: 703 902-5000   Fax: 703 902-3333
Toll-Free:
Address: 8283 Greensboro Dr., McLean, VA 22102 United States

STOCK TICKER/OTHER:

Stock Ticker: BAH   Exchange: NYS
Employees: 27,700   Fiscal Year Ends:
Parent Company: Carlyle Group (The)

SALARIES/BONUSES:

Top Exec. Salary: $ Bonus: $
Second Exec. Salary: $ Bonus: $

OTHER THOUGHTS:

Estimated Female Officers or Directors: 4
Hot Spot for Advancement for Women/Minorities: Y

Boston Consulting Group Inc (The, BCG)   www.bcg.com
NAIC Code: 541610

TYPES OF BUSINESS:
Management Consulting
Management Consulting
Analytics

BRANDS/DIVISIONS/AFFILIATES:

CONTACTS: Note: Officers with more than one job title may be intentionally listed here more than once.
Christopher Schweizer, CEO
Paul Tranter, CFO
Jeremy Barton, General Counsel
Miki Tsusaka, Sr. Partner
Sharon Marcil, Sr. Partner
Matthew Krentz, Sr. Partner
Hans-Paul Burkner, Chmn.
Vaishali Rastogi, Partner

GROWTH PLANS/SPECIAL FEATURES:
The Boston Consulting Group, Inc. (BCG) is a global management consulting firm as well as a world-leading advisor on business strategy. BCG partners with clients from the private, public and nonprofit sectors in all regions to identify their highest-value opportunities, address critical challenges and transform their enterprises. The company's capabilities include big data, advanced analytics, diversity/inclusion, growth, marketing, sales, people/organization, procurement, strategy, transformation, restructuring, change management, enablement, innovation, product development, mergers/acquisitions, post-merger integration, smart simplicity, sustainability, corporate development, finance, globalization, manufacturing, operations, pricing, social impact and technology/digital. Industries served by BCG include automotive, mobility, biopharmaceuticals, consumer products, education, energy, environment, engineered products, infrastructure, financial institutions, health care payers/providers/services, insurance, media, entertainment, medical devices, technology, metals, mining, principal investors, private equity, process industrial materials, building materials, public sector, retail, technology industries, telecommunications, transportation, travel and tourism. BCG has offices in more than 90 cities in 50 countries.

FINANCIAL DATA: Note: Data for latest year may not have been available at press time.

In U.S. $	2020	2019	2018	2017	2016	2015
Revenue	8,600,000,000	8,500,000,000	7,500,000,000	6,300,000,000	5,600,000,000	5,000,000,000
R&D Expense						
Operating Income						
Operating Margin %						
SGA Expense						
Net Income						
Operating Cash Flow						
Capital Expenditure						
EBITDA						
Return on Assets %						
Return on Equity %						
Debt to Equity						

CONTACT INFORMATION:
Phone: 617-973-1200   Fax: 617-973-1399
Toll-Free:
Address: 200 Pier 4 Blvd., Boston, MA 02210 United States

STOCK TICKER/OTHER:
Stock Ticker: Private
Employees: 22,000
Parent Company:

Exchange:
Fiscal Year Ends: 12/31

SALARIES/BONUSES:
Top Exec. Salary: $ Bonus: $
Second Exec. Salary: $ Bonus: $

OTHER THOUGHTS:
Estimated Female Officers or Directors: 4
Hot Spot for Advancement for Women/Minorities: Y

Brightstar Corporation

NAIC Code: 423690

www.brightstar.com

TYPES OF BUSINESS:

Telecommunication Supply Chain & Distribution Services
Wireless Device & Accessories Distribution
Wireless Device Manufacturing
Supply Chain, Marketing and Retail Consultation

BRANDS/DIVISIONS/AFFILIATES:

Brightstar Capital Partners

GROWTH PLANS/SPECIAL FEATURES:

Brightstar Corporation, owned by private equity firm Brightstar Capital Partners, distributes and manages telecommunication devices and accessories globally. The firm serves carrier, retail and enterprise customers across approximately 50 countries worldwide and process millions of devices annually. Brightstar operates at every stage of the device lifecycle to provide an integrated experience with its customer's business, from the moment it is manufactured to the time it is traded in and remarketed. For businesses, Brightstar also operates at every stage of the device lifecycle in order to provide integrated services that link seamlessly. This infrastructure enables businesses to better serve their customers by providing end-to-end service. In December 2020, Brightstar announced plans to sell its 51% stake in Brightstar India to an investment firm in the U.K., to focus on core geographies and streamline operations.

CONTACTS: Note: Officers with more than one job title may be intentionally listed here more than once.

Rod Millar, CEO
Dennis J. Strand, Pres., Brightstar Financial Svcs.
Jack Negro, CFO
Ray Roman, CCO
Catherine Smith, Sr. VP
Bela Lainck, Pres., Buy-Back & Trade-In Solutions
Rafael M. de Guzman, III, VP-Strategy
Oscar J. Fumagali, Chief Treas. Officer
Oscar J. Rojas, Pres., Brightstar Latin America
Arturo A. Osorio, Pres., Asia Pacific, Middle East & Africa
Jeff Gower, Pres., Brightstar U.S. & Canada
David Leach, CEO-eSecuritel
Michael Singer, Sr. VP-Global Strategy & New Bus. Dev.
Ramon Colomina, Pres., Supply Chain Solutions

FINANCIAL DATA: Note: Data for latest year may not have been available at press time.

In U.S. $	2020	2019	2018	2017	2016	2015
Revenue	11,576,250,000	11,025,000,000	10,500,000,000	10,000,000,000	7,750,000,000	7,600,000,000
R&D Expense						
Operating Income						
Operating Margin %						
SGA Expense						
Net Income						
Operating Cash Flow						
Capital Expenditure						
EBITDA						
Return on Assets %						
Return on Equity %						
Debt to Equity						

CONTACT INFORMATION:

Phone: 682-348-0354   Fax:
Toll-Free:
Address: 1900 W. Kirkwood Blvd., Ste. 1600C, Southlake, TX 76092 United States

STOCK TICKER/OTHER:

Stock Ticker: Subsidiary   Exchange:
Employees: 9,000   Fiscal Year Ends: 12/31
Parent Company: Brightstar Capital Partners

SALARIES/BONUSES:

Top Exec. Salary: $ Bonus: $
Second Exec. Salary: $ Bonus: $

OTHER THOUGHTS:

Estimated Female Officers or Directors: 1
Hot Spot for Advancement for Women/Minorities:

Bristol-Myers Squibb Company

www.bms.com

NAIC Code: 325412

TYPES OF BUSINESS:

Drugs-Diversified
Biopharmaceuticals
Manufacturing
Distribution
Marketing

BRANDS/DIVISIONS/AFFILIATES:

MyoKardia Inc

CONTACTS: Note: Officers with more than one job title may be intentionally listed here more than once.

Giovanni Caforio, CEO
Charles Bancroft, CFO
Adam Dubow, Chief Compliance Officer
Paul von Autenried, Chief Information Officer
Thomas Lynch, Chief Scientific Officer
Christopher Boerner, Executive VP
Sandra Leung, General Counsel
Ann Judge, Other Executive Officer
Louis Schmukler, President, Divisional
John Elicker, Senior VP, Divisional
Paul Biondi, Senior VP, Divisional
Karen Santiago, Senior VP

GROWTH PLANS/SPECIAL FEATURES:

Bristol-Myers Squibb Company (BMS) discovers, develops, licenses, manufactures, markets, distributes and sells biopharmaceutical products on a global basis. BMS focuses on discovering, developing and delivering transformational medicines for patients facing serious diseases such as cancer, as well as immunology, cardiovascular and fibrosis. The company's products are sold worldwide, primarily to wholesalers, distributors, specialty pharmacies, and to a lesser extent, directly to retailers, hospitals, clinics and government agencies. BMS manufactures its products in the U.S. and Puerto Rico, with most revenues coming from products in hematology, oncology, cardiovascular and immunology therapeutic classes. More than 60% of annual revenues is derived from the U.S., 23% from Europe and the remainder from the rest of the world. In late-2020, BMS acquired MyoKardia, Inc., a clinical-stage biopharmaceutical company, for $13.1 billion in cash.

BMS offers its employees medical and dental insurance; pension and 401(k) plans; short- and long-term disability coverage; travel accident insurance; an employee assistance plan; and adoption assistance.

FINANCIAL DATA: Note: Data for latest year may not have been available at press time.

In U.S. $	2020	2019	2018	2017	2016	2015
Revenue	42,518,000,000	26,145,000,000	22,561,000,000	20,776,000,000	19,427,000,000	16,560,000,000
R&D Expense	11,143,000,000	6,148,000,000	6,345,000,000	6,411,000,000	4,940,000,000	5,920,000,000
Operating Income	1,647,000,000	5,612,000,000	4,987,000,000	3,157,000,000	4,430,000,000	1,612,000,000
Operating Margin %		.23%	.23%	.17%	.23%	.10%
SGA Expense	7,661,000,000	4,871,000,000	4,551,000,000	4,849,000,000	5,002,000,000	5,001,000,000
Net Income	-9,015,000,000	3,439,000,000	4,920,000,000	1,007,000,000	4,457,000,000	1,565,000,000
Operating Cash Flow	14,052,000,000	8,067,000,000	5,940,000,000	5,275,000,000	2,850,000,000	1,832,000,000
Capital Expenditure	753,000,000	836,000,000	951,000,000	1,055,000,000	1,215,000,000	820,000,000
EBITDA	4,929,000,000	7,377,000,000	6,788,000,000	6,116,000,000	6,464,000,000	2,637,000,000
Return on Assets %		.04%	.14%	.03%	.14%	.05%
Return on Equity %		.10%	.38%	.07%	.29%	.11%
Debt to Equity		0.854	0.402	0.594	0.353	0.459

CONTACT INFORMATION:

Phone: 212 546-4000   Fax: 212 546-4020
Toll-Free:
Address: 430 E. 29th St., 14/Fl, New York, NY 10016 United States

STOCK TICKER/OTHER:

Stock Ticker: BMY   Exchange: NYS
Employees: 30,000   Fiscal Year Ends: 12/31
Parent Company:

SALARIES/BONUSES:

Top Exec. Salary: $ Bonus: $
Second Exec. Salary: $ Bonus: $

OTHER THOUGHTS:

Estimated Female Officers or Directors: 4
Hot Spot for Advancement for Women/Minorities: Y

Broadcom Inc

NAIC Code: 335313

www.broadcom.com

TYPES OF BUSINESS:

Electrical Switches, Sensors, MEMS, Optomechanicals
Semiconductors
Connectivity Technology
Wireless Applications
Optical Products
Mainframe Software
Enterprise Software
Security Software

BRANDS/DIVISIONS/AFFILIATES:

CONTACTS: *Note: Officers with more than one job title may be intentionally listed here more than once.*

Hock Tan, CEO
Thomas Krause, CFO
Kirsten Spears, Chief Accounting Officer
Henry Samueli, Chief Technology Officer
Bryan Ingram, General Manager, Divisional
Mark Brazeal, Other Executive Officer
Charles Kawwas, Other Executive Officer

GROWTH PLANS/SPECIAL FEATURES:

Broadcom, Inc. designs, develops and supplies a broad range of semiconductor and infrastructure software solutions, with a focus on connectivity technologies. The firm develops semiconductor devices with a focus on complex digital and mixed signal complementary metal oxide semiconductor (CMOS) based devices and analog III-V based products. Broadcom's applications include data center, enterprise storage, broadband, wired networking, wireless communications, mobile communications, industrial, automotive and software solutions. Broadcom's products are vast and are grouped into the categories of storage and systems, wireless, wired connectivity, optical products, mainframe software, enterprise software, and security. Storage and systems products include storage adapters, controllers, integrated circuits, fiber channel networking, peripheral component interconnect (PCI) switches and bridges. Wireless products include radio frequency (RF) and microwave demo boards, FBAR devices, handset power amplifiers, Bluetooth system-on-a-chip (SoC), GNSS/GPS functionality, wireless LAN/Bluetooth combos, and wireless LAN infrastructure. Wired connectivity products include Ethernet connectivity, switching, broadband digital subscriber lines, passive optical networking, set-top box solutions, embedded and networking processors, and customized SoCs. Optical products include fiber optic modules and components, LEDs and other displays, motion control encoders, optocouplers, opto-isolators and optical sensors. Mainframe software products span application development, testing/quality, identity, access, compliance, data protection, operational analytics, operations management, workload automation, content management, databases and product portfolio. Enterprise software products span business management, artificial intelligence (AI) capabilities, enterprise automation, continuous testing and application programming interface (API) full lifecycle management. Last, security products include cyber security and payment security.

FINANCIAL DATA: *Note: Data for latest year may not have been available at press time.*

In U.S. $	2020	2019	2018	2017	2016	2015
Revenue	23,888,000,000	22,597,000,000	20,848,000,000	17,636,000,000	13,240,000,000	6,824,000,000
R&D Expense	4,968,000,000	4,696,000,000	3,768,000,000	3,292,000,000	2,674,000,000	1,049,000,000
Operating Income	4,212,000,000	4,180,000,000	5,368,000,000	2,666,000,000	587,000,000	1,769,000,000
Operating Margin %		.18%	.26%	.15%	.04%	.26%
SGA Expense	1,935,000,000	1,709,000,000	1,056,000,000	787,000,000	806,000,000	486,000,000
Net Income	2,960,000,000	2,724,000,000	12,259,000,000	1,692,000,000	-1,739,000,000	1,364,000,000
Operating Cash Flow	12,061,000,000	9,697,000,000	8,880,000,000	6,551,000,000	3,411,000,000	2,318,000,000
Capital Expenditure	463,000,000	432,000,000	635,000,000	1,069,000,000	723,000,000	593,000,000
EBITDA	11,125,000,000	9,478,000,000	9,254,000,000	7,016,000,000	2,520,000,000	2,620,000,000
Return on Assets %		.05%	.23%	.03%	-.06%	.13%
Return on Equity %		.10%	.52%	.09%	-.15%	.34%
Debt to Equity		1.203	0.656	0.859	0.698	0.828

CONTACT INFORMATION:

Phone: 408-433-8000   Fax:
Toll-Free:
Address: 1320 Ridder Park Dr., San Jose, CA 95131 United States

STOCK TICKER/OTHER:

Stock Ticker: AVGO
Employees: 21,000
Parent Company:

Exchange: NAS
Fiscal Year Ends: 10/31

SALARIES/BONUSES:

Top Exec. Salary: $ Bonus: $
Second Exec. Salary: $ Bonus: $

OTHER THOUGHTS:

Estimated Female Officers or Directors: 5
Hot Spot for Advancement for Women/Minorities: Y

Burger King Worldwide Inc

www.bk.com

NAIC Code: 722513

TYPES OF BUSINESS:

Fast Food Restaurants
Franchising

BRANDS/DIVISIONS/AFFILIATES:

3G Capital
Pershing Square Capital Management LP
Restaurant Brands International Inc
Whopper
BK Stacker
BK Veggie Burger
Croissan'wich
BK Fish Filet

CONTACTS: *Note: Officers with more than one job title may be intentionally listed here more than once.*

Jose Cil, CEO-Restaurant Brands International
Alexandre Behring, Director
Bernardo Hees, Director
Jose Dias, Executive VP, Divisional
Jose Cil, Executive VP
Alex Macedo, Executive VP
Jill Granat, General Counsel

GROWTH PLANS/SPECIAL FEATURES:

Burger King Worldwide, Inc., one of the largest fast food restaurant chains in the world, operates over 20,000 restaurants in more than 100 countries and U.S. territories. Of these restaurants, nearly half are located in the U.S., and nearly all of them (99.5%) are privately-owned and -operated. Burger King's products include hamburgers, chicken sandwiches and tenders, fish sandwiches, french fries, onion rings and shakes as well as breakfast items including croissant sandwiches, french toast sticks and hash browns. Brand names include the Whopper, Whopper Jr., BK Stacker, BK Fish Filet, BK Veggie Burger and Croissan'wich. In an effort to provide healthier food choices and broaden its customer appeal, the firm has added a line of salads, real fruit smoothies and fresh wraps in addition to low-fat versions of existing menu items. Burger King restaurants typically offer counter service, a dining room and drive-through service. Burger King operates under Restaurant Brands International, Inc., which itself is majority-owned by 3G Capital and minority-owned by Pershing Square Capital Management, LP.

The company offers employees medical and dental insurance, life insurance and a 401(k) savings plan.

FINANCIAL DATA: *Note: Data for latest year may not have been available at press time.*

In U.S. $	2020	2019	2018	2017	2016	2015
Revenue	20,038,000,000	22,912,000,000	21,624,000,000	20,075,000,000	18,209,000,000	17,303,700,000
R&D Expense						
Operating Income						
Operating Margin %						
SGA Expense						
Net Income	832,000,000	994,000,000	928,000,000	903,000,000	815,000,000	795,500,000
Operating Cash Flow						
Capital Expenditure						
EBITDA						
Return on Assets %						
Return on Equity %						
Debt to Equity						

CONTACT INFORMATION:

Phone: 305 378-3000   Fax:
Toll-Free: 866-394-2493
Address: 5505 Blue Lagoon Dr., Miami, FL 33126 United States

STOCK TICKER/OTHER:

Stock Ticker: Subsidiary   Exchange:
Employees: 10,870   Fiscal Year Ends: 12/31
Parent Company: 3G Capital

SALARIES/BONUSES:

Top Exec. Salary: $ Bonus: $
Second Exec. Salary: $ Bonus: $

OTHER THOUGHTS:

Estimated Female Officers or Directors: 3
Hot Spot for Advancement for Women/Minorities: Y

Burns & McDonnell Inc

www.burnsmcd.com

NAIC Code: 541330

TYPES OF BUSINESS:

Engineering Services
Construction
Consulting
Environmental Consulting
Architecture & Design
Energy Transmission

BRANDS/DIVISIONS/AFFILIATES:

CONTACTS: Note: Officers with more than one job title may be intentionally listed here more than once.

Ray Kowalik, CEO
Mark Taylor, Treas.
Don Greenwood, Pres., Construction
Ray Kowalik, VP
John Nobles, Pres., Process & Industrial

GROWTH PLANS/SPECIAL FEATURES:

Burns & McDonnell, Inc. is a family of companies that provide engineering, architectural, construction, environmental and consulting services across an array of industries on a global scale. Aviation services span every facility and every service related to the customer's commercial or private operation, including airfields, architecture, infrastructure, technology, security, cogeneration, commissioning, construction, environmental, code consulting, and wastewater/stormwater collection. Chemicals, oil and gas services include biorefining, business consulting, construction, electric power generation/exploration/production, industrial cogeneration, water/wastewater, facilities, midstream, pipeline, Tier 3 compliance and unmanned aerial systems/unmanned aerial vehicles (UAS/UAV). Commercial, retail and institutional services consist of planning, design and construction for project success, covering air quality/noise, architecture, business consulting, construction, commissioning, data/switch centers, federal/military, food/beverage, green buildings, mission-critical, smart buildings and more. Environmental services include air quality/noise, coal combustion residuals management, constructed wetland treatment systems, decommissioning/demolition, emerging contaminants, compliance, engineering, health and safety, studies, permitting, mitigation and much more. Government, military and municipal services include aircraft beddowns, airfields, architecture, cybersecurity, power transmission/distribution, planning, intelligent seaports, technology and more. Manufacturing and industrial services include solutions for controlling costs and optimizing systems and processes. Power services include electric vehicles (EVs), energy storage/transmission/distribution, gas turbines, microgrids, nuclear, plant decommissioning and smart energy. Telecommunications services include backup systems, communication shelters, automation, EVs, fiber, local area networks, SCADA systems and much more. Transportation services include planning, designing and constructing ways to keep traffic flowing while saving time and money. Last, water services include water treatment, supply and systems solutions, erosion/sediment control and water program management.

Burns & McDonnell offers employees comprehensive benefits.

FINANCIAL DATA: Note: Data for latest year may not have been available at press time.

In U.S. $	2020	2019	2018	2017	2016	2015
Revenue	5,300,000,000	4,200,000,000	4,000,000,000	3,450,000,000	3,400,000,000	2,700,000,000
R&D Expense						
Operating Income						
Operating Margin %						
SGA Expense						
Net Income						
Operating Cash Flow						
Capital Expenditure						
EBITDA						
Return on Assets %						
Return on Equity %						
Debt to Equity						

CONTACT INFORMATION:

Phone: 816-333-9400   Fax: 816-822-3028
Toll-Free:
Address: 9400 Ward Pkwy., Kansas City, MO 64114 United States

STOCK TICKER/OTHER:

Stock Ticker: Private   Exchange:
Employees: 7,600   Fiscal Year Ends: 12/31
Parent Company:

SALARIES/BONUSES:

Top Exec. Salary: $ Bonus: $
Second Exec. Salary: $ Bonus: $

OTHER THOUGHTS:

Estimated Female Officers or Directors:
Hot Spot for Advancement for Women/Minorities:

Sales, profits and employees may be estimates. Financial information, benefits and other data can change quickly and may vary from those stated here.

C&S Wholesale Grocers Inc

www.cswg.com

NAIC Code: 424410

TYPES OF BUSINESS:

Wholesale Food Distribution
Warehousing
Wholesale Food Distribution
Produce
Meat
Health & Beauty Aids
Dairy Products
Fresh/Frozen Bakery Items

BRANDS/DIVISIONS/AFFILIATES:

GROWTH PLANS/SPECIAL FEATURES:

C&S Wholesale Grocers, Inc. provides grocery retailers with warehousing, distribution and logistics service solutions. C&S delivers food and non-food items to more than 7,700 independent supermarkets, chain stores, military bases and institutions. The company supplies over 137,000 items including private label products, such as produce, meat, dairy products, delicatessen products, frozen products, tobacco, beauty items and candy. C&S also provides licensing trademark services, automated warehouse technologies, business and accounting services, a hybrid pricing strategy for in-store price reductions, marketing and advertising solutions, store design and engineering services, and other related services.

CONTACTS: *Note: Officers with more than one job title may be intentionally listed here more than once.*

Bob Palmer, CEO
Peter Fiore, Chief Supply Chain Officer
Kevin McNamara, CFO
Eric Winn, Pres., Commercial
Miriam Ort, Chief Human Resources Officer
George Dramalis, CIO
Mike Newbold, Chief Admin. Officer
Bruce Johnson, Chief Organization Effectiveness Officer
Peter Fiore, Exec. VP-Distribution Services
Rick Cohen, Chmn.
Bob Palmer, Exec. VP-Procurement & Sales

FINANCIAL DATA: *Note: Data for latest year may not have been available at press time.*

In U.S. $	2020	2019	2018	2017	2016	2015
Revenue	29,767,500,000	28,350,000,000	27,000,000,000	30,500,000,000	30,000,000,000	29,000,000,000
R&D Expense						
Operating Income						
Operating Margin %						
SGA Expense						
Net Income						
Operating Cash Flow						
Capital Expenditure						
EBITDA						
Return on Assets %						
Return on Equity %						
Debt to Equity						

CONTACT INFORMATION:

Phone: 603-354-7000   Fax:
Toll-Free:
Address: 7 Corporate Dr., Keene, NH 03431 United States

STOCK TICKER/OTHER:

Stock Ticker: Private
Employees: 14,000
Parent Company:

Exchange:
Fiscal Year Ends: 09/30

SALARIES/BONUSES:

Top Exec. Salary: $ Bonus: $
Second Exec. Salary: $ Bonus: $

OTHER THOUGHTS:

Estimated Female Officers or Directors:
Hot Spot for Advancement for Women/Minorities:

Cabelas Inc
NAIC Code: 451110

www.cabelas.com

TYPES OF BUSINESS:
Sporting Goods Stores
Hunting & Fishing Supplies
Camping Equipment
Outdoor Apparel
Catalog & Online Sales

BRANDS/DIVISIONS/AFFILIATES:
BPS Direct LLC (Bass Pro Shops)
Cabelas.com
Cabelas.ca

GROWTH PLANS/SPECIAL FEATURES:
Cabela's, Inc., a subsidiary of BPS Direct, LLC (dba Bass Pro Shops), is a leading retailer of outdoor and hunting supply merchandise. The company's products include merchandise and equipment for hunting, fishing, marine use, camping and recreational sport shooting, as well as casual and outdoor apparel, footwear, optics, vehicle accessories and gifts and home furnishings comprising an outdoor theme. Retail stores range in size from 40,000 to 246,000 square feet, which either comprise the company's standard format or its large/tourist format. Cabela's also offers its products via ecommerce websites (Cabelas.com and Cabelas.ca), mobile apps, inbound telemarketing and print catalog distributions.

CONTACTS:
Note: Officers with more than one job title may be intentionally listed here more than once.

Johnny Morris, CEO-BPS
Thomas Millner, CEO
Douglas Means, Executive VP
Scott Williams, President
Brent LaSure, Secretary

FINANCIAL DATA:
Note: Data for latest year may not have been available at press time.

In U.S. $	2020	2019	2018	2017	2016	2015
Revenue	5,093,550,000	4,630,500,000	4,410,000,000	4,200,000,000	4,129,359,104	3,997,701,888
R&D Expense						
Operating Income						
Operating Margin %						
SGA Expense						
Net Income						
Operating Cash Flow						
Capital Expenditure						
EBITDA						
Return on Assets %						
Return on Equity %						
Debt to Equity						

CONTACT INFORMATION:
Phone: 308 254-5505   Fax: 308 254-4800
Toll-Free: 800-237-4444
Address: One Cabela Dr., Sidney, NE 69160 United States

STOCK TICKER/OTHER:
Stock Ticker: Private   Exchange:
Employees: 19,100   Fiscal Year Ends: 12/31
Parent Company: BPS Direct LLC (Bass Pro Shops)

SALARIES/BONUSES:
Top Exec. Salary: $ Bonus: $
Second Exec. Salary: $ Bonus: $

OTHER THOUGHTS:
Estimated Female Officers or Directors: 2
Hot Spot for Advancement for Women/Minorities:

CACI International Inc

www.caci.com

NAIC Code: 541512

TYPES OF BUSINESS:

Consulting-InfoTech Related
Enterprise Technology
Mission Technology
Security
Information Technology
Cloud
Command and Control
Electronic Warfare

BRANDS/DIVISIONS/AFFILIATES:

Ascent Vision Technologies LLC

CONTACTS: Note: Officers with more than one job title may be intentionally listed here more than once.

Gregory Bradford, CEO, Subsidiary
Kenneth Asbury, CEO
Thomas Mutryn, CFO
J. London, Chairman of the Board
Christopher Voci, Chief Accounting Officer
John Mengucci, COO
J. Koegel, Executive VP
DeEtte Gray, President, Divisional

GROWTH PLANS/SPECIAL FEATURES:

CACI International, Inc. is a holding company whose operations are conducted through subsidiaries located in the U.S. and Europe, primarily providing expertise and technology to enterprise and mission customers on a domestic and international basis. The company's products and services support national security missions and government modernization transformation. For enterprises, CACI provides capabilities that enable the internal operations of an agency, including business systems, business process re-engineering and enterprise information technology (IT). The firm also designs, develops, integrates, deploys and sustains enterprise-wide IT systems in a variety of models. CACI's technology division develops and implements business systems, enterprise applications, and end-to-end IT systems, and modernizes infrastructure via migration to the cloud and IT or software-as-a-service (SaaS). For mission customers, CACI provides capabilities that enable the execution of an agency's primary function/mission, such as supporting them in areas such as command and control, communications, intelligence collection and analysis, signals intelligence, electronic warfare, and cyber operations. CACI develops tools and offerings in an open, software-defined architecture with multi-domain and multi-mission capabilities. CACI provides expertise to both enterprise and mission customers, delivering talent with specific technical and functional knowledge to support internal agency operations (for enterprises), and delivers talent with technical and domain knowledge to support the execution of an agency's mission. During 2020, CACI acquired Ascent Vision Technologies, LLC, a provider of technology and solutions that support multi-domain intelligence, surveillance and reconnaissance (ISR), unmanned aircraft systems, air defense, and counter-unmanned aircraft system operations.

FINANCIAL DATA: Note: Data for latest year may not have been available at press time.

In U.S. $	2020	2019	2018	2017	2016	2015
Revenue	5,720,042,000	4,986,341,000	4,467,860,000	4,354,617,000	3,744,053,000	
R&D Expense						
Operating Income	457,696,000	377,867,000	340,700,000	297,261,000	264,750,000	
Operating Margin %		.08%	.08%	.07%	.07%	
SGA Expense						
Net Income	321,480,000	265,604,000	301,171,000	163,671,000	142,799,000	
Operating Cash Flow	518,705,000	555,297,000	325,127,000	281,250,000	242,577,000	
Capital Expenditure	72,303,000	47,902,000	41,594,000	43,268,000	20,835,000	
EBITDA	568,384,000	463,744,000	412,896,000	369,021,000	329,502,000	
Return on Assets %		.06%	.08%	.04%	.04%	
Return on Equity %		.12%	.15%	.10%	.09%	
Debt to Equity		0.682	0.482	0.657	0.872	

CONTACT INFORMATION:

Phone: 703 841-7800   Fax: 703 841-7882
Toll-Free:
Address: 1100 N. Glebe Rd., Arlington, VA 22201 United States

SALARIES/BONUSES:

Top Exec. Salary: $ Bonus: $
Second Exec. Salary: $ Bonus: $

STOCK TICKER/OTHER:

Stock Ticker: CACI   Exchange: NYS
Employees: 22,900   Fiscal Year Ends: 06/30
Parent Company:

OTHER THOUGHTS:

Estimated Female Officers or Directors: 5
Hot Spot for Advancement for Women/Minorities: Y

Cadence Design Systems Inc

www.cadence.com

NAIC Code: 511210N

TYPES OF BUSINESS:

Software-Electronic Design Automation
Training & Support Services
Design & Methodology Services

BRANDS/DIVISIONS/AFFILIATES:

CONTACTS: *Note: Officers with more than one job title may be intentionally listed here more than once.*

Lip-Bu Tan, CEO
John Wall, CFO
John Shoven, Chairman of the Board
James Cowie, General Counsel
Anirudh Devgan, President
Chin-Chi Teng, Senior Executive VP, Divisional
Neil Zaman, Senior VP, Divisional
Surendra Babu Mandava, Senior VP, Divisional
Thomas Beckley, Senior VP, Divisional

GROWTH PLANS/SPECIAL FEATURES:

Cadence Design Systems, Inc. is a leading provider of system design enablement solutions and electronic design automation software/hardware used by semiconductor and electronic system customers to develop and design integrated circuits (ICs) and electronic devices. It licenses, sells and leases its hardware technology and provides design and methodology services throughout the world to help manage and accelerate electronic product development processes. Cadence combines its design technologies into platforms for five major design activities: functional verification, digital IC and signoff, custom IC, system interconnect and analysis and IP. Functional verification products are used to verify that the circuitry designed by customers will perform as intended. Digital IC design offerings are used by customers to create logical representations of a digital circuit or an IC that can be verified for correctness prior to implementation. Once the logic is verified, the design is converted to a format ready for silicon manufacturing. This division's signoff offering is comprised of tools used to signoff the design as ready for manufacture by a silicon foundry, which provides certification for this step. Custom IC design and verification offerings are used to create schematic and physical representations of circuits down to the transistor level for analog, mixed-signal, custom digital, memory and radio frequency designs. System interconnect and analysis offerings are used to develop PCBs and IC packages. IP offerings consist of pre-verified, customizable functional blocks which customers integrate into their system-on-a-chips to accelerate the development process and to reduce the risk of errors in the design process.

FINANCIAL DATA: *Note: Data for latest year may not have been available at press time.*

In U.S. $	2020	2019	2018	2017	2016	2015
Revenue	2,682,891,000	2,336,319,000	2,138,022,000	1,943,032,000	1,816,083,000	1,702,091,000
R&D Expense	1,033,732,000	935,938,000	884,816,000	804,223,000	735,340,000	637,567,000
Operating Income	654,767,000	500,417,000	407,298,000	333,361,000	285,856,000	289,941,000
Operating Margin %		.21%	.19%	.17%	.16%	.17%
SGA Expense	670,885,000	621,479,000	573,075,000	553,342,000	520,300,000	512,414,000
Net Income	590,644,000	988,979,000	345,777,000	204,101,000	203,086,000	252,417,000
Operating Cash Flow	904,922,000	729,600,000	604,751,000	470,740,000	444,879,000	378,200,000
Capital Expenditure	94,813,000	74,605,000	61,503,000	57,901,000	53,712,000	44,808,000
EBITDA	803,633,000	621,148,000	518,250,000	456,234,000	380,411,000	414,072,000
Return on Assets %		.34%	.14%	.09%	.09%	.09%
Return on Equity %		.58%	.30%	.24%	.19%	.19%
Debt to Equity		0.205	0.268	0.651	0.868	0.253

CONTACT INFORMATION:

Phone: 408 943-1234   Fax: 408 428-5001
Toll-Free: 800-746-6223
Address: 2655 Seely Ave., Bldg. 5, San Jose, CA 95134 United States

STOCK TICKER/OTHER:

Stock Ticker: CDNS   Exchange: NAS
Employees: 8,100   Fiscal Year Ends: 12/31
Parent Company:

SALARIES/BONUSES:

Top Exec. Salary: $ Bonus: $
Second Exec. Salary: $ Bonus: $

OTHER THOUGHTS:

Estimated Female Officers or Directors: 2
Hot Spot for Advancement for Women/Minorities:

Campbell Soup Company

www.campbells.com

NAIC Code: 311422

TYPES OF BUSINESS:

Soup & Sauces-Manufacturing
Manufacturer
Convenience Foods
Canned Foods
Processed Foods
Jar Food
Frozen Products
Snack Foods

BRANDS/DIVISIONS/AFFILIATES:

Campbella
Swanson
Pacific Foods
Prego
Pace
V8
Lance
Pepperidge Farm

CONTACTS: *Note: Officers with more than one job title may be intentionally listed here more than once.*

Mark Clouse, CEO
Emily Waldorf, Sr. VP, Divisional
Anthony Disilvestro, CFO
Stanley Polomski, Chief Accounting Officer
Les Vinney, Director
Luca Mignini, Executive VP, Divisional
Adam Ciongoli, General Counsel
Xavier Boza, Other Executive Officer
Carlos Abrams-Rivera, President, Divisional
Roberto Leopardi, President, Divisional
Robert Furbee, Senior VP

GROWTH PLANS/SPECIAL FEATURES:

Campbell Soup Company is a global manufacturer and marketer of convenience food products. The firm operates in two business segments: meals and beverages and snacks. The meals and beverages segment includes the retail and foodservice businesses in the U.S. and Canada. Products within this segment includes the following: Campbell's condensed and ready-to-serve soups; Swanson broth and stocks; Pacific Foods broth, soups and non-dairy beverages; Prego pasta sauces; Pace Mexican sauces; Campbell's gravies, pasta, beans and dinner sauces; Swanson canned poultry; Plum baby food and snacks; V8 juices and beverages; and Campbell's tomato juice. The Snacks segment consists of: Pepperidge Farm cookies, crackers, fresh bakery and frozen products in U.S. retail, including Milano cookies and Goldfish crackers; and Snyder's of Hanover pretzels, Lance sandwich crackers, Cape Cod and Kettle Brand potato chips, Late July snacks, Snack Factory Pretzel Crisps, Pop Secret popcorn, Emerald nuts, and other snacking products in the U.S. and Canada. This division also manages Campbell's snack-related retail business in Latin America. In early-2021, Campbell Soup Company announced plans to close its manufacturing facility in Columbus, Georgia by spring 2022.

FINANCIAL DATA: *Note: Data for latest year may not have been available at press time.*

In U.S. $	2020	2019	2018	2017	2016	2015
Revenue	8,691,000,000	8,107,000,000	8,685,000,000	7,890,000,000	7,961,000,000	8,082,000,000
R&D Expense	93,000,000	91,000,000	110,000,000	98,000,000	124,000,000	113,000,000
Operating Income	1,251,000,000	1,102,000,000	1,116,000,000	1,637,000,000	1,102,000,000	1,204,000,000
Operating Margin %		.14%	.13%	.21%	.14%	.15%
SGA Expense	1,612,000,000	1,452,000,000	1,556,000,000	1,305,000,000	1,534,000,000	1,471,000,000
Net Income	1,628,000,000	211,000,000	261,000,000	887,000,000	563,000,000	691,000,000
Operating Cash Flow	1,396,000,000	1,398,000,000	1,305,000,000	1,291,000,000	1,463,000,000	1,182,000,000
Capital Expenditure	299,000,000	384,000,000	407,000,000	338,000,000	341,000,000	380,000,000
EBITDA	1,439,000,000	1,427,000,000	867,000,000	1,723,000,000	1,272,000,000	1,401,000,000
Return on Assets %		.02%	.02%	.11%	.07%	.09%
Return on Equity %		.17%	.17%	.56%	.39%	.46%
Debt to Equity		6.44	5.864	1.527	1.517	1.849

CONTACT INFORMATION:

Phone: 856 342-4800   Fax: 856 342-3878
Toll-Free: 800-257-8443
Address: 1 Campbell Pl., Camden, NJ 08103 United States

SALARIES/BONUSES:

Top Exec. Salary: $ Bonus: $
Second Exec. Salary: $ Bonus: $

STOCK TICKER/OTHER:

Stock Ticker: CPB   Exchange: NYS
Employees: 14,500   Fiscal Year Ends: 07/31
Parent Company:

OTHER THOUGHTS:

Estimated Female Officers or Directors: 8
Hot Spot for Advancement for Women/Minorities: Y

Camping World Holdings Inc

www.campingworld.com

NAIC Code: 441210

TYPES OF BUSINESS:

Recreational Vehicle Dealers

BRANDS/DIVISIONS/AFFILIATES:

Good Sam
Camping World

CONTACTS: *Note: Officers with more than one job title may be intentionally listed here more than once.*

Melvin Flanigan,
Marcus Lemonis, CEO
Brent Moody, Director
Thomas Wolfe, President, Subsidiary

GROWTH PLANS/SPECIAL FEATURES:

Camping World Holdings, Inc. is a provider of services, protection plans, products and resources for recreational vehicle enthusiast. The company is the largest national network of RV-centric retail locations, with more than 160 in the U.S. Whether customers are ready to buy or trade an RV, in need of service, repair or professional installation for an RV, or in need of specialized accessories designed for an RV, Camping World aims to meet those needs. The firm provides its offerings and services through two iconic brands: Good Sam and Camping World. Good Sam consumer services and plans include extended vehicle service contracts, emergency roadside assistance, property and casualty insurance, membership clubs, vehicle financing/refinancing, travel protection, credit cards, magazines and hosted online forums. Camping World consumer offerings are grouped into three categories: new and used vehicles, including travel trailers, fifth wheel trailers and motorhomes; parts and services, including repair and maintenance, installation, parts, accessories and supplies; and dealership finance and insurance, including vehicle financing and various protection plans. Along with RV parts and accessories the firm also operates services center with over 1,900 bays, over 100 collision centers and RV Spa detail and refurbishment centers. In November 2020, the firm agreed to acquire All RV Needs located in Medford, Oregon.

FINANCIAL DATA: *Note: Data for latest year may not have been available at press time.*

In U.S. $	2020	2019	2018	2017	2016	2015
Revenue	5,446,591,000	4,892,019,000	4,792,017,000	4,285,255,000	3,526,706,000	3,333,261,000
R&D Expense						
Operating Income	494,427,000	85,823,000	244,251,000	361,634,000	282,022,000	245,452,000
Operating Margin %		.02%	.05%	.08%	.08%	.07%
SGA Expense	1,156,071,000	1,141,643,000	1,069,359,000	853,160,000	691,884,000	644,409,000
Net Income	122,345,000	-60,591,000	10,398,000	28,362,000	191,661,000	178,530,000
Operating Cash Flow	747,669,000	251,934,000	136,292,000	-9,094,000	223,710,000	112,143,000
Capital Expenditure	85,099,000	88,356,000	254,359,000	89,515,000	56,859,000	71,709,000
EBITDA	528,317,000	78,684,000	247,337,000	492,150,000	301,011,000	269,791,000
Return on Assets %		-.02%	.00%	.01%	.13%	.14%
Return on Equity %		-10.15%	.21%	.43%		
Debt to Equity			26.871	16.24	8.422	

CONTACT INFORMATION:

Phone: 847-808-3000   Fax:
Toll-Free:
Address: 250 Parkway Dr., Ste. 270, Lincolnshire, IL 60069 United States

STOCK TICKER/OTHER:

Stock Ticker: CWH   Exchange: NYS
Employees: 11,947   Fiscal Year Ends:
Parent Company:

SALARIES/BONUSES:

Top Exec. Salary: $ Bonus: $
Second Exec. Salary: $ Bonus: $

OTHER THOUGHTS:

Estimated Female Officers or Directors:
Hot Spot for Advancement for Women/Minorities:

Cardinal Health Inc

www.cardinalhealth.com

NAIC Code: 424210

TYPES OF BUSINESS:

Healthcare Products & Services
Pharmaceutical Distribution
Pharmacy Operations
Medication Management Solutions
Medical Product Manufacturing
Surgical Products

BRANDS/DIVISIONS/AFFILIATES:

Cardinal.com

CONTACTS: Note: Officers with more than one job title may be intentionally listed here more than once.

Jon Giacomin, CEO, Divisional
Michael Kaufmann, CEO
Jorge Gomez, CFO
Gregory Kenny, Chairman of the Board
Stuart Laws, Chief Accounting Officer
Michele Holcomb, Executive VP, Divisional
Pamela Kimmet, Other Executive Officer

GROWTH PLANS/SPECIAL FEATURES:

Cardinal Health, Inc. is a provider of products and services that improve the safety and productivity of health care. The company operates in two segments: pharmaceuticals and medical products. The pharmaceutical segment distributes a broad line of branded and generic pharmaceutical products, specialty pharmaceutical, over-the-counter health care products and consumer products. It is also a full-service wholesale distributor to retail customers, hospitals and alternate care providers located throughout the U.S. In addition, this segment operates nuclear pharmacies and cyclotron facilities, provides pharmacy operations, medication therapy management and patient outcomes services to hospitals and other healthcare providers. The segment offers a broad range of support services including computerized order entry provided through Cardinal.com; generic sourcing programs; product movement, inventory and management reports; and consultation on store operations and merchandising. Through its medical products segment manufactures and sources Cardinal Health branded general and specialty medical, surgical and laboratory products and devices. These include: exam and surgical gloves; needle, syringe and sharps disposal; compression; incontinence; nutritional delivery; wound care; single-use surgical drapes, gowns and apparel; fluid suction and collection systems; urology; operating room supply; and electrode product lines. Branded products are sold directly through third-party distributors in the U.S., Canada, Europe, Asia and other markets. During 2021, Cardinal Health sold its Cordis business to Hellman & Friedman for approximately $1 billion.

Cardinal Health offers its employees medical, dental, vision short/long-term disability and life insurance; a 401(k); and various employee assistance programs.

FINANCIAL DATA: Note: Data for latest year may not have been available at press time.

In U.S. $	2020	2019	2018	2017	2016	2015
Revenue	152,922,000,000	145,534,000,000	136,809,000,000	129,976,000,000	121,546,000,000	
R&D Expense						
Operating Income	1,772,000,000	1,733,000,000	1,878,000,000	2,242,000,000	2,436,000,000	
Operating Margin %		.01%	.01%	.02%	.02%	
SGA Expense	4,572,000,000	4,480,000,000	4,596,000,000	3,775,000,000	3,648,000,000	
Net Income	-3,696,000,000	1,363,000,000	256,000,000	1,288,000,000	1,427,000,000	
Operating Cash Flow	1,960,000,000	2,722,000,000	2,768,000,000	1,184,000,000	2,971,000,000	
Capital Expenditure	375,000,000	328,000,000	384,000,000	387,000,000	465,000,000	
EBITDA	-2,621,000,000	3,045,000,000	1,133,000,000	2,842,000,000	3,095,000,000	
Return on Assets %		.03%	.01%	.03%	.04%	
Return on Equity %		.22%	.04%	.19%	.22%	
Debt to Equity		1.198	1.322	1.332	0.756	

CONTACT INFORMATION:

Phone: 614 757-5000 Fax:
Toll-Free: 800-234-8701
Address: 7000 Cardinal Pl., Dublin, OH 43017 United States

STOCK TICKER/OTHER:

Stock Ticker: CAH
Employees: 48,000
Parent Company:

Exchange: NYS
Fiscal Year Ends: 06/30

SALARIES/BONUSES:

Top Exec. Salary: $ Bonus: $
Second Exec. Salary: $ Bonus: $

OTHER THOUGHTS:

Estimated Female Officers or Directors: 8
Hot Spot for Advancement for Women/Minorities: Y

Sales, profits and employees may be estimates. Financial information, benefits and other data can change quickly and may vary from those stated here.

Cargill Incorporated

NAIC Code: 311200

TYPES OF BUSINESS:

Crop Production, Milling & Distribution
Meat Processing
Food Ingredients
Fertilizers
Steel
Money Markets & Commodity Trading
Supply Chain Solutions
Risk Management & Financial Services

BRANDS/DIVISIONS/AFFILIATES:

Leman Decoration Group
AnimalBiome

CONTACTS: *Note: Officers with more than one job title may be intentionally listed here more than once.*

David MacLennan, CEO
Brian Sikes, COO
David W. MacLennan, Pres.
Jamie Miller, CFO
Myriam Beatove, Chief Human Resources Officer
Christopher P. Mallett, Corp. VP-R&D
Julian Chase, Chief Transformation Officer
Laura Witte, General Counsel
Thomas M. Hayes, Corp. VP-Oper.
Sarena Lin, Corp. VP-Strategy & Bus. Dev.
Michael A. Fernandez, Corp. VP-Corp. Affairs
Kimberly A. Lattu, Controller
Emery N. Koenig, Chief Risk Officer
Jayme D. Olson, Treas.
David MacLennan, Chmn.

GROWTH PLANS/SPECIAL FEATURES:

Cargill, Incorporated, established in 1865, is a leading provider and marketer of food, agricultural, financial and industrial products and services operating in 70 countries worldwide. The company operates through five business segments: food ingredients & bio-industrial, animal nutrition, protein & salt, agricultural supply chain and metals & shipping. The food ingredients & bio-industrial segment serves food and beverage manufacturers, foodservice companies and retailers with food ingredients, as well as food and non-food applications. Non-food applications encompass specialty ingredients for personal care as well as for pharmaceutical applications. Among these products are sustainable, nature-derived ingredients for a range of bio-industrial applications. The animal nutrition segment helps livestock and aquaculture farmers, feed manufacturers and distributors of all sizes to deliver better animal nutrition via innovative feed and pre-mix products and services, as well as digital modeling and formulation solutions. The protein & salt segment processes beef, poultry, value-added meats and egg products to food makers, food service companies and food retailers. This division's salt is used in food, agriculture, water softening and for deicing winter roads. The agricultural supply chain segment connects producers and users of grains and oilseeds worldwide through origination, trading, processing and distribution. This division also offers a range of farmer services and risk management solutions. Last, the metals & shipping segment offers Cargill customers physical supply and risk management solutions in global ferrous markets, including iron ore and steel. This division also provides ocean freight shipping services through its own sizable fleet, enabling customers to ship their products to global ports via Cargill. In May 2021, Cargill acquired Leman Decoration Group, a supplier of cake decorations across the bakery sector. That July, Cargill announced an investment in AnimalBiome, a California-based startup using innovative microbiome science to restore pet digestive and skin issues.

FINANCIAL DATA: *Note: Data for latest year may not have been available at press time.*

In U.S. $	2020	2019	2018	2017	2016	2015
Revenue	114,600,000,000	113,490,000,000	114,695,000,000	109,700,000,000	109,699,000,000	107,164,000,000
R&D Expense						
Operating Income						
Operating Margin %						
SGA Expense						
Net Income	4,128,040,000	2,564,000,000	3,103,000,000	2,800,000,000	2,835,000,000	2,377,000,000
Operating Cash Flow						
Capital Expenditure						
EBITDA						
Return on Assets %						
Return on Equity %						
Debt to Equity						

CONTACT INFORMATION:

Phone: 952-742-7575   Fax: 952-742-7393
Toll-Free: 800-227-4455
Address: P.O. Box 9300, Minneapolis, MN 55440-9300 United States

STOCK TICKER/OTHER:

Stock Ticker: Private   Exchange:
Employees: 155,000   Fiscal Year Ends: 05/31
Parent Company:

SALARIES/BONUSES:

Top Exec. Salary: $ Bonus: $
Second Exec. Salary: $ Bonus: $

OTHER THOUGHTS:

Estimated Female Officers or Directors: 4
Hot Spot for Advancement for Women/Minorities: Y

Sales, profits and employees may be estimates. Financial information, benefits and other data can change quickly and may vary from those stated here.

CarMax Inc

NAIC Code: 441120

TYPES OF BUSINESS:

Used Auto Dealers
Used Auto Dealers
Online Sales
Vehicle Repair Services
Financial Services

BRANDS/DIVISIONS/AFFILIATES:

CarMax Auto Finance
Edmunds

CONTACTS: Note: Officers with more than one job title may be intentionally listed here more than once.

William Nash, CEO
Thomas Reedy, CFO
Thomas Folliard, Chairman of the Board
Jill Livesay, Chief Accounting Officer
Shamim Mohammad, Chief Information Officer
James Lyski, Chief Marketing Officer
Edwin Hill, COO
Eric Margolin, Executive VP
Diane Cafritz, Other Executive Officer
Jon Daniels, Senior VP, Divisional
Darren Newberry, Senior VP, Divisional
Joe Wilson, Senior VP, Divisional

GROWTH PLANS/SPECIAL FEATURES:

CarMax, Inc. is a leading retailer of used cars in the U.S. The firm purchases, reconditions and sells used vehicles through more than 220 used car superstores across the U.S. CarMax vehicles are typically 0 to 10 years old and range in price from $11,000 to $37,000. The firm also sells new vehicles at two of its locations under franchise agreements with car manufacturers. The company offers a wide selection of makes and models of both domestic and imported vehicles to appeal to diverse consumer preferences and budgets, including popular brands from manufacturers such as Chrysler, Ford, General Motors, Honda, Hyundai, Kia, Mazda, Nissan, Toyota and Volkswagen, and luxury brands such as Acura, BMW, Infiniti, Lexus and Mercedes-Benz. The company will also transfer any used vehicle in its nationwide inventory to a local superstore. Vehicles purchased through the company's in-store appraisal process that fall short of retail standards are sold at onsite wholesale auctions restricted to licensed automobile dealers. All store locations provide vehicle repair service and used-car warranty service. In addition, through the company's web site, customers can search new and used cars as well as find information on Kelley Blue Book figures, car buying tips, rebates and incentives. CarMax offers financing options through CarMax Auto Finance, including revolving credit and automobile installment loans. The firm sold more than 750,000 used vehicles and more than 425,000 wholesale vehicles at its in-store and virtual auctions during fiscal 2021. Vehicles purchased through CarMax's appraisal process that do not meet its retail standards (average age, mileage or vehicle condition) are sold to licensed dealers through onsite wholesale auctions. In June 2021, CarMax acquired the remaining stake it did not own in Edmunds, an online guide for automotive information and a leader in digital car shopping innovations.

FINANCIAL DATA: Note: Data for latest year may not have been available at press time.

In U.S. $	2020	2019	2018	2017	2016	2015
Revenue	20,319,990,000	18,173,100,000	17,120,210,000	15,875,120,000	15,149,670,000	
R&D Expense						
Operating Income	782,240,000	750,291,000	711,808,000	694,794,000	666,860,000	
Operating Margin %	.04%	.04%	.04%	.04%	.04%	
SGA Expense	1,940,100,000	1,730,300,000	1,617,051,000	1,488,500,000	1,351,900,000	
Net Income	888,433,000	842,413,000	664,112,000	626,970,000	623,428,000	
Operating Cash Flow	-236,606,000	162,971,000	-80,550,000	-468,138,000	-148,893,000	
Capital Expenditure	331,896,000	304,636,000	296,816,000	418,144,000	315,584,000	
EBITDA	1,459,804,000	1,370,845,000	1,314,295,000	1,231,696,000	1,183,662,000	
Return on Assets %	.04%	.05%	.04%	.04%	.05%	
Return on Equity %	.25%	.25%	.21%	.21%	.21%	
Debt to Equity	4.082	4.113	3.845	3.804	3.56	

CONTACT INFORMATION:

Phone: 804 747-0422   Fax: 804 747-5848
Toll-Free: 800-519-1511
Address: 12800 Tuckahoe Creek Pkwy., Richmond, VA 23238 United States

STOCK TICKER/OTHER:

Stock Ticker: KMX
Employees: 26,889
Parent Company:

Exchange: NYS
Fiscal Year Ends: 02/28

SALARIES/BONUSES:

Top Exec. Salary: $ Bonus: $
Second Exec. Salary: $ Bonus: $

OTHER THOUGHTS:

Estimated Female Officers or Directors: 9
Hot Spot for Advancement for Women/Minorities: Y

Carriage Services Inc

www.carriageservices.com

NAIC Code: 812210

TYPES OF BUSINESS:

Funeral Homes and Funeral Services
Funeral Home
Cemetery
Burial Services
Cremation

BRANDS/DIVISIONS/AFFILIATES:

CONTACTS: *Note: Officers with more than one job title may be intentionally listed here more than once.*

Melvin Payne, CEO
Adeola Olaniyan, Chief Accounting Officer
Paul Elliott, Other Corporate Officer
Shawn Phillips, Other Corporate Officer
Viki Blinderman, Senior VP
Carl Brink, Senior VP

GROWTH PLANS/SPECIAL FEATURES:

Carriage Services, Inc. is a provider of death care services and merchandise in the U.S. It operates two types of businesses: funeral home operations and cemetery operation. Funeral homes are mainly service businesses that provide burial and cremation services and sells related merchandise, such as caskets and urns. Given the high fixed cost structure associated with funeral home operations, the following are key factors affecting its profitability: demographic trends in terms of population growth and average age, which impact death rates and number of deaths; establishing and maintaining market share positions supported by strong local heritage and relationships; effectively responding to increasing cremation trends by packaging complimentary service and merchandise; controlling salary and merchandise costs; and exercising pricing leverage related to its at-need business to increase average revenues per contract. Cemeteries are mainly a sales business providing interment rights and related merchandise, such as markers and memorials. Carriage Services mainly serves suburban and rural markets, where it competes with smaller, independent operations. The company provides funeral and cemetery services and products on both an at-need (time of death) and preneed (planned prior to death) basis. As of February 2021, Carriage Services operated 176 funeral homes in 26 states and 32 cemeteries in 12 states.

FINANCIAL DATA: *Note: Data for latest year may not have been available at press time.*

In U.S. $	2020	2019	2018	2017	2016	2015
Revenue	329,448,000	274,107,000	267,992,000	258,139,000	248,200,000	242,502,000
R&D Expense						
Operating Income	78,669,000	52,289,000	43,307,000	48,941,000	50,204,000	48,648,000
Operating Margin %		.19%	.16%	.19%	.20%	.20%
SGA Expense	25,827,000	25,880,000	30,827,000	26,253,000	27,944,000	27,114,000
Net Income	16,090,000	14,533,000	11,645,000	37,193,000	19,581,000	20,853,000
Operating Cash Flow	82,915,000	43,216,000	48,994,000	45,230,000	49,457,000	49,904,000
Capital Expenditure	15,198,000	15,379,000	13,526,000	16,395,000	23,104,000	35,824,000
EBITDA	76,762,000	65,950,000	58,997,000	66,038,000	63,270,000	62,383,000
Return on Assets %		.01%	.01%	.04%	.02%	.02%
Return on Equity %		.06%	.06%	.20%	.12%	.12%
Debt to Equity		2.28	1.644	1.735	1.835	2.014

CONTACT INFORMATION:

Phone: 713 332-8400   Fax:
Toll-Free:
Address: 3040 Post Oak Blvd., Ste. 300, Houston, TX 77056 United States

STOCK TICKER/OTHER:

Stock Ticker: CSV   Exchange: NYS
Employees: 2,718   Fiscal Year Ends: 12/31
Parent Company:

SALARIES/BONUSES:

Top Exec. Salary: $ Bonus: $
Second Exec. Salary: $ Bonus: $

OTHER THOUGHTS:

Estimated Female Officers or Directors:
Hot Spot for Advancement for Women/Minorities:

Caterpillar Inc

www.cat.com

NAIC Code: 333120

TYPES OF BUSINESS:

Machinery-Earth Moving & Agricultural
Diesel and Turbine Engines
Financing
Fuel Cell Manufacturing
Rail Car Maintenance
Engine & Equipment Remanufacturing
Locomotive Manufacturing and Maintenance

BRANDS/DIVISIONS/AFFILIATES:

Cat
Caterpillar Financial Services Corporation
Caterpillar Insurance Holdings Inc

CONTACTS:
Note: Officers with more than one job title may be intentionally listed here more than once.

D. Umpleby, CEO
Andrew Bonfield, CFO
Gary Marvel, Chief Accounting Officer
Jananne Copeland, Chief Accounting Officer
Suzette Long, General Counsel
Cheryl Johnson, Other Executive Officer
Denise Johnson, President, Divisional
Bob De Lange, President, Divisional
Ramin Younessi, President, Divisional
William Ainsworth, President, Divisional
Thomas Pellette, President, Subsidiary

GROWTH PLANS/SPECIAL FEATURES:

Caterpillar, Inc. is a leading manufacturer of construction and mining equipment. The company's principal lines of business are machinery, energy and transportation, and financial products. The machinery, energy and transportation segment comprises Caterpillar's construction industries division, the resource industries division, and the energy and transportation division. The construction industries division supports customers via machinery in infrastructure, forestry and building construction. Most of its machine sales are made in the heavy and general construction, rental, quarry and aggregates markets and mining. The resource industries division supports customers using machinery for mining, quarry, waste and material handling applications. This division manufactures high productivity equipment for both surface and underground mining operations worldwide. The equipment is used to extract and haul copper, iron ore, coal, oil sands, aggregates, gold and other minerals and ores. The energy and transportation division supports customers in oil and gas, power generation, marine, rail and industrial applications. Products and services include reciprocating engines, generator sets, marine propulsion systems, gas turbines, the remanufacturing of Cat-branded engines and components, as well as the remanufacturing services for other companies. The financial products segment includes: Caterpillar Financial Services Corporation, which provides retail and wholesale financing alternatives for Caterpillar products to customers and dealers globally; and Caterpillar Insurance Holdings, Inc., which offers property/casualty, life and health insurance products, among other services. Caterpillar's machines are distributed through a worldwide organization of dealers, 44 in the U.S. and 116 outside the U.S., serving 192 countries. Caterpillar has been in business for more than 95 years. In early-2021, Caterpillar acquired the oil and gas division of the Weir Group PLC, a Scotland-based global engineering business.

Caterpillar offers its employees health coverage, 401(k), an employee assistance program and flexible spending accounts.

FINANCIAL DATA:
Note: Data for latest year may not have been available at press time.

In U.S. $	2020	2019	2018	2017	2016	2015
Revenue	41,748,000,000	53,800,000,000	54,722,000,000	45,462,000,000	38,537,000,000	47,011,000,000
R&D Expense	1,415,000,000	1,693,000,000	1,850,000,000	1,905,000,000	1,951,000,000	2,165,000,000
Operating Income	4,553,000,000	8,290,000,000	8,293,000,000	4,406,000,000	1,093,000,000	3,256,000,000
Operating Margin %		.15%	.15%	.10%	.03%	.07%
SGA Expense	4,642,000,000	5,162,000,000	5,478,000,000	5,177,000,000	4,686,000,000	5,199,000,000
Net Income	2,998,000,000	6,093,000,000	6,147,000,000	754,000,000	-67,000,000	2,102,000,000
Operating Cash Flow	6,327,000,000	6,912,000,000	6,558,000,000	5,702,000,000	5,608,000,000	6,675,000,000
Capital Expenditure	2,115,000,000	2,669,000,000	2,916,000,000	2,336,000,000	2,928,000,000	3,261,000,000
EBITDA	6,941,000,000	10,810,000,000	10,992,000,000	7,490,000,000	3,678,000,000	6,408,000,000
Return on Assets %		.08%	.08%	.01%	.00%	.03%
Return on Equity %		.43%	.44%	.06%	.00%	.13%
Debt to Equity		1.802	1.781	1.741	1.737	1.705

CONTACT INFORMATION:

Phone: 309 675-1000 Fax: 309 675-4332
Toll-Free:
Address: 510 Lake Cook Rd., Ste. 100, Deerfield, IL 60015 United States

STOCK TICKER/OTHER:

Stock Ticker: CAT Exchange: NYS
Employees: 102,300 Fiscal Year Ends: 12/31
Parent Company:

SALARIES/BONUSES:

Top Exec. Salary: $ Bonus: $
Second Exec. Salary: $ Bonus: $

OTHER THOUGHTS:

Estimated Female Officers or Directors: 11
Hot Spot for Advancement for Women/Minorities: Y

CDW Corporation

NAIC Code: 423430

www.cdw.com

TYPES OF BUSINESS:

Direct Selling-Computer Products
Online Sales
Custom Installation & Repair-Computers

BRANDS/DIVISIONS/AFFILIATES:

CDW Government LLC
CDW Canada Inc
CDW Ltd
CDW UK
IGNW

CONTACTS: *Note: Officers with more than one job title may be intentionally listed here more than once.*

Christine Leahy, CEO
Mark Chong, Sr. VP, Divisional
Collin Kebo, CFO
Thomas Richards, Chairman of the Board
Neil Fairfield, Chief Accounting Officer
Jonathan Stevens, Chief Information Officer
Christina Corley, COO
Elizabeth Connelly, Other Executive Officer
Frederick Kulevich, Secretary
Robert Kirby, Senior VP, Divisional
Jill Billhorn, Senior VP, Divisional
Christina Rother, Senior VP, Divisional
Matthew Troka, Senior VP, Divisional
Douglas Eckrote, Senior VP, Divisional

GROWTH PLANS/SPECIAL FEATURES:

CDW Corporation is one of the leading providers of multi-branded information technology products and services to business, government, education and healthcare customers in the U.S., Canada and the U.K. The firm offers over 100,000 products from over 1,000 leading technology brands, in addition to customized solution design and management with focus areas including notebooks, desktops, printers, servers and storage, unified communications, security, wireless, power and cooling, networking, software licensing, cloud computing, data center optimization and mobility solutions. The company manages its inventory through a 442,000-square-foot distribution center in Vernon Hills, Illinois; a 513,000-square-foot distribution center in Las Vegas, Nevada; and a 120,000-square foot distribution center in Rugby, Warwickshire, U.K. CDW offers customers free access to certified technicians for telephone support and complete custom installation and repair services via the company's configuration center, in addition to access to a database of frequently asked technical questions and direct links to manufacturers' tech support websites. Its CDW Government, LLC subsidiary provides specialized product offerings and services to federal, state and local governments as well as the educational sector. Subsidiaries CDW Canada, Inc. and CDW Ltd. (doing business as CDW UK) provide IT solutions, serving commercial and public sector customers. During 2020, CDW acquired IGNW, a provider of cloud-native services, software development and data orchestration capabilities.

CDW offers its employees health and wellness coverage, 401(k) and profit sharing plans, and career development opportunities and training.

FINANCIAL DATA: *Note: Data for latest year may not have been available at press time.*

In U.S. $	2020	2019	2018	2017	2016	2015
Revenue	18,467,500,000	18,032,400,000	16,240,500,000	15,191,500,000	13,981,900,000	12,988,700,000
R&D Expense						
Operating Income	1,179,200,000	1,133,600,000	987,300,000	866,100,000	819,200,000	742,000,000
Operating Margin %		.06%	.06%	.06%	.06%	.06%
SGA Expense	2,030,900,000	1,906,300,000	1,719,600,000	1,583,800,000	1,508,000,000	1,373,800,000
Net Income	788,500,000	736,800,000	643,000,000	523,000,000	424,400,000	403,100,000
Operating Cash Flow	1,314,300,000	1,027,200,000	905,900,000	777,700,000	604,000,000	277,500,000
Capital Expenditure	158,000,000	236,300,000	86,100,000	81,100,000	63,500,000	90,100,000
EBITDA	1,582,800,000	1,376,200,000	1,254,700,000	1,071,700,000	1,073,400,000	1,033,900,000
Return on Assets %		.10%	.09%	.08%	.06%	.06%
Return on Equity %		.76%	.66%	.52%	.40%	.40%
Debt to Equity		3.555	3.264	3.266	3.076	2.95

CONTACT INFORMATION:

Phone: 847-465-6000   Fax: 847-465-6800
Toll-Free: 800-750-4239
Address: 75 Tri-State International, Lincolnshire, IL 60069 United States

STOCK TICKER/OTHER:

Stock Ticker: CDW   Exchange: NAS
Employees: 9,900   Fiscal Year Ends: 12/31
Parent Company:

SALARIES/BONUSES:

Top Exec. Salary: $ Bonus: $
Second Exec. Salary: $ Bonus: $

OTHER THOUGHTS:

Estimated Female Officers or Directors: 10
Hot Spot for Advancement for Women/Minorities: Y

Celanese Corporation

www.celanese.com

NAIC Code: 325211

TYPES OF BUSINESS:

Manufacturing-Acetyl Intermediate Chemicals
Industrial Products
Technical & High-Performance Polymers
Sweeteners & Sorbates
Ethanol Production
Food Ingredients
Cellulose Derivative Fibers

BRANDS/DIVISIONS/AFFILIATES:

Celanex
Celstran
Riteflex
Thermx PCT
Sunett
Ateva
VitalDose
Elotex

CONTACTS: Note: Officers with more than one job title may be intentionally listed here more than once.

Mark Rohr, CEO
Scott Richardson, CFO
Benita Casey, Chief Accounting Officer
Shannon Jurecka, Other Executive Officer

GROWTH PLANS/SPECIAL FEATURES:

Celanese Corporation is a producer of industrial chemicals and advanced materials. The firm manufactures acetyl products, which are intermediate chemicals for nearly all major industries, and produces high-performance engineered polymers. The company operates through six business segments: engineered materials, food ingredients, cellulose derivatives, intermediate chemistry, EVA polymers and emulsion polymers. The engineered materials segment engineers high-performance polymers for a variety of industries. Products include Celanex thermoplastic polyester, Celstran long fiber reinforced thermoplastic, GUR ultra-high molecular wright polyethylene, Riteflex thermoplastic polyester elastomer, Thermx PCT thermoplastic polyester alloy and more. The food ingredients segment produces Sunett acesulfame potassium and sorbates. The cellulose derivatives segment manufactures cellulose acetate products for use in filtration, luxury packaging, insultation, acetate granules, the medical industry and nonwovens. The intermediate chemistry segment manufactures intermediate chemistry products. Products include acetic acid, vinyl acetate monomer, acetic anhydride and other specialty derivative products. The EVA polymers segment produces a full range ethylene vinyl acetate (EVA) polymers. Products include Ateva EVA polymers, Ateva G medical-grade EVA copolymers, and VitalDose pharmaceutical EVA-based excipients. Headquartered in Irving, Texas, the company's operations are primarily located in North America, Europe and Asia, consisting of 33 global production facilities and strategic affiliate production facilities. In April 2020, Celanese acquired Nouryon's redispersible polymer powders business offered under the Elotex brand. In October 2020, the firm sold its 45% equity stake in the Polyplastics joint venture to Daicel Corporation for $1.575 billion.

FINANCIAL DATA: Note: Data for latest year may not have been available at press time.

In U.S. $	2020	2019	2018	2017	2016	2015
Revenue	5,655,000,000	6,297,000,000	7,155,000,000	6,140,000,000	5,389,000,000	5,674,000,000
R&D Expense	74,000,000	67,000,000	72,000,000	72,000,000	78,000,000	119,000,000
Operating Income	715,000,000	1,032,000,000	1,330,000,000	967,000,000	902,000,000	682,000,000
Operating Margin %		.16%	.19%	.16%	.17%	.12%
SGA Expense	482,000,000	483,000,000	546,000,000	456,000,000	416,000,000	506,000,000
Net Income	1,985,000,000	852,000,000	1,207,000,000	843,000,000	900,000,000	304,000,000
Operating Cash Flow	1,343,000,000	1,454,000,000	1,558,000,000	803,000,000	893,000,000	862,000,000
Capital Expenditure	364,000,000	370,000,000	337,000,000	267,000,000	246,000,000	520,000,000
EBITDA	2,716,000,000	1,459,000,000	1,984,000,000	1,507,000,000	1,445,000,000	970,000,000
Return on Assets %		.09%	.13%	.09%	.11%	.03%
Return on Equity %		.31%	.41%	.31%	.36%	.12%
Debt to Equity		1.432	0.995	1.148	1.117	1.038

CONTACT INFORMATION:

Phone: 972 443-4000   Fax: 972 332-9373
Toll-Free:
Address: 222 West Las Colinas Blvd, Ste 900N, Irving, TX 75039-5421
United States

STOCK TICKER/OTHER:

Stock Ticker: CE
Employees: 7,658
Parent Company:

Exchange: NYS
Fiscal Year Ends: 12/31

SALARIES/BONUSES:

Top Exec. Salary: $ Bonus: $
Second Exec. Salary: $ Bonus: $

OTHER THOUGHTS:

Estimated Female Officers or Directors: 1
Hot Spot for Advancement for Women/Minorities: Y

Centene Corporation
NAIC Code: 524114

TYPES OF BUSINESS:
Insurance-Medical & Health, HMOs & PPOs
Medicaid Managed Care
Specialty Services
Behavioral Health
Disease Management
Managed Vision
Nurse Triage
Pharmacy Benefit Management

BRANDS/DIVISIONS/AFFILIATES:

CONTACTS: *Note: Officers with more than one job title may be intentionally listed here more than once.*
Michael Neidorff, CEO
Jeffrey Schwaneke, CFO
Mark Brooks, Chief Information Officer
Jesse Hunter, Chief Strategy Officer
Christopher Bowers, Executive VP, Divisional
Brandy Burkhalter, Executive VP, Divisional
Keith Williamson, Executive VP
Christopher Isaak, Senior VP

GROWTH PLANS/SPECIAL FEATURES:
Centene Corporation is a multi-line healthcare plan firm operating in two segments: managed care and specialty services. In the managed care segment, the company provides programs and services to people receiving benefits from foster care, Medicaid, the State Children's Health Insurance Program (CHIP), Medicare special needs plans, supplemental security income (SSI), dual eligible individuals (Duals), long term care (LTC) and federally-facilitated and state-based Marketplaces. This segment accounted for 95% of total annual revenue. Centene's specialty services segment (5%) provides healthcare services to state programs, correctional facilities, healthcare organizations, and to the firm's own subsidiaries. The firm's locally-based staff assists members in accessing care, coordinating referrals to related health and social services and addressing member concerns and questions. Centene's health plans generally provide the following services: primary and specialty physician care, in- and out-patient hospital care, prenatal care, laboratory and x-ray services, home-based primary care, transportation assistance, vision care, dental care, telehealth services, immunizations, prescriptions and limited over-the-counter drugs, specialty pharmacy, provision of durable medical equipment, behavioral health and substance abuse services, 24-hour nurse advice line, therapies, social work services and care coordination. The company also provides a comprehensive set of education and outreach programs to inform and assist members to access healthcare services. During 2021, Centene agreed to acquire Magellan Health Inc., an American for-profit managed health care company. The transaction was expected to close by year's end.

Centene offers its employees comprehensive health benefits, retirement options, life and disability coverage and a variety of employee assistance plans and programs.

FINANCIAL DATA: *Note: Data for latest year may not have been available at press time.*

In U.S. $	2020	2019	2018	2017	2016	2015
Revenue	111,115,000,000	74,639,000,000	60,116,000,000	48,382,000,000	40,607,000,000	22,760,000,000
R&D Expense						
Operating Income	3,154,000,000	2,052,000,000	1,458,000,000	1,199,000,000	1,260,000,000	705,000,000
Operating Margin %		.03%	.02%	.02%	.03%	.03%
SGA Expense	11,343,000,000	6,533,000,000	6,752,000,000	4,446,000,000	4,137,000,000	2,041,000,000
Net Income	1,808,000,000	1,321,000,000	900,000,000	828,000,000	562,000,000	355,000,000
Operating Cash Flow	5,503,000,000	1,483,000,000	1,234,000,000	1,489,000,000	1,851,000,000	658,000,000
Capital Expenditure	869,000,000	730,000,000	675,000,000	422,000,000	306,000,000	150,000,000
EBITDA	4,760,000,000	2,837,000,000	2,206,000,000	1,750,000,000	1,652,000,000	851,000,000
Return on Assets %		.04%	.03%	.04%	.04%	.05%
Return on Equity %		.11%	.10%	.13%	.14%	.18%
Debt to Equity		1.087	0.609	0.685	0.789	0.564

CONTACT INFORMATION:
Phone: 314 725-4477   Fax: 314 725-5180
Toll-Free:
Address: 7700 Forsyth Blvd., St. Louis, MO 63105 United States

STOCK TICKER/OTHER:
Stock Ticker: CNC   Exchange: NYS
Employees: 56,600   Fiscal Year Ends: 12/31
Parent Company:

SALARIES/BONUSES:
Top Exec. Salary: $ Bonus: $
Second Exec. Salary: $ Bonus: $

OTHER THOUGHTS:
Estimated Female Officers or Directors: 4
Hot Spot for Advancement for Women/Minorities: Y

CenterPoint Energy Inc

www.centerpointenergy.com/en-us

NAIC Code: 221112

TYPES OF BUSINESS:

Utilities-Electricity & Natural Gas
Gas Marketing
Pipelines
Field Services
Management Services

BRANDS/DIVISIONS/AFFILIATES:

CenterPoint Energy Home Service Plus

CONTACTS: Note: Officers with more than one job title may be intentionally listed here more than once.

Scott Prochazka, CEO
Xia Liu, CFO
Milton Carroll, Chairman of the Board
Kristie Colvin, Chief Accounting Officer
Susan Ortenstone, Other Executive Officer
Tracy Bridge, President, Divisional
Joseph Vortherms, Senior VP, Divisional
Scott Doyle, Senior VP, Divisional

GROWTH PLANS/SPECIAL FEATURES:

CenterPoint Energy, Inc. is a major combined electricity and natural gas utilities in the U.S., serving residential and commercial customers. Through its subsidiaries, the company operates through five business segments: natural gas, electric transmission and distribution and power generation, energy, CenterPoint Energy Home Service Plus (HSP), and CenterPoint Energy and HomeServe. The natural gas segment sells and delivers natural gas to more than 4.5 million homes and businesses in eight states, including Arkansas, Indiana, Louisiana, Minnesota, Mississippi, Ohio, Oklahoma and Texas. The electric transmission and distribution power generation segment maintains the wires, poles and electric infrastructure that serves the company's metered customers in the greater Houston area and in southwestern Indiana. This division owns and operates approximately 1,300 MW of electric generation capacity in Indiana. The energy segment includes energy-related services; energy efficiency and sustainability solutions; and owns and operates intrastate natural gas pipeline systems, all of which span more than 20 states. HSP provides heating and cooling solutions for Minnesota homeowners, including the sale of gas and electric equipment and repair and maintenance services. CenterPoint Energy and HomeServe provides emergency home repair programs in the company's natural gas markets of Arkansas, Louisiana and Texas.

FINANCIAL DATA: Note: Data for latest year may not have been available at press time.

In U.S. $	2020	2019	2018	2017	2016	2015
Revenue	7,418,000,000	12,301,000,000	10,589,000,000	9,614,000,000	7,528,000,000	7,386,000,000
R&D Expense						
Operating Income	1,224,000,000	1,274,000,000	831,000,000	1,072,000,000	959,000,000	933,000,000
Operating Margin %		.10%	.08%	.11%	.13%	.13%
SGA Expense						
Net Income	-773,000,000	791,000,000	368,000,000	1,792,000,000	432,000,000	-692,000,000
Operating Cash Flow	1,995,000,000	1,638,000,000	2,136,000,000	1,421,000,000	1,928,000,000	1,865,000,000
Capital Expenditure	2,596,000,000	2,506,000,000	1,651,000,000	1,426,000,000	1,414,000,000	1,584,000,000
EBITDA	855,000,000	2,807,000,000	2,177,000,000	2,489,000,000	2,241,000,000	297,000,000
Return on Assets %		.02%	.01%	.08%	.02%	- .03%
Return on Equity %		.10%	.06%	.44%	.12%	- .17%
Debt to Equity		2.152	1.374	1.748	2.177	2.283

CONTACT INFORMATION:

Phone: 713 207-1111   Fax: 713 207-3169
Toll-Free: 800-231-6406
Address: 1111 Louisiana St., Houston, TX 77002 United States

STOCK TICKER/OTHER:

Stock Ticker: CNP   Exchange: NYS
Employees: 15,565   Fiscal Year Ends: 12/31
Parent Company:

SALARIES/BONUSES:

Top Exec. Salary: $ Bonus: $
Second Exec. Salary: $ Bonus: $

OTHER THOUGHTS:

Estimated Female Officers or Directors: 2
Hot Spot for Advancement for Women/Minorities: Y

Cerner Corporation

www.cerner.com

NAIC Code: 511210D

TYPES OF BUSINESS:

Computer Software, Healthcare & Biotechnology
Medical Information Systems
Application Hosting
Integrated Delivery Networks
Access Management
Consulting Services
Safety & Risk Management

BRANDS/DIVISIONS/AFFILIATES:

Cerner Millennium
HealtheIntent
Cerner Health Services Inc
CernerWorks
Kantar Health

CONTACTS: Note: Officers with more than one job title may be intentionally listed here more than once.

Marc Naughton, CFO
David Shafer, Chairman of the Board
Michael Battaglioli, Chief Accounting Officer
Michael Nill, COO
Donald Trigg, Executive VP, Divisional
Jeffrey Townsend, Executive VP
John Peterzalek, Executive VP
Randy Sims, Executive VP
Julia Wilson, Other Executive Officer

GROWTH PLANS/SPECIAL FEATURES:

Cerner Corporation designs, develops, installs and supports information technology and content applications for health care organizations, consumers and physicians. Cerner's applications are designed to help eliminate error, variance and waste in the care process as well as provide appropriate health information and knowledge to care givers, clinicians and consumers, and appropriate management information to healthcare administrations. Cerner solutions are offered on the unified Cerner Millennium architecture and on the HealtheIntent cloud-based platform. Cerner Millennium combines clinical, financial and management information systems and provides secure access to an individual's electronic medical record at the point of care and organizes and proactively delivers information to meet the specific needs of the physician, nurse, laboratory technician, pharmacist or other care provider, front- and back-office professionals as well as consumers. HealtheIntent offers EHR-agnostic (electronic health record) solutions based on sophisticated, statistical algorithms to help providers predict and improve outcomes, control costs, improve quality and manage the health of their patients. Cerner also offers a broad range of services including implementation and training, remote hosting, operational management services, revenue cycle services, support and maintenance, healthcare data analysis, clinical process optimization, transaction processing, employer health centers, employee wellness programs and third-party administrator (TPA) services for employer-based health plans. Cerner Health Services, Inc. offers a portfolio of enterprise-level clinical and financial healthcare information technology solutions, as well as departmental, connectivity, population health and care coordination solutions globally. CernerWorks is the company's remote-hosting business. These facilities include hospitals; physician practices; ambulatory facilities such as laboratories, ambulatory centers, cardiac facilities, radiology clinics and surgery centers; home health facilities; and retail pharmacies. During 2021, Cerner acquired Kantar Health, a division of Kantar Group. Kantar Health was combined with Cerner's data and technology and is expected to accelerate innovation in life sciences research and improve patient outcomes worldwide.

FINANCIAL DATA: Note: Data for latest year may not have been available at press time.

In U.S. $	2020	2019	2018	2017	2016	2015
Revenue	5,505,788,000	5,692,598,000	5,366,325,000	5,142,272,000	4,796,473,000	4,425,267,000
R&D Expense	749,007,000	737,136,000	683,663,000	605,046,000	551,418,000	539,799,000
Operating Income	694,044,000	600,669,000	774,785,000	960,471,000	911,013,000	781,136,000
Operating Margin %		.11%	.14%	.19%	.19%	.18%
SGA Expense	3,074,201,000	3,195,935,000	2,883,165,000	2,632,088,000	2,464,380,000	2,262,024,000
Net Income	780,088,000	529,454,000	630,059,000	866,978,000	636,484,000	539,362,000
Operating Cash Flow	1,436,705,000	1,313,099,000	1,454,009,000	1,307,675,000	1,155,612,000	947,526,000
Capital Expenditure	617,501,000	780,976,000	757,440,000	665,877,000	771,595,000	648,220,000
EBITDA	1,717,976,000	1,356,947,000	1,451,429,000	1,555,864,000	1,427,149,000	1,245,425,000
Return on Assets %		.08%	.10%	.14%	.11%	.11%
Return on Equity %		.11%	.13%	.20%	.16%	.15%
Debt to Equity		0.241	0.089	0.108	0.137	0.146

CONTACT INFORMATION:

Phone: 816 221-1024   Fax:
Toll-Free:
Address: 2800 Rock Creek Pkwy., North Kansas City, MO 64117 United States

STOCK TICKER/OTHER:

Stock Ticker: CERN   Exchange: NAS
Employees: 27,400   Fiscal Year Ends: 12/31
Parent Company:

SALARIES/BONUSES:

Top Exec. Salary: $ Bonus: $
Second Exec. Salary: $ Bonus: $

OTHER THOUGHTS:

Estimated Female Officers or Directors: 13
Hot Spot for Advancement for Women/Minorities: Y

CH Robinson Worldwide Inc

www.chrobinson.com

NAIC Code: 488510

TYPES OF BUSINESS:

3PL Third Party Logistics
Logistics
Freight Transport
Contract Transportation
Truckload
Less Than Truckload
Freight Services
Shipping Technology

BRANDS/DIVISIONS/AFFILIATES:

Robinson Fresh
Prime Distribution Services

CONTACTS: *Note: Officers with more than one job title may be intentionally listed here more than once.*

Robert Biesterfeld, CEO
Scott Hagen, CFO
John Wiehoff, Chairman of the Board
Michael Neill, Chief Technology Officer
Christopher OBrien, Other Executive Officer
Angela Freeman, Other Executive Officer
Ben Campbell, Other Executive Officer
Jereon Eijsink, President, Divisional
Jordan Kass, President, Divisional
Michael Short, President, Divisional
Mac Pinkerton, President, Divisional

GROWTH PLANS/SPECIAL FEATURES:

C.H. Robinson Worldwide, Inc. (CHRW) is one of the world's largest global logistics companies, with consolidated total revenues of $16.2 billion in 2020. CHRW enters into contractual relationships with transportation companies and utilizes them to arrange the transport of its customer's freight. The firm utilized approximately 73,000 contracted transportation companies, including contracted motor carriers, railroads, ocean and air carriers in 2020. CHRW operates through two segments: North American surface transportation and global forwarding. The North American surface transportation segment provides transportation and logistics services across North America through a network of offices in the U.S., Canada and Mexico. Primary services provided by the division are truckload and less-than-truckload (LTL) transportation services. The global forwarding segment provides transportation and logistics services through an international network of offices in North America, Europe, Asia, Oceania and South America, and also contracts with independent agents worldwide. Primary services by this division include ocean freight services, air freight services and customs brokerage. Other activities by CHRW include sourcing services under the trade name Robinson Fresh, managed services and other surface transportation outside of North America. Robinson Fresh's sourcing services primarily include the buying, selling and marketing of fresh fruits, vegetables and other value-added perishable items. During 2020, CHRW acquired Prime Distribution Services, a provider of retail consolidation services in North America. In January 2021, CHRW announced a new technology center in Cork, Ireland to further deliver personalized solutions for shippers and carriers.

FINANCIAL DATA: *Note: Data for latest year may not have been available at press time.*

In U.S. $	2020	2019	2018	2017	2016	2015
Revenue	16,207,110,000	15,309,510,000	16,631,170,000	14,869,380,000	13,144,410,000	13,476,080,000
R&D Expense						
Operating Income	673,268,000	789,976,000	912,083,000	775,119,000	837,531,000	858,310,000
Operating Margin %		.05%	.05%	.05%	.06%	.06%
SGA Expense	496,122,000	497,806,000	449,610,000	413,404,000	375,061,000	358,760,000
Net Income	506,421,000	576,968,000	664,505,000	504,893,000	513,384,000	509,699,000
Operating Cash Flow	499,191,000	835,419,000	792,896,000	384,001,000	529,408,000	718,336,000
Capital Expenditure	54,009,000	70,465,000	63,871,000	57,945,000	91,437,000	44,642,000
EBITDA	774,995,000	890,425,000	1,008,812,000	868,096,000	912,200,000	924,719,000
Return on Assets %		.13%	.15%	.13%	.15%	.16%
Return on Equity %		.35%	.44%	.38%	.43%	.46%
Debt to Equity		0.809	0.841	0.526	0.398	0.435

CONTACT INFORMATION:

Phone: 952 937-8500   Fax: 952 937-6714
Toll-Free:
Address: 14701 Charlson Rd., Eden Prairie, MN 55347 United States

SALARIES/BONUSES:

Top Exec. Salary: $ Bonus: $
Second Exec. Salary: $ Bonus: $

STOCK TICKER/OTHER:

Stock Ticker: CHRW   Exchange: NAS
Employees: 15,788   Fiscal Year Ends: 12/31
Parent Company:

OTHER THOUGHTS:

Estimated Female Officers or Directors: 4
Hot Spot for Advancement for Women/Minorities: Y

Charles River Laboratories International Inc

www.criver.com

NAIC Code: 541711

TYPES OF BUSINESS:
Medical and Drug Research Models
Consulting
Bioactivity Software
Biosafety Testing
Contract Staffing
Laboratory Diagnostics
Intellectual Property Consulting
Analytical Testing

BRANDS/DIVISIONS/AFFILIATES:
Biologics Testing Services

CONTACTS:
Note: Officers with more than one job title may be intentionally listed here more than once.

James Foster, CEO
David Smith, CFO
Michael Knell, Chief Accounting Officer
David Johst, Chief Administrative Officer
Birgit Girshick, Executive VP, Divisional
Joseph LaPlume, Executive VP, Divisional
William Barbo, Executive VP

GROWTH PLANS/SPECIAL FEATURES:

Charles River Laboratories International, Inc. (CRL) is a global provider of solutions that accelerate the drug discovery and development process, including research models and outsourced preclinical services. CRL operates in over 100 facilities in more than 20 countries. The firm's customer base includes global pharmaceutical companies, biotechnology companies, government agencies, hospitals and academic institutions. CRL operates in three segments: research models and services (RMS), discovery and safety assessment (DSA) and manufacturing. RMS supplies research models to the drug development industry, and is a global leader in the production and sale of rodent research model strains, principally genetically and microbiologically defined purpose-bred rats and mice. RMS accounted for 19.6% of 2020 total revenue. DSA (62.8%) provides services that enable clients to outsource their drug discovery research; their critical, regulatory-required safety assessment testing; and related drug discovery and development activities to CRL. Manufacturing (17.6%) helps ensure the safe production and release of products manufactured by the firm's clients. This division's endotoxin and microbial detection business provides non-animal, or in vitro, methods for lot release testing of medical devices and injectable drugs for endotoxin contamination. Its avian vaccine services business provides specific pathogen free (SPF) fertile chicken eggs and chickens for the manufacture of live viruses. Its Biologics Testing Services business provides specialized testing of biologics and devices frequently outsourced by global pharmaceutical and biotechnology companies. In May 2021, CRL agreed to acquire Vigene Biosciences, Inc., a U.S.-based gene therapy contract development and manufacturing organization providing viral vector-based gene delivery solutions.

CRL offers its employees comprehensive benefits that vary by country.

FINANCIAL DATA:
Note: Data for latest year may not have been available at press time.

In U.S. $	2020	2019	2018	2017	2016	2015
Revenue	2,923,933,000	2,621,226,000	2,266,096,000	1,857,601,000	1,681,432,000	1,363,302,000
R&D Expense						
Operating Income	432,729,000	351,151,000	331,383,000	287,498,000	237,419,000	206,449,000
Operating Margin %		.13%	.15%	.15%	.14%	.15%
SGA Expense	528,935,000	517,622,000	443,854,000	373,446,000	367,548,000	300,414,000
Net Income	364,304,000	252,019,000	226,373,000	123,355,000	154,765,000	149,313,000
Operating Cash Flow	546,575,000	480,936,000	441,140,000	316,265,000	298,319,000	286,358,000
Capital Expenditure	166,560,000	140,514,000	140,054,000	82,431,000	55,288,000	63,252,000
EBITDA	768,471,000	563,061,000	507,232,000	457,891,000	377,288,000	305,381,000
Return on Assets %		.06%	.07%	.04%	.06%	.08%
Return on Equity %		.17%	.19%	.13%	.20%	.21%
Debt to Equity		1.203	1.242	1.066	1.443	1.154

CONTACT INFORMATION:
Phone: 781 222-6000   Fax: 978 658-7841
Toll-Free:
Address: 251 Ballardvale St., Wilmington, MA 01887 United States

STOCK TICKER/OTHER:
Stock Ticker: CRL   Exchange: NYS
Employees: 17,100   Fiscal Year Ends: 12/31
Parent Company:

SALARIES/BONUSES:
Top Exec. Salary: $ Bonus: $
Second Exec. Salary: $ Bonus: $

OTHER THOUGHTS:
Estimated Female Officers or Directors: 3
Hot Spot for Advancement for Women/Minorities: Y

Charles Schwab Corporation (The)

www.schwab.com

NAIC Code: 523120

TYPES OF BUSINESS:

Stock Brokerage-Retail, Online & Discount
Investment Services
Physical Branch Investment Offices
Mutual Funds
Wealth Management
Financial Information
Retail Banking
Online Trading Platform

BRANDS/DIVISIONS/AFFILIATES:

Charles Schwab & Co Inc
Charles Schwab Bank
Charles Schwab Investment Management Inc
TD Ameritrade Holding Corporation
TD Ameritrade Inc
TD Ameritrade Clearing Inc

CONTACTS: *Note: Officers with more than one job title may be intentionally listed here more than once.*

Walter Bettinger, CEO
Peter Crawford, CFO
Charles Schwab, Chairman of the Board
Joseph Martinetto, COO
Nigel Murtagh, Executive VP, Divisional
Terri Kallsen, Executive VP, Divisional
Bernard Clark, Executive VP, Divisional
David Garfield, Executive VP
Jonathan Craig, Senior Executive VP

GROWTH PLANS/SPECIAL FEATURES:

The Charles Schwab Corporation (CSC) engages in securities brokerage, banking, money management and related financial advisory services. As of October 31, 2020, the company was managing $5.9 trillion in client assets, 29 million active brokerage accounts, 2.1 million corporate retirement plan participants and 1.5 million banking accounts through its primary subsidiary, securities broker-dealer Charles Schwab & Co., Inc. (Schwab). CSC also engages in futures and commodities trading activities. In addition, subsidiary Charles Schwab Bank is a federal savings bank; and Charles Schwab Investment Management, Inc. is an investment advisor for the company's proprietary mutual and exchange-traded funds. CSC provides its financial services and products such as brokerage, banking, trust, advice and mutual/exchange trade funds to individuals and institutional clients through two segments: investor services and advisor services. Investor services provides retail brokerage and banking services to individual investors, retirement plan services and corporate brokerage services. Advisor services provides custodial, trading and support services to independent investment advisors (IAs), and retirement business services to independent retirement plan advisors and record keepers whose plan assets are held at Schwab Bank. Many products and services are offered through CSC's digital channels. In October 2020, the firm completed its acquisition of TD Ameritrade Holding Corporation and its consolidated subsidiaries, including TD Ameritrade Inc. and TD Ameritrade Clearing Inc.

CSC offers employees health benefits; 401(k) and savings plans; education reimbursement; and on-the-job training and support.

FINANCIAL DATA: *Note: Data for latest year may not have been available at press time.*

In U.S. $	2020	2019	2018	2017	2016	2015
Revenue	11,691,000,000	10,721,000,000	10,132,000,000	8,618,000,000	7,473,000,000	6,369,000,000
R&D Expense						
Operating Income						
Operating Margin %						
SGA Expense	4,796,000,000	4,002,000,000	3,801,000,000	3,415,000,000	2,968,000,000	2,723,000,000
Net Income	3,299,000,000	3,704,000,000	3,507,000,000	2,354,000,000	1,889,000,000	1,447,000,000
Operating Cash Flow	6,852,000,000	9,325,000,000	12,456,000,000	1,263,000,000	2,662,000,000	1,246,000,000
Capital Expenditure	631,000,000	708,000,000	570,000,000	400,000,000	346,000,000	266,000,000
EBITDA						
Return on Assets %		.01%	.01%	.01%	.01%	.01%
Return on Equity %		.19%	.20%	.15%	.14%	.12%
Debt to Equity		0.392	0.385	0.302	0.211	0.242

CONTACT INFORMATION:

Phone: Fax:
Toll-Free: 800-648-5300
Address: TX-114 Circle T Ranch, Westlake, TX 76262 United States

STOCK TICKER/OTHER:

Stock Ticker: SCHW   Exchange: NYS
Employees: 19,700   Fiscal Year Ends: 12/31
Parent Company:

SALARIES/BONUSES:

Top Exec. Salary: $ Bonus: $
Second Exec. Salary: $ Bonus: $

OTHER THOUGHTS:

Estimated Female Officers or Directors: 6
Hot Spot for Advancement for Women/Minorities: Y

Chemed Corporation

NAIC Code: 621610

TYPES OF BUSINESS:
Home Health Care Services
Hospice Care
Plumbing Services
Pressure Washer Jetting
Leak Detection Services
Pipe Inspections
Pipe Repair

BRANDS/DIVISIONS/AFFILIATES:
VITAS Healthcare Corporation
Roto-Rooter Corporation

CONTACTS: *Note: Officers with more than one job title may be intentionally listed here more than once.*
Nicholas Westfall, CEO, Subsidiary
Kevin McNamara, CEO
David Williams, CFO
George Walsh, Chairman of the Board
Michael Witzeman, Chief Accounting Officer
Thomas Hutton, Director
Spencer Lee, Executive VP
Naomi Dallob, Secretary

GROWTH PLANS/SPECIAL FEATURES:
Chemed Corporation, through its wholly-owned subsidiaries VITAS Healthcare Corporation and Roto-Rooter Corporation, offers hospice care and plumbing services, respectively. VITAS is one of the largest national providers of hospice care and end-of-life services. Its team members include registered nurses, licensed practical nurses, home health aides, physicians, social workers, chaplains and other caregiving professionals. VITAS provides hospice care services in the patient's home, including music therapy and pet visits. Additionally, the firm manages inpatient hospice units, providing service in hospitals, nursing homes and assisted living communities/residential care facilities. Approximately 95% of VITAS' service revenues consist of payments from Medicare and Medicaid. Roto-Rooter supports the maintenance needs of residential and commercial markets by providing services such as plumbing, drain cleaning, high-pressure water jetting, underground leak and line detection, video camera pipe inspections, grease trap and liquid waste pumping, backflow protection, emergency services, automated drain care programs and pipe repair and replacement. One of the largest businesses of its type in North America, Roto-Rooter operates hundreds of company-owned and franchises throughout the U.S. Concerning revenues, Roto-Rooter's largest share is generated by plumbing repair and maintenance, followed by sewer and drain cleaning, HVAC (heating, ventilation and air conditioning) repair and other products and services.

FINANCIAL DATA: *Note: Data for latest year may not have been available at press time.*

In U.S. $	2020	2019	2018	2017	2016	2015
Revenue	2,079,583,000	1,938,555,000	1,782,648,000	1,666,724,000	1,576,881,000	1,543,388,000
R&D Expense						
Operating Income	394,810,000	266,512,000	244,932,000	203,915,000	178,749,000	184,458,000
Operating Margin %		.14%	.14%	.12%	.11%	.12%
SGA Expense	330,218,000	305,712,000	270,209,000	276,652,000	243,572,000	237,821,000
Net Income	319,466,000	219,923,000	205,544,000	98,177,000	108,743,000	110,274,000
Operating Cash Flow	489,289,000	301,249,000	287,138,000	162,495,000	135,393,000	171,500,000
Capital Expenditure	58,831,000	53,022,000	52,872,000	64,300,000	39,772,000	44,135,000
EBITDA	454,928,000	311,349,000	283,453,000	156,814,000	215,407,000	217,270,000
Return on Assets %		.20%	.22%	.11%	.13%	.13%
Return on Equity %		.33%	.36%	.18%	.21%	.23%
Debt to Equity		0.243	0.151	0.169	0.191	0.163

CONTACT INFORMATION:
Phone: 513 762-6900   Fax: 513 762-6919
Toll-Free:
Address: 255 E. 5th St., Ste. 2600, Cincinnati, OH 45202 United States

STOCK TICKER/OTHER:
Stock Ticker: CHE   Exchange: NYS
Employees: 15,544   Fiscal Year Ends: 12/31
Parent Company:

SALARIES/BONUSES:
Top Exec. Salary: $ Bonus: $
Second Exec. Salary: $ Bonus: $

OTHER THOUGHTS:
Estimated Female Officers or Directors: 3
Hot Spot for Advancement for Women/Minorities: Y

Chewy Inc (Chewy.com)

www.chewy.com

NAIC Code: 454111

TYPES OF BUSINESS:

Online Pet Supplies Sales
Pharmacy for Pets

BRANDS/DIVISIONS/AFFILIATES:

PetSmart Inc
Chewy.com
Chewy.com Rescue and Shelter Network

CONTACTS: Note: Officers with more than one job title may be intentionally listed here more than once.

Sumit Singh, CEO
Mario Marte, CFO
Raymond Svider, Chairman of the Board
Satish Mehta, Chief Technology Officer
Susan Helfrick, General Counsel

GROWTH PLANS/SPECIAL FEATURES:

Chewy, Inc., commonly referred to as Chewy.com, is an online retailer of pet food and other pet related products. The firm was founded in 2011 and a significant portion of its stock is owned by PetSmart, Inc. With items from over 1,800 brands in stock and ready to ship, Chewy offers pet foods and pet products for dogs; cats; fish; birds; small pets such as rabbits, hamsters, gerbils, guinea pigs and chinchillas; reptiles; and horses. By the end of 2020, the company had more than 16 million customers and continued to grow quickly. Headquartered in Dania Beach, Florida, with fulfillment centers in Nevada, Pennsylvania and Indiana, the firm offers same day shipping on all orders placed before 4 pm and a freshness guarantee combined with a 365-day hassle-free return policy. Customer service agents make up approximately one sixth of the firm's total employees, teams of which are available 24/7/365, and are trained in pet care in order to be better able to address customer questions, concerns and needs. In addition to its online pet food and pet products business, Chewy also operates the Chewy.com Rescue and Shelter Network. This network is free to all registered nonprofit organizations specializing in assisting the needs of pets and grants these organizations access to programs providing donations and fundraising opportunities. A portion of each purchase made on Chewy.com is donated to the organizations within the network.

FINANCIAL DATA: Note: Data for latest year may not have been available at press time.

In U.S. $	2020	2019	2018	2017	2016	2015
Revenue	4,846,743,000	3,532,837,000	2,104,287,000		900,566,000	
R&D Expense						
Operating Income	-252,726,000	-267,766,000	-337,851,000		-107,427,000	
Operating Margin %	- .05%	- .08%	- .16%		- .12%	
SGA Expense	1,396,786,000	982,571,000	705,401,000		257,258,000	
Net Income	-252,370,000	-267,890,000	-338,057,000		-107,164,000	
Operating Cash Flow	46,581,000	-13,415,000	-79,747,000		7,252,000	
Capital Expenditure	48,636,000	44,160,000	40,282,000		22,272,000	
EBITDA	-222,081,000	-244,499,000	-325,315,000		-101,825,000	
Return on Assets %	- .34%	- .51%	-1.39%			
Return on Equity %						
Debt to Equity						

CONTACT INFORMATION:

Phone: 954-793-4144   Fax:
Toll-Free: 800-672-4399
Address: 1855 Griffin Rd., Dania Beach, FL 33004 United States

STOCK TICKER/OTHER:

Stock Ticker: CHWY
Employees: 18,500
Parent Company: PetSmart Inc

Exchange: NYS
Fiscal Year Ends:

SALARIES/BONUSES:

Top Exec. Salary: $ Bonus: $
Second Exec. Salary: $ Bonus: $

OTHER THOUGHTS:

Estimated Female Officers or Directors:
Hot Spot for Advancement for Women/Minorities:

Chick-fil-A Inc

www.chick-fil-a.com

NAIC Code: 722513

TYPES OF BUSINESS:

Fast Food Restaurants
Fast Food Restaurant

BRANDS/DIVISIONS/AFFILIATES:

Chick-fil-A Chicken Sandwich
Chick-fil-A Kid's Meal Program
Truetts Grill
Truetts Luau
Dwarf House
Chick-fil-A One

CONTACTS: *Note: Officers with more than one job title may be intentionally listed here more than once.*

Dan T. Cathy, CEO
William (Woody) F. Faulk, VP-Innovation & Design
Roger H. Shealy, Dir.-Production Design
Tim Boggs, Sr. Dir.-Admin.
Kelly D. Ludwick, Sr. Dir.-Corp. Legal
Timothy Tassopoulos, Exec. VP-Oper.
Roger E. Blythe, Jr., VP-Bus. Analysis
Greg Thompson, Dir.-Corp. Comm.
James (Buck) McCabe, Exec. VP-Finance
Donald M. (Bubba) Cathy, Pres., Dwarf House
Perry Ragsdale, Sr. VP-Real Estate, Design & Construction
Thomas E. Childers, Sr. Dir.-Menu Innovation & Quality
Brent Ragsdale, VP
Onome Okuma, Sr. Dir.-Supply Chain & Business Growth Solutions

GROWTH PLANS/SPECIAL FEATURES:

Chick-fil-A, Inc., headquartered in Atlanta, Georgia, is a fast food chain with a focus on chicken sandwiches and chicken products. The company has more than 2,400 restaurants throughout the U.S. and other countries, including both freestanding buildings with drive-through lanes and mall-based locations. Stores are also licensed to college campuses, hospitals, airports and other similar institutions. Offerings include chicken entrees, sandwiches, salads, waffle fries and fresh-squeezed lemonade and desserts served separately and in combo meals. The company's proprietary menu item is the Chick-fil-A Chicken Sandwich. The firm boasts a trans-fat free menu, cooking all foods in 100% refined peanut oil. The Chick-fil-A Kid's Meal Program includes activities to educate children in math and language arts skills and provides healthy alternatives to fries and soda. Sister restaurants include Truett's Grill, a full-service 50's diner themed restaurant; Truett's Luau, which serves fresh sea food items and Hawaii-inspired dishes; and Dwarf House, a full-service restaurant. The company also offers catering services with large trays of menu items. Chick-fil-A One is a rewards program in which members earn points with every purchase, and can be redeemed in various ways. Chick-fil-A attributes its growth over the past 50 years to dedicated franchisee owners and the company's emphasis on product quality. The company advertises through its signature Eat Mor Chikin campaign, featuring ads with cows trying to convince consumers to eat more chicken.

Chick-fil-A's elgible full-time employees are offered comprehensive health benefits, life and disability insurance, 401(k) and pension plans, as well as a variety of employee assistance programs.

FINANCIAL DATA: *Note: Data for latest year may not have been available at press time.*

In U.S. $	2020	2019	2018	2017	2016	2015
Revenue	13,700,000,000	12,000,000,000	10,460,000,000	8,970,000,000	7,154,000,000	6,600,000,000
R&D Expense						
Operating Income						
Operating Margin %						
SGA Expense						
Net Income						
Operating Cash Flow						
Capital Expenditure						
EBITDA						
Return on Assets %						
Return on Equity %						
Debt to Equity						

CONTACT INFORMATION:

Phone: 404-765-8038   Fax:
Toll-Free: 800-232-2677
Address: 5200 Buffington Rd., Atlanta, GA 30349 United States

STOCK TICKER/OTHER:

Stock Ticker: Private   Exchange:
Employees: 15,000   Fiscal Year Ends: 12/31
Parent Company:

SALARIES/BONUSES:

Top Exec. Salary: $ Bonus: $
Second Exec. Salary: $ Bonus: $

OTHER THOUGHTS:

Estimated Female Officers or Directors: 14
Hot Spot for Advancement for Women/Minorities: Y

Chipotle Mexican Grill Inc

www.chipotle.com

NAIC Code: 722513

TYPES OF BUSINESS:

Restaurants
Restaurants
Mexican Food
Digital Only Concepts
Dine-In

BRANDS/DIVISIONS/AFFILIATES:

Pizzeria Locale
Chipotle Digital Kitchen

CONTACTS: Note: Officers with more than one job title may be intentionally listed here more than once.

John Hartung, CFO
Steve Ells, Chairman of the Board
Curtis Garner, Chief Information Officer
Mark Crumpacker, Chief Marketing Officer

GROWTH PLANS/SPECIAL FEATURES:

Chipotle Mexican Grill, Inc. operates Mexican food restaurants serving a relatively focused menu of burritos, tacos, burrito bowls (burrito ingredients without the tortilla) and salads, with an emphasis on fresh and naturally-sourced meats and produce. Chipotle was majority-owned by McDonald's Corporation from 2001 to 2006, when the firm was spun-off and completed its initial public offering. The company operates more than 2,750 Chipotle branded restaurants located in the U.S., Canada and the U.K. (as of December 31, 2020). Chipotle is also an investor in a consolidated entity that owns and operates three Pizzeria Locale restaurants in Colorado, offering a fast-casual pizza concept. Basic Chipotle ingredients include marinated chicken and steak, carnitas (seasoned and braised pork), barbacoa (spicy shredded beef) and pinto and vegetarian black beans. Chipotle's collection of Lifestyle Bowls include the Paleo Salad Bowl, Keto Salad Bowl, Vegetarian Bowl, Whole30 Salad Bowl and High Protein Bowl. Customers can customize their food with rice (tossed with lime juice and chopped cilantro) as well as shredded cheese, sour cream, lettuce, peppers and onions. Chipotle also provides a variety of extras such as guacamole, salsas and tortilla chips. In addition to sodas and fruit drinks, most locations also offer a selection of beer and margaritas. All items can be ordered through the company's mobile app and website, and can be delivered or picked up in-restaurant. In November 2020, Chipotle announced its first digital-only restaurant called the Chipotle Digital Kitchen, which is located in Highland Falls, New York. The concept only provides pickup and delivery services.

Chipotle offers its employees comprehensive health and wellness benefits.

FINANCIAL DATA: Note: Data for latest year may not have been available at press time.

In U.S. $	2020	2019	2018	2017	2016	2015
Revenue	5,984,634,000	5,586,369,000	4,864,985,000	4,476,412,000	3,904,384,000	4,501,223,000
R&D Expense						
Operating Income	320,741,000	467,052,000	325,007,000	284,139,000	58,444,000	776,783,000
Operating Margin %		.08%	.07%	.06%	.01%	.17%
SGA Expense	466,291,000	451,552,000	375,460,000	296,388,000	276,240,000	250,214,000
Net Income	355,766,000	350,158,000	176,553,000	176,253,000	22,938,000	475,602,000
Operating Cash Flow	663,847,000	721,632,000	621,552,000	467,105,000	349,242,000	683,316,000
Capital Expenditure	373,352,000	333,912,000	287,390,000	216,777,000	258,842,000	257,418,000
EBITDA	743,813,000	843,782,000	526,986,000	447,487,000	204,812,000	907,151,000
Return on Assets %		.10%	.08%	.09%	.01%	.18%
Return on Equity %		.22%	.13%	.13%	.01%	.23%
Debt to Equity		1.591				

CONTACT INFORMATION:

Phone: 303-595-4000 Fax:
Toll-Free:
Address: 610 Newport Center Dr., Ste. 1300, Newport, CA 92660 United States

STOCK TICKER/OTHER:

Stock Ticker: CMG
Employees: 97,000
Parent Company:

Exchange: NYS
Fiscal Year Ends: 12/31

SALARIES/BONUSES:

Top Exec. Salary: $ Bonus: $
Second Exec. Salary: $ Bonus: $

OTHER THOUGHTS:

Estimated Female Officers or Directors: 1
Hot Spot for Advancement for Women/Minorities:

Church & Dwight Company Inc

NAIC Code: 325611

churchdwight.com

TYPES OF BUSINESS:

Soap & Cleaning Compound Manufacturing
Manufacturer
Household Products
Personal Care

BRANDS/DIVISIONS/AFFILIATES:

Arm & Hammer
Trojan
XTRA
OxiClean
VitaFusion
Orajel
Scrub Free Kaboom
Matrixx Initiatives Inc

CONTACTS: Note: Officers with more than one job title may be intentionally listed here more than once.

Rick Dierker, CFO
James Craigie, Chairman of the Board
Steven Katz, Chief Accounting Officer
Britta Bomhard, Chief Marketing Officer
Matthew Farrell, Director
Steven Cugine, Executive VP, Divisional
Paul Wood, Executive VP, Divisional
Paul Wood, Executive VP, Divisional
Judy Zagorski, Executive VP, Divisional
Rick Spann, Executive VP, Divisional
Carlos Linares, Executive VP, Divisional
Patrick De Maynadier, Executive VP

GROWTH PLANS/SPECIAL FEATURES:

Church & Dwight Company, Inc. develops, manufactures and markets a broad range of household, personal care and specialty products. The company focuses its marketing efforts mainly on its power brands. These well-recognized brand names include Arm & Hammer, used in multiple product categories such as baking soda, carpet deodorization and laundry detergent; Trojan condoms, lubricants and vibrators; OxiClean stain removers, cleaning solutions, laundry detergents and bleach alternatives; SpinBrush battery-operated toothbrushes; First Response home pregnancy and ovulation test kits; NAIR depilatories; Orajel oral analgesic; XTRA laundry detergent; the combination of the L'il Critters and VitaFusion brand names for the our gummy dietary supplement business; Batiste dry shampoo; and WaterPik water flossers and showerheads. Church & Dwitgh's business is divided into three primary segments: consumer domestic, consumer international and specialty products. The consumer domestic segment includes the power brands and other household and personal care products such as Scrub Free Kaboom and Orange Glo cleaning products and Arrid antiperspirant. The consumer international segment mainly sells a variety of personal care products, some of which use the same brands as its domestic product lines, in international markets, including France, the U.K., Germany, Canada, Mexico, Australia, China and Brazil. The specialty products segment is one of the largest U.S. producers of sodium bicarbonate, which it sells together with other specialty inorganic chemicals for a variety of industrial, institutional, medical and food applications. This segment also sells a range of animal nutrition and specialty cleaning products. In December 2020, Church & Dwight acquired Matrixx Initiatives, Inc., owner of the ZICAM brand.

FINANCIAL DATA: Note: Data for latest year may not have been available at press time.

In U.S. $	2020	2019	2018	2017	2016	2015
Revenue	4,895,800,000	4,357,700,000	4,145,900,000	3,776,200,000	3,493,100,000	3,394,800,000
R&D Expense						
Operating Income	1,029,700,000	840,200,000	791,700,000	732,700,000	724,200,000	674,200,000
Operating Margin %		.19%	.19%	.19%	.21%	.20%
SGA Expense	1,184,500,000	1,143,800,000	1,049,100,000	996,900,000	866,400,000	837,600,000
Net Income	785,900,000	615,900,000	568,600,000	743,400,000	459,000,000	410,400,000
Operating Cash Flow	990,300,000	864,500,000	763,600,000	681,500,000	655,300,000	606,100,000
Capital Expenditure	98,900,000	73,700,000	60,400,000	45,000,000	49,800,000	61,800,000
EBITDA	1,224,500,000	1,023,700,000	940,000,000	870,700,000	841,200,000	766,900,000
Return on Assets %		.10%	.09%	.14%	.11%	.10%
Return on Equity %		.24%	.24%	.35%	.23%	.20%
Debt to Equity		0.679	0.615	0.948	0.351	0.342

CONTACT INFORMATION:

Phone: 609 806-1200   Fax:
Toll-Free:
Address: 500 Charles Ewing Blvd., Ewing, NJ 08628 United States

STOCK TICKER/OTHER:

Stock Ticker: CHD   Exchange: NYS
Employees: 4,500   Fiscal Year Ends: 12/31
Parent Company:

SALARIES/BONUSES:

Top Exec. Salary: $ Bonus: $
Second Exec. Salary: $ Bonus: $

OTHER THOUGHTS:

Estimated Female Officers or Directors: 4
Hot Spot for Advancement for Women/Minorities: Y

Ciena Corporation

www.ciena.com

NAIC Code: 334210

TYPES OF BUSINESS:
Communications Networking Equipment
Software & Support Services
Consulting Services
Switching Platforms
Packet Interworking Products
Access Products
Network & Service Management Tools

BRANDS/DIVISIONS/AFFILIATES:
Blue Planet Automation
Adaptive Network

CONTACTS: Note: Officers with more than one job title may be intentionally listed here more than once.
Gary Smith, CEO
James Moylan, CFO
Patrick Nettles, Chairman of the Board
Andrew Petrik, Chief Accounting Officer
Stephen Alexander, Chief Technology Officer
David Rothenstein, General Counsel
James Frodsham, Other Executive Officer
Scott McFeely, Senior VP, Divisional
Jason Phipps, Senior VP, Divisional
Rick Hamilton, Senior VP, Divisional

GROWTH PLANS/SPECIAL FEATURES:
Ciena Corporation provides communications networking equipment, software and services that support the transport, switching, aggregation and management of voice, video and data traffic. The firm's solutions include its portfolio of networking platforms, including the converged packet optical and packet networking products, that can be applied from the network core to end user access points, and that allow network operators to scale capacity, increase transmission speeds, allocate traffic and adapt dynamically to changing end-user service demands. Additionally, Ciena offers platform software that provides management and domain control of our hardware solutions and automates network lifecycle operations, including provisioning equipment and services. Through the Blue Planet Automation Software, the firm enables network providers to use network data, analytics and policy-based assurance to achieve closed loop automation across multi-vendor and multi-domain network environments, streamlining key business and network processes. To complement these hardware and software products, Ciena offers a broad range of services that help customers build, operate and improve their networks and associated operational environments. The firm refers to the complete portfolio vision as the Adaptive Network. The Adaptive Network emphasizes a programmable network infrastructure, software control and automation capabilities, and network analytics and intelligence. By transforming network infrastructures into a dynamic, programmable environment driven by automation and analytics, network operators can realize greater business agility, dynamically adapt to changing end user service demands and rapidly introduce new revenue-generating services. They can also gain valuable real-time network insights, allowing them to optimize network operation and maximize the return on their network infrastructure investment. In November 2019, Ciena closed on its acquisition of Centina Systems, a provider of service assurance analytics and network performance management solutions.

FINANCIAL DATA: Note: Data for latest year may not have been available at press time.

In U.S. $	2020	2019	2018	2017	2016	2015
Revenue	3,532,157,000	3,572,131,000	3,094,286,000	2,801,687,000	2,600,573,000	2,445,669,000
R&D Expense	529,888,000	548,139,000	491,564,000	475,329,000	451,794,000	414,201,000
Operating Income	513,647,000	374,674,000	253,196,000	238,655,000	165,715,000	134,613,000
Operating Margin %		.10%	.08%	.09%	.06%	.06%
SGA Expense	585,973,000	597,445,000	554,193,000	498,773,000	482,559,000	457,238,000
Net Income	361,291,000	253,434,000	-344,690,000	1,261,953,000	72,584,000	11,667,000
Operating Cash Flow	493,654,000	413,140,000	229,261,000	234,882,000	289,520,000	262,112,000
Capital Expenditure	82,667,000	62,579,000	67,616,000	94,600,000	107,185,000	62,109,000
EBITDA	619,809,000	473,354,000	314,050,000	334,880,000	285,066,000	210,710,000
Return on Assets %		.07%	- .09%	.37%	.03%	.00%
Return on Equity %		.12%	- .17%	.87%	.10%	.04%
Debt to Equity		0.343	0.391	0.308	1.371	2.07

CONTACT INFORMATION:
Phone: 410 694-5700   Fax: 410 694-5750
Toll-Free: 800-921-1144
Address: 7035 Ridge Rd., Hanover, MD 21076 United States

STOCK TICKER/OTHER:
Stock Ticker: CIEN
Employees: 7,032
Parent Company:

Exchange: NYS
Fiscal Year Ends: 10/31

SALARIES/BONUSES:
Top Exec. Salary: $ Bonus: $
Second Exec. Salary: $ Bonus: $

OTHER THOUGHTS:
Estimated Female Officers or Directors: 2
Hot Spot for Advancement for Women/Minorities:

Cigna Corporation
NAIC Code: 524114

TYPES OF BUSINESS:
Insurance-Medical & Health, HMOs & PPOs
Indemnity Insurance
Investment Management Services
Group Life, Accident & Disability

BRANDS/DIVISIONS/AFFILIATES:
Evernorth
Cigna

CONTACTS: Note: Officers with more than one job title may be intentionally listed here more than once.
David Cordani, CEO
Michael Triplett, Pres., Divisional
Eric Palmer, CFO
Isaiah Harris, Chairman of the Board
Mary Agoglia Hoeltzel, Chief Accounting Officer
Mark Boxer, Chief Information Officer
Lisa Bacus, Chief Marketing Officer
John Murabito, Executive VP, Divisional
Alan Muney, Executive VP
Nicole Jones, Executive VP
Steven Miller, Executive VP
Jason Sadler, President, Divisional
Brian Evanko, President, Divisional
Timothy Wentworth, President, Divisional
Matthew Manders, President, Divisional

GROWTH PLANS/SPECIAL FEATURES:
Cigna Corporation is a global health services organization. The firm offers a differentiated set of pharmacy, medical, behavioral, dental and supplemental products and services, primarily through two brands: Cigna and Evernorth. Cigna operates in three main segments: Evernorth, U.S. Medical and International Markets. Evernorth brings together coordinated and point solution health services including pharmacy solutions, benefits management solutions, care solutions and intelligence solutions, and specialized to deliver custom and flexible solutions that meet the needs of clients and customers. U.S. Medical includes Cigna's U.S. Commercial and U.S. Government businesses that provide comprehensive medical and coordinated solutions. U.S. Commercial products and services include medical, pharmacy, behavioral health, dental, vision, health advocacy programs and other products and services for insured and self-insured customers. U.S. Government solutions include Medicare Advantage, Medicare Supplement, and Medicare Part D plans for seniors, Medicaid plans, and individual health insurance plans both on and off the public exchanges. Cigna's International Markets segment has operations in over 30 countries or jurisdictions providing a full range of comprehensive medical and supplemental health, life and accident benefits to individuals and employers. Products and services include comprehensive health coverage, hospitalization, dental, critical illness, personal accident, term life, medical cost containment and variable universal life. In December 2020, New York Life Insurance Company completed its $6.3 billion acquisition of Cigna's group life, accident, and disability insurance business. In April 2021, Molina Healthcare, Inc. agreed to acquired Cigna's Texas Medicaid and Medicare-Medicaid Plan contracts and certain operating assets for approximately $60 million.

FINANCIAL DATA: Note: Data for latest year may not have been available at press time.

In U.S. $	2020	2019	2018	2017	2016	2015
Revenue	160,577,000,000	153,743,000,000	48,569,000,000	41,616,000,000	39,668,000,000	37,876,000,000
R&D Expense						
Operating Income						
Operating Margin %						
SGA Expense	14,072,000,000	14,053,000,000	11,934,000,000			
Net Income	8,458,000,000	5,104,000,000	2,637,000,000	2,237,000,000	1,867,000,000	2,094,000,000
Operating Cash Flow	10,350,000,000	9,485,000,000	3,770,000,000	4,086,000,000	4,026,000,000	2,717,000,000
Capital Expenditure	1,094,000,000	1,050,000,000	528,000,000	471,000,000	461,000,000	510,000,000
EBITDA						
Return on Assets %		.03%	.02%	.04%	.03%	.04%
Return on Equity %		.12%	.10%	.16%	.14%	.18%
Debt to Equity		0.703	0.963	0.379	0.347	0.417

CONTACT INFORMATION:
Phone: 860 226-6000   Fax: 215 761-3596
Toll-Free: 800-997-1654
Address: 900 Cottage Grove Rd., Bloomfield, CT 06002 United States

STOCK TICKER/OTHER:
Stock Ticker: CI   Exchange: NYS
Employees: 73,700   Fiscal Year Ends: 12/31
Parent Company:

SALARIES/BONUSES:
Top Exec. Salary: $ Bonus: $
Second Exec. Salary: $ Bonus: $

OTHER THOUGHTS:
Estimated Female Officers or Directors: 4
Hot Spot for Advancement for Women/Minorities: Y

Cisco Systems Inc

www.cisco.com

NAIC Code: 334210A

TYPES OF BUSINESS:

Computer Networking Equipment
Routers & Switches
Real-Time Conferencing Technology
Server Virtualization Software
Data Storage Products
Security Products
Teleconference Systems and Technology
Unified Communications Systems

BRANDS/DIVISIONS/AFFILIATES:

AppDynamics Inc
Cicsco Talos
Fluidmesh Networks LLC

CONTACTS: Note: Officers with more than one job title may be intentionally listed here more than once.

Charles Robbins, CEO
Prat Bhatt, Chief Accounting Officer
Geraldine Elliott, Chief Marketing Officer
Kelly Kramer, Executive VP
David Goeckeler, Executive VP
Maria Martinez, Executive VP
Mark Chandler, Executive VP
Irving Tan, Senior VP, Divisional

GROWTH PLANS/SPECIAL FEATURES:

Cisco Systems, Inc. designs and sells a broad range of technologies that power the internet. The company's products and services are grouped into the categories of infrastructure platforms, applications and security. Infrastructure platforms consist of Cisco's core networking technologies of switching, routing, data center products, and wireless that are designed to work together to deliver networking capabilities and transport and/or store data. These technologies consist of both hardware and software that help customers build networks, automate, orchestrate, integrate and digitize data. The firm is moving to software and subscriptions across its core networking portfolio. The applications category primarily includes network security, cloud and email security, identity and access management, advanced threat protection, and unified threat management products. These offerings encompass hardware- and software, including licenses and software-as-a-service (SaaS). Applications include collaboration products/solutions such as unified communications, telepresence and conferencing; and the Internet of Things (IoT) and analytics software from subsidiary AppDynamics, an application intelligence software company. Last, the security category includes Cisco's network security, cloud and email security, identity and access management, advanced threat protection and unified threat management products. Offerings in this category are powered by cloud-delivered threat intelligence based on our Cisco Talos technology. Other products offered primarily consists of Cisco's cloud and system management products. In July 2020, Cisco acquired Fluidmesh Networks, LLC, which has expertise in wireless backhaul systems. As of January 2021, Cisco Systems announced that it was seeking confirmation from the Delaware Court of Chancery that it had met all conditions for closing its acquisition of Acacia Communications, Inc., a public fabless semiconductor company.

FINANCIAL DATA: Note: Data for latest year may not have been available at press time.

In U.S. $	2020	2019	2018	2017	2016	2015
Revenue	49,301,000,000	51,904,000,000	49,330,000,000	48,005,000,000	49,247,000,000	49,161,000,000
R&D Expense	6,347,000,000	6,577,000,000	6,332,000,000	6,059,000,000	6,296,000,000	6,207,000,000
Operating Income	14,101,000,000	14,541,000,000	12,667,000,000	12,729,000,000	12,928,000,000	11,254,000,000
Operating Margin %		.28%	.26%	.27%	.26%	.23%
SGA Expense	11,094,000,000	11,398,000,000	11,386,000,000	11,177,000,000	11,433,000,000	11,861,000,000
Net Income	11,214,000,000	11,621,000,000	110,000,000	9,609,000,000	10,739,000,000	8,981,000,000
Operating Cash Flow	15,426,000,000	15,831,000,000	13,666,000,000	13,876,000,000	13,570,000,000	12,552,000,000
Capital Expenditure	770,000,000	909,000,000	834,000,000	964,000,000	1,146,000,000	1,227,000,000
EBITDA	16,363,000,000	17,327,000,000	16,174,000,000	15,434,000,000	15,746,000,000	14,209,000,000
Return on Assets %		.11%	.00%	.08%	.09%	.08%
Return on Equity %		.30%	.00%	.15%	.17%	.15%
Debt to Equity		0.431	0.471	0.389	0.385	0.359

CONTACT INFORMATION:

Phone: 408 526-4000   Fax: 408 526-4100
Toll-Free: 800-553-6387
Address: 170 W. Tasman Dr., San Jose, CA 95134 United States

STOCK TICKER/OTHER:

Stock Ticker: CSCO
Employees: 77,500
Parent Company:

Exchange: NAS
Fiscal Year Ends: 07/31

SALARIES/BONUSES:

Top Exec. Salary: $ Bonus: $
Second Exec. Salary: $ Bonus: $

OTHER THOUGHTS:

Estimated Female Officers or Directors: 10
Hot Spot for Advancement for Women/Minorities: Y

Citigroup Inc
NAIC Code: 522110

www.citigroup.com

TYPES OF BUSINESS:
Banking
Commercial, Residential & Consumer Lending
Credit Cards
Investment Banking
Insurance
Brokerage Services
Equity
Cash Management

BRANDS/DIVISIONS/AFFILIATES:

GROWTH PLANS/SPECIAL FEATURES:
Citigroup, Inc. is a global diversified financial services holding company and one of the largest banking organizations in the world, with approximately 200 million customer accounts. The firm does business in more than 160 countries and jurisdictions, and operates two primary business segments: global consumer banking and institutional clients. The global consumer banking segment spans North America, Latin America and Asia, offering retail banking, wealth management, debit/credit cards and other retail services. The institutional clients segment offers products and services in two categories: banking, including investment banking, treasury solutions, trade solutions, corporate lending and private banking; and markets and securities services, including fixed income markets, equity markets and securities. Other services and solutions by Citigroup include technological capabilities and features for group-wide and customer-focused purposes.

CONTACTS: Note: Officers with more than one job title may be intentionally listed here more than once.
Stephen Bird, CEO, Divisional
James Forese, CEO, Divisional
William Mills, CEO, Geographical
Jim Cowles, CEO, Geographical
Francisco Aristeguieta, CEO, Geographical
Jane Fraser, CEO, Geographical
Barbara Desoer, CEO, Subsidiary
Michael Corbat, CEO
John Gerspach, CFO
Michael ONeill, Chairman of the Board
Jeffrey Walsh, Chief Accounting Officer
Bradford Hu, Chief Risk Officer
Rohan Weerasinghe, General Counsel

FINANCIAL DATA: Note: Data for latest year may not have been available at press time.

In U.S. $	2020	2019	2018	2017	2016	2015
Revenue	75,494,000,000	75,067,000,000	74,036,000,000	72,698,000,000	71,020,000,000	77,472,000,000
R&D Expense						
Operating Income						
Operating Margin %						
SGA Expense	32,130,000,000	30,880,000,000	31,175,000,000	31,038,000,000	30,636,000,000	31,746,000,000
Net Income	11,047,000,000	19,401,000,000	18,045,000,000	-6,798,000,000	14,912,000,000	17,242,000,000
Operating Cash Flow	-20,621,000,000	-12,837,000,000	36,952,000,000	-8,587,000,000	53,932,000,000	39,737,000,000
Capital Expenditure	3,446,000,000	5,336,000,000	3,774,000,000	3,361,000,000	2,756,000,000	3,198,000,000
EBITDA						
Return on Assets %		.01%	.01%	.00%	.01%	.01%
Return on Equity %		.10%	.09%	- .04%	.07%	.08%
Debt to Equity		1.419	1.305	1.304	1.002	0.981

CONTACT INFORMATION:
Phone: 212 559-1000   Fax: 212 816-8913
Toll-Free: 800-285-3000
Address: 388 Greenwich St., New York, NY 10013 United States

STOCK TICKER/OTHER:
Stock Ticker: C   Exchange: NYS
Employees: 210,000   Fiscal Year Ends: 12/31
Parent Company:

SALARIES/BONUSES:
Top Exec. Salary: $ Bonus: $
Second Exec. Salary: $ Bonus: $

OTHER THOUGHTS:
Estimated Female Officers or Directors: 5
Hot Spot for Advancement for Women/Minorities: Y

Citrix Systems Inc

www.citrix.com

NAIC Code: 511210B

TYPES OF BUSINESS:

Computer Software: Network Management (IT), System Testing & Storage
IT Development
Cloud
Workspace Organization
Application Programming
Collaboration
Security
Delivery Management

BRANDS/DIVISIONS/AFFILIATES:

CONTACTS: Note: Officers with more than one job title may be intentionally listed here more than once.

David Henshall, CEO
Jessica Soisson, CFO
Robert Calderoni, Chairman of the Board
Timothy Minahan, Chief Marketing Officer
Jeroen van Rotterdam, Executive VP, Divisional
Antonio Gomes, Executive VP
Donna Kimmel, Executive VP
Mark Ferrer, Executive VP
Paul Hough, Executive VP

GROWTH PLANS/SPECIAL FEATURES:

Citrix Systems, Inc. designs, develops and markets digital workspace technology for organizations. Users obtain a seamless work experience and information technology (IT) obtains a unified platform to secure, manage and monitor diverse technologies in complex cloud environments. Approximately 100 million users and more than 400,000 organizations across 100 countries (including 98% of the Fortune 500) rely on Citrix. The company's digital workspaces products offer app and desktop virtualization, analytics, content collaboration, unified endpoint management and secure access. Its application delivery controller provides operational consistency and visibility across a multi-cloud, application programming interface (API) protection, app security, application delivery management, and an always-on experience for connected remote and branch locations. Industries served by Citrix include healthcare, financial services, education, government, manufacturing and retail. Headquartered in Florida, USA, Citrix operates from 60 offices in 40 countries worldwide.

Citrix offers its employees health benefits, wellness programs, job development, 401(k), a bonus program and flexible workstyles.

FINANCIAL DATA: Note: Data for latest year may not have been available at press time.

In U.S. $	2020	2019	2018	2017	2016	2015
Revenue	3,236,700,000	3,010,564,000	2,973,903,000	2,824,686,000	3,418,265,000	3,275,594,000
R&D Expense	538,080,000	518,877,000	439,984,000	415,801,000	489,265,000	563,975,000
Operating Income	620,789,000	558,365,000	694,685,000	645,910,000	776,904,000	450,496,000
Operating Margin %		.19%	.23%	.23%	.23%	.14%
SGA Expense	1,576,486,000	1,453,385,000	1,389,577,000	1,308,677,000	1,563,382,000	1,538,027,000
Net Income	504,446,000	681,813,000	575,667,000	-20,719,000	536,112,000	319,361,000
Operating Cash Flow	935,809,000	783,070,000	1,035,345,000	908,276,000	1,115,830,000	1,034,548,000
Capital Expenditure	50,019,000	66,954,000	72,564,000	88,280,000	160,512,000	172,228,000
EBITDA	769,977,000	744,946,000	851,513,000	771,970,000	910,751,000	748,909,000
Return on Assets %		.14%	.11%	.00%	.09%	.06%
Return on Equity %		.98%	.74%	-.01%	.23%	.15%
Debt to Equity		1.137	1.326	2.144		0.671

CONTACT INFORMATION:

Phone: 954 267-3000   Fax: 954 267-9319
Toll-Free: 800-424-8749
Address: 851 W. Cypress Creek Rd., Fort Lauderdale, FL 33309 United States

STOCK TICKER/OTHER:

Stock Ticker: CTXS
Employees: 9,000
Parent Company:

Exchange: NAS
Fiscal Year Ends: 12/31

SALARIES/BONUSES:

Top Exec. Salary: $ Bonus: $
Second Exec. Salary: $ Bonus: $

OTHER THOUGHTS:

Estimated Female Officers or Directors: 2
Hot Spot for Advancement for Women/Minorities:

Clark Construction Group LLC

www.clarkconstruction.com

NAIC Code: 236220

TYPES OF BUSINESS:

Construction & Engineering Services
Building Construction
Civil Construction Services
Advisory Services
Concrete Services
Foundations Services
Water & Wastewater Projects
Technology Solutions

BRANDS/DIVISIONS/AFFILIATES:

Guy F Atkinson Construction LLC
C3M Power Systems
Clark Civil
Clark Concrete
Coda
Edgemoor Infrastructure & Real Estate
S2N Technology Group
Shirley Contracting Company LLC

CONTACTS: *Note: Officers with more than one job title may be intentionally listed here more than once.*

Robert Moser, Jr., CEO
Sameer Bhargava, CFO
Sara Cuthrie, Sr. VP-Mktg. & Communications
Soledad Alamaraz, Sr. VP-Human Resources

GROWTH PLANS/SPECIAL FEATURES:

Clark Construction Group, LLC is a building and civil construction services firm located in the U.S. Clark's portfolio features projects of all sizes and levels of complexity, from intricate interior renovations to some of the most complex civil operations in the country. The company represents the aviation, education, government, healthcare, hospitality, industrial, mass transit, military, office, renovation/restoration, residential, roadways/bridges, science, sports/entertainment, transmission, tunnels/mines and water/wastewater markets in its completed portfolio. Specialized services offered by Clark include: Guy F. Atkinson Construction, LLC, a civil contractor known for its bridge and dam work; the power division, delivering energy infrastructure; Carta, an advisory firm that offers building solutions and risk management services; C3M Power Systems, a full-service transportation systems contractor, specializing in construction, rehabilitation and maintenance of electrical, traction power, overhead catenary, communications and signaling systems for heavy rail, light rail, streetcar, freight rail, automated guideway and bus transit systems; Clark Civil, which works directly with clients to develop innovative, tailor-made civil solutions in all manner of heavy civil construction, from highways and railways to airports and water treatment facilities; Clark Concrete, performing structural concrete work on some of the most technically-sophisticated projects; Clark Foundations, providing sophisticated excavation support systems; Clark Water, a specialized group that constructs water and wastewater infrastructure projects; Coda, a technology company that delivers solutions to accelerate the discovery and availability of the way assets are developed, built and operated; Edgemoor Infrastructure & Real Estate, performing public-private delivery and turnkey development solutions; S2N Technology Group, offering design, installation and support for IT services for new construction and renovations; and Shirley Contracting Company, LLC, performing infrastructure work. The firm is owned by its management team.

FINANCIAL DATA: *Note: Data for latest year may not have been available at press time.*

In U.S. $	2020	2019	2018	2017	2016	2015
Revenue	5,565,000,000	5,250,000,000	5,000,000,000	4,900,000,000	4,400,000,000	4,151,000,000
R&D Expense						
Operating Income						
Operating Margin %						
SGA Expense						
Net Income						
Operating Cash Flow						
Capital Expenditure						
EBITDA						
Return on Assets %						
Return on Equity %						
Debt to Equity						

CONTACT INFORMATION:

Phone: 301-272-8100   Fax:
Toll-Free:
Address: 7500 Old Georgetown Rd., Bethesda, MD 20814 United States

STOCK TICKER/OTHER:

Stock Ticker: Private   Exchange:
Employees: 4,200   Fiscal Year Ends:
Parent Company:

SALARIES/BONUSES:

Top Exec. Salary: $ Bonus: $
Second Exec. Salary: $ Bonus: $

OTHER THOUGHTS:

Estimated Female Officers or Directors:
Hot Spot for Advancement for Women/Minorities:

Clayton Homes Inc

www.claytonhomes.com

NAIC Code: 321992

TYPES OF BUSINESS:

Construction Services
Manufactured Housing
Insurance & Financing
Park Model Recreational Vehicle Homes

BRANDS/DIVISIONS/AFFILIATES:

Berkshire Hathaway Inc
Vanderbilt Mortgage and Finance Inc

CONTACTS: Note: Officers with more than one job title may be intentionally listed here more than once.

Kevin T. Clayton, CEO
Kevin T. Clayton, Pres.
Richard D. Strachan, Pres., Mfg.
Leon Van Tonder, Dir.-Oper.

GROWTH PLANS/SPECIAL FEATURES:

Clayton Homes, Inc., a subsidiary of Berkshire Hathaway, Inc., produces, sells, finances and insures modular and manufactured homes, in addition to commercial and educational relocatable buildings. The company's manufacturing plants produce homes that are marketed throughout the U.S. via independent retailers and company-owned sales centers. Clayton's factory-built manufactured homes are completely-finished dwellings that are constructed under federal code in factories and then transported by truck to its targeted location. The homes are generally designed to be permanent, owner-occupied residential sites with attached utilities, but Clayton does build park model recreational vehicle (PMRV) homes. The firm manufactures a variety of single- and multi-sectional homes from 1,000 to 2,000 square feet and larger. Standard features offered in Clayton homes include central heating, flooring systems and wall and floor treatments. Customers can choose predesigned homes or custom-design a home by size, number of bedrooms and other features. Through financial subsidiary Vanderbilt Mortgage and Finance, Inc. (VMF), the firm offers financing to manufactured home customers as well as customers purchasing homes from certain third parties. VMF's financing products include manufactured home loans, Federal Housing Authority (FHA) loans, Land Home financing and more. Clayton also offers home insurance products, and acts as a reinsurance agent for physical damage, family protection and homebuyer protection insurance and other policies issued by insurance companies in connection with the firm's homes. Affiliates and brands include Schult, Crest, Karsten, Marlette, Golden West, Southern Energy Homes (SEhomes), Norris, Cavalier, Giles and Buccaneer, among others.

Clayton offers its employees medical, dental and vision plans; 401(k); and various employee assistance programs.

FINANCIAL DATA: Note: Data for latest year may not have been available at press time.

In U.S. $	2020	2019	2018	2017	2016	2015
Revenue	8,600,000,000	7,300,000,000	6,046,000,000	5,010,000,000	4,230,000,000	3,580,000,000
R&D Expense						
Operating Income						
Operating Margin %						
SGA Expense						
Net Income	1,250,000,000	1,100,000,000	911,000,000	765,000,000	744,000,000	706,000,000
Operating Cash Flow						
Capital Expenditure						
EBITDA						
Return on Assets %						
Return on Equity %						
Debt to Equity						

CONTACT INFORMATION:

Phone: 865-380-3000   Fax: 865-380-3742
Toll-Free: 800-822-0633
Address: 5000 Clayton Rd., Maryville, TN 37804 United States

SALARIES/BONUSES:

Top Exec. Salary: $ Bonus: $
Second Exec. Salary: $ Bonus: $

STOCK TICKER/OTHER:

Stock Ticker: Subsidiary
Employees: 19,445
Parent Company: Berkshire Hathaway Inc

Exchange:
Fiscal Year Ends: 12/31

OTHER THOUGHTS:

Estimated Female Officers or Directors:
Hot Spot for Advancement for Women/Minorities:

Cleveland Clinic Foundation (The)

www.clevelandclinic.org

NAIC Code: 622110

TYPES OF BUSINESS:

General Medical and Surgical Hospitals

BRANDS/DIVISIONS/AFFILIATES:

CONTACTS: *Note: Officers with more than one job title may be intentionally listed here more than once.*

Tomislav Mihaljevic, CEO
Robert Wyllie, Chief Medical Oper. Officer
Cindy Hundorfean, Chief Admin. Officer-Clinical Svcs.
David W. Rowan, Chief Legal Officer
Michael Harrington, Chief Acct. Officer
Kristen D.W. Morris, Chief Gov't. & Community Rel. Officer
Linda McHugh, Exec. Admin.-CEO & Board of Governors
K. Kelly Hancock, Interim Exec. Chief Nursing Officer
Ann Huston, Chief Strategy Officer

GROWTH PLANS/SPECIAL FEATURES:

The Cleveland Clinic Foundation is a nonprofit corporation in Ohio that combines medical care with education and research. It is noted for very advanced surgical techniques and advanced care. Founded in 1921, Cleveland Clinic cares for millions of patients annually, with nearly 10 million outpatient visits at its locations throughout the world. The firm's health system includes 18 hospitals, more than 220 outpatient locations and over 6,025 beds. The Cleveland Clinic runs a 170-acre campus in Cleveland, as well as affiliated hospitals and family health centers in Ohio, Florida and Nevada. Outside the U.S., the firm operates the Cleveland Clinic Abu Dhabi hospital and an outpatient sports medicine clinic in Toronto. In 2020-21, Cleveland Clinic was ranked as second overall hospital in the U.S. by the U.S. News & World Report, with high-rankings in the fields of cardiology, heart surgery, urology, gastroenterology, nephrology, rheumatology, orthopedic surgery, pulmonology, lung surgery, cancer, diabetes, endocrinology, otolaryngology, geriatrics, gynecology, neurology, ophthalmology and psychiatry. In September 2021, the nonprofit announced the opening of its London hospital and the ground breaking at the future site of Cleveland Clinic Mentor Hospital, set to open in early 2023 in Ohio.

The Cleveland Clinic offers its employees comprehensive health benefits, savings and retirement options and career development resources.

FINANCIAL DATA: *Note: Data for latest year may not have been available at press time.*

In U.S. $	2020	2019	2018	2017	2016	2015
Revenue	10,627,906,000	10,559,521,000	8,900,000,000	8,400,000,000	8,037,207,000	7,156,972,000
R&D Expense						
Operating Income						
Operating Margin %						
SGA Expense						
Net Income	1,325,244,000	2,025,222,000	266,000,000	328,000,000	139,352,000	480,224,000
Operating Cash Flow						
Capital Expenditure						
EBITDA						
Return on Assets %						
Return on Equity %						
Debt to Equity						

CONTACT INFORMATION:

Phone: 216-444-2200   Fax:
Toll-Free: 800-223-2273
Address: 9500 Euclid Ave., Cleveland, OH 44195 United States

STOCK TICKER/OTHER:

Stock Ticker: Nonprofit   Exchange:
Employees: 60,000   Fiscal Year Ends: 12/31
Parent Company:

SALARIES/BONUSES:

Top Exec. Salary: $ Bonus: $
Second Exec. Salary: $ Bonus: $

OTHER THOUGHTS:

Estimated Female Officers or Directors: 22
Hot Spot for Advancement for Women/Minorities: Y

Clorox Company (The)

www.thecloroxcompany.com

NAIC Code: 325611

TYPES OF BUSINESS:

Cleaning/Laundry Products-Manufacturing
Automotive Care Products
Pesticides
Cat Litter
Water Filtration Products
Charcoal
Domestic Plastics
Dressings & Sauces

BRANDS/DIVISIONS/AFFILIATES:

Clorox
Pine-Sol
Green Works
KC Masterpiece
Burts Bees
Fresh Step
RenewLife
Ayudin

CONTACTS: *Note: Officers with more than one job title may be intentionally listed here more than once.*

Benno Dorer, CEO
Andrew Mowery, Other Executive Officer
Kevin Jacobsen, CFO
Jeff Baker, Chief Accounting Officer
John McNulty, Chief Information Officer
Stacey Grier, Chief Marketing Officer
Linda Rendle, Executive VP, Divisional
Eric Reynolds, Executive VP, Divisional
Jon Balousek, Executive VP, Divisional
Laura Stein, Executive VP, Divisional
Kirsten Marriner, Executive VP
Michael Costello, General Manager, Divisional
Diego Barral, General Manager, Divisional
Matthew Laszlo, Other Executive Officer
Denise Garner, Other Executive Officer
William Bailey, Senior VP, Divisional

GROWTH PLANS/SPECIAL FEATURES:

The Clorox Company is a leading producer of consumer and institutional products. Its operations consist of four business segments: cleaning, lifestyle, household and international. The cleaning segment includes: Clorox branded bleaches; Clorox 2 branded color boosters and stain fighters; home-care products sold under the Pine-Sol, S.O.S., Tilex, Liquid-Plumr and Formula 409 brands; natural cleaning products sold under the Green Works brand name; and professional cleaning and disinfecting products under the CloroxPro, Dispatch and Clorox Healthcare brands. The lifestyle segment includes: sauces and dressing food products, as well as charcoal marketed under the KC Masterpiece, Soy Vay, Hidden Valley and Kingsford brands; water filtration systems and filters under the Brita brand; natural personal care products under the Burt's Bees brand; and dietary supplements under the Rainbow Light, Natural Vitality and NeoCell brands. The household segment includes: charcoal products under the Kingsford and Match Light brands; bags, wraps and containers under the Glad brand; cat litter products under the Fresh Step, Scoop Away and Ever Clean brands; and digestive health products under the RenewLife brand. Last, the international segment sells products outside of the U.S., and includes: laundry and home care; water filtration systems and filters; digestive health products; charcoal; cat litter products; food products; bags, wraps and containers; natural personal care products; and professional cleaning and disinfecting products. International brands include, but are not limited to, Ayudin, Poett, Mistolin, Agua Jane, and Chux.

FINANCIAL DATA: *Note: Data for latest year may not have been available at press time.*

In U.S. $	2020	2019	2018	2017	2016	2015
Revenue	6,721,000,000	6,214,000,000	6,124,000,000	5,973,000,000	5,761,000,000	
R&D Expense	145,000,000	136,000,000	132,000,000	135,000,000	141,000,000	
Operating Income	1,261,000,000	1,107,000,000	1,125,000,000	1,117,000,000	1,056,000,000	
Operating Margin %		.18%	.18%	.19%	.18%	
SGA Expense	1,644,000,000	1,468,000,000	1,407,000,000	1,409,000,000	1,393,000,000	
Net Income	939,000,000	820,000,000	823,000,000	701,000,000	648,000,000	
Operating Cash Flow	1,546,000,000	992,000,000	974,000,000	868,000,000	778,000,000	
Capital Expenditure	254,000,000	206,000,000	194,000,000	231,000,000	172,000,000	
EBITDA	1,464,000,000	1,301,000,000	1,305,000,000	1,284,000,000	1,236,000,000	
Return on Assets %		.16%	.17%	.15%	.15%	
Return on Equity %		1.28%	1.30%	1.67%	3.12%	
Debt to Equity		4.091	3.146	2.566	6.051	

CONTACT INFORMATION:

Phone: 510 271-7000   Fax: 510 832-1463
Toll-Free:
Address: 1221 Broadway, Oakland, CA 94612-1888 United States

STOCK TICKER/OTHER:

Stock Ticker: CLX
Employees: 8,800
Parent Company:

Exchange: NYS
Fiscal Year Ends: 06/30

SALARIES/BONUSES:

Top Exec. Salary: $ Bonus: $
Second Exec. Salary: $ Bonus: $

OTHER THOUGHTS:

Estimated Female Officers or Directors: 3
Hot Spot for Advancement for Women/Minorities: Y

Coca-Cola Bottling Consolidated Inc   www.cokeconsolidated.com

NAIC Code: 312111

TYPES OF BUSINESS:

Beverages-Soft Drink Manufacturing
Bottling Services
Beverages

BRANDS/DIVISIONS/AFFILIATES:

Coca-Cola Company (The)
POWERade
Dasani
glaceau vitaminwater
Minute Maid
Gold Peak Tea
Tum-E Yummies

CONTACTS: Note: Officers with more than one job title may be intentionally listed here more than once.

J. Harrison, CEO
F. Anthony, CFO
William Billiard, Chief Accounting Officer
David Katz, COO
Umesh Kasbekar, Co-Vice Chairman of the Board
Henry Flint, Co-Vice Chairman of the Board
Morgan Everett, Director
Robert Chambless, Executive VP, Divisional
E. Fisher, Executive VP
Kimberly Kuo, Senior VP, Divisional
James Matte, Senior VP, Divisional

GROWTH PLANS/SPECIAL FEATURES:

Coca-Cola Bottling Consolidated, Inc. (CCB), founded in 1902, is a nonalcoholic beverage manufacturer and distributor. The firm primarily produces, markets and distributes products of The Coca-Cola Company, which owns approximately 27% of CCB. The company manufactures products in two categories: sparkling beverages, which consist of beverages with carbonation, including energy drinks; and still beverages, including bottled water, tea, ready-to-drink coffee, enhanced water, juices and sports drinks. CCB distributes and markets still beverages of The Coca-Cola Company such as POWERade, Dasani water, glaceau vitaminwater and Minute Maid Juices To Go in certain regions. It markets and distributes certain products which it owns, including Gold Peak Tea; coffee beverages; and Tum-E Yummies, a vitamin C enhanced flavored drink. CCB also distributes products for other beverage companies, including BA Sports Nutrition LLC, Keurig Dr Pepper Inc., and Monster Energy Company. The firm's principal soft drink is Coca-Cola classic, and products of The Coca-Cola Company generate more than 80% of CCB's bottle/can volume to retail customers. CCB's main packaging materials are plastic bottles and aluminum cans. In addition, the company provides restaurants and other immediate consumption outlets with fountain products. CCB has 12 manufacturing facilities and 68 distribution centers.

FINANCIAL DATA: Note: Data for latest year may not have been available at press time.

In U.S. $	2020	2019	2018	2017	2016	2015
Revenue	5,007,357,000	4,826,549,000	4,625,364,000	4,323,668,000	3,156,428,000	2,306,458,000
R&D Expense						
Operating Income	313,378,000	180,754,000	57,902,000	96,179,000	127,859,000	98,144,000
Operating Margin %		.04%	.01%	.02%	.04%	.04%
SGA Expense	1,455,531,000	1,489,748,000	1,497,810,000	1,444,768,000	1,087,863,000	802,888,000
Net Income	172,493,000	11,375,000	-19,930,000	96,535,000	50,146,000	59,002,000
Operating Cash Flow	494,461,000	290,370,000	168,879,000	307,816,000	161,995,000	108,290,000
Capital Expenditure	202,034,000	176,028,000	138,235,000	192,199,000	172,586,000	163,887,000
EBITDA	456,792,000	260,131,000	224,475,000	273,716,000	245,660,000	208,933,000
Return on Assets %		.00%	-.01%	.03%	.02%	.04%
Return on Equity %		.03%	-.05%	.30%	.19%	.28%
Debt to Equity		3.30	3.158	3.063	3.422	2.767

CONTACT INFORMATION:

Phone: 704 557-4400   Fax: 704 551-4451
Toll-Free: 800-777-2653
Address: 4100 Coca-Cola Plaza, Charlotte, NC 28211 United States

STOCK TICKER/OTHER:

Stock Ticker: COKE   Exchange: NAS
Employees: 15,800   Fiscal Year Ends: 12/31
Parent Company:

SALARIES/BONUSES:

Top Exec. Salary: $ Bonus: $
Second Exec. Salary: $ Bonus: $

OTHER THOUGHTS:

Estimated Female Officers or Directors: 3
Hot Spot for Advancement for Women/Minorities: Y

Cognizant Technology Solutions Corporation www.cognizant.com
NAIC Code: 541512

TYPES OF BUSINESS:
Computer Systems Design Services
Outsourced Services
Software Engineering
Artificial Intelligence
Machine Learning
Data Analytics

BRANDS/DIVISIONS/AFFILIATES:
Inawisdom
Linium

CONTACTS: *Note: Officers with more than one job title may be intentionally listed here more than once.*
Brian Humphries, CEO
Sean Middleton, Sr. VP
Karen McLoughlin, CFO
Michael Patsalos-Fox, Chairman of the Board
Srinivasan Veeraraghavachary, COO
Allen Shaheen, Executive VP, Divisional
Malcolm Frank, Executive VP, Divisional
Matthew Friedrich, Executive VP
Gajakarnan Kandiah, Executive VP
Debashis Chatterjee, Executive VP
Ramakrishna Chintamaneni, Executive VP
Dharmendra Sinha, Executive VP
Santosh Thomas, Executive VP
Sumithra Gomatam, Executive VP
James Lennox, Other Executive Officer
Robert Telesmanic, Senior VP
Venkat Krishnaswamy, Vice Chairman, Divisional
Ramakrishnan Chandrasekaran, Vice Chairman, Subsidiary
Ramakrishnan Chandrasekaran, Vice Chairman, Subsidiary

GROWTH PLANS/SPECIAL FEATURES:
Cognizant Technology Solutions Corporation is a leading professional services company. The firm's business segments are categorized into four segments: financial services, healthcare, products and resources, and communications, media and technology (CMT). The financial services segment includes banking, capital markets and insurance companies, with Cognizant offering services in regards to regulatory compliance, and the adoption/integration of digital technologies. The healthcare segment consists of healthcare providers and payers as well as life sciences companies, including pharmaceutical, biotech and medical device entities. Through this division, Cognizant's services include enhanced compliance, integrated health management, claims investigative services, claims processing, enrollment, membership, billing and the adoption/integration of digital technologies. The products and resources segment includes manufacturers, retailers, travel and hospitality companies, and companies that provide logistics, energy and utility services. Products and resource services from this division serve to improve the efficiency of their operations, enable and integrate mobile platforms to support sales and other omni-channel initiatives, and the adoption/integration of digital technologies such as the application of intelligent systems for supply chain management and for enhancing overall customer experiences. Last, the CMT segment includes information, media and entertainment, communications and technology companies, with services by Cognizant relating to digital content management, creating differentiated user experiences, transitioning to agile development methodologies, enhancing networks, and adopting/integrating digital technologies such as cloud enablement and interactive/connected products. Cognizant offers a consultative approach so that customers can envision, build and then run more innovative and efficient businesses. In December 2020, Cognizant acquired Inawisdom, a U.K.-based consultancy specializing in artificial intelligence (AI), machine learning and data analytics. In January 2021, Cognizant agreed to acquire Linium, a cloud transformation consultancy group.

Cognizant offers health plans and employee assistance programs.

FINANCIAL DATA: *Note: Data for latest year may not have been available at press time.*

In U.S. $	2020	2019	2018	2017	2016	2015
Revenue	16,652,000,000	16,783,000,000	16,125,000,000	14,810,000,000	13,487,000,000	12,416,000,000
R&D Expense						
Operating Income	2,329,000,000	2,670,000,000	2,801,000,000	2,481,000,000	2,289,000,000	2,142,000,000
Operating Margin %		.16%	.17%	.17%	.17%	.17%
SGA Expense	3,100,000,000	2,972,000,000	3,026,000,000	2,769,000,000	2,731,000,000	2,508,600,000
Net Income	1,392,000,000	1,842,000,000	2,101,000,000	1,504,000,000	1,553,000,000	1,623,600,000
Operating Cash Flow	3,299,000,000	2,499,000,000	2,592,000,000	2,407,000,000	1,621,000,000	2,153,300,000
Capital Expenditure	398,000,000	392,000,000	377,000,000	284,000,000	300,000,000	272,800,000
EBITDA	2,679,000,000	3,095,000,000	3,322,000,000	3,121,000,000	2,755,000,000	2,511,300,000
Return on Assets %		.11%	.13%	.10%	.11%	.13%
Return on Equity %		.16%	.19%	.14%	.16%	.19%
Debt to Equity		0.131	0.064	0.065	0.074	0.095

CONTACT INFORMATION:
Phone: 201 801-0233   Fax: 201 801-0243
Toll-Free: 888-937-3277
Address: 500 Frank W. Burr Blvd., Teaneck, NJ 07666 United States

STOCK TICKER/OTHER:
Stock Ticker: CTSH   Exchange: NAS
Employees: 289,500   Fiscal Year Ends: 12/31
Parent Company:

SALARIES/BONUSES:
Top Exec. Salary: $ Bonus: $
Second Exec. Salary: $ Bonus: $

OTHER THOUGHTS:
Estimated Female Officers or Directors: 1
Hot Spot for Advancement for Women/Minorities:

Sales, profits and employees may be estimates. Financial information, benefits and other data can change quickly and may vary from those stated here.

Colgate-Palmolive Company

www.colgatepalmolive.com

NAIC Code: 325611

TYPES OF BUSINESS:

Toothpaste & Oral Care Products Manufacturer
Household Cleaning Products
Soap Products
Baby Care Products
Pet Food
Hair Products
Shaving Products

BRANDS/DIVISIONS/AFFILIATES:

Colgate
Softsoap
Palmolive
Protex
Speed Stick
Murphys Oil Soap
Hills Science Diet
Hills Prescription Diet

CONTACTS: *Note: Officers with more than one job title may be intentionally listed here more than once.*

Noel Wallace, CEO
Henning Jakobsen, CFO
Ian Cook, Chairman of the Board
Philip Shotts, Chief Accounting Officer
Jennifer Daniels, Chief Legal Officer
John Kooyman, Chief Marketing Officer
P. Skala, Chief Strategy Officer
Patricia Verduin, Chief Technology Officer
Daniel Marsili, Other Executive Officer
John Huston, Other Executive Officer

GROWTH PLANS/SPECIAL FEATURES:

Colgate-Palmolive Company founded in 1806, is a consumer products company whose merchandise is marketed in over 200 countries and territories throughout the world. The company manages its business in two product segments: oral, personal and home care; and pet nutrition. Within the oral, personal and home care segment, oral care products include toothpaste, toothbrushes and mouthwashes, as well as pharmaceutical products for dentists and other oral health professionals; personal care products consist of soaps, deodorants/antiperspirants, shampoos, conditioners and skin care products; and home care products such as dishwashing liquids, household soaps and cleaners, and fabric cleaners. Brands within this segment include Colgate, Softsoap, Palmolive, Protex, Sanex, Speed Stick, Tom's, Ajax and Murphy's Oil Soap, among others. The pet nutrition segment provides specialty pet nutrition products for dogs and cats, with products marketed under the Hill's brand name in over 80 countries and territories. Two primary brands within this division include Hill's Science Diet (Hill's Science Plan in Europe), and Hill's Prescription Diet. Colgate-Palmolive is engaged in manufacturing and sourcing its products and materials on a global scale; therefore, the company owns or leases approximately 320 properties, which include manufacturing, distribution, research and office facilities.

FINANCIAL DATA: *Note: Data for latest year may not have been available at press time.*

In U.S. $	2020	2019	2018	2017	2016	2015
Revenue	16,471,000,000	15,693,000,000	15,544,000,000	15,454,000,000	15,195,000,000	16,034,000,000
R&D Expense						
Operating Income	3,875,000,000	3,617,000,000	3,772,000,000	3,747,000,000	3,852,000,000	3,896,000,000
Operating Margin %		.23%	.24%	.24%	.25%	.24%
SGA Expense	6,019,000,000	5,575,000,000	5,389,000,000	5,497,000,000	5,249,000,000	5,464,000,000
Net Income	2,695,000,000	2,367,000,000	2,400,000,000	2,024,000,000	2,441,000,000	1,384,000,000
Operating Cash Flow	3,719,000,000	3,133,000,000	3,056,000,000	3,054,000,000	3,141,000,000	2,949,000,000
Capital Expenditure	410,000,000	335,000,000	436,000,000	553,000,000	593,000,000	691,000,000
EBITDA	4,369,000,000	4,012,000,000	4,168,000,000	4,115,000,000	4,330,000,000	3,345,000,000
Return on Assets %		.17%	.19%	.16%	.20%	.11%
Return on Equity %		315.60%				3.27%
Debt to Equity		66.872				

CONTACT INFORMATION:

Phone: 212 310-2000   Fax: 212 310-3284
Toll-Free: 800-468-6502
Address: 300 Park Ave., New York, NY 10022 United States

STOCK TICKER/OTHER:

Stock Ticker: CL
Employees: 34,300
Parent Company:

Exchange: NYS
Fiscal Year Ends: 12/31

SALARIES/BONUSES:

Top Exec. Salary: $ Bonus: $
Second Exec. Salary: $ Bonus: $

OTHER THOUGHTS:

Estimated Female Officers or Directors: 29
Hot Spot for Advancement for Women/Minorities: Y

Sales, profits and employees may be estimates. Financial information, benefits and other data can change quickly and may vary from those stated here.

Collins Aerospace
NAIC Code: 334511

www.collinsaerospace.com

TYPES OF BUSINESS:
Aerospace Electronics
Defense Systems
Avionics
Aviation Technologies

BRANDS/DIVISIONS/AFFILIATES:
Raytheon Technologies Corp

CONTACTS: Note: Officers with more than one job title may be intentionally listed here more than once.
Stephen Timm, Pres.
Kevin Myers, Dir.-Oper. & Quality
Patrick Allen, CFO
Tatum Buse, Dir.-Finance
Isolde Karro, Chief Communications Officer
Natalie Morris, Acting Dir.-Human Resources
Kent Statler, COO, Divisional
Jennifer Schopfer, Dir.-Digital Technology
Robert Perna, General Counsel
Robert Sturgell, Senior VP, Divisional
Colin Mahoney, Senior VP, Divisional
Jeffrey MacLauchlan, Senior VP, Divisional
Bruce King, Senior VP, Divisional
Nan Mattai, Senior VP, Divisional
Jeffrey Standerski, Senior VP, Divisional
David Nieuwsma, Senior VP, Divisional
Mauro Atalla, Dir.-Engineering & Tech

GROWTH PLANS/SPECIAL FEATURES:
Collins Aerospace, a subsidiary of Raytheon Technologies Corp., is a world-leading supplier of aerospace and defense products, with a focus on providing technologically-advanced and intelligent solutions. For the commercial aviation industry, Collins provides aerospace systems, avionics, interior systems and information management services, from cockpit to cabin, nose to tail. These solutions deliver enhanced passenger safety and comfort, maximized operational efficiency, secure and reliable connectivity and improved availability, maintainability and sustainability. For the business aviation industry, Collins creates intelligent and connected cockpits to help pilots fly more safely and efficiently. Its flight support services provide operators with a single resource for flight planning, trip support and flight operations management; and its interiors are luxurious as well as connected for an enhanced experience for travelers. For the military and defense industry, Collins offers a broad spectrum of advanced solutions, whether in the air, on ground or at sea, both in manned and unmanned platforms, to help them complete their missions safely, efficiently and effectively. For the helicopter segment, Collins provides advanced systems for commercial and military helicopters. This division equips rotorcraft from all major manufacturers to help save lives and complete strategic missions. For the space industry, Collins designs, develops and produces systems for spacecraft to help ensure successful missions. For the airport industry, Collins is present at more than 170 global airports, offering integrated and intelligent solutions for passenger processing and facilitation, airport operations and baggage management. Other industries served by Collins include: rail, offering network communications capabilities; marine, offering life rafts and support systems for keeping sailors safe; and communities, offering security and monitoring systems. Based in North Carolina, USA, Collins Aerospace has operations in Iowa, California and Connecticut.

Collins Aerospace offers its employees health coverage and a variety of employee assistance programs.

FINANCIAL DATA: Note: Data for latest year may not have been available at press time.

In U.S. $	2020	2019	2018	2017	2016	2015
Revenue	19,288,000,000	26,028,000,000	16,634,000,000	14,691,000,000	14,465,000,000	
R&D Expense						
Operating Income						
Operating Margin %						
SGA Expense						
Net Income	1,466,000,000	4,508,000,000	2,397,000,000	2,191,000,000	2,167,000,000	
Operating Cash Flow						
Capital Expenditure						
EBITDA						
Return on Assets %						
Return on Equity %						
Debt to Equity						

CONTACT INFORMATION:
Phone: 704-423-7000   Fax: 704-423-7002
Toll-Free:
Address: 2730 W. Tyvola Rd., Charlotte, NC 29217-4578 United States

STOCK TICKER/OTHER:
Stock Ticker: Subsidiary   Exchange:
Employees: 76,000   Fiscal Year Ends: 09/30
Parent Company: Raytheon Technologies Corp

SALARIES/BONUSES:
Top Exec. Salary: $ Bonus: $
Second Exec. Salary: $ Bonus: $

OTHER THOUGHTS:
Estimated Female Officers or Directors:
Hot Spot for Advancement for Women/Minorities:

Sales, profits and employees may be estimates. Financial information, benefits and other data can change quickly and may vary from those stated here.

Comcast Corporation

NAIC Code: 517110

corporate.comcast.com

TYPES OF BUSINESS:

Cable Television
VoIP Service
Cable Network Programming
High-Speed Internet Service
Video-on-Demand
Advertising Services
Streaming TV Programming
Wireless Services

BRANDS/DIVISIONS/AFFILIATES:

Sky Limited
XFINITY
Universal Pictures
Sky News
Sky Sports
Philadelphia Flyers
Universal Studios
Peacock

CONTACTS: *Note: Officers with more than one job title may be intentionally listed here more than once.*

Stephen Burke, CEO, Subsidiary
Dave Watson, CEO, Subsidiary
Brian Roberts, CEO
Michael Cavanagh, CFO
Daniel Murdock, Chief Accounting Officer
Joseph Collins, Director Emeritus
Judith Rodin, Director Emeritus
Arthur Block, Executive VP
David Cohen, Senior Executive VP

GROWTH PLANS/SPECIAL FEATURES:

Comcast Corporation is a global media and technology company with three primary businesses: Comcast Cable, NBCUniversal and Sky. Comcast Cable is a leading provider of high-speed internet, video, voice, wireless and security and automation services to residential customers in the U.S. under the Xfinity brand and to commercial customers as well. NBCUniversal operates in four business segments: Cable Networks, Broadcast Television, Filmed Entertainment and Theme Parks. The Cable Networks segment consists primarily of national cable networks that provide a variety of entertainment, news and information and sports content; regional sports and news networks; international cable networks; cable television studio production operations; and various digital properties. Broadcast Television consists of the NBC and Telemundo broadcast networks; NBC and Telemundo owned local broadcast television stations; the NBC Universo national cable network; broadcast television studio production operations; and various digital properties. Filmed Entertainment consists of the operation of Universal Pictures which produces, acquires, markets and distributes filmed entertainment worldwide (films are also produced under the Illumination, DreamWorks Animation and Focus Features names). Theme Parks consists of Universal Studios theme parks in Orlando, Florida; Hollywood, California; and Osaka Japan. A theme park in Beijing, China is under development in partnership with a consortium of Chinese state-owned companies and a fully owned new park is also under development in Orlando. Sky is a leading European entertainment company which includes a direct-to-consumer business providing video, high-speed internet, voice and wireless phone services and a content business which operates the Sky News broadcast network and Sky Sports networks. Other business interests consist primarily of the operations of Comcast Spectacor, which owns the Philadelphia Flyers and the Wells Fargo Center arena in Philadelphia, Pennsylvania. Peacock, is a direct-to-consumer online streaming service that features NBCUniversal content.

FINANCIAL DATA: *Note: Data for latest year may not have been available at press time.*

In U.S. $	2020	2019	2018	2017	2016	2015
Revenue	103,564,000,000	108,942,000,000	94,507,000,000	84,526,000,000	80,403,000,000	74,510,000,000
R&D Expense						
Operating Income	17,493,000,000	21,125,000,000	19,009,000,000	17,987,000,000	16,859,000,000	15,998,000,000
Operating Margin %		.19%	.20%	.21%	.21%	.21%
SGA Expense	39,850,000,000	40,424,000,000	35,130,000,000	31,330,000,000	29,523,000,000	27,282,000,000
Net Income	10,534,000,000	13,057,000,000	11,731,000,000	22,714,000,000	8,695,000,000	8,163,000,000
Operating Cash Flow	24,737,000,000	25,697,000,000	24,297,000,000	21,403,000,000	19,240,000,000	18,778,000,000
Capital Expenditure	11,634,000,000	12,428,000,000	11,709,000,000	11,297,000,000	10,821,000,000	9,869,000,000
EBITDA	31,753,000,000	34,516,000,000	29,801,000,000	28,675,000,000	26,853,000,000	24,754,000,000
Return on Assets %		.05%	.05%	.12%	.05%	.05%
Return on Equity %		.17%	.17%	.37%	.16%	.16%
Debt to Equity		1.182	1.499	0.866	1.03	0.937

CONTACT INFORMATION:

Phone: 215 286-1700   Fax:
Toll-Free: 800-266-2278
Address: One Comcast Center, Philadelphia, PA 19103 United States

STOCK TICKER/OTHER:

Stock Ticker: CMCSA   Exchange: NAS
Employees: 168,000   Fiscal Year Ends: 12/31
Parent Company:

SALARIES/BONUSES:

Top Exec. Salary: $ Bonus: $
Second Exec. Salary: $ Bonus: $

OTHER THOUGHTS:

Estimated Female Officers or Directors: 16
Hot Spot for Advancement for Women/Minorities: Y

Comfort Systems USA Inc

www.comfortsystemsusa.com

NAIC Code: 238220

TYPES OF BUSINESS:

Mechanical Contractors
Industrial & Commercial HVAC Systems & Services
Electrical Services
Plumbing Services

BRANDS/DIVISIONS/AFFILIATES:

Starr Electric Company Inc
TAS Energy Inc

CONTACTS: Note: Officers with more than one job title may be intentionally listed here more than once.

Brian Lane, CEO
Franklin Myers, Chairman of the Board
William George, Executive VP
Laura Howell, General Counsel
Terry Young, Senior VP, Divisional
Julie Shaeff, Senior VP

GROWTH PLANS/SPECIAL FEATURES:

Comfort Systems USA, Inc. provides mechanical and electrical contracting services. The company builds, installs, maintains, repairs and replaces mechanical, electrical and plumbing (MEP) systems throughout its 37 operating units. Comfort System's mechanical segment includes heating, ventilation and air conditioning (HVAC), plumbing, piping and controls, as well as off-site construction, monitoring and fire protection. This division derives 84.5% of annual revenue. The electrical segment includes the installation and servicing of electrical systems. It derives 15.5% of annual revenue. Comfort System has 139 locations throughout the U.S. The firm operates primarily in the commercial, industrial and institutional MEP markets, and performs most of its services in industrial, healthcare, education, office, technology, retail and government facilities. During 2020, Comfort Systems acquired Starr Electric Company, Inc., based in Greensboro, North Carolina; and TAS Energy, Inc., based in Houston, Texas. In early-2021, Comfort Systems agreed to acquire Tennessee Electric Company, Inc., which does business as TEC Industrial Construction and Maintenance and is headquartered in Kingsport, Tennessee.

FINANCIAL DATA: Note: Data for latest year may not have been available at press time.

In U.S. $	2020	2019	2018	2017	2016	2015
Revenue	2,856,659,000	2,615,277,000	2,182,879,000	1,787,922,000	1,634,340,000	1,580,519,000
R&D Expense						
Operating Income	189,206,000	161,938,000	149,293,000	99,695,000	100,808,000	89,164,000
Operating Margin %		.06%	.07%	.06%	.06%	.06%
SGA Expense	357,777,000	340,005,000	296,986,000	266,586,000	243,201,000	228,965,000
Net Income	150,139,000	114,324,000	112,903,000	55,272,000	64,896,000	49,364,000
Operating Cash Flow	286,510,000	142,028,000	147,190,000	114,090,000	91,188,000	97,867,000
Capital Expenditure	24,131,000	31,750,000	27,268,000	35,467,000	23,217,000	20,808,000
EBITDA	259,180,000	211,732,000	194,218,000	140,621,000	128,548,000	112,797,000
Return on Assets %		.09%	.12%	.07%	.09%	.07%
Return on Equity %		.21%	.25%	.14%	.18%	.15%
Debt to Equity		0.475	0.148	0.143	0.005	0.031

CONTACT INFORMATION:

Phone: 713-830-9600   Fax: 713 830-9696
Toll-Free: 800-723-8431
Address: 675 Bering Dr., Ste. 400, Houston, TX 77057 United States

STOCK TICKER/OTHER:

Stock Ticker: FIX
Employees: 12,000
Parent Company:

Exchange: NYS
Fiscal Year Ends: 12/31

SALARIES/BONUSES:

Top Exec. Salary: $ Bonus: $
Second Exec. Salary: $ Bonus: $

OTHER THOUGHTS:

Estimated Female Officers or Directors: 3
Hot Spot for Advancement for Women/Minorities: Y

CommScope Holding Company Inc

www.commscope.com

NAIC Code: 335921

TYPES OF BUSINESS:

Cable-Coaxial & Fiber Optic
Broadband Networks
Outdoor Wireless Networks
Venue Networks
Campus Networks
Home Networks

BRANDS/DIVISIONS/AFFILIATES:

CommScope NEXT

CONTACTS: Note: Officers with more than one job title may be intentionally listed here more than once.

Alexander Pease, CFO
Frank Drendel, Chairman of the Board
Brooke Clark, Chief Accounting Officer
Bruce McClelland, COO
Morgan Kurk, Executive VP
Frank Wyatt, General Counsel
Robyn Mingle, Other Executive Officer
Marvin Edwards, President
Peter Karlsson, Senior VP, Divisional

GROWTH PLANS/SPECIAL FEATURES:

CommScope Holding Company, Inc., along with its subsidiaries, operate in four business segments: broadband networks, outdoor wireless networks, venue and campus networks, and home networks. The broadband networks segment provides an end-to-end product portfolio serving the telecommunications and cable provider broadband market. This division includes converged cable access, passive optical networking, video systems, access technologies, fiber and coaxial cable, fiber and copper connectivity and hardened closures. The outdoor wireless networks segment focuses on the macro and metro cell markets, and includes base station antennas, radio frequency filters, tower connectivity, microwave antennas, metro cell products, cabinets, steel, accessories, access systems and search solutions. The venue and campus networks segment provides public and private networks for campuses, venues, data centers and buildings. This division combines Wi-Fi and switching, distributed antenna systems, licensed and unlicensed small cells and enterprise fiber and copper infrastructure. Last, the home networks segment includes subscriber-based solutions that support broadband and video applications. In early-2021, CommScope announced and began implementing a business transformation initiative called CommScope NEXT, with plans to spin off its home networks business.

FINANCIAL DATA: Note: Data for latest year may not have been available at press time.

In U.S. $	2020	2019	2018	2017	2016	2015
Revenue	8,435,900,000	8,345,100,000	4,568,507,000	4,560,582,000	4,923,621,000	3,807,828,000
R&D Expense	703,300,000	578,500,000	185,696,000	185,222,000	200,715,000	135,964,000
Operating Income	243,300,000	-44,700,000	508,993,000	521,392,000	656,177,000	301,865,000
Operating Margin %		- .01%	.11%	.11%	.13%	.08%
SGA Expense	1,170,700,000	1,277,100,000	729,032,000	794,291,000	879,495,000	687,389,000
Net Income	-573,400,000	-929,500,000	140,217,000	193,764,000	222,838,000	-70,875,000
Operating Cash Flow	436,200,000	596,400,000	494,144,000	586,286,000	606,225,000	302,060,000
Capital Expenditure	121,200,000	104,100,000	82,347,000	68,721,000	68,314,000	56,501,000
EBITDA	746,600,000	274,100,000	770,187,000	844,803,000	949,156,000	476,160,000
Return on Assets %		- .09%	.02%	.03%	.03%	- .01%
Return on Equity %		- .75%	.08%	.13%	.17%	- .06%
Debt to Equity		11.719	2.269	2.652	3.263	4.278

CONTACT INFORMATION:

Phone: 828-324-2200   Fax:
Toll-Free: 800-982-1708
Address: 1100 CommScope Place SE, Hickory, NC 28602 United States

STOCK TICKER/OTHER:

Stock Ticker: COMM
Employees: 30,000
Parent Company:

Exchange: NAS
Fiscal Year Ends: 12/31

SALARIES/BONUSES:

Top Exec. Salary: $ Bonus: $
Second Exec. Salary: $ Bonus: $

OTHER THOUGHTS:

Estimated Female Officers or Directors: 2
Hot Spot for Advancement for Women/Minorities:

Conagra Brands Inc

www.conagrafoods.com

NAIC Code: 311412

TYPES OF BUSINESS:

Food Products Manufacturing
Food Production
Shelf-Stable Foods
Refrigerated Foods
Frozen Foods
Distribution

BRANDS/DIVISIONS/AFFILIATES:

Slim Jim
gardein
Duncan Hines
Health Choice
earth balance
Hunts
Birds Eye
udis

CONTACTS: *Note: Officers with more than one job title may be intentionally listed here more than once.*

Sean Connolly, CEO
Darren Serrao, Co-COO
Thomas McGough, Co-COO
Robert Wise, Controller
Richard Lenny, Director
David Marberger, Executive VP
Colleen Batcheler, Executive VP
Charisse Brock, Executive VP
David Biegger, Executive VP

GROWTH PLANS/SPECIAL FEATURES:

Conagra Brands, Inc. is a food company serving grocery retailers as well as restaurants and other food service establishments. Types of foods produced and supplied by the company include shelf-stable food products and refrigerated and frozen food products. The firm operates through two business segments: foodservice and international. The foodservice segment offers products to restaurants, retailers, commercial customers and other foodservice suppliers; and the international business segment offers Conagra Brands' products to consumers outside the U.S., primarily Canada and Mexico. Foodservice produces meals, entrees, sauces and a variety of custom-manufactured culinary products that are packaged for sale to foodservice establishments. Among Conagra Brands' 60+ brands include Slim Jim, gardein, Duncan Hines, Healthy Choice, earth balance, Hunts, Marie Callender's, Reddi Wip, vlasic, Birds Eye, udis, and PAM. In January 2021, Conagra Brands sold its Peter Pan peanut butter brand to Post Holdings, Inc. That same fiscal year, Conagra sold its H.K. Anderson peanut butter-filled pretzel and snacks business.

Conagra Brands offers its employees comprehensive health benefits, retirement options and employee assistance plans and programs.

FINANCIAL DATA: *Note: Data for latest year may not have been available at press time.*

In U.S. $	2020	2019	2018	2017	2016	2015
Revenue	11,054,400,000	9,538,400,000	7,938,300,000	7,826,900,000	11,642,900,000	
R&D Expense						
Operating Income	1,447,100,000	1,179,600,000	1,033,500,000	925,000,000	881,400,000	
Operating Margin %	.13%	.12%	.13%	.12%	.08%	
SGA Expense	1,622,500,000	1,473,400,000	1,318,000,000	1,417,100,000	2,209,400,000	
Net Income	840,100,000	678,300,000	808,400,000	639,300,000	-677,000,000	
Operating Cash Flow	1,842,600,000	1,125,500,000	954,200,000	1,175,500,000	1,207,400,000	
Capital Expenditure	369,500,000	353,100,000	251,600,000	242,100,000	440,200,000	
EBITDA	1,849,000,000	1,554,500,000	1,294,300,000	1,196,700,000	1,256,600,000	
Return on Assets %	.04%	.04%	.08%	.05%	-.04%	
Return on Equity %	.11%	.12%	.21%	.17%	-.17%	
Debt to Equity	1.156	1.443	0.879	0.694	1.324	

CONTACT INFORMATION:

Phone: 312-549-5000   Fax:
Toll-Free:
Address: 222 W Merchandise Mart Plaza, Ste 1300, Chicago, IL 60654 United States

STOCK TICKER/OTHER:

Stock Ticker: CAG
Employees: 16,500
Parent Company:

Exchange: NYS
Fiscal Year Ends: 05/31

SALARIES/BONUSES:

Top Exec. Salary: $ Bonus: $
Second Exec. Salary: $ Bonus: $

OTHER THOUGHTS:

Estimated Female Officers or Directors: 4
Hot Spot for Advancement for Women/Minorities: Y

Sales, profits and employees may be estimates. Financial information, benefits and other data can change quickly and may vary from those stated here.

Concentrix Corporation

www.concentrix.com

NAIC Code: 541512

TYPES OF BUSINESS:
Information Technology Outsourcing
Technical Support
Customer Experience Solutions
Office Automation
Analytics
Business Transformation Services

BRANDS/DIVISIONS/AFFILIATES:

CONTACTS: *Note: Officers with more than one job title may be intentionally listed here more than once.*
Christopher Caldwell, Pres.
Dick Rapach, VP-Oper

GROWTH PLANS/SPECIAL FEATURES:
Concentrix Corporation is a global provider of technology-infused customer experience (CX) solutions. The company provides end-to-end capabilities, including CX process optimization, technology innovation, front- and back-office automation, analytics and business transformation services. Concentrix's clients are primarily engaged in industries including automotive, banking, financial services, energy, public sector, healthcare, insurance, media, communications, retail, ecommerce, technology, travel, transportation and tourism. The firm's portfolio of solutions deliver an optimized and consistent brand experience across all channels of communication, such as voice, chat, email, social media, asynchronous messaging and custom applications. Concentrix's integrated solutions support the entirety of the customer lifecycle, and includes CX and user experience (UX) strategy and design services, analytics and actional insight solutions, and innovative approaches to enhancing the customer experience through technological advancements. Based in the U.S., Concentrix has office locations in more than 40 countries, conducting business in over 70 languages. December 2020, Concentrix was spun-off from former parent SYNNEX Corporation into an independent public company, trading on the Nasdaq Stock Market under ticker symbol CNXC.

FINANCIAL DATA: *Note: Data for latest year may not have been available at press time.*

In U.S. $	2020	2019	2018	2017	2016	2015
Revenue	4,719,534,000	4,707,912,000	2,463,151,000	1,990,180,000		
R&D Expense						
Operating Income	308,761,000	294,332,000	144,761,000	114,623,000		
Operating Margin %						
SGA Expense	1,352,764,000	1,454,116,000	792,791,000	634,531,000		
Net Income	164,811,000	117,164,000	48,271,000	72,250,000		
Operating Cash Flow	507,614,000	449,736,000	212,323,000	168,365,000		
Capital Expenditure	171,332,000	111,122,000	92,518,000	78,702,000		
EBITDA	592,774,000	602,392,000	303,745,000	242,165,000		
Return on Assets %						
Return on Equity %						
Debt to Equity						

CONTACT INFORMATION:
Phone: 510-656-3333   Fax:
Toll-Free: 800-747-0583
Address: 44111 Nobel Dr., Freemont, CA 94538 United States

STOCK TICKER/OTHER:
Stock Ticker: CNXC   Exchange: NAS
Employees: 40,000   Fiscal Year Ends: 11/30
Parent Company:

SALARIES/BONUSES:
Top Exec. Salary: $ Bonus: $
Second Exec. Salary: $ Bonus: $

OTHER THOUGHTS:
Estimated Female Officers or Directors:
Hot Spot for Advancement for Women/Minorities:

Concur Technologies Inc

NAIC Code: 511210Q

TYPES OF BUSINESS:

Software Manufacturer-Expense Reporting
Corporate Expense Management Solutions
Invoice Management
Travel Management
Software
Data Analysis
Data Capture

BRANDS/DIVISIONS/AFFILIATES:

SAP SE
SAP Concur

CONTACTS: Note: Officers with more than one job title may be intentionally listed here more than once.

Jim Lucier, Pres.
Tom Lavin, CFO
Chris Juneau, CMO
Kyile Stair, VP-Human Resources
Saju Pillai, CTO
John Torrey, Executive VP, Divisional
Robert Cavanaugh, Executive VP
Elena Donio, Executive VP
Ed Kim, Sr. VP-Strategic Programs & Oper.

GROWTH PLANS/SPECIAL FEATURES:

Concur Technologies, Inc. does business as SAP Concur, and provides travel, expense and invoice management tools that simplify processes and creates enhanced experiences. SAP Concur's travel management solutions enable employees to book business travel on their own. The software along with an extensive network of travel suppliers combine to provide an automated, integrated corporate travel system for achieving travel and expense goals. SAP Concur's expense management solutions automate and integrate so that employee travel spending can be planned and captured through multiple devices to a single source. Business settings can be configured, spending policies can be adjusted and receipts can be automatically captured. Reimbursement to employees is swift and the expense reporting process is simplified across each business trip. SAP Concur's invoice solutions automate accounts payable and invoices, reducing tedious tasks. The invoice software increases compliance, reduces fraud, and captures data for business decision purposes. Its mobile tools enable employees to work from anywhere. Industries served by SAP Concur's products and solutions include financial services, healthcare, higher education, legal services, professional services, life sciences, manufacturing, non-profits, oil and gas, mining, retail, restaurant, technology and more. Concur Technologies is owned by German software giant SAP SE. The company is headquartered in Washington, USA, with global locations spanning the Americas, Europe, Asia Pacific, Middle East and Africa.

FINANCIAL DATA: Note: Data for latest year may not have been available at press time.

In U.S. $	2020	2019	2018	2017	2016	2015
Revenue	1,848,510,000	2,139,255,800	1,767,980,000	1,743,120,000	1,381,972,534	724,603,419
R&D Expense						
Operating Income						
Operating Margin %						
SGA Expense						
Net Income	69,273,000	2,166,597	2,043,960	155,798,000	1,291,875,652	-20,571,530
Operating Cash Flow						
Capital Expenditure						
EBITDA						
Return on Assets %						
Return on Equity %						
Debt to Equity						

CONTACT INFORMATION:

Phone: 425 590-5000   Fax: 425 590-5999
Toll-Free: 800-401-8412
Address: 601 108th Ave. NE, Suite 1000, Bellevue, WA 98004 United States

SALARIES/BONUSES:

Top Exec. Salary: $ Bonus: $
Second Exec. Salary: $ Bonus: $

STOCK TICKER/OTHER:

Stock Ticker: Subsidiary
Employees: 4,000
Parent Company: SAP SE

Exchange:
Fiscal Year Ends: 12/31

OTHER THOUGHTS:

Estimated Female Officers or Directors: 2
Hot Spot for Advancement for Women/Minorities:

Constellation Brands Inc

NAIC Code: 312130

www.cbrands.com

TYPES OF BUSINESS:

Beverages-Wineries
Beer & Distilled Spirits
Wine Distribution
Bottled Water
Import/Export

BRANDS/DIVISIONS/AFFILIATES:

Corona
Modelo
Pacifico
Meiomi
Cooper & Thief
7 Moons
Casa Noble
SVEDKA

CONTACTS: *Note: Officers with more than one job title may be intentionally listed here more than once.*

William Newlands, CEO
David Klein, CFO
Robert Sands, Chairman of the Board
James Sabia, Chief Marketing Officer
Richard Sands, Director
James Bourdeau, Executive VP
Thomas Kane, Executive VP
F. Hetterich, Executive VP
Robert Hanson, Executive VP

GROWTH PLANS/SPECIAL FEATURES:

Constellation Brands, Inc. is one of the largest wine companies in the world as well as a leading alcoholic beverage supplier in the U.S. and Canada, and a major producer and exporter of wine from New Zealand. The firm has more than 100 brands in its portfolio and operates through three business segments: beer, wine and spirits, and corporate operations and other. The beer segment markets and sells popular imported brands, such as Corona, Modelo and Pacifico. The wine and spirits segment produces and markets premium wines in all major categories, including dessert wine, table wine and sparkling wine in the U.S. and Canada, as well as other countries. Wine brands include Kim Crawford, Meiomi, The Prisoner Wine Company, Cooper & Thief, Charles Smith Wines, 7 Moons, Robert Mondavi Winery, Ruffino, and many more. Spirit products include Casa Noble (tequila), High West (whiskey), SVEDKA (vodka), Nelson's Green Brier (bourbon), among others. The corporate and other segment oversees traditional corporate-related activities, such as corporate development, corporate finance, human resources, internal audit, investor relations, legal, public relations and global information technology. During 2020, Constellation Brands acquired Empathy Wines, and sold its Ballast Point craft beer business.

FINANCIAL DATA: *Note: Data for latest year may not have been available at press time.*

In U.S. $	2020	2019	2018	2017	2016	2015
Revenue	8,343,500,000	8,116,000,000	7,585,000,000	7,331,500,000	6,548,400,000	
R&D Expense						
Operating Income	2,530,100,000	2,412,200,000	2,284,500,000	2,137,000,000	1,765,100,000	
Operating Margin %	.30%	.30%	.30%	.29%	.27%	
SGA Expense	1,621,800,000	1,668,100,000	1,532,700,000	1,392,400,000	1,177,200,000	
Net Income	-11,800,000	3,435,900,000	2,318,900,000	1,535,100,000	1,054,900,000	
Operating Cash Flow	2,551,100,000	2,246,300,000	1,931,400,000	1,696,000,000	1,413,700,000	
Capital Expenditure	726,500,000	886,300,000	1,057,600,000	907,400,000	891,300,000	
EBITDA	-190,000,000	4,845,200,000	2,968,500,000	2,720,600,000	2,036,100,000	
Return on Assets %	.00%	.14%	.12%	.09%	.07%	
Return on Equity %	.00%	.33%	.31%	.23%	.17%	
Debt to Equity	0.964	0.937	1.17	1.12	1.039	

CONTACT INFORMATION:

Phone: 585 678-7100   Fax: 585 678-7103
Toll-Free: 888-724-2169
Address: 207 High Point Dr., Bldg. 100, Victor, NY 14564 United States

STOCK TICKER/OTHER:

Stock Ticker: STZ   Exchange: NYS
Employees: 9,300   Fiscal Year Ends: 02/28
Parent Company:

SALARIES/BONUSES:

Top Exec. Salary: $ Bonus: $
Second Exec. Salary: $ Bonus: $

OTHER THOUGHTS:

Estimated Female Officers or Directors: 2
Hot Spot for Advancement for Women/Minorities:

Cooper Companies Inc (The)

www.coopercos.com

NAIC Code: 339100

TYPES OF BUSINESS:

Medical Devices
Contact Lenses
Gynecological Instruments
Diagnostic Products

BRANDS/DIVISIONS/AFFILIATES:

CooperVision
CooperSurgical
Proclear
Phosphorylcholine (PC) Technology
obp Medical Corporation
MiSight

CONTACTS: Note: Officers with more than one job title may be intentionally listed here more than once.

Albert White, CEO
A. Bender, Chairman of the Board
Agostino Ricupati, Chief Accounting Officer
Holly Sheffield, Chief Strategy Officer
Daniel McBride, COO
Allan Rubenstein, Director
Randal Golden, General Counsel
Robert Auerbach, President, Subsidiary
Brian Andrews, Senior VP

GROWTH PLANS/SPECIAL FEATURES:

The Cooper Companies, Inc. develops, manufactures and markets healthcare products, primarily medical devices. The company operates through two business units: CooperVision and CooperSurgical. CooperVision develops, manufactures and markets a broad range of contact lenses, including disposable spherical and specialty contact lenses. It is a leading manufacturer of toric and multifocal lenses, which correct astigmatism; multifocal lenses for presbyopia, the blurring of vision due to advancing age; and spherical lenses, including hydrogel lenses, which correct the most common near- and far-sighted visual defects. CooperVision offers single-use, two-week, monthly and quarterly disposable sphere and toric lenses as well as custom toric lenses to correct a high degree of astigmatism. CooperVision's Proclear line of spherical, toric and multifocal lenses are manufactured with omafilcon, a material that incorporates its proprietary Phosphorylcholine (PC) Technology to enhance tissue-device compatibility. CooperVision's products are primarily manufactured at its facilities in the U.S., the U.K., Hungary, Costa Rico and Puerto Rico. It distributes its products out of its facilities in the U.S., the U.K., Belgium and various smaller international distribution facilities. CooperSurgical develops, manufactures and markets medical devices, diagnostic products and surgical instruments and accessories used primarily by gynecologists and obstetricians. This unit manufactures and distributes its products at its facilities in Connecticut, Texas and New York, USA, as well as in Denmark, Costa Rica and the U.K. In 2021, Cooper Companies announced the creation of a 50/50 joint venture with EssilorLuxottica for the acquisition of SightGlass Vision, a life sciences company focused on developing innovative spectacle lenses to reduce the progression of myopia in children; the acquisition of obp Medical Corporation, a medical device company; and the approval of MiSight one day contact lenses by the Chinese National Medical Products Administration for use within China.

FINANCIAL DATA: Note: Data for latest year may not have been available at press time.

In U.S. $	2020	2019	2018	2017	2016	2015
Revenue	2,430,900,000	2,653,400,000	2,532,800,000	2,139,000,000	1,966,814,000	1,797,060,000
R&D Expense	93,300,000	86,700,000	84,800,000	69,200,000	65,411,000	69,589,000
Operating Income	311,800,000	528,100,000	427,500,000	429,100,000	324,080,000	236,671,000
Operating Margin %		.20%	.17%	.20%	.16%	.13%
SGA Expense	992,500,000	996,200,000	973,300,000	799,100,000	722,798,000	712,543,000
Net Income	238,400,000	466,700,000	139,900,000	372,900,000	273,917,000	203,523,000
Operating Cash Flow	486,600,000	713,200,000	668,900,000	593,600,000	509,637,000	390,970,000
Capital Expenditure	310,400,000	292,100,000	193,600,000	127,200,000	152,640,000	243,023,000
EBITDA	590,400,000	826,200,000	689,700,000	615,800,000	520,097,000	424,991,000
Return on Assets %		.08%	.03%	.08%	.06%	.05%
Return on Equity %		.13%	.04%	.13%	.10%	.08%
Debt to Equity		0.348	0.60	0.362	0.41	0.415

CONTACT INFORMATION:

Phone: 925 460-3600   Fax: 949 597-0662
Toll-Free:
Address: 6140 Stoneridge Mall Rd., Ste. 590, Pleasanton, CA 94588
United States

STOCK TICKER/OTHER:

Stock Ticker: COO
Employees: 12,000
Parent Company:

Exchange: NYS
Fiscal Year Ends: 10/31

SALARIES/BONUSES:

Top Exec. Salary: $ Bonus: $
Second Exec. Salary: $ Bonus: $

OTHER THOUGHTS:

Estimated Female Officers or Directors: 2
Hot Spot for Advancement for Women/Minorities: Y

Cornerstone Building Brands Inc   www.cornerstonebuildingbrands.com
NAIC Code: 326199

TYPES OF BUSINESS:
Windows and Window Frames, Vinyl, Manufacturing
Vinyl Siding & Accessories
Windows & Doors
Fencing, Railing & Decking
Metal Systems

BRANDS/DIVISIONS/AFFILIATES:
Prime Window Systems

CONTACTS: Note: Officers with more than one job title may be intentionally listed here more than once.
Donald Riley, CEO, Divisional
James Metcalf, CEO
Shawn Poe, CFO
Brian Boyle, Chief Accounting Officer
Todd Moore, Chief Compliance Officer
Katy Theroux, Executive VP, Divisional
Arthur Steinhafel, President, Divisional
John Buckley, President, Divisional
Bradley Little, Vice President, Divisional

GROWTH PLANS/SPECIAL FEATURES:
Cornerstone Building Brands, Inc. manufactures exterior building products. Cornerstone offers products and solutions for the commercial and residential construction industries, serving customers and communities across North America. Commercial building solutions include coil coating, metal doors, metal roofing systems, metal wall systems, insulated metal panels and complete building systems. Commercial buildings range from hospitals to hotels to offices and stadiums. Residential building solutions include windows, doors, siding, trim, roofing, gutters, shutters, accents, stone, fencing and railing. These products and solutions provide a way for builders and designers to create varied styles and aesthetics of residential properties. In addition, Cornerstone Building Brands create complete building solutions across a breadth of industries, including agricultural, automotive, aviation, community, distribution/warehouse, educational, healthcare, manufacturing, industrial, office, recreational, residential new/repair, retail, restaurant, storage and more. The firm's vertically-integrated technical team encompasses licensed engineers registered in all U.S. states and Canadian provinces, certifying its customized solutions. Cornerstone also engages in advanced research and development of product innovation that meets or exceeds all required structural, fire, wind, seismic and life safety standards via three dedicated product development centers. It provides consulting services to meet customer needs and requirements, and offers training services for dealers, architects and contractors at its training facilities in Houston and Pittsburgh, as well as off-site locations throughout North America. In May 2021, Cornerstone Building Brands acquired Prime Window Systems, which serves the residential new construction and repair/remodel markets with energy efficient vinyl window and door products.

FINANCIAL DATA: Note: Data for latest year may not have been available at press time.

In U.S. $	2020	2019	2018	2017	2016	2015
Revenue	4,617,369,000	4,889,747,000	2,000,577,000	1,770,278,000	1,684,928,000	1,563,693,000
R&D Expense						
Operating Income	290,126,000	282,981,000	145,928,000	113,436,000	114,059,000	68,573,000
Operating Margin %		.06%	.07%	.06%	.07%	.04%
SGA Expense	579,200,000	627,861,000	307,106,000	293,145,000	302,551,000	286,840,000
Net Income	-482,778,000	-15,390,000	63,106,000	54,724,000	51,027,000	17,818,000
Operating Cash Flow	308,417,000	229,608,000	82,463,000	62,359,000	68,768,000	105,040,000
Capital Expenditure	81,851,000	121,085,000	47,827,000	22,074,000	21,024,000	20,683,000
EBITDA	20,997,000	482,411,000	147,228,000	153,355,000	151,907,000	106,642,000
Return on Assets %		.00%	.06%	.05%	.05%	.02%
Return on Equity %		-.02%	.20%	.19%	.18%	.07%
Debt to Equity		3.636	1.22	1.269	1.437	1.633

CONTACT INFORMATION:
Phone: 866-419-0042   Fax:
Toll-Free:
Address: 5020 Weston Pkwy., Ste. 400, Cary, NC 27513 United States

STOCK TICKER/OTHER:
Stock Ticker: CNR
Employees: 20,100
Parent Company:

Exchange: NYS
Fiscal Year Ends: 10/31

SALARIES/BONUSES:
Top Exec. Salary: $ Bonus: $
Second Exec. Salary: $ Bonus: $

OTHER THOUGHTS:
Estimated Female Officers or Directors:
Hot Spot for Advancement for Women/Minorities:

Corning Incorporated

www.corning.com

NAIC Code: 327212

TYPES OF BUSINESS:

Glass & Optical Fiber Manufacturing
Glass Substrates for LCDs
Optical Switching Products
Photonic Modules & Components
Networking Devices
Semiconductor Materials
Laboratory Supplies
Emissions Control Products

BRANDS/DIVISIONS/AFFILIATES:

Eagle XG
Iris
Vascade
LEAF
ClearCurve
InfiniCor
Gorilla

CONTACTS: Note: Officers with more than one job title may be intentionally listed here more than once.

Wendell Weeks, CEO
Martin Curran, Executive VP
R. Tripeny, CFO
Edward Schlesinger, Chief Accounting Officer
Jeffrey Evenson, Chief Strategy Officer
David Morse, Chief Technology Officer
Clark Kinlin, Executive VP
Christine Pambianchi, Executive VP, Divisional
James Clappin, Executive VP, Divisional
Eric Musser, Executive VP, Divisional
Lewis Steverson, Executive VP
Lawrence McRae, Other Corporate Officer

GROWTH PLANS/SPECIAL FEATURES:

Corning Incorporated, established in 1851, is an international technology-based corporation. The firm operates in five business segments: display technologies, optical communications, specialty materials, environmental technologies and life sciences. The display technologies segment manufactures glass substrates for active matrix liquid crystal displays (LCDs), used in notebook computers, flat panel desktop monitor and LCD televisions. Its Eagle XG glass is an LCD glass substrate free of heavy metals; and its Eagle XG slim glass and Iris glass products enables lighter-weight portable devices and thinner televisions and monitors. The optical communications segment is divided into carrier network and enterprise network. The carrier network products include: Vascade submarine optical fibers for use in submarine networks; LEAF optical fiber for long-haul, regional and metropolitan networks; SMF-28e single mode optical fiber for additional transmission wavelengths in metropolitan and access networks; and ClearCurve fiber for use in multiple dwelling units. Enterprise network products include ClearCurve ultra-bendable multimode fiber for data centers and other enterprise network applications; InfiniCor fibers for local area networks; and ClearCurve VSDN ultra-bendable optical fiber designed to support emerging high-speed interconnects between computers and other consumer electronics devices. The specialty materials segment offers products such as glass windows for space shuttles and optical components for high-tech industries and includes the firm's Gorilla glass product line of protective cover glass for portable display devices. The environmental technologies segment produces ceramic products for emissions and pollution control, such as gasoline/diesel substrate and filter products. The life sciences segment manufactures laboratory products such as consumables (plastic vessels, specialty surfaces and media), as well as general labware and equipment used for cell culture research, bioprocessing, genomics, drug discovery, microbiology and chemistry. Corning manufactures products at 122 plants in 15 countries.

FINANCIAL DATA: Note: Data for latest year may not have been available at press time.

In U.S. $	2020	2019	2018	2017	2016	2015
Revenue	11,303,000,000	11,503,000,000	11,290,000,000	10,116,000,000	9,390,000,000	9,111,000,000
R&D Expense	1,154,000,000	1,031,000,000	993,000,000	860,000,000	742,000,000	769,000,000
Operating Income	509,000,000	1,306,000,000	1,575,000,000	1,630,000,000	1,468,000,000	1,307,000,000
Operating Margin %		.11%	.14%	.16%	.16%	.14%
SGA Expense	1,747,000,000	1,585,000,000	1,799,000,000	1,467,000,000	1,472,000,000	1,523,000,000
Net Income	512,000,000	960,000,000	1,066,000,000	-497,000,000	3,695,000,000	1,339,000,000
Operating Cash Flow	2,180,000,000	2,031,000,000	2,919,000,000	2,004,000,000	2,521,000,000	2,809,000,000
Capital Expenditure	1,377,000,000	1,987,000,000	2,310,000,000	1,804,000,000	1,130,000,000	1,250,000,000
EBITDA	2,419,000,000	2,940,000,000	2,987,000,000	2,970,000,000	5,046,000,000	2,810,000,000
Return on Assets %		.03%	.04%	-.02%	.13%	.04%
Return on Equity %		.08%	.08%	-.04%	.22%	.07%
Debt to Equity		0.771	0.522	0.354	0.234	0.237

CONTACT INFORMATION:

Phone: 607 974-9000   Fax: 607 974-8688
Toll-Free:
Address: 1 Riverfront Plaza, Corning, NY 14831 United States

STOCK TICKER/OTHER:

Stock Ticker: GLW   Exchange: NYS
Employees: 40,700   Fiscal Year Ends: 12/31
Parent Company:

SALARIES/BONUSES:

Top Exec. Salary: $ Bonus: $
Second Exec. Salary: $ Bonus: $

OTHER THOUGHTS:

Estimated Female Officers or Directors: 1
Hot Spot for Advancement for Women/Minorities: Y

Sales, profits and employees may be estimates. Financial information, benefits and other data can change quickly and may vary from those stated here.

Costco Wholesale Corporation

www.costco.com

NAIC Code: 452910

TYPES OF BUSINESS:

Warehouse Clubs, Retail
Food
Health & Beauty Products
Electronics
Furniture
Apparel
Automotive Supplies
Gasoline Sales

BRANDS/DIVISIONS/AFFILIATES:

Costco Wholesale Industries
Kirkland Signature

CONTACTS: Note: Officers with more than one job title may be intentionally listed here more than once.

Hamilton James, Chairman of the Board
James Murphy, COO, Divisional
Roland Vachris, COO, Divisional
Russell Miller, COO, Geographical
James Klauer, COO, Geographical
Joseph Portera, COO, Geographical
W. Jelinek, Director
Franz Lazarus, Executive VP, Divisional
Timothy Rose, Executive VP, Divisional
Richard Galanti, Executive VP
Paul Moulton, Executive VP
Daniel Hines, Senior VP

GROWTH PLANS/SPECIAL FEATURES:

Costco Wholesale Corporation operates membership warehouses based on the concept that offering members very low prices on a limited selection of branded and private-label products will produce high sales volumes and rapid inventory turnover. This rapid turnover, combined with volume purchasing, efficient distribution and reduced handling of merchandise in self-service warehouse facilities, allows the firm to operate at significantly lower margins than traditional discount retailers. Costco buys the majority of its merchandise directly from manufacturers for shipment to warehouses or to consolidation points, minimizing freight and handling costs. Products include health and beauty aids, cleaning supplies, foods, alcohol, appliances, electronics, tools, office supplies, furniture, automotive supplies, apparel, cameras, house wares and books. Stores contain other features, including pharmacies, print shops, photo labs and gas stations. Costco's private products are marketed under the Kirkland Signature label brand. It has three types of memberships: executive, business and gold star. Memberships are designed to build customer loyalty and start at $60 per year (for U.S. and Canadian operations). The firm operates 778 warehouses, including 547 in the U.S. and Puerto Rico; 100 in Canada; 39 in Mexico; 29 in the U.K.; 26 in Japan; 16 in South Korea; 13 in Taiwan; 11 in Australia; two in Spain; and one each in Iceland, France and China (as of March 2020). The stores average approximately 144,000 square feet and stock distinct products including upscale items such as jewelry and wines. Costco Wholesale Industries, a division of the company, operates manufacturing businesses, including special food packaging, optical laboratories, meat processing and jewelry distribution. The company also operates eCommerce websites in several countries.

Costco offers employees health, dental, vision, life insurance, short- and long-term disability and prescription coverage; 401(k); and employee assistance plans.

FINANCIAL DATA: Note: Data for latest year may not have been available at press time.

In U.S. $	2020	2019	2018	2017	2016	2015
Revenue	166,761,000,000	152,703,000,000	141,576,000,000	129,025,000,000	118,719,000,000	116,199,000,000
R&D Expense						
Operating Income	5,435,000,000	4,737,000,000	4,480,000,000	4,111,000,000	3,672,000,000	3,624,000,000
Operating Margin %		.03%	.03%	.03%	.03%	.03%
SGA Expense	16,332,000,000	14,994,000,000	13,876,000,000	12,950,000,000	12,068,000,000	11,445,000,000
Net Income	4,002,000,000	3,659,000,000	3,134,000,000	2,679,000,000	2,350,000,000	2,377,000,000
Operating Cash Flow	8,861,000,000	6,356,000,000	5,774,000,000	6,726,000,000	3,292,000,000	4,285,000,000
Capital Expenditure	2,810,000,000	2,998,000,000	2,969,000,000	2,502,000,000	2,649,000,000	2,393,000,000
EBITDA	7,172,000,000	6,407,000,000	6,038,000,000	5,543,000,000	5,007,000,000	4,855,000,000
Return on Assets %		.08%	.08%	.08%	.07%	.07%
Return on Equity %		.26%	.27%	.23%	.21%	.21%
Debt to Equity		0.336	0.507	0.61	0.336	0.458

CONTACT INFORMATION:

Phone: 425 313-8100   Fax: 425 313-8103
Toll-Free: 800-774-2678
Address: 999 Lake Dr., Issaquah, WA 98027 United States

SALARIES/BONUSES:

Top Exec. Salary: $ Bonus: $
Second Exec. Salary: $ Bonus: $

STOCK TICKER/OTHER:

Stock Ticker: COST
Employees: 273,000
Parent Company:

Exchange: NAS
Fiscal Year Ends: 08/31

OTHER THOUGHTS:

Estimated Female Officers or Directors: 4
Hot Spot for Advancement for Women/Minorities: Y

Crown Castle International Corp

www.crowncastle.com

NAIC Code: 237130

TYPES OF BUSINESS:

Cellular Service Antenna Towers
Antenna Site Leasing
Site Management Services
Construction & Engineering Services
Radio & Television Broadcast Towers

BRANDS/DIVISIONS/AFFILIATES:

CONTACTS: Note: Officers with more than one job title may be intentionally listed here more than once.

Daniel Schlanger, CFO
J. Martin, Chairman of the Board
Robert Collins, Chief Accounting Officer
Robert Ackerman, COO, Divisional
James Young, COO, Divisional
Michael Kavanagh, Other Executive Officer
Jay Brown, President
Philip Kelley, Senior VP, Divisional
Kenneth Simon, Senior VP

GROWTH PLANS/SPECIAL FEATURES:

Crown Castle International Corp. owns, operates and leases towers and other communications structures for wireless communication purposes. Approximately 40,000 towers are dispersed throughout the U.S., and approximately 80,000 route miles of fiber optics primarily supports outdoor/indoor small cell networks and related solutions. Crown Castle's core business is the provision of access, including space or capacity, to its shared communications infrastructure via long-term contracts in various forms, including lease, license, sublease and service agreements. The firm partners with wireless carriers, technology companies, broadband providers and municipalities to design and delivery end-to-end infrastructure solutions to consumers and businesses. Crown Castle's largest tenants include T-Mobile, AT&T and Verizon Wireless, which collectively accounted for 76% of 2020 site rental revenues. Site rental revenues represent 91% of consolidated net revenues, of which approximately 70% and 30% were from the towers segment and the fiber segment, respectively.

Corwn Castle's employee benefits include medical, dental, vision and prescription drug coverage; a 401(k); short- and long-term disability; life insurance; tuition reimbursement; an employee assistance program; and flexible spending accounts.

FINANCIAL DATA: Note: Data for latest year may not have been available at press time.

In U.S. $	2020	2019	2018	2017	2016	2015
Revenue	5,840,000,000	5,763,000,000	5,423,000,000	4,355,605,000	3,921,225,000	3,663,851,000
R&D Expense						
Operating Income	1,947,000,000	1,591,000,000	1,485,000,000	1,122,798,000	1,001,122,000	995,326,000
Operating Margin %		.28%	.27%	.26%	.26%	.27%
SGA Expense	678,000,000	614,000,000	563,000,000	426,698,000	371,031,000	310,921,000
Net Income	1,056,000,000	860,000,000	671,000,000	444,550,000	356,973,000	1,520,992,000
Operating Cash Flow	3,055,000,000	2,698,000,000	2,502,000,000	2,044,186,000	1,782,264,000	1,796,725,000
Capital Expenditure	1,624,000,000	2,057,000,000	1,741,000,000	1,228,071,000	873,883,000	908,892,000
EBITDA	3,350,000,000	3,115,000,000	2,838,000,000	2,282,770,000	1,976,094,000	1,994,175,000
Return on Assets %		.02%	.02%	.01%	.01%	.07%
Return on Equity %		.06%	.05%	.04%	.04%	.21%
Debt to Equity		1.377	1.377	1.30	1.597	1.713

CONTACT INFORMATION:

Phone: 713 570-3050   Fax:
Toll-Free: 877-486-9377
Address: 1220 Augusta Dr., Ste. 600, Houston, TX 77057-2261 United States

STOCK TICKER/OTHER:

Stock Ticker: CCI
Employees: 5,100
Parent Company:

Exchange: NYS
Fiscal Year Ends: 12/31

SALARIES/BONUSES:

Top Exec. Salary: $ Bonus: $
Second Exec. Salary: $ Bonus: $

OTHER THOUGHTS:

Estimated Female Officers or Directors:
Hot Spot for Advancement for Women/Minorities:

Crown Holdings Inc

NAIC Code: 332431

www.crowncork.com

TYPES OF BUSINESS:

Metal Can Manufacturing
Food and Beverage Cans
Plastic Containers
Glass Bottles
Manufacture
Packaging
Distribution
Closures

BRANDS/DIVISIONS/AFFILIATES:

CONTACTS: *Note: Officers with more than one job title may be intentionally listed here more than once.*

Timothy Donahue, CEO
Thomas Kelly, CFO
John Conway, Chairman of the Board
David Beaver, Controller
Gerard Gifford, COO
Caesar Sweitzer, Independent Director
Djalma Novaes, President, Divisional
Robert Bourque, President, Divisional
Hok Goh, President, Divisional
Didier Sourisseau, President, Divisional

GROWTH PLANS/SPECIAL FEATURES:

Crown Holdings, Inc. is a worldwide leader in the design, manufacture and sale of packaging products and equipment for consumer goods and industrial products. Crown has operations in more than 45 countries and is organized by product line and geography within four divisions: Americas, Europe, Asia Pacific and transit packaging. The Americas division includes operations in the U.S., Brazil, Canada, Colombia and Mexico. These operations manufacture aluminum beverage cans and ends, steel crowns, glass bottles and aluminum closures, and supplies its products to a variety of customers. The European division includes operations in Europe, the Middle East and North Africa, manufacturing steel and aluminum beverage cans and ends, and supplies its products to a variety of customers. The Asia Pacific division primarily consists of: beverage can operations in Cambodia, China, Indonesia, Malaysia, Myanmar, Singapore, Thailand and Vietnam; and non-beverage can operations, primarily food cans and specialty packaging. Last, the transit packaging division encompasses the company's global consumables and equipment and tools business. Consumables include steel strap, plastic strap and industrial film and other related products used in a wide range of industries, and transit protection products that help prevent movement during transport for a wide range of industrial and consumer products. Equipment and tools include manual, semi-automatic and automatic equipment and tools used in end-of-line operations to apply industrial solutions consumables. In August 2021, Crown Holdings sold 80% of its European tinplate business to KPS Capital Partners LP, retaining the 20% ownership stake in the business.

FINANCIAL DATA: *Note: Data for latest year may not have been available at press time.*

In U.S. $	2020	2019	2018	2017	2016	2015
Revenue	11,575,000,000	11,665,000,000	11,151,000,000	8,698,000,000	8,284,000,000	8,762,000,000
R&D Expense						
Operating Income	1,298,000,000	1,195,000,000	1,140,000,000	1,125,000,000	1,065,000,000	993,000,000
Operating Margin %		.10%	.10%	.13%	.13%	.11%
SGA Expense	614,000,000	631,000,000	558,000,000	371,000,000	368,000,000	390,000,000
Net Income	579,000,000	510,000,000	439,000,000	323,000,000	496,000,000	393,000,000
Operating Cash Flow	1,315,000,000	1,163,000,000	571,000,000	760,000,000	930,000,000	956,000,000
Capital Expenditure	587,000,000	432,000,000	462,000,000	498,000,000	473,000,000	354,000,000
EBITDA	1,707,000,000	1,654,000,000	1,549,000,000	1,328,000,000	1,259,000,000	1,146,000,000
Return on Assets %		.03%	.03%	.03%	.05%	.04%
Return on Equity %		.38%	.57%	.67%	1.95%	2.99%
Debt to Equity		4.661	9.09	8.681	12.888	36.493

CONTACT INFORMATION:

Phone: 215 698-5100   Fax:
Toll-Free:
Address: 770 Township Line Rd., Yardley, PA 19067-4232 United States

STOCK TICKER/OTHER:

Stock Ticker: CCK   Exchange: NYS
Employees: 33,000   Fiscal Year Ends: 12/31
Parent Company:

SALARIES/BONUSES:

Top Exec. Salary: $ Bonus: $
Second Exec. Salary: $ Bonus: $

OTHER THOUGHTS:

Estimated Female Officers or Directors: 3
Hot Spot for Advancement for Women/Minorities: Y

Curia Inc

NAIC Code: 541711

TYPES OF BUSINESS:

Contract Drug Discovery & Development
Pharmaceutical
Biotechnology
Drug Discovery
Drug Production
Analytical Services
Active Pharmaceutical Ingredients

BRANDS/DIVISIONS/AFFILIATES:

Carlyl Group (The)
GTCR LLC

GROWTH PLANS/SPECIAL FEATURES:

Curia Inc., formerly Albany Molecular Research, Inc., is a global contract research and manufacturing organization that serves the pharmaceutical and biotechnology industries to improve patient outcomes and quality of life. With locations in North America, Europe and Asia, Curia provides scientific expertise and technology to offer discovery, development, analytical services, active pharmaceutical ingredient (API) manufacturing and drug products. The company's capabilities span the entire drug continuum, including target discovery, lead finding, lead optimization, candidate selection, pre-clinical, Phases 1-3, product approval, generic research and development and ANDA development and approval. Curia has locations across seven countries, including API manufacturing plants in the U.S., India, France, Germany and Spain. Curia is privately-owned by The Carlyle Group and affiliates of GTCR, LLC.

CONTACTS: Note: Officers with more than one job title may be intentionally listed here more than once.

Johh Ratliff, CEO
Scott Wagner, Sr. VP-Global Oper.
Jason Knoblauch, CFO
Mike Kleppinger, CCO
Joe Sangregorio, Chief Human Resources Officer
Prakash Pandian, CIO
Margalit Fine, Executive VP, Divisional
Lori Henderson, General Counsel
Milton Boyer, Senior VP, Divisional
Christopher Conway, Senior VP, Divisional
Steven Hagen, Senior VP

FINANCIAL DATA: Note: Data for latest year may not have been available at press time.

In U.S. $	2020	2019	2018	2017	2016	2015
Revenue	801,360,000	756,000,000	630,000,000	600,000,000	570,449,984	402,356,000
R&D Expense						
Operating Income						
Operating Margin %						
SGA Expense						
Net Income		-62,996,015	-69,995,572	-73,679,550	-70,171,000	-2,301,000
Operating Cash Flow						
Capital Expenditure						
EBITDA						
Return on Assets %						
Return on Equity %						
Debt to Equity						

CONTACT INFORMATION:

Phone: 518 512-2000   Fax: 518-512-2020
Toll-Free:
Address: 26 Corporate Cir., Albany, NY 12212 United States

STOCK TICKER/OTHER:

Stock Ticker: Subsidiary
Employees: 3,200
Parent Company: Carlyle Group (The)

Exchange:
Fiscal Year Ends: 12/31

SALARIES/BONUSES:

Top Exec. Salary: $ Bonus: $
Second Exec. Salary: $ Bonus: $

OTHER THOUGHTS:

Estimated Female Officers or Directors: 3
Hot Spot for Advancement for Women/Minorities: Y

CVS Health Corporation

cvshealth.com

NAIC Code: 446110

TYPES OF BUSINESS:

Drug Stores
Pharmacy Benefits Management
Online Pharmacy Services
Healthcare Services
Health Benefits
Pharmacy Retail
Clinic Retail

BRANDS/DIVISIONS/AFFILIATES:

MinuteClinic
Omnicare
SilverScript Insurance Company
CVS Pharmacy
Aetna Inc

CONTACTS: Note: Officers with more than one job title may be intentionally listed here more than once.

Karen Lynch, CEO
Thomas Moriarty, Executive VP
Eva Boratto, CFO
David Dorman, Chairman of the Board
James Clark, Chief Accounting Officer
Troyen Brennan, Chief Medical Officer
Joshua Flum, Executive VP, Divisional
Alan Lotvin, Executive VP, Divisional
Karen Lynch, Executive VP, Divisional
Jonathan Roberts, Executive VP
Derica Rice, Executive VP
Kevin Hourican, Executive VP
Lisa Bisaccia, Other Executive Officer

GROWTH PLANS/SPECIAL FEATURES:

CVS Health Corporation is a leading provider of prescription and related healthcare services in the U.S. It operates in four segments: corporate, retail/LTC, pharmacy services and health care benefits. The corporate segment provides management and administrative services to support the company's overall operations. The retail/LTC (long-term care) segment operated more than 9,900 retail locations, over 1,100 MinuteClinic locations as well as online retail pharmacy websites, LTC pharmacies and onsite pharmacies. LTC pharmacy services are through the Omnicare business. Omnicare provides pharmacy consulting, including monthly patient drug therapy evaluations, to assist in compliance with state and federal regulations and provide proprietary clinical and health management programs. It also provides pharmaceutical case management services for retirees, employees and dependents who have drug benefits under corporate-sponsored health care programs. The pharmacy services segment provides a full range of pharmacy benefit management services, including mail order pharmacy services, plan design and administration, formulary management, claims processing and health management programs. Through subsidiary SilverScript Insurance Company, the division is a national provider of drug benefits to eligible beneficiaries under Medicare Part D. The segment operates a national network of approximately 66,000 retail pharmacies, consisting of approximately 40,000 chain pharmacies (which includes CVS Pharmacy locations) and 26,000 independent pharmacies, in the U.S., including Puerto Rico, the District of Columbia, Guam and the U.S. Virgin Islands. The health care benefits segment is one of the nation's leading diversified health care benefits providers, serving an estimated 34 million people. The segment offers a range of traditional, voluntary and consumer-directed health insurance products and related services.

Employee benefits include medical, dental, vision and prescription coverage; 401(k), stock and savings plans; short- and long-term disability; and a variety of employee assistance plans and programs.

FINANCIAL DATA: Note: Data for latest year may not have been available at press time.

In U.S. $	2020	2019	2018	2017	2016	2015
Revenue	268,706,000,000	256,776,000,000	194,579,000,000	184,765,000,000	177,526,000,000	153,290,000,000
R&D Expense						
Operating Income	13,911,000,000	11,987,000,000	10,170,000,000	9,517,000,000	10,338,000,000	9,454,000,000
Operating Margin %		.05%	.05%	.05%	.06%	.06%
SGA Expense						
Net Income	7,179,000,000	6,634,000,000	-594,000,000	6,622,000,000	5,317,000,000	5,237,000,000
Operating Cash Flow	15,865,000,000	12,848,000,000	8,865,000,000	8,007,000,000	10,069,000,000	8,412,000,000
Capital Expenditure	2,437,000,000	2,457,000,000	2,037,000,000	1,918,000,000	2,224,000,000	2,367,000,000
EBITDA	17,118,000,000	16,403,000,000	6,743,000,000	11,809,000,000	12,190,000,000	11,567,000,000
Return on Assets %		.03%	.00%	.07%	.06%	.06%
Return on Equity %		.11%	-.01%	.18%	.14%	.14%
Debt to Equity		1.309	1.227	0.588	0.695	0.706

CONTACT INFORMATION:

Phone: 401 765-1500   Fax: 401 762-2137
Toll-Free: 888-746-7287
Address: 1 CVS Dr., Woonsocket, RI 02895 United States

STOCK TICKER/OTHER:

Stock Ticker: CVS   Exchange: NYS
Employees: 202,000   Fiscal Year Ends: 12/31
Parent Company:

SALARIES/BONUSES:

Top Exec. Salary: $ Bonus: $
Second Exec. Salary: $ Bonus: $

OTHER THOUGHTS:

Estimated Female Officers or Directors: 4
Hot Spot for Advancement for Women/Minorities: Y

Danaher Corporation

www.danaher.com

NAIC Code: 334510

TYPES OF BUSINESS:

Medical Diagnostic Equipment
Life Science Research Tools
Diagnostic Instruments
Software
Environmental Analytic Instruments
Water Measure Systems
Water Detection Solutions
Biotechnology

BRANDS/DIVISIONS/AFFILIATES:

Aldevron LLC

CONTACTS: Note: Officers with more than one job title may be intentionally listed here more than once.

Thomas Joyce, CEO
Matthew McGrew, CFO
Steven Rales, Chairman of the Board
Robert Lutz, Chief Accounting Officer
Brian Ellis, Chief Compliance Officer
Mitchell Rales, Co-Founder
Rainer Blair, Executive VP
Daniel Comas, Executive VP
William Daniel II, Executive VP
Joakim Weidemanis, Executive VP
Angela Lalor, Senior VP, Divisional
Daniel Raskas, Senior VP, Divisional
William King, Senior VP, Divisional

GROWTH PLANS/SPECIAL FEATURES:

Danaher Corporation designs, manufactures and markets professional, medical, industrial and commercial products and services. The company operates through three segments: life sciences, diagnostics, and environmental & applied solutions. The life sciences segment offers a range of research tools that scientists use to study genes, proteins, metabolites and cells in an effort to understand the cause of disease and identify new therapies and test new drugs and vaccines. The diagnostics segment offers analytical instruments, reagents, consumables, software and services that hospitals, physicians' offices, reference laboratories and other critical care settings use to diagnose disease and make treatment decisions. Last, the environmental & applied solutions segment offers products and services that help protect resources and keep global food and water supplies safe. This division's products include a wide range of analytical instruments, software and related equipment that detect and measure water; ultraviolet disinfection systems; and industrial water treatment solutions. Danaher's manufacturing locations and worldwide presence include North America, Europe, Asia, Australia and Latin America. In August 2021, Danaher acquired Aldevron LLC, which manufactures high-quality plasmid DNA, mRNA and proteins, serving biotechnology and pharmaceutical customers across research, clinical and commercial applications. Aldevron operates as a standalone company, but its business is also included in the life sciences segment.

FINANCIAL DATA: Note: Data for latest year may not have been available at press time.

In U.S. $	2020	2019	2018	2017	2016	2015
Revenue	22,284,000,000	17,911,100,000	19,893,000,000	18,329,700,000	16,882,400,000	20,563,100,000
R&D Expense	1,348,000,000	1,126,000,000	1,231,200,000	1,128,800,000	975,100,000	1,239,100,000
Operating Income	4,231,000,000	3,269,400,000	3,403,800,000	3,021,200,000	2,750,900,000	3,469,100,000
Operating Margin %		.18%	.17%	.16%	.16%	.17%
SGA Expense	6,896,000,000	5,588,300,000	6,472,100,000	6,042,500,000	5,608,600,000	6,054,300,000
Net Income	3,646,000,000	3,008,200,000	2,650,900,000	2,492,100,000	2,553,700,000	3,357,400,000
Operating Cash Flow	6,208,000,000	3,951,600,000	4,022,000,000	3,477,800,000	3,521,800,000	3,801,800,000
Capital Expenditure	791,000,000	635,500,000	655,700,000	619,600,000	589,600,000	633,000,000
EBITDA	6,545,000,000	4,603,400,000	4,757,900,000	4,339,800,000	3,923,800,000	4,538,100,000
Return on Assets %		.05%	.06%	.05%	.05%	.08%
Return on Equity %		.11%	.10%	.10%	.11%	.14%
Debt to Equity		0.773	0.343	0.392	0.421	0.508

CONTACT INFORMATION:

Phone: 202 828-0850   Fax: 202 828-0860
Toll-Free:
Address: 2200 Pennsylvania Ave. NW, Ste. 800W, Washington, WA 20037-1701 United States

SALARIES/BONUSES:

Top Exec. Salary: $ Bonus: $
Second Exec. Salary: $ Bonus: $

STOCK TICKER/OTHER:

Stock Ticker: DHR   Exchange: NYS
Employees: 69,000   Fiscal Year Ends: 12/31
Parent Company:

OTHER THOUGHTS:

Estimated Female Officers or Directors: 2
Hot Spot for Advancement for Women/Minorities: Y

Datalogic SpA

NAIC Code: 334118

www.datalogic.com

TYPES OF BUSINESS:

Optical Readers and Scanners Manufacturing
Data Management Software
Portable Data Collection Terminals
Integrated Sorting Systems

BRANDS/DIVISIONS/AFFILIATES:

ScaleSentry

CONTACTS: Note: Officers with more than one job title may be intentionally listed here more than once.

Valentina Volta, CEO

GROWTH PLANS/SPECIAL FEATURES:

Datalogic SpA, provides integrated bar code scanning and data management equipment for the retail supply chain. The firm created one of the first commercial bar code scanners in 1974. Datalogic's products primarily include high-performance POS (point of sale) on-counter and in-counter scanners as well as industrial/general purpose handheld scanners. The company's scanners combine several functions and innovations designed to increase cashier productivity, including one-step bar code scanning and electronic article surveillance tag deactivation, 3D scanning technology that scans five sides of an item simultaneously, regular software updates and remote diagnostic capabilities. General duty hand-held scanners offer a variety of choices for most data collection activities; industrial hand-held scanners come with unique distinctive features; presentation scanners comprise omni-directional reading capabilities as well as hands-free reading; and original equipment manufacturer (OEM) scanners comprise data collection components and subassemblies based on imaging technology for many applications. Fixed retail scanners come in a variety of shapes, comprise a patented ScaleSentry scale platter, are integrated EAS compatible, and feature both Digimarc decoding software and Sapphire glass windows. Stationary industrial scanners are engineered for applications not permanently monitored by operators. Datalogic's laser marking products provide solutions for automotive, electronics, medical devices and high-precision metal manufacturing. Its sensors and safety products are designed for universal and specific purposes applications. The firm's radio frequency identification systems are developed to satisfy RFID requirements in many industries and applications, including retail in-store, warehouse management and healthcare. In addition, Datalogic's mobile computers range from pocket-sized to full-alpha-keyboard hand-held devices, industrial personal data assistants (PDAs), pistol-grip terminals, vehicle-mounted computers and more. Its machine vision product line encompasses both hardware and software while covering a wide range of performance and price point requirements and include smart cameras as well as embedded vision systems.

FINANCIAL DATA: Note: Data for latest year may not have been available at press time.

In U.S. $	2020	2019	2018	2017	2016	2015
Revenue	586,242,800	748,321,300	770,959,600	740,423,700	704,332,400	653,733,800
R&D Expense	63,696,120	72,544,230	75,773,380	67,883,150	61,751,050	59,184,100
Operating Income	17,244,160	71,972,440	97,260,780	97,761,700	81,824,850	60,490,180
Operating Margin %		.10%	.13%	.13%	.12%	.09%
SGA Expense	181,365,500	210,189,600	197,145,900	182,824,300	177,294,500	181,377,700
Net Income	16,594,180	61,173,150	76,006,740	73,404,360	56,013,590	49,539,390
Operating Cash Flow	83,221,340	89,005,230	83,152,920	88,632,580	67,961,340	75,357,980
Capital Expenditure	52,282,280	46,280,910	35,942,240	19,093,930	20,564,950	26,891,310
EBITDA	52,008,600	109,237,900	121,857,600	119,629,100	107,114,400	88,071,790
Return on Assets %		.06%	.07%	.08%	.06%	.06%
Return on Equity %		.13%	.17%	.18%	.14%	.15%
Debt to Equity		0.287	0.419	0.61	0.414	0.469

CONTACT INFORMATION:

Phone: 39 051 3147011   Fax: 39 051 3147205
Toll-Free: 800-695-5700
Address: Via Cnadini 2, Lippo di Calderara di Reno, Bologna, OR 40012 United States

STOCK TICKER/OTHER:

Stock Ticker: DLGCF   Exchange: GREY
Employees: 2,826   Fiscal Year Ends: 12/31
Parent Company:

SALARIES/BONUSES:

Top Exec. Salary: $ Bonus: $
Second Exec. Salary: $ Bonus: $

OTHER THOUGHTS:

Estimated Female Officers or Directors: 1
Hot Spot for Advancement for Women/Minorities:

DaVita Inc
NAIC Code: 621492

www.davita.com

TYPES OF BUSINESS:
Renal Care Services
Dialysis Services
Laboratory Services
Administrative Services
Integrated Kidney Care
Physician Services
Clinical Research

BRANDS/DIVISIONS/AFFILIATES:

CONTACTS: Note: Officers with more than one job title may be intentionally listed here more than once.
Javier Rodriguez, CEO
Joel Ackerman, CFO
Kent Thiry, Chairman of the Board
James Hilger, Chief Accounting Officer
James Hearty, Chief Compliance Officer
Kathleen Waters, Chief Legal Officer
Leanne Zumwalt, Vice President, Divisional

GROWTH PLANS/SPECIAL FEATURES:
DaVita, Inc. is a leading provider of dialysis services for patients suffering from chronic kidney failure, also known as end stage renal disease (ESRD). The company operates through a network of outpatient dialysis centers located in the U.S. and 10 countries outside the U.S., serving more than 200,000 patients. Loss of kidney function is normally irreversible, and typically caused by Type I and Type II diabetes, hypertension, polycycstic kidney disease, long-term autoimmune attack on the kidneys and prolonged urinary tract obstruction. End stage renal disease or end stage kidney disease (ESRD or ESKD) is the stage of advanced kidney impairment that requires continued dialysis treatments or a kidney transplant to sustain life. Dialysis is the removal of toxins, fluids and salt from the blood of patients by artificial means. DaVita's U.S. dialysis and related lab services business treats patients with chronic kidney failure and ESRD in the U.S. Internationally, DaVita provides dialysis and administrative services to approximately 320 outpatient dialysis centers located in 10 countries outside the U.S., serving approximately 36,200 patients. DaVita also provides ancillary services, consisting primarily of integrated kidney care, physician services, ESCO joint ventures and clinical research programs.

DaVita offers its employees health benefits, 401(k), employee stock purchase plan, career development opportunities and a variety of employee assistance plans and programs.

FINANCIAL DATA: Note: Data for latest year may not have been available at press time.

In U.S. $	2020	2019	2018	2017	2016	2015
Revenue	11,550,600,000	11,388,480,000	11,404,850,000	10,876,630,000	14,745,110,000	13,781,840,000
R&D Expense						
Operating Income	1,683,972,000	1,755,530,000	1,490,149,000	1,619,725,000	1,773,742,000	1,362,604,000
Operating Margin %		.15%	.13%	.15%	.12%	.10%
SGA Expense	1,247,584,000	1,103,312,000	1,135,454,000	1,064,026,000	1,592,698,000	1,452,135,000
Net Income	773,642,000	810,981,000	159,394,000	663,618,000	879,874,000	269,732,000
Operating Cash Flow	1,979,028,000	2,072,355,000	1,771,640,000	1,907,449,000	1,963,444,000	1,557,200,000
Capital Expenditure	674,541,000	766,546,000	987,138,000	905,250,000	829,095,000	707,998,000
EBITDA	2,252,808,000	2,254,415,000	2,126,948,000	2,607,905,000	2,623,529,000	1,769,540,000
Return on Assets %		.04%	.01%	.04%	.05%	.01%
Return on Equity %		.28%	.04%	.14%	.18%	.05%
Debt to Equity		5.016	2.207	1.953	1.925	1.848

CONTACT INFORMATION:
Phone: 303 405-2100   Fax: 310 792-8928
Toll-Free:
Address: 2000 16th St., Denver, CO 80202 United States

STOCK TICKER/OTHER:
Stock Ticker: DVA
Employees: 67,000
Parent Company:

Exchange: NYS
Fiscal Year Ends: 12/31

SALARIES/BONUSES:
Top Exec. Salary: $ Bonus: $
Second Exec. Salary: $ Bonus: $

OTHER THOUGHTS:
Estimated Female Officers or Directors: 3
Hot Spot for Advancement for Women/Minorities: Y

Deere & Company (John Deere)

NAIC Code: 333111

www.deere.com

TYPES OF BUSINESS:

Construction & Agricultural Equipment
Commercial & Consumer Equipment
Forestry Equipment
Financing

BRANDS/DIVISIONS/AFFILIATES:

John Deere

CONTACTS: Note: Officers with more than one job title may be intentionally listed here more than once.

Samuel Allen, CEO
Ryan Campbell, CFO
Marc Howze, Chief Administrative Officer
Rajesh Kalathur, Chief Information Officer
John May, COO
James Field, President, Divisional
Markwart Pentz, President, Divisional
Cory Reed, President, Divisional
Mary Jones, Senior VP

GROWTH PLANS/SPECIAL FEATURES:

Deere & Company is known for its John Deere brand name. The firm conducts business in three divisions: agriculture and turf; construction and forestry; and financial services. The agriculture and turf segment manufactures and distributes farm, lawn and garden equipment including tractors; combines; harvesters; tillage, seeding and soil preparation machinery; sprayers; hay and forage equipment; material handling equipment; integrated agricultural management systems technology; mowers; golf course equipment; utility tractors; landscape and irrigation equipment; sugarcane harvester aftermarket parts; and other outdoor power products. The construction and forestry division offers equipment and service parts used in construction, earthmoving, material handling and timber harvesting, including backhoe loaders, crawler dozers and loaders, four-wheel-drive loaders, excavators and more. The financial services segment primarily finances sales and leases by John Deere dealers of new and used agriculture and turf equipment and construction and forestry equipment. In addition, the segment provides wholesale financing to dealers of the foregoing equipment, finances retail revolving charge accounts and operating loans, and offers crop risk mitigation products and extended equipment warranties. Sales are generally conducted through nearly 2,000 dealer locations (largely independently owned and operated), 1,544 of which sell agricultural equipment and about 435 of which sell construction, earthmoving, material handling and/or forestry equipment.

FINANCIAL DATA: Note: Data for latest year may not have been available at press time.

In U.S. $	2020	2019	2018	2017	2016	2015
Revenue	35,259,000,000	38,941,000,000	37,021,300,000	29,115,600,000	26,363,500,000	28,609,300,000
R&D Expense	1,644,000,000	1,783,000,000	1,657,600,000	1,367,700,000	1,389,100,000	1,425,100,000
Operating Income	3,857,000,000	4,063,000,000	4,056,400,000	2,761,300,000	2,208,100,000	2,754,700,000
Operating Margin %		.10%	.11%	.09%	.08%	.10%
SGA Expense	3,677,000,000	3,694,000,000	3,630,500,000	3,253,600,000	2,951,700,000	3,056,300,000
Net Income	2,751,000,000	3,253,000,000	2,368,400,000	2,159,100,000	1,523,900,000	1,940,000,000
Operating Cash Flow	7,483,000,000	3,412,000,000	1,820,300,000	2,199,800,000	3,764,300,000	3,740,300,000
Capital Expenditure	2,656,000,000	3,449,000,000	2,950,100,000	2,592,300,000	2,955,100,000	2,826,100,000
EBITDA	5,975,000,000	6,082,000,000	5,983,500,000	4,476,800,000	3,767,900,000	4,137,100,000
Return on Assets %		.05%	.03%	.03%	.03%	.03%
Return on Equity %		.29%	.23%	.27%	.23%	.25%
Debt to Equity		2.649	2.413	2.709	3.644	3.534

CONTACT INFORMATION:

Phone: 309 765-8000   Fax: 309 765-9929
Toll-Free:
Address: 1 John Deere Pl., Moline, IL 61265 United States

SALARIES/BONUSES:

Top Exec. Salary: $ Bonus: $
Second Exec. Salary: $ Bonus: $

STOCK TICKER/OTHER:

Stock Ticker: DE   Exchange: NYS
Employees: 73,500   Fiscal Year Ends: 10/31
Parent Company:

OTHER THOUGHTS:

Estimated Female Officers or Directors: 7
Hot Spot for Advancement for Women/Minorities: Y

Dell Technologies Inc
www.delltechnologies.com/en-us/index.htm
NAIC Code: 334111

TYPES OF BUSINESS:

Computer Manufacturing
Direct Sales
Technical & Support Services
Online Music Service
Web Hosting Services
Printers & Accessories
Personal Music Players
Storage Devices

BRANDS/DIVISIONS/AFFILIATES:

VMware Inc
Pivotal Software Inc
SecureWorks Corp
Virtustream Group Holdings Inc
Dell
Dell EMC

CONTACTS: *Note: Officers with more than one job title may be intentionally listed here more than once.*

Michael Dell, CEO
Thomas Sweet, CFO
Maya McReynolds, Chief Accounting Officer
Allison Dew, Chief Marketing Officer
Allison Dew, Chief Marketing Officer
Rory Read, COO, Subsidiary
Richard Rothberg, General Counsel
Karen Quintos, Other Executive Officer
Steven Price, Other Executive Officer
Marius Haas, Other Executive Officer
Howard Elias, President, Divisional
William Scannell, President, Subsidiary
Jeffrey Clarke, Vice President, Divisional

GROWTH PLANS/SPECIAL FEATURES:

Dell Technologies, Inc. is a multinational information technology corporation. The firm provides transformational devices, processes and services in order to modernize data centers, drive progress and help clients thrive within the digital era. Dell organizes its products and services into the following business units: Client Solutions Group (CSG), Infrastructure Solutions Group (ISG) and VMware. Offerings by CSG include branded hardware, such as personal computers (PCs), notebooks, and branded peripherals, such as monitors and projectors, as well as third-party software and peripherals. CSG hardware and services also provide the architecture to enable the Internet of Things and connected ecosystems to securely and efficiently capture massive amounts of data for analytics and actionable insights for commercial customers. CSG also offers attached software, peripherals, and services, including support and deployment, configuration, and extended warranty services. Services and products offered by the ISG includes traditional storage solutions as well as next-generation storage solutions of Dell EMC; high-performance rack, blade, tower, and hyperscale servers; and networking products that help business customers transform and modernize their infrastructure, mobilize and enrich end-user experiences, and accelerate business applications and processes. ISG also includes the cloud software and infrastructure-as-a-service solutions of Virtustream. The VMware reportable segment reflects the operations of VMware, Inc. within Dell Technologies. VMware provides compute, cloud, mobility, networking and security infrastructure software to businesses that provides a flexible digital foundation for the applications that empower businesses to serve their customers globally. Brands by Dell Technologies include Dell, Dell EMC, Pivotal, Secureworks, VirtuStream and VMware. In April 2021, the firm announced plans to spin off its 81% stake in VMware by the end of 2021.

FINANCIAL DATA: *Note: Data for latest year may not have been available at press time.*

In U.S. $	2020	2019	2018	2017	2016	2015
Revenue	92,154,000,000	90,621,000,000	78,660,000,000	61,642,000,000	50,911,000,000	
R&D Expense	4,992,000,000	4,604,000,000	4,384,000,000	2,636,000,000	1,051,000,000	
Operating Income	2,622,000,000	-191,000,000	-3,333,000,000	-3,252,000,000	-514,000,000	
Operating Margin %	.03%	.00%	-.04%	-.05%	-.01%	
SGA Expense	21,319,000,000	20,640,000,000	19,003,000,000	13,575,000,000	7,850,000,000	
Net Income	4,616,000,000	-2,310,000,000	-3,728,000,000	-1,672,000,000	-1,104,000,000	
Operating Cash Flow	9,291,000,000	6,991,000,000	6,810,000,000	2,222,000,000	2,162,000,000	
Capital Expenditure	2,576,000,000	1,497,000,000	1,581,000,000	906,000,000	482,000,000	
EBITDA	8,814,000,000	7,873,000,000	5,352,000,000	1,333,000,000	2,266,000,000	
Return on Assets %	.04%	-.02%	-.03%	-.02%	-.02%	
Return on Equity %		-.90%	-.32%	-.22%	-.70%	
Debt to Equity			4.531	3.196	6.775	

CONTACT INFORMATION:

Phone: 512 338-4400   Fax: 512 283-6161
Toll-Free: 800-289-3355
Address: One Dell Way, Round Rock, TX 78682 United States

STOCK TICKER/OTHER:

Stock Ticker: DELL   Exchange: NYS
Employees: 158,000   Fiscal Year Ends: 01/31
Parent Company:

SALARIES/BONUSES:

Top Exec. Salary: $ Bonus: $
Second Exec. Salary: $ Bonus: $

OTHER THOUGHTS:

Estimated Female Officers or Directors: 1
Hot Spot for Advancement for Women/Minorities: Y

Deloitte LLP

NAIC Code: 541211

www2.deloitte.com/us/en.html

TYPES OF BUSINESS:

Accounting Services
Management Consulting
Risk Management Services
Financial Advisory Services
Outsourcing Services
Legal & Compliance Advisory Services
Consulting Services

BRANDS/DIVISIONS/AFFILIATES:

Deloitte Touche Tohmatsu Lmited

CONTACTS: *Note: Officers with more than one job title may be intentionally listed here more than once.*

Joseph B. Ucuzoglu, CEO
Janet Foutty, Chmn.

GROWTH PLANS/SPECIAL FEATURES:

Deloitte, LLP, the U.S. division of global accounting firm Deloitte Touche Tohmatsu Limited, offers a variety of financial and consulting services. The company divides its services into eight groups: tax, consulting, audit & assurance, private company services, mergers & acquisitions, risk and financial advisory, analytics and cloud. The tax division offers global business tax, global employer tax and multi-state tax services, as well as tax-related operations transformation. The consulting division helps address its client's most challenging issues by providing strategic, financial, operational, human capital and IT services. The audit & assurance division provides independent financial statement and internal control audits, in accordance with the latest professional standards. This division's accounting and reporting advisory services can help organizations navigate financial and non-financial reporting challenges. Services for private companies provide consulting services in relation to investing in emerging technologies, expanding global markets, navigating tax reform and restyling the workforce. The mergers & acquisitions division provides value-added services ranging from strategy and execution through integration and divestiture. The risk and financial advisory division helps organizations navigate a variety of risks and opportunities, including assurance, internal audit, cyber risk, financial risk, transactions, restructuring, forensic, regulatory risk, operations risk and risk intelligence. The analytics division translates the science of analytics and artificial intelligence (AI) into reality for its business customers, helping them to harness the power of analytics and AI for identifying advantages to move faster, improve decision making and creating beneficial connections with customers. Last, the cloud division offers cloud strategy and readiness, software-as-a-service (SaaS) implementation, custom implementation, cloud migration, cloud enablement and managed services. Deloitte serves many industries within segments such as consumer, energy, resources, industrial, financial services, government, public services, life sciences, healthcare, technology, media and telecommunications.

Deloitte offers comprehensive health benefits and various employee assistance programs.

FINANCIAL DATA: *Note: Data for latest year may not have been available at press time.*

In U.S. $	2020	2019	2018	2017	2016	2015
Revenue	23,157,000,000	21,913,000,000	19,897,000,000	18,551,000,000	17,518,000,000	16,147,000,000
R&D Expense						
Operating Income						
Operating Margin %						
SGA Expense						
Net Income						
Operating Cash Flow						
Capital Expenditure						
EBITDA						
Return on Assets %						
Return on Equity %						
Debt to Equity						

CONTACT INFORMATION:

Phone: 212-492-4000   Fax: 212-489-1687
Toll-Free:
Address: 30 Rockefeller Plz., 41/Fl, New York, NY 10112-0015 United States

STOCK TICKER/OTHER:

Stock Ticker: Subsidiary   Exchange:
Employees: 113,257   Fiscal Year Ends: 05/31
Parent Company: Deloitte Touche Tohmatsu Limited

SALARIES/BONUSES:

Top Exec. Salary: $ Bonus: $
Second Exec. Salary: $ Bonus: $

OTHER THOUGHTS:

Estimated Female Officers or Directors: 18
Hot Spot for Advancement for Women/Minorities: Y

Dentsply Sirona Inc

www.dentsplysirona.com/en-us

NAIC Code: 339100

TYPES OF BUSINESS:

Dental Device Manufacturing
Dental Products
Product Manufacture
Dental Product Technologies
Consumable Medical Devices
Imaging Equipment
Dental Implants
Orthodontic Appliances

BRANDS/DIVISIONS/AFFILIATES:

CONTACTS: Note: Officers with more than one job title may be intentionally listed here more than once.

Nick Alexos, CFO
Donald Casey, Director
Eric Brandt, Director
Keith Ebling, Executive VP
Walter Petersohn, Other Executive Officer
Daniel Key, Other Executive Officer
Maureen MacInnis, Other Executive Officer
Markus Boehringer, Senior VP, Divisional
William Newell, Senior VP, Divisional
Henning Mueller, Vice President, Divisional

GROWTH PLANS/SPECIAL FEATURES:

Dentsply Sirona, Inc. is a world-leading manufacturer of professional dental products and technologies. With a 135-year history (since 1886) of innovation and service to the dental industry and to patients worldwide, the firm's products and solutions include dental and oral health products as well as other consumable medical devices under a strong portfolio of renowned brands. Dentsply's products provide innovative, high-quality and effective solutions for the purpose of advancing patient care and for delivering better, safer and faster dentistry. The company's primary products consist of: dental technology and equipment, including imaging equipment, computer aided design and machining (CAD/CAM) systems, dental implants, scanning equipment, treatment software, orthodontic appliances and a variety of dental restoration products; dental consumables, including endodontic (root canal) instruments and materials, dental anesthetics, prophylaxis paste, dental sealants, impression materials, restorative materials, tooth whiteners, topical fluoride, dental handpieces, intraoral curing light systems, dental diagnostic systems and ultrasonic scalers and polishers; and healthcare consumables, including urology catheters, surgical products, medical drills and other non-medical products. Dentsply Sirona's global headquarters are based in Charlotte, North Carolina. Approximately two-thirds of the company's sales are derived from regions outside the U.S.

FINANCIAL DATA: Note: Data for latest year may not have been available at press time.

In U.S. $	2020	2019	2018	2017	2016	2015
Revenue	3,342,000,000	4,029,200,000	3,986,300,000	3,993,400,000	3,745,300,000	2,674,300,000
R&D Expense						
Operating Income	222,000,000	441,600,000	348,700,000	513,800,000	477,900,000	439,900,000
Operating Margin %		.11%	.09%	.13%	.13%	.16%
SGA Expense	1,435,000,000	1,723,500,000	1,719,100,000	1,674,700,000	1,523,000,000	1,077,300,000
Net Income	-83,000,000	262,900,000	-1,011,000,000	-1,550,000,000	429,900,000	251,200,000
Operating Cash Flow	635,000,000	632,800,000	499,800,000	601,900,000	563,400,000	497,400,000
Capital Expenditure	87,000,000	122,900,000	188,000,000	151,000,000	126,100,000	72,000,000
EBITDA	322,000,000	697,600,000	-590,300,000	-1,248,800,000	748,500,000	508,500,000
Return on Assets %		.03%	-.11%	-.14%	.05%	.06%
Return on Equity %		.05%	-.17%	-.21%	.08%	.11%
Debt to Equity		0.305	0.306	0.244	0.186	0.488

CONTACT INFORMATION:

Phone: 844-546-3722   Fax:
Toll-Free: 800-877-0020
Address: 13320 Ballantyne Corporate Pl., Charlotte, NC 28277-3607
United States

STOCK TICKER/OTHER:

Stock Ticker: XRAY
Employees: 15,000
Parent Company:

Exchange: NAS
Fiscal Year Ends: 09/30

SALARIES/BONUSES:

Top Exec. Salary: $ Bonus: $
Second Exec. Salary: $ Bonus: $

OTHER THOUGHTS:

Estimated Female Officers or Directors: 1
Hot Spot for Advancement for Women/Minorities:

Dicks Sporting Goods Inc

NAIC Code: 451110

www.dickssportinggoods.com

TYPES OF BUSINESS:

Sporting Goods Stores
Outdoor Apparel
Footwear
Hunting & Fishing Supplies
Golf Supplies
Bicycles
Online Sales

BRANDS/DIVISIONS/AFFILIATES:

Dicks Sporting Goods
Golf Galaxy
Field & Stream
Public Lands
GameChanger
Alpine Design
CALIA
DSG

CONTACTS: *Note: Officers with more than one job title may be intentionally listed here more than once.*

Edward Stack, CEO
Lee Belitsky, CFO
Lauren Hobart, Director
William Colombo, Director
Paul Gaffney, Executive VP
Holly Tyson, Other Executive Officer
John Hayes, Senior VP

GROWTH PLANS/SPECIAL FEATURES:

Dick's Sporting Goods, Inc. (DSG) is a retail sporting goods chain that operates 728 Dick's Sporting Goods stores throughout the U.S., as well as Golf Galaxy, Field & Stream and Public Lands specialty stores and related ecommerce platforms. DSG also owns and operates the GameChanger youth sports mobile app for video streaming, scorekeeping, scheduling and communications. The company offers a broad assortment of sporting goods equipment, footwear and apparel under national and private-label brands Asics, Brooks, Callaway Golf, Columbia, Easton, Nike, Patagonia, TaylorMade, The North Face, Titleist, Under Armour and Yeti. DSG also offers a wide variety of its own brands sold exclusively at Dick's Sporting Goods stores, including Alpine Design, CALIA, DSG, ETHOS, Field & Stream, Fitness Gear, Lady Hagen, MAXFLI, Nishiki, Quest, Tommy Armour, Top-Flite, VRST and Walter Hagen. Licensed brands from third parties include adidas (baseball and football), Slazenger (golf) and Prince (tennis). Each of the Dick's Sporting Goods location typically contains specialty divisions, such as footwear, team sports, outdoor lodge, golf, fitness and athletic apparel. In addition to apparel and equipment sales, DSG stores offer a variety of services such as golf club fitting, repair and grip replacement; tennis and lacrosse racket stringing; ice skate sharpening; bicycle repair and servicing; scope mounting and bore sighting; and CO2 tank filling for paintball. Subsidiary Golf Galaxy LLC, which operates the Golf Galaxy stores designed for serious golf enthusiasts and include artificial bent grass putting greens, golf simulators and private lessons. Field & Stream and Public Lands retail concepts offer specialized outdoor merchandise. In addition to its retail locations, the firm maintains catalog and ecommerce sites for its branded chains.

FINANCIAL DATA: *Note: Data for latest year may not have been available at press time.*

In U.S. $	2020	2019	2018	2017	2016	2015
Revenue	8,750,743,000	8,436,570,000	8,590,472,000	7,921,981,000	7,270,965,000	
R&D Expense						
Operating Income	375,613,000	444,733,000	477,574,000	449,854,000	535,192,000	
Operating Margin %	.04%	.05%	.06%	.06%	.07%	
SGA Expense	2,173,677,000	1,986,576,000	1,982,363,000	1,875,643,000	1,613,075,000	
Net Income	297,462,000	319,864,000	323,445,000	287,396,000	330,391,000	
Operating Cash Flow	404,612,000	712,755,000	746,310,000	758,983,000	643,514,000	
Capital Expenditure	217,461,000	198,219,000	474,347,000	421,920,000	370,028,000	
EBITDA	695,164,000	685,998,000	747,035,000	698,112,000	728,481,000	
Return on Assets %	.06%	.08%	.08%	.08%	.09%	
Return on Equity %	.16%	.17%	.17%	.15%	.18%	
Debt to Equity	1.546	0.029	0.031	0.002	0.003	

CONTACT INFORMATION:

Phone: 724 273-3400   Fax:
Toll-Free: 877-846-9997
Address: 345 Court St., Coraopolis, PA 15108 United States

STOCK TICKER/OTHER:

Stock Ticker: DKS   Exchange: NYS
Employees: 41,600   Fiscal Year Ends: 02/02
Parent Company:

SALARIES/BONUSES:

Top Exec. Salary: $ Bonus: $
Second Exec. Salary: $ Bonus: $

OTHER THOUGHTS:

Estimated Female Officers or Directors: 4
Hot Spot for Advancement for Women/Minorities: Y.

Diodes Incorporated
NAIC Code: 334413

www.diodes.com

TYPES OF BUSINESS:
Semiconductor Manufacturing
Semiconductor Design
Semiconductor Marketing

BRANDS/DIVISIONS/AFFILIATES:
Diodes FabTech Inc
Shanghai Kaihong Technology Electronic Co Ltd
Diodes Hong Kong Holding Company Limited
Lite-On Semiconductor Corporation

CONTACTS: *Note: Officers with more than one job title may be intentionally listed here more than once.*
Keh-Shew Lu, CEO
Brett Whitmire, CFO
Raymond Soong, Chairman of the Board
Richard White, Secretary
C.H. Chen, Vice Chairman of the Board
Francis Tang, Vice President, Divisional
Emily Yang, Vice President, Divisional
Evan Yu, Vice President, Divisional
Julie Holland, Vice President, Divisional

GROWTH PLANS/SPECIAL FEATURES:
Diodes Incorporated designs, manufactures and markets discrete and analogue semiconductor products. The semiconductors are found in a variety of end-user products in the consumer electronics, computing, industrial, communications and automotive sectors. Diodes' product line includes more than 25,000 offerings such as diodes, rectifiers, transistors, metal oxide semiconductor field-effect transistors (MOSFETs), protection devices and functional specific arrays. The company also produces amplifiers and comparators, Hall effect and temperature sensors, power management devices (including light emitting diode drivers), DC-DC switching and linear voltage regulators, voltage references, special function devices (including USB power switch, load switch, voltage supervisor and motor controllers) and silicon wafers used to manufacture these products. Corporate headquarters are located in Plano, Texas, USA, with sales and marketing offices in Taiwan, China, South Korea, Germany, the U.K. and Japan. The firm conducts a number of operations through its subsidiaries, including Diodes FabTech, Inc., which is responsible for wafer fabrication, research and development, engineering and sales; Shanghai Kaihong Technology Electronic Co. Ltd., which also handles packaging, assembly, testing, research and development and engineering; and Diodes Hong Kong Holding Company Limited, which contains a logistical center and handles sales and marketing. Diodes serves approximately 240 direct customers worldwide, including original equipment manufacturers and electronic manufacturing services providers. The firm also has over 80 distributor customers around the world, through which it indirectly serves tens of thousands of customers. In November 2020, Diodes Incorporated completed its acquisition of Lite-On Semiconductor Corporation, broadening Diodes' discrete product offerings, including glass-passivated bridges and rectifiers for the automotive and industrial markets.

FINANCIAL DATA: *Note: Data for latest year may not have been available at press time.*

In U.S. $	2020	2019	2018	2017	2016	2015
Revenue	1,229,215,000	1,249,130,000	1,213,989,000	1,054,204,000	942,162,000	848,904,000
R&D Expense	94,288,000	88,517,000	86,286,000	77,877,000	69,937,000	57,027,000
Operating Income	134,438,000	176,179,000	155,078,000	92,708,000	38,056,000	43,715,000
Operating Margin %		.14%	.13%	.09%	.04%	.05%
SGA Expense	185,067,000	181,343,000	176,197,000	167,639,000	158,256,000	139,245,000
Net Income	98,088,000	153,250,000	104,021,000	-1,805,000	15,935,000	24,274,000
Operating Cash Flow	187,220,000	229,772,000	185,566,000	181,123,000	124,742,000	118,111,000
Capital Expenditure	75,813,000	98,505,000	87,507,000	111,161,000	58,549,000	133,244,000
EBITDA	240,010,000	315,723,000	264,507,000	171,720,000	137,257,000	124,927,000
Return on Assets %		.10%	.07%	.00%	.01%	.02%
Return on Equity %		.15%	.12%	.00%	.02%	.03%
Debt to Equity		0.083	0.20	0.298	0.532	0.573

CONTACT INFORMATION:
Phone: 972 987-3900   Fax: 972 731-3510
Toll-Free:
Address: 4949 Hedgcoxe Rd., Ste. 200, Plano, TX 75024 United States

STOCK TICKER/OTHER:
Stock Ticker: DIOD
Employees: 7,271
Parent Company:

Exchange: NAS
Fiscal Year Ends: 12/31

SALARIES/BONUSES:
Top Exec. Salary: $ Bonus: $
Second Exec. Salary: $ Bonus: $

OTHER THOUGHTS:
Estimated Female Officers or Directors: 1
Hot Spot for Advancement for Women/Minorities:

Discount Tire Company

www.discounttire.com

NAIC Code: 441320

TYPES OF BUSINESS:

Tire Stores
Mail-Order & Online Tire Sales
Roadside Assistance
Tire Dealer
Tire Retail Stores
Tire Repair Services
Financing

BRANDS/DIVISIONS/AFFILIATES:

Reinalt-Thomas Corporation
Discount Tire
Americas Tire Co
Discount Tire Credit Card

CONTACTS: *Note: Officers with more than one job title may be intentionally listed here more than once.*

Dean Muglia, CEO
Christian Roe, CFO

GROWTH PLANS/SPECIAL FEATURES:

Discount Tire Company, based in Arizona, is one of the largest independent tire dealers in the U.S. The firm operates over 1,065 stores in 36 states (as of May 2020). These stores primarily operate under the Discount Tire name, but also as America's Tire Co. in certain parts of California. Discount Tire carries leading tire brands such as BF Goodrich, Michelin, Goodyear, Pirelli and GT Radial as well as in-house exclusive brands Road Hugger, Arizonian, MB Wheels and Maxxim tires and wheels. Types of tires offered by the company are lawn/garden, ATV/UTV, trailer, temporary spares, winter, performance truck, ribbed, highway all-season, mud-terrain, all-terrain, all-purpose, track and competition, summer performance, all-season performance, grand touring and the standard all-season touring. The company also repairs tires, offers tire rotations and balancing and provides free air pressure checking to its customers. In addition, the firm sells and delivers tires through its mail-order/online division (Discount Tire direct), which provides fast free shipping to a customer's door as well as through its website. This website also provides extensive information for its customers on all aspects of wheel and tire care. The company offers a Discount Tire Credit Card, which can be applied for online and is underwritten by Synchrony Bank. In early-2020, Discount Tire entered the northeast market with a location in Pittsburgh, Pennsylvania.

Discount Tires offers its employees comprehensive health benefits, retirement plans and a variety of employee assistance programs.

FINANCIAL DATA: *Note: Data for latest year may not have been available at press time.*

In U.S. $	2020	2019	2018	2017	2016	2015
Revenue	4,608,000,000	4,800,000,000	4,784,850,000	4,557,000,000	4,340,000,000	4,200,000,000
R&D Expense						
Operating Income						
Operating Margin %						
SGA Expense						
Net Income						
Operating Cash Flow						
Capital Expenditure						
EBITDA						
Return on Assets %						
Return on Equity %						
Debt to Equity						

CONTACT INFORMATION:

Phone: 480-606-6000   Fax: 480-951-8619
Toll-Free:
Address: 20225 N. Scottsdale Rd., Scottsdale, AZ 85254 United States

STOCK TICKER/OTHER:

Stock Ticker: Private   Exchange:
Employees: 22,500   Fiscal Year Ends: 12/31
Parent Company: Reinalt-Thomas Corporation

SALARIES/BONUSES:

Top Exec. Salary: $ Bonus: $
Second Exec. Salary: $ Bonus: $

OTHER THOUGHTS:

Estimated Female Officers or Directors:
Hot Spot for Advancement for Women/Minorities:

Discovery Inc
NAIC Code: 515210

corporate.discovery.com

TYPES OF BUSINESS:

Cable TV Networks
Digital Media
Catalog & Online Sales
Educational Products
E-commerce
Merchandising

BRANDS/DIVISIONS/AFFILIATES:

Discovery Channel
HGTV
Food Network
TLC
Investigation Discovery
Travel Channel
Discovery Kids
Eurosport

CONTACTS: *Note: Officers with more than one job title may be intentionally listed here more than once.*

Peter Faricy, CEO, Divisional
Jean-Briac Perrette, CEO, Divisional
David Zaslav, CEO
Gunnar Wiedenfels, CFO
Robert Miron, Chairman of the Board
Lori Locke, Chief Accounting Officer
Kurt Wehner, Chief Accounting Officer
Bruce Campbell, Chief Legal Officer
Savalle Sims, Executive VP
Adria Romm, Other Corporate Officer
David Leavy, Other Executive Officer

GROWTH PLANS/SPECIAL FEATURES:

Discovery, Inc. is a global media company that provides content across multiple distribution platforms. These platforms include linear such as pay-television (payTV), free-to-air and broadcast television, authenticated GO applications, digital distribution arrangements and content licensing agreements. Discovery also operates a portfolio of digital direct-to-consumer products and production studios. The company operates through three business segments: U.S. networks, consisting primarily of domestic television networks and digital content services; international networks, consisting principally of international television networks and digital content services; and other, consisting of a production studio. Discovery delivers over 8,000 hours of original programming each year across its content genres. Its platform is available in 220 countries and territories and 50 languages. Discovery's portfolio of brands includes Discovery Channel, HGTV, Food Network, TLC, Investigation Discovery, Travel Chanel, MotorTrend, Turbo Discovery, Animal Planet and Science Channel, as well as OWN: Oprah Winfrey Network in the U.S.; Discovery Kids in Latin America; and Eurosport across Europe.

FINANCIAL DATA: *Note: Data for latest year may not have been available at press time.*

In U.S. $	2020	2019	2018	2017	2016	2015
Revenue	10,671,000,000	11,144,000,000	10,553,000,000	6,873,000,000	6,497,000,000	6,394,000,000
R&D Expense						
Operating Income	2,730,000,000	3,190,000,000	2,600,000,000	2,119,000,000	2,053,000,000	2,052,000,000
Operating Margin %		.29%	.25%	.31%	.32%	.32%
SGA Expense	2,722,000,000	2,788,000,000	2,620,000,000	1,768,000,000	1,690,000,000	1,669,000,000
Net Income	1,219,000,000	2,069,000,000	594,000,000	-337,000,000	1,194,000,000	1,034,000,000
Operating Cash Flow	2,739,000,000	3,399,000,000	2,576,000,000	1,629,000,000	1,373,000,000	1,277,000,000
Capital Expenditure	402,000,000	289,000,000	147,000,000	135,000,000	88,000,000	103,000,000
EBITDA	6,691,000,000	7,171,000,000	6,437,000,000	2,578,000,000	4,119,000,000	3,928,000,000
Return on Assets %		.05%	.02%	- .02%	.08%	.06%
Return on Equity %		.17%	.07%	- .07%	.22%	.19%
Debt to Equity		1.497	1.811	3.201	1.518	1.398

CONTACT INFORMATION:

Phone: 240 662-2000   Fax: 240 662-1868
Toll-Free:
Address: 8403 Colesville Rd., Silver Spring, MD 20910 United States

STOCK TICKER/OTHER:

Stock Ticker: DISCA
Employees: 9,200
Parent Company:

Exchange: NAS
Fiscal Year Ends: 12/31

SALARIES/BONUSES:

Top Exec. Salary: $ Bonus: $
Second Exec. Salary: $ Bonus: $

OTHER THOUGHTS:

Estimated Female Officers or Directors: 1
Hot Spot for Advancement for Women/Minorities: Y

DocuSign Inc

NAIC Code: 511210Q

TYPES OF BUSINESS:

Online Signature Management Software
Cloud
Electronic Signature

BRANDS/DIVISIONS/AFFILIATES:

DocuSign Agreement Cloud
DocuSign eSignature
Seal Software Group Limited
Liveoak Technololgies Inc

CONTACTS: *Note: Officers with more than one job title may be intentionally listed here more than once.*

Daniel Springer, CEO
Michael Sheridan, CFO
Mary Agnes Wilderotter, Chairman of the Board
Kirsten Wolberg, Chief Technology Officer
Scott Olrich, Co-COO
Loren Alhadeff, Other Executive Officer

GROWTH PLANS/SPECIAL FEATURES:

DocuSign, Inc. provides a cloud-based electronic signature platform that helps organizations, businesses, enterprises and individuals of all sizes collect information, automate data workflows and sign on various devices. Its platform automates manual and paper-based processes that allow users to manage documented business transactions, including identity management, authentication, digital signature, forms/data collection, collaboration and workflow automation and storage. The DocuSign Agreement Cloud is a category of software designed to safely and securely manage document-based transactions digitally, and removes friction inherent in processes that involve people, documents and data inside and beyond the firewall. Its DocuSign eSignature application programming interface (API) enables the sending of electronic signature requests and the eSign of documents via mobile app. It also tracks documents in real-time. These electronic processes create faster, easier and secure transactions. DocuSign provides training and support services. More than 500,000 companies and hundreds of million users worldwide utilize DocuSign. In 2020, 82% of all successful transactions on DocuSign's eSignature platform were completed in less than 24 hours and 50% within 15 minutes. DocuSign offers transaction management services and is the National Association of REALTORS Official and Exclusive provider of electronic signature services under the REALTOR Benefits Program. DocuSign has domestic offices throughout the U.S. and international offices in Canada, the U.K., France, Germany, Ireland, Israel, Australia, Singapore, Japan and Brazil. During 2020, DocuSign acquired Seal Software Group Limited, and acquired Liveoak Technologies, Inc.

FINANCIAL DATA: *Note: Data for latest year may not have been available at press time.*

In U.S. $	2020	2019	2018	2017	2016	2015
Revenue	973,971,000	700,969,000	518,504,000	381,459,000	250,481,000	
R&D Expense	185,552,000	185,968,000	92,428,000	89,652,000	62,255,000	
Operating Income	-193,509,000	-426,323,000	-51,653,000	-115,817,000	-119,304,000	
Operating Margin %	- .20%	- .61%	- .10%	- .30%	- .48%	
SGA Expense	738,694,000	748,903,000	359,456,000	305,147,000	233,675,000	
Net Income	-208,359,000	-426,458,000	-52,276,000	-115,412,000	-122,559,000	
Operating Cash Flow	115,696,000	76,086,000	54,979,000	-4,790,000	-67,995,000	
Capital Expenditure	72,046,000	30,413,000	18,929,000	43,330,000	28,305,000	
EBITDA	-126,098,000	-379,337,000	-16,798,000	-85,976,000	-101,684,000	
Return on Assets %	- .12%	- .38%	- .09%	- .24%	- .25%	
Return on Equity %	- .36%	-1.04%				
Debt to Equity	1.149	0.714				

CONTACT INFORMATION:

Phone: 866-219-4318   Fax:
Toll-Free:
Address: 221 Main St., Ste. 1550, San Francisco, CA 94105 United States

STOCK TICKER/OTHER:

Stock Ticker: DOCU
Employees: 5,630
Parent Company:

Exchange: NAS
Fiscal Year Ends: 01/31

SALARIES/BONUSES:

Top Exec. Salary: $ Bonus: $
Second Exec. Salary: $ Bonus: $

OTHER THOUGHTS:

Estimated Female Officers or Directors:
Hot Spot for Advancement for Women/Minorities:

Dollar General Corporation

www.dollargeneral.com

NAIC Code: 452112

TYPES OF BUSINESS:

Discount Stores

BRANDS/DIVISIONS/AFFILIATES:

Dollar General
Clover Valley
DG
Forever Pals
OT Sport
Sweet Smiles
Open Trails
Dollar General Literacy Foundation

CONTACTS: Note: Officers with more than one job title may be intentionally listed here more than once.

Todd Vasos, CEO
John Garratt, CFO
Anita Elliott, Chief Accounting Officer
Carman Wenkoff, Chief Information Officer
Michael Calbert, Director
Jeffery Owen, Executive VP, Divisional
Jason Reiser, Executive VP
Rhonda Taylor, General Counsel
Michael Kindy, Senior VP, Divisional

GROWTH PLANS/SPECIAL FEATURES:

Dollar General Corporation operates more than 16,300 discount retail stores in 45 states, primarily in the southern, southwestern, midwestern and eastern United States. The firm runs conveniently sized stores offering a broad range of merchandise at low prices, including consumables, seasonal, home products and apparel. Dollar General focuses on low- and fixed-income customers providing basic packaged and refrigerated food and dairy products, cleaning supplies, paper products, health and beauty care items, greeting cards, basic apparel, housewares, hardware and automotive supplies. Consumables make up 78% of annual items sold, with seasonal items deriving 11.7%, home products deriving 5.8% and apparel deriving 4.5%. The typical Dollar General store averages 7,400 square feet of selling space, and approximately 75% of its stores are in towns of 20,000 or fewer people. The company has 16 distribution facilities. Trademarks owned by Dollar General include Dollar General, Dollar General Market, Clover Valley, DG, DG Deals, Forever Pals, I-Magine, OT Sport, OT Revolutions, Smart & Simple, trueliving, Sweet Smiles, Open Trails and many more. The firm is affiliated with Dollar General Literacy Foundation, which is committed to helping adults and youth achieve educational goals. In 2020, Dollar General announced it was opening a new brand of stores called Popshelf that will sell items such as beauty treatments, home decor and party supplies, mostly proced at under $5; opened its first store in Washington state; and announced plans to build a new distribution center in Blair, Nebraska.

The firm offers employees a 401(k) plan; a retirement plan; medical, dental, vision and prescription plans; flexible spending accounts; short- and long-term disability; wellness programs; business travel accident insurance; and rewards programs.

FINANCIAL DATA: Note: Data for latest year may not have been available at press time.

In U.S. $	2020	2019	2018	2017	2016	2015
Revenue	27,753,970,000	25,625,040,000	23,470,970,000	21,986,600,000	20,368,560,000	
R&D Expense						
Operating Income	2,302,304,000	2,116,306,000	2,007,818,000	2,063,449,000	1,940,294,000	
Operating Margin %	.08%	.08%	.09%	.09%	.10%	
SGA Expense	6,186,757,000	5,687,564,000	5,213,541,000	4,719,189,000	4,365,797,000	
Net Income	1,712,555,000	1,589,472,000	1,538,960,000	1,251,133,000	1,165,080,000	
Operating Cash Flow	2,237,998,000	2,143,550,000	1,802,108,000	1,605,041,000	1,377,988,000	
Capital Expenditure	784,843,000	734,380,000	646,456,000	560,296,000	504,806,000	
EBITDA	2,807,108,000	2,569,421,000	2,408,547,000	2,443,380,000	2,292,399,000	
Return on Assets %	.10%	.12%	.13%	.11%	.10%	
Return on Equity %	.26%	.25%	.27%	.23%	.21%	
Debt to Equity	1.601	0.446	0.425	0.501	0.552	

CONTACT INFORMATION:

Phone: 615 855-4000   Fax: 615 855-5527
Toll-Free:
Address: 100 Mission Ridge, Goodlettsville, TN 37072 United States

STOCK TICKER/OTHER:

Stock Ticker: DG
Employees: 158,000
Parent Company:

Exchange: NYS
Fiscal Year Ends: 01/31

SALARIES/BONUSES:

Top Exec. Salary: $ Bonus: $
Second Exec. Salary: $ Bonus: $

OTHER THOUGHTS:

Estimated Female Officers or Directors: 4
Hot Spot for Advancement for Women/Minorities: Y

Dollar Tree Inc

NAIC Code: 452112

TYPES OF BUSINESS:

Discount Stores
Dollar Stores

BRANDS/DIVISIONS/AFFILIATES:

Dollar Tree
Family Dollar
Dollar Tree Canada

CONTACTS: Note: Officers with more than one job title may be intentionally listed here more than once.

Kevin Wampler, CFO
Gary Philbin, Pres.
Kathleen Mallas, Chief Accounting Officer
Joshua Jewett, Chief Information Officer
William Old, Chief Legal Officer
David Jacobs, Chief Strategy Officer
Thomas OBoyle, COO, Subsidiary
Michael Witynski, COO, Subsidiary
Bob Sasser, Director
Robert Rudman, Other Executive Officer
Gary Maxwell, Other Executive Officer
Betty Click, Other Executive Officer
Duncan Naughton, President, Subsidiary

GROWTH PLANS/SPECIAL FEATURES:

Dollar Tree, Inc. operates 15,288 discount variety retail stores located across 48 U.S. states, the District of Columbia and five Canadian provinces. Types of merchandise sold at the company's stores include consumables, home products (decor, blankets, sheets, towels), apparel, shoes, stationery, school supplies, toys, seasonal items, food, tobacco, health and beauty aids and electronics. The firm's stores operate under the names Dollar Tree, Family Dollar and Dollar Tree Canada. Dollar Tree is a leading operator of discount variety stores that offer merchandise at the fixed price point of $1.00. Stores range from 8,000 to 10,000 square feet in size and carry approximately 7,700 items. This division is comprised of 13 distribution centers in the U.S. and two in Canada, as well as a store support center in Chesapeake, Virginia. Dollar Tree buys approximately 58-60% of its merchandise domestically and imports the rest. Domestic purchases include basic seasonal, home, closeouts and promotional merchandise. Family Dollar operates approximately 7,783 general merchandise discount retail stores that provide consumers a selection of competitively priced merchandise. Stores range from 6,000 to 8,000 square feet of selling space and carry basic items alongside items that are ever-changing and seasonally relevant. Family Dollar purchases approximately 14% of its merchandise through its partnership with McLane Company, Inc.; and approximately 17% of its merchandise is imported. This division is comprised of 11 distribution centers and a store support center in Matthews, North Carolina.

The firm offers employees medical, dental and vision insurance; disability coverage; life insurance; health and dependent care reimbursement accounts; a 401(k) plan; and an employee stock purchase plan.

FINANCIAL DATA: Note: Data for latest year may not have been available at press time.

In U.S. $	2020	2019	2018	2017	2016	2015
Revenue	23,610,800,000	22,823,300,000	22,245,500,000	20,719,200,000	15,498,400,000	
R&D Expense						
Operating Income	1,575,200,000	1,787,500,000	2,017,600,000	1,704,800,000	1,049,700,000	
Operating Margin %	.07%	.08%	.09%	.08%	.07%	
SGA Expense	5,465,500,000	5,160,000,000	5,004,300,000	4,689,900,000	3,607,000,000	
Net Income	827,000,000	-1,590,800,000	1,714,300,000	896,200,000	282,400,000	
Operating Cash Flow	1,869,800,000	1,766,000,000	1,510,200,000	1,673,300,000	780,900,000	
Capital Expenditure	1,036,700,000	817,100,000	632,200,000	565,600,000	480,500,000	
EBITDA	1,906,200,000	-317,900,000	2,617,000,000	2,342,400,000	1,535,200,000	
Return on Assets %	.05%	-.11%	.11%	.06%	.03%	
Return on Equity %	.14%	-.25%	.27%	.18%	.09%	
Debt to Equity	1.408	0.756	0.663	1.145	1.643	

CONTACT INFORMATION:

Phone: 757 321-5000   Fax: 757 857-6848
Toll-Free: 877-530-8733
Address: 500 Volvo Pkwy., Chesapeake, VA 23320 United States

STOCK TICKER/OTHER:

Stock Ticker: DLTR
Employees: 199,327
Parent Company:

Exchange: NAS
Fiscal Year Ends: 01/31

SALARIES/BONUSES:

Top Exec. Salary: $ Bonus: $
Second Exec. Salary: $ Bonus: $

OTHER THOUGHTS:

Estimated Female Officers or Directors: 1
Hot Spot for Advancement for Women/Minorities:

Dominion Energy Inc

www.dom.com

NAIC Code: 221112

TYPES OF BUSINESS:

Utilities-Electricity & Natural Gas
Energy Production
Renewable Energy
Nuclear Energy
Electricity
Natural Gas

BRANDS/DIVISIONS/AFFILIATES:

GROWTH PLANS/SPECIAL FEATURES:

Dominion Energy, Inc. provides energy to more than 7 million customers across 20 U.S. states. The firm produces energy, including nuclear, solar, coal, natural gas and hydroelectric; and delivers electricity and natural gas through electricity lines and natural gas pipelines to its utility and retail energy customers. Dominion Energy comprises a 6,700-mile network of regulated electric transmission lines and 58,510 miles of distribution lines. In November 2020, Dominion Energy sold its gas transmission and storage assets to an affiliate of Berkshire Hathaway, Inc.; and expected to complete the sale of Questar Pipelines to Berkshire Hathaway in early 2021.

CONTACTS: Note: Officers with more than one job title may be intentionally listed here more than once.

Paul Koonce, CEO, Divisional
Robert Blue, CEO, Subsidiary
Diane Leopold, CEO, Subsidiary
Thomas Farrell, CEO
Mark Mcgettrick, CFO
Michele Cardiff, Chief Accounting Officer
David Christian, Executive VP
Mark Webb, Other Executive Officer

FINANCIAL DATA: Note: Data for latest year may not have been available at press time.

In U.S. $	2020	2019	2018	2017	2016	2015
Revenue	14,172,000,000	16,572,000,000	13,366,000,000	12,586,000,000	11,737,000,000	11,683,000,000
R&D Expense						
Operating Income	4,099,000,000	3,887,000,000	3,624,000,000	4,130,000,000	3,627,000,000	3,536,000,000
Operating Margin %		.23%	.27%	.33%	.31%	.30%
SGA Expense						
Net Income	-401,000,000	1,358,000,000	2,447,000,000	2,999,000,000	2,123,000,000	1,899,000,000
Operating Cash Flow	5,227,000,000	5,204,000,000	4,773,000,000	4,549,000,000	4,127,000,000	4,475,000,000
Capital Expenditure	6,020,000,000	4,980,000,000	4,254,000,000	5,504,000,000	6,085,000,000	5,575,000,000
EBITDA	5,624,000,000	6,477,000,000	6,902,000,000	6,497,000,000	5,726,000,000	5,401,000,000
Return on Assets %		.01%	.03%	.04%	.03%	.03%
Return on Equity %		.05%	.13%	.19%	.16%	.16%
Debt to Equity		1.142	1.549	1.805	2.07	1.865

CONTACT INFORMATION:

Phone: 804 819-2000   Fax: 804 775-5819
Toll-Free:
Address: 120 Tredegar St., Richmond, VA 23219 United States

STOCK TICKER/OTHER:

Stock Ticker: D
Employees: 17,300
Parent Company:

Exchange: NYS
Fiscal Year Ends: 12/31

SALARIES/BONUSES:

Top Exec. Salary: $ Bonus: $
Second Exec. Salary: $ Bonus: $

OTHER THOUGHTS:

Estimated Female Officers or Directors: 4
Hot Spot for Advancement for Women/Minorities: Y

Dominos Pizza Inc

NAIC Code: 722513

TYPES OF BUSINESS:

Pizza Delivery Shops
Restaurant
Franchise
Pizza
Retail
Manufacturing
Distribution

BRANDS/DIVISIONS/AFFILIATES:

CONTACTS: *Note: Officers with more than one job title may be intentionally listed here more than once.*

Jeffrey Lawrence, CFO
David Brandon, Chairman of the Board
J. Vasconi, Chief Information Officer
Richard Allison, Director
Scott Hinshaw, Executive VP, Divisional
Timothy McIntyre, Executive VP, Divisional
Joseph Jordan, Executive VP, Divisional
Stuart Levy, Executive VP, Divisional
Thomas Curtis, Executive VP, Geographical
Kevin Morris, Executive VP
Russell Weiner, President, Geographical

GROWTH PLANS/SPECIAL FEATURES:

Domino's Pizza, Inc. is an international pizza restaurant chain and delivery company, with more than 17,600 locations in 90 worldwide markets (as of January 3, 2021). The firm's business model features a delivery-oriented store design with low capital requirements, a focused menu of pizza and complementary side items, committed owner-operator franchisees and a vertically-integrated distribution system. Its earnings are driven largely from retail sales at its franchise stores, which generate royalty payments and distribution revenues to the company. Domino's also generates earnings through retail sales at its company-owned stores. The firm operates its business in three segments: domestic stores, supply chain and international franchise. The domestic stores segment consists of operations through which the company oversees a network of more than 5,992 stores in the U.S., most of which are franchises and 363 company-owned. This segment accounts for approximately 35% of consolidated revenues. The supply chain segment operates 21 regional dough manufacturing and food distribution centers in the U.S., and also operates a thin crust manufacturing center, a vegetable processing center and a center providing equipment and supplies to certain domestic and international stores. In Canada, this division operates five dough manufacturing and food supply chain centers. The international franchise segment is comprised of a network of nearly 11,300 franchised stores in international markets. The principal sources of revenue from this division are derived from royalty payments generated by retail sales from franchised stores.

FINANCIAL DATA: *Note: Data for latest year may not have been available at press time.*

In U.S. $	2020	2019	2018	2017	2016	2015
Revenue	4,117,411,000	3,618,774,000	3,432,867,000	2,787,979,000	2,472,628,000	2,216,528,000
R&D Expense						
Operating Income	725,642,000	629,407,000	571,689,000	521,232,000	454,042,000	405,439,000
Operating Margin %		.17%	.17%	.19%	.18%	.18%
SGA Expense	868,851,000	773,092,000	730,990,000	344,759,000	313,649,000	277,692,000
Net Income	491,296,000	400,709,000	361,972,000	277,905,000	214,678,000	192,789,000
Operating Cash Flow	592,794,000	496,950,000	394,171,000	339,036,000	287,273,000	291,786,000
Capital Expenditure	88,768,000	85,565,000	119,888,000	90,011,000	58,555,000	63,282,000
EBITDA	792,334,000	693,385,000	628,688,000	567,063,000	492,867,000	438,186,000
Return on Assets %		.35%	.42%	.36%	.28%	.27%
Return on Equity %						
Debt to Equity						

CONTACT INFORMATION:

Phone: 734 930-3030   Fax: 734 747-6210
Toll-Free:
Address: 30 Frank Lloyd Wright Dr., Ann Arbor, MI 48106 United States

STOCK TICKER/OTHER:

Stock Ticker: DPZ   Exchange: NYS
Employees: 14,400   Fiscal Year Ends: 12/31
Parent Company:

SALARIES/BONUSES:

Top Exec. Salary: $ Bonus: $
Second Exec. Salary: $ Bonus: $

OTHER THOUGHTS:

Estimated Female Officers or Directors:
Hot Spot for Advancement for Women/Minorities:

DoorDash Inc

www.doordash.com

NAIC Code: 492210

TYPES OF BUSINESS:

Online Restaurant Meals Delivery Services

BRANDS/DIVISIONS/AFFILIATES:

Caviar Inc

CONTACTS: *Note: Officers with more than one job title may be intentionally listed here more than once.*

Tony Xu, CEO
Chris Payne, COO
Stanley Tang, Co-Founder
Andy Fang, Founder

GROWTH PLANS/SPECIAL FEATURES:

DoorDash, Inc. provides on-demand delivery service. The San Francisco-based company's mission is to empower small business owners to offer delivery service in an affordable and convenient way. Customers can purchase goods from local restaurant and convenient store merchants via the DoorDash app or website and have them delivered in less than 45 minutes. Dashers (delivery persons) are background checked, provided basic Dashing training and gear when hired, and must have a smart phone. They are paid directly through the app. DoorDash is available in over 500 cities throughout North America. Investors of the firm include Sequoia, CRV, Kleiner Perkins Caufield Byers, Khosla Ventures, SV Angel and Y. Some of the over 300,000 restaurants that have partnered with DoorDash are Grimaldi's Pizzeria, Jason's Deli, Landry's Restaurants, Saltgrass Steak House, P.F. Changs, Whole Foods Market and California Pizza Kitchen.

The company offers its employees health, dental and vision coverage; unlimited PTO; flexible hours; meal and delivery perks; and gym membership stipends.

FINANCIAL DATA: *Note: Data for latest year may not have been available at press time.*

In U.S. $	2020	2019	2018	2017	2016	2015
Revenue	2,886,000,000	885,000,000	291,000,000			
R&D Expense	321,000,000	107,000,000	51,000,000			
Operating Income	-436,000,000	-616,000,000	-210,000,000			
Operating Margin %						
SGA Expense	1,513,000,000	839,000,000	213,000,000			
Net Income	-461,000,000	-667,000,000	-204,000,000			
Operating Cash Flow	252,000,000	-467,000,000	-159,000,000			
Capital Expenditure	159,000,000	92,000,000	16,000,000			
EBITDA	-306,000,000	-634,000,000	-194,000,000			
Return on Assets %						
Return on Equity %						
Debt to Equity						

CONTACT INFORMATION:

Phone: 650 487-3970   Fax:
Toll-Free: 844-285-0248
Address: 303 2nd St., S. Tower, Fl. 8, San Francisco, CA 94107 United States

STOCK TICKER/OTHER:

Stock Ticker: DASH
Employees: 3,886
Parent Company:

Exchange: NYS
Fiscal Year Ends:

SALARIES/BONUSES:

Top Exec. Salary: $ Bonus: $
Second Exec. Salary: $ Bonus: $

OTHER THOUGHTS:

Estimated Female Officers or Directors:
Hot Spot for Advancement for Women/Minorities:

Sales, profits and employees may be estimates. Financial information, benefits and other data can change quickly and may vary from those stated here.

Dow Inc

NAIC Code: 325199

www.dow.com/en-us.html

TYPES OF BUSINESS:

Specialty Chemicals Manufacturer
Manufacturing
Coatings & Infrastructure
Packaging Products
Industrial Intermediates
Performance Materials
Innovation

BRANDS/DIVISIONS/AFFILIATES:

CONTACTS: Note: Officers with more than one job title may be intentionally listed here more than once.

Jim Fitterling, CEO
Howard Ungerleider, Pres.
Karen S. Carter, Chief Human Resources Officer
James Collins, COO, Divisional
Melanie Kalmar, CIO
James Fitterling, COO, Divisional
Charles Kalil, Executive VP, Subsidiary

GROWTH PLANS/SPECIAL FEATURES:

Dow, Inc. is an American materials science company. The company's portfolio of plastics, industrial intermediates, coatings and silicones businesses deliver a broad range of science-based products and solutions for its customers in market segments such as packaging, infrastructure, mobility and consumer care. Dow operates 106 manufacturing sites in 31 countries (as of March 2021). The firm operates through three segments: packaging & specialty plastics, industrial intermediates & infrastructure, and performance materials & coatings. The packaging & specialty plastics segment consists of two integrated businesses: hydrocarbons & energy, and packaging and specialty plastics. Hydrocarbons & energy is a global producer of ethylene, a key chemical used within the packaging and specialty plastics segment; and a producer of propylene and aromatics products that are used to manufacture consumer materials. Packaging and specialty plastics utilizes technology, and existing and pipeline products to create solutions for the packaging value chain. The industrial intermediates & infrastructure segment has two businesses: industrial solutions and polyurethanes & construction chemicals, which develops intermediate chemicals essential to manufacturing processes, as well as downstream, customized materials and formulations that use advanced development technologies. These businesses primarily produce and market ethylene oxide and propylene oxide derivatives aligned to markets such as appliances, coatings, electronics, surfactants, infrastructure and oil and gas. Last, the performance materials & coatings segment consists of franchises that deliver an array of solutions to consumer and infrastructure end-markets. This division primarily utilizes Dow's acrylics, cellulosics and silicone-based technology platforms to serve architectural and industrial coatings; home care and personal care; consumer and electronics; mobility and transportation; industrial and chemical processing; and building and infrastructure end-markets.

FINANCIAL DATA: Note: Data for latest year may not have been available at press time.

In U.S. $	2020	2019	2018	2017	2016	2015
Revenue	38,542,000,000	42,951,000,000	60,278,000,000	43,730,000,000	48,158,000,000	
R&D Expense	768,000,000	765,000,000	1,536,000,000	803,000,000	1,593,000,000	
Operating Income	2,556,000,000	3,520,000,000	7,569,000,000	4,382,000,000	4,287,000,000	
Operating Margin %		.08%	.13%	.10%	.09%	
SGA Expense	1,471,000,000	1,590,000,000	2,846,000,000	1,795,000,000	4,066,000,000	
Net Income	1,225,000,000	-1,359,000,000	4,499,000,000	465,000,000	4,318,000,000	
Operating Cash Flow	6,226,000,000	5,930,000,000	3,894,000,000	-4,929,000,000	-2,957,000,000	
Capital Expenditure	1,387,000,000	1,970,000,000	2,584,000,000	2,994,000,000	3,991,000,000	
EBITDA	5,772,000,000	2,624,000,000	10,365,000,000	3,697,000,000	8,133,000,000	
Return on Assets %		-.02%	.06%	.01%		
Return on Equity %		-.07%	.17%	.02%		
Debt to Equity		1.308	0.718	0.765		

CONTACT INFORMATION:

Phone: 989 636-1000   Fax: 989 636-3518
Toll-Free: 800-422-8193
Address: 2211 H.H. Dow Way, Midland, MI 48674 United States

STOCK TICKER/OTHER:

Stock Ticker: DOW   Exchange: NYS
Employees: 56,000   Fiscal Year Ends: 12/31
Parent Company:

SALARIES/BONUSES:

Top Exec. Salary: $ Bonus: $
Second Exec. Salary: $ Bonus: $

OTHER THOUGHTS:

Estimated Female Officers or Directors: 3
Hot Spot for Advancement for Women/Minorities: Y

DR Horton Inc

www.drhorton.com

NAIC Code: 236117

TYPES OF BUSINESS:

Construction, Home Building and Residential
Mortgages
Title Insurance
Residential Development

BRANDS/DIVISIONS/AFFILIATES:

DHI Mortgage

CONTACTS: Note: Officers with more than one job title may be intentionally listed here more than once.

David Auld, CEO
Bill Wheat, CFO
Donald Horton, Chairman of the Board
Michael Murray, COO
Thomas Montano, Secretary

GROWTH PLANS/SPECIAL FEATURES:

D.R. Horton, Inc. is a leading national builder of single-family homes with a diversified set of holdings and operating divisions in 91 markets across 29 U.S. states. The firm generally builds homes between 1,000 to more than 4,000 square feet, ranging in price from $150,000 to over $1 million. In fiscal (March 31) 2021, the company closed approximately 76,330 homes, with an average closing sales price approximating $308,800. D.R. Horton divides its business into six regional homebuilding segments and one financial services segment. The homebuilding segments are: East, operating in eight states; Midwest, four states; Southeast, five states; South Central, three states; Southwest, two states; and West, six states. This segment constructs residences, tailored to the particular community where they are being built, including single-family residential homes, townhouses, condominiums, duplexes and triplexes. Detached homes sales accounted for 91% of the firm's 2020 revenues. Subcontractors under the supervision of D. R. Horton do substantially all the actual building. The financial services segment of the company provides mortgage financing and title insurance through its wholly-owned subsidiary, DHI Mortgage. D.R. Horton's current business strategy is to enter new lot option contracts to purchase finished lots in selected communities to potentially increase sales volumes and profitability. The firm plans to renegotiate existing lot option contracts as necessary to reduce lot costs and better match the scheduled lot purchases with new home demand in each community. The company also manages inventory of homes under construction by selectively starting construction on unsold homes to capture new home demand while monitoring the number and aging of unsold homes and aggressively marketing its unsold, completed homes in inventory.

FINANCIAL DATA: Note: Data for latest year may not have been available at press time.

In U.S. $	2020	2019	2018	2017	2016	2015
Revenue	20,311,100,000	17,592,900,000	16,068,000,000	14,091,000,000	12,157,400,000	10,824,000,000
R&D Expense						
Operating Income	2,890,100,000	2,039,500,000	1,993,100,000	1,576,600,000	1,334,500,000	1,102,300,000
Operating Margin %		.12%	.12%	.11%	.11%	.10%
SGA Expense	2,047,800,000	1,832,500,000	1,676,800,000	1,471,600,000	1,320,300,000	1,186,000,000
Net Income	2,373,700,000	1,618,500,000	1,460,300,000	1,038,400,000	886,300,000	750,700,000
Operating Cash Flow	1,421,600,000	892,100,000	545,200,000	435,100,000	618,000,000	700,400,000
Capital Expenditure	286,800,000	224,100,000	68,100,000	157,300,000	86,100,000	56,100,000
EBITDA	2,970,500,000	2,111,500,000	2,055,500,000	1,631,300,000	1,395,500,000	1,177,500,000
Return on Assets %		.11%	.11%	.09%	.08%	.07%
Return on Equity %		.17%	.17%	.14%	.14%	.14%
Debt to Equity		0.339	0.357	0.371	0.482	0.647

CONTACT INFORMATION:

Phone: 817-390-8200   Fax: 817 856-8429
Toll-Free:
Address: 1341 Horton Cir., Arlington, TX 76011 United States

STOCK TICKER/OTHER:

Stock Ticker: DHI
Employees: 8,916
Parent Company:

Exchange: NYS
Fiscal Year Ends: 09/30

SALARIES/BONUSES:

Top Exec. Salary: $ Bonus: $
Second Exec. Salary: $ Bonus: $

OTHER THOUGHTS:

Estimated Female Officers or Directors: 1
Hot Spot for Advancement for Women/Minorities:

DTE Energy Company

NAIC Code: 221112

www.dteenergy.com

TYPES OF BUSINESS:

Utilities-Electricity & Natural Gas
Energy Management
Wholesale Energy Trading
Fuel Supply Services
Hydroelectric Power
Nuclear Power
Coal Shipping-Rail & Boat
Consulting Services

BRANDS/DIVISIONS/AFFILIATES:

DTE Electric
DTE Gas

CONTACTS: *Note: Officers with more than one job title may be intentionally listed here more than once.*

Gerard Anderson, CEO
Peter Oleksiak, CFO
Mark Rolling, Chief Accounting Officer
David Meador, Chief Administrative Officer
Mark Stiers, COO, Subsidiary
Trevor Lauer, COO, Subsidiary
Gerardo Norcia, COO
Bruce Peterson, General Counsel
Lisa Muschong, Other Executive Officer
David Ruud, President, Divisional
David Slater, President, Subsidiary

GROWTH PLANS/SPECIAL FEATURES:

DTE Energy Company is a diversified energy and energy technology company that develops merchant power and industrial energy projects and works in energy trading, selling electricity, natural gas, coal, chilled water, landfill gas and steam. DTE is also one of the nation's largest purchasers, transporters and marketers of coal. The company's operations are divided into four segments: electric, gas, non-utility operations and corporate & other. The electric segment consists of DTE Electric, which is engaged in the generation, purchase, distribution and sale of electricity to approximately 2.2 million residential, commercial and industrial customers in southeastern Michigan. The gas segment is represented by DTE Gas, which buys, stores, transports and distributes natural gas to 1.3 million residential, commercial and industrial customers. The firm's non-utility operations segment include gas storage & pipelines, encompassing DTE's interstate gas transmission pipelines and storage facilities; power and industrial projects, primarily consisting of energy product delivery, coal transportation, as well as marketing and electricity provided by biomass-fueled energy projects; and energy trading, which buys, sells and trades electricity, coal and natural gas, and provides risk management services such as energy marketing and trading operations. The corporate & other segment consists of various holding company activities, certain non-utility debt and energy-related investments. In October 2020, DTE Energy announced plans to spin off its midstream business, which includes its non-utility natural gas pipeline, storage and gathering business. The transaction would transform DTE Energy into a predominantly pure-play regulated electric and natural gas utility. Midstream would become an independent, publicly-traded company.

DTE offers its employees medical, dental and vision coverage; comprehensive wellness programs; a 401(k) plan; flexible spending accounts; an employee assistance program; long-term care insurance; life, disability and AD&D insurance; and flex time.

FINANCIAL DATA: *Note: Data for latest year may not have been available at press time.*

In U.S. $	2020	2019	2018	2017	2016	2015
Revenue	12,177,000,000	12,669,000,000	14,212,000,000	12,607,000,000	10,630,000,000	10,337,000,000
R&D Expense						
Operating Income	2,046,000,000	1,746,000,000	1,649,000,000	1,710,000,000	1,473,000,000	1,345,000,000
Operating Margin %		.14%	.12%	.14%	.14%	.13%
SGA Expense						
Net Income	1,368,000,000	1,169,000,000	1,120,000,000	1,134,000,000	868,000,000	727,000,000
Operating Cash Flow	3,697,000,000	2,649,000,000	2,680,000,000	2,117,000,000	2,084,000,000	1,911,000,000
Capital Expenditure	3,857,000,000	2,997,000,000	2,713,000,000	2,250,000,000	2,045,000,000	2,020,000,000
EBITDA	3,701,000,000	3,228,000,000	2,899,000,000	2,853,000,000	2,553,000,000	2,252,000,000
Return on Assets %		.03%	.03%	.03%	.03%	.03%
Return on Equity %		.11%	.11%	.12%	.10%	.09%
Debt to Equity		1.376	1.185	1.281	1.251	1.007

CONTACT INFORMATION:

Phone: 313 235-4000   Fax: 313 235-6743
Toll-Free: 866-966-5555
Address: 1 Energy Plaza, Detroit, MI 48226 United States

STOCK TICKER/OTHER:

Stock Ticker: DTE   Exchange: NYS
Employees: 10,600   Fiscal Year Ends: 12/31
Parent Company:

SALARIES/BONUSES:

Top Exec. Salary: $ Bonus: $
Second Exec. Salary: $ Bonus: $

OTHER THOUGHTS:

Estimated Female Officers or Directors: 8
Hot Spot for Advancement for Women/Minorities: Y

Duke Energy Corporation

www.duke-energy.com

NAIC Code: 221112

TYPES OF BUSINESS:

Utilities-Electricity & Natural Gas
Merchant Power Generation
Natural Gas Transportation & Storage
Electricity Transmission
Energy Marketing
Real Estate
Telecommunications
Facility & Plant Services

BRANDS/DIVISIONS/AFFILIATES:

Duke Energy Carolinas LLC
Duke Energy Progress LLC
Duke Energy Florida LLC
Duke Energy Indiana LLC
Duke Energy Ohio Inc
Duke-American Transmission Company
Piedmont Natural Gas Company Inc
Duke Energy Kentucky

CONTACTS: *Note: Officers with more than one job title may be intentionally listed here more than once.*

Lynn Good, CEO
Steven Young, CFO
Dwight Jacobs, Chief Accounting Officer
Julie Janson, Chief Legal Officer
Melissa Anderson, Executive VP, Divisional
Douglas Esamann, Executive VP, Divisional
Lloyd Yates, Executive VP, Divisional
Dhiaa Jamil, Executive VP
Franklin Yoho, Executive VP
William Currens, Senior VP, Divisional

GROWTH PLANS/SPECIAL FEATURES:

Duke Energy Corporation is an energy services provider that offers delivery and management of electricity and natural gas throughout the U.S. The company operates in three segments: electric utilities and infrastructure (EUI), gas utilities and infrastructure (GUI), and commercial renewables. EUI conducts operations primarily through the regulated public utilities of Duke Energy Carolinas, LLC; Duke Energy Progress, LLC; Duke Energy Florida, LLC; Duke Energy Indiana, LLC; and Duke Energy Ohio, Inc. This segment provides retail electric service through the generation, transmission, distribution and sale of electricity to approximately 7.8 million customers within the southeast and midwest regions of the U.S. EUI is also a joint owner in certain electric transmission projects; has a 50% ownership interest in Duke-American Transmission Company, a partnership with American Transmission Company, formed to design, build and operate transmission infrastructure; and has a 50% ownership interest in Pioneer Transmission LLC, which builds, owns and operates electric transmission facilities in North America. GUI conducts natural gas operations primarily through the regulated public utilities of Piedmont Natural Gas Company Inc., Duke Energy Ohio and Duke Energy Kentucky. This segment serves 1.6 million residential, commercial, industrial and power generation natural gas customers. GUI also owns, operates and has investments in various pipeline transmission and natural gas storage facilities. The commercial renewables segment primarily acquires, builds, develops, operates and owns wind and solar renewable generation throughout the continental U.S. The portfolio includes nonregulated renewable energy and energy storage businesses. Included within the segment is utility-scale wind and solar generation assets which total 2,282 megawatts (MW) across 19 states from 22 wind farms, 126 solar projects, 11 fuel cell locations and one battery storage facility. In July 2020, Duke and Dominion Energy announced the cancellation of the Atlantic Coast Pipeline due to ongoing delays and increasing cost uncertainty.

FINANCIAL DATA: *Note: Data for latest year may not have been available at press time.*

In U.S. $	2020	2019	2018	2017	2016	2015
Revenue	23,868,000,000	25,079,000,000	24,521,000,000	23,565,000,000	22,743,000,000	23,459,000,000
R&D Expense						
Operating Income	5,527,000,000	5,705,000,000	5,176,000,000	6,035,000,000	5,332,000,000	5,452,000,000
Operating Margin %		.23%	.21%	.26%	.23%	.23%
SGA Expense						
Net Income	1,377,000,000	3,748,000,000	2,666,000,000	3,059,000,000	2,152,000,000	2,816,000,000
Operating Cash Flow	8,856,001,000	8,209,000,000	7,186,000,000	6,634,000,000	6,798,000,000	6,676,000,000
Capital Expenditure	9,907,000,000	11,122,000,000	9,389,000,000	8,052,000,000	7,901,000,000	6,766,000,000
EBITDA	8,487,000,000	11,477,000,000	9,863,000,000	10,298,000,000	9,530,000,000	9,363,000,000
Return on Assets %		.02%	.02%	.02%	.02%	.02%
Return on Equity %		.08%	.06%	.07%	.05%	.07%
Debt to Equity		1.258	1.167	1.175	1.111	0.944

CONTACT INFORMATION:

Phone: 704-382-3853   Fax: 704-382-3814
Toll-Free: 800-873-3853
Address: 550 S. Tryon St., Charlotte, NC 28202 United States

STOCK TICKER/OTHER:

Stock Ticker: DUK
Employees: 28,798
Parent Company:

Exchange: NYS
Fiscal Year Ends: 12/31

SALARIES/BONUSES:

Top Exec. Salary: $ Bonus: $
Second Exec. Salary: $ Bonus: $

OTHER THOUGHTS:

Estimated Female Officers or Directors: 8
Hot Spot for Advancement for Women/Minorities: Y

DUSA Pharmaceuticals Inc

NAIC Code: 325412

www.levulanhcp.com

TYPES OF BUSINESS:
Photodynamic Therapy Products
Dermatology Products

BRANDS/DIVISIONS/AFFILIATES:
Sun Pharmaceutical Industries Ltd
Levulan
Levulan Kerastick
BLU-U

CONTACTS: *Note: Officers with more than one job title may be intentionally listed here more than once.*
Robert F. Doman, Pres.
Stuart Marcus, VP-Scientific Affairs
Nanette W. Mantell, Sec.
Mark Carota, VP-Oper.
Israel Makov, Chmn.-Sun Pharma

GROWTH PLANS/SPECIAL FEATURES:
DUSA Pharmaceuticals, Inc. is a dermatologic pharmaceutical company that develops and markets Levulan photodynamic therapy (PDT) and other products for common skin conditions. The company's marketed products include Levulan Kerastick 20% Topical Solution with PDT and the BLU-U brand light source. The Levulan brand of aminolevulinic acid hydrochloride (HCl) is designed to be utilized when followed by exposure to light, either to treat or to detect a medical condition. The Levulan Kerastick is a single-use, disposable applicator, which follows for uniform application of Levulan topical solution in standardized doses. The Levulan Kerastick 20% topical solution with PDT and the BLU-U light source are used for the treatment of non-hyperkeratotic actinic keratoses, precancerous skin lesions caused by chronic sun exposure of the face or scalp. BLU-U is also used for the treatment of moderate inflammatory acne vulgaris and general dermatological conditions. DUSA is a subsidiary of Sun Pharmaceutical Industries Ltd.

Employee benefits include 401(k); health, dental and vision coverage; life insurance; flexible spending accounts; short- and long-term disability; and tuition reimbursement.

FINANCIAL DATA: *Note: Data for latest year may not have been available at press time.*

In U.S. $	2020	2019	2018	2017	2016	2015
Revenue	104,284,000	94,334,112	87,346,400	137,387,000	103,264,000	
R&D Expense						
Operating Income						
Operating Margin %						
SGA Expense						
Net Income	7,387,310	48,758,976	43,534,800	40,057,800	19,704,400	-746,666
Operating Cash Flow						
Capital Expenditure						
EBITDA						
Return on Assets %						
Return on Equity %						
Debt to Equity						

CONTACT INFORMATION:
Phone: 978 657-7500   Fax: 978 657-9193
Toll-Free:
Address: 25 Upton Dr., Wilmington, MA 01887 United States

STOCK TICKER/OTHER:
Stock Ticker: Subsidiary   Exchange:
Employees: 6,500   Fiscal Year Ends: 03/31
Parent Company: Sun Pharmaceutical Industries Ltd

SALARIES/BONUSES:
Top Exec. Salary: $ Bonus: $
Second Exec. Salary: $ Bonus: $

OTHER THOUGHTS:
Estimated Female Officers or Directors: 1
Hot Spot for Advancement for Women/Minorities:

E & J Gallo Winery

www.gallo.com

NAIC Code: 312130

TYPES OF BUSINESS:

Beverages-Wineries
Wineries
Manufacturing
Distribution
Marketing

BRANDS/DIVISIONS/AFFILIATES:

Gallo Glass Company
Carlo Rossi
Gallo
Clarendon Hills
Gossamer Bay
DaVinci
Whitehaven
Black Box

CONTACTS: Note: Officers with more than one job title may be intentionally listed here more than once.

Joseph E. Gallo, CEO
Joseph E. Gallo, Pres.
Susan Hensley, VP-Public Rel.
James E. Coleman, Co-Chmn.
George Marsden, Head-EMEA Div.

GROWTH PLANS/SPECIAL FEATURES:

E. & J. Gallo Winery (Gallo), family-owned and -operated, is one of the largest wineries in the world. Gallo markets more than 100 brands in more than 110 countries, making it one of California's largest wine exporters. Most noted for its Carlo Rossi and Gallo wines, the company also makes Clarendon Hills and Gossamer Bay premium wines. With thousands of acres of vineyards and wineries in various parts of California, Gallo has access to grapes to produce numerous varieties. Gallo's portfolio includes premium-to moderately-priced table wines; sparkling wines, including Andre and Ballatore; dessert wines; malt beverages; and distilled spirits. Premium table wines include Bridlewood Estate Winery, Frei Brothers Reserve, Mirassou, Rancho Zabaco, Ghost Pines Vineyard, Louis M. Martini and MacMurray Ranch. Its mid-priced table wines include Turning Leaf, Barefoot Cellars and Redwood Creek. The firm's brands of imported table wines include Bella Sera, Black Swan, DaVinci, Ecco Domani and Whitehaven. These wines are imported from South Africa, Australia, New Zealand, Argentina, Spain, France, Germany and Italy. The company's economy wines include Wild Vines, Carlo Rossi, Peter Vella, and Boone's Farm. Gallo also produces a line of wines for hotels and restaurants, including Burlwood, Copperidge by E&J Gallo, Liberty Creek and William Wycliff Vineyards. The firm creates wines using state-of-the-art technology at its micro-winery research facility as well as old-world methods of barrel-aging wines stored in its barrel cellar and research facility. Through Gallo Glass Company, Gallo manufactures approximately 1 billion glass bottles a year for its own use and for outside customers. In January 2021, E. & J. Gallo acquired more than 30 wine brands from Constellation Brands, Inc., including Arbor Mist, Black Box, Clos du Bois, Estancia, Hogue, and Wild Horse. The acquisition also adds five wineries to Gallo's portfolio, located in California, Washington and New York.

FINANCIAL DATA: Note: Data for latest year may not have been available at press time.

In U.S. $	2020	2019	2018	2017	2016	2015
Revenue	5,093,550,000	4,851,000,000	4,620,000,000	4,400,000,000	4,325,000,000	4,200,000,000
R&D Expense						
Operating Income						
Operating Margin %						
SGA Expense						
Net Income						
Operating Cash Flow						
Capital Expenditure						
EBITDA						
Return on Assets %						
Return on Equity %						
Debt to Equity						

CONTACT INFORMATION:

Phone: 209-341-3111   Fax:
Toll-Free: 877-687-9463
Address: 600 Yosemite Blvd., Modesto, CA 95354 United States

STOCK TICKER/OTHER:

Stock Ticker: Private   Exchange:
Employees: 6,500   Fiscal Year Ends: 12/31
Parent Company:

SALARIES/BONUSES:

Top Exec. Salary: $ Bonus: $
Second Exec. Salary: $ Bonus: $

OTHER THOUGHTS:

Estimated Female Officers or Directors: 1
Hot Spot for Advancement for Women/Minorities:

E*Trade Financial LLC

www.etrade.com

NAIC Code: 523120

TYPES OF BUSINESS:

Stock Brokerage/Investment Management-Online
Online Trading
Retail Investing
Stock Plan Administration
Custody
Exchange Traded Funds

BRANDS/DIVISIONS/AFFILIATES:

Morgan Stanley

GROWTH PLANS/SPECIAL FEATURES:

E*TRADE Financial, LLC is a financial services company that provides online trading for retail investors. The firm specializes in digital investing and trading, backed by personal professional guidance. E*TRADE also has a high-tech custody platform for advisors and a stock plan administration platform. Investors can access a full spectrum of offerings via E*TRADE, including non-proprietary exchange traded funds (ETFs) and more than 4,400 no-load, no-transaction-fee mutual funds. Investors also have access to a variety of solutions to help keep them on track for financial goals, including resources for self-directed investors to professional investment management through customizable managed portfolios. In October 2020, E*TRADE Financial Corporation was acquired by Morgan Stanley in a $13 billion, all-stock deal. E*TRADE ceased from being publicly traded and became a limited liability company (LLC).

E*TRADE offers its employees health benefits, a 401(k), flexible spending accounts, life insurance and employee assistance programs.

CONTACTS: Note: Officers with more than one job title may be intentionally listed here more than once.

Sebastiano Visentini, VP
Chad Turner, CFO
Michael Curcio, Executive VP, Divisional

FINANCIAL DATA: Note: Data for latest year may not have been available at press time.

In U.S. $	2020	2019	2018	2017	2016	2015
Revenue	3,030,300,134	2,886,000,128	2,872,999,936	2,366,000,128	1,940,999,936	1,428,000,000
R&D Expense						
Operating Income						
Operating Margin %						
SGA Expense						
Net Income		955,000,000	1,052,000,000	614,000,000	552,000,000	268,000,000
Operating Cash Flow						
Capital Expenditure						
EBITDA						
Return on Assets %						
Return on Equity %						
Debt to Equity						

CONTACT INFORMATION:

Phone: 646 521-4300   Fax:
Toll-Free: 800-387-2331
Address: 671 N. Glebe Rd., Arlington, VA 22203 United States

STOCK TICKER/OTHER:

Stock Ticker: Subsidiary   Exchange:
Employees: 4,100   Fiscal Year Ends: 12/31
Parent Company: Morgan Stanley

SALARIES/BONUSES:

Top Exec. Salary: $ Bonus: $
Second Exec. Salary: $ Bonus: $

OTHER THOUGHTS:

Estimated Female Officers or Directors: 3
Hot Spot for Advancement for Women/Minorities: Y

East Penn Manufacturing Company Inc

www.eastpennmanufacturing.com

NAIC Code: 336300

TYPES OF BUSINESS:

Battery Manufacturing
Battery Recycling
Fuel Cell Technology
Electric Vehicle Battery Manufacturing

BRANDS/DIVISIONS/AFFILIATES:

Deka Battery
Navitas Systems

CONTACTS: *Note: Officers with more than one job title may be intentionally listed here more than once.*

Chris Pruitt, CEO
Christopher E. Pruitt, Exec. VP-Admin.
Christopher E. Pruitt, Exec. VP-Finance

GROWTH PLANS/SPECIAL FEATURES:

East Penn Manufacturing Company, Inc. manufactures lead-acid batteries, battery accessories, wire and cable products for the industrial, automotive, commercial, marine, stationary and specialty markets. The firm markets its products in four segments: transportation, motive power, reserve power, and wire cable and battery accessories. The transportation segment makes batteries for the automotive; marine; power sports; lawn and garden; golf care/electric vehicle (EV); agricultural; floor care equipment; and trucks and buses markets. The motive power segment offers products for industrial lift trucks; airline ground support; automatic guided vehicle (AGV); and rail and locomotive industries. The reserve power segment produces battery lines for telecommunications; uninterruptible power supply; grid optimization services; renewable energy; and community access television (CATV). The wire cable and battery accessories segment offers products that are used in the marine and fleet industries. Products are manufactured under the brand name Deka Battery. East Penn and operates a 520-acre single-site manufacturing complex in Berks County, Pennsylvania. The company safely reuses all parts of used batteries, reclaiming lead, plastic and sulfuric acid and turning sulfur fumes into liquid fertilizer. East Penn also traps its wastewater and separates it into liquid and solids for separate treatment, resulting in an overall reduction of pollution. The firm exports its products worldwide. Moreover, East Penn holds a majority interest in Navitas Systems, a global leader in larger-format lithium battery technology and systems for heavy-duty commercial/industrial and government/defense market segments.

FINANCIAL DATA: *Note: Data for latest year may not have been available at press time.*

In U.S. $	2020	2019	2018	2017	2016	2015
Revenue	1,530,090,844	1,800,106,875	1,714,387,500	1,632,750,000	1,555,000,000	1,500,000,000
R&D Expense						
Operating Income						
Operating Margin %						
SGA Expense						
Net Income						
Operating Cash Flow						
Capital Expenditure						
EBITDA						
Return on Assets %						
Return on Equity %						
Debt to Equity						

CONTACT INFORMATION:

Phone: 610-682-6361   Fax: 610-682-4781
Toll-Free:
Address: Deka Rd., Lyon Station, PA 19536 United States

SALARIES/BONUSES:

Top Exec. Salary: $ Bonus: $
Second Exec. Salary: $ Bonus: $

STOCK TICKER/OTHER:

Stock Ticker: Private
Employees: 10,500
Parent Company:

Exchange:
Fiscal Year Ends: 12/31

OTHER THOUGHTS:

Estimated Female Officers or Directors: 1
Hot Spot for Advancement for Women/Minorities:

Ecolab Inc

NAIC Code: 325611

www.ecolab.com

TYPES OF BUSINESS:

Soap & Cleaning Compound Manufacturing
Product Development
Water Treatment Solutions
Paper Process Applications
Cleaning/Sanitizing Solutions
Infection Control Solutions
Pharmaceuticals
Pest Elimination

BRANDS/DIVISIONS/AFFILIATES:

VanBaerle Hygiene AG
TechTex Holdings Limited

CONTACTS: *Note: Officers with more than one job title may be intentionally listed here more than once.*

Douglas Baker, CEO
Darrell Brown, Exec. VP
Daniel Schmechel, CFO
Bruno Lavandier, Chief Accounting Officer
Larry Berger, Chief Technology Officer
Christophe Beck, COO
Laurie Marsh, Executive VP, Divisional
Angela Busch, Executive VP, Divisional
Elizabeth Simermeyer, Executive VP, Divisional
Michael Hickey, Executive VP, Divisional
Michael McCormick, Executive VP
Alex Blanco, Executive VP
Roberto Inchaustegui, Executive VP
Timothy Mulhere, Executive VP
Jill Wyant, Executive VP

GROWTH PLANS/SPECIAL FEATURES:

Ecolab, Inc. develops and markets premium products and services for the hospitality, foodservice, healthcare and industrial markets. The firm divides its operations into four segments: global industrial, global institutional and specialty, global healthcare and life sciences and other. Global industrial segment offers services associated with water treatment and paper process applications. The global institutional and specialty segment services include cleaning and sanitizing programs and wash process solutions. The global healthcare and life sciences segment offers pharmaceutical, personal care, infection and containment control solutions. The other segment consists of services designed to detect, eliminate and prevent pests. Ecolab is a trusted partner at nearly 3 million customer locations. The firm has more than 9,400 patents. During the first half of 2021, Ecolab acquired VanBaerle Hygiene AG, which sells cleaning products and related services to restaurants, long-term care facilities, hotels and laundries; and acquired TechTex Holdings Limited, a healthcare business that sells wet and dry wipes and other non-woven products to the life sciences and healthcare industries. That August, Ecolab announced the opening of the Ecolab Healthcare Advanced Design Center in Eagan, Minnesota, a 22,000-square-foot facility for partnering with medical device customers focused on infection prevention solutions for their surgical equipment, and to develop new solutions for hospitals and surgery centers.

FINANCIAL DATA: *Note: Data for latest year may not have been available at press time.*

In U.S. $	2020	2019	2018	2017	2016	2015
Revenue	11,790,200,000	14,906,300,000	14,668,200,000	13,838,300,000	13,152,800,000	13,545,100,000
R&D Expense						
Operating Income	1,575,300,000	2,225,400,000	2,073,700,000	2,016,100,000	1,954,500,000	1,976,100,000
Operating Margin %		.15%	.14%	.15%	.15%	.15%
SGA Expense	3,309,100,000	3,957,500,000	3,968,600,000	4,417,100,000	4,299,400,000	4,345,500,000
Net Income	-1,205,100,000	1,558,900,000	1,429,100,000	1,508,400,000	1,229,600,000	1,002,100,000
Operating Cash Flow	1,860,200,000	2,420,700,000	2,277,700,000	2,091,300,000	1,939,700,000	1,999,800,000
Capital Expenditure	489,000,000	800,600,000	847,100,000	868,600,000	756,800,000	815,200,000
EBITDA	2,278,900,000	3,087,500,000	2,980,100,000	2,932,700,000	2,786,500,000	2,430,900,000
Return on Assets %		.08%	.07%	.08%	.07%	.05%
Return on Equity %		.19%	.18%	.21%	.18%	.14%
Debt to Equity		0.737	0.787	0.887	0.891	0.617

CONTACT INFORMATION:

Phone: 800 232-6522   Fax: 612 225-3080
Toll-Free:
Address: 1 Ecolab Pl., St. Paul, MN 55102 United States

STOCK TICKER/OTHER:

Stock Ticker: ECL   Exchange: NYS
Employees: 44,000   Fiscal Year Ends: 12/31
Parent Company:

SALARIES/BONUSES:

Top Exec. Salary: $ Bonus: $
Second Exec. Salary: $ Bonus: $

OTHER THOUGHTS:

Estimated Female Officers or Directors: 2
Hot Spot for Advancement for Women/Minorities:

Edison International

www.edison.com

NAIC Code: 221112

TYPES OF BUSINESS:

Electric Utility
Financial Services
Operations Services
Energy Trading

BRANDS/DIVISIONS/AFFILIATES:

Southern California Edison Company
Edison Energy LLC

GROWTH PLANS/SPECIAL FEATURES:

Edison International is a California-based holding company of companies engaged in electric utilities and related businesses. Subsidiary Southern California Edison Company (SCE) is one of the largest electric utilities in the U.S., and a longtime leader in renewable energy and energy efficiency. SCE serves approximately 15 million people through 5 million member accounts, all within a 50,000-square-mile area. Subsidiary Edison Energy, LLC is an independent advisory and services company with the capabilities to develop and integrate energy solutions for energy users nationwide. Edison Energy has the resources, experience and technology to improve the way commercial, industrial and institutional organizations procure, use and manage energy.

Edison International offers comprehensive benefits, retirement options and employee assistance programs.

CONTACTS: Note: Officers with more than one job title may be intentionally listed here more than once.

Kevin Payne, CEO, Subsidiary
Kevin Walker, Senior VP, Subsidiary
Pedro Pizarro, CEO
William Petmecky, CFO, Subsidiary
Maria Rigatti, CFO
William Sullivan, Chairman of the Board
Aaron Moss, Chief Accounting Officer
Adam Umanoff, Executive VP
Russell Swartz, General Counsel, Subsidiary
Ronald Nichols, President, Subsidiary
J. Murphy, Senior VP, Divisional
Gaddi Vasquez, Senior VP, Divisional
Jacqueline Trapp, Senior VP, Divisional
Caroline Choi, Senior VP, Divisional
Philip Herrington, Senior VP, Subsidiary

FINANCIAL DATA: Note: Data for latest year may not have been available at press time.

In U.S. $	2020	2019	2018	2017	2016	2015
Revenue	13,578,000,000	12,347,000,000	12,657,000,000	12,320,000,000	11,869,000,000	11,524,000,000
R&D Expense						
Operating Income	1,101,000,000	1,959,000,000	-474,000,000	2,231,000,000	2,113,000,000	2,013,000,000
Operating Margin %		.18%	.17%	.18%	.18%	.17%
SGA Expense	1,664,000,000	407,000,000	2,669,000,000			
Net Income	871,000,000	1,405,000,000	-302,000,000	689,000,000	1,434,000,000	1,133,000,000
Operating Cash Flow	1,263,000,000	-307,000,000	3,177,000,000	3,587,000,000	3,256,000,000	4,509,000,000
Capital Expenditure	5,484,000,000	4,877,000,000	4,509,000,000	3,828,000,000	3,734,000,000	4,225,000,000
EBITDA	3,497,000,000	3,771,000,000	1,585,000,000	3,703,000,000	4,269,000,000	4,128,000,000
Return on Assets %		.02%	-.01%	.01%	.03%	.02%
Return on Equity %		.11%	-.04%	.05%	.11%	.09%
Debt to Equity		1.389	1.399	0.998	0.848	0.964

CONTACT INFORMATION:

Phone: 626 302-2222   Fax: 626 302-9935
Toll-Free: 800-655-4555
Address: 2244 Walnut Grove Ave., Rosemead, CA 91770 United States

STOCK TICKER/OTHER:

Stock Ticker: EIX
Employees: 13,351
Parent Company:

Exchange: NYS
Fiscal Year Ends: 12/31

SALARIES/BONUSES:

Top Exec. Salary: $ Bonus: $
Second Exec. Salary: $ Bonus: $

OTHER THOUGHTS:

Estimated Female Officers or Directors: 4
Hot Spot for Advancement for Women/Minorities: Y

Edward D Jones & Co LP

www.edwardjones.com

NAIC Code: 523120

TYPES OF BUSINESS:

Stock Brokerage
Financial Planning
Retirement & Estate Planning
Life Insurance
Banking Services
Annuities

BRANDS/DIVISIONS/AFFILIATES:

Jones Financial Companies LLLP (The)
Edward Jones

GROWTH PLANS/SPECIAL FEATURES:

Edward D. Jones & Co. LP, branded as Edward Jones, is a registered broker-dealer and investment adviser in the U.S. Its subsidiary operates as a registered broker-dealer in Canada. Edward Jones is a retail brokerage business and primarily derives revenues from fees for providing investment advisory and other account services to its clients, fees for assets held by clients, the distribution of mutual fund shares, and commissions for the purchase or sale of securities and the purchase of insurance products. Edward Jones serves over 7 million clients with a total of $1.2 trillion in client assets under care. Investments and services offered by the company include wealth management, retirement savings, retirement planning for business owners, college savings, stocks, bonds, mutual funds, insurance, annuities and cash and credit services. Edward D. Jones & Co. is a wholly owned subsidiary of Jones Financial Companies LLLP.

CONTACTS: Note: Officers with more than one job title may be intentionally listed here more than once.

Penny Pennington, Managing Partner
Norman Eaker, Principal-Firm Admin.
James A. Tricarico, General Counsel

FINANCIAL DATA: Note: Data for latest year may not have been available at press time.

In U.S. $	2020	2019	2018	2017	2016	2015
Revenue	1,006,300,000	9,369,000,000	8,469,000,000	7,506,000,000	6,557,000,000	6,619,000,000
R&D Expense						
Operating Income						
Operating Margin %						
SGA Expense						
Net Income	1,285,000,000	1,092,000,000	990,000,000	872,000,000	746,000,000	838,000,000
Operating Cash Flow						
Capital Expenditure						
EBITDA						
Return on Assets %						
Return on Equity %						
Debt to Equity						

CONTACT INFORMATION:

Phone: 314-515-2000   Fax: 314-515-2622
Toll-Free:
Address: 12555 Manchester Rd., Des Peres, MO 63131 United States

STOCK TICKER/OTHER:

Stock Ticker: Subsidiary   Exchange:
Employees: 50,000   Fiscal Year Ends: 12/31
Parent Company: Jones Financial Companies LLLP (The)

SALARIES/BONUSES:

Top Exec. Salary: $ Bonus: $
Second Exec. Salary: $ Bonus: $

OTHER THOUGHTS:

Estimated Female Officers or Directors: 3
Hot Spot for Advancement for Women/Minorities: Y

Edwards Lifesciences Corporation

www.edwards.com

NAIC Code: 339100

TYPES OF BUSINESS:

Supplies-Cardiovascular Disease Related
Cardiac Surgery Products
Critical Care Products
Vascular Products
Heart Valve Implants
Software

BRANDS/DIVISIONS/AFFILIATES:

Carpentier-Edwards PERIMOUNT
Edwards Intuity
Edwards SAPIEN
PASCAL
Cardioband
PERIMOUNT Magna Ease
INSPIRIS RESILIA

CONTACTS: Note: Officers with more than one job title may be intentionally listed here more than once.

Michael Mussallem, CEO
Scott Ullem, CFO
Donald Bobo, Vice President
Larry Wood, Vice President, Divisional
Catherine Szyman, Vice President, Divisional
Daveen Chopra, Vice President, Divisional
Jean-Luc Lemercier, Vice President, Geographical
Huimin Wang, Vice President, Geographical

GROWTH PLANS/SPECIAL FEATURES:

Edwards Lifesciences Corporation designs products for cardiovascular diseases, such as heart valve disease, coronary artery disease, peripheral vascular disease (PVD) and congestive heart failure. The firm operates in four main areas: surgical structural heart (16% of 2020 net sales), transcatheter aortic valve replacement (65%), transcatheter mitral and tricuspid therapies, and critical care (9%). Surgical structural heart products include the Carpentier-Edwards PERIMOUNT line of pericardial heart valves made from biologically inert porcine tissue, often on a wire-form stent; and valve repair therapies, such as the Edwards Intuity valve system, a minimally-invasive aortic system designed to enable a faster procedure and a smaller incision. Transcatheter aortic valve replacement technologies are designed for the non-surgical replacement of heart valves. Its main products are the Edwards SAPIEN, Edwards Sapien XT, Edwards Sapien 3 and Edwards Sapien 3 Ultra transcatheter aortic heart valves and delivery systems used to treat heart valve disease using catheter-based approaches for patients deemed at high risk for traditional open-heart surgery. The transcatheter mitral and tricuspid therapies division is making investments in the development of transcatheter heart valve repair and replacement technologies designed to treat mitral and tricuspid valve diseases. Many of these technologies are in early development and clinical phases, but the PASCAL transcatheter valve repair system and the Cardioband systems are commercially available in Europe. Surgical structural heart products include annuloplasty rings, cardiac cannula devices and the Carpentier-Edwards PERIMOUNT pericardial valve platform, including the line of PERIMOUNT Magna Ease valves for aortic and mitral surgical valve replacement. This division's INSPIRIS RESILIA aortic valve is built on the PERMOUNT platform and offers RESILIA tissue and VFit technology. In mid-2021, Edwards announced that its Acumen Hypotension Prediction Index software with the Acumen IQ finger cuff received U.S. Food and Drug Administration clearance.

Edwards offers comprehensive benefits and retirement plans.

FINANCIAL DATA: Note: Data for latest year may not have been available at press time.

In U.S. $	2020	2019	2018	2017	2016	2015
Revenue	4,386,300,000	4,348,000,000	3,722,800,000	3,435,300,000	2,963,700,000	2,493,700,000
R&D Expense	760,700,000	752,700,000	622,200,000	552,600,000	477,800,000	383,100,000
Operating Income	1,316,600,000	1,238,700,000	1,072,700,000	1,022,700,000	783,800,000	642,700,000
Operating Margin %		.28%	.29%	.30%	.26%	.26%
SGA Expense	1,228,400,000	1,242,200,000	1,088,500,000	984,700,000	904,700,000	850,700,000
Net Income	823,400,000	1,046,900,000	722,200,000	583,600,000	569,500,000	494,800,000
Operating Cash Flow	1,054,300,000	1,179,400,000	926,800,000	1,000,700,000	704,400,000	549,700,000
Capital Expenditure	407,300,000	278,400,000	241,700,000	175,500,000	217,400,000	106,500,000
EBITDA	1,039,700,000	1,276,500,000	868,700,000	1,140,000,000	828,300,000	705,400,000
Return on Assets %		.18%	.13%	.11%	.13%	.13%
Return on Equity %		.29%	.24%	.21%	.22%	.21%
Debt to Equity		0.157	0.189	0.148	0.314	0.24

CONTACT INFORMATION:

Phone: 949 250-2500   Fax: 949 250-2525
Toll-Free: 800-424-3278
Address: 1 Edwards Way, Irvine, CA 92614 United States

STOCK TICKER/OTHER:

Stock Ticker: EW
Employees: 14,900
Parent Company:

Exchange: NYS
Fiscal Year Ends: 12/31

SALARIES/BONUSES:

Top Exec. Salary: $ Bonus: $
Second Exec. Salary: $ Bonus: $

OTHER THOUGHTS:

Estimated Female Officers or Directors: 3
Hot Spot for Advancement for Women/Minorities: Y

Sales, profits and employees may be estimates. Financial information, benefits and other data can change quickly and may vary from those stated here.

Eli Lilly and Company

NAIC Code: 325412

TYPES OF BUSINESS:

Pharmaceuticals Discovery & Development
Pharmaceuticals
Drug Development
Drug Discovery
Drug Production

BRANDS/DIVISIONS/AFFILIATES:

Humalog
Trulicity
Forteo
Cymbalta
Zyprexa
Alimta
Olumiant
Promoter Technologies

CONTACTS: Note: Officers with more than one job title may be intentionally listed here more than once.

Jeffrey Simmons, CEO, Subsidiary
Anne White, Pres., Divisional
David Ricks, CEO
Joshua Smiley, CFO
Donald Zakrowski, Chief Accounting Officer
Melissa Barnes, Chief Compliance Officer
Aarti Shah, Chief Information Officer
Daniel Skovronsky, Chief Scientific Officer
Michael Harrington, General Counsel
Alfonso Zulueta, President, Divisional
Enrique Conterno, President, Divisional
Myles ONeill, President, Divisional
Leigh Pusey, Senior VP, Divisional
Johna Norton, Senior VP, Divisional
Stephen Fry, Senior VP, Divisional

GROWTH PLANS/SPECIAL FEATURES:

Eli Lilly and Company discovers, develops, manufactures and markets human pharmaceutical products. Human pharmaceutical products are grouped into five divisions: endocrinology, neuroscience, oncology, immunology and other. Endocrinology products include: Humalog, Humulin, Baqsimi, Basaglar, Trajenta, Jardiance and Trulicity, for the treatment of diabetes; and Forteo, for osteoporosis in women. Neuroscience products include: Cymbalta, for major depressive disorder; Zyprexa, for schizophrenia; Strattera, for attention-deficit hyperactivity disorder; Emgality, for migraine prevention; and Reyvow, for acute treatment of migraine. Oncology products include: Alimta, for non-small cell lung cancer; Erbitux, for colorectal cancers; Cyramza, for advanced or metastatic gastric cancer; and Verzenio, for advanced/metastatic breast cancer. Immunology products include: Olumiant, for adults with moderately-to-severe active rheumatoid arthritis; and Taltz, for moderate-to-severe plaque psoriasis and active psoriatic arthritis. The other division consists of Cialis, a product for the treatment of erectile dysfunction and benign prostatic hyperplasia. In July 2021, Eli Lilly acquired Promoter Technologies, a private biotech company whose proprietary peptide- and protein-engineering platform is used to identify and synthesize molecules that can sense glucose or other endogenous modulators of protein activity. That same month, Eli Lilly announced a multi-year, exclusive collaboration with Kumquat Biosciences to discover, develop and commercialize potential novel small molecules that stimulate tumor-specific immune responses.

FINANCIAL DATA: Note: Data for latest year may not have been available at press time.

In U.S. $	2020	2019	2018	2017	2016	2015
Revenue	24,539,800,000	22,319,500,000	24,555,700,000	22,871,300,000	21,222,100,000	19,958,700,000
R&D Expense	6,085,700,000	5,595,000,000	5,307,100,000	5,281,800,000	5,243,900,000	4,796,400,000
Operating Income	6,849,600,000	5,789,500,000	6,186,800,000	4,417,500,000	3,871,300,000	3,592,100,000
Operating Margin %		.25%	.17%	.14%	.18%	.15%
SGA Expense	6,121,200,000	6,213,800,000	6,631,800,000	7,101,800,000	6,452,000,000	6,533,000,000
Net Income	6,193,700,000	8,318,400,000	3,232,000,000	-204,100,000	2,737,600,000	2,408,400,000
Operating Cash Flow	6,499,600,000	4,836,600,000	5,524,500,000	5,615,600,000	4,851,000,000	2,772,800,000
Capital Expenditure	2,029,100,000	1,353,500,000	3,018,200,000	2,163,600,000	1,092,000,000	1,626,200,000
EBITDA	8,913,400,000	6,899,100,000	5,676,800,000	3,989,700,000	5,055,800,000	4,378,900,000
Return on Assets %		.20%	.07%	.00%	.07%	.07%
Return on Equity %		1.34%	.30%	-.02%	.19%	.16%
Debt to Equity		5.487	1.184	0.858	0.597	0.547

CONTACT INFORMATION:

Phone: 317 276-2000   Fax:
Toll-Free:
Address: Lilly Corporate Center, Indianapolis, IN 46285 United States

STOCK TICKER/OTHER:

Stock Ticker: LLY   Exchange: NYS
Employees: 33,625   Fiscal Year Ends: 12/31
Parent Company:

SALARIES/BONUSES:

Top Exec. Salary: $ Bonus: $
Second Exec. Salary: $ Bonus: $

OTHER THOUGHTS:

Estimated Female Officers or Directors: 8
Hot Spot for Advancement for Women/Minorities: Y

EMCOR Group Inc

www.emcorgroup.com

NAIC Code: 238210

TYPES OF BUSINESS:

Electric, Heating and AC Contractors
Mechanical Contracting
Technical Consulting Services
Facilities Management

BRANDS/DIVISIONS/AFFILIATES:

CONTACTS: *Note: Officers with more than one job title may be intentionally listed here more than once.*

Anthony Guzzi, CEO
Mark Pompa, CFO
R. Matz, Executive VP, Divisional
Maxine Mauricio, Executive VP

GROWTH PLANS/SPECIAL FEATURES:

EMCOR Group, Inc. is a global leader in mechanical and electrical contracting and facilities services. The company offers its services through more than 80 operating subsidiaries and joint ventures located in the U.S. and the U.K. Services provided to customers include the design, integration, installation, start up, operation and maintenance of systems for generation and distribution of electrical power; lighting systems; low-voltage systems, such as fire alarm, security, communications and process control systems; voice and data communication systems; heating, ventilation, air conditioning, refrigeration and clean-room process ventilation systems; plumbing, process and high-purity piping systems; water and wastewater treatment systems; and central plant heating and cooling systems. In addition to its construction services, EMCOR offers facilities services, such as site-based operations and maintenance, mobile maintenance and service, facilities management, installation and support for building systems, technical consulting and diagnostic services, small modification and retrofit projects and program development and management for energy systems. Most of the firm's business is done with corporations, municipalities and other government agencies, owner/developers and building tenants. Additional services are provided to a range of general and specialty contractors, with EMCOR operating as a subcontractor.

EMCOR offers its employees benefits including medical, vision and dental coverage; life insurance; flexible spending accounts; disability income; employee wellness and assistance programs; and a 401(k) and stock purchase options.

FINANCIAL DATA: *Note: Data for latest year may not have been available at press time.*

In U.S. $	2020	2019	2018	2017	2016	2015
Revenue	8,797,061,000	9,174,611,000	8,130,631,000	7,686,999,000	7,551,524,000	6,718,726,000
R&D Expense						
Operating Income	491,798,000	462,415,000	406,296,000	389,950,000	312,324,000	287,906,000
Operating Margin %		.05%	.05%	.05%	.04%	.04%
SGA Expense	903,584,000	893,453,000	799,157,000	757,062,000	725,538,000	656,573,000
Net Income	132,943,000	325,140,000	283,531,000	227,196,000	181,935,000	172,286,000
Operating Cash Flow	806,366,000	355,700,000	271,011,000	366,134,000	264,561,000	266,666,000
Capital Expenditure	47,969,000	48,432,000	43,479,000	34,684,000	39,648,000	35,460,000
EBITDA	368,006,000	556,797,000	489,487,000	420,028,000	388,910,000	361,944,000
Return on Assets %		.07%	.07%	.06%	.05%	.05%
Return on Equity %		.17%	.17%	.14%	.12%	.12%
Debt to Equity		0.243	0.161	0.176	0.266	0.203

CONTACT INFORMATION:

Phone: 203 849-7800   Fax: 203 849-7900
Toll-Free: 866-890-7794
Address: 301 Merritt Seven, Norwalk, CT 06851-1092 United States

STOCK TICKER/OTHER:

Stock Ticker: EME
Employees: 36,000
Parent Company:

Exchange: NYS
Fiscal Year Ends: 12/31

SALARIES/BONUSES:

Top Exec. Salary: $ Bonus: $
Second Exec. Salary: $ Bonus: $

OTHER THOUGHTS:

Estimated Female Officers or Directors: 3
Hot Spot for Advancement for Women/Minorities: Y

Envision Healthcare Corporation

NAIC Code: 621610

TYPES OF BUSINESS:

Home Health Care Services
Physician Services
Surgery Services
Home Health Services
Hospice Services
Surgery Centers
Surgical Hospital
Ambulatory Services

BRANDS/DIVISIONS/AFFILIATES:

KKR & Co Inc
Envision Physician Services
Evolution Health
AMSURG

CONTACTS: Note: Officers with more than one job title may be intentionally listed here more than once.

Jim Rechtin, CEO
William Sanger, Chairman of the Board
Henry Howe, CFO
April Zepeda, Sr. VP-Communication
Beth Sweetman, Chief People Officer
Megan Barney, CIO
Karey Witty, Executive VP
Phillip Clendenin, Executive VP
Brian Jackson, Executive VP
Craig Wilson, General Counsel
Patrick Solomon, Other Executive Officer
Christopher Holden, President
Kenneth Zongor, Senior VP
Chan Chuang, Chief Medical Officer

GROWTH PLANS/SPECIAL FEATURES:

Envision Healthcare Corporation, privately-owned by KKR & Co. Inc, is a physician-led organization operating through three primary business units: Envision Physician Services, Evolution Health and AMSURG. The company delivers its services to clinical departments in healthcare facilities throughout the U.S. and the District of Columbia. The Envision Physician Services business unit provides tailored physician services to hospital and health systems, including anesthesia, emergency medicine, hospital medicine, radiology and surgical services, as well as women's and children's services. The Evolution Health business unit provides home health, hospice and home infusion services, which are patient-centered solutions. Evolution Health focuses on hiring compassionate, highly-experienced clinicians to deliver outcomes that will reduce re-hospitalizations and increase patient satisfaction. This division provides comprehensive traditional home health services reimbursed by Medicare, Medicaid and commercial payers or can provide custom solutions to health plans, hospital partners and other care models. Last, AMSURG owns and operates more than 250 surgery centers and one surgical hospital across 34 U.S. states and the District of Columbia. The company's medical specialties range from gastroenterology to ophthalmology and orthopedics. AMSURG is a leader in the ambulatory surgery center quality movement, and therefore provides an approach that combines technology, data analytics, patient engagement and quality reporting for optimal outcomes for patients.

FINANCIAL DATA: Note: Data for latest year may not have been available at press time.

In U.S. $	2020	2019	2018	2017	2016	2015
Revenue	8,478,750,000	8,925,000,000	8,500,000,000	7,819,299,840	3,696,000,000	2,566,884,096
R&D Expense						
Operating Income						
Operating Margin %						
SGA Expense						
Net Income		-214,525,200	-221,160,000	-228,000,000	-18,600,000	162,947,008
Operating Cash Flow						
Capital Expenditure						
EBITDA						
Return on Assets %						
Return on Equity %						
Debt to Equity						

CONTACT INFORMATION:

Phone: 615-665-1283   Fax:
Toll-Free:
Address: 1A Burton Hills Blvd., Nashville, TN 37215 United States

STOCK TICKER/OTHER:

Stock Ticker: Subsidiary   Exchange:
Employees: 48,000   Fiscal Year Ends: 12/31
Parent Company: KKR & Co Inc

SALARIES/BONUSES:

Top Exec. Salary: $ Bonus: $
Second Exec. Salary: $ Bonus: $

OTHER THOUGHTS:

Estimated Female Officers or Directors:
Hot Spot for Advancement for Women/Minorities:

EPAM Systems Inc

NAIC Code: 541511

www.epam.com

TYPES OF BUSINESS:

Software Engineering
Software Product Development
Digital Platform Engineering
Consulting

BRANDS/DIVISIONS/AFFILIATES:

GROWTH PLANS/SPECIAL FEATURES:

EPAM Systems, Inc. is a global software product development and digital platform engineering services provider. The company serves clients worldwide, primarily in North America, Europe, Asia and Australia. EPAM comprises a strong focus on innovative and scalable software solutions, and a continually-evolving mix of advanced capabilities. The firm's key service offerings and solutions include the practice areas of engineering, operations, optimization, consulting and design. EPAM's industry expertise include financial services, travel, consumer, software, high-tech, business information, media, life sciences, healthcare and emerging verticals such as energy, telecommunications, automotive and manufacturing industries.

CONTACTS: *Note: Officers with more than one job title may be intentionally listed here more than once.*

Arkadiy Dobkin, CEO
Jason Peterson, CFO
Gary Abrahams, Chief Accounting Officer
Elaina Shekhter, Chief Marketing Officer
Edward Rockwell, General Counsel
Viktar Dvorkin, Other Corporate Officer
Sergey Yezhkov, Other Corporate Officer
Jason Harman, Other Corporate Officer
Balazs Fejes, Other Corporate Officer
Boris Shnayder, Other Corporate Officer
Lawrence Solomon, Other Executive Officer

FINANCIAL DATA: *Note: Data for latest year may not have been available at press time.*

In U.S. $	2020	2019	2018	2017	2016	2015
Revenue	2,659,478,000	2,293,798,000	1,842,912,000	1,450,448,000	1,160,132,000	914,128,000
R&D Expense						
Operating Income	379,324,000	302,850,000	245,764,000	172,946,000	133,696,000	105,967,000
Operating Margin %		.13%	.13%	.12%	.12%	.12%
SGA Expense	484,758,000	457,433,000	373,587,000	324,855,000	264,658,000	222,759,000
Net Income	327,160,000	261,057,000	240,256,000	72,760,000	99,266,000	84,456,000
Operating Cash Flow	544,407,000	287,453,000	292,218,000	195,364,000	164,817,000	76,393,000
Capital Expenditure	68,793,000	99,308,000	37,574,000	29,806,000	29,317,000	17,964,000
EBITDA	508,567,000	404,026,000	282,404,000	201,508,000	157,083,000	123,362,000
Return on Assets %		.14%	.17%	.07%	.12%	.12%
Return on Equity %		.18%	.21%	.08%	.14%	.16%
Debt to Equity		0.129	0.02	0.026	0.032	0.057

CONTACT INFORMATION:

Phone: 267 759-9000   Fax: 267 759-8989
Toll-Free:
Address: 41 University Dr., Ste. 202, Newtown, PA 18940 United States

STOCK TICKER/OTHER:

Stock Ticker: EPAM
Employees: 41,168
Parent Company:

Exchange: NYS
Fiscal Year Ends: 12/31

SALARIES/BONUSES:

Top Exec. Salary: $ Bonus: $
Second Exec. Salary: $ Bonus: $

OTHER THOUGHTS:

Estimated Female Officers or Directors: 2
Hot Spot for Advancement for Women/Minorities:

Epic Systems Corporation

NAIC Code: 511210D

www.epic.com

TYPES OF BUSINESS:

Computer Software, Healthcare & Biotechnology
Information Networks
Support Services
Software
Clinical Software
Health Records Management

BRANDS/DIVISIONS/AFFILIATES:

Epicenter
EpicCare
Lucy
Community Library Exchange

CONTACTS: Note: Officers with more than one job title may be intentionally listed here more than once.

Judy Faulkner, CEO
Carl Dvorak, Exec. VP

GROWTH PLANS/SPECIAL FEATURES:

Epic Systems Corporation is a developer of health industry clinical, access and revenue software for mid-and large-sized medical groups, hospitals, academic facilities, children's organizations, multi-hospital systems and integrated health care organizations. All Epic software applications are designed to share a single database, called Epicenter, so that each viewer can access available patient data through a single interface from anywhere in the organization. The firm's clinical software products include integrated inpatient and ambulatory systems under the EpicCare brand as well as health information management tools and specialty information systems. The firm's interoperability service, Lucy, personal health record that allows patients to organize and access their medical history independently of any one facility. Other products offer access services, including scheduling, inpatient and ambulatory registration, call management and nurse triage; revenue cycle services, such as hospital and professional billing; health plan and managed care administration systems; clinical and financial data repositories; enterprise reporting; patient medical record access systems; and connectivity tools, including voice recognition, interfacing and patient monitoring devices. In conjunction with its software applications, the company provides extensive client services, including training, process engineering, tailoring of applications to the client's situation and access to network specialists who plan and implement client systems. In addition, Epic hosts Community Library Exchange, an online collection of application tools and pre-made content that allows clients to share report and registration templates, custom forms, enterprise report formats and documentation shortcuts. Epic is headquartered in Wisconsin, USA, with international offices in the Netherlands, Australia, Denmark, Norway, United Arab Emirates, the U.K., Saudi Arabia, Finland and Singapore.

FINANCIAL DATA: Note: Data for latest year may not have been available at press time.

In U.S. $	2020	2019	2018	2017	2016	2015
Revenue	3,300,000,000	3,200,000,000	2,890,000,000	2,740,000,000	2,550,000,000	2,015,000,000
R&D Expense						
Operating Income						
Operating Margin %						
SGA Expense						
Net Income						
Operating Cash Flow						
Capital Expenditure						
EBITDA						
Return on Assets %						
Return on Equity %						
Debt to Equity						

CONTACT INFORMATION:

Phone: 608-271-9000   Fax: 608-271-7237
Toll-Free:
Address: 1979 Milky Way, Verona, WI 53593 United States

STOCK TICKER/OTHER:

Stock Ticker: Private
Employees: 10,000
Parent Company:

Exchange:
Fiscal Year Ends: 12/31

SALARIES/BONUSES:

Top Exec. Salary: $ Bonus: $
Second Exec. Salary: $ Bonus: $

OTHER THOUGHTS:

Estimated Female Officers or Directors: 1
Hot Spot for Advancement for Women/Minorities:

Equinix Inc

NAIC Code: 517110

TYPES OF BUSINESS:

Data Networks
Internet Exchange Services

BRANDS/DIVISIONS/AFFILIATES:

International Business Exchange (IBX)
xScale
Equinix Internet Exchange
Equinix Fabric
Equinix SmartKey
Bare Metal

CONTACTS: Note: Officers with more than one job title may be intentionally listed here more than once.

Charles Meyers, CEO
Keith Taylor, CFO
Peter Van Camp, Chairman of the Board
Simon Miller, Chief Accounting Officer
Brandi Morandi, Chief Legal Officer
Eric Schwartz, Chief Strategy Officer
Michael Campbell, Other Executive Officer
Karl Strohmeyer, Other Executive Officer
Samuel Lee, President, Geographical

GROWTH PLANS/SPECIAL FEATURES:

Equinix, Inc. provides network neutral co-location, interconnection and managed services to enterprises. The company operates data centers in more than 60 markets across the Americas, Europe, Middle East, Africa and Asia Pacific. The firm's proprietary Equinix platform incorporates International Business Exchange (IBX) data centers with unique ecosystems and a global footprint to offer customers accelerated business growth by safeguarding the client's infrastructure, housing their applications and assets closer to the user for improved overall performance and enabling the client to collaborate with numerous customers and partners. The xScale data centers serve the unique core workload deployment needs of a targeted group of hyperscale companies, including cloud service providers. Interconnection solutions connect businesses directly within and between Equinix's data centers across its global platform. Interconnection solutions include: cross connects, providing point-to-point cable link between two customers in the same IBX data center; fabric, offering flexible, on-demand global connection; metro connect, connecting to multiple data centers within a metropolitan area; and Equinix Internet Exchange, which enables networks, content providers and enterprises to exchange internet traffic through a global peering solution. The firm's edge services help businesses deploy-as-a-service networking, security and hardware across its global data footprint as an alternative to buying, owning and managing the physical infrastructure. Edge services include: network edge, allowing customers to modernize networks by deploying network functions virtualization (NFV) from multiple vendors across Equinix metros; Equinix SmartKey, which simplifies data protection across cloud architecture through a global Software-as-a-Service (SaaS)-based, hardware security module management and cryptography service that provides on-premises and hybrid multi-cloud cloud encryption key management; and Bare Metal, which helps enterprises more seamlessly deploy hybrid multi-cloud architectures on the Equinix platform. Equinix also offers remote support and professional services.

Equinix offers its employees health and financial benefit options, depending on location.

FINANCIAL DATA: Note: Data for latest year may not have been available at press time.

In U.S. $	2020	2019	2018	2017	2016	2015
Revenue	5,998,545,000	5,562,140,000	5,071,654,000	4,368,428,000	3,611,989,000	2,725,867,000
R&D Expense						
Operating Income	1,114,868,000	1,165,892,000	1,005,783,000	847,649,000	657,816,000	609,065,000
Operating Margin %		.21%	.20%	.19%	.18%	.22%
SGA Expense	1,809,337,000	1,586,064,000	1,460,396,000	1,327,630,000	1,133,303,000	825,296,000
Net Income	369,777,000	507,450,000	365,359,000	232,982,000	126,800,000	187,774,000
Operating Cash Flow	2,309,826,000	1,992,728,000	1,815,426,000	1,439,233,000	1,016,580,000	894,793,000
Capital Expenditure	2,282,504,000	2,079,521,000	2,096,174,000	1,378,725,000	1,113,365,000	868,120,000
EBITDA	2,346,060,000	2,457,118,000	2,182,021,000	1,808,010,000	1,389,222,000	1,035,633,000
Return on Assets %		.02%	.02%	.01%	.01%	.02%
Return on Equity %		.06%	.05%	.04%	.04%	.07%
Debt to Equity		1.396	1.507	1.451	1.51	2.027

CONTACT INFORMATION:

Phone: 650 598-6000   Fax: 650 513-7900
Toll-Free: 800-322-9280
Address: 1 Lagoon Dr., Redwood City, CA 94065 United States

STOCK TICKER/OTHER:

Stock Ticker: EQIX   Exchange: NAS
Employees: 8,378   Fiscal Year Ends: 12/31
Parent Company:

SALARIES/BONUSES:

Top Exec. Salary: $ Bonus: $
Second Exec. Salary: $ Bonus: $

OTHER THOUGHTS:

Estimated Female Officers or Directors: 3
Hot Spot for Advancement for Women/Minorities: Y

Estes Express Lines Inc

www.estes-express.com

NAIC Code: 484122

TYPES OF BUSINESS:

General Freight Trucking, LTL
Less-Than-Truckload Freight
Logistics Services
Supply Chain Management
Warehousing
Truckload Freight

BRANDS/DIVISIONS/AFFILIATES:

Estes SureMove
Estes Forwarding Worldwide LLC
Estes Leasing LLC
Big E Transportation

CONTACTS: *Note: Officers with more than one job title may be intentionally listed here more than once.*

Rob Estes, CEO
Gary D. Okes, Treas.

GROWTH PLANS/SPECIAL FEATURES:

Estes Express Lines, Inc. is a family-owned and -operated company offering less-than-truckload (LTL) and truckload freight carriage, with additional operational areas targeting time-sensitive and larger-volume shipping and various logistics and related specialty services. The company maintains a fleet of more than 7,000 tractors and 30,000 trailers (which range from 28 to 57 feet in length). Estes' network is composed of over 260 terminal facilities in key regional sites nationwide, providing service to all U.S. states as well as major commercial markets in Mexico and the Caribbean. The firm's divisions include: time-critical services, offering guaranteed and time-sensitive service; level2 logistics, which helps businesses create business-to-business (B2B) and business-to-consumer (B2C) shipping solutions in order to enhance supply chain services; specialized truckload and delivery services, allowing customers to develop regular pickup and delivery solutions for retail, store-to-door and contract deliveries; and Estes SureMove, a lower-cost option for DIY household goods moving, Estes drives. Estes subsidiaries include: Estes Forwarding Worldwide, LLC, which offers a suite of innovative and secure solutions to customers, as well as to the forwarding industry; Estes Leasing, LLC, which provides alternatives to equipment financing and maintenance; and Big E Transportation, which provides nationwide logistics and dedicated fleet services for retail replenishment, home delivery and final mile.

FINANCIAL DATA: *Note: Data for latest year may not have been available at press time.*

In U.S. $	2020	2019	2018	2017	2016	2015
Revenue	2,844,000,000	3,160,000,000	2,740,000,000	2,200,000,000	2,155,000,000	2,135,000,000
R&D Expense						
Operating Income						
Operating Margin %						
SGA Expense						
Net Income						
Operating Cash Flow						
Capital Expenditure						
EBITDA						
Return on Assets %						
Return on Equity %						
Debt to Equity						

CONTACT INFORMATION:

Phone: 804-353-1900   Fax: 804-353-8001
Toll-Free:
Address: 3901 W. Broad St., Richmond, VA 23230 United States

STOCK TICKER/OTHER:

Stock Ticker: Private   Exchange:
Employees: 19,200   Fiscal Year Ends: 12/31
Parent Company:

SALARIES/BONUSES:

Top Exec. Salary: $ Bonus: $
Second Exec. Salary: $ Bonus: $

OTHER THOUGHTS:

Estimated Female Officers or Directors:
Hot Spot for Advancement for Women/Minorities:

Eversource Energy

www.eversource.com

NAIC Code: 221122

TYPES OF BUSINESS:

Electric Power Distribution
Natural Gas Distribution
Electric Power Generation

BRANDS/DIVISIONS/AFFILIATES:

Connecticut Light and Power Company
NSTAR Electric Company
Public Service Company of New Hampshire
NSTAR Gas Company
Yankee Gas Services Company
Eversource Aquarion Holdings Inc

CONTACTS: Note: Officers with more than one job title may be intentionally listed here more than once.

Werner Schweiger, CEO, Subsidiary
James Judge, CEO
Philip Lembo, CFO
Jay Buth, Chief Accounting Officer
Leon Olivier, Executive VP, Divisional
Joseph Nolan, Executive VP, Divisional
Christine Carmody, Executive VP, Divisional
Gregory Butler, General Counsel
Kenneth Leibler, Trustee
Sanford Cloud, Trustee
Francis Doyle, Trustee
William Van Faasen, Trustee
James DiStasio, Trustee
Frederica Williams, Trustee
John Kim, Trustee
Linda Forry, Trustee
David Long, Trustee
Cotton Cleveland, Trustee

GROWTH PLANS/SPECIAL FEATURES:

Eversource Energy is a public utility holding company doing business through its wholly-owned subsidiaries, transmitting and delivering electricity and natural gas, and supplying water to approximately 4.3 million customers. The Connecticut Light and Power Company is a regulated electric utility serving residential, commercial and industrial customers in parts of Connecticut. NSTAR Electric Company serves residential, commercial and industrial customers in parts of eastern and western Massachusetts, and owns solar power facilities. Public Service Company of New Hampshire serves residential, commercial and industrial customers in parts of New Hampshire. NSTAR Gas Company is a regulated natural gas utility that serves residential, commercial and industrial customers in parts of Massachusetts. Yankee Gas Services Company is a regulated natural gas utility that services customers in parts of Connecticut. Eversource Aquarion Holdings, Inc. is a utility holding company that owns three separate regulated water utility subsidiaries and collectively serves residential, commercial, industrial, and municipal and fire protection customers in parts of Connecticut, Massachusetts and New Hampshire.

FINANCIAL DATA: Note: Data for latest year may not have been available at press time.

In U.S. $	2020	2019	2018	2017	2016	2015
Revenue	8,904,430,000	8,526,500,000	8,448,200,000	7,752,000,000	7,639,100,000	7,954,800,000
R&D Expense						
Operating Income	1,988,734,000	1,830,165,000	1,699,929,000	1,918,202,000	1,859,830,000	1,764,137,000
Operating Margin %		.21%	.20%	.25%	.24%	.22%
SGA Expense						
Net Income	1,205,167,000	909,053,000	1,033,000,000	987,996,000	942,302,000	878,485,000
Operating Cash Flow	1,682,572,000	2,009,577,000	1,783,978,000	638,400,000	2,175,052,000	1,424,025,000
Capital Expenditure	2,942,996,000	2,911,489,000	2,523,371,000	719,623,000	1,976,867,000	1,724,139,000
EBITDA	3,256,383,000	2,803,926,000	2,900,252,000	2,769,964,000	2,621,245,000	2,464,247,000
Return on Assets %		.02%	.03%	.03%	.03%	.03%
Return on Equity %		.08%	.09%	.09%	.09%	.09%
Debt to Equity		1.133	1.117	1.062	0.824	0.851

CONTACT INFORMATION:

Phone: 413 785-5871   Fax: 413 665-3652
Toll-Free:
Address: 300 Cadwell Dr., Springfield, MA 01104 United States

SALARIES/BONUSES:

Top Exec. Salary: $ Bonus: $
Second Exec. Salary: $ Bonus: $

STOCK TICKER/OTHER:

Stock Ticker: ES
Employees: 7,943
Parent Company:

Exchange: NYS
Fiscal Year Ends: 12/31

OTHER THOUGHTS:

Estimated Female Officers or Directors:
Hot Spot for Advancement for Women/Minorities:

Exelon Corporation

NAIC Code: 221113

www.exeloncorp.com

TYPES OF BUSINESS:

Electric Power Generation-Nuclear
Energy Generation
Electricity
Natural Gas
Renewable Energy
Distribution
Marketing
Retail

BRANDS/DIVISIONS/AFFILIATES:

Exelon Generation Company LLC
Constellation
Commonwealth Edison Company
PECO Energy Company
Baltimore Gas and Electric Company
Pepco Holdings LLC
Potomac Electric Power Company
Delmarva Power & Light

CONTACTS:
Note: Officers with more than one job title may be intentionally listed here more than once.

Denis OBrien, CEO, Divisional
Christopher Crane, CEO

GROWTH PLANS/SPECIAL FEATURES:

Exelon Corporation is a utility services holding company engaged in the generation, delivery, marketing, distribution and transmission of energy through its subsidiaries. Exelon Generation Company, LLC generates, delivers and markets power across multiple geographic regions through Constellation, which sells electricity to both wholesale and retail customers. Exelon Generation also sells natural gas, renewable energy and other energy-related products and services. Commonwealth Edison Company engages in the purchase and regulated retail sale of electricity, and transmits and distributes electricity to retail customers. PECO Energy Company engages in the purchase and regulated retail sale of electricity and natural gas, transmits and distributes electricity, and distributes natural gas to retail customers. Baltimore Gas and Electric Company engages in the purchase and regulated retail sale of electricity and natural gas, transmits and distributes electricity, and distributes natural gas to retail customers. Pepco Holdings, LLC is a utility services holding company operating through three subsidiaries: Potomac Electric Power Company (Pepco), which engages in the purchase and regulated retail sale of electricity, and transmits and distributes electricity to retail customers; Delmarva Power & Light (DPL), which engages in the purchase and regulated retail sale of electricity and natural gas, transmits and distributes electricity, and distributes natural gas to retail customers; and Atlantic City Electric (ACE), which engages in the purchase and regulated retail sale of electricity, and transmits and distributes electricity to retail customers.

FINANCIAL DATA:
Note: Data for latest year may not have been available at press time.

In U.S. $	2020	2019	2018	2017	2016	2015
Revenue		38,144,098,304	35,984,998,400	33,531,000,832	31,360,000,000	29,447,000,064
R&D Expense						
Operating Income						
Operating Margin %						
SGA Expense						
Net Income		2,510,000,000	2,010,000,000	3,769,999,872	1,134,000,000	2,268,999,936
Operating Cash Flow						
Capital Expenditure						
EBITDA						
Return on Assets %						
Return on Equity %						
Debt to Equity						

CONTACT INFORMATION:

Phone: 312 394-7398   Fax: 312 394-7945
Toll-Free: 800-483-3220
Address: 10 S. Dearborn St., 48/Fl., Chicago, IL 60680-5379 United States

STOCK TICKER/OTHER:

Stock Ticker: EXC
Employees: 34,396
Parent Company:

Exchange: NYS
Fiscal Year Ends: 12/31

SALARIES/BONUSES:

Top Exec. Salary: $ Bonus: $
Second Exec. Salary: $ Bonus: $

OTHER THOUGHTS:

Estimated Female Officers or Directors: 6
Hot Spot for Advancement for Women/Minorities: Y

Expeditors International of Washington Inc www.expeditors.com

NAIC Code: 488510

TYPES OF BUSINESS:

Freight Transportation Arrangement
Online Services
Logistics Software
Freight Consolidation
Customs Brokerage

BRANDS/DIVISIONS/AFFILIATES:

Project Cargo
Transcon

CONTACTS: Note: Officers with more than one job title may be intentionally listed here more than once.

Jeffrey Musser, CEO
Bradley Powell, CFO
Christopher McClincy, Chief Information Officer
Philip Coughlin, Chief Strategy Officer
Robert Wright, Director
Benjamin Clark, General Counsel
Richard Rostan, President, Divisional
Daniel Wall, President, Divisional
Eugene Alger, President, Divisional

GROWTH PLANS/SPECIAL FEATURES:

Expeditors International of Washington, Inc. provides global logistics services through an international network of more than 175 district offices in the Americas, Asia, Europe, Middle East, Africa and India. The company provides a range of transportation services and customer solutions, such as customs brokerage, order management, time-definite transportation, warehousing and distribution, temperature-controlled transit, cargo insurance, specialized cargo monitoring and tracking, and other customized logistics and consulting solutions. Expeditors' Project Cargo unit handles special project shipments that move through a single method or combination of air, ocean and/or ground transportation, and generally requires a high level of specialized attention due to its size or other reason. As an airfreight consolidator, Expeditors purchases cargo capacity from airlines on a volume basis and resells that space to its customers at lower rates than what they would pay directly from the airlines. As a freight forwarder, the company receives and forwards individual, unconsolidated shipments and arranges the transportation with the airline that carries the shipment. As an ocean freight consolidator, Expeditors contracts with ocean shipping carriers to obtain transportation for a fixed number of containers between various ports during a specified time period and agreed-upon rates. The firm handles both full container loads (FCL) and less-than container loads (LCL). Expeditors also generates fees for ancillary services such as shipping and customs documentation, packing, crating, insurance and more. Expeditors' Transcon consists of multi-modal, intra-continental ground transportation and delivery services, and includes value-added, white glove and time-definite services. Last, the firm's distribution and warehouse services include distribution center management, inventory management, order fulfillment, returns programs and other services. Industries served include aerospace, automotive, fashion, healthcare, manufacturing, oil/energy, retail and technology. During 2020, Expeditors acquired Fleet Logistics' digital platform to support Expeditors' online less-than-truckload shipping platform and related digital solutions.

FINANCIAL DATA: Note: Data for latest year may not have been available at press time.

In U.S. $	2020	2019	2018	2017	2016	2015
Revenue	10,116,480,000	8,175,426,000	8,138,365,000	6,920,948,000	6,098,037,000	6,616,632,000
R&D Expense						
Operating Income	940,437,000	766,692,000	796,563,000	700,260,000	670,163,000	721,484,000
Operating Margin %		.09%	.10%	.10%	.11%	.11%
SGA Expense	18,436,000	44,002,000	45,346,000	44,290,000	41,763,000	41,990,000
Net Income	696,140,000	590,395,000	618,199,000	489,345,000	430,807,000	457,223,000
Operating Cash Flow	655,012,000	771,935,000	572,804,000	488,639,000	529,099,000	564,712,000
Capital Expenditure	47,543,000	47,022,000	47,474,000	95,016,000	59,316,000	44,383,000
EBITDA	997,396,000	817,642,000	850,582,000	749,570,000	716,959,000	767,496,000
Return on Assets %		.17%	.19%	.17%	.16%	.17%
Return on Equity %		.28%	.31%	.26%	.24%	.26%
Debt to Equity		0.149				

CONTACT INFORMATION:

Phone: 206 674-3400   Fax: 206 674-3459
Toll-Free:
Address: 1015 3rd Ave., Seattle, WA 98104 United States

STOCK TICKER/OTHER:

Stock Ticker: EXPD
Employees: 18,000
Parent Company:

Exchange: NAS
Fiscal Year Ends: 12/31

SALARIES/BONUSES:

Top Exec. Salary: $ Bonus: $
Second Exec. Salary: $ Bonus: $

OTHER THOUGHTS:

Estimated Female Officers or Directors: 2
Hot Spot for Advancement for Women/Minorities:

Sales, profits and employees may be estimates. Financial information, benefits and other data can change quickly and may vary from those stated here.

EY LLP
NAIC Code: 541211

www.ey.com/us/en/home

TYPES OF BUSINESS:
Accounting
Accounting
Advisory
Tax Services
Audit Assurance
Transaction Services

BRANDS/DIVISIONS/AFFILIATES:
EY

CONTACTS: *Note: Officers with more than one job title may be intentionally listed here more than once.*
Kelly Grier, U.S. Chmn
Michael Inserra, Regional Managing Partner-Financial Svcs.
Tom Hough, Vice Chair-Assurance Svcs.
Richard Jeanneret, Vice Chair-Transaction Advisory Svcs.
Jean-Yves, Vice Chair-Quality & Risk Mgmt.
Tom McGrath, Sr. Vice Chair-Accounts
Ronen Barel, Chmn.

GROWTH PLANS/SPECIAL FEATURES:
EY, LLP, the U.S. branch of the global accounting firm EY, is a professional services company. EY, LLP provides advisory, tax, assurance and transaction services. Advisory services include actuarial, customer, cyber security, finance, risk management, internal audit, people advisory, program management, risk assurance, risk transformation, strategy, supply chain, operations and technology. Tax services include global tax, country tax, cross border tax, global trade, global compliance and reporting, human capital, private client, law, tax accounting, tax performance, tax policy and controversy, transaction tax, sales tax, transfer pricing and operating model effectiveness. Assurance services include accounting compliance, reporting, climate change, sustainability, financial accounting, financial statement audit, fraud investigation and dispute services. Transactions service include corporate development, divesture, lead advisory, operational transaction, restructuring, strategy, transaction support, transaction tax, valuation and business modeling. Industries served by EY, LLP include automotive, transportation, health, oil and gas, technology, consumer products, retail, life sciences, power/utilities, telecommunications, financial services, media/entertainment, private equity, government, public sector, mining/metals, real estate, hospitality and construction.

FINANCIAL DATA: *Note: Data for latest year may not have been available at press time.*

In U.S. $	2020	2019	2018	2017	2016	2015
Revenue	17,187,000,000	16,784,000,000	15,606,000,000	13,000,000,000	12,200,000,000	11,200,000,000
R&D Expense						
Operating Income						
Operating Margin %						
SGA Expense						
Net Income						
Operating Cash Flow						
Capital Expenditure						
EBITDA						
Return on Assets %						
Return on Equity %						
Debt to Equity						

CONTACT INFORMATION:
Phone: 212-773-3000   Fax: 212-773-6350
Toll-Free:
Address: 5 Times Sq., New York, NY 10036-6530 United States

STOCK TICKER/OTHER:
Stock Ticker: Subsidiary   Exchange:
Employees: 75,951   Fiscal Year Ends: 06/30
Parent Company: EY

SALARIES/BONUSES:
Top Exec. Salary: $ Bonus: $
Second Exec. Salary: $ Bonus: $

OTHER THOUGHTS:
Estimated Female Officers or Directors: 5
Hot Spot for Advancement for Women/Minorities: Y

F5 Networks Inc   www.f5.com

NAIC Code: 511210B

TYPES OF BUSINESS:

Computer Software: Network Management (IT), System Testing & Storage
Multi-Cloud
Security
Managed Services
Software
Hardware

BRANDS/DIVISIONS/AFFILIATES:

Shape Security Inc

CONTACTS: Note: Officers with more than one job title may be intentionally listed here more than once.

Francis Pelzer, CFO
Ryan Kearny, CTO
Alan Higginson, Director
Francois Locoh-Donou, Director
Steve McMillan, Executive VP, Divisional
Chad Whalen, Executive VP, Divisional
Scot Rogers, Executive VP
Ana White, Executive VP
Tom Fountain, Executive VP
Kara Sprague, General Manager, Divisional

GROWTH PLANS/SPECIAL FEATURES:

F5 Networks, Inc. is a multi-cloud application security and delivery company. The firm's enterprise-grade solutions are available in a range of consumption models, from on-premises to managed services, optimized for multi-cloud environments. In connection with its solutions, F5 Networks offers a broad range of professional services, including consulting, training, installation, maintenance and other technical support services. Products by F5 Networks span traffic management, application security, infrastructure security, automation, visibility, centralized management, cloud services, cloud software, hardware, application firewall and more. Based in the U.S. F5 Networks has office located in more than 40 countries worldwide. Over 45 of the Fortune 50 rely on F5's products, solutions and services. In early-2020, F5 Networks acquired Shape Security, Inc., a provider of application security against fraud and abuse. In January 2021, F5 Networks agreed to acquire Volterra, a provider of distributed cloud services for deploying, networking and securing applications across multi-cloud and the edge.

F5 Networks offers its employees comprehensive health benefits and a variety of assistance programs.

FINANCIAL DATA: Note: Data for latest year may not have been available at press time.

In U.S. $	2020	2019	2018	2017	2016	2015
Revenue	2,350,822,000	2,242,447,000	2,161,407,000	2,090,041,000	1,995,034,000	1,919,823,000
R&D Expense	441,324,000	408,058,000	366,084,000	350,365,000	334,227,000	296,583,000
Operating Income	400,067,000	518,463,000	609,325,000	577,065,000	556,428,000	552,899,000
Operating Margin %	.23%	.28%	.28%	.28%	.28%	.29%
SGA Expense	1,101,544,000	959,349,000	824,517,000	809,126,000	767,174,000	738,080,000
Net Income	307,441,000	427,734,000	453,689,000	420,761,000	365,855,000	365,014,000
Operating Cash Flow	660,898,000	747,841,000	761,068,000	740,281,000	711,535,000	684,541,000
Capital Expenditure	59,940,000	103,542,000	53,465,000	42,681,000	68,238,000	67,086,000
EBITDA	495,924,000	586,970,000	668,816,000	638,213,000	613,204,000	605,482,000
Return on Assets %		.14%	.18%	.18%	.16%	.16%
Return on Equity %		.28%	.36%	.35%	.29%	.27%
Debt to Equity						

CONTACT INFORMATION:

Phone: 206 272-5555   Fax: 206 272-5556
Toll-Free: 888-882-4447
Address: 801 5th Ave., Seattle, WA 98104 United States

STOCK TICKER/OTHER:

Stock Ticker: FFIV
Employees: 6,109
Parent Company:

Exchange: NAS
Fiscal Year Ends: 09/30

SALARIES/BONUSES:

Top Exec. Salary: $ Bonus: $
Second Exec. Salary: $ Bonus: $

OTHER THOUGHTS:

Estimated Female Officers or Directors: 3
Hot Spot for Advancement for Women/Minorities: Y

Facebook Inc

investor.fb.com

NAIC Code: 519130

TYPES OF BUSINESS:

Social Networking
Advertising Services
Developer Tools
Online Video
3-D Headset Manufacturing
Apps

BRANDS/DIVISIONS/AFFILIATES:

Facebook Platform
Instagram
Messenger
WhatsApp Messenger
Oculus

CONTACTS: Note: Officers with more than one job title may be intentionally listed here more than once.

Mark Zuckerberg, CEO
David Wehner, CFO
Susan Taylor, Chief Accounting Officer
Michael Schroepfer, Chief Technology Officer
Sheryl Sandberg, COO
Christopher Cox, Other Executive Officer
David Fischer, Other Executive Officer
Colin Stretch, Vice President

GROWTH PLANS/SPECIAL FEATURES:

Facebook, Inc. owns and operates a free social networking platform for communicating online with family, friends and acquaintances. The company has 2.5 billion monthly active users in general, and 1.66 billion daily active users who specifically used the company's mobile products. Some of the site's core functions and applications include individual profiles and home pages; friend lists; group pages; and photos, videos, events and other shared items. Communication is enabled through means such as in-site instant messaging, personal messages, public posts and status updates. Third-party applications (such as games, quizzes and personality tests) can also be added to users' pages to further personalize the site. For privacy, the firm gives users the ability to limit, to some extent, who can view their profile, postings and other personal information. The company's Facebook Platform is a set of development tools and application programming interfaces that enable developers to integrate with Facebook to create social apps and websites. Millions of apps and websites have been integrated as part of the platform. Facebook generates the majority of its revenues from advertising, which can be customized to reach specifically targeted audiences by accessing information users provide the company on their individual profiles. Subsidiary Instagram is a mobile phone-based photo-sharing service that makes it simple for users to upload photos to their profiles; Messenger is a mobile-to-mobile messaging application; WhatsApp Messenger is a cross-platform mobile messaging app that allows people to exchange messages on mobile devices; and Oculus, a virtual reality technology and content platform that power products and enable users to immerse and interact in connected environments.

Facebook offers its employees comprehensive benefits.

FINANCIAL DATA: Note: Data for latest year may not have been available at press time.

In U.S. $	2020	2019	2018	2017	2016	2015
Revenue	85,965,000,000	70,697,000,000	55,838,000,000	40,653,000,000	27,638,000,000	17,928,000,000
R&D Expense	18,447,000,000	13,600,000,000	10,273,000,000	7,754,000,000	5,919,000,000	4,816,000,000
Operating Income	32,671,000,000	23,986,000,000	24,913,000,000	20,203,000,000	12,427,000,000	6,225,000,000
Operating Margin %		.34%	.45%	.50%	.45%	.35%
SGA Expense	18,155,000,000	20,341,000,000	11,297,000,000	7,242,000,000	5,503,000,000	4,020,000,000
Net Income	29,146,000,000	18,485,000,000	22,112,000,000	15,934,000,000	10,217,000,000	3,688,000,000
Operating Cash Flow	38,747,000,000	36,314,000,000	29,274,000,000	24,216,000,000	16,108,000,000	8,599,000,000
Capital Expenditure	15,115,000,000	15,102,000,000	13,915,000,000	6,733,000,000	4,491,000,000	2,523,000,000
EBITDA	39,533,000,000	30,573,000,000	29,685,000,000	23,625,000,000	14,870,000,000	8,162,000,000
Return on Assets %		.16%	.24%	.21%	.18%	.08%
Return on Equity %		.20%	.28%	.24%	.20%	.09%
Debt to Equity		0.094				0.002

CONTACT INFORMATION:

Phone: 650 543-4800   Fax:
Toll-Free:
Address: 1601 Willow Rd., Menlo Park, CA 94025 United States

STOCK TICKER/OTHER:

Stock Ticker: FB
Employees: 58,604
Parent Company:

Exchange: NAS
Fiscal Year Ends: 12/31

SALARIES/BONUSES:

Top Exec. Salary: $ Bonus: $
Second Exec. Salary: $ Bonus: $

OTHER THOUGHTS:

Estimated Female Officers or Directors: 2
Hot Spot for Advancement for Women/Minorities: Y

FactSet Research Systems Inc

www.factset.com

NAIC Code: 511120A

TYPES OF BUSINESS:

Online Financial & Economic Data
Financial Software
Consulting Services

BRANDS/DIVISIONS/AFFILIATES:

CONTACTS:
Note: Officers with more than one job title may be intentionally listed here more than once.

F. Snow, CEO
Helen Shan, CFO
Philip Hadley, Chairman of the Board
Brian Daly, Chief Accounting Officer
Gene Fernandez, Chief Technology Officer
John Wiseman, Executive VP, Divisional
Rachel Stern, Executive VP
Robert Robie, Executive VP

GROWTH PLANS/SPECIAL FEATURES:

FactSet Research Systems, Inc. supplies financial information and analytical applications to global investors, including portfolio managers, performance analysts, risk managers, sell-side equity researchers, investment bankers and fixed income professionals. FactSet has more than 133,000 users and 6,225+ clients, with an annual client retention rate at over 95% (as of August 31, 2020). Users and clients have access to data from thousands of third-party data suppliers, news sources, exchanges, brokers and contributors within FactSet's single online service. The company's goal is to provide a seamless user experience spanning idea generation, research, portfolio construction, trade execution, performance measurement, risk management, reporting and portfolio analysis, in which it serves the front, middle and back offices to drive productivity and improved performance. FactSet's flexible, open data and technology solutions can be implemented both across the investment portfolio lifecycle or as standalone components serving different workflows in the organization. FactSet is focused on growing its business throughout the Americas, EMEA and the Asia Pacific. Headquartered in Norwalk, Connecticut, the company operates from more than 45 office locations in 22 countries. In October 2020, FactSet agreed to acquire Truvalue Labs, Inc., a leader in artificial intelligence (AI)-driven environmental, social and governance data.

FINANCIAL DATA:
Note: Data for latest year may not have been available at press time.

In U.S. $	2020	2019	2018	2017	2016	2015
Revenue	1,494,111,000	1,435,351,000	1,350,145,000	1,221,179,000	1,127,092,000	1,006,768,000
R&D Expense						
Operating Income	439,660,000	438,035,000	366,204,000	352,135,000	349,676,000	331,918,000
Operating Margin %		.31%	.27%	.29%	.31%	.33%
SGA Expense	359,005,000	333,870,000	324,645,000	302,464,000	290,007,000	269,511,000
Net Income	372,938,000	352,790,000	267,085,000	258,259,000	338,815,000	241,051,000
Operating Cash Flow	505,840,000	427,136,000	385,668,000	320,527,000	331,140,000	306,442,000
Capital Expenditure	77,642,000	59,370,000	33,520,000	36,862,000	47,740,000	25,682,000
EBITDA	537,762,000	498,498,000	423,489,000	400,429,000	387,728,000	363,267,000
Return on Assets %		.24%	.19%	.21%	.39%	.34%
Return on Equity %		.59%	.49%	.48%	.65%	.46%
Debt to Equity		0.854	1.093	1.027	0.58	0.066

CONTACT INFORMATION:

Phone: 203 810-1000   Fax: 203 810-1001
Toll-Free:
Address: 45 Glover Ave., Norwalk, CT 06850 United States

SALARIES/BONUSES:

Top Exec. Salary: $ Bonus: $
Second Exec. Salary: $ Bonus: $

STOCK TICKER/OTHER:

Stock Ticker: FDS   Exchange: NYS
Employees: 10,484   Fiscal Year Ends: 08/31
Parent Company:

OTHER THOUGHTS:

Estimated Female Officers or Directors: 3
Hot Spot for Advancement for Women/Minorities: Y

Fanatics Inc

www.fanaticsinc.com

NAIC Code: 454111

TYPES OF BUSINESS:

Electronic Shopping of Licensed Sports Merchandise
Ecommerce
Vertical Commerce
Sports Retailer

BRANDS/DIVISIONS/AFFILIATES:

Kynetic LLC
Fanatics.com
FansEdge.com
Kitbag.com
MajesticAthletic.com
FanaticsAuthentic.com
NFLSHOP.ca

CONTACTS: Note: Officers with more than one job title may be intentionally listed here more than once.

Doug Mack, CEO
Jamie Davis, Pres.
Mich Chandlee, CFO
Lonnie Phillips, Chief Customer Officer
Robin Eletto, Chief People Officer
Ramana Thumu, CTO
Jack Boyle, Pres., Merch.
Mitch Trager, Chief Strategy Officer
Meier Raivich, VP-Branding
Gary Gertzog, Exec. VP-Bus. Affairs
Michael Rubin, Exec. Chmn.

GROWTH PLANS/SPECIAL FEATURES:

Fanatics, Inc. is an online retailer of licensed sports merchandise. Customers can purchase items via online sites through the Fanatics (Fanatics.com), FansEdge (FansEdge.com), Kitbag (Kitbag.com) and Majestic (MajesticAthletic.com) brands. The firm also offers a collection of sports collectibles and memorabilia through Fanatics Authentic (FanaticsAuthentic.com). Fanatics operates more than 300 online and offline partner stores, including the eCommerce business for all major professional sports leagues (NFL, MLB, NBA, NHL, NASCAR, MLS, PGA, Premier League); major media brands (NBC Sports, CBS Sports, FOX Sports); and more than 200 collegiate and professional team properties. In addition to eCommerce, the company's capabilities include multichannel-integrated event and team retail across all leagues and major events such as Kentucky Derby, Ryder Cup and NHL's Winder Classic. International capabilities that provide a global sports retail platform is currently growing the licensed sports merchandise business in soccer as well as across all sports worldwide. NFLSHOP.ca is an eCommerce platform for Canadian NFL fans. Fanatics launched an innovative business model called Vertical Commerce (vCommerce), meaning Fanatics will own, design, produce and distribute its own exclusive merchandise, and therefore sell unique, specialized and differentiated products that cannot be commoditized by the internet. As of 2020, Fanatics uses its vCommerce manufacturing capabilities to design, manufacture and distribute all Nike fan gear sold at retail, offering a wider assortment of timely merchandise across categories to fans and retailers at a fast rate. Fanatics is headquartered in Florida, and is privately-owned by Kynetic, LLC. The firm has other headquarter locations in California, USA; Manchester, U.K.; and Tokyo, Japan.

FINANCIAL DATA: Note: Data for latest year may not have been available at press time.

In U.S. $	2020	2019	2018	2017	2016	2015
Revenue	2,887,500,000	2,500,000,000	2,475,375,000	2,415,000,000	2,000,000,000	1,500,000,000
R&D Expense						
Operating Income						
Operating Margin %						
SGA Expense						
Net Income						
Operating Cash Flow						
Capital Expenditure						
EBITDA						
Return on Assets %						
Return on Equity %						
Debt to Equity						

CONTACT INFORMATION:

Phone: 904-421-1897   Fax:
Toll-Free: 877-833-7397
Address: 8100 Nations Way, Jacksonville, FL 32256 United States

STOCK TICKER/OTHER:

Stock Ticker: Subsidiary   Exchange:
Employees: 5,000   Fiscal Year Ends:
Parent Company: Kynetic LLC

SALARIES/BONUSES:

Top Exec. Salary: $ Bonus: $
Second Exec. Salary: $ Bonus: $

OTHER THOUGHTS:

Estimated Female Officers or Directors:
Hot Spot for Advancement for Women/Minorities:

Fannie Mae (Federal National Mortgage Association)

www.fanniemae.com

NAIC Code: 522294

TYPES OF BUSINESS:

Mortgages, Secondary Market
Mortgage Financing
Mortgage-backed Securities

BRANDS/DIVISIONS/AFFILIATES:

CONTACTS: *Note: Officers with more than one job title may be intentionally listed here more than once.*

Hugh Frater, CEO
Celeste Brown, CFO
Jonathan Plutzik, Chairman of the Board
John Forlines, Chief Risk Officer
Chryssa Halley, Controller
Kimberly Johnson, COO
Stephen Mcelhennon, Deputy General Counsel
Andrew Bon Salle, Executive VP, Divisional
Jeffery Hayward, Other Corporate Officer
David Benson, President

GROWTH PLANS/SPECIAL FEATURES:

Federal National Mortgage Association, known as Fannie Mae, is a source of financing for mortgages in the U.S. It is a government-sponsored enterprise chartered by the U.S. Congress, yet shareholder-owned. Fannie Mae's revenues are primarily driven by guaranty fees received for assuming the credit risk on loans underlying the mortgage-backed securities it issues. The association does not originate loans nor lend money directly to borrowers; but instead, primarily works with lenders who originate loans to borrowers. Fannie Me securitizes the loans into Fannie Mae mortgage-backed securities (MBS) that it guarantees. In exchange for assuming credit risk on the loans it acquires, Fannie Mae receives guaranty fees, which take into account the credit risk characteristics of the loans and consist of two primary components: loan-level pricing adjustments, which are upfront fees received when Fannie Mae acquires single-family loans; and base guaranty fees, which are received monthly over the life of the loan. During 2020, Fannie Mae provided over $1.4 trillion in liquidity to the mortgage market, which enabled the financing of approximately 6 million home purchases, refinancings or rental units. In May 2021, Fannie Mae announced the sale of non-performing loans as part of the company's effort to reduce to the size of its retained mortgage portfolio, including its 17th Community Impact Pool (CIP).

Fannie Mae offers its employees comprehensive benefits, retirement options and employee assistance programs.

FINANCIAL DATA: *Note: Data for latest year may not have been available at press time.*

In U.S. $	2020	2019	2018	2017	2016	2015
Revenue	23,734,000,000	21,694,000,000	24,003,000,000	23,271,000,000	22,436,000,000	22,326,000,000
R&D Expense						
Operating Income						
Operating Margin %						
SGA Expense	2,147,000,000	2,056,000,000	2,027,000,000	1,804,000,000	1,600,000,000	1,884,000,000
Net Income	11,805,000,000	14,160,000,000	15,959,000,000	2,463,000,000	12,313,000,000	10,954,000,000
Operating Cash Flow	-72,934,000,000	-4,754,000,000	2,248,000,000	8,256,000,000	-733,000,000	-6,673,000,000
Capital Expenditure						
EBITDA						
Return on Assets %		.00%	.00%	.00%	.00%	.00%
Return on Equity %						
Debt to Equity						

CONTACT INFORMATION:

Phone: 202 752-7000   Fax: 202 752-4934
Toll-Free: 800-232-6643
Address: 1100 15th St. NW, Washington, DC 20005 United States

SALARIES/BONUSES:

Top Exec. Salary: $ Bonus: $
Second Exec. Salary: $ Bonus: $

STOCK TICKER/OTHER:

Stock Ticker: FNMA   Exchange: PINX
Employees: 7,500   Fiscal Year Ends: 12/31
Parent Company:

OTHER THOUGHTS:

Estimated Female Officers or Directors: 5
Hot Spot for Advancement for Women/Minorities: Y

FedEx Corporation

NAIC Code: 492110

www.fedex.com

TYPES OF BUSINESS:

Couriers and Express Delivery Services
Ground Delivery Services
Freight Services
Document Solutions & Business Services
International Trade Services
Ecommerce Shopping Platform

BRANDS/DIVISIONS/AFFILIATES:

Federal Express Corporation
FedEx Ground Package System Inc
FedEx Freight Corporation
FedEx Corporate Services Inc
FedEx SmartPost
FedEx Freight Priority
FedEx Freight Economy
ShopRunner Inc

CONTACTS: Note: Officers with more than one job title may be intentionally listed here more than once.

Rajesh Subramaniam, CEO, Subsidiary
Henry Maier, CEO, Subsidiary
John Smith, CEO, Subsidiary
Frederick Smith, CEO
Robert Carter, Chief Information Officer
Alan Graf, Executive VP
Mark Allen, Executive VP
Donald Colleran, Executive VP
John Merino, Vice President

GROWTH PLANS/SPECIAL FEATURES:

FedEx Corporation is a holding company that offers transportation, ecommerce and business services through four subsidiary segments. The FedEx Express Corporation segment provides time-definitive delivery to more than 220 countries and territories, connecting markets that comprise more than 99% of the world's gross domestic product. The FedEx Ground Package System, Inc. segment is a North American provider of small-package ground delivery services. It provides day-certain service to any business address in the U.S. and Canada, as well as residential delivery to 100% of U.S. residences through its FedEx Home Delivery service. This division's FedEx SmartPost ground service specializes in the consolidation and delivery of high volumes of low-weight, less time-sensitive business-to-consumer packages primarily using the U.S. Postal Service for final delivery to residences. The FedEx Freight Corporation segment is a leading U.S. provider of less-than-truckload freight services across all lengths of haul. This division includes: FedEx Freight Priority, when speed is critical for supply chain needs; and FedEx Freight Economy, for when a customer can trade time for cost savings. This segment also offers freight delivery service to most points in Canada, Mexico, Puerto Rico and the U.S. Virgin Islands. Last, the FedEx Corporate Services, Inc. segment provides sales, marketing, IT, communications, customer service, technical support, billing and collections services, as well as certain back-office functions that support FedEx Corporation's transportation segments. This division includes FedEx Office and Print Services, Inc., which provides of document and business services, as well as retail access to FedEx's package transportation businesses. In December 2020, FedEx acquired ShopRunner, Inc., an ecommerce platform that directly connects brands and merchants with online shoppers.

FedEx Corporation offers comprehensive health benefits and retirement/pension plans.

FINANCIAL DATA: Note: Data for latest year may not have been available at press time.

In U.S. $	2020	2019	2018	2017	2016	2015
Revenue	69,217,000,000	69,693,000,000	65,450,000,000	60,319,000,000	50,365,000,000	
R&D Expense						
Operating Income	2,852,000,000	4,786,000,000	5,250,000,000	5,037,000,000	3,077,000,000	
Operating Margin %	.04%	.07%	.08%	.08%	.06%	
SGA Expense						
Net Income	1,286,000,000	540,000,000	4,572,000,000	2,997,000,000	1,820,000,000	
Operating Cash Flow	5,097,000,000	5,613,000,000	4,674,000,000	4,930,000,000	5,708,000,000	
Capital Expenditure	5,868,000,000	5,490,000,000	5,663,000,000	5,116,000,000	4,818,000,000	
EBITDA	5,956,000,000	4,596,000,000	8,006,000,000	8,086,000,000	5,707,000,000	
Return on Assets %	.02%	.01%	.09%	.06%	.04%	
Return on Equity %	.07%	.03%	.26%	.20%	.13%	
Debt to Equity	1.866	0.936	0.785	0.928	1.004	

CONTACT INFORMATION:

Phone: 901 818-7500   Fax: 901 346-1013
Toll-Free:
Address: 942 S. Shady Grove Rd., Memphis, TN 38120 United States

STOCK TICKER/OTHER:

Stock Ticker: FDX   Exchange: NYS
Employees: 245,000   Fiscal Year Ends: 05/31
Parent Company:

SALARIES/BONUSES:

Top Exec. Salary: $ Bonus: $
Second Exec. Salary: $ Bonus: $

OTHER THOUGHTS:

Estimated Female Officers or Directors: 3
Hot Spot for Advancement for Women/Minorities: Y

FedEx Freight

NAIC Code: 484122

www.fedex.com/us/freight

TYPES OF BUSINESS:

Trucking, Less than Truckload Freight
Express LTL Shipping
Technology Solutions

BRANDS/DIVISIONS/AFFILIATES:

FedEx Corporation
FedEx Freight Priority
Fed Ex Freight Economy
FedEx Ship Manager

CONTACTS: *Note: Officers with more than one job title may be intentionally listed here more than once.*

Frederick W. Smith, CEO
Rajesh Subramaniam, Pres.
Mike Lenz, CFO
Brie Carer, CMO
Robert B. Carter, CIO
Frederick W. Smith, Chmn.

GROWTH PLANS/SPECIAL FEATURES:

FedEx Freight, a subsidiary of FedEx Corporation, is a provider of air and less-than-truckload (LTL) freight service solutions. The firm offers LTL two shipping methods: FedEx Freight Priority, which provides fast-transit delivery of time-sensitive freight; and FedEx Freight Economy, which provides reliable, cost-effective delivery when freight is not time-sensitive. Other freight services include: day/time-definite guaranteed services, when LTL freight must arrive by a certain day and/or a certain time; volume services, for oversized and large-volume freight shipments that are not time-sensitive; international services, between the U.S., Canada and Mexico; and offshore services, providing end-to-end coverage for less-than-container-load freight shipments to Alaska, Hawaii, Puerto Rico and the U.S. Virgin Islands. Freight shipping can be managed with the FedEx Ship Manager, and shipping forms can be viewed, printed or downloaded from the FedEx website for U.S. and international shipping needs. FedEx also engages in technology innovation, such as its Roxo same-day robot delivery service designed to meet ecommerce and last-mile delivery needs; drone small package delivery; supply chain data analytics and inventory management; and SenseAware ID package location solutions via wireless solutions.

FedEx Freight offers its employees comprehensive health and retirement benefits, life and disability insurance and a variety of employee assistance programs.

FINANCIAL DATA: *Note: Data for latest year may not have been available at press time.*

In U.S. $	2020	2019	2018	2017	2016	2015
Revenue	7,102,000,000	7,582,000,000	6,812,000,000	6,070,000,000	5,825,000,000	6,191,000,000
R&D Expense						
Operating Income						
Operating Margin %						
SGA Expense						
Net Income	580,000,000	615,000,000	490,000,000	371,000,000	421,000,000	484,000,000
Operating Cash Flow						
Capital Expenditure						
EBITDA						
Return on Assets %						
Return on Equity %						
Debt to Equity						

CONTACT INFORMATION:

Phone: 901-346-4400   Fax: 901-434-3118
Toll-Free:
Address: 1715 Aaron Brenner Dr., Ste. 600, Memphis, TN 38120 United States

STOCK TICKER/OTHER:

Stock Ticker: Subsidiary   Exchange:
Employees: 49,000   Fiscal Year Ends: 05/31
Parent Company: FedEx Corporation

SALARIES/BONUSES:

Top Exec. Salary: $ Bonus: $
Second Exec. Salary: $ Bonus: $

OTHER THOUGHTS:

Estimated Female Officers or Directors:
Hot Spot for Advancement for Women/Minorities:

FedEx Ground

NAIC Code: 492110

www.fedex.com/us/ground/main

TYPES OF BUSINESS:

Couriers and Express Delivery Services
Home Delivery Services
Courier Services
Trucking

BRANDS/DIVISIONS/AFFILIATES:

FedEx Corporation
FedEx Delivery Manager
FedEx SmartPost
FedEx Ground COLLECT

CONTACTS: *Note: Officers with more than one job title may be intentionally listed here more than once.*

John A. Smith, CEO

GROWTH PLANS/SPECIAL FEATURES:

FedEx Ground, a subsidiary of FedEx Corporation, provides ground delivery of small packages throughout the U.S. and Canada. Packages weigh up to 150 pounds, are up to 108 inches in length and up to 165 inches in length plus girth. FedEx Ground's business is divided into three divisions: U.S., international and home delivery. Small package deliveries to U.S. addresses are generally made within one to five business days in the continental U.S. and in three to seven business days to Alaska and Hawaii, depending on distance. International deliveries are only made to Canada, and are delivered within three to seven business days. The home delivery division serves virtually 100% of the U.S. population, and offers services such as requiring a signature for the delivery, scheduling a specific date for delivery and/or scheduling evening delivery (between 5 and 8pm). The FedEx Delivery Manager offers shipment management options such as delivery, pickup, proof-of-delivery and collect-on-delivery options, all of which can be managed online or by mobile phone. FedEx SmartPost specializes in shipping high volumes of low-weight packages to residential customers for a reduced cost. FedEx Ground COLLECT is a payment platform that enables companies to control inbound shipping charges by allowing them to pay for shipments, bill the recipients or a third party and pay for all inbound shipments. Other payment options include billing to a FedEx account, electronic funds transfer/automatic debit or billing a recipient.

FINANCIAL DATA: *Note: Data for latest year may not have been available at press time.*

In U.S. $	2020	2019	2018	2017	2016	2015
Revenue	22,733,000,000	20,522,000,000	18,395,000,000	16,503,000,000	15,051,000,000	12,568,000,000
R&D Expense						
Operating Income						
Operating Margin %						
SGA Expense						
Net Income	2,014,000,000	2,663,000,000	2,529,000,000	2,243,000,000	2,240,000,000	2,172,000,000
Operating Cash Flow						
Capital Expenditure						
EBITDA						
Return on Assets %						
Return on Equity %						
Debt to Equity						

CONTACT INFORMATION:

Phone: 412-269-1000   Fax: 412-747-4290
Toll-Free:
Address: 1000 FedEx Dr., Coraopolis, PA 15018-9373 United States

STOCK TICKER/OTHER:

Stock Ticker: Subsidiary
Employees: 110,000
Parent Company: FedEx Corporation

Exchange:
Fiscal Year Ends: 05/31

SALARIES/BONUSES:

Top Exec. Salary: $ Bonus: $
Second Exec. Salary: $ Bonus: $

OTHER THOUGHTS:

Estimated Female Officers or Directors:
Hot Spot for Advancement for Women/Minorities:

FedEx Supply Chain

supplychain.fedex.com

NAIC Code: 488510

TYPES OF BUSINESS:

Third Party Logistics Services
Logistics Software
Consulting
Warehousing
Transportation Services
Supply Chain Analysis
Asset Recovery
Pharmaceutical Returns

BRANDS/DIVISIONS/AFFILIATES:

FedEx Corporation
FedEx Logistics

CONTACTS: Note: Officers with more than one job title may be intentionally listed here more than once.

Scott Temple, Pres.
Joseph Salamunovich, General Counsel
Ryan Kelly, Sr. VP-Strategy
Art Smuck, Group Pres., Tech. Solutions & Healthcare Logistic
Val Dodd, Pres., Healthcare Logistics
John McGonigle, III, Pres., Genco Infrastructure Solutions
Laurie Barkmen, CEO-Genco Marketplace
Tom Perry, Pres., Retail Logistics

GROWTH PLANS/SPECIAL FEATURES:

FedEx Supply Chain provides third-party logistics (3PL) and supply chain management solutions for businesses of all sizes. The firm works closely with companies to develop tailored, technology-based logistics solutions for supply chain needs. Its business in divided into ecommerce fulfillment, supply chain solutions and transportation. The ecommerce fulfillment division manages orders and returns, including uploading inventory into the customer's platform, performing integrations with related marketplaces and platforms, scaling ecommerce capabilities, shipping products to warehouses, delivering real-time information and offering support. Supply chain solutions include designing, building and operating logistics ecosystems that are inter-connected and interactive throughout the network, including people, services and technology. This business division's solutions span: supply chain engineering, including network optimization, warehouse location analysis, supply chain analysis, optimal mode selection and shipment consolidation; warehouse operations and distribution, providing dedicated or shared warehouse space, acquiring and developing warehouses, designing/building/starting up a warehouse, managing warehouse staffing and offering warehouse and distribution management; supply chain technology, including a warehouse management system, labor management systems, tracking and visibility, and warehouse automation and other technologies; and packaging, kitting and value-added services, including packaging products, providing customization and postponement; performing kitting and assembly, building and distributing point-of-sale displays, and configuring and packaging electronics. Last, the transportation division consists of a network of more than 10,000 carriers coast-to-coast, all through a non-asset-biased 3PL. Services include outsourced transportation management, one load/one time delivery, inbound/outbound transportation management, time-definite options, truckload brokerage, transportation procurement, single point of contact, online web portal, dry van freight, less-than-truckload (LTL) freight, refrigerated freight, flatbed and heavy freight, intermodal shipment and bulk freight. FedEx Supply Chain operates under FedEx Logistics, a subsidiary of FedEx Corporation.

FINANCIAL DATA: Note: Data for latest year may not have been available at press time.

In U.S. $	2020	2019	2018	2017	2016	2015
Revenue	1,652,757,750	1,739,745,000	1,656,900,000	1,578,000,000	1,524,000,000	
R&D Expense						
Operating Income						
Operating Margin %						
SGA Expense						
Net Income						
Operating Cash Flow						
Capital Expenditure						
EBITDA						
Return on Assets %						
Return on Equity %						
Debt to Equity						

CONTACT INFORMATION:

Phone: Fax:
Toll-Free: 800-463-3339
Address: 700 Cranberry Woods Dr., Cranberry Township, PA 16066
United States

STOCK TICKER/OTHER:

Stock Ticker: Subsidiary
Employees: 13,000
Parent Company: FedEx Corporation

Exchange:
Fiscal Year Ends: 05/31

SALARIES/BONUSES:

Top Exec. Salary: $ Bonus: $
Second Exec. Salary: $ Bonus: $

OTHER THOUGHTS:

Estimated Female Officers or Directors: 1
Hot Spot for Advancement for Women/Minorities:

Sales, profits and employees may be estimates. Financial information, benefits and other data can change quickly and may vary from those stated here.

Ferguson Enterprises Inc

www.ferguson.com

NAIC Code: 444190

TYPES OF BUSINESS:

Plumbing Supplies, Retail
Wholesale Distribution
Construction Supplies, Retail
Waterworks Supplies
HVAC Equipment, Retail
PVF Supplies, Retail

BRANDS/DIVISIONS/AFFILIATES:

Ferguson plc
Ferguson Xpress
FNW Valve
Mirabelle
Monogram Brass
Park Harbor
PROFLO
PROSELECT

CONTACTS: *Note: Officers with more than one job title may be intentionally listed here more than once.*

Kevin Murphy, CEO
Alex Hutcherson, COO
Frank W. Roach, Pres.
Bill Brundage, CFO

GROWTH PLANS/SPECIAL FEATURES:

Ferguson Enterprises, Inc. is one of the largest wholesale distributors of plumbing supplies in the U.S. The company operates as a subsidiary of Ferguson plc, one of largest distributors of plumbing and heating products in the world. Ferguson Enterprises has more than 1,400 locations in all 50 U.S. states, Puerto Rico, the Caribbean and Mexico. Additionally, the firm operates Ferguson Xpress stores, largely self-service locations that market plumbing and light commercial products to contractors. In general, Ferguson Enterprise's customers include homeowners, builders, contractors, engineers and other trade professionals. The company operates in eight business groups: residential, heating and cooling equipment, industrial, commercial and mechanical, waterworks, hospitality, government and integrated services. Ferguson Enterprise's product offerings include plumbing supplies; pipes, valves and fittings; heating, ventilation and air conditioning (HVAC); waterworks; lighting; appliances; tools and safety equipment; gas fireplaces; and fire protection products. An internal delivery service moves products from distribution hubs to Ferguson branches, satellites and customers. Through other divisions, Ferguson Enterprises is involved in nuclear power provision, fire protection supply, valve assembly and testing and geo-synthetic product supply to the mining industry. Ferguson Enterprise's brands include FNW Valve, Mirabelle, Monogram Brass, Park Harbor, Westcraft, PROFLO, PROSELECT and RAPTOR. In November 2020, Ferguson acquired Old Dominion Supply, Inc., a wholesale distributor of HVAC parts and supplies in Maryland and Northern Virginia; and acquired Atlantic Construction Fabrics, Inc, a geotextile company.

Ferguson offers comprehensive benefits, retirement and savings options, and employee assistance programs.

FINANCIAL DATA: *Note: Data for latest year may not have been available at press time.*

In U.S. $	2020	2019	2018	2017	2016	2015
Revenue	18,816,950,000	18,358,000,000	16,670,000,000	15,000,000,000	13,800,000,000	13,004,000,000
R&D Expense						
Operating Income						
Operating Margin %						
SGA Expense						
Net Income						
Operating Cash Flow						
Capital Expenditure						
EBITDA						
Return on Assets %						
Return on Equity %						
Debt to Equity						

CONTACT INFORMATION:

Phone: 757-874-7795   Fax: 757-989-2501
Toll-Free:
Address: 12500 Jefferson Ave, Newport News, VA 23602 United States

STOCK TICKER/OTHER:

Stock Ticker: Subsidiary   Exchange:
Employees: 27,000   Fiscal Year Ends: 07/31
Parent Company: Ferguson plc

SALARIES/BONUSES:

Top Exec. Salary: $ Bonus: $
Second Exec. Salary: $ Bonus: $

OTHER THOUGHTS:

Estimated Female Officers or Directors: 3
Hot Spot for Advancement for Women/Minorities: Y

Fidelity Investments Financial Services

www.fidelity.com

NAIC Code: 523920

TYPES OF BUSINESS:

Mutual Funds
Human Resources Administration Services
Employee Benefits Services
Online Brokerage
Physical Branch Investment Offices
Clearing and Execution Products and Services
Real Estate Investments
Institutional Account Management and Services

BRANDS/DIVISIONS/AFFILIATES:

FMR LLC
Fidelity Insitutional Asset Management
Fidelity Charitable

CONTACTS: Note: Officers with more than one job title may be intentionally listed here more than once.

Abigail Johnson, CEO
Kathleen Murphy, Pres.
Bart Grenier, Asset Mgmt. Chief
Jim Speros, Chief Creative Officer
Brian Hogan, Head, Investment Solutions
Steve A. Scullen, III, Pres., Corp. Oper.
Lori Kalahar Johnson, VP-Online Strategy
Jacques Perold, Pres., Fidelity Management & Research Company
Charles Morrison, Pres., Asset Mgmt.
Nancy D. Prior, Pres., Fixed Income Div.

GROWTH PLANS/SPECIAL FEATURES:

Fidelity Investments Financial Services (FIFS), a subsidiary of FMR LLC, is one of the world's largest providers of financial services, serving 32 million individual customers. With approximately $8.8 trillion total customer assets and $3.5 trillion total discretionary assets under management, the company offers personal investment services, workplace investment services, institutional solutions and asset management. The personal investment division offers financial planning and retirement options such as independent retirement accounts (IRAs), annuities and managed accounts; brokerage and cash management products; college savings accounts; and other financial services for individual investors. The workplace investment division works with employers to build benefit programs for their employees. This segment provides recordkeeping, investments and servicing in relation to contributions, benefits, health and welfare and stock plans. For financial institutions, FIFS provides technology and personalized service such as clearing, custody, investment products, brokerage and trading services to a wide range of financial firms. Fidelity Institutional Asset Management is a distribution organization dedicated to the institutional marketplace. It serves as a gateway to Fidelity's broad and deep institutional investment management capabilities, including U.S. equity, international equity, fixed income and asset allocation. In addition, Fidelity Charitable is an independent public charity that allows donors to establish a dedicated donor-advised fund to support their favorite charities in the short-term and create a systematic plan for longer-term philanthropic goals. Headquartered in Boston, Massachusetts, FIS serves customers through 12 regional offices and more than 190 investor centers in the U.S. Globally, the company spans eight other countries across North America, Europe, Asia and Australia. In February 2020, parent company FMR spun-off its secure application programming interface-based network operator Akoya.

The company is owned approximately 49% by the founding family and 51% by current and former employees.

FINANCIAL DATA: Note: Data for latest year may not have been available at press time.

In U.S. $	2020	2019	2018	2017	2016	2015
Revenue	21,000,000,000	20,790,000,000	20,400,000,000	18,200,000,000	15,900,000,000	15,350,000,000
R&D Expense						
Operating Income						
Operating Margin %						
SGA Expense						
Net Income	7,200,000,000	6,840,000,000	6,300,000,000	5,300,000,000	3,450,000,000	3,000,000,000
Operating Cash Flow						
Capital Expenditure						
EBITDA						
Return on Assets %						
Return on Equity %						
Debt to Equity						

CONTACT INFORMATION:

Phone: 617-563-7000   Fax:
Toll-Free: 800-343-3548
Address: 82 Devonshire St., Boston, MA 02109 United States

STOCK TICKER/OTHER:

Stock Ticker: Private
Employees: 45,000
Parent Company: FMR LLC

Exchange:
Fiscal Year Ends: 12/31

SALARIES/BONUSES:

Top Exec. Salary: $ Bonus: $
Second Exec. Salary: $ Bonus: $

OTHER THOUGHTS:

Estimated Female Officers or Directors: 2
Hot Spot for Advancement for Women/Minorities:

Sales, profits and employees may be estimates. Financial information, benefits and other data can change quickly and may vary from those stated here.

Fidelity National Financial Inc

NAIC Code: 524127

www.fnf.com

TYPES OF BUSINESS:

Title Insurance
Title Insurance
Escrow
Trusts
Home Warranty
Mortgage Loan Management
Annuities
Life Insurance

BRANDS/DIVISIONS/AFFILIATES:

Fidelity National Title Insurance Company
Chicago Title Insurance Company
Commonwealth Land Title Insurance Company
Alamo Title Insurance
National Title Insurance of New York Inc
FGL Holdings Inc

CONTACTS: Note: Officers with more than one job title may be intentionally listed here more than once.

Raymond Quirk, CEO
Anthony Park, CFO
William Foley, Chairman of the Board
Roger Jewkes, COO
Brent Bickett, Executive VP, Divisional
Michael Gravelle, Executive VP
Peter Sadowski, Executive VP
Michael Nolan, President

GROWTH PLANS/SPECIAL FEATURES:

Fidelity National Financial, Inc. is a leading provider of real estate services to the real estate and mortgage industries. The company operates through three business segments: title, F&G and corporate and other. The title segment consists of the operations of title insurance underwriters and related businesses, which provide title insurance and escrow and other title-related services, including trust activities, trustee sales guarantees, and home warranty products. This division also includes Fidelity National's transaction services business, such as title -related services used in the production and management of mortgage loans, including mortgage loans that experience default. Fidelity National's title insurance underwriters include Fidelity National Title Insurance Company, Chicago Title Insurance Company, Commonwealth Land Title Insurance Company, Alamo Title Insurance, and National Title Insurance of New York, Inc. The F&G segment consists of annuities and life insurance related businesses, and issues a broad portfolio of deferred annuities (fixed indexed and fixed rate annuities), immediate annuities and indexed universal life insurance. The corporate and other segment consists of the parent holding company, Fidelity National's real estate technology subsidiaries, non-title businesses and certain unallocated corporate overhead expenses and eliminations of revenues and expenses in relation to the title segment. In mid-2020, Fidelity National acquired FGL Holdings, Inc., which became a new business segment referred to as F&G. That December, Fidelity National and F&G sold F&G Reinsurance Ltd. to Aspida Holdings Ltd.

FINANCIAL DATA: Note: Data for latest year may not have been available at press time.

In U.S. $	2020	2019	2018	2017	2016	2015
Revenue	10,778,000,000	8,469,000,000	7,594,000,000	7,663,000,000	9,554,000,000	9,132,000,000
R&D Expense						
Operating Income						
Operating Margin %						
SGA Expense	2,951,000,000	2,696,000,000	2,538,000,000	2,460,000,000	2,832,000,000	2,671,000,000
Net Income	1,427,000,000	1,062,000,000	628,000,000	771,000,000	650,000,000	527,000,000
Operating Cash Flow	1,578,000,000	1,121,000,000	943,000,000	737,000,000	1,162,000,000	917,000,000
Capital Expenditure	110,000,000	96,000,000	83,000,000	149,000,000	290,000,000	241,000,000
EBITDA						
Return on Assets %		.11%	.07%	.07%	.05%	.04%
Return on Equity %		.21%	.14%	.15%	.11%	.09%
Debt to Equity		0.238	0.181	0.171	0.458	0.485

CONTACT INFORMATION:

Phone: 904 854-8100   Fax: 904 357-1007
Toll-Free: 888-934-3354
Address: 601 Riverside Ave., Jacksonville, FL 32204 United States

STOCK TICKER/OTHER:

Stock Ticker: FNF
Employees: 25,063
Parent Company:

Exchange: NYS
Fiscal Year Ends: 12/31

SALARIES/BONUSES:

Top Exec. Salary: $ Bonus: $
Second Exec. Salary: $ Bonus: $

OTHER THOUGHTS:

Estimated Female Officers or Directors: 1
Hot Spot for Advancement for Women/Minorities:

Fidelity National Information Services Inc   www.fisglobal.com

NAIC Code: 522320

TYPES OF BUSINESS:

Payment & Transaction Processing Services
Banking Technology Solutions
Payment Solutions
Processing Services
Information Services

BRANDS/DIVISIONS/AFFILIATES:

Capco

CONTACTS: *Note: Officers with more than one job title may be intentionally listed here more than once.*

Gary Norcross, CEO
James Woodall, CFO
Katy Thompson, Chief Accounting Officer
Marc Mayo, Chief Legal Officer
Gregory Montana, Chief Risk Officer
Bruce Lowthers, Co-COO
Marianne Brown, Co-COO
Lenore Williams, Executive VP

GROWTH PLANS/SPECIAL FEATURES:

Fidelity National Information Services, Inc. (FIS) offers banking/payments technology solutions, processing services and information-based services. Headquartered in Jacksonville, Florida, FIS maintains a global presence, serving more than 20,000 financial institutions through offices in over 100 countries worldwide. Through its Capco brand, the firm provides core financial institution processing, card issuer and transaction processing services as well as outsourcing services to financial institutions and retailers worldwide. The company operates in three segments: integrated financial solutions (IFS), global financial solutions (GFS) and corporate and other. IFS serves the North America regional and community bank market for transaction and account processing, payment solutions, channel solutions, digital channels, risk and compliance solutions and services. This segment's solutions include core processing and ancillary applications, digital solutions (internet, mobile and eBanking), fraud and risk management, compliance, electronic funds transfer, credit cards, item processing, output services, government payment, ePayment and retail check authorization. GFS serves the largest financial institutions worldwide with banking and payments solutions, as well as consulting and transformation services. This segment also delivers an array of capital markets and asset management solutions and services, as well as insurance and public sector and education solutions and services. GFS solutions include retail banking, payment services, securities processing, finance, asset management, global trading, corporate liquidity, insurance, wealth management, global commercial services, strategic consulting, as well as domain-specific, mission critical enterprise resource planning and administrative software to state and local governments and K-12 educational institutions. The corporate and other segment consists of overhead expense, leveraged functions and miscellaneous expenses not included in the operating segments.

FINANCIAL DATA: *Note: Data for latest year may not have been available at press time.*

In U.S. $	2020	2019	2018	2017	2016	2015
Revenue	12,552,000,000	10,333,000,000	8,423,000,000	9,123,000,000	9,241,000,000	6,595,200,000
R&D Expense						
Operating Income	688,000,000	1,056,000,000	1,553,000,000	1,492,000,000	1,298,000,000	1,099,200,000
Operating Margin %		.10%	.18%	.16%	.14%	.17%
SGA Expense	3,516,000,000	2,667,000,000	1,301,000,000	1,450,000,000	1,710,000,000	1,102,800,000
Net Income	158,000,000	298,000,000	846,000,000	1,319,000,000	568,000,000	631,500,000
Operating Cash Flow	4,442,000,000	2,410,000,000	1,993,000,000	1,741,000,000	1,925,000,000	1,136,900,000
Capital Expenditure	1,129,000,000	828,000,000	622,000,000	613,000,000	616,000,000	415,300,000
EBITDA	4,319,000,000	3,246,000,000	2,838,000,000	2,786,000,000	2,483,000,000	1,905,500,000
Return on Assets %		.01%	.04%	.05%	.02%	.03%
Return on Equity %		.01%	.08%	.13%	.06%	.08%
Debt to Equity		0.358	0.849	0.712	1.042	1.234

CONTACT INFORMATION:

Phone: 904 438-6000   Fax: 904 357-1105
Toll-Free: 888-323-0310
Address: 601 Riverside Ave., Jacksonville, FL 32204 United States

STOCK TICKER/OTHER:

Stock Ticker: FIS   Exchange: NYS
Employees: 55,000   Fiscal Year Ends: 12/31
Parent Company:

SALARIES/BONUSES:

Top Exec. Salary: $ Bonus: $
Second Exec. Salary: $ Bonus: $

OTHER THOUGHTS:

Estimated Female Officers or Directors: 3
Hot Spot for Advancement for Women/Minorities: Y

FireEye Inc

NAIC Code: 511210E

www.fireeye.com

TYPES OF BUSINESS:
Computer Software, Network Security, Managed Access, Digital ID, Cybersecurity & Anti-Virus
Data Security Software

BRANDS/DIVISIONS/AFFILIATES:
Helix Security Platform
Verodin Security Instrumentation Platform
Network Security and Forensics
Endpoint Security
Expertise On Demand
Managed Defense
Threat Intelligence
Respond Software

CONTACTS: Note: Officers with more than one job title may be intentionally listed here more than once.
Kevin Mandia, CEO
Frank Verdecanna, CFO
Enrique Salem, Chairman of the Board
William Robbins, Executive VP, Divisional
Alexa King, General Counsel
Travis Reese, President

GROWTH PLANS/SPECIAL FEATURES:

FireEye, Inc. provides comprehensive cybersecurity solutions for detecting, preventing, analyzing and resolving advanced cyberattacks that evade legacy signature-based security products. The company's technology and solutions include its multi-vector virtual execution (MVX) engine and intelligence-driven analysis, which detect both known and unknown threats. MVX-based detection and prevention solutions encompass web, email, endpoint, cloud and content (file) attack vectors. These products are complemented by FireEye's network forensics, cloud-based intelligence and threat analytics, managed security services, cybersecurity consulting and incident response offerings. FireEye's enterprise solutions include: the Helix Security Platform, which applies threat intelligence, automation and case management to FireEye and third-party solutions in a unified security operations platform; the Verodin Security Instrumentation Platform, a business platform that enables users to understand and communicate cybersecurity effectiveness with quantifiable, evidence-based data; Network Security and Forensics, which provides network visibility and protection against the world's most sophisticated and damaging cyber attacks; Endpoint Security, providing comprehensive endpoint defense, protecting users from threats, detecting advanced attacks and empowering response; Email Security, which detects email-based cyber attacks and blocks dangerous threats such as malicious attachments, phishing sites and impersonation attacks; Expertise On Demand, providing flexible access to FireEye's industry-recognized security expertise and threat intelligence; Managed Defense, which applies frontline knowledge of the attacker and hunting methodologies to detect and respond to covert activity; and Threat Intelligence, which empowers security teams with forward-looking high fidelity, adversary-focused intelligence and actionable advice. In November 2020, FireEye acquired Respond Software, a cybersecurity investigation automation company.

FINANCIAL DATA: Note: Data for latest year may not have been available at press time.

In U.S. $	2020	2019	2018	2017	2016	2015
Revenue	940,584,000	889,152,000	830,950,000	751,086,000	714,114,000	622,967,000
R&D Expense	252,771,000	271,326,000	254,142,000	243,273,000	279,594,000	279,467,000
Operating Income	-128,664,000	-199,769,000	-182,402,000	-258,606,000	-416,686,000	-507,660,000
Operating Margin %		-.22%	-.22%	-.34%	-.58%	-.81%
SGA Expense	482,450,000	508,703,000	486,735,000	497,532,000	579,338,000	617,956,000
Net Income	-207,303,000	-257,409,000	-243,123,000	-303,691,000	-480,129,000	-539,215,000
Operating Cash Flow	94,895,000	67,537,000	17,381,000	17,640,000	-14,585,000	37,015,000
Capital Expenditure	26,326,000	45,605,000	50,831,000	43,779,000	36,314,000	54,549,000
EBITDA	-47,959,000	-86,487,000	-94,668,000	-145,876,000	-321,714,000	-396,053,000
Return on Assets %		-.09%	-.10%	-.13%	-.20%	-.26%
Return on Equity %		-.38%	-.35%	-.38%	-.51%	-.47%
Debt to Equity		1.374	1.48	1.047	0.882	0.676

CONTACT INFORMATION:
Phone: 408-321-6300   Fax: 408-321-9818
Toll-Free:
Address: 601 McCarthy Blvd., Milpitas, CA 95035 United States

SALARIES/BONUSES:
Top Exec. Salary: $ Bonus: $
Second Exec. Salary: $ Bonus: $

STOCK TICKER/OTHER:
Stock Ticker: FEYE
Employees: 3,400
Parent Company:

Exchange: NAS
Fiscal Year Ends:

OTHER THOUGHTS:
Estimated Female Officers or Directors: 4
Hot Spot for Advancement for Women/Minorities: Y

First American Financial Corporation

www.firstam.com

NAIC Code: 524127

TYPES OF BUSINESS:

Title Insurance
Real Estate Services
Escrow Services
Screening Services
Credit Reporting
Property & Casualty Insurance
Trust Services
Internet Services

BRANDS/DIVISIONS/AFFILIATES:

CONTACTS: Note: Officers with more than one job title may be intentionally listed here more than once.

Dennis Gilmore, CEO
Mark Seaton, CFO
Parker Kennedy, Chairman of the Board
Matthew Wajner, Chief Accounting Officer
Christopher Leavell, COO, Subsidiary
Kenneth Degiorgio, Executive VP

GROWTH PLANS/SPECIAL FEATURES:

First American Financial Corporation (FAFC) provides title insurance and settlement services, as well as specialty insurance coverage and risk solutions for the real estate and mortgage industries. The company conducts its operations through two units: title insurance and services, which accounted for 92.2% of the firm's 2020 revenue; and specialty insurance. The title insurance and services division issues title insurance policies on residential and commercial property in the U.S. and internationally. This segment also provides closing and/or escrow services; accommodates tax-deferred exchanges of real estate; provides products, services and solutions involving the use of real property related data designed to mitigate risk or otherwise facilitate real estate transactions; maintains, manages and provides access to title plant records and images; and provides banking, trust and investment advisory services. FAFC's specialty insurance segment includes property and casualty insurance and home warranties. Its property and casualty insurance business provides insurance coverage to residential homeowners and renters for liability losses and typical hazards such as fire, theft, vandalism and other types of property damage. It is licensed to issue policies in all 50 states and Washington, D.C. Its home warranty business provides residential service contracts that cover residential systems such as heating and air conditioning systems, and certain appliances against failures that occur as the result of normal usage during the coverage period. Most of these policies are issued on resale residences, although policies are also available in some instances for new homes.

First American offers its employees medical, dental and vision coverage; wellness programs; stock purchase program; adoption assistance and other perks.

FINANCIAL DATA: Note: Data for latest year may not have been available at press time.

In U.S. $	2020	2019	2018	2017	2016	2015
Revenue	7,080,949,000	6,199,225,000	5,747,844,000	5,772,363,000	5,575,846,000	5,175,456,000
R&D Expense						
Operating Income						
Operating Margin %						
SGA Expense	1,941,477,000	1,806,005,000	1,748,949,000	1,898,551,000	1,756,633,000	1,594,935,000
Net Income	696,429,000	707,410,000	474,496,000	423,049,000	342,993,000	288,086,000
Operating Cash Flow	1,084,659,000	913,089,000	793,165,000	632,134,000	489,416,000	551,323,000
Capital Expenditure	114,084,000	106,979,000	118,170,000	134,206,000	132,265,000	123,697,000
EBITDA						
Return on Assets %	.06%	.05%	.05%	.04%	.04%	
Return on Equity %	.17%	.13%	.13%	.12%	.11%	
Debt to Equity	0.202	0.153	0.165	0.192	0.212	

CONTACT INFORMATION:

Phone: 714 250-3000 Fax:
Toll-Free: 800-854-3643
Address: 1 First American Way, Santa Ana, CA 92707 United States

STOCK TICKER/OTHER:

Stock Ticker: FAF
Employees: 18,412
Parent Company:

Exchange: NYS
Fiscal Year Ends: 12/31

SALARIES/BONUSES:

Top Exec. Salary: $ Bonus: $
Second Exec. Salary: $ Bonus: $

OTHER THOUGHTS:

Estimated Female Officers or Directors: 1
Hot Spot for Advancement for Women/Minorities:

First Solar Inc

NAIC Code: 334413A

www.firstsolar.com

TYPES OF BUSINESS:

Photovoltaic Cell Manufacturing
Thin-Film Solar Modules
Solar Module Collection & Recycling
Photovoltaic Site Operation & Maintenance
Solar Project Engineering, Procurement & Construction
Project Development & Financing

BRANDS/DIVISIONS/AFFILIATES:

CONTACTS: *Note: Officers with more than one job title may be intentionally listed here more than once.*

Mark Widmar, CEO
Alexander Bradley, CFO
Michael Ahearn, Chairman of the Board
Byron Jeffers, Chief Accounting Officer
Raffi Garabedian, Chief Technology Officer
Philip deJong, COO
Christopher Bueter, Executive VP, Divisional
Paul Kaleta, Executive VP
Georges Antoun, Other Executive Officer

GROWTH PLANS/SPECIAL FEATURES:

First Solar, Inc. develops and manufactures thin-film solar modules based on its proprietary thin-film semiconductor technology, and designs, constructs and sells photovoltaic (PV) solar power systems. The firm's single-junction polycrystalline thin-film technology utilizes cadmium telluride (CdTe) as the absorption layer, allowing the company to use about 99% less semiconductor material than traditional crystalline silicon modules. It has developed advanced manufacturing techniques including the use of robotics, in order to cut costs. The solar modules have dimensions up to 6 feet in size, with First Solar's Series 6 modules having an average power output of approximately 430 watts. First Solar operates its business in two segments: modules and systems. The modules segment designs, manufactures and sells solar modules which convert sunlight into electricity. Third-party customers of these components consist of project developers, system integrators and operators of renewable energy projects. The company sells developed projects to system operators who wish to own generating facilities (such as utilities), or to investors looking for long-term investment vehicles that are expected to generate consistent returns. The systems segment provides complete turn-key PV solar power systems. Additionally, it offers project development; engineering, procurement and construction services; operating and maintenance services (O&M); and project finance expertise. First Solar maintains a comprehensive O&M service with more than 8 gigawatts (GW) direct current (DC) of utility-scale PV plants under the O&M program. It maintains a fleet average system effective availability greater than 99%. The firm also has a collection and recycling program for used solar modules. First Solar has manufacturing centers include major locations in Ohio, Malaysia and Vietnam. In August 2020, First Solar agreed to sell its North American O&M business to NovaSource Power Services, a portfolio company of private equity firm Clairvest Group, Inc. of Toronto, Canada.

First Solar offers comprehensive employee benefits.

FINANCIAL DATA: *Note: Data for latest year may not have been available at press time.*

In U.S. $	2020	2019	2018	2017	2016	2015
Revenue	2,711,332,000	3,063,117,000	2,244,044,000	2,941,324,000	2,951,328,000	3,578,995,000
R&D Expense	93,738,000	96,611,000	84,472,000	88,573,000	124,762,000	130,593,000
Operating Income	323,489,000	201,215,000	40,113,000	215,032,000	316,202,000	516,664,000
Operating Margin %		.07%	.02%	.07%	.11%	.14%
SGA Expense	222,918,000	205,471,000	176,857,000	202,699,000	261,994,000	255,192,000
Net Income	398,355,000	-114,933,000	144,326,000	-165,615,000	-357,964,000	546,421,000
Operating Cash Flow	37,120,000	174,201,000	-326,809,000	1,340,677,000	206,753,000	-360,919,000
Capital Expenditure	416,635,000	668,717,000	739,838,000	514,357,000	229,452,000	166,438,000
EBITDA	550,151,000	112,412,000	269,804,000	343,193,000	-220,212,000	784,635,000
Return on Assets %		-.02%	.02%	-.02%	-.05%	.08%
Return on Equity %		-.02%	.03%	-.03%	-.07%	.10%
Debt to Equity		0.111	0.088	0.083	0.031	0.045

CONTACT INFORMATION:

Phone: 602 414-9300   Fax: 602 414-9400
Toll-Free: 877-850-3757
Address: 350 W. Washington St., Ste. 600, Tempe, AZ 85281 United States

STOCK TICKER/OTHER:

Stock Ticker: FSLR
Employees: 5,100
Parent Company:

Exchange: NAS
Fiscal Year Ends: 12/31

SALARIES/BONUSES:

Top Exec. Salary: $ Bonus: $
Second Exec. Salary: $ Bonus: $

OTHER THOUGHTS:

Estimated Female Officers or Directors: 3
Hot Spot for Advancement for Women/Minorities: Y

Sales, profits and employees may be estimates. Financial information, benefits and other data can change quickly and may vary from those stated here.

FirstCash Inc

ir.firstcash.com

NAIC Code: 522298

TYPES OF BUSINESS:

Pawn Shops
Check Cashing
Cash Advance
Credit Services
Money Orders & Transfers
Credit Services Program

BRANDS/DIVISIONS/AFFILIATES:

GROWTH PLANS/SPECIAL FEATURES:

FirstCash, Inc. provides retail and consumer lending services. FirstCash had approximately 2.750 pawn store locations in 24 U.S. states and the District of Columbia, as well as in Mexico, Guatemala, El Salvador and Colombia (as of November 2020). The company focuses on serving cash- and credit-constrained consumers through its retail pawn locations, which buy and sell a variety of jewelry, consumer electronics, power tools, household appliances, sporting goods, musical instruments and other merchandise. It also makes small consumer pawn loans, which are secured by pledged personal property. Nearly all of the firm's revenues are from pawn operations.

CONTACTS: Note: Officers with more than one job title may be intentionally listed here more than once.

Rick Wessel, CEO
R. Orr, CFO
Daniel Feehan, Chairman of the Board
Thomas Stuart, COO
Anna Alvarado, General Counsel
Raul Ramos, Senior VP, Geographical

FINANCIAL DATA: Note: Data for latest year may not have been available at press time.

In U.S. $	2020	2019	2018	2017	2016	2015
Revenue	1,631,284,000	1,864,439,000	1,780,858,000	1,779,822,000	1,088,377,000	704,602,000
R&D Expense						
Operating Income	195,945,000	258,570,000	240,443,000	217,926,000	148,387,000	110,915,000
Operating Margin %		.14%	.14%	.12%	.14%	.16%
SGA Expense	110,931,000	122,334,000	120,042,000	122,473,000	96,537,000	54,758,000
Net Income	106,579,000	164,618,000	153,206,000	143,892,000	60,127,000	60,710,000
Operating Cash Flow	222,264,000	231,596,000	243,429,000	220,357,000	96,854,000	92,749,000
Capital Expenditure	83,045,000	118,972,000	55,673,000	37,135,000	33,863,000	21,073,000
EBITDA	215,148,000	300,550,000	277,443,000	251,580,000	145,632,000	122,507,000
Return on Assets %		.07%	.07%	.07%	.04%	.08%
Return on Equity %		.12%	.11%	.10%	.06%	.14%
Debt to Equity		0.611	0.448	0.273	0.315	0.598

CONTACT INFORMATION:

Phone: 817-335-1100   Fax: 817 461-7019
Toll-Free:
Address: 1600 West 7th St., Fort Worth, TX 76102 United States

STOCK TICKER/OTHER:

Stock Ticker: FCFS   Exchange: NAS
Employees: 17,000   Fiscal Year Ends: 12/31
Parent Company:

SALARIES/BONUSES:

Top Exec. Salary: $ Bonus: $
Second Exec. Salary: $ Bonus: $

OTHER THOUGHTS:

Estimated Female Officers or Directors:
Hot Spot for Advancement for Women/Minorities:

FirstEnergy Corporation

www.firstenergycorp.com

NAIC Code: 221112

TYPES OF BUSINESS:

Electric Utility
Power Generation
Energy Management
Telecommunications

BRANDS/DIVISIONS/AFFILIATES:

Ohio Edison
Illuminating Company (The)
Met-Ed
Penelec
Jersey Central Power & Light
Mon Power
Potomac Edison
FirstEnergy Solutions

CONTACTS: *Note: Officers with more than one job title may be intentionally listed here more than once.*

Charles Jones, CEO
Eileen Mikkelsen, VP, Subsidiary
Donald Misheff, Director
Leila Vespoli, Executive VP, Divisional
Robert Reffner, General Counsel, Subsidiary
Charles Lasky, Other Corporate Officer
Ebony Yeboah-Amankwah, Other Executive Officer
Bennett Gaines, Other Executive Officer
Samuel Belcher, President, Subsidiary
Steven Strah, President, Subsidiary
Gary Benz, Senior VP, Subsidiary
M. Dowling, Senior VP, Subsidiary
Dennis Chack, Senior VP, Subsidiary
Christine Walker, Vice President, Subsidiary
Irena Prezelj, Vice President, Subsidiary
Jason Lisowski, Vice President

GROWTH PLANS/SPECIAL FEATURES:

FirstEnergy Corporation and its subsidiaries are principally involved in the generation, transmission and distribution of electricity. Its 10 utility operating companies serve more than 6 million customers in the Midwest and Mid-Atlantic regions. FirstEnergy's regulated and unregulated generation subsidiaries produce energy from a diverse mix of non-emitting nuclear, scrubbed coal, natural gas, hydroelectric and other renewables. The firm's transmission operations include approximately 24,500 miles of lines and two regional transmission operation centers. Subsidiaries include: Ohio Edison, The Illuminating Company, and Toledo Edison, in Ohio; Met-Ed, Penelec, Penn Power, and West Penn Power, in Pennsylvania; Jersey Central Power & Light, in New Jersey; and Mon Power, and Potomac Edison, in West Virginia and Maryland. FirstEnergy's revenues are primarily derived from: the sale of energy and related products and services by its unregulated competitive subsidiaries; the electric service provided by its utility operating subsidiaries; and its transmission subsidiaries. During 2020, subsidiary FirstEnergy Solutions emerged from Chapter 11 bankruptcy proceedings and became Energy Harbor Corporation, becoming owned by its creditors and no longer a subsidiary of FirstEnergy Corporation. The former subsidiary ran three nuclear coal plants in Ohio and Pennsylvania, as well as coal plants in Ohio, Pennsylvania and West Virginia.

FINANCIAL DATA: *Note: Data for latest year may not have been available at press time.*

In U.S. $	2020	2019	2018	2017	2016	2015
Revenue	10,790,000,000	11,035,000,000	11,261,000,000	14,017,000,000	14,562,000,000	15,026,000,000
R&D Expense						
Operating Income	1,685,000,000	1,836,000,000	2,358,000,000	2,578,000,000	2,403,000,000	2,334,000,000
Operating Margin %		.17%	.21%	.18%	.17%	.16%
SGA Expense	477,000,000	674,000,000	144,000,000	141,000,000	147,000,000	242,000,000
Net Income	1,079,000,000	912,000,000	1,348,000,000	-1,724,000,000	-6,177,000,000	578,000,000
Operating Cash Flow	1,423,000,000	2,467,000,000	1,410,000,000	3,808,000,000	3,371,000,000	3,447,000,000
Capital Expenditure	2,657,000,000	2,665,000,000	2,675,000,000	2,841,000,000	3,067,000,000	2,894,000,000
EBITDA	3,316,000,000	3,296,000,000	3,947,000,000	1,970,000,000	-6,181,000,000	3,744,000,000
Return on Assets %		.02%	.02%	-.04%	-.13%	.01%
Return on Equity %		.13%	.18%	-.34%	-.66%	.05%
Debt to Equity		2.813	2.633	5.38	2.915	1.545

CONTACT INFORMATION:

Phone: 800 736-3402　　Fax:
Toll-Free: 800-633-4766
Address: 76 S. Main St., Akron, OH 44308 United States

STOCK TICKER/OTHER:

Stock Ticker: FE
Employees: 5,362
Parent Company:

Exchange: NYS
Fiscal Year Ends: 12/31

SALARIES/BONUSES:

Top Exec. Salary: $　　　　Bonus: $
Second Exec. Salary: $　　　Bonus: $

OTHER THOUGHTS:

Estimated Female Officers or Directors: 6
Hot Spot for Advancement for Women/Minorities: Y

Fiserv Inc

www.fiserv.com

NAIC Code: 522320

TYPES OF BUSINESS:

Financial Services
Investment Services
Online Banking
Electronic Billing & Payment
Software Applications & Investment Management Solutions

BRANDS/DIVISIONS/AFFILIATES:

First Data
STAR

CONTACTS: Note: Officers with more than one job title may be intentionally listed here more than once.

Jeffery Yabuki, CEO
Frank Bisignano, Pres.
Glenn Renwick, Chairman of the Board
Robert Hua, CFO
Byron Vielehr, Chief Administrative Officer
Lynn McCreary, Chief Legal Officer
Kevin Schultz, Executive VP
Devin McGranahan, President, Divisional
Jeffery Yabuki, Chmn.

GROWTH PLANS/SPECIAL FEATURES:

Fiserv, Inc. provides integrated data processing and information management systems to more than 12,000 financial services providers, including banks, thrifts, credit unions, investment management firms, leasing and finance companies, retailers, merchants and government agencies. It operates in three primary segments: First Data, financial institution services (financial) and payments and industry products (payments). The businesses in the First Data segment primarily provide merchant acquiring, e-commerce, mobile commerce and other business solutions at the point-of-sale to businesses of all sizes and types; credit card and loan account processing, commercial payments, customer communications, plastics solutions, customer service and other products to support issuers; and a range of network solutions and security, risk and fraud management solutions to business and financial institution clients, including U.S. debit card processing, the STAR network, stored value commerce solutions (both closed-loop and open-loop), and our suite of security and fraud products and services. The financial segment provides banks, thrifts and credit unions with account processing services, item processing services, loan origination and servicing products, cash management and consulting services as well as other products and services that support a variety of financial transactions. The payments segment provides products and services that address a range of technology needs for the financial services industry, including internet banking, electronic bill payment, electronic funds transfer and debit processing, fraud and risk management capabilities, card and print personalization services, check imaging and investment account processing services for separately managed accounts. The company operates centers nationwide for full-service data processing, software development, item processing and check imaging, technology support and related product businesses. It operates data, development, item processing and support centers in approximately 95 cities worldwide.

FINANCIAL DATA: Note: Data for latest year may not have been available at press time.

In U.S. $	2020	2019	2018	2017	2016	2015
Revenue	14,852,000,000	10,187,000,000	5,823,000,000	5,696,000,000	5,505,000,000	5,254,000,000
R&D Expense						
Operating Income	1,388,000,000	1,594,000,000	1,526,000,000	1,522,000,000	1,445,000,000	1,311,000,000
Operating Margin %		.16%	.26%	.27%	.26%	.25%
SGA Expense	5,652,000,000	3,284,000,000	1,228,000,000	1,150,000,000	1,101,000,000	1,034,000,000
Net Income	958,000,000	893,000,000	1,187,000,000	1,246,000,000	930,000,000	712,000,000
Operating Cash Flow	4,147,000,000	2,795,000,000	1,552,000,000	1,483,000,000	1,431,000,000	1,346,000,000
Capital Expenditure	900,000,000	721,000,000	360,000,000	287,000,000	290,000,000	359,000,000
EBITDA	5,090,000,000	3,207,000,000	2,304,000,000	1,967,000,000	1,856,000,000	1,643,000,000
Return on Assets %		.02%	.11%	.12%	.10%	.08%
Return on Equity %		.05%	.47%	.47%	.36%	.24%
Debt to Equity		0.655	2.597	1.793	1.758	1.612

CONTACT INFORMATION:

Phone: 262 879-5000   Fax: 262 879-5275
Toll-Free: 800-872-7882
Address: 255 Fiserv Dr., Brookfield, WI 53045 United States

STOCK TICKER/OTHER:

Stock Ticker: FISV
Employees: 44,000
Parent Company:

Exchange: NAS
Fiscal Year Ends: 12/31

SALARIES/BONUSES:

Top Exec. Salary: $ Bonus: $
Second Exec. Salary: $ Bonus: $

OTHER THOUGHTS:

Estimated Female Officers or Directors: 1
Hot Spot for Advancement for Women/Minorities:

Sales, profits and employees may be estimates. Financial information, benefits and other data can change quickly and may vary from those stated here.

Flowers Foods Inc

www.flowersfoods.com

NAIC Code: 311800

TYPES OF BUSINESS:

Food Products-Baked Goods
Baked Bread
Bakery Goods
Tortillas
Snack Cakes
Sweet Treats

BRANDS/DIVISIONS/AFFILIATES:

Natures Own
Wonder
Sunbeam
Daves Killer Bread
Canyon Bakehouse
Mi Casa
TastyKake
Mrs Freshleys

CONTACTS: Note: Officers with more than one job title may be intentionally listed here more than once.

Ryals McMullian, CEO
R. Kinsey, CFO
Karyl Lauder, Chief Accounting Officer
Stephanie Tillman, Chief Compliance Officer
Debo Mukherjee, Chief Marketing Officer
Bradley Alexander, COO
George Deese, Director
Stephen Avera, Other Executive Officer
Tonja Taylor, Other Executive Officer
D. Wheeler, Other Executive Officer
Robert Benton, Other Executive Officer
David Roach, President, Divisional
H. Courtney, President, Divisional

GROWTH PLANS/SPECIAL FEATURES:

Flowers Foods, Inc. is one of the largest producers and marketers of packaged bakery foods in the U.S. Its business units are divided into fresh bakery and specialty/snacking products, which include a variety of breads, buns, rolls, tortillas and snack cakes. Walmart/Sam's Club is Flowers Foods' largest customer, accounting for more than 20% of the firm's sales. Nature's Own is the Flower Foods' top-selling bread brand in the U.S., with other brands including Wonder, Sunbeam, Merita, Captain John Derst's, Evangeline Maid, European Bakers, Butternut, Bunny Bread and Home Pride. Dave's Killer Bread is an organic bread brand that is both USDA organic and non-GMO Project Verified. Canyon Bakehouse produces gluten-free bakery foods. Mi Casa is a brand that offers corn and flour tortillas. TastyKake offers a line of snack cakes, pies, donuts and pastry products available in supermarkets and other retail outlets. Mrs. Freshley's offers a wide array of sweet treats in vending machines, convenience stores and other retail outlets, and primarily come in single-packages or multi-pack boxes.

FINANCIAL DATA: Note: Data for latest year may not have been available at press time.

In U.S. $	2020	2019	2018	2017	2016	2015
Revenue	4,387,991,000	4,123,974,000	3,951,852,000	3,920,733,000	3,926,885,000	3,778,505,000
R&D Expense						
Operating Income	357,078,000	248,915,000	230,432,000	261,084,000	295,413,000	301,650,000
Operating Margin %		.06%	.06%	.06%	.08%	.08%
SGA Expense	1,693,387,000	1,575,122,000	1,507,960,000	1,503,867,000	1,464,236,000	1,381,527,000
Net Income	152,318,000	164,538,000	157,160,000	150,120,000	163,776,000	189,191,000
Operating Cash Flow	454,464,000	366,952,000	295,893,000	297,389,000	346,044,000	324,233,000
Capital Expenditure	97,929,000	103,685,000	99,422,000	75,232,000	101,727,000	95,773,000
EBITDA	380,885,000	395,158,000	376,971,000	332,569,000	425,311,000	452,021,000
Return on Assets %		.05%	.06%	.06%	.06%	.07%
Return on Equity %		.13%	.13%	.12%	.13%	.16%
Debt to Equity		0.955	0.787	0.656	0.782	0.751

CONTACT INFORMATION:

Phone: 229 226-9110   Fax:
Toll-Free:
Address: 1919 Flowers Cir., Thomasville, GA 31757 United States

SALARIES/BONUSES:

Top Exec. Salary: $ Bonus: $
Second Exec. Salary: $ Bonus: $

STOCK TICKER/OTHER:

Stock Ticker: FLO   Exchange: NYS
Employees: 9,700   Fiscal Year Ends: 12/31
Parent Company:

OTHER THOUGHTS:

Estimated Female Officers or Directors: 3
Hot Spot for Advancement for Women/Minorities: Y

Fluor Corporation

www.fluor.com

NAIC Code: 237000

TYPES OF BUSINESS:

Heavy Construction and Engineering
Engineering
Procurement
Fabrication
Construction
Energy Solutions
Urban Solutions
Mission Solutions

BRANDS/DIVISIONS/AFFILIATES:

CONTACTS: Note: Officers with more than one job title may be intentionally listed here more than once.

Carlos Hernandez, CEO
Bruce Stanski, CFO
Alan Boeckmann, Chairman of the Board
Robin Chopra, Controller
Ray Barnard, Executive VP, Divisional
Jose Luis Bustamante, Executive VP, Divisional
Mark Landry, Executive VP, Divisional
Matthew McSorley, Executive VP, Divisional
James Brittain, President, Divisional
Taco de Haan, President, Divisional
Nestoras Koumouris, President, Divisional
Thomas DAgostino, President, Divisional

GROWTH PLANS/SPECIAL FEATURES:

Fluor Corporation is a global engineering, procurement, fabrication and construction company with projects and offices on six continents. The firm operates through three business segments: energy solutions, urban solutions and mission solutions. The energy solutions segment is focused on energy transition, chemicals, liquefied natural gas (LNG) and traditional oil and gas opportunities. It is pursuing new opportunities in the energy transition market including carbon capture, green chemicals, hydrogen, biofuels and other low carbon energy sources. The urban solutions segment pursues opportunities in mining, metals, advanced technologies, manufacturing, life sciences and infrastructure. It also provides professional staffing services. The mission solutions segment focuses on delivering solutions to federal agencies across the U.S. government and to select international opportunities. These include, among others, the Department of Energy, the Department of Defense, the Federal Emergency Management Agency and intelligence agencies. In early 2021, Fluor realigned its business segments and put its maintenance segment and subsidiary, Stork Holding BV, up for sale.

Fluor offers its employees health, dental, vision, life and accident insurance; disability coverage; savings and retirement plans; a tax savings account; and educational assistance.

FINANCIAL DATA: Note: Data for latest year may not have been available at press time.

In U.S. $	2020	2019	2018	2017	2016	2015
Revenue	15,668,480,000	14,348,020,000	19,166,600,000	19,520,970,000	19,036,520,000	18,114,050,000
R&D Expense						
Operating Income	144,559,000	-586,470,000	521,966,000	426,303,000	599,243,000	926,367,000
Operating Margin %			.03%	.02%	.03%	.05%
SGA Expense	240,692,000	159,089,000	147,958,000	192,187,000	191,073,000	168,329,000
Net Income	-435,046,000	-1,522,164,000	224,833,000	191,377,000	281,401,000	412,512,000
Operating Cash Flow	185,884,000	219,018,000	162,164,000	601,971,000	705,919,000	849,132,000
Capital Expenditure	113,442,000	180,842,000	210,998,000	283,107,000	235,904,000	240,220,000
EBITDA	-29,358,000	-1,032,115,000	775,587,000	679,348,000	842,202,000	961,060,000
Return on Assets %			.02%	.02%	.03%	.05%
Return on Equity %			.07%	.06%	.09%	.14%
Debt to Equity			0.561	0.476	0.486	0.331

CONTACT INFORMATION:

Phone: 469 398-7000   Fax: 469 398-7255
Toll-Free:
Address: 6700 Las Colinas Blvd., Irving, TX 75039 United States

STOCK TICKER/OTHER:

Stock Ticker: FLR
Employees: 50,182
Parent Company:

Exchange: NYS
Fiscal Year Ends: 12/31

SALARIES/BONUSES:

Top Exec. Salary: $ Bonus: $
Second Exec. Salary: $ Bonus: $

OTHER THOUGHTS:

Estimated Female Officers or Directors: 3
Hot Spot for Advancement for Women/Minorities: Y

Ford Motor Company

NAIC Code: 336111

www.ford.com

TYPES OF BUSINESS:

Automobile Manufacturing
Automobile Financing
Fuel-Cell & Hybrid Research

BRANDS/DIVISIONS/AFFILIATES:

Ford
Lincoln
Ford Motor Credit Company LLC
E-Series Cutaway
Ford SuperDuty Chassis Cab
Ford Mustang
Ford F150
Ford Focus

CONTACTS: *Note: Officers with more than one job title may be intentionally listed here more than once.*

David McClelland, CEO, Subsidiary
James Hackett, CEO
Cathy O'Callaghan, CFO, Divisional
Tim Stone, CFO
William Ford, Chairman of the Board
Bradley Gayton, Chief Administrative Officer
Hau Thai-Tang, Other Corporate Officer
Kiersten Robinson, Other Executive Officer
Marcy Klevorn, President, Divisional
James Farley, President, Divisional
Joseph Hinrichs, President, Divisional

GROWTH PLANS/SPECIAL FEATURES:

Ford Motor Company is a designer and manufacturer of automobiles and automotive systems. The firm operates in two primary segments: automotive and financial services. The automotive segment designs, manufactures, sells and services cars, trucks, sport utility vehicles (SUVs), electrified vehicles and luxury vehicles under the Ford and Lincoln brand names. The company sells its vehicles to the public via independently owned dealerships, including Ford, Ford-Lincoln and Lincoln dealerships. These dealerships are in North America, South America, Europe, Asia Pacific and Africa. Ford's 2021 E-Series Cutaway commercial vehicle will comprise a 7.3L V8 engine and a redesigned instrument cluster; and the 2021 Ford SuperDuty Chassis Cab would also feature the 7.3-liter V8 engine as well as the standard 10-speed transmission, and automated technologies such as pre-collision assistance with automatic emergency braking and lane-keeping alerts. In addition to new car sales, the firm also sells vehicles to its dealerships for sale to fleet customers, including commercial fleet customers, daily rental car companies and governments, and sells parts and accessories to authorized parts distributors. The firm's financial services segment, operating through Ford Motor Credit Company, LLC, offers vehicle-related financing, leasing and insurance. Some of Ford's most popular vehicles include the Ford Mustang sports car, the Ford F150 truck, the compact Ford Focus, the Lincoln Navigator SUV and the Ford Escape Hybrid SUV. In early-2021, Ford Motor announced that its Brazil operations would cease vehicle production over the course of that year.

FINANCIAL DATA: *Note: Data for latest year may not have been available at press time.*

In U.S. $	2020	2019	2018	2017	2016	2015
Revenue	127,144,000,000	155,900,000,000	160,338,000,000	156,776,000,000	151,800,000,000	149,558,000,000
R&D Expense						
Operating Income	4,199,000,000	10,046,000,000	12,666,000,000	13,917,000,000	13,020,000,000	7,647,000,000
Operating Margin %		.00%	.02%	.03%	.03%	.05%
SGA Expense	10,193,000,000	11,161,000,000	11,403,000,000	11,527,000,000	12,196,000,000	14,999,000,000
Net Income	-1,279,000,000	47,000,000	3,677,000,000	7,602,000,000	4,596,000,000	7,373,000,000
Operating Cash Flow	24,269,000,000	17,639,000,000	15,022,000,000	18,096,000,000	19,792,000,000	16,170,000,000
Capital Expenditure	5,742,000,000	7,632,000,000	7,785,000,000	7,049,000,000	6,992,000,000	7,196,000,000
EBITDA	16,597,000,000	18,371,000,000	23,344,000,000	26,838,000,000	25,311,000,000	18,991,000,000
Return on Assets %		.00%	.01%	.03%	.02%	.03%
Return on Equity %		.00%	.10%	.24%	.16%	.28%
Debt to Equity		3.086	2.803	2.943	3.199	3.137

CONTACT INFORMATION:

Phone: 313 322-3000   Fax: 313 222-4177
Toll-Free: 800-392-3673
Address: 1 American Rd., Dearborn, MI 48126 United States

STOCK TICKER/OTHER:

Stock Ticker: F
Employees: 186,000
Parent Company:

Exchange: NYS
Fiscal Year Ends: 12/31

SALARIES/BONUSES:

Top Exec. Salary: $ Bonus: $
Second Exec. Salary: $ Bonus: $

OTHER THOUGHTS:

Estimated Female Officers or Directors: 4
Hot Spot for Advancement for Women/Minorities: Y

Fortinet Inc

www.fortinet.com

NAIC Code: 334210A

TYPES OF BUSINESS:

Network Security Products
ASIC Network Security Appliances
Security Subscription Services

BRANDS/DIVISIONS/AFFILIATES:

FortiOS
FortiASIC
FortiGuard
Fortinet Security Fabric
Fabric Ready Partners
Client Access Security Broker Solution
FortiCASB
Panopta

CONTACTS: *Note: Officers with more than one job title may be intentionally listed here more than once.*

Ken Xie, CEO
Keith Jensen, CFO
Michael Xie, CTO
John Whittle, Executive VP, Divisional

GROWTH PLANS/SPECIAL FEATURES:

Fortinet, Inc. is a worldwide market leader in unified threat management security systems. The company specializes in protecting computers from web-based threats such as viruses, worms, intrusions and inappropriate web content, among others, while ensuring that network performance is undisturbed. The firm focuses on four areas of business: network security, Fortinet Security Fabric, cloud security and Internet of Things (IoT) and operational technology. Network security appliances include the FortiOS operating system, which provides the foundation for FortiGate security functions, and FortiASIC integrated circuit, which is designed to accelerate the processing of security and networking functions. Network security also offers the FortiGuard subscription services that sends customers threat intelligence updates. The Fortinet Security Fabric platform is an architectural approach that protects the entire digital attack surface, including network core, endpoints, applications, data centers and private and public cloud. Together with the Fabric-Ready Partners network, the Fortinet Security Fabric platform enables disparate security devices to work together as an integrated, automated and collaborative solution. Cloud security helps customers connect securely to and across their cloud environments by offering security through a virtual firewall and other software products in public and private cloud environments. Solutions include Client Access Security Broker Solution, FortiCASB, extend the core capabilities of the Fortinet Security Fabric platform to provide businesses with the same level of cybersecurity and threat intelligence in cloud environments that they receive on their physical networks. IoT and operational technology security protects end-customers from advanced threats that target their devices and the data that are on them. Fortinet's artificial intelligence (AI) security operations develop and provide AI-driven security solutions, endpoint detection, related analytics and reporting capabilities, and more. In December 2020, Fortinet acquired the Panopta software-as-a-service (SaaS)-based hybrid infrastructure monitoring and diagnostics platform.

FINANCIAL DATA: *Note: Data for latest year may not have been available at press time.*

In U.S. $	2020	2019	2018	2017	2016	2015
Revenue	2,594,400,000	2,156,200,000	1,801,200,000	1,494,930,000	1,275,443,000	1,009,268,000
R&D Expense	341,400,000	277,100,000	244,500,000	210,614,000	183,084,000	158,129,000
Operating Income	491,600,000	344,200,000	231,000,000	110,144,000	46,941,000	22,477,000
Operating Margin %		.16%	.13%	.07%	.04%	.02%
SGA Expense	1,191,400,000	1,029,000,000	875,300,000	788,888,000	707,581,000	541,885,000
Net Income	488,500,000	326,500,000	332,200,000	31,399,000	32,187,000	7,987,000
Operating Cash Flow	1,083,700,000	808,000,000	638,900,000	594,405,000	345,708,000	282,547,000
Capital Expenditure	125,900,000	92,200,000	53,000,000	135,312,000	67,182,000	37,358,000
EBITDA	560,400,000	405,800,000	286,700,000	165,620,000	95,461,000	54,066,000
Return on Assets %		.09%	.12%	.01%	.02%	.00%
Return on Equity %		.28%	.42%	.04%	.04%	.01%
Debt to Equity						

CONTACT INFORMATION:

Phone: 866-789-9001   Fax: 408 235-7737
Toll-Free:
Address: 899 Kifer Rd., Sunnyvale, CA 94086 United States

STOCK TICKER/OTHER:

Stock Ticker: FTNT
Employees: 7,082
Parent Company:

Exchange: NAS
Fiscal Year Ends: 12/31

SALARIES/BONUSES:

Top Exec. Salary: $ Bonus: $
Second Exec. Salary: $ Bonus: $

OTHER THOUGHTS:

Estimated Female Officers or Directors: 3
Hot Spot for Advancement for Women/Minorities: Y

Fortune Brands Home & Security Inc

www.fbhs.com

NAIC Code: 337110

TYPES OF BUSINESS:

Wood Kitchen Cabinet and Countertop Manufacturing
Home Products
Security Products
Manufacturing
Cabinets
Plumbing
Doors

BRANDS/DIVISIONS/AFFILIATES:

Aristokraft
Diamond
Kitchen Craft
Moen
Perrin & Rowe
Therma-Tru
Fiberon
SentrySafe

CONTACTS: *Note: Officers with more than one job title may be intentionally listed here more than once.*

Christopher Klein, CEO
Patrick Hallinan, CFO
David Thomas, Chairman of the Board
Danny Luburic, Chief Accounting Officer
Nicholas Fink, COO
Robert Biggart, General Counsel
Brett Finley, President, Divisional
David Randich, President, Divisional
Cheri Phyfer, President, Subsidiary
Sheri Grissom, Senior VP, Divisional
Martin Thomas, Senior VP, Divisional
Tracey Belcourt, Senior VP, Divisional
Brian Lantz, Senior VP, Divisional

GROWTH PLANS/SPECIAL FEATURES:

Fortune Brands Home & Security, Inc. is a home and security products company. The firm operates through three business segments: cabinets, deriving 40.5% of annual net sales; plumbing, 36.2%; and outdoors & security, 23.3%. The cabinet segment manufactures custom, semi-custom and stock cabinetry, as well as vanities, for the kitchen, bath and other parts of the home. Cabinet brands include Aristokraft, Diamond, Kitchen Craft, Mid-Continent, Schrock, Omega, Homecrest, Ultracraft, Kemper, Mantra and StarMark. This division sells substantially all of its products in North America. The plumbing segment manufactures or assembles and sells faucets, kitchen sinks, waste disposals and accessories predominantly under the Moen, ROHL, Riobel, Perrin & Rowe, Victoria + Albert and Shaws brands. This division principally sells products in the U.S., China and Canada, it also sells in Mexico, Southeast Asia, Europe and South America. The outdoors & security segment manufactures fiberglass and steel entry door systems under the Therma-Tru brand name; composite decking, railing and fencing under the Fiberon brand name; and urethan millwork under the Fypon brand name. It manufactures, sources and distributes locks, safety and security devices, and electronic security products under the Master Lock brand; and fire-resistant safes, security containers and commercial cabinets under the SentrySafe brand. This division principally sells its products in the U.S., Canada, Europe, Central America, Japan and Australia. Fortune Brands operates 36 U.S. manufacturing facilities in 19 states, and has 21 international manufacturing facilities located in Mexico (8), Europe (4), Africa (4), Canada (3) and Asia (2). The firm has more than 60 distribution centers and warehouses worldwide, of which 49 are leased.

FINANCIAL DATA: *Note: Data for latest year may not have been available at press time.*

In U.S. $	2020	2019	2018	2017	2016	2015
Revenue	6,090,300,000	5,764,600,000	5,485,100,000	5,283,300,000	4,984,900,000	4,579,400,000
R&D Expense						
Operating Income	841,100,000	722,800,000	688,400,000	706,000,000	646,600,000	512,700,000
Operating Margin %		.13%	.13%	.13%	.13%	.11%
SGA Expense	1,281,300,000	1,288,200,000	1,234,900,000	1,194,800,000	1,129,900,000	1,047,600,000
Net Income	553,100,000	431,900,000	389,600,000	472,600,000	413,200,000	315,000,000
Operating Cash Flow	825,700,000	637,200,000	604,000,000	600,300,000	650,500,000	411,100,000
Capital Expenditure	150,500,000	131,800,000	150,100,000	165,000,000	149,300,000	128,500,000
EBITDA	978,200,000	822,200,000	761,100,000	814,500,000	753,900,000	606,900,000
Return on Assets %		.07%	.07%	.09%	.08%	.07%
Return on Equity %		.19%	.16%	.19%	.17%	.13%
Debt to Equity		0.793	0.831	0.58	0.606	0.478

CONTACT INFORMATION:

Phone: 847 484-4400   Fax:
Toll-Free:
Address: 520 Lake Cook Rd., Deerfield, IL 60015-5611 United States

STOCK TICKER/OTHER:

Stock Ticker: FBHS   Exchange: NYS
Employees: 24,700   Fiscal Year Ends: 12/31
Parent Company:

SALARIES/BONUSES:

Top Exec. Salary: $ Bonus: $
Second Exec. Salary: $ Bonus: $

OTHER THOUGHTS:

Estimated Female Officers or Directors:
Hot Spot for Advancement for Women/Minorities:

Freddie Mac (Federal Home Loan Mortgage Corporation)

www.freddiemac.com

NAIC Code: 522294

TYPES OF BUSINESS:

Mortgages, Secondary Market
Mortgage Loan Purchaser
Mortgage Securitization

BRANDS/DIVISIONS/AFFILIATES:

CONTACTS: Note: Officers with more than one job title may be intentionally listed here more than once.

David Brickman, CEO
Donald Kish, CFO
Sara Mathew, Chairman of the Board
Jerry Weiss, Chief Administrative Officer
Stacey Goodman, Chief Information Officer
Michael Hutchins, Executive VP, Divisional
Deborah Jenkins, Executive VP, Divisional
Ricardo Anzaldua, Executive VP
Anil Hinduja, Executive VP

GROWTH PLANS/SPECIAL FEATURES:

Freddie Mac, officially known as Federal Home Loan Mortgage Corporation, is a public company chartered by the U.S. Congress to create a continuous flow of funds to mortgage lenders in support of home ownership and rental housing. Freddie Mac purchases residential mortgage loans from lenders and then packages them into securities, which are sold to investors worldwide. The firm purchases 30-year, 20-year, 15-year and 10-year fixed-rate single-family mortgages; adjustable-rate mortgages (ARMs); interest-only; and FHA/VA and other governmental mortgages. Freddie Mac's mortgage securitization business receives the mortgage payments from the original lender or loan servicer and deducts a timeliness guarantee fee and other fees, passing the remainder on to the holder or holders of the mortgage-backed securities. The company implements regular public risk-based capital stress tests, initiates public interest-rate risk sensitivity analyses, discloses credit risk sensitivity analyses and obtains annual ratings from statistical rating organizations. Freddie Mac's primary business objectives are to support U.S. homeowners and renters by maintaining mortgage availability with alternatives that allow them to stay in their homes or avoid foreclosure; to reduce taxpayer exposure to losses by increasing the role of private capital in the mortgage market; and to support and improve the secondary mortgage market. In December 2020, Freddie Mac announced a key milestone achieved in 2020 as part of its transition from the London Interbank Offered Rate to the Secured Overnight Financing Rate (SOFR), when it began purchasing and securitizing single-family adjustable-rate mortgage (ARM) loans tied to SOFR.

Freddie Mac provides its employees benefits including medical, dental, disability and vision coverage; a 401(k) plan; parental, medical and military leave; and a variety of employee assistance programs.

FINANCIAL DATA: Note: Data for latest year may not have been available at press time.

In U.S. $	2020	2019	2018	2017	2016	2015
Revenue	16,659,000,000	14,078,000,000	15,565,000,000	20,692,000,000	15,090,000,000	11,587,000,000
R&D Expense						
Operating Income						
Operating Margin %						
SGA Expense	2,137,000,000	2,119,000,000	1,807,000,000	1,654,000,000	1,450,000,000	1,374,000,000
Net Income	7,326,000,000	7,214,000,000	9,235,000,000	5,625,000,000	7,815,000,000	6,376,000,000
Operating Cash Flow	907,000,000	12,197,000,000	674,000,000	5,462,000,000	4,859,000,000	-934,000,000
Capital Expenditure						
EBITDA						
Return on Assets %		.00%	.00%	.00%	.00%	.00%
Return on Equity %						
Debt to Equity						

CONTACT INFORMATION:

Phone: 703 903-2000   Fax: 703 903-2759
Toll-Free: 800-424-5401
Address: 8200 Jones Branch Dr., McLean, VA 22102-3110 United States

STOCK TICKER/OTHER:

Stock Ticker: FMCC
Employees: 6,912
Parent Company:

Exchange: PINX
Fiscal Year Ends: 12/31

SALARIES/BONUSES:

Top Exec. Salary: $ Bonus: $
Second Exec. Salary: $ Bonus: $

OTHER THOUGHTS:

Estimated Female Officers or Directors: 2
Hot Spot for Advancement for Women/Minorities: Y

Sales, profits and employees may be estimates. Financial information, benefits and other data can change quickly and may vary from those stated here.

Frito-Lay North America Inc

NAIC Code: 311919

www.fritolay.com

TYPES OF BUSINESS:

Snack Products
Salsas & Dips
Chips
Cookies

BRANDS/DIVISIONS/AFFILIATES:

PepsiCo Inc
Lays
Doritos
Cheetos
SunChips
Rold Gold
Grandmas
Smartfood

CONTACTS: *Note: Officers with more than one job title may be intentionally listed here more than once.*

Rachel Ferdinando, Sr. VP
Mike Zbuchalski, Sr. VP-R&D
Marc Kesselman, General Counsel
Christopher Wyse, VP-Public Affairs
Randy Melville, Gen. Mgr.-Central Bus. Unit
Vivek Sankaran, Chief Customer Officer
Dave Scalera, Sr. VP-Go-to-Market Capability & Productivity
Ted Herrod, Gen. Mgr.-West Bus. Unit
Marc Guay, Pres., PepsiCo Foods Canada
Leslie Starr Keating, Sr. VP-Supply Chain

GROWTH PLANS/SPECIAL FEATURES:

Frito-Lay North America, Inc., a subsidiary of PepsiCo, Inc., manufactures, markets, sells and distributes branded snacks. The firm's proprietary products include: Lay's potato chips, Doritos tortilla chips, Tostitos tortilla chips and salsas, Cheetos cheese-flavored snacks, Fritos corn chips, Ruffles potato chips, SunChips and multigrain snacks. Additionally, the company's brand portfolio includes: Rold Gold pretzels, Grandma's cookies, Cracker Jack candy-coated popcorn, Matador beef jerky, Funyuns fried onion rings, Sabritones puffed wheat snacks, Isleno plantain chips, Smartfood popcorn, Stacy's pita chips and more. The firm's joint venture with Strauss Group markets refrigerated spreads and dips under the Sabra brand name, including hummus, salsas and guacamole. Over time, the firm updated its Lay's Classic Potato Chips recipe to feature only potatoes, healthier oils such as corn and sunflower oil and a dash of salt; and updated the Tostitos and SunChips brands to feature healthier recipes with no MSG (monosodium glutamate), artificial preservatives or artificial flavorings. The company offers a gluten-free recipe section on its website for customers with Celiac Disease or gluten sensitivities. Frity-Lay operates more than 30 manufacturing facilities in the U.S. and Canada, and over 200 distribution centers.

FINANCIAL DATA: *Note: Data for latest year may not have been available at press time.*

In U.S. $	2020	2019	2018	2017	2016	2015
Revenue	18,189,000,000	17,078,000,000	16,346,000,000	15,798,000,000	15,549,000,000	14,782,000,000
R&D Expense						
Operating Income						
Operating Margin %						
SGA Expense						
Net Income	5,340,000,000	5,258,000,000	5,008,000,000	4,793,000,000	4,612,000,000	4,304,000,000
Operating Cash Flow						
Capital Expenditure						
EBITDA						
Return on Assets %						
Return on Equity %						
Debt to Equity						

CONTACT INFORMATION:

Phone: 972-334-7000   Fax: 972-334-2019
Toll-Free: 800-352-4477
Address: 7701 Legacy Dr., Plano, TX 75024 United States

SALARIES/BONUSES:

Top Exec. Salary: $ Bonus: $
Second Exec. Salary: $ Bonus: $

STOCK TICKER/OTHER:

Stock Ticker: Subsidiary
Employees: 55,000
Parent Company: PepsiCo Inc

Exchange:
Fiscal Year Ends: 12/31

OTHER THOUGHTS:

Estimated Female Officers or Directors: 3
Hot Spot for Advancement for Women/Minorities: Y

Sales, profits and employees may be estimates. Financial information, benefits and other data can change quickly and may vary from those stated here.

FTI Consulting Inc

www.fticonsulting.com

NAIC Code: 541610

TYPES OF BUSINESS:

Bankruptcy & Restructuring Consulting
Consulting
Technology
Management Consulting
Corporate Restructuring
Litigation Consulting
Strategic Communications

BRANDS/DIVISIONS/AFFILIATES:

CONTACTS: Note: Officers with more than one job title may be intentionally listed here more than once.

Steven Gunby, CEO
Ajay Sabherwal, CFO
Gerard Holthaus, Chairman of the Board
Brendan Keating, Chief Accounting Officer
Matthew Pachman, Chief Risk Officer
Curtis Lu, General Counsel
Paul Linton, Other Executive Officer
Holly Paul, Other Executive Officer

GROWTH PLANS/SPECIAL FEATURES:

FTI Consulting, Inc. is a global consulting firm that provides turnaround, technology, change management and many other high-level consulting services. The firm works across a myriad of industries, including aerospace, defense, agriculture, automotive, construction, energy/power, environmental, financial institutions, healthcare, life sciences, hospitality, gaming, leisure, insurance, mining, public sector, government contracts, real estate, retail, consumer products, transportation, telecommunications, media and technology. FTI Consulting operates through five segments: corporate finance & restructuring (including bankruptcy), forensic and litigation consulting, economic consulting, technology, and strategic communications. Collectively, these business segments offer a comprehensive suite of services designed to assist FTI's clients across the business cycle, from proactive risk management to rapid response to unexpected events and dynamic environments. FTI works closely with its clients to help them anticipate, illuminate and overcome complex business challenges and make the most of opportunities arising from factors such as the economy, financial and credit markets, governmental legislation and regulation, and litigation. FTI operates offices worldwide, including the U.S., Canada, Latin America, Asia-Pacific, Europe, Middle East, Africa and the U.K. FTI offers its employees comprehensive benefits, retirement options and a variety of employee assistance programs.

FINANCIAL DATA: Note: Data for latest year may not have been available at press time.

In U.S. $	2020	2019	2018	2017	2016	2015
Revenue	2,461,275,000	2,352,717,000	2,027,877,000	1,807,732,000	1,810,394,000	1,779,149,000
R&D Expense						
Operating Income	283,524,000	305,595,000	226,005,000	111,002,000	144,320,000	163,311,000
Operating Margin %		.13%	.11%	.08%	.09%	.09%
SGA Expense	491,930,000	504,074,000	465,636,000	429,722,000	434,552,000	432,668,000
Net Income	210,682,000	216,726,000	150,611,000	107,962,000	85,520,000	66,053,000
Operating Cash Flow	327,069,000	217,886,000	230,672,000	147,625,000	233,488,000	139,920,000
Capital Expenditure	34,866,000	42,072,000	32,270,000	32,004,000	28,935,000	31,399,000
EBITDA	325,299,000	345,961,000	274,639,000	154,203,000	201,628,000	191,272,000
Return on Assets %		.08%	.06%	.05%	.04%	.03%
Return on Equity %		.15%	.12%	.09%	.07%	.06%
Debt to Equity		0.304	0.197	0.332	0.303	0.431

CONTACT INFORMATION:

Phone: 202-312-9100   Fax: 202-312-9101
Toll-Free: 800-334-5701
Address: 555 12th St. NW, Washington, DC 20004 United States

STOCK TICKER/OTHER:

Stock Ticker: FCN
Employees: 6,321
Parent Company:

Exchange: NYS
Fiscal Year Ends: 12/31

SALARIES/BONUSES:

Top Exec. Salary: $ Bonus: $
Second Exec. Salary: $ Bonus: $

OTHER THOUGHTS:

Estimated Female Officers or Directors: 3
Hot Spot for Advancement for Women/Minorities: Y

Gartner Inc
NAIC Code: 541910

TYPES OF BUSINESS:
Research-Computer Hardware & Software
Industry Research
IT Symposia & Conferences
Measurement & Advisory Services

BRANDS/DIVISIONS/AFFILIATES:
Symposium/Xpo

CONTACTS: Note: Officers with more than one job title may be intentionally listed here more than once.
Eugene Hall, CEO
Craig Safian, CFO
Michael Diliberto, Chief Information Officer
Robin Kranich, Exec. VP-Human Resources
Alwyn Dawkins, Senior VP, Divisional
Per Waern, Senior VP, Divisional
Robin Kranich, Senior VP, Divisional
Peter Sondergaard, Senior VP, Divisional
David McVeigh, Senior VP, Divisional
David Godfrey, Senior VP, Divisional
Thomas Christopher, Senior VP, Divisional
Kendall Davis, Senior VP, Divisional
Daniel Peale, Senior VP
James Smith, Chairman of the Board

GROWTH PLANS/SPECIAL FEATURES:
Gartner, Inc. is a research and advisory firm that offers independent research and analysis on IT, computer hardware, software, communications and related technology industries. With consultants in 100 countries, the firm serves more than 14,000 organizations worldwide. The company operates in three segments: research, consulting and conferences. The research segment, the main service of the company, delivers independent, objective advice to leaders across the technology enterprise, primarily through a subscription-based digital media service. Within the research segment, Global Technology Sales delivers products and services to users and providers of technology, while Global Business Sales delivers products and services to all other functional leaders. The consulting division provides customized solutions to unique client needs through on-site, day-to-day support, as well as proprietary tools for measuring and improving IT performance with a focus on coast, performance, efficiency and quality. Last, the conferences group provides IT, supply chain, digital marketing and other business professionals the opportunity to attend various symposia, conferences and exhibitions to learn, contribute and network with their peers, attracting thousands of business and technology professionals to its annual conferences, including virtual conferences. Its flagship event, Symposium/Xpo, as well as summits, focus on specific technologies and industries and offer experimental workshop-style seminars. This division also provides the latest Gartner research into applicable insight and advice at its events.

FINANCIAL DATA: Note: Data for latest year may not have been available at press time.

In U.S. $	2020	2019	2018	2017	2016	2015
Revenue	4,099,403,000	4,245,321,000	3,975,454,000	3,311,494,000	2,444,540,000	2,163,056,000
R&D Expense						
Operating Income	496,432,000	379,550,000	366,912,000	152,121,000	347,739,000	314,172,000
Operating Margin %		.09%	.09%	.05%	.14%	.15%
SGA Expense	2,038,963,000	2,103,424,000	1,884,141,000	1,599,004,000	1,089,184,000	962,677,000
Net Income	266,745,000	233,290,000	122,456,000	3,279,000	193,582,000	175,635,000
Operating Cash Flow	903,278,000	565,436,000	471,158,000	254,517,000	365,632,000	345,561,000
Capital Expenditure	83,888,000	149,016,000	126,873,000	110,765,000	49,863,000	46,128,000
EBITDA	660,753,000	590,349,000	563,496,000	240,301,000	377,965,000	341,890,000
Return on Assets %		.03%	.02%	.00%	.09%	.09%
Return on Equity %		.26%	.13%	.01%		12.21%
Debt to Equity		3.065	2.682	3.066	10.913	

CONTACT INFORMATION:
Phone: 203 316-1111   Fax:
Toll-Free:
Address: 56 Top Gallant Rd., Stamford, CT 06902-7700 United States

STOCK TICKER/OTHER:
Stock Ticker: IT   Exchange: NYS
Employees: 16,724   Fiscal Year Ends: 12/31
Parent Company:

SALARIES/BONUSES:
Top Exec. Salary: $ Bonus: $
Second Exec. Salary: $ Bonus: $

OTHER THOUGHTS:
Estimated Female Officers or Directors: 3
Hot Spot for Advancement for Women/Minorities: Y

Genentech Inc

NAIC Code: 325412

TYPES OF BUSINESS:

Drug Development & Manufacturing
Genetically Engineered Drugs
Biotechnology

BRANDS/DIVISIONS/AFFILIATES:

Roche Holding AG
www.gene.com
Tecentriq

CONTACTS: *Note: Officers with more than one job title may be intentionally listed here more than once.*

Alexander Hardy, CEO
Ed Harrington, CFO
Cynthia Burks, Sr. VP-Human Resources
Richard H. Scheller, Exec. VP-Research
Frederick C. Kentz, Sec.
Timothy Moore, Head-Pharmaceutical Technical Operation Biologics
Severin Schwan, Chmn.

GROWTH PLANS/SPECIAL FEATURES:

Genentech, Inc., a wholly owned subsidiary of Roche Holding AG, is a biotechnology company that discovers, develops, manufactures and commercializes medicines to treat patients with serious or life-threatening medical conditions. The firm makes medicines by splicing genes into fast-growing bacteria that then produce therapeutic proteins and combat diseases on a molecular level. Genentech uses cutting-edge technologies such as computer visualization of molecules, micro arrays and sensitive assaying techniques to develop, manufacture and market pharmaceuticals for unmet medical needs. For patients, the company's website (www.gene.com) provides access for viewing medicine information, investigational medicines, finding open clinical trials and information on diseases in general. Genentech's range of programs and services help make sure that price is not a barrier for patients. For medical professionals, the website offers information on the medicines that are on the market by Genentech, as well as what is on the current pipeline, compliance, product security and various types of medical resources. There were over 40 medicines on the market by the company, and 54 molecules in the pipeline. These medicines and molecules are in various phases in relation to oncology, metabolism, immunology, infectious disease, neuroscience, ophthalmology or other conditions. Approximately half of Genentech's marketed and pipeline products are derived from collaborations with companies and institutions worldwide; therefore, the firm is open to having partners.

Genentech provides employees benefits including a 401(k); disability, life, AD&D, medical, dental and vision coverage; flexible spending accounts; and paid vacations.

FINANCIAL DATA: *Note: Data for latest year may not have been available at press time.*

In U.S. $	2020	2019	2018	2017	2016	2015
Revenue	21,840,000,000	21,000,000,000	20,000,000,000	19,000,000,000	18,000,000,000	17,000,000,000
R&D Expense						
Operating Income						
Operating Margin %						
SGA Expense						
Net Income						
Operating Cash Flow						
Capital Expenditure						
EBITDA						
Return on Assets %						
Return on Equity %						
Debt to Equity						

CONTACT INFORMATION:

Phone: 650-225-1000   Fax: 650-225-6000
Toll-Free: 800-626-3553
Address: 1 DNA Way, South San Francisco, CA 94080-4990 United States

STOCK TICKER/OTHER:

Stock Ticker: Subsidiary
Employees: 13,500
Parent Company: Roche Holding AG

Exchange:
Fiscal Year Ends: 12/31

SALARIES/BONUSES:

Top Exec. Salary: $ Bonus: $
Second Exec. Salary: $ Bonus: $

OTHER THOUGHTS:

Estimated Female Officers or Directors: 1
Hot Spot for Advancement for Women/Minorities: Y

General Dynamics Corporation

www.generaldynamics.com

NAIC Code: 336411

TYPES OF BUSINESS:

Aircraft Manufacturing
Combat Vehicles & Systems
Telecommunications Systems
Naval Vessels & Submarines
Ship Management Services
Information Systems & Technology
Defense Systems & Services
Business Jets

BRANDS/DIVISIONS/AFFILIATES:

Bath Iron Works
Electric Boat Corporation
General Dynamics NASSCO
Jet Aviation
Gulfstream Aerospace Corporation

CONTACTS: *Note: Officers with more than one job title may be intentionally listed here more than once.*

Phebe Novakovic, CEO
Robert Helm, Sr. VP, Divisional
Jason Aiken, CFO
William Moss, Chief Accounting Officer
Mark Roualet, Executive VP, Divisional
Christopher Marzilli, Executive VP, Divisional
John Casey, Executive VP, Divisional
Gregory Gallopoulos, General Counsel
Marguerite Gilliland, President, Subsidiary
Mark Burns, President, Subsidiary
Gary Whited, President, Subsidiary
Jeffrey Geiger, President, Subsidiary
Christopher Brady, President, Subsidiary
Kimberly Kuryea, Senior VP, Divisional

GROWTH PLANS/SPECIAL FEATURES:

General Dynamics Corporation is one of the world's largest aerospace and defense contractors. Its customers include the U.S. military, other government organizations, armed forces of allied nations and a diverse base of corporate and industrial buyers. The firm's operations are divided into five segments: information technology (IT), marine systems, combat systems, aerospace, and mission systems. The IT group designs, manufactures and delivers tactical and strategic mission systems, information technology and mission services as well as intelligence mission systems to the U.S. Department of Defense and other customers. The marine systems division provides the U.S. Navy with combat vessels, including nuclear submarines, surface combatants and auxiliary ships. The segment also provides ship management services, such as overhaul, repair and lifecycle support services, and builds commercial ships. Subsidiaries within the marine division include Bath Iron Works, Electric Boat Corporation, and General Dynamics NASSCO. The combat systems group provides design, development, production, support and enhancement for tracked and wheeled military vehicles, weapons systems and munitions, with product lines including medium armored vehicles, main battle tanks, munitions, rockets and missile components and armament and detection systems. It is the leading builder of armored vehicles. The aerospace segment comprises two subsidiaries: Jet Aviation provides comprehensive services and offers a network of locations for aircraft owners and operators, spanning Asia, the Caribbean, Europe, the Middle East and North America; and Gulfstream Aerospace Corporation produces technology-advanced aircraft, and offers related support and services globally. Gulfstream's fleet of aircraft comprises the G280, G550, G500, G600, G650, G650ER and G700. The mission systems segment provides and manufactures communications systems, command and control systems, cyber security solutions and products and imagery, signals intelligence and multi-intelligence solutions to multiple defense agencies.

FINANCIAL DATA: *Note: Data for latest year may not have been available at press time.*

In U.S. $	2020	2019	2018	2017	2016	2015
Revenue	37,925,000,000	39,350,000,000	36,193,000,000	30,973,000,000	31,353,000,000	31,469,000,000
R&D Expense						
Operating Income	4,133,000,000	4,648,000,000	4,457,000,000	4,177,000,000	4,309,000,000	4,178,000,000
Operating Margin %		.12%	.12%	.13%	.14%	.13%
SGA Expense	2,192,000,000	2,411,000,000	2,258,000,000	2,010,000,000	1,940,000,000	1,952,000,000
Net Income	3,167,000,000	3,484,000,000	3,345,000,000	2,912,000,000	2,955,000,000	2,965,000,000
Operating Cash Flow	3,858,000,000	2,981,000,000	3,148,000,000	3,879,000,000	2,198,000,000	2,499,000,000
Capital Expenditure	967,000,000	987,000,000	690,000,000	428,000,000	392,000,000	569,000,000
EBITDA	5,105,000,000	5,503,000,000	5,222,000,000	4,635,000,000	4,784,000,000	4,682,000,000
Return on Assets %		.07%	.08%	.09%	.09%	.09%
Return on Equity %		.28%	.29%	.26%	.27%	.26%
Debt to Equity		0.756	0.975	0.348	0.272	0.27

CONTACT INFORMATION:

Phone: 703 876-3000   Fax: 703 876-3125
Toll-Free:
Address: 11011 Sunset Hills Rd., Renton, VA 20190 United States

STOCK TICKER/OTHER:

Stock Ticker: GD   Exchange: NYS
Employees: 100,700   Fiscal Year Ends: 12/31
Parent Company:

SALARIES/BONUSES:

Top Exec. Salary: $ Bonus: $
Second Exec. Salary: $ Bonus: $

OTHER THOUGHTS:

Estimated Female Officers or Directors: 3
Hot Spot for Advancement for Women/Minorities: Y

General Mills Inc

NAIC Code: 311230

www.generalmills.com

TYPES OF BUSINESS:

Cereal Manufacturing
Snack Foods
Frozen Foods
Baking Products
Yogurt
Organic Foods
Convenience Meal Products
Canned and Frozen Vegetables

BRANDS/DIVISIONS/AFFILIATES:

Cereal Partners Worldwide
Haagen-Dazs Japan Inc
Betty Crocker
Cheerios
Gold Medal
Larabar
Pillsbury
Wheaties

CONTACTS: Note: Officers with more than one job title may be intentionally listed here more than once.

Jeffrey Harmening, CEO
Donal Mulligan, CFO
Kofi Bruce, Chief Accounting Officer
Ivan Pollard, Chief Marketing Officer
John Church, Executive VP
Jacqueline Williams-Roll, Other Executive Officer
Jonathon Nudi, President, Divisional
William Bishop, President, Divisional
Shawn OGrady, President, Divisional
Bethany Quam, President, Geographical
Christina Law, President, Geographical
Richard Allendorf, Senior VP

GROWTH PLANS/SPECIAL FEATURES:

General Mills, Inc. is a leading global producer of packaged consumer and pet foods. The company manufactures its products in 13 countries and markets them in more than 100. General Mills offers a variety of food products for consumers with a focus on six large global categories: ready-to-eat cereal; convenient meals, including meal kits, ethnic meals, pizza, soup, side dish mixes, frozen breakfast and frozen entrees; snacks, including grain, fruit and savory snacks, nutrition bars and frozen hot snacks; yogurt; super-premium ice cream; and pet food. Other significant product categories include: baking mixes and ingredients; and refrigerated and frozen dough. General Mills' principal raw materials are grains (wheat, oats and corn), sugar, dairy products, vegetables, fruits, meats, nuts, vegetable oils and other agricultural products. Cereal Partners Worldwide, a joint venture with Nestle SA, offers the ready-to-eat cereal category to markets outside North America; and Haagen-Dazs Japan, Inc., another joint venture, offers the super-premium ice cream category in Japan. During fiscal 2020, Walmart Inc. and its affiliates accounted for 21% of consolidated net sales, as well as 30% of net sales of General Mills' North American retail segment. Among the firm's many trademarks include Annie's, Betty Crocker, Bisquick, Cheerios, Fruit Roll-Ups, Gold Medal, Larabar, Nature Valley, Old El Paso, Pillsbury, Progresso, Wheaties and Yoplait.

FINANCIAL DATA: Note: Data for latest year may not have been available at press time.

In U.S. $	2020	2019	2018	2017	2016	2015
Revenue	17,626,600,000	16,865,200,000	15,740,400,000	15,619,800,000	16,563,100,000	
R&D Expense						
Operating Income	2,978,300,000	2,821,000,000	2,674,900,000	2,762,500,000	2,710,600,000	
Operating Margin %	.17%	.17%	.17%	.18%	.16%	
SGA Expense	3,151,600,000	2,935,800,000	2,752,600,000	2,801,300,000	3,118,900,000	
Net Income	2,181,200,000	1,752,700,000	2,131,000,000	1,657,500,000	1,697,400,000	
Operating Cash Flow	3,676,200,000	2,807,000,000	2,841,000,000	2,313,300,000	2,629,800,000	
Capital Expenditure	460,800,000	537,600,000	622,700,000	684,400,000	729,300,000	
EBITDA	3,667,400,000	3,229,500,000	3,139,800,000	3,177,000,000	3,323,600,000	
Return on Assets %	.07%	.06%	.08%	.08%	.08%	
Return on Equity %	.29%	.27%	.41%	.36%	.34%	
Debt to Equity	1.391	1.648	2.063	1.766	1.432	

CONTACT INFORMATION:

Phone: 763 764-7600   Fax: 763 764-7384
Toll-Free: 800-248-7310
Address: 1 General Mills Blvd., Minneapolis, MN 55426 United States

STOCK TICKER/OTHER:

Stock Ticker: GIS
Employees: 35,000
Parent Company:

Exchange: NYS
Fiscal Year Ends: 05/31

SALARIES/BONUSES:

Top Exec. Salary: $ Bonus: $
Second Exec. Salary: $ Bonus: $

OTHER THOUGHTS:

Estimated Female Officers or Directors: 11
Hot Spot for Advancement for Women/Minorities: Y

General Motors Company (GM)

www.gm.com

NAIC Code: 336111

TYPES OF BUSINESS:

Automobile Manufacturing
Security & Information Services
Automotive Electronics
Financing & Insurance
Parts & Service
Transmissions
Engines
Locomotives

BRANDS/DIVISIONS/AFFILIATES:

Cruise
Buick
Cadillac
Chevrolet
GMC
Baojun
Jiefang
Wuling

CONTACTS: *Note: Officers with more than one job title may be intentionally listed here more than once.*

Daniel Ammann, CEO, Subsidiary
Mary Barra, CEO
Dhivya Suryadevara, CFO
Christopher Hatto, Chief Accounting Officer
Alicia Boler-Davis, Executive VP, Divisional
Craig Glidden, Executive VP
Barry Engle, Executive VP
Alan Batey, Executive VP
Matthew Tsien, Executive VP
Mark Reuss, President

GROWTH PLANS/SPECIAL FEATURES:

General Motors Company (GM) is engaged in the worldwide design, production and marketing of cars, crossovers, trucks and automotive parts. GM's automotive operations are grouped into four segments: GM North America, GM international, Cruise and GM Financial. GMNA meets the demands of customers in North America with vehicles developed, manufactured and/or marketed under the Buick, Cadillac, Chevrolet and GMC brands. GM international primarily meets the demands of customers outside North America with vehicles developed, manufactured and/or marketed under the Buick, Cadillac and GMC brands. This division also has equity ownership stakes in entities that meet the demands of customers in other countries, primarily China, with vehicles developed, manufactured and/or marketed under the Baojun, Buick, Cadillac, Chevrolet, Jiefang and Wuling brands. Cruise is a global segment responsible for the development and commercialization of autonomous vehicle technology, and includes autonomous vehicle-related engineering. GM Financial offers a comprehensive suite of financing products regarding the sale or lease of GM's vehicles. Approximately 70% of this division's total loan originations in North America were prime loans, with other revenues deriving from leased vehicle income, finance charges and other services. In the nine months ending September 30, 2020, GM wound down its Holden sales, design and engineering operations in Australia and New Zealand; and GM agreed to sell its vehicle and powertrain manufacturing facilities in Thailand.

FINANCIAL DATA: *Note: Data for latest year may not have been available at press time.*

In U.S. $	2020	2019	2018	2017	2016	2015
Revenue	122,485,000,000	137,237,000,000	147,049,000,000	145,588,000,000	166,380,000,000	152,356,000,000
R&D Expense						
Operating Income	6,634,000,000	5,481,000,000	4,445,000,000	10,016,000,000	9,545,000,000	4,897,000,000
Operating Margin %		.04%	.03%	.07%	.06%	.03%
SGA Expense	7,038,000,000	8,491,000,000	9,650,000,000	9,575,000,000	11,710,000,000	13,405,000,000
Net Income	6,427,000,000	6,732,000,000	8,014,000,000	-3,864,000,000	9,427,000,000	9,687,000,000
Operating Cash Flow	16,670,000,000	15,021,000,000	15,256,000,000	17,328,000,000	16,545,000,000	11,978,000,000
Capital Expenditure	20,533,000,000	23,996,000,000	25,497,000,000	27,633,000,000	29,166,000,000	23,032,000,000
EBITDA	22,008,000,000	22,336,000,000	22,873,000,000	24,699,000,000	22,664,000,000	16,178,000,000
Return on Assets %		.03%	.04%	-.02%	.05%	.05%
Return on Equity %		.16%	.21%	-.10%	.23%	.26%
Debt to Equity		1.602	1.88	1.921	1.268	1.092

CONTACT INFORMATION:

Phone: 313 556-5000   Fax:
Toll-Free:
Address: 300 Renaissance Ctr., Detroit, MI 48265-3000 United States

STOCK TICKER/OTHER:

Stock Ticker: GM
Employees: 135,000
Parent Company:

Exchange: NYS
Fiscal Year Ends: 12/31

SALARIES/BONUSES:

Top Exec. Salary: $ Bonus: $
Second Exec. Salary: $ Bonus: $

OTHER THOUGHTS:

Estimated Female Officers or Directors: 8
Hot Spot for Advancement for Women/Minorities: Y

Genuine Parts Company

www.genpt.com

NAIC Code: 423120

TYPES OF BUSINESS:

Auto Parts, Distribution
Automotive Replacement Parts
Industrial Replacement Parts
Parts Distributor
Automotive Parts Stores

BRANDS/DIVISIONS/AFFILIATES:

National Automotive Parts Association (NAPA)
NAPA AUTO PARTS
NAPA Canada/UAP Inc
Repco
Alliance Automotive Group
Motion Industries Inc
Motion Industries (Canada) Inc
Motion Mexico S de RL de CV

CONTACTS: *Note: Officers with more than one job title may be intentionally listed here more than once.*

Paul Donahue, CEO
Carol Yancey, CFO
Jerry Nix, Director
Kevin Herron, President, Divisional
Scott Sonnemaker, President, Geographical
Randall Breaux, President, Subsidiary
James Neill, Senior VP, Divisional

GROWTH PLANS/SPECIAL FEATURES:

Genuine Parts Company (GPC) distributes automotive and industrial replacement parts and materials. GPC serves hundreds of thousands of customers from a network of more than 10,000 locations in 14 countries throughout North America, Australasia and Europe. The company's automotive parts division distributes parts and accessories, and offers inventory, catalogue, marketing, training and other programs to the automotive aftermarket sector in select regions. This division includes: National Automotive Parts Association (NAPA) automotive parts distribution centers and automotive parts stores (NAPA AUTO PARTS) in the U.S.; NAPA Canada/UAP, Inc. (Canada); Repco (in Australasia); and Alliance Automotive Group (Europe). Automotive replacement parts are offered for substantially all motor vehicle makes and models in the U.S., including imported vehicles, hybrids, electric vehicles, trucks, SUVs, buses, motorcycles, recreational vehicles and farm vehicles. This division also distributes replacement parts for small engines, farm equipment, marine equipment and heavy-duty equipment. GPC's industrial parts division operates in North America and Australasia. Wholly-owned Motion Industries, Inc. distributes industrial replacement parts and related supplies such as bearings, mechanical and electrical power transmission products, industrial automation and robotics, hoses, hydraulic and pneumatic components, industrial and safety supplies and material handling products to maintenance, repair and operation (MRO) and original equipment manufacturer (OEM) customers throughout the U.S., Canada (via Motion Industries (Canada) Inc., and Mexico via Motion Mexico S de RL de CV.

GPC offers comprehensive health benefits, 401(k) and various employee assistance programs and company perks.

FINANCIAL DATA: *Note: Data for latest year may not have been available at press time.*

In U.S. $	2020	2019	2018	2017	2016	2015
Revenue	16,537,430,000	19,392,310,000	18,735,070,000	16,308,800,000	15,339,710,000	15,280,040,000
R&D Expense						
Operating Income	971,683,000	1,096,909,000	1,109,715,000	1,019,639,000	1,069,772,000	1,124,414,000
Operating Margin %		.06%	.06%	.06%	.07%	.07%
SGA Expense	4,386,739,000	4,934,167,000	4,615,290,000	3,705,136,000	3,370,833,000	3,277,390,000
Net Income	-29,102,000	621,085,000	810,474,000	616,757,000	687,240,000	705,672,000
Operating Cash Flow	2,019,561,000	892,010,000	1,145,164,000	815,043,000	946,078,000	1,159,373,000
Capital Expenditure	153,502,000	297,869,000	232,422,000	156,760,000	160,643,000	109,544,000
EBITDA	745,923,000	1,196,299,000	1,419,172,000	1,218,445,000	1,242,911,000	1,287,018,000
Return on Assets %		.05%	.06%	.06%	.08%	.09%
Return on Equity %		.17%	.24%	.19%	.22%	.22%
Debt to Equity		0.987	0.705	0.764	0.184	0.091

CONTACT INFORMATION:

Phone: 770 953-1700 Fax: 770 956-2211
Toll-Free:
Address: 2999 Wildwood Pkwy., Atlanta, GA 30339 United States

SALARIES/BONUSES:

Top Exec. Salary: $ Bonus: $
Second Exec. Salary: $ Bonus: $

STOCK TICKER/OTHER:

Stock Ticker: GPC   Exchange: NYS
Employees: 55,000   Fiscal Year Ends: 12/31
Parent Company:

OTHER THOUGHTS:

Estimated Female Officers or Directors: 2
Hot Spot for Advancement for Women/Minorities: Y

Georgia Power Company

www.georgiapower.com

NAIC Code: 221112

TYPES OF BUSINESS:

Electric Utility
Fossil-Fuel Plants
Hydroelectric Power
Nuclear Power
Recreational Facilities-Reservoirs

BRANDS/DIVISIONS/AFFILIATES:

Southern Company (The)
SurgeDefender

CONTACTS: *Note: Officers with more than one job title may be intentionally listed here more than once.*

Paul Bowers, CEO
David Poroch, CFO
Sloane Drake, Sr. VP-Human Resources
Joseph A. Miller, Exec. VP-Nuclear Dev.
Thomas P. Bishop, General Counsel
Anthony Wilson, Exec. VP-Oper. & Customer Service
Ronnie R. Labrato, Treas.
Craig Barrs, Exec. VP-External Affairs
Mike Anderson, Sr. VP-Charitable Giving
Monica Caston, VP-Diversity & Inclusion
John L. Pemberton, Sr. VP-Fossil & Hydro Generation
Paul Bowers, Chmn.

GROWTH PLANS/SPECIAL FEATURES:

Georgia Power Company is the largest of the five subsidiaries of The Southern Company, a major U.S. utility holding company. Georgia Power is a regulated utility that provides electricity to more than 2.25 million residential, commercial and industrial customers throughout 155 counties in the state of Georgia. The company also sells wholesale electricity to several cooperatives and municipalities in the region. Georgia Power has a generating capacity of more than 14.3 million kilowatts (kWs) provided by its network of 46 generating plants. These plants include fuel sources such as hydro/renewables, oil, gas, solar, nuclear and coal. Oil and gas account for approximately 6.3 million kWs of generating capacity; nuclear accounts, 1.96 million kWs; hydro power, 1.09 million kWs; coal, 4.8 million kWs; and renewables, 169,006 kW. Georgia Power owns 76,484 miles of distribution lines and 12,622 miles of transmission lines. Georgia Power also offers surge protection, SurgeDefender, for $9.95 per month for energy related products like water heaters and heat pumps that are motor driven. The firm is a major non-government provider of recreation facilities in the state, responsible for several reservoirs throughout Georgia, including approximately 1,400 miles of shoreline and 38,000 acres of wildlife management acres. The firm also operates an online store where customers can purchase thermostats, smart home appliances, lighting, elect vehicle chargers and more.

Southern Company's employee benefits include an employee assistance program; a pension plan; life, prescription, medical and dental insurance; a savings plan; AD&D, accident, long-term disability and business travel insurance; adoption assistance; parenta

FINANCIAL DATA: *Note: Data for latest year may not have been available at press time.*

In U.S. $	2020	2019	2018	2017	2016	2015
Revenue	8,309,000,000	8,408,000,000	8,420,000,000	8,310,000,000	8,383,000,000	8,326,000,000
R&D Expense						
Operating Income						
Operating Margin %						
SGA Expense						
Net Income	1,575,000,000	1,720,000,000	793,000,000	1,414,000,000	1,330,000,000	1,260,000,000
Operating Cash Flow						
Capital Expenditure						
EBITDA						
Return on Assets %						
Return on Equity %						
Debt to Equity						

CONTACT INFORMATION:

Phone: 404 506-6526   Fax:
Toll-Free:
Address: 241 Ralph McGill Blvd., NE, Atlanta, GA 30308 United States

STOCK TICKER/OTHER:

Stock Ticker: Subsidiary   Exchange:
Employees: 6,700   Fiscal Year Ends: 12/31
Parent Company: Southern Company (The)

SALARIES/BONUSES:

Top Exec. Salary: $ Bonus: $
Second Exec. Salary: $ Bonus: $

OTHER THOUGHTS:

Estimated Female Officers or Directors: 2
Hot Spot for Advancement for Women/Minorities: Y

Georgia-Pacific LLC

www.gp.com

NAIC Code: 322121

TYPES OF BUSINESS:

Wood & Paper Products
Lumber
Building Products
Disposable Tableware
Paper & Wood Chemicals
Gypsum Products
Packaging Products
Cleaning Chemicals

BRANDS/DIVISIONS/AFFILIATES:

Koch Industries Inc
GP Pro

CONTACTS: Note: Officers with more than one job title may be intentionally listed here more than once.

Christian Fischer, CEO
Jeff Koeppel, Sr. VP-Operations
Tyler Woolson, CFO
Julie Brehm, Sr. VP-Human Resources
Kathleen A. Walters, Exec. VP-Consumer Prod. Group
Tye Darland, Sr. VP-Gen. Counsel
W. Wesley Jones, Exec. VP-Oper. Excellence & Compliance
David Park, Sr. VP-Strategy & Bus. Dev.
Sheila M. Weidman, Sr. VP-Comm., Gov't and Public Affairs
Mike E. Adam, Sr. VP-Sourcing
Curley M. Dossman, Jr., Pres., Georgia-Pacific Foundation
Christian Fischer, Exec. VP-Packaging
Mark Luetters, Exec. VP-Bldg. Prod.

GROWTH PLANS/SPECIAL FEATURES:

Georgia-Pacific, LLC (GP), a wholly-owned subsidiary of Koch Industries, Inc., is a leading producer of paper and wood products, with production facilities located worldwide. GP's business segments include consumer products, building/construction, chemicals, packaging, cellulose, nonwovens, and GP Pro. Consumer products include branded and private-label tissue/paper-based items such as paper towels, bath tissue, napkins and facial tissue, as well as disposable cups, plates and cutlery. Building/construction products include wood panels made from plywood and oriented strand board, as well as related gypsum products and lumber. The chemicals business manufactures wood adhesives, industrial thermosetting resins, fertilizers, formaldehyde, paper chemicals and tall oil-based chemicals used in applications such as adhesives and coatings, mining chemicals, oilfield and drilling, rubber processing, concrete, detergents, printing inks and surfactants. The packaging division makes folding carton stock, reusable plastic containers, graphic packaging, moisture-resistant packaging, linerboard, corrugated board and containerboard. The cellulose division operates four non-integrated wood pulp mills, one cotton linters pulp mill and one cotton converting plant in the U.S., producing paper pulp, specialty cellulose and customized fibers. Nonwovens are airlaid nonwoven substrates used in everyday products such as wet wipes, baby wipes, absorbent food pads, personal hygiene products, napkins, surgical drops, tray covers and more. GP Pro provides professional-grade paper, tissue and disposable containers and cutlery regarding food service and restroom needs, with sectors including healthcare, food service, manufacturing and office buildings. In May 2021, Georgia-Pacific sold its U.S. nonwovens business to Glatfelter Corporation for $175 million. That July, Georgia-Pacific sold four lumber mills to Interfor Corporation, which were located in Fayette, Alabama; Bay Springs, Mississippi; Philomath, Oregon; and Dequincy, Louisiana.

GP offers employees comprehensive benefits, a 401(k) plan and assistance programs.

FINANCIAL DATA: Note: Data for latest year may not have been available at press time.

In U.S. $	2020	2019	2018	2017	2016	2015
Revenue	13,440,000,000	14,000,000,000				
R&D Expense						
Operating Income						
Operating Margin %						
SGA Expense						
Net Income						
Operating Cash Flow						
Capital Expenditure						
EBITDA						
Return on Assets %						
Return on Equity %						
Debt to Equity						

CONTACT INFORMATION:

Phone: 404-652-4000   Fax: 404-749-2454
Toll-Free:
Address: 133 Peachtree St. NE, Atlanta, GA 30303 United States

STOCK TICKER/OTHER:

Stock Ticker: Subsidiary
Employees: 46,000
Parent Company: Koch Industries Inc

Exchange:
Fiscal Year Ends: 12/31

SALARIES/BONUSES:

Top Exec. Salary: $ Bonus: $
Second Exec. Salary: $ Bonus: $

OTHER THOUGHTS:

Estimated Female Officers or Directors: 3
Hot Spot for Advancement for Women/Minorities: Y

Giant Eagle Inc

www.gianteagle.com

NAIC Code: 445110

TYPES OF BUSINESS:

Grocery Stores
Video Rentals
Pharmacies
Gas Stations

BRANDS/DIVISIONS/AFFILIATES:

Giant Eagle
Market District
Market District Express
getGo
Giant Eagle Advantage Card
Nature's Basket

CONTACTS: Note: Officers with more than one job title may be intentionally listed here more than once.

Laura Shapira Karet, CEO
David S. Shapira, Pres.
Ian Prisuta, Sr. VP-Grocery Merch.
Mark Minnaugh, Chief Admin. Officer
Brett L. Merrell, Sr. VP-Supermarket Strategy & Dev.

GROWTH PLANS/SPECIAL FEATURES:

Giant Eagle, Inc. operates more than 410 corporate and independently owned grocery and convenient stores in the U.S. Giant Eagle branded grocery stores carry 20,000 to over 60,000 products, including more than 10,000 branded products. These stores' offerings are categorized into three broad groups: foods, including bakery, beer/wine/spirits, cheese shop, dairy, deli, frozen, grocery aisles, meat/poultry, prepared foods, produce and seafood; health and home, including baby care, contact lenses, floral, greeting cards, health and wellness products, household needs, personal care and beauty, pet care, pharmacy and equipment rental; and services, including banking, cafes, dietitians, dry cleaning, child care, photos, Port Authority ConnectCard, Western Union and a wireless center. Giant Eagle's Nature's Basket brand offers products without artificial ingredients or preservatives. The company's Market District and Market District Express stores carry primarily the same products as Giant Eagle stores, but include upscale amenities such as a kosher deli, international foods, a WiFi enabled cafe, cooking demonstrations and a focus on natural and organic foods. Market District Express is a smaller version of its signature shopping and dining concept. The firm's getGo retail concept is a convenience store/gas station chain. getGo stores offer fast foods, beverages and convenience items. Over 4.6 million customers are enrolled in the Giant Eagle Advantage Card program, which provides special offers, lifestyle information and tips and electronic offers and discounts online. The company is active in its communities, aiding local food banks, community events, the United Way and other nonprofit organizations. It also recycles over 141 million pounds of material annually.

Giant Eagle offers health, dental, vision, life, long/short-term disability insurance; 401(k) and pension plans; and employee assistance programs.

FINANCIAL DATA: Note: Data for latest year may not have been available at press time.

In U.S. $	2020	2019	2018	2017	2016	2015
Revenue	10,679,090,625	10,418,625,000	9,922,500,000	9,450,000,000	9,300,000,000	9,780,000,000
R&D Expense						
Operating Income						
Operating Margin %						
SGA Expense						
Net Income						
Operating Cash Flow						
Capital Expenditure						
EBITDA						
Return on Assets %						
Return on Equity %						
Debt to Equity						

CONTACT INFORMATION:

Phone: 412-963-6200   Fax: 412-968-1617
Toll-Free: 800-553-2324
Address: 101 Kappa Dr., Pittsburgh, PA 15238 United States

STOCK TICKER/OTHER:

Stock Ticker: Private
Employees: 32,000
Parent Company:

Exchange:
Fiscal Year Ends: 06/30

SALARIES/BONUSES:

Top Exec. Salary: $ Bonus: $
Second Exec. Salary: $ Bonus: $

OTHER THOUGHTS:

Estimated Female Officers or Directors: 2
Hot Spot for Advancement for Women/Minorities:

Gilbane Inc

www.gilbaneco.com

NAIC Code: 236220

TYPES OF BUSINESS:

Construction & Real Estate Services
Real Estate Development
Real Estate Construction
Construction Technology
Property Management

BRANDS/DIVISIONS/AFFILIATES:

Gilbane Building Company
Gilbane Development Company

GROWTH PLANS/SPECIAL FEATURES:

Gilbane, Inc., based in Providence, Rhode Island, is one of the largest privately-held, family-owned real estate development and construction firms in the industry. The firm has office locations worldwide, with several billion square feet of project completions. Gilbane offers a range of construction and facilities-related services, from sustainable building to construction technology for clients across a variety of markets. The company also provides property management services, and creates and implements real estate programs for public, private and non-profit clients primarily in the U.S. Other Gilbane companies include: Gilbane Building Company, a building firm that provides full construction and facilities-related services; and Gilbane Development Company, which is the real estate development, investment and property management arm of Gilbane, serving as a single resource for real estate development, construction, financing, operations and management.

CONTACTS: Note: Officers with more than one job title may be intentionally listed here more than once.

Thomas F. Gilbane, Jr., CEO

FINANCIAL DATA: Note: Data for latest year may not have been available at press time.

In U.S. $	2020	2019	2018	2017	2016	2015
Revenue	6,360,000,000	6,000,000,000	5,800,000,000	4,900,000,000	4,500,000,000	3,850,000,000
R&D Expense						
Operating Income						
Operating Margin %						
SGA Expense						
Net Income						
Operating Cash Flow						
Capital Expenditure						
EBITDA						
Return on Assets %						
Return on Equity %						
Debt to Equity						

CONTACT INFORMATION:

Phone: 401-456-5800   Fax:
Toll-Free: 800-445-2263
Address: 7 Jackson Walkway, Providence, RI 02903 United States

STOCK TICKER/OTHER:

Stock Ticker: Private   Exchange:
Employees: 2,600   Fiscal Year Ends:
Parent Company:

SALARIES/BONUSES:

Top Exec. Salary: $ Bonus: $
Second Exec. Salary: $ Bonus: $

OTHER THOUGHTS:

Estimated Female Officers or Directors:
Hot Spot for Advancement for Women/Minorities:

Gilead Sciences Inc

www.gilead.com

NAIC Code: 325412

TYPES OF BUSINESS:

Viral & Bacterial Infections Drugs
Biopharmaceuticals
Drug Development
Drug Commercialization

BRANDS/DIVISIONS/AFFILIATES:

MYR GmbH
Hepcludex

CONTACTS: *Note: Officers with more than one job title may be intentionally listed here more than once.*

Daniel O'Day, CEO
Robin Washington, CFO
Brett Pletcher, Chief Compliance Officer
John McHutchison, Chief Scientific Officer
Laura Hamill, Executive VP, Divisional
Gregg Alton, Other Executive Officer

GROWTH PLANS/SPECIAL FEATURES:

Gilead Sciences, Inc. is a biopharmaceutical company that discovers, develops and commercializes innovative medicines to prevent and treat life-threatening diseases. The firm's primary areas of focus include human immunodeficiency virus (HIV), acquired immunodeficiency syndrome (AIDS), COVID-19, liver diseases, hematology/oncology/cell therapy, and other. In HIV/AIDS, Gilead offers eight treatments, namely Biktarvy, Genvoya, Descovy, Odefsey, Truvada, Complera/Eviplera, Stribild and Atripla, all of which are oral formulations. In COVID-19, Gilead offers Veklury (remdesivir), an injection for intravenous use. In liver diseases, the firm offers five treatments, including Epclusa, Harvoni, Vosevi, Vemlidy and Viread, each of which are oral formulations. In hematology/oncology/cell therapy, Gilead offers four treatments, including Yescarta, Tecartus, Trodelvy and Zydelig, with the first three being intravenous and Zydelig being an oral formulation. Other medicines include: Letairis, an oral formulation for the treatment of pulmonary arterial hypertension (PAH); Ranexa, an oral formulation for the treatment of chronic angina; and AmBisome, a proprietary liposomal formulation for the treatment of serious invasive fungal infections. In early-2021, Gilead acquired MYR GmbH, which encompasses Hepcludex for the treatment of chronic hepatitis delta virus in adults with compensated liver disease; and Gilead announced that the U.S. Food and Drug Administration accelerated approval for Trodelvy for the treatment of metastatic urothelial cancer.

Gilead offers its employees comprehensive benefits.

FINANCIAL DATA: *Note: Data for latest year may not have been available at press time.*

In U.S. $	2020	2019	2018	2017	2016	2015
Revenue	24,689,000,000	22,449,000,000	22,127,000,000	26,107,000,000	30,390,000,000	32,639,000,000
R&D Expense	5,039,000,000	9,106,000,000	5,018,000,000	3,734,000,000	5,098,000,000	3,014,000,000
Operating Income	9,927,000,000	4,287,000,000	8,200,000,000	14,124,000,000	17,633,000,000	22,193,000,000
Operating Margin %		.19%	.37%	.54%	.58%	.68%
SGA Expense	5,151,000,000	4,381,000,000	4,056,000,000	3,878,000,000	3,398,000,000	3,426,000,000
Net Income	123,000,000	5,386,000,000	5,455,000,000	4,628,000,000	13,501,000,000	18,108,000,000
Operating Cash Flow	8,168,000,000	9,144,001,000	8,400,000,000	11,898,000,000	16,669,000,000	20,329,000,000
Capital Expenditure	650,000,000	825,000,000	924,000,000	590,000,000	748,000,000	747,000,000
EBITDA	4,133,000,000	7,559,000,000	10,305,000,000	15,933,000,000	19,219,000,000	23,445,000,000
Return on Assets %		.09%	.08%	.07%	.25%	.42%
Return on Equity %		.25%	.26%	.24%	.72%	1.07%
Debt to Equity		0.981	1.149	1.506	1.395	1.144

CONTACT INFORMATION:

Phone: 650 574-3000   Fax: 650 578-9264
Toll-Free: 800-445-3235
Address: 333 Lakeside Dr., Foster City, CA 94404 United States

STOCK TICKER/OTHER:

Stock Ticker: GILD   Exchange: NAS
Employees: 11,800   Fiscal Year Ends: 12/31
Parent Company:

SALARIES/BONUSES:

Top Exec. Salary: $ Bonus: $
Second Exec. Salary: $ Bonus: $

OTHER THOUGHTS:

Estimated Female Officers or Directors: 4
Hot Spot for Advancement for Women/Minorities: Y

GoDaddy Inc

www.godaddy.com

NAIC Code: 518210

TYPES OF BUSINESS:

Domain Name Registration
Domain Name Reselling
Research & Development, Internet Services

BRANDS/DIVISIONS/AFFILIATES:

Poynt

CONTACTS: *Note: Officers with more than one job title may be intentionally listed here more than once.*

Scott Wagner, CEO
Ray Winborne, CFO
Charles Robel, Chairman of the Board
Rebecca Morrow, Chief Accounting Officer
Arne Josefsberg, Chief Information Officer
Nima Kelly, Chief Legal Officer
Ah Kee Low, COO
James Carroll, Executive VP, Divisional

GROWTH PLANS/SPECIAL FEATURES:

GoDaddy, Inc. provides domain name registration and related services. The company has approximately 19 million customers made up of individuals and organizations. GoDaddy operates the world's largest domain marketplace where customers can find a domain name to match their concept, with nearly 80 million domains under management. The firm is a leading technology provider to small businesses, web design professionals and individuals, offering easy-to-use cloud-based products. GoDaddy provides website building, hosting and security tools to construct and protect each customer's online presence. Products are developed internally, and include shared website hosting, website hosting on virtual dedicated servers and dedicated services, managed hosting services, cloud services, cloud applications, website builder, ecommerce solutions, search engine visibility, email accounts, office solutions, email marketing solutions and payment solutions. GoDaddy provides localized solutions in over 50 markets, with approximately 32% of its total bookings attributable to customers outside the U.S. During 2020, GoDaddy completed its acquisition of Neustar Inc.'s registry business, which features a high-performance backend registry technology platform and enhanced domain security systems that enable people and brands to seamlessly connect and transact online with speed, security and reliability. In February 2021, GoDaddy acquired Poynt, expanding GoDaddy's ecommerce services to help small businesses grow, online and offline, through a single platform.

GoDaddy offers its employees 100% paid medical and dental premiums, employee appreciation outings, a 401(k) plan, life and disability insurance, maternity and paternity leave, adoption assistance, subsidized lunches and employee discounts.

FINANCIAL DATA: *Note: Data for latest year may not have been available at press time.*

In U.S. $	2020	2019	2018	2017	2016	2015
Revenue	3,316,700,000	2,988,100,000	2,660,100,000	2,231,900,000	1,847,900,000	1,607,300,000
R&D Expense	560,400,000	492,600,000	434,000,000	355,800,000	287,800,000	270,200,000
Operating Income	-358,900,000	211,300,000	164,500,000	190,100,000	37,600,000	-31,000,000
Operating Margin %		.07%	.06%	.03%	.03%	-.02%
SGA Expense	762,300,000	707,700,000	625,400,000	535,600,000	450,000,000	421,900,000
Net Income	-495,100,000	137,000,000	77,100,000	136,400,000	-16,500,000	-75,600,000
Operating Cash Flow	764,600,000	723,400,000	559,800,000	475,600,000	386,500,000	259,400,000
Capital Expenditure	81,500,000	92,300,000	97,000,000	135,200,000	62,800,000	79,300,000
EBITDA	-201,400,000	428,200,000	405,500,000	395,600,000	195,800,000	107,400,000
Return on Assets %		.02%	.01%	.03%	.00%	-.01%
Return on Equity %		.18%	.12%	.26%	-.03%	-.11%
Debt to Equity		3.329	3.02	4.955	1.841	2.442

CONTACT INFORMATION:

Phone: 480-505-8800 Fax: 480-505-8844
Toll-Free:
Address: 2155 E. GoDaddy Way, Tempe, AZ 85284 United States

SALARIES/BONUSES:

Top Exec. Salary: $ Bonus: $
Second Exec. Salary: $ Bonus: $

STOCK TICKER/OTHER:

Stock Ticker: GDDY   Exchange: NYS
Employees: 7,024   Fiscal Year Ends: 12/31
Parent Company:

OTHER THOUGHTS:

Estimated Female Officers or Directors: 3
Hot Spot for Advancement for Women/Minorities: Y

Golden State Foods Corporation

NAIC Code: 424400

www.goldenstatefoods.com

TYPES OF BUSINESS:

Food Products Distribution
Restaurant Supplier
Liquid Products
Dairy
Beverages
Protein
Logistics

BRANDS/DIVISIONS/AFFILIATES:

Quality Custom Distribution Services
KanPak LLC

CONTACTS: *Note: Officers with more than one job title may be intentionally listed here more than once.*

Mark Wetterau, CEO
Brian Dick, Pres.
Joe Heffington, CFO
Shellie Frey, VP-Global Branding & Communications
Ed Rodriguez, Chief Human Resources Officer
Carol Fawcett, CIO
Guilda Javaheri, CTO

GROWTH PLANS/SPECIAL FEATURES:

Golden State Foods Corporation (GSF) is a diversified supplier serving the quick service restaurants and retail industries. The firm's business segments include logistics, liquid products, dairy and beverages, protein products and produce. The logistics segment consists of logistic operations, which include distribution, warehouse and freight management services. Subsidiary Quality Custom Distribution Services (QCD) provides distribution services to thousands of U.S. restaurants, and operates distribution centers located throughout the U.S. The liquid products segment consists of operations of seven international production facilities, which produce approximately 30 million cases of liquid products annually. The sauces, dressings and condiments unit offers products, such as ketchup, mayonnaise, salad dressings, dipping sauces, tartar sauce and a variety of sandwich sauces. GSF has a joint venture partnership, KanPak, LLC, which makes dairy-based products including soft-service ice cream, smoothies, coffee creamers, specialty beverages and extended shelf-life products. The syrups and toppings unit makes a variety of jams, jellies, coffee syrups, pancake syrups and shake syrups. The dairy and beverages segment consists of: dairy and aseptic processing and packaging; and the production of specialty beverages, such as smoothies, iced coffee, coffee creamers and tea, as well as yogurt, desserts, breakfast drinks and protein shakes. The protein products segment consists of operations of meat plant that makes 400,000 hamburger patties each hour. Ground beef is blended to specified leanness, formed to specific patty dimensions, individually quick-frozen, inspected and packaged. The produce segment sources best raw material from certified growers and uses state-of-the-art rapid chilling techniques, offering fresh produce to food service and retail industries. In November 2020, GSF opened a new facility in Wuhan, capable of processing 2.2 million pounds of produce annually. This location will supply GSF customer restaurants in central and northwest China.

GSF offers employees health benefits, life and disability insurance,401(k) and other employee assistance programs.

FINANCIAL DATA: *Note: Data for latest year may not have been available at press time.*

In U.S. $	2020	2019	2018	2017	2016	2015
Revenue	5,000,000,000	8,379,000,000	7,980,000,000	7,600,000,000	7,500,000,000	7,300,000,000
R&D Expense						
Operating Income						
Operating Margin %						
SGA Expense						
Net Income						
Operating Cash Flow						
Capital Expenditure						
EBITDA						
Return on Assets %						
Return on Equity %						
Debt to Equity						

CONTACT INFORMATION:

Phone: 949-247-8000   Fax:
Toll-Free:
Address: 18301 Von Karman Ave., Ste. 1100, Irvine, CA 92612 United States

STOCK TICKER/OTHER:

Stock Ticker: Private
Employees: 6,000
Parent Company:

Exchange:
Fiscal Year Ends: 12/31

SALARIES/BONUSES:

Top Exec. Salary: $ Bonus: $
Second Exec. Salary: $ Bonus: $

OTHER THOUGHTS:

Estimated Female Officers or Directors:
Hot Spot for Advancement for Women/Minorities:

Goldman Sachs Group Inc (The)

www.goldmansachs.com

NAIC Code: 523110

TYPES OF BUSINESS:

Investment Banking
Investment Banking
Global Markets
Asset Management
Wealth Management
Credit Cards
Online Banking

BRANDS/DIVISIONS/AFFILIATES:

CONTACTS: Note: Officers with more than one job title may be intentionally listed here more than once.

David Solomon, CEO
Stephen Scherr, CFO
Brian Lee, Controller
John Waldron, COO
Karen Seymour, Executive VP
Dane Holmes, Executive VP
Sarah Smith, Executive VP
John Rogers, Executive VP

GROWTH PLANS/SPECIAL FEATURES:

The Goldman Sachs Group, Inc. is a financial holding company regulated by the Board of Governors of the Federal Reserve System, operating in over 30 countries. The firm has four main business segments: investment banking, global markets, asset management, and consumer and wealth management. The investment banking segment provides a broad range of services to corporations, financial institutions, investment funds and governments. Services include strategic advisory assignments with respect to mergers and acquisitions, divestitures, corporate defense activities, restructurings, spin-offs, and equity and debt underwriting of public offerings and private placements. This division also provides lending to corporate clients, including relationship lending, middle-market lending and acquisition financing. The global markets segment facilitates client transactions and makes markets in fixed income, equity, currency and commodity products with institutional clients, such as corporations, financial institutions, investment funds and governments. This division also makes markets in and clears institutional client transactions on major stock, options and futures exchanges worldwide and provides prime brokerage and other equities financing activities, including securities lending, margin lending and swaps. The asset management segment manages assets and offers investment products across al major asset classes to a diverse set of institutional clients and a network of third-party distributors worldwide. This division makes equity investments such as alternative investing activities related to public and private equity investments in corporate, real estate and infrastructure assets, as well as investments through consolidated investment entities, most of which are engaged in real estate investment activities. Last, the consumer and wealth management segment provides investing and wealth advisory solutions, including financial planning and counseling, executing brokerage transactions and managing assets for individuals in its wealth management busines. This division also provides loans and accepts deposits through its consumer banking digital platform and through its private bank; and issues credit cards to consumers.

FINANCIAL DATA: Note: Data for latest year may not have been available at press time.

In U.S. $	2020	2019	2018	2017	2016	2015
Revenue	47,980,000,000	34,534,000,000	34,260,000,000	29,721,000,000	28,452,000,000	35,254,000,000
R&D Expense						
Operating Income						
Operating Margin %						
SGA Expense	13,710,000,000	13,092,000,000	13,068,000,000	12,441,000,000	12,104,000,000	13,235,000,000
Net Income	9,459,000,000	8,466,000,000	10,459,000,000	4,286,000,000	7,398,000,000	6,083,000,000
Operating Cash Flow	-13,728,000,000	23,868,000,000	20,421,000,000	-17,742,000,000	5,570,000,000	6,961,000,000
Capital Expenditure	6,309,000,000	8,443,000,000	7,982,000,000	3,185,000,000	2,876,000,000	1,833,000,000
EBITDA						
Return on Assets %		.01%	.01%	.00%	.01%	.01%
Return on Equity %		.10%	.13%	.05%	.09%	.07%
Debt to Equity		2.801	2.988	3.233	2.617	2.469

CONTACT INFORMATION:

Phone: 212 902-1000   Fax: 212 902-3000
Toll-Free:
Address: 200 West St., New York, NY 10282 United States

STOCK TICKER/OTHER:

Stock Ticker: GS
Employees: 34,400
Parent Company:

Exchange: NYS
Fiscal Year Ends: 12/31

SALARIES/BONUSES:

Top Exec. Salary: $ Bonus: $
Second Exec. Salary: $ Bonus: $

OTHER THOUGHTS:

Estimated Female Officers or Directors: 5
Hot Spot for Advancement for Women/Minorities: Y

Sales, profits and employees may be estimates. Financial information, benefits and other data can change quickly and may vary from those stated here.

Golub Corporation

NAIC Code: 445110

www.pricechopper.com

TYPES OF BUSINESS:

Supermarkets
Online Sales & Delivery
Pharmacies

BRANDS/DIVISIONS/AFFILIATES:

Price Chopper
Market 32
Market Bistro
Full Circle Market
Chef's Menu
PICS
www.pricechopper.com

CONTACTS: Note: Officers with more than one job title may be intentionally listed here more than once.

Scott Grimmett, CEO
John J. Endres, CFO
Mona Golub, VP-Mktg.
Karlin Bohnert, CIO
Tony Farah, CTO
John J. Endres, Sr. VP-Finance
Neil M. Golub, Chmn.

GROWTH PLANS/SPECIAL FEATURES:

Golub Corporation, run by the Golub family since 1943, operates supermarket stores under the Price Chopper, Market 32 and Market Bistro brand names. These retail stores are in the U.S. throughout New York, Vermont, Massachusetts, Connecticut and New Hampshire. Golub supports farmers and producers in the Northeast, and partners with local farm families to bring seasonal fruits and vegetables to store customers. Home grown products also include maple syrup, craft beer, hone, pasta sauce and more. Prepared or take-home food items include pizza, soups, chicken, salads, gourmet macaroni and cheese, sushi, stuffing, mashed potatoes, fresh steamed vegetables and more. The company's brands include: Full Circle Market, featuring more than 250 items that are primarily organic and range from grocery to dairy to produce; Chef's Menu, featuring pre-packaged meals that can be ready in less than 15 minutes at home, and include fares such as chicken, fish, shrimp or beef paired with vegetables, sides and sauces; and PICS, featuring quality yet moderately-priced products. Catering is provided, with offerings grouped by departments, including bakery, deli, produce and seafood; and categories such as bagels, cakes, pastries, deli platters, fine cheeses, fresh fruits, side dishes and sandwiches. Market Bistro markets offer cooking classes, as well as private event bookings that feature a cooking classes or cooking demonstrations by a culinary team. In addition, some of the company's supermarkets have in-house pharmacies. Coupons, flyers, list-making and online shopping capabilities can be obtained from the company's www.pricechopper.com website. Golub's private stock is more than 45% employee owned.

The firm offers employees health and life insurance, retirement benfits and a variety of employee assistance programs.

FINANCIAL DATA: Note: Data for latest year may not have been available at press time.

In U.S. $	2020	2019	2018	2017	2016	2015
Revenue	3,982,125,000	3,885,000,000	3,700,000,000	3,412,000,000	3,400,000,000	3,500,000,000
R&D Expense						
Operating Income						
Operating Margin %						
SGA Expense						
Net Income						
Operating Cash Flow						
Capital Expenditure						
EBITDA						
Return on Assets %						
Return on Equity %						
Debt to Equity						

CONTACT INFORMATION:

Phone: 518-355-5000   Fax: 518-379-3536
Toll-Free: 800-666-7667
Address: 461 Nott St., Schenectady, NY 12308 United States

STOCK TICKER/OTHER:

Stock Ticker: Private
Employees: 18,000
Parent Company:

Exchange:
Fiscal Year Ends: 04/30

SALARIES/BONUSES:

Top Exec. Salary: $ Bonus: $
Second Exec. Salary: $ Bonus: $

OTHER THOUGHTS:

Estimated Female Officers or Directors:
Hot Spot for Advancement for Women/Minorities: Y

Goody Goody Liquor Inc

www.goodygoody.com

NAIC Code: 445310

TYPES OF BUSINESS:

Beer, Wine and Liquor Stores

GROWTH PLANS/SPECIAL FEATURES:

Goody Goody Liquor, Inc. owns and operates approximately 20 wine, beer and spirit retail stores in Texas, primarily in Dallas/Fort Worth, Longview and Houston. From fine wines to 20-year-old single malts to recent local lagers, Goody Goody stores are considered a one-stop shop for selections and service. Typical stores are stocked with more than 8,000 wines from around the world; 1,600 domestic, foreign and craft beers; and 5,900 spirits. Any item that may not be stocked (that is distributed in Texas) can be obtained via special orders at no additional charge. The company's Bottle Club is a rewards program that allows registered members to collect points as they shop, which can be redeemed for direct savings. In addition, members have access to their purchase history and can be informed of special events and sales that may be of interest.

BRANDS/DIVISIONS/AFFILIATES:

Bottle Club

CONTACTS: Note: Officers with more than one job title may be intentionally listed here more than once.

Joe Jansen, Pres.

FINANCIAL DATA: Note: Data for latest year may not have been available at press time.

In U.S. $	2020	2019	2018	2017	2016	2015
Revenue	296,076,375	288,855,000	275,100,000	262,000,000	255,000,000	251,000,000
R&D Expense						
Operating Income						
Operating Margin %						
SGA Expense						
Net Income						
Operating Cash Flow						
Capital Expenditure						
EBITDA						
Return on Assets %						
Return on Equity %						
Debt to Equity						

CONTACT INFORMATION:

Phone: Fax:
Toll-Free: 214-350-1525
Address: 10370 Olympic Dr, Dallas, TX 75220 United States

STOCK TICKER/OTHER:

Stock Ticker: Private Exchange:
Employees: 40,400 Fiscal Year Ends:
Parent Company:

SALARIES/BONUSES:

Top Exec. Salary: $ Bonus: $
Second Exec. Salary: $ Bonus: $

OTHER THOUGHTS:

Estimated Female Officers or Directors:
Hot Spot for Advancement for Women/Minorities:

Grant Thornton LLP

www.grantthornton.com

NAIC Code: 541211

TYPES OF BUSINESS:

Accounting & Auditing Services
Advisory Services
Business Consulting
Forensic Services
Risk
Compliance
Restructuring
Transaction Advisory

BRANDS/DIVISIONS/AFFILIATES:

Grant Thornton International Ltd

CONTACTS: Note: Officers with more than one job title may be intentionally listed here more than once.

Bradley J. Preber, CEO
J. Michael McGuire, Nat'l Managing Partner-Oper.
Trent Gazzaway, Managing Partner-Audit Svcs.
Doreen Griffith, Managing Partner-Tax Svcs.
Steve Lukens, Managing Partner-Advisory Svcs.

GROWTH PLANS/SPECIAL FEATURES:

Grant Thornton, LLP is the U.S. member firm of Grant Thornton International Ltd., and provides advisory, audit and tax services to both public and private corporations. The company's advisory services include business consulting; forensic, investigative and dispute services; governance, risk and compliance; restructuring and turnaround; technology solutions; transaction advisory; and valuation. Its audit solutions include employee benefit plan audit, financial statement audit, fresh start accounting, international financial reporting standards reporting and resources and public finance. Tax services include tax, human capital, international tax, private wealth, SALT alerts, state and local tax, strategic federal tax, tax reporting, advisory, tax hot topics, tax innovation and more. Industries served by the firm include construction, distribution, energy, financial services, food and beverage, healthcare, life sciences, hospitality, restaurants, manufacturing, not-for-profit organizations, private equity, public policy, public sector, real estate, retail, technology and transportation. Grant Thornton, LLP has more than 50 offices across the U.S.

Grant Thornton's employee benefits include medical and dental plans, reimbursement accounts and a 401(k) plan.

FINANCIAL DATA: Note: Data for latest year may not have been available at press time.

In U.S. $	2020	2019	2018	2017	2016	2015
Revenue	1,920,000,000	1,900,000,000	1,790,000,000	1,740,000,000	1,650,000,000	1,450,000,000
R&D Expense						
Operating Income						
Operating Margin %						
SGA Expense						
Net Income						
Operating Cash Flow						
Capital Expenditure						
EBITDA						
Return on Assets %						
Return on Equity %						
Debt to Equity						

CONTACT INFORMATION:

Phone: 312-856-0200   Fax: 312-602-8099
Toll-Free:
Address: 171 N. Clark St., Ste. 200, Chicago, IL 60601 United States

STOCK TICKER/OTHER:

Stock Ticker: Private   Exchange:
Employees: 8,122   Fiscal Year Ends: 07/31
Parent Company: Grant Thornton International Ltd

SALARIES/BONUSES:

Top Exec. Salary: $ Bonus: $
Second Exec. Salary: $ Bonus: $

OTHER THOUGHTS:

Estimated Female Officers or Directors: 2
Hot Spot for Advancement for Women/Minorities:

Greenbrier Companies Inc (The)

www.gbrx.com

NAIC Code: 336510

TYPES OF BUSINESS:

Railcar Manufacturing
Railcar Maintenance
Marine Barge Manufacturing
Railcar Leasing
Railcar Management

BRANDS/DIVISIONS/AFFILIATES:

CONTACTS: *Note: Officers with more than one job title may be intentionally listed here more than once.*

William Furman, CEO
Adrian Downes, CFO
Anne Manning, Controller
Lorie Tekorius, COO
Brian Comstock, Executive VP, Divisional
Mark Rittenbaum, Executive VP
Alejandro Centurion, Executive VP
Martin Baker, General Counsel

GROWTH PLANS/SPECIAL FEATURES:

The Greenbrier Companies, Inc. (TGC) designs, manufactures and markets railroad freight car equipment in North America, Europe and South America. TGC also manufactures and markets marine barges in North America. The firm operates in three segments: manufacturing; wheels, repair and parts; and leasing and services. The manufacturing segment is further divided into: North American railcar manufacturing, which produces an array of railcar types (other than coal) such as intermodal, tank, automotive and conventional; European railcar manufacturing, producing a variety of tank, automotive and conventional freight railcar (wagon) types, as well as flat cars, coil cars, gondolas, sliding wall cars and automobile transporter cars; and marine vessel fabrication, with its manufacturing facility located on a deep water port in Portland, Oregon. The wheels, repair and parts segment includes: a large wheel services network that provides services such as the reconditioning of wheels and axles in addition to new axle machining and finishing and axle downsizing; a railcar repair, refurbishment and maintenance network that includes repair shops; and component parts manufacturing, with facilities that manufacture railcar cushioning units, couplers, yokes, side frames, bolsters and various other parts, as well as roofs, doors and associated parts for boxcars. Last, the leasing and services segment owns a lease fleet of approximately 8,300 railcars and provides management services as well as an array of software and services that include railcar maintenance management, railcar accounting services, total fleet management, railcar administration services and railcar re-marketing services. This division provides management services for a fleet of approximately 390,000 railcars for railroads, shippers, carriers, institutional investors and other leasing and transportation companies. In February 2021, TGC announced plans to form GBX Leasing, a leasing joint venture with The Longwood Group to develop an owned portfolio of leased railcars primarily to be built by Greenbrier.

FINANCIAL DATA: *Note: Data for latest year may not have been available at press time.*

In U.S. $	2020	2019	2018	2017	2016	2015
Revenue	2,792,189,000	3,033,591,000	2,519,464,000	2,169,164,000	2,679,524,000	2,605,278,000
R&D Expense						
Operating Income	148,425,000	153,178,000	208,616,000	250,692,000	392,756,000	385,562,000
Operating Margin %		.05%	.08%	.12%	.15%	.15%
SGA Expense	204,706,000	213,308,000	200,439,000	170,607,000	158,681,000	151,791,000
Net Income	48,967,000	71,076,000	151,781,000	116,067,000	183,213,000	192,832,000
Operating Cash Flow	272,261,000	-21,241,000	103,341,000	280,389,000	331,670,000	192,333,000
Capital Expenditure	66,879,000	198,233,000	176,848,000	86,065,000	139,013,000	105,989,000
EBITDA	277,046,000	269,195,000	328,919,000	324,888,000	475,663,000	439,844,000
Return on Assets %		.03%	.06%	.05%	.10%	.12%
Return on Equity %		.06%	.13%	.12%	.23%	.31%
Debt to Equity		0.666	0.371	0.553	0.348	0.515

CONTACT INFORMATION:

Phone: 503 684-7000   Fax: 503 684-7553
Toll-Free:
Address: 1 Centerpointe Dr., Ste. 200, Lake Oswego, OR 97035 United States

STOCK TICKER/OTHER:

Stock Ticker: GBX
Employees: 10,600
Parent Company:

Exchange: NYS
Fiscal Year Ends: 08/31

SALARIES/BONUSES:

Top Exec. Salary: $ Bonus: $
Second Exec. Salary: $ Bonus: $

OTHER THOUGHTS:

Estimated Female Officers or Directors: 5
Hot Spot for Advancement for Women/Minorities: Y

Griffon Corporation

NAIC Code: 332321

TYPES OF BUSINESS:

Garage Doors, Metal, Manufacturing
Garage Door Manufacturing
Installation Services
Plastic Films & Film Laminates
Electronic Information & Communication Systems
Radar Equipment
Integrated Circuits

BRANDS/DIVISIONS/AFFILIATES:

AMES Companies Inc (The)
Clopay Corporation
Telephonics Corporation
True Temper
Ideal
Holmes
CornellCookson

CONTACTS: Note: Officers with more than one job title may be intentionally listed here more than once.

Ronald Kramer, CEO
Brian Harris, CFO
W. Christopher Durborow, Chief Accounting Officer
Robert Mehmel, COO
Seth Kaplan, General Counsel

GROWTH PLANS/SPECIAL FEATURES:

Griffon Corporation is a diversified management and holding company. The firm operates in three segments: consumer and professional products, home and building products, and defense electronics. The consumer and professional products segment conducts its operations through The AMES Companies, Inc., a leading North American manufacturer and provider of branded consumer and professional tools and products for home storage and organization, landscaping and other outdoor purposes. This division's brands include True Temper, AMES and ClosetMaid. The home and building products segment operates through Clopay Corporation, a manufacturer and marketer of garage doors and rolling steel doors in North America. Products are sold through professional dealers and home center retail chains under the brands Clopay, Ideal and Holmes. Rolling steel door and grill products for commercial, industrial, institutional and retail use are sold under the CornellCookson brand. Last, the defense electronics segment operates through Telephonics Corporation, a provider of highly sophisticated intelligence, surveillance and communications solutions for defense, aerospace and commercial customers. In early-2021, Griffon sold System Engineering Group, Inc. to QuantiTech LLC.

FINANCIAL DATA: Note: Data for latest year may not have been available at press time.

In U.S. $	2020	2019	2018	2017	2016	2015
Revenue	2,407,522,000	2,209,289,000	1,977,918,000	1,524,997,000	1,957,161,000	2,016,032,000
R&D Expense						
Operating Income	155,028,000	135,265,000	96,450,000	69,027,000	109,407,000	101,017,000
Operating Margin %		.06%	.05%	.05%	.06%	.05%
SGA Expense	486,398,000	460,004,000	433,110,000	339,089,000	364,027,000	374,761,000
Net Income	53,429,000	37,287,000	125,678,000	14,912,000	30,010,000	34,289,000
Operating Cash Flow	134,008,000	111,835,000	20,822,000	96,344,000	104,383,000	75,219,000
Capital Expenditure	48,998,000	45,361,000	50,138,000	34,937,000	90,759,000	73,620,000
EBITDA	211,710,000	202,092,000	155,181,000	116,089,000	174,626,000	171,609,000
Return on Assets %		.02%	.06%	.01%	.02%	.02%
Return on Equity %		.08%	.29%	.04%	.07%	.07%
Debt to Equity		2.289	2.336	2.427	2.224	1.921

CONTACT INFORMATION:

Phone: 212 957-5000   Fax: 516 938-5644
Toll-Free:
Address: 712 5th Ave., Fl. 18, New York, NY 10019 United States

STOCK TICKER/OTHER:

Stock Ticker: GFF
Employees: 7,400
Parent Company:

Exchange: NYS
Fiscal Year Ends: 09/30

SALARIES/BONUSES:

Top Exec. Salary: $ Bonus: $
Second Exec. Salary: $ Bonus: $

OTHER THOUGHTS:

Estimated Female Officers or Directors:
Hot Spot for Advancement for Women/Minorities:

Group 1 Automotive Inc

www.group1auto.com

NAIC Code: 441110

TYPES OF BUSINESS:

Auto Dealers
Auto Repair Services
Insurance Services
Automotive Replacement Parts
Financing Services
Collision Service Centers

BRANDS/DIVISIONS/AFFILIATES:

CONTACTS:
Note: Officers with more than one job title may be intentionally listed here more than once.

Earl Hesterberg, CEO
John Rickel, CFO
Stephen Quinn, Chairman of the Board
Lincoln Pereira, Director
Daryl Kenningham, President, Divisional
Peter DeLongchamps, Senior VP, Divisional
Frank Grese, Senior VP, Divisional

GROWTH PLANS/SPECIAL FEATURES:

Group 1 Automotive, Inc. is a leading operator in the automotive retail industries, with locations throughout the U.S., the U.K. and Brazil. The company, through its subsidiaries, sells new and used cars and light trucks, provides maintenance and repair services, sells replacement parts and arranges vehicle financing and insurance through its dealerships and franchises. In total, Group 1 owns and operates 188 dealerships, 242 franchises and 48 collision centers (as of September 2021). The dealerships offer approximately 30 brands of automobiles, which may include Toyota, BMW, Ford, Audi, Mercedes-Benz, Honda, Nissan, Lexus, Chevrolet, MINI, Volkswagen, GMC, Hyundai, Jeep, Acura, RAM, Land Rover, Kia, Cadillac, Dodge, Subaru, Jaguar, Buick, Sprinter, Chrysler, SEAT, Lincoln, Mazda, Skoda, Vauxhall, Volvo and Smart. Group 1's dealerships have taken several steps toward building customer confidence in their used vehicle inventory, including participation in manufacturer certification processes. These processes make used vehicles eligible for new vehicle benefits such as new vehicle finance rates and extended manufacturer warranties. In September 2021, Group 1 agreed to acquire Prime Automotive Group, headquartered in Westwood, Massachusetts. Prime has 30 dealership locations and three collision centers in the mid-Atlantic and New England markets.

FINANCIAL DATA:
Note: Data for latest year may not have been available at press time.

In U.S. $	2020	2019	2018	2017	2016	2015
Revenue	10,851,800,000	12,043,800,000	11,601,360,000	11,123,720,000	10,887,610,000	10,632,510,000
R&D Expense						
Operating Income	523,900,000	386,000,000	384,966,000	361,378,000	373,072,000	365,900,000
Operating Margin %		.03%	.03%	.03%	.03%	.03%
SGA Expense	1,169,300,000	1,358,400,000	1,273,057,000	1,226,195,000	1,170,763,000	1,120,833,000
Net Income	286,500,000	174,000,000	157,772,000	213,442,000	147,065,000	93,999,000
Operating Cash Flow	805,400,000	370,900,000	269,978,000	198,925,000	384,857,000	141,047,000
Capital Expenditure	103,200,000	191,800,000	141,033,000	215,832,000	156,521,000	120,252,000
EBITDA	548,200,000	435,400,000	408,153,000	399,808,000	391,468,000	325,577,000
Return on Assets %		.03%	.03%	.04%	.03%	.02%
Return on Equity %		.14%	.14%	.20%	.15%	.10%
Debt to Equity		1.308	1.17	1.172	1.304	1.311

CONTACT INFORMATION:

Phone: 713 647-5700   Fax: 713 647-5858
Toll-Free:
Address: 800 Gessner, Ste. 500, Houston, TX 77024 United States

STOCK TICKER/OTHER:

Stock Ticker: GPI
Employees: 13,500
Parent Company:

Exchange: NYS
Fiscal Year Ends: 12/31

SALARIES/BONUSES:

Top Exec. Salary: $ Bonus: $
Second Exec. Salary: $ Bonus: $

OTHER THOUGHTS:

Estimated Female Officers or Directors:
Hot Spot for Advancement for Women/Minorities: Y

GrubHub Inc

NAIC Code: 492210

www.grubhub.com

TYPES OF BUSINESS:
Online Restaurant Pick-Up and Delivery
Online Food Order
Food Delivery

BRANDS/DIVISIONS/AFFILIATES:
GrubHub
Seamless
MenuPages
Allmenus
LevelUp
Tapingo

CONTACTS:
Note: Officers with more than one job title may be intentionally listed here more than once.
Matthew Maloney, CEO
Adam DeWitt, CFO
Brian Mcandrews, Chairman of the Board
Maria Belousova, Chief Technology Officer
Brandt Kucharski, Controller
Margo Drucker, General Counsel
Samuel Hall, Other Executive Officer

GROWTH PLANS/SPECIAL FEATURES:
GrubHub, Inc. is an online and mobile food ordering company that connects diners with local takeout restaurants. Its online and mobile ordering platforms allow diners to order directly from more than 300,000 takeout restaurants in thousands of cities across the U.S. cities. Every order is supported by the company's 24/7 customer service teams. GrubHub's portfolio of brands include GrubHub, Seamless, MenuPages, AllMenus, LevelUp and Tapingo. GrubHub helps consumers find and order food from wherever they are via GrubHub.com. Customers type in an address and obtain the restaurants that deliver to that locale as well as a list of local pickup restaurants. Seamless allows consumers and businesses to order food for delivery or takeout at Seamless.com or by using the Seamless smartphone app. Once the order is placed, Seamless sends the order to the restaurant, a confirmation email with delivery or pickup time is sent, and either the restaurant delivers it or the consumer picks it up. More than fifty percent of GrubHub and Seamless orders are placed through mobile devices. MenuPages is a New York-based online restaurant menu guide site found at www.menupages.com, and includes international, organic and vegan menus. Allmenus.com provides menus for restaurants in select U.S. states, and includes a map as well as restaurants in nearby cities. LevelUp is a mobile application designed for mobile diner engagement and payment solutions. Tapingo is a leading platform for ordering food to college and university campuses nationwide, integrating mobile ordering into campus meal plans and point-of-sale systems. In June 2020, in a deal that will create one of the world's largest meal-delivery companies, Grubhub Inc. agreed to be acquired by Just Eat Takeaway.com N.V., an Amsterdam-based food delivery service, for $7.3 billion. The transaction is expected to close by mid-2021.

FINANCIAL DATA:
Note: Data for latest year may not have been available at press time.

In U.S. $	2020	2019	2018	2017	2016	2015
Revenue	1,819,981,952	1,312,151,040	1,007,257,024	683,067,008	493,331,008	361,824,992
R&D Expense						
Operating Income						
Operating Margin %						
SGA Expense						
Net Income	-155,860,992	-18,566,000	78,481,000	98,983,000	49,557,000	38,077,000
Operating Cash Flow						
Capital Expenditure						
EBITDA						
Return on Assets %						
Return on Equity %						
Debt to Equity						

CONTACT INFORMATION:
Phone: 877-585-7878   Fax:
Toll-Free:
Address: 111 W. Washington St., Ste. 2100, Chicago, IL 60602 United States

STOCK TICKER/OTHER:
Stock Ticker: GRUB
Employees: 2,841
Parent Company:

Exchange: NYS
Fiscal Year Ends:

SALARIES/BONUSES:
Top Exec. Salary: $ Bonus: $
Second Exec. Salary: $ Bonus: $

OTHER THOUGHTS:
Estimated Female Officers or Directors:
Hot Spot for Advancement for Women/Minorities:

Gulfstream Aerospace Corporation

www.gulfstream.com

NAIC Code: 336411

TYPES OF BUSINESS:

Aircraft Manufacturing
Business Jets
Support Services
Leasing & Financing

BRANDS/DIVISIONS/AFFILIATES:

General Dynamics Corporation
G280
G500
G550
G650ER
G700

CONTACTS: Note: Officers with more than one job title may be intentionally listed here more than once.

Mark Burns, Pres.
Josh Thompson, CFO
Dan Nale, Sr. VP-Programs, Eng. & Test
Ira Berman, Sr. VP-Admin.
Ira Berman, General Counsel
Dennis Stuligross, Sr. VP-Oper.
Joe Lombardo, Exec. VP-Aerospace Group, General Dynamics
Mark Burns, Pres., Product Support
Scott Neal, Sr. VP-Worldwide Sales & Mktg.
Buddy Sams, Sr. VP-Gov't Programs & Sales
Phebe N. Novakovic, Chmn.

GROWTH PLANS/SPECIAL FEATURES:

Gulfstream Aerospace Corporation, a subsidiary of General Dynamics Corporation, designs, develops, manufactures, markets and provides maintenance and support services for technologically advanced business jet aircraft. Established in 1958, Gulfstream operates facilities on four continents. The company is also a leading provider of land and expeditionary combat systems, armaments and munitions; shipbuilding and marine systems; and information systems and technologies. Gulfstream's current aircraft includes six product lines: the mid-size G280; the ultra-long-range G500, G550 and G600; the extended reach G650ER, extending the nonstop reach to 7,500 nautical miles at Mach 0.85; and the spacious G700, offering five living areas and a nonstop reach to 7,500nm at Mach 0.925. Gulfstream also routinely accepts aircraft trade-ins for the sale of new Gulfstream models and resells the used planes on the pre-owned market. The group offers several product enhancements for its planes, including the ultra-high-speed broadband multi-link (BBML) system, which allows customers to access the internet; and the enhanced vision system (EVS), a forward-looking infrared (FLIR) camera that projects an infrared real-world image on the pilot's heads-up display, which allows the flight crew to see in conditions of low light and reduced visibility.

FINANCIAL DATA: Note: Data for latest year may not have been available at press time.

In U.S. $	2020	2019	2018	2017	2016	2015
Revenue	9,313,258,500	9,426,375,000	8,977,500,000	8,550,000,000	8,500,000,000	8,851,000,000
R&D Expense						
Operating Income						
Operating Margin %						
SGA Expense						
Net Income		1,764,000,000	1,680,000,000	1,600,000,000	1,500,000,000	1,706,000,000
Operating Cash Flow						
Capital Expenditure						
EBITDA						
Return on Assets %						
Return on Equity %						
Debt to Equity						

CONTACT INFORMATION:

Phone: 912-965-3000   Fax: 912-965-3084
Toll-Free:
Address: 500 Gulfstream Rd., Savannah, GA 31407 United States

STOCK TICKER/OTHER:

Stock Ticker: Subsidiary
Employees: 15,000
Parent Company: General Dynamics Corporation

Exchange:
Fiscal Year Ends: 12/31

SALARIES/BONUSES:

Top Exec. Salary: $ Bonus: $
Second Exec. Salary: $ Bonus: $

OTHER THOUGHTS:

Estimated Female Officers or Directors:
Hot Spot for Advancement for Women/Minorities:

Harris Teeter Supermarkets Inc

www.harristeeter.com

NAIC Code: 445110

TYPES OF BUSINESS:

Grocery Stores
Dairy Product Manufacturing
Pharmacies
Fuel Centers

BRANDS/DIVISIONS/AFFILIATES:

Kroger Company (TheO
Harris Teeter Inc

CONTACTS: *Note: Officers with more than one job title may be intentionally listed here more than once.*

Rod Antolock, Pres.
Douglas J. Yacenda, Sec.
Ronald H. Volger, Treas.
Rodney C. Antolock, Exec. VP
Jesse B. Libensperger, Assistant Treas.

GROWTH PLANS/SPECIAL FEATURES:

Harris Teeter Supermarkets, Inc. is a holding company that, through its wholly-owned subsidiary Harris Teeter, Inc. (Harris Teeter), operates a regional chain of approximately 260 supermarkets throughout seven southeastern states and Washington, D.C. Harris Teeter stores carry a full assortment of groceries, produce, meat, seafood, delicatessen items, bakery items, wines and non-food products such as health, beauty care and floral items. Retail supermarket operations are supported by two company-owned distribution centers and one company-owned dairy production facility. Aside from the ice cream and dairy products, which are produced by the company, all other items, including the store's own branded product lines, are purchased either directly from manufacturers or from outside suppliers. Most Harris Teeter stores offer online pickup service and some markets also offer a home delivery option. In addition, the company operates more than 50 fuel centers throughout Delaware, Maryland, North Carolina, South Carolina and Virginia (as of October 2020). Harris Teeter Supermarkets is a wholly-owned subsidiary of The Kroger Company.

FINANCIAL DATA: *Note: Data for latest year may not have been available at press time.*

In U.S. $	2020	2019	2018	2017	2016	2015
Revenue	5,876,325,000	5,733,000,000	5,460,000,000	5,200,000,000	5,130,000,000	5,125,000,000
R&D Expense						
Operating Income						
Operating Margin %						
SGA Expense						
Net Income						
Operating Cash Flow						
Capital Expenditure						
EBITDA						
Return on Assets %						
Return on Equity %						
Debt to Equity						

CONTACT INFORMATION:

Phone: 704 844-3100   Fax:
Toll-Free:
Address: 701 Crestdale Rd., Matthews, NC 28105 United States

STOCK TICKER/OTHER:

Stock Ticker: Subsidiary   Exchange:
Employees: 26,000   Fiscal Year Ends: 10/31
Parent Company: Kroger Company (The)

SALARIES/BONUSES:

Top Exec. Salary: $ Bonus: $
Second Exec. Salary: $ Bonus: $

OTHER THOUGHTS:

Estimated Female Officers or Directors:
Hot Spot for Advancement for Women/Minorities:

Hartford Financial Services Group Inc (The) www.thehartford.com

NAIC Code: 524113

TYPES OF BUSINESS:

Life Insurance
Mutual Funds
Property & Casualty Insurance
Group Life & Accident Insurance
Reinsurance
Employee Benefits Administration
Asset Management
Bank Holding Company

BRANDS/DIVISIONS/AFFILIATES:

Hartford Fire Insurance Company

CONTACTS: Note: Officers with more than one job title may be intentionally listed here more than once.

Christopher Swift, CEO
Beth Costello, CFO
Scott Lewis, Chief Accounting Officer
Kathleen Bromage, Chief Marketing Officer
Robert Paiano, Chief Risk Officer
William Bloom, Executive VP, Divisional
Martha Gervasi, Executive VP, Divisional
David Robinson, Executive VP
Brion Johnson, Executive VP
Douglas Elliot, President

GROWTH PLANS/SPECIAL FEATURES:

The Hartford Financial Services Group, Inc. is a diversified insurance and financial services company that offers insurance and investment products. Through Hartford Fire Insurance Company and its many subsidiaries, it is a leading provider of investment products, individual life, group life and group disability insurance products and property and casualty insurance products in the U.S., Canada and select overseas markets. The Hartford is organized into five major divisions: commercial lines, personal lines, property and casualty (P&C) other operations, group benefits, Hartford funds and corporate. The Commercial lines division provides standard workers' compensation, property, automobile, liability, marine, livestock and umbrella coverages as well as a variety of customized insurance products and risk management services. Personal lines provide standard automobile, homeowners and home-based business coverages, including a special program designed for members of AARP. P&C other operations includes certain property and casualty operations that have discontinued writing new business and includes substantially all the firm's asbestos and environmental exposures. Group benefits offers group life, accident and disability coverage as well as group retiree health and voluntary benefits to individual members of employer groups. Mutual funds offer investment management, administration, distribution and related services to investors through financial products in both domestic and international markets. The corporate division includes Hartford's capital raising activities, including debt financing and interest expense; purchase accounting adjustments; and other expenses.

The firm offers employees medical, dental and vision insurance; a wellness program; investment, savings, stock and bond purchase plans; and short- and long-term disability.

FINANCIAL DATA: Note: Data for latest year may not have been available at press time.

In U.S. $	2020	2019	2018	2017	2016	2015
Revenue	20,320,000,000	20,740,000,000	18,955,000,000	16,974,000,000	18,300,000,000	18,377,000,000
R&D Expense						
Operating Income						
Operating Margin %						
SGA Expense						
Net Income	1,737,000,000	2,085,000,000	1,807,000,000	-3,131,000,000	896,000,000	1,682,000,000
Operating Cash Flow	3,871,000,000	3,489,000,000	2,843,000,000	2,186,000,000	2,066,000,000	2,756,000,000
Capital Expenditure	114,000,000	105,000,000	122,000,000	250,000,000	224,000,000	307,000,000
EBITDA						
Return on Assets %		.03%	.01%	-.01%	.00%	.01%
Return on Equity %		.14%	.14%	-.21%	.05%	.09%
Debt to Equity		0.273	0.334	0.347	0.274	0.288

CONTACT INFORMATION:

Phone: 860 547-5000   Fax: 860 720-6097
Toll-Free:
Address: 690 Asylum Ave., 1 Hartford Plaza, Hartford, CT 06115 United States

STOCK TICKER/OTHER:

Stock Ticker: HIG
Employees: 19,500
Parent Company:

Exchange: NYS
Fiscal Year Ends: 12/31

SALARIES/BONUSES:

Top Exec. Salary: $ Bonus: $
Second Exec. Salary: $ Bonus: $

OTHER THOUGHTS:

Estimated Female Officers or Directors: 1
Hot Spot for Advancement for Women/Minorities: Y

HCA Healthcare Inc

NAIC Code: 622110

www.hcahealthcare.com

TYPES OF BUSINESS:

General Medical and Surgical Hospitals
Hospital
Surgery
Emergency Care
Clinics
Diagnostics
Rehabilitation
Psychiatric

BRANDS/DIVISIONS/AFFILIATES:

GROWTH PLANS/SPECIAL FEATURES:

HCA Healthcare, Inc. owns and operates 187 hospitals and approximately 2,000 sites of care, including surgery centers, freestanding emergency rooms, urgent care centers and physician clinics in 20 U.S. states and the U.K. The company's acute care hospitals provide a full range of services, including internal medicine, general surgery, cardiology, oncology, neurosurgery, orthopedics and obstetrics, as well as diagnostic and emergency services. Outpatient and ancillary health care services are provided by HCA's general, acute care hospitals, freestanding surgery centers, freestanding emergency care facilities, urgent care facilities, walk-in clinics, diagnostic centers and rehabilitation facilities. Its psychiatric hospitals provide a full range of mental health care services through inpatient, partial hospitalization and outpatient settings. In September 2021, HCA Healthcare agreed to acquire five Steward Health Care hospitals in Utah, which would become part of HCA Healthcare's mountain division, which includes hospitals in Utah, Idaho and Alaska.

CONTACTS:
Note: Officers with more than one job title may be intentionally listed here more than once.

Samuel Hazen, CEO
Victor Campbell, Senior VP, Divisional
William Rutherford, CFO
Thomas Frist, Chairman of the Board
Kathleen Whalen, Chief Compliance Officer
Martin Paslick, Chief Information Officer
Jonathan Perlin, Chief Medical Officer
Robert Waterman, General Counsel
John Steele, Other Executive Officer
Joseph Sowell, Other Executive Officer
Jane Englebright, Other Executive Officer
Michael Cuffe, President, Divisional
A. Moore, President, Divisional
Jon Foster, President, Geographical
Charles Hall, President, Geographical
Kathryn Torres, Senior VP, Divisional
Sandra Morgan, Senior VP, Divisional
Phillip Billington, Senior VP, Divisional

FINANCIAL DATA:
Note: Data for latest year may not have been available at press time.

In U.S. $	2020	2019	2018	2017	2016	2015
Revenue	51,533,000,000	51,336,000,000	46,677,000,000	43,614,000,000	41,490,000,000	39,678,000,000
R&D Expense						
Operating Income	7,262,000,000	7,218,000,000	6,642,000,000	6,057,000,000	6,198,000,000	5,965,000,000
Operating Margin %		.14%	.14%	.14%	.15%	.15%
SGA Expense	23,874,000,000	23,560,000,000	21,425,000,000	20,059,000,000	18,897,000,000	18,115,000,000
Net Income	3,754,000,000	3,505,000,000	3,787,000,000	2,216,000,000	2,890,000,000	2,129,000,000
Operating Cash Flow	9,232,000,000	7,602,000,000	6,761,000,000	5,426,000,000	5,653,000,000	4,734,000,000
Capital Expenditure	2,835,000,000	4,158,000,000	3,573,000,000	3,015,000,000	2,760,000,000	2,375,000,000
EBITDA	9,735,000,000	9,664,000,000	9,368,001,000	8,202,000,000	8,483,000,000	7,526,000,000
Return on Assets %		.08%	.10%	.06%	.09%	.07%
Return on Equity %						
Debt to Equity						

CONTACT INFORMATION:

Phone: 615 344-9551   Fax: 615 320-2266
Toll-Free:
Address: 1 Park Plaza, Nashville, TN 37203 United States

STOCK TICKER/OTHER:

Stock Ticker: HCA   Exchange: NYS
Employees: 280,000   Fiscal Year Ends: 12/31
Parent Company:

SALARIES/BONUSES:

Top Exec. Salary: $ Bonus: $
Second Exec. Salary: $ Bonus: $

OTHER THOUGHTS:

Estimated Female Officers or Directors: 2
Hot Spot for Advancement for Women/Minorities:

Health Care Service Corporation (HCSC)   www.hcsc.com

NAIC Code: 524114

TYPES OF BUSINESS:

Insurance-Medical & Health, HMOs & PPOs
Traditional Indemnity Plans
Medicare Supplemental Health
Life Insurance
Dental & Vision Insurance
Electronic Claims & Information Network
Workers' Compensation
Retirement Services

BRANDS/DIVISIONS/AFFILIATES:

Blue Cross and Blue Shield
Dental Network of America Inc
Availity LLC
Medicision Inc

CONTACTS: Note: Officers with more than one job title may be intentionally listed here more than once.

Maurice Smith, CEO
Opella Ernest, COO
James Walsh, CFO
James Gibbs, Chief Human Resources Officer
Stephen Ondra, Chief Medical Officer
John Cannon, Chief Admin. Officer
Deborah Dorman-Rodriguez, Corp. Sec.
Martin G. Foster, Pres., Plan Oper.
Paula A. Steiner, Chief Strategy Officer
Ross Blackstone, Contact-Media
Ted Haynes, Pres., Oklahoma Div.
Kurt Shipley, Pres., New Mexico Div.
Karen M. Atwood, Pres., Illinois Div.
Bert E. Marshall, Pres., Texas Div.

GROWTH PLANS/SPECIAL FEATURES:

Health Care Service Corporation (HCSC) is a customer-owned health insurer which operates through its Blue Cross and Blue Shield divisions in Illinois, Montana, New Mexico, Oklahoma and Texas. HCSC is a legal reserve company, meaning that it maintains policy reserves according to the standards established by the insurance laws of the various states it serves. The firm provides preferred provider organizations (PPOs), health maintenance organizations (HMOs), point of service (POS), traditional indemnity and Medicare supplemental health plans to nearly 17 million members. The company also has several subsidiaries that offer a variety of health and life insurance products and related services to employers and individuals. Through its non-Blue Cross and Blue Shield subsidiaries, HCSC offers prescription drug plans, Medicare supplemental insurance, dental and vision coverage, life and disability insurance, workers' compensation, retirement services and medical financial services. One such subsidiary, Dental Network of America, Inc., functions as a third-party administrator for all company dental programs and is registered in every state except Florida. It also offers a dental discount card program. Availity, LLC, a partially-owned subsidiary, operates a health care clearinghouse and provides internet-based health information services. Medicision, Inc. is an integrated health solutions company that partners with other organizations to manage more than 50 million members in commercial, Medicare Advantage and various Medicaid programs.

Employee benefits include: medical, short/long-term disability, AD&D and life insurance; 401(k) and pension plans; and various employee assistance programs.

FINANCIAL DATA: Note: Data for latest year may not have been available at press time.

In U.S. $	2020	2019	2018	2017	2016	2015
Revenue	47,300,000,000	38,600,000,000	35,900,000,000	36,800,000,000	33,000,000,000	35,000,000,000
R&D Expense						
Operating Income						
Operating Margin %						
SGA Expense						
Net Income						
Operating Cash Flow						
Capital Expenditure						
EBITDA						
Return on Assets %						
Return on Equity %						
Debt to Equity						

CONTACT INFORMATION:

Phone: 312-653-6000   Fax: 312-819-1220
Toll-Free: 800-654-7385
Address: 300 E. Randolph St., Chicago, IL 60601 United States

STOCK TICKER/OTHER:

Stock Ticker: Mutual Company
Employees: 24,000
Parent Company:

Exchange:
Fiscal Year Ends: 12/31

SALARIES/BONUSES:

Top Exec. Salary: $ Bonus: $
Second Exec. Salary: $ Bonus: $

OTHER THOUGHTS:

Estimated Female Officers or Directors: 6
Hot Spot for Advancement for Women/Minorities: Y

Heartland Payment Systems Inc
www.heartlandpaymentsystems.com

NAIC Code: 522320

TYPES OF BUSINESS:

Financial Processing Services
Credit/Debit Processing
Payroll Processing Services
Processing Equipment Provider
Point of Sale
Capital Lending
Customer Engagement

BRANDS/DIVISIONS/AFFILIATES:

Global Payments Inc

GROWTH PLANS/SPECIAL FEATURES:

Heartland Payment Systems, Inc. is a wholly-owned subsidiary of Global Payments, Inc. and a provider of credit/debit/prepaid card, payroll and other associated processing and customer/client engagement services to businesses throughout the U.S. Heartland primarily serves liquor, restaurant, retail, service professionals and quick service industries. The firm's products are divided into five categories: payment, offering payment processing, online payments, mobile payments, service professionals and surcharge solutions; payroll, including payroll, human resources and situation room; point of sale, including mobile pay, terminals, register, restaurant, retail, online ordering and integrations; capital lending; and customer engagement, including analytics, customer intelligence and email marketing.

CONTACTS: Note: Officers with more than one job title may be intentionally listed here more than once.

Jeffrey S. Sloan, CEO-Global Payments
Charles Kallenbach, General Counsel
David Gilbert, President, Divisional
Michael Lawler, President, Divisional
Robert Baldwin, Vice Chairman

FINANCIAL DATA: Note: Data for latest year may not have been available at press time.

In U.S. $	2020	2019	2018	2017	2016	2015
Revenue	4,137,241,500	3,940,230,000	2,717,400,000	2,588,000,000	2,550,500,000	2,682,395,904
R&D Expense						
Operating Income						
Operating Margin %						
SGA Expense						
Net Income						
Operating Cash Flow						
Capital Expenditure						
EBITDA						
Return on Assets %						
Return on Equity %						
Debt to Equity						

CONTACT INFORMATION:

Phone: 609 683-3831   Fax: 609 683-3815
Toll-Free: 888-963-3600
Address: 10 Glenlake Pkwy. North Tower, Atlanta, GA 30328-3495 United States

STOCK TICKER/OTHER:

Stock Ticker: Subsidiary
Employees: 3,734
Parent Company: Global Payments Inc

Exchange:
Fiscal Year Ends: 12/31

SALARIES/BONUSES:

Top Exec. Salary: $ Bonus: $
Second Exec. Salary: $ Bonus: $

OTHER THOUGHTS:

Estimated Female Officers or Directors: 2
Hot Spot for Advancement for Women/Minorities:

HEB Grocery Company LP

www.heb.com

NAIC Code: 445110

TYPES OF BUSINESS:

Supermarkets
Grocery Stores
Gourmet Food Stores
Dairy Processing
Bakery
Pharmacy Services

BRANDS/DIVISIONS/AFFILIATES:

H-E-B
H-E-B plus!
Mi Tienda
Central Market
Joe V's Smart Shop
H-E-B Blooms
Temple Retail Support Center

CONTACTS: *Note: Officers with more than one job title may be intentionally listed here more than once.*

Charles Butt, CEO
Judy Lindquist, General Counsel
Lynette Padalecki, VP-Corp. Planning & Analysis
Winell Herron, VP-Public Affairs & Diversity
Scott McClelland, Pres., Houston Food & Drug Stores Div.
Suzanne Wade, Pres., San Antonio Food & Drug Stores Div.
William Fry, VP-Quality Assurance & Environmental Affairs
Roxanne Orsak, Exec. VP-Drug
Mike Graham, Sr. VP-Logistics & Supply Chain

GROWTH PLANS/SPECIAL FEATURES:

HEB Grocery Company, LP operates more than 400 grocery stores in Texas and Mexico under the H-E-B, H-E-B plus! and Mi Tienda brand names. The firm owns one of the largest milk plants in Texas as well as a large bread bakery, a meat plant, a pastry bakery, an ice cream plant, a chip plant and a photo processing lab. H-E-B stores carry a wide variety of merchandise, including a line of products under the H-E-B brand. H-E-B Plus! Stores offer merchandise beyond normal groceries, including toys, housewares, outdoor entertaining products, apparel and baby items (strollers, high chairs, bounces, etc.). Mi Tienda stores offer fresh produce, authentic Mexican grocery products, fish and meats, a bakery, a tortilleria and more. HEB also operates 10 Central Market stores, with locations in Houston, Dallas, Fort Worth, Plano, San Antonio, Southlake and Austin. Central Markets are gourmet specialty stores featuring large prepared foods-to-go areas, eat-in areas, comprehensive wine departments, specialty butcher and fish counters, a European bakery, a deli with meats, a large selection of cheeses from around the globe and a juice and ice cream bar. The firm also owns a series of eight discount stores in the Houston and Baytown, Texas area known as Joe V's Smart Shop; and H-E-B Blooms, a premier flower delivery and floral design center in Houston, which also provides consultation services in regards to weddings and special events. HEB Grocery Company owns and operates a retail support center in Monterrey, Mexico, as well as the Temple Retail Support Center, a 450,000-square-foot warehouse and transportation facility in central Texas.

HEB offers comprehensive benefits, retirement options and employee assistance programs.

FINANCIAL DATA: *Note: Data for latest year may not have been available at press time.*

In U.S. $	2020	2019	2018	2017	2016	2015
Revenue	29,000,000,000	26,000,000,000	25,000,000,000	24,650,000,000	24,000,000,000	23,000,000,000
R&D Expense						
Operating Income						
Operating Margin %						
SGA Expense						
Net Income						
Operating Cash Flow						
Capital Expenditure						
EBITDA						
Return on Assets %						
Return on Equity %						
Debt to Equity						

CONTACT INFORMATION:

Phone: 210-938-8000   Fax: 210-938-8169
Toll-Free: 800-432-3113
Address: 646 S. Main Ave, San Antonio, TX 78204 United States

SALARIES/BONUSES:

Top Exec. Salary: $ Bonus: $
Second Exec. Salary: $ Bonus: $

STOCK TICKER/OTHER:

Stock Ticker: Private   Exchange:
Employees: 116,000   Fiscal Year Ends: 10/31
Parent Company:

OTHER THOUGHTS:

Estimated Female Officers or Directors: 5
Hot Spot for Advancement for Women/Minorities: Y

Hershey Company (The)

NAIC Code: 311352

www.hersheys.com

TYPES OF BUSINESS:

Candy Manufacturing
Baking Supplies
Chocolate Products
Confectionaries & Snacks
Amusement Parks
Resorts/Hotels

BRANDS/DIVISIONS/AFFILIATES:

Reese's
Kit Kat
Hershey Bars
Hershey Kisses
Hershey's Chocolate World
Amplify Snack Brands Inc
SkinnyPop
ONE Brands LLC

CONTACTS: Note: Officers with more than one job title may be intentionally listed here more than once.

Michele Buck, CEO
Steven Voskuil, CFO
Charles Davis, Chairman of the Board
Javier Idrovo, Chief Accounting Officer
Terence ODay, Chief Technology Officer
Damien Atkins, General Counsel
Mary Stone West, Other Executive Officer
Kevin Walling, Other Executive Officer
Todd Tillemans, President, Divisional

GROWTH PLANS/SPECIAL FEATURES:

The Hershey Company is an industry-leading snacks company known for its iconic brands. The company's more than 80 branded products are marketed in approximately 85 countries worldwide. Hershey's principal product groups include confectionery products such as Reese's, Kit Kat, Hershey Bars and Hershey Kisses; packaged items; and grocery products, such as baking ingredients, chocolate drink mixes, peanut butter, dessert toppings and beverages. Its products are sold primarily to wholesale distributors, chain grocery stores, mass merchandisers, chain drug stores, vending companies, wholesale clubs, convenience stores, dollar stores, concessionaires, department stores and natural food stores. Its direct retail operations include Hershey's Chocolate World in Hershey, Pennsylvania, and Hershey's retail stores in New York City, Las Vegas, Niagara Falls (Ontario) and Singapore. The firm's operations are therefore divided into geographical segments: North America and international and other. The North America segment is responsible for Hershey's traditional chocolate and non-chocolate confectionery market position, as well as its grocery and snacks market positions in the U.S. and Canada. The international and other segment is a combination of all other Hershey business. This includes operations and product manufacturing facilities in China, Mexico, Brazil, India and Malaysia, which also distribute and sell confectionery products in the export markets of Asia, Latin America, the Middle East, Europe, Africa and other regions. This segment also includes the Hershey's Chocolate World stores (even the ones in the U.S.); and is responsible for licensing the use of certain of the company's trademarks and products to third parties worldwide.

Hershey offers its employees comprehensive health benefits and retirement plans.

FINANCIAL DATA: Note: Data for latest year may not have been available at press time.

In U.S. $	2020	2019	2018	2017	2016	2015
Revenue	8,149,719,000	7,986,252,000	7,791,069,000	7,515,426,000	7,440,181,000	7,386,626,000
R&D Expense						
Operating Income	1,810,344,000	1,716,549,000	1,700,496,000	1,531,116,000	1,242,513,000	1,413,367,000
Operating Margin %		.21%	.22%	.20%	.17%	.19%
SGA Expense	1,890,925,000	1,905,929,000	1,874,829,000	1,913,403,000	1,915,378,000	1,969,308,000
Net Income	1,278,708,000	1,149,692,000	1,177,562,000	782,981,000	720,044,000	512,951,000
Operating Cash Flow	1,699,657,000	1,763,873,000	1,599,993,000	1,249,515,000	983,475,000	1,214,456,000
Capital Expenditure	441,626,000	318,192,000	328,601,000	257,675,000	269,476,000	356,810,000
EBITDA	1,943,375,000	1,824,450,000	1,852,063,000	1,472,587,000	1,493,266,000	1,227,758,000
Return on Assets %		.15%	.18%	.14%	.13%	.09%
Return on Equity %		.73%	1.02%	.92%	.81%	.42%
Debt to Equity		2.136	2.327	2.252	2.987	1.56

CONTACT INFORMATION:

Phone: 717 534-4200   Fax: 717 531-6161
Toll-Free: 800-468-1714
Address: 19 E. Chocolate AVe., Hershey, PA 17033 United States

STOCK TICKER/OTHER:

Stock Ticker: HSY
Employees: 16,140
Parent Company:

Exchange: NYS
Fiscal Year Ends: 12/31

SALARIES/BONUSES:

Top Exec. Salary: $ Bonus: $
Second Exec. Salary: $ Bonus: $

OTHER THOUGHTS:

Estimated Female Officers or Directors: 4
Hot Spot for Advancement for Women/Minorities: Y

Hill-Rom Holdings Inc

NAIC Code: 339100

www.hillrom.com/

TYPES OF BUSINESS:

Equipment-Hospital Beds & Related Products
Specialized Therapy Products
Rentals

BRANDS/DIVISIONS/AFFILIATES:

Hillrom

CONTACTS: Note: Officers with more than one job title may be intentionally listed here more than once.

John Groetelaars, CEO
Barbara Bodem, CFO
William Dempsey, Chairman of the Board
Richard Wagner, Chief Accounting Officer
Deborah Rasin, Chief Legal Officer
Kenneth Meyers, Other Executive Officer
Francisco Vega, President, Divisional
Paul Johnson, President, Divisional
Andreas Frank, President, Divisional
Carlos Alonso-Marum, President, Subsidiary
Mary Ladone, Senior VP, Divisional
Jason Richardson, Treasurer

GROWTH PLANS/SPECIAL FEATURES:

Hill-Rom Holdings, Inc. (branded as Hillrom) is a global medical technology company. Hillrom partners with healthcare providers in more than 100 countries, with a focus on patient care solutions that improve clinical and economic outcomes. The firm operates through three segments: patient support systems, front line care and surgical solutions. The patient support systems segment globally provides Hillrom's medical surgery and specialty bed systems and surfaces, safe patient handling equipment and mobility solutions, as well as the company's care communications platform that delivers software and information technologies to improve care and deliver insight to caregivers and patients. The front line care segment globally provides patient monitoring and diagnostic technologies, including a diversified portfolio of physical assessment tools that help diagnose, treat and manage a wide variety of illnesses and diseases, including respiratory and a portfolio of vision care health devices. The surgical solutions segment globally provides products that improve safety and efficiency in the surgical space, including tables, lights, pendants, precision positioning devices and other accessories. In September 2021, Hill-Rom agreed to be acquired by Baxter International, Inc., a global medical products company. Hillrom will bring its complementary product portfolio and innovation pipeline that will enable Baxter to provide a broader array of medical products and services. The combination is also expected to accelerate the companies' expansion into digital and connected care solutions. The transaction was expected to close in early-2022.

FINANCIAL DATA: Note: Data for latest year may not have been available at press time.

In U.S. $	2020	2019	2018	2017	2016	2015
Revenue	2,881,000,000	2,907,300,000	2,848,000,000	2,743,700,000	2,655,200,000	1,988,200,000
R&D Expense	136,500,000	139,500,000	135,600,000	133,700,000	133,500,000	91,800,000
Operating Income	409,200,000	344,500,000	367,100,000	310,800,000	270,200,000	124,300,000
Operating Margin %		.12%	.13%	.11%	.10%	.06%
SGA Expense	820,400,000	941,000,000	891,500,000	876,100,000	853,300,000	664,200,000
Net Income	223,000,000	152,200,000	252,400,000	133,600,000	124,100,000	47,700,000
Operating Cash Flow	481,700,000	401,400,000	395,200,000	311,100,000	281,200,000	213,800,000
Capital Expenditure	105,900,000	90,500,000	89,500,000	97,500,000	83,300,000	121,300,000
EBITDA	524,000,000	493,000,000	488,700,000	482,700,000	437,700,000	201,700,000
Return on Assets %		.03%	.06%	.03%	.03%	.02%
Return on Equity %		.10%	.17%	.10%	.10%	.05%
Debt to Equity		1.133	1.108	1.561	1.58	1.897

CONTACT INFORMATION:

Phone: 3120819-7200   Fax:
Toll-Free:
Address: 130 E. Randolph St., Ste. 1000, Chicago, IL 60601 United States

STOCK TICKER/OTHER:

Stock Ticker: HRC
Employees: 10,000
Parent Company:

Exchange: NYS
Fiscal Year Ends: 09/30

SALARIES/BONUSES:

Top Exec. Salary: $ Bonus: $
Second Exec. Salary: $ Bonus: $

OTHER THOUGHTS:

Estimated Female Officers or Directors: 1
Hot Spot for Advancement for Women/Minorities: Y

Home Depot Inc (The)

www.homedepot.com

NAIC Code: 444110

TYPES OF BUSINESS:

Home Centers, Retail
Home Improvement Products
Building Materials
Lawn & Garden Products
Online & Catalog Sales
Tool & Truck Rental
Installation & Design Services

BRANDS/DIVISIONS/AFFILIATES:

Hampton Bay
Husky
Vigoro
HDX
Glacier Bay

CONTACTS: *Note: Officers with more than one job title may be intentionally listed here more than once.*

Carol Tome, CFO
Matthew Carey, Chief Information Officer
Mark Holifield, Executive VP, Divisional
Ann-Marie Campbell, Executive VP, Divisional
Edward Decker, Executive VP, Divisional
William Lennie, Executive VP, Divisional
Timothy Hourigan, Executive VP, Divisional
Teresa Roseborough, Executive VP
Craig Menear, President
Richard McPhail, Senior VP, Divisional

GROWTH PLANS/SPECIAL FEATURES:

The Home Depot, Inc. is one of the world's largest home improvement retailers. The company operates approximately 2,295 Home Depot stores in all 50 U.S. states, the District of Columbia, Canada, Guam, Puerto Rico, the U.S. Virgin Islands and Mexico. A typical store encompasses 104,000-square-feet of enclosed space with a 24,000-square-foot outdoor garden center; these locations usually stock between 30,000 and 40,000 items. Approximately 1 million products can be accessed through the homedepot.com website. These stores sell an assortment of building materials, plumbing materials, electrical materials, kitchen products, hardware, seasonal items, paint, flooring and wall coverings. The firm's proprietary brands include Hampton Bay lighting, Husky hand tools, Vigoro lawn care products, Glacier Bay bath fixtures and HDX storage and cleaning products. Home Depot markets its products primarily to three types of customers: professional customers, such as remodelers, contractors, repairmen and small business owners; do-it-for-me shoppers, who are homeowners that personally purchase Home Depot products but hire third-party individuals for installation and/or project completion; and do-it-yourself (DIY) customers, who are homeowners that both shop for and personally install and/or utilize the firm's materials. In November 2020, Home Depot agreed to acquire HD Supply Holdings, Inc., a national distributor of maintenance, repair and operations (MRO) products in the multifamily and hospitality end markets.

Home Depot offers its employees medical, dental, vision, life, AD&D and disability insurance; a 401(k) plan; a stock purchase plan; adoption, education and relocation assistance; flexible spending accounts; a legal services plan; auto and homeowners insur

FINANCIAL DATA: *Note: Data for latest year may not have been available at press time.*

In U.S. $	2020	2019	2018	2017	2016	2015
Revenue	110,225,000,000	108,203,000,000	100,904,000,000	94,595,000,000	88,519,000,000	
R&D Expense						
Operating Income	15,843,000,000	15,777,000,000	14,681,000,000	13,427,000,000	11,774,000,000	
Operating Margin %	.14%	.15%	.15%	.14%	.13%	
SGA Expense	19,740,000,000	19,513,000,000	17,864,000,000	17,132,000,000	16,801,000,000	
Net Income	11,242,000,000	11,121,000,000	8,630,000,000	7,957,000,000	7,009,000,000	
Operating Cash Flow	13,723,000,000	13,038,000,000	12,031,000,000	9,783,000,000	9,373,000,000	
Capital Expenditure	2,678,000,000	2,442,000,000	1,897,000,000	1,621,000,000	1,503,000,000	
EBITDA	18,212,000,000	17,759,000,000	16,817,000,000	15,436,000,000	13,803,000,000	
Return on Assets %	.24%	.25%	.20%	.19%	.17%	
Return on Equity %			2.98%	1.49%	.90%	
Debt to Equity			16.69	5.158	3.307	

CONTACT INFORMATION:

Phone: 770 433-8211   Fax: 770 431-2707
Toll-Free: 800-553-3199
Address: 2455 Paces Ferry Rd. N.W., Atlanta, GA 30339 United States

STOCK TICKER/OTHER:

Stock Ticker: HD   Exchange: NYS
Employees: 415,700   Fiscal Year Ends: 01/31
Parent Company:

SALARIES/BONUSES:

Top Exec. Salary: $ Bonus: $
Second Exec. Salary: $ Bonus: $

OTHER THOUGHTS:

Estimated Female Officers or Directors: 7
Hot Spot for Advancement for Women/Minorities: Y

Sales, profits and employees may be estimates. Financial information, benefits and other data can change quickly and may vary from those stated here.

Houston Methodist

www.houstonmethodist.org

NAIC Code: 622110

TYPES OF BUSINESS:

General Medical and Surgical Hospitals
Hospitals
Academic Medical Centers
Emergency Care
Imaging Center
Breast Care Center
Outpatient Center
Technologies

BRANDS/DIVISIONS/AFFILIATES:

Houston Methodist Hospital
Houston Methodist Emergency Care
Houston Methodist Imaging
Houston Methodist Breast Care
Houston Methodist Outpatient Center
Houston Methodist Academic Institute
Houston Methodist Institute for Technology
Houston Methodist Hospital Foundation

CONTACTS: Note: Officers with more than one job title may be intentionally listed here more than once.

Marc L. Boom, CEO
Gregory Nelson, Sec.
Carlton Caucum, Treas.
Joseph Walter III, Assistant Treas.
Robert K. Moses, Jr., Assistant Sec.
Gregory V. Nelson, Chmn.

GROWTH PLANS/SPECIAL FEATURES:

Houston Methodist comprises an academic medical center in the Texas Medical Center and six community hospitals serving the greater Houston area. Houston Methodist Hospital is the system's flagship, with other available centers including Houston Methodist Emergency Care Centers, the Houston Methodist Imaging Center, the Houston Methodist Breast Care Center and the Houston Methodist Outpatient Center. These centers offer care in areas of cancer, digestive disorders, heart and vascular disease, neurology, neurosurgery, orthopedics, sports medicine and transplant. Houston Methodist Academic Institute comprises physician-scientists who work in a collaborative environment on more than 800 clinical trials. The Houston Methodist Institute for Technology, Innovation and Education is a 35,000-square-foot surgical training center and virtual hospital that provides ongoing physician education and surgical training in the latest techniques and technologies. Houston Methodist Hospital Foundation accepts all gifts on Houston Methodist's behalf and can assist with choosing an area to apply donations. Houston Methodist Community Benefits provides financial and medical assistance across the group's hospitals. Houston Methodist Specialty Physician Group consist of doctors employed by Houston Methodist who offer academic and research services to support teaching, continued education and collaboration. Houston Methodist Primary Care Group has locations throughout Houston and provides patient care for the entire family.

FINANCIAL DATA: Note: Data for latest year may not have been available at press time.

In U.S. $	2020	2019	2018	2017	2016	2015
Revenue	3,859,500,000	4,150,000,000	4,000,000,000	3,045,000,000	2,900,000,000	2,800,000,000
R&D Expense						
Operating Income						
Operating Margin %						
SGA Expense						
Net Income						
Operating Cash Flow						
Capital Expenditure						
EBITDA						
Return on Assets %						
Return on Equity %						
Debt to Equity						

CONTACT INFORMATION:

Phone: 713-790-3311 Fax:
Toll-Free:
Address: 6565 Fannin St., Houston, TX 77030 United States

STOCK TICKER/OTHER:

Stock Ticker: Nonprofit
Employees: 25,543
Parent Company:

Exchange:
Fiscal Year Ends: 12/31

SALARIES/BONUSES:

Top Exec. Salary: $ Bonus: $
Second Exec. Salary: $ Bonus: $

OTHER THOUGHTS:

Estimated Female Officers or Directors: 5
Hot Spot for Advancement for Women/Minorities: Y

328

Plunkett Research, Ltd.

HTC Global Services Inc

www.htcinc.com

NAIC Code: 541512

TYPES OF BUSINESS:

IT Consulting and Services
Application Development & Management
Business Process Improvement Services
Technical Help Desk Services
Testing Services
Form & Claims Processing
Supply Chain Management
Data Warehousing

BRANDS/DIVISIONS/AFFILIATES:

SoteriaAMS
CareTech
iDoc

CONTACTS:
Note: Officers with more than one job title may be intentionally listed here more than once.

Madhava Reddy, CEO
Laurie Maria, Dir.-Finance
Suresh Subramanian, VP-Human Resources
Chary Mudumby, CTO
Venu Vaishya, Exec. VP-Oper.
Laurie Maria, Dir.-Finance
Vikas Bhutada, Exec. VP
James Joseph, VP-Gov't Svcs.
Vani Prasad, VP-Insurance Svcs.
Girish Arora, VP-Financial Svcs.
Chary Mudumby, VP-Europe & Asia Pacific Oper.

GROWTH PLANS/SPECIAL FEATURES:

HTC Global Services, Inc. is an international IT and business process outsourcing service firm with operation and delivery centers located throughout North America, Europe, Asia Pacific, the Middle East and India. The company is ISO 9001 and ISO 27001 certified, with processes aligned with SEI CMM Level 5. HTC provides sector-specific services for automotive, manufacturing, banking, financial services, higher education, government, healthcare payer services, healthcare provider services, insurance, entertainment, media, publishing, telecommunications, hospitality and retail industries. Services by the firm span application management, data management, data center, digital content management, infrastructure, service desk, SalesForce, SAP, mobile development and testing. HTC also provides services and solution in regards to emerging technologies such as Internet of Things (IoT), DevOps, agile and artificial intelligence (AI). Solutions by HTC include grants management, adult protective services on the cloud (for vulnerable persons, victims of abuse, exploitation, neglect and/or unsafe living conditions), open enterprise resource planning (ERP), the SoteriaAMS library asset management solution, regulatory compliance for banks, CareTech cost management solution for hospitals and healthcare providers, and iDoc medical record document imaging and management solution. The business process division offers end-to-end outsourcing services worldwide. This division's publishing services include microfilm scanning, document scanning, rare collections scanning, archival digitization, content repurposing, eBooks, cataloging, abstraction, indexing, accessibility and audio/video digitization. Its accounting services include accounts payable, accounts receivable, records to report and trade compliance across all manufacturing units.

FINANCIAL DATA:
Note: Data for latest year may not have been available at press time.

In U.S. $	2020	2019	2018	2017	2016	2015
Revenue	760,000,000	800,000,000	630,000,000	600,000,000	340,000,000	320,000,000
R&D Expense						
Operating Income						
Operating Margin %						
SGA Expense						
Net Income						
Operating Cash Flow						
Capital Expenditure						
EBITDA						
Return on Assets %						
Return on Equity %						
Debt to Equity						

CONTACT INFORMATION:

Phone: 248-786-2500 Fax: 248-786-2515
Toll-Free:
Address: 3270 W. Big Beaver Rd., Troy, MI 48084 United States

SALARIES/BONUSES:

Top Exec. Salary: $ Bonus: $
Second Exec. Salary: $ Bonus: $

STOCK TICKER/OTHER:

Stock Ticker: Private
Employees: 13,000
Parent Company:

Exchange:
Fiscal Year Ends: 12/31

OTHER THOUGHTS:

Estimated Female Officers or Directors: 1
Hot Spot for Advancement for Women/Minorities:

Sales, profits and employees may be estimates. Financial information, benefits and other data can change quickly and may vary from those stated here.

Humana Inc

www.humana.com

NAIC Code: 524114

TYPES OF BUSINESS:

Insurance-Medical & Health, HMOs & PPOs
Insurance-Dental
Employee Benefit Plans
Insurance-Group Life
Wellness Programs
Health Benefits
Home Health
Hospice Services

BRANDS/DIVISIONS/AFFILIATES:

Kindred at Home

CONTACTS: Note: Officers with more than one job title may be intentionally listed here more than once.

Bruce Broussard, CEO
Alan Wheatley, Pres., Divisional
Brian Kane, CFO
Kurt Hilzinger, Chairman of the Board
Cynthia Zipperle, Chief Accounting Officer
Brian LeClaire, Chief Information Officer
Joseph Ventura, Chief Legal Officer
Roy Beveridge, Chief Medical Officer
Samir Deshpande, Chief Risk Officer
Vishal Agrawal, Chief Strategy Officer
Christopher Hunter, Other Corporate Officer
Jody Bilney, Other Executive Officer
Timothy Huval, Other Executive Officer
Elizabeth Bierbower, President, Divisional
William Fleming, President, Divisional

GROWTH PLANS/SPECIAL FEATURES:

Humana, Inc. is a leading health benefits company in the U.S., serving millions of medical benefit plan and specialty products members in the U.S. and Puerto Rico. The firm operates in three segments: retail, group and specialty and healthcare services. The retail segment consists of Medicare and commercial fully-insured medical and specialty health insurance benefits, including dental, vision and other supplemental health and financial protection products, marketed directly to individuals. The group and specialty segment consist of employer group commercial fully-insured medical and specialty health insurance benefits marketed to individuals and employer groups, including dental, vision, and other supplemental health and voluntary insurance benefits, as well as administrative services only (ASO) products marketed to employer groups. Humana provides health benefits and related services to companies ranging from fewer than 10 to over 10,000 employees. The healthcare services segment includes services offered to health plan members as well as to third parties that promote health and wellness, including provider services, pharmacies, integrated wellness and home care services. Other businesses consist of military services, Medicaid and closed-block long-term care businesses as well as the firm's contract with the Centers for Medicare and Medicaid Services to administer the Limited Income Newly Eligible Transition program, known as LI-NET. Many of its products are offered through HMOs (health maintenance organizations), private fee-for-service (PFFS) and preferred provider organizations (PPOs). During 2021, Humana fully acquired Kindred at Home, a leading home health and hospice provider in the U.S.

Humana offers its employees comprehensive health benefits, 401(k), life insurance, tuition assistance, career development and a variety of employee assistance plan/programs and company perks.

FINANCIAL DATA: Note: Data for latest year may not have been available at press time.

In U.S. $	2020	2019	2018	2017	2016	2015
Revenue	77,155,000,000	64,888,000,000	56,912,000,000	53,767,000,000	54,379,000,000	54,289,000,000
R&D Expense						
Operating Income						
Operating Margin %						
SGA Expense	10,052,000,000	7,381,000,000	7,525,000,000	6,567,000,000	7,277,000,000	7,318,000,000
Net Income	3,367,000,000	2,707,000,000	1,683,000,000	2,448,000,000	614,000,000	1,276,000,000
Operating Cash Flow	5,639,000,000	5,284,000,000	2,173,000,000	4,051,000,000	1,936,000,000	868,000,000
Capital Expenditure	964,000,000	736,000,000	612,000,000	526,000,000	527,000,000	523,000,000
EBITDA						
Return on Assets %		.10%	.06%	.09%	.02%	.05%
Return on Equity %		.24%	.17%	.24%	.06%	.13%
Debt to Equity		0.413	0.431	0.485	0.355	0.369

CONTACT INFORMATION:

Phone: 502 580-1000   Fax: 502 580-1441
Toll-Free:
Address: 500 W. Main St., Louisville, KY 40202 United States

STOCK TICKER/OTHER:

Stock Ticker: HUM
Employees: 47,200
Parent Company:

Exchange: NYS
Fiscal Year Ends: 12/31

SALARIES/BONUSES:

Top Exec. Salary: $ Bonus: $
Second Exec. Salary: $ Bonus: $

OTHER THOUGHTS:

Estimated Female Officers or Directors: 3
Hot Spot for Advancement for Women/Minorities: Y

Hycor Biomedical LLC

www.hycorbiomedical.com

NAIC Code: 325413

TYPES OF BUSINESS:

Medical Diagnostics Products
Allergy & Autoimmune Diagnostics
Urinalysis Products

BRANDS/DIVISIONS/AFFILIATES:

Linden Capital Partners
HYTEC
Hycor Ultra-Sensitive EIA
Noveos
Autostat II Elisa
HYTEC 288 Plus

CONTACTS: *Note: Officers with more than one job title may be intentionally listed here more than once.*

Fei Li, CEO
Eric Whitters, COO
Victor Miller, CFO
Erik van Megen, Sr. VP-Global Commercial Operations
Megan Andersen, Dir.-Human Resources
Mark Van Cleve, Dir.-R&D
Tommy Chiu, VP-Operations
Steve Johnson, Dir.-Oper.
Fei Li, Chairperson

GROWTH PLANS/SPECIAL FEATURES:

Hycor Biomedical, LLC is a global manufacturer and supplier of high-quality in vitro diagnostics products. The firm is also engaged in allergy products and autoimmune testing used in clinical laboratories, hospitals and doctors' offices worldwide. Hycor's allergy diagnostic product line includes the HYTEC specific IgE tests and the Hycor Ultra-Sensitive EIA system for allergen specific IgE testing, and features radio-immunoassays and enzymatic immunoassays that test for reactions to more than 1,000 allergens. Another allergy testing system, Noveos, features: smaller sample requirements (4uL), on-board reagents that supply sufficient capacity for up to eight hours of continuous testing and utilizes standardized extracts for consistent and accurate results. Noveos is U.S. Food and Drug Administration (FDA) 510(k) approved. Hycor's autoimmune products division manufactures devices (branded as Autostat II Elisa) that test for disorders such as systemic lupus erythematosus and rheumatoid arthritis. Hycor also produces HYTEC 288 Plus, an automated consolidated workstation capable of storing up to 50 allergy and 105 autoimmune samples, conducting 288 tests per run and providing bar-coded sample identification, high precision robotic liquid handling and real-time incubation control. In addition, Hycor tests for infectious diseases, such as: respiratory pathogens; ticks; herpes; gastrointestinal pathogens; mycosis; basic reagents, which include varicella, borrelia, diphtheria, tetanus and echinococcus; and in partnership with NaGene Diagnosis, has developed the Multiple Real-Time PCR kit for the detection of COVID-19. The firm makes vaccines for diphtheria, poliomyelitis and tetanus. Hycor Biomedical operates as a subsidiary of Linden Capital Partners, with offices in California, U.S. and Kassel, Germany.

FINANCIAL DATA: *Note: Data for latest year may not have been available at press time.*

In U.S. $	2020	2019	2018	2017	2016	2015
Revenue	4,417,497,000	4,167,450,000	3,969,000,000	3,780,000,000	3,600,000,000	3,550,000,000
R&D Expense						
Operating Income						
Operating Margin %						
SGA Expense						
Net Income						
Operating Cash Flow						
Capital Expenditure						
EBITDA						
Return on Assets %						
Return on Equity %						
Debt to Equity						

CONTACT INFORMATION:

Phone: Fax: 714-933-3222
Toll-Free: 800-382-2527
Address: 7272 Chapman Ave., Garden Grove, CA 92841 United States

STOCK TICKER/OTHER:

Stock Ticker: Subsidiary   Exchange:
Employees: 12,000   Fiscal Year Ends: 12/31
Parent Company: Linden Capital Partners

SALARIES/BONUSES:

Top Exec. Salary: $ Bonus: $
Second Exec. Salary: $ Bonus: $

OTHER THOUGHTS:

Estimated Female Officers or Directors:
Hot Spot for Advancement for Women/Minorities:

Sales, profits and employees may be estimates. Financial information, benefits and other data can change quickly and may vary from those stated here.

Hy-Vee Inc

NAIC Code: 445110

TYPES OF BUSINESS:

Grocery Stores/Supermarkets
Food Distribution
Florist Services
Construction Services
Specialty Foods
Banking & Wealth Management Services
Drug Stores

BRANDS/DIVISIONS/AFFILIATES:

D & D Foods Inc
Florist Distributing Inc
Lomar Distributing Inc
Amber Pharmacy
Perishable Distributors of Iowa Ltd
Hy-Vee Construction LC
Midwest Heritage Bank FSB
Hy-Vee Drugstore

CONTACTS: Note: Officers with more than one job title may be intentionally listed here more than once.

Randall B. Edeker, CEO
Jay Marshall, COO
Ron Taylor, Exec. VP-North Div.
Tom Watson, Exec. VP-East Div.
Randall B. Edeker, Chmn.

GROWTH PLANS/SPECIAL FEATURES:

Hy-Vee, Inc. is an employee-owned supermarket chain in the U.S., operating more than 240 retail stores throughout Illinois, Iowa, Missouri, Kansas, Minnesota, Missouri, Nebraska, South Dakota and Wisconsin. The majority of its stores are located within Iowa. The firm operates stores under the Hy-Vee, Hy-Vee Drugstore and Hy-Vee Pharmacy names. Hy-Vee's private label brands include Midwest Country Fare, Full Circle, World Classics Trading Company, Hy-Vee Mother's Choice, LeTechniq, Di Lusso, Paws Premium and Hy-Vee HealthMarket. The company maintains two large distribution centers in Chariton and Cherokee, Iowa. Through its various subsidiaries, Hy-Vee has been able to establish a distribution system that enables the firm to remain a contender in a highly competitive market place. Wholly-owned subsidiaries include D & D Foods, Inc.; Florist Distributing, Inc.; Lomar Distributing, Inc.; Amber Pharmacy; and Perishable Distributors of Iowa, Ltd. These firms encompass a wide spectrum of distribution offerings including specialty foods, pharmaceuticals, pet pharmaceuticals, as well as florist and plant supplies, and meat and seafood products. Additionally, the firm owns Hy-Vee Construction LC, which is based in Des Moines, Iowa; and Midwest Heritage Bank, FSB, with branch locations and offices in Iowa. The company's website provides visitors with online shopping, gift cards, information on weekly specials, access to pharmacies and internet banking. In early-2020, Hy-Vee announced that most of its stores would be ending their 24-hour service, and would be closed from midnight to 5am. In February 2020, Hy-Vee acquired four QuikTrip convenience store locations in Des Moines, and reopened them under the Hy-Vee Fast & Fresh Express brand the following month. That September, Hy-Vee announced the opening of its first DSW Designer Shoe Warehouse shop-in-shop in two of its Minneapolis stores, with four more locations scheduled into October. The shop-in-shop concept is the result from Hy-Vees recent partnership with Designer Brands, Inc.

FINANCIAL DATA: Note: Data for latest year may not have been available at press time.

In U.S. $	2020	2019	2018	2017	2016	2015
Revenue	11,550,000,000	10,500,000,000	10,000,000,000	9,350,000,000	9,220,000,000	9,320,000,000
R&D Expense						
Operating Income						
Operating Margin %						
SGA Expense						
Net Income						
Operating Cash Flow						
Capital Expenditure						
EBITDA						
Return on Assets %						
Return on Equity %						
Debt to Equity						

CONTACT INFORMATION:

Phone: 515-267-2800   Fax:
Toll-Free: 800-289-8343
Address: 5820 Westown Pkwy., West Des Moines, IA 50266 United States

STOCK TICKER/OTHER:

Stock Ticker: Private
Employees: 84,000
Parent Company:

Exchange:
Fiscal Year Ends: 09/30

SALARIES/BONUSES:

Top Exec. Salary: $ Bonus: $
Second Exec. Salary: $ Bonus: $

OTHER THOUGHTS:

Estimated Female Officers or Directors:
Hot Spot for Advancement for Women/Minorities:

IAC/InterActiveCorp

NAIC Code: 519130

www.iac.com

TYPES OF BUSINESS:

E-Commerce, Online Advertising & Search Engines
Online Personals & Dating Services
Online Entertainment & Shopping Directories
Service Provider Listings Online

BRANDS/DIVISIONS/AFFILIATES:

ANGI Homeservices Inc
Angie's List
HomeAdvisor
Vimeo
Dotdash
Ask Media Group
Care.com
Daily Beast

CONTACTS: Note: Officers with more than one job title may be intentionally listed here more than once.

Barry Diller, Chairman of the Board
Mark Stein, Chief Strategy Officer
Joseph Levin, Director
Victor Kaufman, Director
Glenn Schiffman, Executive VP
Gregg Winiarski, General Counsel
Michael Schwerdtman, Senior VP

GROWTH PLANS/SPECIAL FEATURES:

IAC/InterActiveCorp is a leading media and internet company organized into five segments: ANGI Homeservices, Vimeo, Dotdash, Search and Emerging & Other.The ANGI Homeservices segment consists of ANGI Homeservices, Inc., which owns and operates HomeAdvisor, Angie's List and Handy. Vimeo operates a global video platform for creative professionals, marketers and enterprises to connect with their audiences, customers and employees. Vimeo provides cloud-based software products to stream, host, distribute and monetize videos online and across devices, as well as premium video tools on a subscription basis. Vimeo also sells live streaming accessories. Dotdash is a portfolio of digital brands providing expert information and inspiration in select vertical content categories to users. The Search segment consists the Desktop business and Ask Media Group. The Desktop business owns and operates a portfolio of desktop browser applications that provide users with access to a wide variety of online content, tools and services. Ask Media Group is a collection of websites providing general search services and information. The Emerging & Other segment primarily includes: Care.com, an online marketplace for finding and managing family care; the Mosaic Group mobile businesses consisting of the of Apalon, iTranslate, TelTech and Daily Burn; BlueCrew, an on-demand staffing platform that connects temporary workers with traditional blue-collar jobs in areas like warehouse, delivery and moving, data entry and customer service; NurseFly, a temporary healthcare staffing platform; the Daily Beast, a website dedicated to news, commentary, culture and entertainment that publishes original reporting; and IAC Films, a provider of production and producer services for feature films.In 2020, IAC completed its acquisition of Care.com for $500 million, completed the separation of Match Group from the businesses of IAC and announced plans to spin-off Vimeo.

FINANCIAL DATA: Note: Data for latest year may not have been available at press time.

In U.S. $	2020	2019	2018	2017	2016	2015
Revenue	3,047,681,000	4,757,055,000	2,533,048,000	3,307,239,000		
R&D Expense	267,359,000	345,417,000	177,298,000	250,879,000		
Operating Income	-307,203,000	584,651,000	35,835,000	188,466,000		
Operating Margin %						
SGA Expense	2,061,927,000	2,518,573,000	1,669,289,000	2,100,478,000		
Net Income	269,726,000	431,131,000	246,772,000	304,924,000		
Operating Cash Flow	154,581,000	937,939,000	369,435,000	416,699,000		
Capital Expenditure	61,570,000	136,652,000	54,680,000	75,523,000		
EBITDA	436,600,000	829,068,000	468,104,000	288,661,000		
Return on Assets %						
Return on Equity %						
Debt to Equity						

CONTACT INFORMATION:

Phone: 212 314-7300   Fax: 212 314-7399
Toll-Free:
Address: 555 W. 18th St., New York, NY 10011 United States

STOCK TICKER/OTHER:

Stock Ticker: IAC   Exchange: NAS
Employees: 8,700   Fiscal Year Ends: 12/31
Parent Company:

SALARIES/BONUSES:

Top Exec. Salary: $ Bonus: $
Second Exec. Salary: $ Bonus: $

OTHER THOUGHTS:

Estimated Female Officers or Directors: 6
Hot Spot for Advancement for Women/Minorities: Y

IDEXX Laboratories Inc

www.idexx.com

NAIC Code: 334510

TYPES OF BUSINESS:

Veterinary Laboratory Testing Equipment
Point-of-Care Diagnostic Products
Veterinary Pharmaceuticals
Information Management Software
Food & Water Testing Products
Laboratory Testing Services
Consulting

BRANDS/DIVISIONS/AFFILIATES:

IDEXX VetLab
VetLyte
VetStat
Catalyst Dx
SNAP Beta-Lactam
Colilert
Pseudalert
Legiolert

CONTACTS: Note: Officers with more than one job title may be intentionally listed here more than once.

Jonathan Ayers, CEO
Brian Mckeon, CFO
Jay Mazelsky, Executive VP
Sharon Underberg, General Counsel
Giovani Twigge, Other Executive Officer
Kathy Turner, Vice President
Michael Lane, Vice President

GROWTH PLANS/SPECIAL FEATURES:

IDEXX Laboratories, Inc. develops, manufactures and distributes products and provides services for the veterinary and the food and water testing markets. The company operates in three business segments: companion animal group, which provides diagnostic and information technology-based products and services for the veterinary markets; livestock, poultry and dairy, which provides diagnostic products and services for animal health, and to ensure the quality and safety of milk and food; and water quality products. IDEXX markets an integrated and flexible suite of in-house laboratory analyzers for use in veterinary practices, which is referred to as the IDEXX VetLab suite. The suite includes in-clinic chemistry, hematology, immunoassay, urinalysis and coagulation analyzers such as the VetTest, VetLyte, VetStat, LaserCyte Dx, Catalyst One, Catalyst Dx, Coag Dx and ProCyte Dx; and the hand-held IDEXX SNAPshot Dx rapid assay test kits which provide quick, accurate and convenient point-of-care diagnostic test results. Catalyst SDMA allows customers to use the Catalyst One and Catalyst Dx to screen for symmetrical dimethyl arginine (SDMA), a biomarker that detects kidney disease. In addition, the company provides assay kits, software and instrumentation for accurate assessment of infectious disease in production animals, such as cattle, swine and poultry. IDEXX's principal product for use in testing for antibiotic residue in milk is the SNAP Beta-Lactam test, which detects penicillin, amoxicillin, ampicillin, ceftiofur and cephapirin residues. SNAPduo Beta-Tetra ST detects certain tetracycline antibiotic residues in addition to those detected by the Beta-Lactam test kits. Last, water quality products include Colilert, Colilert-18 and Colisure tests, which simultaneously detect total coliforms and E. coli in water; Enterolert products detect the presence of enterococci in waters; Pseudalert detects pseudomonas in waters; Filta-Max products detect cryptosporidium and giardia in water; Legiolert detects legionella pneumophila in water; and Quanti-Tray products measure microbial contamination in water. In mid-2021, IDEXX acquired ezyVet.

FINANCIAL DATA: Note: Data for latest year may not have been available at press time.

In U.S. $	2020	2019	2018	2017	2016	2015
Revenue	2,706,655,000	2,406,908,000	2,213,242,000	1,969,058,000	1,775,423,000	1,601,892,000
R&D Expense	141,249,000	133,193,000	117,863,000	109,182,000	101,122,000	99,681,000
Operating Income	694,524,000	552,846,000	491,335,000	413,028,000	350,239,000	308,124,000
Operating Margin %		.23%	.22%	.21%	.20%	.19%
SGA Expense	735,267,000	679,510,000	632,344,000	575,172,000	524,075,000	482,465,000
Net Income	581,776,000	427,720,000	377,031,000	263,144,000	222,045,000	192,078,000
Operating Cash Flow	648,063,000	459,158,000	400,084,000	373,276,000	334,571,000	216,364,000
Capital Expenditure	107,876,000	155,224,000	122,936,000	76,704,000	64,787,000	82,921,000
EBITDA	791,108,000	641,284,000	575,664,000	501,422,000	432,113,000	371,336,000
Return on Assets %		.25%	.23%	.16%	.15%	.13%
Return on Equity %		5.09%				11.50%
Debt to Equity		4.318				

CONTACT INFORMATION:

Phone: 207 556-0300   Fax: 207 856-0346
Toll-Free: 800-548-6733
Address: 1 Idexx Dr., Westbrook, ME 04092 United States

STOCK TICKER/OTHER:

Stock Ticker: IDXX
Employees: 9,300
Parent Company:

Exchange: NAS
Fiscal Year Ends: 12/31

SALARIES/BONUSES:

Top Exec. Salary: $ Bonus: $
Second Exec. Salary: $ Bonus: $

OTHER THOUGHTS:

Estimated Female Officers or Directors: 2
Hot Spot for Advancement for Women/Minorities: Y

II-VI Incorporated

NAIC Code: 334513

TYPES OF BUSINESS:

Infrared Instruments, Industrial Process-Type, Manufacturing
Engineered Materials Manufacturing
Optoelectronic Components Manufacturing

BRANDS/DIVISIONS/AFFILIATES:

Ascatron AB
INNOViON Corporation

CONTACTS: Note: Officers with more than one job title may be intentionally listed here more than once.

Mary Raymond, Assistant Secretary
Vincent Mattera, CEO
Giovanni Barbarossa, Chief Technology Officer
Gary Kapusta, COO
Francis Kramer, Director
Jo Anne Schwendinger, Other Executive Officer
David Wagner, Vice President, Divisional

GROWTH PLANS/SPECIAL FEATURES:

II-VI Incorporated develops, manufactures and market engineered materials, optoelectronic components and devices for precision use in an array of applications and markets. II-VI is pronounced as Two Six, which stands for Groups II and VI on the Periodic Table of Elements and the firm's originally-designed and produced infrared optics for high-power CO2 lasers used in materials processing. The company's products address the applications and markets of industrial materials processing, optical communications, military, consumer electronics, semiconductor equipment, life sciences and automotive electronics. II-VI uses advanced engineered materials growth technologies with proprietary high-precision fabrication, micro-assembly, optical thin-film coating and electronic integration to manufacture complex optoelectronic devices and modules. These products are deployed in applications such as laser cutting, welding, marking, 3D sensing, optical, data/wireless communications, military intelligence/surveillance/reconnaissance, semiconductor processing/tooling, thermoelectric cooling and power generation. II-VI also offers a broad portfolio of compound semiconductor lasers used in most of its end markets, including wireless handsets, tablets and the Internet of Things (IoT). Products are categorized into two business units: photonic solutions and compound semiconductors. Based in Pennsylvania, USA, the firm has R&D, engineering, manufacturing and sales facilities worldwide, including China, Singapore, Vietnam, Philippines, Germany, Switzerland and the U.K. During 2020, II-VI acquired Ascatron AB, which produces silicon carbide (SiC) epitaxial wafers and devices for power electronics; and acquired the remining interest it did not own in INNOViON Corporation, a provider of ion implantation services that support unique capabilities in semiconductor materials processing.

FINANCIAL DATA: Note: Data for latest year may not have been available at press time.

In U.S. $	2020	2019	2018	2017	2016	2015
Revenue	2,380,071,000	1,362,496,000	1,158,794,000	972,046,000	827,216,000	
R&D Expense	339,073,000	139,163,000	117,244,000	96,810,000	60,354,000	
Operating Income	39,479,000	148,668,000	135,287,000	115,541,000	91,813,000	
Operating Margin %		.11%	.12%	.12%	.11%	
SGA Expense	440,998,000	233,518,000	208,757,000	176,002,000	160,646,000	
Net Income	-67,029,000	107,517,000	88,002,000	95,274,000	65,486,000	
Operating Cash Flow	297,292,000	178,475,000	161,014,000	118,616,000	122,970,000	
Capital Expenditure	140,627,000	137,122,000	153,438,000	138,517,000	58,170,000	
EBITDA	246,363,000	243,595,000	221,316,000	189,234,000	149,699,000	
Return on Assets %		.06%	.05%	.07%	.06%	
Return on Equity %		.10%	.09%	.11%	.09%	
Debt to Equity		0.391	0.409	0.384	0.276	

CONTACT INFORMATION:

Phone: 724 352-4455   Fax: 724 352-4980
Toll-Free:
Address: 375 Saxonburg Blvd., Saxonburg, PA 16056 United States

STOCK TICKER/OTHER:

Stock Ticker: IIVI   Exchange: NAS
Employees: 22,969   Fiscal Year Ends: 06/30
Parent Company:

SALARIES/BONUSES:

Top Exec. Salary: $ Bonus: $
Second Exec. Salary: $ Bonus: $

OTHER THOUGHTS:

Estimated Female Officers or Directors:
Hot Spot for Advancement for Women/Minorities:

Illumina Inc

www.illumina.com

NAIC Code: 325413

TYPES OF BUSINESS:

DNA Analysis Technology
Array Technology
Genotyping Services

BRANDS/DIVISIONS/AFFILIATES:

BeadArray

CONTACTS: Note: Officers with more than one job title may be intentionally listed here more than once.

Francis DeSouza, CEO
Sam Samad, CFO
Mostafa Ronaghi, Chief Technology Officer
Jay Flatley, Director
Charles Dadswell, General Counsel
Oene Van, Other Executive Officer
Aimee Hoyt, Other Executive Officer
Malcolm Hampton, Senior VP, Divisional
Omead Ostadan, Senior VP, Divisional
Robert Ragusa, Senior VP, Divisional
Karen McGinnis, Vice President

GROWTH PLANS/SPECIAL FEATURES:

Illumina, Inc. provides sequencing- and array-based solutions for genetic analysis. The firm's products and services enable the adoption of genomics solutions in research and clinical settings. Customers include genomic research centers, academic institutions, government laboratories and hospitals, as well as pharmaceutical, biotechnology, commercial molecular diagnostic and consumer genomics companies. Most of the company's product sales consist of instruments and consumables based on proprietary technology, including reagents, flow cells and microarrays. Illumina's genome discovery platform involves sequencing, arrays and consumables. Sequencing is the process of determining the order of nucleotide bases (A, C, G or T) in a DNA sample. Customers use the platforms to perform whole-genome and exome sequencing, as well as targeted sequencing of specific gene regions and genes. Arrays are used for a broad range of DNA (deoxyribonucleic acid) and RNA (ribonucleic acid) analysis applications, including single nucleotide polymorphism (SNP) genotyping, copy number variations (CNV) analysis, gene expression analysis and methylation analysis. The technology allows for the detection of millions of known genetic markers on a single array. The firm's BeadArray technology combines microscopic beads and a substrate in a proprietary manufacturing process to produce arrays that can perform many assays simultaneously. Consumables involve the array-based genotyping consumables that customers use for analyses, including diverse species, disease-related mutations and genetic characteristics associated with cancer. Customers can select from a range of human, animal and agriculturally-relevant genome panels or create their own. Illumina owns or has exclusive licenses to 901 U.S. patents and 650 pending U.S. patent applications, which cover various aspects of its arrays, assays, oligo synthesis, sequencing technology, instruments, digital microfluidics, software, bioinformatics and chemical-detection technologies.

Illumina offers its employees comprehensive benefits, which vary by location.

FINANCIAL DATA: Note: Data for latest year may not have been available at press time.

In U.S. $	2020	2019	2018	2017	2016	2015
Revenue	3,239,000,000	3,543,000,000	3,333,000,000	2,752,000,000	2,398,373,000	2,219,762,000
R&D Expense	682,000,000	647,000,000	623,000,000	546,000,000	504,415,000	401,527,000
Operating Income	580,000,000	985,000,000	883,000,000	606,000,000	579,028,000	623,106,000
Operating Margin %		.28%	.26%	.22%	.24%	.28%
SGA Expense	941,000,000	835,000,000	794,000,000	674,000,000	583,005,000	524,657,000
Net Income	656,000,000	1,002,000,000	826,000,000	726,000,000	462,649,000	461,559,000
Operating Cash Flow	1,080,000,000	1,051,000,000	1,142,000,000	875,000,000	687,238,000	659,596,000
Capital Expenditure	189,000,000	209,000,000	296,000,000	312,000,000	271,381,000	143,247,000
EBITDA	1,092,000,000	1,358,000,000	1,130,000,000	1,236,000,000	735,274,000	751,682,000
Return on Assets %		.14%	.14%	.15%	.11%	.13%
Return on Equity %		.24%	.25%	.29%	.22%	.28%
Debt to Equity		0.398	0.237	0.43	0.477	0.549

CONTACT INFORMATION:

Phone: 858 202-4500 Fax: 858 587-4297
Toll-Free: 800-809-4566
Address: 5200 Illumina Way, San Diego, CA 92122 United States

STOCK TICKER/OTHER:

Stock Ticker: ILMN
Employees: 7,700
Parent Company:

Exchange: NAS
Fiscal Year Ends: 12/31

SALARIES/BONUSES:

Top Exec. Salary: $ Bonus: $
Second Exec. Salary: $ Bonus: $

OTHER THOUGHTS:

Estimated Female Officers or Directors:
Hot Spot for Advancement for Women/Minorities:

Ingles Markets Incorporated

www.ingles-markets.com

NAIC Code: 445110

TYPES OF BUSINESS:

Grocery Stores
Shopping Centers
Dairy Processing
Juices
Bottled Water
Gas Stations
Pharmacies

BRANDS/DIVISIONS/AFFILIATES:

Ingles
Sav-Mor
Laura Lynn
Milkco Inc

CONTACTS: *Note: Officers with more than one job title may be intentionally listed here more than once.*

James Lanning, CEO
Ronald Freeman, CFO
Robert Ingle, Chairman of the Board
L. Collins, President, Subsidiary
Patricia Jackson, Secretary

GROWTH PLANS/SPECIAL FEATURES:

Ingles Markets, Incorporated operates supermarkets and shopping centers in the southeastern U.S., primarily under the Ingles brand name, but also under the Sav-Mor brand name. As of September 30, 2020, the company operated 197 supermarkets located in North Carolina (73), Georgia (66), South Carolina (35), Tennessee (21), Virginia (1) and Alabama (1). Ingles supermarkets offer a wide variety of nationally advertised food products, including fresh meat, dairy products, produce, frozen foods and non-food products such as health and beauty care items, general merchandise and private-label goods (under the Laura Lynn brand). In addition, Ingles focuses on selling high-growth, high-margin products to its customers through the development of book sections, media centers, floral departments, bakery departments and prepared foods. Ingles operates pharmacies and fuel stations at many of its stores. The firm comprises a 919,000-square-foot warehouse and distribution facility in Asheville, North Carolina; and an 839,000-square-foot warehouse and distribution facility adjacent to the Asheville distribution site. Ingles maintains its own fleet of tractor-trailer trucks for distribution purposes. Milkco, Inc., a fluid dairy processing subsidiary, provides most of the company's supermarkets with dairy products, citrus juices and bottled water products.

Ingles Markets offers its employees medical plans, dental and vision coverage, 401(k), life and short-term disability insurance, and a variety of employee assistance plans, programs and perks.

FINANCIAL DATA: *Note: Data for latest year may not have been available at press time.*

In U.S. $	2020	2019	2018	2017	2016	2015
Revenue	4,610,609,000	4,202,034,000	4,092,805,000	4,002,700,000	3,794,977,000	3,778,644,000
R&D Expense						
Operating Income	276,502,700	148,140,800	124,095,300	126,448,100	129,810,500	136,990,800
Operating Margin %		.04%	.03%	.03%	.03%	.04%
SGA Expense	921,749,200	873,859,500	856,074,100	837,144,800	794,594,600	756,313,000
Net Income	178,601,400	81,580,000	97,364,620	53,873,580	54,189,460	59,353,120
Operating Cash Flow	350,117,100	211,503,200	161,240,100	156,340,300	159,030,800	153,465,200
Capital Expenditure	122,767,200	161,751,000	150,486,500	127,695,600	137,642,100	104,056,000
EBITDA	391,855,800	266,528,200	240,971,000	242,649,000	237,552,400	244,341,900
Return on Assets %		.04%	.05%	.03%	.03%	.04%
Return on Equity %		.13%	.18%	.11%	.12%	.15%
Debt to Equity		1.267	1.432	1.694	1.843	2.058

CONTACT INFORMATION:

Phone: 828 669-2941   Fax: 828 669-3668
Toll-Free:
Address: PO Box 6676, Asheville, NC 28816 United States

SALARIES/BONUSES:

Top Exec. Salary: $ Bonus: $
Second Exec. Salary: $ Bonus: $

STOCK TICKER/OTHER:

Stock Ticker: IMKTA   Exchange: NAS
Employees: 27,000   Fiscal Year Ends: 09/30
Parent Company:

OTHER THOUGHTS:

Estimated Female Officers or Directors: 1
Hot Spot for Advancement for Women/Minorities:

Ingredion Incorporated

www.ingredion.com

NAIC Code: 311221

TYPES OF BUSINESS:

Food Products, Manufacturing
Wet Milling
Food Ingredients
Starch-Based Products
Cornstarch
Liquid Sweeteners

BRANDS/DIVISIONS/AFFILIATES:

CONTACTS: *Note: Officers with more than one job title may be intentionally listed here more than once.*

James Zallie, CEO
Gregory Kenny, Director
Jorgen Kokke, Executive VP, Divisional
James Gray, Executive VP
Elizabeth Adefioye, Other Executive Officer
Larry Fernandes, Other Executive Officer
Robert Stefansic, Other Executive Officer
Anthony Delio, Other Executive Officer
Pierre Perez Landazuri, President, Divisional
Valdirene Bastos-Licht, President, Geographical
Ernesto Peres Pousada, President, Geographical
Stephen Latreille, Vice President

GROWTH PLANS/SPECIAL FEATURES:

Ingredion Incorporated is one of the world's largest corn refiners and a major supplier of food ingredients and industrial products derived from wet milling and processing of corn and other starch-based materials such as tapioca, potatoes and rice. Corn processing is a two-step process. During the front-end process, corn is steeped in a water-based solution and separated into starch and other co-products such as animal feed and germ. The starch is then dried for sale or further processed to make sweeteners and other ingredients that serve the particular needs of various industries. The company's sweetener products include high fructose corn syrup, glucose corn syrups, high maltose corn syrups, caramel color, dextrose, polyols, maltodextrins and glucose and corn syrup solids. Starch-based products include both industrial and food-grade starches. Ingredion's specialty ingredients comprise select starch and sweetener ingredients that provide clean-label solutions that enable front-of-pack claims for customers. The firm serves customers in many diverse industries, including the food and beverage, pharmaceutical, paper products, laminated paper, textile and brewing industries as well as the global animal feed and corn oil markets. Ingredion supplies a broad range of customers, including food, beverage, brewing, pharmaceutical, paper/corrugated products, textile, personal care, animal feed and corn oil markets. Ingredion owns and operates manufacturing facilities and innovation centers worldwide.

FINANCIAL DATA: *Note: Data for latest year may not have been available at press time.*

In U.S. $	2020	2019	2018	2017	2016	2015
Revenue	5,987,000,000	6,209,000,000	6,289,000,000	6,180,000,000	6,022,000,000	5,958,000,000
R&D Expense						
Operating Income	675,000,000	721,000,000	767,000,000	871,000,000	827,000,000	685,000,000
Operating Margin %		.12%	.12%	.14%	.14%	.11%
SGA Expense					579,000,000	555,000,000
Net Income	348,000,000	413,000,000	443,000,000	519,000,000	485,000,000	402,000,000
Operating Cash Flow	829,000,000	680,000,000	703,000,000	769,000,000	771,000,000	686,000,000
Capital Expenditure	340,000,000	328,000,000	350,000,000	314,000,000	284,000,000	280,000,000
EBITDA	787,000,000	886,000,000	949,000,000	1,057,000,000	1,011,000,000	862,000,000
Return on Assets %		.07%	.08%	.09%	.09%	.08%
Return on Equity %		.16%	.17%	.19%	.21%	.19%
Debt to Equity		0.693	0.809	0.603	0.721	0.848

CONTACT INFORMATION:

Phone: 708-551-2600   Fax: 708-551-2700
Toll-Free: 800-443-2746
Address: 5 Westbrook Corporate Ctr., Westchester, IL 60154 United States

STOCK TICKER/OTHER:

Stock Ticker: INGR
Employees: 11,000
Parent Company:

Exchange: NYS
Fiscal Year Ends: 12/31

SALARIES/BONUSES:

Top Exec. Salary: $ Bonus: $
Second Exec. Salary: $ Bonus: $

OTHER THOUGHTS:

Estimated Female Officers or Directors: 7
Hot Spot for Advancement for Women/Minorities: Y

In-N-Out Burgers Inc

in-n-out.com

NAIC Code: 722513

TYPES OF BUSINESS:

Fast-Food Restaurants
Fast Food Restaurants
Hamburgers

BRANDS/DIVISIONS/AFFILIATES:

In-N-Out Burger
Animal Style

CONTACTS: *Note: Officers with more than one job title may be intentionally listed here more than once.*

Lynsi Snyder, Pres.

GROWTH PLANS/SPECIAL FEATURES:

In-N-Out Burgers, Inc. is a chain of fast food restaurants that began in 1948 and primarily serve hamburgers, French fries, ice cream shakes and beverages. Founded in Baldwin Park, California, it has slowly expanded outside of the state and into Arizona, Nevada, Colorado, Utah, Oregon and Texas with over 355 locations (as of early-2020). Hamburgers and cheeseburgers consist of 100% pure beef, American cheese, leaf lettuce, tomato, a special spread, with or without onions and stacked high on a freshly-baked bun. The restaurants have an extras menu where hamburger choices include double meat; 3x3, containing three patties and three slices of cheese; 4x4, four patties and four slices of cheese; protein style, the burger wrapped in lettuce instead of a bun; and Animal Style, which is any size burger choice with the patties cooked with mustard and all the fixings. All hamburger patties are free of additives, fillers and preservatives of any kind. The firm pays a premium to purchase fresh, high quality beef chuck, and has in-house butchers that remove the bones, grind the meat and make every patty ready for cooking. Potatoes are shipped directly from farms, individually cut in the firm's stores, then cooked in 100% pure vegetable oil. Shakes are made with milk and real ice cream. Typical fast-food equipment such as heat lamps, microwaves and freezers are never found in an In-N-Out Burgers kitchen. The company's website offers products for purchase such as apparel and gift cards, as well as limited time offers. In-N-Out cookout trailers can be reserved for parties, weddings or other events.

In-N-Out Burger offers its employees career growth opportunities, 401(k)/profit sharing, paid vacations and company perks.

FINANCIAL DATA: *Note: Data for latest year may not have been available at press time.*

In U.S. $	2020	2019	2018	2017	2016	2015
Revenue	982,437,750	1,034,145,000	984,900,000	938,000,000	870,000,000	740,000,000
R&D Expense						
Operating Income						
Operating Margin %						
SGA Expense						
Net Income		99,807,000	96,900,000	95,000,000	88,000,000	75,000,000
Operating Cash Flow						
Capital Expenditure						
EBITDA						
Return on Assets %						
Return on Equity %						
Debt to Equity						

CONTACT INFORMATION:

Phone: 949-509-6200   Fax: 949-509-6389
Toll-Free: 800-786-1000
Address: 4199 Campus Dr., 9/Fl, Irvine, CA 92612 United States

SALARIES/BONUSES:

Top Exec. Salary: $ Bonus: $
Second Exec. Salary: $ Bonus: $

STOCK TICKER/OTHER:

Stock Ticker: Private
Employees: 26,000
Parent Company:

Exchange:
Fiscal Year Ends: 12/31

OTHER THOUGHTS:

Estimated Female Officers or Directors:
Hot Spot for Advancement for Women/Minorities: Y

Insight Enterprises Inc

www.insight.com

NAIC Code: 423430

TYPES OF BUSINESS:

Computer & Electronic Products, Direct Selling
IT Business Hardware
IT Business Software

BRANDS/DIVISIONS/AFFILIATES:

CONTACTS:
Note: Officers with more than one job title may be intentionally listed here more than once.

Kenneth Lamneck, CEO
Helen Johnson, CFO, Geographical
Timothy Crown, Chairman of the Board
Rachael Bertrandt, Chief Accounting Officer
Michael Guggemos, Chief Information Officer
Samuel Cowley, General Counsel
Steven Dodenhoff, President, Geographical
Wolfgang Ebermann, President, Geographical

GROWTH PLANS/SPECIAL FEATURES:

Insight Enterprises, Inc. provides intelligent information technology (IT) solutions and services to businesses, government, healthcare and educational clients globally. The company's products offer organizations of all sizes insight for maximizing IT business value. Insight Enterprises' products, solutions and services are distributed through three geographical segments: North America, representing approximately 75% of consolidated net sales; and EMEA (Europe, Middle East and Africa) and APAC (Asia-Pacific) each representing the remainder. Offerings in North America and certain countries in EMEA and APAC include hardware, software and services. Offerings in the remainder of EMEA and APAC consist largely of software and software-related services. Insight Enterprises offers hardware products from hundreds of manufacturers to meet its clients' specific business needs. These manufacturers include Cisco, Dell/EMC, HP, Lenovo, NetApp, Apple, Microsoft and IBM. In addition to Insight Enterprises' distribution facilities, the company has direct-ship programs with many partners, including manufacturers and distributors. Insight Enterprises offers software products from hundreds of publishers, including industry leaders such as Microsoft, VMware, Adobe and IBM. Insight Enterprises' services solutions span supply chain optimization, connected workforce, cloud and data center transformation and digital innovation, helping clients innovate and optimize operations so they can run more intelligently. Insight Enterprises has operations in more than 20 countries, and partnerships with 3,500+ software and hardware manufacturers and publishers.

FINANCIAL DATA:
Note: Data for latest year may not have been available at press time.

In U.S. $	2020	2019	2018	2017	2016	2015
Revenue	8,340,579,000	7,731,190,000	7,080,136,000	6,703,623,000	5,485,515,000	5,373,090,000
R&D Expense						
Operating Income	286,177,000	257,361,000	237,189,000	195,242,000	157,859,000	131,426,000
Operating Margin %		.03%	.03%	.03%	.03%	.02%
SGA Expense	950,704,000	834,528,000	719,071,000	723,328,000	585,243,000	584,906,000
Net Income	172,640,000	159,407,000	163,677,000	90,683,000	84,690,000	75,851,000
Operating Cash Flow	355,582,000	127,876,000	292,647,000	-305,426,000	95,805,000	180,510,000
Capital Expenditure	24,184,000	69,086,000	17,251,000	19,230,000	12,266,000	13,416,000
EBITDA	335,606,000	286,403,000	272,172,000	220,871,000	186,216,000	164,357,000
Return on Assets %		.05%	.06%	.04%	.04%	.04%
Return on Equity %		.15%	.18%	.12%	.12%	.11%
Debt to Equity		0.739	0.198	0.352	0.056	0.13

CONTACT INFORMATION:

Phone: 480 902-1001   Fax: 480 902-1180
Toll-Free: 800-467-4448
Address: 6820 South Harl Ave., Tempe, AZ 85283 United States

SALARIES/BONUSES:

Top Exec. Salary: $ Bonus: $
Second Exec. Salary: $ Bonus: $

STOCK TICKER/OTHER:

Stock Ticker: NSIT
Employees: 5,930
Parent Company:

Exchange: NAS
Fiscal Year Ends: 12/31

OTHER THOUGHTS:

Estimated Female Officers or Directors: 4
Hot Spot for Advancement for Women/Minorities: Y

Intel Corporation

NAIC Code: 334413

TYPES OF BUSINESS:

Microprocessors
Semiconductors
Circuit Boards
Flash Memory Products
Software Development
Home Network Equipment
Digital Imaging Products
Healthcare Products

BRANDS/DIVISIONS/AFFILIATES:

Intel Neural Compute Stick 2
Moovit

CONTACTS: Note: Officers with more than one job title may be intentionally listed here more than once.

Robert Swan, CEO
George Davis, CFO
Andy Bryant, Chairman of the Board
Kevin McBride, Chief Accounting Officer
Steven Rodgers, Executive VP
Navin Shenoy, Executive VP
Venkata Renduchintala, Executive VP
Todd Underwood, Other Corporate Officer

GROWTH PLANS/SPECIAL FEATURES:

Intel Corporation designs and manufactures products and technologies that power the cloud and smart connectivity. The company produces computer, networking and communications platforms to a broad set of customers, including original equipment manufacturers (OEMs), original design manufacturers (ODMs), cloud and communications service providers, as well as industrial, communications and automotive equipment manufacturers. Intel's business across the cloud and data center are focused on memory and field-programmable gate array technologies. Its devices include everything smart: personal computers (PCs), sensors, consoles and other edge devices that are connected to the cloud. Memory and programmable solutions make possible new classes of products for the data center and Internet of Things (IoT). Its Intel Neural Compute Stick 2 (Intel NCS 2) is designed to build smarter artificial intelligence (AI) algorithms and for prototyping computer vision at the network edge. Intel is a leader in silicon manufacturing process technology, of which its products are manufactured in the company's own facilities. Its intellectual property can be shared across its platforms and operating segments, providing cost reduction and seamless production capabilities. Intel also offers software and services for consumer and corporate environments, as well as for assisting software developers in creating software applications via Intel platforms. Its client computing product group includes platforms for notebooks, 2-in-1 systems, desktops, tablets, phones, wired/wireless connectivity products and mobile communications components. The firm's non-volatile memory solutions (NAND) flash memory products are primarily used in solid-state drives. In May 2020, Intel acquired Moovit, a mobility-as-a-service solutions company, for approximately $900 million. In October of the same year, the firm announced that it will acquire SigOpt, a provider of a platform for the optimization of AI software models at scale.

FINANCIAL DATA: Note: Data for latest year may not have been available at press time.

In U.S. $	2020	2019	2018	2017	2016	2015
Revenue	77,867,000,000	71,965,000,000	70,848,000,000	62,761,000,000	59,387,000,000	55,355,000,000
R&D Expense	13,556,000,000	13,362,000,000	13,543,000,000	13,098,000,000	12,740,000,000	12,128,000,000
Operating Income	23,876,000,000	22,428,000,000	23,244,000,000	18,320,000,000	14,760,000,000	14,356,000,000
Operating Margin %		.31%	.33%	.29%	.25%	.26%
SGA Expense	6,180,000,000	6,150,000,000	6,750,000,000	7,474,000,000	8,397,000,000	7,930,000,000
Net Income	20,899,000,000	21,048,000,000	21,053,000,000	9,601,000,000	10,316,000,000	11,420,000,000
Operating Cash Flow	35,384,000,000	33,145,000,000	29,432,000,000	22,110,000,000	21,808,000,000	19,017,000,000
Capital Expenditure	14,453,000,000	16,213,000,000	15,181,000,000	11,778,000,000	9,625,000,000	7,446,000,000
EBITDA	37,946,000,000	35,373,000,000	32,870,000,000	29,127,000,000	21,459,000,000	23,260,000,000
Return on Assets %		.16%	.17%	.08%	.10%	.12%
Return on Equity %		.28%	.29%	.14%	.16%	.19%
Debt to Equity		0.326	0.335	0.358	0.308	0.323

CONTACT INFORMATION:

Phone: 408 765-8080   Fax: 408 765-2633
Toll-Free: 800-628-8686
Address: 2200 Mission College Blvd., Santa Clara, CA 95054 United States

STOCK TICKER/OTHER:

Stock Ticker: INTC   Exchange: NAS
Employees: 110,600   Fiscal Year Ends: 12/31
Parent Company:

SALARIES/BONUSES:

Top Exec. Salary: $ Bonus: $
Second Exec. Salary: $ Bonus: $

OTHER THOUGHTS:

Estimated Female Officers or Directors: 10
Hot Spot for Advancement for Women/Minorities: Y

Intuit Inc

NAIC Code: 511210Q

www.intuit.com

TYPES OF BUSINESS:

Computer Software-Financial Management
Business Accounting Software
Consumer Finance Software
Tax Preparation Software
Online Financial Services

BRANDS/DIVISIONS/AFFILIATES:

QuickBooks Online
Mint
Turbo
Turbo Tax
Lacerte
ProSeries
ProConnect Tax Online
Intuit Financial Freedom Foundation

CONTACTS: *Note: Officers with more than one job title may be intentionally listed here more than once.*

Sasan Goodarzi, CEO
Michelle Clatterbuck, CFO
Brad Smith, Chairman of the Board
Mark Flournoy, Chief Accounting Officer
Marianna Tessel, Chief Technology Officer
Alex Chriss, Executive VP, Divisional
Gregory Johnson, Executive VP
Laura Fennell, Executive VP
Scott Cook, Founder
Kerry McLean, General Counsel

GROWTH PLANS/SPECIAL FEATURES:

Intuit, Inc. is a provider of software and web-based services, specializing in financial management and tax solutions. The company has three business segments: small business, consumer and strategic partner. The small business segment targets small businesses, as well as the accounting professionals who serve them. This division's products include QuickBooks financial and business management online services and desktop software, payroll solutions, merchant payment processing solutions, and financing for small businesses. The consumer segment offers the Mint and Turbo brands of financial improvement products. Mint and Turbo help consumers understand and improve their financial lives by offering a view of their financial health. Turbo Tax solutions are designed to enable individuals to prepare and file their own federal and state personal income tax returns quickly and accurately. The strategic partner segment targets professional accountants in the U.S. and Canada, who are essential to both small business success and tax preparation and filing. This division's tax offerings include Lacerte, ProSeries, ProFile and ProConnect Tax Online. Additionally, through the Intuit Financial Freedom Foundation the firm sponsors programs and projects that promote financial literacy and independence among lower and middle-income individuals, families, entrepreneurs and small businesses. In December 2020, Intuit completed its acquisition of Credit Karma, Inc., a consumer technology platform with more than 110 million members in the U.S., Canada and U.K., for approximately $7.1 billion in cash and stock.

FINANCIAL DATA: *Note: Data for latest year may not have been available at press time.*

In U.S. $	2020	2019	2018	2017	2016	2015
Revenue	7,679,000,000	6,784,000,000	5,964,000,000	5,177,000,000	4,694,000,000	4,192,000,000
R&D Expense	1,392,000,000	1,233,000,000	1,186,000,000	998,000,000	881,000,000	798,000,000
Operating Income	2,176,000,000	1,854,000,000	1,497,000,000	1,395,000,000	1,242,000,000	886,000,000
Operating Margin %		.27%	.25%	.27%	.26%	.21%
SGA Expense	2,727,000,000	2,524,000,000	2,298,000,000	1,973,000,000	1,807,000,000	1,771,000,000
Net Income	1,826,000,000	1,557,000,000	1,211,000,000	971,000,000	979,000,000	365,000,000
Operating Cash Flow	2,414,000,000	2,324,000,000	2,112,000,000	1,599,000,000	1,401,000,000	1,504,000,000
Capital Expenditure	137,000,000	155,000,000	124,000,000	230,000,000	522,000,000	261,000,000
EBITDA	2,430,000,000	2,121,000,000	1,776,000,000	1,634,000,000	1,476,000,000	970,000,000
Return on Assets %		.27%	.26%	.23%	.21%	.07%
Return on Equity %		.51%	.65%	.77%	.56%	.13%
Debt to Equity		0.103	0.165	0.323	0.42	0.214

CONTACT INFORMATION:

Phone: 650 944-6000   Fax: 650 944-3060
Toll-Free: 800-446-8848
Address: 2700 Coast Ave., Mountain View, CA 94043 United States

STOCK TICKER/OTHER:

Stock Ticker: INTU
Employees: 10,600
Parent Company:

Exchange: NAS
Fiscal Year Ends: 07/31

SALARIES/BONUSES:

Top Exec. Salary: $ Bonus: $
Second Exec. Salary: $ Bonus: $

OTHER THOUGHTS:

Estimated Female Officers or Directors: 5
Hot Spot for Advancement for Women/Minorities: Y

IQVIA Holdings Inc

NAIC Code: 541711

www.iqvia.com

TYPES OF BUSINESS:
Contract Research
Pharmaceutical, Biotech & Medical Device Research
Consulting & Training Services
Sales & Marketing Services

BRANDS/DIVISIONS/AFFILIATES:
IQVIA CORE
Q2 Solutions

CONTACTS: *Note: Officers with more than one job title may be intentionally listed here more than once.*
Michael Mcdonnell, CFO
Ari Bousbib, Chairman of the Board
Emmanuel Korakis, Chief Accounting Officer
Eric Sherbet, Executive VP
W. Staub, President, Divisional
Kevin Knightly, President, Divisional

GROWTH PLANS/SPECIAL FEATURES:
IQVIA Holdings, Inc. provides advanced analytics, technology solutions and contract research services to the life sciences industry. The firm applies human data science, leveraging analytics and data science to the scope of human science, to enable companies to reimagine and develop new approaches to clinical development and commercialization, speed innovation and accelerate improvements in healthcare outcomes. Its IQVIA CORE platform delivers actionable insights at the intersection of large-scale analytics, transformative technology and extensive domain expertise as well as execution capabilities to help biotech, medical device and pharmaceutical companies, medical researchers, government agencies, payers and other healthcare stakeholders better understand diseases, human behaviors and scientific advances, for the purpose of finding cures. Capabilities of the company include healthcare-specific global IT infrastructure, analytics-driven clinical development, artificial intelligence, machine learning, human data science, decentralized trials, proprietary clinical and commercial applications and more. IQVIA'a product portfolio spans research and development, pre-launch, launch and in-market. The company conducts operations in more than 100 countries worldwide. In April 2021, IQVIA acquired the 40% minority share of Q2 Solutions from Quest Diagnostics, resulting in 100% ownership by IQVIA. Q2 Solutions is a global clinical laboratory services organization that provides comprehensive testing, project management, supply chain, biorepository and biospecimen and consent tracking solutions for clinical trials.

FINANCIAL DATA: *Note: Data for latest year may not have been available at press time.*

In U.S. $	2020	2019	2018	2017	2016	2015
Revenue	11,359,000,000	11,088,000,000	10,412,000,000	9,739,000,000	6,878,000,000	5,737,619,000
R&D Expense						
Operating Income	783,000,000	852,000,000	809,000,000	822,000,000	828,000,000	679,848,000
Operating Margin %		.08%	.08%	.08%	.12%	.12%
SGA Expense	1,789,000,000	1,734,000,000	1,716,000,000	1,605,000,000	1,011,000,000	920,985,000
Net Income	279,000,000	191,000,000	259,000,000	1,309,000,000	115,000,000	387,205,000
Operating Cash Flow	1,959,000,000	1,417,000,000	1,254,000,000	970,000,000	860,000,000	475,691,000
Capital Expenditure	616,000,000	582,000,000	459,000,000	369,000,000	164,000,000	78,391,000
EBITDA	2,076,000,000	2,001,000,000	1,883,000,000	1,688,000,000	912,000,000	768,529,000
Return on Assets %		.01%	.01%	.06%	.01%	.11%
Return on Equity %		.03%	.03%	.16%	.03%	
Debt to Equity		1.989	1.625	1.248	0.823	

CONTACT INFORMATION:
Phone: 919-998-2000   Fax:
Toll-Free: 866-267-4479
Address: 4820 Emperor Blvd., Durham, NC 27703 United States

STOCK TICKER/OTHER:
Stock Ticker: IQV   Exchange: NYS
Employees: 67,000   Fiscal Year Ends: 12/31
Parent Company:

SALARIES/BONUSES:
Top Exec. Salary: $ Bonus: $
Second Exec. Salary: $ Bonus: $

OTHER THOUGHTS:
Estimated Female Officers or Directors: 3
Hot Spot for Advancement for Women/Minorities: Y

Itron Inc

NAIC Code: 334515

www.itron.com

TYPES OF BUSINESS:

Wireless Meter Reading Transmitters
Data Collection Systems & Software
Industrial Internet of Things
Meters
Sensors
Software

BRANDS/DIVISIONS/AFFILIATES:

CONTACTS: Note: Officers with more than one job title may be intentionally listed here more than once.

Philip Mezey, CEO
Joan Hooper, CFO
Lynda Ziegler, Chairman of the Board
Thomas Deitrich, Executive VP
Sarah Hlavinka, General Counsel
Michel Cadieux, Senior VP, Divisional

GROWTH PLANS/SPECIAL FEATURES:

Itron, Inc. is a technology company and leader in the Industrial Internet of Things (IIoT), enabling utilities and cities to deliver critical infrastructure solutions to communities in more than 100 countries. The firm's platform integrates smart networks, software, services, devices and sensors so that customers can better manage their operations in the energy, water and smart city spaces. Itron operates through three segments: device solutions, networked solutions and outcomes. The device solutions segment includes hardware products used for measurement, control or sensing, such as gas, electricity and water meters. The networked solutions segment includes a combination of communicating devices, network infrastructure and associated application software designed and sold as a complete solution for acquiring and transporting application-specific data. Products in this division include software for the implementation, installation and management of communicating devices and data networks. IIoT solutions supported by this segment include automated meter reading, advanced metering infrastructure, smart grid and distribution automation, smart street lighting and gas/water systems. Last, the outcomes segment offers value-added, enhanced software and services in which Itron then manages, organizes, analyzes and interprets data for the goal of improving efficiency and decision making, maximizing operational profitability and delivering results for consumers, utilities and smart cities.

Itron offers its employees retirement and health benefits as well as access to the Itron Employee Emergency Foundation.

FINANCIAL DATA: Note: Data for latest year may not have been available at press time.

In U.S. $	2020	2019	2018	2017	2016	2015
Revenue	2,173,350,000	2,502,470,000	2,376,117,000	2,018,197,000	2,013,186,000	1,883,533,000
R&D Expense	194,101,000	202,200,000	207,905,000	169,977,000	168,209,000	162,334,000
Operating Income	86,435,000	138,961,000	27,491,000	157,844,000	145,301,000	45,583,000
Operating Margin %		.06%	.01%	.08%	.07%	.02%
SGA Expense	276,920,000	346,872,000	423,210,000	326,548,000	321,698,000	317,095,000
Net Income	-57,955,000	49,006,000	-99,250,000	57,298,000	31,770,000	12,678,000
Operating Cash Flow	109,514,000	172,840,000	109,755,000	191,354,000	115,842,000	73,350,000
Capital Expenditure	46,208,000	60,749,000	59,952,000	49,495,000	43,543,000	43,918,000
EBITDA	84,652,000	239,885,000	71,549,000	209,371,000	163,893,000	125,384,000
Return on Assets %		.02%	-.04%	.03%	.02%	.01%
Return on Equity %		.07%	-.13%	.08%	.05%	.02%
Debt to Equity		1.29	1.387	0.755	0.46	0.595

CONTACT INFORMATION:

Phone: 509 924-9900   Fax:
Toll-Free: 800 635-5641
Address: 2111 N. Molter Rd., Liberty Lake, WA 99019 United States

STOCK TICKER/OTHER:

Stock Ticker: ITRI   Exchange: NAS
Employees: 7,900   Fiscal Year Ends: 12/31
Parent Company:

SALARIES/BONUSES:

Top Exec. Salary: $ Bonus: $
Second Exec. Salary: $ Bonus: $

OTHER THOUGHTS:

Estimated Female Officers or Directors: 6
Hot Spot for Advancement for Women/Minorities: Y

J2 Global Inc

NAIC Code: 517110

www.j2global.com

TYPES OF BUSINESS:

Unified Messaging & Communication Services
Internet-Based Faxing
Internet Conferencing
Cloud-Based Communications Services
Customer Relationship Management Solutions

BRANDS/DIVISIONS/AFFILIATES:

MyFax
eVoice
LiveDrive
IPVanish
Campaigner
IGN
Mashable
Everyday Health

CONTACTS: *Note: Officers with more than one job title may be intentionally listed here more than once.*

Vivek Shah, CEO
R. Turicchi, CFO
Richard Ressler, Chairman of the Board
Steve Dunn, Chief Accounting Officer
Jeremy Rossen, General Counsel

GROWTH PLANS/SPECIAL FEATURES:

J2 Global, Inc. is a global provider of internet information and services. Through its cloud services division, the company provides cloud services to consumers and businesses (any size), and licenses intellectual property (IP) to third parties. This segment's cloud-based eFax, MyFax and sFax online fax services enable users to receive faxes in their email inboxes and to send faxes via the internet. eVoice and Line2 provide customers a virtual phone system with various available enhancements. LiveDrive enables customers to back up data and dispose tape or other physical systems. IPVanish and Encrypt.me provide virtual private networks that encrypt customers' data and activity on the internet. Campaigner, iContact and SMTP provide enhanced email marketing and delivery solutions. J2's digital media division operates a portfolio of web properties that provide reviews of technology, gaming and lifestyle products and services; news and commentary related to their vertical markets; professional networking tools, targeted emails and white papers for IT professionals; speed testing for internet and mobile network connections; online deals and discounts for consumers; interactive tools and mobile applications that enable consumers to manage an array of health and wellness needs, such as medical conditions, pregnancy, diet and fitness news; and tools and information for healthcare professionals to stay informed about industry, legislative and regulatory developments in major medical specialties. This division's web properties and apps include IGN, Mashable, PC Mag, Humble Bundle, Speedtest, Offers, Black Friday, MedPageToday, Everyday Health, and What to Expect, among others. During the first half of 2021, J2 Global completed two acquisitions that provide access to new markets and expand J2's product line, they include Moz Inc. and Daily OM. J2 Global also announced plans to separate into two independent publicly-traded companies, J2 Global Inc. and Consensus, through a spin-off.

FINANCIAL DATA: *Note: Data for latest year may not have been available at press time.*

In U.S. $	2020	2019	2018	2017	2016	2015
Revenue	1,489,593,000	1,372,054,000	1,207,295,000	1,117,838,000	874,255,000	720,815,000
R&D Expense	64,295,000	54,396,000	48,370,000	46,004,000	38,046,000	34,329,000
Operating Income	334,611,000	277,080,000	244,280,000	245,708,000	242,566,000	199,382,000
Operating Margin %		.20%	.20%	.22%	.28%	.28%
SGA Expense	858,905,000	803,255,000	713,571,000	653,813,000	446,543,000	364,146,000
Net Income	150,668,000	218,806,000	128,687,000	139,425,000	152,439,000	133,636,000
Operating Cash Flow	480,079,000	412,539,000	401,325,000	264,419,000	282,387,000	229,061,000
Capital Expenditure	95,670,000	70,634,000	57,048,000	41,835,000	29,067,000	18,752,000
EBITDA	591,111,000	522,595,000	426,748,000	429,784,000	374,900,000	292,590,000
Return on Assets %		.07%	.05%	.06%	.08%	.08%
Return on Equity %		.18%	.12%	.14%	.17%	.15%
Debt to Equity		0.89	0.978	0.982	0.658	0.675

CONTACT INFORMATION:

Phone: 323 860-9200   Fax: 323 860-9201
Toll-Free:
Address: 700 S. Flower St., Fl. 15, Los Angeles, CA 90017 United States

STOCK TICKER/OTHER:

Stock Ticker: JCOM
Employees: 3,090
Parent Company:

Exchange: NAS
Fiscal Year Ends: 12/31

SALARIES/BONUSES:

Top Exec. Salary: $ Bonus: $
Second Exec. Salary: $ Bonus: $

OTHER THOUGHTS:

Estimated Female Officers or Directors: 2
Hot Spot for Advancement for Women/Minorities:

Jabil Inc

NAIC Code: 334418

www.jabil.com

TYPES OF BUSINESS:

Contract Electronics Manufacturing
Electronic Manufacturing Services
Engineering Solutions

BRANDS/DIVISIONS/AFFILIATES:

CONTACTS: Note: Officers with more than one job title may be intentionally listed here more than once.

Michael Loparco, CEO, Divisional
Alessandro Parimbelli, CEO, Divisional
Steven Borges, CEO, Divisional
Kenneth Wilson, CEO, Divisional
Brenda Chamulak, CEO, Divisional
Mark Mondello, CEO
Meheryar Dastoor, CFO
Timothy Main, Chairman of the Board
Thomas Sansone, Director
Courtney Ryan, Executive VP, Divisional
Robert Katz, Executive VP
Bruce Johnson, Other Executive Officer
Daryn Smith, Senior VP, Divisional
Sergio Cadavid, Senior VP

GROWTH PLANS/SPECIAL FEATURES:

Jabil, Inc. is a provider of worldwide electronic manufacturing services and solutions. Through its 100 locations in 30 countries, the firm develops and manufactures products that help to connect people, advance technology and more. Jabil divides its operations into two segments: diversified manufacturing services (DMS) and electronics manufacturing services (EMS). DMS is focused on providing engineering solutions and on material sciences and technologies. This segment includes customers primarily in the consumer lifestyles and wearable technologies, defense & aerospace, emerging growth, healthcare, mobility and packaging industries. EMS is focused around leveraging information technology, supply chain design and engineering, technologies largely centered on core electronics, sharing of Jabil's large-scale manufacturing infrastructure and the ability to serve a broad range of end markets. This segment includes customers primarily in the automotive, digital home, industrial and energy, networking and telecommunications, point of sale, printing and storage industries. As of fiscal 2020, Jabil's five largest accounted for approximately 47% of net revenue and 73 customers accounted for approximately 90% of net revenue, Apple, Inc. alone accounted for 20%.

FINANCIAL DATA: Note: Data for latest year may not have been available at press time.

In U.S. $	2020	2019	2018	2017	2016	2015
Revenue	27,266,440,000	25,282,320,000	22,095,420,000	19,063,120,000	18,353,090,000	17,899,200,000
R&D Expense	44,143,000	42,861,000	38,531,000	29,680,000	31,954,000	27,645,000
Operating Income	656,432,000	727,270,000	579,055,000	572,737,000	534,202,000	588,477,000
Operating Margin %		.03%	.03%	.03%	.03%	.03%
SGA Expense	1,174,694,000	1,111,347,000	1,050,716,000	907,702,000	924,427,000	862,647,000
Net Income	53,912,000	287,111,000	86,330,000	129,090,000	254,095,000	284,019,000
Operating Cash Flow	1,257,275,000	1,193,066,000	933,850,000	1,256,643,000	916,207,000	1,240,282,000
Capital Expenditure	983,035,000	1,005,480,000	1,036,651,000	716,485,000	924,239,000	963,145,000
EBITDA	1,229,196,000	1,411,267,000	1,296,107,000	1,154,712,000	1,220,333,000	1,088,913,000
Return on Assets %		.02%	.01%	.01%	.03%	.03%
Return on Equity %		.15%	.04%	.05%	.11%	.12%
Debt to Equity		1.124	1.279	0.694	0.851	0.582

CONTACT INFORMATION:

Phone: 727 577-9749   Fax: 727 579-8529
Toll-Free:
Address: 10560 Dr. Martin Luther King Jr. St. N., St. Petersburg, FL 33716 United States

STOCK TICKER/OTHER:

Stock Ticker: JBL
Employees: 240,000
Parent Company:

Exchange: NYS
Fiscal Year Ends: 08/31

SALARIES/BONUSES:

Top Exec. Salary: $ Bonus: $
Second Exec. Salary: $ Bonus: $

OTHER THOUGHTS:

Estimated Female Officers or Directors:
Hot Spot for Advancement for Women/Minorities: Y

Jack Henry & Associates Inc

NAIC Code: 511210Q

www.jackhenry.com

TYPES OF BUSINESS:

Software-Data Processing
Financial Services Software
Data Processing
Integrated Computer Systems
Bank
Credit Union
Corporation

BRANDS/DIVISIONS/AFFILIATES:

Jack Henry Banking
Symitar
ProfitStars

CONTACTS: Note: Officers with more than one job title may be intentionally listed here more than once.

David Foss, CEO
Kevin Williams, CFO
John Prim, Chairman of the Board
Mark Forbis, Chief Technology Officer
Matthew Flanigan, Director
Craig Morgan, General Counsel
Gregory Adelson, General Manager, Divisional
Ronald Moses, General Manager, Divisional
Russell Bernthal, President, Divisional
Teddy Bilke, President, Divisional
Stacey Zengel, President, Divisional

GROWTH PLANS/SPECIAL FEATURES:

Jack Henry & Associates, Inc. is a provider of integrated computer systems relating to data processing and management information for banks, credit unions and other financial institutions in the U.S. The company serves nearly 8,700 financial institutions and corporate entities. It provides products and services through three marketed brands: Jack Henry Banking, Symitar and ProfitStars. Jack Henry Banking provides integrated data processing systems to approximately 1,000 banks, ranging from community banks to multi-billion-dollar institutions with assets of up to $50 billion. Jack Henry Banking's solutions support both in-house and outsources environments with core processing platforms and more than 140 integrated complementary solutions. Symitar provides core data processing solutions for credit unions of all sizes, with nearly 840 credit union customers. It markets two distinct core processing platforms and more than 100 integrated complementary solutions that support both in-house and outsourced environments. ProfitStars provides highly specialized core agnostic products and services to financial institutions that are primarily not core customers of Jack Henry & Associates. Its more than 100 integrated complementary solutions offer highly specialized financial performance, imaging and payments processing, information security and risk management, retail delivery, and online and mobile solutions. ProfitStars serves more than 8,600 customers, including 6,800 non-core customers. All of the company's products and services can be tailored to support the customer's unique goals. Jack Henry & Associates focuses on establishing long-term customer relationships.

FINANCIAL DATA: Note: Data for latest year may not have been available at press time.

In U.S. $	2020	2019	2018	2017	2016	2015
Revenue	1,697,067,000	1,552,691,000	1,536,603,000	1,431,117,000	1,354,646,000	1,256,190,000
R&D Expense	109,988,000	96,378,000	90,340,000	84,753,000	81,234,000	71,495,000
Operating Income	380,627,000	347,285,000	390,475,000	364,432,000	342,168,000	317,865,000
Operating Margin %		.22%	.25%	.25%	.25%	.25%
SGA Expense	197,988,000	185,998,000	182,146,000	162,898,000	157,593,000	146,494,000
Net Income	296,668,000	271,885,000	376,660,000	245,793,000	248,867,000	211,221,000
Operating Cash Flow	510,532,000	431,128,000	412,142,000	357,322,000	365,116,000	373,790,000
Capital Expenditure	177,510,000	170,781,000	149,920,000	148,186,000	164,562,000	145,301,000
EBITDA	553,569,000	508,794,000	544,930,000	507,736,000	491,614,000	437,030,000
Return on Assets %		.13%	.19%	.13%	.14%	.12%
Return on Equity %		.20%	.33%	.24%	.25%	.21%
Debt to Equity				0.048		0.051

CONTACT INFORMATION:

Phone: 417 235-6652   Fax:
Toll-Free: 800-299-4222
Address: 663 W. Highway 60, Monett, MO 65708 United States

SALARIES/BONUSES:

Top Exec. Salary: $ Bonus: $
Second Exec. Salary: $ Bonus: $

STOCK TICKER/OTHER:

Stock Ticker: JKHY   Exchange: NAS
Employees: 6,717   Fiscal Year Ends: 06/30
Parent Company:

OTHER THOUGHTS:

Estimated Female Officers or Directors: 3
Hot Spot for Advancement for Women/Minorities: Y

Jacobs Engineering Group Inc

www.jacobs.com

NAIC Code: 237000

TYPES OF BUSINESS:

Engineering & Design Services
Facility Management
Construction & Field Services
Technical Consulting Services
Environmental Services

BRANDS/DIVISIONS/AFFILIATES:

PA Consulting

CONTACTS: Note: Officers with more than one job title may be intentionally listed here more than once.

Steven Demetriou, CEO
Kevin Berryman, CFO
Joanne Caruso, Chief Administrative Officer
Michael Tyler, Chief Compliance Officer
Robert Pragada, COO
Dawne Hickton, Executive VP
Vinayak Pai, President, Divisional
William Allen, Senior VP

GROWTH PLANS/SPECIAL FEATURES:

Jacobs Engineering Group, Inc. offers technical, professional and construction services to industrial, commercial and governmental clients throughout the Americas, Europe, Asia, India, the Middle East, Africa, the U.K. and Australia. Jacobs provides project services, which include engineering, design and architecture; process, scientific and systems consulting services; operations and maintenance services; and construction services, which include direct-hire construction and management services. Services are offered to industry groups such as buildings, which includes projects in the fields of health care and education as well as civic, governmental and other buildings; infrastructure; technology; energy; consumer and forest products; automotive and industrial; and environmental programs. Jacobs also provides pricing studies, project feasibility reports and automation and control system analysis for U.S. government agencies involved in defense and aerospace programs. In addition, the company is one of the leading providers of environmental engineering and consulting services in the U.S. and abroad, providing support in such areas as underground storage tank removal, contaminated soil and water remediation and long-term groundwater monitoring. Jacobs also designs, builds, installs, operates and maintains various types of soil and groundwater cleanup systems. In March 2021, Jacobs acquired a 65% stake in PA Consulting, a U.K.-based innovation and transformation consulting firm.

Jacobs offers its employees medical, disability, life and AD&D insurance; an employee stock purchase plan; and tuition reimbursement.

FINANCIAL DATA: Note: Data for latest year may not have been available at press time.

In U.S. $	2020	2019	2018	2017	2016	2015
Revenue	13,566,970,000	12,737,870,000	14,984,650,000	10,022,790,000	10,964,160,000	12,114,830,000
R&D Expense						
Operating Income	535,973,000	404,851,000	647,971,000	392,269,000	338,598,000	445,527,000
Operating Margin %		.03%	.04%	.04%	.03%	.04%
SGA Expense	2,050,695,000	2,072,177,000	2,180,399,000	1,379,983,000	1,429,233,000	1,522,811,000
Net Income	491,845,000	847,979,000	163,431,000	293,727,000	210,463,000	302,971,000
Operating Cash Flow	806,849,000	-366,436,000	481,152,000	574,881,000	680,173,000	484,572,000
Capital Expenditure	118,269,000	135,977,000	94,884,000	118,060,000	77,715,000	88,404,000
EBITDA	685,042,000	604,075,000	830,052,000	527,765,000	431,954,000	598,932,000
Return on Assets %		.07%	.02%	.04%	.03%	.04%
Return on Equity %		.15%	.03%	.07%	.05%	.07%
Debt to Equity		0.21	0.367	0.053	0.09	0.136

CONTACT INFORMATION:

Phone: 214-583-8500   Fax:
Toll-Free:
Address: 1999 Bryan St., Ste. 1200, Dallas, TX 75201 United States

STOCK TICKER/OTHER:

Stock Ticker: J
Employees: 48,000
Parent Company:

Exchange: NYS
Fiscal Year Ends: 09/30

SALARIES/BONUSES:

Top Exec. Salary: $ Bonus: $
Second Exec. Salary: $ Bonus: $

OTHER THOUGHTS:

Estimated Female Officers or Directors: 1
Hot Spot for Advancement for Women/Minorities: Y

Jayco Inc

NAIC Code: 336214

www.jayco.com

TYPES OF BUSINESS:

Travel Trailer and Camper Manufacturing
Motor Homes
Camping Trailers
Manufacture

BRANDS/DIVISIONS/AFFILIATES:

Thor Industries Inc

CONTACTS: *Note: Officers with more than one job title may be intentionally listed here more than once.*

Ken Walters, Pres.

GROWTH PLANS/SPECIAL FEATURES:

Jayco, Inc. is a leading manufacturer of recreational vehicles (RVs). The company began in a farmhouse in 1968, and now consists of a large-scale production operation with dealerships throughout the U.S. Jayco's recreational vehicles include travel trailers, fifth wheels, toy haulers and motorhomes. Jayco's travel trailers offer modern kitchen designs, spacious living areas and relaxing bedroom features, with weights ranging up to 9,500 or more pounds. Fifth wheels can include lightweight and luxurious features, with some models sleeping up to 11 people. Toy haulers are built to be durable and can haul small recreational vehicles such as motorcycles, quads, ATVS and more, with some models sleeping up to 8 people. Class C motorhomes include a 7,500-lb hitch and sleep up to 10 people; and some models come with a Freightliner S2RV chassis chasses and diesel engine. Jayco has one Class B motorhome for release in 2022 that sleeps up to two people and are 20-feet, 11-inches in length. Class A motorhomes feature wide windshields, premium handling and ride features, recessed lighting and more, and range in price up to more than $345,000. Jayco's craftmanship includes its Magnum roof systems, Climate Shield heating and air system, custom-manufactured frames, and JRide precision handling. The firm operates as a subsidiary of Thor Industries, Inc., a manufacturer of recreational vehicles.

FINANCIAL DATA: *Note: Data for latest year may not have been available at press time.*

In U.S. $	2020	2019	2018	2017	2016	2015
Revenue	2,072,264,512	2,031,631,875	1,934,887,500	1,842,750,000	1,755,000,000	1,500,000,000
R&D Expense						
Operating Income						
Operating Margin %						
SGA Expense						
Net Income						
Operating Cash Flow						
Capital Expenditure						
EBITDA						
Return on Assets %						
Return on Equity %						
Debt to Equity						

CONTACT INFORMATION:

Phone: 574-825-5861   Fax: 574-825-7354
Toll-Free:
Address: 903 S. Main St., Middlebury, IN 46540 United States

STOCK TICKER/OTHER:

Stock Ticker: Subsidiary   Exchange:
Employees: 4,000   Fiscal Year Ends: 08/31
Parent Company: Thor Industries Inc

SALARIES/BONUSES:

Top Exec. Salary: $ Bonus: $
Second Exec. Salary: $ Bonus: $

OTHER THOUGHTS:

Estimated Female Officers or Directors:
Hot Spot for Advancement for Women/Minorities:

JB Hunt Transport Services Inc

www.jbhunt.com

NAIC Code: 484121

TYPES OF BUSINESS:

General Freight Trucking
Truckload Transportation
Logistics
Intermodal
Contract Services
Final Mile Services
Warehousing
Supply Chain Solutions

BRANDS/DIVISIONS/AFFILIATES:

Mass Movement Inc

CONTACTS: Note: Officers with more than one job title may be intentionally listed here more than once.

Kevin Bracy, Assistant Secretary
John Roberts, CEO
David Mee, CFO
Kirk Thompson, Chairman of the Board
John Kuhlow, Chief Accounting Officer
Stuart Scott, Chief Information Officer
Shelley Simpson, Chief Medical Officer
Craig Harper, Executive VP
Darren Field, Executive VP, Divisional
Bradley Hicks, Executive VP, Divisional
Eric McGee, Executive VP, Divisional
Nicholas Hobbs, Executive VP
Terrence Matthews, Executive VP
Jennifer Boattini, General Counsel

GROWTH PLANS/SPECIAL FEATURES:

J.B. Hunt Transport Services, Inc. is a North American truckload transportation and logistics company serving the U.S., Canada and Mexico. The firm's operations are organized into five business segments: intermodal (JBI), dedicated contract services (DCS), truckload (JBT), integrated capacity solutions (ICS) and final mile services (FMS). The JBI segment utilizes agreements with rail carriers to provide intermodal freight solutions to customers. It operates more than 98,600 pieces of company-owned trailing equipment and 83,259 chassis fleet units, and manages a fleet of 5,166 company-owned tractors, 497 independent contractor trucks and 6,745 company drivers. The DCS segment focuses on private fleet conversion and specialized equipment, and offers supply chain solutions that support a variety of transportation networks. This division operates 9,408 company-owned trucks, 498 customer-owned trucks and five independent contractor trucks, as well as related trailing equipment and trailers. The JBT segment offers full-load, dry van freight services, utilizing tractors and trailers operating over roads and highways. It picks up freight at the dock or other specified locations of the shipper and transports the load directly to the location of the consignee. The ICS segment provides freight brokerage and transportation logistics solutions to customers, including flatbed, refrigerated, expedited and less-than truckload, as well as a variety of dry van and intermodal solutions. It also offers an online multi-modal marketplace for matching loads with appropriate carriers, and provides outsource transportation services. Last, the FMS segment provides final-mile delivery services through its nationwide network of cross-dock and other delivery system network locations. It provides both asset and non-asset big and bulky delivery and installation services, as well as fulfillment and retail-pooling distribution services. In late-2020, J.B. Hunt acquired Mass Movement, Inc., offering final mile delivery of big and bulky products, primarily serving customers in the commercial health and fitness industry.

FINANCIAL DATA: Note: Data for latest year may not have been available at press time.

In U.S. $	2020	2019	2018	2017	2016	2015
Revenue	9,636,573,000	9,165,258,000	8,614,874,000	7,189,568,000	6,555,459,000	6,187,646,000
R&D Expense						
Operating Income	713,119,000	733,825,000	681,021,000	623,789,000	721,020,000	715,694,000
Operating Margin %		.08%	.08%	.09%	.11%	.12%
SGA Expense	348,076,000	383,981,000	323,587,000	273,440,000	185,436,000	166,799,000
Net Income	506,035,000	516,320,000	489,585,000	686,263,000	432,090,000	427,235,000
Operating Cash Flow	1,122,859,000	1,098,347,000	1,087,841,000	855,153,000	854,143,000	873,308,000
Capital Expenditure	738,545,000	854,115,000	995,650,000	526,928,000	638,430,000	725,122,000
EBITDA	1,240,980,000	1,234,724,000	1,117,138,000	1,007,542,000	1,082,601,000	1,055,393,000
Return on Assets %		.10%	.10%	.17%	.12%	.12%
Return on Equity %		.24%	.25%	.42%	.32%	.34%
Debt to Equity		0.572	0.428	0.59	0.697	0.773

CONTACT INFORMATION:

Phone: 479 820-0000   Fax:
Toll-Free: 800-643-3622
Address: 615 J.B. Hunt Corporate Dr., Lowell, AR 72745-0130 United States

STOCK TICKER/OTHER:

Stock Ticker: JBHT
Employees: 29,056
Parent Company:

Exchange: NAS
Fiscal Year Ends: 12/31

SALARIES/BONUSES:

Top Exec. Salary: $ Bonus: $
Second Exec. Salary: $ Bonus: $

OTHER THOUGHTS:

Estimated Female Officers or Directors: 4
Hot Spot for Advancement for Women/Minorities: Y

JM Family Enterprises Inc

NAIC Code: 423110

www.jmfamily.com

TYPES OF BUSINESS:
Automobile Distribution-Wholesale
Automobile Dealer
Parts Distribution
Financing & Insurance
Dealership Financing
Consulting Services

BRANDS/DIVISIONS/AFFILIATES:
Southeast Toyota Distributors LLC
Southeast Toyota Finance
JM Lexus
JM&A Group
Home Franchise Concepts
Budget Blinds
Concrete Craft
AdvantaClean

CONTACTS: *Note: Officers with more than one job title may be intentionally listed here more than once.*
Brent Burns, Pres.
Eric Gebhard, Interim CFO
Carmen Johnson, VP-Human Resources
Carmen Johnson, General Counsel
Frank Armstrong, Exec. VP
Ron Coombs, Sr. VP
Forrest Heathcott, Exec. VP
Ed Sheehy, Exec. VP
Colin Brown, Chmn.

GROWTH PLANS/SPECIAL FEATURES:

JM Family Enterprises, Inc. is a leading family-owned diversified automotive company. Through its subsidiaries, JM is a distributor of Toyotas, operates a Lexus dealership, provides finance and insurance products, and operates a franchise network in the home improvement goods and services space. Subsidiary Southeast Toyota Distributors, LLC is an independent distributor of Toyotas, distributing vehicles, parts and accessories to more than 175 independent Toyota dealers in Alabama, Florida, Georgia, North Carolina and South Carolina. JM Lexus is located in Margate, Florida, and is a Lexus Plus dealership which also maintains state-of-the-art service and parts departments as well as a Lexus Certified Collision Center. Southeast Toyota Finance is a finance company for JM's Toyota dealers, servicing finance and lease accounts. The finance firm is part of World Omni Financial Corporation, a global leader in wholesale floorplan accounting and risk management systems. JM&A Group is an independent provider of finance and insurance products to more than 3,800 automobile dealerships, including protection programs for new and used vehicles. Last, Home Franchise Concepts is among the world's largest franchise businesses, encompassing four brands: Budget Blinds, a provider of custom window coverings; Tailored Living, providing whole-home organization solutions; Concrete Craft, offering decorative concrete products; and AdvantaClean, offering professional home cleaning services. Through these brands, Home Franchise Concepts has nearly 1,700 franchises located in the U.S., Canada and Mexico.

JM offers its employees comprehensive health and retirement benefits, and a variety of employee assistance plans and programs.

FINANCIAL DATA: *Note: Data for latest year may not have been available at press time.*

In U.S. $	2020	2019	2018	2017	2016	2015
Revenue	15,087,500,000	17,750,000,000	16,300,000,000	15,100,000,000	14,900,000,000	14,500,000,000
R&D Expense						
Operating Income						
Operating Margin %						
SGA Expense						
Net Income						
Operating Cash Flow						
Capital Expenditure						
EBITDA						
Return on Assets %						
Return on Equity %						
Debt to Equity						

CONTACT INFORMATION:
Phone: 954-429-2000   Fax: 954-429-2300
Toll-Free:
Address: 100 Jim Moran Blvd., Deerfield Beach, FL 33442 United States

STOCK TICKER/OTHER:
Stock Ticker: Private
Employees: 4,200
Parent Company:

Exchange:
Fiscal Year Ends: 12/31

SALARIES/BONUSES:
Top Exec. Salary: $ Bonus: $
Second Exec. Salary: $ Bonus: $

OTHER THOUGHTS:
Estimated Female Officers or Directors: 1
Hot Spot for Advancement for Women/Minorities:

JM Smucker Company (The)

www.jmsmucker.com

NAIC Code: 311421

TYPES OF BUSINESS:
Food Products, Manufacturing
Manufacturer
Marketing
Pet Food
Coffee
Sandwiches
Spreads
Retail

BRANDS/DIVISIONS/AFFILIATES:
Rachael Ray Nutrish
Meow Mix
Milk-Bone
Folgers
CafÃ© Bustelo
Smuckers
Jif

CONTACTS: *Note: Officers with more than one job title may be intentionally listed here more than once.*
Mark Belgya, CFO
Timothy Smucker, Chairman Emeritus
Richard Smucker, Chairman of the Board
Mark Smucker, Director
Jeannette Knudsen, General Counsel
Tina Floyd, General Manager, Divisional
Joseph Stanziano, General Manager, Divisional
David Lemmon, President, Divisional
Jill Penrose, Senior VP, Divisional
Kevin Jackson, Senior VP, Divisional
Amy Held, Senior VP, Divisional

GROWTH PLANS/SPECIAL FEATURES:
The J.M. Smucker Company manufactures and markets food and beverage products. The company operates through three core segments: U.S. retail pet foods, U.S. retail coffee and U.S. retail consumer foods. The U.S. retail pet foods segment includes the domestic sales of Rachael Ray Nutrish, Meow Mix, Milk-Bone, Kibbles 'n Bits, 9Lives, Nature's Recipe and Pup-Peroni branded products. The U.S retail coffee segment primarily includes the domestic sales of Folgers, Dunkin' and Cafe Bustelo branded coffee. The U.S. retail consumer foods segment primarily includes the domestic sales of Smucker's and Jif branded products, such as frozen sandwiches, peanut butter and fruit spreads. Other operations by J.M. Smucker consists of the sale of products distributed domestically and in foreign countries via retail channels and foodservice distributors and operators, such as health care operators, restaurants, lodging and hospitality establishments, offices, educational entities and convenience stores. In December 2020, J.M. Smucker sold its Crisco oil and shortening business to B&G Foods, Inc. In January 2021, the firm sold its Natural Balance pet food business to Nexus Capital Management LP.

FINANCIAL DATA: *Note: Data for latest year may not have been available at press time.*

In U.S. $	2020	2019	2018	2017	2016	2015
Revenue	7,801,000,000	7,838,000,000	7,357,100,000	7,392,300,000	7,811,200,000	
R&D Expense						
Operating Income	1,292,000,000	1,197,800,000	1,258,400,000	1,241,600,000	1,281,200,000	
Operating Margin %	.17%	.15%	.17%	.17%	.16%	
SGA Expense	1,474,300,000	1,508,600,000	1,370,800,000	1,390,700,000	1,510,300,000	
Net Income	779,500,000	514,400,000	1,338,600,000	592,300,000	688,700,000	
Operating Cash Flow	1,254,800,000	1,141,200,000	1,218,000,000	1,059,000,000	1,458,300,000	
Capital Expenditure	269,300,000	359,800,000	321,900,000	192,400,000	201,400,000	
EBITDA	1,662,400,000	1,355,800,000	1,448,200,000	1,460,500,000	1,579,100,000	
Return on Assets %	.05%	.03%	.09%	.04%	.04%	
Return on Equity %	.10%	.06%	.18%	.09%	.10%	
Debt to Equity	0.671	0.588	0.594	0.649	0.734	

CONTACT INFORMATION:
Phone: 330 682-3000   Fax: 330 682-3370
Toll-Free: 888-550-9555
Address: 1 Strawberry Ln., Orrville, OH 44667-0280 United States

STOCK TICKER/OTHER:
Stock Ticker: SJM
Employees: 7,300
Parent Company:

Exchange: NYS
Fiscal Year Ends: 04/30

SALARIES/BONUSES:
Top Exec. Salary: $ Bonus: $
Second Exec. Salary: $ Bonus: $

OTHER THOUGHTS:
Estimated Female Officers or Directors: 7
Hot Spot for Advancement for Women/Minorities: Y

John Hancock Financial

NAIC Code: 524113

www.johnhancock.com

TYPES OF BUSINESS:

Life Insurance
Mortgages
Annuities
Retirement Products
Mutual Funds
Asset Management

BRANDS/DIVISIONS/AFFILIATES:

Manulife Financial Corporation
John Hancock Life Insurance

CONTACTS: Note: Officers with more than one job title may be intentionally listed here more than once.

Marianne Harrison, CEO
Sebastian Pariath, COO
Martin Sheerin, CFO
Barbara Goose, CMO
James Gallagher, Chief Admin. Officer
James Gallagher, General Counsel
Andrew G. Arnott, CEO/Pres., John Hancock Funds LLC
Peter Gordon, Pres., John Hancock Retirement Plan Svcs.
Michael Doughty, Pres.

GROWTH PLANS/SPECIAL FEATURES:

John Hancock Financial, a subsidiary of Canada-based Manulife Financial Corporation, includes John Hancock Life Insurance, one of the largest life insurers in the U.S. Overall, the company offers a wide range of insurance products including annuities, individual and group long-term care insurance, 401(k) plans, multiple life insurance policies, securitized investments, benefit payment services, retiree health care solutions, 529 college savings plans and fixed income and equity services. The firm's core retail products include life insurance, long-term care insurance, annuities and mutual funds. John Hancock also specializes in institutional investment, providing opportunities for pension funds and endowments to invest. Corporate employers are among the firm's largest customers. John Hancock's products and services are separated into three categories: life insurance, planning and advice and retirement.

The firm offers comprehensive benefits, retirement plans and employee assistance programs.

FINANCIAL DATA: Note: Data for latest year may not have been available at press time.

In U.S. $	2020	2019	2018	2017	2016	2015
Revenue	8,487,706,500	9,029,475,000	8,599,500,000	8,190,000,000	7,800,000,000	7,780,000,000
R&D Expense						
Operating Income						
Operating Margin %						
SGA Expense						
Net Income						
Operating Cash Flow						
Capital Expenditure						
EBITDA						
Return on Assets %						
Return on Equity %						
Debt to Equity						

CONTACT INFORMATION:

Phone: 617-663-3000   Fax: 617-572-6015
Toll-Free: 800-225-5291
Address: 601 Congress St., Boston, MA 02110 United States

STOCK TICKER/OTHER:

Stock Ticker: Subsidiary   Exchange:
Employees: 34,000   Fiscal Year Ends: 12/31
Parent Company: Manulife Financial Corporation

SALARIES/BONUSES:

Top Exec. Salary: $ Bonus: $
Second Exec. Salary: $ Bonus: $

OTHER THOUGHTS:

Estimated Female Officers or Directors:
Hot Spot for Advancement for Women/Minorities: Y

Johnson & Johnson

www.jnj.com

NAIC Code: 325412

TYPES OF BUSINESS:

Personal Health Care & Hygiene Products
Sterilization Products
Surgical Products
Pharmaceuticals
Skin Care Products
Baby Care Products
Contact Lenses
Medical Equipment

BRANDS/DIVISIONS/AFFILIATES:

Motrin
Band-Aid
Listerine
Tylenol
Neosporin
Risperdal Consta
Remicade
Momenta Pharmaceuticals Inc

CONTACTS: Note: Officers with more than one job title may be intentionally listed here more than once.

Alex Gorsky, CEO
Joaquin Duato, Vice Chairman
Joseph Wolk, CFO
Jorge Mesquita, Chairman of the Board, Divisional
Ronald Kapusta, Chief Accounting Officer
Paulus Stoffels, Chief Scientific Officer
Thibaut Mongon, Executive VP, Divisional
Ashley McEvoy, Executive VP, Divisional
Jennifer Taubert, Executive VP, Divisional
Michael Sneed, Executive VP, Divisional
Kathy Wengel, Executive VP
Peter Fasolo, Executive VP
Michael Ullmann, General Counsel

GROWTH PLANS/SPECIAL FEATURES:

Johnson & Johnson, founded in 1886, is one of the world's most comprehensive and well-known researchers, developers and manufacturers of healthcare products. Johnson & Johnson's worldwide operations are divided into three segments: consumer, pharmaceuticals and medical devices. The company's principal consumer goods are personal care and hygiene products, including baby care, skin care, oral care, wound care and women's healthcare products as well as nutritional and over-the-counter pharmaceutical products. Major consumer brands include Motrin, Band-Aid, Listerine, Tylenol, Neosporin, Aveeno and Pepcid AC. The pharmaceutical segment covers a wide spectrum of health fields, including anti-infective, antipsychotic, contraceptive, dermatology, gastrointestinal, hematology, immunology, neurology, oncology, pain management and virology. Among its pharmaceutical products are Risperdal Consta, an antipsychotic used to treat schizophrenia, and Remicade for the treatment of immune mediated inflammatory diseases. In the medical devices segment, Johnson & Johnson makes a number of products including orthopedic joint reconstruction devices, surgical care, glucose monitoring devices, diagnostic products and disposable contact lenses. The firm owns more than 260 companies in virtually all countries of the world, and is headquartered in New Brunswick, New Jersey. In October 2020, Johnson & Johnson completed its acquisition of Momenta Pharmaceuticals, Inc., a company that discovers and develops novel therapies for immune-mediated diseases, for $6.5 billion. The firm developed a one-dose vaccine for COVID-19 which began administration in 2021.

FINANCIAL DATA: Note: Data for latest year may not have been available at press time.

In U.S. $	2020	2019	2018	2017	2016	2015
Revenue	82,584,000,000	82,059,000,000	81,581,000,000	76,450,000,000	71,890,000,000	70,074,000,000
R&D Expense	12,159,000,000	11,355,000,000	10,775,000,000	10,554,000,000	9,095,000,000	9,046,000,000
Operating Income	19,914,000,000	20,970,000,000	21,175,000,000	19,122,000,000	21,165,000,000	18,289,000,000
Operating Margin %		.24%	.25%	.24%	.29%	.26%
SGA Expense	22,084,000,000	22,178,000,000	22,540,000,000	21,420,000,000	19,945,000,000	21,203,000,000
Net Income	14,714,000,000	15,119,000,000	15,297,000,000	1,300,000,000	16,540,000,000	15,409,000,000
Operating Cash Flow	23,536,000,000	23,416,000,000	22,201,000,000	21,056,000,000	18,767,000,000	19,279,000,000
Capital Expenditure	3,347,000,000	3,498,000,000	3,670,000,000	3,279,000,000	3,226,000,000	3,463,000,000
EBITDA	23,929,000,000	24,655,000,000	25,933,000,000	24,249,000,000	24,283,000,000	23,494,000,000
Return on Assets %		.10%	.10%	.01%	.12%	.12%
Return on Equity %		.25%	.26%	.02%	.23%	.22%
Debt to Equity		0.445	0.463	0.51	0.319	0.181

CONTACT INFORMATION:

Phone: 732 524-0400   Fax: 732 214-0332
Toll-Free:
Address: 1 Johnson & Johnson Plaza, New Brunswick, NJ 08933 United States

STOCK TICKER/OTHER:

Stock Ticker: JNJ
Employees: 134,500
Parent Company:

Exchange: NYS
Fiscal Year Ends: 12/31

SALARIES/BONUSES:

Top Exec. Salary: $ Bonus: $
Second Exec. Salary: $ Bonus: $

OTHER THOUGHTS:

Estimated Female Officers or Directors: 4
Hot Spot for Advancement for Women/Minorities: Y

JPMorgan Chase & Co Inc

www.jpmorganchase.com

NAIC Code: 522110

TYPES OF BUSINESS:

Banking
Mortgages
Investment Banking
Stock Brokerage
Credit Cards
Business Finance
Mutual Funds
Annuities

BRANDS/DIVISIONS/AFFILIATES:

JPMorgan Chase Bank NA
JP Morgan Securities LLC
MP Morgan Securities plc

CONTACTS: *Note: Officers with more than one job title may be intentionally listed here more than once.*

Mary Erdoes, CEO, Divisional
Douglas Petno, CEO, Divisional
Marianne Lake, CEO, Divisional
James Dimon, CEO
Jennifer Piepszak, CFO
Nicole Giles, Chief Accounting Officer
Lori Beer, Chief Information Officer
Ashley Bacon, Chief Risk Officer
Daniel Pinto, Co- President
Gordon Smith, Co- President
Stacey Friedman, General Counsel
Peter Scher, Other Corporate Officer
Robin Leopold, Other Corporate Officer

GROWTH PLANS/SPECIAL FEATURES:

JPMorgan Chase & Co., Inc. (JPM) is one of the largest banking institutions in the world, with operations in over 60 countries and $3.2 trillion in assets (as of November 2020). JPM's principal subsidiaries include: JPMorgan Chase Bank, NA, a national banking association that is JPM's principal credit card-issuing bank; and J.P. Morgan Securities LLC, a non-bank subsidiary of the bank, is a broker-dealer investment firm serving the U.S., while J.P. Morgan Securities plc operates in the U.K. JPM operates its business through four segments: consumer and community banking (CCB), corporate and investment banking (CIB), commercial banking, and asset and wealth management (AWM). The CCB segment serves consumers and businesses through personal service at bank branches and through ATMs, online, mobile and telephone banking. The CIB segment, comprised of banking and markets and investor services, offers a broad range of investment banking, market-making, prime brokerage, and treasury and securities products and services to a global client base. The commercial banking segment provides local expertise and service to U.S. and U.S. multinational clients, including corporations, municipalities, financial institutions and nonprofit entities, with annual revenue generally ranging from $20 million to $2 billion. This division also provides financing to real estate investors and owners. Solutions within the commercial banking segment include lending, treasury services, investment banking and more. The AWM segment manages client assets and offers investment management across most major asset classes such as equities, fixed income, alternatives and money market funds. This division also offers multi-asset investment management, retirement products and services, brokerage and banking services, including trusts, estates, loans, mortgages and deposits.

JPMorgan Chase offers its employees comprehensive benefits, retirement options and assistance programs.

FINANCIAL DATA: *Note: Data for latest year may not have been available at press time.*

In U.S. $	2020	2019	2018	2017	2016	2015
Revenue	119,543,000,000	115,627,000,000	109,029,000,000	98,979,000,000	95,668,000,000	93,029,000,000
R&D Expense						
Operating Income						
Operating Margin %						
SGA Expense	47,802,000,000	47,555,000,000	45,209,000,000	41,615,000,000	39,722,000,000	38,651,000,000
Net Income	29,131,000,000	36,431,000,000	32,474,000,000	24,441,000,000	24,733,000,000	24,442,000,000
Operating Cash Flow	-79,910,000,000	6,046,000,000	14,187,000,000	-2,501,000,000	20,196,000,000	73,466,000,000
Capital Expenditure						
EBITDA						
Return on Assets %		.01%	.01%	.01%	.01%	.01%
Return on Equity %		.15%	.13%	.10%	.10%	.10%
Debt to Equity		1.244	1.224	1.237	1.294	1.303

CONTACT INFORMATION:

Phone: 212 270-6000   Fax: 212 270-1648
Toll-Free: 877-242-7372
Address: 383 Madison Ave., New York, NY 10179 United States

STOCK TICKER/OTHER:

Stock Ticker: JPM   Exchange: NYS
Employees: 251,196   Fiscal Year Ends: 12/31
Parent Company:

SALARIES/BONUSES:

Top Exec. Salary: $ Bonus: $
Second Exec. Salary: $ Bonus: $

OTHER THOUGHTS:

Estimated Female Officers or Directors: 3
Hot Spot for Advancement for Women/Minorities: Y

Juniper Networks Inc

www.juniper.net

NAIC Code: 334210A

TYPES OF BUSINESS:

Networking Equipment
IP Networking Systems
Internet Routers
Network Security Products
Internet Software
Intrusion Prevention
Application Acceleration

BRANDS/DIVISIONS/AFFILIATES:

ACX
MX
PTX
EX
SRX
Juniper
Netrounds

CONTACTS: Note: Officers with more than one job title may be intentionally listed here more than once.

Rami Rahim, CEO
Kenneth Miller, CFO
Scott Kriens, Chairman of the Board
Terrance Spidell, Chief Accounting Officer
Bikash Koley, Chief Technology Officer
Manoj Leelanivas, Executive VP
Anand Athreya, Executive VP
Brian Martin, Senior VP

GROWTH PLANS/SPECIAL FEATURES:

Juniper Networks, Inc. designs, develops and sells products and services for high-performance networks. These products help customers build highly scalable, reliable, secure and cost-effective networks for their businesses. Juniper sells its products in more than 150 countries across three geographic regions: Americas; Europe, Middle East and Africa (EMEA); and Asia Pacific. The company's offerings address high-performance network requirements for global service providers, cloud environments, enterprises, governments and research and public-sector organizations who view the network as critical to its business success. Routing products include the firm's ACX universal metro routers, MX universal routing platform, PTX packet transport routers, CTP circuit to pack platforms and JRR200 route reflector appliance. Switching products include the EX ethernet and QFX series switches, as well as data center switching architectures. Security products include the SRX series firewalls; vSRX firewalls for private, hybrid or public cloud environments; cSRX container firewall; next-generation firewall services; Juniper advanced threat prevention products; Juniper security intelligence (SecIntel); Junos space security director; a policy enforcer; Juniper secure analytics; integrate real-time threat intelligence; and Juniper identity management service. Other products include cloud services, network automation, network Edge, network operating system, packet optical, SDN and related management/operations, wireless access points and more. Juniper Networks owns nearly 4,000 issued or pending technology patents. In late-2021, Juniper Networks acquired Netrounds, which provides a programmable, software-based active test and service platform for fixed and mobile networks; and agreed to acquire 128 Technology, Inc. and Apstra, Inc.

Juniper Networks offers medical, dental, prescription and vision insurance; paid time off; and stock/savings plans.

FINANCIAL DATA: Note: Data for latest year may not have been available at press time.

In U.S. $	2020	2019	2018	2017	2016	2015
Revenue	4,445,100,000	4,445,400,000	4,647,500,000	5,027,200,000	4,990,100,000	4,857,800,000
R&D Expense	958,400,000	955,700,000	1,003,200,000	980,700,000	1,013,700,000	994,500,000
Operating Income	421,100,000	477,500,000	579,500,000	913,700,000	893,000,000	911,400,000
Operating Margin %		.11%	.12%	.18%	.18%	.19%
SGA Expense	1,194,200,000	1,183,600,000	1,158,500,000	1,177,700,000	1,197,800,000	1,172,700,000
Net Income	257,800,000	345,000,000	566,900,000	306,200,000	592,700,000	633,700,000
Operating Cash Flow	612,000,000	528,900,000	861,100,000	1,260,100,000	1,106,000,000	892,500,000
Capital Expenditure	100,400,000	109,600,000	147,400,000	151,200,000	214,700,000	210,300,000
EBITDA	554,600,000	713,400,000	846,400,000	1,138,600,000	1,131,800,000	1,112,000,000
Return on Assets %		.04%	.06%	.03%	.06%	.07%
Return on Equity %		.07%	.12%	.06%	.12%	.13%
Debt to Equity		0.40	0.371	0.456	0.43	0.36

CONTACT INFORMATION:

Phone: 408 745-2000   Fax: 408 745-2100
Toll-Free: 888-586-4737
Address: 1133 Innovation Way, Sunnyvale, CA 94089 United States

STOCK TICKER/OTHER:

Stock Ticker: JNPR
Employees: 9,950
Parent Company:

Exchange: NYS
Fiscal Year Ends: 12/31

SALARIES/BONUSES:

Top Exec. Salary: $ Bonus: $
Second Exec. Salary: $ Bonus: $

OTHER THOUGHTS:

Estimated Female Officers or Directors: 3
Hot Spot for Advancement for Women/Minorities: Y

Kaiser Permanente

NAIC Code: 622110

www.kaiserpermanente.org

TYPES OF BUSINESS:

General Medical and Surgical Hospitals
Telemedicine
Outpatient Facilities
HMO
Medical School
Integrated Health Care System
Physician Networks
Clinical Record Management

BRANDS/DIVISIONS/AFFILIATES:

Kaiser Foundation Health Plan Inc
Kaiser Foundation Hospitals
Permanente Medical Groups
Kaiser Permanente Center for Health Research
KP HealthConnect
Kaiser Permanente Bernard J Tyson School of Med

CONTACTS: *Note: Officers with more than one job title may be intentionally listed here more than once.*

Gregory A. Adams, CEO
Janet A. Liang, COO
Kathy Lancaster, CFO
Catherine Hernandez, CCO
Christian Meisner, Sr. VP-Chief Human Resources Officer
Raymond J. Baxter, Sr. VP-Community Benefit, Research & Health Policy
Diane Comer, Interim CIO
Mark S. Zemelman, General Counsel
Arthur M. Southam, Exec. VP-Health Plan Oper.
Chris Grant, Sr. VP-Corp. Dev. & Care Delivery Strategy
Diane Gage Lofgren, Sr. VP
Cynthia Powers Overmyer, Sr. VP-Internal Audit Svcs.
Daniel P. Garcia, Chief Compliance Officer
Anthony Barrueta, Sr. VP-Gov't Rel.
Amy Compton-Phillips, Associate Exec. Dir.-Quality, Permanente
Gregory A. Adams, Chmn.

GROWTH PLANS/SPECIAL FEATURES:

Kaiser Permanente is a nonprofit company dedicated to providing integrated health care coverage. The firm operates in California, Colorado, Georgia, Hawaii, Maryland, Washington D.C., Oregon, Virginia and Washington. It serves 12.4 million members, most of which are in California. Kaiser has three main operating divisions: Kaiser Foundation Health Plan, Inc., which contracts with individuals and groups to provide medical coverage; Kaiser Foundation Hospitals and their subsidiaries, operating community hospitals and outpatient facilities in several states; and Permanente Medical Groups, the company's network of physicians providing healthcare to its members. As of mid-2020, the company's assets consist of 39 medical centers, including hospitals and outpatient facilities; 715 medical offices; and more than 23,270 physicians. Kaiser Permanente is one of the largest health plans serving the Medicare program. Kaiser Foundation Hospitals also fund medical- and health-related research. The Kaiser Permanente Center for Health Research, founded in 1964, is a single research center that spans two regions of Kaiser Permanente: Northwest and Hawaii. The center pursues a vigorous agenda of public health research within large, diverse populations, and specializes in the disciplines of biostatistics, clinical research support services, data resources, evidence-based practices and qualitative research. In addition, the company's KP HealthConnect platform integrates clinical records with appointments, registration and billing, thereby significantly improving care delivery and patient satisfaction. In mid-2020, Kaiser inaugurated its first class of medical students at the new Kaiser Permanente Bernard J. Tyson School of Medicine, located in Pasadena, California. The school will offer conventional medical education as well as ground-breaking integrated health care to prepare future physicians to become collaborative and transformative in the health care sector.

Kaiser offers its employees comprehensive health benefits, retirement options, life and disability insurance and a variety of employee assistance plans and programs.

FINANCIAL DATA: *Note: Data for latest year may not have been available at press time.*

In U.S. $	2020	2019	2018	2017	2016	2015
Revenue	88,700,000,000	84,500,000,000	79,700,000,000	72,700,000,000	64,600,000,000	60,700,000,000
R&D Expense						
Operating Income						
Operating Margin %						
SGA Expense						
Net Income	6,400,000,000	7,400,000,000	2,500,000,000	3,800,000,000	3,100,000,000	1,900,000,000
Operating Cash Flow						
Capital Expenditure						
EBITDA						
Return on Assets %						
Return on Equity %						
Debt to Equity						

CONTACT INFORMATION:

Phone: 510-271-5910   Fax:
Toll-Free:
Address: 1 Kaiser Plaza, 19/Fl, Oakland, CA 94612 United States

SALARIES/BONUSES:

Top Exec. Salary: $ Bonus: $
Second Exec. Salary: $ Bonus: $

STOCK TICKER/OTHER:

Stock Ticker: Nonprofit   Exchange:
Employees: 217,000   Fiscal Year Ends: 12/31
Parent Company:

OTHER THOUGHTS:

Estimated Female Officers or Directors: 9
Hot Spot for Advancement for Women/Minorities: Y

Sales, profits and employees may be estimates. Financial information, benefits and other data can change quickly and may vary from those stated here.

Kansas City Southern

www.kcsouthern.com/en-us

NAIC Code: 482111

TYPES OF BUSINESS:

Line-Haul Railroads
Locomotive Leasing
Insurance
Railroad Ties
Bulk Materials Handling

BRANDS/DIVISIONS/AFFILIATES:

Kansas City Southern Railway Company
Kansas City Southern de Mexico SA de CV
Mexrail Inc
Texas Mexican Railway Company (The)
Panama Canal Railway Company
Panarail Tourism Company
Pabtex Inc

CONTACTS: Note: Officers with more than one job title may be intentionally listed here more than once.

Michael Upchurch, CFO
Suzanne Grafton, Chief Accounting Officer
Brian Hancock, Chief Marketing Officer
Michael Naatz, Chief Marketing Officer
Robert Druten, Director
Warren Erdman, Executive VP, Divisional
Jeffrey Songer, Executive VP
Adam Godderz, General Counsel
Jose Delano, Other Corporate Officer
William Wochner, Other Executive Officer
Patrick Ottensmeyer, President
Lora Cheatum, Senior VP, Divisional

GROWTH PLANS/SPECIAL FEATURES:

Kansas City Southern (KCS) is a holding company that, through its subsidiaries, owns and operates rail transportation companies in North America. The company owns and operates Kansas City Southern Railway Company (KCSR); Kansas City Southern de Mexico, SA de CV (KCSM); and Mexrail, Inc., which owns The Texas Mexican Railway Company (Tex-Mex). Additionally, the firm maintains the Panama Canal Railway Company (PCRC) as a joint venture with Mi-Jack Products, Inc. The firm's first railway, KCSR, was founded in 1887 and provides one of the shortest north-to-south rail routes between Kansas City, Missouri and significant ports along the Gulf of Mexico in Texas, Mississippi, Louisiana and Alabama. KCSR, KCSM and Tex-Mex together operate tracks extending from the Southeast and Midwest regions of the U.S. into Mexico, connecting with all other Class I railroads along the corridor. By a special concession from the Government of Panama, PCRC operates a 47-mile railroad located adjacent to the Panama Canal, providing international container shipping companies with a railway transportation option across the isthmus. Panarail Tourism Company, a subsidiary of PCRC, offers commuter and tourist passenger service over the Panama Canal Railway. In addition to its primary railways, KCS also holds interests in Pabtex, Inc., a bulk handling facility in Port Arthur, Texas specializing in exporting petroleum coke and coal. Moreover, the company ships via maritime to the western shores of South America and various Asia Pacific markets. In May 2021, KCS agreed to be acquired by Canadian National Railway for $33.6 billion. The combined entity would be the first rail network connecting the U.S., Mexico and Canada, and would be headquartered in Calgary, Canada.

FINANCIAL DATA: Note: Data for latest year may not have been available at press time.

In U.S. $	2020	2019	2018	2017	2016	2015
Revenue	2,632,600,000	2,866,000,000	2,751,700,000	2,627,000,000	2,397,000,000	2,418,800,000
R&D Expense						
Operating Income	1,033,600,000	1,055,100,000	968,400,000	921,600,000	818,500,000	813,400,000
Operating Margin %		.37%	.35%	.35%	.34%	.34%
SGA Expense						
Net Income	617,000,000	538,900,000	627,400,000	962,000,000	478,100,000	483,500,000
Operating Cash Flow	1,080,000,000	1,103,500,000	945,700,000	1,028,400,000	913,300,000	909,300,000
Capital Expenditure	490,100,000	626,200,000	619,200,000	628,000,000	590,500,000	832,200,000
EBITDA	1,332,000,000	1,255,000,000	1,343,600,000	1,295,400,000	1,065,400,000	1,039,100,000
Return on Assets %		.06%	.07%	.11%	.06%	.06%
Return on Equity %		.12%	.13%	.22%	.12%	.13%
Debt to Equity		0.75	0.557	0.492	0.556	0.523

CONTACT INFORMATION:

Phone: 816 983-1303   Fax: 816 556-0297
Toll-Free: 800-468-6527
Address: 427 W. 12th St., Kansas City, MO 64105 United States

SALARIES/BONUSES:

Top Exec. Salary: $ Bonus: $
Second Exec. Salary: $ Bonus: $

STOCK TICKER/OTHER:

Stock Ticker: KSU
Employees: 6,522
Parent Company:

Exchange: NYS
Fiscal Year Ends: 12/31

OTHER THOUGHTS:

Estimated Female Officers or Directors: 1
Hot Spot for Advancement for Women/Minorities: Y

KBR Inc
NAIC Code: 237000

TYPES OF BUSINESS:
Heavy Construction and Engineering
Engineering
Technology
Test and Evaluation
Software
Petrochemicals
Licensing
Energy

BRANDS/DIVISIONS/AFFILIATES:

CONTACTS: Note: Officers with more than one job title may be intentionally listed here more than once.
Mark Sopp, CFO
Raymond Carney, Chief Accounting Officer
Eileen Akerson, Executive VP
Ian Mackey, Executive VP
Gregory Conlon, Other Executive Officer
William Bright, President, Divisional
John Derbyshire, President, Divisional
J. Ibrahim, President, Divisional
Farhan Mujib, President, Divisional
Stuart Bradie, President
Adam Kramer, Secretary

GROWTH PLANS/SPECIAL FEATURES:
KBR, Inc. delivers scientific, technology and engineering solutions to governments and companies worldwide. The firm's core business segments include government solutions, technology solutions and energy solutions. The government solutions business segment provides full lifecycle support solutions to defense, intelligence, space, aviation and other programs and missions for military and other government agencies in the U.S., U.K. and Australia. Services range from research and development to systems engineering, test and evaluation, systems integration and program management to operations support, readiness and logistics. This business segment also provides software and engineering solutions to critical national security missions across space, cyber, intelligence, surveillance and reconnaissance, mission defense and intelligence domains to the U.S. government and related defense agencies. The technology solutions segment offers a sustainability focus when developing its technologies in areas such as refining, petrochemicals, inorganic chemicals, specialty chemicals, gasification, syngas, ammonia, nitric acid and fertilizers. Licensing and engineering/design services are typically provided during the front-end planning stage of both green-and brown-field capital projects, and proprietary equipment is delivered and installed as part of this segment's facility construction services. Last, the energy solutions business segment provides full lifecycle support solutions across the upstream, midstream and downstream energy markets, including advisory services focused on energy transition and net-zero carbon objectives; technology-led industrial solutions focused on advanced remote operations capabilities; digitally-enabled professional services such as program management, engineering, design and advanced project integration; and other construction services. In May 2021, KBR signed a memorandum of understanding with Cummins, Inc. to offer a complete and integrated solution to produce ammonia from renewable sources, commonly referred to as green ammonia.

FINANCIAL DATA: Note: Data for latest year may not have been available at press time.

In U.S. $	2020	2019	2018	2017	2016	2015
Revenue	5,767,000,000	5,639,000,000	4,913,000,000	4,171,000,000	4,268,000,000	5,096,000,000
R&D Expense						
Operating Income	331,000,000	312,000,000	290,000,000	195,000,000	-31,000,000	170,000,000
Operating Margin %		.06%	.06%	.05%	-.01%	.03%
SGA Expense	335,000,000	341,000,000	166,000,000	147,000,000	143,000,000	155,000,000
Net Income	-72,000,000	202,000,000	281,000,000	434,000,000	-61,000,000	203,000,000
Operating Cash Flow	367,000,000	256,000,000	165,000,000	193,000,000	61,000,000	47,000,000
Capital Expenditure	20,000,000	20,000,000	17,000,000	8,000,000	11,000,000	10,000,000
EBITDA	173,000,000	471,000,000	527,000,000	318,000,000	14,000,000	209,000,000
Return on Assets %		.04%	.06%	.11%	-.02%	.05%
Return on Equity %		.11%	.19%	.44%	-.07%	.20%
Debt to Equity		0.75	0.724	0.405	0.904	0.048

CONTACT INFORMATION:
Phone: 713 753-2000   Fax: 713 753-5353
Toll-Free:
Address: 601 Jefferson St., Ste. 3400, Houston, TX 77002 United States

STOCK TICKER/OTHER:
Stock Ticker: KBR   Exchange: NYS
Employees: 28,000   Fiscal Year Ends: 12/31
Parent Company:

SALARIES/BONUSES:
Top Exec. Salary: $ Bonus: $
Second Exec. Salary: $ Bonus: $

OTHER THOUGHTS:
Estimated Female Officers or Directors: 2
Hot Spot for Advancement for Women/Minorities: Y

Kellogg Company

www.kelloggs.com

NAIC Code: 311230

TYPES OF BUSINESS:

Cereal Manufacturing
Ready-to-Eat Cereal
Snack Foods
Frozen Foods
Processed Foods
Manufacturer
Marketer

BRANDS/DIVISIONS/AFFILIATES:

Kelloggs
Cheez-It
Pringles
Austin
RXBAR
Eggo
Morningstar Farms
Menuvation Center at The Hatchery

CONTACTS: *Note: Officers with more than one job title may be intentionally listed here more than once.*

Steven Cahillane, CEO
Kurt Forche, Chief Accounting Officer
Monica McGurk, Other Executive Officer
Gary Pilnick, Other Executive Officer
David Lawlor, President, Geographical
Amit Banati, President, Geographical
Christopher Hood, President, Geographical
Maria Mejia, President, Geographical
Alistair Hirst, Senior VP, Divisional
Melissa Howell, Senior VP, Divisional
Fareed Khan, Senior VP

GROWTH PLANS/SPECIAL FEATURES:

Kellogg Company and its subsidiaries are engaged in the manufacture and marketing of ready-to-eat cereal and convenience foods. The company's principal products are snacks such as crackers, toaster pastries, cereal bars and granola bars; and convenience foods such as cereals, frozen waffles, vegetable-based foods and noodles. These products are manufactured in 21 countries and marketed in more than 180 countries. They are sold to retailers through direct sales forces for resale to consumers. Cereals and cereal bars are generally marketed under the Kellogg's name, with some under the Kashi and Bear Naked brands. Crackers, crisps and snack brands include Kellogg's, Cheez-It, Pringles, Austin, Parati and RXBAR. Frozen foods are marketed under the Eggo and Morningstar Farms brands. In December 2020, Kellogg Company announced a new, state-of-the-art Menuvation Center at The Hatchery, a food and beverage business incubator located in Chicago, to help non-commercial and commercial foodservice operators develop new menus.

FINANCIAL DATA: *Note: Data for latest year may not have been available at press time.*

In U.S. $	2020	2019	2018	2017	2016	2015
Revenue	13,770,000,000	13,578,000,000	13,547,000,000	12,923,000,000	13,014,000,000	13,525,000,000
R&D Expense						
Operating Income	1,761,000,000	1,401,000,000	1,706,000,000	1,946,000,000	1,395,000,000	1,091,000,000
Operating Margin %		.10%	.13%	.15%	.11%	.08%
SGA Expense	2,966,000,000	2,980,000,000	3,020,000,000	3,076,000,000	3,360,000,000	3,590,000,000
Net Income	1,251,000,000	960,000,000	1,336,000,000	1,269,000,000	694,000,000	614,000,000
Operating Cash Flow	1,986,000,000	1,176,000,000	1,536,000,000	1,646,000,000	1,628,000,000	1,691,000,000
Capital Expenditure	505,000,000	586,000,000	578,000,000	501,000,000	507,000,000	553,000,000
EBITDA	2,361,000,000	2,073,000,000	2,132,000,000	2,411,000,000	1,850,000,000	1,534,000,000
Return on Assets %		.05%	.08%	.08%	.05%	.04%
Return on Equity %		.36%	.56%	.62%	.34%	.25%
Debt to Equity		2.777	3.155	3.542	3.507	2.485

CONTACT INFORMATION:

Phone: 269 961-2000   Fax: 616 961-2871
Toll-Free: 800-962-1413
Address: One Kellogg Sq., Battle Creek, MI 49016 United States

STOCK TICKER/OTHER:

Stock Ticker: K
Employees: 31,000
Parent Company:

Exchange: NYS
Fiscal Year Ends: 12/31

SALARIES/BONUSES:

Top Exec. Salary: $ Bonus: $
Second Exec. Salary: $ Bonus: $

OTHER THOUGHTS:

Estimated Female Officers or Directors: 10
Hot Spot for Advancement for Women/Minorities: Y

KEMET Corporation

NAIC Code: 334413

TYPES OF BUSINESS:

Electronic Equipment-Capacitors

BRANDS/DIVISIONS/AFFILIATES:

KEMET Blue Powder Corporation
Evox Rifa Group Oyj
Arcotronics Italia SpA
KEMET Foil Manufacturing LLC
KEMET Charged
TOKIN
Yageo Corporation

CONTACTS: Note: Officers with more than one job title may be intentionally listed here more than once.

William Lowe, CEO
Gregory Thompson, CFO
Frank Brandenberg, Chairman of the Board
Philip Lessner, Chief Technology Officer
Michael Raynor, Controller
Shigenori Oyama, Executive VP, Divisional
Charles Meeks, Executive VP, Divisional
R. Assaf, General Counsel
Stefano Vetralla, Other Executive Officer
Susan Barkal, Other Executive Officer
Robert Willoughby, Senior VP, Divisional
Claudio Lollini, Senior VP, Divisional
Andreas Meier, Senior VP, Divisional
Richard Vatinelle, Vice President

GROWTH PLANS/SPECIAL FEATURES:

KEMET Corporation is a global manufacturer of passive electronic components. These components are used in virtually all electronic applications and products, including communication systems, data processing equipment, personal computers, cellular phones, power management systems, automotive electronic systems and defense and aerospace systems as well as most consumer electronics. KEMET also makes solid aluminum capacitors for high-frequency applications. The company is organized into three business divisions: solid capacitors, film and electrolytic and electro-magnetic, sensors and actuators. The solid capacitors business group operates 10 manufacturing sites in the U.S. Mexico and Asia. This division primarily produces tantalum, aluminum, polymer and ceramic capacitors which are sold globally. It also produces tantalum powder used in the production of tantalum capacitors. The tantalum portfolio includes computing, telecommunications, consumer, medical, military, automotive and general industries products. Ceramics include high temperature and capacitance stable products for markets such as medical, industrial, defense and aerospace. Subsidiary KEMET Blue Powder Corporation, as well as the tantalum business unit of EPCOS AG, manufacture solid capacitor products. The film and electrolytic business group produces film, paper and wet aluminum electrolytic capacitors from 10 film and electrolytic manufacturing sites throughout Europe and Asia. This segment primarily serves the industrial, automotive, consumer and telecom markets. The electro-magnetic, sensors and actuators segment operates in four manufacturing sites through Asia. The segment primarily produces EMC materials and devices, piezo materials and actuators and various types of sensors. The firm holds more than 1,600 patents and trademarks worldwide. In June 2020, KEMET was acquired by Yageo Corporation for approximately $1.8 billion.

FINANCIAL DATA: Note: Data for latest year may not have been available at press time.

In U.S. $	2020	2019	2018	2017	2016	2015
Revenue	1,260,000,000	1,382,818,048	1,199,926,016	757,790,976	734,822,976	823,192,000
R&D Expense						
Operating Income						
Operating Margin %						
SGA Expense						
Net Income		206,587,008	254,528,992	47,989,000	-53,629,000	-14,143,000
Operating Cash Flow						
Capital Expenditure						
EBITDA						
Return on Assets %						
Return on Equity %						
Debt to Equity						

CONTACT INFORMATION:

Phone: 864 963-6300   Fax: 864 963-6322
Toll-Free: 877-695-3638
Address: 2835 Kemet Way, Simpsonville, SC 29681 United States

SALARIES/BONUSES:

Top Exec. Salary: $ Bonus: $
Second Exec. Salary: $ Bonus: $

STOCK TICKER/OTHER:

Stock Ticker: KEM
Employees: 9,100
Parent Company: Yageo Corporation

Exchange: NYS
Fiscal Year Ends: 02/28

OTHER THOUGHTS:

Estimated Female Officers or Directors: 3
Hot Spot for Advancement for Women/Minorities: Y

Kenco Group Inc

www.kencogroup.com

NAIC Code: 541614

TYPES OF BUSINESS:

Logistics Outsourcing
Third Party Logistics
Distribution
Transportation Management
Material Handling
Engineering
Consulting
Technology

BRANDS/DIVISIONS/AFFILIATES:

Kenco FleetCloud
Kenco STARR

CONTACTS: Note: Officers with more than one job title may be intentionally listed here more than once.

Denis Reilly, CEO
David Caines, COO
David Caines, Pres.
John Lamb, Sr. VP-Oper.
Sam Smartt, Jr., Vice Chmn.
Kristi Montgomery, VP-Technology, Kenco Management
Jimmy Glascock, Pres., JDK Real Estate LLC
Jane Kennedy Greene, Chmn.

GROWTH PLANS/SPECIAL FEATURES:

Kenco Group, Inc. is a third-party logistics company. The firm's integrated logistics solutions include distribution and ecommerce fulfillment, comprehensive transportation management services, material handling equipment services, engineering and innovation consulting, and information technology. Kenco manages 90 distribution facilities, comprises 30 million square feet of space. The company offers a full range of transportation services, including transportation management, freight brokerage and dedicated contract carriage. Kenco's material handling equipment fleet management software solution helps businesses maintain, optimize and standardize their total fleet. Kenco FleetCloud product is a proprietary telematics solution that automates material handling equipment service processes and monitors equipment performance to drive efficiency, safety and compliance. FleetCloud provides real-time visibility into a wide range of metrics that impact material handling equipment operations. Kenco STARR is the company's innovative technology solution that helps customers improve their supply chain performance. STARR encompasses technology, resources and freight rates for small-to-mid-sized shippers. Kenco's supply chain solutions span engineering, consulting, innovation, continuous improvement and advanced analytics. Kenco Group serves more than 200 clients across a wide range of industries, including industrial, durable consumer goods, fast-moving consumer goods and healthcare.

FINANCIAL DATA: Note: Data for latest year may not have been available at press time.

In U.S. $	2020	2019	2018	2017	2016	2015
Revenue	753,816,000	673,050,000	641,000,000	571,000,000	550,000,000	530,000,000
R&D Expense						
Operating Income						
Operating Margin %						
SGA Expense						
Net Income						
Operating Cash Flow						
Capital Expenditure						
EBITDA						
Return on Assets %						
Return on Equity %						
Debt to Equity						

CONTACT INFORMATION:

Phone: 423-622-1113   Fax:
Toll-Free: 800-758-3289
Address: 2001 Riverside Dr., Chattanooga, TN 37406 United States

STOCK TICKER/OTHER:

Stock Ticker: Private
Employees: 5,000
Parent Company:

Exchange:
Fiscal Year Ends: 12/31

SALARIES/BONUSES:

Top Exec. Salary: $ Bonus: $
Second Exec. Salary: $ Bonus: $

OTHER THOUGHTS:

Estimated Female Officers or Directors: 2
Hot Spot for Advancement for Women/Minorities: Y

Kiewit Corporation

NAIC Code: 237310

TYPES OF BUSINESS:

Construction & Engineering Services

BRANDS/DIVISIONS/AFFILIATES:

CONTACTS: *Note: Officers with more than one job title may be intentionally listed here more than once.*

Tom Shelby, Exec. VP

GROWTH PLANS/SPECIAL FEATURES:

Kiewit Corporation, based in Omaha, Nebraska and employee-owned, is one of the largest general contractors in the world. The firm is organized into seven business divisions: building; industrial; mining; oil, gas and chemical; power; transportation; and water/wastewater. The building division focuses on office buildings, industrial complexes, education and sports facilities, hotels, hospitals, transportation terminals, science and technology facilities and manufacturing plants, as well as retail and special-use facilities. The segment is Leadership in Energy and Environmental Design (LEED) certified. The industrial division has extensive experience in industrial engineering and construction with work including mineral processing; cement; bulk manufacturing; industrial water; metals; pulp and paper; specialty chemicals; food and beverage; pharmaceuticals and advanced manufacturing. The mining division specializes in mine management, production, maintenance, contract mining, ore processing and mine infrastructure. The oil, gas and chemical division partners with domestic and international oil and gas firms to develop energy sources. It offers clients a fully integrated delivery model for engineer-procure-construct (EPC) and startup services for their energy needs. This division focuses on the market sectors of offshore, oil sands, midstream and downstream. The power division helps clients meet the challenge of changing power consumption trends by building run-of-the-river hydroelectric, nuclear and geothermal power plants, as well as cogeneration, combined-cycle and waste-to-energy generation and resource facilities. The transportation division builds highways, bridges, rails and runways in order to connect the world. Its transportation projects deliver engineering solutions and construction services for air, bridge, marine/port, rail, roads and tunnels sectors, among others. Last, water/wastewater performs water supply projects such as roller-compacted concrete, earth-fill and rock-fill dams, reservoirs, water tunnels and canals across North America. Kiewet has hundreds of subsidiaries and offices located in the U.S., Canada and Mexico.

FINANCIAL DATA: *Note: Data for latest year may not have been available at press time.*

In U.S. $	2020	2019	2018	2017	2016	2015
Revenue	12,500,000,000	10,300,000,000	8,900,000,000	8,700,000,000	8,600,000,000	10,380,000,000
R&D Expense						
Operating Income						
Operating Margin %						
SGA Expense						
Net Income						
Operating Cash Flow						
Capital Expenditure						
EBITDA						
Return on Assets %						
Return on Equity %						
Debt to Equity						

CONTACT INFORMATION:

Phone: 402-342-2052   Fax: 402-271-2829
Toll-Free:
Address: 1550 Mike Fahey St., Omaha, NE 68102 United States

STOCK TICKER/OTHER:

Stock Ticker: Private   Exchange:
Employees: 27,000   Fiscal Year Ends:
Parent Company:

SALARIES/BONUSES:

Top Exec. Salary: $ Bonus: $
Second Exec. Salary: $ Bonus: $

OTHER THOUGHTS:

Estimated Female Officers or Directors:
Hot Spot for Advancement for Women/Minorities:

Kimberly-Clark Corporation

www.kimberly-clark.com

NAIC Code: 322291

TYPES OF BUSINESS:

Personal Care Products-Paper
Consumer Tissue Products
Safety Products
Healthcare Products

BRANDS/DIVISIONS/AFFILIATES:

Depend
Little Swimmers
Huggies
U by Kotex
Intimus
Scott
Kleenex
Jackson Safety

CONTACTS: Note: Officers with more than one job title may be intentionally listed here more than once.

Michael Hsu, CEO
Sergio Cruz, Pres., Geographical
Maria Henry, CFO
Thomas Falk, Chairman of the Board
Andrew Drexler, Controller
Jeffrey Melucci, General Counsel
Sandra MacQuillan, Other Executive Officer
Scott Boston, Other Executive Officer
Aaron Powell, President, Divisional
Tristram Wilkinson, President, Divisional
Kimberly Underhill, President, Divisional
Achal Agarwal, President, Geographical

GROWTH PLANS/SPECIAL FEATURES:

Kimberly-Clark Corporation is a health and hygiene company that manufactures a wide range of products worldwide. Kimberly-Clark operates in three segments: personal care, consumer tissue and K-C professional. The personal care segment manufactures and markets products such as feminine and incontinence care products; baby wipes; training, youth and swim pants; and disposable diapers. Items in this segment are sold under brand names such as Kotex, Depend, Poise, Little Swimmers, Pull-Ups, Huggies, DryNites, U by Kotex, Plenitud, Intimus and GoodNites. The consumer tissue segment manufactures and markets napkins, paper towels, facial and bathroom tissue and related products for household use. Products in this division are sold under brands such as Scott, Kleenex, Viva, Andrex, Scottex, Cottonelle and Neve. The K-C professional segment manufactures and markets paper towels, napkins, wipes, facial and bathroom tissue and a range of safety products for the away-from-home marketplace. Brand names in this segment include Kimtech, Scott, WypAll, Kleenex and Jackson Safety. Kimberly-Clark's largest customer is Wal-Mart, Inc., accounting for 15% of net sales in 2020. The firm has manufacturing facilities in 34 countries and sells products in a substantial majority of countries around the world. In October 2020, Kimberly-Clark completed its $1.2 billion acquisition of Softex Indonesia, a leader in the fast-growing Indonesian personal care market.

FINANCIAL DATA: Note: Data for latest year may not have been available at press time.

In U.S. $	2020	2019	2018	2017	2016	2015
Revenue	19,140,000,000	18,450,000,000	18,486,000,000	18,259,000,000	18,202,000,000	18,591,000,000
R&D Expense						
Operating Income	3,244,000,000	2,991,000,000	2,229,000,000	3,299,000,000	3,317,000,000	1,613,000,000
Operating Margin %		.16%	.12%	.18%	.18%	.09%
SGA Expense	3,632,000,000	3,254,000,000	3,367,000,000	3,227,000,000	3,326,000,000	3,443,000,000
Net Income	2,352,000,000	2,157,000,000	1,410,000,000	2,278,000,000	2,166,000,000	1,013,000,000
Operating Cash Flow	3,729,000,000	2,736,000,000	2,970,000,000	2,929,000,000	3,232,000,000	2,306,000,000
Capital Expenditure	1,217,000,000	1,209,000,000	877,000,000	785,000,000	771,000,000	1,056,000,000
EBITDA	3,978,000,000	3,828,000,000	2,958,000,000	4,033,000,000	4,033,000,000	2,376,000,000
Return on Assets %		.14%	.10%	.15%	.15%	.07%
Return on Equity %			8.25%	8.65%		3.65%
Debt to Equity				10.289		

CONTACT INFORMATION:

Phone: 972 281-1200 Fax:
Toll-Free: 888-525-8388
Address: PO Box 619100, Dallas, TX 75261 United States

STOCK TICKER/OTHER:

Stock Ticker: KMB
Employees: 46,000
Parent Company:

Exchange: NYS
Fiscal Year Ends: 12/31

SALARIES/BONUSES:

Top Exec. Salary: $ Bonus: $
Second Exec. Salary: $ Bonus: $

OTHER THOUGHTS:

Estimated Female Officers or Directors: 7
Hot Spot for Advancement for Women/Minorities: Y

KLA Corporation

NAIC Code: 333242

TYPES OF BUSINESS:

Semiconductor Test Equipment
Process Control & Yield Management Software & Services
Support Services

BRANDS/DIVISIONS/AFFILIATES:

CONTACTS: Note: Officers with more than one job title may be intentionally listed here more than once.

Richard Wallace, CEO
Bren Higgins, CFO
Edward Barnholt, Chairman of the Board
Virendra Kirloskar, Chief Accounting Officer
Ahmad Khan, Executive VP, Divisional
Brian Trafas, Executive VP, Divisional
Teri Little, Executive VP
Brian Lorig, General Manager, Divisional

GROWTH PLANS/SPECIAL FEATURES:

KLA Corporation is a supplier of process control and yield management products to the semiconductor and related nanoelectronics industries. The firm's products are categorized into the four groups: semiconductor process control (SPC); specialty semiconductor process (SSP); printed circuit board (PCB), display and component inspection (PDC); and other. The SPC's portfolio of defect inspection, review, metrology, patterning simulation, in situ process monitoring and data analytics products, and related service, software and other offerings, helps substrate and chip manufacturers manage yield throughout the wafer and chip fabrication processes, from research and development to final volume production. These offerings are designed to provide comprehensive solutions to help accelerate development and production ramp cycles, achieve higher and more stable semiconductor die yields and improve overall profitability. The SSP segment is conducted by the subsidiary SPTS Technologies, Inc. SPTS provides etch and deposition processes on a range of single wafer handling platforms for wafer sizes up to 330mm, as well as 400mm taped frame assemblies. These products include etch and deposition equipment designed to address advanced IC packaging manufacturing, and manufacturing of devices such as MEMS, LEDs, high speed RF and power semiconductors. The PDC segment enables electronic device manufacturers to inspect, test and measure printed circuit boards and flat panel displays and ICs to verify their quality, pattern the desired electronic circuitry on the relevant substrate and perform three-dimensional shaping of metalized circuits on multiple surfaces. The other segment encompasses KLA's research, development and marketing of products for the deposition of thin film coating of various materials on crystalline silicon photovoltaic wafers for solar energy panels.

FINANCIAL DATA: Note: Data for latest year may not have been available at press time.

In U.S. $	2020	2019	2018	2017	2016	2015
Revenue	5,806,424,000	4,568,904,000	4,036,701,000	3,480,014,000	2,984,493,000	
R&D Expense	863,864,000	711,030,000	608,712,000	526,870,000	481,258,000	
Operating Income	1,758,850,000	1,389,373,000	1,537,194,000	1,276,261,000	960,445,000	
Operating Margin %		.30%	.38%	.37%	.32%	
SGA Expense	734,149,000	599,124,000	443,426,000	389,336,000	379,399,000	
Net Income	1,216,785,000	1,175,617,000	802,265,000	926,076,000	704,422,000	
Operating Cash Flow	1,778,850,000	1,152,632,000	1,229,120,000	1,079,665,000	759,696,000	
Capital Expenditure	152,675,000	130,498,000	66,961,000	38,594,000	31,741,000	
EBITDA	1,825,034,000	1,654,059,000	1,632,991,000	1,353,558,000	1,048,011,000	
Return on Assets %		.16%	.14%	.18%	.14%	
Return on Equity %		.55%	.54%	.92%	1.27%	
Debt to Equity		1.193	1.381	2.021	4.437	

CONTACT INFORMATION:

Phone: 408 875-3000   Fax: 408 434-4266
Toll-Free:
Address: One Technology Dr., Milpitas, CA 95035 United States

STOCK TICKER/OTHER:

Stock Ticker: KLAC
Employees: 10,600
Parent Company:

Exchange: NAS
Fiscal Year Ends: 06/30

SALARIES/BONUSES:

Top Exec. Salary: $ Bonus: $
Second Exec. Salary: $ Bonus: $

OTHER THOUGHTS:

Estimated Female Officers or Directors:
Hot Spot for Advancement for Women/Minorities:

KPMG LLP

home.kpmg/us/en/home.html

NAIC Code: 541211

TYPES OF BUSINESS:

Accounting Services
Accounting
Audit Services
Advisory
Tax Services

BRANDS/DIVISIONS/AFFILIATES:

KPMG International
Audit Committee Institute
KPMG TaxWatch

CONTACTS: *Note: Officers with more than one job title may be intentionally listed here more than once.*

Paul Knopp, CEO
George Ledwith, Dir.-Global Comm.

GROWTH PLANS/SPECIAL FEATURES:

KPMG LLP, a subsidiary of global accounting cooperative KPMG International, is a leading provider of audit, advisory and tax services within the U.S. The firm's audit operations are based on a multidisciplinary approach focused on compliance tools, technological assistance and cultural values. KPMG founded and maintains the Audit Committee Institute, designed to educate audit committee members about governance, accounting, financial reporting and other audit issues. KPMG's tax services segment provides tax assistance in the following areas: economic and valuation services, exempt organizations tax, federal tax, inbound tax services, international corporate tax, international executive services, legislative and regulatory services, mergers and acquisitions, state and local tax and trade and customs. The company also provides tax-related news through its KPMG TaxWatch podcast series and tax-related newsletters and publications. The firm's advisory services division assists its clients in achieving strengthened governance, reporting and internal controls; early identification and assessment of risk and control issues; improved efficiency and effectiveness of key business processes; and informed responses to existing and proposed regulatory requirements. With offices across the country, KPMG serves companies and organizations in such major industry sectors as alternative investments, private capital, communications/media, consumer markets, energy, financial services, government, healthcare, life sciences, middle market and technology. The firm also maintains a special focus group that has industry experience with the issues Japanese companies face in the U.S., as well as both Japanese and U.S. business cultures, practices and standards.

KPMG offers its employees comprehensive health benefits, retirement and savings plans and a variety of employee assistance programs.

FINANCIAL DATA: *Note: Data for latest year may not have been available at press time.*

In U.S. $	2020	2019	2018	2017	2016	2015
Revenue	11,220,000,000	11,720,000,000	11,100,000,000	10,480,000,000	9,100,000,000	7,890,000,000
R&D Expense						
Operating Income						
Operating Margin %						
SGA Expense						
Net Income						
Operating Cash Flow						
Capital Expenditure						
EBITDA						
Return on Assets %						
Return on Equity %						
Debt to Equity						

CONTACT INFORMATION:

Phone: 212-758-9700   Fax: 212-758-9819
Toll-Free:
Address: 345 Park Ave., New York, NY 10154-0102 United States

STOCK TICKER/OTHER:

Stock Ticker: Subsidiary
Employees: 57,000
Parent Company: KPMG International

Exchange:
Fiscal Year Ends: 09/30

SALARIES/BONUSES:

Top Exec. Salary: $ Bonus: $
Second Exec. Salary: $ Bonus: $

OTHER THOUGHTS:

Estimated Female Officers or Directors:
Hot Spot for Advancement for Women/Minorities:

Kraft Heinz Company (The)   www.kraftheinzcompany.com/company.htm

NAIC Code: 311421

TYPES OF BUSINESS:

Food Products-Manufacturing
Manufacturer
Packaging
Distribution
Condiments
Frozen Foods
Soups & Snack Foods
Cheese

BRANDS/DIVISIONS/AFFILIATES:

3G Capital
Berkshire Hathaway Inc
Kraft
Heinz
Jell-O
Maxwell House
Oscar Mayer
Velveeta

CONTACTS: *Note: Officers with more than one job title may be intentionally listed here more than once.*

Miguel Patricio, CEO
John Cahill, Vice Chairman of the Board
Vince Garlati, Chief Accounting Officer
Alexandre Behring, Director
David Knopf, Executive VP
Rashida La Lande, General Manager, Divisional
Joao Araujo, Other Corporate Officer
Carlos Piani, Other Corporate Officer
Paulo Basilio, Other Executive Officer
Nina Barton, President, Divisional
Pedro Drevon, President, Geographical
Rodrigo Wickbold, President, Geographical
Rafael Oliveira, President, Geographical

GROWTH PLANS/SPECIAL FEATURES:

The Kraft Heinz Company is one of the largest food and beverage companies in the world, with sales in more than 190 countries and territories. Some of the many iconic brands of the firm include Kraft, Heinz, Oscar Mayer, Ore-Ida, Classico, Velveeta, Smart Ones, ABC, CapriSun, Wattie's, Kool-Aid, Weight Watchers frozen Heinz, Jell-O, Philadelphia, golden circle, Lunchables, Planters, Pudliszki, Maxwell House, Grey Poupon, Cracker Barrel, Master, Honig, Plasmon and Quero. Together, the company manufactures and markets products such as cheese, meats, refreshment beverages, coffee, packaged dinners, refrigerated meals, snack nuts, dressings, ketchup, sauces and infant nutrition. Kraft Heinz is majority-owned by 3G Capital and minority-owned by Berkshire Hathaway, Inc. late-2020, Kraft Heinz agreed to sell certain assets in its global cheese business, as well as to license certain trademarks, to Groupe Lactalis for approximately $3.3 billion. In February 2021, Kraft Heinz agreed to sell certain assets in its global nuts business to Hormel Foods Corporation for approximately $3.4 billion, including rights to the Planters and Corn Nuts brands, three manufacturing facilities in the U.S., and associated inventories.

FINANCIAL DATA: *Note: Data for latest year may not have been available at press time.*

In U.S. $	2020	2019	2018	2017	2016	2015
Revenue	26,185,000,000	24,977,000,000	26,268,000,000	26,232,000,000	26,487,000,000	18,338,000,000
R&D Expense						
Operating Income	5,728,000,000	4,969,000,000	5,716,000,000	6,773,000,000	6,142,000,000	2,639,000,000
Operating Margin %		.20%	.22%	.26%	.23%	.14%
SGA Expense	3,449,000,000	3,178,000,000	3,205,000,000	2,930,000,000	3,444,000,000	3,122,000,000
Net Income	356,000,000	1,935,000,000	-10,192,000,000	10,999,000,000	3,632,000,000	634,000,000
Operating Cash Flow	4,929,000,000	3,552,000,000	2,574,000,000	527,000,000	5,238,000,000	2,467,000,000
Capital Expenditure	596,000,000	768,000,000	826,000,000	1,217,000,000	1,247,000,000	648,000,000
EBITDA	3,393,000,000	5,016,000,000	-9,054,000,000	7,800,000,000	7,494,000,000	3,074,000,000
Return on Assets %		.02%	-.09%	.09%	.03%	.00%
Return on Equity %		.04%	-.17%	.18%	.06%	-.01%
Debt to Equity		0.547	0.596	0.429	0.518	0.436

CONTACT INFORMATION:

Phone: 412 456-5700   Fax: 412 456-6128
Toll-Free: 800-255-5750
Address: 1 PPG Pl., Pittsburgh, PA 15222 United States

SALARIES/BONUSES:

Top Exec. Salary: $ Bonus: $
Second Exec. Salary: $ Bonus: $

STOCK TICKER/OTHER:

Stock Ticker: KHC   Exchange: NAS
Employees: 37,000   Fiscal Year Ends: 12/31
Parent Company: 3G Capital

OTHER THOUGHTS:

Estimated Female Officers or Directors: 1
Hot Spot for Advancement for Women/Minorities: Y

Kratos Defense & Security Solutions Inc   www.kratosdefense.com

NAIC Code: 541512

TYPES OF BUSINESS:

IT Consulting
System Design & Engineering Services
Consulting Services
Network Management

BRANDS/DIVISIONS/AFFILIATES:

CONTACTS: Note: Officers with more than one job title may be intentionally listed here more than once.

Eric Demarco, CEO
Deanna Lund, CFO
William Hoglund, Chairman of the Board
Maria Cervantes de Burgreen, Controller
Thomas Mills, President, Divisional
Jonah Adelman, President, Divisional
Phillip Carrai, President, Divisional
David Carter, President, Divisional
Steve Fendley, President, Divisional
Stacey Rock, President, Divisional
Benjamin Goodwin, Senior VP, Divisional
Marie Mendoza, Vice President

GROWTH PLANS/SPECIAL FEATURES:

Kratos Defense & Security Solutions, Inc. is a mid-tier government contractor for the U.S. Department of Defense. The firm develops strategic weapon systems to address peer and near peer threats, with a focus on the U.S. and its allies' national security. Kratos operates through two business segments: government solutions and unmanned systems. The government solutions segment includes the company's microwave electronic products, space and satellite communications, modular systems and defense and rocket support services. Microwave electronics include radio frequency (RF) and microwave assemblies and subassemblies to support high-end requirements of radar, simulators, communications, test and other equipment for various platforms such as fighter aircraft, missiles, smart munition and naval. Space and satellite communication products offer the reliability and security of satellite and terrestrial networks and boost the readiness of human teams via simulations, game-based and full-fidelity training solutions. Modular systems and subsystems encompass missile and radar systems, combat systems, unmanned systems and related technical services. Defense and rocket support services include logistics, engineering, target operations support, international programs, rocket program services and advanced weapon system research and engineering. The unmanned systems segment consists of two divisions: unmanned aerial systems, offering high-performance aerial targets, aerial target services, ancillary target equipment and advanced composite solutions; and unmanned ground and seaborne systems, offering avionics, transponders, payloads, advanced command and control (C2) systems, ground vehicle automation solutions, flight termination systems and autonomous impact protection solutions.

Kratos offers its employees benefits including a 401(k) plan and a stock purchase program.

FINANCIAL DATA: Note: Data for latest year may not have been available at press time.

In U.S. $	2020	2019	2018	2017	2016	2015
Revenue	747,700,000	717,500,000	618,000,000	751,900,000	668,700,000	657,100,000
R&D Expense	27,000,000	18,000,000	15,600,000	17,800,000	13,900,000	16,200,000
Operating Income	31,700,000	41,200,000	34,300,000	18,900,000	-6,600,000	-5,100,000
Operating Margin %		.06%	.06%	.03%	-.01%	-.01%
SGA Expense	144,500,000	130,800,000	119,800,000	160,600,000	146,300,000	150,700,000
Net Income	79,600,000	12,500,000	-3,500,000	-42,700,000	-60,500,000	19,800,000
Operating Cash Flow	46,600,000	30,000,000	10,400,000	-27,000,000	-12,300,000	-26,900,000
Capital Expenditure	35,900,000	26,300,000	22,600,000	26,500,000	9,200,000	11,300,000
EBITDA	64,400,000	74,300,000	48,200,000	800,000	5,200,000	16,900,000
Return on Assets %		.01%	.00%	-.04%	-.07%	.02%
Return on Equity %		.02%	-.01%	-.11%	-.23%	.08%
Debt to Equity		0.58	0.567	0.574	1.559	1.747

CONTACT INFORMATION:

Phone: 512-238-9840   Fax:
Toll-Free:
Address: 1 Chisholm Trail, Ste. 3200, Round Rock, TX 78681 United States

STOCK TICKER/OTHER:

Stock Ticker: KTOS
Employees: 3,200
Parent Company:

Exchange: NAS
Fiscal Year Ends: 12/31

SALARIES/BONUSES:

Top Exec. Salary: $ Bonus: $
Second Exec. Salary: $ Bonus: $

OTHER THOUGHTS:

Estimated Female Officers or Directors: 4
Hot Spot for Advancement for Women/Minorities: Y

Sales, profits and employees may be estimates. Financial information, benefits and other data can change quickly and may vary from those stated here.

Kroger Co (The)

NAIC Code: 445110

TYPES OF BUSINESS:

Grocery Stores
Supermarkets
Convenience Stores
Fuel Stations
Pharmacies
Food Manufacturing

BRANDS/DIVISIONS/AFFILIATES:

Kroger
City Market
Dillons
JayC
Food 4 Less
Smiths

CONTACTS: Note: Officers with more than one job title may be intentionally listed here more than once.

W. Mcmullen, CEO
Alessandro Tosolini, Sr. VP, Divisional
J. Schlotman, CFO
Christopher Hjelm, Chief Information Officer
Yael Cosset, Chief Information Officer
Todd Foley, Controller
Michael Donnelly, Executive VP
Christine Wheatley, General Counsel
Mark Tuffin, Senior VP
Calvin Kaufman, Senior VP
Stuart Aitken, Senior VP
Stephen McKinney, Senior VP
Timothy Massa, Senior VP, Divisional
Robert Clark, Senior VP, Divisional
Carin Fike, Treasurer
Jessica Adelman, Vice President, Divisional

GROWTH PLANS/SPECIAL FEATURES:

The Kroger Co. is one of the largest supermarket operators in the U.S. The company operates approximately 2,750 supermarkets under a variety of names such as Kroger, City Market, Dillons, JayC, Food 4 Less and Smith's (as of November 2020). Nearly 1,600 of these stores have fuel centers, and approximately 2,255 have pharmacies. Kroger's supermarkets operate under one of four store formats: combination food and drug stores, multi-department stores, marketplace stores and price impact warehouses. The combo stores are the primary food store format and typically draw customers from a 2- to 2.5-mile radius; multi-department stores are larger in size than combos and sell merchandise such as apparel, home furnishings, decor, outdoor living, electronics, automotive products, toys and fine jewelry; marketplace stores offer full-service grocery, pharmacy and beauty care departments, as well as general merchandise; and price impact warehouses offer low cost promotions for grocery, health and beauty items. Kroger manages many walk-in medical clinics located in its stores. The company operates 35 manufacturing plants, which supply approximately 30% of the corporate brand units sold in its retail outlets. They consist of dairy, deli, grocery product, beverage, meat and cheese manufacturing facilities.

FINANCIAL DATA: Note: Data for latest year may not have been available at press time.

In U.S. $	2020	2019	2018	2017	2016	2015
Revenue	122,286,000,000	121,162,000,000	122,662,000,000	115,337,000,000	109,830,000,000	
R&D Expense						
Operating Income	2,251,000,000	2,614,000,000	2,085,000,000	3,436,000,000	3,576,000,000	
Operating Margin %	.02%	.02%	.02%	.03%	.03%	
SGA Expense	22,092,000,000	21,189,000,000	22,479,000,000	20,059,000,000	18,669,000,000	
Net Income	1,659,000,000	3,110,000,000	1,907,000,000	1,975,000,000	2,039,000,000	
Operating Cash Flow	4,664,000,000	4,164,000,000	3,413,000,000	4,272,000,000	4,833,000,000	
Capital Expenditure	3,128,000,000	2,967,000,000	2,809,000,000	3,699,000,000	3,349,000,000	
EBITDA	5,873,000,000	7,063,000,000	4,521,000,000	5,776,000,000	5,665,000,000	
Return on Assets %	.04%	.08%	.05%	.06%	.06%	
Return on Equity %	.20%	.42%	.28%	.29%	.33%	
Debt to Equity	2.164	1.531	1.736	1.765	1.424	

CONTACT INFORMATION:

Phone: 513 762-4000   Fax: 513 762-1575
Toll-Free: 866-221-4141
Address: 1014 Vine St., Cincinnati, OH 45202 United States

STOCK TICKER/OTHER:

Stock Ticker: KR
Employees: 465,000
Parent Company:

Exchange: NYS
Fiscal Year Ends: 01/31

SALARIES/BONUSES:

Top Exec. Salary: $ Bonus: $
Second Exec. Salary: $ Bonus: $

OTHER THOUGHTS:

Estimated Female Officers or Directors: 5
Hot Spot for Advancement for Women/Minorities: Y

L3Harris Technologies Inc

www.l3harris.com

NAIC Code: 334220

TYPES OF BUSINESS:

Communications Equipment Manufacturing
Aerospace and Defense Technology
Communication Systems
Electronic Systems
Space Systems
Intelligence Systems

BRANDS/DIVISIONS/AFFILIATES:

GROWTH PLANS/SPECIAL FEATURES:

L3Harris Technologies, Inc. is an agile global aerospace and defense technology innovator that designs and builds systems for safety purposes. The company anticipates and mitigates risk with end-to-end solutions that meet its customers' mission-critical needs across air, land, sea, space and cyber domains. L3Harris serves customers in more than 100 countries. During 2020, L3Harris sold its security and detection systems, its MacDonald Humfrey automation solutions business, its applied kilovolts and analytical instruments business, and its EOTech holographic sighting systems, magnified field optics and related accessories business.

CONTACTS: Note: Officers with more than one job title may be intentionally listed here more than once.

William Brown, CEO
Christopher E. Kubasik, Pres.
Jesus Malave Jr., CFO
James P. Girard, VP-Human Resources
Scott Mikuen, General Counsel
Dana Mehnert, Other Executive Officer
Christopher Young, President, Divisional
Edward Zoiss, President, Divisional
William Gattle, President, Divisional
Robert Duffy, Senior VP, Divisional
Sheldon Fox, Senior VP, Divisional

FINANCIAL DATA: Note: Data for latest year may not have been available at press time.

In U.S. $	2020	2019	2018	2017	2016	2015
Revenue	18,194,000,000	6,801,000,000	6,182,000,000	5,900,000,000	7,467,000,000	
R&D Expense						
Operating Income	1,993,000,000	1,092,000,000	1,122,000,000	1,073,000,000	1,149,000,000	
Operating Margin %		.16%	.18%	.18%	.15%	
SGA Expense	3,315,000,000	1,242,000,000	1,129,000,000	1,016,000,000	1,186,000,000	
Net Income	1,119,000,000	949,000,000	718,000,000	553,000,000	324,000,000	
Operating Cash Flow	2,790,000,000	1,185,000,000	751,000,000	569,000,000	924,000,000	
Capital Expenditure	368,000,000	161,000,000	136,000,000	119,000,000	152,000,000	
EBITDA	2,624,000,000	1,540,000,000	1,355,000,000	1,388,000,000	1,155,000,000	
Return on Assets %		.10%	.07%	.05%	.03%	
Return on Equity %		.28%	.23%	.18%	.10%	
Debt to Equity		0.822	1.026	1.16	1.348	

CONTACT INFORMATION:

Phone: 321 727-9100   Fax: 321 724-3973
Toll-Free: 800-442-7747
Address: 1025 West NASA Blvd., Melbourne, FL 32919 United States

STOCK TICKER/OTHER:

Stock Ticker: LHX
Employees: 48,000
Parent Company:

Exchange: NYS
Fiscal Year Ends: 06/30

SALARIES/BONUSES:

Top Exec. Salary: $ Bonus: $
Second Exec. Salary: $ Bonus: $

OTHER THOUGHTS:

Estimated Female Officers or Directors: 2
Hot Spot for Advancement for Women/Minorities: Y

Laboratory Corporation of America Holdings   www.labcorp.com

NAIC Code: 621511

TYPES OF BUSINESS:

Clinical Laboratory Testing
Diagnostics
Urinalyses
Blood Cell Counts
Blood Chemistry Analysis
HIV Tests
Genetic Testing
Specialty & Niche Tests

BRANDS/DIVISIONS/AFFILIATES:

LabCorp
LabCorp Diagnositcs
Covance Drug Development

CONTACTS: Note: Officers with more than one job title may be intentionally listed here more than once.

John Ratliff, CEO, Divisional
David King, CEO
Glenn Eisenberg, CFO
Peter Wilkinson, Chief Accounting Officer
Sandra van der Vaart, Chief Compliance Officer
Lance Berberian, Chief Information Officer
Brian Caveney, Chief Medical Officer
Lisa Uthgenannt, Other Executive Officer

GROWTH PLANS/SPECIAL FEATURES:

Laboratory Corporation of America Holdings (LabCorp) is a global life sciences company deeply integrated in guiding patient care. LabCorp provides comprehensive clinical laboratory and end-to-end drug development services through LabCorp Diagnostics (LCD) and Covance Drug Development (CDD). The company provides diagnostic, drug development and technology-enabled solutions for more than 120 million patient encounters each year. The firm typically processes tests on more than 2.5 million patient specimens per week and supports clinical trial activity in about 100 countries through its central laboratory and preclinical development businesses. LCD is an independent clinical laboratory business, offering a comprehensive array of testing through an integrated network of primary and specialty laboratories across the U.S. This network is supported by an IT system, with more than 65,000 electronic interfaces to deliver test results, nimble and efficient logistics and local labs offering rapid response testing. LCD's online LabCorp patient portal and mobile app offer access to new and historical test results, information about tests and an option to receive information about clinical trials. CDD provides end-to-end drug development, medical devices and diagnostic development solutions from early-stage research to clinical development and commercial market access. CDD collaborated on 85% of the novel drugs approved by the U.S. Food and Drug Administration (FDA) in 2019, including 100% of the novel oncology drugs and 86% of the rare and orphan disease drugs. In addition, CDD has been involved in the development of all the current top 50 drugs on the market as measured by sales revenue. In March 2020, LabCorp received emergency use authorization from the FDA for a test for COVID-19 to help mitigate the pandemic. That September, LabCorp acquired Franciscan Missionaries of Our Lady Health System's clinical ambulatory business and select assets, and will provide reference testing for all FMOHS facilities and clinics.

FINANCIAL DATA: Note: Data for latest year may not have been available at press time.

In U.S. $	2020	2019	2018	2017	2016	2015
Revenue	13,978,500,000	11,554,800,000	11,333,400,000	10,441,400,000	9,641,800,000	8,680,100,000
R&D Expense						
Operating Income	2,948,100,000	1,384,800,000	1,373,800,000	1,435,100,000	1,370,800,000	1,116,800,000
Operating Margin %		.12%	.12%	.14%	.14%	.13%
SGA Expense	1,729,300,000	1,624,500,000	1,570,900,000	1,812,400,000	1,630,200,000	1,622,000,000
Net Income	1,556,100,000	823,800,000	883,700,000	1,268,200,000	732,100,000	436,900,000
Operating Cash Flow	2,135,300,000	1,444,700,000	1,305,400,000	1,459,400,000	1,175,900,000	982,400,000
Capital Expenditure	381,700,000	400,200,000	379,800,000	315,400,000	278,900,000	255,800,000
EBITDA	3,051,200,000	1,922,800,000	2,064,600,000	1,903,200,000	1,823,800,000	1,464,800,000
Return on Assets %		.05%	.05%	.08%	.05%	.04%
Return on Equity %		.11%	.13%	.21%	.14%	.11%
Debt to Equity		0.856	0.867	0.929	0.963	1.212

CONTACT INFORMATION:

Phone: 336 229-1127   Fax: 336 229-7717
Toll-Free:
Address: 358 S. Main St., Burlington, NC 27215 United States

STOCK TICKER/OTHER:

Stock Ticker: LH   Exchange: NYS
Employees: 65,000   Fiscal Year Ends: 12/31
Parent Company:

SALARIES/BONUSES:

Top Exec. Salary: $ Bonus: $
Second Exec. Salary: $ Bonus: $

OTHER THOUGHTS:

Estimated Female Officers or Directors: 3
Hot Spot for Advancement for Women/Minorities: Y

Lam Research Corporation

www.lamresearch.com

NAIC Code: 333242

TYPES OF BUSINESS:

Semiconductor Manufacturing Equipment
Etch Processing Systems
Chemical Mechanical Planarization Systems
Wafer Cleaning Equipment & Services
Support Services

BRANDS/DIVISIONS/AFFILIATES:

Flex
Versys
Kiyo
Syndion
VECTOR
Metryx
SABRE
SOLA

CONTACTS: Note: Officers with more than one job title may be intentionally listed here more than once.

Timothy Archer, CEO
Douglas Bettinger, CFO
Stephen Newberry, Chairman of the Board
Richard Gottscho, Chief Technology Officer
Vahid Vahedi, General Manager, Divisional
Seshasayee Varadarajan, General Manager, Divisional
Patrick Lord, General Manager, Divisional
Sarah ODowd, Other Executive Officer
Kevin Jennings, Senior VP, Divisional
Scott Meikle, Senior VP, Divisional

GROWTH PLANS/SPECIAL FEATURES:

Lam Research Corporation supplies wafer fabrication equipment and services to semiconductor companies worldwide. The firm designs, manufactures, markets and services semiconductor processing equipment used in semiconductor device fabrication. The company's etch products are used to deposit special films on silicon wafers and to selectively etch away portions of these films utilizing plasma-based technologies, creating an integrated circuit (IC). Its products include the Flex product family for dielectric etch, the Versys metal and Kiyo product families for conductor etch and the Syndion product family for three-dimensional ICs. Lam's VECTOR family of plasma-enhanced chemical vapor deposition and atomic layer deposition systems delivers superior thin film quality, wafer-to-water uniformity, productivity and low cost of ownership. The firm also offers wafer cleaning services and equipment that employs proprietary technology and can be used throughout the semiconductor manufacturing process. The Metryx family of mass metrology systems provide high precision in-line mass measurement for semiconductor wafer manufacturing. Lam's ALTUS product family deposits a highly conformal atomic layer for advanced tungsten metallization applications. The patented multi-station sequential deposition architecture enables a layer to be formed using pulsed nucleation layer technology. The SABRE electrochemical deposition (ECD) product family is a system for copper damascene manufacturing. SABRE 3D addresses through-silicon via (TSV) and wafer-level packaging (WLP) applications, such as copper pillar, redistribution layers, high-density fanout, underbump metallization, bumping and microbumps used in post-TSV processing. The SPEED family of products are designed to provide void-free gap-fill of high-quality dielectric films with throughput and reliability. The SOLA product family is used for treatment of back-end-of-line low-k dielectric films and front-end-of-line silicon nitride strained films.

Lam Research offers its employees comprehensive health, financial and income protection benefits, as well as employee assistance programs.

FINANCIAL DATA: Note: Data for latest year may not have been available at press time.

In U.S. $	2020	2019	2018	2017	2016	2015
Revenue	10,044,740,000	9,653,559,000	11,077,000,000	8,013,620,000	5,885,893,000	
R&D Expense	1,252,412,000	1,191,320,000	1,189,514,000	1,033,742,000	913,712,000	
Operating Income	2,673,802,000	2,464,732,000	3,213,299,000	1,902,132,000	1,074,256,000	
Operating Margin %		.26%	.29%	.24%	.18%	
SGA Expense	682,479,000	702,407,000	762,219,000	667,485,000	630,954,000	
Net Income	2,251,753,000	2,191,430,000	2,380,681,000	1,697,763,000	914,049,000	
Operating Cash Flow	2,126,451,000	3,176,013,000	2,655,747,000	2,029,282,000	1,350,277,000	
Capital Expenditure	203,239,000	303,491,000	273,469,000	157,419,000	175,330,000	
EBITDA	3,020,943,000	2,873,115,000	3,575,571,000	2,236,312,000	1,385,918,000	
Return on Assets %		.18%	.19%	.14%	.08%	
Return on Equity %		.39%	.35%	.26%	.16%	
Debt to Equity		0.809	0.275	0.255	0.554	

CONTACT INFORMATION:

Phone: 510 572-0200   Fax: 510 572-6454
Toll-Free: 800-526-7678
Address: 4650 Cushing Pkwy., Fremont, CA 94538 United States

SALARIES/BONUSES:

Top Exec. Salary: $ Bonus: $
Second Exec. Salary: $ Bonus: $

STOCK TICKER/OTHER:

Stock Ticker: LRCX
Employees: 11,300
Parent Company:

Exchange: NAS
Fiscal Year Ends: 06/30

OTHER THOUGHTS:

Estimated Female Officers or Directors: 3
Hot Spot for Advancement for Women/Minorities: Y

Legg Mason Inc
NAIC Code: 523110

www.leggmason.com

TYPES OF BUSINESS:
Stock Brokerage/Investment Banking
Mutual Funds

BRANDS/DIVISIONS/AFFILIATES:
Western Asset Management Company
ClearBridge Investments
Brandywine Global Investment Management
Clarion Partners
EnTrust
RARE Infrastructure
Legg Mason Funds
Royce Funds

CONTACTS: Note: Officers with more than one job title may be intentionally listed here more than once.
Joseph Sullivan, CEO
Peter Nachtwey, CFO
Ursula Schliessler, Chief Administrative Officer
Thomas Merchant, Executive VP
Terence Johnson, Executive VP
John Kenney, Other Corporate Officer
Frances Cashman, Other Corporate Officer
Thomas Hoops, Other Corporate Officer
Patricia Lattin, Other Corporate Officer

GROWTH PLANS/SPECIAL FEATURES:
Legg Mason, Inc. is a global asset management company with more than $790 billion in consolidated assets under management (as of October 31, 2019). Operating through its subsidiaries, the firm provides investment management and related services to institutional and individual clients, company-sponsored mutual funds and other pooled investment vehicles. Legg Mason offers these products and services directly and through various financial intermediaries. The firm conducts its business primarily through several asset managers, housed in independent subsidiaries owned by Legg Mason. Asset managers provide a range of separate account investment management services to institutional clients, including pension and other retirement plans, corporations, insurance companies, endowments, foundations and governments as well as to high-net-worth individuals and families. They also sponsor and manage various groups of U.S. mutual funds and exchange-traded funds (ETFs), including equity, fixed income, liquidity and balanced funds. Asset managers include Western Asset Management Company, ClearBridge Investments, Brandywine Global Investment Management, Clarion Partners, EnTrust, Royce & Associates, Martin Currie, QS Investors and RARE Infrastructure. U.S. funds primarily consist of proprietary mutual and closed-end funds, the Legg Mason Funds and the Royce Funds, totaling 106 mutual funds and 26 close-ended funds. Legg Mason Funds invest in a range of domestic and international equity and fixed income securities utilizing various investment styles; and the Royce Funds invest primarily in smaller-cap company stocks using a value investment approach. International funds include a broad range of cross border funds that are domiciled in Ireland and are sold in a number of countries across Asia, Europe and Latin America.

Legg Mason offers its employees heal benefits, 401(k) and other financial benefits, as well as a variety of employee assistance programs.

FINANCIAL DATA: Note: Data for latest year may not have been available at press time.

In U.S. $	2020	2019	2018	2017	2016	2015
Revenue		2,903,258,880	3,140,322,048	2,886,902,016	2,660,844,032	2,819,106,048
R&D Expense						
Operating Income						
Operating Margin %						
SGA Expense						
Net Income		-28,508,000	285,075,008	227,256,000	-25,032,000	237,080,000
Operating Cash Flow						
Capital Expenditure						
EBITDA						
Return on Assets %						
Return on Equity %						
Debt to Equity						

CONTACT INFORMATION:
Phone: 410 539-0000   Fax: 410 454-4174
Toll-Free: 800-822-5544
Address: 100 International Dr., Baltimore, MD 21202 United States

STOCK TICKER/OTHER:
Stock Ticker: LM
Employees: 3,059
Parent Company:

Exchange: NYS
Fiscal Year Ends: 02/28

SALARIES/BONUSES:
Top Exec. Salary: $ Bonus: $
Second Exec. Salary: $ Bonus: $

OTHER THOUGHTS:
Estimated Female Officers or Directors: 2
Hot Spot for Advancement for Women/Minorities:

Lennar Corporation

www.lennar.com

NAIC Code: 236117

TYPES OF BUSINESS:
Construction, Home Building and Residential
Home Development
Home Construction
Land Real Estate
Financial Services
Rental Properties
Property Management

BRANDS/DIVISIONS/AFFILIATES:
Lennar Mortgage LLC
Upward America Venture

CONTACTS: Note: Officers with more than one job title may be intentionally listed here more than once.
Stuart Miller, Chairman of the Board
David Collins, Chief Accounting Officer
Richard Beckwitt, Director
Jonathan Jaffe, Director
Mark Sustana, Secretary
Jeffrey McCall, Senior VP
Diane Bessette, Vice President

GROWTH PLANS/SPECIAL FEATURES:
Lennar Corporation is a U.S. homebuilder and related financial services provider. The firm sells single-family attached and detached homes and, to a lesser extent, multi-level residential buildings primarily under the Lennar brand name in communities targeted to first-time, move-up and active adult homebuyers. The company also purchases, develops and sells residential land. Lennar divides its homebuilding operations into five segments: East (which includes Florida, New Jersey, North Carolina, Pennsylvania and South Carolina); Central (including Georgia, Illinois, Indiana, Maryland, Minnesota, Tennessee and Virginia); Texas; West (including Arizona, California, Colorado, Nevada, Oregon, Utah and Washington); and Other (including urban divisions and other homebuilding-related investments). Lennar's financial services are provided through subsidiary Lennar Mortgage, LLC, offering conforming conventional, FHA-insured and VA-guaranteed residential mortgage loan products and other home mortgage products to buyers of Lennar homes. Approximately 80% of Lennar homebuyers utilize its related mortgage services. In addition, Lennar's multi-family operations develop, construct and manage apartment communities across the U.S., with interests in more than 60 communities. During 2021, Lennar announced the formation of the Upward America Venture, alongside Centerbridge Partners, Allianz Real Estate and other investors, which will acquire single family homes for rent in high growth markets throughout the U.S. The venture will acquire over $4 billion of new single-family homes and townhomes from Lennar and potentially other homebuilders, making the single family lifestyle available to a broader social and economic array of families.

Lennar offers its employees medical, dental, vision, life and short-/long-term insurance; home and auto insurance; and mortgage and title perks.

FINANCIAL DATA: Note: Data for latest year may not have been available at press time.

In U.S. $	2020	2019	2018	2017	2016	2015
Revenue	22,488,850,000	22,259,560,000	20,571,630,000	12,646,370,000	10,950,000,000	9,474,008,000
R&D Expense						
Operating Income	3,115,690,000	2,461,181,000	1,990,251,000	1,338,995,000	1,262,363,000	1,086,016,000
Operating Margin %		.11%	.10%	.11%	.12%	.11%
SGA Expense	358,418,000	341,114,000	343,934,000	285,889,000	232,562,000	216,244,000
Net Income	2,465,036,000	1,849,052,000	1,695,831,000	810,480,000	911,844,000	802,894,000
Operating Cash Flow	4,190,819,000	1,482,343,000	1,711,609,000	996,864,000	507,804,000	-419,646,000
Capital Expenditure	72,752,000	86,497,000	130,439,000	111,773,000	76,439,000	91,355,000
EBITDA	3,240,742,000	2,553,381,000	2,365,123,000	1,263,099,000	1,385,314,000	1,265,736,000
Return on Assets %	.06%	.07%	.05%	.06%	.06%	
Return on Equity %	.12%	.15%	.11%	.14%	.15%	
Debt to Equity	0.60	0.694	1.013	0.893	1.178	

CONTACT INFORMATION:
Phone: 305 559-4000 Fax: 305 227-7115
Toll-Free: 800-741-4663
Address: 700 NW 107th Ave., Miami, FL 33172 United States

STOCK TICKER/OTHER:
Stock Ticker: LEN
Employees: 9,495
Parent Company:

Exchange: NYS
Fiscal Year Ends: 11/30

SALARIES/BONUSES:
Top Exec. Salary: $ Bonus: $
Second Exec. Salary: $ Bonus: $

OTHER THOUGHTS:
Estimated Female Officers or Directors: 3
Hot Spot for Advancement for Women/Minorities: Y

LHC Group Inc

NAIC Code: 621610

TYPES OF BUSINESS:

Home Health Care Services
Hospices
Long-Term Acute Care Hospitals

BRANDS/DIVISIONS/AFFILIATES:

Mederi Caretenders
Mederi Private Care

GROWTH PLANS/SPECIAL FEATURES:

LHC Group, Inc. is a national provider of high-quality, affordable in-home healthcare services and innovations. The firm's services cover a wide range of healthcare needs for patients and families dealing with illness, injury or chronic conditions. LHC delivers home health, hospice, home- and community-based services, and facility-based care in 35 U.S. states and the District of Columbia, reaching 60% of the U.S. population aged 65 and older. In August 2020, LHC Group announced a joint venture with Orlando Health System in Orlando, Florida, which will include six locations: three current Orlando Health providers and three current LHC Group providers in Orlando, Clermont, Kissimmee and Altamonte Springs. They home health providers will operate under the name Mederi Caretenders, and the home and community based services location will operate under the name Mederi Private Care.

CONTACTS: Note: Officers with more than one job title may be intentionally listed here more than once.

Keith Myers, CEO
Joshua Proffitt, CFO
Collin McQuiddy, Chief Accounting Officer
Bruce Greenstein, Chief Strategy Officer
Donald Stelly, COO
Nicholas Gachassin, Executive VP

FINANCIAL DATA: Note: Data for latest year may not have been available at press time.

In U.S. $	2020	2019	2018	2017	2016	2015
Revenue	2,063,204,000	2,080,241,000	1,809,963,000	1,072,086,000	914,823,000	816,366,000
R&D Expense						
Operating Income	179,954,000	159,348,000	115,690,000	76,253,000	71,761,000	67,616,000
Operating Margin %		.08%	.06%	.07%	.08%	.08%
SGA Expense	632,847,000	596,006,000	537,916,000	310,539,000	270,622,000	248,629,000
Net Income	111,596,000	95,726,000	63,574,000	50,112,000	36,583,000	32,335,000
Operating Cash Flow	529,247,000	130,462,000	108,585,000	32,326,000	67,472,000	59,934,000
Capital Expenditure	65,875,000	33,609,000	32,993,000	74,774,000	39,165,000	83,855,000
EBITDA	233,900,000	203,236,000	127,363,000	88,628,000	83,214,000	78,755,000
Return on Assets %		.05%	.05%	.07%	.06%	.06%
Return on Equity %		.07%	.07%	.12%	.10%	.10%
Debt to Equity		0.228	0.179	0.321	0.222	0.278

CONTACT INFORMATION:

Phone: 337 233-1307		Fax: 337 235-8037
Toll-Free:
Address: 901 Hugh Wallis Rd. S., Lafayette, LA 70508 United States

STOCK TICKER/OTHER:

Stock Ticker: LHCG				Exchange: NAS
Employees: 27,959				Fiscal Year Ends: 12/31
Parent Company:

SALARIES/BONUSES:

Top Exec. Salary: $		Bonus: $
Second Exec. Salary: $		Bonus: $

OTHER THOUGHTS:

Estimated Female Officers or Directors: 6
Hot Spot for Advancement for Women/Minorities: Y

Liberty Mutual Group Inc
www.libertymutualgroup.com

NAIC Code: 524126

TYPES OF BUSINESS:
Insurance, Direct Property & Casualty
Rehabilitation Services
Disability Care Management
Homeowners' Insurance
Auto Insurance
Group Life Insurance
Asset Management & Investment Products
Workers' Compensation

BRANDS/DIVISIONS/AFFILIATES:
Liberty Mutual Insurance Company
Liberty Mutual Fire Insurance Company
Employers Insurance of Wausau
Liberty Corporate Services LLC

CONTACTS: Note: Officers with more than one job title may be intentionally listed here more than once.
David H. Long, CEO
Christopher L. Peirce, CFO
Neeti Bhalla Johnson, CIO
Melanie M. Foley, Sr. VP-Admin.
James F. Kelleher, Sr. VP
Paul G. Alexander, Mgr.-Comm.
Laurance H.S. Yahia, Treas.
J. Paul Condrin III, Exec. VP
A. Alexander Fontanes, Exec. VP
Christopher L. Peirce, Exec. VP
Timothy M. Sweeney, Exec. VP
David H. Long, Chmn.
Luis Bonell, Exec. VP

GROWTH PLANS/SPECIAL FEATURES:
Liberty Mutual Group, Inc. offers a wide range of insurance products and services globally. The firm's global network provides personal automobile, homeowners, specialty lines, reinsurance, commercial multiple-peril, workers compensation, commercial automobile, general liability, surety and commercial property insurance. Liberty Mutual's principal stock insurance companies include: Liberty Mutual Insurance Company, Liberty Mutual Fire Insurance Company and Employers Insurance of Wausau. Its related service subsidiary is Liberty Corporate Services, LLC. Together the group operates from over 800 offices worldwide and conducts substantially all of its business through two units: global retail markets and global risk solutions. These units operate independently of the other in certain areas such as sales, underwriting and claims; but, as appropriate, collaborates in other areas such as actuarial and financial. The global retail markets business consists of four segments: U.S., offering personal and business insurance products; West, selling property and casualty, health and life insurance products and services to customers in Brazil, Colombia, Chile, Ecuador, Spain, Portugal and Ireland; East, selling property and casualty, health and life insurance products and services to customers in Thailand, Singapore, Hong Kong, Vietnam, Malaysia, India, and China; and GRM Reinsurance, offering certain internal reinsurance programs. The global risk solutions business offers a wide range of property, casualty, specialty and reinsurance coverage distributed through brokers and independent agents globally. This business operates four segments: Liberty Specialty Markets, offering global risk solutions outside of North America, and global reinsurance; National Insurance, offering U.S. admitted and non-admitted property and casualty insurance in excess of $150,000 annual premium; North America Specialty, offering specialty lines and non-admitted property and casualty in North America; Global Surety, providing contract and commercial surety bonds to businesses of all sizes; and other global risk solutions, primarily consisting of internal reinsurance programs.

Comprehensive benefits, 401(k) and other employee benefits are offered.

FINANCIAL DATA: Note: Data for latest year may not have been available at press time.

In U.S. $	2020	2019	2018	2017	2016	2015
Revenue	43,796,000,000	43,228,000,000	41,568,000,000	39,409,000,000	38,308,000,000	37,617,000,000
R&D Expense						
Operating Income						
Operating Margin %						
SGA Expense						
Net Income	760,000,000	1,038,000,000	2,161,000,000	17,000,000	1,006,000,000	514,000,000
Operating Cash Flow						
Capital Expenditure						
EBITDA						
Return on Assets %						
Return on Equity %						
Debt to Equity						

CONTACT INFORMATION:
Phone: 617-357-9500   Fax: 617-350-7648
Toll-Free: 800-837-5254
Address: 175 Berkeley St., Boston, MA 02116 United States

STOCK TICKER/OTHER:
Stock Ticker: Mutual Company
Employees: 45,000
Parent Company:

Exchange:
Fiscal Year Ends: 12/31

SALARIES/BONUSES:
Top Exec. Salary: $ Bonus: $
Second Exec. Salary: $ Bonus: $

OTHER THOUGHTS:
Estimated Female Officers or Directors: 4
Hot Spot for Advancement for Women/Minorities: Y

Sales, profits and employees may be estimates. Financial information, benefits and other data can change quickly and may vary from those stated here.

Lincoln National Corporation

NAIC Code: 524113

TYPES OF BUSINESS:

Life Insurance
Investment Management
Retirement Plans
Mutual Funds
Financial Planning
Annuities

BRANDS/DIVISIONS/AFFILIATES:

Lincoln Financial Group

CONTACTS: *Note: Officers with more than one job title may be intentionally listed here more than once.*

Wilford Fuller, CEO, Subsidiary
Dennis Glass, CEO
Randal Freitag, CFO
Christine Janofsky, Chief Accounting Officer
Kenneth Solon, Chief Information Officer
William Cunningham, Director
Leon Roday, Executive VP
Jamie Ohl, Executive VP
Ellen Cooper, Executive VP
Lisa Buckingham, Executive VP
Richard Mucci, Executive VP

GROWTH PLANS/SPECIAL FEATURES:

Lincoln National Corporation is a holding company operating multiple insurance and retirement businesses. The operations of the firm's subsidiaries, collectively known as Lincoln Financial Group, are divided into four operating businesses: retirement plan services, life insurance, annuities and group protection. Retirement plan services provides employers with retirement plan products and services, with a focus on defined contribution retirement plans. The life insurance segment offers life insurance products including term insurances, a linked-benefit product, indexed universal life (UL) insurance and both single and survivorship versions of UL and variable UL (VUL) products. In a UL contract, contract holders typically have flexibility in the timing and amount of premium payments and the amount of death benefit, provided there is sufficient account value to cover all policy charges. VUL products are UL products that provide a return on account values linked to an underlying investment portfolio of variable funds offered through the products. The annuities segment offers fixed and variable annuities to its clients. Group protection offers employers non-medical insurance products, principally term life, disability and dental. The company's other operations include financial data for operations that are not directly related to the business segments, investment income and its run-off institutional pension business. In addition, Lincoln National's retail and wholesale distributors include: Lincoln Financial Network, which offers the group's and non-proprietary products and advisory services through a national network of more than 9,000 producers; and Lincoln Financial Distributors, which distributes the group's individual products and services, retirement plans, as well as corporate-owned UL insurance, corporate-owned VUL insurance, bank-owned UL insurance and bank-owned VUL insurance products and services. LFD has approximately 660 internal and external wholesalers.

Lincoln National offers medical, dental, vision, disability and life insurance; 401(k); and a variety of employee assistance programs.

FINANCIAL DATA: *Note: Data for latest year may not have been available at press time.*

In U.S. $	2020	2019	2018	2017	2016	2015
Revenue	17,556,000,000	17,258,000,000	16,424,000,000	14,257,000,000	13,330,000,000	13,572,000,000
R&D Expense						
Operating Income						
Operating Margin %						
SGA Expense	2,072,000,000	2,210,000,000	1,953,000,000	1,766,000,000	1,687,000,000	1,730,000,000
Net Income	499,000,000	886,000,000	1,641,000,000	2,079,000,000	1,192,000,000	1,154,000,000
Operating Cash Flow	534,000,000	-2,686,000,000	1,943,000,000	788,000,000	1,272,000,000	2,243,000,000
Capital Expenditure						
EBITDA						
Return on Assets %		.00%	.01%	.01%	.00%	.00%
Return on Equity %		.05%	.10%	.13%	.08%	.08%
Debt to Equity		0.308	0.407	0.283	0.369	0.41

CONTACT INFORMATION:

Phone: 484 583-1400   Fax: 215 448-3962
Toll-Free: 877-275-5462
Address: 150 N. Radnor Chester Rd., Ste. A305, Radnor, PA 19087
United States

STOCK TICKER/OTHER:

Stock Ticker: LNC
Employees: 12,732
Parent Company:

Exchange: NYS
Fiscal Year Ends: 12/31

SALARIES/BONUSES:

Top Exec. Salary: $ Bonus: $
Second Exec. Salary: $ Bonus: $

OTHER THOUGHTS:

Estimated Female Officers or Directors: 2
Hot Spot for Advancement for Women/Minorities: Y

LinkedIn Corporation

www.linkedin.com

NAIC Code: 519130

TYPES OF BUSINESS:

Business-Oriented Social Networking
Advertising Services
Recruiting Tools

BRANDS/DIVISIONS/AFFILIATES:

Microsoft Corporation
LinkedIn.com
Open for Business

CONTACTS: Note: Officers with more than one job title may be intentionally listed here more than once.

Ryan Roslansky, CEO
Reid Hoffman, Chairman of the Board
Michael Gamson, Senior VP, Divisional
Patricia Wadors, Senior VP, Divisional
James Scott, Senior VP, Divisional
Shannon Stubo, Senior VP, Divisional
Steven Sordello, Senior VP
Michael Callahan, Senior VP

GROWTH PLANS/SPECIAL FEATURES:

LinkedIn Corporation operates an online social networking site targeting the business and professional community. On LinkedIn.com users can post profiles, connect with co-workers, post resumes and search for job openings. Other features on the site include company pages, which allows companies to showcase brands and products; and a suite of products for corporate recruitment initiatives, including sourcing and pipelining, a referral engine, career pages and recruitment ads. The company's Open for Business platform enables freelancers to be discovered on the platform. The LinkedIn website generates revenue through ad sales, user subscription fees on premium accounts and enterprise hiring software licensing fees. The company offers a range of solutions to its members, including free solutions, such as stay connected and informed, advance my career and ubiquitous access; and monetized solutions, such as talent, marketing and premium subscription. Its membership base had more than 722 million users across 200 countries (as of January 2021), and is available in multiple languages including English, French, German, Italian, Portuguese, Spanish, Japanese, Korean, Russian, Arabic and Turkish. LinkedIn operates as a subsidiary of Microsoft Corporation.

FINANCIAL DATA: Note: Data for latest year may not have been available at press time.

In U.S. $	2020	2019	2018	2017	2016	2015
Revenue	7,140,000,000	6,800,000,000	5,300,000,000	3,859,000,000	3,500,000,000	2,990,910,976
R&D Expense						
Operating Income						
Operating Margin %						
SGA Expense						
Net Income						
Operating Cash Flow						
Capital Expenditure						
EBITDA						
Return on Assets %						
Return on Equity %						
Debt to Equity						

CONTACT INFORMATION:

Phone: 650 687-3600 Fax:
Toll-Free:
Address: 1000 W. Maude, Sunnyvale, CA 94085 United States

STOCK TICKER/OTHER:

Stock Ticker: Subsidiary
Employees: 13,000
Parent Company: Microsoft Corporation

Exchange:
Fiscal Year Ends: 06/30

SALARIES/BONUSES:

Top Exec. Salary: $ Bonus: $
Second Exec. Salary: $ Bonus: $

OTHER THOUGHTS:

Estimated Female Officers or Directors: 4
Hot Spot for Advancement for Women/Minorities: Y

Sales, profits and employees may be estimates. Financial information, benefits and other data can change quickly and may vary from those stated here.

LKQ Corporation

NAIC Code: 336300

www.lkqcorp.com

TYPES OF BUSINESS:

Remanufactured OEM Parts
Aftermarket Replacement Parts
Vehicle Salvage
Scrap/Bulk Automotive Parts
Refurbished Aluminum Wheels

BRANDS/DIVISIONS/AFFILIATES:

Green Bean Battery, LLC

CONTACTS: Note: Officers with more than one job title may be intentionally listed here more than once.

John Quinn, CEO, Geographical
Dominick Zarcone, CEO
Varun Laroyia, CFO
Ashley Brooks, Chief Information Officer
Michael Clark, Controller
Joseph Holsten, Director
Victor Casini, General Counsel
Walter Hanley, Senior VP, Divisional
Justin Jude, Senior VP, Divisional
Matthew McKay, Senior VP, Divisional

GROWTH PLANS/SPECIAL FEATURES:

LKQ Corporation is a global distributor of vehicle products, including replacement parts, components and systems used in the repair and maintenance of vehicles. The company also distributes specialty products and accessories that improve the performance, functionality and appearance of vehicles. LKQ operates through four segments: North America, Europe, specialty and self-service. The North America segment comprises the company's wholesale operations, which include aftermarket, recycled, remanufactured, refurbished and original equipment manufacturer (OEM) parts supplied to professional collision and mechanical automobile repair businesses throughout the U.S. and Canada. The Europe segment provides mechanical aftermarket parts for the repair of vehicles 3 to 15 years old. Top-selling products within this division include brake pads, discs, sensors, clutches, spark plugs, batteries, steering systems and components, suspension systems and components, filters, and oil/automotive fluids. The specialty segment sells and distributes recreational vehicle appliances, vehicle air conditioners, tow hitches, truck bed covers, vehicle protection products, cargo management products, wheels, tires and suspension products. This division primarily supplies small- to medium-sized businesses that focus on a narrow product or market niche. Last, the self-service segment generates scrap metal, alloys and other materials that are sold to recyclers. Vehicles LKQ no longer make available to the public and crush-only vehicles acquired from other companies are typically crushed using equipment on site. Damaged and unusable wheel cores are melted in LKQ's aluminum furnace and sold to consumers of aluminum ingot and used for the production of various automotive products, including wheels In December 2019, LKQ acquired Auto Data Labels, Inc., a manufacturer and distributor of replacement vehicle information labels in North America.

FINANCIAL DATA: Note: Data for latest year may not have been available at press time.

In U.S. $	2020	2019	2018	2017	2016	2015
Revenue	11,628,830,000	12,506,110,000	11,876,670,000	9,736,909,000	8,584,031,000	7,192,633,000
R&D Expense						
Operating Income	1,054,914,000	980,724,000	947,913,000	866,990,000	801,160,000	724,138,000
Operating Margin %		.08%	.08%	.09%	.09%	.10%
SGA Expense	3,266,065,000	3,580,300,000	3,352,731,000	1,915,699,000	1,670,192,000	1,431,230,000
Net Income	638,423,000	541,260,000	480,118,000	533,744,000	463,975,000	423,223,000
Operating Cash Flow	1,443,870,000	1,064,033,000	710,739,000	518,900,000	635,014,000	529,837,000
Capital Expenditure	172,695,000	265,730,000	250,027,000	179,090,000	207,074,000	170,490,000
EBITDA	1,281,248,000	1,243,932,000	1,183,885,000	1,098,470,000	971,630,000	835,082,000
Return on Assets %		.04%	.05%	.06%	.07%	.08%
Return on Equity %		.11%	.11%	.14%	.14%	.15%
Debt to Equity		0.969	0.876	0.781	0.951	0.491

CONTACT INFORMATION:

Phone: 312 621-1950   Fax: 312 621-1969
Toll-Free: 877-557-2677
Address: 500 W. Madison St., Ste. 2800, Chicago, IL 60661 United States

STOCK TICKER/OTHER:

Stock Ticker: LKQ
Employees: 44,000
Parent Company:

Exchange: NAS
Fiscal Year Ends: 12/31

SALARIES/BONUSES:

Top Exec. Salary: $ Bonus: $
Second Exec. Salary: $ Bonus: $

OTHER THOUGHTS:

Estimated Female Officers or Directors:
Hot Spot for Advancement for Women/Minorities:

Lockheed Martin Corporation

www.lockheedmartin.com

NAIC Code: 336411

TYPES OF BUSINESS:

Aircraft Manufacturing
Military Aircraft
Defense Electronics
Systems Integration & Technology Services
Communications Satellites & Launch Services
Undersea, Shipboard, Land & Airborne Systems & Subsystems

BRANDS/DIVISIONS/AFFILIATES:

F-35 Lightning
F-22
F-16
C-130
Orion Artemis I

CONTACTS:
Note: Officers with more than one job title may be intentionally listed here more than once.

Marillyn Hewson, CEO
Kenneth Possenriede, CFO
Brian Colan, Chief Accounting Officer
Richard Edwards, Executive VP, Divisional
Dale Bennett, Executive VP, Divisional
Richard Ambrose, Executive VP, Divisional
Michele Evans, Executive VP, Divisional
Frank St John, Executive VP, Divisional
Maryanne Lavan, General Counsel
John Mollard, Treasurer

GROWTH PLANS/SPECIAL FEATURES:

Lockheed Martin Corporation is a global security and aerospace company engaged in the research, design, development, manufacture, integration and sustainment of advanced technology systems, products and services. It serves domestic and international customers with products and services that have defense, civil and commercial applications, with principal customers including agencies of the U.S. government (approximately 70% of annual sales). The company operates in four segments: aeronautics, missiles and fire control (MFC), rotary and mission systems (RMS) and space. The aeronautics segment is engaged in the design, R&D, systems integration, production, sustainment, support and upgrade of advanced military aircraft, air and unmanned vehicles and related technologies. Major products include the F-35 Lightning strike fighter, the F-22 stealth fighter, the F-16 multi-role fighter and the C-130 tactical airlifter. The MFC segment provides: air and missile defense systems; tactical missiles and air-to-ground precision strike weapon systems; logistics; fire control systems; mission operations support, readiness, engineering support and integration services; manned and unmanned ground vehicles; and energy management solutions. The RMS division provides: design, manufacture, service and support for a variety of military and commercial helicopters; ship and submarine mission and combat systems; mission systems and sensors for rotary and fixed-wing aircraft; sea and land-based missile defense systems; radar systems; the Littoral Combat Ship; simulation and training services; and unmanned systems and technologies. Last, the space segment is engaged in the R&D, design, engineering and production of satellites, strategic and defensive missile systems and space transportation systems. In December 2020, Lockheed Martin agreed to acquire Aerojet Rocketdyne Holdings, Inc., with the expected closing date to occur in March 2021. In January 2021, Lockheed Martin completed the assembly and testing of its Orion Artemis I spacecraft, and transferred Orion to NASA's exploration ground systems division for its mission to the Moon later in 2021.

FINANCIAL DATA:
Note: Data for latest year may not have been available at press time.

In U.S. $	2020	2019	2018	2017	2016	2015
Revenue	65,398,000,000	59,812,000,000	53,762,000,000	51,048,000,000	47,248,000,000	46,132,000,000
R&D Expense						
Operating Income	8,644,000,000	8,367,000,000	7,370,000,000	5,548,000,000	5,142,000,000	5,302,000,000
Operating Margin %		.14%	.14%	.11%	.11%	.11%
SGA Expense						
Net Income	6,833,000,000	6,230,000,000	5,046,000,000	2,002,000,000	5,302,000,000	3,605,000,000
Operating Cash Flow	8,183,000,000	7,311,000,000	3,138,000,000	6,476,000,000	5,189,000,000	5,101,000,000
Capital Expenditure	1,766,000,000	1,484,000,000	1,278,000,000	1,177,000,000	1,063,000,000	939,000,000
EBITDA	10,116,000,000	9,083,000,000	7,667,000,000	7,115,000,000	6,764,000,000	6,492,000,000
Return on Assets %		.13%	.11%	.04%	.11%	.08%
Return on Equity %		2.76%	14.19%	4.84%	2.30%	1.11%
Debt to Equity		3.647	9.042		9.452	4.619

CONTACT INFORMATION:

Phone: 301 897-6000   Fax: 301 897-6083
Toll-Free:
Address: 6801 Rockledge Dr., Bethesda, MD 20817 United States

STOCK TICKER/OTHER:

Stock Ticker: LMT   Exchange: NYS
Employees: 114,000   Fiscal Year Ends: 12/31
Parent Company:

SALARIES/BONUSES:

Top Exec. Salary: $ Bonus: $
Second Exec. Salary: $ Bonus: $

OTHER THOUGHTS:

Estimated Female Officers or Directors: 5
Hot Spot for Advancement for Women/Minorities: Y

Sales, profits and employees may be estimates. Financial information, benefits and other data can change quickly and may vary from those stated here.

Logitech International SA

NAIC Code: 334118

www.logitech.com

TYPES OF BUSINESS:

Keyboards & Mouse Devices, Computer Peripheral Equipment,
Manufacturing
Keyboards & Mice
Imaging Devices
Control Devices
Interface Devices
Cordless Technology
Video Conferencing
Streaming

BRANDS/DIVISIONS/AFFILIATES:

Logitech
Jaybird
Logitech G
Ultimate Ears
ASTRO Gaming
Blue Microphones

CONTACTS: *Note: Officers with more than one job title may be intentionally listed here more than once.*

Bracken Darrell, CEO
Prakash Arunkundrum, Head of Global Ops
Guerrino De Luca, Chairman of the Board
Nate Olmstead, CFO
Nate Olmstead, Vice President, Divisional
Wendy Becker, Chairperson of the Board

GROWTH PLANS/SPECIAL FEATURES:

Logitech International SA designs, manufactures and markets products that connect people to digital experiences via computer, mobile device or the cloud. The company's brands include Logitech, Jaybird, Logitech G, Ultimate Ears, ASTRO Gaming and Blue Microphones. Its products fall into the categories of music, gaming, video collaboration, streaming, smart home and creativity/productivity. Music offerings include: mobile speakers, specifically portable wireless Bluetooth speakers; microphones, recording tools and accessories for audio professionals, musicians and consumers; and audio-PC and wearables, which includes PC speakers, PC headsets, in-ear headphones and premium wireless audio wearables designed to enhance the audio experience. Gaming offerings include keyboards, mice, headsets, mousepads and simulation products such as steering wheels and flight sticks. Video collaboration products include conference cameras and video-related equipment. Streaming includes a selection of webcams and microphones. Smart home products include the company's Logitech Harmony line of advanced home entertainment controllers, as well as products dedicated to controlling emerging categories of connected smart home devices such as lighting, thermostats and door locks. Last, creativity/productivity offerings include: pointing devices, keyboards, keyboard-and-mouse combinations, tablets, web cams and related accessories. Logitech primarily sells its products to a network of distributors and retailers, supporting these channels with third-party distribution centers located in North America, South America, Europe and Asia Pacific.

Logitech employees receive comprehensive health benefits, insurance, retirement options and other assistance programs.

FINANCIAL DATA: *Note: Data for latest year may not have been available at press time.*

In U.S. $	2020	2019	2018	2017	2016	2015
Revenue	2,975,851,000	2,788,322,000	2,566,863,000	2,221,427,000	2,018,100,000	
R&D Expense	177,593,000	161,230,000	143,760,000	130,525,000	113,624,000	
Operating Income	299,886,000	274,496,000	224,709,000	203,791,000	146,860,000	
Operating Margin %	.10%	.10%	.09%	.09%	.07%	
SGA Expense	627,339,000	586,995,000	531,842,000	479,911,000	420,563,000	
Net Income	449,723,000	257,573,000	208,542,000	205,876,000	119,317,000	
Operating Cash Flow	425,000,000	305,181,000	346,261,000	278,728,000	183,111,000	
Capital Expenditure	39,484,000	35,930,000	39,748,000	31,804,000	56,615,000	
EBITDA	373,637,000	342,147,000	281,611,000	254,279,000	184,465,000	
Return on Assets %	.20%	.14%	.13%	.15%	.09%	
Return on Equity %	.34%	.23%	.22%	.25%	.16%	
Debt to Equity	0.013					

CONTACT INFORMATION:

Phone: 510-795-8500　　Fax:
Toll-Free: 800-231-7717
Address: 7700 Gateway Blvd., Newark, CA 94560 United States

STOCK TICKER/OTHER:

Stock Ticker: LOGI
Employees: 9,000
Parent Company:

Exchange: NAS
Fiscal Year Ends: 03/31

SALARIES/BONUSES:

Top Exec. Salary: $　　Bonus: $
Second Exec. Salary: $　　Bonus: $

OTHER THOUGHTS:

Estimated Female Officers or Directors: 4
Hot Spot for Advancement for Women/Minorities: Y

Lowes Companies Inc

www.lowes.com

NAIC Code: 444110

TYPES OF BUSINESS:

Home Centers, Retail
Home Improvement Products
Home Installation Services
Special Order Sales
Smarthome Products

BRANDS/DIVISIONS/AFFILIATES:

CONTACTS: Note: Officers with more than one job title may be intentionally listed here more than once.

Marvin Ellison, CEO
David Denton, CFO
Richard Dreiling, Chairman of the Board
Seemantini Godbole, Chief Information Officer
Donald Frieson, Executive VP, Divisional
William Boltz, Executive VP, Divisional
Joseph Mcfarland, Executive VP, Divisional
Ross Mccanless, Executive VP
Jennifer Weber, Executive VP
Tiffany Mason, Senior VP, Divisional
Matthew Hollifield, Senior VP

GROWTH PLANS/SPECIAL FEATURES:

Lowe's Companies, Inc. is one of the largest home improvement retailers in the world. The company owns nearly 2,000 stores in 50 U.S. states and Canada (as of July 31, 2020), each carrying thousands of products and 208 million square feet of total retail space. Hundreds of thousands of items are also available through the firm's special-order system. Lowe's stores chiefly serve do-it-yourself (DIY) homeowners and commercial business customers, including contractors, landscapers, electricians, painters and plumbers. Its home improvement product categories include building materials, lighting, cabinets and countertops, seasonal living, millwork, lumber, flooring, lawn and landscaping items, hardware, fashion and rough plumbing, appliances, paint, tools, plants and plant pots, outdoor power equipment, rough electrical, home environment and organization and windows and walls. Each Lowe's store carries a wide selection of national brand name merchandise such as Samsung, Whirlpool, Stainmaster, GE, Valspar, Dewalt and Owens Corning; and private brand names such as Kobalt, allen+roth and Utilitech. The company's Lowes.com website facilitates customers researching, comparing and buying Lowe's products, and also allows customers to special order products not carried in its physical store locations. Lowe's entered the smarthome market with Iris, an affordable, cloud-based home management system, which allows users to interact and control their home's security cameras, thermostat, locks, lighting and appliances remotely from a smart phone or computer.

Lowe's offers comprehensive benefits, retirement and savings options, and employee assistance programs.

FINANCIAL DATA: Note: Data for latest year may not have been available at press time.

In U.S. $	2020	2019	2018	2017	2016	2015
Revenue	72,148,000,000	71,309,000,000	68,619,000,000	65,017,000,000	59,074,000,000	
R&D Expense						
Operating Income	6,314,000,000	4,018,000,000	6,586,000,000	5,846,000,000	4,971,000,000	
Operating Margin %	.09%	.06%	.10%	.09%	.08%	
SGA Expense	15,367,000,000	17,413,000,000	15,376,000,000	15,129,000,000	14,115,000,000	
Net Income	4,281,000,000	2,314,000,000	3,447,000,000	3,091,000,000	2,546,000,000	
Operating Cash Flow	4,296,000,000	6,193,000,000	5,065,000,000	5,617,000,000	4,784,000,000	
Capital Expenditure	1,484,000,000	1,174,000,000	1,123,000,000	1,167,000,000	1,197,000,000	
EBITDA	7,751,000,000	5,653,000,000	7,678,000,000	7,448,000,000	6,562,000,000	
Return on Assets %	.12%	.07%	.10%	.09%	.08%	
Return on Equity %	1.52%	.48%	.56%	.43%	.29%	
Debt to Equity	10.503	3.949	2.65	2.237	1.508	

CONTACT INFORMATION:

Phone: 704 758-1000   Fax: 336 658-4766
Toll-Free: 800-445-6937
Address: 1000 Lowe's Blvd., Mooresville, NC 28117 United States

SALARIES/BONUSES:

Top Exec. Salary: $ Bonus: $
Second Exec. Salary: $ Bonus: $

STOCK TICKER/OTHER:

Stock Ticker: LOW
Employees: 340,000
Parent Company:

Exchange: NYS
Fiscal Year Ends: 01/31

OTHER THOUGHTS:

Estimated Female Officers or Directors: 3
Hot Spot for Advancement for Women/Minorities: Y

Lubrizol Corporation (The)

NAIC Code: 325110

www.lubrizol.com

TYPES OF BUSINESS:
Manufacturing-Specialty Chemicals
Fuel & Lubricant Additives
Polymers
Performance Coatings, Resins & Additives
Plastic Plumbing, Automobile Molded Parts & Film
Rubber, Plastic & Lubricants Additives

BRANDS/DIVISIONS/AFFILIATES:
Berkshire Hathaway Inc
Lubrizol Additives
Lubrizol Advanced Materials
Lubrizol Corporate Ventures

CONTACTS: Note: Officers with more than one job title may be intentionally listed here more than once.
Eric R. Schnur, CEO
J. Brian Pitts, CFO
Ana G. Rodriguez, Chief Human Resources Officer
John J. King, CIO
Eric R. Schnur, Chmn.

GROWTH PLANS/SPECIAL FEATURES:

The Lubrizol Corporation, a subsidiary of Berkshire Hathaway, Inc., is a manufacturer and marketer of specialty chemicals and additives for the transportation, consumer and industrial markets. The company maintains production facilities throughout the Americas, Europe, the Middle East & Africa and Asia Pacific. It operates through three segments: Lubrizol Additives, Lubrizol Advanced Materials and Lubrizol Corporate Ventures. The Lubrizol Additives segment partners with customers and original equipment manufacturers to solve end-user challenges through additives for engine oils, driveline applications, gasoline and diesel fuel, and other transportation-related fluids and industrial applications. Engine oil additives are useful in heavy duty diesel vehicles, passenger cars, marine vehicles, motorcycles, recreational vehicles, power tools and stationary natural gas equipment. Driveline additives are useful in axle oil, transmission fluids, construction and mining fluids and agriculture processes. Industrial lubricant additives are useful in grease, metalworking, industrial gear oil, hydraulic fluids, emulsion explosives, turbine and circulating oils and compressor lubricants. Fuel additives are useful in diesel, home heating oil, gasoline, industrial, marine and biofuel processes and applications. The Lubrizol Advanced Materials segment (and subsidiary) provides formulations that enable the distinct characteristics in customer's products, such as enhanced durability, nourishment in products and better quality in digital printing. Products lines include: engineered polymers, personal and home care, performance coatings, CPVC (chlorinated polyvinyl chloride) piping systems (flexible and withstand temperatures) and life sciences (such as medical devices and pharmaceuticals). Lubrizol Corporate Ventures (established in 2020) partners with industries to develop, test, commercialize and scale breakthrough opportunities in emerging, high-impact industries such as energy solutions and thermal management.

Lubrizol employee benefits vary by country but include healthcare and disability coverage and retirement planning.

FINANCIAL DATA: Note: Data for latest year may not have been available at press time.

In U.S. $	2020	2019	2018	2017	2016	2015
Revenue	5,950,000,000	6,500,000,000	6,800,000,000	6,300,000,000	6,100,000,000	6,300,000,000
R&D Expense						
Operating Income						
Operating Margin %						
SGA Expense						
Net Income						
Operating Cash Flow						
Capital Expenditure						
EBITDA						
Return on Assets %						
Return on Equity %						
Debt to Equity						

CONTACT INFORMATION:
Phone: 440-943-4200   Fax: 440-943-5337
Toll-Free:
Address: 29400 Lakeland Blvd., Wickliffe, OH 44092 United States

STOCK TICKER/OTHER:
Stock Ticker: Subsidiary   Exchange:
Employees: 8,636   Fiscal Year Ends: 12/31
Parent Company: Berkshire Hathaway Inc

SALARIES/BONUSES:
Top Exec. Salary: $ Bonus: $
Second Exec. Salary: $ Bonus: $

OTHER THOUGHTS:
Estimated Female Officers or Directors: 1
Hot Spot for Advancement for Women/Minorities:

Lumentum Operations LLC

www.lumentum.com

NAIC Code: 334220

TYPES OF BUSINESS:

Optical Components & Modules
Telecommunications Equipment
Lasers

BRANDS/DIVISIONS/AFFILIATES:

Lumentum Holdings Inc

CONTACTS: Note: Officers with more than one job title may be intentionally listed here more than once.

Alan Lowe, CEO
Wajid Ali, CFO
Jason Reinhardt, Exec. VP-Global Sales
Sharon Parker, Sr. VP-Human Resources
Ralph Loura, CIO
Harold Covert, Chmn.

GROWTH PLANS/SPECIAL FEATURES:

Lumentum Operations, LLC designs and manufactures innovative photonics for the purpose of accelerating the speed and scale of cloud, networking, advanced manufacturing and 3D sensing applications. The company's products are categorized into three groups: optical communications, commercial lasers and diode lasers. Optical communications products include dense wavelength division multiplexing (DWDM) and coherent optical transceivers, DWDM transmission components, reconfigurable optical add-drop multiplexers (ROADMs) and wavelength management, software-defined networking (SDN) elements, optical amplifiers, passive components and modules, pump lasers, source lasers and photodiodes, and submarine components. Commercial lasers include kW fiber and direct-diode lasers, ultra-fast lasers, Q-switched lasers, and low power continuous wave lasers. Diode lasers include edge-emitting diode lasers and fiber-coupled diode lasers. Based in California, USA, the firm has additional offices in North America, Europe and Asia. Lumentum operates as a subsidiary of Lumentum Holdings, Inc.

Lumentum offers its employees benefits programs and wellness initiatives, as well as performance incentives.

FINANCIAL DATA: Note: Data for latest year may not have been available at press time.

In U.S. $	2020	2019	2018	2017	2016	2015
Revenue	1,678,600,000	1,565,300,000	1,247,700,000	1,001,600,000	903,000,000	837,100,000
R&D Expense						
Operating Income						
Operating Margin %						
SGA Expense						
Net Income	135,500,000	-36,400,000	248,100,000	-102,500,000	9,300,000	-3,400,000
Operating Cash Flow						
Capital Expenditure						
EBITDA						
Return on Assets %						
Return on Equity %						
Debt to Equity						

CONTACT INFORMATION:

Phone: 408-546-5483   Fax: 408-546-4300
Toll-Free:
Address: 1001 Ridder Park Dr., San Jose, CA 95131 United States

STOCK TICKER/OTHER:

Stock Ticker: Subsidiary
Employees: 5,473
Parent Company: Lumentum Holdings Inc

Exchange:
Fiscal Year Ends: 06/30

SALARIES/BONUSES:

Top Exec. Salary: $ Bonus: $
Second Exec. Salary: $ Bonus: $

OTHER THOUGHTS:

Estimated Female Officers or Directors:
Hot Spot for Advancement for Women/Minorities:

Magellan Health Inc

www.magellanhealth.com

NAIC Code: 621999

TYPES OF BUSINESS:

Specialty Managed Health Care Services
Psychiatric Hospitals
Residential Treatment Centers

BRANDS/DIVISIONS/AFFILIATES:

Magellan Complete Care

CONTACTS: *Note: Officers with more than one job title may be intentionally listed here more than once.*

Mostafa Kamal, CEO, Subsidiary
Barry Smith, CEO
Jonathan Rubin, CFO
Caskie Lewis-Clapper, Other Executive Officer
Daniel Gregoire, Secretary
Jeffrey West, Senior VP

GROWTH PLANS/SPECIAL FEATURES:

Magellan Health, Inc. is engaged in the healthcare management business. Magellan develops innovative solutions that combine advanced analytics, agile technology and clinical excellence to promote best decision-making capabilities for its clients. The firm serves health plans, managed care organizations, employers, labor unions, various military and governmental agencies and third-party administrators. Magellan operates in two business segments: Magellan healthcare and Magellan pharmacy management. Magellan healthcare includes the firm's management of behavioral healthcare services and employee assistance program services; management of specialty areas such as diagnostic imaging and musculoskeletal management; and the integrated management of physical, behavioral and pharmaceutical health care for special populations delivered via Magellan Complete Care. Special populations include individuals with serious mental illness, dual eligible, long-term services and supports and other populations with unique and often complex health care needs. Magellan pharmacy management comprises products and solutions that provide clinical and financial management of pharmaceuticals paid under medical and pharmacy benefit programs. Its services include pharmacy benefit management, pharmacy benefit administration for state Medicaid and other government-sponsored programs, pharmaceutical dispensing operations, clinical and formulary management programs, medical pharmacy management programs, as well as programs for the integrated management of specialty drugs across both the medical and pharmacy benefit that treat complex conditions.

FINANCIAL DATA: *Note: Data for latest year may not have been available at press time.*

In U.S. $	2020	2019	2018	2017	2016	2015
Revenue	4,577,531,000	7,159,423,000	7,314,151,000	5,838,583,000	4,836,884,000	4,597,400,000
R&D Expense						
Operating Income	20,404,000	97,781,000	64,522,000	155,314,000	152,892,000	75,532,000
Operating Margin %		.01%	.01%	.03%	.03%	.02%
SGA Expense						
Net Income	382,335,000	55,902,000	24,181,000	110,207,000	77,879,000	31,413,000
Operating Cash Flow	450,761,000	115,846,000	164,844,000	162,273,000	66,699,000	239,185,000
Capital Expenditure	75,480,000	60,402,000	68,275,000	57,232,000	60,881,000	71,584,000
EBITDA	109,125,000	248,479,000	211,250,000	276,907,000	261,756,000	180,541,000
Return on Assets %		.02%	.01%	.04%	.03%	.02%
Return on Equity %		.04%	.02%	.09%	.07%	.03%
Debt to Equity		0.486	0.567	0.58	0.195	0.224

CONTACT INFORMATION:

Phone: 602-572-6050   Fax:
Toll-Free: 800-410-8312
Address: 4800 Scottsdale Rd, Ste. 4000, Scottsdale, AZ 85251 United States

STOCK TICKER/OTHER:

Stock Ticker: MGLN   Exchange: NAS
Employees: 9,000   Fiscal Year Ends: 12/31
Parent Company:

SALARIES/BONUSES:

Top Exec. Salary: $ Bonus: $
Second Exec. Salary: $ Bonus: $

OTHER THOUGHTS:

Estimated Female Officers or Directors: 3
Hot Spot for Advancement for Women/Minorities: Y

ManTech International Corporation

www.mantech.com

NAIC Code: 541512

TYPES OF BUSINESS:

Information Technology Services
Technology and Software Development

BRANDS/DIVISIONS/AFFILIATES:

Tapestry Technologies
Minerva Engineering

CONTACTS: Note: Officers with more than one job title may be intentionally listed here more than once.

Kevin Phillips, CEO
Judith Bjornaas, CFO
George Pedersen, Chairman of the Board
Richard Wagner, President, Divisional
Matthew Tait, President, Divisional

GROWTH PLANS/SPECIAL FEATURES:

ManTech International Corporation is a provider of mission-focused technology solutions and services for U.S. defense, intelligence community and federal civilian agencies. The company specializes in full-spectrum cyber, data collection & analytics, enterprise IT, systems engineering and software application development solutions that support national and homeland security. Cyber solutions encompass defense, resilience, offence, analytics and compliance. Data collection and analytics include predictive and other types of analytics. The enterprise IT division develops, implements and maintains solutions that leverage technology across an enterprise, delivering services that improve mission performance and reduce costs for our customers. Solutions primarily involve hardware and software to support the core technology infrastructure, such as data centers, cloud services, email or desktop computing and managed services. Systems engineering encompasses ManTech's expertise across major domains such as land, sea, air, space and cyberspace. This division applies systems engineering across a wide array of large-scale system development and acquisition programs used by government and industry. Its test and evaluation services are closely interlinked with its systems engineering capabilities, and include specific competencies in test engineering, preparation and planning, modeling and simulation, test range operations/management, systems and cyber vulnerability, and independent validation and verification. The software application division develops, modifies and maintains software solutions and complex systems that link different computing systems and software applications to act as a coordinated whole. It includes an array of lifecycle services, and supports all major software development lifecycle methodologies: agile, DevOps, DevSecOps and hybrid. ManTech delivers advanced training solutions using a range of environments, including live, virtual, constructive, immersive and gaming scenarios. Training services are leveraged according to subject matter. In late-2020, ManTech acquired Tapestry Technologies, as well as Minvera Engineering, to expand its advanced cyber capabilities.

ManTech offers its employees comprehensive health and retirement benefits.

FINANCIAL DATA: Note: Data for latest year may not have been available at press time.

In U.S. $	2020	2019	2018	2017	2016	2015
Revenue	2,518,384,000	2,222,559,000	1,958,557,000	1,717,018,000	1,601,596,000	1,550,117,000
R&D Expense						
Operating Income	158,049,000	138,325,000	112,742,000	98,194,000	90,963,000	84,886,000
Operating Margin %		.06%	.06%	.06%	.06%	.05%
SGA Expense	221,544,000	190,773,000	167,715,000	155,225,000	140,858,000	144,534,000
Net Income	120,530,000	113,890,000	82,097,000	114,141,000	56,391,000	51,127,000
Operating Cash Flow	247,244,000	221,406,000	93,439,000	152,958,000	95,764,000	153,883,000
Capital Expenditure	76,322,000	58,472,000	35,132,000	38,862,000	10,410,000	6,227,000
EBITDA	228,597,000	194,571,000	165,552,000	132,409,000	121,358,000	116,823,000
Return on Assets %		.06%	.05%	.07%	.04%	.03%
Return on Equity %		.08%	.06%	.09%	.05%	.04%
Debt to Equity		0.094	0.005	0.023		

CONTACT INFORMATION:

Phone: 703 218-6000   Fax: 703 218-6301
Toll-Free:
Address: 2251 Corporate Park Dr., Herndon, VA 20171 United States

STOCK TICKER/OTHER:

Stock Ticker: MANT
Employees: 8,900
Parent Company:

Exchange: NAS
Fiscal Year Ends: 12/31

SALARIES/BONUSES:

Top Exec. Salary: $ Bonus: $
Second Exec. Salary: $ Bonus: $

OTHER THOUGHTS:

Estimated Female Officers or Directors: 2
Hot Spot for Advancement for Women/Minorities: Y

Mars Incorporated
NAIC Code: 311351

TYPES OF BUSINESS:
Chocolate & Confectionery Manufacturing
Snack Foods & Candy Bars
Pet Nutrition
Drink Vending Systems
Prepared Foods
Information Technology Services

BRANDS/DIVISIONS/AFFILIATES:
AniCura
Cesar
Eukanuba
M&Ms
Snickers
Orbit
Uncle Bens
CocaVia

CONTACTS: Note: Officers with more than one job title may be intentionally listed here more than once.
Grant F. Reid, CEO
Claus Aagaard, CFO
Eric Minvielle, VP-Human Resources
Richard Ware, VP-R&D
John Donofrio, General Counsel
David Kamenetzky, VP-Corp. Affairs
Frank Mars, Pres., Symbioscience
Martin Radvan, Pres., Wrigley
Grant Reid, Pres., Chocolate
Poul Weihrauch, Pres., Food
Richard Ware, VP-Supply & Procurement

GROWTH PLANS/SPECIAL FEATURES:
Mars Incorporated, founded in 1911, is a family-owned company that operates through four segments: Mars petcare, Mars Wrigley confectionery, Mars food and Mars edge. Mars petcare is a diverse business comprising brands that serve the health and nutrition needs of pets, including AniCura, API, Banfield Pet Hospital, bluepearl, Cesar, Dreamies, Eukanuba, IAMS, Pedigree, Sheba, Waltham Petcare Science Institute, whiskas and Wisdom Panel. Mars Wrigley manufactures a range of chocolate, chewing gum, mints and fruit-based confections, which are enjoyed in more than 180 countries. Some of its brands include M&Ms, Snickers, Orbit, Extra and Skittles. Mars food is based in London, U.K. and operates more than 10 manufacturing sites. This division's leading food brands are available in more than 30 countries, and include the Uncle Ben's brand of rice products, with the brand having been in business for more than 70 years. Other food brands include Dolmio, KanTong, MasterFoods, Royco, Seeds of Change and Tasty Bite, among others. Mars edge builds partnerships with academia, startup companies and philanthropic organizations to provide nutrition solutions. For example, this division's GoMo is a nutritious product for nutritional deficient populations, such as school-aged children in India; and its CocoaVia dietary supplement for heart and brain health, which promotes blood flow and supplies high levels of oxygen and nutrients to the body's organs.

FINANCIAL DATA: Note: Data for latest year may not have been available at press time.

In U.S. $	2020	2019	2018	2017	2016	2015
Revenue	40,425,229,688	39,827,812,500	37,931,250,000	36,125,000,000	36,000,000,000	35,500,000,000
R&D Expense						
Operating Income						
Operating Margin %						
SGA Expense						
Net Income						
Operating Cash Flow						
Capital Expenditure						
EBITDA						
Return on Assets %						
Return on Equity %						
Debt to Equity						

CONTACT INFORMATION:
Phone: 703-821-4900   Fax: 703-448-9678
Toll-Free: 800-627-7852
Address: 6885 Elm St., McLean, VA 22101 United States

STOCK TICKER/OTHER:
Stock Ticker: Private
Employees: 130,000
Parent Company:

Exchange:
Fiscal Year Ends: 12/31

SALARIES/BONUSES:
Top Exec. Salary: $ Bonus: $
Second Exec. Salary: $ Bonus: $

OTHER THOUGHTS:
Estimated Female Officers or Directors: 1
Hot Spot for Advancement for Women/Minorities:

Mass General Brigham Incorporated   www.massgeneralbrigham.org

NAIC Code: 622110

TYPES OF BUSINESS:

General Medical and Surgical Hospitals
Teaching Hospitals
Mental Health
Radiology
Lab Services
Emergency Care

BRANDS/DIVISIONS/AFFILIATES:

Brigham and Women's Hospital
Massachusetts General Hospital
Brigham and Women's Health Care Center
Brigham and Women's Faulkner Hospital
Brigham and Women's Urgent Care Center
Brigham Health Fast Care
BWH
Cooley Dickinson

CONTACTS: Note: Officers with more than one job title may be intentionally listed here more than once.

Anne Klibanski, CEO
Ron M. Walls, COO
Peter K. Markell, CFO
Mark Bohen, CMO
Rosemary R. Sheehan, Chief Human Resources Officer
Elizabeth Mort, Sr. Medical Dir.
Peter K. Markell, Exec. VP-Admin.
Brent L. Henry, General Counsel
Lynne J. Eickholt, Chief Strategy Officer
Sara Andrews, Chief Dev. Officer
Rich Copp, VP-Comm.
Peter K. Markell, Exec. VP-Finance
David E.Storto, VP-Non-Acute Care Svcs.
Peter R. Brown, Chief of Staff
Kathryn E. West, VP-Real Estate & Facility
Tejal K. Gandhi, Chief Quality & Safety Officer
Scott M. Sperling, Chmn.

GROWTH PLANS/SPECIAL FEATURES:

Mass General Brigham Incorporated (formerly Partners HealthCare) is a non-profit hospital and physician network with more than 15 member institutions and several affiliates. Brigham and Women's Hospital is a 793-bed teaching hospital of Harvard Medical School. Massachusetts General Hospital offers diagnostic and therapeutic care in virtually every specialty and subspecialty of medicine and surgery. Brigham and Women's Health Care Center (Westwood) is a state-of-the-art health care center that provides primary and specialty care, as well as on-site diagnostic radiology and lab services. Brigham and Women's Faulkner Hospital is a 171-bed community teaching hospital offering medical, surgical and psychiatric care, as well as emergency, ambulatory and diagnostic services. Brigham and Women's Health Care Center (Chestnut Hill) provides multi-specialty care. Brigham and Women's Health Care Center (Pembroke) offers comprehensive services ranging from annual physical exams to the management of complex medical conditions, on-site diagnostic radiology and lab services and more. Other institutions include Brigham and Women's Urgent Care Center (Foxborough), Brigham Health and Brigham and Women's/Mass General Health Care Center, Brigham Health Fast Care (Pembroke), BWH Brookside Community Health Center, BWH Southern Jamaica Plain Health Center, Cooley Dickinson Hospital, Harbor Medical Associates Urgent Care Center, and many more. In late-2019, Partners HealthCare rebranded as Mass General Brigham to reflect and unify the organization's best-known assets, Massachusetts General Hospital and Brigham and Women's Hospital.

Mass General Brigham offers its employees health, drug, dental and vision coverage; retirement savings and financial counseling; optional life and disability insurance; and flexibla savings accounts.

FINANCIAL DATA: Note: Data for latest year may not have been available at press time.

In U.S. $	2020	2019	2018	2017	2016	2015
Revenue	13,020,000,000	14,000,000,000	13,307,269,000	13,371,063,000	12,517,887,000	11,665,645,000
R&D Expense						
Operating Income						
Operating Margin %						
SGA Expense						
Net Income		867,935,250	826,605,000	659,097,000	-249,011,000	-91,989,000
Operating Cash Flow						
Capital Expenditure						
EBITDA						
Return on Assets %						
Return on Equity %						
Debt to Equity						

CONTACT INFORMATION:

Phone: 617-278-1000   Fax:
Toll-Free:
Address: 800 Boylston St., 11/Fl, Boston, MA 02199 United States

STOCK TICKER/OTHER:

Stock Ticker: Nonprofit
Employees: 78,000
Parent Company:

Exchange:
Fiscal Year Ends: 09/30

SALARIES/BONUSES:

Top Exec. Salary: $ Bonus: $
Second Exec. Salary: $ Bonus: $

OTHER THOUGHTS:

Estimated Female Officers or Directors: 11
Hot Spot for Advancement for Women/Minorities: Y

MassMutual Financial Group

NAIC Code: 524113

www.massmutual.com

TYPES OF BUSINESS:

Life Insurance
Pension Products
Real Estate Equity Management
Disability Insurance
Investment Management Products
Mutual Fund Management
Investor Services

BRANDS/DIVISIONS/AFFILIATES:

Massachusetts Mutual Life Insurance Company
CM Life Insurance Company
MML Bay State Life Insurance Company
Oppenheimer Funds Inc
Barings LLC
MassMutual Ventures LLC

CONTACTS: *Note: Officers with more than one job title may be intentionally listed here more than once.*

Roger Crandall, CEO
Elizabeth Ward, CFO
Susan Cicco, Head-Human Resources
Timothy Corbett, Chief Investment Officer
Mark D. Roellig, General Counsel
Sharmaine Miller, VP-New Bus. Oper.
Douglas G. Russell, Sr. VP-Strategy & Corp. Dev.
Elizabeth A. Ward, Chief Enterprise Risk Officer
William F. Glavin, Jr., CEO/Pres./Chmn-OppenheimerFunds, Inc.
Susan M. Cicco, VP
Roger Crandall, Chmn.
Elaine A. Sarsynski, CEO/Chmn.-MassMutual Int'l LLC

GROWTH PLANS/SPECIAL FEATURES:

MassMutual Financial Group, a marketing name for Massachusetts Mutual Life Insurance Company and its affiliated companies, is a global, growth oriented, diversified financial services organization. The mutually-owned company offers financial protection, accumulation and income management by providing life insurance, annuities, disability income insurance, long-term care insurance, retirement planning products, income management and other products and services for individuals, business owners, corporations and institutions. It operates through several subsidiaries, including CM Life Insurance Company and MML Bay State Life Insurance Company. MassMutual's investment group provides investment management products, such as securities and real estate as well as mutual fund management primarily through Oppenheimer Funds, Inc. and Barings, LLC. MassMutual Ventures, LLC is a venture capital firm with the mandate to back startups and entrepreneurial businesses. In December 2020, MassMutual agreed to acquire Flourish, a fintech platform for RIAs, from Stone Ridge Holdings Group. The transaction was expected to be complete in early-2021.

The firm offers employees life, health, dental, disability and vision insurance; flexible spending accounts; and a 401(k).

FINANCIAL DATA: *Note: Data for latest year may not have been available at press time.*

In U.S. $	2020	2019	2018	2017	2016	2015
Revenue	23,259,000,000	32,603,000,000	32,484,000,000	26,113,000,000	29,560,000,000	29,488,000,000
R&D Expense						
Operating Income						
Operating Margin %						
SGA Expense						
Net Income	128,000,000	524,000,000	-716,000,000	137,000,000	70,000,000	546,000,000
Operating Cash Flow						
Capital Expenditure						
EBITDA						
Return on Assets %						
Return on Equity %						
Debt to Equity						

CONTACT INFORMATION:

Phone: 413-744-1000   Fax: 413-744-6005
Toll-Free: 800-767-1000
Address: 1295 State St., Springfield, MA 01111 United States

STOCK TICKER/OTHER:

Stock Ticker: Mutual Company   Exchange:
Employees: 9,500   Fiscal Year Ends: 12/31
Parent Company:

SALARIES/BONUSES:

Top Exec. Salary: $ Bonus: $
Second Exec. Salary: $ Bonus: $

OTHER THOUGHTS:

Estimated Female Officers or Directors: 8
Hot Spot for Advancement for Women/Minorities: Y

MasterCard Incorporated

www.mastercard.com

NAIC Code: 522320

TYPES OF BUSINESS:

Credit Card Issuer
Transaction Processing Services
Global Payment Solutions
Credit Cards
Debit Cards

BRANDS/DIVISIONS/AFFILIATES:

MasterCard
Maestro
Cirrus

CONTACTS: *Note: Officers with more than one job title may be intentionally listed here more than once.*

Ajay Banga, CEO
Michael Miebach, Other Executive Officer
Sachin Mehra, CFO
Richard Haythornthwaite, Chairman of the Board
Sandra Arkell, Chief Accounting Officer
Raja Rajamannar, Chief Marketing Officer
Timothy Murphy, General Counsel
Michael Fraccaro, Other Executive Officer
Kevin Stanton, Other Executive Officer
Ajay Bhalla, President, Divisional
Gilberto Caldart, President, Divisional

GROWTH PLANS/SPECIAL FEATURES:

MasterCard Incorporated is a global payment solutions company that provides services to support the credit, debit and related payment programs of thousands of financial institutions. The company develops and markets payment solutions and processes payment transactions; it also provides consulting services to customers and merchants. MasterCard manages payment card brands including MasterCard, Maestro and Cirrus. A typical transaction processed over the MasterCard network involves four parties in addition to the firm: the cardholder, the merchant, the issuer (the cardholder's financial institution) and the acquirer (the merchant's financial institution). The company's customers are the financial institutions that act as issuers and acquirers. MasterCard generates revenues from the fees that it charges customers for providing these transaction processing and other payment-related services by assessing their customers based on their volume of dollar activity. The firm's credit and debit cards are accepted at more than 150 currencies in 210+ countries and territories worldwide. In September 2021, MasterCard agreed to acquire CipherTrace, a cryptocurrency intelligence company with insight into more than 900 cryptocurrencies.

MasterCard offers its employees medical, dental and vision coverage; life, disability and AD&D insurance; child care options; flexible work hours; adoption assistance; financial wellness programs; and personal services and discounts.

FINANCIAL DATA: *Note: Data for latest year may not have been available at press time.*

In U.S. $	2020	2019	2018	2017	2016	2015
Revenue	15,301,000,000	16,883,000,000	14,950,000,000	12,497,000,000	10,776,000,000	9,667,000,000
R&D Expense						
Operating Income	8,163,000,000	9,696,000,000	8,374,000,000	6,743,000,000	5,912,000,000	5,057,000,000
Operating Margin %		.57%	.56%	.54%	.55%	.52%
SGA Expense	2,771,000,000	3,128,000,000	2,903,000,000	2,631,000,000	2,266,000,000	2,139,000,000
Net Income	6,411,000,000	8,118,000,000	5,859,000,000	3,915,000,000	4,059,000,000	3,808,000,000
Operating Cash Flow	7,224,000,000	8,183,000,000	6,223,000,000	5,555,000,000	4,484,000,000	4,043,000,000
Capital Expenditure	708,000,000	728,000,000	504,000,000	423,000,000	382,000,000	342,000,000
EBITDA	8,720,000,000	10,477,000,000	7,849,000,000	7,113,000,000	6,114,000,000	5,385,000,000
Return on Assets %		.30%	.25%	.20%	.23%	.24%
Return on Equity %		1.44%	1.08%	.70%	.69%	.59%
Debt to Equity		1.447	1.081	0.992	0.916	0.545

CONTACT INFORMATION:

Phone: 914 249-2000   Fax: 914 249-4206
Toll-Free: 800-627-8372
Address: 2000 Purchase St., Purchase, NY 10577 United States

STOCK TICKER/OTHER:

Stock Ticker: MA
Employees: 21,000
Parent Company:

Exchange: NYS
Fiscal Year Ends: 12/31

SALARIES/BONUSES:

Top Exec. Salary: $ Bonus: $
Second Exec. Salary: $ Bonus: $

OTHER THOUGHTS:

Estimated Female Officers or Directors: 2
Hot Spot for Advancement for Women/Minorities: Y

MAXIMUS Inc

NAIC Code: 541512

www.maximus.com

TYPES OF BUSINESS:

Consulting-Government Agencies
Business Process Services
Health Services
Human Services

BRANDS/DIVISIONS/AFFILIATES:

Veterans Evaluation Services Inc

CONTACTS: Note: Officers with more than one job title may be intentionally listed here more than once.

Bruce Caswell, CEO
Richard Nadeau, CFO
Peter Pond, Chairman of the Board
Richard Montoni, Director
Raymond Ruddy, Director
David Francis, General Counsel
Mark Andrekovich, Other Executive Officer

GROWTH PLANS/SPECIAL FEATURES:

MAXIMUS, Inc. provides business process services (BPS) to government health and human services agencies. The company's operations are divided into three segments: U.S. health and human services, U.S. federal services, and outside the U.S. The U.S. health and human services segment provides BPS programs such as administration, appeals and assessments work and related consulting work for U.S. state and local government programs. These services support a variety of programs including the Affordable Care Act, Medicaid and the Children's Health Insurance Program (CHIP). This division also serves as administrators in state-based welfare-to-work and child support programs. The U.S. federal services segment provides program administration, appeals and assessments services and technology solutions, including system and software development and maintenance services, for various U.S. federal civilian programs. This division also contains certain state-based assessments and appeals work that is part of its Medicare appeals portfolio and is managed within this segment. Outside the U.S., MAXIMUS offers clients welfare-to-work programs in the U.K., Australia, Canada, Saudi Arabia, Singapore, Italy, Sweden and South Korea. In June 2021, MAXIMUS acquired Veterans Evaluation Services, Inc., a premier provider of medical disability examinations to the U.S. Department of Veterans Affairs.

FINANCIAL DATA: Note: Data for latest year may not have been available at press time.

In U.S. $	2020	2019	2018	2017	2016	2015
Revenue	3,461,537,000	2,886,815,000	2,392,236,000	2,450,961,000	2,403,360,000	2,099,821,000
R&D Expense						
Operating Income	288,278,000	317,107,000	298,836,000	315,187,000	280,555,000	264,577,000
Operating Margin %		.11%	.12%	.13%	.12%	.13%
SGA Expense	387,090,000	321,023,000	285,241,000	284,510,000	268,259,000	238,792,000
Net Income	214,509,000	240,824,000	220,751,000	209,426,000	178,362,000	157,772,000
Operating Cash Flow	244,592,000	356,727,000	323,525,000	337,200,000	180,026,000	206,217,000
Capital Expenditure	40,707,000	66,846,000	26,520,000	24,154,000	46,391,000	105,149,000
EBITDA	389,282,000	405,735,000	362,401,000	384,374,000	361,883,000	317,414,000
Return on Assets %		.15%	.16%	.16%	.14%	.14%
Return on Equity %		.21%	.22%	.25%	.26%	.27%
Debt to Equity				0.001	0.221	0.344

CONTACT INFORMATION:

Phone: 703 251-8500   Fax:
Toll-Free: 800-629-4687
Address: 1891 Metro Center Dr., Reston, VA 20190 United States

STOCK TICKER/OTHER:

Stock Ticker: MMS
Employees: 34,300
Parent Company:

Exchange: NYS
Fiscal Year Ends: 09/30

SALARIES/BONUSES:

Top Exec. Salary: $ Bonus: $
Second Exec. Salary: $ Bonus: $

OTHER THOUGHTS:

Estimated Female Officers or Directors: 3
Hot Spot for Advancement for Women/Minorities: Y

Mayo Clinic

www.mayo.edu

NAIC Code: 622110

TYPES OF BUSINESS:

General Medical and Surgical Hospitals
Physician Practice Management
Medical Research
Health Care Education

BRANDS/DIVISIONS/AFFILIATES:

Mayo Clinic
Mayo Clinic Hospital
Saint Marys Campus
Mayo Clinic Building
Samuel C Johnson Research
Mayo Clinic Collaborative Research
Mayo Clinic Specialty
Civica Rx

CONTACTS: *Note: Officers with more than one job title may be intentionally listed here more than once.*

Gianrico Farrugia, CEO
Dennis E. Dahlen, CFO
Shirley A. Weis, Chief Admin. Officer
Jonathan J. Oviatt, Chief Legal Officer
Harry N. Hoffman, Treas.
William C. Rupp, VP
Wyatt W. Decker, VP
Robert F. Brigham, Assistant Sec.
Sherry L. Hubert, Assistant Sec.
Samuel A. Di Piazza Jr., Chmn.

GROWTH PLANS/SPECIAL FEATURES:

Mayo Clinic is a nonprofit healthcare organization founded in 1864, and part of the Mayo Foundation for Medical Education and Research. Mayo Clinic provides medical treatment, physician management, healthcare education, research and other specialized medical services through a network of clinics and hospitals in Minnesota, Arizona and Florida. The organization's primary clinics are located in Rochester, Minnesota; Jacksonville, Florida; and Scottsdale and Phoenix, Arizona. The Rochester campus has been in business for more than 100 years, and includes the Mayo Clinic, the Mayo Clinic Hospital, Saint Mary's Campus and Mayo Clinic Hospital-Methodist Campus, which together provide comprehensive diagnosis and treatment in virtually every medical and surgical specialty. The Mayo Clinic Hospital, located on the Jacksonville campus, offers over 260 beds and represents more than 40 medical and surgical specialties. In Arizona, Mayo Clinic focuses on adult specialty and surgical disciplines, supported by programs in medical education and research. The original Scottsdale campus opened in 1987, and includes the Mayo Clinic Building, the Samuel C. Johnson Research building and the Mayo Clinic Collaborative Research building. The Phoenix campus includes the Mayo Clinic Specialty building and Mayo Clinic Hospital. Mayo Clinic schools offer more than 400 educational programs across its campuses, which include five schools under the Mayo Clinic name. Mayo Clinic partnered with other health organizations in the 2018 creation of Civica Rx, a not-for-profit generic drug and pharmaceutical company focused on combating life-saving drug shortages and affordability.

Doctors are paid by salary, rather than fee for service. Employees are offered comprehensive benefits, retirement plans and employee assistance programs.

FINANCIAL DATA: *Note: Data for latest year may not have been available at press time.*

In U.S. $	2020	2019	2018	2017	2016	2015
Revenue	13,910,000,000	13,708,000,000	12,603,000,000	11,984,000,000	10,990,000,000	10,315,000,000
R&D Expense						
Operating Income						
Operating Margin %						
SGA Expense						
Net Income	1,971,000,000	1,242,000,000	1,129,000,000	856,000,000	475,000,000	526,000,000
Operating Cash Flow						
Capital Expenditure						
EBITDA						
Return on Assets %						
Return on Equity %						
Debt to Equity						

CONTACT INFORMATION:

Phone: 507-284-2511   Fax: 507-284-0161
Toll-Free: 800-660-4582
Address: 200 First St. SW, Rochester, MN 55905 United States

STOCK TICKER/OTHER:

Stock Ticker: Nonprofit
Employees: 71,350
Parent Company:

Exchange:
Fiscal Year Ends: 12/31

SALARIES/BONUSES:

Top Exec. Salary: $ Bonus: $
Second Exec. Salary: $ Bonus: $

OTHER THOUGHTS:

Estimated Female Officers or Directors: 5
Hot Spot for Advancement for Women/Minorities: Y

McAfee Corp

NAIC Code: 511210E

www.mcafee.com

TYPES OF BUSINESS:
Computer Software: Network Security, Managed Access, Digital ID,
Cybersecurity & Anti-Virus
Virus Protection Software
Network Management Software
Cybersecurity
Malware Protection

BRANDS/DIVISIONS/AFFILIATES:
Thoma Bravo LLC
Intel Corporation
Foundation Technology Worldwide LLC
McAfee LLC
McAfee Global Threat Intelligence
MVISION Device

CONTACTS: Note: Officers with more than one job title may be intentionally listed here more than once.
Peter Leav, CEO
Venkat Bhamidipati, CFO
Lynne Doherty, Exec. VP-Global Sales & Mktg.
Chatelle Lynch, Chief Human Resources Officer
Steven Grobman, CTO
Bryan Reed Barney, Exec. VP-Prod. Dev.
Ari Jaaksi, Sr. VP
Louis Riley, General Counsel
Tom Fountain, Sr. VP
Edward Hayden, Sr. VP-Finance & Acct.
Steve Redman, Exec. VP-Global Sales
Ken Levine, Sr. VP
Gert-Jan Schenk, Pres., EMEA
Barry McPherson, Exec. VP-Worldwide Delivery & Support Svcs.
Jean-Claude Broido, Pres., McAfee Japan
Barry McPherson, Exec. VP-Supply Chain & Facilities

GROWTH PLANS/SPECIAL FEATURES:
McAfee Corp. is engaged in designing and delivering global
computer security software and is the holding company of
Foundation Technology Worldwide, LLC (FTW) and its
subsidiaries. FTW wholly-owns McAfee LLC, a cybersecurity
company that provides advanced security solutions to
consumers, small- and medium-sized businesses, large
enterprises and governments. Security technologies from
McAfee use a predictive capability powered by McAfee Global
Threat Intelligence, which enables home users and businesses
to stay ahead of fileless attacks, viruses, malware and other
online threats. McAfee's products protect over 600 million
devices. The company's personal protection services cover
device security, online privacy, comprehensive internet
security and identity protection. For enterprises and
governments, McAfee offers the MVISION Device, which offers
next-generation endpoint solutions offering comprehensive
threat detection and data protection for both modern and
legacy devices, such as traditional endpoints, mobile and fixed-
function systems. McAfee Corp. is a joint venture between
Thoma Bravo, LLC and Intel Corporation. In late-2020, McAfee
filed a registration statement with the U.S. Securities and
Exchange Commission to a proposed initial public offering of
its Class A common stock. The firm was approved and is listed
on Nasdaq under ticker symbol MCFE.

FINANCIAL DATA: Note: Data for latest year may not have been available at press time.

In U.S. $	2020	2019	2018	2017	2016	2015
Revenue	2,906,000,000	2,635,000,000	2,409,000,000			
R&D Expense	475,000,000	380,000,000	406,000,000			
Operating Income	178,000,000	148,000,000	-137,000,000			
Operating Margin %						
SGA Expense	1,158,000,000	1,042,000,000	1,068,000,000			
Net Income	-289,000,000	-236,000,000	-512,000,000			
Operating Cash Flow	760,000,000	496,000,000	319,000,000			
Capital Expenditure	42,000,000	56,000,000	61,000,000			
EBITDA	540,000,000	682,000,000	400,000,000			
Return on Assets %						
Return on Equity %						
Debt to Equity						

CONTACT INFORMATION:
Phone: 866-622-3911   Fax:
Toll-Free:
Address: 6220 America Center Dr., San Jose, CA 95002 United States

STOCK TICKER/OTHER:
Stock Ticker: MCFE   Exchange: NAS
Employees: 6,916   Fiscal Year Ends: 12/31
Parent Company:

SALARIES/BONUSES:
Top Exec. Salary: $ Bonus: $
Second Exec. Salary: $ Bonus: $

OTHER THOUGHTS:
Estimated Female Officers or Directors: 3
Hot Spot for Advancement for Women/Minorities: Y

McCarthy Building Companies Inc
www.mccarthy.com
NAIC Code: 236220

TYPES OF BUSINESS:
Construction & Engineering Services
Commercial Builder
Pre-Construction Services
Construction Services
Post-Construction Services

BRANDS/DIVISIONS/AFFILIATES:

CONTACTS: Note: Officers with more than one job title may be intentionally listed here more than once.
Ray Sedey, CEO
Scott Wittkop, COO
Doug Audiffred, CFO
Mike Bolen, Chmn.

GROWTH PLANS/SPECIAL FEATURES:
McCarthy Building Companies, Inc. is an employee-owned firm, and one of the oldest and highly regarded commercial builders in the U.S. The company is headquartered in St. Louis, Missouri, and has offices in Atlanta, Austin, Dallas, Denver, Houston, Illinois, Kansas City, Las Vegas, Los Angeles, Newport Beach, Omaha, Phoenix, Sacramento, San Diego, San Francisco and San Jose. McCarthy has undertaken projects in the markets of advanced technology, manufacturing, aviation, commercial, education, government, healthcare, heavy civil, transportation, hospitality, entertainment, industrial, justice, mission critical, parking, ports/marine terminals, renewable energy, research laboratory and water/wastewater. The firm's services include preconstruction, construction and post-construction. The preconstruction services offered include budget development and estimating, value analysis, LEED/green construction, constructability and virtual design and construction technology. Construction services offered are project scheduling, equipment and material procurement, self-performance, minority mentoring, quality assurance/quality planning and commissioning. Post-construction services offered are quality checks, closing out contractors, definition of an occupancy plan and following up on warranties and guarantees.

FINANCIAL DATA: Note: Data for latest year may not have been available at press time.

In U.S. $	2020	2019	2018	2017	2016	2015
Revenue	4,118,100,000	3,885,000,000	3,700,000,000	3,100,000,000	3,000,000,000	2,800,000,000
R&D Expense						
Operating Income						
Operating Margin %						
SGA Expense						
Net Income						
Operating Cash Flow						
Capital Expenditure						
EBITDA						
Return on Assets %						
Return on Equity %						
Debt to Equity						

CONTACT INFORMATION:
Phone: 314-968-3300   Fax: 314-968-4780
Toll-Free:
Address: 12851 Manchester Rd., St. Louis, MO 63131 United States

STOCK TICKER/OTHER:
Stock Ticker: Private   Exchange:
Employees: 3,506   Fiscal Year Ends:
Parent Company:

SALARIES/BONUSES:
Top Exec. Salary: $ Bonus: $
Second Exec. Salary: $ Bonus: $

OTHER THOUGHTS:
Estimated Female Officers or Directors:
Hot Spot for Advancement for Women/Minorities:

McCormick & Company Incorporated

www.mccormick.com

NAIC Code: 311940

TYPES OF BUSINESS:

Herbs, Spices & Seasonings
Manufacturer
Distributor
Spices
Seasonings
Flavorings

BRANDS/DIVISIONS/AFFILIATES:

McCormick
Frenchs
Franks RedHot
Lawrys
Zatarains
Ducros
Drogheria & Alimatari
Kohinoor

CONTACTS: Note: Officers with more than one job title may be intentionally listed here more than once.

Lawrence Kurzius, CEO
Christina Mcmullen, Chief Accounting Officer
Michael Smith, Executive VP
Malcolm Swift, President, Divisional
Brendan Foley, President, Divisional
Lisa Manzone, Senior VP, Divisional
Nneka Rimmer, Senior VP, Divisional
Jeffery Schwartz, Vice President

GROWTH PLANS/SPECIAL FEATURES:

McCormick & Company, Incorporated is a global manufacturer, marketer and distributor of spices, seasonings and flavorings to the entire food industry, including retail outlets, food manufacturers and food service businesses. The firm operates in two segments: consumer and flavor solutions. The consumer segment consists of brands that reach consumers in approximately 160 countries and territories. Leading brands in the Americas include McCormick, French's, Frank's RedHot, Lawry's and Club House, as well as Gourmet Garden and OLD BAY. Ethnic brands marketed by this division include Zatarain's, Stubbs, Thai Kitchen and Simply Asia. In the Europe, Middle East and Africa (EMEA) region, this division's major brands include Ducros, Schwartz, Kamis and Drogheria & Alimentari, as well as Vahine dessert items. In China the consumer segment markets products under the McCormick and DaQiao brands; in Australia, under the McCormick, Aeroplane and Gourmet Garden brands; in India, under the Kohinoor brand; and elsewhere in the Asia/Pacific region under the McCormick and other brands. Approximately half of this division's sales are derived from spices, herbs and seasonings. The flavor solutions segment provides a wide range of products to multinational food manufacturers and foodservice customers, which are supplied with branded, packaged products both directly and indirectly through distributors. Supplies include customized flavor solutions, including seasoning blends, spices, herbs, condiments, coating systems and compound flavors. This division continually engages in sensory testing, culinary research, food safety and flavor application. In December 2020, McCormick & Company acquired FONA International LLC, a manufacturer of natural flavors that provide solutions for a diverse customer base across various applications for the food, beverage and nutritional markets.

McCormick offers its employees a comprehensive benefit program.

FINANCIAL DATA: Note: Data for latest year may not have been available at press time.

In U.S. $	2020	2019	2018	2017	2016	2015
Revenue	5,601,300,000	5,347,400,000	5,408,900,000	4,834,100,000	4,411,500,000	4,296,300,000
R&D Expense						
Operating Income	1,018,800,000	978,500,000	942,100,000	765,400,000	656,700,000	609,900,000
Operating Margin %		.18%	.17%	.15%	.15%	.13%
SGA Expense	1,281,600,000	1,166,800,000	1,429,500,000	1,244,800,000	1,175,000,000	1,127,400,000
Net Income	747,400,000	702,700,000	933,400,000	477,400,000	472,300,000	401,600,000
Operating Cash Flow	1,041,300,000	946,800,000	821,200,000	815,300,000	658,100,000	590,000,000
Capital Expenditure	225,300,000	173,700,000	169,100,000	182,400,000	153,800,000	128,400,000
EBITDA	1,182,100,000	1,143,200,000	1,066,600,000	815,700,000	753,900,000	655,400,000
Return on Assets %		.07%	.09%	.06%	.10%	.09%
Return on Equity %		.21%	.33%	.23%	.29%	.23%
Debt to Equity		1.053	1.278	1.736	0.648	0.63

CONTACT INFORMATION:

Phone: 410-771-7301　　Fax:
Toll-Free:
Address: 24 Schilling Rd., Ste. 1, Hunt Valley, MD 21031 United States

STOCK TICKER/OTHER:

Stock Ticker: MKC
Employees: 13,000
Parent Company:

Exchange: NYS
Fiscal Year Ends: 11/30

SALARIES/BONUSES:

Top Exec. Salary: $　　Bonus: $
Second Exec. Salary: $　　Bonus: $

OTHER THOUGHTS:

Estimated Female Officers or Directors: 1
Hot Spot for Advancement for Women/Minorities: Y

McDermott International Ltd

www.mcdermott.com

NAIC Code: 541330

TYPES OF BUSINESS:

Engineering Services
Energy Engineering
Energy Procurement
Energy Construction
Energy Installation
Energy Technology

BRANDS/DIVISIONS/AFFILIATES:

CONTACTS:
Note: Officers with more than one job title may be intentionally listed here more than once.

Stuart Spence, CFO
Tareq Kawash, Sr. VP, Geographical
Gary Luquette, Chairman of the Board
Christopher Krummel, Chief Accounting Officer
David Dickson, Director
Daniel McCarthy, Executive VP, Divisional
Samik Mukherjee, Executive VP
John Freeman, Executive VP
Brian McLaughlin, Other Executive Officer
Stephen Allen, Other Executive Officer
Scott Munro, Other Executive Officer
Neil Gunnion, Senior VP, Divisional
Mark Coscio, Senior VP, Geographical
Linh Austin, Senior VP, Geographical
Ian Prescott, Senior VP, Geographical

GROWTH PLANS/SPECIAL FEATURES:

McDermott International Ltd. is a fully integrated provider of engineering, procurement, construction, installation (EPCI) and technology solutions to the energy industry. The firm operates through five segments: North, Central and South America (NCSA); Europe, Africa, Russia and Caspian (EARC); the Middle East and North Africa (MENA); Asia Pacific (APAC); and technology. Through these segments McDermott delivers a broad offering of services that addresses for key end markets: offshore and subsea, offering a comprehensive range of EPCI and technology services for the upstream oil and gas sector; liquefied natural gas (LNG), offering a full range of technology and engineering, procurement, fabrication and construction services for the LNG industry, with a focus on natural gas liquefaction plants and LNG regasification terminals; downstream, which designs, builds and offers technology licenses and services for state-of-the-art petrochemical and refinery process units and plants; and power, which designs and builds new combined-cycle and simple-cycle gas-fired power generation projects and provides related engineering, procurement, construction and commissioning services.

FINANCIAL DATA:
Note: Data for latest year may not have been available at press time.

In U.S. $	2020	2019	2018	2017	2016	2015
Revenue		8,431,000,000	6,704,999,936	2,984,768,000	2,635,983,104	3,070,275,072
R&D Expense						
Operating Income						
Operating Margin %						
SGA Expense						
Net Income		-2,884,000,000	-2,687,000,064	178,546,000	34,117,000	-17,983,000
Operating Cash Flow						
Capital Expenditure						
EBITDA						
Return on Assets %						
Return on Equity %						
Debt to Equity						

CONTACT INFORMATION:

Phone: 281 870-5000   Fax: 281 870-5095
Toll-Free:
Address: 757 N. Eldridge Pkwy., Houston, TX 77079 United States

SALARIES/BONUSES:

Top Exec. Salary: $ Bonus: $
Second Exec. Salary: $ Bonus: $

STOCK TICKER/OTHER:

Stock Ticker: MCDIF   Exchange: PINX
Employees: 42,600   Fiscal Year Ends: 12/31
Parent Company:

OTHER THOUGHTS:

Estimated Female Officers or Directors: 4
Hot Spot for Advancement for Women/Minorities: Y

McDonalds Corporation

www.mcdonalds.com

NAIC Code: 722513

TYPES OF BUSINESS:

Fast Food Restaurants
Home-Meal Replacement Restaurants
Franchising
Fast Food
Hamburgers

BRANDS/DIVISIONS/AFFILIATES:

Big Mac
Quarter Pounder
Filet O'Fish
Happy Meal
Egg McMuffin

CONTACTS: *Note: Officers with more than one job title may be intentionally listed here more than once.*

Kevin Ozan, CFO
Daniel Henry, Chief Information Officer
Enrique Hernandez, Director
Stephen Easterbrook, Director
Francesca DeBiase, Executive VP, Divisional
Silvia Lagnado, Executive VP
Jerome Krulewitch, Executive VP
David Fairhurst, Executive VP
Robert Gibbs, Executive VP
Joseph Erlinger, President, Divisional
Ian Borden, President, Divisional
Christopher Kempczinski, President, Geographical
Catherine Hoovel, Vice President

GROWTH PLANS/SPECIAL FEATURES:

McDonald's Corporation operates approximately 39,200 fast-food restaurants in 119 countries, serving tens of millions of customers per day. Of these restaurants, 36,521 are franchised (93%) and the remainder are company-operated. McDonald's franchise model consists of independent businessmen and women providing capital by initially investing in equipment, signs, seating and restaurant decor and then personally operating them. The company shares the investment by owning or leasing the land and buildings. McDonald's menu includes items such as hamburgers, cheeseburgers, fish and chicken sandwiches, chicken nuggets, French fries, salads, milkshakes, desserts and soft drinks. McDonald's restaurants are also open during breakfast hours and offer egg sandwiches, hotcakes, biscuit and bagel sandwiches and muffins. Brand names include the Big Mac, Quarter Pounder, Filet O'Fish, Happy Meal and Egg McMuffin. As part of a multi-year beverage business strategy designed to take advantage of the significant and growing beverage category, the company offers hot specialty coffee offerings on a market-by-market basis, all of which serve as a platform for the recent introduction of smoothies, frappes and other beverage options in a number of markets. The company is continually working to provide nutritious additions to its menu, including salads, apple slices, oatmeal and low-fat yogurt.

McDonald's offers qualified employees comprehensive health benefits; life and disability insurance; and various employee assistance programs.

FINANCIAL DATA: *Note: Data for latest year may not have been available at press time.*

In U.S. $	2020	2019	2018	2017	2016	2015
Revenue	19,207,800,000	21,076,500,000	21,025,200,000	22,820,400,000	24,621,900,000	25,413,000,000
R&D Expense						
Operating Income	7,206,500,000	8,885,900,000	8,585,800,000	8,389,500,000	7,820,200,000	7,354,900,000
Operating Margin %		.42%	.41%	.37%	.32%	.29%
SGA Expense	2,245,000,000	2,229,400,000	2,200,200,000	2,231,300,000	2,384,500,000	2,434,300,000
Net Income	4,730,500,000	6,025,400,000	5,924,300,000	5,192,300,000	4,686,500,000	4,529,300,000
Operating Cash Flow	6,265,200,000	8,122,100,000	6,966,700,000	5,551,200,000	6,059,600,000	6,539,100,000
Capital Expenditure	1,640,800,000	2,393,700,000	2,741,700,000	1,853,700,000	1,821,100,000	1,813,900,000
EBITDA	9,110,200,000	10,757,900,000	10,279,300,000	10,858,200,000	9,267,300,000	8,749,700,000
Return on Assets %		.15%	.18%	.16%	.14%	.13%
Return on Equity %					1.92%	.45%
Debt to Equity						3.403

CONTACT INFORMATION:

Phone: 630 623-3000   Fax: 630 623-5700
Toll-Free: 800-244-6227
Address: 110 N. Carpenter St., Chicago, IL 60607 United States

STOCK TICKER/OTHER:

Stock Ticker: MCD   Exchange: NYS
Employees: 200,000   Fiscal Year Ends: 12/31
Parent Company:

SALARIES/BONUSES:

Top Exec. Salary: $ Bonus: $
Second Exec. Salary: $ Bonus: $

OTHER THOUGHTS:

Estimated Female Officers or Directors: 4
Hot Spot for Advancement for Women/Minorities: Y

McKesson Corporation

www.mckesson.com

NAIC Code: 424210

TYPES OF BUSINESS:

Pharmaceutical Distribution
Medical-Surgical Products Distribution
Health Care Management Software
Consulting
Outsourcing

BRANDS/DIVISIONS/AFFILIATES:

McKesson Canada
McKesson Prescription Technology Solutions

CONTACTS: Note: Officers with more than one job title may be intentionally listed here more than once.

Brian Tyler, CEO
Britt Vitalone, CFO
Edward Mueller, Chairman of the Board
Sundeep Reddy, Chief Accounting Officer
Lori Schechter, Chief Compliance Officer
Kathleen McElligott, Chief Information Officer
Bansi Nagji, Executive VP, Divisional
Jorge Figueredo, Executive VP
Michele Lau, Secretary
Paul Smith, Senior VP, Divisional
Brian Moore, Senior VP

GROWTH PLANS/SPECIAL FEATURES:

McKesson Corporation provides healthcare management solutions, retail pharmacy, healthcare technology, community oncology and specialty care. McKesson operates through four business segments: U.S. pharmaceutical and specialty solutions, European pharmaceutical solutions, medical-surgical solutions and other. The U.S. pharmaceutical and specialty solutions segment distributes branded, generic, specialty, biosimilar and over-the-counter (OTC) pharmaceutical drugs and other healthcare-related products. It provides practice management, clinical support and business solutions to community-based oncology and other specialty practices. This division also provides solutions for life sciences companies, including offering multiple distribution channels and clinical trials access to specific patient populations through McKesson's network of oncology physicians. This segment also sells financial, operational and clinical solutions to pharmacies (retail, hospital and alternate sites) and provides consulting, outsourcing and other services. The European pharmaceutical solutions segment provides distribution and related services to wholesale, institutional and retail customers in 13 European countries through McKesson's own pharmacies and participating pharmacies that operate under the brand partnership and franchise arrangements. The medical-surgical solutions segment distributes medical-surgical supplies and provides logistics and other services to healthcare providers in the U.S. The other segment primarily consists of the following: McKesson Canada; a distributor of pharmaceutical and medical products, and an operator of Rexall Health retail pharmacies; and McKesson Prescription Technology Solutions, a provider of innovative technologies that support retail pharmacies. In March 2020, the firm announced the completion of the split-off and subsequent merger of PF2 SpinCo, Inc., which held McKesson's interest in Change Healthcare LLC, into Change Healthcare Inc.

Employee benefits include medical, dental, vision, AD&D and dependent life insurance; an employee assistance program; and flexible spending accounts.

FINANCIAL DATA: Note: Data for latest year may not have been available at press time.

In U.S. $	2020	2019	2018	2017	2016	2015
Revenue	231,051,000,000	214,319,000,000	208,357,000,000	198,533,000,000	190,884,000,000	
R&D Expense	96,000,000	71,000,000	125,000,000	341,000,000	392,000,000	
Operating Income	2,759,000,000	3,280,000,000	2,921,000,000	3,464,000,000	3,748,000,000	
Operating Margin %	.01%	.02%	.01%	.02%	.02%	
SGA Expense	9,168,000,000	8,403,000,000	8,138,000,000	7,466,000,000	7,276,000,000	
Net Income	900,000,000	34,000,000	67,000,000	5,070,000,000	2,258,000,000	
Operating Cash Flow	4,374,000,000	4,036,000,000	4,345,000,000	4,744,000,000	3,672,000,000	
Capital Expenditure	506,000,000	557,000,000	580,000,000	562,000,000	677,000,000	
EBITDA	2,315,000,000	1,823,000,000	1,473,000,000	8,109,000,000	4,488,000,000	
Return on Assets %	.01%	.00%	.00%	.09%	.04%	
Return on Equity %	.14%	.00%	.01%	.51%	.27%	
Debt to Equity	1.57	0.898	0.689	0.658	0.732	

CONTACT INFORMATION:

Phone: 972-446-4800   Fax:
Toll-Free: 800-826-9360
Address: 6555 State Hwy. 161, Irving, TX 75039 United States

STOCK TICKER/OTHER:

Stock Ticker: MCK
Employees: 76,000
Parent Company:

Exchange: NYS
Fiscal Year Ends: 03/31

SALARIES/BONUSES:

Top Exec. Salary: $ Bonus: $
Second Exec. Salary: $ Bonus: $

OTHER THOUGHTS:

Estimated Female Officers or Directors: 4
Hot Spot for Advancement for Women/Minorities: Y

McKinsey & Company Inc

www.mckinsey.com

NAIC Code: 541610

TYPES OF BUSINESS:

Management Consulting
Management Consulting
Business Consulting
Organization Consulting
Analytics
Digital Technology
Transformation Services
Risk

BRANDS/DIVISIONS/AFFILIATES:

McKinsey Global Institute
McKinsey Quarterly

CONTACTS: *Note: Officers with more than one job title may be intentionally listed here more than once.*

Kevin Sneader, Managing Dir.

GROWTH PLANS/SPECIAL FEATURES:

McKinsey & Company, Inc. is a privately-held international management consulting firm established in 1926. Headquartered in New York, the firm maintains approximately 130 offices in 65 countries. McKinsey provides consulting services for leading businesses, governments, non-governmental organizations and non-profits. The company helps clients make improvements to their performance at every level of their organization. Business functions include analytics, diagnostics, business technology, digital technology, implementation, learning programs for clients, marketing and sales, operations, organization, recover and transformation services, risk, strategy and corporate finance, as well as sustainability and resource productivity. Industries served by McKinsey include advanced electronics, aerospace and defense, automotive and assembly, chemicals, consumer packaged goods, electric power and natural gas, financial services, healthcare systems and services, high tech, infrastructure, media and entertainment, metals and mining, oil and gas, paper and forest products, pharmaceuticals and medical products, private equity and principal investors, public sector, retail, semiconductors, social sector, telecommunications and travel/transport/logistics. The McKinsey Global Institute helps leaders in multiple sectors develop deeper understanding of the global economy. The firm's flagship business publication, McKinsey Quarterly, has been defining and informing the senior-management agenda since 1964.

FINANCIAL DATA: *Note: Data for latest year may not have been available at press time.*

In U.S. $	2020	2019	2018	2017	2016	2015
Revenue	10,900,000,000	10,500,000,000	10,000,000,000	8,800,000,000	8,590,500,000	8,300,000,000
R&D Expense						
Operating Income						
Operating Margin %						
SGA Expense						
Net Income						
Operating Cash Flow						
Capital Expenditure						
EBITDA						
Return on Assets %						
Return on Equity %						
Debt to Equity						

CONTACT INFORMATION:

Phone: 212-446-7000   Fax: 212-446-8575
Toll-Free:
Address: 3 World Trade Center, 175 Greenwich St., New York, NY 10007 United States

STOCK TICKER/OTHER:

Stock Ticker: Private   Exchange:
Employees: 30,000   Fiscal Year Ends: 12/31
Parent Company:

SALARIES/BONUSES:

Top Exec. Salary: $ Bonus: $
Second Exec. Salary: $ Bonus: $

OTHER THOUGHTS:

Estimated Female Officers or Directors: 2
Hot Spot for Advancement for Women/Minorities: Y

McLane Company Inc

www.mclaneco.com

NAIC Code: 424410

TYPES OF BUSINESS:

Food & Grocery Wholesale Distribution
Supply Chain Services
Distribution Center Operations
Logistics Software & Services
Third-Party Solutions
Retail Services

BRANDS/DIVISIONS/AFFILIATES:

Berkshire Hathaway Inc
CD Hartnett Company
Empire Distributors Inc
KINEXO
Vantix Logistics
Consumer Value Products
CVP Home
CVP Health

CONTACTS: Note: Officers with more than one job title may be intentionally listed here more than once.

William Grady Rosier, CEO
Neftalia Garcia, Dir.-Gov't Affairs

GROWTH PLANS/SPECIAL FEATURES:

McLane Company, Inc., owned by Berkshire Hathaway, Inc., is a supply chain services company, providing grocery and foodservice supply chain solutions to thousands of convenience stores, mass merchants, drug stores, military locations and chain restaurants across the U.S. McLane operates more than 80 grocery and food distribution centers, which offer supply chain, procurement, logistics, merchandising and technology solutions and services to approximately 110,000 locations. Subsidiary C.D. Hartnett Company is a full-line grocery distributor serving the convenience store and foodservice industries. Through wholly-owned Empire Distributors, Inc., McLane distributes spirits, wine, beer and non-alcoholic beverages in Georgia, North Carolina and Tennessee. McLane's foodservice distribution division provides quick-service restaurants with food and nonfood products through a range of logistics, technology, promotion management and rapid response solutions. Subsidiary KINEXO provides highly-customized supply chain solutions designed to reduce costs, increase transactional visibility and maximize operating efficiency. Vantix Logistics provides third-party logistics, supply chain development and freight management services, including transportation management, shipment optimization, warehousing and multi-temperature product handling. Consumer Value Products is a family of products designed to provide a value-based alternative for retailers, including home, health, baby, snacks, pet treats, automotive items and more, with brands including CVP Home, CVP Health, CVP Baby, Excursion Jerky, and YumBees, among others.

McLane offers its employees comprehensive health benefits, life and disability insurance, 401(k) plans and an employee assistance program.

FINANCIAL DATA: Note: Data for latest year may not have been available at press time.

In U.S. $	2020	2019	2018	2017	2016	2015
Revenue	46,840,000,000	50,458,000,000	49,987,000,000	49,775,000,000	48,075,000,000	48,223,000,000
R&D Expense						
Operating Income						
Operating Margin %						
SGA Expense						
Net Income						
Operating Cash Flow						
Capital Expenditure						
EBITDA						
Return on Assets %						
Return on Equity %						
Debt to Equity						

CONTACT INFORMATION:

Phone: 254-771-7500   Fax: 254-771-7244
Toll-Free: 800-299-1401
Address: 4747 McLane Parkway, Temple, TX 76504 United States

STOCK TICKER/OTHER:

Stock Ticker: Subsidiary   Exchange:
Employees: 24,304   Fiscal Year Ends: 12/31
Parent Company: Berkshire Hathaway Inc

SALARIES/BONUSES:

Top Exec. Salary: $ Bonus: $
Second Exec. Salary: $ Bonus: $

OTHER THOUGHTS:

Estimated Female Officers or Directors: 1
Hot Spot for Advancement for Women/Minorities:

MDU Resources Group Inc

NAIC Code: 221210

www.mdu.com

TYPES OF BUSINESS:

Gas and Electric Utility
Construction Materials & Mining
Oil & Gas Exploration & Production
Pipelines & Storage
Energy Products & Services
Equipment & Maintenance-Electric & HVAC
Utility Construction
Energy Management Services

BRANDS/DIVISIONS/AFFILIATES:

Cascade Natural Gas Corporation
Intermountain Gas Company
Great Plains Natural Gas Company
Centennial Energy Holdings Inc
Knife River Corporation
MDU Construction Services Group Inc
WBI Holdings Inc
PerLectric Inc

CONTACTS: *Note: Officers with more than one job title may be intentionally listed here more than once.*

Nicole Kivisto, CEO, Subsidiary
David Barney, CEO, Subsidiary
Jeffrey Thiede, CEO, Subsidiary
Trevor Hastings, CEO, Subsidiary
David Goodin, CEO
Stephanie Barth, Chief Accounting Officer
Margaret Link, Chief Information Officer
Dennis Johnson, Director
Daniel Kuntz, General Counsel
Jason Vollmer, Treasurer
Anne Jones, Vice President, Divisional

GROWTH PLANS/SPECIAL FEATURES:

MDU Resources Group, Inc. is a diversified natural resources company. MDU stands for Montana-Dakota utilities. Through the company's electric and natural gas distribution segments, MDU generates, transmits and distributes electricity and distributes natural gas in Montana, North Dakota, South Dakota and Wyoming. Subsidiary Cascade Natural Gas Corporation distributes natural gas in Oregon and Washington; Intermountain Gas Company distributes natural gas in Idaho; and Great Plains Natural Gas Company distributes natural gas in western Minnesota and southeastern North Dakota. Through wholly owned Centennial Energy Holdings, Inc., MDU owns WBI Holdings, Inc., a pipeline and midstream company; Knife River Corporation, a construction material and contracting provider; and MDU Construction Services Group, Inc., a construction services provider. Knife River mines aggregates and markets crushed stone, sand, gravel and related construction materials, including ready-mix concrete, cement, asphalt, liquid asphalt and other value-added products. MDU Construction provides utility construction services specializing in constructing and maintaining electric and communications lines, gas pipelines, fire suppression systems and external lighting and traffic signalization equipment. In February 2020, the firm acquired PerLectric, Inc., a provider of electrical construction to government, mission critical, commercial and health care customers, and the assets of Oldcastle Infrastructure Spokane, the Washington-based prestressed-construction business previously owned by Oldcastle Infrastructure.

The company offers employees benefits including medical, dental and vision insurance; life insurance, disability coverage and AD&D insurance; flexible spending accounts; a 401(k) plan; an employee assistance plan; education assistance; and employee discou

FINANCIAL DATA: *Note: Data for latest year may not have been available at press time.*

In U.S. $	2020	2019	2018	2017	2016	2015
Revenue	5,532,750,000	5,336,776,000	4,531,552,000	4,443,351,000	4,128,828,000	4,191,549,000
R&D Expense						
Operating Income	544,925,000	481,220,000	401,723,000	428,712,000	409,120,000	254,133,000
Operating Margin %		.09%	.09%	.10%	.10%	.06%
SGA Expense						
Net Income	390,205,000	335,453,000	272,318,000	281,203,000	64,433,000	-622,435,000
Operating Cash Flow	768,374,000	542,280,000	499,881,000	448,011,000	462,209,000	641,144,000
Capital Expenditure	558,007,000	576,065,000	568,230,000	341,382,000	388,183,000	625,375,000
EBITDA	856,736,000	753,049,000	621,690,000	640,301,000	630,394,000	501,095,000
Return on Assets %		.05%	.04%	.04%	.01%	-.09%
Return on Equity %		.12%	.11%	.12%	.03%	-.23%
Debt to Equity		0.811	0.723	0.645	0.759	0.683

CONTACT INFORMATION:

Phone: 701 530-1000   Fax: 701 222-7607
Toll-Free: 866-760-4852
Address: 1200 W. Century Ave., Bismarck, ND 58506 United States

STOCK TICKER/OTHER:

Stock Ticker: MDU
Employees: 13,359
Parent Company:

Exchange: NYS
Fiscal Year Ends: 12/31

SALARIES/BONUSES:

Top Exec. Salary: $ Bonus: $
Second Exec. Salary: $ Bonus: $

OTHER THOUGHTS:

Estimated Female Officers or Directors: 2
Hot Spot for Advancement for Women/Minorities: Y

Meijer Inc

NAIC Code: 445110

www.meijer.com

TYPES OF BUSINESS:

Grocery Stores
General Merchandise
Hardware
Photo Services
Pharmacies
In-Store Restaurants
Gasoline, Retail
Home Decor

BRANDS/DIVISIONS/AFFILIATES:

Meijer Real Estate
Purple Cow Creamery
Meijer
Meijer Gold
True Goodness by Meijer
True Goodness by Meijer Organics
Meijer Ecowise
Misfits

CONTACTS: *Note: Officers with more than one job title may be intentionally listed here more than once.*

Janet Emerson, VP-Retail Oper.
Stacie Behler, VP-Corp. Comm. & Public Rel.
Doug Meijer, Co-Chmn.
Hank Meijer, Co-Chmn.

GROWTH PLANS/SPECIAL FEATURES:

Meijer, Inc. is a leading grocery retailer in the Midwest, with over 255 superstores throughout Illinois, Indiana, Kentucky, Michigan, Ohio and Wisconsin. Each Meijer store carries brand-name and private-label products, including bulk foods, fresh produce, frozen items, seafood and meat products. Most stores feature nearly 40 departments, such as electronics, hardware, toys, garden, entertainment, jewelry, photo, banking, pharmacy, books, apparel, automotive and furniture. Meijer Real Estate provides leasing and internal licenses on adjacent properties, former Meijer properties and in-store tenant space. Company brands include Meijer, Meijer Gold, True Goodness by Meijer, True Goodness by Meijer Organics, Meijer Ecowise, Markets of Meijer, At Home with Meijer, Falls Creek, MTA Sport, Shop Force, Fun Club, Studio M, Wave Zone, GFM, Baby Beginnings, Simple Pleasures and Lake & Trail. The Misfits produce line features cosmetically-challenged fruit and vegetables at reduced prices. The pre-packaged produce may be discolored, scarred or odd in size, but saves customers money and reduces food waste. Meijer stores are open 24-hours-a-day and close only on Christmas. Its superstores offer several in-store restaurants, including delis and cafes, as well as gas stations at select locations. In addition to retail stores, the firm operates a website that features a baby club, wine guides, contests, advertisements, pharmaceutical help and gardening tips. The firm also owns the Purple Cow Creamery dairy production facility in Ohio.

Meijer offers its employees medical, dental and vision insurance; short-/long-term disability, life and AD&D protection; 401(k); and a variety of employee assistance programs.

FINANCIAL DATA: *Note: Data for latest year may not have been available at press time.*

In U.S. $	2020	2019	2018	2017	2016	2015
Revenue	18,726,750,000	18,270,000,000	17,400,000,000	15,450,000,000	15,300,000,000	15,550,000,000
R&D Expense						
Operating Income						
Operating Margin %						
SGA Expense						
Net Income						
Operating Cash Flow						
Capital Expenditure						
EBITDA						
Return on Assets %						
Return on Equity %						
Debt to Equity						

CONTACT INFORMATION:

Phone: 616-453-6711   Fax: 616-791-2572
Toll-Free: 877-363-4537
Address: 2929 Walker Ave. NW, Grand Rapids, MI 49544 United States

SALARIES/BONUSES:

Top Exec. Salary: $ Bonus: $
Second Exec. Salary: $ Bonus: $

STOCK TICKER/OTHER:

Stock Ticker: Private
Employees: 74,000
Parent Company:

Exchange:
Fiscal Year Ends: 01/31

OTHER THOUGHTS:

Estimated Female Officers or Directors:
Hot Spot for Advancement for Women/Minorities: Y

Memorial Hermann Healthcare System   www.memorialhermann.org

NAIC Code: 622110

TYPES OF BUSINESS:

General Medical and Surgical Hospitals
Long-Term Care
Retirement & Nursing Homes
Wellness Centers
Rehabilitation Services
Home Health Services
Air Ambulance Services
Sports Medicine

BRANDS/DIVISIONS/AFFILIATES:

Children's Memorial Hermann Pediatrics

CONTACTS: *Note: Officers with more than one job title may be intentionally listed here more than once.*

David L. Callender, CEO
M. Michael Shabot, Chief Medical Officer
Craig Cordola, CEO-Children's Memorial Hermann Hospital
Sean L. Richardson, COO-Memorial Hermann Northeast Hospital

GROWTH PLANS/SPECIAL FEATURES:

Memorial Hermann Healthcare System is a leading provider of healthcare in greater Houston and southeast Texas. Memorial Hermann owns and operates 14 hospitals and has joint ventures with three other hospital facilities, including Memorial Hermann Surgical Hospital First Colony, Memorial Hermann Surgical Hospital Kingwood and Memorial Hermann Rehabilitation Hospital-Katy. Specialties by the healthcare system include neck pain and spine care, cancer, children's health, digestive health, emergency services, heart and vascular care, neurosurgery, neurology, stroke, orthopedics, sports medicine, rehabilitation, physical therapy, sleep medicine, transplant, weight loss, women's health, maternity and more. Services offered by the group include alcohol and drug rehabilitation, diabetes education, durable medical equipment, home care, hospice, Memorial Hermann Medical Group, mental health, pelvic floor health, senior living and specialty pharmacy. Imaging and diagnostic services span breast care centers, imaging, magnetic resonance imaging (MRI), X-ray and lab tests. Care services encompass everyday wellness, convenient care centers, doctor's offices, emergency rooms, urgent care, walk-in clinics and virtual care. The integrated system has 6,700 affiliated physicians. Memorial Hermann Pearland Hospital was designated as a Level IV Trauma Center by the Texas Department State Health Services in 2019 after consistently demonstrating its ability to provide advanced trauma life support, evaluation, stabilization and diagnostic services. During 2020, Memorial Hermann announced a new brand, Children's Memorial Hermann Pediatrics, offering pediatric clinics across the Greater Houston area.

Employees receive comprehensive benefits, retirement plans and employee assistance programs.

FINANCIAL DATA: *Note: Data for latest year may not have been available at press time.*

In U.S. $	2020	2019	2018	2017	2016	2015
Revenue	5,747,742,387	5,580,332,415	5,260,000,000	5,061,526,000	4,894,244,000	4,422,334,000
R&D Expense						
Operating Income						
Operating Margin %						
SGA Expense						
Net Income				315,904,000	106,815,000	249,338,000
Operating Cash Flow						
Capital Expenditure						
EBITDA						
Return on Assets %						
Return on Equity %						
Debt to Equity						

CONTACT INFORMATION:

Phone: 713-448-5555   Fax: 713-448-5665
Toll-Free:
Address: 929 Gessner Dr., Ste 2600, Houston, TX 77024 United States

STOCK TICKER/OTHER:

Stock Ticker: Nonprofit   Exchange:
Employees: 28,000   Fiscal Year Ends: 06/30
Parent Company:

SALARIES/BONUSES:

Top Exec. Salary: $ Bonus: $
Second Exec. Salary: $ Bonus: $

OTHER THOUGHTS:

Estimated Female Officers or Directors:
Hot Spot for Advancement for Women/Minorities:

Sales, profits and employees may be estimates. Financial information, benefits and other data can change quickly and may vary from those stated here.

Memorial Sloan Kettering Cancer Center   www.mskcc.org

NAIC Code: 622310

TYPES OF BUSINESS:

Cancer Hospitals
Cancer Research

BRANDS/DIVISIONS/AFFILIATES:

Sloan-Kettering Institute
Rockefeller Outpatient Pavilion
Sidney Kimmel Center
Evelyn H Lauder Breast Cancer
MSK Bergen

CONTACTS: Note: Officers with more than one job title may be intentionally listed here more than once.

Craig B. Thompson, CEO
Kathryn Martin, COO
Michael P. Harrington, CFO
Kerry Bessey, Chief HR Officer
Atefeh Riazi, CIO
Norman C. Selby, Sec.
Clifton S. Robbins, Treas.

GROWTH PLANS/SPECIAL FEATURES:

Memorial Sloan Kettering Cancer Center (MSKCC), a nonprofit organization, provides cancer treatment, research and education. The organization can accurately screen for mutations in more than 400 genes. MSKCC operates one hospital, several outpatient facilities, as well as three research facilities, primarily located in New York, but also in New Jersey. Today, MSKCC is one of 51 National Cancer Institute-designated comprehensive cancer centers, with nearly 500 inpatient beds, a 72,000-square-foot surgical center, as well as a state-of-the-art treatment hub for outpatient procedures. The Sloan-Kettering Institute is the hospital's research arm, with specific focus on cell biology, cancer biology genetics, biochemistry, molecular biology, structural biology, computational and developmental biology, immunology and therapeutics. The institute provides research training in conjunction with Louis V. Gerstner, Jr. Graduate School of Biomedical Sciences, Rockefeller University, Cornell University and Weill Medical College of Cornell University for PhD and MD students. Several of the firm's leading researchers are members of the Institute of Medicine and the National Academy of Science, and some are Howard Hughes Medical Institute investigators. MSKCC also operates the Rockefeller Outpatient Pavilion for the provision of outpatient services, including medical consultation, diagnostic imaging, chemotherapy, pharmacy services, cancer screening and integrative medicine services; and the Sidney Kimmel Center for Prostate and Urologic Cancers, which provides treatment for genitourinary cancers. MSKCC's Evelyn H. Lauder Breast Cancer center provides breast and cervical cancer screening.

Memorial Sloan Kettering offers comprehensive benefits, retirement plans and employee assistance programs.

FINANCIAL DATA: Note: Data for latest year may not have been available at press time.

In U.S. $	2020	2019	2018	2017	2016	2015
Revenue	5,407,196,000	5,483,376,000	4,909,854,000	4,409,320,000	3,954,488,000	3,611,291,000
R&D Expense						
Operating Income						
Operating Margin %						
SGA Expense						
Net Income	-417,172,000	194,479,000	219,060,000	239,765,000	189,937,000	169,169,000
Operating Cash Flow						
Capital Expenditure						
EBITDA						
Return on Assets %						
Return on Equity %						
Debt to Equity						

CONTACT INFORMATION:

Phone: 212-639-2000   Fax: 212-639-3576
Toll-Free: 800-525-2225
Address: 1275 York Ave., New York, NY 10065 United States

STOCK TICKER/OTHER:

Stock Ticker: Nonprofit   Exchange:
Employees: 17,301   Fiscal Year Ends: 12/31
Parent Company:

SALARIES/BONUSES:

Top Exec. Salary: $ Bonus: $
Second Exec. Salary: $ Bonus: $

OTHER THOUGHTS:

Estimated Female Officers or Directors: 1
Hot Spot for Advancement for Women/Minorities: Y

Sales, profits and employees may be estimates. Financial information, benefits and other data can change quickly and may vary from those stated here.

Menard Inc

NAIC Code: 444110

www.menards.com

TYPES OF BUSINESS:

Home Improvement Stores
Lumber
Housing Materials
Building Materials Manufacturing
Prefabricated Houses

BRANDS/DIVISIONS/AFFILIATES:

Menards
Menard Real Estate
Midwest Manufacturing
Menards Transportation
NailPlant.com
Menards Self Storage

CONTACTS: *Note: Officers with more than one job title may be intentionally listed here more than once.*

John R. Menard, Jr., Pres.

GROWTH PLANS/SPECIAL FEATURES:

Menard, Inc. is a family-owned company that began in 1960, which is headquartered in Eau Claire, Wisconsin and has 300 home improvement stores. The company's Menards-branded stores are located throughout the Midwest region: Illinois, Indiana, Iowa, Kansas, Kentucky, Michigan, Minnesota, Missouri, Nebraska, North Dakota, Ohio, South Dakota, West Virginia, Wisconsin and Wyoming. Menards operates five subsidiaries: Menard Real Estate, Midwest Manufacturing, Menards Transportation, NailPlant.com and Menards Self Storage. The firm's departments include appliances; bath; building materials; doors, windows and millwork; electrical; flooring and rugs; grocery and pet; heating and cooling; home and decor; kitchen; lighting and ceiling fans; maintenance, repair and operations; outdoors; paint; plumbing; home and patio; storage and organization; and tools and hardware. Menards provides a number of quality brands such as Midwest Manufacturing, Masterforce, Dakota, Mastercraft, Grip Fast, Tuscany, Tool Shop and Enchanted Garden/Enchanted Forest. Menard Real Estate is responsible for selling its properties. Midwest Manufacturing, operates a number of manufacturing facilities in Wisconsin, Illinois, Ohio, Nebraska, Iowa and Minnesota. Menards Transportation ships Menards products throughout its distribution area and operates its own fleet as well as through owner-operators. NailPlant.com is an eCommerce site that sells nails and other nail-like products and has a manufacturing plant in Rochester, Minnesota. Menards Self Storage has five locations, three in Wisconsin and two in Iowa.

Menard offers its employees medical, dental and disability insurance; a profit sharing program; advancement opportunities; a 401(k); store discounts and other incentives.

FINANCIAL DATA: *Note: Data for latest year may not have been available at press time.*

In U.S. $	2020	2019	2018	2017	2016	2015
Revenue	10,762,500,000	11,497,500,000	10,950,000,000	9,878,000,000	9,500,000,000	8,970,000,000
R&D Expense						
Operating Income						
Operating Margin %						
SGA Expense						
Net Income						
Operating Cash Flow						
Capital Expenditure						
EBITDA						
Return on Assets %						
Return on Equity %						
Debt to Equity						

CONTACT INFORMATION:

Phone: 715-876-5911   Fax: 715-876-2868
Toll-Free:
Address: 5101 Menard Dr., Eau Claire, WI 54703 United States

STOCK TICKER/OTHER:

Stock Ticker: Private
Employees: 45,000   Exchange:
Parent Company: Fiscal Year Ends: 01/31

SALARIES/BONUSES:

Top Exec. Salary: $ Bonus: $
Second Exec. Salary: $ Bonus: $

OTHER THOUGHTS:

Estimated Female Officers or Directors:
Hot Spot for Advancement for Women/Minorities:

Mercer LLC

www.mercer.com

NAIC Code: 541612

TYPES OF BUSINESS:

Consulting-Human Resources
Human Resource Advisory
Human Resource Solutions
Benefits
Investments
Retirement
Workforce
Mergers/Acquisitions

BRANDS/DIVISIONS/AFFILIATES:

Marsh & McLennan Companies Inc
MercerInsight

CONTACTS: Note: Officers with more than one job title may be intentionally listed here more than once.

Martine Ferland, CEO
Rian Miller, General Counsel
David Rahill, Pres., Health & Benefits
Phil de Cristo, Pres., Investments
Patricia Milligan, Pres., North America
Orlando Ashford, Pres., Talent
Simon O'Regan, Pres., EuroPac

GROWTH PLANS/SPECIAL FEATURES:

Mercer, LLC, a subsidiary of Marsh & McLennan Companies, Inc., offers a broad range of human resource advice and solutions to clients worldwide. The firm divides its services into four categories: health and benefits, investments and retirement, workforce and careers, and mergers and acquisitions. Health and benefits include private health exchange, employee benefits, global benefits, health benefits administration and affinity benefits. Investments and retirement include investments, retirement and benefit plan administration, defined benefit pension plans, pension risk management, defined contribution plans, employee financial wellness, endowments and foundations, and the MercerInsight platform which offers investment insights and analytics. Workforce and careers include talent strategy, executive compensation, workforce rewards, talent mobility, human resource transformation and employee communication. Mergers and acquisitions (MA) include M&A due diligence, M&A project management office, post-merger integration and private equity consulting and advisory. Mercer provides its solutions and services for those in business roles such as CEOs, boards, CFOs, talent leaders, benefits managers, financial advisors, trustees and fiduciaries and employees; for organizations such as corporations, multinational corporations, endowments and foundations, affinity, public sector, wealth management and private equity; and for industries such as energy, insurance, healthcare, financial services, higher education and retail. Based in New York, USA, the firm has offices throughout the world, including North America, Latin America, Europe, the Middle East, Africa, Asia-Pacific, Australia and New Zealand.

Mercer offers its employees comprehensive health benefits, retirement and savings options and a variety of assistance programs, which may vary across locations.

FINANCIAL DATA: Note: Data for latest year may not have been available at press time.

In U.S. $	2020	2019	2018	2017	2016	2015
Revenue	4,828,320,000	5,021,000,000	4,745,300,000	4,487,680,000	4,359,630,000	4,313,000,000
R&D Expense						
Operating Income						
Operating Margin %						
SGA Expense						
Net Income						
Operating Cash Flow						
Capital Expenditure						
EBITDA						
Return on Assets %						
Return on Equity %						
Debt to Equity						

CONTACT INFORMATION:

Phone: 212-345-7000   Fax: 212-345-7414
Toll-Free:
Address: 1166 Ave. of the Americas, New York, NY 10036 United States

STOCK TICKER/OTHER:

Stock Ticker: Subsidiary   Exchange:
Employees: 24,700   Fiscal Year Ends: 12/31
Parent Company: Marsh & McLennan Companies Inc

SALARIES/BONUSES:

Top Exec. Salary: $ Bonus: $
Second Exec. Salary: $ Bonus: $

OTHER THOUGHTS:

Estimated Female Officers or Directors: 2
Hot Spot for Advancement for Women/Minorities: Y

Merck & Co Inc

NAIC Code: 325412

TYPES OF BUSINESS:

Drugs-Diversified
Prescription Medicines
Vaccines
Biologic Therapies
Animal Health Products

BRANDS/DIVISIONS/AFFILIATES:

CONTACTS: Note: Officers with more than one job title may be intentionally listed here more than once.

Kenneth Frazier, CEO
Robert Davis, CFO
Rita Karachun, Chief Accounting Officer
Jim Scholefield, Chief Information Officer
Michael Nally, Chief Marketing Officer
Jennifer Zachary, Executive VP
Frank Clyburn, Executive VP
Steven Mizell, Executive VP
Julie Gerberding, Executive VP
Sanat Chattopadhyay, Executive VP
Roger Perlmutter, Executive VP
Richard DeLuca, Executive VP

GROWTH PLANS/SPECIAL FEATURES:

Merck & Co., Inc., known as MSD outside the U.S. and Canada, is a global healthcare company. The firm delivers innovative health solutions through its prescription medicines, vaccines, biologic therapies and animal health products. Merck operates through two business segments: pharmaceutical and animal health. The pharmaceutical segment includes human health pharmaceutical and vaccine products. Human pharmaceutical products consist of therapeutic and preventive agents, generally sold by prescription, for the treatment of human disorders. This division sells its products to drug wholesalers and retailers, hospitals, government agencies and managed healthcare providers. Human health vaccine products consist of preventive pediatric, adolescent and adult vaccines, primarily administered at physician offices. These vaccines are primarily sold to physicians, wholesalers, physician distributors and government entities. The animal health segment discovers, develops, manufactures and markets a wide range of veterinary pharmaceutical and vaccine products, as well as health management solutions and services, for the prevention, treatment and control of disease in all major livestock and companion animal species. This division also offers an extensive suite of digitally-connected identification, traceability and monitoring products. It sells these products to veterinarians, distributors and animal producers. In May 2021, Merck announced the spinoff of Organon & Co. into an independent, publicly-traded company and global healthcare company. The transaction was expected to finalize on June 2, 2021.

FINANCIAL DATA: Note: Data for latest year may not have been available at press time.

In U.S. $	2020	2019	2018	2017	2016	2015
Revenue	47,994,000,000	46,840,000,000	42,294,000,000	40,122,000,000	39,807,000,000	39,498,000,000
R&D Expense	13,558,000,000	9,872,000,000	9,752,001,000	10,208,000,000	10,124,000,000	6,704,000,000
Operating Income	8,483,000,000	12,241,000,000	8,931,000,000	7,309,000,000	6,030,000,000	7,547,000,000
Operating Margin %		.26%	.21%	.18%	.15%	.19%
SGA Expense	10,468,000,000	10,615,000,000	10,102,000,000	9,830,000,000	9,762,000,000	10,313,000,000
Net Income	7,067,000,000	9,843,000,000	6,220,000,000	2,394,000,000	3,920,000,000	4,442,000,000
Operating Cash Flow	10,253,000,000	13,440,000,000	10,922,000,000	6,447,000,000	10,376,000,000	12,421,000,000
Capital Expenditure	4,684,000,000	3,473,000,000	2,615,000,000	1,888,000,000	1,614,000,000	1,283,000,000
EBITDA	13,247,000,000	16,009,000,000	13,992,000,000	11,912,000,000	10,793,000,000	12,448,000,000
Return on Assets %		.12%	.07%	.03%	.04%	.04%
Return on Equity %		.37%	.20%	.06%	.09%	.10%
Debt to Equity		0.878	0.742	0.622	0.606	0.536

CONTACT INFORMATION:

Phone: 908 423-1000   Fax: 908 735-1253
Toll-Free:
Address: 2000 Galloping Hill Rd., Kenilworth, NJ 07033 United States

STOCK TICKER/OTHER:

Stock Ticker: MRK   Exchange: NYS
Employees: 71,000   Fiscal Year Ends: 12/31
Parent Company:

SALARIES/BONUSES:

Top Exec. Salary: $ Bonus: $
Second Exec. Salary: $ Bonus: $

OTHER THOUGHTS:

Estimated Female Officers or Directors: 4
Hot Spot for Advancement for Women/Minorities: Y

Merrill

NAIC Code: 523110

TYPES OF BUSINESS:

Stock Brokerage & Investment Banking
Research Services
Financial Planning Services

BRANDS/DIVISIONS/AFFILIATES:

Bank of America Corporation

CONTACTS: Note: Officers with more than one job title may be intentionally listed here more than once.

Alexandre Bettamio, CEO-Brazilian Oper.
Manuel Ebner, CEO-Merrill Lynch Capital Markets AG
Brian Moynihan, Chmn.-BofA

GROWTH PLANS/SPECIAL FEATURES:

Merrill is the wealth management arm of Bank of America Corporation. The firm provides investment insights in regards to investing and financial strategies and goals. Merrill's advisors build tailored strategies based on each client's need, and help guide them throughout the entire process. Merrill utilizes six tools for determining the proper wealth management approach for the client: social security, determining the effects of taking it too early; healthcare, looking at potential out-of-pocket healthcare expenses now and in retirement; lifetime income, considering the impact that income, inflation and life expectancy have on retirement; trust, which helps address goals such as protecting one's assets and providing for family; sequence of returns, considering the risk of experiencing poor market returns early in retirement; and longevity, considering opportunities and challenges that come with living longer in retirement. Merrill's advisors meet with clients often and offer in-depth annual reviews, one-on-one; goals are revisited and adjustments are made when needed.

FINANCIAL DATA: Note: Data for latest year may not have been available at press time.

In U.S. $	2020	2019	2018	2017	2016	2015
Revenue	15,300,000,000	16,100,000,000	15,900,000,000	15,293,000,000	16,000,000,000	14,898,000,000
R&D Expense						
Operating Income						
Operating Margin %						
SGA Expense						
Net Income						
Operating Cash Flow						
Capital Expenditure						
EBITDA						
Return on Assets %						
Return on Equity %						
Debt to Equity						

CONTACT INFORMATION:

Phone: 212-449-100   Fax:
Toll-Free: 800-937-0605
Address: 225 Liberty St., 41/Fl, 2 World Financial Center, New York, NY 10281 United States

STOCK TICKER/OTHER:

Stock Ticker: Subsidiary
Employees: 52,000
Parent Company: Bank of America Corporation

Exchange:
Fiscal Year Ends: 12/31

SALARIES/BONUSES:

Top Exec. Salary: $ Bonus: $
Second Exec. Salary: $ Bonus: $

OTHER THOUGHTS:

Estimated Female Officers or Directors: 2
Hot Spot for Advancement for Women/Minorities:

MetLife Inc
NAIC Code: 524113

TYPES OF BUSINESS:
Insurance
Banking
Investment Products
Mutual Funds
Life Insurance
Property & Casualty Insurance
Auto Insurance

BRANDS/DIVISIONS/AFFILIATES:

CONTACTS: Note: Officers with more than one job title may be intentionally listed here more than once.
Michel Khalaf, CEO
John McCallion, CFO
Esther Lee, CMO
Susan Podlogar, Chief Human Resources Officer
Esther Lee, Chief Marketing Officer
Stephen Gauster, Executive VP
Susan Podlogar, Executive VP
Steven Goulart, Executive VP
Oscar Schmidt, President, Geographical
Kishore Ponnavolu, President, Geographical
R. Hubbard, Chairman of the Board

GROWTH PLANS/SPECIAL FEATURES:
MetLife, Inc. is a provider of insurance and other financial services with operations throughout the world. Through its domestic and international subsidiaries and affiliates, the company provides insurance, annuities and employee benefit programs. The firm is organized into five segments: U.S.; Asia; Latin America; Europe, the Middle East and Africa (EMEA); and MetLife Holdings. The U.S. segment is organized into three businesses: group benefits, retirement and income solutions (R&I) and property and casualty (P&C). The group benefits business offers life, dental, group short- and long-term disability, individual disability, accidental death and dismemberment, vision and accident & health coverages, as well as prepaid legal plans; additionally, the firm also sell administrative services-only arrangements to some employers. The R&I business provides funding and financing solutions that help institutional customers mitigate and manage liabilities primarily associated with their qualified, nonqualified and welfare employee benefit programs using a spectrum of life and annuity-based insurance and investment products. The P&C business offers personal and commercial lines of P&C insurance, including private passenger automobile, homeowners' and personal excess liability insurance. The Asia, Latin America and EMEA segments offer a broad range of products (life, dental, accident and health, retirement and savings and credit insurance) to both individuals and corporations, as well as other institutions and their respective employees. The MetLife Holdings segment consists of operations relating to products and businesses that are no longer actively marketed in the U.S., such as variable, universal, term and whole life insurance, variable, fixed and index-linked annuities, long-term care insurance, as well as the assumed variable annuity guarantees from the former operating joint venture in Japan. In December 2019, MetLife agreed to acquire PetFirst Healthcare, LLC, a pet insurance administrator. In September 2020, the firm agreed to acquire Versant Health for $1.675 billion.

FINANCIAL DATA: Note: Data for latest year may not have been available at press time.

In U.S. $	2020	2019	2018	2017	2016	2015
Revenue	67,842,000,000	69,620,000,000	67,941,000,000	62,308,000,000	63,476,000,000	69,951,000,000
R&D Expense						
Operating Income						
Operating Margin %						
SGA Expense	5,775,000,000	6,554,000,000	6,462,000,000	6,724,000,000	7,114,000,000	7,177,000,000
Net Income	5,407,000,000	5,899,000,000	5,123,000,000	4,010,000,000	800,000,000	5,310,000,000
Operating Cash Flow	11,639,000,000	13,786,000,000	11,738,000,000	12,283,000,000	14,827,000,000	14,129,000,000
Capital Expenditure						
EBITDA						
Return on Assets %		.01%	.01%	.00%	.00%	.01%
Return on Equity %		.10%	.09%	.06%	.01%	.07%
Debt to Equity		0.251	0.303	0.321	0.292	0.312

CONTACT INFORMATION:
Phone: 212 578-2211　　　Fax: 212 578-3320
Toll-Free: 800-638-5433
Address: 200 Park Ave., New York, NY 10166 United States

STOCK TICKER/OTHER:
Stock Ticker: MET　　　　　　　　Exchange: NYS
Employees: 49,000　　　　　　　　Fiscal Year Ends: 12/31
Parent Company:

SALARIES/BONUSES:
Top Exec. Salary: $　　　　Bonus: $
Second Exec. Salary: $　　　Bonus: $

OTHER THOUGHTS:
Estimated Female Officers or Directors: 5
Hot Spot for Advancement for Women/Minorities: Y

Microchip Technology Incorporated

www.microchip.com

NAIC Code: 334413

TYPES OF BUSINESS:

Semiconductors-Specialized
Microcontrollers
Battery Management & Interface Devices
Development Tools
Memory Products

BRANDS/DIVISIONS/AFFILIATES:

SuperFlash
Smartbits
Tekron International Limited

CONTACTS: *Note: Officers with more than one job title may be intentionally listed here more than once.*

Steve Sanghi, CEO
J. Bjornholt, CFO
Ganesh Moorthy, COO
Mitchell Little, Senior VP, Divisional
Richard Simoncic, Senior VP, Divisional
Stephen Drehobl, Senior VP, Divisional

GROWTH PLANS/SPECIAL FEATURES:

Microchip Technology Incorporated develops, manufactures and sells specialized semiconductor products used for a wide variety of embedded control applications. The company focuses on embedded control functions, including microcontrollers, development tools, analog and interface products and memory products. Microchip offers a broad family of microcontroller products featuring its proprietary architecture branded as PIC, with a variety of memory technology configurations, low voltage and power and a small footprint. The company targets the 8-bit, 16-bit and 32-bit microcontroller markets. It is able to incorporate non-volatile memory, such as reprogrammable Flash memory, into its microcontrollers and offers reprogrammable microcontroller products. The development tools enable system designers to program PIC microcontrollers and digital signal controllers for specific applications. These tools range from entry-level systems, which include an assembler and programmer or in-circuit debugging hardware, to fully configured systems that provide in-circuit emulation hardware. Analog and interface products consist of several families with over 7,800 power management, linear, mixed-signal, high voltage, thermal management, discrete diodes, metal oxide silicon field effect transistors (MOSFETs), radio frequency (RF), drivers, safety, security, timing, USB, ethernet, wireless and other interface products. Memory products consists primarily of serial electrically erasable programmable read-only memory, referred to as Serial EEPROMs. Serial EEPROM products are used for non-volatile program and data storage systems where such data must be either modified frequently or retained for long periods. Additionally, the firm's technology licensing business includes license fees and royalties associated with technology licenses for the use of its SuperFlash and Smartbits one-time programmable non-volatile memory (NVM) technologies. Manufacturing facilities are located in Arizona, Oregon, Colorado, Thailand and Philippines. In late-2020, Microchip acquired Tekron International Limited.

Microchip offers its employees health benefits, and shared profit and training opportunities.

FINANCIAL DATA: *Note: Data for latest year may not have been available at press time.*

In U.S. $	2020	2019	2018	2017	2016	2015
Revenue	5,274,200,000	5,349,500,000	3,980,800,000	3,407,807,000	2,173,334,000	
R&D Expense	877,800,000	826,300,000	529,300,000	545,293,000	372,596,000	
Operating Income	693,800,000	748,000,000	953,800,000	374,425,000	356,302,000	
Operating Margin %	.13%	.14%	.24%	.11%	.16%	
SGA Expense	676,600,000	682,900,000	452,100,000	499,811,000	301,670,000	
Net Income	570,600,000	355,900,000	255,400,000	164,639,000	324,132,000	
Operating Cash Flow	1,543,800,000	1,674,800,000	1,419,600,000	1,059,452,000	744,483,000	
Capital Expenditure	67,600,000	228,900,000	206,800,000	75,310,000	97,895,000	
EBITDA	1,863,300,000	1,583,800,000	1,552,200,000	705,341,000	668,482,000	
Return on Assets %	.03%	.03%	.03%	.02%	.06%	
Return on Equity %	.10%	.08%	.08%	.06%	.15%	
Debt to Equity	1.606	1.692	0.536	0.887	1.154	

CONTACT INFORMATION:

Phone: 480 792-7200   Fax: 480 899-9210
Toll-Free:
Address: 2355 W. Chandler Blvd., Chandler, AZ 85224-6199 United States

STOCK TICKER/OTHER:

Stock Ticker: MCHP
Employees: 19,500
Parent Company:

Exchange: NAS
Fiscal Year Ends: 02/28

SALARIES/BONUSES:

Top Exec. Salary: $ Bonus: $
Second Exec. Salary: $ Bonus: $

OTHER THOUGHTS:

Estimated Female Officers or Directors: 3
Hot Spot for Advancement for Women/Minorities: Y

Microsoft Corporation

www.microsoft.com

NAIC Code: 511210H

TYPES OF BUSINESS:

Computer Software, Operating Systems, Languages & Development Tools
Enterprise Software
Game Consoles
Operating Systems
Software as a Service (SAAS)
Search Engine and Advertising
E-Mail Services
Instant Messaging

BRANDS/DIVISIONS/AFFILIATES:

Office 365
Exchange
SharePoint
Microsoft Teams
Skype for Business
Outlook.com
OneDrive
LinkedIn

CONTACTS: *Note: Officers with more than one job title may be intentionally listed here more than once.*

Satya Nadella, CEO
Amy Hood, CFO
John Thompson, Chairman of the Board
Frank Brod, Chief Accounting Officer
Christopher Capossela, Chief Marketing Officer
William Gates, Co-Founder
Kathleen Hogan, Executive VP, Divisional
Margaret Johnson, Executive VP, Divisional
Jean-Philippe Courtois, Executive VP
Bradford Smith, Other Executive Officer

GROWTH PLANS/SPECIAL FEATURES:

Microsoft Corporation develops, license and supports software products, services and devices. Microsoft's services include cloud-based solutions that provide customers with software, services, platforms and content, and it provides solution support and consulting services. The company also delivers online advertising on a global scale. Microsoft's products include operating systems, cross-device productivity applications, server applications, business solution applications, desktop and server management tools, software development tools, and video games. The firm designs, manufactures and sells personal computers, tablets, gaming and entertainment consoles, and other intelligent devices and related accessories. Microsoft operates through three business segments: productivity and business processes, intelligent cloud, and personal computing. The productivity and business processes segment primarily comprises the following products and services: office commercial, including Office 365 subscriptions and Office licensed on-premises (Office, Exchange, SharePoint, Microsoft Teams, Office 365 Security and Compliance, and Skype for Business; office consumer, including Office 365 subscriptions and Office licensed on-premises, and Skype, Outlook.com and OneDrive; LinkedIn, including talent solutions, marketing solutions and premium subscriptions; and dynamic business solutions such as cloud-based applications across enterprise resource planning (ERP) and customer relationship management (CRM). The intelligent cloud segment offers digital technology products, solutions and services to businesses and organizations for empowering employees, customer engagement and optimizing operations. The personal computing segment offers products and solutions that enable users to interact with technology in intuitive, engaging and dynamic ways. Windows 10 offers artificial-intelligence-first interfaces such as voice-activated commands, inking, immersive 3D content storytelling and mixed reality experiences. In September 2020, Microsoft agreed to acquire ZeniMax Media and its game publisher Bethesda Softworks for $7.5 billion

Microsoft offers its employees comprehensive benefits, a 401(k) and employee stock purchase plans; and employee assistance programs.

FINANCIAL DATA: *Note: Data for latest year may not have been available at press time.*

In U.S. $	2020	2019	2018	2017	2016	2015
Revenue	143,015,000,000	125,843,000,000	110,360,000,000	89,950,000,000	85,320,000,000	
R&D Expense	19,269,000,000	16,876,000,000	14,726,000,000	13,037,000,000	11,988,000,000	
Operating Income	52,959,000,000	42,959,000,000	35,058,000,000	22,632,000,000	21,292,000,000	
Operating Margin %	.37%	.34%	.32%	.25%	.25%	
SGA Expense	24,709,000,000	23,098,000,000	22,223,000,000	20,020,000,000	19,260,000,000	
Net Income	44,281,000,000	39,240,000,000	16,571,000,000	21,204,000,000	16,798,000,000	
Operating Cash Flow	60,675,000,000	52,185,000,000	43,884,000,000	39,507,000,000	33,325,000,000	
Capital Expenditure	15,441,000,000	13,925,000,000	11,632,000,000	8,129,000,000	8,343,000,000	
EBITDA	68,423,000,000	58,056,000,000	49,468,000,000	34,149,000,000	27,616,000,000	
Return on Assets %	.15%	.14%	.07%	.10%	.09%	
Return on Equity %	.40%	.42%	.21%	.29%	.22%	
Debt to Equity	0.568	0.712	0.941	1.051	0.566	

CONTACT INFORMATION:

Phone: 425 882-8080   Fax: 425 936-7329
Toll-Free: 800-642-7676
Address: One Microsoft Way, Redmond, WA 98052 United States

STOCK TICKER/OTHER:

Stock Ticker: MSFT   Exchange: NAS
Employees: 163,000   Fiscal Year Ends: 06/30
Parent Company:

SALARIES/BONUSES:

Top Exec. Salary: $ Bonus: $
Second Exec. Salary: $ Bonus: $

OTHER THOUGHTS:

Estimated Female Officers or Directors: 4
Hot Spot for Advancement for Women/Minorities: Y

Molex LLC

www.molex.com

NAIC Code: 334417

TYPES OF BUSINESS:

Electronic Connector Manufacturing
Transportation Products
Commercial Products
Micro Products
Automation & Electrical Products
Integrated Products
Global Sales & Marketing Organization

BRANDS/DIVISIONS/AFFILIATES:

Koch Industries Inc
Fiberguide Industries

CONTACTS: Note: Officers with more than one job title may be intentionally listed here more than once.

Joseph Nelligan, CEO
Robert J. Zeitler, General Counsel
Tim Ruff, Sr. VP-Bus. Dev. & Corp. Strategy
David D. Johnson, Treas.
John H. Krehbiel, Jr., Co-Chmn.
Junichi Kaji, Pres., Global Micro Prod. Div.
J. Michael Nauman, Pres., Global Integrated Prod. Div.
Joseph Nelligan, Pres., Commercial Prod. Division

GROWTH PLANS/SPECIAL FEATURES:

Molex, LLC, a subsidiary of Koch Industries, Inc., manufactures and supplies electronic components. The firm designs, manufactures and sells thousands of products, including 3D semiconductors, 3D custom circuitry, antennas, application tooling, audio-balanced armature, automation, cables, cable assemblies, capillary tubing, micro components, connectors, edgecards, sockets, electrical rubber solutions, power distribution electricals, grips, portable lighting, reels, test and control electronics, wiring devices, noise suppression sheets, flexible circuit solutions, FPGA computing systems, hoods, IT infrastructure solutions, lighting products, optical solutions, printed circuit board (PCB) assemblies, product traceability, sensor solutions, user interface and wireless solutions. Molex also provides manufacturing services to integrate specific components into a customer's product. The company's products are utilized across a wide range of industries, including data communications, consumer electronics, industrial, automotive, commercial vehicle, medical and other. As of January 2021, Molex's technology focus is on 5G, connected health, connected home, connected mobility, data center, Industry 4.0 and Internet of Things (IoT). Molex is present in more than 40 countries. In December 2020, Molex acquired Fiberguide Industries, a manufacturer of customized optical fiber solutions. Fiberguide will merge into Molex's polymicro business unit.

FINANCIAL DATA: Note: Data for latest year may not have been available at press time.

In U.S. $	2020	2019	2018	2017	2016	2015
Revenue	4,095,000,000	4,200,000,000	4,150,000,000	4,100,000,000	4,000,000,000	3,900,000,000
R&D Expense						
Operating Income						
Operating Margin %						
SGA Expense						
Net Income						
Operating Cash Flow						
Capital Expenditure						
EBITDA						
Return on Assets %						
Return on Equity %						
Debt to Equity						

CONTACT INFORMATION:

Phone: 630 969-4550   Fax: 630 969-1352
Toll-Free: 800-786-6539
Address: 2222 Wellington Ct., Lisle, IL 60532-1682 United States

SALARIES/BONUSES:

Top Exec. Salary: $ Bonus: $
Second Exec. Salary: $ Bonus: $

STOCK TICKER/OTHER:

Stock Ticker: Subsidiary
Employees: 40,200
Parent Company: Koch Industries Inc

Exchange:
Fiscal Year Ends: 06/30

OTHER THOUGHTS:

Estimated Female Officers or Directors: 2
Hot Spot for Advancement for Women/Minorities:

Molina Healthcare Inc

NAIC Code: 524114

www.molinahealthcare.com

TYPES OF BUSINESS:

HMO-Low Income Patients
Medicaid HMO
SCHIP HMO

BRANDS/DIVISIONS/AFFILIATES:

CONTACTS:
Note: Officers with more than one job title may be intentionally listed here more than once.

Thomas Tran, CFO
Dale Wolf, Chairman of the Board
Maurice Hebert, Chief Accounting Officer
Jeff Barlow, Chief Legal Officer
Ronna Romney, Director
Mark Keim, Executive VP, Divisional
Pamela Sedmak, Executive VP, Divisional
James Woys, Executive VP, Divisional
Joseph Zubretsky, President

GROWTH PLANS/SPECIAL FEATURES:

Molina Healthcare, Inc. is a multi-stage, managed care organization participating in government-sponsored health care programs for low-income persons, such as the Medicaid program and Children's Health Insurance Program (CHIP, including Perinatal). The company also focuses on a small number of persons who are dually eligible under the Medicaid and Medicare programs. Molina operates in two segments: health plans and other. Health plans consists of operational health plans in 14 states and Puerto Rico and Molina's direct delivery business. The health plans, serving approximately 3.8 million, are operated by the firm's wholly owned subsidiaries in those states, each of which is licensed as a health maintenance organization (HMO). Molina manages the vast majority of its operations through the health plans segment.

Molina offers employees medical, dental and vision plans; life insurance; disability; employee assistance; flexible spending accounts; 401(k); and an employee stock purchase plan.

FINANCIAL DATA:
Note: Data for latest year may not have been available at press time.

In U.S. $	2020	2019	2018	2017	2016	2015
Revenue	19,423,000,000	16,829,000,000	18,890,000,000	19,883,000,000	17,782,000,000	14,178,000,000
R&D Expense						
Operating Income	1,078,000,000	1,050,000,000	1,192,000,000	149,000,000	306,000,000	387,000,000
Operating Margin %		.05%	.06%	.00%	.02%	.03%
SGA Expense	1,480,000,000	1,296,000,000	1,333,000,000	1,594,000,000	1,393,000,000	1,146,000,000
Net Income	673,000,000	737,000,000	707,000,000	-512,000,000	52,000,000	143,000,000
Operating Cash Flow	1,890,000,000	427,000,000	-314,000,000	804,000,000	673,000,000	1,125,000,000
Capital Expenditure	74,000,000	57,000,000	30,000,000	86,000,000	176,000,000	132,000,000
EBITDA	1,151,000,000	1,148,000,000	1,241,000,000	-316,000,000	488,000,000	514,000,000
Return on Assets %		.11%	.09%	-.06%	.01%	.03%
Return on Equity %		.41%	.47%	-.34%	.03%	.11%
Debt to Equity		0.749	0.739	1.134	0.711	0.745

CONTACT INFORMATION:

Phone: 562 435-3666   Fax: 562 499-0790
Toll-Free: 888-562-5442
Address: 200 Oceangate, Ste. 100, Long Beach, CA 90802 United States

STOCK TICKER/OTHER:

Stock Ticker: MOH   Exchange: NYS
Employees: 10,000   Fiscal Year Ends: 12/31
Parent Company:

SALARIES/BONUSES:

Top Exec. Salary: $ Bonus: $
Second Exec. Salary: $ Bonus: $

OTHER THOUGHTS:

Estimated Female Officers or Directors: 2
Hot Spot for Advancement for Women/Minorities: Y

Mondelez International Inc

www.mondelezinternational.com

NAIC Code: 311821

TYPES OF BUSINESS:

Cookie and Cracker Manufacturing
Manufacturer
Distributor
Snack Products
Chocolate
Gum
Candy

BRANDS/DIVISIONS/AFFILIATES:

Cadbury
Milka
Toblerone
Oreo
belVita
Halls
Trident
Tang

CONTACTS: *Note: Officers with more than one job title may be intentionally listed here more than once.*

Dirk Van de Put, CEO
Maurizio Brusadelli, Exec. VP
Nelson Urdaneta, Chief Accounting Officer
Robin Hargrove, Executive VP, Divisional
Daniel Myers, Executive VP, Divisional
Luca Zaramella, Executive VP
Gerhard Pleuhs, Executive VP
Timothy Cofer, Executive VP
Paulette Alviti, Executive VP
Vinzenz Gruber, Executive VP
Alejandro Lorenzo, Executive VP
Henry Walter, Executive VP

GROWTH PLANS/SPECIAL FEATURES:

Mondelez International, Inc. is a leading manufacturer of snack products. These items consist of cookies, crackers, salted snacks, chocolate, gum and candy. Mondelez also makes and sells various cheese, grocery and powdered beverage products. The firm has operations in approximately 80 countries. It makes its products at its 133 manufacturing and processing facilities in 45 countries (as of December 31, 2020), and sells its products in over 150 countries worldwide. Popular brands of Mondelez include Cadbury, Milka and Toblerone chocolate; Oreo, belVita and LU cookies/biscuits; Halls candy; Trident gum; and Tang powdered beverages. Mondelez's operations and management structure are organized geographically into Latin America, which represents 9% of annual income; AMEA (Asia, Middle East and Africa), 22%; Europe, 38%; and North America, 31%. Products are generally sold to supermarket chains, wholesalers, supercenters, club stores, mass merchandisers, distributors, convenience stores, gasoline stations, drug stores, value stores and other retail food outlets. Mondelez also sells through eCommerce channels worldwide. During 2020, Mondelez acquired a majority stake in Toronto-based Give & Go, which manufactures sweet baked goods, including two-bite brownies, and is known for its Create-A-Treat brand of cookie and gingerbread house decorating kits. In January 2021, Mondelez acquired Hu Master Holdings, which manufactures premium chocolate in the U.S.

FINANCIAL DATA: *Note: Data for latest year may not have been available at press time.*

In U.S. $	2020	2019	2018	2017	2016	2015
Revenue	26,581,000,000	25,868,000,000	25,938,000,000	25,896,000,000	25,923,000,000	29,636,000,000
R&D Expense						
Operating Income	4,154,000,000	4,027,000,000	3,701,000,000	3,976,000,000	3,412,000,000	3,754,000,000
Operating Margin %		.16%	.14%	.15%	.13%	.13%
SGA Expense	6,098,000,000	6,136,000,000	6,475,000,000	5,911,000,000	6,540,000,000	7,577,000,000
Net Income	3,555,000,000	3,870,000,000	3,381,000,000	2,922,000,000	1,659,000,000	7,267,000,000
Operating Cash Flow	3,964,000,000	3,965,000,000	3,948,000,000	2,593,000,000	2,838,000,000	3,728,000,000
Capital Expenditure	863,000,000	925,000,000	1,095,000,000	1,014,000,000	1,224,000,000	1,514,000,000
EBITDA	4,922,000,000	4,978,000,000	4,115,000,000	4,336,000,000	2,792,000,000	9,387,000,000
Return on Assets %		.06%	.05%	.05%	.03%	.11%
Return on Equity %		.15%	.13%	.11%	.06%	.26%
Debt to Equity		0.536	0.489	0.497	0.525	0.52

CONTACT INFORMATION:

Phone: 847-943-4000   Fax:
Toll-Free: 855-535-5648
Address: 905 W. Fulton Market, Ste. 200, Chicago, IL 60607 United States

STOCK TICKER/OTHER:

Stock Ticker: MDLZ
Employees: 79,000
Parent Company:

Exchange: NAS
Fiscal Year Ends: 12/31

SALARIES/BONUSES:

Top Exec. Salary: $ Bonus: $
Second Exec. Salary: $ Bonus: $

OTHER THOUGHTS:

Estimated Female Officers or Directors: 5
Hot Spot for Advancement for Women/Minorities: Y

Monro Inc

NAIC Code: 811100

TYPES OF BUSINESS:

Automotive Repair & Maintenance
Under-Car Repair Services
Inspection Services
Automobile Tires
Automobile Maintenance Services
Vehicle Alignment

BRANDS/DIVISIONS/AFFILIATES:

Monro Auto Service and Tire Centers
Tire Choice Auto Service Centers
Mr Tire Auto Service Centers
Car-X Tire & Auto
Tire Warehouse Tires for Less
Ken Towerys Tire & Auto Care
Tire Barn Warehouse
Free Service Tire & Auto Centers

CONTACTS: Note: Officers with more than one job title may be intentionally listed here more than once.

Brett Ponton, CEO
Brian DAmbrosia, CFO
Robert Mellor, Chairman of the Board
Maureen Mulholland, General Counsel
Deborah Brundage, Senior VP, Divisional
Samuel Senuk, Vice President, Divisional
Raymond Pickens, Vice President, Divisional

GROWTH PLANS/SPECIAL FEATURES:

Monro, Inc. is a nation-wide operator of retail tire and automotive repair stores in the U.S. The company offers replacement tires and tire-related services, as well as automotive undercar repair services and a broad range of routine maintenance services primarily on cars, light trucks and vans. Monro also provides brake products, muffler and exhaust systems, and vehicle alignment services. Company-operated store brands (as of March 27, 2021) include Monro Auto Service and Tire Centers, Tire Choice Auto Service Centers, Mr. Tire Auto Service Centers, Car-X Tire & Auto, Tire Warehouse Tires for Less, Ken Towery's Tire & Auto Care, Tire Barn Warehouse, Free Service Tire & Auto Centers, and others. The firm operates more than 1,260 stores. During 2021, Monro acquired 30 retail tire and automotive repair stores located in California from Mountain View Tire & Service, Inc. for $62.1 million. The stores will operate under the Mountain View Tire & Service name.

Monro offers its employees a 401(k) plan, an employee stock purchase plan, long-term disability and basic life insurance options, voluntary benefits, company discounts and other benefits.

FINANCIAL DATA: Note: Data for latest year may not have been available at press time.

In U.S. $	2020	2019	2018	2017	2016	2015
Revenue	1,256,524,000	1,200,230,000	1,127,815,000	1,021,511,000	943,651,000	
R&D Expense						
Operating Income	101,702,000	126,743,000	127,296,000	116,384,000	120,589,000	
Operating Margin %	.08%	.11%	.11%	.11%	.13%	
SGA Expense	374,956,000	338,485,000	308,278,000	280,505,000	265,114,000	
Net Income	58,024,000	79,752,000	63,935,000	61,526,000	66,805,000	
Operating Cash Flow	121,329,000	152,891,000	121,235,000	129,935,000	126,504,000	
Capital Expenditure	55,918,000	44,468,000	39,122,000	34,640,000	36,834,000	
EBITDA	166,688,000	182,274,000	176,631,000	161,013,000	160,358,000	
Return on Assets %	.03%	.06%	.05%	.06%	.07%	
Return on Equity %	.08%	.12%	.11%	.11%	.13%	
Debt to Equity	1.41	0.537	0.597	0.68	0.502	

CONTACT INFORMATION:

Phone: 585-647-6400   Fax: 585-647-0945
Toll-Free:
Address: 200 Holleder Pkwy., Rochester, NY 14615 United States

STOCK TICKER/OTHER:

Stock Ticker: MNRO
Employees: 7,800
Parent Company:

Exchange: NAS
Fiscal Year Ends: 03/31

SALARIES/BONUSES:

Top Exec. Salary: $ Bonus: $
Second Exec. Salary: $ Bonus: $

OTHER THOUGHTS:

Estimated Female Officers or Directors: 1
Hot Spot for Advancement for Women/Minorities:

Monster Beverage Corporation

monsterbevcorp.com

NAIC Code: 312111

TYPES OF BUSINESS:

Beverages-Natural Sodas
Energy Drinks
Fruit Juice
Manufacture
Distribution
Marketing

BRANDS/DIVISIONS/AFFILIATES:

Monster Energy
Burn
NOS
Full Throttle
Relentless
Mother

CONTACTS: Note: Officers with more than one job title may be intentionally listed here more than once.

Rodney Sacks, CEO
Hilton Schlosberg, CFO
Thomas Kelly, Controller, Subsidiary
Emelie Tirre, President, Geographical
Guy Carling, President, Geographical

GROWTH PLANS/SPECIAL FEATURES:

Monster Beverage Corporation markets and distributes a range of energy drinks and alternative beverages. Its products include natural sodas, fruit juices, juice drinks, energy drinks, dairy-based coffee drinks, fruit juice smoothies, functional drinks, iced teas, juice cocktails, children's multi-vitamin juice drinks, lightly flavored sparkling waters and powdered drink mixes. The company maintains several brands, including Monster Energy, Burn, NOS, Full Throttle, Relentless and Mother. Monster Beverage outsources its manufacturing needs to third-party bottlers and contract packers, whom it supplies with juices, flavors, vitamins, minerals, nutrients, herbs, supplements, caps, labels, trays and ingredients. Distribution levels vary from state to state and a limited range of products are marketed abroad. Domestic customers are usually retail and specialty chains, club stores, mass merchandisers, convenience chains, food service and full-service beverage distributors and health food distributors. Major customers include Costco, Sam's Club and Wal-Mart. The company has more than 14,200 registered trademarks and pending applications worldwide. The firm and The Coca-Cola Co. (TCCC) have a strategic partnership where TCCC controls a minority stake in Monster Beverage. As a result of the partnership, TCC transferred its energy brands to Monster Beverage and Monster Beverage transferred its non-energy brands to TCCC. Therefore, the Monster Beverage drinks segment represents more than 90% of annual net sales.

FINANCIAL DATA: Note: Data for latest year may not have been available at press time.

In U.S. $	2020	2019	2018	2017	2016	2015
Revenue	4,598,638,000	4,200,819,000	3,807,183,000	3,369,045,000	3,049,393,000	2,722,564,000
R&D Expense						
Operating Income	1,633,153,000	1,402,939,000	1,283,619,000	1,198,787,000	1,085,338,000	732,183,000
Operating Margin %		.33%	.34%	.36%	.36%	.27%
SGA Expense						
Net Income	1,409,594,000	1,107,835,000	993,004,000	820,678,000	712,685,000	546,733,000
Operating Cash Flow	1,364,163,000	1,113,762,000	1,161,881,000	987,731,000	701,355,000	207,986,000
Capital Expenditure	67,272,000	110,398,000	74,925,000	93,128,000	105,337,000	42,493,000
EBITDA	1,694,126,000	1,467,753,000	1,340,598,000	1,247,674,000	1,126,183,000	763,043,000
Return on Assets %		.23%	.21%	.18%	.15%	.14%
Return on Equity %		.28%	.26%	.23%	.18%	.17%
Debt to Equity						

CONTACT INFORMATION:

Phone: 951 739-6200   Fax: 909 739-6210
Toll-Free: 800-426-7367
Address: 1 Monster Way, Corona, CA 92879 United States

SALARIES/BONUSES:

Top Exec. Salary: $ Bonus: $
Second Exec. Salary: $ Bonus: $

STOCK TICKER/OTHER:

Stock Ticker: MNST   Exchange: NAS
Employees: 3,666   Fiscal Year Ends: 12/31
Parent Company:

OTHER THOUGHTS:

Estimated Female Officers or Directors:
Hot Spot for Advancement for Women/Minorities:

Sales, profits and employees may be estimates. Financial information, benefits and other data can change quickly and may vary from those stated here.

Moody's Corporation

NAIC Code: 561450

www.moodys.com

TYPES OF BUSINESS:

Credit Bureau
Credit Risk Assessment Products & Services
Credit Processing Software
Credit Training Services

BRANDS/DIVISIONS/AFFILIATES:

Regulatory DataCorp
RBA International
Acquire Media
ZM Financial Systems
Malaysian Rating Corporation Berhad
MioTech

CONTACTS: Note: Officers with more than one job title may be intentionally listed here more than once.

Raymond Mcdaniel, CEO
Mark Kaye, CFO
Henry McKinnell, Chairman of the Board
Caroline Sullivan, Chief Accounting Officer
Richard Cantor, Chief Risk Officer
John Goggins, Executive VP
Melanie Hughes, Other Executive Officer
Mark Almeida, President, Subsidiary
Robert Fauber, President, Subsidiary

GROWTH PLANS/SPECIAL FEATURES:

Moody's Corporation is a provider of credit ratings; credit and economic related research, data and analytical tools; risk management software; quantitative credit risk measures, credit portfolio management solutions, training and financial credentialing and certification services; and outsourced research and analytical services to institutional customers. Moody's operates in two segments: Moody's investors service (MIS) and Moody's analytics (MA). MIS publishes rating opinions on a range of credit obligors and credit obligations issued in domestic and international markets, including various corporate and governmental obligations, structured finance securities and commercial paper programs. MIS has ratings relationships with approximately non-financial 4,900 corporate issuers, 4,100 financial institution issuers, approximately 17,200 public finance issuers, 1,000 infrastructure and project finance issuers and approximately 9,500 structured finance transactions. MA offers a range of products that support the risk management activities of institutional participants in global financial markets. These products and services include in-depth research on major debt issuers, industry studies and commentary on topical credit related events as well as economic research, credit data and analytical tools such as quantitative credit risk scores. MA's customers represent more than 11,000 institutions worldwide operating in approximately 155 countries. During 2019, Moody's research website was accessed by over 306,000 individuals including 41,000 client users. In 2020, Moody's acquired Regulatory DataCorp, a provider of anti-money laundering and know-your-customer data and due diligence services; RBA International, a provider of online retail bank training and certifications; Acquire Media, an aggregator and distributor of curated media; ZM Financial Systems, a provider of risk and financial management software; and minority stakes in Malaysian Rating Corporation Berhad and MioTech.

FINANCIAL DATA: Note: Data for latest year may not have been available at press time.

In U.S. $	2020	2019	2018	2017	2016	2015
Revenue	5,371,000,000	4,829,000,000	4,442,700,000	4,204,100,000	3,604,200,000	3,484,500,000
R&D Expense						
Operating Income	2,447,000,000	2,075,000,000	1,925,200,000	1,831,600,000	1,516,100,000	1,479,800,000
Operating Margin %		.43%	.43%	.44%	.42%	.42%
SGA Expense	1,229,000,000	1,167,000,000	1,080,100,000	991,400,000	936,400,000	921,300,000
Net Income	1,778,000,000	1,422,000,000	1,309,600,000	1,000,600,000	266,600,000	941,300,000
Operating Cash Flow	2,146,000,000	1,675,000,000	1,461,100,000	747,500,000	1,226,100,000	1,153,600,000
Capital Expenditure	103,000,000	69,000,000	90,400,000	90,600,000	115,200,000	89,000,000
EBITDA	2,665,000,000	2,235,000,000	2,093,600,000	2,149,500,000	833,400,000	1,617,900,000
Return on Assets %		.14%	.14%	.14%	.05%	.19%
Return on Equity %		2.65%	19.81%			
Debt to Equity		9.912	11.364			

CONTACT INFORMATION:

Phone: 212 553-0300   Fax: 212 553-4820
Toll-Free:
Address: 250 Greenwich St., 7 World Trade Center, New York, NY 10007 United States

STOCK TICKER/OTHER:

Stock Ticker: MCO
Employees: 11,000
Parent Company:

Exchange: NYS
Fiscal Year Ends: 12/31

SALARIES/BONUSES:

Top Exec. Salary: $ Bonus: $
Second Exec. Salary: $ Bonus: $

OTHER THOUGHTS:

Estimated Female Officers or Directors: 2
Hot Spot for Advancement for Women/Minorities: Y

Morgan Stanley

NAIC Code: 523110

www.morganstanley.com

TYPES OF BUSINESS:

Stock Brokerage/Investment Banking
Institutional Securities
Wealth Management
Investment Management

BRANDS/DIVISIONS/AFFILIATES:

E*TRADE Financial LLC
E*TRADE Financial Corp

CONTACTS: *Note: Officers with more than one job title may be intentionally listed here more than once.*

James Gorman, CEO
Jonathan Pruzan, CFO
Paul Wirth, Chief Accounting Officer
Keishi Hotsuki, Chief Risk Officer
Jeffrey Brodsky, Executive VP
Eric Grossman, Executive VP
Daniel Simkowitz, Other Corporate Officer
Thomas Kelleher, President

GROWTH PLANS/SPECIAL FEATURES:

Morgan Stanley provides global financial services to clients worldwide including corporations, governments, institutions and individuals, with offices in more than 40 countries. The firm operates through three segments: institutional securities, wealth management, and investment management. The institutional securities segment provides investment banking, sales and trading, lending and other services to corporations, governments, financial institutions and high to ultra-high net worth clients. This division offers advice on mergers and acquisitions, restructurings, real estate and project finance. The wealth management segment provides comprehensive financial services and solutions to individual investors and small-to-medium-sized businesses and institutions covering: brokerage and investment advisory services; financial and wealth planning services; stock plan administration services; annuity and insurance products; securities-based lending; residential real estate loans and other lending products; banking; and retirement plan services. The investment management segment provides a range of investment strategies and products that span geographies, asset classes and public and private markets to a diverse group of clients across institutional and intermediary channels. Strategies and products are offered through a variety of investment vehicles, including equity, fixed income, liquidity and alternative/other products. In October 2020, Morgan Stanley acquired E*TRADE Financial Corp. in a $13 billion, all-stock deal, which became E*TRADE Financial LLC. That same month, Morgan Stanley agreed to acquire fund manager Eaton Vance Corp.

FINANCIAL DATA: *Note: Data for latest year may not have been available at press time.*

In U.S. $	2020	2019	2018	2017	2016	2015
Revenue	45,269,000,000	38,926,000,000	37,714,000,000	35,852,000,000	32,711,000,000	33,263,000,000
R&D Expense						
Operating Income						
Operating Margin %						
SGA Expense	23,753,000,000	21,691,000,000	20,339,000,000	19,566,000,000	18,252,000,000	18,464,000,000
Net Income	10,996,000,000	9,042,000,000	8,748,000,000	6,111,000,000	5,979,000,000	6,127,000,000
Operating Cash Flow	-25,231,000,000	40,773,000,000	7,305,000,000	-4,505,000,000	2,447,000,000	3,674,000,000
Capital Expenditure	1,444,000,000	1,826,000,000	1,865,000,000	1,629,000,000	1,276,000,000	1,373,000,000
EBITDA						
Return on Assets %		.01%	.01%	.01%	.01%	.01%
Return on Equity %		.12%	.12%	.08%	.08%	.09%
Debt to Equity		2.603	2.623	2.774	2.404	2.273

CONTACT INFORMATION:

Phone: 212 761-4000   Fax: 212 761-0086
Toll-Free:
Address: 1585 Broadway, New York, NY 10036 United States

STOCK TICKER/OTHER:

Stock Ticker: MS   Exchange: NYS
Employees: 68,000   Fiscal Year Ends: 12/31
Parent Company:

SALARIES/BONUSES:

Top Exec. Salary: $ Bonus: $
Second Exec. Salary: $ Bonus: $

OTHER THOUGHTS:

Estimated Female Officers or Directors: 3
Hot Spot for Advancement for Women/Minorities: Y

Mutual of Omaha Insurance Company   www.mutualofomaha.com
NAIC Code: 524113

TYPES OF BUSINESS:
Life Insurance
Insurance
Medicare
Financial Services

GROWTH PLANS/SPECIAL FEATURES:
Mutual of Omaha Insurance Company provides insurance, Medicare and financial products and services through its subsidiaries. Insurance offered by Mutual of Omaha includes term life, whole life, universal life, accidental death, long-term care, disability income, critical illness, cancer, heart attack and stroke coverage. Medicare offerings include Medicare solutions, Medicare supplement insurance, a prescription drug plan and dental insurance. Financial services include a wide range of annuities, investments and mortgage products. Mutual of Omaha offers its products and services to individuals, businesses and groups throughout the U.S. The firm is owned by its policyholders. In December 2019, Mutual of Omaha Bank was sold to CIT Group, Inc. for $1 billion.

Mutual of Omaha offers its employees medical, dental, vision and pharmacy coverage; life, short- and long-term disability and AD&D insurance; 401(k); tuition reimbursement; and learning/career development.

BRANDS/DIVISIONS/AFFILIATES:

CONTACTS: Note: Officers with more than one job title may be intentionally listed here more than once.
James T. Blackledge, CEO
Richard C. Anderl, General Counsel
Stacy A. Scholtz, Exec. VP-Corp. Oper.
David A. Diamond, Treas.
Daniel P. Martin, Exec. VP-Group Benefit Svcs.
Michael C. Weekly, Exec. VP-Individual Financial Svcs.
Richard A. Witt, Chief Investment Officer
Kenneth R. Cook, Pres., East Campus Realty

FINANCIAL DATA: Note: Data for latest year may not have been available at press time.

In U.S. $	2020	2019	2018	2017	2016	2015
Revenue	10,306,206,441	8,588,645,770	7,737,582,461	8,249,301,176	7,898,472,000	7,235,734,000
R&D Expense						
Operating Income						
Operating Margin %						
SGA Expense						
Net Income	844,799,395	5,567,374	-102,044,942	54,640,997	356,558,000	333,006,000
Operating Cash Flow						
Capital Expenditure						
EBITDA						
Return on Assets %						
Return on Equity %						
Debt to Equity						

CONTACT INFORMATION:
Phone: 402-342-7600   Fax: 402-351-2775
Toll-Free: 800-775-6000
Address: Mutual of Omaha Plz., Omaha, NE 68175 United States

STOCK TICKER/OTHER:
Stock Ticker: Mutual Company   Exchange:
Employees: 5,500   Fiscal Year Ends: 12/31
Parent Company:

SALARIES/BONUSES:
Top Exec. Salary: $ Bonus: $
Second Exec. Salary: $ Bonus: $

OTHER THOUGHTS:
Estimated Female Officers or Directors: 3
Hot Spot for Advancement for Women/Minorities: Y

National Instruments Corporation

www.ni.com

NAIC Code: 511210N

TYPES OF BUSINESS:

Software-Instrumentation
Virtual Instrumentation
Signal Conditioning Hardware
Test & Measurement Software
Motion Control Products
Analysis & Visualization Software
Automation Software
Image Acquisition Products

BRANDS/DIVISIONS/AFFILIATES:

LabVIEW
LabVIEW Real-Time
LabVIEW Communications System Design Suite
LabWindows/CVI and Measurement Studio
NI DIAdem
NI SystemLink
OptimalPlus

CONTACTS: Note: Officers with more than one job title may be intentionally listed here more than once.

Karen Rapp, CFO
Michael McGrath, Chairman of the Board
John Roiko, Chief Accounting Officer
Jeffrey Kodosky, Co-Founder
Eric Starkloff, COO
Alexander Davern, Director
Royal Dixon, General Counsel
Scott Rust, Senior VP, Divisional

GROWTH PLANS/SPECIAL FEATURES:

National Instruments Corporation (NI) supplies test, measurement and automation products used by engineers and scientists from numerous industries. Its key markets range from the automotive, aerospace, electronics, semiconductors and defense sectors, to the education, government, medical research and telecommunications industries, among others. Products and services include system design software; programming tools; application software; hardware products and related driver software; the Ni education platform, including software and hardware products for teaching; NI services, including hardware services and maintenance; software maintenance services; and training and certification. The company's flagship product is LabVIEW, a system design software for measurement and control. With LabVIEW, users program graphically and can design custom virtual instruments by connecting icons with software wires to create block diagrams, which are natural design notations for scientists and engineers. Users can customize front panels with knobs, buttons, dials and graphs to emulate control panels of instruments or add custom graphics to visually represent the control and operation of processes. Add-ons LabVIEW Real-Time enables users to easily configure their application program to execute using a real-time operating system kernel instead of a general-purpose operating system. LabVIEW Communications System Design Suite is specifically for wireless prototyping, and also provides a plug-in architecture to offer productive starting points with open application frameworks for LTE, 802.11 and other key standards. LabWindows/CVI and Measurement Studio is designed for alternative programming environments. NI software products are complimentary to LabVIEW. Systems and data management products include NI DIAdem and NI SystemLink. During 2020, NI acquired OptimalPlus, a global leader in data analytics software for the semiconductor, automotive and electronics industries.

FINANCIAL DATA: Note: Data for latest year may not have been available at press time.

In U.S. $	2020	2019	2018	2017	2016	2015
Revenue	1,286,671,000	1,353,215,000	1,359,132,000	1,289,386,000	1,228,179,000	1,225,456,000
R&D Expense	280,381,000	272,452,000	261,072,000	231,761,000	235,706,000	225,131,000
Operating Income	39,797,000	147,712,000	172,879,000	145,778,000	119,726,000	137,172,000
Operating Margin %		.11%	.13%	.11%	.10%	.11%
SGA Expense	595,372,000	596,160,000	591,454,000	583,523,000	559,626,000	546,197,000
Net Income	143,659,000	162,151,000	155,057,000	52,411,000	82,734,000	95,262,000
Operating Cash Flow	180,767,000	224,405,000	274,580,000	224,442,000	195,840,000	162,637,000
Capital Expenditure	55,147,000	71,131,000	54,266,000	74,302,000	78,626,000	68,154,000
EBITDA	287,709,000	221,253,000	243,546,000	218,473,000	193,116,000	210,501,000
Return on Assets %		.10%	.10%	.03%	.06%	.07%
Return on Equity %		.13%	.13%	.05%	.08%	.09%
Debt to Equity		0.035			0.022	0.034

CONTACT INFORMATION:

Phone: 512 338-9119   Fax: 512 683-9300
Toll-Free: 800-433-3488
Address: 11500 N. Mopac Expressway, Austin, TX 78759-3504 United States

STOCK TICKER/OTHER:

Stock Ticker: NATI
Employees: 7,300
Parent Company:

Exchange: NAS
Fiscal Year Ends: 12/31

SALARIES/BONUSES:

Top Exec. Salary: $ Bonus: $
Second Exec. Salary: $ Bonus: $

OTHER THOUGHTS:

Estimated Female Officers or Directors: 1
Hot Spot for Advancement for Women/Minorities:

Sales, profits and employees may be estimates. Financial information, benefits and other data can change quickly and may vary from those stated here.

Nationwide Mutual Insurance Company   www.nationwide.com

NAIC Code: 524126

TYPES OF BUSINESS:

Insurance, Direct Property & Casualty
Life Insurance
Investment Products
Liability Insurance
Workers' Compensation
Health Insurance
Asset Management
Specialty Insurance

BRANDS/DIVISIONS/AFFILIATES:

CONTACTS: Note: Officers with more than one job title may be intentionally listed here more than once.

Kirt Walker, CEO
Mark Berven, Chief Prod. Officer
Gale V. King, Chief Admin. Officer
Patricia R. Hatler, Chief Legal Officer
Mark Berven, Chief Strategy Officer
Jeffrey W. Zellers, Chmn.

GROWTH PLANS/SPECIAL FEATURES:

Nationwide Mutual Insurance Company, operating through its subsidiaries, is one of the largest insurance and financial services companies in the world. The firm offers three types of services: financial, commercial lines and personal lines. The financial services division offers individual life, annuities, retirement plans, corporate life, mutual funds and banking. The commercial lines division offers standard commercial, farm/ranch, commercial agribusiness, excess and surplus (E&S) and specialty insurance products. The personal lines division offers standard auto, homeowners, renter, pet, sport vehicles and personal liability insurance products. The company's investments include fixed maturity securities, mortgage loans, policy loans, real estate, short-term and other types of investments. Revenues are primarily derived from property and casualty insurance premiums, with investment income coming in second, life insurance related business coming in third and other various revenues deriving the remainder. The firm has more than 30 Nationwide office locations throughout the U.S., with leading locations in Columbus, Ohio; Des Moines, Iowa; San Antonio, Texas; and Scottsdale, Arizona.

Nationwide employees are offered benefits such as life, long-term disability, accident and group legal insurance; flexible spending accounts; tuition reimbursement; a 401(k); and a retirement plan.

FINANCIAL DATA: Note: Data for latest year may not have been available at press time.

In U.S. $	2020	2019	2018	2017	2016	2015
Revenue	48,067,500,000	49,300,000,000	46,900,000,000	46,500,000,000	43,000,000,000	42,900,000,000
R&D Expense						
Operating Income						
Operating Margin %						
SGA Expense						
Net Income		1,900,000,000	1,300,000,000	600,000,000	910,000,000	1,230,000,000
Operating Cash Flow						
Capital Expenditure						
EBITDA						
Return on Assets %						
Return on Equity %						
Debt to Equity						

CONTACT INFORMATION:

Phone: 614-249-6349   Fax: 614-249-7705
Toll-Free: 800-882-2822
Address: One Nationwide Plaza, Columbus, OH 43215-2220 United States

STOCK TICKER/OTHER:

Stock Ticker: Mutual Company
Employees: 32,110
Parent Company:

Exchange:
Fiscal Year Ends: 12/31

SALARIES/BONUSES:

Top Exec. Salary: $ Bonus: $
Second Exec. Salary: $ Bonus: $

OTHER THOUGHTS:

Estimated Female Officers or Directors: 2
Hot Spot for Advancement for Women/Minorities: Y

Sales, profits and employees may be estimates. Financial information, benefits and other data can change quickly and may vary from those stated here.

NCH Corporation

www.nch.com

NAIC Code: 325611

TYPES OF BUSINESS:

Specialty Chemicals
Cleaning Chemicals
Water Treatment Equipment & Supplies
Industrial Tools & Supplies
Plumbing Hardware
Parts Washing Solutions

BRANDS/DIVISIONS/AFFILIATES:

Certified
Chemsearch
NCH
Chem-Aqua
Danco
LSP

CONTACTS: *Note: Officers with more than one job title may be intentionally listed here more than once.*

Lester A. Levy Jr., Co-VP
Walter M Levy, Co-VP
Robert M Levy, Co-VP
Walter Levy, Co-CEO
Ann Levy, Co-VP

GROWTH PLANS/SPECIAL FEATURES:

NCH Corporation, founded in 1919, is a global provider of industrial, commercial and institutional maintenance solutions. The company operates through its subsidiaries located on six continents, distributing in more than 50 countries. NCH is organized into six segments: industrial & institutional maintenance, water treatment solutions, plumbing, parts washing, lubrication and biologicals. Industrial & institutional maintenance provides products used in industrial and commercial cleaning; industrial and repair maintenance; drains, grease traps and lift stations; lubrication and coolants; equipment and supplies; parts washing; grounds care; and personal hygiene. Water treatment offers polymer technology-based products such as boilers, cooling towers, closed recirculation systems, cleaners/de-scalers, wastewater and bio-remediation and biocides and algaecides. Plumbing manufactures and distributes a wide array of plumbing products for repair, replacement, remodeling and new construction, which include sinks, faucets, toilets, drains, tubs and showers. Parts washing provides cleaning, washing and degreasing solutions of parts, spill/hazardous waste management and specialty chemical supplies. Lubrication manufactures lubricants through the Certified and NCH brands. Last, the biologicals segment develops solutions to clean water and promote a healthy environment. Brands of the firm include Certified, Chemsearch, NCH, Chem-Aqua, Danco and LSP.

FINANCIAL DATA: *Note: Data for latest year may not have been available at press time.*

In U.S. $	2020	2019	2018	2017	2016	2015
Revenue	1,169,792,400	1,244,460,000	1,185,200,000	1,102,500,000	1,050,000,000	1,000,000,000
R&D Expense						
Operating Income						
Operating Margin %						
SGA Expense						
Net Income						
Operating Cash Flow						
Capital Expenditure						
EBITDA						
Return on Assets %						
Return on Equity %						
Debt to Equity						

CONTACT INFORMATION:

Phone: 972-438-0211   Fax: 972-438-0707
Toll-Free: 800-527-9919
Address: 2727 Chemsearch Blvd., Irving, TX 75062 United States

SALARIES/BONUSES:

Top Exec. Salary: $ Bonus: $
Second Exec. Salary: $ Bonus: $

STOCK TICKER/OTHER:

Stock Ticker: Private   Exchange:
Employees: 8,500   Fiscal Year Ends: 04/30
Parent Company:

OTHER THOUGHTS:

Estimated Female Officers or Directors:
Hot Spot for Advancement for Women/Minorities:

NetApp Inc

NAIC Code: 334112

www.netapp.com

TYPES OF BUSINESS:
Data Management Solutions
Storage Solutions
Data Protection Software Products
Data Protection Platform Products
Storage Security Products
Data Retention & Archive Software Products
Storage Management & Application Software
Management Tools

BRANDS/DIVISIONS/AFFILIATES:
NetApp Keystone

CONTACTS: Note: Officers with more than one job title may be intentionally listed here more than once.
George Kurian, CEO
Mike Berry, CFO
James Whitemore, Sr. VP-Mktg.
Debra McCowan, Chief Human Resources Officer
Joel Reich, Executive VP, Divisional
Henri Richard, Executive VP, Divisional
Matthew Fawcett, General Counsel

GROWTH PLANS/SPECIAL FEATURES:
NetApp, Inc. provides software, systems and services to manage, store and share data across on-premises, private and public clouds. The company enables enterprises, service providers, governmental organizations and partners to deploy and evolve their IT environments. NetApp's cloud services are used for data migration, data protection, databases, block storage, cloud native applications, file services, high-performance computing and analytics. Its flash storage products and solutions accelerate workloads and analytics, gaining data center efficiencies, and protecting and securing data. This division's storage products include: all-flash arrays, such as AFF A-series, AFF C190, NVMe storage, SolidFire, EF-series and ONTAP artificial intelligence (AI); and hybrid arrays, including FAS, E-series and FlexPod. The NetApp Keystone cloud solution is a pay-as-you-go program that lets customers choose a performance tier, pick a storage service such as file/block/object, and manage it themselves or lets NetApp manage it. NetApp's suite of data management products enables customers to manage data no matter where it is within the hybrid cloud environment, and to use software management tools for optimizing operations, delivering automated services and monitoring data. NetApp's data storage software is designed to speed delivery of IT services to application owners, offering flexible configurations and agile deployment options. And the company's backup and recovery solutions help protect data cross the hybrid cloud. NetApp offers related support and training services, product documentation, installation and configuration support, troubleshooting support and other related services. Based in California, the firm has domestic offices throughout the U.S., including Colorado, Oregon, Pennsylvania, North Carolina, Virginia, Massachusetts and Kansas. In July 2020, NetApp acquired Spot, a computer management and cost optimization software provider for public clouds. In April 2020, the company acquired CloudJumper, a cloud software company in the virtual desktop infrastructure and remote desktop services markets.

NetApp offers employees healthcare, insurance, financial, saving and income protection programs.

FINANCIAL DATA: Note: Data for latest year may not have been available at press time.

In U.S. $	2020	2019	2018	2017	2016	2015
Revenue	5,412,000,000	6,146,000,000	5,911,000,000	5,519,000,000	5,546,000,000	
R&D Expense	847,000,000	827,000,000	783,000,000	779,000,000	861,000,000	
Operating Income	928,000,000	1,183,000,000	907,000,000	707,000,000	413,000,000	
Operating Margin %	.17%	.19%	.15%	.13%	.07%	
SGA Expense	1,848,000,000	1,935,000,000	2,009,000,000	1,904,000,000	2,099,000,000	
Net Income	819,000,000	1,169,000,000	76,000,000	509,000,000	229,000,000	
Operating Cash Flow	1,060,000,000	1,341,000,000	1,478,000,000	986,000,000	974,000,000	
Capital Expenditure	124,000,000	173,000,000	145,000,000	175,000,000	160,000,000	
EBITDA	1,192,000,000	1,523,000,000	1,426,000,000	943,000,000	673,000,000	
Return on Assets %	.10%	.13%	.01%	.05%	.02%	
Return on Equity %	1.23%	.74%	.03%	.18%	.07%	
Debt to Equity	5.12	1.05	0.746	0.268	0.517	

CONTACT INFORMATION:
Phone: 408 822-6000   Fax: 408 822-4501
Toll-Free: 877-263-8277
Address: 1395 Crossman Ave., Sunnyvale, CA 94089 United States

STOCK TICKER/OTHER:
Stock Ticker: NTAP
Employees: 10,800
Parent Company:

Exchange: NAS
Fiscal Year Ends: 04/30

SALARIES/BONUSES:
Top Exec. Salary: $ Bonus: $
Second Exec. Salary: $ Bonus: $

OTHER THOUGHTS:
Estimated Female Officers or Directors: 4
Hot Spot for Advancement for Women/Minorities: Y

Netflix Inc
NAIC Code: 515210

TYPES OF BUSINESS:
Streaming Movies and TV Shows
DVD Rentals by Mail
Motion Picture Production
Original Filmed Entertainment

BRANDS/DIVISIONS/AFFILIATES:

CONTACTS: Note: Officers with more than one job title may be intentionally listed here more than once.
Reed Hastings, CEO
Spencer Neumann, CFO
Kelly Bennett, Chief Marketing Officer
David Hyman, General Counsel
Ted Sarandos, Other Executive Officer
Rachel Whetstone, Other Executive Officer
Jessica Neal, Other Executive Officer
Greg Peters, Other Executive Officer

GROWTH PLANS/SPECIAL FEATURES:
Netflix, Inc. is one of the largest online movie rental subscription services, providing access to a library of movie, television and other filmed entertainment titles to more than 195 million subscribers in over 190 countries, as of September 30, 2020. The company's domestic and international streaming segments derive revenues from monthly membership fees for services consisting solely of streaming content. The domestic DVD segment derives revenues from monthly membership fees for services consisting solely of DVD-by-mail, a service offered to U.S. subscribers. Members can watch as much as they want, anytime, anywhere, on any internet-connected screen. Members can play, pause and resume watching, all without commercials or commitments. Additionally, through its Netflix Studios division, the company produces original content available exclusively on Netflix. During 2020, Netflix acquired approximately 16 million new subscribers due to the COVID-19 pandemic.

FINANCIAL DATA: Note: Data for latest year may not have been available at press time.

In U.S. $	2020	2019	2018	2017	2016	2015
Revenue	24,996,060,000	20,156,450,000	15,794,340,000	11,692,710,000	8,830,669,000	6,779,511,000
R&D Expense						
Operating Income	4,585,289,000	2,604,254,000	1,605,226,000	838,679,000	379,793,000	305,826,000
Operating Margin %		.13%	.10%	.07%	.04%	.05%
SGA Expense	5,134,448,000	5,111,980,000	4,221,577,000	3,194,368,000	2,420,975,000	1,882,209,000
Net Income	2,761,395,000	1,866,916,000	1,211,242,000	558,929,000	186,678,000	122,641,000
Operating Cash Flow	2,427,077,000	-2,887,322,000	-2,680,479,000	-1,785,948,000	-1,473,984,000	-749,439,000
Capital Expenditure	497,923,000	253,035,000	212,532,000	227,022,000	184,830,000	169,206,000
EBITDA	15,507,910,000	12,008,080,000	9,303,408,000	7,169,064,000	5,335,599,000	3,852,871,000
Return on Assets %		.06%	.05%	.03%	.02%	.01%
Return on Equity %		.29%	.27%	.18%	.08%	.06%
Debt to Equity		1.947	1.978	1.814	1.255	1.067

CONTACT INFORMATION:
Phone: 408 540-3700   Fax: 408 540-3737
Toll-Free: 1-877-742-1480
Address: 100 Winchester Cir., Los Gatos, CA 95032 United States

SALARIES/BONUSES:
Top Exec. Salary: $ Bonus: $
Second Exec. Salary: $ Bonus: $

STOCK TICKER/OTHER:
Stock Ticker: NFLX
Employees: 9,400
Parent Company:

Exchange: NAS
Fiscal Year Ends: 12/31

OTHER THOUGHTS:
Estimated Female Officers or Directors: 3
Hot Spot for Advancement for Women/Minorities: Y

New York Life Insurance Company

www.newyorklife.com

NAIC Code: 524113

TYPES OF BUSINESS:

Life Insurance
Annuities
Mutual Funds
Asset Management
Life Insurance
Real Estate

BRANDS/DIVISIONS/AFFILIATES:

MainStay Investments

CONTACTS: *Note: Officers with more than one job title may be intentionally listed here more than once.*

Theodore A. Mathas, CEO
Craig L. De Santo, Pres.
Eric A. Feldstein, Exec. VP
Carla T. Rutigliano, Sr. VP-Human Resources
David J. Castellani, Sr. VP
Frank M. Boccio, Chief Admin. Officer
Sheila K. Davidson, General Counsel
Barry Schub, Sr. VP-Strategy & Communications
George Nichols, III, Sr. VP-Office of Gov't Affairs
Christopher O. Blunt, Exec. VP
Mark W. Pfaff, Exec. VP
Susan A. Thrope, Deputy General Counsel
Theodore A. Mathas, Chmn.

GROWTH PLANS/SPECIAL FEATURES:

New York Life Insurance Company provides life insurance, investments, retirement income and long-term care insurance. The firm operates through two segments: insurance products and investment products. Insurance products include life insurance and long-term care insurance. Types of life insurance includes term life, whole life, universal life, variable universal life, corporate sponsored plans and group membership associations. Long-term insurance helps provide for the cost of long-term care generally not covered by health insurance, Medicare or Medicaid. Investment products include retirement income, investment annuities and mutual funds. Retirement income offers several guaranteed income annuity products such as lifetime income annuities, future income annuities, lifetime mutual income annuities and future mutual income annuities. Investment annuities are types of savings plans that help prepare individuals for retirement and come in the form of variable annuities and fixed deferred annuities. Mutual funds are provided under New York Life's MainStay Investments registered service mark and name, offering a broad selection of mutual funds across multiple asset classes and investment styles. These investments include U.S./international/global stock funds; investment grade, high yield and municipal bond funds; and asset allocation funds that invest in a mix of asset classes and investment styles. In addition, New York Life offers premier services, helping premier clients and small business owners reach their retirement, estate planning and business goals. This division has professionals in law, taxation, accounting, business, insurance and philanthropic planning who can work with the clients' financial advisor.

FINANCIAL DATA: *Note: Data for latest year may not have been available at press time.*

In U.S. $	2020	2019	2018	2017	2016	2015
Revenue	32,054,000,000	34,499,000,000	28,770,000,000	30,328,000,000	27,908,000,000	26,127,000,000
R&D Expense						
Operating Income						
Operating Margin %						
SGA Expense						
Net Income	1,501,000,000	3,117,000,000	1,789,000,000	3,039,000,000	1,638,000,000	1,785,000,000
Operating Cash Flow						
Capital Expenditure						
EBITDA						
Return on Assets %						
Return on Equity %						
Debt to Equity						

CONTACT INFORMATION:

Phone: 212-576-7000 Fax: 212-576-8145
Toll-Free: 800-692-3086
Address: 51 Madison Ave., New York, NY 10010 United States

STOCK TICKER/OTHER:

Stock Ticker: Mutual Company
Employees: 11,388
Parent Company:

Exchange:
Fiscal Year Ends: 12/31

SALARIES/BONUSES:

Top Exec. Salary: $ Bonus: $
Second Exec. Salary: $ Bonus: $

OTHER THOUGHTS:

Estimated Female Officers or Directors: 4
Hot Spot for Advancement for Women/Minorities: Y

Newfold Digital Inc

newfold.com

NAIC Code: 518210

TYPES OF BUSINESS:

Web Hosting Products & Services
Web Design Services
Search Engine
eCommerce
Advertising
Domain Name

BRANDS/DIVISIONS/AFFILIATES:

Siris Capital Group LLC
Clearlake Capital Group LP
Web.com Online Marketing
Web.com Contractor Services
Network Solutions
Register.com
Name Jet
bluehost inc.

CONTACTS: Note: Officers with more than one job title may be intentionally listed here more than once.

Sharon Rowlands, CEO
Christine Barry, COO
Christina Clohecy, CFO
Paula Drum, CMO
Deb Myers, Chief People Officer
Michael Bouchet, CIO
Roseann Duran, Executive VP

GROWTH PLANS/SPECIAL FEATURES:

Newfold Digital Inc, a result of the combination of Web.com Group, Inc. and Endurance Web Presence, is a web technology company servicing millions of customers worldwide. The firm's portfolio of brands include Web.com, Network Solutions, Register.com, Name Jet, bluehost inc. Web.com Online Marketing Agency offers search engine optimization and placement solutions. Web.com Contractor Services is a online networking platform that displays over 3,000 remodeling contractors who carry out bathroom remodeling, kitchen remodeling, attic remodeling and basement remodeling projects, from which homeowners can locate and hire. Network Solutions helps small businesses to start and market their businesses on the web, offering a full range of web-related services. Register.com is a leading provider of global domain name registration, website design and management services. The platform is also a business web hosting provider. NameJet is the premier aftermarket domain name service. Bluehost inc. is a web hosting solutions company. In February 2021, Siris Capital Group, LLC and Clearlake Capital Group, L.P. announced the formation of Newfold Digital through the combination of Endurance Web Presence and Web.com Group, Inc.

FINANCIAL DATA: Note: Data for latest year may not have been available at press time.

In U.S. $	2020	2019	2018	2017	2016	2015
Revenue	833,250,000	825,000,000	798,000,000	749,260,992	710,505,024	543,460,992
R&D Expense						
Operating Income						
Operating Margin %						
SGA Expense						
Net Income		55,795,611	54,701,580	53,629,000	3,990,000	89,961,000
Operating Cash Flow						
Capital Expenditure						
EBITDA						
Return on Assets %						
Return on Equity %						
Debt to Equity						

CONTACT INFORMATION:

Phone: 904 680-6600   Fax: 904 880-0350
Toll-Free:
Address: 5335 Gate Pkwy., Jacksonville, FL 32256 United States

STOCK TICKER/OTHER:

Stock Ticker: Private
Employees: 3,600
Parent Company: Siris Capital Group LLC

Exchange:
Fiscal Year Ends: 12/31

SALARIES/BONUSES:

Top Exec. Salary: $ Bonus: $
Second Exec. Salary: $ Bonus: $

OTHER THOUGHTS:

Estimated Female Officers or Directors: 3
Hot Spot for Advancement for Women/Minorities: Y

Sales, profits and employees may be estimates. Financial information, benefits and other data can change quickly and may vary from those stated here.

NextEra Energy Inc

NAIC Code: 221115

www.nexteraenergy.com

TYPES OF BUSINESS:

Wind Electric Power Generation
Fiber-Optic Services
Financial Services
Nuclear Power
Energy Trading & Marketing
Electric Power
Solar Power
Electricity Distribution

BRANDS/DIVISIONS/AFFILIATES:

Florida Power & Light Company
NextEra Energy Resources LLC
NextEra Energy Capital Holdings Inc
Gulf Power Company

CONTACTS: Note: Officers with more than one job title may be intentionally listed here more than once.

Paul Cutler, Assistant Secretary
Manoochehr Nazar, Other Executive Officer
Eric Silagy, CEO, Subsidiary
John Ketchum, CEO, Subsidiary
James Robo, CEO
Rebecca Kujawa, CFO
James May, Chief Accounting Officer, Subsidiary
Joseph Kelliher, Executive VP, Divisional
William Yeager, Executive VP, Divisional
Deborah Caplan, Executive VP, Divisional
Miguel Arechabala, Executive VP, Divisional
Charles Sieving, Executive VP
Terrell Crews, Vice President, Subsidiary

GROWTH PLANS/SPECIAL FEATURES:

NextEra Energy, Inc. is one of the largest electric power companies in North America and a leader in the renewable energy industry. The firm has approximately 54,400 megawatts (MW) of generating capacity, with electric generation capacity across 37 states in the U.S., four provinces in Canada and in Spain. NextEra provides retail and wholesale electric services to more than 10 million customers. It owns generation, transmission and distribution facilities to support its services. The company also has investments in gas infrastructure assets. NextEra's business strategy emphasizes the development, acquisition and operation of renewable, nuclear and natural gas-fired generation facilities in response to long-term federal policy trends supportive of zero and low air emission sources of power. Nearly 100% of the company's generation comes from renewable, nuclear and natural gas-fired facilities. The firm conducts its operations principally through two wholly owned subsidiaries: Florida Power & Light Company (FPL) and NextEra Energy Resources, LLC (NEER). In addition, subsidiary NextEra Energy Capital Holdings, Inc. owns and provides funding for NEER and all NextEra subsidiaries other than FPL. FPL is the largest electric utility in the state of Florida and one of the largest electric utilities in the U.S. NEER is the world's largest operator of wind and solar projects. Additionally, NextEra also operates the recently acquired Gulf Power Company. Gulf Power serves approximately 470,000 customers in eight counties throughout northwest Florida and had approximately 2,300 MW of fossil-fueled electric net generating capacity and 9,500 miles of transmission and distribution lines located primarily in Florida. In September 2020, the firm agreed to acquire GridLiance Holdco, LP and GridLiance GP, LLC from Blackstone for approximately $660 million.

NextEra Energy offers employees medical, dental and vision benefits; flexible spending plans; life insurance and dependent life insurance; vacation time; and education and adoption assistance.

FINANCIAL DATA: Note: Data for latest year may not have been available at press time.

In U.S. $	2020	2019	2018	2017	2016	2015
Revenue	17,997,000,000	19,204,000,000	16,727,000,000	17,195,000,000	16,155,000,000	17,486,000,000
R&D Expense						
Operating Income	4,763,000,000	5,054,000,000	4,243,000,000	4,730,000,000	4,297,000,000	4,660,000,000
Operating Margin %		.26%	.25%	.28%	.27%	.27%
SGA Expense						
Net Income	2,919,000,000	3,769,000,000	6,638,000,000	5,378,000,000	2,912,000,000	2,752,000,000
Operating Cash Flow	7,983,000,000	8,155,000,000	6,593,000,000	6,413,000,000	6,336,000,000	6,116,000,000
Capital Expenditure	7,759,000,000	11,077,000,000	6,010,000,000	5,445,000,000	4,240,000,000	3,872,000,000
EBITDA	8,678,000,000	10,563,000,000	12,997,000,000	8,854,000,000	8,858,000,000	8,404,000,000
Return on Assets %		.03%	.07%	.06%	.03%	.03%
Return on Equity %		.11%	.21%	.20%	.12%	.13%
Debt to Equity		1.015	0.784	1.115	1.143	1.182

CONTACT INFORMATION:

Phone: 561 694-4000   Fax: 561 694-4620
Toll-Free: 888-218-4392
Address: 700 Universe Blvd., Juno Beach, FL 33408 United States

STOCK TICKER/OTHER:

Stock Ticker: NEE
Employees: 14,900
Parent Company:

Exchange: NYS
Fiscal Year Ends: 12/31

SALARIES/BONUSES:

Top Exec. Salary: $ Bonus: $
Second Exec. Salary: $ Bonus: $

OTHER THOUGHTS:

Estimated Female Officers or Directors: 5
Hot Spot for Advancement for Women/Minorities: Y

Nielsen Holdings plc

www.nielsen.com

NAIC Code: 541910

TYPES OF BUSINESS:

Market Research
Magazine Publishing
Media/Entertainment Audience Research
Trade Publications
Directories
Business Consulting
Internet Audience Research

BRANDS/DIVISIONS/AFFILIATES:

Nielsen Global Connect
Nielsen Global Media
Precima

CONTACTS: Note: Officers with more than one job title may be intentionally listed here more than once.

David Kenny, CEO
David Anderson, CFO
George Callard, Chief Legal Officer
Giovanni Tavolieri, Chief Technology Officer
James Attwood, Director
Nancy Phillips, Other Executive Officer

GROWTH PLANS/SPECIAL FEATURES:

Nielsen Holdings plc is a leading global provider of marketing information, audience measurement and business media products and services with operations in over 100 countries and data measurements of millions of consumers worldwide. The firm has two major segments: Nielsen Global Connect (watch) and Nielsen Global Media (buy). Accounting for about half (47% in 2019) of Nielsen's annual revenues, the watch segment provides viewership data and analytics primarily to the media industry, and advertising across three primary platforms that include mobile screens, online and television. Clients of this segment use Nielsen's data to plan and optimize their advertising spending and to better ensure that their advertisements reach the intended audience. The buy segment (53%) provides consumer behavior information and analytics primarily to businesses in the consumer-packaged goods industry. Clients use the data to manage their brands, find new sources of demand, launch and grow new products, improve their marketing mix and establish more effective consumer relationships. In January 2020, the firm acquired Precima, a software-as-a-service provider of retail and customer data applications and analytics, from Alliance Data Systems Corp. IN November of the same year, Nielsen agreed to sell its Nielsen Global Connect business to affilates of Advent International for $2.7 billion.

FINANCIAL DATA: Note: Data for latest year may not have been available at press time.

In U.S. $	2020	2019	2018	2017	2016	2015
Revenue	6,290,000,000	6,498,000,000	6,515,000,000	6,572,000,000	6,309,000,000	6,172,000,000
R&D Expense						
Operating Income	794,000,000	991,000,000	1,077,000,000	1,305,000,000	1,248,000,000	1,144,000,000
Operating Margin %		.15%	.17%	.20%	.20%	.19%
SGA Expense	1,872,000,000	1,929,000,000	1,958,000,000	1,862,000,000	1,851,000,000	1,915,000,000
Net Income	-6,000,000	-415,000,000	-712,000,000	429,000,000	502,000,000	570,000,000
Operating Cash Flow	999,000,000	1,066,000,000	1,058,000,000	1,310,000,000	1,296,000,000	1,179,000,000
Capital Expenditure	519,000,000	519,000,000	520,000,000	489,000,000	433,000,000	408,000,000
EBITDA	1,309,000,000	490,000,000	187,000,000	1,842,000,000	1,752,000,000	1,846,000,000
Return on Assets %		-.03%	-.04%	.03%	.03%	.04%
Return on Equity %		-.16%	-.20%	.10%	.12%	.12%
Debt to Equity		3.538	2.908	1.969	1.886	1.585

CONTACT INFORMATION:

Phone: 646 654-5000   Fax:
Toll-Free: 800-864-1224
Address: 85 Broad St., New York, NY 10004 United States

STOCK TICKER/OTHER:

Stock Ticker: NLSN
Employees: 43,000
Parent Company:

Exchange: NYS
Fiscal Year Ends: 12/31

SALARIES/BONUSES:

Top Exec. Salary: $ Bonus: $
Second Exec. Salary: $ Bonus: $

OTHER THOUGHTS:

Estimated Female Officers or Directors: 4
Hot Spot for Advancement for Women/Minorities: Y

NiSource Inc

NAIC Code: 221210

www.nisource.com

TYPES OF BUSINESS:

Utilities-Electricity & Natural Gas
Energy Marketing
Electricity Generation & Distribution
Gas Transmission & Storage
Gas Distribution

BRANDS/DIVISIONS/AFFILIATES:

NiSource Gas Distribution Group Inc
Northern Indiana Public Service Company

CONTACTS: *Note: Officers with more than one job title may be intentionally listed here more than once.*

Joseph Hamrock, CEO
Joseph Mulpas, Chief Accounting Officer
Carrie Hightman, Chief Legal Officer
Kevin Kabat, Director
Donald Brown, Executive VP
Pablo Vegas, Executive VP
Violet Sistovaris, Executive VP
Suzanne Surface, Other Corporate Officer
Peter Disser, Vice President, Divisional

GROWTH PLANS/SPECIAL FEATURES:

NiSource, Inc. is an energy holding company with subsidiaries that provide natural gas, electricity and other products and services to approximately 3.9 million customers in the U.S. NiSource operates in two segments: gas distribution and electric. The gas distribution segment serves approximately 3.5 million customers in seven states and operates approximately 60,000 miles of pipeline. Through wholly owned subsidiary NiSource Gas Distribution Group, Inc., NiSource owns six distribution subsidiaries that provide natural gas to approximately 2.7 million residential, commercial and industrial customers in Ohio, Pennsylvania, Virginia, Kentucky, Maryland and Massachusetts. Additionally, this division distributes natural gas to 839,000 customers in northern Indiana through wholly owned subsidiary Northern Indiana Public Service Company (NIPSCO). The electric segment generates, transmits and distributes electricity through NIPSCO to approximately 476,000 customers in 20 counties in the northern part of Indiana and engages in wholesale and transmission transactions. NIPSCO owns and operates two coal-fired electric generating stations, having a net capacity of 2,080 megawatts (MW); owns and operates Sugar Creek, a combined cycle gas turbine plant with a net capacity of 571 MW; owns and operates three gas-fired generating units with a net capability of 186 MW; and two hydroelectric generating plants with a net capability of 10 MW.

The firm offers employees a 401(k) plan and profit sharing plan; life insurance; medical, dental, vision, disability and prescription drug coverage; flexible spending accounts; tuition reimbursement; an employee assistance program; work-at-home opportunit

FINANCIAL DATA: *Note: Data for latest year may not have been available at press time.*

In U.S. $	2020	2019	2018	2017	2016	2015
Revenue	4,681,700,000	5,208,900,000	5,114,500,000	4,874,600,000	4,492,500,000	4,651,800,000
R&D Expense						
Operating Income	961,400,000	1,305,200,000	125,900,000	916,100,000	857,200,000	801,500,000
Operating Margin %		.25%	.02%	.19%	.19%	.17%
SGA Expense						
Net Income	-17,600,000	383,100,000	-50,600,000	128,500,000	331,500,000	286,500,000
Operating Cash Flow	1,104,000,000	1,583,300,000	540,100,000	742,200,000	803,300,000	1,456,800,000
Capital Expenditure	1,758,100,000	1,802,400,000	1,818,200,000	1,695,800,000	1,475,200,000	1,360,700,000
EBITDA	1,056,500,000	1,595,000,000	733,900,000	1,376,900,000	1,413,200,000	1,238,600,000
Return on Assets %		.01%	.00%	.01%	.02%	.01%
Return on Equity %		.07%	-.01%	.03%	.08%	.06%
Debt to Equity		1.538	1.459	1.739	1.488	1.548

CONTACT INFORMATION:

Phone: 877 647-5990   Fax: 219 647-6085
Toll-Free: 877-647-5990
Address: 801 E. 86th Ave., Merrillville, IN 46410 United States

STOCK TICKER/OTHER:

Stock Ticker: NI
Employees: 7,389
Parent Company:

Exchange: NYS
Fiscal Year Ends: 12/31

SALARIES/BONUSES:

Top Exec. Salary: $ Bonus: $
Second Exec. Salary: $ Bonus: $

OTHER THOUGHTS:

Estimated Female Officers or Directors: 5
Hot Spot for Advancement for Women/Minorities: Y

North Highland Company (The)   www.northhighland.com

NAIC Code: 541610

TYPES OF BUSINESS:

Management & Technology Consulting Services
Consulting
Data
Analytics
Change Management
Process Analysis
Program Management
Technology

BRANDS/DIVISIONS/AFFILIATES:

CONTACTS: Note: Officers with more than one job title may be intentionally listed here more than once.

Daniel Reardon, CEO
Lauren Childers, CFO
Matthew Klein, CMO
Jennifer Mancuso, VP-Human Resources
Paul Falor, CIO
Richard Dobb, General Counsel
Maria Bothwell, Pres., New Ventures
Daniel Durham, Lead-Global Financial Svcs.
Nancy Schultz, Lead-Global Health Care
Albert Rees, Pres., Northeast Region
Bob Lamont, Pres., West Region
David Deiters, Pres., South Region
Daniel Reardon, Chmn.
Tony Doocey, Group VP-London

GROWTH PLANS/SPECIAL FEATURES:

The North Highland Company, in business for nearly 30 years, is a global consulting firm that serves clients through office across the Americas, Europe, the Middle East, Africa and Asia-Pacific. North Highland specializes in data, analytics, change management, process analysis, business analysis, program management, project management, strategy and technology. The company's solutions include accelerated service design, change economics, managed services and transformation momentum. North Highland serves a wide range of industries, including energy, utilities, financial services, healthcare, hospitality, leisure, life sciences, media/entertainment, communications, public sector, retail, consumer products and transportation.

North Highland offers its employees medical, dental, life and disability insurance; a 401(k) plan; an employee stock ownership plan; health and child care spending accounts; tuition reimbursement; and an employee assistance program.

FINANCIAL DATA: Note: Data for latest year may not have been available at press time.

In U.S. $	2020	2019	2018	2017	2016	2015
Revenue	555,000,000	546,000,000	520,000,000	510,000,000	500,000,000	474,150,000
R&D Expense						
Operating Income						
Operating Margin %						
SGA Expense						
Net Income						
Operating Cash Flow						
Capital Expenditure						
EBITDA						
Return on Assets %						
Return on Equity %						
Debt to Equity						

CONTACT INFORMATION:

Phone: 404-233-1015   Fax: 404-233-4930
Toll-Free:
Address: 3333 Piedmont Rd. NE, Ste. 1000, Atlanta, GA 30305 United States

STOCK TICKER/OTHER:

Stock Ticker: Private
Employees: 3,000
Parent Company:

Exchange:
Fiscal Year Ends:

SALARIES/BONUSES:

Top Exec. Salary: $ Bonus: $
Second Exec. Salary: $ Bonus: $

OTHER THOUGHTS:

Estimated Female Officers or Directors: 6
Hot Spot for Advancement for Women/Minorities: Y

Northrop Grumman Corporation
NAIC Code: 336411

www.northropgrumman.com

TYPES OF BUSINESS:
Aircraft Manufacturing
Shipbuilding & Engineering
Aircraft Manufacturing
Electronic Systems & Components
Hardware & Software Manufacturing
Design & Engineering Services
IT Systems & Services
Nuclear-Powered Aircraft Carriers & Submarines

BRANDS/DIVISIONS/AFFILIATES:
Northrop Grumman Innovation Systems

CONTACTS: *Note: Officers with more than one job title may be intentionally listed here more than once.*
Kathy Warden, CEO
Jennifer McGarey, Sec.
Kenneth Bedingfield, CFO
Wesley Bush, Chairman of the Board
Michael Hardesty, Chief Accounting Officer
Patrick Antkowiak, Chief Technology Officer
Sheila Cheston, General Counsel
Denise Peppard, Other Executive Officer
David Perry, Other Executive Officer
Christopher Jones, President, Divisional
Mark Caylor, President, Divisional
Janis Pamiljans, President, Divisional
Shawn Purvis, President, Divisional
Lesley Kalan, Vice President, Divisional
Lisa Davis, Vice President, Divisional

GROWTH PLANS/SPECIAL FEATURES:
Northrop Grumman Corporation (NGC) is a global aerospace and defense technology company. It has three primary segments: aerospace systems, mission systems, technology services and innovation systems. The aerospace systems segment designs, develops, integrates and produces manned aircraft, autonomous systems, spacecraft, high-energy laser systems, microelectronics and other systems/subsystems. This division's customers, primarily the Department of Defense (DoD) and other U.S. government agencies, use these systems in mission areas such as intelligence, surveillance and reconnaissance, strike operations, communications, earth observation, space science and space exploration. This division also produces autonomous aircraft systems for tactical and strategic intelligence, surveillance and reconnaissance (ISR) missions. The mission systems segment provides advanced end-to-end mission solutions and multifunction systems for DoD, intelligence community, international, federal civil and commercial customers. Its major products and services include C4ISR (command, control, communications and computer (C4)/ISR) systems; radar, electro-optical/infrared and acoustic sensors; electronic warfare systems; cyber solutions; space systems; intelligence processing systems; air and missile defense integration; navigation; and shipboard missile and encapsulated payload launch systems. Last, the technology services segment provides logistics solutions supporting the full life cycle of platforms and systems for global defense and federal-civil customers. Its offerings include software and system sustainment, modernization of platforms and associated subsystems, advanced training solutions and integrated logistics support. Northrop Grumman Innovation Systems designs, builds and delivers space, defense and aviation-related systems. The segments main products include launch vehicles, propulsion systems, missile products, defense electronics, armament systems and ammunition. In December 2020, NGC agreed to sell its federal IT and mission support services business for $3.4 billion in cash to Veritas Capital. The transaction was expected to close by mid-2021.

FINANCIAL DATA: *Note: Data for latest year may not have been available at press time.*

In U.S. $	2020	2019	2018	2017	2016	2015
Revenue	36,799,000,000	33,841,000,000	30,095,000,000	25,803,000,000	24,508,000,000	23,526,000,000
R&D Expense						
Operating Income	4,065,000,000	3,969,000,000	3,780,000,000	3,299,000,000	3,193,000,000	3,076,000,000
Operating Margin %		.12%	.13%	.13%	.13%	.13%
SGA Expense	3,413,000,000	3,290,000,000	3,011,000,000	2,655,000,000	2,584,000,000	2,566,000,000
Net Income	3,189,000,000	2,248,000,000	3,229,000,000	2,015,000,000	2,200,000,000	1,990,000,000
Operating Cash Flow	4,305,000,000	4,297,000,000	3,827,000,000	2,613,000,000	2,813,000,000	2,162,000,000
Capital Expenditure	1,420,000,000	1,264,000,000	1,249,000,000	928,000,000	920,000,000	471,000,000
EBITDA	5,588,000,000	4,094,000,000	5,104,000,000	3,884,000,000	3,680,000,000	3,558,000,000
Return on Assets %		.06%	.09%	.07%	.09%	.08%
Return on Equity %		.26%	.42%	.33%	.41%	.31%
Debt to Equity		1.596	1.696	2.043	1.342	1.162

CONTACT INFORMATION:
Phone: 703 280-2900   Fax: 310 201-3023
Toll-Free:
Address: 2980 Fairview Park Dr., Falls Church, VA 22042 United States

SALARIES/BONUSES:
Top Exec. Salary: $ Bonus: $
Second Exec. Salary: $ Bonus: $

STOCK TICKER/OTHER:
Stock Ticker: NOC   Exchange: NYS
Employees: 97,000   Fiscal Year Ends: 12/31
Parent Company:

OTHER THOUGHTS:
Estimated Female Officers or Directors: 9
Hot Spot for Advancement for Women/Minorities: Y

Sales, profits and employees may be estimates. Financial information, benefits and other data can change quickly and may vary from those stated here.

Northwestern Mutual Life Insurance Company (The)

www.northwesternmutual.com
NAIC Code: 524113

TYPES OF BUSINESS:

Life Insurance
Disability Insurance
Employee Benefit Plans
Long-Term Care Insurance
Investment Products & Services
Financial Planning Services

BRANDS/DIVISIONS/AFFILIATES:

Northwestern Long Term Care Insurance Company
Northwestern Mutual Investment Services LLC
Northwestern Mutual Investment Management Co LLC
Northwestern Mutual Wealth Management Company
Mason Street Advisors LLC

CONTACTS: *Note: Officers with more than one job title may be intentionally listed here more than once.*

John E. Schlifske, CEO
Souheil Badran, COO
Michael G. Carter, CFO
Christian W. Mitchell, CCO
Don J. Robertson, Exec. VP
Neal J. Sample, CIO
Jean M. Maier, Exec. VP-Tech.
Raymond J. Manista, General Counsel
Jean M. Maier, Exec. VP-Enterprise Oper.
Ronald P. Joelson, Exec. VP
Todd M. Schoon, Exec. VP-Agencies
John E. Schlifske, Chmn.

GROWTH PLANS/SPECIAL FEATURES:

Northwestern Mutual Life Insurance Company (NMLIC) is a financial network that, together with its subsidiaries, offers network services, insurance products, investment products and advisory services. Its network services include asset and income protection, personal needs analysis, investment services, education funding and retirement products. NMLIC itself issues life and disability insurance, annuities, and life insurance with long-term care benefits. Subsidiary Northwestern Long Term Care Insurance Company issues long-term care insurance. Northwestern Mutual Investment Services, LLC is a broker-dealer and registered investment advisor that serves the investment planning and product needs of individuals and businesses. This company's special account services include electronic transfers, dividend reinvestment, a mutual fund purchase program, account protection, direct deposit, check writing privileges and online account access. It also offers a variety of individual investment services such as college education funding and IRA (individual retirement account) solutions. Northwestern Mutual Investment Management Company, LLC manages NMLIC's investments in publicly-traded debt and equity securities, privately-placed debt and equity securities, interests in private equity funds, mortgage loans and real estate equity. Northwestern Mutual Wealth Management Company is a limited purpose federal savings bank that also provides investment management, trust services and fee-based financial planning. This subsidiary is not a broker-dealer or insurance company. Mason Street Advisors, LLC is an investment advisor for Northwestern Mutual Series Fund variable annuity and variable life products.

FINANCIAL DATA: *Note: Data for latest year may not have been available at press time.*

In U.S. $	2020	2019	2018	2017	2016	2015
Revenue	31,124,000,000	29,855,000,000	28,482,000,000	28,087,000,000	28,158,000,000	27,880,000,000
R&D Expense						
Operating Income						
Operating Margin %						
SGA Expense						
Net Income	425,000,000	1,268,000,000	783,000,000	1,017,000,000	818,000,000	815,000,000
Operating Cash Flow						
Capital Expenditure						
EBITDA						
Return on Assets %						
Return on Equity %						
Debt to Equity						

CONTACT INFORMATION:

Phone: 414-271-1444   Fax: 414-299-7022
Toll-Free:
Address: 720 E. Wisconsin Ave., Milwaukee, WI 53202 United States

STOCK TICKER/OTHER:

Stock Ticker: Mutual Company
Employees: 5,900
Parent Company:

Exchange:
Fiscal Year Ends: 12/31

SALARIES/BONUSES:

Top Exec. Salary: $ Bonus: $
Second Exec. Salary: $ Bonus: $

OTHER THOUGHTS:

Estimated Female Officers or Directors: 5
Hot Spot for Advancement for Women/Minorities: Y

NortonLifeLock Inc

NAIC Code: 511210E

www.nortonlifelock.com

TYPES OF BUSINESS:

Computer Software: Network Security, Managed Access, Digital ID,
Cybersecurity & Anti-Virus
Cybersecurity
Identity Security

BRANDS/DIVISIONS/AFFILIATES:

NortonLifeLock
Norton 360

CONTACTS: *Note: Officers with more than one job title may be intentionally listed here more than once.*

Richard Hill, CEO
Vincent Pilette, CFO
Daniel Schulman, Chairman of the Board
Matthew Brown, Chief Accounting Officer
Samir Kapuria, Executive VP, Divisional
Scott Taylor, Executive VP
Amy Cappellanti-Wolf, Senior VP

GROWTH PLANS/SPECIAL FEATURES:

NortonLifeLock, Inc. provides cyber safety solutions for consumers worldwide. The company's business is built around the prevention, detection and restoration of potential damages caused by cyber criminals. The firm's solutions help secure the devices, identities, online privacy, and home and family needs of nearly 50 million consumers globally. NortonLifeLock offers subscription-based cyber safety solutions marketed under the NortonLifeLock brand, which integrates with its cyber safety platform Norton 360. The company sells its products primarily direct-to-consumer through its in-house eCommerce platform, and indirectly through partner relationships with retailers, telecommunication service providers, hardware original equipment manufacturers (OEMs), and employee benefit providers. Most subscriptions are sold on either annual or monthly terms. In December 2020, NortonLifeLock agreed to acquire Avira in an all-cash transaction for approximately $360 million. Avira provides a consumer-focused portfolio of cybersecurity and privacy solutions primarily within the European market, as well as emerging markets. In August 2021, NortonLifeLock agreed to acquire and combine with cybersecurity firm Avast in a cash-and-stock deal that has an equity value between $8.1 billion and $8.6 billion.

NortonLifeLock offers its employees health and financial benefits, including medical/dental/vision insurance and an employee stock purchase program.

FINANCIAL DATA: *Note: Data for latest year may not have been available at press time.*

In U.S. $	2020	2019	2018	2017	2016	2015
Revenue	2,490,000,000	4,731,000,000	4,834,000,000	4,019,000,000	3,600,000,000	
R&D Expense	328,000,000	913,000,000	956,000,000	823,000,000	748,000,000	
Operating Income	621,000,000	621,000,000	459,000,000	173,000,000	593,000,000	
Operating Margin %	.25%	.13%	.09%	.04%	.16%	
SGA Expense	1,069,000,000	1,940,000,000	2,167,000,000	2,023,000,000	1,587,000,000	
Net Income	3,887,000,000	31,000,000	1,138,000,000	-106,000,000	2,488,000,000	
Operating Cash Flow	-861,000,000	1,495,000,000	950,000,000	-220,000,000	796,000,000	
Capital Expenditure	89,000,000	207,000,000	142,000,000	70,000,000	272,000,000	
EBITDA	1,376,000,000	931,000,000	1,333,000,000	476,000,000	766,000,000	
Return on Assets %	.33%	.00%	.07%	-.01%	.20%	
Return on Equity %	1.35%	.01%	.27%	-.03%	.52%	
Debt to Equity	353.80	0.69	1.001	1.972	0.60	

CONTACT INFORMATION:

Phone: 650 527-8000   Fax:
Toll-Free:
Address: 60 E. Rio Salado Pkwy, Ste. 1000, Tempe, AZ 85281 United States

STOCK TICKER/OTHER:

Stock Ticker: NLOK
Employees: 2,800
Parent Company:

Exchange: NAS
Fiscal Year Ends: 03/31

SALARIES/BONUSES:

Top Exec. Salary: $ Bonus: $
Second Exec. Salary: $ Bonus: $

OTHER THOUGHTS:

Estimated Female Officers or Directors: 3
Hot Spot for Advancement for Women/Minorities: Y

Nutanix Inc

www.nutanix.com

NAIC Code: 511210B

TYPES OF BUSINESS:

Computer Software: Network Management (IT), System Testing & Storage
Cloud-Based Data Storage

BRANDS/DIVISIONS/AFFILIATES:

Nutanix Core
Acropolis
Nutanix Essentials
Calm
Nutanix Enterprise
Karbon
Xi Cloud Services

CONTACTS: Note: Officers with more than one job title may be intentionally listed here more than once.

Dheeraj Pandey, CEO
Duston Williams, CFO
Aaron Boynton, Controller
David Sangster, Executive VP, Divisional
Sunil Potti, Other Executive Officer
Tyler Wall, Other Executive Officer

GROWTH PLANS/SPECIAL FEATURES:

Nutanix, Inc. provides a leading enterprise cloud platform with software solutions that power business applications by digitizing the traditional silos of enterprise computing. The company's software solutions run on a variety of underlying hardware platforms, which decouples the software from its Nutanix-branded hardware appliances and creates a true enterprise cloud operating system that can power a variety of on-premises private cloud deployment. Nutanix's enterprise cloud platform encompasses its hyperconverged infrastructure (HCI) products. The Nutanix Core modernizes IT infrastructures, migrating them from a traditional one to an integrated on-premises enterprise cloud platform via: Acropolis, a software-defined HCI product; Prism, an HCI control plane and management console; and AHV, a hypervisor that provides free virtualization. Nutanix Essentials builds on the Core offerings and enhances security, automation, data management and operational efficiencies. Essentials is comprised of: Calm, which adds native application orchestration, automation and lifecycle management to the cloud platform; Files, a software-defined storage consolidation solution; Flow, an application-centric network and policy management solution; and Prism Pro, a set of features that provide customers with advanced analytics and intelligent insights into their Nutanix environments. Last, Nutanix Enterprise provides a suite of products and services that give customers additional choice, enabling new capabilities as customers advance from on-premises deployments into the hybrid and multi-cloud deployment stage of their enterprise cloud journey. Enterprise is composed of: Objects, a scalable, software-defined object storage solution; Karbon, a turn-key, enterprise-grade Kubernetes service that simplifies the provisioning, operations and lifecycle management of Kubernetes; Move, which simplifies and streamlines the enterprise cloud transition by enabling the mobility of applications across public and private cloud environments; Era, a database services software that automates and simplifies database provisioning and lifecycle management; Volumes, a scale-out storage solution; and Xi Cloud Services, a suite of cloud-based services for multi-cloud management.

FINANCIAL DATA: Note: Data for latest year may not have been available at press time.

In U.S. $	2020	2019	2018	2017	2016	2015
Revenue	1,307,682,000	1,236,143,000	1,155,457,000	766,869,000	444,928,000	241,432,000
R&D Expense	553,978,000	500,719,000	313,777,000	288,619,000	116,400,000	73,510,000
Operating Income	-828,921,000	-598,041,000	-280,408,000	-426,951,000	-165,017,000	-118,765,000
Operating Margin %		-.48%	-.24%	-.56%	-.37%	-.49%
SGA Expense	1,295,936,000	1,029,337,000	736,058,000	577,870,000	322,758,000	185,728,000
Net Income	-872,883,000	-621,179,000	-297,161,000	-458,011,000	-168,499,000	-126,127,000
Operating Cash Flow	-159,885,000	42,168,000	92,555,000	13,822,000	3,636,000	-25,694,000
Capital Expenditure	89,488,000	118,452,000	62,372,000	50,181,000	42,294,000	23,308,000
EBITDA	-735,148,000	-520,429,000	-230,106,000	-388,552,000	-138,609,000	-102,198,000
Return on Assets %		-.37%	-.26%	-.81%	-.52%	-.68%
Return on Equity %		-2.42%	-1.58%			
Debt to Equity		2.455	1.315			

CONTACT INFORMATION:

Phone: 855-688-2649   Fax: 408-916-4039
Toll-Free:
Address: 1740 Technology Dr., Ste. 150, San Jose, CA 95110 United States

STOCK TICKER/OTHER:

Stock Ticker: NTNX
Employees: 6,170
Parent Company:

Exchange: NAS
Fiscal Year Ends: 07/31

SALARIES/BONUSES:

Top Exec. Salary: $ Bonus: $
Second Exec. Salary: $ Bonus: $

OTHER THOUGHTS:

Estimated Female Officers or Directors:
Hot Spot for Advancement for Women/Minorities:

Sales, profits and employees may be estimates. Financial information, benefits and other data can change quickly and may vary from those stated here.

NVIDIA Corporation

NAIC Code: 334413

TYPES OF BUSINESS:

Printed Circuit & Chips Manufacturing
Graphics Processors
Graphics Software
Artificial Intelligence
Compute
Networking
Data Center
Robotics

BRANDS/DIVISIONS/AFFILIATES:

GeForce
Quadro
Mellanox
DRIVE
Jetson

CONTACTS: *Note: Officers with more than one job title may be intentionally listed here more than once.*

Jen-Hsun Huang, CEO
Colette Kress, CFO
Michael Mccaffery, Chairman of the Board
Donald Robertson, Chief Accounting Officer
Ajay Puri, Executive VP, Divisional
Debora Shoquist, Executive VP, Divisional
Timothy Teter, Executive VP
Michael Byron, Vice President, Divisional

GROWTH PLANS/SPECIAL FEATURES:

NVIDIA Corporation designs, develops and markets a family of 3D graphics processors, graphics processing units (GPUs), artificial intelligence (AI) and related software. The company specializes in products and platforms for the large, growing markets of gaming, professional visualization, data center, and automotive. NVIDIA operates through two business segments: graphics and compute & networking. The graphics segment includes GeForce GPUs for gaming and PCs, the GeForce NOW game streaming service and related infrastructure, and solutions for gaming platforms. This division's Quadro GPUs are for enterprise design; its GRID software is for cloud-based visual and virtual computing; and its automotive platforms include infotainment systems. The compute & networking segment includes data center platforms and systems for artificial intelligence (AI)-based, high-performing and accelerated computing; Mellanox networking and interconnect solutions; DRIVE for autonomous vehicles; and Jetson for robotics and other embedded platforms. During the first half of 2020, Nvidia completed its acquisition of networking firm Mellanox Technologies Ltd. In September of the same year, the firm agreed to acquire Arm Limited from SoftBank Group Corp. for approximately $40 billion. The transaction, still subject to regulatory approval, is expected to close in 18 months.

NVIDIA offers its employees medical benefits, an employee stock purchase plan and flexible paid leave of absence.

FINANCIAL DATA: *Note: Data for latest year may not have been available at press time.*

In U.S. $	2020	2019	2018	2017	2016	2015
Revenue	10,918,000,000	11,716,000,000	9,714,000,000	6,910,000,000	5,010,000,000	
R&D Expense	2,829,000,000	2,376,000,000	1,797,000,000	1,463,000,000	1,331,000,000	
Operating Income	2,846,000,000	3,804,000,000	3,210,000,000	1,937,000,000	878,000,000	
Operating Margin %	.26%	.32%	.33%	.28%	.18%	
SGA Expense	1,093,000,000	991,000,000	815,000,000	663,000,000	602,000,000	
Net Income	2,796,000,000	4,141,000,000	3,047,000,000	1,666,000,000	614,000,000	
Operating Cash Flow	4,761,000,000	3,743,000,000	3,502,000,000	1,672,000,000	1,175,000,000	
Capital Expenditure	489,000,000	600,000,000	593,000,000	176,000,000	86,000,000	
EBITDA	3,403,000,000	4,216,000,000	3,456,000,000	2,150,000,000	987,000,000	
Return on Assets %	.18%	.34%	.29%	.19%	.08%	
Return on Equity %	.26%	.49%	.46%	.33%	.14%	
Debt to Equity	0.209	0.213	0.266	0.345	0.002	

CONTACT INFORMATION:

Phone: 408 486-2000   Fax: 408 486-2200
Toll-Free:
Address: 2788 San Tomas Expressway, Santa Clara, CA 95051 United States

STOCK TICKER/OTHER:

Stock Ticker: NVDA
Employees: 18,975
Parent Company:

Exchange: NAS
Fiscal Year Ends: 01/31

SALARIES/BONUSES:

Top Exec. Salary: $ Bonus: $
Second Exec. Salary: $ Bonus: $

OTHER THOUGHTS:

Estimated Female Officers or Directors: 3
Hot Spot for Advancement for Women/Minorities: Y

NVR Inc

NAIC Code: 236117

TYPES OF BUSINESS:

Construction, Home Building and Residential
Mortgage Solutions
Townhouse Construction
Condominium Construction
Single-Family Homes

BRANDS/DIVISIONS/AFFILIATES:

NVR Mortgage Finance Inc
Ryan Homes
NVHomes
Heartland Homes

CONTACTS: Note: Officers with more than one job title may be intentionally listed here more than once.

Paul Saville, CEO
Daniel Malzahn, CFO
Dwight Schar, Chairman of the Board
Matthew Kelpy, Chief Accounting Officer
Paul Praylo, COO
Jeffrey Martchek, President, Divisional
Eugene Bredow, President, Subsidiary

GROWTH PLANS/SPECIAL FEATURES:

NVR, Inc. is primarily engaged in the construction and sale of single-family detached homes, townhomes and condominium buildings. Additionally, NVR offers mortgage banking services through its subsidiary NVR Mortgage Finance, Inc. (NVRM). NVRM originates mortgage loans for NVR's homebuilding customers and sells all mortgage loans it closes to investors in the secondary markets on a servicing released basis. The company operates in 14 states, with concentration in the Washington, D.C. and Baltimore, Maryland metropolitan areas, which accounted for 42% and 10% of its 2020 homebuilding revenues. NVR's homebuilding operations include the sale and construction of single-family detached homes, townhomes and condominium buildings under three brand names: Ryan Homes, NVHomes and Heartland Homes. The Ryan Homes products are moderately priced and marketed primarily to first-time homeowners and first-time move-up buyers. Ryan Homes are currently sold in 33 metropolitan areas located primarily in the eastern U.S. NVHomes and Heartland Homes are marketed primarily to move-up and upscale buyers. NVHomes are sold in Delaware, Washington, D.C., Baltimore and Philadelphia metropolitan areas. Heartland Homes are sold in Pittsburgh. The firm's houses range from approximately 1,000 to 9,000 square feet, typically including two to four bedrooms, and are priced between $140,000 and $1.5 million. NVR also provides mortgage-related services through its mortgage banking operations, which include subsidiaries that broker title insurance and perform title searches.

FINANCIAL DATA: Note: Data for latest year may not have been available at press time.

In U.S. $	2020	2019	2018	2017	2016	2015
Revenue	7,545,853,000	7,400,806,000	7,175,267,000	6,313,690,000	5,830,113,000	5,165,493,000
R&D Expense						
Operating Income	1,115,656,000	1,048,318,000	982,267,000	869,048,000	681,752,000	625,658,000
Operating Margin %		.14%	.14%	.14%	.12%	.12%
SGA Expense	509,734,000	527,405,000	512,712,000	460,800,000	443,320,000	424,009,000
Net Income	901,248,000	878,539,000	797,197,000	537,521,000	425,262,000	382,927,000
Operating Cash Flow	925,269,000	866,535,000	723,126,000	568,904,000	384,465,000	203,391,000
Capital Expenditure	16,119,000	22,699,000	19,665,000	20,269,000	22,369,000	18,277,000
EBITDA	1,140,897,000	1,071,993,000	1,004,981,000	893,763,000	705,673,000	648,305,000
Return on Assets %		.25%	.26%	.19%	.16%	.16%
Return on Equity %		.42%	.47%	.37%	.33%	.32%
Debt to Equity		0.292	0.33	0.372	0.457	0.484

CONTACT INFORMATION:

Phone: 703 956-4000   Fax: 703 956-4750
Toll-Free:
Address: 11700 Plaza America Dr., Ste. 500, Reston, VA 20190 United States

STOCK TICKER/OTHER:

Stock Ticker: NVR
Employees: 6,100
Parent Company:

Exchange: NYS
Fiscal Year Ends: 12/31

SALARIES/BONUSES:

Top Exec. Salary: $ Bonus: $
Second Exec. Salary: $ Bonus: $

OTHER THOUGHTS:

Estimated Female Officers or Directors:
Hot Spot for Advancement for Women/Minorities:

Old Dominion Freight Line Inc

www.odfl.com

NAIC Code: 484122

TYPES OF BUSINESS:

Trucking
LTL Trucking
Freight Logistics

BRANDS/DIVISIONS/AFFILIATES:

CONTACTS: *Note: Officers with more than one job title may be intentionally listed here more than once.*

Adam Satterfield, Assistant Secretary
Greg Gantt, CEO
David Congdon, Chairman of the Board
Earl Congdon, Chairman of the Board
Kimberly Maready, Chief Accounting Officer
Kevin Freeman, COO
Ross Parr, General Counsel
Christopher Brooks, Senior VP, Divisional
Gregory Plemmons, Senior VP, Divisional
Cecil Overbey, Senior VP, Divisional
David Bates, Senior VP, Divisional

GROWTH PLANS/SPECIAL FEATURES:

Old Dominion Freight Line, Inc. is a less-than-truckload (LTL) carrier providing regional, inter-regional and national services. These services include ground and air expedited transportation, as well as consumer household pickup and delivery (P&D), through a single integrated organization. In addition to Old Dominion's core LTL services, the company offers a range of value-added services, including container drayage, truckload brokerage, supply chain consulting and warehousing. More than 98% of revenue is derived from transporting LTL shipments for customers. Old Dominion conducts its operations through approximately 244 U.S. service center locations throughout the continental U.S., with major break-bulk facilities in Atlanta, Georgia; Columbus, Ohio; Indianapolis, Indiana; Greensboro, North Carolina; Harrisburg, Pennsylvania; Memphis and Morristown, Tennessee; Dallas, Texas; and Salt Lake City, Utah. The firm comprises about 45,938 tractors and trailers, with more than 24,500 trailers being 28 feet in length for line haul operations. These trailers are often combined into tractor-trailer-trailer combinations, allowing goods to be shipped with minimal unload/reload handling. Tractors are generally used in long-distance operations for roughly three to five years and are then transferred to less demanding pickup and delivery operations.

FINANCIAL DATA: *Note: Data for latest year may not have been available at press time.*

In U.S. $	2020	2019	2018	2017	2016	2015
Revenue	4,015,129,000	4,109,111,000	4,043,695,000	3,358,112,000	2,991,517,000	2,972,442,000
R&D Expense						
Operating Income	906,882,000	818,706,000	817,051,000	575,886,000	483,835,000	498,240,000
Operating Margin %		.20%	.20%	.17%	.16%	.17%
SGA Expense	184,185,000	206,125,000	194,368,000	177,205,000	152,391,000	153,589,000
Net Income	672,682,000	615,518,000	605,668,000	463,774,000	295,765,000	304,690,000
Operating Cash Flow	933,024,000	983,888,000	900,116,000	536,294,000	565,583,000	553,880,000
Capital Expenditure	225,081,000	479,325,000	588,292,000	382,125,000	417,941,000	462,059,000
EBITDA	1,165,413,000	1,078,007,000	1,046,059,000	783,749,000	671,786,000	660,570,000
Return on Assets %		.16%	.18%	.16%	.11%	.13%
Return on Equity %		.21%	.24%	.22%	.17%	.19%
Debt to Equity		0.015	0.017	0.02	0.057	0.064

CONTACT INFORMATION:

Phone: 336 889-5000   Fax: 336 822-5239
Toll-Free: 800-432-6335
Address: 500 Old Dominion Way, Thomasville, NC 27360 United States

STOCK TICKER/OTHER:

Stock Ticker: ODFL   Exchange: NAS
Employees: 20,105   Fiscal Year Ends: 12/31
Parent Company:

SALARIES/BONUSES:

Top Exec. Salary: $ Bonus: $
Second Exec. Salary: $ Bonus: $

OTHER THOUGHTS:

Estimated Female Officers or Directors:
Hot Spot for Advancement for Women/Minorities:

Oliver Wyman Group

www.oliverwyman.com/index.html

NAIC Code: 541610

TYPES OF BUSINESS:

Management Consulting
Business Strategy Consulting
Financial Services Consulting
Risk Management & Insurance Consulting

BRANDS/DIVISIONS/AFFILIATES:

Marsh & McLennan Companies Inc

CONTACTS: Note: Officers with more than one job title may be intentionally listed here more than once.

Nick Studer, CEO
Paula McGlarry, General Counsel
Simon Harris, Chief Strategy & Corp. Dev. Officer
David Fishbaum, Actuarial
Rachel Kirsh, Chief Risk Officer

GROWTH PLANS/SPECIAL FEATURES:

Oliver Wyman Group, a subsidiary of Marsh & McLennan Companies, Inc., is a global consulting group with offices in 60 cities across 29 countries. Oliver Wyman's expertise is grouped into three categories: industries, capabilities and insights. Industry expertise includes the following sectors: automotive, aviation, aerospace, business services, communications, consumer goods, defense, distribution, education, energy, financial services, health, industrial products, leisure, life sciences, media, public sector, retail, surface transportation, technology, travel and wholesale. Oliver Wyman's capabilities span actuarial, corporate finance, restructuring, digital, brand, innovation, operations, innovative approaches to technology, organizational effectiveness, payments, pricing, sales, marketing, risk management, strategy and sustainability. The firm's insights division offers expert perspectives on issues that are reshaping businesses, economies and societies, and include insights on areas such as biometrics, trends, operational resilience, banks and recession, millennials, smart investments, airline economic analysis, diversity, merchant payments and much more. Oliver Wyman is known for scheduling worldwide events, where industry leaders and experts gather to share experiences and spread knowledge. Upcoming events can be located on the firm's website.

FINANCIAL DATA: Note: Data for latest year may not have been available at press time.

In U.S. $	2020	2019	2018	2017	2016	2015
Revenue	2,069,280,000	2,122,000,000	2,033,700,000	1,963,360,000	1,803,530,000	1,751,000,000
R&D Expense						
Operating Income						
Operating Margin %						
SGA Expense						
Net Income						
Operating Cash Flow						
Capital Expenditure						
EBITDA						
Return on Assets %						
Return on Equity %						
Debt to Equity						

CONTACT INFORMATION:

Phone: 212-345-8000   Fax: 212-345-8075
Toll-Free:
Address: 1166 Ave. of the Americas, New York, NY 10036 United States

STOCK TICKER/OTHER:

Stock Ticker: Subsidiary
Employees: 5,000
Parent Company: Marsh & McLennan Companies Inc

Exchange:
Fiscal Year Ends: 12/31

SALARIES/BONUSES:

Top Exec. Salary: $ Bonus: $
Second Exec. Salary: $ Bonus: $

OTHER THOUGHTS:

Estimated Female Officers or Directors: 3
Hot Spot for Advancement for Women/Minorities: Y

Oracle Corporation

NAIC Code: 511210H

www.oracle.com

TYPES OF BUSINESS:

Computer Software, Data Base & File Management
Enterprise Software
Enterprise Technology
Enterprise Applications
Artificial Intelligence
Internet of Things
Cloud

BRANDS/DIVISIONS/AFFILIATES:

CONTACTS: *Note: Officers with more than one job title may be intentionally listed here more than once.*

Lawrence Ellison, Chairman of the Board
William West, Chief Accounting Officer
Mark Hurd, Co-CEO
Safra Catz, Co-CEO
Jeffrey Henley, Director
Dorian Daley, Executive VP
Edward Screven, Executive VP

GROWTH PLANS/SPECIAL FEATURES:

Oracle Corporation is a leading enterprise software company, providing hardware products and services to over 430,000 customers in 175 countries. The firm's innovative products are categorized into two segments: infrastructure and applications. The infrastructure segment encompasses applications server, database, database on Linux, database on Unix, database management tools, database warehouse, engineered systems, integrated platforms, middleware and structural data management software. The applications segment spans applications development and deployment, analytics data management, big data and analytics, business software, cloud core financial management, deployment-centric application platforms, enterprise performance management, home energy management, human capital management, talent management, inventory management, life insurance policy administration, logistics, lead management automation, marketing automation, project management and portfolio management. In addition, Oracle offers various development tools and pre-packaged artificial intelligence (AI) solutions that help customers accelerate their adoption of AI and machine learning, and enable businesses to speed time-to-value or custom-build AI-powered applications and more. Faster time-to-value occurs through Oracle's ready-to-use Internet of Things (IoT) solutions, which are designed to address interoperability gaps between operations technology and information technology, and are built on a highly-scalable IoT technology platform that runs on Oracle cloud infrastructure. Oracle's products and solutions are utilized by a wide range of industries, including automotive, communications, consumer goods, education, research, financial services, healthcare, high-technology, insurance, life sciences, public sector, retail and utilities.

Oracle offers employees health, life and disability benefits, a 401(k) plan and an employee stock purchase plan.

FINANCIAL DATA: *Note: Data for latest year may not have been available at press time.*

In U.S. $	2020	2019	2018	2017	2016	2015
Revenue	39,068,000,000	39,506,000,000	39,831,000,000	37,728,000,000	37,047,000,000	
R&D Expense	6,067,000,000	6,026,000,000	6,091,000,000	6,159,000,000	5,787,000,000	
Operating Income	14,202,000,000	14,022,000,000	14,319,000,000	13,276,000,000	13,104,000,000	
Operating Margin %	.36%	.35%	.36%	.35%	.35%	
SGA Expense	9,275,000,000	9,774,000,000	9,720,001,000	9,373,000,000	9,039,000,000	
Net Income	10,135,000,000	11,083,000,000	3,825,000,000	9,335,000,000	8,901,000,000	
Operating Cash Flow	13,139,000,000	14,551,000,000	15,386,000,000	14,126,000,000	13,561,000,000	
Capital Expenditure	1,564,000,000	1,660,000,000	1,736,000,000	2,021,000,000	1,189,000,000	
EBITDA	17,026,000,000	17,269,000,000	17,701,000,000	15,766,000,000	15,418,000,000	
Return on Assets %	.09%	.09%	.03%	.08%	.08%	
Return on Equity %	.60%	.33%	.08%	.18%	.19%	
Debt to Equity	5.733	2.372	1.227	0.893	0.848	

CONTACT INFORMATION:

Phone: 650 506-7000   Fax: 650 506-7200
Toll-Free: 800-392-2999
Address: 500 Oracle Pkwy., Redwood City, CA 94065 United States

STOCK TICKER/OTHER:

Stock Ticker: ORCL
Employees: 135,000
Parent Company:

Exchange: NYS
Fiscal Year Ends: 05/31

SALARIES/BONUSES:

Top Exec. Salary: $ Bonus: $
Second Exec. Salary: $ Bonus: $

OTHER THOUGHTS:

Estimated Female Officers or Directors: 6
Hot Spot for Advancement for Women/Minorities: Y

Oracle NetSuite
www.netsuite.com

NAIC Code: 511210H

TYPES OF BUSINESS:

Business Management Application Suites
Enterprise Resource Planning
Customer Relationship Management
eCommerce
Automation
Marketing
Analytics
Business Intelligence

BRANDS/DIVISIONS/AFFILIATES:

Oracle Corporation

CONTACTS: Note: Officers with more than one job title may be intentionally listed here more than once.

Sam Levy, Sr. VP-Sales
Douglas Solomon, General Counsel
Marc Huffman, President, Divisional

GROWTH PLANS/SPECIAL FEATURES:

Oracle NetSuite is a global business unit of Oracle Corporation and a leading vendor of cloud-based financials, enterprise resource planning (ERP) and omnichannel commerce software. The firm's solutions run the business of more than 24,000 customers worldwide. Oracle NetSuite's cloud ERP, customer relationship management (CRM) and eCommerce products enable customers to manage their back-office, front-office and web operations in a single application. Products by the company also include global business management, human capital management, professional services automation, omnichannel commerce, email marketing, analytics, business intelligence and user experience. Industries served by the company include advertising and digital marketing agencies, apparel/footwear/accessories, campus store, education, energy, financial services, food and beverage, health and beauty, IT services, manufacturing, media and publishing, nonprofit, professional services, restaurants, hospitality, retail, software and technology companies, transportation, logistics and wholesale distribution.

FINANCIAL DATA: Note: Data for latest year may not have been available at press time.

In U.S. $	2020	2019	2018	2017	2016	2015
Revenue	1,008,291,375	960,277,500	914,550,000	871,000,000	855,000,000	741,148,992
R&D Expense						
Operating Income						
Operating Margin %						
SGA Expense						
Net Income						
Operating Cash Flow						
Capital Expenditure						
EBITDA						
Return on Assets %						
Return on Equity %						
Debt to Equity						

CONTACT INFORMATION:

Phone: 877-638-7848   Fax:
Toll-Free:
Address: 2300 Oracle Way, Austin, TX 78741 United States

SALARIES/BONUSES:

Top Exec. Salary: $ Bonus: $
Second Exec. Salary: $ Bonus: $

STOCK TICKER/OTHER:

Stock Ticker: Subsidiary
Employees: 3,357
Parent Company: Oracle Corporation

Exchange:
Fiscal Year Ends: 12/31

OTHER THOUGHTS:

Estimated Female Officers or Directors: 3
Hot Spot for Advancement for Women/Minorities: Y

Owens Corning

NAIC Code: 326199

www.owenscorning.com

TYPES OF BUSINESS:

Building Materials (e.g., Fascia, Panels, Siding, Soffit), Plastics, Manufacturing
Glass Fiber Reinforcements
Manufactured Stone Veneer Products
Glass Fiber Fabrics
Construction Services

BRANDS/DIVISIONS/AFFILIATES:

Owens Corning PINK FIBERGLAS Insulation
vliepa GmbH

CONTACTS: Note: Officers with more than one job title may be intentionally listed here more than once.

Brian Chambers, CEO
Michael McMurray, CFO
Michael Thaman, Chairman of the Board
Kelly Schmidt, Controller
Ava Harter, General Counsel
Marcio Sandri, President, Divisional
Gunner Smith, President, Divisional
Julian Francis, President, Divisional
Daniel Smith, Senior VP, Divisional

GROWTH PLANS/SPECIAL FEATURES:

Owens Corning is a producer of residential and commercial building materials and glass fiber reinforcements and other similar materials for composite systems. The company operates through three business segments: composites, insulation and roofing. Composites includes the firm's reinforcements and downstream businesses, and accounted for 27% of total net sales in 2020. This division's glass fiber materials can be found in over 40,000 end-use applications primarily within the following five markets: building and construction, transportation, consumer, industrial, and power and energy. End-use applications include pipe, roofing shingles, sporting goods, consumer electronics, telecommunications cables, boats, aviation, defense, automotive, industrial containers and wind-energy. Composites manufactures, fabricates and sells glass reinforcements in the form of fiber and of fabrics. Insulation comprises 36% net sales, and its products help customers conserve energy, provide improved acoustical performance and offer convenience of installation and use for new home construction and remodeling purposes. These products include thermal and acoustical batts, loosefill insulation, foam sheathing and accessories, and are sold under the brand and trademark name Owens Corning PINK FIBERGLASS Insulation. Roofing products (37%) include laminate and strip asphalt roofing shingles, as well as oxidized asphalt and roofing components and accessories. Owens Corning has operations in more than 30 countries. In July 2021, Owens Corning acquired vliepa GmbH, which specializes in the coating, printing and finishing of nonwovens, paper and film for the building materials industry.

Owens Corning offers its employees health and wellness benefits, life insurance, financial growth options and other employee incentives.

FINANCIAL DATA: Note: Data for latest year may not have been available at press time.

In U.S. $	2020	2019	2018	2017	2016	2015
Revenue	7,055,000,000	7,160,000,000	7,057,000,000	6,384,000,000	5,677,000,000	5,350,000,000
R&D Expense	82,000,000	87,000,000	89,000,000	85,000,000	82,000,000	73,000,000
Operating Income	806,000,000	787,000,000	807,000,000	737,000,000	699,000,000	548,000,000
Operating Margin %		.11%	.11%	.12%	.12%	.10%
SGA Expense	664,000,000	698,000,000	700,000,000	620,000,000	584,000,000	525,000,000
Net Income	-383,000,000	405,000,000	545,000,000	289,000,000	393,000,000	330,000,000
Operating Cash Flow	1,135,000,000	1,037,000,000	803,000,000	1,016,000,000	943,000,000	742,000,000
Capital Expenditure	307,000,000	447,000,000	537,000,000	337,000,000	373,000,000	393,000,000
EBITDA	369,000,000	1,178,000,000	1,254,000,000	1,037,000,000	1,041,000,000	853,000,000
Return on Assets %		.04%	.06%	.04%	.05%	.04%
Return on Equity %		.09%	.13%	.07%	.10%	.09%
Debt to Equity		0.675	0.785	0.578	0.545	0.455

CONTACT INFORMATION:

Phone: 419 248-8000   Fax: 419 248-8445
Toll-Free: 800-438-7465
Address: 1 Owens Corning Pkwy., Toledo, OH 43659 United States

STOCK TICKER/OTHER:

Stock Ticker: OC
Employees: 19,000
Parent Company:

Exchange: NYS
Fiscal Year Ends: 12/31

SALARIES/BONUSES:

Top Exec. Salary: $ Bonus: $
Second Exec. Salary: $ Bonus: $

OTHER THOUGHTS:

Estimated Female Officers or Directors: 2
Hot Spot for Advancement for Women/Minorities: Y

Palo Alto Networks Inc

www.paloaltonetworks.com

NAIC Code: 511210E

TYPES OF BUSINESS:

Computer Software: Network Security, Managed Access, Digital ID,
Cybersecurity & Anti-Virus
Cybersecurity
Cloud
Hybrid Cloud
Internet of Things
Software-as-a-Service

BRANDS/DIVISIONS/AFFILIATES:

Prisma
Prisma Cloud
Prisma Software-as-a-Service
Prisma Access
Cortex XDR
Cortex XSOAR
Cortex Data Lake

CONTACTS: Note: Officers with more than one job title may be intentionally listed here more than once.

Nikesh Arora, CEO
Kathleen Bonanno, CFO
Jean Compeau, Chief Accounting Officer
Rene Bonvanie, Chief Marketing Officer
Nir Zuk, Chief Technology Officer
Mark McLaughlin, Director
Lee Klarich, Other Executive Officer
Amit Singh, President

GROWTH PLANS/SPECIAL FEATURES:

Palo Alto Networks, Inc. is a global cybersecurity provider. The firm's solutions focus on delivering value in three core areas: secure the enterprise, secure the cloud and secure the future. The secure the enterprise solution secures the network through Palo Alto's machine-learning-powered firewalls. These are available in a number of form factors, including physical, virtual and containerized appliances, as well as a cloud-delivered service. It offers panorama management as an appliance or as a virtual machine for the public and private cloud. This solution also includes services such as threat prevention, URL filtering, targeted malware, domain name system (DNS) security, Internet of Things (IoT) security, global protection, software-defined networking in a wide area network (SD-WAN), and data loss prevention. The secure the cloud solution utilizes Palo Alto's Prisma security offerings, such as: Prisma Cloud, a comprehensive cloud native security platform, protecting applications, data and the entire cloud native technology stack throughout the full development lifecycle and across multi- and hybrid-cloud environments; Prisma Software-as-a-Service (SaaS), for protecting SaaS applications; and Prisma Access, a comprehensive secure access service edge that secures SD-WAN to enable cloud delivery and for in-line network security in multi- and hybrid-cloud environments. Last, the secure the future solution secures security operations via: Cortex XDR, for prevention, detection and response; Cortex XSOAR, for security orchestration, automation and response: AutoFocus, for threat intelligence; and Cortex Data Lake, to collect and integrate security data for analytics purposes. These products are delivered as software or SaaS subscriptions. Palo Alto's global operations span the U.S., Europe, the Middle East, Africa, Asia and Australasia.

FINANCIAL DATA: Note: Data for latest year may not have been available at press time.

In U.S. $	2020	2019	2018	2017	2016	2015
Revenue	3,408,400,000	2,899,600,000	2,273,100,000	1,761,600,000	1,378,500,000	928,052,000
R&D Expense	768,100,000	539,500,000	400,700,000	347,400,000	284,200,000	185,828,000
Operating Income	-179,000,000	-54,100,000	-129,100,000	-179,800,000	-190,100,000	-133,536,000
Operating Margin %		- .02%	- .06%	- .10%	- .14%	- .14%
SGA Expense	1,819,800,000	1,605,800,000	1,356,200,000	1,117,400,000	914,400,000	624,261,000
Net Income	-267,000,000	-81,900,000	-147,900,000	-216,600,000	-225,900,000	-164,982,000
Operating Cash Flow	1,035,700,000	1,055,600,000	1,037,000,000	868,500,000	658,100,000	350,304,000
Capital Expenditure	214,400,000	131,200,000	112,000,000	163,400,000	72,500,000	33,828,000
EBITDA	110,400,000	163,100,000	-4,200,000	-109,800,000	-138,900,000	-104,371,000
Return on Assets %		- .01%	- .03%	- .07%	- .10%	- .10%
Return on Equity %		- .06%	- .17%	- .28%	- .33%	- .32%
Debt to Equity		0.901	1.386	0.691	0.643	

CONTACT INFORMATION:

Phone: 408 753-4000 Fax: 408 753-4001
Toll-Free:
Address: 3000 Tannery Way, Santa Clara, CA 95054 United States

SALARIES/BONUSES:

Top Exec. Salary: $ Bonus: $
Second Exec. Salary: $ Bonus: $

STOCK TICKER/OTHER:

Stock Ticker: PANW Exchange: NYS
Employees: 8,014 Fiscal Year Ends: 07/31
Parent Company:

OTHER THOUGHTS:

Estimated Female Officers or Directors:
Hot Spot for Advancement for Women/Minorities:

PAREXEL International Corporation

www.parexel.com

NAIC Code: 541711

TYPES OF BUSINESS:

Clinical Trial & Data Management
Clinical Research Organization
Biopharmaceuticals
Outsourcing Services
Consulting

BRANDS/DIVISIONS/AFFILIATES:

Pamplona Capital Management LP
Calyx

CONTACTS: *Note: Officers with more than one job title may be intentionally listed here more than once.*

Jamie Macdonald, CFO
Sy Pretorius, Pres., Chief Medical & Scientific Officer
Sybrand Pretorius, Chief Scientific Officer
Greg Rush, Exec. VP
Peyton Howell, Pres., Chief Commercial & Strategy Officer
MaryJo Zaborowski, Sr. VP
Josef Von Rickenbach, Founder
Michelle Graham, Other Executive Officer
Xavier Flinois, President, Divisional
Gadi Saarony, Senior VP, Divisional
Roland Andersson, Senior VP, Divisional
Joshua Schultz, Senior VP, Divisional
David Godwin, Senior VP, Divisional
Douglas Batt, Senior VP

GROWTH PLANS/SPECIAL FEATURES:

PAREXEL International Corporation is a leading global clinical research organization (CRO) that provides biopharmaceutical services that help clients transform discoveries into new treatments. The company's wide range of solutions are categorized into clinical development, outsourcing services, consulting, medical affairs, and evidence and late phase. PAREXEL's expertise spans patient centricity, precision medicine, adaptive and flexible trials, real world data trials, and innovation, as well as therapeutic areas such as oncology, cardiovascular, metabolic, central nervous system, infectious disease, ophthalmology, respiratory, rheumatology, immunology, rare diseases and regenerative medicine. Headquartered in Massachusetts and North Carolina, PAREXEL supports clients in more than 100 countries. The firm is privately-owned by Pamplona Capital Management, LLP. In early-2021, PAREXEL announced that it completed the separation of its informatics and medical imaging business to simplify and streamline its business strategy. Parexel Informatics became Calyx.

FINANCIAL DATA: *Note: Data for latest year may not have been available at press time.*

In U.S. $	2020	2019	2018	2017	2016	2015
Revenue	2,665,000,000	2,500,000,000	2,221,000,000	2,117,600,000	2,094,300,000	2,016,000,000
R&D Expense						
Operating Income						
Operating Margin %						
SGA Expense						
Net Income				107,300,000	154,900,000	147,800,000
Operating Cash Flow						
Capital Expenditure						
EBITDA						
Return on Assets %						
Return on Equity %						
Debt to Equity						

CONTACT INFORMATION:

Phone: 617-454-9300   Fax:
Toll-Free:
Address: 275 Grove St., Ste. 101C, Newton, MA 02466 United States

STOCK TICKER/OTHER:

Stock Ticker: Private   Exchange:
Employees: 17,000   Fiscal Year Ends: 06/30
Parent Company: Pamplona Capital Management LLP

SALARIES/BONUSES:

Top Exec. Salary: $ Bonus: $
Second Exec. Salary: $ Bonus: $

OTHER THOUGHTS:

Estimated Female Officers or Directors: 1
Hot Spot for Advancement for Women/Minorities: Y

Parsons Corporation

www.parsons.com

NAIC Code: 541330

TYPES OF BUSINESS:

Civil Engineering
Construction Management
Facility Operations and Maintenance
Environmental Services
Analytical, Technical and Training Services
Transportation Infrastructure Project Design and Construction

BRANDS/DIVISIONS/AFFILIATES:

Braxton Science and Technology Group LLC

CONTACTS: Note: Officers with more than one job title may be intentionally listed here more than once.

Charles Harrington, CEO
George Ball, CFO
Adam Taylor, Chief Administrative Officer
Michael Kolloway, Chief Legal Officer
Carey Smith, COO

GROWTH PLANS/SPECIAL FEATURES:

Parsons Corporation provides technology-driven solutions in the defense, intelligence and critical infrastructure markets. The firm's software and hardware products, technical services and integrated solutions support its customers' missions. Parsons has developed significant expertise and capabilities in key areas of cybersecurity, intelligence, missile defense, C5ISR (command, control, communications, computers, combat systems, intelligence, surveillance and reconnaissance), space, geospatial and connected communities. The company's federal solutions division derives 49% of annual revenue, and its critical infrastructure division derives the majority 51%. The federal solutions division provides high-end technology to the U.S. government, and the critical infrastructure division provides integrated design and engineering services for complex physical and digital infrastructure worldwide. In late-2020, Parsons acquired Braxton Science and Technology Group, LLC, which offers products that provide mission critical solutions.

Parsons offers its employees medical and life insurance, tuition reimbursement, an ESOP for eligible employees, a 401(k) and membership to a Federal Credit Union.

FINANCIAL DATA: Note: Data for latest year may not have been available at press time.

In U.S. $	2020	2019	2018	2017	2016	2015
Revenue	3,918,946,000	3,954,812,000	3,560,508,000	3,017,011,000	3,039,191,000	
R&D Expense						
Operating Income	147,756,000	50,342,000	168,093,000	110,616,000	85,078,000	
Operating Margin %		.01%	.05%	.04%	.03%	
SGA Expense	729,103,000	781,408,000	597,410,000	506,255,000	522,920,000	
Net Income	98,541,000	120,534,000	167,949,000	97,326,000	-13,147,000	
Operating Cash Flow	289,161,000	220,240,000	284,634,000	265,029,000	198,559,000	
Capital Expenditure	34,036,000	67,597,000	29,283,000	27,939,000	30,079,000	
EBITDA	310,349,000	216,671,000	350,514,000	183,997,000	70,671,000	
Return on Assets %		.04%	.07%	.04%		
Return on Equity %		.09%	.20%	.13%		
Debt to Equity		0.279	0.464	0.321		

CONTACT INFORMATION:

Phone: 703-988-8500   Fax:
Toll-Free:
Address: 5875 Trinity Pkwy. #300, Centreville, VA 20120 United States

STOCK TICKER/OTHER:

Stock Ticker: PSN
Employees: 15,879
Parent Company:

Exchange: NYS
Fiscal Year Ends: 12/31

SALARIES/BONUSES:

Top Exec. Salary: $ Bonus: $
Second Exec. Salary: $ Bonus: $

OTHER THOUGHTS:

Estimated Female Officers or Directors:
Hot Spot for Advancement for Women/Minorities:

PayPal Holdings Inc

NAIC Code: 522320

www.paypal.com

TYPES OF BUSINESS:
Payment Processing-Intermediary
Online Payment Systems
Web-Enabled Payments
Online Auction Technology
Credit Cards
Debit Cards
Account Management
Money Transfer

BRANDS/DIVISIONS/AFFILIATES:
PayPal
PayPal Credit
Braintree
Venmo
Xoom
iZettle
GoPay
Honey Science Corporation

CONTACTS: Note: Officers with more than one job title may be intentionally listed here more than once.
Daniel Schulman, CEO
John Rainey, CFO
John Donahoe, Chairman of the Board
Aaron Karczmer, Chief Compliance Officer
Louise Pentland, Chief Legal Officer
Allison Johnson, Chief Marketing Officer
Jonathan Auerbach, Chief Strategy Officer
William Ready, COO
Mark Britto, Executive VP, Divisional
Brian Yamasaki, Secretary
Aaron Anderson, Vice President

GROWTH PLANS/SPECIAL FEATURES:

PayPal Holdings, Inc. is a leading technology platform and global online payment processing company. The firm's products allow businesses and consumers to cost-effectively send and receive payments within and between more than 200 markets and 100 currencies worldwide. The company has about 300 million active customer accounts worldwide. The PayPal system extends the existing financial infrastructure of bank accounts and credit cards, and can also be used to collect subscriptions, recurring payments and donations. Moreover, the firm is a leading payment processing provider for online auction services, with the bulk of the company's business coming from eBay. PayPal's combined payment solution capabilities are comprised of the PayPal, PayPal Credit, Braintree, Venmo, Xoom and iZettle proprietary payments platform. These products make it safer and simpler for friends and family to transfer funds to each other, including cross border transfers. Merchants are provided an end-to-end payments solution that provides authorization and settlement capabilities, as well as instant access to funds. PayPal Credit provides the ability for consumers to receive a line of credit; Braintree specializes in mobile and web payment systems for eCommerce companies; Venmo is a mobile application which moves money between friends and family via mobile devices; Xoom enables consumers to send money, pay bills and send mobile phone reloads to family and friends around the world via mobile devices; and iZettle offers a card acceptance service that enables small businesses to take credit and debit card payments, as well as a software solution to record, manage and analyze sales. In December 2019, PayPal acquired a 70% equity interest in Guofubao Information Technology Co., Ltd. (GoPay). In January 2020, the firm completed the acquisition of Honey Science Corporation for approximately $4 billion.

FINANCIAL DATA: Note: Data for latest year may not have been available at press time.

In U.S. $	2020	2019	2018	2017	2016	2015
Revenue	21,454,000,000	17,772,000,000	15,451,000,000	13,094,000,000	10,842,000,000	9,248,000,000
R&D Expense			1,071,000,000	953,000,000	834,000,000	947,000,000
Operating Income	3,428,000,000	2,790,000,000	2,503,000,000	2,259,000,000	1,586,000,000	1,509,000,000
Operating Margin %		.16%	.16%	.17%	.15%	.16%
SGA Expense	6,573,000,000	5,197,000,000	2,764,000,000	3,647,000,000	3,264,000,000	2,765,000,000
Net Income	4,202,000,000	2,459,000,000	2,057,000,000	1,795,000,000	1,401,000,000	1,228,000,000
Operating Cash Flow	5,854,000,000	4,561,000,000	5,483,000,000	2,531,000,000	3,158,000,000	2,546,000,000
Capital Expenditure	866,000,000	704,000,000	823,000,000	667,000,000	669,000,000	722,000,000
EBITDA	6,463,000,000	4,025,000,000	3,229,000,000	3,064,000,000	2,310,000,000	2,117,000,000
Return on Assets %		.05%	.05%	.05%	.05%	.05%
Return on Equity %		.15%	.13%	.12%	.10%	.11%
Debt to Equity		0.294				

CONTACT INFORMATION:
Phone: 408-967-1000   Fax: 650-864-8001
Toll-Free:
Address: 2211 N. First St., San Jose, CA 95131 United States

STOCK TICKER/OTHER:
Stock Ticker: PYPL
Employees: 26,500
Parent Company:

Exchange: NAS
Fiscal Year Ends: 12/31

SALARIES/BONUSES:
Top Exec. Salary: $ Bonus: $
Second Exec. Salary: $ Bonus: $

OTHER THOUGHTS:
Estimated Female Officers or Directors: 1
Hot Spot for Advancement for Women/Minorities: Y

Penske Automotive Group Inc

www.penskeautomotive.com

NAIC Code: 441110

TYPES OF BUSINESS:

Auto Dealers
Automotive Leasing
Parts & Service
Commercial Truck Dealerships
Automotive Dealerships
Ecommerce

BRANDS/DIVISIONS/AFFILIATES:

CarSense
CarShop
Penske Australia
Penske Truck Leasing Co LP
Penske Corporation
Kansas City Freightliner

CONTACTS: *Note: Officers with more than one job title may be intentionally listed here more than once.*

Roger Penske, CEO
J. Carlson, Chief Accounting Officer
Robert Kurnick, Director
Bud Denker, Executive VP, Divisional
Shane Spradlin, Executive VP

GROWTH PLANS/SPECIAL FEATURES:

Penske Automotive Group, Inc. (PAG) is an international transportation services company operating automotive and commercial truck dealerships primarily in the U.S., Canada and western Europe. PAG also distributes commercial vehicles, diesel engines, gas engines, power systems and related parts and services principally in Australia and New Zealand. As of June 30, 2021, PAG operated 305 automotive retail franchises, of which 144 are located in the U.S. and 161 outside of the U.S. The franchises outside the U.S. are located primarily in the U.K. This division also operates stand-alone used vehicle supercenters in the U.S. and U.K., which retail and wholesale pre-owned vehicles under a one price, no haggle methodology. Through subsidiary CarSense operates U.S. retail and ecommerce locations, and retail and ecommerce locations in the U.K. under the CarShop name. In the six months ended June 30, 2021, PAG retailed and wholesaled more than 290,000 vehicles. During 2020, the company retailed and wholesaled more than 500,000 vehicles. The commercial vehicle is the exclusive importer and distributor of Western Star heavy-duty trucks (a Daimler brand), MAN heavy- and medium-duty trucks and buses (a Volkswagen brand), and Dennis Eagle refuse collection vehicles across Australia and New Zealand, as well as portions of the Pacific. In these same markets, the company is also a leading distributor of diesel and gas engines and power systems, principally representing MTU, Detroit Diesel, Allison Transmission, MTU Onsite Energy, and Rolls Royce Power Systems. This business is known as Penske Australia, and also offers products across the on- and off-highway markets, including the construction, mining, marine and defense sectors. Minority-owned (28.9%) Penske Truck Leasing Co., LP provides transportation and supply chain services. Penske Corporation and Mitsui & Co. Ltd. owns the remaining 41.1% and 30%, of Penske Truck Leasing, respectively. During 2021, PAG acquired Kansas City Freightliner.

FINANCIAL DATA: *Note: Data for latest year may not have been available at press time.*

In U.S. $	2020	2019	2018	2017	2016	2015
Revenue	20,443,900,000	23,179,400,000	22,785,100,000	21,386,900,000	20,118,500,000	19,284,900,000
R&D Expense						
Operating Income	704,500,000	652,700,000	664,900,000	611,400,000	574,900,000	566,500,000
Operating Margin %		.03%	.03%	.03%	.03%	.03%
SGA Expense	2,364,500,000	2,693,200,000	2,646,300,000	2,516,000,000	2,302,000,000	2,223,000,000
Net Income	543,600,000	435,800,000	471,000,000	613,300,000	342,900,000	326,100,000
Operating Cash Flow	1,201,800,000	518,600,000	614,700,000	623,500,000	367,100,000	386,000,000
Capital Expenditure	185,900,000	245,300,000	305,600,000	247,000,000	203,100,000	199,500,000
EBITDA	989,000,000	909,800,000	903,400,000	814,100,000	734,100,000	683,800,000
Return on Assets %		.04%	.04%	.06%	.04%	.04%
Return on Equity %		.16%	.19%	.30%	.19%	.19%
Debt to Equity		1.632	0.814	0.873	1.044	0.701

CONTACT INFORMATION:

Phone: 248 648-2500   Fax: 248 648-2525
Toll-Free:
Address: 2555 Telegraph Rd., Bloomfield Hills, MI 48302-0954 United States

STOCK TICKER/OTHER:

Stock Ticker: PAG
Employees: 27,000
Parent Company:

Exchange: NYS
Fiscal Year Ends: 12/31

SALARIES/BONUSES:

Top Exec. Salary: $ Bonus: $
Second Exec. Salary: $ Bonus: $

OTHER THOUGHTS:

Estimated Female Officers or Directors: 2
Hot Spot for Advancement for Women/Minorities:

PerkinElmer Inc

NAIC Code: 325413

www.perkinelmer.com

TYPES OF BUSINESS:

Diagnostic Systems
Mechanical Components
Optoelectronics
Pharmaceutical Manufacturing
Life Science Systems
Environmental Safety Equipment

BRANDS/DIVISIONS/AFFILIATES:

Tri-carb
Opera Phenix
EnSight
PerkinElmer
Clarus
NexION
DELFIA
Chitas

CONTACTS: Note: Officers with more than one job title may be intentionally listed here more than once.

Robert Friel, CEO
James Mock, CFO
Andrew Okun, Chief Accounting Officer
Prahlad Singh, COO
James Corbett, Executive VP
Joel Goldberg, General Counsel
Deborah Butters, Other Executive Officer
Daniel Tereau, Senior VP, Divisional
Tajinder Vohra, Senior VP, Divisional

GROWTH PLANS/SPECIAL FEATURES:

PerkinElmer, Inc. provides products, services and solutions for the diagnostics, life sciences and applied markets. The company's technologies and solutions address critical issues that help to improve lives. The company operates through two segments: discovery and analytical solutions, and diagnostics. The discovery and analytical solutions segment comprises a portfolio of technologies that help life sciences researchers better understand diseases and develop treatments. This division also serves applied markets such as environmental, food and industrial, offering products and solutions that detect, monitor and manage contaminants and toxic chemicals impacting the environment and food supply. Just a few of the many product, services and application solutions developed by this segment include: gas chromatographs, mass spectrometers, sample-handling equipment, advanced liquid chromatography systems, analyzers, quantitative pathology research solutions, radiometric detection solutions, screening systems and plate readers. The diagnostics segment offers instruments, reagents, assay platforms and software to hospitals, medical labs, clinicians and medical research professionals. This division focuses on reproductive health, emerging market diagnostics and applied genomics. Products, services and application solutions include screening platforms, in vitro diagnostic kits, blood analyzing kits, informatics data management, X-ray detectors, umbilical cord blood banking services, automated liquid handling platforms, next-generation sequencing automation and nucleic acid quantitation and automated small-scale purification. Brand names include Tri-carb, Opera Phenix, EnSight, PerkinElmer, Clarus, NexION, DELFIA, Chitas, JANUS and PG-Seq, among many others. PerkinElmer is headquartered in Waltham, Massachusetts, and markets its products and services in more than 190 countries.

FINANCIAL DATA: Note: Data for latest year may not have been available at press time.

In U.S. $	2020	2019	2018	2017	2016	2015
Revenue	3,782,745,000	2,883,673,000	2,777,996,000	2,256,982,000	2,115,517,000	2,262,359,000
R&D Expense	205,389,000	189,336,000	193,998,000	139,404,000	124,278,000	125,928,000
Operating Income	986,594,000	391,401,000	335,028,000	317,460,000	288,190,000	299,724,000
Operating Margin %		.14%	.12%	.14%	.14%	.13%
SGA Expense	917,894,000	815,318,000	811,913,000	616,167,000	600,885,000	598,848,000
Net Income	727,887,000	227,558,000	237,927,000	292,633,000	234,299,000	212,425,000
Operating Cash Flow	892,177,000	363,469,000	311,038,000	288,453,000	350,615,000	287,098,000
Capital Expenditure	77,506,000	81,331,000	93,253,000	39,089,000	31,702,000	29,632,000
EBITDA	1,202,583,000	514,794,000	505,247,000	445,658,000	385,568,000	394,019,000
Return on Assets %		.04%	.04%	.06%	.06%	.05%
Return on Equity %		.08%	.09%	.13%	.11%	.10%
Debt to Equity		0.786	0.726	0.715	0.485	0.479

CONTACT INFORMATION:

Phone: 781 663-6900   Fax:
Toll-Free: 800-762-4000
Address: 940 Winter St., Waltham, MA 02451 United States

STOCK TICKER/OTHER:

Stock Ticker: PKI
Employees: 14,000
Parent Company:

Exchange: NYS
Fiscal Year Ends: 01/31

SALARIES/BONUSES:

Top Exec. Salary: $ Bonus: $
Second Exec. Salary: $ Bonus: $

OTHER THOUGHTS:

Estimated Female Officers or Directors: 1
Hot Spot for Advancement for Women/Minorities: Y

Petco Animal Supplies Inc

www.petco.com

NAIC Code: 453910

TYPES OF BUSINESS:

Pets & Pet Supplies, Retail
Online Sales
Pet Grooming
Veterinary Services
Obedience Training
Pet Photography

BRANDS/DIVISIONS/AFFILIATES:

CVC Capital Partners
Canada Pension Plan Investment Board
Petco
Unleashed by Petco
PALS

CONTACTS: Note: Officers with more than one job title may be intentionally listed here more than once.

Ron Coughlin, CEO
Thomas A. Farello, Sr. VP-Oper.
Lisa Epstein, Sr. Comm. Specialist
Jim Myers, Chmn.

GROWTH PLANS/SPECIAL FEATURES:

Petco Animal Supplies, Inc. is a leading specialty retailer of premium pet food, supplies and services. The company currently operates over 1,500 Petco and Unleashed by Petco locations across the U.S., Mexico and Puerto Rico. Petco's superstores carry more than 10,000 products including premium pet food and treats; small animals such as fish, birds and reptiles as well as related supplies; collars and leashes; grooming products; toys; pet carriers; cat furniture; dog houses and beds; vitamins; and veterinary supplies. Most stores also provide a variety of pet services, including professional grooming, veterinary clinics, vaccinations, obedience training and pet photography. Several services are performed in glass-walled stations in order to increase customer awareness and confidence in the services. In light of overpopulation problems, Petco chooses not to sell dogs and cats, though it does support adoption programs such as Petfinder.com through in-store Think Adoption First kiosks in many stores. The firm also operates the P.A.L.S. (Petco animal lovers save) customer loyalty program. Members receive special benefits and savings through the use of the P.A.L.S. card, which allows Petco to target customers and track shopping habits. In addition to its retail stores, the company operates an e-commerce site, which offers Petco merchandise, pet tips, a community forum, online specials and information about The Petco Foundation, an animal welfare and rights group. Petco Animal Supplies is privately-owned by CVC Capital Partners and Canada Pension Plan Investment Board. Petco has an exclusive partnership with Canada-based retailer, Canadian Tire, which makes Petco's assortment of food, treats, supplies and accessories available to pet parents in Canada, both online and in stores. In November 2020, Petco announced that it submitted a draft registration statement to the U.S. Securities and Exchange Commission to the proposed public offering of its common stock.

FINANCIAL DATA: Note: Data for latest year may not have been available at press time.

In U.S. $	2020	2019	2018	2017	2016	2015
Revenue	4,574,062,500	4,462,500,000	4,250,000,000	4,200,000,000	4,100,000,000	3,995,368,000
R&D Expense						
Operating Income						
Operating Margin %						
SGA Expense						
Net Income						
Operating Cash Flow						
Capital Expenditure						
EBITDA						
Return on Assets %						
Return on Equity %						
Debt to Equity						

CONTACT INFORMATION:

Phone: 858-453-7845   Fax:
Toll-Free:
Address: 9125 Rehco Rd., San Diego, CA 92121 United States

STOCK TICKER/OTHER:

Stock Ticker: Private
Employees: 27,000
Parent Company: CVC Capital Partners

Exchange:
Fiscal Year Ends: 01/31

SALARIES/BONUSES:

Top Exec. Salary: $ Bonus: $
Second Exec. Salary: $ Bonus: $

OTHER THOUGHTS:

Estimated Female Officers or Directors: 2
Hot Spot for Advancement for Women/Minorities:

PetSmart Inc

NAIC Code: 453910

www.petsmart.com

TYPES OF BUSINESS:

Pets & Pet Supplies, Retail
Online & Catalog Sales
Pet Training
In-Store Adoption Centers
Veterinary Services
Pet Boarding
Pet Grooming

BRANDS/DIVISIONS/AFFILIATES:

Argos Holdings Inc
PetSmart.com
PetPerks
Medical Management International Inc
Banfield Pet Hospital
PetSmart PetHotels
Chewy Inc
Chewy.com

CONTACTS: *Note: Officers with more than one job title may be intentionally listed here more than once.*

J.K. Symancyk, CEO
Alan Schnaid, CFO
Donald Beaver, Chief Information Officer
Paulette Dodson, General Counsel
Erick Goldberg, Senior VP, Divisional
Bruce Thorn, Senior VP, Divisional
Jaye Perricone, Senior VP, Divisional
Matthew McAdam, Senior VP, Divisional
Melvin Tucker, Senior VP, Divisional
Gene Burt, Senior VP, Divisional

GROWTH PLANS/SPECIAL FEATURES:

PetSmart, Inc. is a leading operator of superstores specializing in pet food, supplies and services. The company operates over 1,650 stores in the U.S., Puerto Rico and Canada, which offer an assortment of pet services and products. Its stores range in size from 12,000 to 27,500 square feet and carry roughly 11,000 distinct items in store and 9,000 additional items online through PetSmart.com. These items include nationally recognized brand names and a selection of proprietary or private label brands. PetSmart stores sell supplies for dogs, cats, fresh-water tropical fish, reptiles, birds and other small pets. The firm offers a PetPerks loyalty program to its customers. PetSmart stores also offer value-added pet services including grooming, training, boarding and day camp; and it operates full-service veterinary hospitals in many of its stores. Medical Management International, Inc., an operator of veterinary hospitals, operates more than 800 of PetSmart's hospitals under the name Banfield Pet Hospital. The remaining seven hospitals are located in Canada and operated by other third parties. PetSmart offers pet boarding in more than 200 stores through its PetSmart PetsHotels. PetsHotels provide boarding for dogs and cats, which includes 24-hour supervision by caregivers who are PetSmart-trained to provide personalized pet care, temperature-controlled rooms and suites and play time as well as day camp for dogs. The company also actively supports pet adoption through its in-store adoption centers. Independent subsidiary Chewy, Inc. operates an eCommerce pet platform at chewy.com, offering thousands of products and 24/7 support services. PetSmart is privately-owned by Argos Holdings, Inc.

PetSmart offers employees medical, dental and vision insurance; life and AD&D insurance; short- and long-term disability; a 401(k) plan; and various employee assistance programs.

FINANCIAL DATA: *Note: Data for latest year may not have been available at press time.*

In U.S. $	2020	2019	2018	2017	2016	2015
Revenue	6,150,000,000	6,000,000,000	9,912,500,000	7,125,000,000	7,050,000,000	7,000,000,000
R&D Expense						
Operating Income						
Operating Margin %						
SGA Expense						
Net Income						
Operating Cash Flow						
Capital Expenditure						
EBITDA						
Return on Assets %						
Return on Equity %						
Debt to Equity						

CONTACT INFORMATION:

Phone: 623 580-6100   Fax:
Toll-Free: 800-738-1385
Address: 19601 N. 27th Ave., Phoenix, AZ 85027 United States

STOCK TICKER/OTHER:

Stock Ticker: Private
Employees: 56,000
Parent Company: Argos Holdings Inc

Exchange:
Fiscal Year Ends: 01/31

SALARIES/BONUSES:

Top Exec. Salary: $ Bonus: $
Second Exec. Salary: $ Bonus: $

OTHER THOUGHTS:

Estimated Female Officers or Directors: 3
Hot Spot for Advancement for Women/Minorities: Y

Pfizer Inc

NAIC Code: 325412

www.pfizer.com

TYPES OF BUSINESS:

Pharmaceuticals
Biopharmaceutical
Therapeutics
Drug Development

BRANDS/DIVISIONS/AFFILIATES:

Viatris Inc

GROWTH PLANS/SPECIAL FEATURES:

Pfizer, Inc. is a research-based, global biopharmaceutical company. The firm applies science and global resources to bring therapies for extending and improving the lives of people through the discovery, development, manufacture, marketing, sales and distribution of biopharmaceutical products worldwide. Pfizer works across developed and emerging markets to advance wellness, prevention, treatments and cures. The company's therapeutic areas include internal medicine, oncology, hospital, vaccines, inflammation, immunology and rare disease. Pfizer collaborates with healthcare providers, governments and local communities to support and expand access to healthcare around the globe. In November 2020, Pfizer spun off its off-patent branded and generics business, which included a portfolio of 20 globally recognized solid oral dose brands as well as its U.S.-based Greenstone generics platform, and combined it with Mylan to create Viatris, Inc. Viatris trades on the NASDAQ under ticker symbol VTRS. In August 2021, Pfizer received FDA approval for its Coronavirus vaccine which was developed in partnership with BioNTech SE.

CONTACTS: *Note: Officers with more than one job title may be intentionally listed here more than once.*

Albert Bourla, CEO
Michael Goettler, Pres., Divisional
Frank DAmelio, CFO
Ian Read, Chairman of the Board
Loretta Cangialosi, Chief Accounting Officer
Rady Johnson, Chief Risk Officer
Mikael Dolsten, Chief Scientific Officer
Lidia Fonseca, Chief Technology Officer
Sally Susman, Executive VP, Divisional
Douglas Lankler, Executive VP
Freda Lewis-Hall, Executive VP
Alexander Mackenzie, Executive VP
Dawn Rogers, Executive VP
John Young, Other Executive Officer
Margaret Madden, Other Executive Officer
Angela Hwang, President, Divisional

FINANCIAL DATA: *Note: Data for latest year may not have been available at press time.*

In U.S. $	2020	2019	2018	2017	2016	2015
Revenue	41,908,000,000	51,750,000,000	53,647,000,000	52,546,000,000	52,824,000,000	48,851,000,000
R&D Expense	9,405,000,000	8,650,000,000	8,006,000,000	7,657,000,000	7,872,000,000	7,690,000,000
Operating Income	8,760,001,000	13,921,000,000	15,045,000,000	14,107,000,000	13,730,000,000	12,976,000,000
Operating Margin %		.27%	.28%	.27%	.26%	.27%
SGA Expense	11,615,000,000	14,350,000,000	14,455,000,000	14,784,000,000	14,837,000,000	14,809,000,000
Net Income	9,616,000,000	16,273,000,000	11,153,000,000	21,308,000,000	7,215,000,000	6,960,000,000
Operating Cash Flow	14,403,000,000	12,588,000,000	15,827,000,000	16,470,000,000	15,901,000,000	14,512,000,000
Capital Expenditure	2,791,000,000	2,594,000,000	2,196,000,000	2,217,000,000	1,999,000,000	1,496,000,000
EBITDA	13,723,000,000	25,266,000,000	19,585,000,000	19,844,000,000	15,294,000,000	15,321,000,000
Return on Assets %		.10%	.07%	.12%	.04%	.04%
Return on Equity %		.26%	.17%	.33%	.12%	.10%
Debt to Equity		0.57	0.519	0.47	0.528	0.445

CONTACT INFORMATION:

Phone: 212 733-2323   Fax: 212 573-7851
Toll-Free:
Address: 235 E. 42nd St., New York, NY 10017 United States

STOCK TICKER/OTHER:

Stock Ticker: PFE
Employees: 93,000
Parent Company:

Exchange: NYS
Fiscal Year Ends: 12/31

SALARIES/BONUSES:

Top Exec. Salary: $ Bonus: $
Second Exec. Salary: $ Bonus: $

OTHER THOUGHTS:

Estimated Female Officers or Directors: 7
Hot Spot for Advancement for Women/Minorities: Y

PG&E Corporation

NAIC Code: 221111

www.pgecorp.com

TYPES OF BUSINESS:

Hydroelectric Power Generation
Electric and Gas Utility
Transmission
Distribution

GROWTH PLANS/SPECIAL FEATURES:

PG&E Corporation markets energy services and products in northern and central California through subsidiary Pacific Gas and Electric Company. The subsidiary is one of the largest electric and natural gas utilities in the U.S., serving customers throughout a 70,000-square-mile service area. PG&E's utility assets include 106,681 circuit miles of electric distribution lines and 18,466 circuit miles of interconnected transmission lines, serving more than 5 million electric customer accounts; and 42,141 miles of natural gas distribution pipelines and 6,438 miles of transmission pipelines, serving approximately 4.4 million natural gas customer accounts. In mid-2020, PG&E emerged from Chapter 11 bankruptcy protection.

BRANDS/DIVISIONS/AFFILIATES:

Pacific Gas and Electric Company

CONTACTS:
Note: Officers with more than one job title may be intentionally listed here more than once.

William L. Smith, Interim CEO
Michael Lewis, Senior VP, Divisional
David Thomason, CFO, Subsidiary
Jason Wells, CFO
Nora Brownell, Chairman of the Board
Julie Kane, Chief Compliance Officer
John Simon, Executive VP
Janet Loduca, General Counsel
Dinyar Mistry, Other Executive Officer
Loraine Giammona, Other Executive Officer
Kathleen Kay, Other Executive Officer
Fong Wan, Senior VP, Subsidiary

FINANCIAL DATA:
Note: Data for latest year may not have been available at press time.

In U.S. $	2020	2019	2018	2017	2016	2015
Revenue	18,469,000,000	17,129,000,000	16,759,000,000	17,135,000,000	17,666,000,000	16,833,000,000
R&D Expense						
Operating Income	2,419,000,000	1,341,000,000	2,071,000,000	2,956,000,000	2,177,000,000	1,508,000,000
Operating Margin %		.08%	.12%	.17%	.12%	.09%
SGA Expense						
Net Income	-1,304,000,000	-7,642,000,000	-6,837,000,000	1,660,000,000	1,407,000,000	888,000,000
Operating Cash Flow	-19,047,000,000	4,816,000,000	4,752,000,000	5,977,000,000	4,409,000,000	3,753,000,000
Capital Expenditure	7,690,000,000	6,313,000,000	6,514,000,000	5,641,000,000	5,709,000,000	5,173,000,000
EBITDA	3,787,000,000	-6,874,000,000	-6,164,000,000	5,913,000,000	5,046,000,000	4,246,000,000
Return on Assets %		-.09%	-.09%	.02%	.02%	.01%
Return on Equity %		-.86%	-.43%	.09%	.08%	.05%
Debt to Equity		0.337		0.924	0.904	0.967

CONTACT INFORMATION:

Phone: 415 973-8200   Fax: 415 973-8719
Toll-Free: 800-719-9056
Address: 77 Beale Street, 24/F, San Francisco, CA 94177 United States

STOCK TICKER/OTHER:

Stock Ticker: PCG
Employees: 24,000
Parent Company:

Exchange: NYS
Fiscal Year Ends: 12/31

SALARIES/BONUSES:

Top Exec. Salary: $ Bonus: $
Second Exec. Salary: $ Bonus: $

OTHER THOUGHTS:

Estimated Female Officers or Directors: 15
Hot Spot for Advancement for Women/Minorities: Y

Philips Healthcare

www.usa.philips.com/healthcare

NAIC Code: 334510

TYPES OF BUSINESS:

Manufacturing-Medical Equipment
Diagnostic & Treatment Equipment
Imaging Equipment
Equipment Repair & Maintenance
Healthcare Consulting

BRANDS/DIVISIONS/AFFILIATES:

Koninklijke Philips NV

CONTACTS: Note: Officers with more than one job title may be intentionally listed here more than once.

Frans van Houten, CEO-Koninklijke Philips
Eric Silfen, Chief Medical Officer
Clement Revetti, Chief Legal Officer
Michael Dreher, Global Head-Oper. & Customer Svcs.
Diego Olego, Chief Strategy & Innovation Officer
Rachel Bloom-Baglin, Media Contact-Global
Frans van Houten, CEO-Royal Philips Electronics NV
Steve Laczynski, Pres., Americas
Desmond Thio, Pres., China
Brent Shafer, CEO-Home Health Care Solutions
Arjen Radder, Pres., Asia Pacific

GROWTH PLANS/SPECIAL FEATURES:

Philips Healthcare, a subsidiary of Koninklijke Philips NV, manufactures medical diagnostic and treatment solutions, distributing its products to more than 100 countries worldwide. The company's many products and services address advanced molecular imaging, breathing/respiratory care, clinical informatics, computed tomography machines/solutions, customer service solutions, diagnostic electrocardiogram (ECG), electroencephalogram (EEG) neuroimaging, emergency care and resuscitation solutions, enterprise telehealth, fluoroscopy, hospital respiratory care, image-guided therapy devices, interventional X-ray systems and solutions, medical parts and related supplies, mother/child care, magnetic resonance imaging (MRI) systems and solutions, pathology, patient monitoring, radiation oncology, radiography, refurbished systems, sleep and ultrasounds. Philips Healthcare provides integrated solutions across the health continuum, from healthy living and prevention to diagnosis, treatment and home care. In August 2020, Philips agreed to acquire Intact Vascular, Inc., a U.S.-based developer of medical devices for minimally-invasive peripheral vascular procedures.

FINANCIAL DATA: Note: Data for latest year may not have been available at press time.

In U.S. $	2020	2019	2018	2017	2016	2015
Revenue	24,021,030,000	21,837,300,000	20,726,700,000	21,298,000,000	20,196,679,771	14,406,749,346
R&D Expense						
Operating Income						
Operating Margin %						
SGA Expense						
Net Income		1,343,830,000	1,254,740,000	2,240,000,000	1,570,860,000	697,041,000
Operating Cash Flow						
Capital Expenditure						
EBITDA						
Return on Assets %						
Return on Equity %						
Debt to Equity						

CONTACT INFORMATION:

Phone: 978-659-4278   Fax:
Toll-Free: 800-722-9377
Address: 222 Jacobs St., Cambridge, MA 02141 United States

STOCK TICKER/OTHER:

Stock Ticker: Subsidiary
Employees: 80,495
Parent Company: Koninklijke Philips NV

Exchange:
Fiscal Year Ends: 12/31

SALARIES/BONUSES:

Top Exec. Salary: $ Bonus: $
Second Exec. Salary: $ Bonus: $

OTHER THOUGHTS:

Estimated Female Officers or Directors: 2
Hot Spot for Advancement for Women/Minorities:

Pilgrims Pride Corporation

NAIC Code: 311615

TYPES OF BUSINESS:

Poultry Production
Poultry Production
Pork Production
Pet Food Production
Manufacturing
Distribution

BRANDS/DIVISIONS/AFFILIATES:

JBS SA

GROWTH PLANS/SPECIAL FEATURES:

Pilgrim's Pride Corporation produces, processes, markets and distributes fresh, frozen and value-added chicken and pork products. The company markets its portfolio to over 6,100 customers across the U.S., Mexico, the U.K. and Europe, including retailers, distributors and foodservice operators. Pilgrim's Pride's network consists of approximately 5,100 growers, 39 feed mills, 48 hatcheries, 39 processing plants, 27 prepared foods cook plants, 25 distribution centers, 10 rendering facilities and four pet food plants. The firm's chicken and pork products come as whole or cut up, pre-marinated or non-marinated. Case-ready options include various combinations of refrigerated, parts in trays, bags or other consumer packs labeled and priced for the retail grocer. Fresh chicken sales accounted for nearly 86% of the company's total U.S., U.K., Europe and Mexico chicken sales in 2020. Prepared products include portion-controlled chicken or pork, which come as fillets, strips, in salads, formed as nuggets or patties, and either boneless or bone-in. Other prepared meats include smoked, sausages, bacon, gammon joints, deli meats, meatballs and more. JBS SA owns a 78.31% share of Pilgrim's Pride.

CONTACTS:
Note: Officers with more than one job title may be intentionally listed here more than once.

Jayson Penn, CEO
Fabio Sandri, CFO
Gilberto Tomazoni, Chairman of the Board

FINANCIAL DATA:
Note: Data for latest year may not have been available at press time.

In U.S. $	2020	2019	2018	2017	2016	2015
Revenue	12,091,900,000	11,409,220,000	10,937,780,000	10,767,860,000	7,931,123,000	8,180,104,000
R&D Expense						
Operating Income	245,586,000	690,484,000	500,451,000	1,082,097,000	714,579,000	1,050,496,000
Operating Margin %		.06%	.05%	.10%	.09%	.13%
SGA Expense	592,610,000	379,910,000	343,025,000	389,517,000	199,781,000	203,881,000
Net Income	94,757,000	455,924,000	247,945,000	718,065,000	440,532,000	645,914,000
Operating Cash Flow	724,247,000	666,521,000	491,650,000	801,321,000	755,483,000	976,828,000
Capital Expenditure	354,762,000	348,120,000	348,666,000	339,872,000	272,467,000	175,764,000
EBITDA	625,047,000	1,037,405,000	774,696,000	1,367,041,000	899,071,000	1,189,281,000
Return on Assets %		.07%	.04%	.15%	.14%	.20%
Return on Equity %		.20%	.13%	.51%	.41%	.37%
Debt to Equity		0.994	1.142	1.428	1.14	0.783

CONTACT INFORMATION:

Phone: 970 506-8000   Fax: 903 856-7505
Toll-Free: 800-727-5366
Address: 1770 Promontory Cir., Greeley, CO 80634 United States

SALARIES/BONUSES:

Top Exec. Salary: $ Bonus: $
Second Exec. Salary: $ Bonus: $

STOCK TICKER/OTHER:

Stock Ticker: PPC
Employees: 56,400
Parent Company:

Exchange: NAS
Fiscal Year Ends: 12/31

OTHER THOUGHTS:

Estimated Female Officers or Directors: 1
Hot Spot for Advancement for Women/Minorities: Y

Plantronics Inc

www.poly.com

NAIC Code: 334210

TYPES OF BUSINESS:

Communications Headsets
Communications Accessories
Specialty Telephone Products
Wireless Headsets

BRANDS/DIVISIONS/AFFILIATES:

Poly
RealPresence

CONTACTS: *Note: Officers with more than one job title may be intentionally listed here more than once.*

Joseph Burton, CEO
Charles Boynton, CFO
Mary Huser, Chief Compliance Officer
Robert Hagerty, Director
Marvin Tseu, Director
Jeff Loebbaka, Executive VP, Divisional
Tom Puorro, Executive VP, Divisional

GROWTH PLANS/SPECIAL FEATURES:

Plantronics, Inc. does business as Poly, and designs, manufactures and markets integrated communication and collaboration solutions. Poly's primary product categories include: enterprise headsets, encompassing corded and cordless communication headsets; consumer headsets, including Bluetooth and corded products for mobile device applications, personal computer and gaming; and voice, video and content sharing solutions, such as open session initiation protocol (SIP) desktop phones, conference room phones and video endpoints (cameras, speakers and microphones). Poly's solutions are designed to work in a wide range of Unified Communications & Collaboration, Unified Communication-as-a-Service and Video-as-a-Service environments. Poly's RealPresence collaboration solutions range from infrastructure to endpoints and allow people to connect and collaborate globally and naturally. The firm also offers comprehensive support services, including support on its solutions and hardware devices, as well as professional, hosted and managed services. Enterprise products are sold through sales representatives, global distributors, channel partners, service providers and resellers. Consumer products are sold through traditional and online consumer electronics retailers, consumer products retailers, office supply distributors, wireless carriers, catalog and mail order companies, and mass merchants. Manufacturing operations are conducted through Plantronics' facility in Tijuana, Mexico, and through contract manufacturers and original design manufacturers in Asia. Plantronics' distribution centers are located in Mexico (serving the U.S., Canada and Latin America regions), Thailand (serving the Asia Pacific region, excluding mainland China), Czech Republic (serving Europe, Africa and Middle East regions), China (serving mainland China), and the U.S. (serving the Americas region).

FINANCIAL DATA: *Note: Data for latest year may not have been available at press time.*

In U.S. $	2020	2019	2018	2017	2016	2015
Revenue	1,696,990,000	1,674,535,000	856,903,000	881,176,000	856,907,000	
R&D Expense	218,277,000	201,886,000	84,193,000	88,318,000	90,408,000	
Operating Income	-261,505,000	-75,626,000	125,532,000	129,222,000	122,967,000	
Operating Margin %						
SGA Expense	595,463,000	567,879,000	229,390,000	223,830,000	221,299,000	
Net Income	-827,182,000	-135,561,000	-869,000	82,599,000	68,392,000	
Operating Cash Flow	78,019,000	116,047,000	121,148,000	137,971,000	146,869,000	
Capital Expenditure	22,880,000	26,797,000	12,468,000	23,176,000	30,661,000	
EBITDA	-573,681,000	125,743,000	146,710,000	150,199,000	143,109,000	
Return on Assets %						
Return on Equity %						
Debt to Equity						

CONTACT INFORMATION:

Phone: 831 426-5858   Fax: 831 426-6098
Toll-Free: 800-544-4660
Address: 345 Encinal St., Santa Cruz, CA 95060 United States

STOCK TICKER/OTHER:

Stock Ticker: POLY
Employees: 8,200
Parent Company:

Exchange: NYS
Fiscal Year Ends: 03/31

SALARIES/BONUSES:

Top Exec. Salary: $ Bonus: $
Second Exec. Salary: $ Bonus: $

OTHER THOUGHTS:

Estimated Female Officers or Directors: 4
Hot Spot for Advancement for Women/Minorities: Y

PPD Inc
NAIC Code: 541711

TYPES OF BUSINESS:
Contract Research
Clinical Development
Laboratory Services
Advanced Testing
Therapeutics

BRANDS/DIVISIONS/AFFILIATES:

GROWTH PLANS/SPECIAL FEATURES:

PPD, Inc. provides a comprehensive suite of clinical development and laboratory services to the pharmaceutical, biotechnology, medical device and government organizations, as well as other industry participants. The company's clinical development division encompasses all phases of development (Phases 1-4), peri- and post-approval and site and patient access services. Laboratory services include a range of high-value, advanced testing services, including bioanalytical, biomarker, vaccine, good manufacturing practice (GMP) and central laboratory services. PPD has developed significant expertise in the design and execution of complex global clinical trials, a result on conducting studies on global, national, regional and local levels across a wide spectrum of therapeutic areas in more than 100 countries. PPD is headquartered in North Carolina, USA, with offices in 46 countries. In April 2021, PPD agreed to be acquired by Thermo Fisher Scientific, Inc.

CONTACTS:
Note: Officers with more than one job title may be intentionally listed here more than once.

David Simmons, CEO
Christine A. Dingivan, Chief Medical Officer
B. Judd Hartman, General Counsel
William W. Richardson, Sr. VP-Global Bus. Dev.
Randy Buckwalter, Head-Media
Luke Heagle, Head-Investor Rel.
Lee E. Babiss, Chief Science Officer
David Johnston, Exec. VP-Global Lab Svcs.
Paul Colvin, Exec. VP-Global Clinical Dev.

FINANCIAL DATA:
Note: Data for latest year may not have been available at press time.

In U.S. $	2020	2019	2018	2017	2016	2015
Revenue	4,681,474,000	4,031,017,000	3,748,971,000	3,001,050,000	2,679,565,000	
R&D Expense						
Operating Income	509,431,000	418,489,000	402,237,000	261,328,000	314,264,000	
Operating Margin %		.10%	.11%	.09%	.12%	
SGA Expense	1,010,127,000	938,806,000	813,035,000	809,333,000	718,139,000	
Net Income	153,691,000	47,821,000	104,186,000	296,027,000	183,095,000	
Operating Cash Flow	251,334,000	432,946,000	423,406,000	359,079,000	407,995,000	
Capital Expenditure	163,331,000	125,928,000	116,145,000	105,135,000	90,258,000	
EBITDA	683,596,000	635,849,000	669,222,000	549,426,000	630,674,000	
Return on Assets %		.01%	.02%	.04%		
Return on Equity %						
Debt to Equity						

CONTACT INFORMATION:
Phone: 910-251-0081   Fax: 910-762-5820
Toll-Free:
Address: 929 N. Front St., Wilmington, NC 28401-3331 United States

STOCK TICKER/OTHER:
Stock Ticker: PPD   Exchange: NAS
Employees: 23,000   Fiscal Year Ends: 12/31
Parent Company:

SALARIES/BONUSES:
Top Exec. Salary: $ Bonus: $
Second Exec. Salary: $ Bonus: $

OTHER THOUGHTS:
Estimated Female Officers or Directors: 2
Hot Spot for Advancement for Women/Minorities:

PRA Health Sciences Inc

prahs.com

NAIC Code: 541711

TYPES OF BUSINESS:

Clinical Research & Testing Services
Contract Research
Clinical Drug Development
Data Management
Clinical Trial Management
Medical Writing
Regulatory Consulting
Drug Development Consulting

BRANDS/DIVISIONS/AFFILIATES:

ICON plc

GROWTH PLANS/SPECIAL FEATURES:

PRA Health Sciences is a contract research organization
(CRO) that provides clinical drug development and data
solution services to pharmaceutical and biotechnology
companies worldwide. The firm helps develop drugs with its
comprehensive clinical development services, including data
management, statistical analysis, clinical trial management,
medical writing, and regulatory and drug development
consulting. PRAH has more than 75 offices globally, serving
more than 80 countries. In July 2021, PRAH Health Sciences
was acquired by ICON plc and ceased from being publicly
traded.

CONTACTS: *Note: Officers with more than one job title may be intentionally listed here more than once.*

Michael Bonello, CFO
Ciaran Murray, Chmn.-ICON

FINANCIAL DATA: *Note: Data for latest year may not have been available at press time.*

In U.S. $	2020	2019	2018	2017	2016	2015
Revenue	3,183,365,120	3,066,262,016	2,871,921,920	2,259,388,928	1,811,710,976	1,613,883,008
R&D Expense						
Operating Income						
Operating Margin %						
SGA Expense						
Net Income	197,043,008	243,020,000	153,904,992	86,927,000	68,175,000	81,765,000
Operating Cash Flow						
Capital Expenditure						
EBITDA						
Return on Assets %						
Return on Equity %						
Debt to Equity						

CONTACT INFORMATION:

Phone: 919-786-8200   Fax: 919-786-8201
Toll-Free:
Address: 4130 Parklake Ave, Suite 400, Raleigh, NC 27612 United
States

STOCK TICKER/OTHER:

Stock Ticker: Subsidiary
Employees: 17,500
Parent Company: ICON plc

Exchange:
Fiscal Year Ends: 12/31

SALARIES/BONUSES:

Top Exec. Salary: $ Bonus: $
Second Exec. Salary: $ Bonus: $

OTHER THOUGHTS:

Estimated Female Officers or Directors: 2
Hot Spot for Advancement for Women/Minorities: Y

PriceSmart Inc

NAIC Code: 452910

www.pricesmart.com

TYPES OF BUSINESS:
Warehouse Clubs, Retail
Merchandise
Warehouse Club Membership

BRANDS/DIVISIONS/AFFILIATES:

CONTACTS: *Note: Officers with more than one job title may be intentionally listed here more than once.*
Sherry Bahrambeygui, CEO
Maarten Jager, CFO
Robert Price, Chairman of the Board
William Naylon, COO
Frank Diaz, Executive VP, Divisional
Rodrigo Calvo, Executive VP, Divisional
Brud Drachman, Executive VP, Divisional
John Hildebrandt, Executive VP, Divisional
Laura Santana, Executive VP, Divisional
Jesus Von Chong, Executive VP, Geographical
Francisco Velasco, Executive VP
Ana Bianchi, Executive VP

GROWTH PLANS/SPECIAL FEATURES:
PriceSmart, Inc. is one of the largest operators of warehouse membership clubs in Central America, the Caribbean and Colombia. The company serves more than 3 million cardholders at 46 owned and operated warehouse clubs (as of August 2020). PriceSmart's typical warehouse buildings range in sales floor size from 40,000 to 60,000 square feet, and are located primarily in and around the major cities of its markets. The firm also constructs smaller sales floor warehouse clubs so as to reach additional geographic areas. PriceSmart's membership club model is similar to U.S. clubs like Costco and Sam's, with some differences: smaller store size, lower membership fees (average $35), and merchandise is tailored to local preferences as well as for retail and wholesale customers. PriceSmart warehouse clubs can be found in Colombia, 7; Costa Rica, 8; Panama, 7; Dominican Republic, 5; Trinidad and Tobago, 4; Guatemala, 4; Honduras, 3; El Salvador, 2; Nicaragua, 2; and one each in Aruba, Barbados, Jamaica and the U.S. Virgin Islands. Online shopping is available to its members in all countries. Merchandise departments include electronics, computers, baby, automotive, restaurant/institutional, sporting goods, outdoor, hardware, toys and games, appliances, housewares, bed and bath, luggage, healthcare, furniture, office and fashion accessories.

FINANCIAL DATA: *Note: Data for latest year may not have been available at press time.*

In U.S. $	2020	2019	2018	2017	2016	2015
Revenue	3,329,188,000	3,223,918,000	3,166,702,000	2,996,628,000	2,905,176,000	2,802,603,000
R&D Expense						
Operating Income	122,911,000	116,115,000	129,320,000	138,431,000	137,885,000	148,371,000
Operating Margin %		.04%	.04%	.05%	.05%	.05%
SGA Expense	429,954,000	409,386,000	379,949,000	338,401,000	316,474,000	297,656,000
Net Income	78,109,000	73,191,000	74,328,000	90,724,000	88,723,000	89,124,000
Operating Cash Flow	259,268,000	170,332,000	119,454,000	122,856,000	139,862,000	110,503,000
Capital Expenditure	100,320,000	140,061,000	98,109,000	135,294,000	77,700,000	89,185,000
EBITDA	184,890,000	170,007,000	180,299,000	185,812,000	176,925,000	177,481,000
Return on Assets %		.06%	.06%	.08%	.08%	.09%
Return on Equity %		.09%	.10%	.13%	.14%	.16%
Debt to Equity		0.08	0.116	0.124	0.115	0.129

CONTACT INFORMATION:
Phone: 858 404-8800   Fax: 858 404-8848
Toll-Free:
Address: 9740 Scranton Rd., San Diego, CA 92121 United States

STOCK TICKER/OTHER:
Stock Ticker: PSMT   Exchange: NAS
Employees: 9,500   Fiscal Year Ends: 08/31
Parent Company:

SALARIES/BONUSES:
Top Exec. Salary: $ Bonus: $
Second Exec. Salary: $ Bonus: $

OTHER THOUGHTS:
Estimated Female Officers or Directors: 4
Hot Spot for Advancement for Women/Minorities: Y

PricewaterhouseCoopers (PwC)

www.pwc.com

NAIC Code: 541211

TYPES OF BUSINESS:

Accounting Services
Business Advisory
Corporate Finance Services
Employee Benefits Services
Tax Services
Business Publications
Management Consulting

BRANDS/DIVISIONS/AFFILIATES:

CONTACTS: *Note: Officers with more than one job title may be intentionally listed here more than once.*

Martyn Curragh, CFO
J.C. Lapierre, CCO
Mike Fenlon, Chief People Officer
Joe Atkinson, CTO
Gary Price, Chief Admin. Officer
Diana Weiss, General Counsel
Robert E. Moritz, Chmn.
Mitch Cohen, Vice Chmn.
Terri McClements, Head-U.S. Human Capital & Public Policy
Laura Cox Kaplan, Head-Regulation Affairs & Public Policy
Tim Ryan, Chmn.

GROWTH PLANS/SPECIAL FEATURES:

PricewaterhouseCoopers (PwC) is a global accounting firm with offices in 155 countries. PwC provides the following services: audit/assurance, consulting, entrepreneurial/private clients, family business, IFRS (a global financial reporting language), legal, people/organization, sustainability/climate change and tax. PwC covers such areas as cybersecurity and privacy, human resources, deals and forensics. The company serves a wide array of industry sectors, including aerospace/defense, asset and wealth management, automotive, banking/capital markets, capital projects, infrastructure, chemicals, communications, energy, utilities, mining, engineering, construction, entertainment/media, financial services, forest/paper/packaging, government services, public services, healthcare, hospitality/leisure, industrial manufacturing, insurance, metals, pharmaceuticals, life sciences, private equity, real estate, retail, consumer, sovereign wealth funds, technology and transportation and logistics. PwC is very active in the consulting business, including management consulting and technology consulting, representing a substantial portion of total revenues for the firm.

PwC offers its employees comprehensive health benefits, retirement and savings options, and a variety of employee assistance programs, which may vary by country.

FINANCIAL DATA: *Note: Data for latest year may not have been available at press time.*

In U.S. $	2020	2019	2018	2017	2016	2015
Revenue	43,032,000,000	42,488,000,000	41,280,000,000	37,695,000,000	35,900,000,000	35,400,000,000
R&D Expense						
Operating Income						
Operating Margin %						
SGA Expense						
Net Income						
Operating Cash Flow						
Capital Expenditure						
EBITDA						
Return on Assets %						
Return on Equity %						
Debt to Equity						

CONTACT INFORMATION:

Phone: 646-471-3000   Fax: 813-286-6000
Toll-Free:
Address: 300 Madison Ave., New York, NY 10017-6204 United States

STOCK TICKER/OTHER:

Stock Ticker: Private
Employees: 284,258
Parent Company:

Exchange:
Fiscal Year Ends: 06/30

SALARIES/BONUSES:

Top Exec. Salary: $ Bonus: $
Second Exec. Salary: $ Bonus: $

OTHER THOUGHTS:

Estimated Female Officers or Directors: 5
Hot Spot for Advancement for Women/Minorities: Y

Principal Financial Group Inc

NAIC Code: 524113

www.principal.com

TYPES OF BUSINESS:

Asset Management
Life Insurance
Health Insurance
Annuities
Disability Insurance
Investment Services
Specialty Benefits Insurance

BRANDS/DIVISIONS/AFFILIATES:

CONTACTS: *Note: Officers with more than one job title may be intentionally listed here more than once.*

Patrick Halter, CEO, Subsidiary
Daniel Houston, CEO
Deanna Strable-Soethout, CFO
Gary Scholten, Chief Information Officer
Julia Lawler, Chief Risk Officer
Karen Shaff, Executive VP
Timothy Dunbar, Executive VP
Amy Friedrich, President, Divisional
Luis Valdes, President, Divisional
Nora Everett, President, Divisional

GROWTH PLANS/SPECIAL FEATURES:

The Principal Financial Group is a leading provider of retirement savings, investment and insurance products and services. It holds a total of $626.8 billion in assets and serves 24.2 million customers globally. The company is organized into four segments: retirement and income solutions, principal global investors, principal international and U.S. insurance solutions. The retirement and income solutions segment offers products and services for retirement savings and retirement income to small- and medium-sized businesses (companies with less than 1,000 employees), including 401(k) and 403(b) plans, benefit pension plans, non-qualified executive benefit plants, employee stock ownership plans, as well as SIMPLE individual retirement accounts (IRA) and payroll deduction plans. For large institutional clients, it offers investment-only products such as guaranteed investment contracts; and for employees of businesses and other individuals, it offers accumulate savings for retirement plans, as well as mutual funds, individual annuities and bank products. The principal global investors segment manages assets for sophisticated investors worldwide, including equity, fixed income, real estate and other alternative investments. This division maintains offices worldwide, including Australia, Brazil, China, France, Germany, Hong Kong, Ireland, Italy, Japan, Luxembourg, the Netherlands, Portugal, Singapore, Spain, Switzerland, the UAE, the U.K. and the U.S. The principal international segment focuses on countries and territories with growing middle classes, favorable demographics and increasing long-term savings. This division has operations in Latin America and Asia. The U.S. insurance solutions segment offers group and individual insurance solutions, providing comprehensive insurance solutions for small- and medium-sized businesses and their owners and executives. These include both group and individual dental, vision, life and disability insurance; and both group and individual life insurance options.

Employee benefits include medical, dental and vision coverage; and 401(k), employee stock and retirement plans.

FINANCIAL DATA: *Note: Data for latest year may not have been available at press time.*

In U.S. $	2020	2019	2018	2017	2016	2015
Revenue	14,741,700,000	16,222,100,000	14,237,200,000	14,093,200,000	12,394,100,000	11,964,400,000
R&D Expense						
Operating Income						
Operating Margin %						
SGA Expense	4,646,500,000	4,503,900,000	4,136,700,000	3,893,800,000	3,732,600,000	3,672,400,000
Net Income	1,395,800,000	1,394,200,000	1,546,500,000	2,310,400,000	1,316,500,000	1,234,000,000
Operating Cash Flow	3,738,600,000	5,493,200,000	5,156,500,000	4,188,000,000	3,857,800,000	4,377,100,000
Capital Expenditure	108,800,000	132,400,000	92,300,000	164,800,000	154,900,000	136,400,000
EBITDA						
Return on Assets %		.01%	.01%	.01%	.01%	.01%
Return on Equity %		.11%	.13%	.20%	.13%	.12%
Debt to Equity		0.255	0.286	0.247	0.306	0.353

CONTACT INFORMATION:

Phone: 515 247-5111   Fax:
Toll-Free: 800-986-3343
Address: 711 High St., Des Moines, IA 50392 United States

SALARIES/BONUSES:

Top Exec. Salary: $ Bonus: $
Second Exec. Salary: $ Bonus: $

STOCK TICKER/OTHER:

Stock Ticker: PFG
Employees: 17,400
Parent Company:

Exchange: NAS
Fiscal Year Ends: 12/31

OTHER THOUGHTS:

Estimated Female Officers or Directors: 10
Hot Spot for Advancement for Women/Minorities: Y

Procter & Gamble Company (The)

www.pg.com

NAIC Code: 325620

TYPES OF BUSINESS:

Personal Care Products
Beauty Products
Household Products and Cleansers
Personal Care Products
Fabric Care Products
Franchising, Dry Cleaners and Car Washes
Pet Products
Diapers and Toilet Paper

BRANDS/DIVISIONS/AFFILIATES:

Head & Shoulders
Olay
Braun
Crest
Metamucil
Downy
Swiffer
Pampers

CONTACTS: Note: Officers with more than one job title may be intentionally listed here more than once.

Jon Moeller, CFO
Mary Ferguson-McHugh, Pres., Divisional
Valarie Sheppard, Chief Accounting Officer
David Taylor, Director
Jeffrey Schomburger, Other Corporate Officer
Ioannis Skoufalos, Other Corporate Officer
M. Grabowski, Other Executive Officer
Kathleen Fish, Other Executive Officer
Marc Pritchard, Other Executive Officer
Deborah Majoras, Other Executive Officer
Gary Coombe, President, Divisional
Matthew Price, President, Divisional
Shailesh Jejurikar, President, Divisional
Fama Francisco, President, Divisional
Steven Bishop, President, Divisional
R. Keith, President, Divisional
Loic Tassel, President, Geographical

GROWTH PLANS/SPECIAL FEATURES:

The Procter & Gamble Company develops and manufactures a wide range of consumer packaged goods, which are marketed in more than 180 countries and territories. The firm operates in five reportable segments: beauty, grooming, health care, fabric and home care, and baby, feminine and family care. The beauty segment consists of two product categories: hair care such as conditioners, shampoo, styling aids and treatments; and skin and personal care such as antiperspirants, deodorants, personal cleansing and skin care. Major brands within this division include: (hair care) Head & Shoulders, Herbal Essences, Pantene and Rejoice; and (skin/personal care) Olay, Old Spice, Safeguard, SK-II and Secret. The grooming segment consists of shave products such as razors, blades, pre- and post-shave products, and related appliances. Brands include Braun, Gillette and Venus. The health care segment consists of: oral care such as toothbrushes, toothpaste and other oral care products; and personal health care such as gastrointestinal products, respiratory products, rapid diagnostics, vitamins/minerals/supplements, pain relievers and other personal health care products. Brands include: (oral care) Crest and Oral-B; and (personal health care) Metamucil, Neurobion, Pepto Bismol and Vicks. The fabric and home care segment consists of: fabric care such as fabric enhancers, laundry additives and laundry detergents; and home care such as air care, dish care, surface care and more. Brands include (fabric care) Airel, Downy, Gain and Tide; and (home care) Cascade, Dawn, Fairy, Febreeze, Mr. Clean and Swiffer. Last, the baby, feminine and family care segment consists of: baby care products such as wipes and diapers; feminine care products addressing adult incontinence and feminine care; and family care such as paper towels, tissues and toilet paper. Brands within this division include (baby care) Luvs and Pampers; (feminine care) Always, Always Discreet and Tampax; and (family care) Bounty, Charmin and Puffs.

FINANCIAL DATA: Note: Data for latest year may not have been available at press time.

In U.S. $	2020	2019	2018	2017	2016	2015
Revenue	70,950,000,000	67,684,000,000	66,832,000,000	65,058,000,000	65,299,000,000	
R&D Expense						
Operating Income	15,706,000,000	13,832,000,000	13,711,000,000	13,955,000,000	13,441,000,000	
Operating Margin %		.20%	.21%	.21%	.21%	
SGA Expense	19,994,000,000	19,084,000,000	18,853,000,000	18,568,000,000	18,949,000,000	
Net Income	13,027,000,000	3,897,000,000	9,750,000,000	15,326,000,000	10,508,000,000	
Operating Cash Flow	17,403,000,000	15,242,000,000	14,867,000,000	12,753,000,000	15,435,000,000	
Capital Expenditure	3,073,000,000	3,347,000,000	3,717,000,000	3,384,000,000	3,314,000,000	
EBITDA	19,312,000,000	9,402,000,000	16,666,000,000	16,542,000,000	17,026,000,000	
Return on Assets %		.03%	.08%	.12%	.08%	
Return on Equity %		.07%	.18%	.27%	.17%	
Debt to Equity		0.441	0.406	0.333	0.336	

CONTACT INFORMATION:

Phone: 513 983-1100   Fax: 513 983-9369
Toll-Free:
Address: One Procter & Gamble Plz., Cincinnati, OH 45202 United States

STOCK TICKER/OTHER:

Stock Ticker: PG
Employees: 99,000
Parent Company:

Exchange: NYS
Fiscal Year Ends: 06/30

SALARIES/BONUSES:

Top Exec. Salary: $ Bonus: $
Second Exec. Salary: $ Bonus: $

OTHER THOUGHTS:

Estimated Female Officers or Directors: 18
Hot Spot for Advancement for Women/Minorities: Y

Protiviti Inc

NAIC Code: 541610

www.protiviti.com

TYPES OF BUSINESS:

Risk Consulting
Financial Consulting
Technology Consulting
Business Consulting
Litigation, Restructuring and Investigative Services
Governance Consulting

BRANDS/DIVISIONS/AFFILIATES:

Robert Half International Inc
Bulletin (The)
KnowledgeLeader

CONTACTS: Note: Officers with more than one job title may be intentionally listed here more than once.

Joseph A. Tarantino, CEO
Andrew Clinton, Exec. VP-International Operations
Barbara Rothenstein, Exec. VP-Global Finance & Operations
Patrick Scott, Exec. VP-Mktg. & Client Programs
Scott Redfearn, Exec. VP-Global Human Resources
Carol M. Beaumier, Exec. VP-Global Strategic Planning
Patrick Scott, Exec. VP-Global Industry & Client Programs
Brian Christensen, Exec. VP-Global Internal Audit
James Pajakowski, Exec. VP-Global Services
Shaheen Dil, Managing Dir.-Risk & Compliance
Andrew Clinton, Exec. VP-Int'l Oper.

GROWTH PLANS/SPECIAL FEATURES:

Protiviti, Inc., a wholly-owned subsidiary of Robert Half International, Inc., is a global business consulting and internal audit firm specializing in risk, advisory and transactional services. The firm advises clients concerning critical business problems, including business performance, enterprise data and analytics, internal audit, financial advisory, managed solutions, operational resilience, risk and compliance, robotic process automation, technology consulting and transaction services. Protiviti serves a variety of industries, including consumer products and services, energy, utilities, financial services, healthcare, manufacturing, distribution, private equity, technology, media and telecommunications. Protiviti's products include publications such as The Bulletin newsletter, white papers and research reports; software such as the firm's GRC (governance/risk/compliance) portal; and the KnowledgeLeader website, which is a subscription-based tool that provides audit programs, checklists, tools, resources and best practices to internal auditors and risk management professionals. Based in the U.S., the firm has offices throughout the Americas, Asia Pacific, Europe, the Middle East and Africa.

Protiviti offers its employees comprehensive health benefits, retirement and savings options, and a variety of employee assistance programs.

FINANCIAL DATA: Note: Data for latest year may not have been available at press time.

In U.S. $	2020	2019	2018	2017	2016	2015
Revenue	1,144,000,000	1,100,000,000	958,000,000	816,533,000	804,000,000	742,700,000
R&D Expense						
Operating Income						
Operating Margin %						
SGA Expense						
Net Income						
Operating Cash Flow						
Capital Expenditure						
EBITDA						
Return on Assets %						
Return on Equity %						
Debt to Equity						

CONTACT INFORMATION:

Phone: 650-234-6000   Fax: 650-234-6999
Toll-Free:
Address: 2884 Sand Hill Rd., Ste 200, Menlo Park, CA 94025 United States

STOCK TICKER/OTHER:

Stock Ticker: Subsidiary   Exchange:
Employees: 7,000   Fiscal Year Ends:
Parent Company: Robert Half International Inc

SALARIES/BONUSES:

Top Exec. Salary: $ Bonus: $
Second Exec. Salary: $ Bonus: $

OTHER THOUGHTS:

Estimated Female Officers or Directors: 1
Hot Spot for Advancement for Women/Minorities:

Prudential Financial Inc

www.prudential.com

NAIC Code: 524113

TYPES OF BUSINESS:

Insurance-Life
Property & Casualty Insurance
Asset Management
Life Insurance
Retirement
Group Insurance
Individual Insurance
Technology

BRANDS/DIVISIONS/AFFILIATES:

PGIM
Assurance IQ

CONTACTS: *Note: Officers with more than one job title may be intentionally listed here more than once.*

Charles Lowrey, CEO
Robert Falzon, Vice Chairman
Kenneth Tanji, CFO
John Strangfeld, Chairman of the Board
Robert Axel, Chief Accounting Officer
Barbara Koster, Chief Information Officer
Timothy Schmidt, Chief Investment Officer
Nicholas Silitch, Chief Risk Officer
Scott Sleyster, COO, Divisional
Stephen Pelletier, COO, Geographical
Mark Grier, Director
Timothy Harris, Executive VP
Lucien Alziari, Other Executive Officer
Candace Woods, Other Executive Officer

GROWTH PLANS/SPECIAL FEATURES:

Prudential Financial, Inc. provides a wide range of insurance, investment management and other financial products and services to individual and institutional customers throughout the U.S., as well as in many other countries. The company operates through four divisions: PGIM, U.S. businesses, U.S. individual solutions, and Assurance IQ. PGIM provides asset management services related to public and private fixed income, public equity and real estate, commercial mortgage origination and servicing, and mutual funds and other retail services. The U.S. businesses division consists of two business units: the retirement solutions unit develops and distributes retirement and income products and services to retirement plan sponsors in the public, private and not-for-profit sectors; the group insurance solutions unit develops and distributes group life, long-term and short-term group disability, and group corporate-, bank- and trust-owned life insurance in the U.S. primarily to institutional clients for use in connection with employee and membership benefits plans, and also sells accidental death and dismemberment and other ancillary coverages, and provides plan administrative services in connection with its insurance coverages. The U.S. individual division consists of two business units: the individual annuities unit develops and distributes individual variable and fixed annuity products primarily to U.S. mass affluent (households with investable assets or annual income in excess of $100,000) and affluent ($250,000+) customers; and the individual life unit develops and distributes variable life, universal life and term life insurance products primarily to U.S. mass middle (assets $25,000+ or annual income $50,000+), mass affluent ($100,000+) and affluent ($250,000+) customers. Last, the Assurance IQ division leverages data science and technology to distribute third-party life, health, Medicare and property and casualty products directly to retail shoppers primarily through its digital and independent agent channels.

Prudential offers employees comprehensive benefits and retirement plans.

FINANCIAL DATA: *Note: Data for latest year may not have been available at press time.*

In U.S. $	2020	2019	2018	2017	2016	2015
Revenue	57,033,000,000	64,807,000,000	62,992,000,000	59,689,000,000	58,779,000,000	57,119,000,000
R&D Expense						
Operating Income						
Operating Margin %						
SGA Expense	13,913,000,000	13,416,000,000	11,949,000,000	11,915,000,000	11,779,000,000	10,912,000,000
Net Income	-374,000,000	4,186,000,000	4,074,000,000	7,863,000,000	4,368,000,000	5,642,000,000
Operating Cash Flow	8,368,000,000	19,625,000,000	21,664,000,000	13,445,000,000	14,778,000,000	13,895,000,000
Capital Expenditure						
EBITDA						
Return on Assets %		.00%	.00%	.01%	.01%	.01%
Return on Equity %		.07%	.08%	.16%	.10%	.13%
Debt to Equity		0.311	0.377	0.346	0.44	0.676

CONTACT INFORMATION:

Phone: 973 802-6000   Fax: 973 367-6476
Toll-Free: 877-998-7625
Address: 751 Broad St., Newark, NJ 07102 United States

STOCK TICKER/OTHER:

Stock Ticker: PRU   Exchange: NYS
Employees: 51,511   Fiscal Year Ends: 12/31
Parent Company:

SALARIES/BONUSES:

Top Exec. Salary: $ Bonus: $
Second Exec. Salary: $ Bonus: $

OTHER THOUGHTS:

Estimated Female Officers or Directors: 6
Hot Spot for Advancement for Women/Minorities: Y

Publicis Sapient

NAIC Code: 541512

www.publicissapient.com

TYPES OF BUSINESS:

IT Consulting
Internet Strategy Consulting
Interactive Marketing Software

BRANDS/DIVISIONS/AFFILIATES:

Publicis Groupe SA
Publicis.Sapient

CONTACTS: *Note: Officers with more than one job title may be intentionally listed here more than once.*

Nigel Vaz, CEO
Nathalie Le Bos, CFO
Teresa Barreira, CMO
Kameshwari Rao, Interim Chief Talent Officer
Alan Wexler, Executive VP
J. Moore, Founder
Joseph LaSala, General Counsel
Harry Register, Managing Director, Divisional
Christian Oversohl, Managing Director, Geographical
Laurie MacLaren, Senior VP, Divisional

GROWTH PLANS/SPECIAL FEATURES:

Publicis Sapient, a subsidiary of Publicis Groupe SA, is a business consulting and technology services firm focused on digital transformation and the dynamics of an always-on world. The firm's Publicis.Sapient platform is designed to help clients reimagine core business activities via transformation in order to drive growth and improve operating efficiency. The platform's digital transformation technology helps businesses in three keyways: creates business opportunities by rapidly reaching, meeting and/or changing customer expectations and behavior; creates new value via ongoing technological advances in marketing, sales, service, supply chain, IT and more; and stays ahead of competitors through smart/connected products and an enterprise-wide open ecosystem. According to Publicis Sapient, digital is at the core of transformation because the entire business eventually needs to be wired for the digital world, primarily change-sensitive technology architectures and rapid development methods. The Publicis.Sapient platform's data and analytics on customers provide strategy and direction to Sapient Corporation's business consulting services to its clients. Therefore, Sapient combines these technology capabilities with consulting expertise for the best outcomes for its business clients. Publicis Sapient serves financial services, retail, technology, communications, consumer packaged goods, travel/leisure, automotive, energy services, government, health and education sectors, among others. Based in the USA, the firm has operations worldwide, including the Americas, Europe and Asia-Pacific.

FINANCIAL DATA: *Note: Data for latest year may not have been available at press time.*

In U.S. $	2020	2019	2018	2017	2016	2015
Revenue	1,877,871,996	1,805,646,150	1,765,050,000	1,681,000,000	1,625,000,000	1,562,781,000
R&D Expense						
Operating Income						
Operating Margin %						
SGA Expense						
Net Income						
Operating Cash Flow						
Capital Expenditure						
EBITDA						
Return on Assets %						
Return on Equity %						
Debt to Equity						

CONTACT INFORMATION:

Phone: 617 621-0200   Fax: 617 621-1300
Toll-Free: 877-454-9860
Address: 131 Dartmouth St., Boston, MA 02116 United States

STOCK TICKER/OTHER:

Stock Ticker: Subsidiary   Exchange:
Employees: 20,000   Fiscal Year Ends: 12/31
Parent Company: Publicis Groupe SA

SALARIES/BONUSES:

Top Exec. Salary: $ Bonus: $
Second Exec. Salary: $ Bonus: $

OTHER THOUGHTS:

Estimated Female Officers or Directors: 2
Hot Spot for Advancement for Women/Minorities:

Publix Super Markets Inc

investors.pricesmart.com/home-page

NAIC Code: 445110

TYPES OF BUSINESS:

Grocery Stores
Dairy, Deli & Bakery Products
Convenience Stores
Liquor Stores
Restaurants

BRANDS/DIVISIONS/AFFILIATES:

GROWTH PLANS/SPECIAL FEATURES:

Publix Super Markets, Inc. Is a food retailer that operates more than 1,250 stores throughout the U.S. (as of September 26, 2020). These supermarkets are located in the states of Florida, Georgia, Alabama, South Carolina, Tennessee, North Carolina and Virginia. Publix sells grocery items such as dairy, produce, floral, deli, bakery, meat and seafood, as well as health and beauty care, general merchandise, pharmacy and other products. The firm's merchandise includes a variety of nationally advertised and private label brands and unbranded products. Products are delivered to the supermarkets through Publix's distribution centers or directly from the suppliers.

Publix offers its employees health, dental and vision coverage;401(k); and a variety of employee assistance programs.

CONTACTS: *Note: Officers with more than one job title may be intentionally listed here more than once.*

Sharon Miller, Assistant Secretary
David Bornmann, VP
William Crenshaw, CEO
David Phillips, CFO
Laurie Zeitlin, Chief Information Officer
Charles Jenkins, Director
Hoyt Barnett, Director
Randall Jones, President
John Hrabusa, Senior VP
John Attaway, Senior VP
Linda Hall, Vice President
Dale Myers, Vice President
David Duncan, Vice President
David Bridges, Vice President
Michael Smith, Vice President
Thomas Mclaughlin, Vice President
William Fauerbach, Vice President
Alfred Ottolino, Vice President
Mark Irby, Vice President
John Frazier, Vice President
Marc Salm, Vice President

FINANCIAL DATA: *Note: Data for latest year may not have been available at press time.*

In U.S. $	2020	2019	2018	2017	2016	2015
Revenue	44,863,507,000	38,215,502,438	36,395,716,608	34,836,836,352	34,274,109,440	32,618,758,144
R&D Expense						
Operating Income						
Operating Margin %						
SGA Expense						
Net Income	3,971,838,000	3,005,395,000	2,381,167,104	2,291,894,016	2,025,688,064	1,965,048,064
Operating Cash Flow						
Capital Expenditure						
EBITDA						
Return on Assets %						
Return on Equity %						
Debt to Equity						

CONTACT INFORMATION:

Phone: 863 688-1188   Fax: 863 688-5532
Toll-Free: 800-242-1227
Address: 3300 Publix Corporate Pkwy., Lakeland, FL 33811 United States

STOCK TICKER/OTHER:

Stock Ticker: Private
Employees: 227,000
Parent Company:

Exchange:
Fiscal Year Ends: 12/31

SALARIES/BONUSES:

Top Exec. Salary: $ Bonus: $
Second Exec. Salary: $ Bonus: $

OTHER THOUGHTS:

Estimated Female Officers or Directors: 5
Hot Spot for Advancement for Women/Minorities: Y

Puget Energy Inc

NAIC Code: 221111

www.pugetenergy.com

TYPES OF BUSINESS:

Hydroelectric Power Generation
Electric Utility
Wind Generation
Solar Generation

BRANDS/DIVISIONS/AFFILIATES:

Puget Holdings LLC
Puget Sound Energy Inc
Puget LNG LLC

CONTACTS: Note: Officers with more than one job title may be intentionally listed here more than once.

Kimberly Harris, CEO
William Ayers, Chmn.-Puget Sound Energy, Inc.
Susan McLain, Sr. VP-Delivery Oper., Puget Sound Energy, Inc.
Donald E. Gaines, VP-Finance
Steven W. Hooper, Chmn.

GROWTH PLANS/SPECIAL FEATURES:

Puget Energy, Inc. is an energy services holding company whose operations are conducted through Puget Sound Energy, Inc. (PSE), a regulated utility company. Puget Energy also has a wholly owned non-regulated subsidiary, Puget LNG, LLC, which owns, develops and finances the non-regulated activity of a liquefied natural gas (LNG) facility at the Port of Tacoma, Washington. PSE furnishes electric and natural gas service in a territory covering approximately 6,000 square miles, principally in the Puget Sound region, serving 1.1 million electric customers and 790,000 natural gas customers. PSE's electric power resources are either company-owned or -controlled, or obtained via long-term contracts, had a total capacity of 4,696 megawatts (MW). Company-controlled resources are made up of hydroelectric, coal, natural gas, oil, wind and other. PSE purchases natural gas supplies for its power portfolio to meet demand for its combustion turbine generators. These supplies range from long-term to daily agreements, and purchases are made from a diverse group of major and independent natural gas producers and marketers in Canada and the U.S. Puget Energy, Inc. itself is an indirect, wholly owned subsidiary of Puget Holdings, LLC.

FINANCIAL DATA: Note: Data for latest year may not have been available at press time.

In U.S. $	2020	2019	2018	2017	2016	2015
Revenue	3,326,450,000	3,401,130,000	3,346,496,000	3,460,276,000	3,164,301,000	3,092,700,000
R&D Expense						
Operating Income						
Operating Margin %						
SGA Expense						
Net Income	182,717,000	292,924,000	235,622,000	175,194,000	312,889,000	241,179,000
Operating Cash Flow						
Capital Expenditure						
EBITDA						
Return on Assets %						
Return on Equity %						
Debt to Equity						

CONTACT INFORMATION:

Phone: 425-454-6363   Fax:
Toll-Free:
Address: 10885 NE 4th St., Ste. 1200, Bellevue, WA 98004 United States

STOCK TICKER/OTHER:

Stock Ticker: Subsidiary
Employees: 3,150
Parent Company: Puget Holdings LLC

Exchange:
Fiscal Year Ends: 12/31

SALARIES/BONUSES:

Top Exec. Salary: $ Bonus: $
Second Exec. Salary: $ Bonus: $

OTHER THOUGHTS:

Estimated Female Officers or Directors: 3
Hot Spot for Advancement for Women/Minorities: Y

PulteGroup Inc

pultegroupinc.com

NAIC Code: 236117

TYPES OF BUSINESS:

Construction, Home Building and Residential
Financial Services
Mortgages
Land Development
Home Building

BRANDS/DIVISIONS/AFFILIATES:

Pulte Mortgage LLC
Centex
Pulte Homes
Del Webb
DiVosta Homes
John Wieland Homes and Neighborhoods
American West

CONTACTS: Note: Officers with more than one job title may be intentionally listed here more than once.

Ryan Marshall, CEO
Robert OShaughnessy, CFO
James Ossowski, Chief Accounting Officer
Todd Sheldon, Executive VP
John Chadwick, President, Divisional
Stephen Schlageter, Senior VP, Divisional
Michelle Hairston, Senior VP, Divisional

GROWTH PLANS/SPECIAL FEATURES:

PulteGroup, Inc. is a leading homebuilder in the U.S. The firm's subsidiaries primarily engage in the homebuilding business, and Pulte Mortgage, LLC handles the mortgage banking and title operations of the group. PulteGroup builds a wide variety of homes targeted for first-time, first and second move-up and active adult home buyers, including detached units, townhouses, condominium apartments and duplexes, with varying prices, models, options and lot sizes. Homebuilding brands include Centex, Pulte Homes, Del Webb, DiVosta Homes, John Wieland Homes and Neighborhoods, and American West. The company operates in more than 40 homebuilding markets throughout the U.S., offering homes in about 880 active communities. During 2020, the firm closed 24,624 homes, with the average unit selling price of $430,000, compared with $427,000 in 2019. Sales prices range from $150,000 to more than $2,500,000, with 92% falling between $200,000 and $750,000. PulteGroup's homes are located six geographic segments: Northeast (Connecticut, Maryland, Massachusetts, New Jersey, Pennsylvania and Virginia); Southeast (Georgia, North Carolina, South Carolina and Tennessee); Florida; Midwest (Illinois, Indiana, Kentucky, Michigan, Minnesota and Ohio); Texas; and West (Arizona, California, Nevada, New Mexico and Washington). The firm's strategy is based on extensive market research that reveals well-defined buying profiles, job demographics and lifestyle choices. During 2021, PulteGroup announced plans to enter the Denver, Colorado market and to expand into the Triad area of North Carolina.

FINANCIAL DATA: Note: Data for latest year may not have been available at press time.

In U.S. $	2020	2019	2018	2017	2016	2015
Revenue	11,036,080,000	10,212,960,000	10,188,330,000	8,573,250,000	7,668,476,000	5,981,964,000
R&D Expense						
Operating Income	1,747,025,000	1,338,852,000	1,347,589,000	952,979,000	968,864,000	820,486,000
Operating Margin %		.13%	.13%	.11%	.13%	.14%
SGA Expense	1,011,442,000	1,044,337,000	1,012,023,000	891,581,000	957,150,000	589,780,000
Net Income	1,406,839,000	1,016,700,000	1,022,023,000	447,221,000	602,703,000	494,090,000
Operating Cash Flow	1,784,342,000	1,077,545,000	1,449,744,000	663,077,000	68,270,000	-348,129,000
Capital Expenditure	58,354,000	58,119,000	59,039,000	32,051,000	39,295,000	45,440,000
EBITDA	1,799,023,000	1,394,159,000	1,397,587,000	990,329,000	988,543,000	863,033,000
Return on Assets %		.10%	.10%	.04%	.06%	.06%
Return on Equity %		.20%	.23%	.10%	.13%	.10%
Debt to Equity		0.583	0.701	0.829	0.743	0.502

CONTACT INFORMATION:

Phone: 404-978-6400   Fax:
Toll-Free: 866-785-8325
Address: 3350 Peachtree Rd. NE, Ste 150, Atlanta, GA 30326 United States

STOCK TICKER/OTHER:

Stock Ticker: PHM
Employees: 5,249
Parent Company:

Exchange: NYS
Fiscal Year Ends: 12/31

SALARIES/BONUSES:

Top Exec. Salary: $ Bonus: $
Second Exec. Salary: $ Bonus: $

OTHER THOUGHTS:

Estimated Female Officers or Directors: 4
Hot Spot for Advancement for Women/Minorities: Y

Qualcomm Incorporated

NAIC Code: 334413

www.qualcomm.com

TYPES OF BUSINESS:

Telecommunications Equipment
Digital Wireless Communications Products
Integrated Circuits
Mobile Communications Systems
Wireless Software & Services
E-Mail Software
Code Division Multiple Access

BRANDS/DIVISIONS/AFFILIATES:

CONTACTS: Note: Officers with more than one job title may be intentionally listed here more than once.

Steven Mollenkopf, CEO
David Wise, CFO
Jeffrey Henderson, Chairman of the Board
Erin Polek, Chief Accounting Officer
James Thompson, Chief Technology Officer
Michelle Sterling, Executive VP, Divisional
Brian Modoff, Executive VP, Divisional
Donald Rosenberg, Executive VP
Alexander Rogers, Executive VP
Cristiano Amon, President

GROWTH PLANS/SPECIAL FEATURES:

Qualcomm Incorporated provides digital wireless communications products, technologies and services. Its operations are divided into three segments: Qualcomm CDMA Technologies (QCT), Qualcomm Technology Licensing (QTL) and Qualcomm Strategic Initiatives (QSI). QCT designs application-specific integrated circuits based on Code Division Multiple Access (CDMA), Orthogonal Frequency-Division Multiple Access (OFDMA), Time Division Multiple Access (TDMA) and other technologies for use in voice and data communications, networking, application processing, multimedia functions and GPS products. QTL grants licenses and provides rights to use portions of Qualcomm's intellectual property portfolio to third-party manufacturers of wireless products and networking equipment. QSI makes strategic investments in various companies and technologies that Qualcomm believes will open new opportunities for its technologies. Subsidiary RF360 Holdings Singapore Pte. Ltd. (RF360), delivers radio frequency (RF) front-end modules and RF filters into fully integrated systems for mobile devices and fast-growing business segments such as the Internet of Things, drones, robotics, automotive applications and more. Qualcomm Incorporated has pioneered in 3G, 4G and 5G wireless technologies, not just for smartphones and mobile devices, but also for industries and applications including automotive, Internet of Things (IoT), networking, computing and artificial intelligence (AI). The company's non-reporting segments include cyber security solutions, mobile health, small cells and other wireless technology and service initiatives.

U.S. employees of the company receive medical, dental and vision insurance; dependent/health care reimbursement accounts; tuition reimbursement; a 401(k); and an employee stock purchase plan.

FINANCIAL DATA: Note: Data for latest year may not have been available at press time.

In U.S. $	2020	2019	2018	2017	2016	2015
Revenue	23,531,000,000	24,273,000,000	22,732,000,000	22,291,000,000	23,554,000,000	25,281,000,000
R&D Expense	5,975,000,000	5,398,000,000	5,625,000,000	5,485,000,000	5,151,000,000	5,490,000,000
Operating Income	6,255,000,000	7,667,000,000	742,000,000	2,614,000,000	6,495,000,000	5,776,000,000
Operating Margin %		.32%	.03%	.12%	.28%	.23%
SGA Expense	2,074,000,000	2,195,000,000	2,986,000,000	2,658,000,000	2,385,000,000	2,344,000,000
Net Income	5,198,000,000	4,386,000,000	-4,864,000,000	2,466,000,000	5,705,000,000	5,271,000,000
Operating Cash Flow	5,814,000,000	7,286,000,000	3,895,000,000	4,693,000,000	7,400,000,000	5,506,000,000
Capital Expenditure	1,407,000,000	887,000,000	784,000,000	690,000,000	539,000,000	994,000,000
EBITDA	7,714,000,000	9,509,000,000	2,842,000,000	4,975,000,000	8,558,000,000	7,805,000,000
Return on Assets %		.13%	-.10%	.04%	.11%	.11%
Return on Equity %		1.50%	-.31%	.08%	.18%	.15%
Debt to Equity		2.737	16.557	0.631	0.315	0.317

CONTACT INFORMATION:

Phone: 858 587-1121   Fax: 858 658-2100
Toll-Free:
Address: 5775 Morehouse Dr., San Diego, CA 92121 United States

STOCK TICKER/OTHER:

Stock Ticker: QCOM
Employees: 41,000
Parent Company:

Exchange: NAS
Fiscal Year Ends: 09/30

SALARIES/BONUSES:

Top Exec. Salary: $ Bonus: $
Second Exec. Salary: $ Bonus: $

OTHER THOUGHTS:

Estimated Female Officers or Directors: 2
Hot Spot for Advancement for Women/Minorities: Y

Quest Diagnostics Incorporated

www.questdiagnostics.com

NAIC Code: 621511

TYPES OF BUSINESS:

Services-Testing & Diagnostics
Clinical Laboratory Testing
Clinical Trials Testing
Esoteric Testing Laboratories

BRANDS/DIVISIONS/AFFILIATES:

Quanum
Mid America Clinical Laboratories

CONTACTS: Note: Officers with more than one job title may be intentionally listed here more than once.

Stephen Rusckowski, CEO
Mark Guinan, CFO
Michael Deppe, Chief Accounting Officer
James Davis, Executive VP, Divisional
Michael Prevoznik, General Counsel
Catherine Doherty, Other Corporate Officer
Everett Cunningham, Senior VP, Divisional
Carrie Eglinton Manner, Senior VP, Divisional

GROWTH PLANS/SPECIAL FEATURES:

Quest Diagnostics Incorporated is a world-leading provider of diagnostic information services. The firm's diagnostic insights reveal new avenues to identify and treat disease, inspire healthy behaviors and improve health care management. Diagnostic testing services range from routine blood tests (such as total cholesterol, Pap testing and white blood cell count) to complex, gene-based and molecular testing. These tests are grouped into two categories: general diagnostics, consisting of routine and non-routine testing; and advanced diagnostics, consisting of genetic and advanced molecular testing. These services enable healthcare partners to deliver health care more efficiently, and help support population health via data analytics and extended care services. Quest Diagnostics is also a global clinical trials laboratory services organization that helps biopharmaceutical, medical device and diagnostics customers improve human health through innovation that transforms science and data into medical insights. Quest Diagnostics offers healthcare information technology (IT) solutions, including its Quanum suite of technology and analytics solutions so that physicians can order lab tests, receive test results, share clinical information quickly and securely, and prescribe drugs. Employer solutions include pre-employment drugs-of-abuse screening, and risk assessment services based on health and wellness laboratory testing. Based in New Jersey, Quest Diagnostics' laboratories, patient service centers, offices and other facilities are located throughout the U.S., as well as select locations outside the U.S. During 2020, Quest Diagnostics wholly-acquired Mid America Clinical Laboratories, a leading independent clinical laboratory provider in Indiana. In June 2021, Quest acquired the outreach laboratory business of Mercy in an all-cash transaction.

FINANCIAL DATA: Note: Data for latest year may not have been available at press time.

In U.S. $	2020	2019	2018	2017	2016	2015
Revenue	9,437,000,000	7,726,000,000	7,531,000,000	7,709,000,000	7,515,000,000	7,493,000,000
R&D Expense						
Operating Income	1,971,000,000	1,231,000,000	1,105,000,000	1,165,000,000	1,159,000,000	1,065,000,000
Operating Margin %		.16%	.15%	.15%	.15%	.14%
SGA Expense	1,550,000,000	1,457,000,000	1,424,000,000	1,750,000,000	1,681,000,000	1,679,000,000
Net Income	1,431,000,000	858,000,000	736,000,000	772,000,000	645,000,000	709,000,000
Operating Cash Flow	2,005,000,000	1,243,000,000	1,200,000,000	1,175,000,000	1,069,000,000	810,000,000
Capital Expenditure	418,000,000	400,000,000	383,000,000	252,000,000	293,000,000	263,000,000
EBITDA	2,411,000,000	1,585,000,000	1,404,000,000	1,453,000,000	1,479,000,000	1,561,000,000
Return on Assets %		.07%	.07%	.07%	.06%	.07%
Return on Equity %		.16%	.14%	.16%	.14%	.16%
Debt to Equity		0.776	0.657	0.762	0.806	0.746

CONTACT INFORMATION:

Phone: 973 520-2700   Fax:
Toll-Free: 800-222-0446
Address: 500 Plaza Dr., Secaucus, NJ 07094 United States

STOCK TICKER/OTHER:

Stock Ticker: DGX
Employees: 47,000
Parent Company:

Exchange: NYS
Fiscal Year Ends: 12/31

SALARIES/BONUSES:

Top Exec. Salary: $ Bonus: $
Second Exec. Salary: $ Bonus: $

OTHER THOUGHTS:

Estimated Female Officers or Directors: 3
Hot Spot for Advancement for Women/Minorities: Y

Sales, profits and employees may be estimates. Financial information, benefits and other data can change quickly and may vary from those stated here.

Rackspace Technology Inc

NAIC Code: 517110

www.rackspace.com

TYPES OF BUSINESS:

Web Hosting Services
Data Centers
Cloud Computing Services
Server Farms

BRANDS/DIVISIONS/AFFILIATES:

Apollo Global Management LLC
Onica

CONTACTS: *Note: Officers with more than one job title may be intentionally listed here more than once.*

Kevin Jones, CEO
Subroto Mukerji, COO
Amar Maletira, CFO
Amanda Samuels, CMO
Holly Windham, Chief People Officer
Tolga Tarhan, CTO

GROWTH PLANS/SPECIAL FEATURES:

Rackspace Technology, Inc. provides managed cloud services in the business information technology (IT) market worldwide. The firm actively offers four service categories: Cloud, Applications, Data and Security. It delivers advice and integrated managed services across public and private clouds, managed hosting and enterprise applications. The company partners with leading technology platform providers, including VMware, Alibaba Cloud, Amazon Web Services, Google Cloud Platform, Microsoft, OpenStack, Pivotal Cloud Foundry, Oracle and SAP. Rackspace's solutions include application management, business intelligence, database management, digital experience, email hosting, enterprise resource planning (ERP), productivity and collaboration and website hosting. Industries served by the firm include automotive, business services, education, energy, financial services, government, healthcare, manufacturing and retail. Rackspace is owned by private equity firm, Apollo Global Management, LLC. Based in Texas, the company serves approximately 150,000 business customers, including most of the Fortune 100, from data centers on five continents. In November 2020, Rackspace announced it acquired Bright Skies GmbH, a service provider for cloud transformation in Germany with a focus on the modernization of data centers, cloud managed services and artificial intelligence.

FINANCIAL DATA: *Note: Data for latest year may not have been available at press time.*

In U.S. $	2020	2019	2018	2017	2016	2015
Revenue	2,707,100,000	2,438,100,000	2,452,800,000	2,144,700,000		
R&D Expense						
Operating Income	24,700,000	99,500,000	57,800,000	-122,800,000		
Operating Margin %		.04%	.02%	-.06%		
SGA Expense	959,700,000	911,700,000	949,300,000	942,200,000		
Net Income	-245,800,000	-102,300,000	-470,600,000	-59,900,000		
Operating Cash Flow	116,700,000	292,900,000	429,800,000	291,700,000		
Capital Expenditure	116,500,000	198,000,000	294,300,000	189,500,000		
EBITDA	493,300,000	774,100,000	391,600,000	620,600,000		
Return on Assets %		-.02%	-.08%			
Return on Equity %		-.11%	-.52%			
Debt to Equity		4.659	4.651			

CONTACT INFORMATION:

Phone: 210 312-4000   Fax: 210 312-4300
Toll-Free: 800-961-2888
Address: 1 Fanatical Pl., City of Windcrest, San Antonio, TX 78218 United States

STOCK TICKER/OTHER:

Stock Ticker: RXT   Exchange: NAS
Employees: 7,200   Fiscal Year Ends: 12/31
Parent Company: Apollo Global Management LLC

SALARIES/BONUSES:

Top Exec. Salary: $ Bonus: $
Second Exec. Salary: $ Bonus: $

OTHER THOUGHTS:

Estimated Female Officers or Directors: 1
Hot Spot for Advancement for Women/Minorities:

Raymond James Financial Inc

www.raymondjames.com

NAIC Code: 523110

TYPES OF BUSINESS:

Stock Brokerage/Investment Banking
Trust Services
Asset Management
Banking

BRANDS/DIVISIONS/AFFILIATES:

Raymond James Bank

CONTACTS: Note: Officers with more than one job title may be intentionally listed here more than once.

Paul Allison, CEO, Subsidiary
Scott Curtis, Pres., Divisional
Dennis Zank, CEO, Subsidiary
Steven Raney, CEO, Subsidiary
Tashtego Elwyn, CEO, Subsidiary
Paul Reilly, CEO
Jennifer Ackart, CFO, Subsidiary
Jeffrey Julien, CFO
Thomas James, Chairman Emeritus
Jeffrey Dowdle, Chief Administrative Officer
George Catanese, Chief Risk Officer
Francis Godbold, Director
Bella Allaire, Executive VP, Subsidiary
Jonathan Santelli, Executive VP
James Bunn, President, Subsidiary
Jodi Perry, President, Subsidiary
John Carson, President

GROWTH PLANS/SPECIAL FEATURES:

Raymond James Financial, Inc. (RJF) is a diversified financial services holding company that provides private client group, capital markets, asset management, banking and other services to individuals, corporations and municipalities. The firm manages approximately $930 billion of total client assets under management, as of September 30, 2020. The private client group segment provides financial planning and securities transaction services through a branch office network. The capital markets segment conducts institutional sales, securities trading, equity research, investment banking and the syndication and management of investments that qualify for tax credits. The asset management segment earns asset management and related administrative fees for providing portfolio management and related administrative services for retail and institutional clients. Raymond James Bank (RJ Bank) is a national bank that provides various types of loans, including corporate loans (commercial and industrial), commercial real estate, commercial real estate construction, tax-exempt loans, residential loans, securities-based loans and other loans. RJ Bank is active in corporate loan syndications and participations, and also provides Federal Deposit Insurance Corporation (FDIC)-insured deposit accounts, including to clients of RJF's broker-dealer subsidiaries. Last, the other segment includes RJF's private equity investments, interest income on certain corporate cash balances and certain corporate overhead costs not allocated to RJF's core business segments. The company primarily operates in the U.S., and to a lesser extent in Canada, the U.K. and other parts of Europe.

FINANCIAL DATA: Note: Data for latest year may not have been available at press time.

In U.S. $	2020	2019	2018	2017	2016	2015
Revenue	7,889,000,000	7,646,000,000	7,181,930,000	6,243,855,000	5,300,605,000	5,097,893,000
R&D Expense						
Operating Income						
Operating Margin %						
SGA Expense	5,992,000,000	5,654,000,000	5,342,724,000	4,694,274,000	4,052,906,000	3,950,740,000
Net Income	818,000,000	1,034,000,000	856,695,000	636,235,000	529,350,000	502,140,000
Operating Cash Flow	4,054,000,000	577,000,000	1,903,327,000	1,305,936,000	-518,324,000	899,177,000
Capital Expenditure	124,000,000	138,000,000	133,586,000	189,994,000	121,733,000	74,111,000
EBITDA						
Return on Assets %		.03%	.02%	.02%	.02%	.02%
Return on Equity %		.16%	.14%	.12%	.11%	.12%
Debt to Equity		0.371	0.385	0.439	0.468	0.39

CONTACT INFORMATION:

Phone: 727 567-1000   Fax:
Toll-Free: 800-248-8863
Address: 880 Carillon Pkwy., St. Petersburg, FL 33716 United States

STOCK TICKER/OTHER:

Stock Ticker: RJF
Employees: 14,800
Parent Company:

Exchange: NYS
Fiscal Year Ends: 09/30

SALARIES/BONUSES:

Top Exec. Salary: $ Bonus: $
Second Exec. Salary: $ Bonus: $

OTHER THOUGHTS:

Estimated Female Officers or Directors: 1
Hot Spot for Advancement for Women/Minorities: Y

Red Hat Inc

NAIC Code: 511210I

www.redhat.com

TYPES OF BUSINESS:

Computer Software-Linux Operating Systems
Open-Source Software

BRANDS/DIVISIONS/AFFILIATES:

International Business Machines Corporation (IBM)
Red Hat Enterprise Linux
Red Hat OpenShift Container Storage
Red Hat OpenShift Container Platform
Red Hat OpenStack Platform

CONTACTS: Note: Officers with more than one job title may be intentionally listed here more than once.

Paul Cormier, CEO
Eric Shander, CFO
Arun Oberoi, Executive VP, Divisional
Michael Cunningham, Executive VP
DeLisa Alexander, Executive VP
Paul Cormier, President, Divisional

GROWTH PLANS/SPECIAL FEATURES:

Red Hat, Inc. is a provider of open-source software solutions. The firm's core enterprise platform is Red Hat Enterprise Linux, the foundation for an enterprise hybrid cloud. Linux is an opensource operating system from which enterprises can scale existing apps and roll out emerging technologies across bare-metal, virtual, container and other types of cloud environments. Red Hat OpenShift Container Storage is a software-defined storage for hybrid cloud and multi-cloud container deployments. Red Hat OpenShift Container Platform is an enterprise-ready Kubernetes container platform with full-stack automated operations to manage hybrid cloud and multi-cloud deployments. Red Hat OpenStack Platform is a cloud computing platform that virtualizes resources from industry-standard hardware, organizes those resources into clouds and manages them so users can access what they need as they need it. Red Hat also offers related tools for customers, partners and developers, and its website provides a resource library for information purposes. Red Hat is owned by multinational information technology company, IBM, and has more than 100 offices in 40+ countries.

FINANCIAL DATA: Note: Data for latest year may not have been available at press time.

In U.S. $	2020	2019	2018	2017	2016	2015
Revenue	3,315,000,000	3,400,000,000	2,920,461,056	2,411,802,880	2,052,230,016	1,789,489,024
R&D Expense						
Operating Income						
Operating Margin %						
SGA Expense						
Net Income						
Operating Cash Flow			258,803,008	253,703,008	199,364,992	180,200,992
Capital Expenditure						
EBITDA						
Return on Assets %						
Return on Equity %						
Debt to Equity						

CONTACT INFORMATION:

Phone: 919 754-3700   Fax: 919 754-3701
Toll-Free: 888-733-4281
Address: 100 East Davie St., Raleigh, NC 27601 United States

SALARIES/BONUSES:

Top Exec. Salary: $ Bonus: $
Second Exec. Salary: $ Bonus: $

STOCK TICKER/OTHER:

Stock Ticker: Subsidiary   Exchange:
Employees: 10,500   Fiscal Year Ends: 02/28
Parent Company: International Business Machines Corporation (IBM)

OTHER THOUGHTS:

Estimated Female Officers or Directors: 3
Hot Spot for Advancement for Women/Minorities: Y

Regal-Beloit Corporation

www.regal-beloit.com

NAIC Code: 335312

TYPES OF BUSINESS:

Mechanical Products Manufacturing
Electric Motors
Motion Controls
Generators
Power Transmission

BRANDS/DIVISIONS/AFFILIATES:

CONTACTS: *Note: Officers with more than one job title may be intentionally listed here more than once.*

Louis Pinkham, CEO
Robert Rehard, CFO
Rakesh Sachdev, Chairman of the Board
Jason Longley, Chief Accounting Officer
Jonathan Schlemmer, COO
Thomas Valentyn, General Counsel
Timothy Oswald, Vice President, Divisional
John Avampato, Vice President

GROWTH PLANS/SPECIAL FEATURES:

Regal-Beloit Corporation is a U.S.-based multinational corporation that manufactures electric motors and motion controls, electric generators and power transmission products. The company operates through four segments: commercial systems, industrial systems, climate solutions and power transmission solutions. The commercial systems segment designs, manufactures and sells AC/DC motors from fractional to approximately 5 horsepower, electronic variable speed controls, fans and blowers for commercial applications. These products are sold directly to original equipment manufacturers (OEMs) and end-user customers. Typical applications for these products include commercial building ventilation and HVAC, fan, blower and compressor motors, fans, blowers, water pumps for pools, spas, irrigation, and dewatering, and general commercial equipment. The industrial systems segment designs, manufactures and sells: integral and large AC motors from approximately 3 to 12,000 horsepower (up to 10,000 volts) for general industrial applications, along with aftermarket parts and kits to support such products; electric alternators for prime and standby power applications from 5 kilowatts through 4 megawatts (in 50 and 60 Hz); and power generation switchgear for prime power, standby power, distributed generation and cogeneration applications and residential, automatic and bypass isolation transfer switches. The climate solutions segment designs, manufactures and sells fractional motors, electronic variable speed controls and blowers used in a variety of residential and light commercial air moving applications including HVAC systems and commercial refrigeration. Last, the power transmission solutions segment designs, manufactures and markets: mounted and unmounted bearings; high-quality conveyor products such as chains, belts, sprockets, components, guide rails and wear strips; high-performance disc, diaphragm and gear couplings; mechanical power transmission drives and components; and gearboxes for motion control within complex equipment and systems used for a variety of applications. Regal-Beloit's manufacturing, sales and service facilities are located in the U.S., Mexico, China, Europe, India, Thailand and Australia, as well as other locations worldwide.

FINANCIAL DATA: *Note: Data for latest year may not have been available at press time.*

In U.S. $	2020	2019	2018	2017	2016	2015
Revenue	2,907,000,000	3,238,000,000	3,645,600,000	3,360,300,000	3,224,500,000	3,509,700,000
R&D Expense						
Operating Income	295,800,000	316,400,000	365,200,000	330,100,000	320,600,000	332,700,000
Operating Margin %		.10%	.10%	.10%	.10%	.09%
SGA Expense						
Net Income	189,300,000	238,900,000	231,200,000	213,000,000	203,400,000	143,300,000
Operating Cash Flow	435,400,000	408,500,000	362,700,000	291,900,000	439,600,000	381,100,000
Capital Expenditure	47,500,000	92,400,000	77,600,000	65,200,000	65,200,000	92,200,000
EBITDA	421,800,000	491,300,000	489,800,000	470,500,000	480,500,000	416,500,000
Return on Assets %		.05%	.05%	.05%	.05%	.04%
Return on Equity %		.10%	.10%	.10%	.10%	.07%
Debt to Equity		0.505	0.566	0.447	0.643	0.886

CONTACT INFORMATION:

Phone: 608 364-8800   Fax: 608 364-8818
Toll-Free:
Address: 200 State St., Beloit, WI 53511 United States

STOCK TICKER/OTHER:

Stock Ticker: RBC
Employees: 23,000
Parent Company:

Exchange: NYS
Fiscal Year Ends: 12/31

SALARIES/BONUSES:

Top Exec. Salary: $ Bonus: $
Second Exec. Salary: $ Bonus: $

OTHER THOUGHTS:

Estimated Female Officers or Directors:
Hot Spot for Advancement for Women/Minorities:

Regeneron Pharmaceuticals Inc

NAIC Code: 325412

www.regeneron.com

TYPES OF BUSINESS:

Drugs-Diversified
Protein-Based Drugs
Small-Molecule Drugs
Genetics & Transgenic Mouse Technologies

BRANDS/DIVISIONS/AFFILIATES:

Arcalyst
Praluent
EYLEA
Dupixent
ZALTRAP
VelociGene
VelociMouse
VelocImmune

CONTACTS: *Note: Officers with more than one job title may be intentionally listed here more than once.*

Leonard Schleifer, CEO
Robert Landry, CFO
P. Vagelos, Chairman of the Board
Christopher Fenimore, Chief Accounting Officer
George Yancopoulos, Chief Scientific Officer
Neil Stahl, Executive VP, Divisional
Joseph Larosa, Executive VP
Daniel Van Plew, Executive VP
Marion McCourt, Senior VP, Divisional

GROWTH PLANS/SPECIAL FEATURES:

Regeneron Pharmaceuticals, Inc. is a biopharmaceutical company that discovers, develops, manufactures and commercializes pharmaceutical drugs. The company's commercialized medicines and product candidates in development are designed to help patients with eye diseases, allergic and inflammatory diseases, cancer, cardiovascular and metabolic diseases, neuromuscular diseases, infectious diseases and rare diseases. Regeneron's marketed-approved products include: Arcalyst (rilonacept), a therapy for cryopyrin-associated periodic syndromes (CAPS), a rare, inherited inflammatory condition; Praluent (alirocumab) injection, an adjunct to diet and maximally-tolerated statin therapy for adults who require additional lowering of LDL cholesterol; EYLEA (aflibercept), an injection treatment for neovascular age-related macular degeneration patients; Dupixent (dupilumab), an injection for the treatment of adult patients with moderate-to-severe atopic dermatitis; Kevzara (sarilumab), a solution for subcutaneous injection for the treatment of rheumatoid arthritis in adults; Inmazeb (atoltivimab, maftivimab and odesivmab-ebgn), an injection for the treatment of infection caused by Zaire ebolavirus; Libtayo (cemiplimab), an injection for the treatment of metastatic or locally-advanced cutaneous squamous cell carcinoma; and ZALTRAP (ziv-aflibercept), an injection, in combination with 5-fluorouracil, leucovorin, irinotecan, for patients with metastatic colorectal cancer. Regeneron's proprietary technologies include VelociGene, VelociMouse and VelocImmune. The VelociGene technology allows precise DNA manipulation and gene staining, helping to identify where a particular gene is active in the body. VelociMouse technology allows for the direct and immediate generation of genetically altered mice from embryonic stem cells, avoiding the lengthy process involved in generating and breeding knock-out mice from chimeras. VelocImmune is a novel mouse technology platform for producing fully human monoclonal antibodies. Additionally, VelociMab technologies allow rapid screenings of therapeutic antibodies; VelociT produces fully-human therapeutic T-cell receptors against tumor and viral antigens; Veloci-Bi allows for the generation of full-length bi-specific antibodies; and VelociHum is used to test human therapeutics against human immune cells.

FINANCIAL DATA: *Note: Data for latest year may not have been available at press time.*

In U.S. $	2020	2019	2018	2017	2016	2015
Revenue	8,497,100,000	7,863,400,000	6,710,800,000	5,872,227,000	4,860,427,000	4,103,728,000
R&D Expense	2,735,000,000	3,036,600,000	2,186,100,000	2,075,142,000	2,052,295,000	1,620,577,000
Operating Income	3,576,600,000	2,209,800,000	2,534,400,000	2,079,591,000	1,330,741,000	1,251,916,000
Operating Margin %		.28%	.38%	.35%	.27%	.31%
SGA Expense	1,346,000,000	1,834,800,000	1,556,200,000	1,320,433,000	1,177,697,000	838,526,000
Net Income	3,513,200,000	2,115,800,000	2,444,400,000	1,198,511,000	895,522,000	636,056,000
Operating Cash Flow	2,618,100,000	2,430,000,000	2,195,100,000	1,307,112,000	1,473,396,000	1,330,780,000
Capital Expenditure	614,600,000	429,600,000	383,100,000	272,626,000	511,941,000	677,933,000
EBITDA	4,103,200,000	2,669,600,000	2,729,900,000	2,249,097,000	1,441,755,000	1,314,247,000
Return on Assets %		.16%	.24%	.15%	.14%	.13%
Return on Equity %		.21%	.33%	.23%	.22%	.21%
Debt to Equity		0.064	0.081	0.114	0.079	0.099

CONTACT INFORMATION:

Phone: 914 847-7000   Fax:
Toll-Free:
Address: 777 Old Saw Mill River Rd., Tarrytown, NY 10591-6707 United States

STOCK TICKER/OTHER:

Stock Ticker: REGN
Employees: 9,123
Parent Company:

Exchange: NAS
Fiscal Year Ends: 12/31

SALARIES/BONUSES:

Top Exec. Salary: $ Bonus: $
Second Exec. Salary: $ Bonus: $

OTHER THOUGHTS:

Estimated Female Officers or Directors:
Hot Spot for Advancement for Women/Minorities:

REI (Recreational Equipment Inc)

www.rei.com

NAIC Code: 451110

TYPES OF BUSINESS:

Outdoor Gear & Clothing, Retail
Sporting Equipment Retail & Rental
Adventure Travel Services
Catalog & Online Sales

BRANDS/DIVISIONS/AFFILIATES:

REI
REI Adventures
REI Gear and Apparel
www.rei.com
www.rei.com/rei-garage

CONTACTS: Note: Officers with more than one job title may be intentionally listed here more than once.

Eric Artz, CEO
Susan Viscon, VP-Merch.
Catherine Walker, General Counsel
Brad Brown, Sr. VP-e-Commerce & Direct Sales
Michael Collins, VP-Public Affairs
Sue Sallee, VP-Finance & Acct.
Tim Spangler, Sr. VP-Retail
Kathleen Peterson, VP-REI Private Brands
Anthony Truesdale, Chmn.
Rick Bingle, VP-Supply Chain

GROWTH PLANS/SPECIAL FEATURES:

Recreational Equipment, Inc. (REI) is one of the largest consumer cooperatives in the U.S. The firm offers quality outdoor gear, clothing and footwear selected for performance and durability in outdoor recreation, including hiking, climbing, camping, bicycling, paddling and winter sports. Today, REI has approximately 20 million members served by over 165 retail stores across 39 U.S. states and Washington DC, as well as ecommerce sites www.rei.com and www.rei.com/rei-garage (outlet). Stores include a variety of facilities for testing equipment, including bike test trails, climbing pinnacles and camp stove demonstration tables. While anyone may shop at the stores, customers who pay a small fee to become members receive special discounts and a share in the company's profits through an annual patronage refund based on their purchases. REI's ecommerce sites offer a comprehensive library of product information, expert gear advice and outdoor recreation information. In addition to nationally-recognized brands, the company sells private label apparel and accessories under the REI Gear and Apparel brand. It also offers mountain, road, specialty, hybrid, electric and kid's bikes under various brand names. Through REI Adventures, the company has been operating small group tours throughout the world for decades, avoiding standard tourist routes and emphasizing outdoor activities. Each year, REI Adventures plans domestic and international bicycling, trekking, kayaking, hiking, camping and mountaineering adventures. The firm invests millions of dollars on an annual basis to build trails, clean up the environment and teach children outdoor ethics.

REI offers its employees comprehensive health benefits, retirement and profit-sharing plans, tuition reimbursement and a variety of assistance plans and programs.

FINANCIAL DATA: Note: Data for latest year may not have been available at press time.

In U.S. $	2020	2019	2018	2017	2016	2015
Revenue	2,754,714,000	3,122,994,000	2,781,909,000	2,622,776,000	2,423,221,000	2,217,130,000
R&D Expense						
Operating Income						
Operating Margin %						
SGA Expense						
Net Income	-33,543,000	22,137,000	46,753,000	30,525,000	38,275,000	44,183,000
Operating Cash Flow						
Capital Expenditure						
EBITDA						
Return on Assets %						
Return on Equity %						
Debt to Equity						

CONTACT INFORMATION:

Phone: 253-891-2500   Fax: 253-891-2523
Toll-Free: 800-426-4840
Address: 6750 S. 228th St., Kent, WA 98032 United States

STOCK TICKER/OTHER:

Stock Ticker: Private
Employees: 15,000
Parent Company:

Exchange:
Fiscal Year Ends: 01/02

SALARIES/BONUSES:

Top Exec. Salary: $ Bonus: $
Second Exec. Salary: $ Bonus: $

OTHER THOUGHTS:

Estimated Female Officers or Directors: 7
Hot Spot for Advancement for Women/Minorities: Y

Rent-A-Center Inc

www.rentacenter.com

NAIC Code: 532210

TYPES OF BUSINESS:

Consumer Electronics and Appliances Rental
Retail
Financing

BRANDS/DIVISIONS/AFFILIATES:

Rent-A-Center Franchising International Inc
Rent-A-Center
Get It Now
Home Choice

CONTACTS: Note: Officers with more than one job title may be intentionally listed here more than once.

Maureen Short, CFO
Jeffrey Brown, Chairman of the Board
Mike Santimaw, Chief Information Officer
Ann Davids, Chief Marketing Officer
Mitchell Fadel, Director
Catherine Skula, Executive VP
James York, Executive VP, Divisional
Christopher Crocker, Executive VP, Divisional
Dawn Wolverton, General Counsel

GROWTH PLANS/SPECIAL FEATURES:

Rent-A-Center, Inc. is a rent-to-own operator in North America, providing customers the opportunity to obtain ownership of high-quality durable products such as consumer electronics, appliances, computers, furniture and accessories, under flexible rental purchase agreements with no long-term obligation. There are approximately 2,100 company-owned Rent-A-Center stores in the U.S., Mexico and Puerto Rico; and approximately 370 franchise locations. Operations are conducted through the company's four segments: Rent-A-Center, preferred lease, Mexico and franchising. The Rent-A-Center segment consists of company-owned lease-to-own stores in the U.S. and Puerto Rico, which lease household durable goods to customers on a lease-to-own basis. This division also offers merchandise on an installment sales basis in certain stores under the names Get It Now and Home Choice. This segment operates through the firm's company-owned stores and eCommerce platform via rentacenter.com. The preferred lease segment operates in the U.S. and Puerto Rico, and includes the operations of Merchants Preferred, which generally offers the lease-to-own transactions to consumers who do not qualify for financing from the traditional retailer. Transactions take place through kiosks located within the retail stores, and include staffed options, unstaffed or virtual options, or a combination of the two. The Mexico segment consists of company-owned lease-to-own stores in Mexico that lease household durable goods to customers on a lease-to-own basis. The franchising segment is operated through wholly-owned subsidiary Rent-A-Center Franchising International, Inc., a franchisor of lease-to-own stores. This division's primary source of revenue is the sale of rental merchandise to its franchisees, who in turn offer the merchandise to the general public for rent or purchase under a lease-to-own transaction

Rent-A-Center offers employee benefits, retirement options and employee assistance programs.

FINANCIAL DATA: Note: Data for latest year may not have been available at press time.

In U.S. $	2020	2019	2018	2017	2016	2015
Revenue	2,814,191,000	2,669,852,000	2,660,465,000	2,702,540,000	2,963,252,000	3,278,420,000
R&D Expense						
Operating Income	237,336,000	253,859,000	56,137,000	-63,059,000	84,724,000	162,112,000
Operating Margin %		.10%	.02%	-.02%	.03%	.05%
SGA Expense	732,233,000	772,730,000	846,867,000	903,556,000	957,956,000	1,020,712,000
Net Income	208,115,000	173,546,000	8,492,000	6,653,000	-105,195,000	-866,628,000
Operating Cash Flow	236,502,000	215,416,000	227,505,000	110,533,000	353,735,000	230,488,000
Capital Expenditure	34,545,000	21,157,000	27,962,000	65,460,000	61,143,000	80,870,000
EBITDA	928,466,000	935,482,000	742,395,000	632,779,000	670,534,000	-209,392,000
Return on Assets %		.12%	.01%	.00%	-.06%	-.33%
Return on Equity %		.47%	.03%	.02%	-.29%	-.93%
Debt to Equity		1.124	1.885	2.449	2.734	2.027

CONTACT INFORMATION:

Phone: 972 801-1100   Fax: 866 260-1424
Toll-Free: 800-275-2996
Address: 5501 Headquarters Dr., Plano, TX 75024 United States

STOCK TICKER/OTHER:

Stock Ticker: RCII   Exchange: NAS
Employees: 14,320   Fiscal Year Ends: 12/31
Parent Company:

SALARIES/BONUSES:

Top Exec. Salary: $ Bonus: $
Second Exec. Salary: $ Bonus: $

OTHER THOUGHTS:

Estimated Female Officers or Directors: 1
Hot Spot for Advancement for Women/Minorities: Y

Republic Services Inc

www.republicservices.com

NAIC Code: 562111

TYPES OF BUSINESS:

Solid Waste Collection
Recycling
Solid Waste Collection
Landfills

BRANDS/DIVISIONS/AFFILIATES:

CONTACTS: Note: Officers with more than one job title may be intentionally listed here more than once.

Donald Slager, CEO
Charles Serianni, CFO
Brian Goebel, Chief Accounting Officer
Jeffrey Hughes, Chief Administrative Officer
Catharine Ellingsen, Chief Compliance Officer
Timothy Stuart, COO
Manuel Kadre, Director
Brian Bales, Executive VP
Jon Ark, President

GROWTH PLANS/SPECIAL FEATURES:

Republic Services, Inc. provides non-hazardous solid waste collection services for commercial, industrial, municipal and residential customers through collection operations in 42 states and Puerto Rico. It owns or operates transfer stations, active landfills, recycling centers, treatment/recovery/disposal facilities, saltwater disposal wells, deep injection wells and landfill gas and renewable energy projects. Republic Services was responsible for approximately 130 closed landfills during 2020, and owned or operated nearly 190 active solid waste landfills. The company's operations primarily consist of providing collection, transfer station and disposal of non-hazardous solid waste and the recovery and recycling of certain materials. The firm provides solid waste collection services to commercial, industrial, municipal and residential customers through its collection operations. Republic Services generates approximately 74% of its revenue from collection services. Republic Services deposits waste at its transfer stations, as do other private haulers and municipal haulers. The waste is compacted and then transferred to trailers for transport to disposal sites or recycling facilities. The company's disposal and materials recovery activities generate revenue through the collection, processing and sale of corrugated cardboard, newspaper, aluminum, glass and other materials. Republic Services' facilities and operations are subject to a variety of federal, state and local requirements that regulate the environment, public health, safety, zoning and land use.

FINANCIAL DATA: Note: Data for latest year may not have been available at press time.

In U.S. $	2020	2019	2018	2017	2016	2015
Revenue	10,153,600,000	10,299,400,000	10,040,900,000	10,041,500,000	9,387,700,000	9,115,000,000
R&D Expense						
Operating Income	1,841,300,000	1,802,600,000	1,717,300,000	1,617,400,000	1,537,900,000	1,523,600,000
Operating Margin %		.18%	.17%	.16%	.16%	.17%
SGA Expense	1,025,200,000	1,042,000,000	1,024,700,000	1,026,800,000	949,400,000	960,400,000
Net Income	967,200,000	1,073,300,000	1,036,900,000	1,278,400,000	612,600,000	749,900,000
Operating Cash Flow	2,471,600,000	2,352,100,000	2,242,800,000	1,910,700,000	1,847,800,000	1,679,700,000
Capital Expenditure	1,194,600,000	1,207,100,000	1,071,800,000	989,800,000	927,800,000	945,600,000
EBITDA	2,657,100,000	2,810,200,000	2,818,800,000	2,724,100,000	2,361,600,000	2,571,100,000
Return on Assets %		.05%	.05%	.06%	.03%	.04%
Return on Equity %		.13%	.13%	.16%	.08%	.10%
Debt to Equity		0.982	0.965	0.94	0.995	0.974

CONTACT INFORMATION:

Phone: 480 627-2700   Fax:
Toll-Free:
Address: 18500 North Allied Way, Phoenix, AZ 85054 United States

STOCK TICKER/OTHER:

Stock Ticker: RSG
Employees: 33,000
Parent Company:

Exchange: NYS
Fiscal Year Ends: 12/31

SALARIES/BONUSES:

Top Exec. Salary: $ Bonus: $
Second Exec. Salary: $ Bonus: $

OTHER THOUGHTS:

Estimated Female Officers or Directors:
Hot Spot for Advancement for Women/Minorities:

ResMed Inc

NAIC Code: 334510

TYPES OF BUSINESS:
Sleep Disordered Breathing Medical Equipment
Diagnosis & Treatment Products

BRANDS/DIVISIONS/AFFILIATES:
AirSense 10
AirCurve 10
AirMini
Stellar
Astral
Lumis
Mobi

CONTACTS: *Note: Officers with more than one job title may be intentionally listed here more than once.*
Michael Farrell, CEO
Brett Sandercock, CFO
Peter Farrell, Chairman of the Board
David Pendarvis, Chief Administrative Officer
Robert Douglas, COO
James Hollingshead, President, Divisional
Rajwant Sodhi, President, Divisional
Richie McHale, President, Divisional

GROWTH PLANS/SPECIAL FEATURES:

ResMed, Inc. is an Australia-founded company that develops, manufactures, distributes and markets medical devices and cloud-based software applications for treating, diagnosing and managing sleep disordered breathing (SDB) and other respiratory disorders. SDB includes obstructive sleep apnea (OSA) and other related respiratory disorders that occur during sleep. Other respiratory disorders include chronic obstructive pulmonary disease (COPD) and neuromuscular disease. ResMed was originally founded to commercialize a continuous positive airway pressure (CPAP) treatment for OSA, which delivers pressurized air, typically through a nasal mask, to prevent collapse of the upper airway during sleep. Since the introduction of nasal CPAP, the firm has developed a number of innovative products, including related mask systems, headgear, airflow generators, diagnostic products and other accessories. The firm's recent CPAP products include AirSense 10 Elite and AirSense 10 CPAP. Its variable positive airway pressure (VPAP) products include the AirCurve 10S, AirCurve 10 V Auto, AirCurve 10 ST, AirCurve 10 ASV and the AirCurve 10 CS. Autoset products include the AirSense 10 Auto and the AirMini. Ventilation products include the Stellar 100 and 150, Astral 100 and 150, Lumis 100 and 150, Lumis ST-A and Mobi. ResMed's business strategy includes expanding into new clinical applications by seeking to identify new uses for its technologies, as well as increasing consumer awareness of little-known conditions. The firm sells products in over 140 countries through wholly-owned subsidiaries and independent distributors. Through various subsidiaries, ResMed owns or has licensed rights to over 6,200 pending patents.

FINANCIAL DATA: *Note: Data for latest year may not have been available at press time.*

In U.S. $	2020	2019	2018	2017	2016	2015
Revenue	2,957,013,000	2,606,572,000	2,340,196,000	2,066,737,000	1,838,713,000	
R&D Expense	201,946,000	180,651,000	155,149,000	144,467,000	118,651,000	
Operating Income	809,059,000	635,986,000	560,263,000	456,732,000	435,866,000	
Operating Margin %		.24%	.24%	.22%	.24%	
SGA Expense	676,689,000	645,010,000	600,369,000	553,968,000	488,057,000	
Net Income	621,674,000	404,592,000	315,588,000	342,284,000	352,409,000	
Operating Cash Flow	802,255,000	459,051,000	505,026,000	414,053,000	547,933,000	
Capital Expenditure	105,938,000	77,342,000	71,457,000	71,476,000	67,829,000	
EBITDA	954,838,000	705,798,000	669,627,000	559,136,000	537,621,000	
Return on Assets %		.11%	.10%	.10%	.13%	
Return on Equity %		.20%	.16%	.19%	.21%	
Debt to Equity		0.608	0.131	0.55	0.516	

CONTACT INFORMATION:
Phone: 858 836-5000   Fax: 858 746-2900
Toll-Free: 800-424-0737
Address: 9001 Spectrum Ctr. Blvd., San Diego, CA 92123 United States

STOCK TICKER/OTHER:
Stock Ticker: RMD
Employees: 7,770
Parent Company:

Exchange: NYS
Fiscal Year Ends: 06/30

SALARIES/BONUSES:
Top Exec. Salary: $ Bonus: $
Second Exec. Salary: $ Bonus: $

OTHER THOUGHTS:
Estimated Female Officers or Directors: 2
Hot Spot for Advancement for Women/Minorities:

REV Group Inc

www.revgroup.com

NAIC Code: 336120

TYPES OF BUSINESS:

Trucks, RVs & Misc. Automotive, Manufacturing
Buses
Ambulances
Terminal Trucks
Road Construction Equipment
Sweeper Equipment

BRANDS/DIVISIONS/AFFILIATES:

KME
Collins Bus
Capacity
Lay-Mor
REV Recreation Group
Midwest
Goldshield
Spartan Emergency Response

CONTACTS: *Note: Officers with more than one job title may be intentionally listed here more than once.*

Timothy Sullivan, CEO
Dean Nolden, CFO
Ian Walsh, COO
Paul Bamatter, Director
Stephen Boettinger, General Counsel

GROWTH PLANS/SPECIAL FEATURES:

REV Group, Inc. designs, manufactures and distributes specialty vehicles and related aftermarket parts and services. The company operates through three business segments: fire and emergency, commercial and recreation. The fire and emergency segment manufactures and markets commercial and custom fire and emergency vehicles primarily for fire departments, airports, governmental units, contractors, hospitals and other care providers in the U.S. and other countries. This division's brands include KME, E-One, Ferrara, Spartan ER, Smeal, Ladder Tower, American Emergency Vehicles, Leader Emergency Vehicles, Horton Emergency Vehicles, Road Rescue and Wheeled Coach. The commercial segment consists of: Collins Bus, which manufactures, markets and distributes school buses; ENC, which manufactures heavy-duty transit buses; Capacity manufactures, markets and distributes trucks used in terminal type operations such as rail yards, warehouses, rail terminals and shipping terminals/ports; and Lay-Mor manufactures, markets and distributes industrial sweepers for the commercial and rental markets. The recreation segment consists of: REV Recreation Group manufactures, markets and distributes Class A RVs in both gas and diesel models; Renegade manufactures, markets and distributes Class C and Super C RVs; Midwest manufactures, markets and distributes Class B RVs and luxury vans; Lance manufactures, markets and distributes truck campers, towable campers and toy haulers; and Goldshield manufactures, markets and distributes fiberglass reinforced molded parts to original equipment manufacturers and other commercial and industrial customers. In March of 2021, REV announced it had been awarded a contract for 44 additional thirty-foot clean diesel Axess model heavy-duty transit buses to its subsidiary ElDorado.

FINANCIAL DATA: *Note: Data for latest year may not have been available at press time.*

In U.S. $	2020	2019	2018	2017	2016	2015
Revenue	2,277,600,000	2,403,700,000	2,381,300,000	2,267,783,000	1,925,999,000	1,735,081,000
R&D Expense	5,800,000	4,800,000	6,500,000	4,219,000	4,815,000	5,106,000
Operating Income	4,100,000	30,500,000	70,600,000	87,204,000	75,922,000	65,953,000
Operating Margin %		.01%	.03%	.04%	.04%	.04%
SGA Expense	204,900,000	199,300,000	182,800,000	188,257,000	139,771,000	102,309,000
Net Income	-30,500,000	-12,300,000	13,000,000	31,371,000	30,193,000	22,877,000
Operating Cash Flow	55,700,000	52,500,000	-19,200,000	33,175,000	75,570,000	25,639,000
Capital Expenditure	16,800,000	23,800,000	60,700,000	79,345,000	48,542,000	15,430,000
EBITDA	19,800,000	61,600,000	73,800,000	108,580,000	96,994,000	81,168,000
Return on Assets %		-.01%	.01%	.03%	.05%	.03%
Return on Equity %		-.02%	.02%	.08%	.17%	.10%
Debt to Equity		0.746	0.791	0.40	0.984	0.885

CONTACT INFORMATION:

Phone: 414-290-0190   Fax:
Toll-Free:
Address: 245 S. Executive Dr., Brookfield, WI 53005 United States

STOCK TICKER/OTHER:

Stock Ticker: REVG
Employees: 7,060
Parent Company:

Exchange: NYS
Fiscal Year Ends: 10/31

SALARIES/BONUSES:

Top Exec. Salary: $ Bonus: $
Second Exec. Salary: $ Bonus: $

OTHER THOUGHTS:

Estimated Female Officers or Directors:
Hot Spot for Advancement for Women/Minorities:

Roadrunner Transportation Systems Inc

www.rrts.com

NAIC Code: 484122

TYPES OF BUSINESS:

Trucking
LTL Trucking
Expedited Shipping
Regional Shipping

BRANDS/DIVISIONS/AFFILIATES:

GROWTH PLANS/SPECIAL FEATURES:

Roadrunner Transportation Systems, Inc. is a Wisconsin-based trucking company that provides less-than-truckload (LTL) services to shippers in major cities across the U.S. Roadrunner's LTL services are powered by over 900 independent contractors. The company operates its business from more than 20 service centers, and its network consists of rail partnerships and over 100 pickup and delivery partners. Roadrunner offers long-haul shipping services for freight of all sizes, 1-3 day regional shipping, and next-day shipping. In March 2021, Roadrunner announced that it raised $50 million in new equity for technology investments. The round was led by Andrew Leto, founder of GlobalTranz and Emerge, with other participants including affiliates of Elliott Investment Management, Fox Hill Capital, Memento SA, and Solas Capital, among others.

CONTACTS: Note: Officers with more than one job title may be intentionally listed here more than once.

Curtis Stoelting, CEO
Terence Rogers, CFO
James Staley, Chairman of the Board
Robert Milane, Chief Compliance Officer
Michael Rapken, Chief Information Officer
Michael Gettle, COO
William Goodgion, President, Subsidiary
Frank Hurst, President, Subsidiary
Patrick McKay, Senior VP, Divisional

FINANCIAL DATA: Note: Data for latest year may not have been available at press time.

In U.S. $	2020	2019	2018	2017	2016	2015
Revenue		1,847,862,000	2,216,141,000	2,091,291,000	2,033,200,000	1,995,019,000
R&D Expense						
Operating Income		-141,461,000	-52,262,000	-67,490,000	-30,113,000	97,237,000
Operating Margin %		-.08%	-.02%	-.03%	-.01%	.05%
SGA Expense						
Net Income		-340,937,000	-165,597,000	-91,186,000	-360,320,000	48,000,000
Operating Cash Flow		-97,075,000	5,594,000	-45,552,000	29,401,000	73,362,000
Capital Expenditure		27,745,000	25,495,000	14,517,000	17,573,000	54,859,000
EBITDA		-264,431,000	-14,952,000	-13,448,000	-363,054,000	131,281,000
Return on Assets %		-.45%	-.19%	-.10%	-.32%	.04%
Return on Equity %		-185.44%	-5.64%	-.59%	-.89%	.08%
Debt to Equity		6.053		1.709		0.692

CONTACT INFORMATION:

Phone: 414 615-1500　　　　Fax:
Toll-Free:
Address: 1431 Opus Place, Downers Grove, IL 60515 United States

STOCK TICKER/OTHER:

Stock Ticker: RRTS　　　　　　　　Exchange: PINX
Employees: 4,600　　　　　　　　　Fiscal Year Ends: 12/31
Parent Company:

SALARIES/BONUSES:

Top Exec. Salary: $　　　　Bonus: $
Second Exec. Salary: $　　　Bonus: $

OTHER THOUGHTS:

Estimated Female Officers or Directors: 1
Hot Spot for Advancement for Women/Minorities:

Rockwell Automation Inc
www.rockwellautomation.com
NAIC Code: 334513

TYPES OF BUSINESS:
Architecture & Software Products
Industrial Automation
Digital Transformation
Intelligent Devices
Software
Control Systems
Security Infrastructure
Digital Oilfield Automation Solutions

BRANDS/DIVISIONS/AFFILIATES:
Sensia
Allen-Bradley
PlantPAx
ControlLogix
PowerFlex
Rockwell Software
FactoryTalk
Fiix Inc

CONTACTS: *Note: Officers with more than one job title may be intentionally listed here more than once.*
Blake Moret, CEO
Steven Etzel, VP
Patrick Goris, CFO
David Dorgan, Chief Accounting Officer
Christopher Nardecchia, Chief Information Officer
Sujeet Chand, Chief Technology Officer
Rebecca House, General Counsel
Fran Wlodarczyk, Senior VP
Frank Kulaszewicz, Senior VP
Elik Fooks, Senior VP
Michael Laszkiewicz, Senior VP, Divisional
Thomas Donato, Senior VP, Divisional
John Genovesi, Senior VP, Divisional
Robert Murphy, Senior VP, Divisional
John Miller, Vice President

GROWTH PLANS/SPECIAL FEATURES:
Rockwell Automation, Inc. is a global leader in industrial automation and digital transformation. The firm operates through three business segments: intelligent devices, software and control, and lifecycle services. The intelligent devices segment includes drives, motion, safety, sensing, industrial components, and configured-to-order products. The software and control segment includes control and visualization software and hardware, information software, and network and security infrastructure. The lifecycle services segment includes consulting, professional services and solutions, connected services, and maintenance services, as well as the Sensio joint venture. Sensia is a fully integrated digital oilfield automation solutions provider that leverages Schlumberger's (47%) oil and gas domain knowledge and Rockwell Automation's (53%) automation and information expertise. In early-2021, Rockwell Automation acquired Fiix, Inc., an artificial intelligence (AI)-enabled computerized maintenance management system company based in Canada.

FINANCIAL DATA: *Note: Data for latest year may not have been available at press time.*

In U.S. $	2020	2019	2018	2017	2016	2015
Revenue	6,329,800,000	6,694,800,000	6,666,000,000	6,311,300,000	5,879,500,000	6,307,900,000
R&D Expense						
Operating Income	1,115,400,000	1,361,600,000	1,273,200,000	1,032,700,000	1,008,100,000	1,196,700,000
Operating Margin %		.20%	.19%	.16%	.17%	.19%
SGA Expense	1,479,800,000	1,538,500,000	1,599,000,000	1,591,500,000	1,467,400,000	1,506,400,000
Net Income	1,023,400,000	695,800,000	535,500,000	825,700,000	729,700,000	827,600,000
Operating Cash Flow	1,120,500,000	1,182,000,000	1,300,000,000	1,034,000,000	947,300,000	1,187,700,000
Capital Expenditure	113,900,000	132,800,000	125,500,000	141,700,000	116,900,000	122,900,000
EBITDA	1,412,300,000	1,151,400,000	1,568,400,000	1,282,500,000	1,186,600,000	1,353,700,000
Return on Assets %		.11%	.08%	.12%	.11%	.13%
Return on Equity %		.69%	.25%	.35%	.34%	.34%
Debt to Equity		4.84	0.757	0.467	0.762	0.665

CONTACT INFORMATION:
Phone: 414 382-2000   Fax: 414 382-8520
Toll-Free:
Address: 1201 S. Second St., Milwaukee, WI 53204 United States

SALARIES/BONUSES:
Top Exec. Salary: $ Bonus: $
Second Exec. Salary: $ Bonus: $

STOCK TICKER/OTHER:
Stock Ticker: ROK
Employees: 23,000
Parent Company:

Exchange: NYS
Fiscal Year Ends: 09/30

OTHER THOUGHTS:
Estimated Female Officers or Directors: 1
Hot Spot for Advancement for Women/Minorities:

Roper Technologies Inc

NAIC Code: 334513

www.ropertech.com

TYPES OF BUSINESS:
Controls Manufacturing
Energy Controls
Medical Systems
Flow Controls

BRANDS/DIVISIONS/AFFILIATES:
Aderant
Strata
ConstructConnect
TransCore
Alpha
Verathon
AMOT
Zetec

CONTACTS:
Note: Officers with more than one job title may be intentionally listed here more than once.

L. Neil Hunn, CEO
Robert Crisci, CFO
Wilbur Prezzano, Chairman of the Board
Jason Conley, Chief Accounting Officer
John Stipancich, Executive VP
Paul Soni, Vice President

GROWTH PLANS/SPECIAL FEATURES:

Roper Technologies, Inc. is a diversified technology company that designs and develops software, as well as engineered products and solutions for a variety of niche and end markets. Roper operates through four segments: Application Software, consisting of the Aderant, CBORD, CliniSys, Data Innovations, Deltek, Horizon, IntelliTrans, PowerPlan, Strata and Sunquest businesses; Network Software & Systems, consisting of the ConstructConnect, DAT, Foundry, Inovonics, iPipeline, iTradeNetwork, Link Logistics, MHA, RF IDeas, SHP, SoftWriters and TransCore businesses; Measurement & Analytical Solutions, consisting of the Alpha, CIVCO Medical Solutions, CIVCO Radiotherapy, Dynisco, FMI, Hansen, Hardy, IPA, Logitech, Neptune, Northern Digital, Struers, Technolog, Uson and Verathon; and Process Technologies, consisting of the AMOT, CCC, Cornell, FTI, Metrix, PAC, Roper Pump, Viatran and Zetec businesses. In September 2020, Roper completed its acquisition of Vertafore, a cloud-based insurance software provider, in an all-cash transaction valued at $5.35 billion.

FINANCIAL DATA:
Note: Data for latest year may not have been available at press time.

In U.S. $	2020	2019	2018	2017	2016	2015
Revenue	5,527,100,000	5,366,800,000	5,191,200,000	4,607,471,000	3,789,925,000	3,582,395,000
R&D Expense						
Operating Income	1,431,100,000	1,498,400,000	1,396,400,000	1,210,244,000	1,054,563,000	1,027,918,000
Operating Margin %		.28%	.27%	.26%	.28%	.29%
SGA Expense	2,111,900,000	1,928,700,000	1,883,100,000	1,654,552,000	1,277,847,000	1,136,728,000
Net Income	949,700,000	1,767,900,000	944,400,000	971,772,000	658,645,000	696,067,000
Operating Cash Flow	1,525,100,000	1,461,800,000	1,430,100,000	1,234,482,000	963,785,000	928,825,000
Capital Expenditure	48,900,000	62,900,000	58,600,000	59,536,000	40,106,000	36,260,000
EBITDA	1,949,000,000	2,830,000,000	1,747,500,000	1,560,254,000	1,292,664,000	1,290,831,000
Return on Assets %		.11%	.06%	.07%	.05%	.07%
Return on Equity %		.21%	.13%	.15%	.12%	.14%
Debt to Equity		0.492	0.638	0.634	1.003	0.616

CONTACT INFORMATION:
Phone: 941 556-2601   Fax: 941 556-2670
Toll-Free:
Address: 6901 Professional Parkway East, Sarasota, FL 34240 United States

STOCK TICKER/OTHER:
Stock Ticker: ROP   Exchange: NYS
Employees: 16,460   Fiscal Year Ends: 12/31
Parent Company:

SALARIES/BONUSES:
Top Exec. Salary: $ Bonus: $
Second Exec. Salary: $ Bonus: $

OTHER THOUGHTS:
Estimated Female Officers or Directors:
Hot Spot for Advancement for Women/Minorities:

Roundys Supermarkets Inc

www.roundys.com

NAIC Code: 445110

TYPES OF BUSINESS:

Grocery Stores & Supermarkets
Private Label Merchandise Manufacturing

BRANDS/DIVISIONS/AFFILIATES:

Kroger Company (The)
Pick 'n Save
Copps
Metro Market
Mariano's
Roundy's Select
Roundy's Private Label
Clear Value

CONTACTS: *Note: Officers with more than one job title may be intentionally listed here more than once.*

Christine S. Wheatley, Pres.
Kurt Kappeler, Chief Accounting Officer
Donald Rosanova, Executive VP, Divisional
Jessie Terry, Other Executive Officer
Edward Kitz, Secretary
John Boyle, Vice President, Divisional
Patrick Mullarkey, Vice President, Divisional
Timothy Grabar, Vice President, Divisional
James Hyland, Vice President, Divisional
Michael Turzenski, Vice President

GROWTH PLANS/SPECIAL FEATURES:

Roundy's Supermarkets, Inc. is one of the oldest and largest grocers in midwestern USA. Historically, the firm was active in the wholesale distribution of groceries to independent retailers in the upper midwest. Today, Roundy's operates solely in the retail grocery market, and its network encompasses more than 150 grocery stores under the Pick 'n Save, Copps, Metro Market and Mariano's retail banners. In addition to national brands, Roundy's stores stock premium Roundy's Select and mid-tier Roundy's Private Label merchandise as well as its Clear Value line of entry-level items. Product categories offered by stores include grocery, frozen and dairy; produce; meat and seafood; bakery; deli, cheese and prepared foods; floral; general merchandise; alcohol; pharmacy; and health and beauty care. Roundy's operates as a wholly-owned subsidiary of The Kroger Company.

FINANCIAL DATA: *Note: Data for latest year may not have been available at press time.*

In U.S. $	2020	2019	2018	2017	2016	2015
Revenue	4,793,862,938	4,338,337,500	4,131,750,000	3,935,000,000	3,925,000,000	3,888,000,000
R&D Expense						
Operating Income						
Operating Margin %						
SGA Expense						
Net Income						
Operating Cash Flow						
Capital Expenditure						
EBITDA						
Return on Assets %						
Return on Equity %						
Debt to Equity						

CONTACT INFORMATION:

Phone: 414 231-5000   Fax:
Toll-Free:
Address: 875 E. Wisconsin Ave., Milwaukee, WI 53202 United States

STOCK TICKER/OTHER:

Stock Ticker: Subsidiary
Employees: 21,802
Parent Company: Kroger Company (The)

Exchange:
Fiscal Year Ends: 12/31

SALARIES/BONUSES:

Top Exec. Salary: $ Bonus: $
Second Exec. Salary: $ Bonus: $

OTHER THOUGHTS:

Estimated Female Officers or Directors:
Hot Spot for Advancement for Women/Minorities:

RPM International Inc
NAIC Code: 325510

TYPES OF BUSINESS:
Home & Industrial Maintenance Products
Specialty Paints
Protective Coatings
Roofing Systems
Sealants & Adhesives

BRANDS/DIVISIONS/AFFILIATES:
Bison Innovative Products

CONTACTS: *Note: Officers with more than one job title may be intentionally listed here more than once.*
Frank Sullivan, CEO
Russell Gordon, CFO
Keith Smiley, Chief Accounting Officer
Edward Moore, Chief Compliance Officer
Matthew Ratajczak, Treasurer
Janeen Kastner, Vice President, Divisional
Barry Slifstein, Vice President, Divisional

GROWTH PLANS/SPECIAL FEATURES:
RPM International, Inc., through its subsidiaries, manufactures, markets and sells specialty paints, protective coatings, sealants, adhesives and building materials. The company operates through four business segments: consumer packaged goods (CPG), performance coatings group (PCG), consumer and specialty. The CPG segment produces construction sealants and adhesives, coatings and chemicals, roofing systems, concrete admixture and repair products, building envelope solutions, insulated cladding, flooring systems and weatherproofing solutions. Its products are sold throughout North America, and this division also accounts for the majority of RPM international sales. The PCG segment produces high-performance flooring solutions, corrosion control and fireproofing coatings, infrastructure repair systems, fiberglass reinforced plastic gratings and drainage systems. These products are sold directly to contractors, distributors and end-users such as industrial manufacturing facilities, public institutions and other commercial customers. The consumer segment manufactures and markets professional use and do-it-yourself (DIY) products for a variety of consumer applications, including home improvement and personal leisure activities. Products include specialty, hobby and professional paints; caulks; adhesives; silicone sealants; and wood stains. Last, the specialty segment offers products that include industrial cleaners, restoration services equipment, colorants, nail enamels, exterior finishes, edible coatings and specialty glazes for pharmaceutical and food industries, and other specialty original equipment manufacturer (OEM) coatings. In March 2021, RPM acquired Bison Innovative Products, a manufacturer of raised flooring systems based in Denver, Colorado.

FINANCIAL DATA: *Note: Data for latest year may not have been available at press time.*

In U.S. $	2020	2019	2018	2017	2016	2015
Revenue	5,506,994,000	5,564,551,000	5,321,643,000	4,958,175,000	4,813,649,000	
R&D Expense						
Operating Income	544,202,000	492,277,000	518,069,000	522,168,000	566,071,000	
Operating Margin %	.10%	.09%	.10%	.11%	.12%	
SGA Expense	1,548,653,000	1,769,630,000	1,663,143,000	1,643,520,000	1,520,977,000	
Net Income	304,385,000	266,558,000	337,770,000	181,823,000	354,725,000	
Operating Cash Flow	549,919,000	292,941,000	390,383,000	386,127,000	474,706,000	
Capital Expenditure	147,756,000	136,757,000	114,619,000	126,109,000	117,183,000	
EBITDA	665,609,000	583,979,000	650,094,000	458,060,000	686,188,000	
Return on Assets %	.05%	.05%	.06%	.04%	.07%	
Return on Equity %	.23%	.17%	.22%	.13%	.26%	
Debt to Equity	2.141	1.404	1.331	1.279	1.20	

CONTACT INFORMATION:
Phone: 330 273-5090   Fax: 330 225-8743
Toll-Free:
Address: 2628 Pearl Rd., Medina, OH 44258 United States

SALARIES/BONUSES:
Top Exec. Salary: $ Bonus: $
Second Exec. Salary: $ Bonus: $

STOCK TICKER/OTHER:
Stock Ticker: RPM
Employees: 14,621
Parent Company:
Exchange: NYS
Fiscal Year Ends: 05/31

OTHER THOUGHTS:
Estimated Female Officers or Directors: 2
Hot Spot for Advancement for Women/Minorities:

Russell Stover Candies Inc

www.russellstover.com

NAIC Code: 311351

TYPES OF BUSINESS:

Sugar & Confectioneries Manufacturing
Boxed Chocolates
Sugar-Free Candies
Low-Carb Candies
Gift Baskets
Online Sales
Production
Distribution

BRANDS/DIVISIONS/AFFILIATES:

Chocoladefabriken Lindt & Sprungli AG
Whitmans Candies Company
www.russellstover.com
Millionaires Brand
Pangburn Candy Company

CONTACTS: Note: Officers with more than one job title may be intentionally listed here more than once.

Andrew Deister, CEO

GROWTH PLANS/SPECIAL FEATURES:

Russell Stover Candies, Inc. has been in business since 1932, and is one of the largest candy makers in the U.S. The company, a subsidiary of Swiss chocolatier Chocoladefabriken Lindt & Sprungli AG, hand dips over 20 million pieces of candy per year. Russell Stover sells candy through 19 company-owned retail locations in the U.S., as well as through approximately 70,000 wholesalers such as drug stores, grocery stores and department stores throughout the world. The company's candy products include milk chocolate, dark chocolate, creams, caramels and toffee, marshmallows, nuts, chews and crisps, truffles, whips, cherries, hard candies and jellies. Website www.russellstover.com offers gift cards and allows customers to build a customized box of chocolates in one-, two-, three- and five-pound selections. Customers can also purchase pre-packaged candy assortments of boxed, bagged and bar chocolates in a variety of packages and tins. The website also enables customers to store their chocolate and packaging preferences in a personal online account. Customer accounts feature an address book, which stores shipping addresses, order histories and a reminder service, highlighting upcoming personal gift-giving events. Russell Stover offers low-carbohydrate and sugar-free versions of candy selections, including pecan delights, toffee squares, mint patties, miniature peanut clusters, s'mores cups and caramel cups. Whitman's Candies Company operates as an affiliate of Russell Stover and owns the trademarks of Millionaires Brand candy manufacturer as well as Pangburn Candy Company. Whitman's also offers WeightWatchers candies, including packaged single servings of caramels, toffee squares, chocolates and dessert bars. Russell Stover operates four chocolate factories located in Colorado (1), Kansas (2) and Texas (1).

Russell Stover offers its employees medical, dental and vision coverage; life and disability insurance; a 401(k) plan; and discounts on company products.

FINANCIAL DATA: Note: Data for latest year may not have been available at press time.

In U.S. $	2020	2019	2018	2017	2016	2015
Revenue	360,000,000	413,000,000	619,500,000	590,000,000	585,000,000	580,000,000
R&D Expense						
Operating Income						
Operating Margin %						
SGA Expense						
Net Income						
Operating Cash Flow						
Capital Expenditure						
EBITDA						
Return on Assets %						
Return on Equity %						
Debt to Equity						

CONTACT INFORMATION:

Phone: 816-842-9240   Fax: 816-561-4350
Toll-Free: 800-777-4004
Address: 4900 Oak St., Kansas City, MO 64112 United States

SALARIES/BONUSES:

Top Exec. Salary: $ Bonus: $
Second Exec. Salary: $ Bonus: $

STOCK TICKER/OTHER:

Stock Ticker: Subsidiary
Employees: 3,000
Parent Company: Chocoladefabriken Lindt & Sprungli AG

Exchange:
Fiscal Year Ends: 02/28

OTHER THOUGHTS:

Estimated Female Officers or Directors:
Hot Spot for Advancement for Women/Minorities:

Safeway Inc

NAIC Code: 445110

www.safeway.com

TYPES OF BUSINESS:

Grocery Stores
Food Processing & Packaging
Online Grocery Sales & Home Delivery
Pharmacies
Gift Cards & Payment Processing Technology

BRANDS/DIVISIONS/AFFILIATES:

Cerberus Capital Management LP
Albertsons Companies LLC
GroceryWorks
O Organics
Eating Right
Bright Green
Open Nature

CONTACTS: Note: Officers with more than one job title may be intentionally listed here more than once.

Robert G. Miller, CEO
Larree Renda, Executive VP
Kelly Griffith, Executive VP, Divisional
Diane Dietz, Executive VP
Melissa Plaisance, Senior VP, Divisional
David Stern, Senior VP, Divisional
Donald Wright, Senior VP, Divisional
Jerry Tidwell, Senior VP, Divisional
Russell Jackson, Senior VP, Divisional
Robert Gordon, Senior VP

GROWTH PLANS/SPECIAL FEATURES:

Safeway, Inc. is a leading food retailer in the U.S., operating nearly 900 Safeway stores in 17 states and the District of Columbia. These states include Alaska, Arizona, California, Colorado, Delaware, Hawaii, Idaho, Maryland, Montana, Nebraska, Nevada, New Mexico, Oregon, South Dakota, Virginia, Washington and Wyoming. The company's stores offer a wide selection of both food and general merchandise and feature a variety of special departments such as bakery, delicatessen, pharmacy and floral departments. In addition, Safeway offers online grocery shopping and home delivery through its wholly-owned subsidiary GroceryWorks. Safeway's own line of Safeway SELECT branded products range from packaged foods to laundry detergent. The firm's corporate-branded products include the O Organics, Eating Right, Bright Green and Open Nature brand names. Safeway is a wholly-owned subsidiary of Albertsons Companies, LLC, a Cerberus Capital Management LP company.

Safeway offers its employees comprehensive benefits, retirement options and employee assistance programs.

FINANCIAL DATA: Note: Data for latest year may not have been available at press time.

In U.S. $	2020	2019	2018	2017	2016	2015
Revenue	43,625,400,000	39,480,000,000	37,600,000,000	37,500,000,000	36,000,000,000	36,980,000,000
R&D Expense						
Operating Income						
Operating Margin %						
SGA Expense						
Net Income						
Operating Cash Flow						
Capital Expenditure						
EBITDA						
Return on Assets %						
Return on Equity %						
Debt to Equity						

CONTACT INFORMATION:

Phone: 925 467-3000   Fax: 925 467-3323
Toll-Free: 877-723-3929
Address: 5918 Stoneridge Mall Rd., Pleasanton, CA 94588-3229 United States

STOCK TICKER/OTHER:

Stock Ticker: Private   Exchange:
Employees: 265,000   Fiscal Year Ends: 12/31
Parent Company: Cerberus Capital Management LP

SALARIES/BONUSES:

Top Exec. Salary: $ Bonus: $
Second Exec. Salary: $ Bonus: $

OTHER THOUGHTS:

Estimated Female Officers or Directors: 4
Hot Spot for Advancement for Women/Minorities: Y

Saker ShopRites Inc

www.shoprite.com/sakershoprites

NAIC Code: 445110

TYPES OF BUSINESS:

Grocery Stores
Liquor Stores
Garden Centers
Food Processing
Pharmacies

BRANDS/DIVISIONS/AFFILIATES:

Saker Holdings Corporation
ShopRite
Wakefern Food Corporation

GROWTH PLANS/SPECIAL FEATURES:

Saker ShopRites, Inc. comprises approximately 30 ShopRite-branded supermarkets located in central New Jersey, including Monmouth, Ocean, Middlesex, Somerset and Mercer counties. The company's stores offer food and non-food items, including grocery products, fresh produce, baked products, pharmaceuticals, meat products, floral items, seafood, craft beers and much more. Groceries can be ordered online or by telephone from home or office, and delivered as well. Prescriptions can be filled and refilled through the store's pharmacies, and managed online. ShopRite also provides digital receipts, digital coupons, gift cards, catering services, as well as health and wellness products. Saker ShopRite is a subsidiary of Saker Holdings Corporation. Wakefern Food Corporation is the merchandising and distribution arm for ShopRite, and is the largest retailer-owner cooperative in the U.S. as well as the largest employer in New Jersey. The cooperative consists of 50 members who individually own and operate the ShopRite line of supermarkets.

CONTACTS: Note: Officers with more than one job title may be intentionally listed here more than once.

Richard J. Saker, CEO
Carl L. Montanaro, Sr. VP-Merch.

FINANCIAL DATA: Note: Data for latest year may not have been available at press time.

In U.S. $	2020	2019	2018	2017	2016	2015
Revenue	2,128,698,731	2,006,550,000	1,911,000,000	1,820,000,000	1,810,000,000	1,800,000,000
R&D Expense						
Operating Income						
Operating Margin %						
SGA Expense						
Net Income						
Operating Cash Flow						
Capital Expenditure						
EBITDA						
Return on Assets %						
Return on Equity %						
Debt to Equity						

CONTACT INFORMATION:

Phone: 732-462-4700   Fax: 732-294-2317
Toll-Free:
Address: 922 Hwy. 33, Bldg. 6, Ste. 1, Freehold, NJ 07728 United States

SALARIES/BONUSES:

Top Exec. Salary: $ Bonus: $
Second Exec. Salary: $ Bonus: $

STOCK TICKER/OTHER:

Stock Ticker: Private
Employees: 51,000
Parent Company: Saker Holdings Corporation

Exchange:
Fiscal Year Ends: 10/31

OTHER THOUGHTS:

Estimated Female Officers or Directors:
Hot Spot for Advancement for Women/Minorities:

salesforce.com Inc
NAIC Code: 511210K

www.salesforce.com

TYPES OF BUSINESS:
Software, Sales & Marketing Automation
Customer Relationship Management Software
Software Subscription Services

BRANDS/DIVISIONS/AFFILIATES:
Sales Cloud
Service Cloud
Marketing Cloud
Community Cloud
Industries
IoT Cloud
Tableau Software Inc
myTrailhead

CONTACTS: *Note: Officers with more than one job title may be intentionally listed here more than once.*
Mark Hawkins, CFO
Marc Benioff, Chairman of the Board
Joe Allanson, Chief Accounting Officer
Alexandre Dayon, Chief Strategy Officer
Parker Harris, Chief Technology Officer
Keith Block, Co-CEO
Amy Weaver, General Counsel
Cynthia Robbins, Other Executive Officer
Bret Taylor, Other Executive Officer
Srinivas Tallapragada, President, Divisional

GROWTH PLANS/SPECIAL FEATURES:
Salesforce.com, Inc. builds and delivers customer relationship management (CRM) applications through an on-demand web services platform. The firm's web-based services enable clients to track sales and marketing by delivering enterprise software as an online service, making software purchases like paying for a utility as opposed to a packaged product. The firm offers core cloud-based services such as sales force automation, customer service and support, marketing automation, community management, analytics, as well as a platform for building custom application. Products include Sales Cloud, Service Cloud, Marketing Cloud, Community Cloud, Industries, IoT (Internet of Things) Cloud, Commerce Cloud, Salesforce Quip and Salesforce Platform. Sales Cloud is a platform for sales force automation and solutions for partner relationship management; Service Cloud addresses customer service and support needs; Marketing Cloud is a digital marketing platform that manages customer interactions across email, mobile, social, web and connected products; Community Cloud creates destinations for customers, partners and employees to collaborate; Industries, offers cloud products that meet the specific needs of certain industries; IoT Cloud connects billions of events from devices, sensors, apps and more from the IoT to Salesforce; Commerce Cloud empowers brands to deliver a comprehensive digital commerce experience across web, mobile, social and store; Salesforce Quip is a next-generation productivity solution designed for teams with a mobile-first strategy; and Salesforce Platform is for building enterprise apps quickly via tools, frameworks and services. The Salesforce Platform also offers artificial intelligence (AI), no-code, low-code and code development and integration services including Trailhead, Einstein, AI, Lightning, IoT, Heroku, analytics and the AppExchange. In December 2020, salesforce.com agreed to acquire Slack Technologies, Inc., the developer of Slack messaging service, for $27.7 billion.

FINANCIAL DATA: *Note: Data for latest year may not have been available at press time.*

In U.S. $	2020	2019	2018	2017	2016	2015
Revenue	17,098,000,000	13,282,000,000	10,480,010,000	8,391,984,000	6,667,216,000	
R&D Expense	2,766,000,000	1,886,000,000	1,553,073,000	1,208,127,000	946,300,000	
Operating Income	463,000,000	535,000,000	235,768,000	64,228,000	114,923,000	
Operating Margin %	.03%	.04%	.02%	.01%	.02%	
SGA Expense	9,634,000,000	7,410,000,000	5,917,649,000	4,885,590,000	3,951,445,000	
Net Income	126,000,000	1,110,000,000	127,478,000	179,632,000	-47,426,000	
Operating Cash Flow	4,331,000,000	3,398,000,000	2,737,965,000	2,162,198,000	1,612,585,000	
Capital Expenditure	643,000,000	595,000,000	534,027,000	463,958,000	709,852,000	
EBITDA	2,598,000,000	2,099,000,000	1,041,651,000	746,616,000	662,514,000	
Return on Assets %	.00%	.04%	.01%	.01%	.00%	
Return on Equity %	.01%	.09%	.02%	.03%	-.01%	
Debt to Equity	0.151	0.203	0.146	0.359	0.408	

CONTACT INFORMATION:
Phone: 415 901-7000   Fax: 415 901-7040
Toll-Free:
Address: Salesforce Tower, 415 Mission St., 3/Fl, San Francisco, CA 94105 United States

STOCK TICKER/OTHER:
Stock Ticker: CRM
Employees: 49,000
Parent Company:

Exchange: NYS
Fiscal Year Ends: 01/31

SALARIES/BONUSES:
Top Exec. Salary: $ Bonus: $
Second Exec. Salary: $ Bonus: $

OTHER THOUGHTS:
Estimated Female Officers or Directors: 4
Hot Spot for Advancement for Women/Minorities: Y

Sams Club

NAIC Code: 452910

TYPES OF BUSINESS:

Warehouse Clubs, Retail

BRANDS/DIVISIONS/AFFILIATES:

Wal-Mart Stores Inc
Members Mark
Bakers & Chefs
Sams Club

CONTACTS: Note: Officers with more than one job title may be intentionally listed here more than once.

Kathryn McLay, CEO
Lance de la Rosa, COO
Brandi Joplin, CFO
Eddie Garcio, Sr. VP
Christopher Shyrock, Sr. VP
Vinod Bidarkoppa, Sr. VP-IT
Charles Redfield, Exec. VP-Merch.
Whitney Head, General Counsel
P. Todd Harbaugh, Exec. VP-Oper.
Don Frieson, Sr. VP-Planning & Replenishment
John Boswell, Sr. VP-e-Commerce
Bill Durling, Sr. Dir.-Corp. Comm.
Mike Turner, Sr. VP-Sam's Club Membership
Whitney Head, Sr. VP- Asset Protection & Compliance

GROWTH PLANS/SPECIAL FEATURES:

Sam's Club, a subsidiary of Wal-Mart Stores, Inc., is an American chain of membership-only retail warehouse clubs. Sam's Club operated 599 clubs in 44 U.S. states, Puerto Rico and the U.S. Virgin Islands (as of October 31, 2020). In-club benefits include pharmacy, fuel stations, optical centers, hearing aid centers, photo centers, tire and battery centers, daily taste sampling, demonstrations and free monthly health screenings. Sam's Club offers discounted prices on items, including appliances, electronics, office supplies, food, clothing, optical and pharmacy services, home furnishings, books and auto supplies. It also sells selected private-label items under the Member's Mark, Bakers & Chefs and Sam's Club brands. Most locations also offer fresh departments such as bakery, meat, produce, floral and Sam's Cafe. Sam's Club requires a customer to become a member, providing two options for an annual fee: Sam's Club ($45) and Sam's Plus ($100). In addition to merchandise discounts, the firm offers its members discounted services that include various types of insurance, a travel club, an auto purchase program, discount credit card processing, mail-order pharmacy services, internet access and long-distance services. The Sam's Club MasterCard option is a credit card cash back program issued by Synchrony Financial. Sam's Club stores, averaging 70,000-190,000 square feet, are designed to resemble a warehouse, with merchandise displayed on shipping pallets or in large freezer/cooler units. The company's merchandise consists of five categories: grocery and consumables; fuel and other categories; technology, office and entertainment; home and apparel; and health and wellness. Sam's Club has a partnership with Instacart for same-day delivery of all Sam's Clubs products; a Sam's Club membership is not required to purchase from Sam's Club via Instacart.

FINANCIAL DATA: Note: Data for latest year may not have been available at press time.

In U.S. $	2020	2019	2018	2017	2016	2015
Revenue	59,284,975,000	57,839,000,000	59,216,000,000	57,365,000,000	56,828,000,000	58,020,000,000
R&D Expense						
Operating Income						
Operating Margin %						
SGA Expense						
Net Income	1,580,800,000	1,520,000,000	915,000,000	1,628,000,000	1,820,000,000	1,976,000,000
Operating Cash Flow						
Capital Expenditure						
EBITDA						
Return on Assets %						
Return on Equity %						
Debt to Equity						

CONTACT INFORMATION:

Phone: 479-277-7000   Fax:
Toll-Free: 888-746-7726
Address: 2101 S. E. Simple Savings Dr., Bentonville, AR 72716 United States

STOCK TICKER/OTHER:

Stock Ticker: Subsidiary
Employees: 114,000
Parent Company: Wal-Mart Stores Inc

Exchange:
Fiscal Year Ends: 01/31

SALARIES/BONUSES:

Top Exec. Salary: $ Bonus: $
Second Exec. Salary: $ Bonus: $

OTHER THOUGHTS:

Estimated Female Officers or Directors: 3
Hot Spot for Advancement for Women/Minorities: Y

Sanderson Farms Inc

NAIC Code: 311615

www.sandersonfarms.com

TYPES OF BUSINESS:

Poultry Production
Poultry Processing
Prepared Foods

BRANDS/DIVISIONS/AFFILIATES:

CONTACTS: Note: Officers with more than one job title may be intentionally listed here more than once.

Joe Sanderson, CEO
D. Cockrell, CFO
Timothy Rigney, Chief Accounting Officer
Lampkin Butts, COO

GROWTH PLANS/SPECIAL FEATURES:

Sanderson Farms, Inc. is a poultry processing company engaged in the production, processing, marketing and distribution of fresh and frozen chicken products. It sells ice pack, chill pack, bulk pack and frozen chicken in whole, cut-up and boneless form primarily under the Sanderson Farms brand name to retailers, distributors and casual dining operators principally in the southeastern, southwestern, northeastern and western U.S. Through its food division, the company sells approximately 90 prepared chicken items nationally and regionally, primarily to distributors, national food service accounts and retailers. The production division, which has facilities in Mississippi, Texas, North Carolina and Georgia, is engaged in the production of chickens to the broiler stage. The processing division, with facilities in Mississippi, Louisiana, North Carolina, Georgia and Texas, is engaged in the processing, sale and distribution of chickens. The company's chicken operations encompass 11 hatcheries, nine feed mills, 12 processing plants and one prepared chicken plant. The firm processes approximately 4.8 billion dressed pounds annually. Sanderson Farms has contracts with operators of about 823 grow-out farms that provide it with sufficient housing capacity for its current operations. The company also has contracts with operators of 231 breeder farms.

FINANCIAL DATA: Note: Data for latest year may not have been available at press time.

In U.S. $	2020	2019	2018	2017	2016	2015
Revenue	3,564,267,000	3,440,258,000	3,236,004,000	3,342,226,000	2,816,057,000	2,803,480,000
R&D Expense						
Operating Income	1,112,000	67,994,000	29,700,000	428,275,000	294,111,000	336,925,000
Operating Margin %		.02%	.01%	.13%	.11%	.12%
SGA Expense	180,966,000	178,459,000	202,770,000	208,842,000	151,445,000	148,913,000
Net Income	28,274,000	53,294,000	61,431,000	279,745,000	188,961,000	216,001,000
Operating Cash Flow	222,009,000	206,800,000	131,413,000	408,953,000	292,849,000	297,806,000
Capital Expenditure	202,437,000	249,503,000	308,875,000	166,768,000	200,882,000	158,289,000
EBITDA	145,650,000	203,423,000	143,519,000	526,753,000	378,968,000	410,888,000
Return on Assets %		.03%	.04%	.17%	.14%	.18%
Return on Equity %		.04%	.04%	.21%	.17%	.22%
Debt to Equity		0.039				

CONTACT INFORMATION:

Phone: 601 649-4030   Fax: 601 426-1461
Toll-Free: 800-844-4030
Address: 127 Flynt Rd., Laurel, MS 39441 United States

STOCK TICKER/OTHER:

Stock Ticker: SAFM
Employees: 17,445
Parent Company:

Exchange: NAS
Fiscal Year Ends: 10/31

SALARIES/BONUSES:

Top Exec. Salary: $ Bonus: $
Second Exec. Salary: $ Bonus: $

OTHER THOUGHTS:

Estimated Female Officers or Directors: 4
Hot Spot for Advancement for Women/Minorities: Y

Sanmina Corporation

www.sanmina.com

NAIC Code: 334418

TYPES OF BUSINESS:

Printed Circuit Assembly (Electronic Assembly) Manufacturing
Assembly & Testing
Logistics Services
Support Services
Product Design & Engineering
Repair & Maintenance Services
Printed Circuit Boards

BRANDS/DIVISIONS/AFFILIATES:

CONTACTS: Note: Officers with more than one job title may be intentionally listed here more than once.

Michael Clarke, CEO
David Anderson, CFO
Jure Sola, Chairman of the Board
Brent Billinger, Chief Accounting Officer
Alan Reid, Executive VP, Divisional

GROWTH PLANS/SPECIAL FEATURES:

Sanmina Corporation is a global provider of integrated manufacturing solutions, components, products and repair, along with related logistics and after-market services. With production facilities in 21 countries on six continents, the firm is a world-leading electronics manufacturing services (EMS) provider. Sanmina's end-to-end solutions, combined with its expertise in supply chain management, enable the management of customer products throughout their life cycles. These solutions include: product design and engineering, the manufacturing of components, subassemblies and complete systems, final system assembly and test; direct order fulfillment and logistics services; after-market product service and support; and global supply chain management. Sanmina's integrated manufacturing solutions consists of printed circuit board assembly and test, final system assembly and test, and direct-order fulfillment. Components, products and services by Sanmina include interconnect systems (printed circuit board fabrication, backplane, cable assemblies and plastic injection molding) and mechanical systems (enclosures and precision machining). Services include design, logistics, repair and after-market service and support.

FINANCIAL DATA: Note: Data for latest year may not have been available at press time.

In U.S. $	2020	2019	2018	2017	2016	2015
Revenue	6,960,370,000	8,233,859,000	7,110,130,000	6,868,619,000	6,481,181,000	6,374,541,000
R&D Expense	22,564,000	27,552,000	30,754,000	33,716,000	37,746,000	33,083,000
Operating Income	262,212,000	299,870,000	179,197,000	230,955,000	228,486,000	209,431,000
Operating Margin %		.04%	.03%	.03%	.04%	.03%
SGA Expense	240,931,000	260,032,000	250,924,000	251,568,000	244,604,000	239,288,000
Net Income	139,713,000	141,515,000	-95,533,000	138,833,000	187,838,000	377,261,000
Operating Cash Flow	300,555,000	382,965,000	156,424,000	250,961,000	390,116,000	174,896,000
Capital Expenditure	65,982,000	134,674,000	118,881,000	111,833,000	120,400,000	119,097,000
EBITDA	343,879,000	393,331,000	244,093,000	354,165,000	341,438,000	301,771,000
Return on Assets %		.04%	-.02%	.04%	.05%	.11%
Return on Equity %		.09%	-.06%	.09%	.12%	.27%
Debt to Equity		0.211	0.01	0.238	0.27	0.279

CONTACT INFORMATION:

Phone: 408-964-3500   Fax: 408-964-3636
Toll-Free:
Address: 2700 N. First St., San Jose, CA 95134 United States

STOCK TICKER/OTHER:

Stock Ticker: SANM   Exchange: NAS
Employees: 37,000   Fiscal Year Ends: 09/30
Parent Company:

SALARIES/BONUSES:

Top Exec. Salary: $ Bonus: $
Second Exec. Salary: $ Bonus: $

OTHER THOUGHTS:

Estimated Female Officers or Directors:
Hot Spot for Advancement for Women/Minorities:

Sanofi Genzyme
NAIC Code: 325412

www.sanofi.com/en/your-health/specialty-care

TYPES OF BUSINESS:
Pharmaceuticals Discovery & Development
Genetic Disease Treatments
Surgical Products
Diagnostic Products
Genetic Testing Services
Oncology Products
Biomaterials
Medical Devices

BRANDS/DIVISIONS/AFFILIATES:
Sanofi SA

CONTACTS: Note: Officers with more than one job title may be intentionally listed here more than once.
David Meeker, Pres.
Richard J. Gregory, Head-R&D
William Aitchison, Head-Global Mfg.
Tracey L. Quarles, General Counsel
Charles Thyne, Head-Global Quality, Industrial Oper.
G. Andre Turenne, Head- Strategy & Bus. Dev.
Caren P. Arnstein, Head-Corp. Comm.
Ron C. Branning, Chief Quality Officer
Nicholas Grund, Sr. VP-Asia Pacific & Canada
Carlo Incerti, Head-Global Medical Affairs
Yoshi Nakamura, Pres., Japan-Asia Pacific
Serge Weinberg, Chmn.
Robin Kenselaar, Head-EMEA

GROWTH PLANS/SPECIAL FEATURES:
Sanofi Genzyme is the specialty care global business unit of Sanofi SA, with a focus on rare diseases, rare blood disorders, neurology, immunology and oncology. The rare diseases segment develops therapeutic products to treat patients suffering from genetic and other chronic debilitating diseases, including lysosomal storage disorders (LSDs) and endocrinology. More than 7,000 different rare disease collectively affect over 350 million people worldwide. The rare blood disorders segment comprises a hemophilia portfolio, an approved treatment for acquired thrombotic thrombocytopenic purpura (aTTP). The neurology segment develops new treatment options for people living with neurological disorders, and is a leader in multiple sclerosis, bringing therapies to patients in more than 80 countries worldwide. The immunology segment researches and develops new therapeutic candidates that may have a significant impact on people affected by immune system disorders, including atopic dermatitis, rheumatoid arthritis, asthma, nasal polyposis and eosinophilic esophagitis. Last, the oncology segment builds on Sanofi Genzyme's established legacy in cancer treatment by researching potential new options to offer in this area of medicine. This division is building a pipeline of future therapies in immune-oncology, in which a patient's immune system is used to fight cancer cells. As of March 2021, Sanofi Genzyme's research and development pipeline contained 80 projects, including 36 new molecular entities in clinical development. More than 35 projects are in phase 3 or have been submitted to the regulatory authorities for approval. In May 2021, Sanofi Genzyme announced that it entered into a three-year research collaboration with Stanford University School of Medicine, which together the organizations and their scientists will work to advance the understanding of immunology and inflammation via open scientific exchange.

Sanofi offers comprehensive employee benefits.

FINANCIAL DATA: Note: Data for latest year may not have been available at press time.

In U.S. $	2020	2019	2018	2017	2016	2015
Revenue	13,443,100,000	8,827,062,720	8,265,040,000	6,796,680,000	5,287,820,000	4,097,534,726
R&D Expense						
Operating Income						
Operating Margin %						
SGA Expense						
Net Income						
Operating Cash Flow						
Capital Expenditure						
EBITDA						
Return on Assets %						
Return on Equity %						
Debt to Equity						

CONTACT INFORMATION:
Phone: 617-252-7500   Fax: 617-252-7600
Toll-Free:
Address: 50 Binney St., Cambridge, MA 02142 United States

STOCK TICKER/OTHER:
Stock Ticker: Subsidiary
Employees: 4,700
Parent Company: Sanofi SA

Exchange:
Fiscal Year Ends: 12/31

SALARIES/BONUSES:
Top Exec. Salary: $ Bonus: $
Second Exec. Salary: $ Bonus: $

OTHER THOUGHTS:
Estimated Female Officers or Directors: 4
Hot Spot for Advancement for Women/Minorities: Y

SAS Institute Inc

www.sas.com

NAIC Code: 511210H

TYPES OF BUSINESS:

Computer Software, Statistical Analysis
Business Intelligence Software
Data Warehousing
Online Bookstore
Consulting

BRANDS/DIVISIONS/AFFILIATES:

CONTACTS: Note: Officers with more than one job title may be intentionally listed here more than once.

James Goodnight, CEO
Bryan Harris, CTO
Wm. David Davis, CFO
Paula Henderson, Chief Sales Officer, Americas
Jenn Mann, Chief Human Resources Officer
Jay Upchurch, CIO
John Boswell, Chief Legal Officer
Carl Farrell, Exec. VP-SAS Americas
John Sall, Exec. VP
Riad Gydien, Chief Sales Officer, EMEA & AP
Mikael Hagstrom, Exec. VP-EMEA & Asia Pacific

GROWTH PLANS/SPECIAL FEATURES:

SAS Institute, Inc. provides statistical analysis software. The company's products are designed to extract, manage and analyze large volumes of data, often assisting in financial reporting and credit analysis. Individual contracts can be tailored to specific global and local industries, such as banking, manufacturing and government. SAS' advanced analytics software is infused with cutting-edge, innovative algorithms that help its clients solve their most intractable problems, make the best decisions possible and capture new opportunities. The software comprises data mining, statistical analysis, forecasting, text analysis, optimization and stimulation features. Other products that provide enterprise solutions include artificial intelligence, Internet of Things (IoT), business intelligence, cloud analytics, customer intelligence, data management, fraud and security intelligence, in-memory analytics, performance management, risk management, solutions for Hadoop and supply chain intelligence. Industries that utilize SAS products and solutions include banking, capital markets, casinos, communications, consumer goods, defense/security, government, healthcare, P-12 education, higher education, hotels, insurance, life science, manufacturing, media, oil and gas, retail, small/midsize business, sports, travel, transportation and utilities. SAS serves more than 83,000 business, government and university sites in 147 different countries, including 92 of the top 100 companies on the 2018 Fortune Global 1000 list.

FINANCIAL DATA: Note: Data for latest year may not have been available at press time.

In U.S. $	2020	2019	2018	2017	2016	2015
Revenue	3,000,000,000	3,100,000,000	3,270,000,000	3,240,000,000	3,200,000,000	3,160,000,000
R&D Expense						
Operating Income						
Operating Margin %						
SGA Expense						
Net Income						
Operating Cash Flow						
Capital Expenditure						
EBITDA						
Return on Assets %						
Return on Equity %						
Debt to Equity						

CONTACT INFORMATION:

Phone: 919-677-8000   Fax: 919-677-4444
Toll-Free: 800-727-0025
Address: 100 SAS Campus Dr., Cary, NC 27513 United States

STOCK TICKER/OTHER:

Stock Ticker: Private
Employees: 13,939
Parent Company:

Exchange:
Fiscal Year Ends: 12/31

SALARIES/BONUSES:

Top Exec. Salary: $ Bonus: $
Second Exec. Salary: $ Bonus: $

OTHER THOUGHTS:

Estimated Female Officers or Directors: 1
Hot Spot for Advancement for Women/Minorities: Y

SC Johnson & Son Inc

NAIC Code: 325600

www.scjohnson.com

TYPES OF BUSINESS:

Household Products Manufacturing
Household Products
Cleaning Products
Auto Care Products
Insect Repellents

BRANDS/DIVISIONS/AFFILIATES:

Drano
Pledge
Shout
Mr Muscle
SC Johnson Professional
Scrubbing Bubbles
Duck
Ziploc

CONTACTS: Note: Officers with more than one job title may be intentionally listed here more than once.

H. Fisk Johnson III, CEO

GROWTH PLANS/SPECIAL FEATURES:

SC Johnson & Son, Inc. is one of the world's largest manufacturers of household chemical products, with many proprietary brand names. The firm was established in 1886 as a flooring company and has since been managed by the Johnson family. SC Johnson produces home cleaning, home storage, pest control, auto care and air care products. Its home cleaning products include the Drano home drain cleaner, Pledge dust and pet hair cleaner, Shout stain remover for clothes and fabrics, Mr. Muscle surface and household cleaner, SC Johnson Professional all-purpose cleaner, Scrubbing Bubbles bathroom cleaner, Windex glass and window cleaner and Duck bathroom cleaner. Other products include Saran plastic wrap and Ziploc plastic bags for home storage; Kiwi shoe care, Off!, Raid, Baygon, Autan and ALLOUT for insect repellency; Grand Prix waxes, protectants and cleaners for auto care; Glade candles and home fragrances for the air care market; babyganics organic detergents, sunscreen and body care for babies; and Mrs. Meyer's plant-derived cleaning products. The company's patented Greenlist process allows scientific and environmental organizations to review and rate ingredients for use in the firm's products. This system allows SC Johnson to improve and update its products by health and environmental standards. The firm has operations in more than 70 countries worldwide. SC Johnson & Son also operates an online mail order service, which allows customers to order a select number of company products, available for shipping anywhere in the U.S.

FINANCIAL DATA: Note: Data for latest year may not have been available at press time.

In U.S. $	2020	2019	2018	2017	2016	2015
Revenue	6,489,000,000	10,815,000,000	10,300,000,000	10,500,000,000	10,000,000,000	9,800,000,000
R&D Expense						
Operating Income						
Operating Margin %						
SGA Expense						
Net Income						
Operating Cash Flow						
Capital Expenditure						
EBITDA						
Return on Assets %						
Return on Equity %						
Debt to Equity						

CONTACT INFORMATION:

Phone: 262-260-2000   Fax: 262-260-6004
Toll-Free: 800-494-4855
Address: 1525 Howe St., Racine, WI 53403 United States

STOCK TICKER/OTHER:

Stock Ticker: Private
Employees: 13,200
Parent Company:

Exchange:
Fiscal Year Ends: 06/30

SALARIES/BONUSES:

Top Exec. Salary: $ Bonus: $
Second Exec. Salary: $ Bonus: $

OTHER THOUGHTS:

Estimated Female Officers or Directors:
Hot Spot for Advancement for Women/Minorities: Y

Schreiber Foods Inc

www.schreiberfoods.com

NAIC Code: 311500

TYPES OF BUSINESS:

Dairy Products, Manufacturing
Cheese Processing Equipment
Dairy-Based Ingredients
Food Product Packaging
Supply Chain Management

BRANDS/DIVISIONS/AFFILIATES:

CONTACTS: Note: Officers with more than one job title may be intentionally listed here more than once.

Ron Dunford, CEO
Jon Derouchey, VP-Oper.
Matt Mueller, CFO
Shari Antonissen, VP-Global Chain Sales
Dave Coble, Sr. VP-Human Resources
Tom Andreoli, CIO
Jerry Smyth, General Counsel
Matt Mueller, VP-Finance
Staci Kring, Sr. VP-Retail Sales
Trevor Farrell, CCO
Harley Skidmore, VP-Int'l Oper.

GROWTH PLANS/SPECIAL FEATURES:

Schreiber Foods, Inc. is one of the world's largest employee-owned consumer brand dairy companies. The firm manufactures a wide variety of natural, processed and specialty cheeses; cream cheese; yogurt; dairy-based powders; and other dairy foods such as ghee, butter, ice cream, reduced-fat cheese curd, condensed milk, sour cream and desserts. Schreiber supplies the foodservice and restaurant industries, as well as schools, colleges and universities, healthcare organizations, entertainment customers and businesses. Shelf-stable products, including juice and milk, do not require refrigeration and still provide the vitamins and nutrition people need. Schreiber's variety of natural cheese includes hard, semi-hard, semi-soft, soft and fresh. Its processed cheese is made from natural cheese that are blended with other ingredients and pasteurized. Cream cheese is a fresh, natural cheese that can be used as a spread or dip, or in dishes. Yogurt is made from fresh milk and cultures, and is provided in many different flavors and styles, including Greek, blended, fruit on the bottom, drinkable, organic, fermented, kefir and more. Dry dairy-based powders are good for cooking and baking, and are convenient to store, and include casein protein, whole milk powder, skim milk powder, whey, and a dairy whitener. Schreiber is a global company with more than 30 locations worldwide.

FINANCIAL DATA: Note: Data for latest year may not have been available at press time.

In U.S. $	2020	2019	2018	2017	2016	2015
Revenue	6,058,690,980	5,910,918,029	5,766,749,297	5,626,096,875	5,488,875,000	5,355,000,000
R&D Expense						
Operating Income						
Operating Margin %						
SGA Expense						
Net Income						
Operating Cash Flow						
Capital Expenditure						
EBITDA						
Return on Assets %						
Return on Equity %						
Debt to Equity						

CONTACT INFORMATION:

Phone: 920-437-7601   Fax: 920-437-1617
Toll-Free: 800-344-0333
Address: 400 N. Washington St., Green Bay, WI 54301 United States

STOCK TICKER/OTHER:

Stock Ticker: Private
Employees: 8,000
Parent Company:

Exchange:
Fiscal Year Ends: 09/30

SALARIES/BONUSES:

Top Exec. Salary: $ Bonus: $
Second Exec. Salary: $ Bonus: $

OTHER THOUGHTS:

Estimated Female Officers or Directors: 1
Hot Spot for Advancement for Women/Minorities:

Science Applications International Corporation (SAIC)

www.saic.com
NAIC Code: 541512

TYPES OF BUSINESS:

IT Consulting
IT Infrastructure Management
Research & Development
Software Development
Engineering

BRANDS/DIVISIONS/AFFILIATES:

CONTACTS: Note: Officers with more than one job title may be intentionally listed here more than once.

Anthony Moraco, CEO
Charles Mathis, CFO
Donna Morea, Chairman of the Board
Nazzic Keene, COO
Steven Mahon, Executive VP
Karen Wheeler, Other Executive Officer

GROWTH PLANS/SPECIAL FEATURES:

Science Applications International Corporation (SAIC) provides technical, engineering and enterprise IT services to commercial operations and government agencies. The company's clients include all four branches of the U.S. military (Army, Air Force, Navy and Marines), the U.S. Defense Logistics Agency, the National Aeronautics and Space Administration, the U.S. Department of State and the U.S. Department of Homeland Security. In fiscal 2020, 98% of total revenues were derived from contracts with the U.S. government or from subcontracts with other contractors engaged in work for the U.S. government, all of which were entities located in the U.S. The firm's offerings include: engineering; technology and equipment platform integration; maintenance of ground and maritime systems; logistics; training and simulation; operation and program support services; and end-to-end services that span design, development, integration, deployment, management and operations, sustainment and security of customers' entire IT infrastructure. SAIC serves customers through approximately 1,800 active contracts and task orders via thousands of employees.

FINANCIAL DATA: Note: Data for latest year may not have been available at press time.

In U.S. $	2020	2019	2018	2017	2016	2015
Revenue	6,379,000,000	4,659,000,000	4,454,000,000	4,450,000,000	4,315,000,000	
R&D Expense						
Operating Income	418,000,000	306,000,000	256,000,000	281,000,000	253,000,000	
Operating Margin %	.07%	.07%	.06%	.06%	.06%	
SGA Expense	288,000,000	158,000,000	155,000,000	166,000,000	158,000,000	
Net Income	226,000,000	137,000,000	179,000,000	148,000,000	117,000,000	
Operating Cash Flow	458,000,000	184,000,000	217,000,000	273,000,000	226,000,000	
Capital Expenditure	21,000,000	28,000,000	22,000,000	15,000,000	20,000,000	
EBITDA	514,000,000	272,000,000	304,000,000	325,000,000	289,000,000	
Return on Assets %	.05%	.04%	.09%	.07%	.07%	
Return on Equity %	.16%	.15%	.53%	.40%	.32%	
Debt to Equity	1.428	1.391	3.006	2.887	2.666	

CONTACT INFORMATION:

Phone: 703 676-4300   Fax:
Toll-Free:
Address: 12010 Sunset Hills Rd., Reston, VA 20190 United States

STOCK TICKER/OTHER:

Stock Ticker: SAIC
Employees: 26,000
Parent Company:

Exchange: NYS
Fiscal Year Ends: 01/31

SALARIES/BONUSES:

Top Exec. Salary: $ Bonus: $
Second Exec. Salary: $ Bonus: $

OTHER THOUGHTS:

Estimated Female Officers or Directors: 5
Hot Spot for Advancement for Women/Minorities: Y

SecureWorks Corporation

www.secureworks.com

NAIC Code: 511210E

TYPES OF BUSINESS:

Computer Software, Network Security, Managed Access, Digital ID,
Cybersecurity & Anti-Virus
Cyber Security

BRANDS/DIVISIONS/AFFILIATES:

Dell Inc
Dell Technologies Inc
SecureWorks Counter Threat Platform
Delve Laboratories Inc

CONTACTS: Note: Officers with more than one job title may be intentionally listed here more than once.

Roger Jackson, CFO
Michael Dell, Chairman of the Board
Michael Cote, Director
Teri Miller, Vice President

GROWTH PLANS/SPECIAL FEATURES:

SecureWorks Corporation is a global provider of intelligence-driven information security solutions. The firm is exclusively focused on protecting its clients from cyberattacks by providing them with an early warning system called SecureWorks Counter Threat Platform. The platform is a software-as-a-service-based early warning system that delivers insights and deploys countermeasures derived from analytics and applied intelligence. Counter Threat provides full visibility, and its analytics, intelligence and operations components work seamlessly together, which enables clients to prevent, detect and rapidly respond to and predict cyberattacks. SecureWorks' solutions include advanced threat protection, compliance management, critical asset protection, cybersecurity risk management and security of operations, including cloud security. The company provides its managed security solution to customers in more than 55 countries (as of October 30, 2020). SecureWorks is based in the U.S., with offices throughout the country as well as in the U.K., France, United Arab Emirates, Australia, India, Japan and Romania. The company is majority-owned by Dell Technologies, Inc., which itself is a subsidiary of Dell, Inc. In September 2020, SecureWorks acquired Delve Laboratories, Inc., which offers a software-as-a-service (SaaS) solution that uses artificial intelligence (AI) and machine learning to automate vulnerability detection and prioritization across an organizations' network, endpoint or cloud environment.

FINANCIAL DATA: Note: Data for latest year may not have been available at press time.

In U.S. $	2020	2019	2018	2017	2016	2015
Revenue	552,765,000	518,709,000	467,904,000	429,502,000	339,522,000	
R&D Expense	94,964,000	87,608,000	80,164,000	71,030,000	49,747,000	
Operating Income	-52,174,000	-48,732,000	-83,045,000	-65,953,000	-106,008,000	
Operating Margin %	-.09%	-.09%	-.18%	-.15%	-.31%	
SGA Expense	257,179,000	233,716,000	244,067,000	211,826,000	211,974,000	
Net Income	-31,666,000	-39,101,000	-28,077,000	-38,213,000	-72,381,000	
Operating Cash Flow	78,839,000	57,199,000	787,000	-6,838,000	-9,843,000	
Capital Expenditure	12,590,000	10,200,000	13,819,000	19,361,000	9,023,000	
EBITDA	-9,242,000	-7,525,000	-40,874,000	-26,528,000	-65,370,000	
Return on Assets %	-.03%	-.04%	-.03%	-.04%	-.08%	
Return on Equity %	-.05%	-.06%	-.04%	-.06%	-.11%	
Debt to Equity	0.037					

CONTACT INFORMATION:

Phone: 404-327-6339   Fax:
Toll-Free: 877-838-7947
Address: One Concourse Pkwy NE #500, Atlanta, GA 30328 United States

SALARIES/BONUSES:

Top Exec. Salary: $ Bonus: $
Second Exec. Salary: $ Bonus: $

STOCK TICKER/OTHER:

Stock Ticker: SCWX
Employees: 2,696
Parent Company: Dell Inc

Exchange: NAS
Fiscal Year Ends: 02/01

OTHER THOUGHTS:

Estimated Female Officers or Directors:
Hot Spot for Advancement for Women/Minorities:

Sempra Energy
NAIC Code: 221112

TYPES OF BUSINESS:

Utilities-Electricity & Natural Gas
Energy Management
Energy Marketing
Power Generation-Natural Gas Plants
LNG Pipelines, Storage & Terminals
Power Generation-Solar Power Plants
Power Generation-Wind Farms

BRANDS/DIVISIONS/AFFILIATES:

Southern California Gas Company
San Diego Gas & Electric Company
Sempra Texas Utility
Oncor
Chilqinta Energia SA
Luz del Sur SAA
Sempra Mexico

CONTACTS: Note: Officers with more than one job title may be intentionally listed here more than once.

Patricia Wagner, CEO, Subsidiary
Kevin Sagara, CEO, Subsidiary
Jeffrey Martin, CEO
Bruce Folkmann, CFO, Subsidiary
Trevor Mihalik, CFO
Peter Wall, Chief Accounting Officer
Caroline Winn, COO, Subsidiary
Jimmie Cho, COO, Subsidiary
J. Lane, COO, Subsidiary
Joseph Householder, COO
Dennis Arriola, Executive VP
Diana Day, General Counsel, Subsidiary
David Barrett, General Counsel, Subsidiary

GROWTH PLANS/SPECIAL FEATURES:

Sempra Energy provides electric, natural gas and other energy products and services primarily in California as well as internationally. The company operates through two California-based regulated utilities: Southern California Gas Company (SoCalGas), a natural gas distribution utility that serves customers in southern and central California; and San Diego Gas & Electric Company (SDG&E), which provides electricity distribution and transmission and natural gas distribution services to customers in southern Orange County and San Diego. SoCalGas' natural gas facilities include 3,058 miles of transmission and storage pipelines, 51,079 miles of distribution pipelines, 48,315 miles of service pipelines and nine transmission compressor stations; and SDG&E's facilities consist of 168 miles of transmission pipelines, 8,961 miles of distribution pipelines, 6,582 miles of service pipelines and one compressor station. Sempra Texas Utility owns an 80.25% interest in Oncor, a regulated electric transmission and distribution utility that operates in select regions of Texas, with an estimated population of approximately 10 million. Other subsidiaries include: Chilqinta Energia SA, an electric distribution utility in central Chile; Luz del Sur SAA, an electric distribution utility in the southern zone of Lima, Peru; and Sempra Mexico, which owns a natural gas-fired power plant in Mexico, as well as related pipelines, compressor stations and an LPG storage terminal. During 2019, the firm sold its remaining wind assets and investments to American Electric Power; agreed to sell its equity interests in its Peruvian businesses, including its 83.6% in Luz del Sur SAA to China Yangtze Power International (Hong Kong) Co., Limited; and agreed to sell its equity interests in its Chilean businesses, including wholly-owned Chilquinta Energia, to State Grid International Development Limited.

Benefits provided!

FINANCIAL DATA: Note: Data for latest year may not have been available at press time.

In U.S. $	2020	2019	2018	2017	2016	2015
Revenue	11,370,000,000	10,829,000,000	11,687,000,000	11,207,000,000	10,183,000,000	10,231,000,000
R&D Expense						
Operating Income	2,833,000,000	2,627,000,000	2,393,000,000	2,330,000,000	1,621,000,000	1,910,000,000
Operating Margin %		.24%	.20%	.21%	.16%	.19%
SGA Expense						
Net Income	3,933,000,000	2,198,000,000	1,050,000,000	257,000,000	1,371,000,000	1,350,000,000
Operating Cash Flow	2,591,000,000	3,088,000,000	3,447,000,000	3,625,000,000	2,319,000,000	2,905,000,000
Capital Expenditure	4,676,000,000	3,708,000,000	3,784,000,000	3,949,000,000	4,214,000,000	3,156,000,000
EBITDA	4,236,000,000	4,380,000,000	3,520,000,000	3,734,000,000	3,695,000,000	3,515,000,000
Return on Assets %		.03%	.02%	.01%	.03%	.03%
Return on Equity %		.13%	.07%	.02%	.11%	.12%
Debt to Equity		1.175	1.45	1.296	1.112	1.11

CONTACT INFORMATION:

Phone: 619 696-2000   Fax: 619 696-2374
Toll-Free: 877-773-6397
Address: 488 Eighth Ave, San Diego, CA 92101 United States

SALARIES/BONUSES:

Top Exec. Salary: $ Bonus: $
Second Exec. Salary: $ Bonus: $

STOCK TICKER/OTHER:

Stock Ticker: SRE   Exchange: NYS
Employees: 14,706   Fiscal Year Ends: 12/31
Parent Company:

OTHER THOUGHTS:

Estimated Female Officers or Directors: 6
Hot Spot for Advancement for Women/Minorities: Y

Service Corporation International Inc

www.sci-corp.com

NAIC Code: 812210

TYPES OF BUSINESS:

Funeral Homes and Funeral Services
Funeral Services
Cemetery Services

BRANDS/DIVISIONS/AFFILIATES:

Dignity Memorial
Dignity Planning
National Cremation Society
Advantage Funeral and Cremation Services
Funeraria del Angel
Making Everlasting Memories
Neptune Society
Trident Society

CONTACTS: Note: Officers with more than one job title may be intentionally listed here more than once.

Thomas Ryan, CEO
Tammy Moore, Chief Accounting Officer
Sumner Waring, COO
Robert Waltrip, Founder
Gregory Sangalis, General Counsel
Elisabeth Nash, Senior VP, Divisional
Steven Tidwell, Senior VP, Divisional
Eric Tanzberger, Senior VP

GROWTH PLANS/SPECIAL FEATURES:

Service Corporation International, Inc. is a provider of deathcare products and services in North America. The company is geographically diversified across 44 U.S. states, eight Canadian provinces, the District of Columbia and Puerto Rico. As of December 31, 2020, Service Corporation's funeral service and cemetery operations consisted of 1,470 funeral service locations and 483 cemeteries (including 297 funeral service/cemetery combination locations), as well as crematoria and related businesses. The firm provides all professional services relating to funerals and cremations, including the use of funeral facilities and motor vehicles and preparation and embalming services. Funeral related merchandise, including caskets, burial vaults, cremation receptacles, flowers and other ancillary products and services are sold at funeral service locations. Service Corporation's cemeteries provide cemetery property interment rights, including mausoleum spaces, lots and lawn crypts, and sell cemetery related merchandise and services, including stone and bronze memorials, burial vaults, casket and cremation memorialization products, merchandise installations and burial openings and closings. Service Corporation has branded the company's funeral operations in North America under the name Dignity Memorial. Other brands include Dignity Planning, National Cremation Society, Advantage Funeral and Cremation Services, Funeraria del Angel, Making Everlasting Memories, Neptune Society and Trident Society.

FINANCIAL DATA: Note: Data for latest year may not have been available at press time.

In U.S. $	2020	2019	2018	2017	2016	2015
Revenue	3,511,509,000	3,230,785,000	3,190,174,000	3,095,031,000	3,031,137,000	2,986,380,000
R&D Expense						
Operating Income	835,761,000	633,694,000	614,823,000	567,766,000	538,704,000	543,757,000
Operating Margin %		.20%	.19%	.18%	.18%	.18%
SGA Expense	141,066,000	126,886,000	145,499,000	154,423,000	137,730,000	128,188,000
Net Income	515,907,000	369,596,000	447,208,000	546,663,000	177,038,000	233,772,000
Operating Cash Flow	804,351,000	628,755,000	615,830,000	502,340,000	463,595,000	472,186,000
Capital Expenditure	222,211,000	239,957,000	250,070,000	214,501,000	193,446,000	150,986,000
EBITDA	1,083,269,000	897,254,000	871,773,000	818,276,000	733,685,000	778,570,000
Return on Assets %		.03%	.03%	.04%	.01%	.02%
Return on Equity %		.21%	.29%	.44%	.16%	.18%
Debt to Equity		1.956	2.151	2.225	2.925	2.593

CONTACT INFORMATION:

Phone: 713 522-5141   Fax: 713 525-5586
Toll-Free:
Address: 1929 Allen Parkway, Houston, TX 77019 United States

SALARIES/BONUSES:

Top Exec. Salary: $ Bonus: $
Second Exec. Salary: $ Bonus: $

STOCK TICKER/OTHER:

Stock Ticker: SCI
Employees: 23,463
Parent Company:

Exchange: NYS
Fiscal Year Ends: 12/31

OTHER THOUGHTS:

Estimated Female Officers or Directors:
Hot Spot for Advancement for Women/Minorities:

ServiceNow Inc
NAIC Code: 511210B

www.service-now.com

TYPES OF BUSINESS:
Computer Software: Network Management (IT), System Testing & Storage
Cloud-Based Workflow Software

BRANDS/DIVISIONS/AFFILIATES:
Loom Systems Ltd
Rupert Labs Inc
Passage AI
Sweagle NV

CONTACTS: Note: Officers with more than one job title may be intentionally listed here more than once.
Michael Scarpelli, CFO
Fay Goon, Chief Accounting Officer
Frederic Luddy, Director
John Donahoe, Director
Russell Elmer, General Counsel
Patricia Wadors, Other Executive Officer
Chirantan Desai, Other Executive Officer
David Schneider, President, Divisional

GROWTH PLANS/SPECIAL FEATURES:
ServiceNow, Inc. is a provider of cloud-based services that automate enterprise IT operations. The company's service includes a suite of applications built on its proprietary platform that automates workflow and provides integration between related business processes. The firm focuses on transforming enterprise IT by automating and standardizing business processes and consolidating IT across the global enterprise. Organizations deploy its service to create a single system of record for enterprise IT, lower operational costs and enhance efficiency. Additionally, customers use its extensible platform to build custom applications for automating activities unique to their business requirements. ServiceNow helps transform IT organizations from reactive, manual and task-oriented, to pro-active, automated and service-oriented organizations. The company's on-demand service enables organizations to define their IT strategy, design the systems and infrastructure that will support that strategy, and implement, manage and automate that infrastructure throughout its lifecycle while leveraging its self-service capability. The firm provides a broad set of integrated functionality that is highly configurable and extensible and can be efficiently implemented and upgraded. Its multi-instance architecture has proven scalability for global enterprises as well as having advantages in security, reliability and deployment location. The company offers its service under a Software-as-a-Service (SaaS) business model. Customers can rapidly deploy its service in a modular fashion, allowing them to solve immediate business needs and access, configure and build new applications as their requirements evolve. The firm's service, which is accessed through an intuitive web-based interface, can be easily configured to adapt to customer workflow and processes. ServiceNow serves thousands of enterprise customers worldwide. During 2020, ServiceNow acquired Loom Systems Ltd.; Rupert Labs, Inc. (dba Passage AI); and Sweagle NV. That November, the company agreed to acquire Element AI, which is based in Quebec, Canada.

FINANCIAL DATA: Note: Data for latest year may not have been available at press time.

In U.S. $	2020	2019	2018	2017	2016	2015
Revenue	4,519,484,000	3,460,437,000	2,608,816,000	1,933,026,000	1,390,513,000	1,005,480,000
R&D Expense	1,024,327,000	748,369,000	529,501,000	377,518,000	285,239,000	217,389,000
Operating Income	198,863,000	42,123,000	-42,426,000	-101,414,000	-152,808,000	-166,365,000
Operating Margin %		.01%	-.02%	-.05%	-.11%	-.17%
SGA Expense	2,309,181,000	1,873,300,000	1,499,083,000	1,157,150,000	859,400,000	625,043,000
Net Income	118,503,000	626,698,000	-26,704,000	-149,130,000	-451,804,000	-198,426,000
Operating Cash Flow	1,786,599,000	1,235,972,000	811,089,000	642,825,000	159,921,000	315,091,000
Capital Expenditure	432,517,000	337,581,000	248,862,000	157,180,000	124,312,000	89,231,000
EBITDA	518,312,000	350,976,000	160,651,000	15,494,000	-335,476,000	-103,227,000
Return on Assets %		.13%	-.01%	-.05%	-.24%	-.12%
Return on Equity %		.39%	-.03%	-.31%	-.95%	-.40%
Debt to Equity		0.507	0.595	1.079	1.312	0.837

CONTACT INFORMATION:
Phone: 408-501-8550   Fax:
Toll-Free:
Address: 2225 Lawson Ln., Santa Clara, CA 95054 United States

STOCK TICKER/OTHER:
Stock Ticker: NOW
Employees: 13,096
Parent Company:

Exchange: NYS
Fiscal Year Ends: 12/31

SALARIES/BONUSES:
Top Exec. Salary: $ Bonus: $
Second Exec. Salary: $ Bonus: $

OTHER THOUGHTS:
Estimated Female Officers or Directors:
Hot Spot for Advancement for Women/Minorities:

Shake Shack Inc

www.shakeshack.com

NAIC Code: 722513

TYPES OF BUSINESS:

Fast Food Restaurants
Restaurants
Fast-Casual
Hamburgers
Frozen Custards

BRANDS/DIVISIONS/AFFILIATES:

Shake Shack

CONTACTS: Note: Officers with more than one job title may be intentionally listed here more than once.

Randy Garutti, CEO
Tara Comonte, CFO
Daniel Meyer, Chairman of the Board
Zach Koff, COO

GROWTH PLANS/SPECIAL FEATURES:

Shake Shack, Inc. is an American fast casual restaurant chain based in New York City. It started out as a hot dog cart in Madison Square Park in 2001, and Shack fans lined up daily for three summers afterward. In 2004, the company opened a permanent kiosk in the Park and Shake Shack was born. Currently, Shake Shack serves hamburgers, chicken sandwiches, chicken bites, hot dogs, frozen custard, shakes, beer, wine and more. Some Shacks offer breakfast sandwiches. All burgers are made from 100% all-natural Angus beef, with no hormones and no antibiotics, and placed in a non-GMO Martin's Potato Roll. Chicken offerings are made from 100% all-natural cage free chicken; hot dogs are 100% all-natural Vienna beef with no hormones and no antibiotics; and fries are crinkle cut style, made from Yukon potatoes and no artificial ingredients. Shakes are made from hand-spun ice cream in vanilla, chocolate, caramel, black & white, strawberry, peanut butter or coffee flavors, and often provide a shake-of-the-week specialty flavor. As of April 2021, there were approximately 320 Shake Shack locations, including more than 105 international locations such as London, Hong Kong, Shanghai, Singapore, Philippines, Mexico, Istanbul, Dubai, Tokyo and Seoul.

FINANCIAL DATA: Note: Data for latest year may not have been available at press time.

In U.S. $	2020	2019	2018	2017	2016	2015
Revenue	522,867,000	594,519,000	459,310,000	358,810,000	268,475,000	190,592,000
R&D Expense						
Operating Income	-33,725,000	27,037,000	32,628,000	34,421,000	27,839,000	6,770,000
Operating Margin %		.05%	.07%	.10%	.10%	.04%
SGA Expense	115,842,000	114,100,000	85,430,000	67,200,000	52,376,000	53,032,000
Net Income	-42,158,000	19,827,000	15,179,000	-320,000	12,446,000	-8,776,000
Operating Cash Flow	37,350,000	89,857,000	85,395,000	70,878,000	54,285,000	41,258,000
Capital Expenditure	69,038,000	106,507,000	87,525,000	61,533,000	54,433,000	32,117,000
EBITDA	5,583,000	68,652,000	62,225,000	183,640,000	43,372,000	16,992,000
Return on Assets %		.03%	.03%	.00%	.03%	-.04%
Return on Equity %		.08%	.08%	.00%	.10%	-.16%
Debt to Equity		1.033		0.092	0.086	0.013	0.003

CONTACT INFORMATION:

Phone: 646 747-7200   Fax:
Toll-Free:
Address: 225 Varick St., Ste. 301, New York, NY 10014 United States

STOCK TICKER/OTHER:

Stock Ticker: SHAK
Employees: 7,603
Parent Company:

Exchange: NYS
Fiscal Year Ends: 12/31

SALARIES/BONUSES:

Top Exec. Salary: $ Bonus: $
Second Exec. Salary: $ Bonus: $

OTHER THOUGHTS:

Estimated Female Officers or Directors:
Hot Spot for Advancement for Women/Minorities:

Sherwin-Williams Company (The)

NAIC Code: 325510   **www.sherwin-williams.com**

TYPES OF BUSINESS:

Paints & Coatings Manufacturing
Retail Paint Stores
Wall Coverings
Automotive Finishing Products
Design Consulting

BRANDS/DIVISIONS/AFFILIATES:

Sherwin-Williams

CONTACTS: *Note: Officers with more than one job title may be intentionally listed here more than once.*

John Morikis, CEO
Allen Mistysyn, CFO
Jane Cronin, Chief Accounting Officer
David Sewell, COO
Mary Garceau, General Counsel
Joel Baxter, General Manager, Divisional
Robert Lynch, President, Divisional
Aaron Erter, President, Divisional
Peter Ippolito, President, Divisional
Thomas Gilligan, Senior VP, Divisional
Robert Wells, Senior VP, Divisional

GROWTH PLANS/SPECIAL FEATURES:

The Sherwin-Williams Company is one of the largest international manufacturers, distributors and retailers of paint and related products to professional, industrial, commercial and retail customers. The company operates in three reportable segments: Americas, consumer brands and performance coatings. The Americas segment consists of more than 4,500 company-operated stores in the U.S., Canada, Latin America and the Caribbean region. These company-operated stores sell Sherwin-Williams and other controlled brands architectural paint, coatings and other associated products and brands. The consumer brands segment supplies a broad portfolio of branded and private-label architectural paints, stains, varnishes, industrial products, wood finishes products, wood preservatives, applicators, corrosion inhibitors, aerosols, caulks and adhesives to retailers and distributors throughout North America, as well as in China and Europe. Additionally, this division supports the other segments with new product research and development, manufacturing, distribution and logistics. The consumer brands division consists of operations in the U.S. and subsidiaries in 6 foreign countries. The performance coatings segment develops and sells industrial coatings for wood finishing and general industrial (metal and plastic) applications, automotive refinish, protective and marine coatings, coil coatings, packaging coatings and performance-based resins and colorants worldwide. This division consists of operations in the U.S. and subsidiaries in 45 foreign countries. Its products are distributed through the Americas segment and its company-operated branches. In March 2021, Sherwin-Williams sold Wattyl, an Australian and New Zealand manufacturer and seller of architectural and protective paint and coatings.

FINANCIAL DATA: *Note: Data for latest year may not have been available at press time.*

In U.S. $	2020	2019	2018	2017	2016	2015
Revenue	18,361,700,000	17,900,800,000	17,534,490,000	14,983,790,000	11,855,600,000	11,339,300,000
R&D Expense						
Operating Income	2,854,200,000	2,425,400,000	1,890,373,000	1,773,589,000	1,719,898,000	1,614,637,000
Operating Margin %		.14%	.11%	.12%	.15%	.14%
SGA Expense	5,477,900,000	5,274,900,000	5,033,780,000	4,785,415,000	4,159,435,000	3,913,518,000
Net Income	2,030,400,000	1,541,300,000	1,108,746,000	1,772,262,000	1,132,703,000	1,053,849,000
Operating Cash Flow	3,408,600,000	2,321,300,000	1,943,700,000	1,883,968,000	1,308,572,000	1,447,463,000
Capital Expenditure	303,800,000	328,900,000	250,957,000	222,767,000	239,026,000	234,340,000
EBITDA	3,441,000,000	2,906,000,000	2,322,665,000	2,283,451,000	1,947,032,000	1,809,319,000
Return on Assets %		.08%	.06%	.13%	.18%	.18%
Return on Equity %		.39%	.30%	.64%	.82%	1.13%
Debt to Equity		2.285	2.334	2.677	0.645	2.212

CONTACT INFORMATION:

Phone: 216 566-2000   Fax:
Toll-Free: 800-474-3794
Address: 101 W. Prospect Ave., Cleveland, OH 44115 United States

SALARIES/BONUSES:

Top Exec. Salary: $ Bonus: $
Second Exec. Salary: $ Bonus: $

STOCK TICKER/OTHER:

Stock Ticker: SHW   Exchange: NYS
Employees: 61,111   Fiscal Year Ends: 12/31
Parent Company:

OTHER THOUGHTS:

Estimated Female Officers or Directors: 2
Hot Spot for Advancement for Women/Minorities: Y

Skyline Champion Corporation

ir.skylinechampion.com/overview/default.aspx

NAIC Code: 321992

TYPES OF BUSINESS:

Prefabricated Wood Building Manufacturing (Manufactured Housing)
Home Building
Manufacturing Facilities
Manufactured Homes
Modular Homes
Park Model Recreational Vehicle Homes
Retail Operations

BRANDS/DIVISIONS/AFFILIATES:

Skyline Corporation
Champion Enterprises Holdings LLC
Titan Factory Direct
Star Fleet Trucking
Skyline Homes
Champion Home Builders
Athens Park Models
ScotBilt Homes

CONTACTS: Note: Officers with more than one job title may be intentionally listed here more than once.

Mark Yost, CEO
Laurie Hough, CFO
Timothy Bernlohr, Chairman of the Board
Timothy Burkhardt, Chief Accounting Officer
Roger Scholten, General Counsel
Joe Kimmell, Vice President, Geographical
Wade Lyall, Vice President, Geographical

GROWTH PLANS/SPECIAL FEATURES:

Skyline Champion Corporation is a leading homebuilder in North America, with approximately 70 years of homebuilding experience and 40 manufacturing facilities throughout the U.S. and western Canada. Skyline Champion offers a wide variety of manufactured and modular homes, park model recreational vehicles and module buildings for the multi-family, hospitality, senior and workforce housing sectors. Skyline Champion builds homes under well-known brands such as Skyline Homes, Champion Home Builders, Genesis Homes, Athens Park Models, Dutch Housing, Excel Homes, Homes of Merit, New Era, Redman Homes, ScotBilt Homes, Shore Park, Silvercrest, and Titan Homes in the U.S.; and Moduline and SRI Homes in western Canada. In addition, Skyline Champion operates a factory-direct retail business, Titan Factory Direct, with 18 retail locations across the southern U.S. Subsidiary Star Fleet Trucking provides transportation services to the manufactured housing and RV industries from several dispatch locations across the U.S. During 2021, Skyline Champion acquired ScotBilt Homes LLC from SHI Group Holdings, Inc. ScotBilt has two manufacturing facilities in Georgia, providing affordable housing throughout Alabama, Florida, Georgia and the Carolinas.

FINANCIAL DATA: Note: Data for latest year may not have been available at press time.

In U.S. $	2020	2019	2018	2017	2016	2015
Revenue	1,369,730,000	1,360,043,000	1,064,722,000	861,319,000		
R&D Expense						
Operating Income	86,690,000	-29,619,000	54,042,000	38,338,000		
Operating Margin %	.06%	-.02%	.05%	.04%		
SGA Expense	186,855,000	270,158,000	122,582,000	105,175,000		
Net Income	58,160,000	-58,208,000	15,800,000	51,910,000		
Operating Cash Flow	76,743,000	65,228,000	31,623,000	33,459,000		
Capital Expenditure	15,389,000	12,092,000	9,442,000	6,955,000		
EBITDA	108,232,000	-19,891,000	56,509,000	39,897,000		
Return on Assets %	.08%	-.11%	.04%			
Return on Equity %	.13%	-.21%	.10%			
Debt to Equity	0.163	0.132	0.384			

CONTACT INFORMATION:

Phone: 248-614-8211   Fax:
Toll-Free:
Address: 755 W. Big Beaver Rd., Ste. 1000, Troy, MI 48084 United States

STOCK TICKER/OTHER:

Stock Ticker: SKY
Employees: 7,700
Parent Company:

Exchange: NYS
Fiscal Year Ends: 03/31

SALARIES/BONUSES:

Top Exec. Salary: $ Bonus: $
Second Exec. Salary: $ Bonus: $

OTHER THOUGHTS:

Estimated Female Officers or Directors:
Hot Spot for Advancement for Women/Minorities:

Smithfield Foods Inc

www.smithfieldfoods.com

NAIC Code: 311612

TYPES OF BUSINESS:

Meat Processing, Pork
Hog Production

BRANDS/DIVISIONS/AFFILIATES:

WH Group Limited
Smithfield
Eckrich
Nathan's Famous
Armour
Cook's
Healthy Ones
Pure Farmland

CONTACTS: *Note: Officers with more than one job title may be intentionally listed here more than once.*

Dennis Organ, CEO
Glenn T. Nunziata, CFO
Russ Dokken, Chief Sales Officer
Kiera Lombardo, Chief Administrative Officer
Henry L. Morris, Sr. Corp. VP-Eng.
Michael H. Cole, Chief Legal Officer
Henry L. Morris, Sr. Corp. VP-Oper.
Keira L. Lombardo, VP-Corp. Comm.
Keira L. Lombardo, VP-Investor Rel.
Jeffrey A. Deel, Corp. Controller
George H. Richter, Pres.
Parul Stevens, VP-Risk Mgmt.
Timothy Dykstra, Treas.
Dennis H. Treacy, Chief Sustainability Officer
Dariusz Nowakowski, Pres., Smithfield Europe

GROWTH PLANS/SPECIAL FEATURES:

Smithfield Foods, Inc. is a leading hog producer and one of the largest processors and suppliers of fresh pork and processed meat products in the world, exporting to more than 40 countries. The firm is a leader in numerous packaged meats categories with popular brands including Smithfield, Eckrich, Nathan's Famous, Farmland, Armour, Farmer John, Kretschmar, John Morrell, Cook's, Gwaltney, Crando, Margherita, Curly's, HealthyOnes, Morlinky, Krakus and Berlinki. The company's products include fresh meats, packaged meats, dry meat products, ready-to-eat products and prepared foods. Its meat offerings also include beef and poultry, in addition to pork. The Smithfield Renewables division implements a wide range of renewable projects across the group's farms and facilities, including the conversion of hog manure into renewable natural gas and commercial-grade fertilizer. Smithfield Foods is a subsidiary of WH Group Limited.

FINANCIAL DATA: *Note: Data for latest year may not have been available at press time.*

In U.S. $	2020	2019	2018	2017	2016	2015
Revenue	16,446,543,750	16,868,250,000	16,065,000,000	15,300,000,000	14,300,000,000	14,400,000,000
R&D Expense						
Operating Income						
Operating Margin %						
SGA Expense						
Net Income						
Operating Cash Flow						
Capital Expenditure						
EBITDA						
Return on Assets %						
Return on Equity %						
Debt to Equity						

CONTACT INFORMATION:

Phone: 757 365-3000   Fax: 757 365-3017
Toll-Free: 888-366-6767
Address: 200 Commerce St., Smithfield, VA 23430 United States

STOCK TICKER/OTHER:

Stock Ticker: Subsidiary   Exchange:
Employees: 54,000   Fiscal Year Ends: 04/30
Parent Company: WH Group Lmited

SALARIES/BONUSES:

Top Exec. Salary: $ Bonus: $
Second Exec. Salary: $ Bonus: $

OTHER THOUGHTS:

Estimated Female Officers or Directors: 1
Hot Spot for Advancement for Women/Minorities: Y

Sales, profits and employees may be estimates. Financial information, benefits and other data can change quickly and may vary from those stated here.

Sonic Corp

www.sonicdrivein.com

NAIC Code: 722513

TYPES OF BUSINESS:

Restaurants
Drive-Ins
Franchising

BRANDS/DIVISIONS/AFFILIATES:

Roark Capital Management LLC
Inspire Brands Inc
Sonic Drive-Ins

CONTACTS: Note: Officers with more than one job title may be intentionally listed here more than once.

Claudia San Pedro, Pres.
Tanisha Beacham, Sr. VP-Oper.
J. Hudson, CEO
Ted Tetrick, VP-Finance
Lori Abou Habib, Sr. VP
Jennifer Buxton, VP-Human Resources
John Budd, Executive VP
Jose Duenas, Executive VP
Claudia San Pedro, President
Christina Vaughan, President, Subsidiary
Carolyn Cummins, Secretary
E. Saroch, Senior VP, Divisional

GROWTH PLANS/SPECIAL FEATURES:

Sonic Corp. operates and franchises one of the largest chains of drive-in restaurants (Sonic Drive-Ins) in the U.S. The firm is owned by Inspire Brands, Inc., itself owned by Roark Capital Management, LLC, a private equity firm. Currently, Sonic owns or franchises approximately 3,500 locations, most of which are franchised, throughout the U.S. Together, these establishments serve approximately 3 million customers every day. At a standard Sonic Drive-In restaurant, a customer drives into one of 16 to 24 covered drive-in spaces, orders through an intercom speaker system and has the food delivered by a carhop. Many locations also include a drive-thru lane and patio seating. Sonic Drive-Ins feature Sonic signature items, such as specialty drinks including cherry limeades and slushes, frozen desserts, made-to-order sandwiches and hamburgers, extra-long chili cheese coneys, hand-battered onion rings, tater tots, salads and wraps. Sonic Drive-Ins also offer breakfast items that include breakfast sandwiches and breakfast burritos. Sonic's average restaurant generates about $1.26 million in annual revenues. The firm operates as a subsidiary of Inspire Brands, Inc. the holding company of the Arby's, Buffalo Wild Wings, Jimmy John's and Rusty Taco restaurant chains.

FINANCIAL DATA: Note: Data for latest year may not have been available at press time.

In U.S. $	2020	2019	2018	2017	2016	2015
Revenue	448,875,000	472,500,000	423,590,000	477,267,008	606,320,000	606,089,024
R&D Expense						
Operating Income						
Operating Margin %						
SGA Expense						
Net Income			71,205,000	63,663,000	64,067,000	64,485,000
Operating Cash Flow						
Capital Expenditure						
EBITDA						
Return on Assets %						
Return on Equity %						
Debt to Equity						

CONTACT INFORMATION:

Phone: 405 225-5000   Fax: 405 280-7568
Toll-Free:
Address: 300 Johnny Bench Dr., Oklahoma City, OK 73104 United States

STOCK TICKER/OTHER:

Stock Ticker: Private
Employees: 5,000
Parent Company: Roark Capital Management LLC

Exchange:
Fiscal Year Ends: 08/31

SALARIES/BONUSES:

Top Exec. Salary: $ Bonus: $
Second Exec. Salary: $ Bonus: $

OTHER THOUGHTS:

Estimated Female Officers or Directors:
Hot Spot for Advancement for Women/Minorities:

Southeastern Grocers LLC

www.segrocers.com

NAIC Code: 445110

TYPES OF BUSINESS:

Grocery Stores
Food Processing
Distribution Services
Liquor Stores
Pharmacies
Fuel Centers

BRANDS/DIVISIONS/AFFILIATES:

BI-LO LLC
J H Harvey Co LLC
Winn-Dixie Stores Inc
Fresco Y Mas
Flavor
Whiskers & Tails
www.harveyssupermarkets.com
www.frescosymas.com

CONTACTS: *Note: Officers with more than one job title may be intentionally listed here more than once.*

Anthony Hucker, CEO
D. Mark Prestridge, Exec. VP-Oper.

GROWTH PLANS/SPECIAL FEATURES:

Southeastern Grocers, LLC is a U.S. supermarket chain. It is the parent of BI-LO, LLC; J.H. Harvey Co., LLC; Winn-Dixie Stores, Inc.; and Fresco Y Mas, which are all supermarket chains under the BI-LO, Harveys, Winn-Dixie and Fresco Y Mas banners. Together, Southeastern operates approximately 550 stores, including grocery and liquor stores and in-store pharmacies, primarily within the states of Alabama, Florida, Georgia, Louisiana, Mississippi, North Carolina and South Carolina. The company's stores provide non-perishable products including grocery, dairy, frozen food, general merchandise, alcoholic beverages, tobacco and fuel products; perishable products such as fresh & packaged meat, seafood, deli, bakery, produce and floral items; and pharmaceuticals. Fresco Y Mas is the company's Hispanic banner, featuring Hispanic grocery items and products, as well as a Latin butcher shop and kitchen. Southeastern's monthly publication, Flavor, aims to inspire readers with fresh ideas, seasonal recipes and planning affordable meals. The firm's pet food brand, Whiskers & Tails, is made with high-quality protein and nutritionally-balanced vitamin and mineral ingredients for both dogs and cats. Company websites include www.segrocers.com, www.harveyssupermarkets.com, www.winndixie.com and www.frescosymas.com.

FINANCIAL DATA: *Note: Data for latest year may not have been available at press time.*

In U.S. $	2020	2019	2018	2017	2016	2015
Revenue	9,250,625,000	9,025,000,000	9,500,000,000	10,110,000,000	10,050,000,000	10,080,000,000
R&D Expense						
Operating Income						
Operating Margin %						
SGA Expense						
Net Income						
Operating Cash Flow						
Capital Expenditure						
EBITDA						
Return on Assets %						
Return on Equity %						
Debt to Equity						

CONTACT INFORMATION:

Phone: 904-783-5000   Fax: 904-783-5294
Toll-Free:
Address: 8928 Prominence Parkway, Ste. 200, Jacksonville, FL 32256
United States

STOCK TICKER/OTHER:

Stock Ticker: Private
Employees: 66,000
Parent Company:

Exchange:
Fiscal Year Ends: 06/30

SALARIES/BONUSES:

Top Exec. Salary: $ Bonus: $
Second Exec. Salary: $ Bonus: $

OTHER THOUGHTS:

Estimated Female Officers or Directors:
Hot Spot for Advancement for Women/Minorities: Y

Southern California Edison Company

www.sce.com

NAIC Code: 221112

TYPES OF BUSINESS:

Electric Utility
Nuclear Generation
Hydroelectric Generation

GROWTH PLANS/SPECIAL FEATURES:

Southern California Edison Company (SCE) is one of the largest electric utilities in the U.S. The firm is the largest subsidiary of Edison International, an electric power generator and distributor as well as an investor in infrastructure and renewable energy projects. SCE serves around 15 million individuals in a 50,000-square-mile service area within central, coastal and southern California, excluding Los Angeles.

The company offers employees AD&D, disability, life, medical, dental and vision insurance; a 401(k) plan with company match; an employee assistance program; a retirement pension plan; wellness programs; and educational reimbursements.

BRANDS/DIVISIONS/AFFILIATES:

Edison International

CONTACTS: Note: Officers with more than one job title may be intentionally listed here more than once.

Kevin M. Payne, CEO
Steven D. Powell, Exec. VP-Oper.
William (Tres) Petmecky, CFO
Jacqueline Trapp, Chief Human Resources Officer
Peter T. Dietrich, Chief Nuclear Officer
Todd L. Inlander, CIO
Kevin M. Payne, VP-Eng.
Russell C. Swartz, General Counsel
Chris Dominski, VP-Planning & Performance Reporting
Janet Clayton, Sr. VP-Corp. Comm.
Chris C. Dominski, Controller
Lynda L. Ziegler, Exec. VP-Power Delivery Svcs.
Barbara E. Mathews, Chief Governance Officer
Gaddi H. Vasquez, Sr. VP-Govt Affairs
Stephen E. Pickett, Exec. VP-External Rel.
Pedro J. Pizarro, Chmn.
Douglas R. Bauder, Chief Procurement Officer

FINANCIAL DATA: Note: Data for latest year may not have been available at press time.

In U.S. $	2020	2019	2018	2017	2016	2015
Revenue	13,546,000,000	12,306,000,000	12,611,000,000	12,254,000,000	11,830,000,000	11,485,000,000
R&D Expense						
Operating Income						
Operating Margin %						
SGA Expense						
Net Income	942,000,000	1,530,000,000	-189,000,000	668,000,000	1,499,000,000	1,111,000,000
Operating Cash Flow						
Capital Expenditure						
EBITDA						
Return on Assets %						
Return on Equity %						
Debt to Equity						

CONTACT INFORMATION:

Phone: 626 302-1212   Fax:
Toll-Free: 800-655-4555
Address: 2244 Walnut Grove Ave., Rosemead, CA 91770 United States

STOCK TICKER/OTHER:

Stock Ticker: Subsidiary
Employees: 13,000
Parent Company: Edison International

Exchange:
Fiscal Year Ends: 12/31

SALARIES/BONUSES:

Top Exec. Salary: $ Bonus: $
Second Exec. Salary: $ Bonus: $

OTHER THOUGHTS:

Estimated Female Officers or Directors: 10
Hot Spot for Advancement for Women/Minorities: Y

Sales, profits and employees may be estimates. Financial information, benefits and other data can change quickly and may vary from those stated here.

Southern Company
NAIC Code: 221112

www.southerncompany.com

TYPES OF BUSINESS:

Electric Utility
Wireless Communications Services
Fiber Optic Solutions
Nuclear Power Operating Services
Consulting Services
Power Generation Construction
Biomass

BRANDS/DIVISIONS/AFFILIATES:

Alabama Power Company
Georgia Power Company
Mississippi Power Company
Southern Power Company
Southern Company Gas

CONTACTS: *Note: Officers with more than one job title may be intentionally listed here more than once.*

Mark Crosswhite, CEO, Subsidiary
W. Bowers, CEO, Subsidiary
Kimberly Greene, CEO, Subsidiary
Mark Lantrip, CEO, Subsidiary
Stephen Kuczynski, CEO, Subsidiary
Anthony Wilson, CEO, Subsidiary
Thomas Fanning, CEO
Xia Liu, CFO, Subsidiary
Philip Raymond, CFO, Subsidiary
Daniel Tucker, CFO, Subsidiary
William Grantham, CFO, Subsidiary
Moses Feagin, CFO, Subsidiary
Andrew Evans, CFO
Cynthia Shaw, Chief Accounting Officer, Subsidiary
Elliott Spencer, Chief Accounting Officer, Subsidiary
Anita Allcorn-Walker, Chief Accounting Officer, Subsidiary
David Poroch, Chief Accounting Officer, Subsidiary
Grace Kolvereid, Chief Accounting Officer, Subsidiary
Ann Daiss, Chief Accounting Officer
James Kerr, Chief Compliance Officer

GROWTH PLANS/SPECIAL FEATURES:

Southern Company, through its subsidiaries, is a producer and distributor of electricity in the U.S. Its three main subsidiaries, Alabama Power Company, Georgia Power Company and Mississippi Power Company, are each an operating public utility company. These electric operating companies are vertically integrated utilities that own generation, transmission and distribution facilities, and serve the states in which they are based. Southern Company also owns Southern Power Company, which develops, constructs, acquires, owns and manages power generation assets, including renewable energy facilities, and sells electricity at market-based rates in the wholesale market; and Southern Company Gas, which owns and operates a natural gas storage facility consisting of two salt dome caverns in Louisiana. In January 2020, the firm, through Sothern Power, completed its sale of the Mankato Energy Center to Xcel Energy for $650 million. In May of the same year, Southern Power, a Southern Company subsidiary, acquired the 56-megawatt Beech Ridge II Wind Facility from Invenergy.

FINANCIAL DATA: *Note: Data for latest year may not have been available at press time.*

In U.S. $	2020	2019	2018	2017	2016	2015
Revenue	20,375,000,000	21,419,000,000	23,495,000,000	23,031,000,000	19,896,000,000	17,489,000,000
R&D Expense						
Operating Income	4,820,000,000	5,335,000,000	4,110,000,000	2,551,000,000	4,629,000,000	4,282,000,000
Operating Margin %		.25%	.17%	.11%	.23%	.24%
SGA Expense						
Net Income	3,134,000,000	4,754,000,000	2,242,000,000	880,000,000	2,493,000,000	2,435,000,000
Operating Cash Flow	6,696,000,000	5,781,000,000	6,945,000,000	6,395,000,000	4,894,000,000	6,274,000,000
Capital Expenditure	7,441,000,000	7,555,000,000	8,001,000,000	7,423,000,000	7,310,000,000	7,393,000,000
EBITDA	9,222,000,000	11,609,000,000	8,140,000,000	6,219,000,000	7,720,000,000	6,864,000,000
Return on Assets %		.04%	.02%	.01%	.03%	.03%
Return on Equity %		.18%	.09%	.03%	.11%	.12%
Debt to Equity		1.578	1.648	1.84	1.722	1.199

CONTACT INFORMATION:

Phone: 404 506-5000   Fax: 404 506-0344
Toll-Free:
Address: 30 Ivan Allen Jr. Blvd., NW, Atlanta, GA 30308 United States

STOCK TICKER/OTHER:

Stock Ticker: SO   Exchange: NYS
Employees: 32,015   Fiscal Year Ends: 12/31
Parent Company:

SALARIES/BONUSES:

Top Exec. Salary: $ Bonus: $
Second Exec. Salary: $ Bonus: $

OTHER THOUGHTS:

Estimated Female Officers or Directors: 3
Hot Spot for Advancement for Women/Minorities: Y

Southern Glazers Wine & Spirits LLC   www.southernglazers.com

NAIC Code: 424800

TYPES OF BUSINESS:

Alcoholic Beverage Wholesaler/Distributor
Wine Warehousing
Online Wine Education Resources

BRANDS/DIVISIONS/AFFILIATES:

Southern Wine University

GROWTH PLANS/SPECIAL FEATURES:

Southern Glazer's Wine & Spirits, LLC is a leading distributor of alcoholic beverages, primarily wine and spirits. The firm also provides supply chain solutions such as selling, logistics and data insights for its customers and suppliers. Southern Glazer's territory spans 44 U.S. markets, the District of Columbia and Canada. The Southern Wine University is a resource for its own employees and for employees of its customers and suppliers to the study and analysis of wine, spirits and other beverages. Glazer's university offers four degree plans for employees, customers or supplier partners: Bachelor of Wine, Bachelor of Spirits, Bachelor of Malts and Bachelor of Career Development.

CONTACTS: Note: Officers with more than one job title may be intentionally listed here more than once.

Wayne Chaplin, CEO
Brad Vassar, Exec. VP
Steven R. Becker, Exec. VP-Finance
Gene Sullivan, CSO
Alan Greenspan, General Counsel
Pete Carr, Exec. VP-Mktg. & Sales
Phil Meachan, Exec. VP-Malt Beverages
Harvey Chaplin, Chmn.

FINANCIAL DATA: Note: Data for latest year may not have been available at press time.

In U.S. $	2020	2019	2018	2017	2016	2015
Revenue	20,304,375,000	18,375,000,000	17,500,000,000	16,845,000,000	16,450,000,000	15,000,000,000
R&D Expense						
Operating Income						
Operating Margin %						
SGA Expense						
Net Income						
Operating Cash Flow						
Capital Expenditure						
EBITDA						
Return on Assets %						
Return on Equity %						
Debt to Equity						

CONTACT INFORMATION:

Phone: 305-625-4171   Fax:
Toll-Free:
Address: 1600 NW 163rd St., Miami, FL 33169 United States

SALARIES/BONUSES:

Top Exec. Salary: $ Bonus: $
Second Exec. Salary: $ Bonus: $

STOCK TICKER/OTHER:

Stock Ticker: Private
Employees: 22,000
Parent Company:

Exchange:
Fiscal Year Ends: 12/31

OTHER THOUGHTS:

Estimated Female Officers or Directors: 1
Hot Spot for Advancement for Women/Minorities:

SpaceX (Space Exploration Technologies Corporation)

www.spacex.com
NAIC Code: 336414

TYPES OF BUSINESS:

Missile and Space Vehicle Manufacturing
Satellite Launch Services
Rockets, Reusable
Communications Satellites
Satellite Internet Access
Spaceships

BRANDS/DIVISIONS/AFFILIATES:

Falcon
SpaceX Merlin Engine
Falcon Heavy
Dragon
Starlink
Starship
Falcon 9
Dragon

CONTACTS: *Note: Officers with more than one job title may be intentionally listed here more than once.*

Elon Musk, CEO
Gwynne Shotwell, Pres.
Andy Lambert, VP-Prod.
Timothy Hughes, General Counsel
Barry Matsumori, VP-Bus. Dev.
Elon Musk, Chief Designer
Tim Buzza, VP-Launch & Test
James Henderson, VP-Quality Assurance
Hans Koenigsmann, VP-Mission Assurance

GROWTH PLANS/SPECIAL FEATURES:

Space Exploration Technologies Corporation (SpaceX) designs, manufactures and launches rockets and spacecraft. The firm is private and majority-owned by the Elon Musk Trust. SpaceX is one of the few private companies to return a spacecraft from low-Earth orbit (2010) and conduct official cargo resupply missions for NASA to the International Space Station (ISS in 2012). SpaceX has since flown many missions to the ISS under a cargo resupply contract. The firm's launch vehicles consist of the Falcon family of rockets, offering medium and heavy lift launch capabilities. The firm's medium rocket, the Falcon 9, is a two-stage rocket powered by the SpaceX Merlin Engine. This model is used for the ISS resupply mission and is capable of carrying other spacecraft. The Falcon Heavy, its heavy lift rocket, has a liftoff thrust of 5 million pounds and carries spacecraft or satellites weighing over 64 metric tons, making it one of the most powerful rockets in the world. Falcon Heavy successfully lifted off from Launch Complex 39A at Kennedy Space Center in February 2018. SpaceX offers a free-flying reusable spacecraft, the Dragon. Developed by SpaceX under NASA's Commercial Orbital Transportation Services program, Dragon was the craft used in conjunction with the Falcon 9 for the ISS resupply mission. Starlink is the firm's effort to put as many as 12,000 satellites into low-Earth orbit in a massive communications system. By November 2020, SpaceX had launched 955 Starlink satellites. Starship is a spacecraft and super heavy rocket undergoing high-altitude flight tests through a Starship prototype from SpaceX's Starbase in Texas. These tests help to improve the company's understanding and development of a fully reusable transportation system designed to carry both crew and cargo on long-duration interplanetary flights, and help humanity return to the Moon, and travel to Mars and beyond.

FINANCIAL DATA: *Note: Data for latest year may not have been available at press time.*

In U.S. $	2020	2019	2018	2017	2016	2015
Revenue	1,200,000,000	2,500,000,000	2,000,000,000	1,500,000,000	1,250,000,000	1,000,000,000
R&D Expense						
Operating Income						
Operating Margin %						
SGA Expense						
Net Income						
Operating Cash Flow						
Capital Expenditure						
EBITDA						
Return on Assets %						
Return on Equity %						
Debt to Equity						

CONTACT INFORMATION:

Phone: 310-363-6000   Fax:
Toll-Free:
Address: 1 Rocket Rd., Hawthorne, CA 90250 United States

STOCK TICKER/OTHER:

Stock Ticker: Private   Exchange:
Employees: 8,000   Fiscal Year Ends:
Parent Company:

SALARIES/BONUSES:

Top Exec. Salary: $ Bonus: $
Second Exec. Salary: $ Bonus: $

OTHER THOUGHTS:

Estimated Female Officers or Directors: 1
Hot Spot for Advancement for Women/Minorities: Y

SpartanNash Company

www.spartanstores.com

NAIC Code: 445110

TYPES OF BUSINESS:

Grocery Wholesale Distribution
Grocery Stores
Discount Food & Drug Stores
Marketing & Management Services
Business & Financial Services
Pharmacies
Gas Stations

BRANDS/DIVISIONS/AFFILIATES:

Family Fare Supermarkets
Martin's Super Markets
VGs Grocery
D&W Fresh Market
Dans Supermarket

CONTACTS: *Note: Officers with more than one job title may be intentionally listed here more than once.*

Mark Shamber, CFO
Tammy Hurley, Chief Accounting Officer
Arif Dar, Chief Information Officer
Lori Raya, Chief Marketing Officer
Dennis Eidson, Director
Larry Pierce, Executive VP, Divisional
Yvonne Trupiano, Executive VP
Patrick Weslow, General Manager, Divisional
Thomas Swanson, General Manager, Divisional
Kathleen Mahoney, Other Executive Officer
David Staples, President

GROWTH PLANS/SPECIAL FEATURES:

SpartanNash Company is a Fortune 400 company that distributes grocery products to a diverse group of independent and chain retailers, its corporate-owned retail stores, and military commissaries and exchanges. SpartanNash serves customer locations in all 50 U.S. states, the District of Columbia, Europe, Cuba, Puerto Rico, Honduras, Bahrain, Djibouti and Egypt. The firm operates through three segments: food distribution, military and retail. The food distribution segment uses a multi-channel sales approach to distribute grocery products to retailers, distributors, eCommerce providers and the company's corporate-owned retail stores. It provides a selection of approximately 52,000 stock-keeping units (SKUs) of branded and private brand grocery products, including dry groceries, produce, dairy, meat, delicatessen items, bakery goods, frozen food, seafood, floral products, general merchandise, beverages, tobacco products, health and beauty care products and pharmacy products. The military segment contracts with manufacturers and brokers to distribute a wide variety of grocery products, including dry groceries, beverages, meat and frozen foods, primarily to U.S. military commissaries and exchanges. The retail segment operates 155 corporate-owned retail stores in U.S. states, predominantly in the midwest, under the banners of Family Fare Supermarkets, Martin's Super Markets, VG's Grocery, D&W Fresh Market, and Dan's Supermarket. This division also offered pharmacy services in 97 of its corporate-owned retail stores, and operated 37 fuel centers. These corporate-owned stores range in size from 14,000 to 90,000 total square feet, or on average, approximately 44,000 total sf.

SpartanNash offers comprehensive benefits, retirement and savings options, and employee assistance programs.

FINANCIAL DATA: *Note: Data for latest year may not have been available at press time.*

In U.S. $	2020	2019	2018	2017	2016	2015
Revenue	9,348,485,000	8,536,065,000	8,064,552,000	8,128,082,000	7,734,600,000	7,651,973,000
R&D Expense						
Operating Income	127,225,000	71,429,000	112,995,000	130,244,000	147,842,000	140,110,000
Operating Margin %		.01%	.01%	.02%	.02%	.02%
SGA Expense	1,297,740,000	1,172,401,000	997,411,000	1,014,665,000	963,652,000	975,572,000
Net Income	75,914,000	5,742,000	33,572,000	-52,845,000	56,828,000	62,710,000
Operating Cash Flow	306,716,000	179,978,000	171,374,000	52,706,000	153,786,000	218,749,000
Capital Expenditure	67,298,000	74,815,000	71,495,000	70,906,000	73,429,000	79,394,000
EBITDA	193,658,000	128,720,000	155,371,000	-21,911,000	188,228,000	206,984,000
Return on Assets %		.00%	.02%	- .03%	.03%	.03%
Return on Equity %		.01%	.05%	- .07%	.07%	.08%
Debt to Equity		1.381	0.95	1.026	0.501	0.602

CONTACT INFORMATION:

Phone: 616 878-2000   Fax: 616 878-8092
Toll-Free: 800-343-4422
Address: 850 76th St. SW, Grand Rapids, MI 49518 United States

STOCK TICKER/OTHER:

Stock Ticker: SPTN
Employees: 18,000
Parent Company:

Exchange: NAS
Fiscal Year Ends: 03/31

SALARIES/BONUSES:

Top Exec. Salary: $ Bonus: $
Second Exec. Salary: $ Bonus: $

OTHER THOUGHTS:

Estimated Female Officers or Directors: 3
Hot Spot for Advancement for Women/Minorities: Y

Spectrum Brands Holdings Inc

www.spectrumbrands.com

NAIC Code: 335912

TYPES OF BUSINESS:

Primary Battery Manufacturing
Hardware
Home Improvement Products
Personal Care Products
Small Kitchen Appliances
Pet Supplies
Insecticides
Manufacture

BRANDS/DIVISIONS/AFFILIATES:

Kwikset
Weiser
Tetra
GloFish
Dingo
IAMS
Black Flag
LiquidFence

CONTACTS: *Note: Officers with more than one job title may be intentionally listed here more than once.*

David Maura, CEO
Douglas Martin, CFO
Randal Lewis, COO
Ehsan Zargar, Executive VP

GROWTH PLANS/SPECIAL FEATURES:

Spectrum Brands Holdings, Inc. is a diversified branded consumer products company that primarily operates through wholly-owned subsidiary, SB/RH Holdings, LLC. The firm manufactures, markets and/or distributes its products in 160 countries throughout North America, Europe, the Middle East, Africa, Latin America and Asia-Pacific. Spectrum Brands' products are sold and distributed through retailers, wholesalers, distributors, original equipment manufacturers (OEMs), construction companies and hearing aid professionals. The company's products are divided into four groups: hardware and home improvement, home and personal care, global pet supplies, and home and garden. Hardware and home improvement products include residential and commercial locksets, door hardware, garage hardware, window hardware, floor protection, faucets and plumbing products. Home and personal care products include: small kitchen appliances such as toaster ovens, coffee makers, blenders, mixers, grills, food processors, juicers, toasters, bread makers and irons; and personal care items such as hair dryers, hair irons and straighteners, electric shavers, personal groomers and trimmers, haircut kits and intense pulse light hair removal systems. Products within the global pet supplies division include small animal food and treats, cleanup and training aid products, pet health and grooming products and aquarium and aquatic health supplies. Home and garden products include household insecticides, repellent products and weed control solutions. Brands of the firm include Kwikset, Weiser, Baldwin, Black & Decker, Remington, Marineland, Tetra, Instant Ocean, GloFish, Dingo, FURminator, Nature's Miracle, Wild Harvest, IAMS, Spectracide, Black Flag, EcoLogic and LiquidFence, among others. In September 2021, Spectrum Brands agreed to sell its hardware and home improvement segment to ASSA ABLOY AB for $4.3 billion in cash.

FINANCIAL DATA: *Note: Data for latest year may not have been available at press time.*

In U.S. $	2020	2019	2018	2017	2016	2015
Revenue	3,964,200,000	3,802,100,000	3,145,900,000	5,008,500,000	5,215,400,000	5,815,900,000
R&D Expense	41,800,000	43,500,000	28,300,000			
Operating Income	375,800,000	308,300,000	309,100,000	516,300,000	655,100,000	447,500,000
Operating Margin %		.08%	.10%	.10%	.13%	.08%
SGA Expense	952,300,000	955,100,000	816,200,000	1,359,600,000	1,243,600,000	1,476,500,000
Net Income	97,800,000	471,900,000	768,300,000	106,000,000	-198,800,000	-556,800,000
Operating Cash Flow	80,200,000	1,100,000	343,100,000	840,100,000	913,300,000	283,600,000
Capital Expenditure	61,000,000	58,400,000	64,700,000	115,000,000	95,400,000	116,200,000
EBITDA	448,400,000	209,100,000	240,000,000	710,600,000	812,700,000	252,600,000
Return on Assets %		.07%	.04%	.00%	-.01%	-.02%
Return on Equity %		.29%	.66%	.15%	-.32%	-.55%
Debt to Equity		1.304	2.941	7.382	8.251	10.806

CONTACT INFORMATION:

Phone: 608 275-3340   Fax:
Toll-Free:
Address: 3001 Deming Way, Middleton, WI 53562 United States

STOCK TICKER/OTHER:

Stock Ticker: SPB   Exchange: NYS
Employees: 12,100   Fiscal Year Ends: 09/30
Parent Company:

SALARIES/BONUSES:

Top Exec. Salary: $ Bonus: $
Second Exec. Salary: $ Bonus: $

OTHER THOUGHTS:

Estimated Female Officers or Directors:
Hot Spot for Advancement for Women/Minorities:

Splunk Inc

www.splunk.com

NAIC Code: 511210B

TYPES OF BUSINESS:

Computer Software: Network Management (IT), System Testing & Storage
Data Analysis
Application Management
Security and Compliance Management

BRANDS/DIVISIONS/AFFILIATES:

Splunk Enterprise
Splunk Apps
Splunk Cloud
Splunk Enterprise Security
Splunk for Industrial Internet of Things
Rigor Inc
Flowmill Inc

CONTACTS: *Note: Officers with more than one job title may be intentionally listed here more than once.*

Jason Child, CFO
Graham Smith, Chairman of the Board
Timothy Tully, Chief Technology Officer
Douglas Merritt, Director
Scott Morgan, General Counsel
Jacob Loomis, Other Executive Officer
Susan St.Ledger, President, Divisional
Leonard Stein, Senior VP, Divisional

GROWTH PLANS/SPECIAL FEATURES:

Splunk, Inc. is an enterprise software company that specializes in analyzing the increasing amount of machine data generated by cellphones, computers, digital cameras, smart meters and GPS devices, among others, which is referred to as big data. This data serves as operational intelligence, which organizations can monitor and analyze to gain real-time business insight, study user behavior, reconcile third-party service provider fees, follow patterns and make better informed operational plans of action. The firm's flagship product is Splunk Enterprise, a proprietary machine data engine, comprised of collection, indexing, search, reporting analysis and data management capabilities. The firm complements Splunk Enterprise with apps and add-ons that can be deployed directly on top of the core platform and are generally available for download via its Splunk Apps website. Many apps and add-ons are free, but the company also develops and sells premium apps that enable users to leverage data from their salesforce environment along with other machine data within Splunk Cloud. The firm's Splunk Cloud service delivers the core functionalities of Splunk Enterprise as a scalable, reliable cloud service. Splunk's cybersecurity solutions modernize IT security infrastructure and strengthen cyber defense. Splunk Enterprise Security addresses emerging security threats and security information and event management via monitoring, alert and analytic features. Splunk for Industrial Internet of Things (IIoT) offers real-time and predictive insights from industrial operational data to ensure uptime and reduce cost. More than 90 of the Fortune 100 use Splunk. In late-2020, Splunk acquired Rigor, Inc, which offers advanced synthetic monitoring and optimization tools; and acquired Flowmill, Inc., which specializes in network performance monitoring.

FINANCIAL DATA: *Note: Data for latest year may not have been available at press time.*

In U.S. $	2020	2019	2018	2017	2016	2015
Revenue	2,358,926,000	1,803,010,000	1,270,788,000	949,955,000	668,435,000	
R&D Expense	619,800,000	441,969,000	301,114,000	295,850,000	215,309,000	
Operating Income	-287,137,000	-251,173,000	-254,295,000	-343,831,000	-287,923,000	
Operating Margin %	-.12%	-.14%	-.20%	-.36%	-.43%	
SGA Expense	1,596,475,000	1,267,538,000	967,560,000	806,883,000	626,927,000	
Net Income	-336,668,000	-275,577,000	-259,103,000	-355,189,000	-278,772,000	
Operating Cash Flow	-287,636,000	296,454,000	262,904,000	201,834,000	155,622,000	
Capital Expenditure	103,708,000	23,160,000	20,503,000	45,349,000	51,332,000	
EBITDA	-167,741,000	-168,798,000	-213,354,000	-308,979,000	-268,432,000	
Return on Assets %	-.07%	-.08%	-.14%	-.22%	-.20%	
Return on Equity %	-.19%	-.24%	-.32%	-.43%	-.33%	
Debt to Equity	0.975	1.075				

CONTACT INFORMATION:

Phone: 415 848-8400   Fax: 415 738-5456
Toll-Free:
Address: 270 Brannan St., San Francisco, CA 94107 United States

STOCK TICKER/OTHER:

Stock Ticker: SPLK
Employees: 6,500
Parent Company:

Exchange: NAS
Fiscal Year Ends: 01/31

SALARIES/BONUSES:

Top Exec. Salary: $ Bonus: $
Second Exec. Salary: $ Bonus: $

OTHER THOUGHTS:

Estimated Female Officers or Directors: 2
Hot Spot for Advancement for Women/Minorities:

Sprouts Farmers Market Inc

www.sprouts.com

NAIC Code: 445110

TYPES OF BUSINESS:

Supermarkets
Natural Foods
Grocer
Retail
eCommerce

BRANDS/DIVISIONS/AFFILIATES:

Sprouts.com

CONTACTS: *Note: Officers with more than one job title may be intentionally listed here more than once.*

Bradley Lukow, CFO
Joseph Fortunato, Chairman of the Board
Brandon Lombardi, Chief Legal Officer
James Nielsen, Co-CEO
Theodore Frumkin, Other Executive Officer
Dan Sanders, Other Executive Officer
Shawn Gensch, Other Executive Officer
David McGlinchey, Other Executive Officer

GROWTH PLANS/SPECIAL FEATURES:

Sprouts Farmers Market, Inc. is an Arizona-based independent natural foods retailer. The firm operated 360 stores in 23 states (as of October 28, 2020), and is one of the largest specialty retailers of natural and organic foods in the U.S. Perishable and non-perishable items constitute 58.2% and 41.8% of Sprouts' annual sales. The company's products include baked goods, beer, wine, bulk food bins (rice and other grains, nuts, spices, dried fruit and old-fashioned candies), dairy products, meat, poultry, produce, seafood, vitamins and supplements. In addition to Sprouts' own private label natural and organic foods, the firm acquires products primarily from U.S. suppliers, emphasizing local buying practices. However, Sprouts purchases certain seasonal fruits and vegetables from growers around the world. The stores host a variety of events, such as cooking classes, health screenings and health information sessions. eCommerce site, Sprouts.com, offers recipes, gift cards, nutritional information and a health guide.

The company offers comprehensive benefits, retirement and savings options, and employee assistance programs.

FINANCIAL DATA: *Note: Data for latest year may not have been available at press time.*

In U.S. $	2020	2019	2018	2017	2016	2015
Revenue	6,468,759,000	5,634,835,000	5,207,336,000	4,664,612,000	4,046,385,000	3,593,031,000
R&D Expense						
Operating Income	391,296,000	224,620,000	234,987,000	227,196,000	213,160,000	230,556,000
Operating Margin %		.04%	.05%	.05%	.05%	.06%
SGA Expense	1,863,869,000	1,549,707,000	1,404,443,000	148,408,000	126,929,000	106,412,000
Net Income	287,450,000	149,629,000	158,536,000	158,440,000	124,306,000	128,991,000
Operating Cash Flow	494,035,000	355,210,000	294,379,000	309,567,000	254,351,000	239,898,000
Capital Expenditure	121,968,000	183,232,000	177,083,000	198,624,000	181,509,000	131,020,000
EBITDA	616,873,000	421,442,000	333,980,000	323,439,000	293,800,000	292,885,000
Return on Assets %		.07%	.10%	.10%	.09%	.09%
Return on Equity %		.26%	.26%	.24%	.17%	.17%
Debt to Equity		2.798	0.972	0.728	0.553	0.335

CONTACT INFORMATION:

Phone: 480-814-8016   Fax: 480-814-8017
Toll-Free: 888-577-7688
Address: 5455 East High St., Ste. 111, Phoenix, AZ 85054 United States

STOCK TICKER/OTHER:

Stock Ticker: SFM   Exchange: NAS
Employees: 33,000   Fiscal Year Ends:
Parent Company:

SALARIES/BONUSES:

Top Exec. Salary: $ Bonus: $
Second Exec. Salary: $ Bonus: $

OTHER THOUGHTS:

Estimated Female Officers or Directors: 1
Hot Spot for Advancement for Women/Minorities:

Square Inc

www.squareup.com

NAIC Code: 522320

TYPES OF BUSINESS:

Mobile Credit Card Processing
Credit Card Readers
Point-of-Sale Terminals
Payment Hardware
Payment Software
Analytics
Marketing
Developer Platform

BRANDS/DIVISIONS/AFFILIATES:

Square
Tidal
Crew

CONTACTS: Note: Officers with more than one job title may be intentionally listed here more than once.

Jack Dorsey, CEO
Amrita Ahuja, CFO
Ajmere Dale, Chief Accounting Officer
Sivan Whiteley, General Counsel
Jacqueline Reses, Other Corporate Officer
Alyssa Henry, Other Corporate Officer

GROWTH PLANS/SPECIAL FEATURES:

Square, Inc. develops tools that help businesses, sellers and individuals to participate in the economy. The firm's hardware consists of in-house-built payment terminals and registers, chip/contactless readers and magstripe readers. These products accept every kind of payment, securely, whether in-person or online. Square offers a business toolkit for every kind of business, which encompass virtual terminals, gift cards, marketing capability, dashboard, analytics, retail point-of-sale (POS), restaurant POS, appointments, customizable POS software, a Square business debit card, payroll, business loans and checkout links. Other tools include team management, short message system (SMS) marketing, loyalty programs, customer directory, inventory management, photo studio and more. For developers, Square offers a developer platform, reader SDK, in-app payments SDK, online payments APIs, documentation and developer dashboard. Based in the U.S., Square has international offices in Canada, Japan, Australia, Ireland, Spain, Norway and the U.K. During the first half of 2021, Square acquired a majority stake in the music streaming platform Tidal for $297 million, extending the firm's purpose of providing economic empowerment to musicians; and acquired Crew, a frontline employee platform for consolidating and streamlining day-to-day operations of hourly workforces.

FINANCIAL DATA: Note: Data for latest year may not have been available at press time.

In U.S. $	2020	2019	2018	2017	2016	2015
Revenue	9,497,578,000	4,713,500,000	3,298,177,000	2,214,253,000	1,708,721,000	1,267,118,000
R&D Expense	881,826,000	670,606,000	497,479,000	321,888,000	268,537,000	199,638,000
Operating Income	-18,815,000	26,557,000	-36,614,000	-54,206,000	-170,453,000	-174,458,000
Operating Margin %		.01%	-.01%	-.02%	-.10%	-.14%
SGA Expense	1,688,873,000	1,061,082,000	750,396,000	503,723,000	425,869,000	289,084,000
Net Income	213,105,000	375,446,000	-38,453,000	-62,813,000	-171,590,000	-179,817,000
Operating Cash Flow	381,603,000	465,699,000	295,080,000	127,711,000	23,131,000	27,584,000
Capital Expenditure	138,402,000	62,498,000	62,787,000	26,097,000	25,833,000	38,718,000
EBITDA	357,122,000	102,155,000	24,347,000	-16,927,000	-132,708,000	-146,832,000
Return on Assets %		.10%	-.01%	-.04%	-.16%	-.30%
Return on Equity %		.26%	-.04%	-.09%	-.32%	-1.59%
Debt to Equity		0.611	0.936	0.456		

CONTACT INFORMATION:

Phone: 415-281-3976   Fax:
Toll-Free:
Address: 1455 Market St., Ste. 600, San Francisco, CA 94103 United States

STOCK TICKER/OTHER:

Stock Ticker: SQ
Employees: 3,835
Parent Company:

Exchange: NYS
Fiscal Year Ends: 12/31

SALARIES/BONUSES:

Top Exec. Salary: $ Bonus: $
Second Exec. Salary: $ Bonus: $

OTHER THOUGHTS:

Estimated Female Officers or Directors: 1
Hot Spot for Advancement for Women/Minorities:

Sales, profits and employees may be estimates. Financial information, benefits and other data can change quickly and may vary from those stated here.

SS&C Technologies Holdings Inc

www.ssctech.com

NAIC Code: 511210Q

TYPES OF BUSINESS:

Financial and Investment Management Software
Business Process Outsourcing Services
Application Service Provider Solutions
Financial Education & Simulation Products
Hedge Fund Management Services

BRANDS/DIVISIONS/AFFILIATES:

SS&C Technologies Inc

CONTACTS: Note: Officers with more than one job title may be intentionally listed here more than once.

William Stone, CEO
Patrick Pedonti, CFO
Joseph Frank, Chief Legal Officer
Rahul Kanwar, COO
Normand Boulanger, Vice Chairman

GROWTH PLANS/SPECIAL FEATURES:

SS&C Technologies Holdings, Inc., operating through SS&C Technologies, Inc., offers a suite of highly specialized, mission-critical software and services. These services help automate and simplify information management, analysis, accounting, reporting and compliance for investment professionals in a broad range of financial services segments. The company's products allow clients to rapidly access, manage and analyze large amounts of transactions-based data both in the aggregate and in detail. SS&C's global clients principally comprise the vertical markets of institutional asset and wealth management, alternative investment management, financial advisory and financial institutions. Other clients include commercial lenders, real estate investment trusts (REITs), corporate treasury groups, insurance and pension funds, municipal finance groups and real estate property managers. SS&C provides the global financial services industry with a range of software-enabled services such as outsourcing and subscription-based on-demand software that are managed and hosted at SS&C facilities, as well as specialized software products which are deployed at the clients' facilities. Approximately 75% of annual revenues are derived from North American clients. During 2020, SS&C acquired Innovest Systems, a provider of web-based technology systems for trust accounting, payments and unique asset servicing.

FINANCIAL DATA: Note: Data for latest year may not have been available at press time.

In U.S. $	2020	2019	2018	2017	2016	2015
Revenue	4,667,900,000	4,632,900,000	3,421,100,000	1,675,295,000	1,481,436,000	1,000,285,000
R&D Expense	399,400,000	383,700,000	318,200,000	153,334,000	152,689,000	110,415,000
Operating Income	985,800,000	914,400,000	526,900,000	396,913,000	288,695,000	164,738,000
Operating Margin %		.20%	.15%	.24%	.19%	.16%
SGA Expense	708,600,000	723,100,000	524,900,000	238,623,000	239,563,000	192,782,000
Net Income	625,200,000	438,500,000	103,200,000	328,864,000	130,996,000	42,862,000
Operating Cash Flow	1,184,700,000	1,328,300,000	640,100,000	470,362,000	418,407,000	230,624,000
Capital Expenditure	106,400,000	130,400,000	89,100,000	45,974,000	37,547,000	17,873,000
EBITDA	1,751,000,000	1,716,500,000	923,700,000	628,458,000	522,241,000	291,009,000
Return on Assets %		.03%	.01%	.06%	.02%	.01%
Return on Equity %		.09%	.03%	.13%	.06%	.02%
Debt to Equity		1.452	1.784	0.747	1.052	1.291

CONTACT INFORMATION:

Phone: 860 298-4500   Fax: 860 298-4900
Toll-Free: 800-234-0556
Address: 80 Lamberton Rd., Windsor, CT 06095 United States

STOCK TICKER/OTHER:

Stock Ticker: SSNC   Exchange: NAS
Employees: 24,600   Fiscal Year Ends: 12/31
Parent Company:

SALARIES/BONUSES:

Top Exec. Salary: $ Bonus: $
Second Exec. Salary: $ Bonus: $

OTHER THOUGHTS:

Estimated Female Officers or Directors: 2
Hot Spot for Advancement for Women/Minorities:

Stanley Black & Decker Inc

www.stanleyblackanddecker.com

NAIC Code: 333991

TYPES OF BUSINESS:

Power Tools & Accessories Manufacturer
Security Solutions
Household Appliances
Home Improvement Products
Fastening & Assembly Systems
Plumbing Products
Automotive Machinery

BRANDS/DIVISIONS/AFFILIATES:

DeWALT
Porter-Cable
Bostitch
Guaranteed Tough
Mac Tools
LaBounty
Dubuis
WanderGuard

CONTACTS: Note: Officers with more than one job title may be intentionally listed here more than once.

James Loree, CEO
Donald Allan, CFO
Jocelyn Belisle, Chief Accounting Officer
George Buckley, Director
Jeffery Ansell, Executive VP
Janet Link, General Counsel
Joseph Voelker, Other Executive Officer
John Wyatt, President, Divisional
Jaime Ramirez, President, Divisional

GROWTH PLANS/SPECIAL FEATURES:

Stanley Black & Decker, Inc. is a global manufacturer and marketer of hand tools, power tools and accessories, as well as hardware and home improvement products, security solutions and technology-based fastening systems. The firm is also a worldwide supplier of engineered fastening and assembly systems. Stanley Black & Decker products and services are marketed in hardware and home improvement stores around the globe. The firm operates in three reportable business segments: tools & storage, security and industrial. The tools & storage segment includes professional and consumer power tools and accessories, lawn and garden tools, consumer mechanics tools, storage systems and pneumatic tools and fasteners. The security segment provides both mechanical and electric access and security systems primarily for retailers; educational, financial and health care institutions; and commercial, government and industrial customers. The industrial segment manufactures and markets professional industrial and automotive mechanics tools and storage systems; metal and plastic fasteners and engineered fastening systems; hydraulic tools and accessories; plumbing, heating and air conditioning tools; assembly tools and systems; and specialty tools. The company sells these products to industrial clients in the automotive, transportation, aerospace, electronics and machine tool industries primarily through third-party distributors. Brand names include DeWALT, Porter-Cable, Bostitch, Proto, Powers, Guaranteed Tough, FatMax, Craftsman and Black & Decker as well as Mac Tools, CRC, LaBounty, Dubuis, Stanley, WanderGuard and many more. In September 2021, Stanley Black & Decker agreed to acquire Excel Industries for $375 million in cash. Excel designs and manufactures premium commercial and residential turf-care equipment under the Hustler Turf Equipment and BigDog Mower Co. brands.

Stanley Black & Decker offers its employees medical, dental, life and disability insurance; and a 401(k).

FINANCIAL DATA: Note: Data for latest year may not have been available at press time.

In U.S. $	2020	2019	2018	2017	2016	2015
Revenue	14,534,600,000	14,442,200,000	13,982,400,000	12,747,200,000	11,406,900,000	11,171,800,000
R&D Expense						
Operating Income	1,878,300,000	1,764,500,000	1,679,400,000	1,797,900,000	1,643,300,000	1,585,600,000
Operating Margin %		.12%	.12%	.14%	.14%	.14%
SGA Expense	3,048,500,000	3,008,000,000	3,143,700,000	2,965,700,000	2,602,000,000	2,459,100,000
Net Income	1,233,800,000	955,800,000	605,200,000	1,226,000,000	1,485,200,000	1,182,300,000
Operating Cash Flow	2,022,100,000	1,505,700,000	1,260,900,000	1,418,600,000	965,300,000	883,700,000
Capital Expenditure	348,100,000	424,700,000	492,100,000	442,400,000	347,000,000	311,400,000
EBITDA	2,068,200,000	1,974,500,000	1,806,500,000	2,209,400,000	1,828,600,000	1,745,200,000
Return on Assets %		.05%	.03%	.07%	.06%	.06%
Return on Equity %		.13%	.08%	.18%	.16%	.14%
Debt to Equity		0.416	0.539	0.377	0.599	0.66

CONTACT INFORMATION:

Phone: 860 225-5111   Fax: 860 827-3895
Toll-Free:
Address: 1000 Stanley Dr., New Britain, CT 06053 United States

STOCK TICKER/OTHER:

Stock Ticker: SWK
Employees: 59,438
Parent Company:

Exchange: NYS
Fiscal Year Ends: 12/31

SALARIES/BONUSES:

Top Exec. Salary: $ Bonus: $
Second Exec. Salary: $ Bonus: $

OTHER THOUGHTS:

Estimated Female Officers or Directors: 5
Hot Spot for Advancement for Women/Minorities: Y

Starbucks Corporation

NAIC Code: 722515   www.starbucks.com

TYPES OF BUSINESS:

Coffee Houses & Coffee Stores
Coffee-Related Accessories & Equipment
Wholesale Coffee Distribution
Tea and Accessories

BRANDS/DIVISIONS/AFFILIATES:

Starbucks Coffee Korea Co Ltd
Tata Starbucks Limited (India)
North American Coffee Partnership (The)
Starbucks
Teavana
Seattle's Best Coffee
Evolution Fresh
Ethos

CONTACTS: Note: Officers with more than one job title may be intentionally listed here more than once.

Paul Mutty, Assistant Secretary
Patrick Grismer, CFO
Howard Schultz, Chairman Emeritus
Myron Ullman, Chairman of the Board
Jill Walker, Chief Accounting Officer
Rosalind Brewer, COO
Kevin Johnson, Director
Vivek Varma, Executive VP, Divisional
Rachel Gonzalez, Executive VP
Lucy Helm, Executive VP
Clifford Burrows, On Leave
John Culver, President, Divisional
Mellody Hobson, Vice Chairman of the Board

GROWTH PLANS/SPECIAL FEATURES:

Starbucks Corporation is a roaster, marketer and retailer of specialty coffee, operating in 83 markets worldwide. Of the total 32,000+ retail stores in existence, 15,834 are company-operated stores and 15,422 are licensed stores. The firm purchases and roasts high-quality coffees that it sells, along with handcrafted coffee, tea and other beverages and a variety of fresh food items, through company-operated stores. Starbucks also licenses its trademarks through other channels such as grocery stores and national foodservice accounts. In addition to its flagship Starbucks brand, the company's portfolio includes goods and services offered under the following brands: Teavana, Seattle's Best Coffee, Evolution Fresh, Ethos, Starbucks Reserve and Princi. The firm has three operating segments: Americas inclusive of the U.S., Canada and Latin America, and accounting for 69% of total 2019 net revenues; International, inclusive of China, Japan, Asia Pacific, Europe, Middle East, and Africa, 23%; and channel development, 8%. The Americas and International segments include both company-operated and licensed stores, as well as certain food service accounts. Starbucks owns a 50% interest in each of the following companies: Starbucks Coffee Korea Co. Ltd. and Tata Starbucks Limited (India). It also licenses the rights to produce and distribute Starbucks-branded products to its 50% joint venture with Pepsi-Cola Company, The North American Coffee Partnership, which develops and distributes bottled Starbucks beverages.

Starbucks offers employee health benefits, 401(k) and various assistance programs.

FINANCIAL DATA: Note: Data for latest year may not have been available at press time.

In U.S. $	2020	2019	2018	2017	2016	2015
Revenue	23,518,000,000	26,508,600,000	24,719,500,000	22,386,800,000	21,315,900,000	19,162,700,000
R&D Expense						
Operating Income	1,517,900,000	3,915,700,000	3,806,500,000	3,896,800,000	3,853,700,000	3,351,100,000
Operating Margin %		.15%	.15%	.17%	.18%	.17%
SGA Expense	1,679,600,000	1,824,100,000	1,759,000,000	1,393,300,000	1,360,600,000	1,196,700,000
Net Income	928,300,000	3,599,200,000	4,518,300,000	2,884,700,000	2,817,700,000	2,757,400,000
Operating Cash Flow	1,597,800,000	5,047,000,000	11,937,800,000	4,174,300,000	4,575,100,000	3,749,100,000
Capital Expenditure	1,483,600,000	1,806,600,000	1,976,400,000	1,519,400,000	1,440,300,000	1,303,700,000
EBITDA	3,104,600,000	6,246,500,000	7,256,200,000	5,477,100,000	5,310,000,000	4,907,300,000
Return on Assets %		.17%	.23%	.20%	.21%	.24%
Return on Equity %			1.37%	.51%	.48%	.50%
Debt to Equity			7.773	0.722	0.544	0.403

CONTACT INFORMATION:

Phone: 206 447-1575   Fax: 206 447-0828
Toll-Free: 800-782-7282
Address: 2401 Utah Ave. S., Seattle, WA 98134 United States

SALARIES/BONUSES:

Top Exec. Salary: $ Bonus: $
Second Exec. Salary: $ Bonus: $

STOCK TICKER/OTHER:

Stock Ticker: SBUX   Exchange: NAS
Employees: 346,000   Fiscal Year Ends: 09/30
Parent Company:

OTHER THOUGHTS:

Estimated Female Officers or Directors: 5
Hot Spot for Advancement for Women/Minorities: Y

State Farm Insurance Companies

www.statefarm.com

NAIC Code: 524126

TYPES OF BUSINESS:

Insurance, Direct Property & Casualty
Accident Insurance
Health Insurance
Life Insurance
Annuities
Automobile Insurance
Banking/Savings Association
Mutual Funds

BRANDS/DIVISIONS/AFFILIATES:

CONTACTS: Note: Officers with more than one job title may be intentionally listed here more than once.

Michael L. Tipsord, CEO
Michael L. Tipsord, Chmn.

GROWTH PLANS/SPECIAL FEATURES:

State Farm Insurance Companies is a mutual company providing personal property and casualty insurance, as well as banking and investment products through State Farm agents located across the U.S. Insurance products include car, motorcycle, boat, off-road vehicles, motorhomes, home/property, life, health, disability, liability, identity restoration and small business. Home and property insurance encompasses home, condominium, renters insurance, rental property, personal articles and far and ranch. Life insurance spans term life, whole life and universal life. Health insurance includes supplemental health, Medicare supplement, individual medical and more. Disability insurance includes both short- and long-term coverage. Liability products include personal, business and professional. Banking products include vehicle loans, home loans, checking and savings accounts and credit cards. Investment products span retirement options, mutual funds, educational savings, estate planning and annuities. In September 2020, State Farm agreed to acquire GAINSCO, Inc., which focuses on the non-standard personal automobile market, specializing in minimum-limits personal auto insurance.

Employee benefits include medical, dental and life coverage; a 401(k); a company retirement plan; and a wellness program.

FINANCIAL DATA: Note: Data for latest year may not have been available at press time.

In U.S. $	2020	2019	2018	2017	2016	2015
Revenue	78,900,000,000	79,400,000,000	81,700,000,000	78,300,000,000	76,100,000,000	75,700,000,000
R&D Expense						
Operating Income						
Operating Margin %						
SGA Expense						
Net Income	3,700,000,000	5,600,000,000	8,800,000,000	2,200,000,000	400,000,000	6,200,000,000
Operating Cash Flow						
Capital Expenditure						
EBITDA						
Return on Assets %						
Return on Equity %						
Debt to Equity						

CONTACT INFORMATION:

Phone: 309-766-2311   Fax: 459-766-3621
Toll-Free: 877-734-2265
Address: 1 State Farm Plaza, Bloomington, IL 61710 United States

SALARIES/BONUSES:

Top Exec. Salary: $ Bonus: $
Second Exec. Salary: $ Bonus: $

STOCK TICKER/OTHER:

Stock Ticker: Mutual Company
Employees: 57,500
Parent Company:

Exchange:
Fiscal Year Ends: 12/31

OTHER THOUGHTS:

Estimated Female Officers or Directors: 3
Hot Spot for Advancement for Women/Minorities: Y

State Street Corporation

NAIC Code: 523920

www.statestreet.com

TYPES OF BUSINESS:

Investment Management & Mutual Fund Services
Investment Company Services
Hedge Funds
Trust, Custodial & Transfer Services
Mutual Fund Services
Back Office Services
Foreign Exchange Services
Trading Services

BRANDS/DIVISIONS/AFFILIATES:

State Street Bank and Trust Company
State Street Global Advisors

CONTACTS: Note: Officers with more than one job title may be intentionally listed here more than once.

Ronald OHanley, CEO
Kathryn Horgan, Exec. VP
Joseph Hooley, Chairman of the Board
Ian Appleyard, Chief Accounting Officer
Karen Keenan, Chief Administrative Officer
Antoine Shagoury, Chief Information Officer
Andrew Kuritzkes, Chief Risk Officer
Louis Maiuri, COO
Jeffrey Conway, Executive VP, Divisional
Andrew Erickson, Executive VP, Divisional
Elizabeth Nolan, Executive VP
Eric Aboaf, Executive VP
Hannah Grove, Executive VP
Donna Milrod, Executive VP
Jeffrey Carp, Executive VP
Cyrus Taraporevala, President, Subsidiary
Jeffrey Carp, Executive VP

GROWTH PLANS/SPECIAL FEATURES:

State Street Corporation (SSC) is a global financial holding company. With $3.15 trillion under management as of September 30, 2020, the firm provides a full range of products and services for global investors through its subsidiaries. The company conducts its business primarily through subsidiary State Street Bank and Trust Company (State Street Bank). Clients include mutual funds and other collective investment funds, corporate and public pension funds, insurance companies, foundations, endowments and investment managers. SSC operates in more than 100 geographic markets worldwide, including the U.S., Canada, Europe, the Middle East and Asia. The firm has two main lines of business: investment servicing and investment management. The investment servicing business offers products and services such as master trust and master custody; foreign exchange; brokerage; securities finance; loan & lease financing; investment manager and alternative investment manager operations outsourcing; and performance, risk and compliance analytics. The investment management business, operating via State Street Global Advisors, offers strategies for managing financial assets such as enhanced indexing and hedge fund strategies; provides an array of investment management, investment research and other services, such as securities finance; and offers exchange-traded funds. This division provides these services for corporations, public funds and other sophisticated investors.

SSC offers comprehensive benefits, retirement options and employee assistance programs.

FINANCIAL DATA: Note: Data for latest year may not have been available at press time.

In U.S. $	2020	2019	2018	2017	2016	2015
Revenue	10,623,000,000	10,625,000,000	10,957,000,000	10,226,000,000	9,283,000,000	9,373,000,000
R&D Expense						
Operating Income						
Operating Margin %						
SGA Expense	6,109,000,000	6,182,000,000	6,386,000,000	5,826,000,000	5,551,000,000	5,209,000,000
Net Income	2,420,000,000	2,242,000,000	2,599,000,000	2,177,000,000	2,143,000,000	1,980,000,000
Operating Cash Flow	3,532,000,000	5,690,000,000	10,457,000,000	6,933,000,000	2,290,000,000	-1,403,000,000
Capital Expenditure	560,000,000	730,000,000	609,000,000	637,000,000	613,000,000	703,000,000
EBITDA						
Return on Assets %		.01%	.01%	.01%	.01%	.01%
Return on Equity %		.09%	.12%	.11%	.11%	.10%
Debt to Equity		0.583	0.526	0.608	0.634	0.627

CONTACT INFORMATION:

Phone: 617 786-3000   Fax: 617 985-8055
Toll-Free:
Address: 1 Lincoln St., Boston, MA 02111 United States

STOCK TICKER/OTHER:

Stock Ticker: STT
Employees: 39,439
Parent Company:

Exchange: NYS
Fiscal Year Ends: 12/31

SALARIES/BONUSES:

Top Exec. Salary: $ Bonus: $
Second Exec. Salary: $ Bonus: $

OTHER THOUGHTS:

Estimated Female Officers or Directors: 2
Hot Spot for Advancement for Women/Minorities: Y

Stewart Information Services Corporation   www.stewart.com

NAIC Code: 524127

TYPES OF BUSINESS:

Title Insurance
Real Estate Information Services & Software
Title Insurance
Real Estate Closing Services
Real Estate Settlement Services
Property Appraisal Services

BRANDS/DIVISIONS/AFFILIATES:

Stewart Lender Services Inc

CONTACTS: Note: Officers with more than one job title may be intentionally listed here more than once.

Steven Lessack, CEO, Subsidiary
Matthew Morris, CEO
David Hisey, CFO
Thomas Apel, Chairman of the Board
Brian Glaze, Chief Accounting Officer
Brad Rable, Chief Information Officer
Ann Manal, Other Executive Officer
John Killea, Other Executive Officer
John Magness, President, Divisional
Tara Smith, President, Divisional
David Fauth, Senior VP, Subsidiary

GROWTH PLANS/SPECIAL FEATURES:

Stewart Information Services Corporation is a global real estate services company. The firm offers residential and commercial title insurance, as well as closing and settlement services for the mortgage industry. Internationally, Stewart delivers products and services that protect and promote private land ownership, with offices in Australia, Canada, the Caribbean, Europe, Mexico and the U.K. The company operates in two main segments: title insurance and related services (title), and ancillary services and corporate. The title segment includes searching, examining, closing and insuring the condition of the title to real property. It also includes centralized title services such as title and closing services, post-closing services, default and REO (real estate owned) title services, home and professional insurance services and Internal Revenue Code Section 1031 tax-deferred exchanges. The ancillary services and corporate segment provides appraisal and valuation services to the mortgage industry through Stewart Lender Services, Inc. This division's customers primarily include mortgage lenders and services, mortgage brokers and mortgage investors. During 2021, Stewart agreed to acquire Informative Research (IR), a leader in providing credit, consumer and real estate data and technology services. IR serves more than 3,000 customers throughout the U.S., and offers a wide range of mission critical solutions through its proprietary platform to streamline the loan cycle.

Stewart offers its employees medical, dental and vision insurance; life insurance; short- and long-term disability; flexible spending accounts; a 401(k) plan; a stock purchase program; and employee as well as educational assistance programs.

FINANCIAL DATA: Note: Data for latest year may not have been available at press time.

In U.S. $	2020	2019	2018	2017	2016	2015
Revenue	2,288,432,000	1,940,008,000	1,907,672,000	1,955,724,000	2,006,640,000	2,033,885,000
R&D Expense						
Operating Income						
Operating Margin %						
SGA Expense	988,383,000	912,522,000	907,776,000	917,689,000	968,339,000	1,040,220,000
Net Income	154,905,000	78,615,000	47,523,000	48,659,000	55,478,000	-6,204,000
Operating Cash Flow	275,806,000	166,359,000	84,177,000	108,068,000	122,962,000	80,514,000
Capital Expenditure	14,992,000	17,075,000	10,675,000	16,396,000	18,155,000	19,658,000
EBITDA						
Return on Assets %		.05%	.03%	.04%	.04%	.00%
Return on Equity %		.11%	.07%	.07%	.09%	-.01%
Debt to Equity		0.168	0.014	0.163	0.167	0.163

CONTACT INFORMATION:

Phone: 713 625-8100   Fax: 713 629-2244
Toll-Free: 800-729-1900
Address: 1360 Post Oak Blvd., Ste. 100, Houston, TX 77056 United States

STOCK TICKER/OTHER:

Stock Ticker: STC
Employees: 5,800
Parent Company:

Exchange: NYS
Fiscal Year Ends: 12/31

SALARIES/BONUSES:

Top Exec. Salary: $ Bonus: $
Second Exec. Salary: $ Bonus: $

OTHER THOUGHTS:

Estimated Female Officers or Directors: 3
Hot Spot for Advancement for Women/Minorities: Y

Stifel Financial Corp

NAIC Code: 523110

www.stifel.com

TYPES OF BUSINESS:

Stock Brokerage/Investment Banking
Underwriting
Broker-Dealer
Investment Advisory Services
Research
Insurance
Annuities

BRANDS/DIVISIONS/AFFILIATES:

Stifel Nicolaus & Company Incorporated
Century Securities Associates Inc
Keefe Bruyette & Woods Inc
Miller Buckfire & Co LLC
Stifel Nicolaus Europe Limited
Stifel Bank & Trust
Stifel Trust Company NA
Ziegler Capital Management LLC

CONTACTS: Note: Officers with more than one job title may be intentionally listed here more than once.

Ronald Kruszewski, CEO
James Marischen, CFO
Thomas Weisel, Co-Chairman
David Sliney, COO
James Zemlyak, Co-President
Victor Nesi, Co-President
Richard Himelfarb, Executive VP, Subsidiary
Ben Plotkin, Executive VP, Subsidiary
Mark Fisher, General Counsel
Thomas Michaud, Senior VP

GROWTH PLANS/SPECIAL FEATURES:

Stifel Financial Corp. is a financial services holding company. The firm's principal subsidiary is Stifel, Nicolaus & Company, Incorporated, a full-service retail and institutional wealth management and investment banking firm. Other subsidiaries include: Century Securities Associates, Inc., an independent contractor broker-dealer; Keefe, Bruyette & Woods, Inc. and Miller Buckfire & Co., LLC, broker-dealers; Stifel Nicolaus Europe Limited, serving Europe; Stifel Nicolaus Canada, Inc., serving Canada; Stifel Bank & Trust and Stifel Bank, retail and commercial banks; Stifel Trust Company NA and Stifel Trust Company Delaware, NA, trust companies; and 1919 Investment Counsel, LLC and Ziegler Capital Management, LLC, asset management firms. Stifel Financial operates its business in two primary segments: global wealth management and institutional group. The global wealth management segment provides securities transaction, brokerage and investment services to clients through the Stifel branch system, consisting of: the private client group, with a network of more than 2,125 financial advisors located in 382 branch offices in 47 U.S. states and the District of Columbia; customer financing, offering securities-based lending; asset management, offering specialized investment management solutions for institutions, private clients and investment advisors; and Stifel Bancorp, offering retail and commercial banking services to private and corporate clients, including a wide variety of loans. The institutional group segment consists of: research publications, offering clients with timely, insightful and actionable research aimed at improving investment performance; institutional sales and trading, which executes trades across municipal, corporate, government agency and mortgage-backed securities; investment banking, offering financial advisory services principally with respect to mergers and acquisitions and the execution of public offerings and private placements of debt and equity securities; public finance, acting as an underwriter and dealer in bonds issued by states, cities and other political subdivisions; and syndicate, which coordinates marketing, distribution, pricing and stabilization of Stifel's managed equity and debt offerings.

FINANCIAL DATA: Note: Data for latest year may not have been available at press time.

In U.S. $	2020	2019	2018	2017	2016	2015
Revenue	3,696,101,000	3,293,019,000	2,982,914,000	2,882,300,000	2,531,181,000	2,289,076,000
R&D Expense						
Operating Income						
Operating Margin %						
SGA Expense	2,444,071,000	2,125,544,000	1,911,016,000	2,092,422,000	1,865,660,000	1,699,540,000
Net Income	503,472,000	448,396,000	393,968,000	182,871,000	81,520,000	92,336,000
Operating Cash Flow	1,661,816,000	626,861,000	529,526,000	662,349,000	-349,175,000	-326,829,000
Capital Expenditure	73,364,000	157,897,000	108,207,000	28,217,000	28,211,000	69,822,000
EBITDA						
Return on Assets %		.02%	.02%	.01%	.00%	.01%
Return on Equity %		.14%	.13%	.07%	.03%	.04%
Debt to Equity		0.402	0.595	0.768	0.672	0.429

CONTACT INFORMATION:

Phone: 314 342-2000   Fax: 314 342-1159
Toll-Free: 800-679-5446
Address: 501 N. Broadway, St. Louis, MO 63102 United States

STOCK TICKER/OTHER:

Stock Ticker: SF   Exchange: NYS
Employees: 8,300   Fiscal Year Ends: 12/31
Parent Company:

SALARIES/BONUSES:

Top Exec. Salary: $ Bonus: $
Second Exec. Salary: $ Bonus: $

OTHER THOUGHTS:

Estimated Female Officers or Directors:
Hot Spot for Advancement for Women/Minorities:

Strategy&

www.strategyand.pwc.com

NAIC Code: 541610

TYPES OF BUSINESS:

Management Consulting
Management Consulting
Business Strategy
Customer Strategy
Operations Strategy
Organization Strategy
Product Strategy
Technology Strategy

BRANDS/DIVISIONS/AFFILIATES:

PricewaterhouseCoopers (PWC)

GROWTH PLANS/SPECIAL FEATURES:

Strategy& is a management consulting firm that provides services to businesses and government institutions worldwide. Strategy& serves industries as diverse as aerospace, chemicals, consumer products, entertainment/media, financial services, health, industrials, oil & gas, power/utilities, public sector, steels/metals, technology, telecommunications and transportation. The firm's functional expertise span business strategy, customer strategy, operations strategy, organization strategy, product and service innovation and technology strategy. The company has offices in more than 40 countries, spanning Africa, Asia-Pacific, Europe, the Middle East and the Americas. Strategy& is owned by PricewaterhouseCoopers.

The firm offers employees a formal work-life balance program; substantial sick leave and family care leave; flexible work arrangements that may include job-sharing, flex time, sabbaticals and a compressed work week; and access to training at the PwC Open

CONTACTS: Note: Officers with more than one job title may be intentionally listed here more than once.

Jonathan Cawood, Lead Partner
Mark Berlind, General Counsel
Jochim Rotering, Sr. Partner-Oper.
Peter B. Mensing, Managing Dir.-Europe
Mike Connolly, Sr. Partner-Health Svcs.
Leslie Moeller, Sr. Partner
Jay Davis, Global Dir.-Oper.
Ivan de Souza, Managing Dir.-Global Markets

FINANCIAL DATA: Note: Data for latest year may not have been available at press time.

In U.S. $	2020	2019	2018	2017	2016	2015
Revenue	1,528,800,000	1,470,000,000	1,400,000,000	1,300,000,000	1,194,027,000	1,147,000,000
R&D Expense						
Operating Income						
Operating Margin %						
SGA Expense						
Net Income						
Operating Cash Flow						
Capital Expenditure						
EBITDA						
Return on Assets %						
Return on Equity %						
Debt to Equity						

CONTACT INFORMATION:

Phone: 212-697-1900   Fax: 212-551-6732
Toll-Free:
Address: 90 Park Ave., Ste. 400, New York, NY 10016 United States

STOCK TICKER/OTHER:

Stock Ticker: Subsidiary   Exchange:
Employees: 3,000   Fiscal Year Ends:
Parent Company: PricewaterhouseCoopers (PWC)

SALARIES/BONUSES:

Top Exec. Salary: $ Bonus: $
Second Exec. Salary: $ Bonus: $

OTHER THOUGHTS:

Estimated Female Officers or Directors: 1
Hot Spot for Advancement for Women/Minorities:

Stryker Corporation

www.stryker.com

NAIC Code: 339100

TYPES OF BUSINESS:

Equipment-Orthopedic Implants
Powered Surgical Instruments
Endoscopic Systems
Patient Care & Handling Equipment
Imaging Software
Small Bone Innovations

BRANDS/DIVISIONS/AFFILIATES:

Wright Medical Group NV

CONTACTS: *Note: Officers with more than one job title may be intentionally listed here more than once.*

Kevin Lobo, CEO
Glenn Boehnlein, CFO
William Berry, Chief Accounting Officer
Robert Fletcher, Chief Legal Officer
Timothy Scannell, COO
Michael Hutchinson, Other Corporate Officer
Bijoy Sagar, Other Executive Officer
M. Fink, Other Executive Officer
Viju Menon, President, Divisional
Yin Becker, Vice President, Divisional
Katherine Owen, Vice President, Divisional

GROWTH PLANS/SPECIAL FEATURES:

Stryker Corporation develops, manufactures and markets innovative products and services that help improve patient and hospital outcomes. The firm's products are sold in over 80 countries through company-owned subsidiaries and branches, as well as by third-party dealers and distributors. Stryker's products include implants used in joint replacement and trauma surgeries, surgical equipment, surgical navigation systems, endoscopic systems, communications systems, patient handling equipment, emergency medical equipment, intensive care disposable products, neurosurgical devices, spinal devices, neurovascular devices and other products used in a variety of medical specialties. These products are segregated within the three business segments of: MedSurg, deriving 45% of 2020 net sales; orthopedics, 34%; and neurotechnology and spine, 21%. Stryker owns approximately 4,045 U.S. patents and approximately 6,407 international patents. During 2020, Stryker completed its acquisition of Wright Medical Group NV, a global medical device company focused on extremities and biologics. Wright was integrated into Stryker's trauma and extremities business within the orthopedics segment.

Stryker offers employees health insurance, retirement programs, tuition reimbursement and wellness programs.

FINANCIAL DATA: *Note: Data for latest year may not have been available at press time.*

In U.S. $	2020	2019	2018	2017	2016	2015
Revenue	14,351,000,000	14,884,000,000	13,601,000,000	12,444,000,000	11,325,000,000	9,946,000,000
R&D Expense	984,000,000	971,000,000	862,000,000	787,000,000	715,000,000	625,000,000
Operating Income	2,240,000,000	2,905,000,000	2,560,000,000	2,463,000,000	2,324,000,000	2,157,000,000
Operating Margin %		.20%	.19%	.20%	.21%	.22%
SGA Expense	5,361,000,000	5,356,000,000	5,099,000,000	4,552,000,000	4,137,000,000	3,610,000,000
Net Income	1,599,000,000	2,083,000,000	3,553,000,000	1,020,000,000	1,647,000,000	1,439,000,000
Operating Cash Flow	3,277,000,000	2,191,000,000	2,610,000,000	1,559,000,000	1,812,000,000	899,000,000
Capital Expenditure	487,000,000	649,000,000	572,000,000	598,000,000	490,000,000	270,000,000
EBITDA	3,052,000,000	3,683,000,000	3,283,000,000	3,105,000,000	2,870,000,000	2,554,000,000
Return on Assets %		.07%	.14%	.05%	.09%	.08%
Return on Equity %		.17%	.33%	.10%	.18%	.17%
Debt to Equity		0.799	0.723	0.661	0.70	0.382

CONTACT INFORMATION:

Phone: 269 385-2600   Fax: 269 385-1062
Toll-Free:
Address: 2825 Airview Blvd., Kalamazoo, MI 49002 United States

STOCK TICKER/OTHER:

Stock Ticker: SYK
Employees: 43,000
Parent Company:

Exchange: NYS
Fiscal Year Ends: 12/31

SALARIES/BONUSES:

Top Exec. Salary: $ Bonus: $
Second Exec. Salary: $ Bonus: $

OTHER THOUGHTS:

Estimated Female Officers or Directors: 7
Hot Spot for Advancement for Women/Minorities: Y

SunPower Corporation

us.sunpower.com

NAIC Code: 334413A

TYPES OF BUSINESS:

Photovoltaic Solar Cells
Solar Panels & Modules
Power Plant Operations

BRANDS/DIVISIONS/AFFILIATES:

Equinox
InvisiMount
Helix
Oasis
Maxeon Solar Technologies Ltd

CONTACTS: Note: Officers with more than one job title may be intentionally listed here more than once.

Thomas Werner, CEO
Charles Boynton, CFO
Douglas Richards, Executive VP, Divisional
Bill Mulligan, Executive VP, Divisional
Kenneth Mahaffey, Executive VP

GROWTH PLANS/SPECIAL FEATURES:

SunPower Corporation is a solar products and services firm. The company provides complete solar solutions to residential, commercial and power plant customers worldwide. Its products and offerings include solar module technology and solar power systems designed to generate electricity over a system life typically exceeding 25 years; integrated smart energy software solutions that enable customers to manage and optimize their cost of energy measurement; construction, installation, maintenance and monitoring services; and financing solutions. For residential customers, SunPower offers Equinox trademarked panels with factory-integrated microinverters; and the InvisiMount residential mounting systems via pre-assembled parts and integrated grounding. For commercial customers, SunPower offers the Helix commercial system. Both Equinox and Helix systems are pre-engineered modular solutions that combines the firm's solar module technology with integrated plug-and-play power stations, cable management systems and mounting hardware. For power plants, the company's Oasis system combines SunPower's solar panels and tracker technology into a scalable 2.5 megawatt (MW) solar power block, which streamlines the construction process by conforming to the contours of the production site. The power blocks are shipped pre-assembled to the job site for installation. The Oasis system is designed to support future grid interconnection requirements for large-scale solar power plants. SunPower holds more than 500 patents for solar technology in the U.S. and over 650 internationally. In August 2020, the firm announced it had completed the spin-off Maxeon Solar Technologies, Ltd. (NASDAQ:MAXN), a global technology innovator, manufacturer and marketer of premium solar panels.

The firm offers U.S. employees health and wellness programs, a 401(k) and employee assistance programs.

FINANCIAL DATA: Note: Data for latest year may not have been available at press time.

In U.S. $	2020	2019	2018	2017	2016	2015
Revenue	1,124,829,000	1,864,225,000	1,726,085,000	1,871,813,000	2,559,562,000	1,576,473,000
R&D Expense	22,381,000	67,515,000	81,705,000	80,785,000	116,130,000	99,063,000
Operating Income	-13,697,000	-202,053,000	-638,897,000	-373,089,000	-255,225,000	-199,903,000
Operating Margin %		-.11%	-.37%	-.20%	-.10%	-.13%
SGA Expense	164,703,000	260,443,000	260,111,000	277,033,000	329,061,000	345,486,000
Net Income	475,048,000	22,159,000	-811,091,000	-851,163,000	-471,064,000	-187,019,000
Operating Cash Flow	-187,391,000	-270,413,000	-543,389,000	-267,412,000	-312,283,000	-726,231,000
Capital Expenditure	21,105,000	111,602,000	183,330,000	282,878,000	310,650,000	338,370,000
EBITDA	736,026,000	159,402,000	-663,456,000	-838,612,000	-329,651,000	-60,508,000
Return on Assets %		.01%	-.27%	-.21%	-.10%	-.04%
Return on Equity %				-1.48%	-.38%	-.13%
Debt to Equity		96.445		12.286	1.785	1.204

CONTACT INFORMATION:

Phone: 408 240-5500   Fax: 408 739-7713
Toll-Free: 800-786-7693
Address: 77 Rio Robles, San Jose, CA 95134 United States

STOCK TICKER/OTHER:

Stock Ticker: SPWR
Employees: 8,902
Parent Company:

Exchange: NAS
Fiscal Year Ends: 12/31

SALARIES/BONUSES:

Top Exec. Salary: $ Bonus: $
Second Exec. Salary: $ Bonus: $

OTHER THOUGHTS:

Estimated Female Officers or Directors: 1
Hot Spot for Advancement for Women/Minorities: Y

Sunrun Inc

NAIC Code: 221114

www.sunrunhome.com

TYPES OF BUSINESS:

Solar Electric Power Generation

BRANDS/DIVISIONS/AFFILIATES:

BrightBox

CONTACTS: *Note: Officers with more than one job title may be intentionally listed here more than once.*

Lynn Jurich, CEO
Bob Komin, CFO
Edward Fenster, Chairman of the Board
Christopher Dawson, COO
Jeanna Steele, General Counsel

GROWTH PLANS/SPECIAL FEATURES:

SunRun, Inc., based in California, is a leading residential solar power firm. The firm's solar services operate by allowing the customer to choose between a lease and a power purchase agreement (PPA) plan. In the solar lease plan, homeowners pay a fixed rate each month for solar panel usage, independent of the electricity generated from the panels. In the PPA plan, homeowners pay a fixed monthly rate for the panel usage but only pay for the electricity that the panels generate each month. In both situations, SunRun covers all of the upfront costs for the solar panels, power inverter, permits and installation. Homeowners are locked into the agreement for 20 years but have the assurance of no fixed rate fluctuations and no maintenance fees for any necessary repairs of the panels. The firm provides its products and services through multiple channels, including direct-to-consumer and via partnerships. SunRun has more than 270,000 customers across the U.S., as well as the District of Columbia and Puerto Rico, and deployed an aggregate of over 1,980 megawatts (MW). SunRun's BrightBox solar battery storage product allows residences to generate solar power during the day and store excess electricity for use at night. BrightBox uses lithium ion battery technology. In October 2020, SunRun completed its acquisition of competitor Vivint Solar, Inc. for an enterprise value of $3.2 billion in an all-stock deal.

FINANCIAL DATA: *Note: Data for latest year may not have been available at press time.*

In U.S. $	2020	2019	2018	2017	2016	2015
Revenue	922,191,000	858,578,000	759,981,000	529,699,000	453,898,000	304,606,000
R&D Expense	19,548,000	23,563,000	18,844,000	15,079,000	10,199,000	9,657,000
Operating Income	-465,108,000	-215,740,000	-121,881,000	-182,204,000	-214,904,000	-219,200,000
Operating Margin %		-.25%	-.16%	-.34%	-.47%	-.72%
SGA Expense	619,045,000	400,171,000	323,891,000	244,535,000	255,158,000	229,919,000
Net Income	-173,394,000	26,335,000	26,657,000	124,525,000	91,687,000	-28,246,000
Operating Cash Flow	-317,972,000	-204,487,000	-62,461,000	-61,011,000	-150,580,000	-105,266,000
Capital Expenditure	969,675,000	840,533,000	811,316,000	812,327,000	740,112,000	607,914,000
EBITDA	-213,978,000	-37,831,000	36,914,000	-47,717,000	-109,959,000	-149,596,000
Return on Assets %		.00%	.01%	.03%	.03%	-.02%
Return on Equity %		.03%	.03%	.17%	.15%	-.12%
Debt to Equity		2.654	2.172	1.746	1.538	1.265

CONTACT INFORMATION:

Phone: 415-982-9000   Fax: 415-982-9021
Toll-Free: 855-478-6786
Address: 595 Market St., 29/Fl, San Francisco, CA 94105 United States

STOCK TICKER/OTHER:

Stock Ticker: RUN
Employees: 8,500
Parent Company:

Exchange: NAS
Fiscal Year Ends: 12/31

SALARIES/BONUSES:

Top Exec. Salary: $ Bonus: $
Second Exec. Salary: $ Bonus: $

OTHER THOUGHTS:

Estimated Female Officers or Directors: 4
Hot Spot for Advancement for Women/Minorities: Y

Supervalu Inc

www.supervalu.com

NAIC Code: 445110

TYPES OF BUSINESS:

Grocery Stores
Food Distribution & Logistics

BRANDS/DIVISIONS/AFFILIATES:

United Natural Foods Inc
Cub Foods
Shoppers Food & Pharmacy
Shop n Save
Farm Fresh

CONTACTS: Note: Officers with more than one job title may be intentionally listed here more than once.

Sean F. Griffin, CEO
Randy Burdick, Chief Information Officer
Donald Chappel, Director
Karla Robertson, Executive VP
Michael Stigers, Executive VP, Divisional
Anne Dament, Executive VP, Divisional
James Weidenheimer, Executive VP, Divisional
Robert Woseth, Executive VP
Mark Gross, President
Stuart McFarland, Senior VP

GROWTH PLANS/SPECIAL FEATURES:

Supervalu, Inc. is a grocery distributor to wholesale customers throughout the U.S. The firm operates through two business segments: wholesale and retail. The wholesale segment distributes groceries and other products, logistics services and professional service solutions to retail stores and other customers. This division's distribution centers maintain an assortment of approximately 175,000 stock-keeping units (SKUs). Its network supplies 3,000 owned, franchised and affiliated stores. The retail segment sells groceries and other products at retail locations operated by Supervalu. Its operations are primarily conducted through stores under the retail banners of: Cub Foods, Shoppers Food & Pharmacy, Shop 'n Save, and Farm Fresh. The stores offer grocery items, general merchandise, home items, health and beauty care, and pharmaceutical items. A typical retail store carries 16,000 to 21,000 core SKUs, and range in size from 50,000 to 70,000 square feet. In addition, Supervalu offers professional services such as grocery development, grocery marketing, grocery merchandising, grocery business, systems supply and more. Supervalu operates as a subsidiary of United Natural Foods, Inc., a leading distributor of natural foods in the U.S. and Canada.

FINANCIAL DATA: Note: Data for latest year may not have been available at press time.

In U.S. $	2020	2019	2018	2017	2016	2015
Revenue	16,530,000,000	10,470,000,000	14,156,999,680	12,480,000,000	17,528,999,936	17,820,000,256
R&D Expense						
Operating Income						
Operating Margin %						
SGA Expense						
Net Income			45,000,000	650,000,000	178,000,000	192,000,000
Operating Cash Flow						
Capital Expenditure						
EBITDA						
Return on Assets %						
Return on Equity %						
Debt to Equity						

CONTACT INFORMATION:

Phone: 952 828-4000   Fax: 952 828-8998
Toll-Free:
Address: 11840 Valley View Rd., Eden Prairie, MN 55344 United States

STOCK TICKER/OTHER:

Stock Ticker: Subsidiary   Exchange:
Employees: 29,000   Fiscal Year Ends: 02/28
Parent Company: United Natural Foods Inc

SALARIES/BONUSES:

Top Exec. Salary: $ Bonus: $
Second Exec. Salary: $ Bonus: $

OTHER THOUGHTS:

Estimated Female Officers or Directors: 3
Hot Spot for Advancement for Women/Minorities: Y

Sutter Health Inc
NAIC Code: 622110

TYPES OF BUSINESS:
General Medical and Surgical Hospitals
Neonatal Care
Pregnancy & Birth
Training Programs
Medical Research Facilities
Home Health Services
Hospice Networks
Long-Term Care

BRANDS/DIVISIONS/AFFILIATES:

GROWTH PLANS/SPECIAL FEATURES:
Sutter Health, Inc. is a non-profit healthcare network that delivers personalized care in more than 100 northern California communities. This network includes physician organizations, acute care hospitals, surgery centers, home health and hospice programs, medical research facilities, training programs and specialty services. As a non-profit, Sutter Health invests all of its earnings back into the communities it serves. There are more than 12,000 physicians within the network, 2,000 advanced practice clinicians, 14,500 nurses, 5,000 volunteers, 24 hospitals, 36 ambulatory surgery centers, seven cardiac centers, nine cancer centers, four acute rehabilitation centers, eight behavioral health centers, five trauma centers, 4,188 licensed general acute-care beds and eight neonatal intensive care units.

CONTACTS: Note: Officers with more than one job title may be intentionally listed here more than once.
Sarah Krevans, CEO

FINANCIAL DATA: Note: Data for latest year may not have been available at press time.

In U.S. $	2020	2019	2018	2017	2016	2015
Revenue	13,220,000,000	13,304,000,000	12,700,000,000	12,444,000,000	11,873,000,000	10,998,000,000
R&D Expense						
Operating Income						
Operating Margin %						
SGA Expense						
Net Income	200,000,000	189,000,000	-200,000,000	958,000,000	622,000,000	145,000,000
Operating Cash Flow						
Capital Expenditure						
EBITDA						
Return on Assets %						
Return on Equity %						
Debt to Equity						

CONTACT INFORMATION:
Phone: 916-733-8800   Fax:
Toll-Free:
Address: 2200 River Plaza Dr., Sacramento, CA 95833 United States

STOCK TICKER/OTHER:
Stock Ticker: Nonprofit   Exchange:
Employees: 55,000   Fiscal Year Ends: 12/31
Parent Company:

SALARIES/BONUSES:
Top Exec. Salary: $ Bonus: $
Second Exec. Salary: $ Bonus: $

OTHER THOUGHTS:
Estimated Female Officers or Directors: 3
Hot Spot for Advancement for Women/Minorities: Y

Sykes Enterprises Incorporated

www.sykes.com

NAIC Code: 541512

TYPES OF BUSINESS:

Computer Integrated Systems Design
Outsourcing Services
Customer Engagement Solutions
Management Services
Consulting
Hosting Services

BRANDS/DIVISIONS/AFFILIATES:

CONTACTS:
Note: Officers with more than one job title may be intentionally listed here more than once.

Charles Sykes, CEO
John Chapman, CFO
James Macleod, Chairman of the Board
David Pearson, Chief Information Officer
William Rocktoff, Controller
Jenna Nelson, Executive VP, Divisional
James Holder, Executive VP
Lawrence Zingale, Executive VP

GROWTH PLANS/SPECIAL FEATURES:

Sykes Enterprises, Incorporated provides multichannel demand generation customer engagement solutions and services primarily to Global 2000 companies and their end customers. These companies and customers are principally engaged in the financial services, communications, technology, transportation, leisure and healthcare industries. Sykes' differentiated full lifecycle management services platform engages customers at every touchpoint within the customer journey, including digital marketing, digital acquisition, sales expertise, customer service, technical support, and retention, many of which can be optimized by a suite of robotic process automation (RPA) and artificial intelligence (AI) solutions. The firm serves clients in the EMEA (Europe, Middle East and Africa) region, with an emphasis on inbound multichannel demand generation, customer service and technical support. These services are delivered through communication channels such as phone, email, social media, text messaging, chat and digital self-services. In Europe, Sykes also provides fulfillment services such as order processing, payment processing, inventory control, product delivery and product returns handling. Moreover, Sykes provides a suite of solutions such as consulting, implementation, hosting and managed services, all of which generate demand, enhance the customer service experience, promote brand loyalty and brings about high levels of performance and profitability. In June 2021, Sykes Enterprises agreed to be acquired by Sitel Group, a provider of customer experience products and solutions.

FINANCIAL DATA:
Note: Data for latest year may not have been available at press time.

In U.S. $	2020	2019	2018	2017	2016	2015
Revenue	1,710,261,000	1,614,762,000	1,625,687,000	1,586,008,000	1,460,037,000	1,286,340,000
R&D Expense						
Operating Income	123,337,000	91,511,000	72,603,000	92,301,000	92,562,000	94,645,000
Operating Margin %		.06%	.04%	.06%	.06%	.07%
SGA Expense	421,910,000	412,407,000	407,285,000	376,863,000	351,408,000	297,257,000
Net Income	56,432,000	64,081,000	48,926,000	32,216,000	62,390,000	68,597,000
Operating Cash Flow	175,742,000	101,283,000	109,094,000	134,789,000	130,728,000	120,464,000
Capital Expenditure	52,683,000	38,990,000	55,040,000	68,169,000	78,352,000	49,662,000
EBITDA	148,122,000	159,020,000	135,019,000	166,560,000	163,431,000	151,133,000
Return on Assets %		.05%	.04%	.03%	.06%	.07%
Return on Equity %		.08%	.06%	.04%	.09%	.10%
Debt to Equity		0.274	0.123	0.345	0.369	0.103

CONTACT INFORMATION:

Phone: 813 274-1000   Fax: 813 273-0148
Toll-Free:
Address: 400 N. Ashley Dr., Ste. 2800, Tampa, FL 33602 United States

STOCK TICKER/OTHER:

Stock Ticker: SYKE
Employees: 61,100
Parent Company:

Exchange: NAS
Fiscal Year Ends: 12/31

SALARIES/BONUSES:

Top Exec. Salary: $ Bonus: $
Second Exec. Salary: $ Bonus: $

OTHER THOUGHTS:

Estimated Female Officers or Directors: 3
Hot Spot for Advancement for Women/Minorities: Y

Syneos Health Inc

NAIC Code: 541711

www.syneoshealth.com

TYPES OF BUSINESS:

Research and Development in Biotechnology
Biopharmaceutical Marketing
Medical Device Marketing
Commercialization

BRANDS/DIVISIONS/AFFILIATES:

Biopharmaceutical Acceleration Model
Dynamic Assembly
Data Lake Ecosystem
Syneos One
Illingworth Research Group
Syneract

CONTACTS: Note: Officers with more than one job title may be intentionally listed here more than once.

Alistair Macdonald, CEO
Jason Meggs, CFO
Robert Parks, Chief Accounting Officer
Larry A. Pickett, Jr., CIO
Jonathan Olefson, General Counsel
Michelle Keefe, President, Divisional
Paul Colvin, President, Divisional
John Dineen, Chairman of the Board

GROWTH PLANS/SPECIAL FEATURES:

Syneos Health, Inc. is a leading global biopharmaceutical services organization. The firm serves small-to-large companies in the biopharmaceutical, biotechnology and medical device industries with services and solutions designed to enable them to successfully develop, launch and market their products. Syneos offers both standalone and integrated biopharmaceutical solutions, from early phase clinical trials to the full commercialization of biopharmaceutical products. Its end-to-end solutions are based on a Biopharmaceutical Acceleration Model where Syneos synchronizes its clinical and commercial capabilities via sharing knowledge, data and insights. Dynamic Assembly is a an open, source agnostic and highly flexible architecture. It uses the Data Lake Ecosystem, which links vast amounts of data from various sources using the designed data ingestion process. Syneos One is an end-to-end offering which ensures that data, knowledge and insights move back and forth easily. The company's clinical solutions comprise a variety of clinical development services spanning Phase 1 to Phase IV, including full-service global studies as well as clinical monitoring, investigator recruitment, patient recruitment, data management and study startup to assist customers with their drug development process. Commercial solutions include a range of commercialization services such as outsources field selling solutions, medication adherence, communications (advertising and public relations) and consulting. Syneos' insights-driven approach provides customers with a single source, integrated end-to-end solution that spans the entire product lifecycle. Services are offered in either a full service or individual, unbundled bases, depending on the customer's needs. In October 2020, Syneos announced it had acquired Syneract, a full-service CRO focused on the rapidly growing biopharma segment. And shortly after in December 2020, Syneos announced it had acquired Illingworth Research Group, a provider of clinical research home health services.

FINANCIAL DATA: Note: Data for latest year may not have been available at press time.

In U.S. $	2020	2019	2018	2017	2016	2015
Revenue	4,415,777,000	4,675,815,000	4,390,116,000	2,672,064,000	1,610,596,000	1,399,239,000
R&D Expense						
Operating Income	352,799,000	341,164,000	275,816,000	158,264,000	172,114,000	159,713,000
Operating Margin %		.07%	.06%	.06%	.11%	.11%
SGA Expense	442,484,000	446,281,000	406,305,000	282,620,000	172,386,000	156,609,000
Net Income	192,787,000	131,258,000	24,284,000	-138,469,000	112,630,000	117,047,000
Operating Cash Flow	425,493,000	318,481,000	303,448,000	198,258,000	109,332,000	204,740,000
Capital Expenditure	50,010,000	63,973,000	54,595,000	43,896,000	31,353,000	21,111,000
EBITDA	517,155,000	473,994,000	461,644,000	131,784,000	205,338,000	202,628,000
Return on Assets %		.02%	.00%	-.03%	.09%	.10%
Return on Equity %		.04%	.01%	-.08%	.43%	.38%
Debt to Equity		0.926	0.968	0.981	1.612	2.171

CONTACT INFORMATION:

Phone: 919 876-9300   Fax: 919 876-9360
Toll-Free: 866 462-7373
Address: 1030 Sync St., Morrisville, NC 27650 United States

STOCK TICKER/OTHER:

Stock Ticker: SYNH
Employees: 6,800
Parent Company:

Exchange: NAS
Fiscal Year Ends: 12/31

SALARIES/BONUSES:

Top Exec. Salary: $ Bonus: $
Second Exec. Salary: $ Bonus: $

OTHER THOUGHTS:

Estimated Female Officers or Directors:
Hot Spot for Advancement for Women/Minorities:

SYNNEX Corporation

www.synnex.com

NAIC Code: 423430

TYPES OF BUSINESS:

IT Supply Chain Services
Distribution Services
Logistics Services
Technology Integration
Information Technology
Servers
Software
Security Equipment

BRANDS/DIVISIONS/AFFILIATES:

Hyve
Concentrix Corporation

CONTACTS: Note: Officers with more than one job title may be intentionally listed here more than once.

Dennis Polk, CEO
Marshall Witt, CFO
Matthew Miau, Chairman Emeritus
Kevin Murai, Chairman of the Board
Christopher Caldwell, Executive VP
Simon Leung, General Counsel
Peter Larocque, President, Divisional

GROWTH PLANS/SPECIAL FEATURES:

SYNNEX Corporation is a leading business process services company. The firm provides a comprehensive range of distribution, logistics and integration services for the technology industry to enterprises. SYNNEX's technology solutions include information technology (IT) peripherals, IT systems and servers, system components, software, communication and security equipment, consumer electronics and other complementary products and services. The company maintains relationships with IT reseller and retail customers, including value-added resellers, corporate resellers, government resellers, systems integrators, direct marketers and national and regional retailers. SYNNEX's Hyve solutions division has created a paradigm for scale computing with purpose-built, large-scale data center solutions, integrating hardware, software and services. Hyve's open compute platform provides solutions for leading datacenter customers, including those engaged in public cloud computing and social networking. Headquartered in the U.S., SYNNEX has operations in Canada, Japan and Latin America. In December 2020, SYNNEX spun off Concentrix Corporation into a separate, publicly-traded entity.

FINANCIAL DATA: Note: Data for latest year may not have been available at press time.

In U.S. $	2020	2019	2018	2017	2016	2015
Revenue	24,675,560,000	23,757,290,000	20,053,760,000	17,045,700,000	14,061,840,000	13,338,400,000
R&D Expense						
Operating Income	830,102,000	813,761,000	551,035,000	508,965,000	379,596,000	354,552,000
Operating Margin %		.03%	.03%	.03%	.03%	.03%
SGA Expense	2,017,502,000	2,084,156,000	1,376,664,000	1,041,975,000	903,369,000	837,239,000
Net Income	529,160,000	500,712,000	300,598,000	301,173,000	234,946,000	208,525,000
Operating Cash Flow	1,834,366,000	549,919,000	100,706,000	176,764,000	326,951,000	643,609,000
Capital Expenditure	197,965,000	137,423,000	125,305,000	97,546,000	123,233,000	100,106,000
EBITDA	1,173,015,000	1,216,232,000	767,339,000	669,974,000	506,350,000	457,001,000
Return on Assets %		.04%	.03%	.05%	.05%	.05%
Return on Equity %		.14%	.10%	.14%	.12%	.12%
Debt to Equity		0.718	0.764	0.497	0.305	0.355

CONTACT INFORMATION:

Phone: 510 656-3333   Fax: 510 668-3777
Toll-Free: 800-756-9888
Address: 44201 Nobel Dr., Fremont, CA 94538 United States

SALARIES/BONUSES:

Top Exec. Salary: $ Bonus: $
Second Exec. Salary: $ Bonus: $

STOCK TICKER/OTHER:

Stock Ticker: SNX
Employees: 240,000
Parent Company:

Exchange: NYS
Fiscal Year Ends: 11/30

OTHER THOUGHTS:

Estimated Female Officers or Directors: 2
Hot Spot for Advancement for Women/Minorities:

Synopsys Inc

NAIC Code: 511210N

www.synopsys.com

TYPES OF BUSINESS:

Computer Software-Electronic Design Automation
Electronics Software
Integrated Circuit Testing
Semiconductor IP
Hardware
Software Security

BRANDS/DIVISIONS/AFFILIATES:

Light Tec

CONTACTS: *Note: Officers with more than one job title may be intentionally listed here more than once.*

Trac Pham, CFO
Aart De Geus, Chairman of the Board
Sudhindra Kankanwadi, Chief Accounting Officer
Chi-Foon Chan, Co-CEO
John Runkel, General Counsel
Joseph Logan, Other Corporate Officer

GROWTH PLANS/SPECIAL FEATURES:

Synopsys, Inc. provides products and services across the entire silicon-to-software spectrum. The firm is a global leader in supplying the electronic design automation (EDA) software that engineers use to design and test integrated circuits (ICs), also known as chips. Synopsys also offers semiconductor intellectual property (IP) products, which are pre-designed circuits that engineers use as components of larger chip designs. The company provides the hardware used to validate electronic systems that incorporate chips and the software that runs on them. Synopsys provides related technical services and support to help customers develop advanced chips and electronic systems. Moreover, the firm provides software tools and services that improve the security, quality and compliance of software in a variety of industries, including electronics, financial services, automotive, medicine, energy and industrials. Headquartered in the U.S., Synopsys has global locations across the Americas, Europe, the Middle East, Japan and Asia Pacific. In late-2020, Synopsys acquired Light Tec, a global provider of optical scattering measurements and measurement equipment.

Synopsys offers its employees comprehensive health benefits, retirement accounts, stock purchase plans, among other assistance programs.

FINANCIAL DATA: *Note: Data for latest year may not have been available at press time.*

In U.S. $	2020	2019	2018	2017	2016	2015
Revenue	3,685,281,000	3,360,694,000	3,121,058,000	2,724,880,000	2,422,532,000	2,242,211,000
R&D Expense	1,279,022,000	1,136,932,000	1,084,822,000	908,841,000	856,705,000	776,229,000
Operating Income	656,200,000	567,417,000	373,170,000	384,149,000	327,028,000	281,554,000
Operating Margin %		.17%	.12%	.14%	.13%	.13%
SGA Expense	916,540,000	862,108,000	885,538,000	746,092,000	668,330,000	639,504,000
Net Income	664,347,000	532,367,000	432,518,000	136,563,000	266,826,000	225,934,000
Operating Cash Flow	991,313,000	800,513,000	424,232,000	634,565,000	586,635,000	495,160,000
Capital Expenditure	158,762,000	202,388,000	101,926,000	73,554,000	71,040,000	90,647,000
EBITDA	853,285,000	758,841,000	588,357,000	579,843,000	540,351,000	496,245,000
Return on Assets %		.08%	.07%	.03%	.05%	.05%
Return on Equity %		.14%	.13%	.04%	.08%	.08%
Debt to Equity		0.029	0.036	0.041		.07%

CONTACT INFORMATION:

Phone: 650 584-5000   Fax: 650 965-8637
Toll-Free: 800-541-7737
Address: 690 E. Middlefield Rd., Mountain View, CA 94043 United States

STOCK TICKER/OTHER:

Stock Ticker: SNPS
Employees: 15,036
Parent Company:

Exchange: NAS
Fiscal Year Ends: 10/31

SALARIES/BONUSES:

Top Exec. Salary: $ Bonus: $
Second Exec. Salary: $ Bonus: $

OTHER THOUGHTS:

Estimated Female Officers or Directors: 3
Hot Spot for Advancement for Women/Minorities: Y

T Rowe Price Group Inc

www.troweprice.com

NAIC Code: 523920

TYPES OF BUSINESS:
Investment Management & Mutual Funds
Retirement Accounts
Advisory Services

BRANDS/DIVISIONS/AFFILIATES:
T Rowe Price Associates Inc
T Rowe Price International Ltd

CONTACTS: *Note: Officers with more than one job title may be intentionally listed here more than once.*
Celine Dufetel, CFO
Jessica Hiebler, Chief Accounting Officer
Robert Sharps, Chief Investment Officer
William Stromberg, Director
Christopher Alderson, Other Corporate Officer
Andrew McCormick, Other Corporate Officer
Eric Veiel, Other Corporate Officer
Robert Higginbotham, Other Corporate Officer
Sebastien Page, Other Corporate Officer
Scott David, Other Corporate Officer
David Oestreicher, Other Executive Officer

GROWTH PLANS/SPECIAL FEATURES:
T. Rowe Price Group, Inc. is a financial services holding company. The firm provides an array of U.S. mutual funds, separately-managed accounts, sub-advised funds, collective investment trusts, target date retirement trusts, open-ended investment products offered to investors outside the U.S., and products offered through variable annuity life insurance plans in the U.S. T. Rowe Price also provides certain investment advisory clients with related administrative services, including distribution, mutual fund transfer agent, accounting and shareholder services; participant recordkeeping and transfer agent services for defined contribution retirement plans; brokerage; and trust services. The company derives the majority of its consolidated net revenue and net income from investment advisory services provided by its subsidiaries, primarily T. Rowe Price Associates and T. Rowe Price International Ltd. The firm's revenues depend largely on the total value of composition of assets under management. As of October 31, 2020, T. Rowe Price managed approximately $1.3 trillion in assets. T. Rowe Price's products are distributed in countries located within three broad geographical regions: Americas, Europe Middle East and Africa (EMEA) and Asia Pacific. The group serves clients in 50 countries worldwide.

T. Rowe Price offers its employees comprehensive health benefits, a retirement plan and employee assistance options.

FINANCIAL DATA: *Note: Data for latest year may not have been available at press time.*

In U.S. $	2020	2019	2018	2017	2016	2015
Revenue	6,206,700,000	5,617,900,000	5,372,600,000	4,793,000,000	4,222,900,000	4,200,600,000
R&D Expense						
Operating Income	2,745,700,000	2,387,000,000	2,346,200,000	2,058,800,000	1,799,600,000	1,898,900,000
Operating Margin %		.42%	.44%	.43%	.43%	.45%
SGA Expense	844,600,000	846,000,000	779,500,000	286,900,000	252,700,000	238,900,000
Net Income	2,372,700,000	2,131,300,000	1,837,500,000	1,497,800,000	1,215,000,000	1,223,000,000
Operating Cash Flow	1,918,900,000	1,522,700,000	1,619,900,000	229,500,000	170,500,000	1,506,400,000
Capital Expenditure	214,600,000	204,600,000	168,500,000	186,100,000	148,300,000	151,300,000
EBITDA	2,935,300,000	2,577,800,000	2,505,700,000	2,202,400,000	1,933,000,000	2,025,200,000
Return on Assets %		.24%	.24%	.22%	.21%	.23%
Return on Equity %		.31%	.31%	.28%	.25%	.24%
Debt to Equity		0.021				

CONTACT INFORMATION:
Phone: 410 345-2000   Fax: 410 345-2394
Toll-Free: 800-638-7890
Address: 100 E. Pratt St., Baltimore, MD 21202 United States

SALARIES/BONUSES:
Top Exec. Salary: $ Bonus: $
Second Exec. Salary: $ Bonus: $

STOCK TICKER/OTHER:
Stock Ticker: TROW   Exchange: NAS
Employees: 7,678   Fiscal Year Ends: 12/31
Parent Company:

OTHER THOUGHTS:
Estimated Female Officers or Directors:
Hot Spot for Advancement for Women/Minorities:

Sales, profits and employees may be estimates. Financial information, benefits and other data can change quickly and may vary from those stated here.

Take-Two Interactive Software Inc

www.take2games.com

NAIC Code: 511210G

TYPES OF BUSINESS:
Computer Software, Electronic Games, Apps & Entertainment
Software Distribution
Apps

BRANDS/DIVISIONS/AFFILIATES:
Rockstar Games
2K
Grand Theft Auto
Battleborn
BioShock
Private Division
Social Point
Cloud Chamber

CONTACTS: *Note: Officers with more than one job title may be intentionally listed here more than once.*
Strauss Zelnick, CEO
Lainie Goldstein, CFO
Daniel Emerson, Executive VP
Karl Slatoff, President

GROWTH PLANS/SPECIAL FEATURES:
Take-Two Interactive Software, Inc. is a global publisher, developer and distributor of interactive entertainment software. The firm develops, markets and publishes software titles for leading gaming and entertainment hardware platforms, including Sony's PlayStation (PS4), Microsoft's Xbox One and Nintendo's Switch, as well as handheld gaming devices, personal computers and mobile devices. The company distributes its software through retail stores and online through digital download stores, online platforms and cloud streaming devices. Its business strategy is to capitalize on the success of popular games by creating sequels and perpetuating its consistently popular franchises while continuing to appeal to a broad range of demographics, from game enthusiasts to casual gamers and families. A majority of Take-Two's leading games are developed internally with intellectual property owned by the company, although it selectively markets and publishes externally developed titles and software based on licensed property. The firm wholly-owns the labels Rockstar Games and 2K, and publishes titles under 2K Games, 2K Sports and 2K Play. 2K publishes owned and licensed titles across a range of genres including shooter, action, role-playing, strategy, sports and family/casual. Cloud Chamber, a wholly-owned game development studio within the 2K division, has operations in California, USA and Quebec, Canada. Rockstar Games titles are primarily internally developed and include the Grand Theft Auto series. Other published franchises include Battleborn, BioShock, Borderlands, Carnival Games, Evolve, Mafia, NBA 2K, Sid Meier's Civilization, WWE 2K, Red Dead and XCOM. Take-Two's Private Division label is dedicated to bringing titles from top independent developers to market. Social Point develops and publishes free-to-play mobile games, which includes Dragon City and Monster Legends.

FINANCIAL DATA: *Note: Data for latest year may not have been available at press time.*

In U.S. $	2020	2019	2018	2017	2016	2015
Revenue	3,088,970,000	2,668,394,000	1,792,892,000	1,779,748,000	1,413,698,000	
R&D Expense	296,398,000	230,170,000	196,373,000	137,915,000	119,807,000	
Operating Income	425,350,000	201,714,000	150,319,000	91,305,000	60,457,000	
Operating Margin %	.14%	.08%	.08%	.05%	.04%	
SGA Expense	776,659,000	672,634,000	503,920,000	496,862,000	390,761,000	
Net Income	404,459,000	333,837,000	173,533,000	67,303,000	-8,302,000	
Operating Cash Flow	685,678,000	843,515,000	393,947,000	331,429,000	261,305,000	
Capital Expenditure	53,384,000	66,969,000	87,522,000	21,167,000	37,280,000	
EBITDA	697,619,000	505,643,000	295,238,000	350,661,000	223,889,000	
Return on Assets %	.09%	.08%	.05%	.02%	.00%	
Return on Equity %	.18%	.19%	.14%	.08%	-.01%	
Debt to Equity	0.06		0.005	0.251	0.856	

CONTACT INFORMATION:
Phone: 646 536-2842   Fax: 646 536-2926
Toll-Free:
Address: 110 West 44th St., New York, NY 10036 United States

STOCK TICKER/OTHER:
Stock Ticker: TTWO
Employees: 6,495
Parent Company:

Exchange: NAS
Fiscal Year Ends: 03/31

SALARIES/BONUSES:
Top Exec. Salary: $ Bonus: $
Second Exec. Salary: $ Bonus: $

OTHER THOUGHTS:
Estimated Female Officers or Directors: 1
Hot Spot for Advancement for Women/Minorities:

Sales, profits and employees may be estimates. Financial information, benefits and other data can change quickly and may vary from those stated here.

Target Corporation

www.target.com

NAIC Code: 452910

TYPES OF BUSINESS:

Supercenters
Online Sales
Catalog Sales
Groceries
Credit Cards

BRANDS/DIVISIONS/AFFILIATES:

SuperTarget
Target
Cat & Jack
Hearth & Hand
Market Pantry
Room Essentials
Xhilaration
Target.com

CONTACTS: *Note: Officers with more than one job title may be intentionally listed here more than once.*

Brian Cornell, CEO
Melissa Kremer, Exec. VP
Catherine Smith, CFO
Robert Harrison, Chief Accounting Officer
Michael McNamara, Chief Information Officer
Don Liu, Chief Legal Officer
Rick Gomez, Chief Marketing Officer
Minsok Pak, Chief Strategy Officer
John Mulligan, Executive VP
Janna Potts, Executive VP
Mark Tritton, Executive VP
Laysha Ward, Executive VP
Stephanie Lundquist, Executive VP

GROWTH PLANS/SPECIAL FEATURES:

Target Corporation operates general merchandise and food discount stores in the U.S., which include SuperTarget, Target and flexible format stores. SuperTarget stores combine grocery and general merchandise in a single format and feature coffee bars, bakeries, banking areas, CVS-branded pharmacies and photo services. Target Corporation operates more than 1,870 stores in the U.S. (as of August 1, 2020). Owned brands of Target include A New Day, Cat & Jack, Good & Gather, Hearth & Hand (with Magnolia), Market Pantry, Prologue, Room Essentials, Simply Balanced, Threshold and Xhilaration, among many others. Exclusive brands include California Roots, Defy & Inspire, Fieldcrest, Hand Made Modern, Isabel Maternity (by Ingrid & Isabel), Just One You (by carter's), Kristin Ess, Rose Bae, The Collection, Wine Cube and Who What Wear. Target stores derive the largest percentage of sales from beauty and household essential items, with apparel and accessories coming in second, food and beverage items next, home furnishings and decor next and hardlines and other next. The company's proprietary credit card products, called REDcards, provide discounts to gain customer loyalty. REDcards are sold under the Target Credit Card, Target MasterCard Credit Card and Target Debit Card names. Target also sells merchandise via its eCommerce site, Target.com. SuperTarget stores typically average more than 170,000 square feet in size, while general Target stores average 130,000 square feet in size. Smaller, flexible format stores are primarily located in dense, urban areas, generally smaller than 50,000 square feet in size, and are aimed at millennial shoppers.

Target offers employees comprehensive benefits. The firm promotes women and minorities at an above average rate. About 50% of executives are female.

FINANCIAL DATA: *Note: Data for latest year may not have been available at press time.*

In U.S. $	2020	2019	2018	2017	2016	2015
Revenue	78,112,000,000	75,356,000,000	71,879,000,000	69,495,000,000	73,785,000,000	
R&D Expense						
Operating Income	4,658,000,000	4,110,000,000	4,312,000,000	4,969,000,000	4,910,000,000	
Operating Margin %	.06%	.05%	.06%	.07%	.07%	
SGA Expense	16,233,000,000	15,723,000,000	14,248,000,000	13,356,000,000	14,665,000,000	
Net Income	3,281,000,000	2,937,000,000	2,934,000,000	2,737,000,000	3,363,000,000	
Operating Cash Flow	7,117,000,000	5,973,000,000	6,923,000,000	5,436,000,000	5,844,000,000	
Capital Expenditure	3,027,000,000	3,516,000,000	2,533,000,000	1,547,000,000	1,438,000,000	
EBITDA	7,271,000,000	6,611,000,000	6,757,000,000	7,267,000,000	7,743,000,000	
Return on Assets %	.08%	.07%	.08%	.07%	.08%	
Return on Equity %	.28%	.26%	.26%	.23%	.25%	
Debt to Equity	1.15	1.082	0.967	1.007	0.922	

CONTACT INFORMATION:

Phone: 612 304-6073   Fax: 612 370-5502
Toll-Free:
Address: 1000 Nicollet Mall, Minneapolis, MN 55403 United States

STOCK TICKER/OTHER:

Stock Ticker: TGT   Exchange: NYS
Employees: 409,000   Fiscal Year Ends: 01/31
Parent Company:

SALARIES/BONUSES:

Top Exec. Salary: $ Bonus: $
Second Exec. Salary: $ Bonus: $

OTHER THOUGHTS:

Estimated Female Officers or Directors: 9
Hot Spot for Advancement for Women/Minorities: Y

TD Ameritrade Holding Corporation

NAIC Code: 523120

www.amtd.com

TYPES OF BUSINESS:

Discount Stock Brokerage
Online Brokerage
Financial Planning
Clearing Services

BRANDS/DIVISIONS/AFFILIATES:

Charles Schwab Corporation (The)
TD Ameritrade Inc
TD Ameritrade Clearing Inc

CONTACTS: Note: Officers with more than one job title may be intentionally listed here more than once.

Jon C. Peterson, Interim CFO
Timothy Hockey, Director
Thomas Nally, Executive VP, Divisional
Steven Quirk, Executive VP, Divisional
Peter deSilva, Executive VP, Divisional
Ellen Koplow, Executive VP

GROWTH PLANS/SPECIAL FEATURES:

TD Ameritrade Holding Corporation and its subsidiaries provide securities brokerage services and technology-based financial services to retail investors and independent registered investment advisors. The company provides its services through online, telephone, branch and mobile channels. Products and services include: common and preferred stock, purchasing common and preferred stocks, American Depository Receipts and closed-end funds traded on any U.S. exchange or quotation system; exchange-traded funds (ETFs), offering ETFs from leading providers; mutual funds, from a portfolio of mutual funds from leading fund families; options, offering a range of option trades; futures, in a wide variety of commodities, stock indices and currencies; foreign exchange, with access to trading in over 75 different currency pairs; fixed income, offering a variety of Treasury, corporate, government agency and municipal bonds as well as certificates of deposit; annuities, both fixed and variable; education, offering a suite of free education for beginner, intermediate and advanced investors that is designed to teach investors how to approach the selection process for investment securities and actively manage their investment portfolios; new and secondary issue securities, offering primary and secondary offerings of fixed income securities, closed-end funds, common stock and preferred stock; margin lending, extending credit to clients who maintain margin accounts; cash management services, via third-party banking relationships offering FDIC-insured deposit accounts and money market mutual funds to clients as cash sweep alternatives; and U.S. market access in Asia, offering Singapore and Hong Kong access to U.S. markets and the ability to trade stocks, ETFs, options, futures and options of futures. In October 2020, the firm was acquired by The Charles Schwab Corporation, and began operating as a wholly-owned subsidiary of Schwab. Primary subsidiaries of TD Ameritrade include TD Ameritrade, Inc. and TD Ameritrade Clearing, Inc.

FINANCIAL DATA: Note: Data for latest year may not have been available at press time.

In U.S. $	2020	2019	2018	2017	2016	2015
Revenue	5,989,440,000	5,872,000,000	5,342,000,128	3,604,999,936	3,273,999,872	3,211,000,064
R&D Expense						
Operating Income						
Operating Margin %						
SGA Expense						
Net Income	2,252,160,000	2,208,000,000	1,472,999,936	872,000,000	842,000,000	813,000,000
Operating Cash Flow						
Capital Expenditure						
EBITDA						
Return on Assets %						
Return on Equity %						
Debt to Equity						

CONTACT INFORMATION:

Phone: 402 331-7856   Fax:
Toll-Free: 800-237-8692
Address: 200 S. 108th Ave., Omaha, NE 68154 United States

SALARIES/BONUSES:

Top Exec. Salary: $ Bonus: $
Second Exec. Salary: $ Bonus: $

STOCK TICKER/OTHER:

Stock Ticker: Subsidiary   Exchange:
Employees: 9,226   Fiscal Year Ends: 09/30
Parent Company: Charles Schwab Corporation (The)

OTHER THOUGHTS:

Estimated Female Officers or Directors: 4
Hot Spot for Advancement for Women/Minorities: Y

Tech Data Corporation

www.techdata.com

NAIC Code: 423430

TYPES OF BUSINESS:

Computer & Software Products, Distribution
Training
Assembly Services
Information Technology
Logistics

BRANDS/DIVISIONS/AFFILIATES:

DLT Solutions
Apollo Global Management
Innovix Distribution

CONTACTS: Note: Officers with more than one job title may be intentionally listed here more than once.

Richard Hume, CEO
Charles Dannewitz, CFO
Robert Dutkowsky, Chairman of the Board
Michael Rabinovitch, Chief Accounting Officer
John Tonnison, Chief Information Officer
David Vetter, Chief Legal Officer
Bonnie Smith, CIO
Beth Simonetti, Executive VP
Joseph Quaglia, President, Geographical
Patrick Zammit, President, Geographical

GROWTH PLANS/SPECIAL FEATURES:

Tech Data Corporation is a worldwide distributor of information technology (IT) products, logistics management and other value-added services. The company serves more than 125,000 value-added resellers (VARs), direct marketers, retailers and corporate resellers in over 100 countries throughout North America, South America, Europe, the Middle East and Africa. Products are typically purchased directly from manufacturers or software publishers on a non-exclusive basis and then shipped to customers from one of Tech Data's 20+ strategically-located logistics centers. The company's vendor agreements do not restrict it from selling similar products manufactured by competitors. The firm also provides resellers with extensive pre- and post-sale training, service and support as well as configuration and assembly services and e-commerce tools. Tech Data provides products and services to the online reseller channel and does business with thousands of resellers through its website. The firm's entire electronic catalog is available online, and its electronic software distribution initiative allows resellers and vendors to easily access software titles directly from a secure location on the website. In June of 2020, Tech Data Corporation was acquired by Apollo Global Management. After the announcement Tech Data Corporation revealed plans to invest $750 million in digital transformation initiatives over the next five years. In September 2020, the firm completed its acquisition of Innovix Distribution, a technology distributor in Asia.

FINANCIAL DATA: Note: Data for latest year may not have been available at press time.

In U.S. $	2020	2019	2018	2017	2016	2015
Revenue		37,238,951,936	36,775,010,304	26,234,875,904	26,379,782,144	27,670,632,448
R&D Expense						
Operating Income						
Operating Margin %						
SGA Expense						
Net Income		340,580,000	116,641,000	195,095,008	265,736,000	175,172,000
Operating Cash Flow						
Capital Expenditure						
EBITDA						
Return on Assets %						
Return on Equity %						
Debt to Equity						

CONTACT INFORMATION:

Phone: 727 539-7429   Fax: 727 538-7808
Toll-Free: 800-237-8931
Address: 5350 Tech Data Dr., Clearwater, FL 33760 United States

STOCK TICKER/OTHER:

Stock Ticker: TECD
Employees: 15,000
Parent Company: Apollo Global Management

Exchange: NAS
Fiscal Year Ends: 01/31

SALARIES/BONUSES:

Top Exec. Salary: $ Bonus: $
Second Exec. Salary: $ Bonus: $

OTHER THOUGHTS:

Estimated Female Officers or Directors: 1
Hot Spot for Advancement for Women/Minorities:

Tellabs Inc

www.tellabs.com

NAIC Code: 334210

TYPES OF BUSINESS:

Wireline & Wireless Products & Services
Consulting

BRANDS/DIVISIONS/AFFILIATES:

Marlin Equity Partners LLC

CONTACTS: *Note: Officers with more than one job title may be intentionally listed here more than once.*

Rich Schroder, CEO
Norm Burke, CFO
James M. Sheehan, Chief Admin. Officer
James M. Sheehan, General Counsel
John M. Brots, Exec. VP-Global Oper.
Kenneth G. Craft, Exec. VP-Product Dev.

GROWTH PLANS/SPECIAL FEATURES:

Tellabs, Inc. provides products and services that enable customers to deliver wireline and wireless voice, data and video services to business and residential customers. It operates in two segments: enterprise and broadband. The enterprise segment offers a passive optical local area network (LAN) infrastructure, which is secure, scalable and sustainable. This division serves the business enterprise, federal government, hospitality, higher education, K-12 education, healthcare and transportation industries. The broadband segment offers solutions to service providers that deliver stability and scalability while increasing flexibility. These broadband solutions help telecommunications companies grow HSI (high-speed internet) subscribers, extend service area coverage and offer faster internet service speeds. They also enable Ethernet business services while continuing to support time-division multiplexing (TDM) and automated teller machine (ATM) services. Tellabs offers services such as technical support, professional network services and training. Tellabs is a subsidiary of Marlin Equity Partners, LLC.

FINANCIAL DATA: *Note: Data for latest year may not have been available at press time.*

In U.S. $	2020	2019	2018	2017	2016	2015
Revenue	1,610,256,375	1,533,577,500	1,460,550,000	1,391,000,000	1,372,000,000	1,375,000,000
R&D Expense						
Operating Income						
Operating Margin %						
SGA Expense						
Net Income						
Operating Cash Flow						
Capital Expenditure						
EBITDA						
Return on Assets %						
Return on Equity %						
Debt to Equity						

CONTACT INFORMATION:

Phone: 972-588-7000   Fax:
Toll-Free:
Address: 4240 International Pkwy, St. 105, Carrollton, TX 75007 United States

STOCK TICKER/OTHER:

Stock Ticker: Private
Employees: 9,400
Parent Company: Marlin Equity Partners LLC

Exchange:
Fiscal Year Ends: 12/31

SALARIES/BONUSES:

Top Exec. Salary: $ Bonus: $
Second Exec. Salary: $ Bonus: $

OTHER THOUGHTS:

Estimated Female Officers or Directors: 1
Hot Spot for Advancement for Women/Minorities: Y

Terex Corporation

NAIC Code: 333120

TYPES OF BUSINESS:

Heavy Equipment
Cranes
Mining Equipment
Aerial Work Platforms
Road Building Equipment
Utility Products
Construction Equipment
Materials Handling Equipment

BRANDS/DIVISIONS/AFFILIATES:

Terex Financial Services
Murray Design & Engineering Ltd

CONTACTS: Note: Officers with more than one job title may be intentionally listed here more than once.

John Garrison, CEO
John Sheehan, CFO
Mark Clair, Chief Accounting Officer
Eric Cohen, General Counsel
Kieran Hegarty, President, Divisional
Matthew Fearon, President, Divisional
Stoyan Filipov, President, Divisional
Kevin Barr, Senior VP, Divisional
Brian Henry, Senior VP, Divisional

GROWTH PLANS/SPECIAL FEATURES:

Terex Corporation is a global manufacturer of lifting and materials processing products. The company operates through two business segments: aerial work platforms and materials processing. The aerial work platforms segment designs, manufactures, services and markets aerial work platform equipment, telehandlers, light towers and utility equipment, as well as their related components and replacement parts. Customers use these to: construct and maintain industrial, commercial and residential buildings and facilities; maintain utility and telecommunication lines, tree trimming, and certain construction and foundation drilling applications; and for other commercial and infrastructure projects. The materials processing segment designs, manufactures and markets materials processing and specialty equipment, including crushers, washing systems, screens, apron feeders, material handlers, pick and carry cranes, wood processing, biomass and recycling equipment, concrete mixer trucks, concrete pavers, conveyors and their related components and replacement parts. Customers use these products in: construction, infrastructure and recycling projects; various quarrying and mining applications; landscaping and biomass production; material handling applications; maintenance applications to lift equipment and material; and building roads and bridges. In addition, subsidiary Terex Financial Services offers financial products and services to assist in the acquisition of Terex equipment. In mid-2021, Terex acquired Murray Design & Engineering Ltd., a manufacturer of heavy-duty aggregate and recycling trommels, apron feeders and conveyor systems, based in Ireland.

FINANCIAL DATA: Note: Data for latest year may not have been available at press time.

In U.S. $	2020	2019	2018	2017	2016	2015
Revenue	3,076,400,000	4,353,100,000	5,125,000,000	4,363,400,000	4,443,100,000	6,543,100,000
R&D Expense						
Operating Income	68,400,000	335,000,000	293,300,000	173,600,000	28,200,000	389,900,000
Operating Margin %		.08%	.06%	.04%	.01%	.06%
SGA Expense	470,900,000	552,800,000	673,500,000	642,400,000	684,200,000	918,600,000
Net Income	-10,600,000	54,400,000	113,700,000	128,700,000	-176,100,000	145,900,000
Operating Cash Flow	225,400,000	173,400,000	94,200,000	153,000,000	367,000,000	212,900,000
Capital Expenditure	64,500,000	108,900,000	103,800,000	43,500,000	73,000,000	103,800,000
EBITDA	126,600,000	385,000,000	281,500,000	246,000,000	-72,000,000	459,400,000
Return on Assets %		.02%	.03%	.03%	-.03%	.03%
Return on Equity %		.06%	.11%	.10%	-.10%	.08%
Debt to Equity		1.254	1.412	0.802	1.052	0.933

CONTACT INFORMATION:

Phone: 203 222-7170   Fax: 203 222-7976
Toll-Free:
Address: 45 Glover Ave., Fl. 4, Norwalk, CT 06850 United States

SALARIES/BONUSES:

Top Exec. Salary: $ Bonus: $
Second Exec. Salary: $ Bonus: $

STOCK TICKER/OTHER:

Stock Ticker: TEX   Exchange: NYS
Employees: 8,200   Fiscal Year Ends: 12/31
Parent Company:

OTHER THOUGHTS:

Estimated Female Officers or Directors: 1
Hot Spot for Advancement for Women/Minorities:

Tesla Inc

NAIC Code: 336111

www.teslamotors.com

TYPES OF BUSINESS:

Automobile Manufacturing, All-Electric
Battery Manufacturing
Lithium Ion Battery Storage Technologies
Energy Storage Systems
Automobile Manufacturing
Electric Vehicles

BRANDS/DIVISIONS/AFFILIATES:

Model S
Model X
Model 3
Model Y
Roadster
Tesla Semi
Tesla Cybertruck
Gigafactory

CONTACTS: *Note: Officers with more than one job title may be intentionally listed here more than once.*

Elon Musk, CEO
Zachary Kirkhorn, CFO
Vaibhav Taneja, Chief Accounting Officer
Jeffrey Straubel, Chief Technology Officer
Jerome Guillen, President, Divisional

GROWTH PLANS/SPECIAL FEATURES:

Tesla, Inc. manufactures high-performance, all-electric automobiles and energy storage products. The Model S features a lightweight aluminum body and has a 335-mile range, as well as 360-degree cameras for maximum visibility. The Model X sport utility vehicle has a 295-mile range and room to seat up to seven adult passengers. The Model 3 is an all-wheel drive vehicle with a 310-mile range. Model Y has up to three rows of seats (up to seven people) and a range of up to 300 miles. The Roadster (second generation), slated for 2022 production, will have a 620-mile range and will achieve 0-60 miles per haour in 1.9 seconds and 0-100 mph in 4.2 seconds. The Tesla Semi (was due for release in 2021) is a commercial truck that goes from 0-60 mph in 20 seconds. The Tesla Cybertruck is a pickup truck due for a 2022 release and is made of steel. Battery-wise, each Tesla car has thousands of small, lithium-ion batteries linked together, similar to the batteries found in consumer electronics. The firm's network of car charging stations can fully-charge a Tesla in 75 minutes and are located in North America, Europe and Asia; but Tesla vehicles can be charged anywhere with standard equipment and convenient options. In addition to vehicles, Tesla manufactures solar panels and solar roofs for converting sunlight into energy; manufactures an easy-to-install home-sized energy storage system intended to store local, solar-generated power for later use; and manufactures a giant battery designed for commercial and utility purposes. The company comprises a Gigafactory is in Reno, Nevada, USA and in Shanghai, China. Gigafactories under construction (as of mid-2021) are located in Berlin, Germany and Austin, Texas, USA.

FINANCIAL DATA: *Note: Data for latest year may not have been available at press time.*

In U.S. $	2020	2019	2018	2017	2016	2015
Revenue	31,536,000,000	24,578,000,000	21,461,270,000	11,758,750,000	7,000,132,000	4,046,025,000
R&D Expense	1,491,000,000	1,343,000,000	1,460,370,000	1,378,073,000	834,408,000	717,900,000
Operating Income	1,994,000,000	80,000,000	-252,840,000	-1,632,086,000	-667,340,000	-716,629,000
Operating Margin %		.00%	-.01%	-.14%	-.10%	-.18%
SGA Expense	3,145,000,000	2,646,000,000	2,834,491,000	2,476,500,000	1,432,189,000	922,232,000
Net Income	690,000,000	-862,000,000	-976,091,000	-1,961,400,000	-674,914,000	-888,663,000
Operating Cash Flow	5,943,000,000	2,405,000,000	2,097,802,000	-60,654,000	-123,829,000	-524,499,000
Capital Expenditure	3,242,000,000	1,437,000,000	2,319,516,000	4,081,354,000	1,440,471,000	1,634,850,000
EBITDA	4,224,000,000	2,174,000,000	1,559,376,000	-101,770,000	399,561,000	-334,183,000
Return on Assets %		-.03%	-.03%	-.08%	-.04%	-.13%
Return on Equity %		-.15%	-.21%	-.44%	-.23%	-.89%
Debt to Equity		1.902	2.248	2.616	1.536	1.912

CONTACT INFORMATION:

Phone: 650 681-5000   Fax:
Toll-Free:
Address: 3500 Deer Creek Rd., Palo Alto, CA 94304 United States

STOCK TICKER/OTHER:

Stock Ticker: TSLA   Exchange: NAS
Employees: 70,757   Fiscal Year Ends: 12/31
Parent Company:

SALARIES/BONUSES:

Top Exec. Salary: $ Bonus: $
Second Exec. Salary: $ Bonus: $

OTHER THOUGHTS:

Estimated Female Officers or Directors: 1
Hot Spot for Advancement for Women/Minorities:

Texas Instruments Incorporated

www.ti.com

NAIC Code: 334413

TYPES OF BUSINESS:

Chips-Digital Signal Processors
Semiconductors
Calculators
Educational Software
Power Management Products
Broadband RF/IF & Digital Radio
MEMS
Microcontrollers (MCU)

BRANDS/DIVISIONS/AFFILIATES:

CONTACTS: Note: Officers with more than one job title may be intentionally listed here more than once.

Richard Templeton, CEO
Rafael Lizardi, CFO
Ahmad Bahai, Senior VP
Hagop Kozanian, Senior VP
Kyle Flessner, Senior VP
Niels Anderskouv, Senior VP
Bing Xie, Senior VP
R. Delagi, Senior VP
Darla Whitaker, Senior VP
Julie Van Haren, Senior VP
Haviv Ilan, Senior VP
Ellen Barker, Senior VP
Cynthia Trochu, Senior VP

GROWTH PLANS/SPECIAL FEATURES:

Texas Instruments Incorporated (TI), founded in 1930, is a global designer and manufacturer of semiconductors, serving 100,000 customers worldwide. The firm has 14 manufacturing sites, with 10 wafer fabrications, seven assembly and test factories, and multiple bump and probe facilities. TI operates in three segments: analog, embedded processing and other. Analog semiconductors change real-world signals, such as sound, temperature, pressure or images, by conditioning them, amplifying them and often converting them to a stream of digital data that can be processed by other semiconductors, such as embedded processors. Analog semiconductors are also used to manage power in every electronic device, whether plugged into a wall or running off a battery. Product lines include power supply controls, switches, interfaces, protection devices, high-voltage products, mobile lighting, display products, signal chain products, and high-volume integrated analog and standard products. Embedded processors are designed to handle specific tasks and can be optimized for various combinations of performance, power and cost, depending on the application. The devices vary from simple, low-cost products used in electric toothbrushes to highly specialized, complex devices used in wireless base station communications infrastructure equipment. Products include processors, microcontrollers and connectivity. Last, the other division includes semiconductors such as the firm's proprietary digital light processing (DLP) optical semiconductor products, which enable clear video and microprocessors that serve as the brains of everything from high-end computer servers to high-definition televisions (HDTVs). This segment also includes educational products, such as handheld graphing calculators, business calculators and scientific calculators as well as a wide range of advanced classroom tools and professional development resources, including educational software.

FINANCIAL DATA: Note: Data for latest year may not have been available at press time.

In U.S. $	2020	2019	2018	2017	2016	2015
Revenue	14,461,000,000	14,383,000,000	15,784,000,000	14,961,000,000	13,370,000,000	13,000,000,000
R&D Expense	1,530,000,000	1,544,000,000	1,559,000,000	1,508,000,000	1,370,000,000	1,280,000,000
Operating Income	6,116,000,000	5,975,000,000	7,034,000,000	6,531,000,000	5,103,000,000	4,532,000,000
Operating Margin %		.42%	.45%	.44%	.38%	.35%
SGA Expense	1,623,000,000	1,645,000,000	1,684,000,000	1,694,000,000	1,767,000,000	1,748,000,000
Net Income	5,595,000,000	5,017,000,000	5,580,000,000	3,682,000,000	3,595,000,000	2,986,000,000
Operating Cash Flow	6,139,000,000	6,649,000,000	7,189,000,000	5,363,000,000	4,614,000,000	4,268,000,000
Capital Expenditure	649,000,000	847,000,000	1,131,000,000	695,000,000	531,000,000	551,000,000
EBITDA	7,199,000,000	6,948,000,000	7,765,000,000	7,062,000,000	5,965,000,000	5,439,000,000
Return on Assets %		.29%	.32%	.21%	.22%	.17%
Return on Equity %		.56%	.57%	.35%	.35%	.29%
Debt to Equity		0.624	0.48	0.346	0.284	0.314

CONTACT INFORMATION:

Phone: 972 995-3773   Fax: 972 995-4360
Toll-Free: 800-336-5236
Address: 12500 TI Blvd., Dallas, TX 75266-0199 United States

SALARIES/BONUSES:

Top Exec. Salary: $ Bonus: $
Second Exec. Salary: $ Bonus: $

STOCK TICKER/OTHER:

Stock Ticker: TXN
Employees: 30,000
Parent Company:

Exchange: NAS
Fiscal Year Ends: 12/31

OTHER THOUGHTS:

Estimated Female Officers or Directors: 3
Hot Spot for Advancement for Women/Minorities: Y

Sales, profits and employees may be estimates. Financial information, benefits and other data can change quickly and may vary from those stated here.

Textron Inc

NAIC Code: 336411

www.textron.com

TYPES OF BUSINESS:

Helicopters & General Aviation Aircraft Manufacturing
Aerospace
Electrical Test & Measurement Equipment
Fiber Optic Equipment
Off-Road Vehicles
Financing

BRANDS/DIVISIONS/AFFILIATES:

Bell Helicopter Textron Inc
Textron Systems
Textron Aviation
TRU Simulation + Training Inc
Textron Specialized Vehicles Inc
Beechcraft
Cessna
Response Technologies LLC

CONTACTS: Note: Officers with more than one job title may be intentionally listed here more than once.

Scott Donnelly, CEO
Frank Connor, CFO
Mark Bamford, Chief Accounting Officer
Julie Duffy, Executive VP, Divisional
Robert Lupone, Executive VP

GROWTH PLANS/SPECIAL FEATURES:

Textron, Inc. is a multi-industry company active in the aircraft, defense, industrial and finance industries. The company operates through five core subsidiaries: Bell Helicopter Textron Inc., Textron Systems, Textron Aviation, TRU Simulation + Training Inc., and Textron Specialized Vehicles Inc. Bell Helicopter supplies helicopters, tilt rotor aircraft and helicopter-related spare parts and services for military and commercial applications. It also offers commercially-certified helicopters to corporate; offshore petroleum exploration; utility; charter; and police, fire, rescue and emergency medical helicopter operators. This segment also offers support and services for their vehicles. Textron Systems manufactures weapons systems and surveillance and intelligence products for the defense, aerospace, homeland security and general aviation markets. It sells most of its products to U.S. government customers, but also to customers outside the U.S. through foreign military sales sponsored by the U.S. government and directly through commercial sales channels. Textron Aviation is home to the Beechcraft and Cessna brands, which account for more than half of all general aviation aircraft flying. Its product portfolio includes five business lines: business jets, general aviation and special mission turboprop aircraft, high performance piston aircraft, military trainer and defense aircraft and a customer service organization. TRU Simulation designs, develops, manufactures, installs and provides maintenance of flight training devices, including full-flight simulators (rotary- and fixed-wing) for commercial airlines, aircraft original equipment manufacturers, flight training centers and training organizations worldwide. Textron Specialized Vehicles designs, manufactures and sells golf cars, off-road utility vehicles, recreational side-by-side and all-terrain vehicles, snowmobiles, light transportation vehicles, aviation ground support equipment and professional turf-maintenance equipment, among other vehicles. In late-2020, Textron agreed to sell certain non-U.S. businesses within TRU Simulation + Training, Inc. to CAE, Inc.; and acquired Response Technologies, LLC, a composite solutions and fuel cell company, which was merged into Bell Textron.

Textron offers its employees comprehensive benefits.

FINANCIAL DATA: Note: Data for latest year may not have been available at press time.

In U.S. $	2020	2019	2018	2017	2016	2015
Revenue	11,651,000,000	13,630,000,000	13,972,000,000	14,198,000,000	13,788,000,000	13,423,000,000
R&D Expense						
Operating Income	512,000,000	1,072,000,000	1,103,000,000	1,066,000,000	1,173,000,000	1,140,000,000
Operating Margin %		.08%	.08%	.08%	.09%	.08%
SGA Expense	1,045,000,000	1,152,000,000	1,275,000,000	1,337,000,000	1,304,000,000	1,304,000,000
Net Income	309,000,000	815,000,000	1,222,000,000	307,000,000	962,000,000	697,000,000
Operating Cash Flow	768,000,000	1,014,000,000	1,107,000,000	953,000,000	1,012,000,000	1,090,000,000
Capital Expenditure	317,000,000	339,000,000	369,000,000	423,000,000	446,000,000	420,000,000
EBITDA	839,000,000	1,529,000,000	1,987,000,000	1,383,000,000	1,499,000,000	1,601,000,000
Return on Assets %		.06%	.08%	.02%	.06%	.05%
Return on Equity %		.15%	.23%	.05%	.18%	.15%
Debt to Equity		0.589	0.679	0.69	0.595	0.674

CONTACT INFORMATION:

Phone: 401 421-2800   Fax: 401 421-2878
Toll-Free:
Address: 40 Westminster St., Providence, RI 02903 United States

STOCK TICKER/OTHER:

Stock Ticker: TXT   Exchange: NYS
Employees: 35,000   Fiscal Year Ends: 12/31
Parent Company:

SALARIES/BONUSES:

Top Exec. Salary: $ Bonus: $
Second Exec. Salary: $ Bonus: $

OTHER THOUGHTS:

Estimated Female Officers or Directors: 10
Hot Spot for Advancement for Women/Minorities: Y

Sales, profits and employees may be estimates. Financial information, benefits and other data can change quickly and may vary from those stated here.

Thermo Fisher Scientific Inc

www.thermofisher.com

NAIC Code: 423450

TYPES OF BUSINESS:

Laboratory Equipment & Supplies Distribution
Contract Manufacturing
Equipment Calibration & Repair
Clinical Trial Services
Laboratory Workstations
Clinical Consumables
Diagnostic Reagents
Custom Chemical Synthesis

BRANDS/DIVISIONS/AFFILIATES:

Thermo Scientific
Applied Biosystems
Invitrogen
Fisher Scientific
Unity Lab Services
Patheon
TaqPath

CONTACTS: Note: Officers with more than one job title may be intentionally listed here more than once.

Marc Casper, CEO
Jim Manzi, Chairman of the Board
Mark Stevenson, COO
Michael Boxer, General Counsel
Gregory Herrema, President, Divisional
Patrick Durbin, President, Divisional
Michel Lagarde, President, Divisional
Stephen Williamson, Senior VP
Peter Hornstra, Vice President

GROWTH PLANS/SPECIAL FEATURES:

Thermo Fisher Scientific, Inc. is a distributor of products and services principally to the scientific-research and clinical laboratory markets. The firm serves over 400,000 customers including biotechnology and pharmaceutical companies; colleges and universities; medical-research institutions; hospitals; reference, quality control, process-control and research and development labs in various industries; as well as government agencies. It operates in four segments: life sciences solutions, analytical instruments, specialty diagnostics and laboratory products and services. Life sciences solutions provides a portfolio of reagents, instruments and consumables used in biological and medical research, discover and production of new drugs and vaccines. This division also provides diagnosis of disease. Analytical instruments provides a broad offering of instruments, consumables, software and services used for a range of applications in the laboratory, on the production line and in the field. These products are used by customers in pharmaceutical, biotechnology, academic, government, environmental, research, industrial markets, as well as clinical laboratories. Specialty diagnostics offers a range of diagnostic test kits, reagents, culture media, instruments and associated products in order to serve customers in healthcare, clinical, pharmaceutical, industrial and food safety laboratories. Laboratory products and services offers everything needed for the laboratory. This segment's products are used primarily for drug discovery and development, as well as for life science research. The company's primary brands include Thermo Scientific, Applied Biosystems, Invitrogen, Fisher Scientific, Unity Lab Services and Patheon. In August 2021, Thermo Fisher Scientific announced that the U.S. Food and Drug Administration granted emergency use authorization for its TaqPath COVID-19 Fast PCR Combo Kit 2.0 and the TaqPath COVID-19 RNase P Combo Kit 2.0, both highly accurate assays designed with increased targe redundancy to compensate for current mutations and emerging SARS-CoV-2 variants.

Employees receive comprehensive benefits.

FINANCIAL DATA: Note: Data for latest year may not have been available at press time.

In U.S. $	2020	2019	2018	2017	2016	2015
Revenue	32,218,000,000	25,542,000,000	24,358,000,000	20,918,000,000	18,274,100,000	16,965,400,000
R&D Expense	1,181,000,000	1,003,000,000	967,000,000	888,000,000	754,800,000	692,300,000
Operating Income	7,893,000,000	4,181,000,000	3,833,000,000	3,065,000,000	2,638,400,000	2,451,500,000
Operating Margin %		.16%	.16%	.15%	.14%	.14%
SGA Expense	6,930,000,000	6,144,000,000	6,057,000,000	5,492,000,000	4,975,900,000	4,612,100,000
Net Income	6,375,000,000	3,696,000,000	2,938,000,000	2,225,000,000	2,021,800,000	1,975,400,000
Operating Cash Flow	8,289,000,000	4,973,000,000	4,543,000,000	4,005,000,000	3,156,300,000	2,816,900,000
Capital Expenditure	1,474,000,000	926,000,000	758,000,000	508,000,000	444,400,000	422,900,000
EBITDA	10,103,000,000	7,023,000,000	6,196,000,000	5,054,000,000	4,251,500,000	4,039,500,000
Return on Assets %		.06%	.05%	.04%	.05%	.05%
Return on Equity %		.13%	.11%	.09%	.09%	.09%
Debt to Equity		0.575	0.642	0.743	0.714	0.537

CONTACT INFORMATION:

Phone: 781 622-1000   Fax: 781 933-4476
Toll-Free: 800-678-5599
Address: 168 Third Ave., Waltham, MA 02451 United States

SALARIES/BONUSES:

Top Exec. Salary: $ Bonus: $
Second Exec. Salary: $ Bonus: $

STOCK TICKER/OTHER:

Stock Ticker: TMO
Employees: 80,000
Parent Company:

Exchange: NYS
Fiscal Year Ends: 12/31

OTHER THOUGHTS:

Estimated Female Officers or Directors: 1
Hot Spot for Advancement for Women/Minorities: Y

Thor Industries Inc
NAIC Code: 336214

www.thorindustries.com

TYPES OF BUSINESS:
Recreational Vehicle Manufacturing
Motor Homes
Automotive Parts & Accessories
Recreational Vehicles

BRANDS/DIVISIONS/AFFILIATES:
Airstream
CrossRoads Recreational Vehicles
Dutchmen
Entegra Coach
Erwin Hymer Group
Highland Ridge RV
Starcraft
Thor Motor Coach

CONTACTS: Note: Officers with more than one job title may be intentionally listed here more than once.
Robert Martin, CEO
Colleen Zuhl, CFO
Peter Orthwein, Chairman of the Board
W. Woelfer, General Counsel
Kenneth Julian, Senior VP, Divisional

GROWTH PLANS/SPECIAL FEATURES:
Thor Industries, Inc. is a leading manufacturer of a wide range of recreational vehicles (RVs). The company's branded subsidiaries include Airstream, CrossRoads Recreational Vehicles, Cruiser RV, DRV Luxury Suites, Dutchmen, Entegra Coach, Erwin Hymer Group, Heartland Recreational Vehicles, Highland Ridge RV, Hymer USA, Jayco, Keystone RV Company, KZ Recreational Vehicles, Redwood Recreational Vehicles, Starcraft, Thor Motor Coach, and Venture RV. Other companies of Thor include Roadtrippers, TOGO RV and Postle Aluminum Co. Together these businesses produce towable RVs, which account for approximately 70% of annual net sales, as well as motorized RVs, which account for 30% of sales. Towable RVs include conventional travel trailers, fifth wheels and park models; truck and folding campers; and equestrian and other specialty towable vehicles. Park models are recreational dwellings towed to a permanent site such as a lake, woods or park, with the maximum size of park models in the U.S. being 400 square feet. Motorized RVs include Class A, B and C motorhomes, which are self-powered vehicles built on a chassis and self-contained with their own lighting, heating, cooking, refrigeration, sewage holding and water storage facilities. Thor also manufactures and sells related parts and accessories. In December 2020, Thor announced it acquired luxury RV manufacturer Tiffin Motorhomes. And in September 2021, Thor announced it had acquired Airxcel, a leading supplier of original equipment manufacturers (OEMs) and aftermarket RV parts and accessories.

FINANCIAL DATA: Note: Data for latest year may not have been available at press time.

In U.S. $	2020	2019	2018	2017	2016	2015
Revenue	8,167,933,000	7,864,758,000	8,328,909,000	7,246,952,000	4,582,112,000	4,006,819,000
R&D Expense						
Operating Income	386,854,000	361,412,000	632,104,000	559,811,000	392,094,000	290,639,000
Operating Margin %		.05%	.08%	.08%	.09%	.07%
SGA Expense	634,119,000	536,044,000	477,444,000	419,847,000	306,269,000	250,891,000
Net Income	222,974,000	133,275,000	430,151,000	374,254,000	256,519,000	199,385,000
Operating Cash Flow	540,941,000	508,019,000	466,508,000	419,333,000	341,209,000	247,860,000
Capital Expenditure	106,697,000	130,224,000	138,197,000	115,027,000	51,976,000	42,283,000
EBITDA	576,385,000	401,555,000	731,439,000	664,374,000	437,480,000	324,456,000
Return on Assets %		.03%	.16%	.15%	.13%	.14%
Return on Equity %		.07%	.24%	.26%	.22%	.20%
Debt to Equity		0.904		0.092	0.285	

CONTACT INFORMATION:
Phone: 574-970-7460   Fax:
Toll-Free:
Address: 601 E. Beardsley Ave., Elkhart, IN 46514-3305 United States

STOCK TICKER/OTHER:
Stock Ticker: THO
Employees: 22,250
Parent Company:

Exchange: NYS
Fiscal Year Ends: 07/31

SALARIES/BONUSES:
Top Exec. Salary: $ Bonus: $
Second Exec. Salary: $ Bonus: $

OTHER THOUGHTS:
Estimated Female Officers or Directors:
Hot Spot for Advancement for Women/Minorities:

TIAA
NAIC Code: 523920

www.tiaa-cref.org

TYPES OF BUSINESS:
Investment Management
Retirement & Supplemental Retirement Plans
College Savings Plans
Mutual Funds
Annuities & Pension Funds
Trust Services
Life Insurance

BRANDS/DIVISIONS/AFFILIATES:
TIAA Bank
TIAA FSB
TIAA-CREF Trust Company
Nuveen

CONTACTS: Note: Officers with more than one job title may be intentionally listed here more than once.
Roger Ferguson, CEO
Glenn Richter, Sr. VP
Marty Willis, Sr. VP
Sean Woodroffe, Sr. VP
Rahul Merchant, Exec. VP
Brandon Becker, Chief Legal Officer
Doug Chittenden, Exec. VP-Individual Bus.
Carol Deckbar, Exec. VP
Stephen B. Gruppo, Exec. VP-Risk Mgmt.
Teresa Hassara, Exec. VP-Institutional Bus.
Vijay Advani, Chmn.

GROWTH PLANS/SPECIAL FEATURES:
TIAA (Teachers Insurance and Annuity Association of America) is a nonprofit private retirement system. The firm has been in business for more than 100 years. TIAA's products include investment, banking/loans and insurance. TIAA also offers advisory and performance data services, and its asset management services and solutions are provided through the Nuveen division and brand name. Investment products include retirement plans, individual retirement accounts (IRAs), mutual funds, retirement annuities, brokerage/trading, 529 education savings and managed investment accounts, as well as TIAA's personal portfolio. Banking and loan products and services include interest-building checking accounts, money market, certificates of deposit (CDs), mortgage loans and home loans. These products and services are provided through TIAA Bank, a division of TIAA, FSB. TIAA's insurance products are life insurance, offering both term and permanent options. Performance data and advisory services are provided through TIAA-CREF Trust Company, which presents performance data quotes and activities in relation to mutual funds, fixed annuities, variable annuities and FDIC-insured products. Asset classes include guaranteed, equities, real estate, fixed income, money market, multi-asset and more. Nuveen manages $1.1 trillion in total assets, which are comprised of private capital, multi-assets, fixed-income, equities, real estate and real assets. Nuveen's clients include institutional investors such as corporations, public funds, insurance, Sovereign Wealth funds, endowments and foundations.

TIAA offers comprehensive benfits, retirement options and employee assistance programs.

FINANCIAL DATA: Note: Data for latest year may not have been available at press time.

In U.S. $	2020	2019	2018	2017	2016	2015
Revenue	32,661,000,000	30,305,000,000	30,910,000,000	32,000,000,000	30,797,000,000	26,857,000,000
R&D Expense						
Operating Income						
Operating Margin %						
SGA Expense						
Net Income	604,000,000	1,618,000,000	1,453,000,000	1,020,000,000	1,490,000,000	1,254,000,000
Operating Cash Flow						
Capital Expenditure						
EBITDA						
Return on Assets %						
Return on Equity %						
Debt to Equity						

CONTACT INFORMATION:
Phone: 212-490-9000   Fax: 212-916-4840
Toll-Free: 800-842-2252
Address: 730 Third Ave., New York, NY 10017 United States

SALARIES/BONUSES:
Top Exec. Salary: $ Bonus: $
Second Exec. Salary: $ Bonus: $

STOCK TICKER/OTHER:
Stock Ticker: Private
Employees: 12,997
Parent Company:

Exchange:
Fiscal Year Ends: 12/31

OTHER THOUGHTS:
Estimated Female Officers or Directors: 6
Hot Spot for Advancement for Women/Minorities: Y

T-Mobile US Inc

NAIC Code: 517210

www.t-mobile.com

TYPES OF BUSINESS:
Mobile Phone and Wireless Services
Wireless Services
Cellular
Mobile Devices
5G

BRANDS/DIVISIONS/AFFILIATES:
Deutsche Telekom AG
T-Mobile International AG
T-Mobile
Metro by T-Mobile
Sprint Corporation

CONTACTS: Note: Officers with more than one job title may be intentionally listed here more than once.
J. Carter, CFO
Timotheus Hottges, Chairman of the Board
Neville Ray, Chief Technology Officer
G. Sievert, COO
John Legere, Director
Peter Ewens, Executive VP, Divisional
Elizabeth McAuliffe, Executive VP, Divisional
David Carey, Executive VP, Divisional
David Miller, Executive VP
Thomas Keys, President, Subsidiary
Peter Osvaldik, Senior VP, Divisional

GROWTH PLANS/SPECIAL FEATURES:
T-Mobile US, Inc. (T-Mobile) is a national provider of wireless voice, messaging and data services, and is one of the largest cellular companies in America. T-Mobile's network is powered by its nationwide 4G long-term evolution (LTE) network, which covers more than 325 million consumers. The firm's 5G network covers 1.6 million square miles, 280 million people and 9,100 cities and towns across the U.S., Puerto Rico and the U.S. Virgin Islands. T-Mobile provides wireless services to 102.1 million postpaid, prepaid and wholesale customers. The company also sells a full range of devices and accessories across its flagship brands, including T-Mobile and Metro by T-Mobile, through its owned and operated retail stores, eCommerce websites, mobile app and customer care channels. Moreover, T-Mobile sells devices to dealers and other third-party distributors for resale through independent third-party retail outlets and a variety of third-party websites. T-Mobile operates as a subsidiary of T-Mobile International AG, which itself is the mobile communications subsidiary of Deutsche Telekom AG. During 2020, T-Mobile completed the acquisition of Sprint Corporation, creating a third giant wireless network operator to compete against AT&T, Inc. and Verizon Communications, Inc.

FINANCIAL DATA: Note: Data for latest year may not have been available at press time.

In U.S. $	2020	2019	2018	2017	2016	2015
Revenue	68,397,000,000	44,998,000,000	43,310,000,000	40,604,000,000	37,242,000,000	32,053,000,000
R&D Expense						
Operating Income	7,054,000,000	5,722,000,000	5,309,000,000	4,653,000,000	3,071,000,000	2,278,000,000
Operating Margin %		.13%	.12%	.11%	.08%	.07%
SGA Expense	18,926,000,000	14,139,000,000	13,161,000,000	12,259,000,000	11,378,000,000	10,189,000,000
Net Income	3,064,000,000	3,468,000,000	2,888,000,000	4,536,000,000	1,460,000,000	733,000,000
Operating Cash Flow	8,640,000,000	6,824,000,000	3,899,000,000	7,962,000,000	6,135,000,000	5,414,000,000
Capital Expenditure	12,367,000,000	7,358,000,000	5,668,000,000	11,065,000,000	8,670,000,000	6,659,000,000
EBITDA	20,411,000,000	12,354,000,000	11,760,000,000	10,816,000,000	10,300,000,000	7,162,000,000
Return on Assets %		.04%	.04%	.07%	.02%	.01%
Return on Equity %		.13%	.12%	.22%	.08%	.04%
Debt to Equity		0.793	1.08	0.537	1.197	1.237

CONTACT INFORMATION:
Phone: 425-378-4000   Fax: 425-378-4040
Toll-Free: 800-318-9270
Address: 12920 SE 38th St., Bellevue, WA 98006-1350 United States

STOCK TICKER/OTHER:
Stock Ticker: TMUS
Employees: 50,000
Parent Company: Deutsche Telekom AG

Exchange: NAS
Fiscal Year Ends: 12/31

SALARIES/BONUSES:
Top Exec. Salary: $ Bonus: $
Second Exec. Salary: $ Bonus: $

OTHER THOUGHTS:
Estimated Female Officers or Directors:
Hot Spot for Advancement for Women/Minorities:

Toll Brothers Inc

www.tollbrothers.com

NAIC Code: 236117

TYPES OF BUSINESS:

Construction, Home Building and Residential
Mortgages & Insurance
Property Management
Landscaping
Country Club Communities
Golf Courses
Security Monitoring
Lumber Distribution

BRANDS/DIVISIONS/AFFILIATES:

Keller Homes

CONTACTS: Note: Officers with more than one job title may be intentionally listed here more than once.

Douglas Yearley, CEO
Martin Connor, CFO
Robert Toll, Chairman Emeritus
Richard Hartman, COO
Michael Grubb, Senior VP

GROWTH PLANS/SPECIAL FEATURES:

Toll Brothers, Inc. designs, builds, markets and arranges financing for single-family detached and attached homes in luxury residential communities. The firm is also involved, both directly and through joint ventures, in building or converting existing rental apartment buildings into high-, mid- and low-rise luxury homes. Toll Brothers markets its services to move-up, empty-nester, active-adult, age-qualified and second-home buyers through its operations in more than 20 U.S. states. The company is present in major suburban and urban residential areas including the: Eastern Region, encompassing Connecticut, Delaware, Illinois, Massachusetts, Michigan, Pennsylvania, New Jersey, New York, Georgia, Maryland, North Carolina, Tennessee, Virginia, Florida, South Carolina and Texas; and Western Region, encompassing Arizona, Colorado, Idaho, Nevada, Utah, California, Oregon and Washington. The average selling price of the company's homes was more than $873,000 in 2019, up from $864,300 in 2018. Toll Brothers operates its own land development, architectural, engineering, mortgage, title, landscaping, lumber distribution, house component assembly and manufacturing operations. In addition, the company owns and operates golf courses in conjunction with several of its master planned communities. The company operates a portfolio of communities with approximately 62,000 total homes sites. In 2020, Toll Brothers announced it had acquired Keller Homes, a private home building company based in Colorado Springs.

Toll Brothers offers its employees medical, dental and vision plans, life and disability insurance, 401(k), employee stock purchase plan, adoption assistance, and a variety of company perks.

FINANCIAL DATA: Note: Data for latest year may not have been available at press time.

In U.S. $	2020	2019	2018	2017	2016	2015
Revenue	7,077,659,000	7,223,966,000	7,143,258,000	5,815,058,000	5,169,508,000	4,171,248,000
R&D Expense						
Operating Income	550,260,000	680,800,000	795,153,000	650,737,000	495,927,000	452,094,000
Operating Margin %		.10%	.11%	.11%	.10%	.11%
SGA Expense	867,442,000	734,548,000	684,035,000	607,819,000	535,382,000	455,108,000
Net Income	446,624,000	590,007,000	748,151,000	535,495,000	382,095,000	363,167,000
Operating Cash Flow	1,008,117,000	437,661,000	602,401,000	959,719,000	148,771,000	60,182,000
Capital Expenditure	109,564,000	86,971,000	28,232,000	28,872,000	28,426,000	9,447,000
EBITDA	658,214,000	752,949,000	820,412,000	676,098,000	519,048,000	475,651,000
Return on Assets %		.06%	.08%	.06%	.04%	.04%
Return on Equity %		.12%	.16%	.12%	.09%	.09%
Debt to Equity		0.773	0.777	0.711	0.893	0.898

CONTACT INFORMATION:

Phone: 215 938-8000   Fax: 215 938-8023
Toll-Free:
Address: 250 Gibraltar Rd., Horsham, PA 19044 United States

SALARIES/BONUSES:

Top Exec. Salary: $ Bonus: $
Second Exec. Salary: $ Bonus: $

STOCK TICKER/OTHER:

Stock Ticker: TOL   Exchange: NYS
Employees: 5,100   Fiscal Year Ends: 10/31
Parent Company:

OTHER THOUGHTS:

Estimated Female Officers or Directors:
Hot Spot for Advancement for Women/Minorities:

Tractor Supply Company

www.tractorsupplyco.com

NAIC Code: 444130

TYPES OF BUSINESS:

Farming Supplies, Retail
Work Apparel
Light Truck Equipment
Footwear
Animal Care Products
Private Label Credit Cards

BRANDS/DIVISIONS/AFFILIATES:

Petsense
Tractor Supply Company
Del's Feed & Farm Supply
TractorSupply.com
petsense.com

CONTACTS: *Note: Officers with more than one job title may be intentionally listed here more than once.*

Gregory Sandfort, CEO
Kurt Barton, CFO
Cynthia Jamison, Chairman of the Board
Robert Mills, Chief Technology Officer
Benjamin Parrish, Executive VP
Steve Barbarick, President
Chad Frazell, Senior VP, Divisional

GROWTH PLANS/SPECIAL FEATURES:

Tractor Supply Company (TSC) is one of the largest operators of retail farm and ranch stores in the U.S. and focuses on supplying the needs of recreational farmers and ranchers, tradesmen and small businesses. TSC also owns and operates Petsense, a pet supply and pet service chain retail outlet. Petsenses are found in outlet malls and rural markets across the country. As of September 2020, TSC operated 1,904 stores Tractor Supply Company and Del's Feed & Farm Supply retail stores in 49 states, as well as 183 Petsense pet specialty stores. These stores range from 15,000 to 20,000 square feet of inside selling space, along with additional outside selling space, and are primarily in towns outlying major metropolitan markets and in rural communities. TSC also operates two eCommerce sites: TractorSupply.com and petsense.com. The firm's market niche supplies the needs of recreational farmers and ranchers, as well as tradesmen, small businesses and those who enjoy the rural lifestyle. Types of merchandise in TSC's stores and online include equine, livestock, pet and small animal products, including items necessary for their health, growth and containment; hardware, truck towing and tool products; seasonal products such as heating, lawn and garden items, power equipment, gifts and toys; work/recreational clothing and footwear; and maintenance products for agricultural and rural use. Livestock and pet products account for 48% of company annual sales; hardware, tools, truck and towing, 23%; seasonal, gift and toy products, 19%; clothing and footwear, 5%; and agriculture, 5%. TSC's long-term plan is to grow by about 120 new stores per year until it reaches a total of 2,500 stores.

TSC offers comprehensive benefits, retirement and savings options, and employee assistance programs.

FINANCIAL DATA: *Note: Data for latest year may not have been available at press time.*

In U.S. $	2020	2019	2018	2017	2016	2015
Revenue	10,620,350,000	8,351,931,000	7,911,046,000	7,256,382,000	6,779,579,000	6,226,507,000
R&D Expense						
Operating Income	1,065,901,000	743,220,000	701,737,000	686,382,000	694,080,000	650,508,000
Operating Margin %		.09%	.09%	.09%	.10%	.10%
SGA Expense	2,478,524,000	1,932,572,000	1,823,440,000	1,639,749,000	1,488,164,000	1,369,097,000
Net Income	748,958,000	562,354,000	532,357,000	422,599,000	437,120,000	410,395,000
Operating Cash Flow	1,394,515,000	811,716,000	694,394,000	631,450,000	639,040,000	429,180,000
Capital Expenditure	294,002,000	217,450,000	278,530,000	250,401,000	226,017,000	236,496,000
EBITDA	1,214,052,000	939,198,000	879,088,000	852,216,000	837,038,000	774,077,000
Return on Assets %		.13%	.18%	.15%	.17%	.19%
Return on Equity %		.36%	.36%	.29%	.31%	.31%
Debt to Equity		1.53	0.263	0.306	0.199	0.12

CONTACT INFORMATION:

Phone: 615 440-4000   Fax:
Toll-Free: 800-872-7721
Address: 5401 Virginia Way, Brentwood, TN 37027 United States

STOCK TICKER/OTHER:

Stock Ticker: TSCO   Exchange: NAS
Employees: 26,000   Fiscal Year Ends: 12/31
Parent Company:

SALARIES/BONUSES:

Top Exec. Salary: $ Bonus: $
Second Exec. Salary: $ Bonus: $

OTHER THOUGHTS:

Estimated Female Officers or Directors: 3
Hot Spot for Advancement for Women/Minorities: Y

Trader Joes Company Inc

www.traderjoes.com

NAIC Code: 445110

TYPES OF BUSINESS:

Grocery Stores
Specialty Groceries
Vitamins & Dietary Supplements
Organic Foods

BRANDS/DIVISIONS/AFFILIATES:

CONTACTS: Note: Officers with more than one job title may be intentionally listed here more than once.

Daniel T. Bane, CEO
Charles Pillitier, Sr. VP-Oper.
Brandt Sharrock, VP-Real Estate

GROWTH PLANS/SPECIAL FEATURES:

Trader Joe's Company, Inc. operates a chain of approximately 500 company-owned and -operated specialty grocery stores throughout the U.S. and the District of Columbia, with about half of the stores located in California, where the company was founded. Although the stores sell some brand-name products, the vast majority of the selection is comprised of more than 3,000 Trader Joe's private-label products, including specialty vegetarian, kosher, organic food and vitamin supplement products as well as regional fare, such as Thai and Mexican foods. Prices tend to be comparable to or lower than traditional groceries, as a result of Trader Joe's efforts to buy many items and ingredients directly from suppliers and the chain's focus on its private label lines. The company also keeps costs down by eliminating service departments and using spaces of 15,000 square feet or less for its stores. Selections and inventory tend to vary from state to state and store to store because of the company's commitment to experimentation, regional and seasonal products and bringing variety to its customers. The firm is privately owned by a trust created by Theo Albrecht, co-founder of German supermarket chain ALDI Group.

Trader Joe's offers employees medical, dental and vision plans; a company-paid retirement contribution; employee discounts; and paid time off.

FINANCIAL DATA: Note: Data for latest year may not have been available at press time.

In U.S. $	2020	2019	2018	2017	2016	2015
Revenue	14,246,475,000	13,899,000,000	13,560,000,000	13,400,000,000	13,325,000,000	13,000,000,000
R&D Expense						
Operating Income						
Operating Margin %						
SGA Expense						
Net Income						
Operating Cash Flow						
Capital Expenditure						
EBITDA						
Return on Assets %						
Return on Equity %						
Debt to Equity						

CONTACT INFORMATION:

Phone: 626-599-3700   Fax: 626-301-4431
Toll-Free:
Address: 800 S. Shamrock Ave., Monrovia, CA 91016 United States

STOCK TICKER/OTHER:

Stock Ticker: Private
Employees: 41,000
Parent Company:

Exchange:
Fiscal Year Ends: 06/30

SALARIES/BONUSES:

Top Exec. Salary: $ Bonus: $
Second Exec. Salary: $ Bonus: $

OTHER THOUGHTS:

Estimated Female Officers or Directors: 2
Hot Spot for Advancement for Women/Minorities:

Travelers Companies Inc (The)

NAIC Code: 524126

TYPES OF BUSINESS:

Direct Property & Casualty Insurance
Property & Casualty
Business Insurance
Bond Insurance
Specialty Insurance
Personal Insurance

BRANDS/DIVISIONS/AFFILIATES:

InsuraMatch LLC

CONTACTS: *Note: Officers with more than one job title may be intentionally listed here more than once.*

Alan Schnitzer, CEO
Daniel Frey, CFO
Douglas Russell, Chief Accounting Officer
Andy Bessette, Chief Administrative Officer
Maria Olivo, Executive VP, Divisional
Christine Kalla, Executive VP
Diane Bengston, Executive VP
Mojgan Lefebvre, Executive VP
Gregory Toczydlowski, Executive VP
Michael Klein, Executive VP
Thomas Kunkel, Executive VP
Avrohom Kess, Other Executive Officer
William Heyman, Other Executive Officer
Jay Benet, Vice Chairman

GROWTH PLANS/SPECIAL FEATURES:

The Travelers Companies, Inc. is an insurance company that operates in three segments: business insurance, bond & specialty insurance and personal insurance. The business insurance segment offers an array of property and casualty insurance and insurance-related services to its customers, primarily in the U.S., but also in Canada, the U.K., Ireland and other parts of the world as a corporate member of Lloyd's. The bond & specialty insurance segment provides surety, fidelity, management liability, professional liability and other property and casualty coverages and related risk management services to its customers in the U.S. This division also offers certain specialty insurance products in Canada, the U.K. and Ireland, utilizing various financial-based underwriting approaches. The personal insurance segment writes a range of property and casualty insurance covering individual personal risks, primarily in the U.S., as well as in Canada. This division's primary products of automobile and homeowners insurance are complemented by a broad suite of related coverages. In December 2020, Travelers agreed to acquire InsuraMatch LLC, a digital independent insurance agency.

FINANCIAL DATA: *Note: Data for latest year may not have been available at press time.*

In U.S. $	2020	2019	2018	2017	2016	2015
Revenue	31,981,000,000	31,581,000,000	30,282,000,000	28,902,000,000	27,625,000,000	26,800,000,000
R&D Expense						
Operating Income						
Operating Margin %						
SGA Expense	4,509,000,000	4,365,000,000	4,297,000,000	4,170,000,000	4,154,000,000	4,079,000,000
Net Income	2,697,000,000	2,622,000,000	2,523,000,000	2,056,000,000	3,014,000,000	3,439,000,000
Operating Cash Flow	6,519,000,000	5,205,000,000	4,380,000,000	3,762,000,000	4,202,000,000	3,434,000,000
Capital Expenditure						
EBITDA						
Return on Assets %		.02%	.02%	.02%	.03%	.03%
Return on Equity %		.11%	.11%	.09%	.13%	.14%
Debt to Equity		0.23	0.261	0.252	0.254	0.248

CONTACT INFORMATION:

Phone: 917 778-6000 Fax:
Toll-Free: 800-328-2189
Address: 485 Lexington Ave., New York, NY 10017 United States

STOCK TICKER/OTHER:

Stock Ticker: TRV   Exchange: NYS
Employees: 30,600   Fiscal Year Ends: 12/31
Parent Company:

SALARIES/BONUSES:

Top Exec. Salary: $ Bonus: $
Second Exec. Salary: $ Bonus: $

OTHER THOUGHTS:

Estimated Female Officers or Directors: 7
Hot Spot for Advancement for Women/Minorities: Y

Trimble Inc

www.trimble.com

NAIC Code: 334511

TYPES OF BUSINESS:

GPS Technologies
Surveying & Mapping Equipment
Navigation Tools
Autopilot Systems
Data Collection Products
Fleet Management Systems
Outdoor Recreation Information Service
Telecommunications & Automotive Components

BRANDS/DIVISIONS/AFFILIATES:

Applanix
AXIO-NET GmbH
Beena Vision Systems Inc
e-Builder
HHK Datentechnik GmbH
Innovative Software Engineering
MyTopo
Viewpoint

CONTACTS: Note: Officers with more than one job title may be intentionally listed here more than once.

Steven Berglund, CEO
Robert Painter, CFO
Ulf Johansson, Chairman of the Board
Julie Shepard, Chief Accounting Officer
Darryl Matthews, Other Corporate Officer
Sachin Sankpal, Senior VP, Divisional
Bryn Fosburgh, Senior VP, Divisional
Michael Bank, Senior VP, Divisional
Ronald Bisio, Senior VP, Divisional
Rosalind Buick, Senior VP, Divisional
Thomas Fansler, Senior VP, Divisional
James Kirkland, Senior VP

GROWTH PLANS/SPECIAL FEATURES:

Trimble, Inc. provides technology solutions used in positioning, modeling, connectivity and data analytics to enable customers to improve productivity, quality, safety and sustainability. These products are sold in more than 150 countries and include more than 2,000 unique patents. Trimble's global operations consist of offices and subsidiaries in nearly 40 countries. The company's subsidiaries include: Applanix, an industry leader in the development and manufacture of integrated Inertial/GPS technology; AXIO-NET GmbH, a provider of reference networked services that deliver highly-accurate, satellite-based positioning and navigation information; Beena Vision Systems, Inc., a manufacturer of vision-based automatic wayside inspection systems for the railroad industry; e-Builder, a provider of integrated, cloud-based construction program management software for facility owners and the companies that act on their behalf; HHK Datentechnik GmbH; a developer and marketer of specialized office management, computer-aided design (CAD) and geographic information system (GIS) software solutions for municipal and cadastral offices, utility suppliers and engineering organizations; Innovative Software Engineering, an engineering and systems integration firm; MyTopo, a provider of navigation-ready mapping services, data and software; Muller-Elektronik GmbH & Co., KG, which develops, produces and sells electronic solutions for agricultural machinery; Stabiplan, which develops and sells design software for MEP engineering in Europe; Trade Service, a provider of standardized product and price information to the mechanical, electrical, plumbing, industrial, automotive and office products industries; and Viewpoint, a global provider of integrated software solutions for the construction industry In February 2020, the firm acquired Kuebix, a privately held transportation management systems provider. In October 2020, Trimble sold its construction logistics business to Command and Alcon, a Thoma Bravo company.

FINANCIAL DATA: Note: Data for latest year may not have been available at press time.

In U.S. $	2020	2019	2018	2017	2016	2015
Revenue	3,147,700,000	3,264,300,000	3,108,400,000	2,654,200,000	2,362,200,000	2,290,400,000
R&D Expense	475,900,000	469,700,000	446,100,000	370,200,000	349,600,000	336,700,000
Operating Income	445,600,000	402,700,000	328,900,000	252,900,000	192,600,000	165,800,000
Operating Margin %	.12%	.11%		.10%	.08%	.07%
SGA Expense	767,900,000	834,800,000	829,600,000	706,500,000	633,600,000	629,900,000
Net Income	389,900,000	514,300,000	282,800,000	121,100,000	132,400,000	121,100,000
Operating Cash Flow	672,000,000	585,000,000	486,700,000	411,900,000	407,100,000	354,900,000
Capital Expenditure	56,800,000	69,000,000	67,600,000	43,700,000	26,300,000	44,000,000
EBITDA	670,100,000	634,400,000	566,400,000	467,500,000	390,400,000	376,500,000
Return on Assets %	.08%	.06%		.03%	.04%	.03%
Return on Equity %	.18%	.11%		.05%	.06%	.05%
Debt to Equity	0.557	0.64		0.332	0.212	0.275

CONTACT INFORMATION:

Phone: 408 481-8000   Fax: 408 481-2218
Toll-Free: 800-874-6253
Address: 935 Stewart Dr., Sunnyvale, CA 94085 United States

SALARIES/BONUSES:

Top Exec. Salary: $ Bonus: $
Second Exec. Salary: $ Bonus: $

STOCK TICKER/OTHER:

Stock Ticker: TRMB
Employees: 11,402
Parent Company:

Exchange: NAS
Fiscal Year Ends: 12/31

OTHER THOUGHTS:

Estimated Female Officers or Directors: 5
Hot Spot for Advancement for Women/Minorities: Y

Trinity Industries Inc

www.trin.net

NAIC Code: 336510

TYPES OF BUSINESS:
Railroad Car Manufacturing
Railroad Car Leasing & Management
Railcar Products
Manufacture

BRANDS/DIVISIONS/AFFILIATES:
Trinity Industries Leasing Company
TRIP Rail Holdings LLC
RIV 2013 Rail Holdings LLC
TrinityRail
BayWorks

CONTACTS: Note: Officers with more than one job title may be intentionally listed here more than once.
E. Jean Savage, CEO
Brian D. Madison, Exec. VP-Oper.
Melendy Lovett, CFO
Eric R. Marchetto, CFO
Sarah Teachout, Chief Legal Officer
W. Relle Howard, CIO
Eric Marchetto, Other Executive Officer
Paul Mauer, President, Divisional
Brian Madison, President, Subsidiary

GROWTH PLANS/SPECIAL FEATURES:
Trinity Industries, Inc. owns an integrated platform of businesses that provide railcar products and services in North America, including the U.S., Canada and Mexico. The platform is called TrinityRail, with business activities being grouped into three segments: railcar leasing and management services, railcar products and all other. The railcar leasing and management services segment consists of Trinity Industries Leasing Company, TRIP Rail Holdings LLC and RIV 2013 Rail Holdings LLC, which offer operating leases for freight and tank railcars. The division coordinates its sales and marketing activities via TrinityRail, offering a single point of contact for railroads and shippers seeking rail equipment and services. This segment also originates and manages railcar leases for third-party investors and provides fleet maintenance and management services to industrial shippers. The rail products segment manufactures freight and tank railcars in North America, which are used for transporting a wide variety of liquids, gases and dry cargo. This division holds patents of varying duration for use in its manufacture of railcars and components. Last, the all other segment includes Trinity's highway products business in the U.S., which manufactures guardrail, crash cushions and other highway barriers; logistics business, which primarily provides support services to Trinity; and other peripheral businesses. In February 2021, Trinity announced it had acquired Bay Worx Rail, a maintenance service that safely cleans tank cars using robotics.

FINANCIAL DATA: Note: Data for latest year may not have been available at press time.

In U.S. $	2020	2019	2018	2017	2016	2015
Revenue	1,999,400,000	3,005,100,000	2,509,100,000	3,662,800,000	4,588,300,000	6,392,700,000
R&D Expense						
Operating Income	111,100,000	376,600,000	273,700,000	462,500,000	724,800,000	1,260,100,000
Operating Margin %		.13%	.11%	.13%	.16%	.20%
SGA Expense	379,900,000	262,800,000	296,600,000	454,800,000	407,400,000	476,400,000
Net Income	-147,300,000	137,600,000	159,300,000	702,500,000	343,600,000	796,500,000
Operating Cash Flow	651,700,000	393,600,000	379,100,000	761,600,000	1,090,200,000	939,700,000
Capital Expenditure	704,500,000	1,219,200,000	985,600,000	712,700,000	933,400,000	1,029,800,000
EBITDA	-9,300,000	706,100,000	582,800,000	851,400,000	1,031,700,000	1,713,100,000
Return on Assets %		.02%	.02%	.07%	.04%	.09%
Return on Equity %		.06%	.05%	.16%	.09%	.23%
Debt to Equity		2.405	1.823	0.72	0.78	0.875

CONTACT INFORMATION:
Phone: 214 631-4420   Fax: 214 589-8501
Toll-Free:
Address: 2525 Stemmons Fwy., Dallas, TX 75207-2401 United States

STOCK TICKER/OTHER:
Stock Ticker: TRN
Employees: 11,875
Parent Company:
Exchange: NYS
Fiscal Year Ends: 12/31

SALARIES/BONUSES:
Top Exec. Salary: $ Bonus: $
Second Exec. Salary: $ Bonus: $

OTHER THOUGHTS:
Estimated Female Officers or Directors: 2
Hot Spot for Advancement for Women/Minorities: Y

Turner Corporation (The)

NAIC Code: 236220

TYPES OF BUSINESS:
Commercial & Institutional Building Construction

BRANDS/DIVISIONS/AFFILIATES:
Hochtief AG
Turner Construction Company
Turner International LLC
Clark Builders
EZ Cruz and Company

CONTACTS: Note: Officers with more than one job title may be intentionally listed here more than once.
Peter Davoren, CEO

GROWTH PLANS/SPECIAL FEATURES:
The Turner Corporation, a subsidiary of Hochtief AG, is an American-based, international construction services company. Turner completes approximately $12 billion of construction on 1,500 projects every year. Its construction business is operated through Turner Construction Company, one of the largest construction companies in the U.S. Services offered by the firm include design and build, logistics procurement, medical planning and procurement, building information modeling and lean construction. Turner is a leader in all major market segments, including aviation/transportation, commercial, cultural and entertainment, data center, education, government, green building, healthcare, infrastructure, interiors, industrial/manufacturing, pharmaceutical, public assembly, religious, research & development, residential/hotel, retail, restaurant and sports. The firm holds a majority share of Clark Builders, a leading general contractor in Canada; and owns a joint venture with Flatiron called EE Cruz and Company, which specializes in infrastructure improvement projects in the New York and New Jersey region. In North America, Turner Corporation has offices in 24 U.S. states as well as offices in Vancouver and Toronto, Canada. Turner's international presence, via Turner International, LLC, has offices in Europe, India, Latin America, the Caribbean, the Middle East and Asia.

FINANCIAL DATA: Note: Data for latest year may not have been available at press time.

In U.S. $	2020	2019	2018	2017	2016	2015
Revenue	13,992,000,000	13,200,000,000	12,000,000,000	11,500,000,000	11,000,000,000	10,797,500,000
R&D Expense						
Operating Income						
Operating Margin %						
SGA Expense						
Net Income						
Operating Cash Flow						
Capital Expenditure						
EBITDA						
Return on Assets %						
Return on Equity %						
Debt to Equity						

CONTACT INFORMATION:
Phone: 212-229-6000   Fax:
Toll-Free:
Address: 375 Hudson St., New York, NY 10014 United States

STOCK TICKER/OTHER:
Stock Ticker: Subsidiary
Employees: 10,000
Parent Company: Hochtief AG

Exchange:
Fiscal Year Ends:

SALARIES/BONUSES:
Top Exec. Salary: $ Bonus: $
Second Exec. Salary: $ Bonus: $

OTHER THOUGHTS:
Estimated Female Officers or Directors:
Hot Spot for Advancement for Women/Minorities:

Tyson Foods Inc

www.tysonfoods.com

NAIC Code: 311615

TYPES OF BUSINESS:

Poultry Processing
Beef & Pork Products
Ethnic Foods
Soups & Sauces
Frozen & Refrigerated Food

BRANDS/DIVISIONS/AFFILIATES:

Cobb-Vantress inc
MFG (USA) Holdings Inc
McKey Luxembourg Holdings sarl
Tyson
Hillshire Farm
Jimmy Dean
State Fair
Ballpark

CONTACTS: Note: Officers with more than one job title may be intentionally listed here more than once.

Dean Banks, CEO
Stewart F. Glendinning, CFO
Steve Gibbs, Chief Accounting Officer
Jay Spradley, Chief Technology Officer
Justin Whitmore, Executive VP, Divisional
Amy Tu, Executive VP
Scott Rouse, Executive VP
Mary Oleksiuk, Executive VP
Sally Grimes, President, Divisional
Douglas Ramsey, President, Divisional
Stephen Stouffer, President, Divisional
Curt Calaway, Senior VP, Divisional

GROWTH PLANS/SPECIAL FEATURES:

Tyson Foods, Inc. is a producer, distributor and marketer of chicken, beef, pork, prepared foods and related products. The company operates in four segments: chicken, beef, pork and prepared foods. The chicken operations include breeding and raising chickens as well as processing live chickens into fresh, frozen and value-added chicken products. This segment also includes logistics operations to move products through the supply chain. The beef operations include processing live cattle and fabricating dressed beef carcasses into primal and sub-primal meat cuts and case-ready products. This segment also includes sales from allied products, such as hides and variety meats. The pork operations include processing live market hogs and fabricating pork carcasses into primal and sub-primal cuts and case-ready products. This segment also includes the live swine group and related allied product processing activities. Prepared food operations include the manufacture and marketing of frozen and refrigerated food products. Products include pepperoni, bacon, beef and pork pizza toppings, pizza crusts, flour and corn tortilla products, appetizers, prepared meals, ethnic foods, soups, sauces, side dishes, meat dishes and processed meats. Products are marketed domestically to food retailers, foodservice distributors, restaurant operators and noncommercial foodservice establishments such as schools, hotel chains, healthcare facilities, the military and other food processors as well as to international markets. International business includes Tyson's foreign operations in Australia, China, South Korea, Malaysia, Mexico, Netherlands, Thailand and the U.K. Wholly-owned Cobb-Vantress, Inc. is a leading poultry breeding stock supplier, serving global markets. Tyson brands include, Tyson, Hillshire Farm, Jimmy Dean, State Fair and Ballpark.

FINANCIAL DATA: Note: Data for latest year may not have been available at press time.

In U.S. $	2020	2019	2018	2017	2016	2015
Revenue	43,185,000,000	42,405,000,000	40,052,000,000	38,260,000,000	36,881,000,000	41,373,000,000
R&D Expense						
Operating Income	3,114,000,000	2,827,000,000	3,055,000,000	2,931,000,000	2,833,000,000	2,169,000,000
Operating Margin %		.07%	.08%	.08%	.08%	.05%
SGA Expense	2,270,000,000	2,195,000,000	2,071,000,000	2,152,000,000	1,864,000,000	1,748,000,000
Net Income	2,140,000,000	2,022,000,000	3,024,000,000	1,774,000,000	1,768,000,000	1,220,000,000
Operating Cash Flow	3,874,000,000	2,513,000,000	2,963,000,000	2,599,000,000	2,716,000,000	2,570,000,000
Capital Expenditure	1,199,000,000	1,259,000,000	1,200,000,000	1,069,000,000	695,000,000	854,000,000
EBITDA	4,447,000,000	3,991,000,000	4,038,000,000	3,668,000,000	3,552,000,000	2,925,000,000
Return on Assets %		.07%	.11%	.07%	.08%	.05%
Return on Equity %		.15%	.26%	.18%	.18%	.13%
Debt to Equity		0.698	0.622	0.882	0.645	0.62

CONTACT INFORMATION:

Phone: 479 290-4000   Fax: 479 290-7984
Toll-Free: 800-643-3410
Address: 2200 W. Don Tyson Pkwy., Springdale, AR 72762 United States

STOCK TICKER/OTHER:

Stock Ticker: TSN   Exchange: NYS
Employees: 139,000   Fiscal Year Ends: 09/30
Parent Company:

SALARIES/BONUSES:

Top Exec. Salary: $ Bonus: $
Second Exec. Salary: $ Bonus: $

OTHER THOUGHTS:

Estimated Female Officers or Directors: 4
Hot Spot for Advancement for Women/Minorities: Y

Union Pacific Corporation

www.up.com

NAIC Code: 482111

TYPES OF BUSINESS:

Line-Haul Railroads

BRANDS/DIVISIONS/AFFILIATES:

Union Pacific Railroad Company

CONTACTS: Note: Officers with more than one job title may be intentionally listed here more than once.

Lance Fritz, CEO
Vincenzo Vena, COO
Robert Knight, CFO
Todd Rynaski, Chief Accounting Officer
Scott Moore, Chief Administrative Officer
Rahul Jalali, CIO
Thomas Lischer, Executive VP, Subsidiary
Kenyatta Rocker, Executive VP, Subsidiary
Elizabeth Whited, Executive VP
Rhonda Ferguson, Executive VP
Clark Ponthier, Senior VP, Subsidiary
Jon Panzer, Treasurer
Bryan Clark, Vice President, Divisional
Prentiss Bolin, Vice President, Divisional

GROWTH PLANS/SPECIAL FEATURES:

Union Pacific Corporation is a provider of rail freight transportation. The company operates primarily through Union Pacific Railroad Company (UPRC), one of the largest railroads in North America. UPRC's operating base covers 23 states across the western two-thirds of the U.S. It is a Class I railroad with approximately 32,200 route miles linking Pacific Coast and Gulf Coast ports with the Midwest and eastern U.S. gateways and providing several north/south corridors to key Mexican gateways. The firm handles freight The firm handles freight in three commodity groups: industrial, which accounted for 36% of 2020 freight revenue; bulk 33%' and premium 31%. Union Pacific's premium franchise includes three divisions: international intermodal, consisting of import/export traffic moving in 20- or 40-foot shipping containers; domestic intermodal, consisting of container and trailer traffic picked up and delivered within North America for intermodal marketing companies and truckload carriers; and finished vehicles, consisting of automotive distribution, including vehicles and automotive parts destined for Mexico, the U.S. and Canada. The industrial group facilitates the movement of numerous commodities between thousands of origin and destination points throughout North America, including categories of construction, industrial chemicals, plastics, forest products, specialized products, metals/ores and soda ash. The agricultural products group transports grain, commodities produced from these grains, fertilizer and food and beverage products. The energy group ships coal, sand, petroleum, liquid petroleum gases (PLG) and renewables. Union Pacific's rail fleet comprises 7,310 locomotives (6,255 owned); and 52,933 freight cars (30,575 owned), including 21,626 covered hoppers, 6,964 open hoppers, 7,432 gondolas, 4,743 refrigerated cars, 8,926 boxcars, 2,972 flat cars and 270 other railcars.

Union Pacific employees receive benefits including healthcare coverage, a 401(k) and maternity leave.

FINANCIAL DATA: Note: Data for latest year may not have been available at press time.

In U.S. $	2020	2019	2018	2017	2016	2015
Revenue	19,533,000,000	21,708,000,000	22,832,000,000	21,240,000,000	19,941,000,000	21,813,000,000
R&D Expense						
Operating Income	7,834,000,000	8,554,000,000	8,517,000,000	8,061,000,000	7,272,000,000	8,052,000,000
Operating Margin %		.39%	.37%	.38%	.36%	.37%
SGA Expense						
Net Income	5,349,000,000	5,919,000,000	5,966,000,000	10,712,000,000	4,233,000,000	4,772,000,000
Operating Cash Flow	8,540,000,000	8,609,000,000	8,686,000,000	7,230,000,000	7,525,000,000	7,344,000,000
Capital Expenditure	2,927,000,000	3,453,000,000	3,437,000,000	3,238,000,000	3,505,000,000	4,650,000,000
EBITDA	10,331,000,000	11,013,000,000	10,802,000,000	10,456,000,000	9,502,000,000	10,290,000,000
Return on Assets %		.10%	.10%	.19%	.08%	.09%
Return on Equity %		.31%	.26%	.48%	.21%	.23%
Debt to Equity		1.402	1.025	0.65	0.715	0.657

CONTACT INFORMATION:

Phone: 402 544-5000   Fax: 402 271-6408
Toll-Free:
Address: 1400 Douglas St., Omaha, NE 68179 United States

STOCK TICKER/OTHER:

Stock Ticker: UNP
Employees: 30,960
Parent Company:

Exchange: NYS
Fiscal Year Ends: 12/31

SALARIES/BONUSES:

Top Exec. Salary: $ Bonus: $
Second Exec. Salary: $ Bonus: $

OTHER THOUGHTS:

Estimated Female Officers or Directors: 4
Hot Spot for Advancement for Women/Minorities: Y

United Natural Foods Inc

NAIC Code: 424410

www.unfi.com

TYPES OF BUSINESS:

Food Distribution
Natural & Organic Food Distribution
Nutritional Supplement Distribution
Personal Care Product Distribution
Wholesale
Retail Stores

BRANDS/DIVISIONS/AFFILIATES:

Culinary Circle
Wild Harvest
Essential Everyday
Equaline
Springfield
Arctic Shores Seafood Company
Baby Basic
Stone Ridge Creamery

CONTACTS: Note: Officers with more than one job title may be intentionally listed here more than once.

Sean Griffin, CEO, Subsidiary
Michael Stigers, CEO, Subsidiary
Steven Spinner, CEO
Michael Zechmeister, CFO
Eric Dorne, Chief Administrative Officer
Christopher Testa, Chief Marketing Officer
Michael Funk, Co-Founder
Jill Sutton, General Counsel
Danielle Benedict, Other Executive Officer
Paul Green, Other Executive Officer

GROWTH PLANS/SPECIAL FEATURES:

United Natural Foods, Inc. (UNFI) is a national distributor of natural and organic foods and related products. The company, which is a Certified Organic Distributor, carries more than 275,000 natural and organic products. Product types include: grocery and general merchandise; personal care items; produce; nutritional supplements; sports nutrition perishables; and frozen foods and bulk and food service products. UNFI serves approximately 30,000 customers, including supernatural chains (large chains of natural foods supermarkets), independently owned natural products retailers and conventional supermarkets located across the U.S. and Canada. The company has 55 distribution centers and warehouses, representing 29 million square feet of warehouse space. UNFI operates through two segments: wholesale and retail. The wholesale segment offers customers a variety of food and non-food products, as well as UNFI's own lines of private label products. It also provides professional services such as logistics, marketing and technology. Leading wholesale customers of UNFI include Whole Foods Market, The Fresh Market, Coborn's, Vitamin Cottage, Wegmans, Sprouts Farmers Market and many more. The retail segment consists of stores that carry approximately 17,000 to 21,000 core stock-keeping units (SKUs) and ranges in size from approximately 50,000 to 70,000 square feet. These stores offer national and regional brands as well as UNFI's own private label products. This division's distribution centers also supply the group's wholesale customers. Retail grocery store names include 71 Club Foods and Shoppers. Private label products of UNFI include brands such as Culinary Circle, Wild Harvest, Essential Everyday, Equaline, Springfield, Arctic Shores Seafood Company, Baby Basics, Stone Ridge Creamery and Super Chill, among others.

UNFI offers employees medical, dental, life and disability insurance; an assistance program; and educational assistance.

FINANCIAL DATA: Note: Data for latest year may not have been available at press time.

In U.S. $	2020	2019	2018	2017	2016	2015
Revenue	26,514,270,000	21,387,070,000	10,226,680,000	9,274,471,000	8,470,286,000	8,184,978,000
R&D Expense						
Operating Income	333,305,000	155,297,000	243,238,000	232,889,000	229,661,000	242,760,000
Operating Margin %		.01%	.02%	.03%	.03%	.03%
SGA Expense						
Net Income	-274,140,000	-284,990,000	165,670,000	130,155,000	125,766,000	138,734,000
Operating Cash Flow	456,536,000	284,530,000	109,472,000	280,776,000	296,609,000	48,864,000
Capital Expenditure	172,568,000	207,817,000	44,608,000	56,112,000	41,375,000	129,134,000
EBITDA	115,427,000	-25,273,000	316,847,000	317,588,000	295,487,000	308,067,000
Return on Assets %		-.06%	.06%	.05%	.05%	.06%
Return on Equity %		-.17%	.09%	.08%	.09%	.11%
Debt to Equity		1.934	0.188	0.222	0.387	0.388

CONTACT INFORMATION:

Phone: 401 528-8634   Fax:
Toll-Free:
Address: 313 Iron Horse Way, Providence, RI 02908 United States

STOCK TICKER/OTHER:

Stock Ticker: UNFI
Employees: 28,300
Parent Company:

Exchange: NYS
Fiscal Year Ends: 07/31

SALARIES/BONUSES:

Top Exec. Salary: $ Bonus: $
Second Exec. Salary: $ Bonus: $

OTHER THOUGHTS:

Estimated Female Officers or Directors: 3
Hot Spot for Advancement for Women/Minorities: Y

United Parcel Service Inc (UPS)

www.ups.com

NAIC Code: 492110

TYPES OF BUSINESS:

Couriers and Express Delivery Services
Logistics Services
Supply Chain Services
International Products & Services
Ground & Air Delivery Services
Visibility & Technology Services

BRANDS/DIVISIONS/AFFILIATES:

UPS Hundredweight Services
UPS Next Day Air

CONTACTS: Note: Officers with more than one job title may be intentionally listed here more than once.

David Abney, CEO
Richard Peretz, CFO
Juan Perez, Chief Information Officer
Kevin Warren, Chief Marketing Officer
James Barber, COO
Kate Gutmann, Other Executive Officer
Scott Price, Other Executive Officer
Teri Mcclure, Other Executive Officer
Nando Cesarone, President, Divisional
George Willis, President, Geographical
Norman Brothers, Senior VP

GROWTH PLANS/SPECIAL FEATURES:

United Parcel Service, Inc. (UPS) is one of the world's largest package delivery companies and a global provider of supply chain management. It delivers packages each business day to approximately 11.5 million receivers in over 220 countries and territories. The firm delivers an average of 21.9 million pieces per day worldwide. It is also a major provider of less-than-truckload (LTL) transportation services. Offerings include domestic and international package products and services and supply chain and freight services. The U.S. domestic package products and services business delivers packages traveling by ground or air transportation. In addition to the standard ground delivery products, UPS Hundredweight Services offers guaranteed, time-definite service to customers sending multiple package shipments. UPS Next Day Air offers several service options guaranteeing next business day delivery by 8:00AM, 10:30AM, noon, 3-4:30PM or by the end of the day in the 48 contiguous U.S. states and limited areas of Alaska. International services include guaranteed early morning, morning and noon delivery to major cities around the world as well as scheduled day-definite air and ground services. The supply chain and freight segment consists of its forwarding and logistics operations, UPS Freight and other related businesses. The division's worldwide services include supply chain design and management, freight distribution, customs brokerage, mail and consulting services. UPS Freight offers a variety of LTL/truckload services to customers in North America. UPS' supply chain solutions division is based in Alpharetta, Georgia, and its information technology division is located in Parsippany, New Jersey. In January 2021, UPS announced it had reached an agreement to sell their freight division UPS Freight, to TFI International Inc.

U.S. employees at UPS receive health coverage and other benefits.

FINANCIAL DATA: Note: Data for latest year may not have been available at press time.

In U.S. $	2020	2019	2018	2017	2016	2015
Revenue	84,628,000,000	74,094,000,000	71,861,000,000	65,872,000,000	60,906,000,000	58,363,000,000
R&D Expense						
Operating Income	7,684,000,000	7,798,000,000	7,024,000,000	7,529,000,000	5,467,000,000	7,668,000,000
Operating Margin %		.11%	.10%	.11%	.09%	.13%
SGA Expense						
Net Income	1,343,000,000	4,440,000,000	4,791,000,000	4,910,000,000	3,431,000,000	4,844,000,000
Operating Cash Flow	10,459,000,000	8,639,000,000	12,711,000,000	1,479,000,000	6,473,000,000	7,430,000,000
Capital Expenditure	5,412,000,000	6,380,000,000	6,283,000,000	5,227,000,000	2,965,000,000	2,379,000,000
EBITDA	5,243,000,000	8,665,000,000	8,831,000,000	9,883,000,000	7,741,000,000	9,767,000,000
Return on Assets %		.08%	.10%	.11%	.09%	.13%
Return on Equity %		1.41%	2.38%	6.99%	2.39%	2.10%
Debt to Equity		7.41	6.597	20.278	30.602	4.581

CONTACT INFORMATION:

Phone: 404 828-6000   Fax: 404 828-6562
Toll-Free: 800-874-5877
Address: 55 Glenlake Parkway, NE, Atlanta, GA 30328 United States

STOCK TICKER/OTHER:

Stock Ticker: UPS
Employees: 495,000
Parent Company:

Exchange: NYS
Fiscal Year Ends: 12/31

SALARIES/BONUSES:

Top Exec. Salary: $ Bonus: $
Second Exec. Salary: $ Bonus: $

OTHER THOUGHTS:

Estimated Female Officers or Directors: 4
Hot Spot for Advancement for Women/Minorities: Y

United States Cellular Corporation
www.uscellular.com
NAIC Code: 517210

TYPES OF BUSINESS:
Mobile Phone and Wireless Services
Wireless Services
Telecommunications
Voice
Data Services

BRANDS/DIVISIONS/AFFILIATES:
Telephone and Data Systems Inc

CONTACTS: Note: Officers with more than one job title may be intentionally listed here more than once.
Kenneth Meyers, CEO
Steven Campbell, CFO
Leroy Carlson, Chairman of the Board
Douglas Chambers, Chief Accounting Officer
Michael Irizarry, Chief Technology Officer
Paul-Henri Denuit, Director Emeritus
James Barr, Director Emeritus
Jay Ellison, Executive VP
Deirdre Drake, Executive VP

GROWTH PLANS/SPECIAL FEATURES:

United States Cellular Corporation (U.S. Cellular) is a leading U.S. wireless telecommunications firm. U.S. Cellular provides wireless voice and data services to 5 million customers nationwide, including 4.4 million postpaid, 0.5 million prepaid and 0.1 million reseller and other connections. The company maintains interests in consolidated and investment wireless licenses that cover portions of 21 states. U.S. Cellular offers a range of wireless devices such as handsets, modems, mobile hotspots, home phone and tablets for use by its customers. The firm has also installed service repair programs at certain facilities, which assist customers with over-the-counter exchanges, Smartphone advance exchanges, loaner phones, device recycling and device returns. U.S. Cellular sells wireless devices to agents and other third-party distributors for resale. The wireless services segment provides a variety of packaged voice and data pricing plans. The company offers post-pay plans and prepaid plans. Moreover, U.S. Cellular services include connected home, a self-installed home security and automation system for home monitoring purposes. U.S. Cellular also offers data-services and app-like experiences to non-smartphone devices via a technology known as binary runtime environment for wireless (BREW). These enhanced data services include downloading news, weather, sports information, games, ring tones and other services. In addition, U.S. Cellular has recently engaged in VoLTE (voice over long-term evolution) trials, with plans to upgrade equipment in select markets to allow the trial processes to continue following the services official launch. Telephone and Data Systems, Inc. owns approximately 82% of the company.

U.S. Cellular offers its employees medical, dental and vision coverage; life insurance and AD&D; short- and long-term disability; a 401(k) and Roth IRA; a pension plan; and tuition reimbursement.

FINANCIAL DATA: Note: Data for latest year may not have been available at press time.

In U.S. $	2020	2019	2018	2017	2016	2015
Revenue	4,037,000,000	4,022,000,000	3,967,000,000	3,890,000,000	3,939,000,000	3,996,853,000
R&D Expense						
Operating Income	193,000,000	130,000,000	150,000,000	60,000,000		68,816,000
Operating Margin %		.03%	.04%	.02%		.02%
SGA Expense	1,368,000,000	1,406,000,000	1,388,000,000	1,412,000,000	1,480,000,000	1,493,730,000
Net Income	229,000,000	127,000,000	150,000,000	12,000,000	48,000,000	241,347,000
Operating Cash Flow	1,237,000,000	724,000,000	709,000,000	469,000,000	501,000,000	555,114,000
Capital Expenditure	1,190,000,000	916,000,000	520,000,000	654,000,000	496,000,000	866,400,000
EBITDA	1,045,000,000	997,000,000	971,000,000	456,000,000	813,000,000	1,096,278,000
Return on Assets %		.02%	.02%	.00%	.01%	.04%
Return on Equity %		.03%	.04%	.00%	.01%	.07%
Debt to Equity		0.564	0.396	0.441	0.445	0.457

CONTACT INFORMATION:
Phone: 773 399-8900　　　Fax: 773 399-8936
Toll-Free: 888-944-9400
Address: 8410 W. Bryn Mawr Ave., Chicago, IL 60631 United States

STOCK TICKER/OTHER:
Stock Ticker: USM　　　　　　　　Exchange: NYS
Employees: 5,500　　　　　　　　Fiscal Year Ends: 12/31
Parent Company: Telephone and Data Systems Inc

SALARIES/BONUSES:
Top Exec. Salary: $　　　　Bonus: $
Second Exec. Salary: $　　　Bonus: $

OTHER THOUGHTS:
Estimated Female Officers or Directors: 6
Hot Spot for Advancement for Women/Minorities: Y

United States Steel Corporation

www.ussteel.com

NAIC Code: 331110

TYPES OF BUSINESS:

Steel Manufacturing
Integrated Steel Production
Flat-Rolled Steel
Tubular Steel Products

BRANDS/DIVISIONS/AFFILIATES:

US Steel Kosice

CONTACTS: *Note: Officers with more than one job title may be intentionally listed here more than once.*

Kimberly Fast, Assistant Controller
David Burritt, CEO
Kevin Bradley, CFO
David Sutherland, Chairman of the Board
Duane Holloway, Chief Compliance Officer
Douglas Matthews, Other Corporate Officer
A. Melnkovic, Other Executive Officer
Christine Breves, Other Executive Officer
James Bruno, President, Geographical
Scott Buckiso, Senior VP, Divisional
Sara Greenstein, Senior VP, Divisional

GROWTH PLANS/SPECIAL FEATURES:

United States Steel Corporation is an integrated steel producer of flat-rolled and tubular products with major production operations in North America and Europe. The firm has an annual raw steel production capability of 22.9 million net tons (17.9 million tons in the U.S. and 5 million tons in Europe). United States Steel has three reportable operating segments: flat-rolled products (flat-rolled), United States Steel Europe (USSE) and tubular products (tubular). The flat-rolled segment includes the operating results of United States Steel's North American integrated steel mills and equity investees involved in the production of slabs, rounds, strip mill plates, sheets and tin mill products, as well as all iron ore and coke production facilities in the U.S. Flat-rolled has annual raw steel production capability of 17 million tons. The USSE segment, consisting solely of U.S. Steel Kosice in Slovakia, produced 3.4 million ton of raw steel in 2020. The tubular segment includes the operating results of United States Steel's tubular production facilities, primarily in the U.S., and equity investees in the U.S. and Brazil. These operations produce and sell seamless and electric resistance welded steel casing and tubing, standard and line pipe and mechanical tubing and primarily serve customers in the oil, gas and petrochemical markets. Tubular's total production capability is 1.9 million tons. As an integrated producer, United States Steel's primary raw materials are iron units in the form of iron ore pellets and sinter ore, carbon units in the form of coal and coke, and steel scrap. During 2021, United States Steel agreed to sell Transtar, LLC to an affiliate of Fortress Transportation and Infrastructure Investors LLC for $640 million. Transtar is engaged in railroad operations, and the transaction was expected to close by year's end.

United States Steel offers its employees health and retirement benefits.

FINANCIAL DATA: *Note: Data for latest year may not have been available at press time.*

In U.S. $	2020	2019	2018	2017	2016	2015
Revenue	9,741,000,000	12,937,000,000	14,178,000,000	12,250,000,000	10,261,000,000	11,574,000,000
R&D Expense						
Operating Income	-737,000,000	-35,000,000	1,019,000,000	518,000,000	-122,000,000	-528,000,000
Operating Margin %		.00%	.07%	.04%	-.01%	-.05%
SGA Expense	274,000,000	289,000,000	336,000,000	375,000,000	255,000,000	415,000,000
Net Income	-1,165,000,000	-630,000,000	1,115,000,000	387,000,000	-440,000,000	-1,642,000,000
Operating Cash Flow	138,000,000	682,000,000	938,000,000	802,000,000	727,000,000	359,000,000
Capital Expenditure	725,000,000	1,252,000,000	1,001,000,000	505,000,000	306,000,000	500,000,000
EBITDA	-384,000,000	306,000,000	1,501,000,000	1,028,000,000	321,000,000	-698,000,000
Return on Assets %		-.06%	.11%	.04%	-.05%	-.15%
Return on Equity %		-.15%	.30%	.14%	-.19%	-.53%
Debt to Equity		0.93	0.551	0.813	1.311	1.279

CONTACT INFORMATION:

Phone: 412 433-1121   Fax: 412 433-1167
Toll-Free:
Address: 600 Grant St., Pittsburgh, PA 15219-2800 United States

STOCK TICKER/OTHER:

Stock Ticker: X
Employees: 23,350
Parent Company:

Exchange: NYS
Fiscal Year Ends: 12/31

SALARIES/BONUSES:

Top Exec. Salary: $ Bonus: $
Second Exec. Salary: $ Bonus: $

OTHER THOUGHTS:

Estimated Female Officers or Directors: 2
Hot Spot for Advancement for Women/Minorities:

UnitedHealth Group Inc

NAIC Code: 524114

www.unitedhealthgroup.com

TYPES OF BUSINESS:

Medical Insurance
Wellness Plans
Dental & Vision Insurance
Health Information Technology
Physician Practice Groups
Pharmacy Benefits Management
PBM

BRANDS/DIVISIONS/AFFILIATES:

UnitedHealthcare
Optum
UnitedHealthcare Employer
UnitedHealthcare Medicare & Retirement
UnitedHealthcare Global
OptumHealth
OptumInsight
OptumRx

CONTACTS: *Note: Officers with more than one job title may be intentionally listed here more than once.*

Steven Nelson, CEO, Subsidiary
Andrew Witty, CEO, Subsidiary
David Wichmann, CEO
John Rex, CFO
Stephen Hemsley, Chairman of the Board
Thomas Roos, Chief Accounting Officer
Marianne Short, Executive VP
D. Wilson, Executive VP

GROWTH PLANS/SPECIAL FEATURES:

UnitedHealth Group, Inc. is a diversified health care company. Through its family of businesses, the firm offers core competencies in data and health information, advanced technology and clinical expertise, which are deployed into two platforms: health benefits, operating under UnitedHealthcare; and health services, operating under Optum. UnitedHealthcare provides health care benefits to an array of customers and markets. UnitedHealthcare Employer and Individual serves employers ranging from sole proprietorships to large, multi-site and national employers, public sector employers and individual customers. UnitedHealthcare Medicare & Retirement delivers health and well-being benefits for Medicare beneficiaries and retirees. UnitedHealthcare Community & State manages health care benefit programs on behalf of state Medicaid and community programs and their participants. UnitedHealthcare Global provides health and dental benefits and hospital and clinical services to employer groups and individuals in South America and other diversified global health businesses. Optum is a health services business serving the health care marketplace, including payers, care providers, employers, governments, life sciences companies and consumers, through its OptumHealth, OptumInsight and OptumRx businesses. These businesses have dedicated units that help improve overall health system performance through optimizing care quality, reducing costs and improving consumer experience and care provider performance, leveraging capabilities in data and analytics, pharmacy care services, population health, health care delivery and health care operations.

UnitedHealth Group offers comprehensive benefits, retirement options, tuition reimbursement and a variety of employee assistance programs.

FINANCIAL DATA: *Note: Data for latest year may not have been available at press time.*

In U.S. $	2020	2019	2018	2017	2016	2015
Revenue	255,639,000,000	240,269,000,000	224,871,000,000	200,136,000,000	184,012,000,000	156,397,000,000
R&D Expense						
Operating Income	20,903,000,000	17,799,000,000	15,968,000,000	14,186,000,000	12,102,000,000	10,311,000,000
Operating Margin %		.07%	.07%	.07%	.07%	.07%
SGA Expense						
Net Income	15,403,000,000	13,839,000,000	11,986,000,000	10,558,000,000	7,017,000,000	5,813,000,000
Operating Cash Flow	22,174,000,000	18,463,000,000	15,713,000,000	13,596,000,000	9,795,000,000	9,740,000,000
Capital Expenditure	2,051,000,000	2,071,000,000	2,063,000,000	2,023,000,000	1,705,000,000	1,556,000,000
EBITDA	25,296,000,000	22,405,000,000	19,772,000,000	17,454,000,000	14,985,000,000	12,714,000,000
Return on Assets %		.08%	.08%	.08%	.06%	.06%
Return on Equity %		.25%	.24%	.25%	.19%	.18%
Debt to Equity		0.639	0.669	0.604	0.673	0.753

CONTACT INFORMATION:

Phone: 952 936-1300   Fax: 952 936-0044
Toll-Free: 800-328-5979
Address: 9900 Bren Rd. E., Minnetonka, MN 55343 United States

SALARIES/BONUSES:

Top Exec. Salary: $ Bonus: $
Second Exec. Salary: $ Bonus: $

STOCK TICKER/OTHER:

Stock Ticker: UNH
Employees: 330,000
Parent Company:

Exchange: NYS
Fiscal Year Ends: 12/31

OTHER THOUGHTS:

Estimated Female Officers or Directors: 4
Hot Spot for Advancement for Women/Minorities: Y

Universal Health Services Inc

www.uhsinc.com

NAIC Code: 622110

TYPES OF BUSINESS:

General Medical and Surgical Hospitals
Acute Care Hospitals
Behavioral Health Hospitals
Outpatient Facilities
Ambulatory Care
Real Estate Investment Trust

BRANDS/DIVISIONS/AFFILIATES:

Universal Health Realty Income Trust

GROWTH PLANS/SPECIAL FEATURES:

Universal Health Services, Inc. (UHS), in business for more than 40 years, owns and operates through its subsidiaries acute care hospitals, outpatient facilities and behavioral healthcare facilities. UHS operates 26 acute care hospitals, 330 behavioral health facilities, 41 outpatient facilities and ambulatory care access points, an insurance offering, a physician network and various related services in more than 35 U.S. states, Washington DC, Puerto Rico and the U.K. The firm also acts as the advisor to Universal Health Realty Income Trust, a real estate investment trust.

CONTACTS: Note: Officers with more than one job title may be intentionally listed here more than once.

Alan Miller, CEO
Steve Filton, CFO
Marc Miller, Director
Marvin Pember, Executive VP

FINANCIAL DATA: Note: Data for latest year may not have been available at press time.

In U.S. $	2020	2019	2018	2017	2016	2015
Revenue	11,558,900,000	11,378,260,000	10,772,280,000	10,409,870,000	9,766,210,000	9,043,451,000
R&D Expense						
Operating Income	1,358,354,000	1,215,908,000	1,175,262,000	1,280,178,000	1,276,072,000	1,243,580,000
Operating Margin %		.11%	.11%	.12%	.13%	.14%
SGA Expense	5,729,156,000	5,696,702,000	5,360,630,000	5,083,764,000	4,682,854,000	4,307,360,000
Net Income	943,953,000	814,854,000	779,705,000	752,303,000	702,409,000	680,528,000
Operating Cash Flow	2,360,169,000	1,438,469,000	1,340,893,000	1,182,581,000	1,288,474,000	1,020,898,000
Capital Expenditure	786,218,000	663,518,000	811,669,000	609,431,000	1,155,217,000	912,976,000
EBITDA	1,866,727,000	1,718,213,000	1,641,671,000	1,716,807,000	1,681,473,000	1,640,952,000
Return on Assets %		.07%	.07%	.07%	.07%	.07%
Return on Equity %		.15%	.15%	.16%	.16%	.17%
Debt to Equity		0.757	0.73	0.70	0.889	0.797

CONTACT INFORMATION:

Phone: 610 768-3300 Fax: 610 768-3336
Toll-Free:
Address: 367 S. Gulph Rd., King Of Prussia, PA 19406 United States

STOCK TICKER/OTHER:

Stock Ticker: UHS
Employees: 89,000
Parent Company:

Exchange: NYS
Fiscal Year Ends: 12/31

SALARIES/BONUSES:

Top Exec. Salary: $ Bonus: $
Second Exec. Salary: $ Bonus: $

OTHER THOUGHTS:

Estimated Female Officers or Directors: 2
Hot Spot for Advancement for Women/Minorities: Y

US Bancorp (US Bank)

NAIC Code: 522110

TYPES OF BUSINESS:

Banking
Lease Financing
Consumer Finance
Credit Cards
Discount Brokerage
Investment Advisory Services
Trust Services
Insurance

BRANDS/DIVISIONS/AFFILIATES:

US Bank NA
Elavon Inc

CONTACTS: Note: Officers with more than one job title may be intentionally listed here more than once.

Andrew Cecere, CEO
Ismat Aziz, Exec. VP
Terrance Dolan, CFO
Craig Gifford, Chief Accounting Officer
Katherine Quinn, Chief Administrative Officer
Mark Runkel, Chief Credit Officer
Jodi Richard, Chief Risk Officer
James Chosy, Executive VP
Gunjan Kedia, Vice Chairman, Divisional
Leslie Godridge, Vice Chairman, Divisional
Shailesh Kotwal, Vice Chairman, Divisional

GROWTH PLANS/SPECIAL FEATURES:

U.S. Bancorp is a multi-state financial services holding company. The firm provides a full range of financial services, including loans and deposits, cash management, capital markets, and trust and investment management. U.S. Bancorp also engages in credit card services, merchant and automated teller machine (ATM) processing, mortgage banking, insurance, brokerage and leasing. Subsidiary U.S. Bank NA is engaged in the general banking business, primarily in domestic markets. U.S. Bank had more than $540 billion in assets as of September 30, 2020. It provides its banking services to individuals, businesses, institutional organizations, governmental entities and financial institutions. U.S. Bank's commercial and consumer lending services are offered to customers within U.S. Bancorp's domestic markets, to domestic customers with foreign operations and to large national customers operating in specific industries targeted by U.S. Bancorp. Non-banking subsidiaries offer investment offer investment and insurance products to U.S. Bancorp's customers, principally within its domestic markets, and fund administration services to a broad range of mutual and other funds. Banking and investment services are provided through a network for more than 2,700 banking offices located in the U.S., as well as through online and mobile devices. U.S. Bancorp operations over 4,450 automated teller machines (ATMs) and provides 24/7 telephone customer service. Mortgage banking services are provided through banking offices and loan production offices throughout the company's domestic markets; and lending products may be originated through banking offices, indirect correspondents, brokers or other lending sources. Wholly-owned Elavon, Inc. provides domestic merchant processing services in the U.S., Canada and Mexico, as well as segments of Europe.

U.S. Bancorp offers comprehensive benefits, retirement options and employee assistance programs.

FINANCIAL DATA: Note: Data for latest year may not have been available at press time.

In U.S. $	2020	2019	2018	2017	2016	2015
Revenue	23,226,000,000	22,883,000,000	22,181,000,000	21,852,000,000	21,105,000,000	20,093,000,000
R&D Expense						
Operating Income						
Operating Margin %						
SGA Expense	8,256,000,000	8,037,000,000	7,822,000,000	7,474,000,000	6,766,000,000	6,340,000,000
Net Income	4,959,000,000	6,914,000,000	7,096,000,000	6,218,000,000	5,888,000,000	5,879,000,000
Operating Cash Flow	3,716,000,000	4,889,000,000	10,564,000,000	6,472,000,000	5,336,000,000	8,782,000,000
Capital Expenditure						
EBITDA						
Return on Assets %		.01%	.01%	.01%	.01%	.01%
Return on Equity %		.14%	.15%	.14%	.14%	.14%
Debt to Equity		0.876	0.918	0.74	0.797	0.79

CONTACT INFORMATION:

Phone: 651 466-3000   Fax:
Toll-Free:
Address: 800 Nicollet Mall, Minneapolis, MN 55402 United States

STOCK TICKER/OTHER:

Stock Ticker: USB
Employees: 69,651
Parent Company:

Exchange: NYS
Fiscal Year Ends: 12/31

SALARIES/BONUSES:

Top Exec. Salary: $ Bonus: $
Second Exec. Salary: $ Bonus: $

OTHER THOUGHTS:

Estimated Female Officers or Directors: 5
Hot Spot for Advancement for Women/Minorities: Y

USAA

www.usaa.com

NAIC Code: 524126

TYPES OF BUSINESS:

Insurance, Direct Property & Casualty
Banking
Insurance
Investment
Real Estate
Retirement
Annuities

BRANDS/DIVISIONS/AFFILIATES:

CONTACTS: Note: Officers with more than one job title may be intentionally listed here more than once.

Wayne Peacock, CEO
Shon Manasco, Chief Admin. Officer
Steven A. Bennett, General Counsel
Wendi E. Strong, Exec. VP-Enterprise Affairs
F. David Bohne, Pres., USAA Federal Savings Bank
Kevin J. Bergner, Pres., USAA Property & Casualty Insurance Group
Christopher W. Claus, Exec. VP-Enterprise Advice Group
Wayne Peacock, Pres., USAA Capital Corporation
Thomas B. Fargo, Chmn.

GROWTH PLANS/SPECIAL FEATURES:

USAA (United Services Automobile Association) is a diversified financial services group of companies. The association is a leading provider of insurance, banking, investment, real estate, retirement and health insurance products to members of the U.S. military, veterans, their spouses and their children. Insurance products include auto, renters, homeowner, rental property, valuable personal property, condo, flood, life, annuities, umbrella, motorcycle, boat, recreational vehicle, small business and other solutions. Banking products include checking and savings accounts, credit cards, vehicle and boat loans, certified deposits, home mortgages, personal loans, youth banking and account services. Investment products include brokerage, trading, mutual funds, exchange traded funds (ETFs), IRAs, rollovers, education 529 plans, automated investing, and planning services. Real estate products include mortgage rates, mortgages, VA loans, refinancing and payment assistance. Retirement products include retirement income, IRAs, rollovers, annuities and long-term care. Health insurance products include dental, vision and Medicare. Other products and discounts by USAA include home solutions, travel deals, online shopping, vehicle maintenance, and health and wellness options.

FINANCIAL DATA: Note: Data for latest year may not have been available at press time.

In U.S. $	2020	2019	2018	2017	2016	2015
Revenue	36,296,000,000	35,617,000,000	31,367,800,000	30,000,000,000	27,131,000,000	24,361,000,000
R&D Expense						
Operating Income						
Operating Margin %						
SGA Expense						
Net Income	3,915,000,000	4,007,000,000	2,291,900,000	2,400,000,000	1,779,000,000	2,266,000,000
Operating Cash Flow						
Capital Expenditure						
EBITDA						
Return on Assets %						
Return on Equity %						
Debt to Equity						

CONTACT INFORMATION:

Phone: 210-498-2211   Fax: 210-498-9940
Toll-Free: 800-531-8722
Address: 9800 Fredericksburg Rd., San Antonio, TX 78288 United States

STOCK TICKER/OTHER:

Stock Ticker: Mutual Company
Employees: 36,000
Parent Company:

Exchange:
Fiscal Year Ends: 12/31

SALARIES/BONUSES:

Top Exec. Salary: $ Bonus: $
Second Exec. Salary: $ Bonus: $

OTHER THOUGHTS:

Estimated Female Officers or Directors: 4
Hot Spot for Advancement for Women/Minorities: Y

Vanguard Group Inc (The)

NAIC Code: 523920

TYPES OF BUSINESS:

Investment Management/Mutual Funds
Financial Planning
Brokerage
Annuities
Investment Services-Retirement Plans
Exchange Traded Funds (ETFs)

BRANDS/DIVISIONS/AFFILIATES:

CONTACTS: Note: Officers with more than one job title may be intentionally listed here more than once.

Mortimer J. Buckley, CEO
Michael Rollings, CFO
John James, Chief Human Resources Officer
John T. Mercante, Dir.-IT
Heidi Stam, General Counsel
Michael S. Miller, Managing Dir.-Planning & Dev. Group
Glenn Reed, Managing Dir.-Finance & Strategy Group
Paul Heller, Managing Dir.-Retail Investor Group
Mortimer J. Buckley, Chief Investment Officer
Chris D. McIsaac, Managing Dir.-Institutional Investor Group
Martha King, Head-Financial Svcs. Div.
Mortimer J. Buckley, Chmn.
James M. Norris, Managing Dir.-Int'l Oper.

GROWTH PLANS/SPECIAL FEATURES:

The Vanguard Group, Inc. is an investment manager, holding more than $6 trillion in global assets under management (as of late-2020). The company offers its services through hundreds of domestic U.S. and foreign market funds. Not only does Vanguard provide services to investment companies, it also caters to pooled investment vehicles, corporations, individuals, retirement plan sponsors, institutional investors, separate account institutional clients and financial advisors. Vanguard manages separate client-focused equity, fixed income and balanced portfolios. It manages mutual funds, variable annuities and exchange traded funds (ETFs). Vanguard invests in the public equity and fixed income markets worldwide. It utilizes both a fundamental and quantitative analysis approach to create its portfolio; and employs a combination of in-house and external research to make its investments. Based in the U.S., the firm has approximately 20 locations worldwide.

Vanguard offers employees medical, dental, life and vision insurance; flexible spending accounts; retiree programs; paid time off; leave of absence; legal services; an onsite health clinic and fitness center; and a 401(k).

FINANCIAL DATA: Note: Data for latest year may not have been available at press time.

In U.S. $	2020	2019	2018	2017	2016	2015
Revenue	4,576,000,000	4,400,000,000	4,000,000,000			
R&D Expense						
Operating Income						
Operating Margin %						
SGA Expense						
Net Income						
Operating Cash Flow						
Capital Expenditure						
EBITDA						
Return on Assets %						
Return on Equity %						
Debt to Equity						

CONTACT INFORMATION:

Phone: 610-648-6000   Fax: 610-669-6605
Toll-Free: 877-662-7447
Address: 100 Vanguard Blvd., Malvern, PA 19355 United States

STOCK TICKER/OTHER:

Stock Ticker: Private   Exchange:
Employees: 17,300   Fiscal Year Ends: 12/31
Parent Company:

SALARIES/BONUSES:

Top Exec. Salary: $ Bonus: $
Second Exec. Salary: $ Bonus: $

OTHER THOUGHTS:

Estimated Female Officers or Directors: 3
Hot Spot for Advancement for Women/Minorities: Y

Varian Medical Systems Inc

www.varian.com

NAIC Code: 334510

TYPES OF BUSINESS:

Radiation Oncology Systems
X-Ray Equipment
Software Systems
Security & Inspection Products

BRANDS/DIVISIONS/AFFILIATES:

CONTACTS: Note: Officers with more than one job title may be intentionally listed here more than once.

Dow Wilson, CEO
Gary Bischoping, CFO
R. Eckert, Chairman of the Board
Magnus Momsen, Chief Accounting Officer
Timothy Guertin, Director
John Kuo, General Counsel
Kolleen Kennedy, Other Executive Officer
Christopher Toth, President, Divisional
Chris Toth, President, Divisional

GROWTH PLANS/SPECIAL FEATURES:

Varian Medical Systems, Inc. develops and manufactures medical devices and software for treating cancer and other medical conditions. Varian operates through two segments: oncology systems and proton systems. The oncology systems segment designs, manufactures, sells and services hardware and software products for treating cancer with conventional radiotherapy, and advanced treatments such as fixed field intensity-modulated radiation therapy (IMRT), image-guided radiation therapy (IGRT), volumetric modulated arc therapy (VMAT), stereotactic radiosurgery (SRS), stereotactic body radiotherapy (SBRT) and brachytherapy, as well as associated quality assurance equipment. This segment's software solutions also include informatics software for information management, clinical knowledge exchange, patient care management, practice management and decision-making support for comprehensive cancer clinics, radiotherapy centers and medical oncology practices. Hardware products include linear accelerators, brachytherapy after-loaders, treatment accessories and quality assurance software. The proton solutions segment develops, designs, manufactures, sells and services products and systems for delivering proton therapy, another form of external beam therapy using proton beams, for the treatment of cancer. Varian's current focus is bringing its expertise in X-ray beam radiation therapy to proton therapy to improve its clinical utility and to reduce its cost of treatment per patient. In August 2020, Varian agreed to be acquired by Siemens Healthineers AG, the parent of several European medical technology companies, for $16.4 billion. The transaction is expected to close in the first half of 2021, and upon completion Varian will continue to operate under the Varian name, as a Siemens Healthineers brand.

Varian offers its employees medical, life, AD&D, disability, dental and vision plans; a 401(k); educational reimbursement; an employee assistance program; and a stock purchase plan.

FINANCIAL DATA: Note: Data for latest year may not have been available at press time.

In U.S. $	2020	2019	2018	2017	2016	2015
Revenue		3,225,100,032	2,919,099,904	2,668,199,936	3,217,799,936	3,099,110,912
R&D Expense						
Operating Income						
Operating Margin %						
SGA Expense						
Net Income		291,900,000	149,900,000	249,600,000	402,300,000	411,484,992
Operating Cash Flow						
Capital Expenditure						
EBITDA						
Return on Assets %						
Return on Equity %						
Debt to Equity						

CONTACT INFORMATION:

Phone: 650 493-4000   Fax:
Toll-Free: 800-544-4636
Address: 3100 Hansen Way, Palo Alto, CA 94304 United States

STOCK TICKER/OTHER:

Stock Ticker: VAR
Employees: 10,062
Parent Company:

Exchange: NYS
Fiscal Year Ends: 09/30

SALARIES/BONUSES:

Top Exec. Salary: $ Bonus: $
Second Exec. Salary: $ Bonus: $

OTHER THOUGHTS:

Estimated Female Officers or Directors: 6
Hot Spot for Advancement for Women/Minorities: Y

VCA Inc

NAIC Code: 541940

TYPES OF BUSINESS:

Animal Health Care Services
Veterinary Diagnostic Laboratories
Full-Service Animal Hospitals
Veterinary Equipment
Ultrasound Imaging

BRANDS/DIVISIONS/AFFILIATES:

Mars Incorporated
VCA Animal Hospital
VCA Canada
Companion Animal Practices of North America
Antech Diagnostics
South Technologies Inc
Camp Bow Wow

CONTACTS: Note: Officers with more than one job title may be intentionally listed here more than once.

Arthur J. Antin, COO
Josh Drake, President, Subsidiary

GROWTH PLANS/SPECIAL FEATURES:

VCA, Inc. is a leading animal healthcare company operating in the U.S. and Canada. The firm provides services and diagnostic testing to support veterinary care, and sells diagnostic equipment and other medical technology products to the veterinary market. VCA's hospitals offer a full range of general medical and surgical services for companion animals, as well as specialized treatments, including advanced diagnostic services, internal medicine, oncology, ophthalmology, dermatology and cardiology. In addition, the company provides pharmaceutical products and performs a variety of pet wellness programs such as health examinations, diagnostic testing, routine vaccinations, spaying, neutering and dental care. VCA's network of more than 1,000 animal hospitals provides service to over 10 million patients annually, which are located in 46 U.S. states and five Canadian provinces. In addition, VCA provides diagnostic services to more than 17,000 independent hospitals. Dog day care and boarding services are also offered at more than 130 locations. Brands and subsidiaries of VCA include: VCA Animal Hospital; VCA Canada; Companion Animal Practices of North America (CAPNA); Antech Diagnostics; South Technologies, Inc.; and Camp Bow Wow. VCA, Inc. operates as a distinct and separate business unit within Mars Incorporated's pet care segment.

FINANCIAL DATA: Note: Data for latest year may not have been available at press time.

In U.S. $	2020	2019	2018	2017	2016	2015
Revenue	3,213,000,000	3,150,000,000	3,000,000,000	2,700,000,000	2,516,863,000	2,133,675,008
R&D Expense						
Operating Income						
Operating Margin %						
SGA Expense						
Net Income						
Operating Cash Flow						
Capital Expenditure						
EBITDA						
Return on Assets %						
Return on Equity %						
Debt to Equity						

CONTACT INFORMATION:

Phone: 310 571-6500   Fax: 310 571-6700
Toll-Free: 800-966-1822
Address: 12401 W. Olympic Blvd., Los Angeles, CA 90064 United States

STOCK TICKER/OTHER:

Stock Ticker: Subsidiary
Employees: 30,000
Parent Company: Mars Incorporated

Exchange:
Fiscal Year Ends: 12/31

SALARIES/BONUSES:

Top Exec. Salary: $ Bonus: $
Second Exec. Salary: $ Bonus: $

OTHER THOUGHTS:

Estimated Female Officers or Directors:
Hot Spot for Advancement for Women/Minorities:

Verizon Communications Inc

www.verizon.com

NAIC Code: 517110

TYPES OF BUSINESS:

Mobile Phone and Wireless Services
Telecommunications Services
Cable TV Subscriptions
Long-Distance Services
High-Speed Internet Access
Video-on-Demand Services
e-Commerce & Online Services

BRANDS/DIVISIONS/AFFILIATES:

Verizon Wireless
BlueJeans Network Inc

CONTACTS: Note: Officers with more than one job title may be intentionally listed here more than once.

Kumara Gowrappan, CEO, Divisional
Hans Vestberg, CEO
Matthew Ellis, CFO
Anthony Skiadas, Chief Accounting Officer
Marc Reed, Chief Administrative Officer
Kyle Malady, Chief Technology Officer
Craig Silliman, Executive VP, Divisional
Rima Qureshi, Executive VP
Ronan Dunne, Executive VP
Tami Erwin, Executive VP

GROWTH PLANS/SPECIAL FEATURES:

Verizon Communications, Inc. is a world-leading provider of communications services. The company operates through its subsidiaries, with products and services categorized into two primary segments: wireless and wireline. The wireless segment consists of wireless voice and data services and equipment sales, which are provided to consumer, business and government customers throughout the U.S. This division does business as Verizon Wireless and represents approximately 70% of Verizon's aggregate revenues. Wireless' network technology platform is currently 4G LTE (long-term evolution), but the segment is engaged in 5G wireless technology development and its ecosystems for fixed and mobile 5G wireless services are intact. This division offers various post-paid account service plans, including unlimited plans, shared data plans, single connection plans and other plans tailored to the customer's need. Pre-paid connection plans are available and feature domestic unlimited voice and unlimited domestic/international text. Access to the internet is available on all smartphones and nearly all basic phones; and network access needed to deliver various Internet of Things (IoT) products and services is also provided. The wireline segment consists of video and data services, corporate networking solutions, security and managed network services, and local and long-distance voice services. Wireline products and services are provided to consumers in the U.S., as well as to carriers, businesses and government customers both in the U.S. and worldwide. These products are built around a fiber-based network (as well as a copper-based one, to a lesser degree), supporting data, video and advanced business services in areas where high-speed connections is needed. During 2020, Verizon acquired video conferencing service BlueJeans Network, Inc.; agreed to acquire Tracfone Wireless, Inc. from America Movil, which provides pre-paid and mobile services in the U.S.; and agreed to acquire Bluegrass Cellular, a rural wireless operator serving central Kentucky. In May 2021, the firm agrees to sell Yahoo and AOL to Apollo Global Management, Inc. for $5 billion.

Verizon offers comprehensive employee benefits.

FINANCIAL DATA: Note: Data for latest year may not have been available at press time.

In U.S. $	2020	2019	2018	2017	2016	2015
Revenue	128,292,000,000	131,868,000,000	130,863,000,000	126,034,000,000	125,980,000,000	131,620,000,000
R&D Expense						
Operating Income	28,798,000,000	30,470,000,000	26,869,000,000	29,188,000,000	27,059,000,000	33,060,000,000
Operating Margin %		.23%	.21%	.23%	.21%	.25%
SGA Expense	31,573,000,000	29,990,000,000	31,083,000,000	28,336,000,000	31,569,000,000	29,986,000,000
Net Income	17,801,000,000	19,265,000,000	15,528,000,000	30,101,000,000	13,127,000,000	17,879,000,000
Operating Cash Flow	41,768,000,000	35,746,000,000	34,339,000,000	25,305,000,000	22,715,000,000	38,930,000,000
Capital Expenditure	20,318,000,000	18,837,000,000	18,087,000,000	17,830,000,000	17,593,000,000	27,717,000,000
EBITDA	44,934,000,000	44,145,000,000	41,859,000,000	42,281,000,000	41,290,000,000	49,177,000,000
Return on Assets %		.07%	.06%	.12%	.05%	.07%
Return on Equity %		.34%	.32%	.92%	.67%	1.24%
Debt to Equity		1.94	1.992	2.637	4.681	6.313

CONTACT INFORMATION:

Phone: 212 395-1000   Fax:
Toll-Free: 800-837-4966
Address: 1095 Avenue of the Americas, New York, NY 10036 United States

STOCK TICKER/OTHER:

Stock Ticker: VZ
Employees: 132,200
Parent Company:

Exchange: NYS
Fiscal Year Ends: 12/31

SALARIES/BONUSES:

Top Exec. Salary: $ Bonus: $
Second Exec. Salary: $ Bonus: $

OTHER THOUGHTS:

Estimated Female Officers or Directors: 5
Hot Spot for Advancement for Women/Minorities: Y

ViaSat Inc
NAIC Code: 334220

www.viasat.com

TYPES OF BUSINESS:
Telecommunications Equipment-Digital Satellite
Networking & Wireless Signal Processing
Satellite Broadband Internet Service Provider

BRANDS/DIVISIONS/AFFILIATES:

CONTACTS: *Note: Officers with more than one job title may be intentionally listed here more than once.*
Mark Dankberg, CEO
Shawn Duffy, Chief Accounting Officer
Keven Lippert, Chief Administrative Officer
Mark Miller, Chief Technology Officer
Girish Chandran, Chief Technology Officer
Robert Blair, General Counsel
Melinda Del Toro, Other Executive Officer
Ken Peterman, President, Divisional
Kevin Harkenrider, President, Divisional
David Ryan, President, Divisional
Richard Baldridge, President
Bruce Dirks, Senior VP, Divisional
Doug Abts, Vice President, Divisional
Marc Agnew, Vice President, Divisional

GROWTH PLANS/SPECIAL FEATURES:
ViaSat, Inc. provides advanced satellite and wireless communications and secure networking systems, products and services. The company operates in three segments: government systems, commercial networks and satellite services. The government systems segment encompasses products serving defense customers, including its tactical data link product line; tactical networking and information assurance, enabling the government and military to secure information up to top secret levels; and government satellite communication systems. Current defense products include multifunctional information distribution system (MIDS) terminals for military fighter jets and their successor, MIDS joint tactical radio system (MIDS-JTRS) terminals, 'disposable' weapon data links and portable small tactical terminals. The commercial networks develop and produce a variety of advanced end-to-end satellite and other wireless communication systems and ground networking equipment and products that address five key markets: consumer, enterprise, in-flight, maritime and ground mobile applications. Satellite communication systems for this segment include fixed satellite networks, mobile broadband satellite communication systems, antenna systems and satellite networking development. The satellite services segment, like the commercial networks segment, offers wholesale and retail broadband services, as well as managed broadband wireless networking services, and mobile satellite broadband services to airborne- and marine-based customers. Launched satellites by the firm include: ViaSat-1, in 2011; and ViaSat-2, in 2017; with three ViaSat-3 class satellites under construction. In addition, ViaSat has a joint venture with Eutelsat which operates two businesses: one operates Eutelsat's KA-SAT satellite and wholesale broadband business, and the other purchases KA-SAT capacity and markets retail broadband internet services throughout Europe and the Mediterranean.

ViaSat offers employee benefits such as health, 401(k) and tuition reimbursement, depending on the location.

FINANCIAL DATA: *Note: Data for latest year may not have been available at press time.*

In U.S. $	2020	2019	2018	2017	2016	2015
Revenue	2,309,238,000	2,068,258,000	1,594,625,000	1,559,337,000	1,417,431,000	
R&D Expense	130,434,000	123,044,000	168,347,000	129,647,000	77,184,000	
Operating Income	38,421,000	-60,620,000	-92,187,000	36,459,000	41,119,000	
Operating Margin %	.02%	-.03%	-.06%	.02%	.03%	
SGA Expense	523,085,000	458,458,000	385,420,000	333,468,000	298,345,000	
Net Income	-212,000	-67,623,000	-67,305,000	23,767,000	21,741,000	
Operating Cash Flow	436,936,000	327,551,000	358,633,000	411,298,000	296,937,000	
Capital Expenditure	761,078,000	686,820,000	584,487,000	585,658,000	450,625,000	
EBITDA	382,247,000	258,142,000	154,208,000	283,389,000	285,421,000	
Return on Assets %	.00%	-.02%	-.02%	.01%	.01%	
Return on Equity %	.00%	-.04%	-.04%	.02%	.02%	
Debt to Equity	1.04	0.73	0.533	0.489	0.845	

CONTACT INFORMATION:
Phone: 760 476-2200   Fax: 760 929-3941
Toll-Free:
Address: 6155 El Camino Real, Carlsbad, CA 92009 United States

STOCK TICKER/OTHER:
Stock Ticker: VSAT
Employees: 5,800
Parent Company:

Exchange: NAS
Fiscal Year Ends: 03/31

SALARIES/BONUSES:
Top Exec. Salary: $ Bonus: $
Second Exec. Salary: $ Bonus: $

OTHER THOUGHTS:
Estimated Female Officers or Directors:
Hot Spot for Advancement for Women/Minorities:

Viavi Solutions Inc

NAIC Code: 334220

TYPES OF BUSINESS:

Communications and Commercial Optical Products
Network Systems
Security Products
Systems Enablement and Consulting

BRANDS/DIVISIONS/AFFILIATES:

Optically Variable Pigment
Optically Variable Magnetic Pigment

CONTACTS: Note: Officers with more than one job title may be intentionally listed here more than once.

Oleg Khaykin, CEO
Amar Maletira, CFO
Paul McNab, Chief Marketing Officer
Richard Belluzzo, Director
Kevin Siebert, General Counsel
Luke Scrivanich, General Manager, Divisional
Ralph Rondinone, Senior VP, Divisional
Gary Staley, Senior VP, Divisional

GROWTH PLANS/SPECIAL FEATURES:

Viavi Solutions, Inc. is a global provider of network test, monitoring and assurance solutions to communications service providers, enterprises and their ecosystems. The company's solutions deliver end-to-end visibility across physical, virtual and hybrid networks, which enables Viavi customers to optimize connectivity, quality of experience and profitability. The firm also produces thin film coatings, which provide light management solutions to various markets. Viavi operates through three business segments: network enablement, service enablement and optical security and performance products. Together, the network enablement and service enablement segments enable networks to provide agile, flexible, programmable and cost-effective transmission capacity and speed to their customers. These segments provide products and solutions for the deployment of next-generation network technologies, including optical fiber-to-the-home and to everywhere. The optical security and performance products segment produces and provides Viavi's anti-counterfeiting products and solutions, including its Optically Variable Pigment (OVP) and Optically Variable Magnetic Pigment (OVMP) technologies. These technologies protect the integrity of banknotes and other high-value documents by delivering optical effects which are very easy for consumers to recognize but difficult for counterfeiters to reproduce. This division also provides optical technologies for government, healthcare, consumer electronics and industrial markets. In early-2021, Viavi relocated its headquarters from California to Arizona, and announced that its optical security and performance products segment plans to establish a new manufacturing facility in Chandler, Arizona. The company's San Jose, California office continues to operate as a center of excellence and sales office.

Viavi offers its employees medical, dental and vision benefits, wellness initiatives, retirement benefits, stock compensation and an employee stock purchase plan.

FINANCIAL DATA: Note: Data for latest year may not have been available at press time.

In U.S. $	2020	2019	2018	2017	2016	2015
Revenue	1,136,300,000	1,130,300,000	880,400,000	811,400,000	906,300,000	
R&D Expense	193,600,000	187,000,000	133,300,000	136,300,000	166,400,000	
Operating Income	121,600,000	82,800,000	13,400,000	35,200,000	17,600,000	
Operating Margin %		.07%	.02%	.04%	.02%	
SGA Expense	315,000,000	343,500,000	324,500,000	300,500,000	351,100,000	
Net Income	28,700,000	5,400,000	-46,000,000	166,900,000	-99,200,000	
Operating Cash Flow	135,600,000	138,800,000	66,000,000	80,000,000	52,900,000	
Capital Expenditure	31,900,000	45,000,000	42,500,000	38,600,000	35,500,000	
EBITDA	235,500,000	185,800,000	98,100,000	287,500,000	60,400,000	
Return on Assets %		.00%	-.02%	.09%	-.05%	
Return on Equity %		.01%	-.06%	.23%	-.11%	
Debt to Equity		0.833	0.811	1.22	0.895	

CONTACT INFORMATION:

Phone: 408-404-3600   Fax: 408-404-4500
Toll-Free:
Address: 7047 E. Greenway Pkwy., Ste. 250, Scottsdale, AZ 85254 United States

STOCK TICKER/OTHER:

Stock Ticker: VIAV
Employees: 3,600
Parent Company:

Exchange: NAS
Fiscal Year Ends: 06/27

SALARIES/BONUSES:

Top Exec. Salary: $ Bonus: $
Second Exec. Salary: $ Bonus: $

OTHER THOUGHTS:

Estimated Female Officers or Directors:
Hot Spot for Advancement for Women/Minorities:

Visa Inc

NAIC Code: 522320

TYPES OF BUSINESS:

Credit Cards
Payments Technology
Payments Solutions
Chip Payment Technology
Debit Solutions
Prepaid Solutions
Credit Payment Solutions

BRANDS/DIVISIONS/AFFILIATES:

Visa Canada Corporaiton
CyberSource Corporation
Visa USA Inc
Visa International Service Association
Visa Worldwide Pte Limited
Visa Europe Limited
Visa Technology & Operations LLC
VisaNet

CONTACTS: Note: Officers with more than one job title may be intentionally listed here more than once.

Alfred Kelly, CEO
Vasant Prabhu, CFO
Robert Matschullat, Chairman of the Board
James Hoffmeister, Chief Accounting Officer
Lynne Biggar, Chief Marketing Officer
Mary Richey, Chief Risk Officer
Rajat Taneja, Executive VP, Divisional
William Sheedy, Executive VP, Divisional
Kelly Tullier, Executive VP
Ryan McInerney, President

GROWTH PLANS/SPECIAL FEATURES:

Visa, Inc. is a global payments technology company that connects consumers, businesses, financial institutions and governments in over 200 countries. The company's processing network, VisaNet, facilitates authorization, clearing and settlement of payment transactions worldwide. It also offers fraud protection for account holders and rapid payment for merchants. Visa is not a bank and does not issue cards, extend credit or set rates and fees for account holders in Visa-branded cards and payment products. In most cases, account holder and merchant relationships belong to, and are managed by, Visa's financial institution clients. Visa's tokenization replaces account numbers with digital tokens for online and mobile payments, benefiting merchants and issuers by removing sensitive account information and reducing fraud risk. Visa's chip payment technology addresses fraud at the physical point-of-sale by working with merchants and Visa financial institution clients in the U.S. The company's core products and services can be condensed into three divisions: debit, providing debit solutions that support issuers' payment products that draw on demand deposit accounts; prepaid, providing prepaid payment solutions that support issuer's products that access a pre-funded amount; and credit, providing credit payment solutions that support issuers' deferred payment and customized financing products. Subsidiaries of the company include Visa Canada Corporation, CyberSource Corporation, Visa USA Inc., Visa International Service Association, Visa Worldwide Pte. Limited, Visa Europe Limited, and Visa Technology & Operations LLC. During 2021, Visa agreed to acquire Currencycloud, a global platform that enables banks and fintechs to provide innovative foreign exchange solutions for cross-border payments. The Currencycloud platform supports nearly 500 banking and technology clients with reach in over 180 countries.

FINANCIAL DATA: Note: Data for latest year may not have been available at press time.

In U.S. $	2020	2019	2018	2017	2016	2015
Revenue	21,846,000,000	22,977,000,000	20,609,000,000	18,358,000,000	15,082,000,000	13,880,000,000
R&D Expense						
Operating Income	14,092,000,000	15,401,000,000	13,561,000,000	12,163,000,000	9,762,000,000	9,078,000,000
Operating Margin %		.67%	.66%	.66%	.65%	.65%
SGA Expense	2,475,000,000	2,755,000,000	2,579,000,000	2,391,000,000	2,054,000,000	1,755,000,000
Net Income	10,866,000,000	12,080,000,000	10,301,000,000	6,699,000,000	5,991,000,000	6,328,000,000
Operating Cash Flow	10,440,000,000	12,784,000,000	12,713,000,000	9,208,001,000	5,574,000,000	6,584,000,000
Capital Expenditure	736,000,000	756,000,000	718,000,000	707,000,000	523,000,000	414,000,000
EBITDA	15,073,000,000	16,057,000,000	14,031,000,000	12,813,000,000	8,941,000,000	9,572,000,000
Return on Assets %		.17%	.14%	.10%	.11%	.16%
Return on Equity %		.42%	.36%	.24%	.21%	.22%
Debt to Equity		0.572	0.583	0.61	0.584	

CONTACT INFORMATION:

Phone: 650-432-3200   Fax:
Toll-Free: 800-847-2911
Address: P.O. Box 8999, San Francisco, CA 94128-8999 United States

STOCK TICKER/OTHER:

Stock Ticker: V
Employees: 20,500
Parent Company:

Exchange: NYS
Fiscal Year Ends: 09/30

SALARIES/BONUSES:

Top Exec. Salary: $ Bonus: $
Second Exec. Salary: $ Bonus: $

OTHER THOUGHTS:

Estimated Female Officers or Directors: 6
Hot Spot for Advancement for Women/Minorities: Y

Vivint Solar Inc

www.vivintsolar.com/en

NAIC Code: 221114

TYPES OF BUSINESS:

Solar Electric Power Generation

BRANDS/DIVISIONS/AFFILIATES:

Sunrun Inc

CONTACTS: Note: Officers with more than one job title may be intentionally listed here more than once.

Lynn Jurich, CEO-Sunrun, Inc.
Dana Russell, CFO
Alex Dunn, Director
Todd Pedersen, Director
Thomas Plagemann, Executive VP, Divisional
L. Chance Allred, Other Executive Officer
Paul Dickson, Other Executive Officer

GROWTH PLANS/SPECIAL FEATURES:

Vivint Solar, Inc., a subsidiary of Sunrun, Inc., offers distributed solar energy to residential customers primarily through a direct-to-home sales model. Distributed solar energy refers to electricity generated by a solar energy system install at or near the customer's location. Vivint owns a substantial majority of the solar energy systems it installs and provides solar electricity pursuant to long-term contracts with customers. Under these contracts, customers pay little to no money up-front, typically receive savings on solar-generated electricity rates relative to utility-generated electricity rates following system interconnection to the power grid and continue to benefit from locked-in energy prices for the term of their contracts, insulating them against unpredictable increases in utility rates. The majority of customers sign 20-year contracts for solar electricity and by Vivint's systems, pay Vivint directly over the term of the contract. Customers are also offered the option to purchase solar energy systems for cash or through third-party loan financing. Vivint has developed an integrated approach to providing residential distributed solar energy where the company fully controls the lifecycle of the customer's experience, including the initial consultation, design and engineering process, installation, and ongoing monitoring and service. Vivint has installed solar energy systems with an aggregate of more than 1,294 megawatts (MW) of capacity at approximately 188,000 homes for an average solar energy system capacity of about 6.9 kilowatts. In October 2020, Vivint announced that it had been acquired by competitor Sunrun for an enterprise value of $3.2 billion in an all-stock deal.

FINANCIAL DATA: Note: Data for latest year may not have been available at press time.

In U.S. $	2020	2019	2018	2017	2016	2015
Revenue	360,000,000	341,040,992	290,320,992	268,028,000	135,167,008	64,182,000
R&D Expense						
Operating Income						
Operating Margin %						
SGA Expense						
Net Income		-102,175,000	-15,592,000	209,098,000	17,986,000	13,080,000
Operating Cash Flow						
Capital Expenditure						
EBITDA						
Return on Assets %						
Return on Equity %						
Debt to Equity						

CONTACT INFORMATION:

Phone: 801-377-9111   Fax: 801-377-4116
Toll-Free: 877-404-4129
Address: 1800 W. Ashton Blvd., Lehi, UT 84043 United States

SALARIES/BONUSES:

Top Exec. Salary: $ Bonus: $
Second Exec. Salary: $ Bonus: $

STOCK TICKER/OTHER:

Stock Ticker: Subsidiary
Employees: 2,998
Parent Company: Sunrun Inc

Exchange:
Fiscal Year Ends:

OTHER THOUGHTS:

Estimated Female Officers or Directors:
Hot Spot for Advancement for Women/Minorities:

VMware Inc

NAIC Code: 511210B

www.vmware.com

TYPES OF BUSINESS:

Computer Software: Network Management (IT), System Testing & Storage
Virtual Infrastructure Automation
Virtual Infrastructure Management

BRANDS/DIVISIONS/AFFILIATES:

vSphere
VMware Horizon
VMware AirWatch
Nyansa
Octarine
Lastline
Blue Medora TVS
Datrium

CONTACTS: Note: Officers with more than one job title may be intentionally listed here more than once.

Patrick Gelsinger, CEO
Zane Rowe, CFO
Michael Dell, Chairman of the Board
Kevan Krysler, Chief Accounting Officer
Sanjay Poonen, COO, Divisional
Rangarajan Raghuram, COO, Divisional
Rajiv Ramaswami, COO, Divisional
Maurizio Carli, Executive VP, Divisional
Amy Olli, General Counsel

GROWTH PLANS/SPECIAL FEATURES:

VMware, Inc. is a leader in virtualization infrastructure software. The firm develops and markets its products through three areas: software-defined data center (SDDC), end-user computing and hybrid cloud computing. SDDC consists of four main product categories: compute, providing a hypervisor layer of software that enables compute virtualization through its flagship, vSphere; storage and availability, offering cost-effective holistic data storage and protection options to all applications running on vSphere; network and security, which abstracts physical networks and simplifies the provisioning and consumption of networking resources; and management and automation, which automates overarching IT processes involved in provisioning IT services and resources to users from initial deployment to retirement. The firm's end-user computing products enable IT organizations to deliver secure access to data, applications and devices to end-users. This segment's solutions include desktop streamlining applications through its VMware Horizon brand, which controls and delivers data, stores images, and provides cloud delivery and virtualization solutions; mobile solutions through VMware AirWatch, which offer enterprise mobile management and security solutions; and Workspace ONE, which integrates VMware's silos to streamline the delivery of new applications and experiences and is offered as both an on-premises installed platform or as-a-service. VMware's hybrid cloud computing cross-cloud architecture enables consistent deployment models, security policies, visibility and governance for all applications, running on-premises and off-premises, regardless of the underlying cloud, hardware platform or hypervisor. During 2020, VMware acquired Nyansa, Octarine, Lastline, Blue Medora TVS, Datrium, Mode.net and SaltStack. In April 2021, Dell Technologies, Inc. announced plans to spin off its 81% stake in VMware by the end of 2021.

FINANCIAL DATA: Note: Data for latest year may not have been available at press time.

In U.S. $	2020	2019	2018	2017	2016	2015
Revenue	10,811,000,000	8,974,000,000	7,922,000,000		7,093,000,000	6,571,000,000
R&D Expense	2,522,000,000	1,975,000,000	1,755,000,000		1,503,000,000	1,300,000,000
Operating Income	1,520,000,000	2,059,000,000	1,779,000,000		1,491,000,000	1,220,000,000
Operating Margin %	.14%	.23%	.22%		.21%	.19%
SGA Expense	4,970,000,000	3,682,000,000	3,247,000,000		3,046,000,000	3,033,000,000
Net Income	6,412,000,000	2,422,000,000	570,000,000		1,186,000,000	997,000,000
Operating Cash Flow	3,872,000,000	3,663,000,000	3,211,000,000		2,381,000,000	1,899,000,000
Capital Expenditure	279,000,000	245,000,000	263,000,000		153,000,000	333,000,000
EBITDA	2,460,000,000	3,647,000,000	2,211,000,000		1,844,000,000	1,574,000,000
Return on Assets %	.31%	.14%	.03%		.07%	.06%
Return on Equity %	1.70%	.58%	.07%		.15%	.13%
Debt to Equity	0.535	7.699	0.544		0.185	0.189

CONTACT INFORMATION:

Phone: 650 427-5000   Fax: 650 475-5005
Toll-Free: 877-486-9273
Address: 3401 Hillview Ave., Palo Alto, CA 94304 United States

SALARIES/BONUSES:

Top Exec. Salary: $ Bonus: $
Second Exec. Salary: $ Bonus: $

STOCK TICKER/OTHER:

Stock Ticker: VMW
Employees: 34,000
Parent Company:

Exchange: NYS
Fiscal Year Ends: 12/31

OTHER THOUGHTS:

Estimated Female Officers or Directors: 3
Hot Spot for Advancement for Women/Minorities: Y

Sales, profits and employees may be estimates. Financial information, benefits and other data can change quickly and may vary from those stated here.

Wabtec Corporation

www.wabteccorp.com

NAIC Code: 336510

TYPES OF BUSINESS:

Railroad Equipment Manufacturing
Bus and Subway Equipment Manufacturing

BRANDS/DIVISIONS/AFFILIATES:

Westinghouse Air Brake Technologies Corporation
GE Transportation
RELCO Locomotives
Nordco

CONTACTS: Note: Officers with more than one job title may be intentionally listed here more than once.

Rafael Santana, CEO, Divisional
Raymond Betler, CEO
Patrick Dugan, CFO
Albert Neupaver, Chairman of the Board
John Mastalerz, Chief Accounting Officer
Scott Wahlstrom, Executive VP, Divisional
David DeNinno, Executive VP
Dominique Malefant, Other Corporate Officer
Greg Sbrocco, Senior VP, Divisional
Emilio Fernandez, Vice Chairman of the Board
Timothy Wesley, Vice President, Divisional

GROWTH PLANS/SPECIAL FEATURES:

Wabtec Corporation, formerly Westinghouse Air Brake Technologies Corporation, is a provider of technology-based equipment and services for the global freight rail and passenger transit industries. Wabtec provides its products and services through two business segments: freight and transit. The freight segment primarily manufactures and provides aftermarket parts and services for new locomotives; provides components for new and existing locomotives and freight cars; builds new commuter locomotives; supplies rail control and productivity in the transportation and mining industries; overhauls locomotives; and provides heat exchangers and cooling systems for rail and other industrial markets. This segment's customers include large, publicly-traded railroads, leasing companies, manufacturers of original equipment such as locomotives and freight cars, and utilities. Due to Wabtec's GE Transportation acquisition, this division is the largest global manufacturer of diesel-electric locomotives for freight railroads. The transit segment primarily manufactures and services components for new and existing passenger transit vehicles, typically regional trains, high-speed trains, subway cars, light-rail vehicles and buses, supplies rail control and infrastructure products including electronics, signal design and engineering services; and refurbishes passenger transit vehicles. This division's customers include public transit authorities and municipalities, leasing companies, and manufacturers of passenger transit vehicles and buses worldwide. During 2020 announced it had acquired RELCO Locomotives, a long-established player in the locomotive overhaul and maintenance industry. In 2021, Wabtec announced it had signed an agreement to acquire Nordco, a leading North American supplier of new, rebuilt and used maintenance of way equipment with a broad product and service portfolio including mobile railcar movers and ultrasonic rail flaw detection technologies, from Greenbriar Equity Group LP.

FINANCIAL DATA: Note: Data for latest year may not have been available at press time.

In U.S. $	2020	2019	2018	2017	2016	2015
Revenue	7,556,100,000	8,200,000,000	4,363,547,000	3,881,756,000	2,931,188,000	3,307,998,000
R&D Expense	162,100,000	209,900,000	87,450,000	95,166,000	71,375,000	71,213,000
Operating Income	744,500,000	663,100,000	473,437,000	421,733,000	458,361,000	607,567,000
Operating Margin %		.08%	.11%	.11%	.16%	.18%
SGA Expense	948,100,000	1,166,600,000	633,244,000	511,898,000	371,805,000	347,373,000
Net Income	414,400,000	326,700,000	294,944,000	262,261,000	304,887,000	398,628,000
Operating Cash Flow	783,700,000	1,015,500,000	314,671,000	188,811,000	449,307,000	448,260,000
Capital Expenditure	136,400,000	185,300,000	93,305,000	89,466,000	50,216,000	49,428,000
EBITDA	1,141,200,000	985,100,000	589,114,000	524,015,000	525,193,000	666,990,000
Return on Assets %		.02%	.04%	.04%	.06%	.12%
Return on Equity %		.05%	.10%	.10%	.16%	.23%
Debt to Equity		0.435	1.324	0.649	0.799	0.409

CONTACT INFORMATION:

Phone: 412 825-1000   Fax: 412 825-1019
Toll-Free:
Address: 30 Isabella St., Pittsburgh, PA 15212 United States

STOCK TICKER/OTHER:

Stock Ticker: WAB
Employees: 27,500
Parent Company:

Exchange: NYS
Fiscal Year Ends: 12/31

SALARIES/BONUSES:

Top Exec. Salary: $ Bonus: $
Second Exec. Salary: $ Bonus: $

OTHER THOUGHTS:

Estimated Female Officers or Directors: 1
Hot Spot for Advancement for Women/Minorities:

Walgreens Boots Alliance Inc

www.walgreens.com

NAIC Code: 446110

TYPES OF BUSINESS:

Drug Stores
Mail-Order Pharmacy Services
Pharmacy Benefit Management
Health Care Center Management
Online Pharmacy Services
Photo Printing Services
Specialty Pharmacy Services
Home Infusion Services

BRANDS/DIVISIONS/AFFILIATES:

Boots
Walgreens
Duane Reade
Boots
No7
Botanics
Well Beginnings

CONTACTS: *Note: Officers with more than one job title may be intentionally listed here more than once.*

Stefano Pessina, CEO
James Kehoe, CFO
James Skinner, Chairman of the Board
Heather Dixon, Chief Accounting Officer
Marco Pagni, Chief Administrative Officer
Ornella Barra, Co-COO
Alexander Gourlay, Co-COO
Kathleen Wilson-Thompson, Executive VP
Ken Murphy, Executive VP

GROWTH PLANS/SPECIAL FEATURES:

Walgreens Boots Alliance, Inc. is a global pharmacy-led health and wellbeing enterprise, with more than 18,500 stores worldwide. The company's pharmaceutical wholesale and distribution network is comprised of more than 425 distribution centers delivering to over 250,000 pharmacies, doctors, health centers and hospitals on an annual basis. The firm operates through segments that include retail pharmacy USA and retail pharmacy international. Retail pharmacy USA oversees pharmacy-led health and beauty retail businesses in 50 states, the District of Columbia, Puerto Rico and the U.S. Virgin Islands. It operates more than 9,020 retail stores and fills over 815 million prescriptions (including immunizations) annually. The retail pharmacy international segment oversees pharmacy-led health and beauty retail businesses in eight countries, operating more than 4,425 retail stores across the U.K., Thailand, Norway, Ireland, the Netherlands, Mexico and Chile. Walgreens' portfolio of retail and business global brands include Walgreens, Duane Reade, Boots and Alliance Healthcare, as well as global health and beauty product brands such as No7, NICE!, Botanics, Sleek MakeUP, Liz Earle, Well Beginnings, YourGoodSkin and Soap & Glory. In September 2020, Walgreens launched the Walgreens Test & Program to aid businesses in their COVID-19 work plans and strategies. In early 2021, Walgreens agreed to sell its Allied Healthcare wholesale pharmacy distribution business to AmerisourceBergen.

FINANCIAL DATA: *Note: Data for latest year may not have been available at press time.*

In U.S. $	2020	2019	2018	2017	2016	2015
Revenue	139,537,000,000	136,866,000,000	131,537,000,000	118,214,000,000	117,351,000,000	103,444,000,000
R&D Expense						
Operating Income	972,000,000	4,834,000,000	6,223,000,000	5,422,000,000	5,964,000,000	4,353,000,000
Operating Margin %		.04%	.05%	.05%	.05%	.04%
SGA Expense	27,045,000,000	25,242,000,000	24,569,000,000	23,740,000,000	23,910,000,000	22,571,000,000
Net Income	456,000,000	3,982,000,000	5,024,000,000	4,078,000,000	4,173,000,000	4,220,000,000
Operating Cash Flow	5,484,000,000	5,594,000,000	8,265,000,000	7,251,000,000	7,847,000,000	5,664,000,000
Capital Expenditure	1,374,000,000	1,702,000,000	1,367,000,000	1,351,000,000	1,325,000,000	1,251,000,000
EBITDA	3,309,000,000	7,269,000,000	8,361,000,000	7,200,000,000	7,458,000,000	7,658,000,000
Return on Assets %		.06%	.07%	.06%	.06%	.08%
Return on Equity %		.16%	.19%	.14%	.14%	.16%
Debt to Equity		0.472	0.478	0.462	0.626	0.431

CONTACT INFORMATION:

Phone: 847 315-2500   Fax: 847 914-2804
Toll-Free: 800-925-4733
Address: 108 Wilmot Rd., Deerfield, IL 60015 United States

STOCK TICKER/OTHER:

Stock Ticker: WBA   Exchange: NAS
Employees: 331,000   Fiscal Year Ends: 08/31
Parent Company:

SALARIES/BONUSES:

Top Exec. Salary: $ Bonus: $
Second Exec. Salary: $ Bonus: $

OTHER THOUGHTS:

Estimated Female Officers or Directors: 7
Hot Spot for Advancement for Women/Minorities: Y

Walmart Inc

NAIC Code: 452910

TYPES OF BUSINESS:

Discount Stores
Supermarkets
Warehouse Membership Clubs
Online Sales
Pharmacies
Vision Centers
Auto Repair Centers

BRANDS/DIVISIONS/AFFILIATES:

Walmart
Sams Club
Marketside
Walmart Neighborhood Market
walmart.com
Aspectiva
Delivery Unlimited

CONTACTS: *Note: Officers with more than one job title may be intentionally listed here more than once.*

Gregory Foran, CEO, Divisional
Marc Lore, CEO, Divisional
John Furner, CEO, Subsidiary
C. McMillon, CEO
M. Biggs, CFO
Rachel Brand, Chief Legal Officer
David Chojnowski, Controller
Gregory Penner, Director
Jacqueline Canney, Executive VP, Divisional
Daniel Bartlett, Executive VP, Divisional
Judith McKenna, Executive VP

GROWTH PLANS/SPECIAL FEATURES:

Walmart, Inc. is one of the world's largest retailers, operating through a massive base of Walmart stores, supercenters, Sam's Clubs, Marketsides, Walmart Neighborhood Markets and related ecommerce sites. As of October 31, 2020, Walmart, Inc. had approximately 11,510 stores worldwide. The company operates in three business segments: Walmart U.S., Walmart international and Sam's Club. Walmart U.S. is a mass merchandiser of consumer products, groceries and drugs, operating under the Walmart brand, as well as walmart.com. This segment operates retail stores in the U.S., including all 50 states, Washington D.C. and Puerto Rico, with supercenters in 49 states, Washington D.C. and Puerto Rico and Walmart discount stores in 42 states and Puerto Rico. Wal-Mart U.S. also operates a relatively small number Neighborhood Markets, which are about 42,000 square feet each. Its main line of business, the Walmart supercenters, average 178,000 square feet each. Walmart International consists of operations in over 25 countries outside the U.S., and includes numerous formats divided into three major categories: retail, wholesale and other. These categories consist of formats such as supercenters, supermarkets, hypermarkets, warehouse clubs (including Sam's Clubs), cash & carry, home improvement, specialty electronics, restaurants, apparel stores, drug stores and convenience stores. Sam's Club operates membership-only warehouse clubs, as well as samsclub.com in the U.S. All memberships include a spouse/household card at no additional cost and Plus Members are eligible for cash rewards.

The firm promotes women and minorities at an above average rate. About 50% of its store managers are women.

FINANCIAL DATA: *Note: Data for latest year may not have been available at press time.*

In U.S. $	2020	2019	2018	2017	2016	2015
Revenue	523,964,000,000	514,405,000,000	500,343,000,000	485,873,000,000	482,130,000,000	
R&D Expense						
Operating Income	20,568,000,000	21,957,000,000	20,437,000,000	22,764,000,000	24,105,000,000	
Operating Margin %	.04%	.04%	.04%	.05%	.05%	
SGA Expense	108,791,000,000	107,147,000,000	106,510,000,000	101,853,000,000	97,041,000,000	
Net Income	14,881,000,000	6,670,000,000	9,862,000,000	13,643,000,000	14,694,000,000	
Operating Cash Flow	25,255,000,000	27,753,000,000	28,337,000,000	31,530,000,000	27,389,000,000	
Capital Expenditure	10,705,000,000	10,344,000,000	10,051,000,000	10,619,000,000	11,477,000,000	
EBITDA	33,702,000,000	24,484,000,000	27,982,000,000	32,944,000,000	33,640,000,000	
Return on Assets %	.07%	.03%	.05%	.07%	.07%	
Return on Equity %	.20%	.09%	.13%	.17%	.18%	
Debt to Equity	0.86	0.692	0.473	0.54	0.547	

CONTACT INFORMATION

Phone: 479 273-4000   Fax: 479 273-1986
Toll-Free: 800-925-6278
Address: 702 SW 8th St., Bentonville, AR 72716 United States

STOCK TICKER/OTHER:

Stock Ticker: WMT
Employees: 2,200,000
Parent Company:

Exchange: NYS
Fiscal Year Ends: 01/31

SALARIES/BONUSES:

Top Exec. Salary: $ Bonus: $
Second Exec. Salary: $ Bonus: $

OTHER THOUGHTS:

Estimated Female Officers or Directors: 13
Hot Spot for Advancement for Women/Minorities: Y

Waste Management Inc

NAIC Code: 562000

www.wm.com

TYPES OF BUSINESS:

Waste Disposal
Recycling Services
Landfill Operation
Hazardous Waste Management
Transfer Stations
Recycled Commodity Trading
Waste Methane Generation

BRANDS/DIVISIONS/AFFILIATES:

Think Green

CONTACTS: *Note: Officers with more than one job title may be intentionally listed here more than once.*

James Fish, CEO
Devina Rankin, CFO
Thomas Weidemeyer, Chairman of the Board
Charles Boettcher, Chief Legal Officer
John Morris, COO
Michael Watson, Other Executive Officer
Tamla Oates-Forney, Other Executive Officer
Nikolaj Sjoqvist, Other Executive Officer
Tara Hemmer, Senior VP, Divisional
Steven Batchelor, Senior VP, Divisional
Leslie Nagy, Vice President

GROWTH PLANS/SPECIAL FEATURES:

Waste Management, Inc. provides comprehensive waste management services to municipal, commercial, industrial and residential customers throughout North America. Waste Management is the nation's largest collector of recyclables from businesses and households, collecting recyclable materials and depositing them at about a hundred local materials recovery facilities. The firm recycles several different materials including plastics, rubber, electronics and commodities. The company also has a pulp and paper trading group that reduces paper's overall long-term commodity price exposure. Waste Management owns or operates 249 landfill sites, as well as 302 transfer stations that consolidate, compact and transport waste. Its hazardous waste management services include geosynthetic manufacturing, radioactive waste services and landfill liner installation. Additionally, Waste Management promotes environmental initiatives such as Keep America Beautiful and Wildlife Habitat Council, as well as its own Think Green.

Waste Management offers comprehensive benefits, retirement and savings options, and employee assistance programs.

FINANCIAL DATA: *Note: Data for latest year may not have been available at press time.*

In U.S. $	2020	2019	2018	2017	2016	2015
Revenue	15,218,000,000	15,455,000,000	14,914,000,000	14,485,000,000	13,609,000,000	12,961,000,000
R&D Expense						
Operating Income	2,478,000,000	2,754,000,000	2,735,000,000	2,620,000,000	2,412,000,000	2,142,000,000
Operating Margin %		.18%	.18%	.18%	.18%	.17%
SGA Expense	1,674,000,000	1,593,000,000	1,400,000,000	1,426,000,000	1,370,000,000	1,307,000,000
Net Income	1,496,000,000	1,670,000,000	1,925,000,000	1,949,000,000	1,182,000,000	753,000,000
Operating Cash Flow	3,403,000,000	3,874,000,000	3,570,000,000	3,180,000,000	2,960,000,000	2,498,000,000
Capital Expenditure	1,632,000,000	1,818,000,000	1,694,000,000	1,509,000,000	1,339,000,000	1,233,000,000
EBITDA	3,989,000,000	4,090,000,000	4,227,000,000	3,930,000,000	3,499,000,000	2,690,000,000
Return on Assets %		.07%	.09%	.09%	.06%	.04%
Return on Equity %		.25%	.31%	.34%	.22%	.13%
Debt to Equity		1.879	1.529	1.454	1.679	1.633

CONTACT INFORMATION:

Phone: 713 512-6200   Fax:
Toll-Free:
Address: 1001 Fannin St., Ste. 4000, Houston, TX 77002 United States

STOCK TICKER/OTHER:

Stock Ticker: WM   Exchange: NYS
Employees: 44,900   Fiscal Year Ends: 12/31
Parent Company:

SALARIES/BONUSES:

Top Exec. Salary: $ Bonus: $
Second Exec. Salary: $ Bonus: $

OTHER THOUGHTS:

Estimated Female Officers or Directors: 1
Hot Spot for Advancement for Women/Minorities: Y

Wayfair LLC

www.wayfair.com

NAIC Code: 454111

TYPES OF BUSINESS:

Online Furniture Store

BRANDS/DIVISIONS/AFFILIATES:

CastleGate
Wayfair
Joss & Main
AllModern
Perigold
Birch Lane

CONTACTS:
Note: Officers with more than one job title may be intentionally listed here more than once.

Niraj Shah, CEO
Michael Fleisher, CFO
John Mulliken, Chief Technology Officer
Steven Conine, Co-Chairman of the Board
James Savarese, COO
Jim Miller, CTO
Steve Oblak, Other Executive Officer

GROWTH PLANS/SPECIAL FEATURES:

Wayfair, LLC is an eCommerce home furnishings company. The firm offers more than 18 million products from over 11,000 suppliers. These products include furniture, decor, decorative accents, housewares, seasonal decor and other home goods. Wayfair is able to offer this vast selection of products because it holds minimal inventory. Products are shipped to customers directly from the suppliers, or from Wayfair's CastleGate fulfillment network. The company's CastleGate solution enables suppliers to forward-position their inventory, allowing faster delivery to the customer with lower rates of damage and lowering Wayfair's cost per order over time. Wayfair offers five distinct sites, including websites, mobile websites and mobile applications, with each site comprising a unique brand identity that offers a tailored shopping experience. Sites and Brands include: Wayfair, offering home furnishings; Joss & Main, offering furniture; AllModern, offering modern home design merchandise; Perigold, offering fine home decor and furnishings; and Birch Lane, a collection of classic furnishings and timeless home decor. Based in the U.S., the firm operates internationally in Canada, the U.K., Ireland, Germany and the British Virgin Islands.

FINANCIAL DATA:
Note: Data for latest year may not have been available at press time.

In U.S. $	2020	2019	2018	2017	2016	2015
Revenue	14,145,160,000	9,127,057,000	6,779,174,000	4,720,895,000	3,380,360,000	2,249,885,000
R&D Expense						
Operating Income	360,349,000	-929,941,000	-473,279,000	-235,453,000	-196,217,000	-81,350,000
Operating Margin %		-.10%	-.07%	-.05%	-.06%	-.04%
SGA Expense	3,751,822,000	3,077,273,000	2,060,002,000	1,354,276,000	1,004,028,000	621,183,000
Net Income	184,996,000	-984,584,000	-504,080,000	-244,614,000	-194,375,000	-77,443,000
Operating Cash Flow	1,416,731,000	-196,818,000	84,861,000	33,634,000	62,814,000	135,121,000
Capital Expenditure	334,434,000	400,880,000	221,955,000	146,879,000	128,086,000	62,184,000
EBITDA	637,427,000	-737,522,000	-349,737,000	-148,433,000	-140,645,000	-48,904,000
Return on Assets %		-.41%	-.32%	-.25%	-.27%	-.12%
Return on Equity %				-15.75%	-1.21%	-.28%
Debt to Equity					0.867	0.113

CONTACT INFORMATION:

Phone: 866-263-8325   Fax:
Toll-Free: 877-929-3247
Address: 4 Copley Pl., Fl. 7, Boston, MA 02116 United States

SALARIES/BONUSES:

Top Exec. Salary: $ Bonus: $
Second Exec. Salary: $ Bonus: $

STOCK TICKER/OTHER:

Stock Ticker: W
Employees: 16,122
Parent Company:

Exchange: NYS
Fiscal Year Ends:

OTHER THOUGHTS:

Estimated Female Officers or Directors: 5
Hot Spot for Advancement for Women/Minorities: Y

Wegmans Food Markets Inc

NAIC Code: 445110

www.wegmans.com

TYPES OF BUSINESS:

Grocery Stores/Supermarkets
Home Improvement Stores
Restaurants
Photo Processing
Pharmacies

BRANDS/DIVISIONS/AFFILIATES:

Market Cafe
Buzz Coffee Shop (The)

CONTACTS: Note: Officers with more than one job title may be intentionally listed here more than once.

Colleen Wegman, CEO
Nicole Wegman, Sr. VP
Danny Wegman, Chmn.

GROWTH PLANS/SPECIAL FEATURES:

Wegmans Food Markets, Inc., founded in 1916, is a regional supermarket chain in the northeastern U.S. The company operates 104 stores in New York (48), Pennsylvania (18), Virginia (13), New Jersey (9), Maryland (8) and North Carolina (2). Wegmans supermarkets are larger than average, ranging from 75,000 to 140,000 square feet in size. They offer an average of 40,000 products per store, the largest ones carrying 50,000-70,000 products; other store amenities include photo labs, pharmacies, in-store dining and child play centers. More than 4,000 organic products are offered throughout the stores. Typical selections includes produce, artisan breads and other baked goods, seafood, meat, deli products, international foods and specialty cheeses in addition to standard groceries and household items. Customers can also find the following concepts at its stores: a Market Cafe, which offers take-out or in-store dining, featuring entrees, soups, appetizers, sandwiches and side dishes; sushi made fresh daily; a sub shop, offering hot and cold sandwiches, wraps, party trays and cookies; The Buzz Coffee Shop, with specialty coffee, tea and breakfast sandwiches; organic salad bar, veggie bar, homestyle bar and Asian bar; pizza shop, featuring thin-crust pizza, calzones and chicken wings; bakery, offering European breads and rolls, water-boiled bagels, muffins, pies, cakes and pastries; pharmacy, offering free home shipping, automated refills and pet medications; housewares and seasonal merchandise; floral shop; greeting cards; gifts; and health and beauty care products, including cosmetics and bath and body items.

Wegmans offers employees benefits including medical and dental insurance, life insurance, flexible spending accounts, retirement and savings options, and employee assistance programs.

FINANCIAL DATA: Note: Data for latest year may not have been available at press time.

In U.S. $	2020	2019	2018	2017	2016	2015
Revenue	10,497,500,000	9,500,000,000	9,000,000,000	8,700,000,000	8,300,000,000	7,600,000,000
R&D Expense						
Operating Income						
Operating Margin %						
SGA Expense						
Net Income						
Operating Cash Flow						
Capital Expenditure						
EBITDA						
Return on Assets %						
Return on Equity %						
Debt to Equity						

CONTACT INFORMATION:

Phone: 585-328-2550   Fax:
Toll-Free: 800-934-6267
Address: 1500 Brooks Ave., Rochester, NY 14603 United States

SALARIES/BONUSES:

Top Exec. Salary: $ Bonus: $
Second Exec. Salary: $ Bonus: $

STOCK TICKER/OTHER:

Stock Ticker: Private
Employees: 32,000
Parent Company:

Exchange:
Fiscal Year Ends: 12/31

OTHER THOUGHTS:

Estimated Female Officers or Directors: 1
Hot Spot for Advancement for Women/Minorities:

Weis Markets Inc

www.weismarkets.com

NAIC Code: 445110

TYPES OF BUSINESS:

Grocery Stores
Ice Manufacturing
Ice Cream Manufacturing
Milk Processing
Meat Processing

BRANDS/DIVISIONS/AFFILIATES:

Weis Markets
Weis Club Preferred Shopper

CONTACTS: Note: Officers with more than one job title may be intentionally listed here more than once.

Jonathan Weis, CEO
Scott Frost, CFO
Jeanette Rogers, Chief Accounting Officer
Kurt Schertle, COO
Harold Graber, Director
David Gose, Senior VP, Divisional
Richard Gunn, Senior VP, Divisional
Wayne Bailey, Senior VP, Divisional
James Marcil, Senior VP, Divisional

GROWTH PLANS/SPECIAL FEATURES:

Weis Markets, Inc. operates 196 retail supermarkets, as of November 2020. Founded in 1912, the company is a grocer in Pennsylvania and surrounding states, including Maryland, Virginia, New York, New Jersey, Delaware and West Virginia. Each store has an average size of 48,500 square feet. Its retail food stores offer groceries, dairy products, frozen foods, meats, seafood, fresh produce, floral items, pharmacy services, deli/bakery products, prepared foods, fuel, beer and wine and general merchandise (health, beauty, and household products). In addition, many locations offer services such as in-store banks, laundry services and take-out restaurants, as well as beer-wine cafes. These cafes sell 550 varieties of domestic, imported and craft beer, including a local beer selection, and also offer more than 300 varieties of imported and domestic wines. There are more than 60 beer-wine cafes in Weis' Pennsylvania stores. The company's loyalty card program, Weis Club Preferred Shopper, provides members with an opportunity to receive discounts, promotions and rewards. Weis Markets also operates an ice cream plant, an ice plant, a meat processing plant and a milk processing plant at its warehouse in Sunbury, Pennsylvania, which together utilize a total of 258,000 square feet out of the 541,000-square-foot warehouse. These operations allow Weis Markets to offer private label products. The company's distribution facilities include a 1.3 million square-foot center in Milton, Pennsylvania, and a 76,000 square-foot center in Northumberland.

FINANCIAL DATA: Note: Data for latest year may not have been available at press time.

In U.S. $	2020	2019	2018	2017	2016	2015
Revenue	4,112,601,000	3,543,299,000	3,509,270,000	3,466,807,000	3,136,720,000	2,876,748,000
R&D Expense						
Operating Income	163,178,000	84,639,000	83,590,000	76,425,000	98,325,000	90,779,000
Operating Margin %		.02%	.02%	.02%	.03%	.03%
SGA Expense	937,256,000	853,555,000	851,411,000	850,034,000	773,830,000	695,953,000
Net Income	118,917,000	67,983,000	62,738,000	98,414,000	87,162,000	59,330,000
Operating Cash Flow	277,990,000	171,686,000	148,380,000	165,814,000	151,593,000	136,733,000
Capital Expenditure	131,118,000	102,945,000	99,236,000	99,422,000	144,712,000	92,859,000
EBITDA	262,548,000	178,345,000	177,157,000	161,840,000	175,187,000	160,893,000
Return on Assets %		.04%	.04%	.07%	.07%	.05%
Return on Equity %		.07%	.06%	.10%	.10%	.07%
Debt to Equity		0.17		0.035	0.07	

CONTACT INFORMATION:

Phone: 570 286-4571   Fax:
Toll-Free: 866-999-9347
Address: 1000 S. Second St., Sunbury, PA 17801 United States

STOCK TICKER/OTHER:

Stock Ticker: WMK
Employees: 24,000
Parent Company:

Exchange: NYS
Fiscal Year Ends: 12/31

SALARIES/BONUSES:

Top Exec. Salary: $ Bonus: $
Second Exec. Salary: $ Bonus: $

OTHER THOUGHTS:

Estimated Female Officers or Directors:
Hot Spot for Advancement for Women/Minorities:

Sales, profits and employees may be estimates. Financial information, benefits and other data can change quickly and may vary from those stated here.

WellCare Health Plans Inc

www.wellcare.com

NAIC Code: 524114

TYPES OF BUSINESS:

Insurance-Medical & Health, HMOs & PPOs

BRANDS/DIVISIONS/AFFILIATES:

Centene Corporation

GROWTH PLANS/SPECIAL FEATURES:

WellCare Health Plans, Inc. manages government-sponsored healthcare programs. The company offers plans for beneficiaries of temporary assistance, children's health insurance programs, managed care health plans and other related services. WellCare serves families, children, seniors and individuals in the U.S. In early-2020, WellCare Health Plans was acquired by Centene Corporation, a multi-line healthcare plan firm operating in two segments: managed care and specialty services, for $15.3 billion. WellCare ceased from being publicly traded. Together, WellCare and Centene provides access to affordable healthcare to m ore than 24 million members across all 50 states.

CONTACTS: *Note: Officers with more than one job title may be intentionally listed here more than once.*

Andrew Asher, CFO
Mark Leenay, Chief Medical Officer
Christian Michalik, Director
Michael Polen, Executive VP, Divisional
Kelly Munson, Executive VP, Divisional
Michael Radu, Executive VP, Divisional
Anat Hakim, Executive VP
Rhonda Mims, Executive VP
Timothy Trodden, Executive VP
Michael Neidorff, Chmn.

FINANCIAL DATA: *Note: Data for latest year may not have been available at press time.*

In U.S. $	2020	2019	2018	2017	2016	2015
Revenue	36,644,650,000	27,901,000,000	20,414,099,456	17,007,200,256	14,237,100,032	13,890,199,552
R&D Expense						
Operating Income						
Operating Margin %						
SGA Expense						
Net Income		583,000,000	439,800,000	373,700,000	242,100,000	118,600,000
Operating Cash Flow						
Capital Expenditure						
EBITDA						
Return on Assets %						
Return on Equity %						
Debt to Equity						

CONTACT INFORMATION:

Phone: 813 290-6200   Fax:
Toll-Free: 800-795-3432
Address: 8725 Henderson Rd., Renaissance 1, Tampa, FL 33634 United States

STOCK TICKER/OTHER:

Stock Ticker: Subsidiary
Employees: 14,700
Parent Company: Centene Coropration

Exchange:
Fiscal Year Ends: 12/31

SALARIES/BONUSES:

Top Exec. Salary: $ Bonus: $
Second Exec. Salary: $ Bonus: $

OTHER THOUGHTS:

Estimated Female Officers or Directors: 3
Hot Spot for Advancement for Women/Minorities: Y

Wells Fargo & Company

www.wellsfargo.com

NAIC Code: 522110

TYPES OF BUSINESS:

Banking
Credit & Debit Cards
Personal Trust Accounts Management
Mutual Fund Administration
Mortgages
Insurance Services
Investment Banking
Asset Management

BRANDS/DIVISIONS/AFFILIATES:

Wells Fargo Bank NA

CONTACTS: Note: Officers with more than one job title may be intentionally listed here more than once.

C. Allen Parker, CEO
John Shrewsberry, CFO
Richard Levy, Chief Accounting Officer
Amanda Norton, Chief Risk Officer
Elizabeth Duke, Director
David Galloreese, Other Corporate Officer
Avid Modjtabai, Senior Executive VP, Divisional
Perry Pelos, Senior Executive VP, Divisional
Mary Mack, Senior Executive VP, Divisional
Jonathan Weiss, Senior Executive VP, Divisional

GROWTH PLANS/SPECIAL FEATURES:

Wells Fargo & Company (WFC), with $1.92 trillion in assets, is a holding company that provides diversified financial services. The San Francisco-based company operates throughout the U.S., as well as in over 30 countries and territories to support customers who conduct business in the global economy. The firm operates primarily through Wells Fargo Bank, NA. WFC operates in three business segments: community banking, wholesale banking and wealth and investment management. Through these segments WFC provides retail, commercial and corporate banking services through banking locations and offices, the internet and other distribution channels to individuals, businesses and institutions. Other financial services include wholesale banking, mortgage banking, consumer finance, equipment leasing, agricultural finance, commercial finance, securities brokerage, investment banking, insurance agency and brokerage services, computer and data processing services, trust services, investment advisory services, mortgage-backed securities servicing and venture capital investment. In December 2020, WFC filed to remove its listing and registration of matured, redeemed or retired securities from the New York Stock Exchange.

Wells Fargo offers its employees a 401(k) plan, tuition reimbursement, adoption assistance, discounted checking and savings accounts and scholarships for dependent children.

FINANCIAL DATA: Note: Data for latest year may not have been available at press time.

In U.S. $	2020	2019	2018	2017	2016	2015
Revenue	72,340,000,000	85,063,000,000	86,408,000,000	86,273,000,000	86,728,000,000	83,942,000,000
R&D Expense						
Operating Income						
Operating Margin %						
SGA Expense	35,411,000,000	37,841,000,000	34,134,000,000	34,658,000,000	33,061,000,000	31,654,000,000
Net Income	3,301,000,000	19,549,000,000	22,393,000,000	22,183,000,000	21,938,000,000	22,894,000,000
Operating Cash Flow	2,051,000,000	6,730,000,000	36,073,000,000	18,722,000,000	169,000,000	14,772,000,000
Capital Expenditure						
EBITDA						
Return on Assets %		.01%	.01%	.01%	.01%	.01%
Return on Equity %		.11%	.12%	.12%	.12%	.13%
Debt to Equity		1.378	1.324	1.239	1.457	1.168

CONTACT INFORMATION:

Phone: 866 249-3302 Fax:
Toll-Free: 800-869-3557
Address: 420 Montgomery St., San Francisco, CA 94163 United States

STOCK TICKER/OTHER:

Stock Ticker: WFC
Employees: 268,531
Parent Company:

Exchange: NYS
Fiscal Year Ends: 12/31

SALARIES/BONUSES:

Top Exec. Salary: $ Bonus: $
Second Exec. Salary: $ Bonus: $

OTHER THOUGHTS:

Estimated Female Officers or Directors: 8
Hot Spot for Advancement for Women/Minorities: Y

Westlake Chemical Corporation

www.westlake.com

NAIC Code: 325110

TYPES OF BUSINESS:

Plastics & Rubber, Manufacturing
PVC Piping
Vinyls
Olefins

BRANDS/DIVISIONS/AFFILIATES:

Westlake Chemical Partners LP
Suzhou Huasu Plastic Co Ltd
Westlake Chemical OpCo LP
NAPCO Pipe & Fittings
LASCO Fittings Inc

CONTACTS: Note: Officers with more than one job title may be intentionally listed here more than once.

Albert Chao, CEO
M. Bender, CFO
James Chao, Chairman of the Board
George Mangieri, Chief Accounting Officer
L. Ederington, Chief Administrative Officer
Robert Buesinger, Executive VP, Divisional
Lawrence Teel, Executive VP, Divisional
Roger Kearns, Executive VP, Divisional
Andrew Kenner, Senior VP, Divisional

GROWTH PLANS/SPECIAL FEATURES:

Westlake Chemical Corporation manufactures and markets vinyls, basic chemicals and fabricated products for use in the packaging, automotive, construction and coatings industries. The company operates in two business segments: olefins and vinyls. The olefins business provides ethylene, polyethylene, styrene and co-products. These olefins are used to create a variety of petrochemical products including packaging film, coatings, injection molding and complex chemicals. Principal products for the vinyls business include polyvinyl chloride (PVC), vinyl chloride monomer (VCM), chlorine, caustic soda and ethylene. Westlake manufactures and markets specialty pipe and fittings, water, sewer, irrigation and conduit pipe products under the North American Pipe and Royal Building Products brand names. Westlake maintains manufacturing facilities in North America, Europe and Asia, producing approximately 44 billion pounds of aggregate in fiscal 2019-20. Principal manufacturing facilities are located in Louisiana, Texas, Kentucky and West Virginia, USA; and Bavaria and North Rhine-Westphalia, Germany. Additionally, subsidiary Westlake Chemical Partners LP operates, acquires and develops facilities for the processing of natural gas liquids and related assets; Suzhou Huasu Plastic Co. Ltd. operates a PVC fabrication facility in China; and Westlake Chemical OpCo LP operates an olefins facility in Lake Charles, Louisiana, an ethylene production facility in Calvert City, Kentucky, and a 200-mile common carrier ethylene pipeline that runs from Mont Belvieu, Texas to Westlake's Longview, Texas site. In July 2021, NAPCO Pipe & Fittings a Westlake subsidiary, announced it had acquired LASCO Fittings, Inc.

Westlake offers employees life, AD&D, medical, dental, vision and long-term disability insurance; a 401(k); paid time off; and an assistance program.

FINANCIAL DATA: Note: Data for latest year may not have been available at press time.

In U.S. $	2020	2019	2018	2017	2016	2015
Revenue	7,504,000,000	8,118,000,000	8,635,000,000	8,041,000,000	5,075,456,000	4,463,336,000
R&D Expense						
Operating Income	465,000,000	693,000,000	1,441,000,000	1,262,000,000	685,126,000	959,827,000
Operating Margin %		.09%	.17%	.16%	.13%	.22%
SGA Expense	449,000,000	458,000,000	445,000,000	399,000,000	295,436,000	225,364,000
Net Income	330,000,000	421,000,000	996,000,000	1,304,000,000	398,859,000	646,010,000
Operating Cash Flow	1,297,000,000	1,301,000,000	1,409,000,000	1,538,000,000	833,852,000	1,078,836,000
Capital Expenditure	525,000,000	787,000,000	702,000,000	577,000,000	628,483,000	491,426,000
EBITDA	1,246,000,000	1,407,000,000	2,101,000,000	1,841,000,000	1,015,518,000	1,243,854,000
Return on Assets %		.03%	.08%	.11%	.05%	.12%
Return on Equity %		.07%	.19%	.31%	.12%	.21%
Debt to Equity		0.648	0.477	0.642	1.044	0.234

CONTACT INFORMATION:

Phone: 713 960-9111   Fax:
Toll-Free:
Address: 2801 Post Oak Blvd., Ste. 600, Houston, TX 77056 United States

STOCK TICKER/OTHER:

Stock Ticker: WLK
Employees: 9,430
Parent Company:

Exchange: NYS
Fiscal Year Ends: 12/31

SALARIES/BONUSES:

Top Exec. Salary: $ Bonus: $
Second Exec. Salary: $ Bonus: $

OTHER THOUGHTS:

Estimated Female Officers or Directors:
Hot Spot for Advancement for Women/Minorities:

Sales, profits and employees may be estimates. Financial information, benefits and other data can change quickly and may vary from those stated here.

Whole Foods Market Inc

www.wholefoodsmarket.com

NAIC Code: 445110

TYPES OF BUSINESS:

Natural Foods Grocery Stores
Nutritional Supplements
Seafood Processing
Coffee Roasting
Supermarkets
Bakeries
Prepared Meals to Go

BRANDS/DIVISIONS/AFFILIATES:

Amazon.com Inc
365-Whole Foods Market
365 Everyday Value
Whole Catch
Whole Foods Market
Allegro Coffee
Engine 2 Plant-Strong
Whole Paws

CONTACTS: Note: Officers with more than one job title may be intentionally listed here more than once.

John Mackey, CEO
Gabrielle Sulzberger, Chairman of the Board
Keith Manbeck, CFO
Kenneth Meyer, Executive VP, Divisional
David Lannon, Executive VP, Divisional
James Sud, Executive VP, Divisional
Keith Manbeck, Executive VP

GROWTH PLANS/SPECIAL FEATURES:

Whole Foods Market, Inc. owns and operates a chain of natural organic food supermarkets in the U.S. and internationally, with 487 stores in the U.S., 14 in Canada and seven in the U.K. The firm's stores generally feature foods made from natural ingredients and free of chemical additives. Whole Foods' merchandise items include organically-grown and high-grade commercial produce; grocery products; environmentally safe household items; hormone- and antibiotic-free meats; bulk foods; fresh bakery goods; soups, salads, entrees and sandwiches; vitamins; cosmetics; and miscellaneous items. Merchandise is sold through its private-label brands such as 365 Everyday Value, Whole Catch and Whole Foods Market, which are chef quality, all-natural foods and products. Its stores, averaging 38,000 square feet in size, are supplemented by regional distribution centers, bakeries, commissary kitchens, seafood-processing facilities, produce procurement centers and a coffee roasting operation. Smaller, value-focused stores are branded under the 365-Whole Foods Market name, bringing fresh, healthy and affordable food as well as unique products in a fun and convenient retail format. In addition, the company operates a website that offers features such as online recipes, health information and environmental issue information. Other brands include Allegro Coffee, Engine 2 Plant-Strong and Whole Paws. In November 2020, Whole Foods announced that it would be opening a new 38,000-square-foot store in Asheville, North Carolina the following month, December.

FINANCIAL DATA: Note: Data for latest year may not have been available at press time.

In U.S. $	2020	2019	2018	2017	2016	2015
Revenue	18,977,516,250	17,252,287,500	16,831,500,000	16,030,000,000	15,724,000,256	15,388,999,680
R&D Expense						
Operating Income						
Operating Margin %						
SGA Expense						
Net Income				245,000,000	507,000,000	536,000,000
Operating Cash Flow						
Capital Expenditure						
EBITDA						
Return on Assets %						
Return on Equity %						
Debt to Equity						

CONTACT INFORMATION:

Phone: 512 477-4455   Fax: 512 477-1069
Toll-Free:
Address: 550 Bowie St., Austin, TX 78703 United States

SALARIES/BONUSES:

Top Exec. Salary: $ Bonus: $
Second Exec. Salary: $ Bonus: $

STOCK TICKER/OTHER:

Stock Ticker: Subsidiary   Exchange:
Employees: 86,000   Fiscal Year Ends: 09/30
Parent Company: Amazon.com Inc

OTHER THOUGHTS:

Estimated Female Officers or Directors: 9
Hot Spot for Advancement for Women/Minorities: Y

WinCo Foods Inc

NAIC Code: 445110

www.wincofoods.com

TYPES OF BUSINESS:

Discount Warehouse Stores
Grocery Stores

BRANDS/DIVISIONS/AFFILIATES:

WinCo Food
Waremart by WinCo

CONTACTS: Note: Officers with more than one job title may be intentionally listed here more than once.

Grant Haag, CEO
Rich Charrier, COO
Steven L. Goddard, Pres.
David Butler, CFO
Gary Piva, Chmn.

GROWTH PLANS/SPECIAL FEATURES:

WinCo Foods, Inc. operates a chain of supermarkets throughout the western U.S. region. The company was founded as a discount warehouse grocery store in Boise, Idaho in 1967, and currently has 131 employee-owned WinCo Food stores throughout Washington, Arizona, Idaho, Oklahoma, Oregon, Utah, California, Texas, Montana and Nevada. WinCo focuses on large stores offering a wide variety of nationally branded products, with each store providing a diverse selection of groceries. Its outlets also feature several in-store departments, including a bakery, bulk food items, a meat and produce department and a selection of health and beauty items. WinCo's stores range from 90,000 to 120,000 square feet and are open 24 hours a day. Waremart by WinCo are smaller format stores, with the first stores located in Independence, Ontario and Keizer, Oregon. Unlike WinCo, these stores are not open 24 hours-a-day. The company's distribution centers are located in Woodburn and Myrtle Creek, Oregon; Boise, Idaho; Phoenix, Arizona; Denton, Texas; and Modesto, California. WinCo is one of the largest employee-owned companies in the Pacific Northwest.

FINANCIAL DATA: Note: Data for latest year may not have been available at press time.

In U.S. $	2020	2019	2018	2017	2016	2015
Revenue	6,615,493,500	6,014,085,000	5,867,400,000	5,588,000,000	5,565,050,000	5,500,000,000
R&D Expense						
Operating Income						
Operating Margin %						
SGA Expense						
Net Income						
Operating Cash Flow						
Capital Expenditure						
EBITDA						
Return on Assets %						
Return on Equity %						
Debt to Equity						

CONTACT INFORMATION:

Phone: 208-377-0110   Fax: 208-377-0474
Toll-Free:
Address: 650 N. Armstrong Pl., Boise, ID 83704 United States

STOCK TICKER/OTHER:

Stock Ticker: Private
Employees: 20,000
Parent Company:

Exchange:
Fiscal Year Ends: 03/31

SALARIES/BONUSES:

Top Exec. Salary: $ Bonus: $
Second Exec. Salary: $ Bonus: $

OTHER THOUGHTS:

Estimated Female Officers or Directors:
Hot Spot for Advancement for Women/Minorities:

Woodward Inc

NAIC Code: 334513

TYPES OF BUSINESS:

Industrial Controls
Energy Controls
Power System Equipment

BRANDS/DIVISIONS/AFFILIATES:

CONTACTS: Note: Officers with more than one job title may be intentionally listed here more than once.

Thomas Gendron, CEO
Robert Weber, CFO
Thomas Cromwell, COO
A. Fawzy, General Counsel
Matthew Taylor, President, Divisional
Sagar Patel, President, Divisional
Chad Preiss, President, Divisional
Jonathan Thayer, Vice Chairman, Divisional
James Rudolph, Vice President
Steven Meyer, Vice President, Divisional
John Tysver, Vice President, Divisional
Dan Bowman, Vice President, Divisional

GROWTH PLANS/SPECIAL FEATURES:

Woodward, Inc. is an independent designer, manufacturer and service provider of energy control and optimization solutions for commercial and military aircraft and ground vehicles, turbines, reciprocating engines and electrical power system equipment. Woodward's innovative fluid energy, combustion control, electrical energy and motion control systems help customers offer cleaner, more reliable and more cost-effective equipment. Leading original equipment manufacturers (OEMs) use Woodward's products and services in aerospace, power generation and distribution and transportation markets. It operates in two segments: Aerospace and Industrial. The Aerospace segment designs, manufactures, and services systems and products for the management of fuel, air, combustion and motion control. These products include fuel pumps, metering units, actuators, air valves, specialty valves, fuel nozzles, and thrust reverser actuation systems for turbine engines and nacelles, as well as flight deck controls, actuators, motors and sensors for aircraft. These products are used on commercial and private aircraft and rotorcraft, as well as on military fixed-wing aircraft and rotorcraft, guided weapons, and other defense systems. The Industrial segment designs, produces, and services systems and products for the management of fuel, air, fluids, gases, motion, combustion and electricity. These products include actuators, pumps, fuel injection systems, solenoids, ignition systems, speed controls, electronics and software, power converters, sensors and other devices that measure, communicate and protect electrical distribution systems. The products are used on industrial gas turbines (including heavy frame, aeroderivative and small industrial gas turbines), steam turbines, reciprocating engines (including low speed, medium speed and high speed engines, natural gas vehicles and diesel, heavy fuel oil and dual-fuel engines), electric power generation and power distribution systems, wind turbines, and compressors. During 2020, the agreement and plan of merger between Woodward and Hexcel Corp. was terminated, with no liability to either party.

FINANCIAL DATA: Note: Data for latest year may not have been available at press time.

In U.S. $	2020	2019	2018	2017	2016	2015
Revenue	2,495,665,000	2,900,197,000	2,325,873,000	2,098,685,000	2,023,078,000	2,038,303,000
R&D Expense	133,134,000	159,107,000	148,279,000	126,519,000	126,170,000	134,485,000
Operating Income	289,399,000	337,231,000	265,162,000	269,407,000	238,931,000	263,864,000
Operating Margin %		.12%	.11%	.13%	.12%	.13%
SGA Expense	217,710,000	211,205,000	192,757,000	176,633,000	154,951,000	156,995,000
Net Income	240,395,000	259,602,000	180,378,000	200,507,000	180,838,000	181,452,000
Operating Cash Flow	349,491,000	390,608,000	299,292,000	307,537,000	435,379,000	287,429,000
Capital Expenditure	47,087,000	99,066,000	127,140,000	92,336,000	175,692,000	286,612,000
EBITDA	448,850,000	506,617,000	367,479,000	361,094,000	322,298,000	341,048,000
Return on Assets %		.07%	.06%	.07%	.07%	.07%
Return on Equity %		.16%	.12%	.16%	.15%	.16%
Debt to Equity		0.501	0.71	0.423	0.476	0.737

CONTACT INFORMATION:

Phone: 970 482-5811   Fax: 815 636-6033
Toll-Free:
Address: 1081 Woodward Way, Fort Collins, CO 80524 United States

STOCK TICKER/OTHER:

Stock Ticker: WWD
Employees: 7,100
Parent Company:

Exchange: NAS
Fiscal Year Ends: 09/30

SALARIES/BONUSES:

Top Exec. Salary: $ Bonus: $
Second Exec. Salary: $ Bonus: $

OTHER THOUGHTS:

Estimated Female Officers or Directors:
Hot Spot for Advancement for Women/Minorities:

Workday Inc

NAIC Code: 511210H

www.workday.com

TYPES OF BUSINESS:

Human Resources Software
Enterprise Financial Planning Software (ERF)
Analytics Software

BRANDS/DIVISIONS/AFFILIATES:

Scout REP
Workday Strategic Sourcing

CONTACTS: Note: Officers with more than one job title may be intentionally listed here more than once.

Aneel Bhusri, CEO
Philip Wilmington, Vice Chairman
Robynne Sisco, CFO
Sheri Rhodes, Chief Information Officer
Christine Cefalo, Chief Marketing Officer
David Clarke, Chief Technology Officer
David Duffield, Co-Founder
James Bozzini, COO
Chano Fernandez, Co-Pres.
Thomas Bogan, Executive VP, Divisional
Petros Dermetzis, Other Executive Officer
Ashley Goldsmith, Other Executive Officer
Sayan Chakraborty, Senior VP, Divisional
Emily McEvilly, Senior VP, Divisional
Doug Robinson, Senior VP, Divisional
James Shaughnessy, Senior VP
Michael Stankey, Vice Chairman of the Board

GROWTH PLANS/SPECIAL FEATURES:

Workday, Inc. provides financial management, human capital management, planning and analytics applications for global companies, educational institutions and government agencies. The firm offers innovative and adaptable technology focused on the consumer internet experience and cloud delivery model. Workday's applications are designed for global enterprises to manage complex and dynamic operating environments. Workday provides highly-adaptable, accessible and reliable applications to manage critical business functions that enable customers to optimize their financial and human capital resources. Industries served by Workday include communications, energy, resources, financial services, government, healthcare, K-12 education, higher education, hospitality, insurance, life sciences, manufacturing, media/entertainment, non-profits, professional services, business services, retail and technology. Organizations ranging from medium-sized businesses to Fortune 500 enterprises have selected Workday. Subsidiary Workday Strategic Sourcing is the result of the 2019 acquisition of Scout REP, a cloud-based platform for strategic sourcing and supplier engagement.

Workday offers its employees health plans, retirement plans and employee assistance programs.

FINANCIAL DATA: Note: Data for latest year may not have been available at press time.

In U.S. $	2020	2019	2018	2017	2016	2015
Revenue	3,627,206,000	2,822,180,000	2,143,050,000	1,569,407,000	1,162,346,000	
R&D Expense	1,549,906,000	1,211,832,000	910,584,000	680,531,000	469,944,000	
Operating Income	-502,230,000	-463,284,000	-303,223,000	-376,665,000	-264,659,000	
Operating Margin %	-.14%	-.16%	-.14%	-.24%	-.23%	
SGA Expense	1,514,272,000	1,238,682,000	906,276,000	781,996,000	582,634,000	
Net Income	-480,674,000	-418,258,000	-321,222,000	-408,278,000	-289,918,000	
Operating Cash Flow	864,598,000	606,658,000	465,727,000	348,655,000	258,637,000	
Capital Expenditure	244,544,000	212,957,000	152,536,000	120,813,000	133,667,000	
EBITDA	-147,484,000	-165,432,000	-133,263,000	-263,104,000	-171,030,000	
Return on Assets %	-.08%	-.08%	-.08%	-.14%	-.11%	
Return on Equity %	-.22%	-.24%	-.23%	-.36%	-.26%	
Debt to Equity	0.506	0.496	0.728	0.46	0.447	

CONTACT INFORMATION:

Phone: 925-951-9000   Fax:
Toll-Free: 877-967-5329
Address: 6230 Stoneridge Mall Rd., Ste. 200, Pleasanton, CA 94588 United States

STOCK TICKER/OTHER:

Stock Ticker: WDAY
Employees: 12,500
Parent Company:

Exchange: NAS
Fiscal Year Ends:

SALARIES/BONUSES:

Top Exec. Salary: $ Bonus: $
Second Exec. Salary: $ Bonus: $

OTHER THOUGHTS:

Estimated Female Officers or Directors: 2
Hot Spot for Advancement for Women/Minorities:

Xilinx Inc

www.xilinx.com

NAIC Code: 334413

TYPES OF BUSINESS:

Integrated Circuits
Development System Software
Engineering & Technical Services
Design Services & Field Engineering
Customer Training & Tech. Support

BRANDS/DIVISIONS/AFFILIATES:

Virtex Ultrascale+
Kintex Ultrascale+
Zynq Ultrascale+
Spartan-7
Atrix-7
Alveo
Solarflare
Vitis

CONTACTS: Note: Officers with more than one job title may be intentionally listed here more than once.

Victor Peng, CEO
Lorenzo Flores, CFO
Dennis Segers, Director
Vincent Tong, Executive VP, Divisional
William Madden, Executive VP
Salil Raje, Executive VP
Catia Hagopian, General Counsel
Emre Ã—nder, Senior VP, Divisional
Mark Wadlington, Senior VP, Divisional

GROWTH PLANS/SPECIAL FEATURES:

Xilinx, Inc. designs, develops and provides programmable logic devices (PLDs) and related products. Logic devices are used to manage the interchange and manipulation of digital signals within an electronic system. PLDs can be programmed to perform whatever function the user requires, whereas the operations of other like-kind devices are fixed. The PLDs produced include field programmable gate arrays (FPGAs) and complex programmable devices (CPLDs), which have applications in a variety of industries, including automotive, 5G wireless, data center, aerospace/defense, broadcast, audio/visual, consumer, industrial, medical, science, test/measurement, wired communications and wireless infrastructure. The firm's leading PLD and FPGA brands include the Virtex UltraScale+, Kintex UltraScale+, Zynq UltraScale+, Virtex UltraScale, Spartan-7, Artix-7 and Alveo family lines. Xilinx's portfolio of software and hardware solutions include computer- and IP-based design tools that support the development of software-defined-hardware, as well as the development of software-defined-systems. The company enables breakthroughs in data center technology by building user-friendly development tools for machine learning, video and image processing, data analytics and genomics, among others. In October 2020, Xilinx agreed to be acquired by rival chip maker Advanced Micro Devices, Inc. for $35 billion. The transaction still must pass regulatory scrutiny.

Xilinx offers comprehensive benefit programs.

FINANCIAL DATA: Note: Data for latest year may not have been available at press time.

In U.S. $	2020	2019	2018	2017	2016	2015
Revenue	3,162,666,000	3,059,040,000	2,539,004,000	2,349,330,000	2,213,881,000	
R&D Expense	853,589,000	743,027,000	639,750,000	601,443,000	533,891,000	
Operating Income	820,250,000	956,799,000	778,405,000	699,394,000	669,881,000	
Operating Margin %	.26%	.31%	.31%	.30%	.30%	
SGA Expense	432,308,000	398,416,000	362,329,000	335,150,000	331,652,000	
Net Income	792,721,000	889,750,000	512,381,000	622,512,000	550,867,000	
Operating Cash Flow	1,190,836,000	1,091,215,000	820,027,000	934,131,000	730,102,000	
Capital Expenditure	129,289,000	89,045,000	49,918,000	72,051,000	34,004,000	
EBITDA	1,031,337,000	1,125,575,000	893,002,000	807,659,000	760,722,000	
Return on Assets %	.16%	.17%	.10%	.13%	.11%	
Return on Equity %	.31%	.34%	.21%	.24%	.21%	
Debt to Equity	0.323	0.432	0.521	0.397	0.383	

CONTACT INFORMATION:

Phone: 408 559-7778　　Fax: 408 559-7114
Toll-Free:
Address: 2100 Logic Dr., San Jose, CA 95124 United States

STOCK TICKER/OTHER:

Stock Ticker: XLNX
Employees: 4,890
Parent Company:

Exchange: NAS
Fiscal Year Ends: 02/28

SALARIES/BONUSES:

Top Exec. Salary: $　　Bonus: $
Second Exec. Salary: $　　Bonus: $

OTHER THOUGHTS:

Estimated Female Officers or Directors: 1
Hot Spot for Advancement for Women/Minorities:

XPO Logistics Inc

www.xpologistics.com

NAIC Code: 488510

TYPES OF BUSINESS:

Freight Transportation Arrangement
Logistics
Supply Chain Solutions
Transportation Fleet

BRANDS/DIVISIONS/AFFILIATES:

CONTACTS: *Note: Officers with more than one job title may be intentionally listed here more than once.*

Bradley Jacobs, CEO
Sarah Glickman, CFO
Lance Robinson, Chief Accounting Officer
Mario Harik, Chief Information Officer
AnnaMaria DeSalva, Director
Troy Cooper, President

GROWTH PLANS/SPECIAL FEATURES:

XPO Logistics, Inc. is a global logistics provider of supply chain solutions to companies worldwide, serving more than 50,000 customers via 1,500 locations in 30 countries. XPO operates its business in two segments: transportation and logistics. The transportation segment offers customers a network of multiple modes, flexible capacity and route density to swiftly and cost-effectively transport goods from origin to destination. This division provides freight brokerage, dedicated, non-dedicated, freight forwarding, last mile logistics, expedited shipment, truckload (TL), less-than-truckload (LTL) and intermodal services through its network of ocean, air, ground and cross-border capabilities. Globally, this segment's road fleet encompass approximately 15,500 tractors and 40,000 trailers, primarily related to its TL and LTL operations. The logistics segment, which is also referred to as supply chain or contract logistics by XPO, provides differentiated and data-intensive services, including highly-engineered and customized solutions, value-added warehousing and distribution, cold chain distribution and other inventory management solutions. This division performs eCommerce fulfillment, reverse logistics, recycling, storage, factory support, aftermarket support, manufacturing, distribution, packaging and labeling, as well as customized solutions. In addition, this segment offers supply chain optimization services such as production flow management and transportation management. Globally, XPO operates approximately 200 million square feet (19 million square meters) of contract logistics facility space, with about 104 million sf (10 million square meters) of that space located in the U.S.

FINANCIAL DATA: *Note: Data for latest year may not have been available at press time.*

In U.S. $	2020	2019	2018	2017	2016	2015
Revenue	16,252,000,000	16,648,000,000	17,279,000,000	15,380,800,000	14,619,400,000	7,623,200,000
R&D Expense						
Operating Income	391,000,000	821,000,000	704,000,000	623,200,000	488,100,000	-28,600,000
Operating Margin %		.05%	.04%	.04%	.03%	.00%
SGA Expense	2,172,000,000	1,845,000,000	1,837,000,000	1,656,500,000	1,651,200,000	183,900,000
Net Income	110,000,000	419,000,000	422,000,000	340,200,000	69,000,000	-191,100,000
Operating Cash Flow	885,000,000	791,000,000	1,102,000,000	798,600,000	625,400,000	90,800,000
Capital Expenditure	526,000,000	601,000,000	551,000,000	503,800,000	483,400,000	249,000,000
EBITDA	1,239,000,000	1,600,000,000	1,499,000,000	1,203,400,000	1,111,300,000	299,100,000
Return on Assets %		.03%	.03%	.03%	.01%	-.03%
Return on Equity %		.12%	.11%	.10%	.02%	-.11%
Debt to Equity		2.575	1.104	1.24	1.78	1.971

CONTACT INFORMATION:

Phone: 855-976-4636   Fax:
Toll-Free:
Address: Five American Ln., Greenwich, CT 06831 United States

STOCK TICKER/OTHER:

Stock Ticker: XPO   Exchange: NYS
Employees: 102,000   Fiscal Year Ends: 12/31
Parent Company:

SALARIES/BONUSES:

Top Exec. Salary: $ Bonus: $
Second Exec. Salary: $ Bonus: $

OTHER THOUGHTS:

Estimated Female Officers or Directors: 2
Hot Spot for Advancement for Women/Minorities:

Yellow Corporation

www.yrcw.com

NAIC Code: 484122

TYPES OF BUSINESS:

Specialized Freight, Less-Than-Truckload
Freight Transportation
Next-Day Delivery Services
Transportation Technology Services

BRANDS/DIVISIONS/AFFILIATES:

YRC Inc
YRC Freight Canada
HNRY Logistics Inc
USF Holland LLC
New Penn Motor Express LLC
USF Reddaway Inc

CONTACTS: Note: Officers with more than one job title may be intentionally listed here more than once.

Darren Hawkins, CEO
Stephanie Fisher, CFO
James Hoffman, Chairman of the Board
Jason Ringgenberg, Chief Information Officer
Brianne Simoneau, Controller
Thomas OConnor, COO
James Fry, General Counsel
Justin Hall, Other Executive Officer
Scott Ware, President, Divisional
Howard Moshier, President, Subsidiary
Loren Stone, President, Subsidiary
Mitch Lilly, Senior VP, Divisional
Mark Boehmer, Vice President

GROWTH PLANS/SPECIAL FEATURES:

Yellow Corporation, formerly known as YRC Worldwide, Inc., is a holding company that offers a wide range of transportation services through its subsidiaries. The group has a comprehensive less-than-truckload (LTL) network in North America, with local, regional, national and international capabilities. YRC offers LTL shipments and flexible supply chain solutions, enabling its customers to ship industrial, commercial and retail goods worldwide. The firm operates in two business segments: freight and regional transportation. The freight segment focuses on longer hauls, offering national, regional and international services. This division includes LTL subsidiaries YRC, Inc.; YRC Freight Canada; and HNRY Logistics, Inc., which serves the U.S., Canada and parts of Mexico and Puerto Rico. The regional transportation segment serves the regional and next-day delivery markets. This division is comprised of USF Holland, LLC; New Penn Motor Express, LLC; and USF Reddaway, Inc., each of which provide ground services in their respective regions through a network of facilities located throughout the U.S., Canada and Puerto Rico. In February 2021, the company changed its name from YRC Worldwide, Inc. to Yellow Corporation.

Yellow Corporation offers employees medical, dental and vision coverage; life insurance; a prescription drug plan; and a 401(k) plan.

FINANCIAL DATA: Note: Data for latest year may not have been available at press time.

In U.S. $	2020	2019	2018	2017	2016	2015
Revenue	4,513,700,000	4,871,200,000	5,092,000,000	4,891,000,000	4,697,500,000	4,832,400,000
R&D Expense						
Operating Income	11,200,000	10,700,000	122,100,000	97,800,000	109,700,000	94,900,000
Operating Margin %						
SGA Expense						
Net Income	-53,500,000	-104,000,000	20,200,000	-10,800,000	21,500,000	700,000
Operating Cash Flow	122,500,000	21,500,000	224,800,000	60,700,000	103,100,000	140,800,000
Capital Expenditure	140,600,000	143,200,000	145,400,000	103,300,000	100,600,000	108,000,000
EBITDA	197,700,000	155,300,000	284,800,000	232,400,000	287,800,000	266,900,000
Return on Assets %						
Return on Equity %						
Debt to Equity						

CONTACT INFORMATION:

Phone: 913 696-6100   Fax:
Toll-Free: 800-846-4300
Address: 10990 Roe Ave., Overland Park, KS 66211 United States

SALARIES/BONUSES:

Top Exec. Salary: $ Bonus: $
Second Exec. Salary: $ Bonus: $

STOCK TICKER/OTHER:

Stock Ticker: YELL
Employees: 30,000
Parent Company:

Exchange: NAS
Fiscal Year Ends: 12/31

OTHER THOUGHTS:

Estimated Female Officers or Directors: 1
Hot Spot for Advancement for Women/Minorities: Y

YouTube LLC

NAIC Code: 519130

TYPES OF BUSINESS:

Online Video Services
Video Subscriptions
Online Video Advertising Services

BRANDS/DIVISIONS/AFFILIATES:

Alphabet Inc
Google LLC
YouTube Partner
YouTube Insight
YouTube Premium
YouTube Music
YouTube Music Premium
YouTube Studio

CONTACTS: Note: Officers with more than one job title may be intentionally listed here more than once.

Susan Wojcicki, CEO
Hunter Walk, Head-Product
Kevin Donahue, VP-Content
Julie Supan, Sr. Dir.-Mktg.

GROWTH PLANS/SPECIAL FEATURES:

YouTube, LLC, a subsidiary of Alphabet, Inc.'s Google LLC, is a leading online video-sharing site, featuring significant amounts of user-generated content. More than 500 hours of video content is uploaded to YouTube every minute. The site has more than 2 billion users, is localized in over 100 countries and can be accessed in 80 languages. YouTube derives most of its revenue through in-video advertising, sponsorships and brand channels. Advertisers have the option of purchasing promoted videos, which offer more visibility; 24-hour video banner ads on the website's homepage; the ability to hand-pick videos to advertise against; mobile advertisements; and the ability to advertise with content partners. The YouTube Partner program allows producers of original content that targets a wide audience to upload ad-supported videos, rentals, high quality content and live-streaming videos. Advertisers can track the impact of these advertisements with YouTube Insight, which counts page views, video popularity, demographics and audience attention. YouTube is also available through Apple TV and a variety of mobile devices. YouTube Premium is a monthly subscription that enables users to watch without seeing ads on most types of videos. YouTube Music is a music streaming service; and YouTube Music Premium offers ad-free and offline features for a monthly subscription fee. YouTube Go is an app that makes it easier to access YouTube via mobile devices in emerging markets. YouTube Studio is for creators, where they can manage their presence, grow their channels, interact with audiences and earn money. YouTube Shorts is a beta version of a 15-second video platform, giving users access to creative tools. YouTube Kids is a children's video app with curated selections of content, parental control features and more.

Alphabet offers its employees comprehensive health benefits, retirement plans and a variety of employee assistance programs.

FINANCIAL DATA: Note: Data for latest year may not have been available at press time.

In U.S. $	2020	2019	2018	2017	2016	2015
Revenue	19,772,000,000	15,149,000,000	15,000,000,000	13,250,000,000	11,750,000,000	9,450,000,000
R&D Expense						
Operating Income						
Operating Margin %						
SGA Expense						
Net Income						
Operating Cash Flow						
Capital Expenditure						
EBITDA						
Return on Assets %						
Return on Equity %						
Debt to Equity						

CONTACT INFORMATION:

Phone: 650-253-0000   Fax: 650-253-0001
Toll-Free:
Address: 901 Cherry Ave., San Bruno, CA 94066 United States

STOCK TICKER/OTHER:

Stock Ticker: Subsidiary
Employees: 20,000
Parent Company: Alphabet Inc

Exchange:
Fiscal Year Ends: 12/31

SALARIES/BONUSES:

Top Exec. Salary: $ Bonus: $
Second Exec. Salary: $ Bonus: $

OTHER THOUGHTS:

Estimated Female Officers or Directors: 2
Hot Spot for Advancement for Women/Minorities:

Yum! Brands Inc

www.yum.com

NAIC Code: 722513

TYPES OF BUSINESS:

Fast Food Restaurants

BRANDS/DIVISIONS/AFFILIATES:

KFC
Pizza Hut
Taco Bell
Habit Resaurants
Healthstyles

CONTACTS: *Note: Officers with more than one job title may be intentionally listed here more than once.*

David Gibbs, CEO
David Gibbs, CFO
Brian Cornell, Chairman of the Board
David Russell, Chief Accounting Officer
Scott Catlett, General Counsel
Tracy Skeans, Other Executive Officer

GROWTH PLANS/SPECIAL FEATURES:

Yum! Brands, Inc. is a restaurant company with nearly 50,000 restaurants in more than 150 countries and territories, marketed under the KFC, Pizza Hut and Taco Bell brand names. Practically all (95%) of these restaurants are owned and operated by franchisees. Yum! Brands develops, franchises or operates its worldwide system of fast-food and dine-in restaurants, which prepare and sell competitively-priced food items. Most restaurants in each concept offer the ability to dine in and/or carry out food. KFC and Taco Bell offer a drive-thru option in most of its stores. Pizza Hut offers the drive-thru option on a much more limited basis, but typically offers delivery service. KFC was founded in Corbin, Kentucky by Colonel Harland D. Sanders, who created a secret blend of 11 herbs and spices used for making Kentucky Fried Chicken (KFC). Its menu items include fried and non-fried chicken products, as well as side items and beverages. Pizza Hut began in 1958 in Wichita, Kansas, and is the largest restaurant chain in the world specializing in the sale of ready-to-eat pizza products. Last, Taco Bell began in 1962 in Downey, California, and specializes in Mexican-style food products such as tacos, burritos, quesadillas, salads, nachos and other related items. In March 2020, Yum Brands announced it had acquired Heartstyles, a company offering a leadership development program.

Yum! offers its employees receive health and retirement benefits.

FINANCIAL DATA: *Note: Data for latest year may not have been available at press time.*

In U.S. $	2020	2019	2018	2017	2016	2015
Revenue	5,652,000,000	5,597,000,000	5,688,000,000	5,878,000,000	6,366,000,000	13,105,000,000
R&D Expense						
Operating Income	1,623,000,000	1,897,000,000	1,763,000,000	1,688,000,000	1,505,000,000	2,000,000,000
Operating Margin %		.34%	.31%	.29%	.24%	.15%
SGA Expense	1,064,000,000	917,000,000	895,000,000	999,000,000	1,161,000,000	1,504,000,000
Net Income	904,000,000	1,294,000,000	1,542,000,000	1,340,000,000	1,619,000,000	1,293,000,000
Operating Cash Flow	1,305,000,000	1,315,000,000	1,176,000,000	1,030,000,000	1,204,000,000	2,139,000,000
Capital Expenditure	160,000,000	196,000,000	234,000,000	318,000,000	422,000,000	973,000,000
EBITDA	1,709,000,000	1,971,000,000	2,428,000,000	2,967,000,000	1,934,000,000	2,668,000,000
Return on Assets %		.28%	.33%	.25%	.24%	.16%
Return on Equity %						1.05%
Debt to Equity						3.352

CONTACT INFORMATION:

Phone: 502 874-8300   Fax:
Toll-Free:
Address: 1441 Gardiner Ln., Louisville, KY 40213 United States

SALARIES/BONUSES:

Top Exec. Salary: $ Bonus: $
Second Exec. Salary: $ Bonus: $

STOCK TICKER/OTHER:

Stock Ticker: YUM
Employees: 90,000
Parent Company:

Exchange: NYS
Fiscal Year Ends: 12/31

OTHER THOUGHTS:

Estimated Female Officers or Directors: 3
Hot Spot for Advancement for Women/Minorities: Y

Zillow Group Inc

www.zillow.com

NAIC Code: 519130

TYPES OF BUSINESS:

Online Real Estate Information
Real Estate Platform
Mortgage Loans
Artificial Intelligence
Machine Learning
Broker

BRANDS/DIVISIONS/AFFILIATES:

Zillow
Trulia
StreetEasy
HotPads
OutEast.com
Zestimates
Mortech
dotloop

CONTACTS: *Note: Officers with more than one job title may be intentionally listed here more than once.*

Richard Barton, CEO
Allen Parker, CFO
Lloyd Frink, Chairman of the Board
Jennifer Rock, Chief Accounting Officer
David Beitel, Chief Technology Officer
Arik Prawer, Other Corporate Officer
Dan Spaulding, Other Executive Officer
Stanley Humphries, Other Executive Officer
Errol Samuelson, Other Executive Officer
Greg Schwartz, President, Divisional
Jeremy Wacksman, President, Divisional

GROWTH PLANS/SPECIAL FEATURES:

Zillow Group, Inc. operates a real estate information marketplace dedicated to providing information about homes, real estate listings and mortgages and enabling homeowners, buyers, sellers and renters to connect with real estate and mortgage professionals. The company maintains a database of over 135 million homes in the U.S. that are either for sale, for rent or not currently on the market. Individuals and businesses that utilize the Zillow platform for showcasing properties provide information and photos when creating exclusive home profiles for viewers to search. These property profiles include detailed information such as property descriptions, types of communities (gated, HOA, etc.), listing information, purchase/rent histories and more. Zillow's real estate and rental marketplaces comprise consumer brands such as Zillow, Trulia, Mortgage Lenders of America, StreetEasy, HotPads and OutEast.com. In conjunction with the database, the firm offers users its proprietary automated valuation models, Zestimates and Rent Zestimatesk, which has a median absolute percent error of 1.8% for homes listed for sale and 7.4% for off-market homes. Zillow enables interested purchasers to check on interest rates, search for lenders, and apply for a pre-approved loan. Zillow also owns and operates a number of brands for real estate and mortgage professionals, including Mortech, dotloop, Bridge Interactive and New Home Feed. Zillow's platforms and software solutions encompass artificial intelligence (AI) and machine learning technologies, as well as data and analytic capabilities.

FINANCIAL DATA: *Note: Data for latest year may not have been available at press time.*

In U.S. $	2020	2019	2018	2017	2016	2015
Revenue	3,339,817,000	2,742,837,000	1,333,554,000	1,076,794,000	846,589,000	644,677,000
R&D Expense	518,072,000	477,347,000	410,818,000	319,985,000	273,066,000	198,565,000
Operating Income	35,412,000	-246,835,000	-45,628,000	12,589,000	-192,682,000	-93,036,000
Operating Margin %		-.09%	-.03%	.01%	-.23%	-.14%
SGA Expense	1,029,938,000	1,080,304,000	814,774,000	659,017,000	694,614,000	477,534,000
Net Income	-162,115,000	-305,361,000	-119,858,000	-94,420,000	-220,438,000	-148,874,000
Operating Cash Flow	424,197,000	-612,174,000	3,850,000	258,191,000	8,645,000	22,659,000
Capital Expenditure	108,517,000	86,635,000	78,535,000	78,635,000	71,722,000	68,108,000
EBITDA	119,958,000	-97,218,000	-10,314,000	-46,334,000	-112,310,000	-72,644,000
Return on Assets %		-.06%	-.03%	-.03%	-.07%	-.08%
Return on Equity %		-.09%	-.04%	-.04%	-.08%	-.09%
Debt to Equity		0.513	0.214	0.145	0.145	0.086

CONTACT INFORMATION:

Phone: 206 470-7000   Fax:
Toll-Free:
Address: 1301 Second Ave., Fl. 31, Seattle, WA 98101 United States

STOCK TICKER/OTHER:

Stock Ticker: Z
Employees: 5,504
Parent Company:

Exchange: NAS
Fiscal Year Ends: 12/31

SALARIES/BONUSES:

Top Exec. Salary: $ Bonus: $
Second Exec. Salary: $ Bonus: $

OTHER THOUGHTS:

Estimated Female Officers or Directors: 2
Hot Spot for Advancement for Women/Minorities: Y

Zoetis Inc

NAIC Code: 325414

www.zoetis.com

TYPES OF BUSINESS:

Veterinary Drugs
Veterinary Vaccines
Animal Health Medicines
Diagnostic Products

BRANDS/DIVISIONS/AFFILIATES:

CONTACTS: Note: Officers with more than one job title may be intentionally listed here more than once.

Glenn David, CFO
Michael McCallister, Chairman of the Board
Andrew Fenton, Chief Technology Officer
Juan Alaix, Director
Roxanne Lagano, Executive VP
Clinton Lewis, Executive VP
Catherine Knupp, Executive VP
Kristin Peck, Executive VP
Roman Trawicki, Executive VP
Heidi Chen, Executive VP

GROWTH PLANS/SPECIAL FEATURES:

Zoetis, Inc. discovers, develops, manufactures and commercializes animal health medicines, vaccines and diagnostic products, with a focus on livestock and companion animals. The firm organizes and operates its business in two segments: the USA, (accounting for 53% of annual revenue) and international (46%). Medicines are developed for eight core species: cattle, swine, poultry, sheep and fish (collectively, livestock), and dogs, cats and horses (companion animals). Products are divided into six major categories: anti-infectives, vaccines, parasiticides, medicated feed additives, animal health diagnostics, dermatology products and other pharmaceutical products. Anti-infectives prevent, kill or slow the growth of bacteria, fungi or protozoa; vaccines are biological preparations that prevent diseases of the respiratory, gastrointestinal and reproductive tracts or induce a specific immune response; parasiticides prevent or eliminate external and internal parasites such as fleas, ticks and worms; medicated feed additives are products added to animal feed that provide medicines, nutrients and probiotics to livestock; animal health diagnostics include portable blood and urine analysis systems and point-of-care diagnostic products, including instruments and reagents, rapid immunoassay tests, reference laboratory kits and blood glucose monitors; dermatology products relieve itch associated with allergic conditions and atopic dermatitis; and other pharmaceutical products include pain and sedation, oncology and antiemetic products. Livestock products are sold directly to livestock producers, including beef and dairy farmers as well as pork, poultry and aquaculture operations, and to veterinarians, third-party veterinary distributors and retail outlets that typically then sell the products to livestock producers. The company primarily sells its companion animal products to veterinarians or to third-party veterinary distributors that then sell the products to veterinarians, and in each case veterinarians then typically sell products to pet owners. In August 2021, Zoetis agreed to acquire Jurox, which develops, manufactures and markets veterinary medicines for treating companion animals and livestock.

FINANCIAL DATA: Note: Data for latest year may not have been available at press time.

In U.S. $	2020	2019	2018	2017	2016	2015
Revenue	6,675,000,000	6,260,000,000	5,825,000,000	5,307,000,000	4,888,000,000	4,765,000,000
R&D Expense	463,000,000	457,000,000	432,000,000	382,000,000	376,000,000	364,000,000
Operating Income	2,269,000,000	2,018,000,000	1,881,000,000	1,725,000,000	1,397,000,000	1,070,000,000
Operating Margin %		.32%	.32%	.33%	.29%	.22%
SGA Expense	1,726,000,000	1,638,000,000	1,484,000,000	1,334,000,000	1,364,000,000	1,532,000,000
Net Income	1,638,000,000	1,500,000,000	1,428,000,000	864,000,000	821,000,000	339,000,000
Operating Cash Flow	2,126,000,000	1,795,000,000	1,790,000,000	1,346,000,000	713,000,000	664,000,000
Capital Expenditure	453,000,000	460,000,000	338,000,000	224,000,000	216,000,000	224,000,000
EBITDA	2,668,000,000	2,436,000,000	2,204,000,000	1,942,000,000	1,634,000,000	868,000,000
Return on Assets %		.13%	.15%	.11%	.11%	.05%
Return on Equity %		.61%	.72%	.53%	.64%	.28%
Debt to Equity		2.257	2.949	2.798	3.005	4.179

CONTACT INFORMATION:

Phone: 973-822-7000 Fax:
Toll-Free: 888-963-8471
Address: 10 Sylvan Way, Parsippany, NJ 07054 United States

SALARIES/BONUSES:

Top Exec. Salary: $ Bonus: $
Second Exec. Salary: $ Bonus: $

STOCK TICKER/OTHER:

Stock Ticker: ZTS Exchange: NYS
Employees: 11,300 Fiscal Year Ends:
Parent Company:

OTHER THOUGHTS:

Estimated Female Officers or Directors: 6
Hot Spot for Advancement for Women/Minorities: Y

ADDITIONAL INDEXES

CONTENTS:

INDEX OF FIRMS NOTED AS HOT SPOTS FOR ADVANCEMENT FOR WOMEN & MINORITIES

3M Company
Abbott Laboratories
Adobe Inc
Advanced Micro Devices Inc (AMD)
AdventHealth
AECOM
AES Corporation (The)
aetnaCVSHealth
AFLAC Incorporated
Alcoa Corporation
Alexion Pharmaceuticals Inc
Allscripts Healthcare Solutions Inc
Allstate Corporation (The)
Alphabet Inc (Google)
Amazon.com Inc
Amedisys Inc
American Express Company
American Financial Group Inc
American International Group Inc (AIG)
American Tower Corporation (REIT)
Amerigroup Corporation
AmerisourceBergen Corporation
Amgen Inc
Anixter International Inc
ANSYS Inc
Anthem Inc
Applied Materials Inc
Archer-Daniels-Midland Company (ADM)
Arrow Electronics Inc
AT&T Inc
Avnet Inc
B&G Foods Inc
Ball Corporation
Bank of America Corporation
Bank of New York Mellon Corporation
Baxter International Inc
Bechtel Group Inc
Beckman Coulter Inc
Becton Dickinson and Company
Belden Inc
Best Buy Co Inc
Biogen Inc
Bio-Rad Laboratories Inc
Black & Veatch Holding Company
BlackRock Inc
Blackstone Group Inc (The)
Bloomberg LP
Blue Shield of California
BMC Software Inc
BNSF (Burlington Northern Santa Fe LLC)
Bonneville Power Administration
Booz Allen Hamilton Holding Corporation
Boston Consulting Group Inc (The, BCG)
Bristol-Myers Squibb Company
Broadcom Inc
Burger King Worldwide Inc
CACI International Inc
Campbell Soup Company

Cardinal Health Inc
Cargill Incorporated
CarMax Inc
Caterpillar Inc
CDW Corporation
Celanese Corporation
Centene Corporation
CenterPoint Energy Inc
Cerner Corporation
CH Robinson Worldwide Inc
Charles River Laboratories International Inc
Charles Schwab Corporation (The)
Chemed Corporation
Chick-fil-A Inc
Church & Dwight Company Inc
Cigna Corporation
Cisco Systems Inc
Citigroup Inc
Cleveland Clinic Foundation (The)
Clorox Company (The)
Coca-Cola Bottling Consolidated Inc
Colgate-Palmolive Company
Comcast Corporation
Comfort Systems USA Inc
Conagra Brands Inc
Cooper Companies Inc (The)
Corning Incorporated
Costco Wholesale Corporation
Crown Holdings Inc
Curia Inc
CVS Health Corporation
Danaher Corporation
DaVita Inc
Deere & Company (John Deere)
Dell Technologies Inc
Deloitte LLP
Dicks Sporting Goods Inc
Discovery Inc
Dollar General Corporation
Dominion Energy Inc
Dow Inc
DTE Energy Company
Duke Energy Corporation
E*Trade Financial LLC
Edison International
Edward D Jones & Co LP
Edwards Lifesciences Corporation
Eli Lilly and Company
EMCOR Group Inc
Equinix Inc
Exelon Corporation
EY LLP
F5 Networks Inc
Facebook Inc
FactSet Research Systems Inc
Fannie Mae (Federal National Mortgage Association)
FedEx Corporation
Ferguson Enterprises Inc
Fidelity National Information Services Inc
FireEye Inc
First Solar Inc
FirstEnergy Corporation
Flowers Foods Inc

Fluor Corporation
Ford Motor Company
Fortinet Inc
Freddie Mac (Federal Home Loan Mortgage Corporation)
Frito-Lay North America Inc
FTI Consulting Inc
Gartner Inc
Genentech Inc
General Dynamics Corporation
General Mills Inc
General Motors Company (GM)
Genuine Parts Company
Georgia Power Company
Georgia-Pacific LLC
Gilead Sciences Inc
GoDaddy Inc
Goldman Sachs Group Inc (The)
Golub Corporation
Greenbrier Companies Inc (The)
Group 1 Automotive Inc
Hartford Financial Services Group Inc (The)
Health Care Service Corporation (HCSC)
HEB Grocery Company LP
Hershey Company (The)
Hill-Rom Holdings Inc
Home Depot Inc (The)
Houston Methodist
Humana Inc
IAC/InterActiveCorp
IDEXX Laboratories Inc
Ingredion Incorporated
In-N-Out Burgers Inc
Insight Enterprises Inc
Intel Corporation
Intuit Inc
IQVIA Holdings Inc
Itron Inc
Jabil Inc
Jack Henry & Associates Inc
Jacobs Engineering Group Inc
JB Hunt Transport Services Inc
JM Smucker Company (The)
John Hancock Financial
Johnson & Johnson
JPMorgan Chase & Co Inc
Juniper Networks Inc
Kaiser Permanente
Kansas City Southern
KBR Inc
Kellogg Company
KEMET Corporation
Kenco Group Inc
Kimberly-Clark Corporation
Kraft Heinz Company (The)
Kratos Defense & Security Solutions Inc
Kroger Co (The)
L3Harris Technologies Inc
Laboratory Corporation of America Holdings
Lam Research Corporation
Lennar Corporation
LHC Group Inc
Liberty Mutual Group Inc

Lincoln National Corporation
LinkedIn Corporation
Lockheed Martin Corporation
Logitech International SA
Lowes Companies Inc
Magellan Health Inc
ManTech International Corporation
Mass General Brigham Incorporated
MassMutual Financial Group
MasterCard Incorporated
MAXIMUS Inc
Mayo Clinic
McAfee Corp
McCormick & Company Incorporated
McDermott International Ltd
McDonalds Corporation
McKesson Corporation
McKinsey & Company Inc
MDU Resources Group Inc
Meijer Inc
Memorial Sloan Kettering Cancer Center
Mercer LLC
Merck & Co Inc
MetLife Inc
Microchip Technology Incorporated
Microsoft Corporation
Molina Healthcare Inc
Mondelez International Inc
Moody's Corporation
Morgan Stanley
Mutual of Omaha Insurance Company
Nationwide Mutual Insurance Company
NetApp Inc
Netflix Inc
New York Life Insurance Company
Newfold Digital Inc
NextEra Energy Inc
Nielsen Holdings plc
NiSource Inc
North Highland Company (The)
Northrop Grumman Corporation
Northwestern Mutual Life Insurance
Company (The)
NortonLifeLock Inc
NVIDIA Corporation
Oliver Wyman Group
Oracle Corporation
Oracle NetSuite
Owens Corning
PAREXEL International Corporation
PayPal Holdings Inc
PerkinElmer Inc
PetSmart Inc
Pfizer Inc
PG&E Corporation
Pilgrims Pride Corporation
Plantronics Inc
PRA Health Sciences Inc
PriceSmart Inc
PricewaterhouseCoopers (PwC)
Principal Financial Group Inc
Procter & Gamble Company (The)
Prudential Financial Inc
Publix Super Markets Inc
Puget Energy Inc

PulteGroup Inc
Qualcomm Incorporated
Quest Diagnostics Incorporated
Raymond James Financial Inc
Red Hat Inc
REI (Recreational Equipment Inc)
Rent-A-Center Inc
Safeway Inc
salesforce.com Inc
Sams Club
Sanderson Farms Inc
Sanofi Genzyme
SAS Institute Inc
SC Johnson & Son Inc
Science Applications International
Corporation (SAIC)
Sempra Energy
Sherwin-Williams Company (The)
Smithfield Foods Inc
Southeastern Grocers LLC
Southern California Edison Company
Southern Company
SpaceX (Space Exploration Technologies
Corporation)
SpartanNash Company
Stanley Black & Decker Inc
Starbucks Corporation
State Farm Insurance Companies
State Street Corporation
Stewart Information Services Corporation
Stryker Corporation
SunPower Corporation
Sunrun Inc
Supervalu Inc
Sutter Health Inc
Sykes Enterprises Incorporated
Synopsys Inc
Target Corporation
TD Ameritrade Holding Corporation
Tellabs Inc
Texas Instruments Incorporated
Textron Inc
Thermo Fisher Scientific Inc
TIAA
Tractor Supply Company
Travelers Companies Inc (The)
Trimble Inc
Trinity Industries Inc
Tyson Foods Inc
Union Pacific Corporation
United Natural Foods Inc
United Parcel Service Inc (UPS)
United States Cellular Corporation
UnitedHealth Group Inc
Universal Health Services Inc
US Bancorp (US Bank)
USAA
Vanguard Group Inc (The)
Varian Medical Systems Inc
Verizon Communications Inc
Visa Inc
VMware Inc
Walgreens Boots Alliance Inc
Walmart Inc
Waste Management Inc

Wayfair LLC
WellCare Health Plans Inc
Wells Fargo & Company
Whole Foods Market Inc
Yellow Corporation
Yum! Brands Inc
Zillow Group Inc
Zoetis Inc

INDEX OF SUBSIDIARIES, BRAND NAMES AND AFFILIATIONS

INDEX OF SUBSIDIARIES, BRAND NAMES AND AFFILIATIONS, CONT.

INDEX OF SUBSIDIARIES, BRAND NAMES AND AFFILIATIONS, CONT.

INDEX OF SUBSIDIARIES, BRAND NAMES AND AFFILIATIONS, CONT.

INDEX OF SUBSIDIARIES, BRAND NAMES AND AFFILIATIONS, CONT.

INDEX OF SUBSIDIARIES, BRAND NAMES AND AFFILIATIONS, CONT.

INDEX OF SUBSIDIARIES, BRAND NAMES AND AFFILIATIONS, CONT.

INDEX OF SUBSIDIARIES, BRAND NAMES AND AFFILIATIONS, CONT.

INDEX OF SUBSIDIARIES, BRAND NAMES AND AFFILIATIONS, CONT.

INDEX OF SUBSIDIARIES, BRAND NAMES AND AFFILIATIONS, CONT.

Navitas Systems; **East Penn Manufacturing Company Inc**
NCH; **NCH Corporation**
Neosporin; **Johnson & Johnson**
Neovia SAS; **Archer-Daniels-Midland Company (ADM)**
Neptune Society; **Service Corporation International Inc**
NetApp Keystone; **NetApp Inc**
Netrounds; **Juniper Networks Inc**
Network Security and Forensics; **FireEye Inc**
Network Solutions; **Newfold Digital Inc**
Neulasta; **Amgen Inc**
New Penn Motor Express LLC; **Yellow Corporation**
NexION; **PerkinElmer Inc**
NextEra Energy Capital Holdings Inc; **NextEra Energy Inc**
NextEra Energy Resources LLC; **NextEra Energy Inc**
NFLSHOP.ca; **Fanatics Inc**
NI DIAdem; **National Instruments Corporation**
NI SystemLink; **National Instruments Corporation**
Nielsen Global Connect; **Nielsen Holdings plc**
Nielsen Global Media; **Nielsen Holdings plc**
NiSource Gas Distribution Group Inc; **NiSource Inc**
No7; **Walgreens Boots Alliance Inc**
Nordco; **Wabtec Corporation**
North American Coffee Partnership (The); **Starbucks Corporation**
Northern Indiana Public Service Company; **NiSource Inc**
Northern Natural Gas Company; **Berkshire Hathaway Energy Company**
Northern Powergrid; **Berkshire Hathaway Energy Company**
Northrop Grumman Innovation Systems; **Northrop Grumman Corporation**
Northwestern Long Term Care Insurance Company; **Northwestern Mutual Life Insurance Company (The)**
Northwestern Mutual Investment Management Co LLC; **Northwestern Mutual Life Insurance Company (The)**
Northwestern Mutual Investment Services LLC; **Northwestern Mutual Life Insurance Company (The)**
Northwestern Mutual Wealth Management Company; **Northwestern Mutual Life Insurance Company (The)**
Norton 360; **NortonLifeLock Inc**
NortonLifeLock; **NortonLifeLock Inc**
NOS; **Monster Beverage Corporation**
Noveos; **Hycor Biomedical LLC**

NSTAR Electric Company; **Eversource Energy**
NSTAR Gas Company; **Eversource Energy**
Number Holdings Inc; **99 Cents Only Stores LLC**
Nutanix Core; **Nutanix Inc**
Nutanix Enterprise; **Nutanix Inc**
Nutanix Essentials; **Nutanix Inc**
Nuveen; **TIAA**
NV Energy Inc; **Berkshire Hathaway Energy Company**
NVHomes; **NVR Inc**
NVR Mortgage Finance Inc; **NVR Inc**
Nyansa; **VMware Inc**
O Organics; **Safeway Inc**
Oasis; **SunPower Corporation**
obp Medical Corporation; **Cooper Companies Inc (The)**
OCREVUS; **Biogen Inc**
Octarine; **VMware Inc**
Oculus; **Facebook Inc**
Office 365; **Microsoft Corporation**
Offshore Angler; **Bass Pro Shops Inc**
Ohio Edison; **FirstEnergy Corporation**
Olay; **Procter & Gamble Company (The)**
Olumiant; **Eli Lilly and Company**
Omnicare; **CVS Health Corporation**
Oncor; **Sempra Energy**
ONE Brands LLC; **Hershey Company (The)**
One Day Pay; **AFLAC Incorporated**
OneDrive; **Microsoft Corporation**
Onica; **Rackspace Technology Inc**
Open for Business; **LinkedIn Corporation**
Open Nature; **Safeway Inc**
Open Trails; **Dollar General Corporation**
Opera Phenix; **PerkinElmer Inc**
Oppenheimer Funds Inc; **MassMutual Financial Group**
Optically Variable Magnetic Pigment; **Viavi Solutions Inc**
Optically Variable Pigment; **Viavi Solutions Inc**
OptimalPlus; **National Instruments Corporation**
Optimum HealthCare; **Anthem Inc**
Optum; **UnitedHealth Group Inc**
OptumHealth; **UnitedHealth Group Inc**
OptumInsight; **UnitedHealth Group Inc**
OptumRx; **UnitedHealth Group Inc**
Oracle Corporation; **Oracle NetSuite**
Orajel; **Church & Dwight Company Inc**
Orbit; **Mars Incorporated**
Oreo; **Mondelez International Inc**
Orion Artemis I; **Lockheed Martin Corporation**
Ortega; **B&G Foods Inc**
OrthoCAD; **Align Technology Inc**
Oscar Mayer; **Kraft Heinz Company (The)**

OT Sport; **Dollar General Corporation**
Otezla; **Amgen Inc**
OTN Systems NV; **Belden Inc**
OutEast.com; **Zillow Group Inc**
Outlook.com; **Microsoft Corporation**
Overland Contracting; **Black & Veatch Holding Company**
Overwatch League; **Activision Blizzard Inc**
Owens Corning PINK FIBERGLAS Insulation; **Owens Corning**
Oxford Life Insurance Company; **AMERCO (U-Haul)**
OxiClean; **Church & Dwight Company Inc**
PA Consulting; **Jacobs Engineering Group Inc**
Pabtex Inc; **Kansas City Southern**
Pace; **Campbell Soup Company**
Pacific Foods; **Campbell Soup Company**
Pacific Gas and Electric Company; **PG&E Corporation**
Pacific Kitchen and Home; **Best Buy Co Inc**
Pacifico; **Constellation Brands Inc**
Pacificor; **Archer-Daniels-Midland Company (ADM)**
PacifiCorp; **Berkshire Hathaway Energy Company**
Palmolive; **Colgate-Palmolive Company**
PALS; **Petco Animal Supplies Inc**
Palynziq; **BioMarin Pharmaceutical Inc**
Pampers; **Procter & Gamble Company (The)**
Pamplona Capital Management LP; **PAREXEL International Corporation**
Panama Canal Railway Company; **Kansas City Southern**
Panarail Tourism Company; **Kansas City Southern**
Pangburn Candy Company; **Russell Stover Candies Inc**
Panopta; **Fortinet Inc**
Paragon; **Allscripts Healthcare Solutions Inc**
Park Harbor; **Ferguson Enterprises Inc**
PASCAL; **Edwards Lifesciences Corporation**
Passage AI; **ServiceNow Inc**
Patheon; **Thermo Fisher Scientific Inc**
Pavilions; **Albertsons Companies Inc**
PayPal; **PayPal Holdings Inc**
PayPal Credit; **PayPal Holdings Inc**
Peacock; **Comcast Corporation**
PECO Energy Company; **Exelon Corporation**
Penelec; **FirstEnergy Corporation**
Penske Australia; **Penske Automotive Group Inc**
Penske Corporation; **Penske Automotive Group Inc**

INDEX OF SUBSIDIARIES, BRAND NAMES AND AFFILIATIONS, CONT.

INDEX OF SUBSIDIARIES, BRAND NAMES AND AFFILIATIONS, CONT.

INDEX OF SUBSIDIARIES, BRAND NAMES AND AFFILIATIONS, CONT.

INDEX OF SUBSIDIARIES, BRAND NAMES AND AFFILIATIONS, CONT.

INDEX OF SUBSIDIARIES, BRAND NAMES AND AFFILIATIONS, CONT.

CPSIA information can be obtained
at www.ICGtesting.com
Printed in the USA
FSHW020526271021
85661FS

3 0053 01358 8119

9 781628 316018